GRADE 8 | TEACHER'S EDITION

myPerspectives™
ENGLISH LANGUAGE ARTS

Pearson

NEW YORK, NEW YORK • BOSTON, MASSACHUSETTS
CHANDLER, ARIZONA • GLENVIEW, ILLINOIS

Photo locators denoted as follows: Top (T), Center (C), Bottom (B), Left (L), Right (R), Background (Bkgd)

COVER: © Lee Powers/Stone/Getty Images; T3: londoneye/Getty Images; T5B: PathDoc/Shutterstock; T5B: Franck Boston/Shutterstock; T19: Victoria Kisel/Shutterstock; T20: karandaev/fotolia; T23: Jojje/Shutterstock; T25: Nikada/Getty Images; T26B: Creativa Images/Shutterstock; T32: Monkey Business Images/Shutterstock; T33B: Hocus Focus Studio/Getty Images; T34: artagent/Fotolia; T4: Artishok/Shutterstock; T5B: Derek Latta/ E+/Getty Images; T5B: OJO Images Ltd/Alamy

Acknowledgments of third-party content appear on page R75, which constitutes an extension of this copyright page.

Copyright © 2017 by Pearson Education, Inc., or its affiliates. All Rights Reserved. Printed in the United States of America. This publication is protected by copyright, and permission should be obtained from the publisher prior to any prohibited reproduction, storage in a retrieval system, or transmission in any form or by any means, electronic, mechanical, photocopying, recording, or otherwise. For information regarding permissions, request forms, and the appropriate contacts within the Pearson Education Global Rights & Permissions department, please visit www.pearsoned.com/permissions.

This work is solely for the use of instructors and administrators for the purpose of teaching courses and assessing student learning. Unauthorized dissemination, publication, or sale of the work, in whole or in part (including posting on the internet) will destroy the integrity of the work and is strictly prohibited.

PEARSON, ALWAYS LEARNING, and myPerspectives are exclusive trademarks owned by Pearson Education, Inc. or its affiliates, in the U.S. and/or other countries.

Unless otherwise indicated herein, any third-party trademarks that may appear in this work are the property of their respective owners and any references to third-party trademarks, logos, or other trade dress are for demonstrative or descriptive purposes only. Such references are not intended to imply any sponsorship, endorsement, authorization, or promotion of Pearson's products by the owners of such marks, or any relationship between the owner and Pearson Education, Inc. or its affiliates, authors, licensees, or distributors.

Common Core State Standards: © Copyright 2010. National Governors Association Center for Best Practices and Council of Chief State School Officers. All rights reserved.

ISBN-13: 978-0-13-333867-6
ISBN-10:   0-13-333867-3
8   17

Welcome!

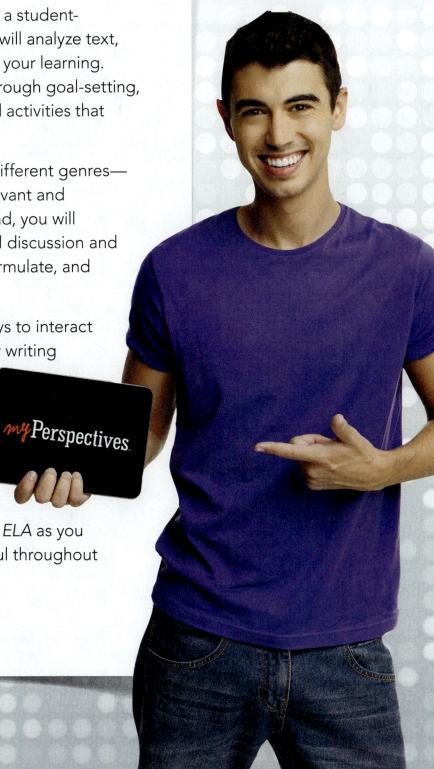

*my*Perspectives™ *English Language Arts* is a student-centered learning environment where you will analyze text, cite evidence, and respond critically about your learning. You will take ownership of your learning through goal-setting, reflection, independent text selection, and activities that allow you to collaborate with your peers.

Each unit of study includes selections of different genres—including multimedia—all related to a relevant and meaningful Essential Question. As you read, you will engage in activities that inspire thoughtful discussion and debate with your peers allowing you to formulate, and defend, your own perspectives.

*my*Perspectives *ELA* offers a variety of ways to interact directly with the text. You can annotate by writing in your print consumable, or you can annotate in your digital Student Edition. In addition, exciting technology allows you to access multimedia directly from your mobile device and communicate using an online discussion board!

We hope you enjoy using *my*Perspectives *ELA* as you develop the skills required to be successful throughout college and career.

Authors' Perspectives

*my*Perspectives is informed by a team of respected experts whose experiences working with students and study of instructional best practices have positively impacted education. From the evolving role of the teacher to how students learn in a digital age, our authors bring new ideas, innovations, and strategies that transform teaching and learning in today's competitive and interconnected world.

" The teaching of English needs to focus on engaging a new generation of learners. How do we get them excited about reading and writing? How do we help them to envision themselves as readers and writers? And, how can we make the teaching of English more culturally, socially, and technologically relevant? Throughout the curriculum, we've created spaces that enhance youth voice and participation and that connect the teaching of literature and writing to technological transformations of the digital age."

Ernest Morrell, Ph.D.

is the Macy professor of English Education at Teachers College, Columbia University, a class of 2014 Fellow of the American Educational Research Association, and the Past-President of the National Council of Teachers of English (NCTE). He is also the Director of Teachers College's Institute for Urban and Minority Education (IUME). He is an award-winning author and in his spare time he coaches youth sports and writes poems and plays. Dr. Morrell has influenced the development of *my*Perspectives in Assessment, Writing & Research, Student Engagement, and Collaborative Learning.

Elfrieda Hiebert, Ph.D.

is President and CEO of TextProject, a nonprofit that provides resources to support higher reading levels. She is also a research associate at the University of California, Santa Cruz. Dr. Hiebert has worked in the field of early reading acquisition for 45 years, first as a teacher's aide and teacher of primary-level students in California and, subsequently, as a teacher and researcher. Her research addresses how fluency, vocabulary, and knowledge can be fostered through appropriate texts. Dr. Hiebert has influenced the development of *my*Perspectives in Vocabulary, Text Complexity, and Assessment.

> "The signature of complex text is challenging vocabulary. In the systems of vocabulary, it's important to provide ways to show how concepts can be made more transparent to students. We provide lessons and activities that develop a strong vocabulary and concept foundation—a foundation that permits students to comprehend increasingly more complex text."

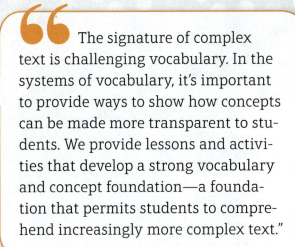

Kelly Gallagher, M.Ed.

teaches at Magnolia High School in Anaheim, California, where he is in his thirty-first year. He is the former co-director of the South Basin Writing Project at California State University, Long Beach. Mr. Gallagher has influenced the development of *my*Perspectives in Writing, Close Reading, and the Role of Teachers.

> "The *my*Perspectives classroom is dynamic. The teacher inspires, models, instructs, facilitates, and advises students as they evolve and grow. When teachers guide students through meaningful learning tasks and then pass them ownership of their own learning, students become engaged and work harder. This is how we make a difference in student achievement—by putting students at the center of their learning and giving them the opportunities to choose, explore, collaborate, and work independently."

> "It's critical to give students the opportunity to read a wide range of highly engaging texts and to immerse themselves in exploring powerful ideas and how these ideas are expressed. In *my*Perspectives, we focus on building up students' awareness of how academic language works, which is especially important for English language learners."

Jim Cummins, Ph.D.

is a Professor Emeritus in the Department of Curriculum, Teaching and Learning of the University of Toronto. His research focuses on literacy development in multilingual school contexts as well as on the potential roles of technology in promoting language and literacy development. In recent years, he has been working actively with teachers to identify ways of increasing the literacy engagement of learners in multilingual school contexts. Dr. Cummins has influenced the development of *my*Perspectives in English Language Learner and English Language Development support.

Each unit focuses on an engaging topic related to the Essential Question.

UNIT 1 Rites of Passage

UNIT INTRODUCTION

UNIT ACTIVITY AND VIDEO 2

LAUNCH TEXT:
NONFICTION NARRATIVE MODEL
Red Roses 6

WHOLE-CLASS LEARNING

COMPARE

ANCHOR TEXT: SHORT STORY
The Medicine Bag
Virginia Driving Hawk Sneve 13

MEDIA: VIDEO
Apache Girl's Rite of Passage
National Geographic 29

PERFORMANCE TASK
WRITING FOCUS
Write a Nonfiction Narrative 34

SMALL-GROUP LEARNING

LETTERS
You Are the Electric Boogaloo
Geoff Herbach 46
Just Be Yourself!
Stephanie Pellegrin 48

POETRY COLLECTION
Hanging Fire
Audre Lorde 56
Translating Grandfather's House
E.J. Vega 58

SHORT STORY
The Setting Sun and the Rolling World
Charles Mungoshi 67
  MEDIA CONNECTION:
  Stories of Zimbabwean Women

PERFORMANCE TASK
SPEAKING AND LISTENING FOCUS
Present Nonfiction Narratives 76

ESSENTIAL QUESTION: What are some milestones on the path to growing up?

> An Essential Question frames all unit activities and discussions.

 INDEPENDENT LEARNING

MEMOIR
Cub Pilot on the Mississippi
Mark Twain

AUTOBIOGRAPHY
from I Know Why the Caged Bird Sings
Maya Angelou

NEWS ARTICLE
Quinceañera Birthday Bash Preserves Tradition, Marks Passage to Womanhood
Natalie St. John

REFLECTIVE ESSAY
Childhood and Poetry
Pablo Neruda

SHORT STORY
The Winter Hibiscus
Minfong Ho

These selections can be accessed via the Interactive Student Edition.

PERFORMANCE-BASED ASSESSMENT PREP
Review Evidence for a Nonfiction Narrative 83

PERFORMANCE-BASED ASSESSMENT
Narration:
Nonfiction Narrative and
Oral Presentation 84

UNIT REFLECTION
Reflect on the Unit 87

> All unit activities are backwards-designed to the Performance-Based Assessment.

DIGITAL PERSPECTIVES

 Use the BouncePage app whenever you see "Scan for Multimedia" to access:

- Unit Introduction Videos
- Media Selections
- Modeling Videos
- Selection Audio Recordings

Additional digital resources can be found in:
- Interactive Student Edition
- *my*Perspectives+

> Grades 6–8 are intentionally designed with five units allowing students ample opportunity to learn the routines of the program. Doing so allows students to develop skills in preparation for the rigor and expectations of high school, which is critical at these grades.

UNIT 2 The Holocaust

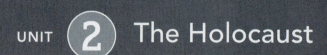

The Launch Text introduces a perspective on the unit topic.

UNIT INTRODUCTION

UNIT ACTIVITY AND VIDEO 88

LAUNCH TEXT: EXPLANATORY MODEL
The Grand Mosque of Paris 92

WHOLE-CLASS LEARNING

HISTORICAL PERSPECTIVES
The Holocaust 98

COMPARE

ANCHOR TEXT: DRAMA
The Diary of Anne Frank, Act I
*Frances Goodrich and
Albert Hackett* 101

ANCHOR TEXT: DRAMA
The Diary of Anne Frank, Act II
*Frances Goodrich and
Albert Hackett* 157

MEDIA: TIMELINE
Frank Family and World War II
Timelines 195

Teachers lead the shared reading experience, providing modeling and support, as students begin exploring perspectives on the unit topic.

SMALL-GROUP LEARNING

DIARY ENTRIES
from Anne Frank: The Diary of a Young Girl
Anne Frank 213

SPEECH
Acceptance Speech for the Nobel Peace Prize
Elie Wiesel 223

MEDIA: GRAPHIC NOVEL
from Maus
Art Spiegelman 231

Students encounter diverse perspectives on the unit topic, working in collaborative teams.

PERFORMANCE TASK

WRITING FOCUS
Write an Explanatory Essay 202

PERFORMANCE TASK

SPEAKING AND LISTENING FOCUS
Deliver a Multimedia Presentation ... 242

ESSENTIAL QUESTION: How do we remember the past?

INDEPENDENT LEARNING

TELEVISION TRANSCRIPT
Saving the Children
Bob Simon

REFLECTIVE ESSAY
A Great Adventure in the Shadow of War
Mary Helen Dirkx

INFORMATIVE ARTICLE
Irena Sendler: Rescuer of the Children of Warsaw
Chana Kroll

HISTORICAL WRITING
Quiet Resistance
from Courageous Teen Resisters
Ann Byers

NEWS ARTICLE
Remembering a Devoted Keeper of Anne Frank's Legacy
Moni Basu

FIRST-PERSON ACCOUNT
I'll Go Fetch Her Tomorrow
from Hidden Like Anne Frank
Bloeme Emden with Marcel Prins

These selections can be accessed via the Interactive Student Edition.

PERFORMANCE-BASED ASSESSMENT PREP
Review Evidence for an Explanatory Essay 249

PERFORMANCE-BASED ASSESSMENT

Explanatory Text:
Essay and Oral Presentation 250

UNIT REFLECTION

Reflect on the Unit 253

DIGITAL PERSPECTIVES

Use the BouncePage app whenever you see "Scan for Multimedia" to access:

- Unit Introduction Videos
- Media Selections
- Modeling Videos
- Selection Audio Recordings

Additional digital resources can be found in:
- Interactive Student Edition
- *my*Perspectives+

> Students self-select a text to explore an aspect of the unit topic and share their learning with the class.

UNIT 3 What Matters

The Launch Text models the mode of writing that will be at the core of the Performance-Based Assessment.

UNIT INTRODUCTION

UNIT ACTIVITY AND VIDEO 254
• LAUNCH TEXT: ARGUMENT MODEL
Freedom of the Press? 258

WHOLE-CLASS LEARNING

ANCHOR TEXT: MAGAZINE ARTICLE
Barrington Irving, Pilot and Educator
National Geographic 265
 MEDIA CONNECTION: Barrington Irving: Got 30 Dollars in My Pocket

ANCHOR TEXT: OPINION PIECE
Three Cheers for the Nanny State
Sarah Conly 277

ANCHOR TEXT: OPINION PIECES
Ban the Ban!
SidneyAnne Stone
Soda's a Problem, but . . .
Karin Klein 287

● PERFORMANCE TASK
WRITING FOCUS
Write an Argument 296

SMALL-GROUP LEARNING

PERSUASIVE SPEECH
Words Do Not Pay
Chief Joseph 307

NONFICTION NARRATIVE
from Follow the Rabbit-Proof Fence
Doris Pilkington 315

MEDIA: VIDEO
The Moth Presents: Aleeza Kazmi 325

PERFORMANCE TASK
SPEAKING AND LISTENING FOCUS
Present an Argument 328

Performance Tasks build toward and prepare students for the Unit Performance-Based Assessment.

ESSENTIAL QUESTION: When is it right to take a stand?

INDEPENDENT LEARNING

MEMOIR
from Through My Eyes
Ruby Bridges

POETRY
The Unknown Citizen
W. H. Auden

BIOGRAPHY
Harriet Tubman: Conductor on the Underground Railroad
Ann Petry

These selections can be accessed via the Interactive Student Edition.

PERFORMANCE-BASED ASSESSMENT PREP

Review Evidence for an Argument 335

PERFORMANCE-BASED ASSESSMENT

Argument:
Essay and Oral Presentation 336

UNIT REFLECTION

Reflect on the Unit 339

DIGITAL PERSPECTIVES

Use the BouncePage app whenever you see "Scan for Multimedia" to access:

- Unit Introduction Videos
- Media Selections
- Modeling Videos
- Selection Audio Recordings

Additional digital resources can be found in:

- Interactive Student Edition
- myPerspectives+

Students pull together their notes, evidence, completed activities, and Performance Tasks to prepare for the Performance-Based Assessment.

UNIT 4 Human Intelligence

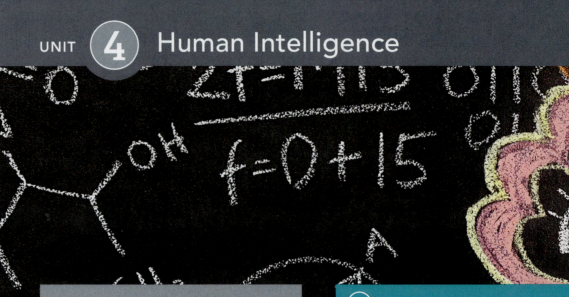

UNIT INTRODUCTION

UNIT ACTIVITY AND VIDEO 340

LAUNCH TEXT:
INFORMATIVE MODEL
The Human Brain 344

WHOLE-CLASS LEARNING

COMPARE

ANCHOR TEXT: SHORT STORY
Flowers for Algernon
Daniel Keyes. 351

SCRIPT
from Flowers for Algernon
David Rogers 385

> Comparing a text and media version of classic literature deepens the learning experience and develops critical skills.

> A rich array of media selections engage students in multi-modal learning.

PERFORMANCE TASK
WRITING FOCUS
Write an Informative Speech. 390

SMALL-GROUP LEARNING

MEMOIR
from Blue Nines and Red Words
from Born on a Blue Day
Daniel Tammet. 401

MEDIA: INFOGRAPHIC
The Theory of Multiple
Intelligences Infographic
Howard Gardner. 413

POETRY COLLECTION
Retort
Paul Laurence Dunbar 418

from The People, Yes
Carl Sandburg 420

PERFORMANCE TASK
SPEAKING AND LISTENING FOCUS
Deliver a Multimedia Presentation . . . 426

xii

ESSENTIAL QUESTION: In what different ways can people be intelligent?

INDEPENDENT LEARNING

ARGUMENT
Is Personal Intelligence Important?
John D. Mayer

BLOG POST
Why Is Emotional Intelligence Important for Teens?
Divya Parekh

EXPLANATORY ESSAY
The More You Know, the Smarter You Are?
Jim Vega

EXPOSITORY NONFICTION
from The Future of the Mind
Michio Kaku

These selections can be accessed via the Interactive Student Edition.

PERFORMANCE-BASED ASSESSMENT PREP

Review Evidence for an an Informative Essay 433

PERFORMANCE-BASED ASSESSMENT

Informative Text:
Essay and Speech 434

UNIT REFLECTION

Reflect on the Unit 437

DIGITAL PERSPECTIVES

 Use the BouncePage app whenever you see "Scan for Multimedia" to access:

- Unit Introduction Videos
- Media Selections
- Modeling Videos
- Selection Audio Recordings

Additional digital resources can be found in:
- Interactive Student Edition
- *my*Perspectives+

Access multimedia resources directly from print by using your mobile or tablet device.

Digital resources, including editable worksheets, can be found in *my*Perspectives+.

xiii

T13

UNIT 5 Invention

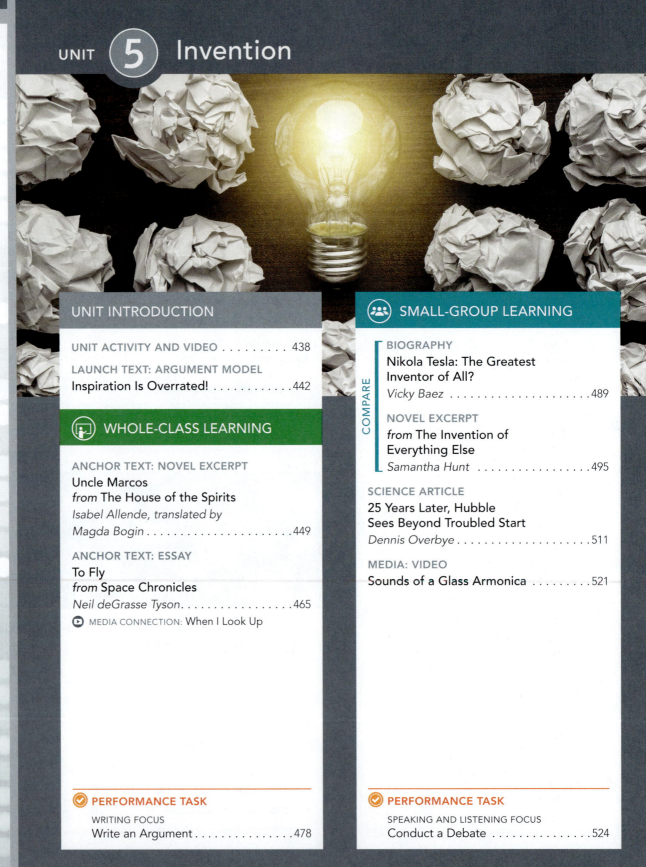

UNIT INTRODUCTION

UNIT ACTIVITY AND VIDEO 438

LAUNCH TEXT: ARGUMENT MODEL
Inspiration Is Overrated! 442

WHOLE-CLASS LEARNING

ANCHOR TEXT: NOVEL EXCERPT
Uncle Marcos
from The House of the Spirits
Isabel Allende, translated by
Magda Bogin 449

ANCHOR TEXT: ESSAY
To Fly
from Space Chronicles
Neil deGrasse Tyson 465
▶ MEDIA CONNECTION: When I Look Up

PERFORMANCE TASK
WRITING FOCUS
Write an Argument 478

SMALL-GROUP LEARNING

COMPARE

BIOGRAPHY
Nikola Tesla: The Greatest
Inventor of All?
Vicky Baez 489

NOVEL EXCERPT
from The Invention of
Everything Else
Samantha Hunt 495

SCIENCE ARTICLE
25 Years Later, Hubble
Sees Beyond Troubled Start
Dennis Overbye 511

MEDIA: VIDEO
Sounds of a Glass Armonica 521

PERFORMANCE TASK
SPEAKING AND LISTENING FOCUS
Conduct a Debate 524

xiv

ESSENTIAL QUESTION: Are inventions realized through inspiration or perspiration?

INDEPENDENT LEARNING

WEB ARTICLE
Ada Lovelace: A Science Legend
James Essinger

WEB ARTICLE
Fermented Cow Dung Air Freshener Wins Two Students Top Science Prize
Kimberley Mok

NEWS ARTICLE
Scientists Build Robot That Runs, Call It "Cheetah"
Rodrique Ngowi

NOVEL EXCERPT
from The Time Machine
H. G. Wells

MYTH
Icarus and Daedalus
retold by Josephine Preston Peabody

These selections can be accessed via the Interactive Student Edition.

PERFORMANCE-BASED ASSESSMENT PREP

Review Evidence for an Argument.................531

PERFORMANCE-BASED ASSESSMENT

Argument:
Essay and Speech..................532

UNIT REFLECTION

Reflect on the Unit................535

Unit Reflection allows students to revisit learning goals and review skills and content learned.

DIGITAL PERSPECTIVES

Use the BouncePage app whenever you see "Scan for Multimedia" to access:

- Unit Introduction Videos
- Media Selections
- Modeling Videos
- Selection Audio Recordings

Additional digital resources can be found in:
- Interactive Student Edition
- *my*Perspectives+

Student-Centered Learning

*my*Perspectives promotes student-centered learning through a unit organization that:

▶ gives students increasing responsibility for the learning process as they understand expectations, set goals, use self-assessment measures, and monitor and reflect on their learning.

▶ supports active learning in which students annotate texts, answer questions, pose questions of their own, and construct knowledge as they search for meaning.

▶ promotes social collaboration and interaction among learners in ways that strengthen positive interdependence and individual accountability.

▶ engages students in making choices in their learning and work they are producing.

▶ provides flexibility for teachers to manage resources to match learner needs.

UNIT INTRODUCTION

▶ An open-ended Essential Question is posed to stimulate thoughtful student inquiry into the richness of a topic.

▶ The Launch Text, unit opener video, and discussion board engage students by provoking and generating interest in the unit topic.

▶ Unit goals link directly to the demands of the Performance-Based Assessment.

WHOLE-CLASS LEARNING

▶ Teachers model, instruct, and support with anchor texts as the class broadens its perspective of the unit topic.

▶ Activities focus on making meaning, language development, and effective expression.

▶ Students develop and share their perspectives on the unit topic through writing in a targeted mode.

SMALL-GROUP LEARNING

▶ Students work collaboratively to broaden their perspectives on the unit topic.

▶ Teachers facilitate and encourage collaboration as students work in groups.

▶ Students develop presentations, participate in group discussions and debates, and share their learning with the class in an array of speaking and listening activities.

INDEPENDENT LEARNING

▶ Students select one online text to read independently.

▶ Teachers advise and encourage students as they implement close-reading strategies.

PERFORMANCE-BASED ASSESSMENT

Students are required to demonstrate their learning by pulling together the content knowledge, process skills, and learning habits they acquired, practiced, and engaged in throughout the unit.

Interactive Student Edition

Whether your students use the print or digital version, the Student Edition is interactive!

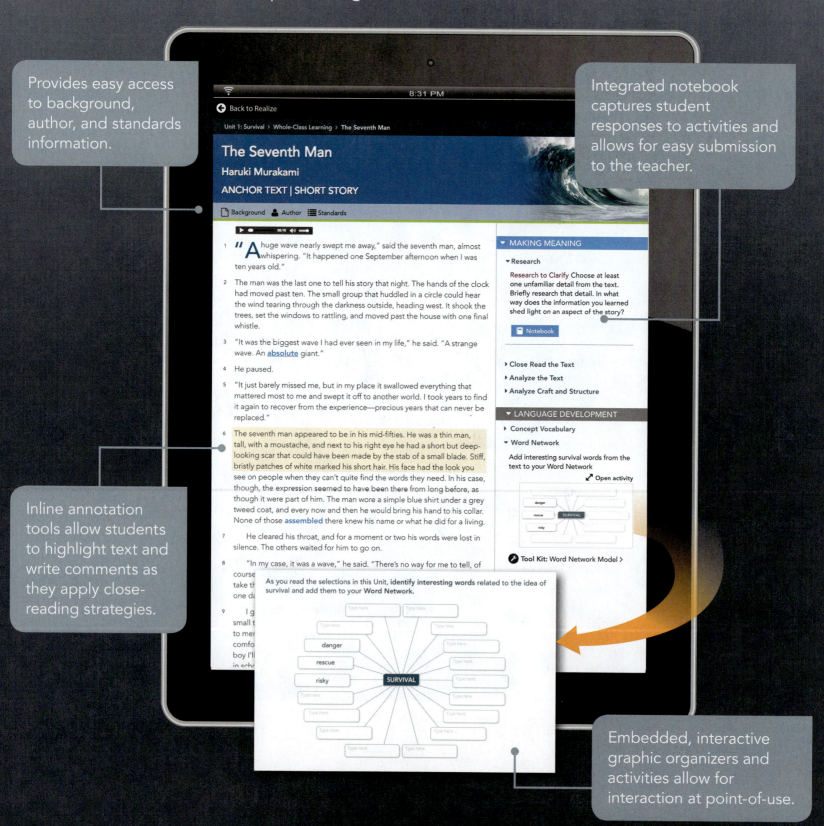

Provides easy access to background, author, and standards information.

Integrated notebook captures student responses to activities and allows for easy submission to the teacher.

Inline annotation tools allow students to highlight text and write comments as they apply close-reading strategies.

Embedded, interactive graphic organizers and activities allow for interaction at point-of-use.

Download the Pearson BouncePages App to access audio, video, and multimedia selections through your mobile device!

A write-in Student Edition allows students to annotate the text and respond to questions.

Close-Reading Routine

myPerspectives motivates students to read a text thoughtfully, apply strategies as they read, and critically examine the text.

Students apply first-read routines as they independently read and annotate texts.

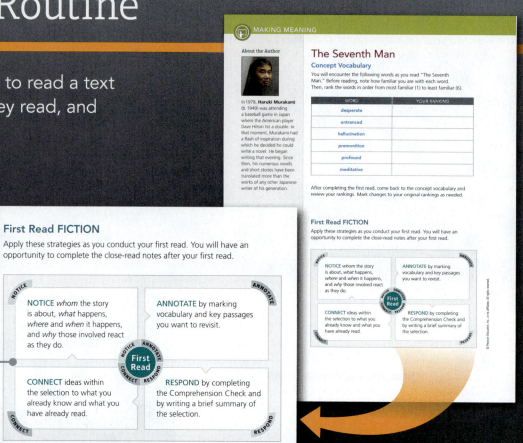

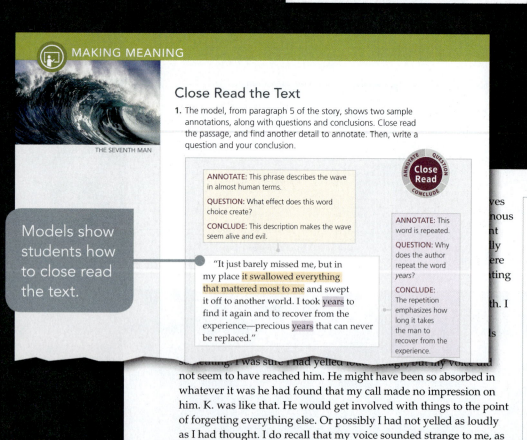

Students close read complex and rich text passages, studying structures, diction, and other elements of author's craft.

Models show students how to close read the text.

Closer Look notes, found only in the Teacher's Edition, provide additional close-reading opportunities.

Digital Annotation Highlights focus on passages in the Interactive Teacher's Edition.

TEACHING

🗨 CLOSER LOOK

Analyze Character

Students may have marked paragraph 10 during their first read. Use this paragraph to help students understand the seventh man's friendship with K.

ANNOTATE: Have students mark details in the paragraph that describe K.'s appearance and personality.

QUESTION: What overall impression does the author create of K.? How does the author characterize the relationship between K. and the seventh man?

Possible response: K. is an artistic, sensitive boy who is often picked on because he is physically different from most boys his age. His speech impediment and difficulty with academics lead most people to think something is wrong with him. K. and the seventh man are best friends. The seventh man feels protective of K., and often stands up for him when he is picked on by others.

CONCLUDE: How does the author's characterization of K. and his friendship with the seventh man help you understand the impact of K.'s death?

Possible response: The seventh man viewed himself as K.'s protector. When K. was lost to the wave the seventh man lost his best friend, and he blamed himself for failing to protect K., carrying that guilt with him for most of his life.

Remind students that there are two types of characterization. In **direct characterization**, a character's traits. **ion**, an author aracter by describing e, does, and says, as rs react to him or o draw conclusions this indirect looks like, feels like, or sounds like. You may wish to model the close read using the following think-aloud format. Possible responses to questions on the student page are included. You may also want to print copies of the Close-Read Guide for students to use.

ANNOTATE: As I read paragraph 2, I notice and highlight the details *the hands of the clock had moved past ten* and *the wind tearing through the darkness outside*. These details suggest to me that the story is set at night during a storm.

● Hide Annotation Highlights

NOTES

Unit 2: Survival > Whole-Class Learning: The Seventh Man

▶ 36:18 🔊 ━━━

1 "A huge wave nearly swept me away," said the seventh man, almost whispering. "It happened one September afternoon when I was ten years old."

2 The men was the last one to tell his story that night. *The hands of the clock had moved past ten*. The small group that huddled in a circle could hear *the wind tearing through the darkness outside*, heading west. It shook the trees, set the windows to rattling, and moved past the house with one final whistle.

3 "It was the biggest wave I had ever seen in my life," he said. "A strange wave. An absolute giant."

4 He paused.

5 "It just barely missed me, but in my place it swallowed everything that mattered most to me and swept it off to another world. I took years to find it again and to recover from the experience—precious years that can never be replaced."

6 The seventh man appeared to be in his mid-fifties. He was a thin man, tall, with a moustache, and next to his right eye he had a short but deep-looking scar that could have been made by the stab of a small blade. Stiff, bristly patches of white marked his short

Building Literacy

For each selection, students **Make Meaning** through first- and close-read routines and by analyzing author's craft and structure. Students also complete **Language Development** activities with concept vocabulary and conventions practice tasks. **Effective Expression** activities provide students with opportunities to share their learning through written and oral projects.

MAKING MEANING
Students make meaning of the text through close reading and analysis.

LANGUAGE DEVELOPMENT
Concept Vocabulary words are taught in conjunction with each text. The selected words enable students to study words within meaningful clusters.

Assessments to Inform Instruction

Assessments can be administered in print and/or online.

Pearson Realize™ provides powerful data reporting.

YEAR-LONG ASSESSMENT

Beginning-of-Year Test
- Tests all standards that will be taught in the school year.
- Allows you to use test data to plan which standards need focus.

Mid-Year Test
- Tests mastery of standards taught in the first half of the year.
- Provides an opportunity to remediate; if administered online, remediation is assigned automatically.

End-of-Year Test
- Allows you to use results to determine mastery of standards, place students in classes for the following school year, and to capture final assessment data.

UNIT-LEVEL ASSESSMENT

Selection Activities
- Instructional activities can be used to assess students' grasp of critical concepts.

Formative Assessments
- Selection activities can be used as formative checks.
- Notes in the Teacher's Edition offer suggestions for reteaching.

Selection Tests
- Test items track student progress toward mastering standards taught with the selection.

Performance Tasks
- Each unit includes both a writing and a speaking and listening performance task.
- Performance Tasks prepare students for success on the end-of-unit Performance-Based Assessment.

Unit Tests
- Students apply standards taught in the unit with new texts.
- These tests provide an opportunity to remediate; if administered online, remediation is assigned automatically.

Performance-Based Assessments
- All unit activities are backwards-mapped to the end-of-unit Performance-Based Assessment.
- Students use their notes, knowledge, and skills learned to complete a project.

Technology-enhanced items allow students to experience next-generation assessment formats.

Personalize for Learning

The Teacher's Edition provides support before, during, and after each selection to help you personalize learning for your students.

> A continuous improvement loop is built in to help teachers perform formative assessment and remediation.

> A full range of reading supports is provided for each text, based on text complexity rubrics.

PERSONALIZE FOR LEARNING WHOL...

Reading Support

Text Complexity Rubric: The Seventh Man

Quantitative Measures

Lexile: 910   Text Length: 5,860 words

Qualitative Measures

Knowledge Demands ①—❷—③—④—⑤	Life experience demands: The situations may be unfamiliar to some readers (experiencing a typhoon, tragedy of losing someone in a natural disaster), but the situations and emotions are clearly explained.
Structure ①—❷—③—④—⑤	Use of flash-back, flash-forward (transitions from narration in third person and the seventh man's story told in first person)
Language Conventionality and Clarity ①—②—❸—④—⑤	Figurative language; complex descriptions
Levels of Meaning/Purpose ①—②—❸—④—⑤	Multiple levels of meaning (events are described that also signify emotions of guilt or of self-forgiveness); concepts and meanings are mostly explained and easy to grasp.

DECIDE AND PLAN

English Language Support
Provide English Learners with support for context and vocabulary as they read the selection. PI.8; PI.12

Knowledge Demands Tell students that this short story is about an event that occurred during a typhoon. They should expect to see language that describes weather and the sea. (high tide, low tide,...)

Language Conventiality and Clarity Students may find the use of sensory language difficult to grasp. Explain that the author often uses words in a figurative way to create feelings or sensations. Figurative language is language that is used imaginatively rather than literally. Such expressions can be difficult for second-language learners.

Strategic Support
Provide students with strategic support to ensure that they can successfully read the text.

Knowledge Demands Use the background information to discuss typhoons. Determine students' prior knowledge and experience with natural disasters. Provide additional background if needed.

Structure Discuss what it means to flash-back or flash-forward in a text. Point out that a story might switch back and forth to different time periods. If students continue to have difficulty with the time sequence, point out clues to transitions between past and present; for example, sentences that say that the man is telling a story, or use of first and third person. When students reread, have them note each transition from past to present.

Challenge
Provide students who need to be challenged with ideas for how they can go beyond a simple interpretation of the text.

Text Analysis For students that grasp the time transitions, have them identify the use of first person when the seventh man is speaking, and descriptions in third person when the story moves to the present.

Written Response Ask students to speculate on what might have happened if the seventh man had made different choices in his life. Have them analyze each choice he made and determine how his life might have differed if he had chosen differently. Have them rewrite the story with reflection the choices.

TEACH

Read and Respond
Have the class do their first read of the selection. Then have them complete their close read. Finally, work with them on the Making Meaning, Language Development, and Effective Expression activities.

> Text complexity rubrics provide targeted suggestions for learner levels, including English Language supports that are based on the demands of the text.

Standards Support Through T...

IDENTIFY NEEDS
Analyze results of the Beginning-of-Year Assessment, focusing on the items relating to Unit 2. Also take into consideration student performance to this point and your observations of where particular students struggle.

- If students have perfo... scaffolds before assig...
- If students have done... keep progressing and...
- Use the Selection Res... students continually i...

Instructional Standa...

	Catching U...
Reading	Review con... students to... understand... have differe... different co... You may wi... the Order o... to help stud... the basic se... narrative.
Writing	You may wi... the Reteach... Anecdotes... students un... anecdote ca... an argumen...
Speaking and Listening	You may wi... the Reteach... worksheet... help studen... to plan and... excerpt.
Language	You may wi... the Clauses... help studen... function of... Review con... students to... understand... have differe... different co...

ANALYZE AND REVISE
- Analyze student work for evidence of student learning.
- Identify whether or not students have met the expectations in the standards.
- Identify implications for future instruction.

TEACH
Implement the planned lesson, and gather evidence of student learning.

PERSONALIZE FOR LEARNING

Challenge
Encourage interested students to expand the Research to Explore activity by learning about the motto of other branches of the U.S. military, including the Air Force, Army, Coast Guard, and Navy, in addition to the Marines. Students can also choose one branch and present their results in a poster.

PERSONALIZE FOR LEARNING

English Language Support
Idioms Explain to students that *eye of the storm* in paragraph 15 is an idiomatic expression—the words used are not meant literally. If students struggle to understand idioms, encourage them to look for context clues. Instruct students to keep reading to get clues about the meaning of this expression (*No such "eye" existed, of course: we were just in that momentary quiet spot at the center of the pool of whirling air*). Make sure students understand that eye of the storm means "a calm in the middle of a turbulent situation." **ALL LEVELS**

English Language Support notes provide support for skills and concepts such as idioms, figurative language, and multiple-meaning words.

Practical and easy-to-implement supports ensure that all students' needs are met as they practice and apply standards with each text.

Customize and Enrich

DIGITAL PERSPECTIVES

Enriching the Text In 2013, the environmental scientist Tim Jarvis re-created Shackleton's voyage from Elephant Island to South Georgia in a replica of the *James Caird*. Jarvis and his crew used the same clothing, food, and navigational equipment that Shackleton had. The documentary *Shackleton: Death or Glory* chronicles the journey. Find a clip from the documentary online and show students (after previewing it yourself). Then, have students write a paragraph explaining how the clip enhances their understanding of the selection "The Voyage of the *James Caird*." For example, students might gain a better understanding of the size of the boat and the harsh conditions Shackleton and his men endured.

Digital Perspectives offers suggestions for using digital resources to strengthen concepts being taught.

AUTHOR'S PERSPECTIVE Jim Cummins

Importance of Background Knowledge It is important for all students, and especially English Language Learners, to tap into background knowledge when they read a text. It is incumbent on teachers to help students access this knowledge and integrate it with new textual information. One way to do this is to encourage groups to share what they know about the topic of the text before they begin reading. For example, on a superficial level, some students may have prior knowledge about sailing, which can help to scaffold understanding of "The Voyage of the *James Caird*." On a deeper level, more students may be able to relate to the idea of forcing oneself to go to extremes or taking risks in order to help others. After students have completed their first read, have them discuss how their background knowledge helped them understand the text.

Author's Perspective notes offer expert insights on topics, including incorporating first-language knowledge, building background knowledge, and academic and conversational vocabulary.

FORMATIVE ASSESSMENT

Analyze Craft and Structure

- **If** students fail to identify the frame, **then** have them look for clues that indicate the point of view. For example, the person narrating the frame may not be involved in the interior story.
- **If** students are unable to identify the point of view, **then** remind them to pay close attention to pronoun usage.

A formative assessment opportunity with recommended prescriptive activities is provided with each skill lesson.

T27

English Language Support

myPerspectives provides supports for English Language Learners at the Emerging, Expanding, and Bridging levels. Various resources can be used flexibly in print and online to meet your students' individual needs.

Selection audio can be found in the Interactive Student Edition and via BouncePages in the print Student Edition.

Glossary terms are defined at point of use and include English and Spanish audio.

Concept and Academic Vocabulary words are defined in Spanish.

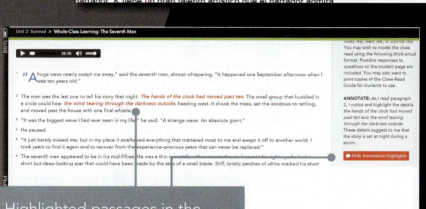

Online selection summaries with both English and Spanish audio and text are assignable.

Highlighted passages in the Interactive Teacher's Edition focus on a key element of the text type or illustrate how language choices develop cohesion and link ideas, events, and concepts within a text.

Printable English Language Support Lessons provide additional instructional opportunities.

ENGLISH LANGUAGE SUPPORT LESSON

The Seventh Man
Analyze Craft and Structure

Author's Choices: Order of Events
Objective Students will learn to describe a sequence of events using a variety of words and sentence structures.

JUMP START
Tell students to listen as you describe the following order of events. *My friend Julio came to my house. Then we walked to the pizza shop. Then we played soccer. Then we went home.*

Ask students for their evaluation of the sentences. Point out that your description used the word *then* many times to describe sequence. Ask: *How can we put more variety into our language when we're talking about sequence of events?*

TEACH
Display this sample sentence:
First, the sky began to change. Next, the wind began to howl and the rain began to beat against the house.

Ask students which words indicate the order of events.

Next, display the second sample sentence. Point out that it's a variation of the first sentence.
After the sky began to change, the wind began to howl and the rain began to beat against the house.

Ask students which word tells about the order of events.

Introduce these other words that show time order: *last, afterward, subsequently, when, before, before long, as soon as, later, finally*.

To challenge students, have them rewrite the sentence one more time to show a different sequence.

Possible response: *When the sky began to change, the wind began to howl and the rain began to beat against the house.*

Remind students that when they read, it's important to pay attention to the order of events. The order of events presented in the story may not be the order in which the events actually happened. Stories can flash back and flash forward.

For example, read aloud the following events from "The Seventh Man."

a. The Seventh Man is telling his story.

b. K. was swept off by a wave.

c. The Seventh Man got past his guilt.

Ask students in what order the events are told in the story. (*a, b, c*) Then ask in what order the events happened. (*b, c, a*) Point out that the events are told in that order because "The Seventh Man" is a frame story—a story within a story. In "The Seventh Man," the narrator is telling his story, which occurred at an

Personalize for Teaching

Lesson planning is easy and efficient with clearly labeled support at point of use in the Teacher's Edition.

A trade book alignment with suggestions for integrating longer works within the unit is provided. Lesson plans for recommended titles are available online.

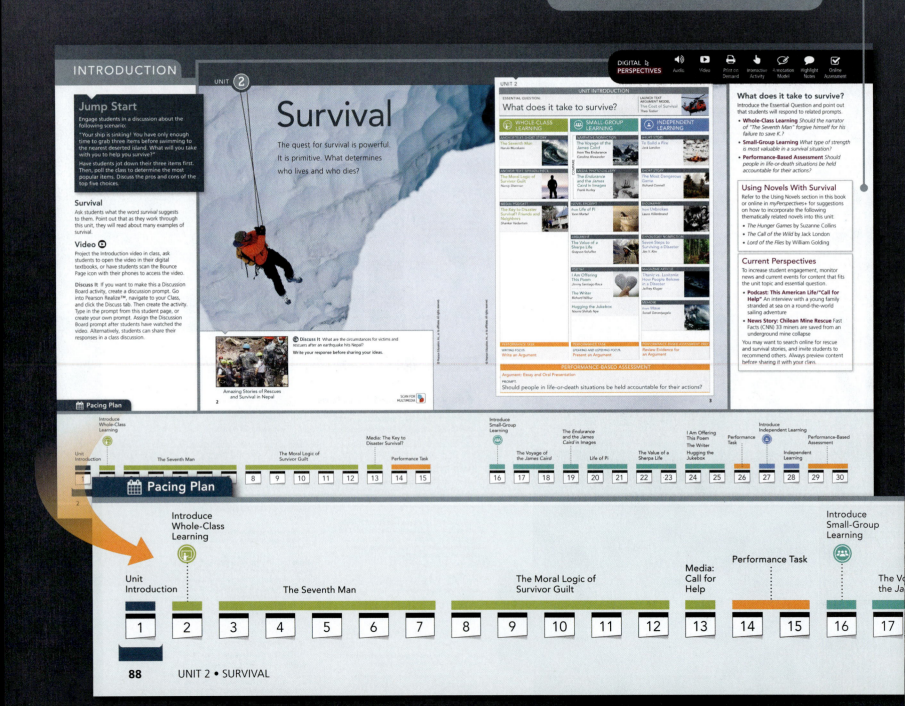

PLANNING WHOLE-CLASS LEARNING • THE SEVENTH MAN

The Seventh Man

AUDIO SUMMARIES
Audio summaries of "The Seventh Man" are available in both English and Spanish and can be assigned to students in Pearson Realize™. Assigning these summaries prior to reading the selection may help students build additional background knowledge and set a context for their first read.

Summary
"The Seventh Man" begins on a stormy night in a house where a group of people is sharing stories. The unnamed seventh man tells his story last and describes a huge wave that changed his life forever. He explains that he grew up in a seaside town in Japan, where he and his best friend, described only as K., were as close as brothers. A typhoon strikes and when the eye of the storm passes over, the seventh man's father allows the boys to go outside. They go down to the beach to play. When the tsunami strikes, the seventh man runs for his life, leaving K. behind. He struggles with guilt for into his adult life. Forty years later, the seventh man makes an important realization.

Insight
The choices survivors make are not always easy or clear. Reading "The Seventh Man" will help students begin their reflections on how complicated survival can be. Although a survivor may have escaped with his or her life, that life may never be the same.

Some students may find "The Seventh Man" disturbing. The realization that a childhood decision might color someone's whole life is sobering and may require support.

> Planning pages provide essential information, including selection summaries, insights, and links to the Essential Question.

> Digital Perspectives identifies online resources.

DIGITAL PERSPECTIVES Audio   Video   Print on Demand   Interactive Activity   Annotation Model   Highlight Notes   Online Assessment

LESSON RESOURCES

	Making Meaning	Language Development	Effective Expression
Lesson	First Read Close Read Analyze the Text Analyze Craft and Structure	Concept Vocabulary Word Study Conventions	Writing to Sources Speaking and Listening
Instructional Standards	RL.9–10.4 RL.9–10.5 PI.5 PI.6a	L.9–10.1b L.9–10.4a PII.3, PII.4, PII.5	W.9–10.3.a–e SL.9–10.4.b PI.1, PI.5, PI.11
STUDENT RESOURCES	Search for these resources in myPerspectives Digital Student Edition or myPerspectives+		
Selection Resources	Audio Selection Student Modeling Video Close-Read Guide First-Read Guide	Word Network	Evidence Log
TEACHER RESOURCES	Search for these resources in myPerspectives Digital Teacher's Edition or myPerspectives+		
Selection Resources	Annotation Model Audio Summaries Additional English Language Support Analyze Text Frame Story Graphic Organizer Order of Events	Dependent Clause Tree Concept Vocabulary Suffixes Clauses	Anecdotes Recitations
Reteach and Practice	Analyze the Text Frame Story	Concept Vocabulary Suffixes Clauses	Anecdotes Recitations
Assessment			Selection Test
My Resources*	• Map of Japan • _____ • _____	• Sentence Strips • Tree diagram for dependent clauses • _____	• _____ • _____ • _____

* These resources are suggested at point of use in this lesson.

> Lesson Resources provides at-a-glance listings of standards, student-facing resources, on-level and reteaching support, and even a place for you to write in your own resources!

Whole-Class Learning 98B

19	20	21	22	23	24	25	26	27	28	29	30
The *Endurance* and the *James Caird* in Images	from *Life of Pi*	The Value of a Sherpa Life		I Am Offering This Poem The Writer Hugging the Jukebox		Performance Task	Introduce Independent Learning		Performance-Based Assessment	

Independent Learning

> A Pacing Plan provides recommended pacing.

Unit Introduction **89**

Resources for Flexibility

myPerspectives+ includes hundreds of additional teacher resources you can use to customize your lessons. Interactive lessons, grammar tutorials, digital novels, and more are student-facing to allow students to work independently.

- interactive lessons
- grammar tutorials
- graphic organizers and rubrics
- trade book lesson plans
- digital novels

- Digital novels, including classics such as *Great Expectations, Pride and Prejudice, The Adventures of Tom Sawyer, Alice in Wonderland, The Scarlet Letter,* and *Romeo and Juliet*

- Novel lesson plans for over 100 titles, including those aligned to each unit

- Interactive lessons to help students develop critical writing, speaking, and listening skills

- High-interest readings and resources for struggling students

- Engaging grammar and academic vocabulary tutorials

- Writing Whiteboard Activities for an interactive and engaging classroom experience

- Editable grammar worksheets for extra practice with this crucial skill

- Generic graphic organizers and rubrics that can be used with any lesson

Pearson Realize™ is your online destination for digital resources, assessments, and data. Flexible classroom management tools give you an amazing amount of freedom and control.

Easily manage your classes and data.

YOU HAVE THE POWER
Customize the program to make it your own.

- Rearrange content
- Upload your own content
- Add links to online media
- Edit resources and assessment

All program-specific resources, flexible agnostic resources, and assessments are available in one location for easy lesson planning and presentation.

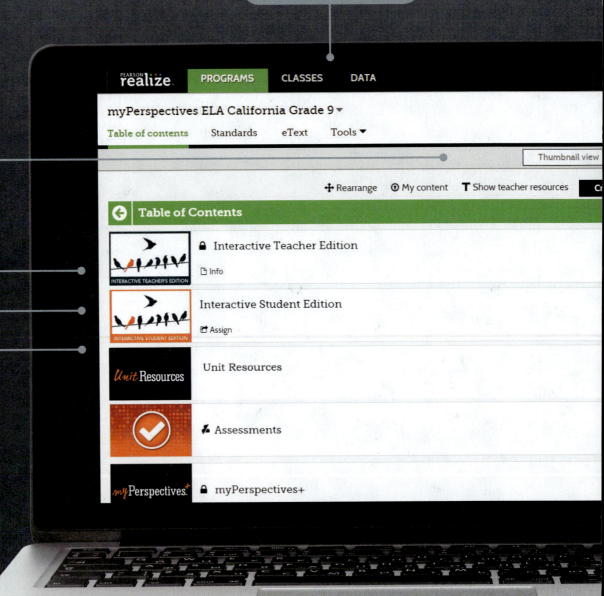

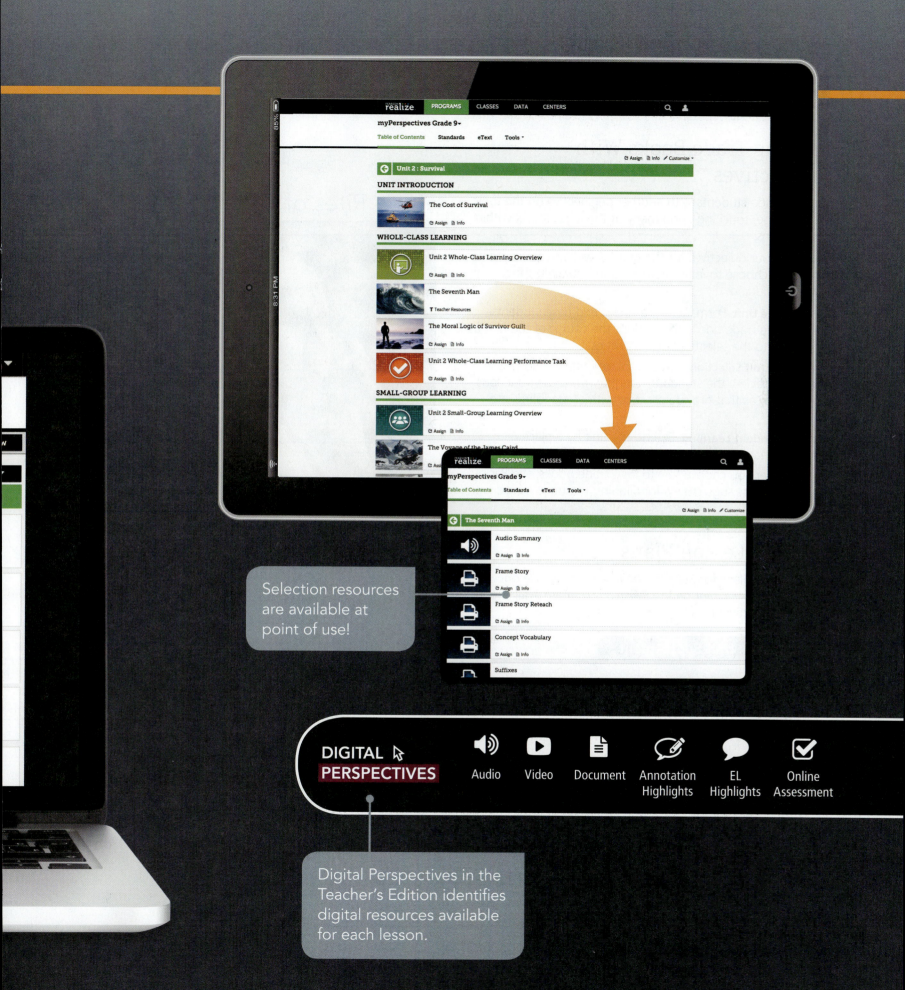

TEACHING WITH TRADE BOOKS

UNIT 1: Rites of Passage

Integrating Trade Books With *myPerspectives*

These titles provide students with another perspective on the topic of rites of passage, touching upon many of the ideas found within the unit selections.

Depending on your objectives for the unit, as well as your students' needs, you may choose to integrate the trade book into the unit in several ways, including:

- **Supplement the Unit** Form literature circles and have students read one of the trade books throughout the course of the unit as a supplement to the selections and activities.
- **Substitute for Unit Selections** If you replace unit selections with a trade book, review the standards taught with those selections. Teacher Resources that provide practice with all standards are available.
- **Extend Independent Learning** Extend the unit by replacing independent reading selections with one of these trade books.
- **Pacing** However you choose to integrate trade books, the Pacing Guide below offers suggestions for aligning the trade books with this unit.

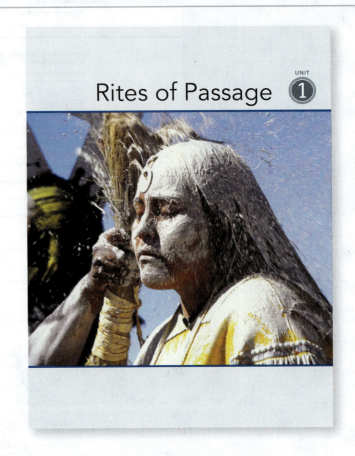

Trade Book Lesson Plans

Trade book lesson plans for *Rules of the Road, The House on Mango Street,* and *All Quiet on the Western Front* are available online in *myPerspectives+*.

Pacing Guide: Unit Supplement

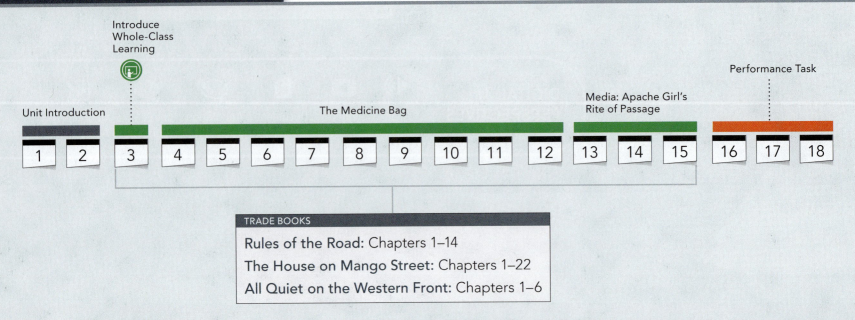

TRADE BOOKS

Rules of the Road: Chapters 1–14

The House on Mango Street: Chapters 1–22

All Quiet on the Western Front: Chapters 1–6

Suggested Trade Books

Rules of the Road
Joan Bauer
Lexile: 850
Sixteen-year-old Jenna goes on a road trip with her elderly boss, Mrs. Gladstone, to save the store where they work from a takeover.

Connection to Essential Question
During cross-country drive, Jenna gets a front-row seat to the workings of business and family, and takes a closer look at her own life and experiences. Along the way, she deals with divorce, loneliness, and her parent's troubles, but learns to rely on herself as readers explore the Essential Question: *What are some milestones on the path to growing up?*

The House on Mango Street
Sandra Cisneros
Lexile: 870
Esperanza aspires to move out of the poor neighborhood where her family lives.

Connection to Essential Question
Esperanza sees a new house as a key symbol of a new life, a there are many steps along the way to her independence. Particularly important are her insights into what she wants from relationships and her final vow to return to the people she leaves behind. Cisneros's text offer readers unique insights into the Essential Question: *What are some milestones on the path to growing up?*

All Quiet on the Western Front
Erich Maria Remarque
Lexile: 830
A young man and his friends enlist in the army. They face more than they expected as they fight the battles of World War I.

Connection to Essential Question
This classic novel provides a pessimistic answer to the Essential Question: *What are some milestones on the path to growing up?* Paul and his comrades become thoroughly disillusioned with the notion of war's glory, and they come to accept the role of random chance in their lives.

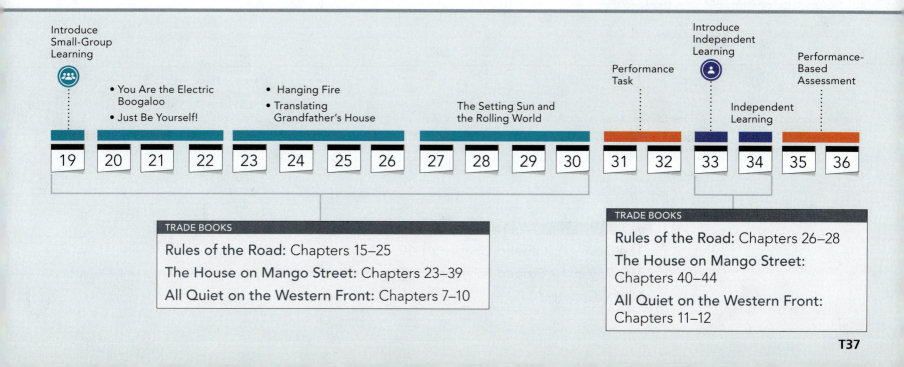

TEACHING WITH TRADE BOOKS

UNIT 2: The Holocaust

Integrating Trade Books With *myPerspectives*

These titles provide students with another perspective on the topic of the Holocaust, touching upon many of the ideas found within the unit selections.

Depending on your objectives for the unit, as well as your students' needs, you may choose to integrate the trade book into the unit in several ways, including:

- **Supplement the Unit** Form literature circles and have students read one of the trade books throughout the course of the unit as a supplement to the selections and activities.
- **Substitute for Unit Selections** If you replace unit selections with a trade book, review the standards taught with those selections. Teacher Resources that provide practice with all standards are available.
- **Extend Independent Learning** Extend the unit by replacing independent reading selections with one of these trade books.
- **Pacing** However you choose to integrate trade books, the Pacing Guide below offers suggestions for aligning the trade books with this unit.

Trade Book Lesson Plans

Trade book lesson plans for *The Devil's Arithmetic, The Boy in the Striped Pajamas,* and *Night* are available online in *myPerspectives+*.

📅 Pacing Guide: Unit Supplement

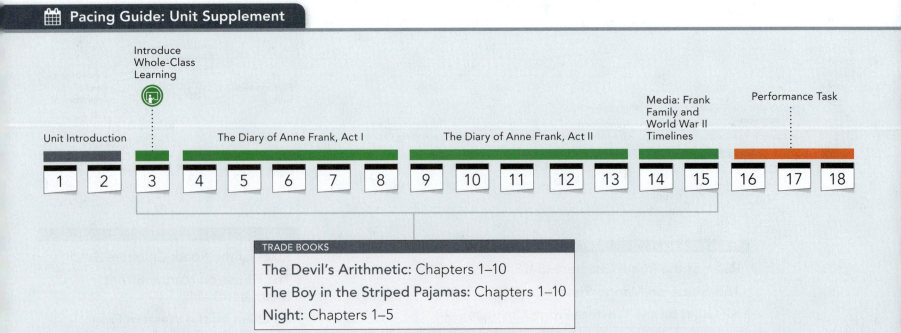

TRADE BOOKS

The Devil's Arithmetic: Chapters 1–10
The Boy in the Striped Pajamas: Chapters 1–10
Night: Chapters 1–5

Suggested Trade Books

The Devil's Arithmetic
Jane Yolen
Lexile: 730

Hannah, a young girl who doesn't want to study the Holocaust, is swept back in time from the present to 1942 Poland.

Connection to Essential Question
Reliving the worst experiences her family suffered gives Hannah a new belief in heroism and a stronger appreciation of what she has. Through the use of a fantastical element, time travel, the book asks the Essential Question: *How do we remember the past?*

The Boy in the Striped Pajamas
John Boyne
Lexile: 1080

In this tragic story, two boys meet at the fence of a concentration camp—one inside, one out.

Connection to Essential Question
This fable emphasizes that any of us can be trapped in a terrible situation. The tragedy provides powerful insight into the Essential Question: *How do we remember the past?*

Night
Elie Wiesel
Lexile: 570

A devastating memoir, *Night* is the documentation of Wiesel's time in a concentration camp and his father's fate.

Connection to Essential Question
Regarding such immense tragedy, Wiesel emphasizes how suddenly life changed. The text shows how the situation in the camp was an utter reversal from the values that had previously governed life, revealing the difficulty in answering the Essential Question: *How do we remember the past?*

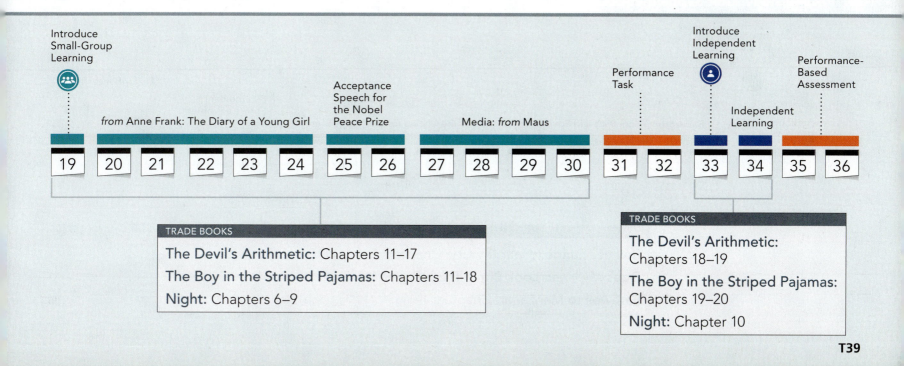

TEACHING WITH TRADE BOOKS

UNIT 3: What Matters

Integrating Trade Books With *myPerspectives*

These titles provide students with another perspective on the topic of what matters in life, touching upon many of the ideas found within the unit selections.

Depending on your objectives for the unit, as well as your students' needs, you may choose to integrate the trade book into the unit in several ways, including:

- **Supplement the Unit** Form literature circles and have students read one of the trade books throughout the course of the unit as a supplement to the selections and activities.
- **Substitute for Unit Selections** If you replace unit selections with a trade book, review the standards taught with those selections. Teacher Resources that provide practice with all standards are available.
- **Extend Independent Learning** Extend the unit by replacing independent reading selections with one of these trade books.
- **Pacing** However you choose to integrate trade books, the Pacing Guide below offers suggestions for aligning the trade books with this unit.

Trade Book Lesson Plans

Trade book lesson plans for *Roll of Thunder, Hear My Cry*; *Does My Head Look Big in This?*; and *Farewell to Manzanar* are available online in *myPerspectives+*.

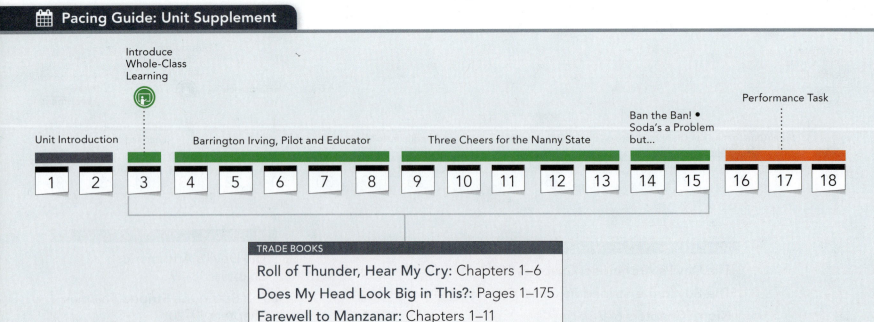

Pacing Guide: Unit Supplement

TRADE BOOKS

Roll of Thunder, Hear My Cry: Chapters 1–6
Does My Head Look Big in This?: Pages 1–175
Farewell to Manzanar: Chapters 1–11

Suggested Trade Books

Roll of Thunder, Hear My Cry
Mildred Taylor
Lexile: 920
A family deals with racism during the Great Depression.

Connection to Essential Question
Papa leads the boycott of a store owned by racists, and sets a fire that prevents a lynching by distracting those involved. In each of these cases, he offers his answer to the Essential Question: *When is it right to take a stand?*

Does My Head Look Big in This?
Randa Abdel-Fattah
Lexile: 850
A teenage Muslim girl decides to start wearing a hijab regularly.

Connection to Essential Question
Amal's decision has quick and major implications. She stands up for her beliefs, refusing to kiss a boy who's interested in her because she doesn't want to do such things before she's married. Her experiences provide the Essential Question: *When is it right to take a stand?*

Farewell to Manzanar
Jeanne Wakatsuki Houston
Lexile: 1010
During World War II, the American government imprisons Jeanne and her family for their Japanese ancestry.

Connection to Essential Question
In this true story, the people in an internment camp hold a wide range of beliefs. Many of them take risks to uphold their ideals, and as a result, they come into conflict with each other. This account illustrates the complexity of the Essential Question: *When is it right to take a stand?*

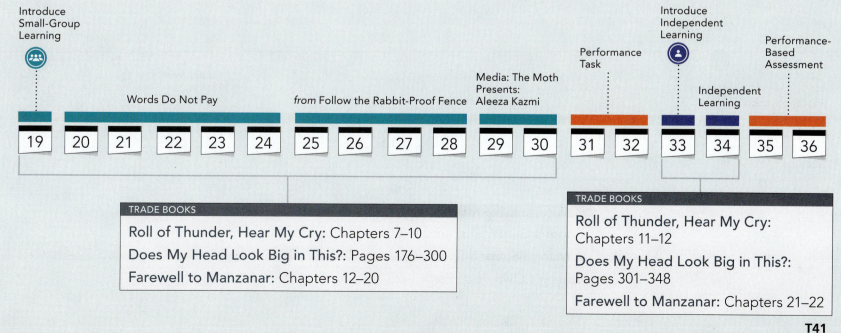

TRADE BOOKS

Roll of Thunder, Hear My Cry: Chapters 7–10

Does My Head Look Big in This?: Pages 176–300

Farewell to Manzanar: Chapters 12–20

TRADE BOOKS

Roll of Thunder, Hear My Cry: Chapters 11–12

Does My Head Look Big in This?: Pages 301–348

Farewell to Manzanar: Chapters 21–22

TEACHING WITH TRADE BOOKS

UNIT 4: Human Intelligence

Integrating Trade Books With *myPerspectives*

These titles provide students with another perspective on the topic of human intelligence, touching upon many of the ideas found within the unit selections.

Depending on your objectives for the unit, as well as your students' needs, you may choose to integrate the trade book into the unit in several ways, including:

- **Supplement the Unit** Form literature circles and have students read one of the trade books throughout the course of the unit as a supplement to the selections and activities.
- **Substitute for Unit Selections** If you replace unit selections with a trade book, review the standards taught with those selections. Teacher Resources that provide practice with all standards are available.
- **Extend Independent Learning** Extend the unit by replacing independent reading selections with one of these trade books.
- **Pacing** However you choose to integrate trade books, the Pacing Guide below offers suggestions for aligning the trade books with this unit.

Trade Book Lesson Plans

Trade book lesson plans for *Ender's Game*, *A Mango-Shaped Space*, and *Queen's Own Fool* are available online in *my*Perspectives+.

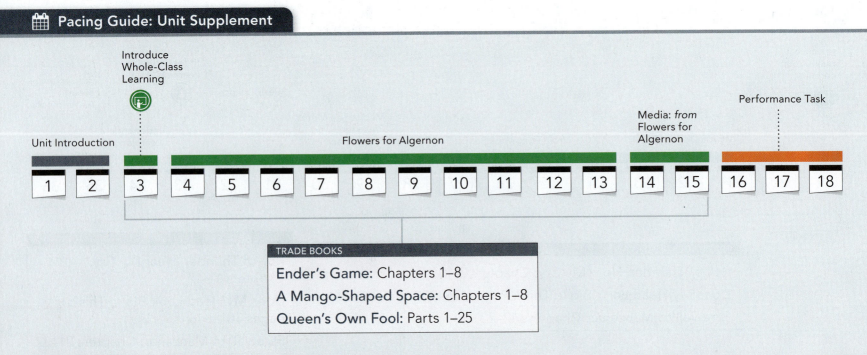

Pacing Guide: Unit Supplement

TRADE BOOKS

Ender's Game: Chapters 1–8
A Mango-Shaped Space: Chapters 1–8
Queen's Own Fool: Parts 1–25

Suggested Trade Books

Ender's Game
Orson Scott Card
Lexile: 780

Recruited into a military school in a futuristic world, Ender Wiggin trains to prevent alien invasion and save the world.

Connection to Essential Question
Ender is a tactical genius but he fails to see how he has been manipulated. This, in addition to his relationship with the other students provides a compelling look into the Essential Question: *In what different ways can people be intelligent?*

A Mango-Shaped Space
Wendy Mass
Lexile: 770

Mia has a condition called synesthesia, in which sounds and numbers seem to have color to her.

Connection to Essential Question
Mia's synesthesia initially causes her trouble with learning math and Spanish. However, it also seems to heighten her senses and helps her enjoy life. By revealing a unique form of intelligence, the novel answers the Essential Question: *In what different ways can people be intelligent?*

Queen's Own Fool
Jane Yolen
Lexile: 740

Nicola, a court jester, helps Mary Queen of Scots during her troubled reign.

Connection to Essential Question
Nicola's nimble mind and excellent emotional intelligence help her comfort Mary and outwit scheming members of the court. Her wit, despite being a "fool," sheds light on the Essential Question: *In what different ways can people be intelligent?*

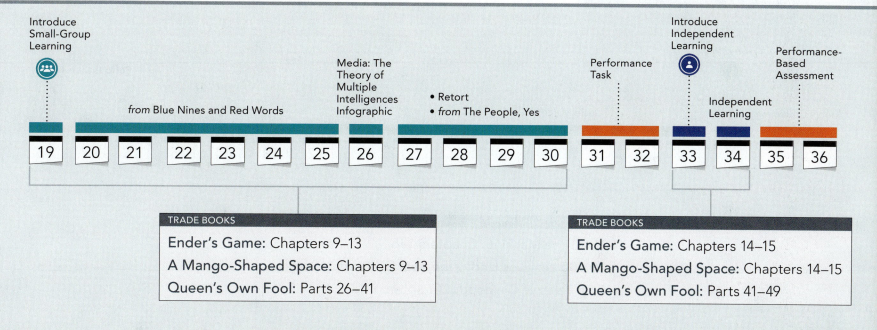

TEACHING WITH TRADE BOOKS

UNIT 5: Invention

Integrating Trade Books With *myPerspectives*

These titles provide students with another perspective on the topic of invention, touching upon many of the ideas found within the unit selections.

Depending on your objectives for the unit, as well as your students' needs, you may choose to integrate the trade book into the unit in several ways, including:

- **Supplement the Unit** Form literature circles and have students read one of the trade books throughout the course of the unit as a supplement to the selections and activities.
- **Substitute for Unit Selections** If you replace unit selections with a trade book, review the standards taught with those selections. Teacher Resources that provide practice with all standards are available.
- **Extend Independent Learning** Extend the unit by replacing independent reading selections with one of these trade books.
- **Pacing** However you choose to integrate trade books, the Pacing Guide below offers suggestions for aligning the trade books with this unit.

Trade Book Lesson Plans

Trade book lesson plans for *The Time Machine*, *20,000 Leagues Under the Sea*, and *Boy: Tales of Childhood* are available online in *my*Perspectives+.

📅 Pacing Guide: Unit Supplement

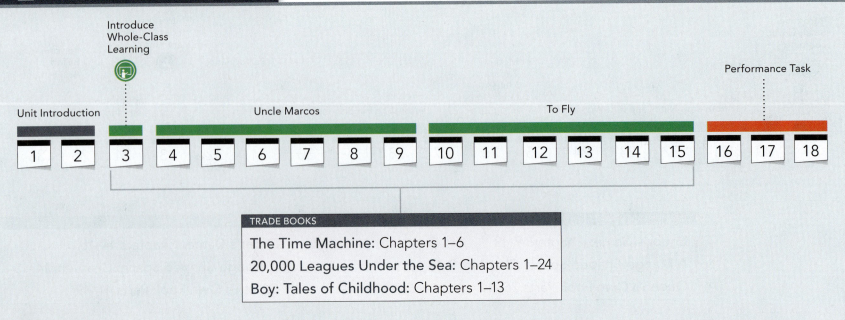

TRADE BOOKS

The Time Machine: Chapters 1–6

20,000 Leagues Under the Sea: Chapters 1–24

Boy: Tales of Childhood: Chapters 1–13

Suggested Trade Books

The Time Machine
H.G. Wells
Lexile: 1070

A man invents a time machine and takes it into the far future, where he encounters a superficially heavenly but truly horrifying civilization.

Connection to Essential Question
The machine's development takes time and runs into a few holdups. There are plenty of hidden steps between the Time Traveler's insights into the fourth dimension and the completion of the machine. The process suggests an answer to the Essential Question: *Are inventions realized through inspiration or perspiration?*

20,000 Leagues Under the Sea
Jules Verne
Lexile: 860

In the late 1800s, a professor is captured by a man who has built an incredibly advanced submarine. Together, they embark on adventures across the ocean.

Connection to Essential Question
During its planning, the *Nautilus's* special capabilities receive great detail, but its construction is left largely mysterious. However, Nemo's reasons for building the submarine include bitterness about his lost country and the desire for revenge. This powerful motivation gives insight into the Essential Question: *Are inventions realized through inspiration or perspiration?*

Boy: Tales of Childhood
Roald Dahl
Lexile: 1090

Roald Dahl tells stories of his childhood and how his experiences led him to become a writer.

Connection to Essential Question
Dahl was creative as a boy, with plenty of brief and short-lived schemes. The varying success and dedication of these adventures provide plenty of contrast to answer the Essential Question: *Are inventions realized through inspiration or perspiration?*

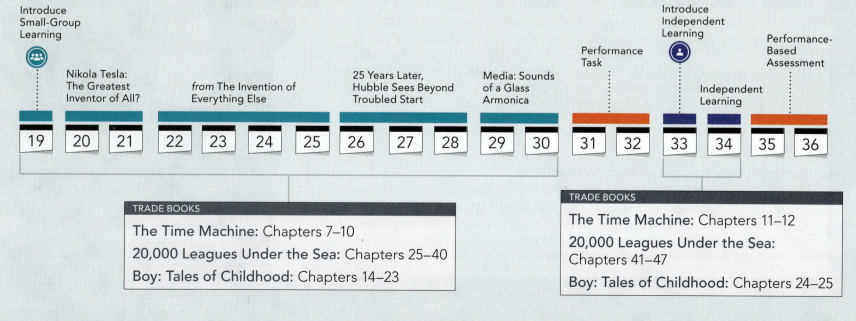

Standards Correlation

Key Features of the Standards

The following summary of key features is from the Introduction to the Common Core State Standards for English Language Arts © 2010, National Governors Association for Best Practices and Council of Chief State School Officers. All rights reserved.

Reading
Text Complexity and the Growth of Comprehension

The Reading standards place equal emphasis on the sophistication of what students read and the skill with which they read. Standard 10 defines a grade-by-grade "staircase" of increasing text complexity that rises from beginning reading to the college and career readiness level. Whatever they are reading, students must also show a steadily growing ability to discern more from and make fuller use of text. This process should include making an increasing number of connections among ideas and between texts, considering a wider range of textual evidence, and becoming more sensitive to inconsistencies, ambiguities, and poor reasoning in texts.

Writing
Text Types, Responding to Reading, and Research

The Standards acknowledge the fact that whereas some writing skills, such as the ability to plan, revise, edit, and publish, are applicable to many types of writing, other skills are more properly defined in terms of specific writing types: arguments, informative/explanatory texts, and narratives. Standard 9 stresses the importance of the writing-reading connection by requiring students to draw upon and write about evidence from literary and informational texts. Because of the centrality of writing to most forms of inquiry, research standards are prominently included in this strand, though skills important to research are infused throughout the document.

Speaking and Listening
Flexible Communication and Collaboration

Including but not limited to skills necessary for formal presentations, the Speaking and Listening standards require students to develop a range of broadly useful oral communication and interpersonal skills. Students must learn to work together, express and listen carefully to ideas, integrate information from oral, visual, quantitative, and media sources, evaluate what they hear, use media and visual displays strategically to help achieve communicative purposes, and adapt speech to context and task.

Language
Conventions, Effective Use, and Vocabulary

The Language standards include the essential "rules" of standard written and spoken English, but they also approach language as a matter of craft and informed choice among alternatives. The vocabulary standards focus on understanding words and phrases, their relationships, and their nuances and on acquiring new vocabulary, particularly general academic and domain-specific words and phrases.

Correlation to *myPerspectives*™ English Language Arts

The following correlation shows points at which focused standards instruction is provided in the Student Edition. The Teacher's Edition provides further opportunity to address standards through Personalize for Learning notes and additional resources available only in the Interactive Teacher's Edition.

Standards for Reading

College and Career Readiness Anchor Standards for Reading

Key Ideas and Details

1. Read closely to determine what the text says explicitly and to make logical inferences from it; cite specific textual evidence when writing or speaking to support conclusions drawn from the text.
2. Determine central ideas or themes of a text and analyze their development; summarize the key supporting details and ideas.
3. Analyze how and why individuals, events, and ideas develop and interact over the course of a text.

Craft and Structure

4. Interpret words and phrases as they are used in a text, including determining technical, connotative, and figurative meanings, and analyze how specific word choices shape meaning or tone.
5. Analyze the structure of texts, including how specific sentences, paragraphs, and larger portions of the text (e.g., a section, chapter, scene, or stanza) relate to each other and the whole.
6. Assess how point of view or purpose shapes the content and style of a text.

Integration of Knowledge and Ideas

7. Integrate and evaluate content presented in diverse formats and media, including visually and quantitatively, as well as in words.
8. Delineate and evaluate the argument and specific claims in a text, including the validity of the reasoning as well as the relevance and sufficiency of the evidence.
9. Analyze how two or more texts address similar themes or topics in order to build knowledge or to compare the approaches the authors take.

Range of Reading and Level of Text Complexity

10. Read and comprehend complex literary and informational texts independently and proficiently.

Standards Correlation

Grade 8 Reading Standards for Literature

STANDARD CODE	Standard	Print and Interactive Editions
Key Ideas and Details		
RL.8.1	Cite the textual evidence that most strongly supports an analysis of what the text says explicitly as well as inferences drawn from the text.	**SE/TE:** *The Diary of Anne Frank,* Act II, 188; "Flowers for Algernon," 380; "Uncle Marcos," 458; Students will address this standard in *Analyze the Text* features which appear with every literature selection.
RL.8.2	Determine a theme or central idea of a text and analyze its development over the course of the text, including its relationship to the characters, setting, and plot; provide an objective summary of the text.	**SE/TE:** "The Medicine Bag," 21; "Hanging Fire" / "Translating Grandfather's House," 62–63; "Uncle Marcos," 457, 463; "Flowers for Algernon," 380–381
RL.8.3	Analyze how particular lines of dialogue or incidents in a story or drama propel the action, reveal aspects of a character, or provoke a decision.	**SE/TE:** *The Diary of Anne Frank,* Act I, 152; *The Diary of Anne Frank,* Act II, 188; "Uncle Marcos," 458
Craft and Structure		
RL.8.4	Determine the meaning of words and phrases as they are used in a text, including figurative and connotative meanings; analyze the impact of specific word choices on meaning and tone, including analogies or allusions to other texts.	**SE/TE:** "The Medicine Bag," 22; "Hanging Fire" / "Translating Grandfather's House," 64; "Retort" / "The People, Yes," 422; "The Invention of Everything Else," 506
RL.8.5	Compare and contrast the structure of two or more texts and analyze how the differing structure of each text contributes to its meaning and style.	**SE/TE:** "Hanging Fire" / "Translating Grandfather's House," 62; *Flowers for Algernon* (video), 388; "Retort" / "The People, Yes," 422
RL.8.6	Analyze how differences in the points of view of the characters and the audience or reader (e.g., created through the use of dramatic irony) create such effects as suspense or humor.	**SE/TE:** "The Setting Sun and the Rolling World," 72; *The Diary of Anne Frank,* Act I, 152; "Flowers for Algernon," 380
Integration of Knowledge and Ideas		
RL.8.7	Analyze the extent to which a filmed or live production of a story or drama stays faithful to or departs from the text or script, evaluating the choices made by the director or actors.	**SE/TE:** *The Diary of Anne Frank,* Act II, 193; *Flowers for Algernon* (video), 387
RL.8.8	(Not applicable to literature)	
RL.8.9	Analyze how a modern work of fiction draws on themes, patterns of events, or character types from myths, traditional stories, or religious works such as the Bible, including describing how the material is rendered new.	**SE/TE:** "Flowers for Algernon," 380-381; "Uncle Marcos," 463; Whole-Group Performance Task, Unit 5: 478–479
Range of Reading and Level of Text Complexity		
RL.8.10	By the end of the year, read and comprehend literature, including stories, dramas, and poems, at the high end of grades 6–8 text complexity band independently and proficiently.	**SE/TE:** "The Medicine Bag," 12; "Hanging Fire" / "Translating Grandfather's House," 54; "The Setting Sun and the Rolling World," 66; First-Read Guide, Unit 1: 80, Unit 2: 246, Unit 3: 332, Unit 4: 430, Unit 5: 528; Close-Read Guide, Unit 1: 81, Unit 2: 247, Unit 3: 333, Unit 4: 431, Unit 5: 529; *The Diary of Anne Frank,* Act I, 100; *The Diary of Anne Frank,* Act II, 156; *Maus,* 230; "Flowers for Algernon," 350; *Flowers for Algernon* (video), 384; "Retort" / "The People, Yes," 416; "Uncle Marcos," 448; "The Invention of Everything Else," 494

Grade 8 Reading Standards for Informational Text

STANDARD CODE	Standard	Print and Interactive Editions
Key Ideas and Details		
RI.8.1	Cite the textual evidence that most strongly supports an analysis of what the text says explicitly as well as inferences drawn from the text.	**SE/TE:** *Anne Frank: The Diary of a Young Girl,* 218; "Acceptance Speech for the Nobel Peace Prize," 226; "Barrington Irving, Pilot and Educator," 270; "Ban the Ban!" / "Soda's a Problem but…", 290; Students will address this standard in Analyze the Text features which appear with every informational text selection.
RI.8.2	Determine a central idea of a text and analyze its development over the course of the text, including its relationship to supporting ideas; provide an objective summary of the text.	**SE/TE:** *Anne Frank: The Diary of a Young Girl,* 218–219; "Acceptance Speech for the Nobel Peace Prize," 225; *Blue Nines and Red Words,* 408
RI.8.3	Analyze how a text makes connections among and distinctions between individuals, ideas, or events (e.g., through comparisons, analogies, or categories).	**SE/TE:** "Barrington Irving, Pilot and Educator," 270; *Blue Nines and Red Words,* 408; "To Fly," 472; "Nikola Tesla: The Greatest Inventor of All?", 491–492
Craft and Structure		
RI.8.4	Determine the meaning of words and phrases as they are used in a text, including figurative, connotative, and technical meanings; analyze the impact of specific word choices on meaning and tone, including analogies or allusions to other texts.	**SE/TE:** "You Are the Electric Boogaloo" / "Just Be Yourself!", 50; *Anne Frank: The Diary of a Young Girl,* 220; "Acceptance Speech for the Nobel Peace Prize," 226; "Words Do Not Pay," 310; *Follow the Rabbit-Proof Fence,* 320; "To Fly," 472
RI.8.5	Analyze in detail the structure of a specific paragraph in a text, including the role of particular sentences in developing and refining a key concept.	**SE/TE:** *Anne Frank: The Diary of a Young Girl,* 218; *Follow the Rabbit-Proof Fence,* 320; "To Fly," 472; "Nikola Tesla: The Greatest Inventor of All?", 492
RI.8.6	Determine an author's point of view or purpose in a text and analyze how the author acknowledges and responds to conflicting evidence or viewpoints.	**SE/TE:** "Acceptance Speech for the Nobel Peace Prize," 226; "Three Cheers for the Nanny State," 282; *Follow the Rabbit-Proof Fence,* 320; *Blue Nines and Red Words,* 408; "25 Years Later, Hubble Sees Beyond Troubled Start," 517
Integration of Knowledge and Ideas		
RI.8.7	Evaluate the advantages and disadvantages of using different mediums (e.g., print or digital text, video, multimedia) to present a particular topic or idea.	**SE/TE:** "The Medicine Bag" / "Apache Girl's Rite of Passage," 33; *The Diary of Anne Frank* / "Frank Family and World War II Timeline," 201; "The Theory of Multiple Intelligences Infographic," 414
RI.8.8	Delineate and evaluate the argument and specific claims in a text, assessing whether the reasoning is sound and the evidence is relevant and sufficient; recognize when irrelevant evidence is introduced.	**SE/TE:** "Three Cheers for the Nanny State," 282–283; "Ban the Ban!" / "Soda's a Problem but…", 290–291; "Three Cheers for the Nanny State" / "Ban the Ban!" / "Soda's a Problem but…", 294–295
RI.8.9	Analyze a case in which two or more texts provide conflicting information on the same topic and identify where the texts disagree on matters of fact or interpretation.	**SE/TE:** "Ban the Ban!" / "Soda's a Problem but…", 290; "Three Cheers for the Nanny State" / "Ban the Ban!" / "Soda's a Problem but…", 294
Range of Reading and Level of Text Complexity		
RI.8.10	By the end of the year, read and comprehend literary nonfiction at the high end of the grades 6–8 text complexity band independently and proficiently.	**SE/TE:** "Apache Girl's Rite of Passage," 28; "You Are the Electric Boogaloo" / "Just Be Yourself!", 44; First-Read Guide, Unit 1: 80, Unit 2: 246, Unit 3: 332, Unit 4: 430, Unit 5: 528; Close-Read Guide, Unit 1: 81, Unit 2: 247, Unit 3: 333, Unit 4: 431, Unit 5: 529; "Frank Family and World War II Timeline," 194; *Anne Frank: The Diary of a Young Girl,* 212; "Acceptance Speech for the Nobel Peace Prize," 222; "Barrington Irving, Pilot and Educator," 264; "Three Cheers for the Nanny State," 276; "Ban the Ban!" / "Soda's a Problem but…", 286; "Words Do Not Pay," 306; *Follow the Rabbit-Proof Fence,* 314; "The Moth Presents: Aleeza Kazmi," 324; *Blue Nines and Red Words,* 400; "The Theory of Multiple Intelligences Infographic," 412; "To Fly," 464; "Nikola Tesla: The Greatest Inventor of All?", 488; "25 Years Later, Hubble Sees Beyond Troubled Start," 510; "Sounds of a Glass Armonica," 520

Standards Correlation

Standards for Writing

College and Career Readiness Anchor Standards for Writing

Key Ideas and Details

1. Write arguments to support claims in an analysis of substantive topics or texts, using valid reasoning and relevant and sufficient evidence.
2. Write informative/explanatory texts to examine and convey complex ideas and information clearly and accurately through the effective selection, organization, and analysis of content.
3. Write narratives to develop real or imagined experiences or events using effective technique, well-chosen details, and well-structured event sequences.

Production and Distribution of Writing

4. Produce clear and coherent writing in which the development, organization, and style are appropriate to task, purpose, and audience.
5. Develop and strengthen writing as needed by planning, revising, editing, rewriting, or trying a new approach.
6. Use technology, including the Internet, to produce and publish writing and to interact and collaborate with others.

Research to Build and Present Knowledge

7. Conduct short as well as more sustained research projects based on focused questions, demonstrating understanding of the subject under investigation.
8. Gather relevant information from multiple print and digital sources, assess the credibility and accuracy of each source, and integrate the information while avoiding plagiarism.
9. Draw evidence from literary or informational texts to support analysis, reflection, and research.

Range of Writing

10. Write routinely over extended time frames (time for research, reflection, and revision) and shorter time frames (a single sitting or a day or two) for a range of tasks, purposes, and audiences.

Grade 8 Writing Standards

STANDARD CODE	Standard	Print and Interactive Editions
Text Types and Purposes		
W.8.1	Write arguments to support claims with clear reasons and relevant evidence.	**SE/TE:** "Barrington Irving, Pilot and Educator," 274; "Three Cheers for the Nanny State" / "Ban the Ban!" / "Soda's a Problem but…", 295; "Uncle Marcos," 462; "To Fly," 476; Whole-Class Performance Task, Unit 3: 296–300, Unit 5: 478–480, 482–483; Performance-Based Assessment, Unit 3: 335–337, Unit 5: 531–532
W.8.1.a	Introduce claim(s), acknowledge and distinguish the claim(s) from alternate or opposing claims, and organize the reasons and evidence logically.	**SE/TE:** "Barrington Irving, Pilot and Educator," 274; "Three Cheers for the Nanny State" / "Ban the Ban!" / "Soda's a Problem but…", 295; "Uncle Marcos," 462; "To Fly," 476; Whole-Class Performance Task, Unit 3: 297–298, Unit 5: 479; Performance-Based Assessment, Unit 3: 335–337, Unit 5: 531–532
W.8.1.b	Support claim(s) with logical reasoning and relevant evidence, using accurate, credible sources and demonstrating an understanding of the topic or text.	**SE/TE:** "Barrington Irving, Pilot and Educator," 274; "Three Cheers for the Nanny State" / "Ban the Ban!" / "Soda's a Problem but…", 295; "Uncle Marcos," 462; "To Fly," 476; Whole-Class Performance Task, Unit 3: 297, 300, Unit 5: 479; Performance-Based Assessment, Unit 3: 335–337, Unit 5: 531–532
W.8.1.c	Use words, phrases, and clauses to create cohesion and clarify the relationships among claim(s), counterclaims, reasons, and evidence.	**SE/TE:** "Barrington Irving, Pilot and Educator," 274; "Three Cheers for the Nanny State" / "Ban the Ban!" / "Soda's a Problem but…", 295; "Uncle Marcos," 462; "To Fly," 476; Whole-Class Performance Task, Unit 3: 298, Unit 5: 482; Performance-Based Assessment, Unit 3: 337, Unit 5: 532
W.8.1.d	Establish and maintain a formal style.	**SE/TE:** "Barrington Irving, Pilot and Educator," 274; "Three Cheers for the Nanny State" / "Ban the Ban!" / "Soda's a Problem but…", 295; "Uncle Marcos," 462; "To Fly," 476; Whole-Class Performance Task, Unit 3: 300, Unit 5: 483; Performance-Based Assessment, Unit 3: 337, Unit 5: 532
W.8.1.e	Provide a concluding statement or section that follows from and supports the argument presented.	**SE/TE:** "Barrington Irving, Pilot and Educator," 274; "Three Cheers for the Nanny State" / "Ban the Ban!" / "Soda's a Problem but…", 295; "Uncle Marcos," 462; "To Fly," 476; Whole-Class Performance Task, Unit 3: 298, Unit 5: 480, 482; Performance-Based Assessment, Unit 3: 337, Unit 5: 532
W.8.2	Write informative/explanatory texts to examine a topic and convey ideas, concepts, and information through the selection, organization, and analysis of relevant content.	**SE/TE:** "The Medicine Bag" / "Apache Girl's Rite of Passage," 33; "The Setting Sun and the Rolling World," 74; *The Diary of Anne Frank*, Act II, 193; *The Diary of Anne Frank* / "Frank Family and World War II Timeline," 201; *Maus*, 241; "Words Do Not Pay," 312; *Flowers for Algernon* (video), 388; *Blue Nines and Red Words*, 411; "Nikola Tesla: The Greatest Inventor of All?" / "The Invention of Everything Else," 509; Whole-Class Performance Task, Unit 2: 202–204, 206, Unit 4: 390–392, 394; Performance-Based Assessment, Unit 2: 249–250, Unit 4: 433–434
W.8.2.a	Introduce a topic clearly, previewing what is to follow; organize ideas, concepts, and information into broader categories; include formatting (e.g., headings), graphics (e.g., charts, tables), and multimedia when useful to aiding comprehension.	**SE/TE:** "The Medicine Bag" / "Apache Girl's Rite of Passage," 33; *The Diary of Anne Frank* / "Frank Family and World War II Timeline," 201; *Maus*, 241; "Words Do Not Pay," 312; "Flowers for Algernon" (script), 388; Whole-Class Performance Task, Unit 2: 203, Unit 4: 391–392, 394
W.8.2.b	Develop the topic with relevant, well-chosen facts, definitions, concrete details, quotations, or other information and examples.	**SE/TE:** "The Setting Sun and the Rolling World," 74; *The Diary of Anne Frank*, Act II, 193; *The Diary of Anne Frank* / "Frank Family and World War II Timeline," 201; *Maus*, 241; "Words Do Not Pay," 312; *Flowers for Algernon* (video), 388; *Blue Nines and Red Words*, 411; Whole-Class Performance Task, Unit 2: 203–204, Unit 4: 391; Performance-Based Assessment, Unit 2: 249, Unit 4: 433

Standards Correlation

Grade 8 Writing Standards (continued)

STANDARD CODE	Standard	Print and Interactive Editions
Text Types and Purposes (continued)		
W.8.2.c	Use appropriate and varied transitions to create cohesion and clarify the relationships among ideas and concepts.	**SE/TE:** *The Diary of Anne Frank* / "Frank Family and World War II Timeline," 201; *Maus,* 241; "Words Do Not Pay," 312; *Flowers for Algernon* (video), 388; Whole-Class Performance Task, Unit 2: 206, Unit 4: 394
W.8.2.d	Use precise language and domain-specific vocabulary to inform about or explain the topic.	**SE/TE:** *The Diary of Anne Frank* / "Frank Family and World War II Timeline," 201; *Maus,* 241; "Words Do Not Pay," 312; *Flowers for Algernon* (video), 388; "Blue Nines and Red Words," 411; Whole-Class Performance Task, Unit 2: 206, Unit 4: 394
W.8.2.e	Establish and maintain a formal style.	**SE/TE:** *The Diary of Anne Frank* / "Frank Family and World War II Timeline," 201; *Maus,* 241; "Words Do Not Pay," 312; *Flowers for Algernon* (video), 388; Whole-Class Performance Task, Unit 2: 206, Unit 4: 394
W.8.2.f	Provide a concluding statement or section that follows from and supports the information or explanation presented.	**SE/TE:** "The Setting Sun and the Rolling World," 74; *The Diary of Anne Frank,* Act II, 193; *The Diary of Anne Frank* / "Frank Family and World War II Timeline," 201; *Maus,* 241; "Words Do Not Pay," 312; *Flowers for Algernon* (video), 388; Whole-Class Performance Task, Unit 2: 204; , Unit 4: 395
W.8.3	Write narratives to develop real or imagined experiences or events using effective technique, relevant descriptive details, and well-structured event sequences.	**SE/TE:** "The Medicine Bag," 26; *Follow the Rabbit-Proof Fence,* 323; Whole-Class Performance Task, Unit 1: 34–36, 38; Performance-Based Assessment, Unit 1: 83–84
W.8.3.a	Engage and orient the reader by establishing a context and point of view and introducing a narrator and/or characters; organize an event sequence that unfolds naturally and logically.	**SE/TE:** "The Medicine Bag," 26; *Follow the Rabbit-Proof Fence,* 323; Whole-Class Performance Task, Unit 1: 34–36
W.8.3.b	Use narrative techniques, such as dialogue, pacing, description, and reflection, to develop experiences, events, and/or characters.	**SE/TE:** "The Medicine Bag," 26; *Follow the Rabbit-Proof Fence,* 323; Whole-Class Performance Task, Unit 1: 34–35
W.8.3.c	Use a variety of transition words, phrases, and clauses to convey sequence, signal shifts from one time frame or setting to another, and show the relationships among experiences and events.	**SE/TE:** "The Medicine Bag," 26; *Follow the Rabbit-Proof Fence,* 323; Whole-Class Performance Task, Unit 1: 34, 36–37
W.8.3.d	Use precise words and phrases, relevant descriptive details, and sensory language to capture the action and convey experiences and events.	**SE/TE:** "The Medicine Bag," 26; *Follow the Rabbit-Proof Fence,* 323; Whole-Class Performance Task, Unit 1: 34, 38
W.8.3.e	Provide a conclusion that follows from and reflects on the narrated experiences or events.	**SE/TE:** "The Medicine Bag," 26; *Follow the Rabbit-Proof Fence,* 323; Whole-Class Performance Task, Unit 1: 34, 38
Production and Distribution of Writing		
W.8.4	Produce clear and coherent writing in which the development, organization, and style are appropriate to task, purpose, and audience.	**SE/TE:** "Three Cheers for the Nanny State" / "Ban the Ban!" / "Soda's a Problem but…", 295; Whole-Class Performance Task, Unit 1, Unit 2, Unit 3, Unit 4, Unit 5; Performance-Based Assessment, Unit 1: 84, Unit 4: 395
W.8.5	With some guidance and support from peers and adults, develop and strengthen writing as needed by planning, revising, editing, rewriting, or trying a new approach, focusing on how well purpose and audience have been addressed.	**SE/TE:** *Follow the Rabbit-Proof Fence,* 323; Whole-Class Performance Task, Unit 1: 39, Unit 2: 207, Unit 3: 301, Unit 4: 395, Unit 5: 483
W.8.6	Use technology, including the Internet, to produce and publish writing and present the relationships between information and ideas efficiently as well as to interact and collaborate with others.	**SE/TE:** "You Are the Electric Boogaloo" / "Just Be Yourself!", 53; "Sounds of a Glass Armonica," 523; Small-Group Performance Task, Unit 2, 242–243, Unit 4, 426–427; Whole-Class Performance Task, Unit 3: 301

Grade 8 Writing Standards (continued)

STANDARD CODE	Standard	Print and Interactive Editions
Research to Build and Present Knowledge		
W.8.7	Conduct short research projects to answer a question (including a self-generated question), drawing on several sources and generating additional related, focused questions that allow for multiple avenues of exploration.	**SE/TE:** "You Are the Electric Boogaloo" / "Just Be Yourself!", 52; "The Setting Sun and the Rolling World," 74; Maus, 241; "Barrington Irving, Pilot and Educator," 274; "Words Do Not Pay," 312; Follow the Rabbit-Proof Fence, 323; Blue Nines and Red Words, 411; "Sounds of a Glass Armonica," 523
W.8.8	Gather relevant information from multiple print and digital sources, using search terms effectively; assess the credibility and accuracy of each source; and quote or paraphrase the data and conclusions of others while avoiding plagiarism and following a standard format for citation.	**SE/TE:** "The Setting Sun and the Rolling World," 74; Maus, 241; "Words Do Not Pay," 312; Blue Nines and Red Words, 411
W.8.9	Draw evidence from literary or informational texts to support analysis, reflection, and research.	**SE/TE:** "Three Cheers for the Nanny State" / "Ban the Ban!" / "Soda's a Problem but…", 294; "Nikola Tesla: The Greatest Inventor of All?" / "The Invention of Everything Else," 509; Performance-Based Assessment, Unit 3: 336, Unit 4: 434
W.8.9.a	Apply *grade 8 Reading standards* to literature (e.g., "Analyze how a modern work of fiction draws on themes, patterns of events, or character types from myths, traditional stories, or religious works such as the Bible, including describing how the material is rendered new").	**SE/TE:** Flowers for Algernon (video), 388; "Uncle Marcos," 463; Whole-Group Performance Task, Unit 5: 478–479
W.8.9.b	Apply *grade 8 Reading standards* to literary nonfiction (e.g., "Delineate and evaluate the argument and specific claims in a text, assessing whether the reasoning is sound and the evidence is relevant and sufficient; recognize when irrelevant evidence is introduced").	**SE/TE:** "Barrington Irving, Pilot and Educator," 274; "Three Cheers for the Nanny State" / "Ban the Ban!" / "Soda's a Problem but…", 294–295
Range of Writing		
W.8.10	Write routinely over extended time frames (time for research, reflection, and revision) and shorter time frames (a single sitting or a day or two) for a range of discipline-specific tasks, purposes, and audiences.	**SE/TE:** Whole-Class Performance Task, Unit 2: 202, Unit 4: 390; Performance-Based Assessment, Unit 1: 84, Unit 2: 250, Unit 3: 336, Unit 4: 434

Standards Correlation

Standards for Speaking and Listening

College and Career Readiness Anchor Standards for Speaking and Listening

Comprehension and Collaboration

1. Prepare for and participate effectively in a range of conversations and collaborations with diverse partners, building on others' ideas and expressing their own clearly and persuasively.
2. Integrate and evaluate information presented in diverse media and formats, including visually, quantitatively, and orally.
3. Evaluate a speaker's point of view, reasoning, and use of evidence and rhetoric.

Presentation of Knowledge and Ideas

4. Present information, findings, and supporting evidence such that listeners can follow the line of reasoning and the organization, development, and style are appropriate to task, purpose, and audience.
5. Make strategic use of digital media and visual displays of data to express information and enhance understanding of presentations.
6. Adapt speech to a variety of contexts and communicative tasks, demonstrating command of formal English when indicated or appropriate.

Grade 8 Speaking and Listening Standards

STANDARD CODE	Standard	Print and Interactive Editions
Comprehension and Collaboration		
SL.8.1	Engage effectively in a range of collaborative discussions (one-on-one, in groups, and teacher-led) with diverse partners on *grade 8 topics, texts, and issues,* building on others' ideas and expressing their own clearly.	**SE/TE:** "Hanging Fire" / "Translating Grandfather's House," 64; *The Diary of Anne Frank,* Act II, 192; *Anne Frank: The Diary of a Young Girl,* 221; "Acceptance Speech for the Nobel Peace Prize," 229; "The Moth Presents: Aleeza Kazmi," 327; "The Theory of Multiple Intelligences Infographic," 415; "Retort" / "The People, Yes," 425; "Uncle Marcos," 463; "25 Years Later, Hubble Sees Beyond Troubled Start," 519; "Sounds of a Glass Armonica," 522, 523; Share Your Independent Learning, Unit 1: 82, Unit 2: 248, Unit 3: 334, Unit 4: 432, Unit 5: 530; Small-Group Performance Task, Unit 3: 328, Unit 4: 426–427, Unit 5: 524–525
SL.8.1.a	Come to discussions prepared, having read or researched material under study; explicitly draw on that preparation by referring to evidence on the topic, text, or issue to probe and reflect on ideas under discussion.	**SE/TE:** "Hanging Fire" / "Translating Grandfather's House," 64; *The Diary of Anne Frank,* Act II, 192; *Anne Frank: The Diary of a Young Girl,* 221; "Acceptance Speech for the Nobel Peace Prize," 229; "The Moth Presents: Aleeza Kazmi," 327; "The Theory of Multiple Intelligences Infographic," 415; "Retort" / "The People, Yes," 425; "Uncle Marcos," 463; "25 Years Later, Hubble Sees Beyond Troubled Start," 519; "Sounds of a Glass Armonica," 523; Small-Group Performance Task, Unit 3: 328, Unit 4: 426, Unit 5: 524
SL.8.1.b	Follow rules for collegial discussions and decision-making, track progress toward specific goals and deadlines, and define individual roles as needed.	**SE/TE:** *The Diary of Anne Frank,* Act II, 192; "Acceptance Speech for the Nobel Peace Prize," 229; "The Theory of Multiple Intelligences Infographic," 415; "25 Years Later, Hubble Sees Beyond Troubled Start," 519; "Sounds of a Glass Armonica," 523; Small-Group Performance Task, Unit 4: 426, Unit 5: 524; Students will address this standard in Working as a Team features which appear in the Small Group Learning Overview lessons.
SL.8.1.c	Pose questions that connect the ideas of several speakers and respond to others' questions and comments with relevant evidence, observations, and ideas.	**SE/TE:** "Hanging Fire" / "Translating Grandfather's House," 64; *Anne Frank: The Diary of a Young Girl,* 221; "The Moth Presents: Aleeza Kazmi," 327; "The Theory of Multiple Intelligences Infographic," 415; "Uncle Marcos," 463; "25 Years Later, Hubble Sees Beyond Troubled Start," 519; Small-Group Performance Task, Unit 4: 426, Unit 5: 525; Students will address this standard in Launch Activity features which appear in the Unit Introduction and in Working as a Team features which appear in the Small Group Learning Overview lessons.
SL.8.1.d	Acknowledge new information expressed by others, and, when warranted, qualify or justify their own views in light of the evidence presented.	**SE/TE:** "Hanging Fire" / "Translating Grandfather's House," 64; *Anne Frank: The Diary of a Young Girl,* 221; "The Moth Presents: Aleeza Kazmi," 327; "The Theory of Multiple Intelligences Infographic," 415; "25 Years Later, Hubble Sees Beyond Troubled Start," 519; Small-Group Performance Task, Unit 4: 427, Unit 5: 525; Students will address this standard in *Launch Activity* features which appear in the Unit Introduction, in Working as a Team features which appear in the Small Group Learning Overview lessons, and *Group Discussion Tips* which appear throughout the program.
SL.8.2	Analyze the purpose of information presented in diverse media and formats (e.g., visually, quantitatively, orally) and evaluate the motives (e.g., social, commercial, political) behind its presentation.	**SE/TE:** "The Medicine Bag" / "Apache Girl's Rite of Passage," 32; *Maus,* 240; "The Moth Presents: Aleeza Kazmi," 326–327
SL.8.3	Delineate a speaker's argument and specific claims, evaluating the soundness of the reasoning and relevance and sufficiency of the evidence and identifying when irrelevant evidence is introduced.	**SE/TE:** "Barrington Irving, Pilot and Educator," 274; "25 Years Later, Hubble Sees Beyond Troubled Start," 519; Small-Group Performance Task, Unit 5: 524; Performance-Based Assessment, Unit 5: 534

Standards Correlation

Standards for Language

College and Career Readiness Anchor Standards for Language

Conventions of Standard English

1. Demonstrate command of the conventions of standard English grammar and usage when writing or speaking.
2. Demonstrate command of the conventions of standard English capitalization, punctuation, and spelling when writing.

Knowledge of Language

3. Apply knowledge of language to understand how language functions in different contexts, to make effective choices for meaning or style, and to comprehend more fully when reading or listening.

Vocabulary Acquisition and Use

4. Determine or clarify the meaning of unknown and multiple-meaning words and phrases by using context clues, analyzing meaningful word parts, and consulting general and specialized reference materials, as appropriate.
5. Demonstrate understanding of figurative language, word relationships, and nuances in word meanings.
6. Acquire and use accurately a range of general academic and domain-specific words and phrases sufficient for reading, writing, speaking, and listening at the college and career readiness level; demonstrate independence in gathering vocabulary knowledge when considering a word or phrase important to comprehension or expression.

Grade 8 Speaking and Listening Standards (continued)

STANDARD CODE	Standard	Print and Interactive Editions
Presentation of Knowledge and Ideas		
SL.8.4	Present claims and findings, emphasizing salient points in a focused, coherent manner with relevant evidence, sound valid reasoning, and well-chosen details; use appropriate eye contact, adequate volume, and clear pronunciation.	**SE/TE:** "The Medicine Bag," 26; "You Are the Electric Boogaloo" / "Just Be Yourself!", 52; *The Diary of Anne Frank*, Act II, 192; "Barrington Irving, Pilot and Educator," 274; "To Fly," 476; Small-Group Performance Task, Unit 1: 76, Unit 2: 243, Unit 3: 329, Unit 4: 427, Unit 5: 525; Performance-Based Assessment, Unit 1: 86, Unit 2: 252, Unit 3: 338, Unit 4: 436, Unit 5: 534
SL.8.5	Integrate multimedia and visual displays into presentations to clarify information, strengthen claims and evidence, and add interest.	**SE/TE:** "You Are the Electric Boogaloo" / "Just Be Yourself!", 52; "Retort" / "The People, Yes," 425; "To Fly," 476; "Sounds of a Glass Armonica," 523; Small-Group Performance Task, Unit 1: 76, Unit 2: 243, Unit 4: 426–427; Performance-Based Assessment, Unit 1: 86, Unit 3: 338
SL.8.6	Adapt speech to a variety of contexts and tasks, demonstrating command of formal English when indicated or appropriate.	**SE/TE:** "The Medicine Bag," 27; *The Diary of Anne Frank*, Act II, 192; Barrington Irving, Pilot and Educator," 275; "To Fly," 477; Small-Group Performance Task, Unit 2: 243, Unit 4: 427

Standards Correlation

Grade 8 Language Standards

STANDARD CODE	Standard	Print and Interactive Editions
Conventions of Standard English		
L.8.1	Demonstrate command of the conventions of standard English grammar and usage when writing or speaking.	**SE/TE:** "The Medicine Bag," 25; "You Are the Electric Boogaloo" / "Just Be Yourself!", 52; "The Setting Sun and the Rolling World," 74; *The Diary of Anne Frank,* Act I, 154; *The Diary of Anne Frank,* Act II, 190; "Acceptance Speech for the Nobel Peace Prize," 228; "Barrington Irving, Pilot and Educator," 272; "Three Cheers for the Nanny State," 284; "Words Do Not Pay," 312; *Follow the Rabbit-Proof Fence,* 322; "Flowers for Algernon," 382; *Blue Nines and Red Words,* 410; "Retort" / "The People, Yes," 424; "Uncle Marcos," 460; "The Invention of Everything Else," 507; Whole-Class Performance Task, Unit 2: 205, Unit 3: 299, Unit 4: 393, Unit 5: 481
L.8.1.a	Explain the function of verbals (gerunds, participles, infinitives) in general and their function in particular sentences.	**SE/TE:** "Retort" / "The People, Yes," 424; Whole-Class Performance Task, Unit 5: 481
L.8.1.b	Form and use verbs in the active and passive voice.	**SE/TE:** "The Medicine Bag," 25–26; Whole-Class Performance Task, Unit 4: 393
L.8.1.c	Form and use verbs in the indicative, imperative, interrogative, conditional, and subjunctive mood.	**SE/TE:** "You Are the Electric Boogaloo" / "Just Be Yourself!", 52; "The Setting Sun and the Rolling World," 74
L.8.1.d	Recognize and correct inappropriate shifts in verb voice and mood.	**SE/TE:** "You Are the Electric Boogaloo" / "Just Be Yourself!", 52; "The Setting Sun and the Rolling World," 74
L.8.2	Demonstrate command of the conventions of standard English capitalization, punctuation, and spelling when writing.	**SE/TE:** "Barrington Irving, Pilot and Educator," 272; "Three Cheers for the Nanny State," 284; "Ban the Ban!" / "Soda's a Problem but…", 292; "To Fly," 474; "Nikola Tesla: The Greatest Inventor of All?", 493; "25 Years Later, Hubble Sees Beyond Troubled Start," 518; Whole-Class Performance Task, Unit 2: 205, Unit 3: 299, 301, Unit 5: 481
L.8.2.a	Use punctuation (comma, ellipsis, dash) to indicate a pause or break.	**SE/TE:** "Nikola Tesla: The Greatest Inventor of All?", 493; "25 Years Later, Hubble Sees Beyond Troubled Start," 518
L.8.2.b	Use an ellipsis to indicate an omission.	**SE/TE:** "25 Years Later, Hubble Sees Beyond Troubled Start," 518; Resources, R64
L.8.2.c	Spell correctly.	**SE/TE:** "Barrington Irving, Pilot and Educator," 272; "To Fly," 474; Whole-Class Performance Task, Unit 3: 299, 301, Unit 5: 481
Knowledge of Language		
L.8.3	Use knowledge of language and its conventions when writing, speaking, reading, or listening.	**SE/TE:** "The Medicine Bag," 25; *The Diary of Anne Frank,* Act II, 190; "Ban the Ban!" / "Soda's a Problem but…", 292; "Words Do Not Pay," 312; Whole-Class Performance Task, Unit 2: 205
L.8.3.a	Use verbs in the active and passive voice and in the conditional and subjunctive mood to achieve particular effects (e.g., emphasizing the actor or the action; expressing uncertainty or describing a state contrary to fact).	**SE/TE:** "The Medicine Bag," 25–26; "The Setting Sun and the Rolling World," 74; Whole-Class Performance Task, Unit 4: 393
Vocabulary Acquisition and Use		
L.8.4	Determine or clarify the meaning of unknown and multiple-meaning words or phrases based on *grade 8 reading and content,* choosing flexibly from a range of strategies.	**SE/TE:** "The Medicine Bag," 24; "You Are the Electric Boogaloo" / "Just Be Yourself!", 44, 50; "Hanging Fire" / "Translating Grandfather's House," 54, 62; "The Setting Sun and the Rolling World," 72; *The Diary of Anne Frank,* Act I, 154; *The Diary of Anne Frank,* Act II, 190; *Anne Frank: The Diary of a Young Girl,* 212, 218; "Acceptance Speech for the Nobel Peace Prize," 222, 226; "Barrington Irving, Pilot and Educator," 272; "Three Cheers for the Nanny State," 284; "Ban the Ban!" / "Soda's a Problem but…", 292; "Words Do Not Pay," 306, 310; *Follow the Rabbit-Proof Fence,* 314; *Blue Nines and Red Words,* 400; "Retort" / "The People, Yes," 416; "Retort" / "The People, Yes," 422; "Uncle Marcos," 460; "To Fly," 474; "Nikola Tesla: The Greatest Inventor of All?", 491; "The Invention of Everything Else," 505; "25 Years Later, Hubble Sees Beyond Troubled Start," 510, 516

Grade 8 Language Standards (continued)

STANDARD CODE	Standard	Print and Interactive Editions
Vocabulary Acquisition and Use (continued)		
L.8.4.a	Use context (e.g., the overall meaning of a sentence or paragraph; a word's position or function in a sentence) as a clue to the meaning of a word or phrase.	**SE/TE:** "You Are the Electric Boogaloo" / "Just Be Yourself!", 44; "Hanging Fire" / "Translating Grandfather's House," 54; *Anne Frank: The Diary of a Young Girl,* 212; "Words Do Not Pay," 306; "Retort" / "The People, Yes," 416; "25 Years Later, Hubble Sees Beyond Troubled Start," 510
L.8.4.b	Use common, grade-appropriate Greek or Latin affixes and roots as clues to the meaning of a word (e.g., *precede, recede, secede*).	**SE/TE:** "You Are the Electric Boogaloo" / "Just Be Yourself!", 50; "Hanging Fire" / "Translating Grandfather's House," 62; "The Setting Sun and the Rolling World," 72; *The Diary of Anne Frank,* Act I, 154; *The Diary of Anne Frank,* Act II, 190; *Anne Frank: The Diary of a Young Girl,* 218; "Acceptance Speech for the Nobel Peace Prize," 226; "Three Cheers for the Nanny State," 284; "Ban the Ban!" / "Soda's a Problem but…", 292; "Flowers for Algernon," 382; "Uncle Marcos," 460; "To Fly," 474; "25 Years Later, Hubble Sees Beyond Troubled Start," 516
L.8.4.c	Consult general and specialized reference materials (e.g., dictionaries, glossaries, thesauruses), both print and digital, to find the pronunciation of a word or determine or clarify its precise meaning or its part of speech.	**SE/TE:** "The Medicine Bag," 24; "You Are the Electric Boogaloo" / "Just Be Yourself!", 50; "The Setting Sun and the Rolling World," 72; *The Diary of Anne Frank,* Act II, 190; "Acceptance Speech for the Nobel Peace Prize," 222; *Follow the Rabbit-Proof Fence,* 314; "Retort" / "The People, Yes," 422; "Nikola Tesla: The Greatest Inventor of All?", 491; "25 Years Later, Hubble Sees Beyond Troubled Start," 516
L.8.4.d	Verify the preliminary determination of the meaning of a word or phrase (e.g., by checking the inferred meaning in context or in a dictionary).	**SE/TE:** "The Medicine Bag," 24; *The Diary of Anne Frank,* Act I, 154; *The Diary of Anne Frank,* Act II, 190; *Anne Frank: The Diary of a Young Girl,* 218; "Acceptance Speech for the Nobel Peace Prize," 222; "Three Cheers for the Nanny State," 284; "Words Do Not Pay," 306
L.8.5	Demonstrate understanding of figurative language, word relationships, and nuances in word meanings.	**SE/TE:** "You Are the Electric Boogaloo" / "Just Be Yourself!", 50; "The Setting Sun and the Rolling World," 66; *The Diary of Anne Frank,* Act I, 154; "Barrington Irving, Pilot and Educator," 272; "Three Cheers for the Nanny State," 284; "Ban the Ban!" / "Soda's a Problem but…", 292; "Words Do Not Pay," 310; *Follow the Rabbit-Proof Fence,* 320; "Flowers for Algernon," 382; "Retort" / "The People, Yes," 422; "Nikola Tesla: The Greatest Inventor of All?", 488; "The Invention of Everything Else," 494, 505–506
L.8.5.a	Interpret figures of speech (e.g. verbal irony, puns) in context.	**SE/TE:** "To Fly," 472; "The Invention of Everything Else," 506; Resources R45–46
L.8.5.b	Use the relationship between particular words to better understand each of the words.	**SE/TE:** "The Setting Sun and the Rolling World," 66; *The Diary of Anne Frank,* Act I, 154; "Barrington Irving, Pilot and Educator," 272; "Three Cheers for the Nanny State," 284; "Ban the Ban!" / "Soda's a Problem but…", 292; "Retort" / "The People, Yes," 422; "Nikola Tesla: The Greatest Inventor of All?", 488
L.8.5.c	Distinguish among the connotations (associations) of words with similar denotations (definitions) (e.g., *bullheaded, willful, firm, persistent, resolute*).	**SE/TE:** "You Are the Electric Boogaloo" / "Just Be Yourself!", 50; "Words Do Not Pay," 310; "The Invention of Everything Else," 494, 505
L.8.6	Acquire and use accurately grade-appropriate general academic and domain-specific words and phrases; gather vocabulary knowledge when considering a word or phrase important to comprehension or expression.	**SE/TE:** Unit Goals, Unit 1: 4, Unit 2: 90, Unit 3: 256, Unit 4: 342, Unit 5: 440; "Apache Girl's Rite of Passage," 28; *Maus,* 230, 240; "The Moth Presents: Aleeza Kazmi," 324; "Flowers for Algernon," 382; "The Theory of Multiple Intelligences Infographic," 412; "Nikola Tesla: The Greatest Inventor of All?", 488; "Sounds of a Glass Armonica," 520

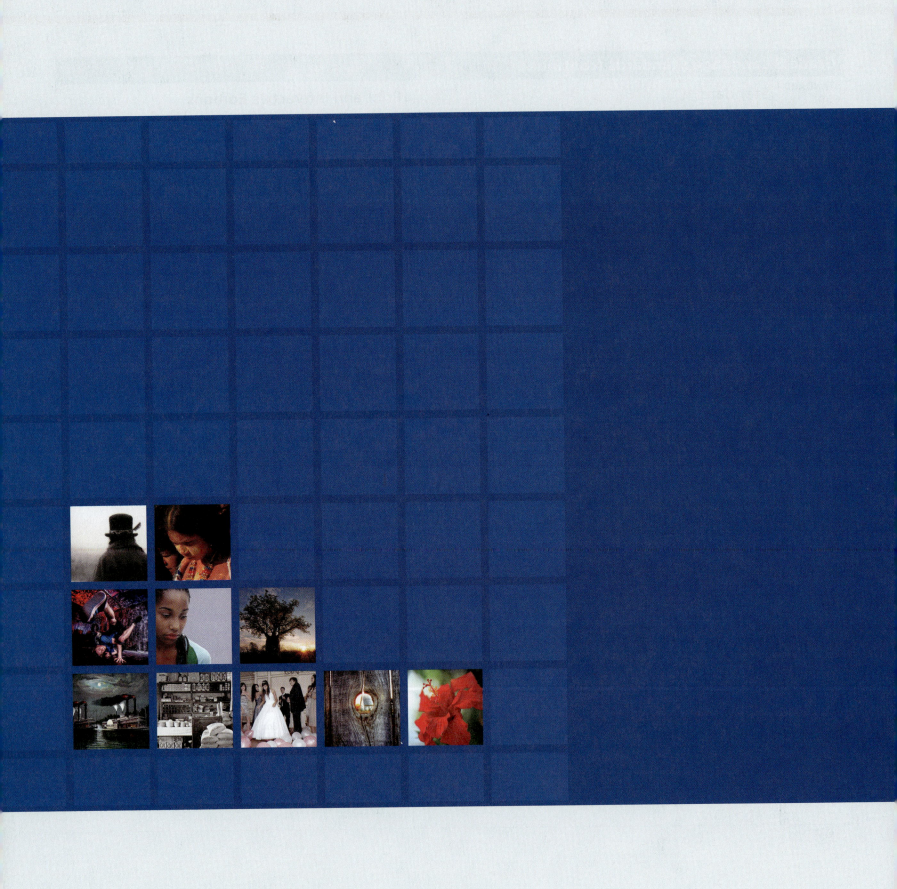

Rites of Passage

UNIT 1

INTRODUCTION

Jump Start

Engage students in a discussion based on the following questions:

"What's the difference between a child and a teenager? Is it as simple as a person's age and physical appearance? Or is it more of a mental transformation, a way of looking at the world?"

Have students jot down three ideas first. Then poll the class to determine the three most popular ideas. Discuss how the transformation might be different in other cultures.

Rites of Passage

Ask students what the phrase *rites of passage* suggests to them. Point out that as they work through this unit, they will read many examples about the experiences that are part of growing up.

Video ▶

Project the introduction video in class, ask students to open the video in their digital textbooks, or have students scan the Bounce Page icon with their phones to access the video.

Discuss It If you want to make this a digital activity, go online and navigate to the Discussion Board. Alternatively, students can share their responses in a class discussion.

Block Scheduling

Each day in this pacing calendar represents a 40- to 50-minute class period. Teachers using block scheduling may combine days to reflect their class schedule. In addition, teachers may revise pacing to differentiate and support core instruction by integrating components and resources as students require.

📅 **Pacing Plan**

UNIT 1

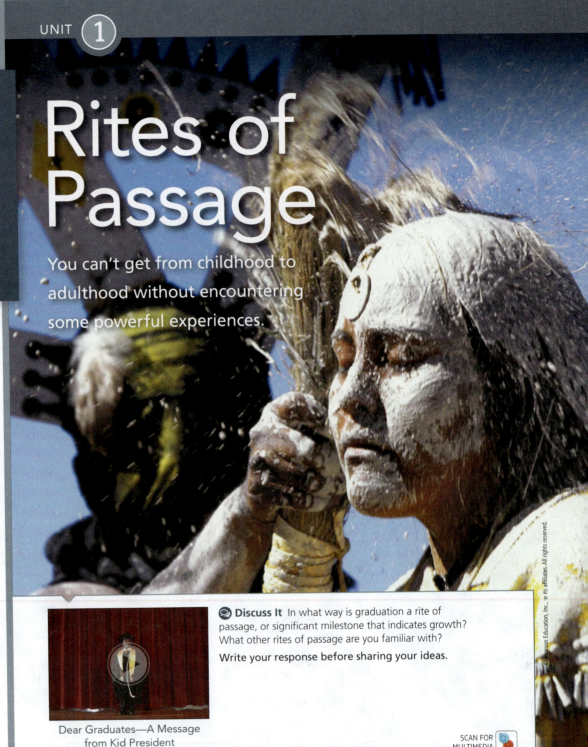

Rites of Passage

You can't get from childhood to adulthood without encountering some powerful experiences.

Discuss It In what way is graduation a rite of passage, or significant milestone that indicates growth? What other rites of passage are you familiar with?

Write your response before sharing your ideas.

Dear Graduates—A Message from Kid President

SCAN FOR MULTIMEDIA

Unit Introduction | Introduce Whole-Class Learning | The Medicine Bag | Media: Apache Girl's Rite of Passage | Performance Task

1 · 2 · 3 · 4 · 5 · 6 · 7 · 8 · 9 · 10 · 11 · 12 · 13 · 14 · 15 · 16 · 17 · 18

2 UNIT 1 • RITES OF PASSAGE

DIGITAL PERSPECTIVES

 Audio Video Document Annotation Highlights EL Highlights Online Assessment

UNIT 1

UNIT INTRODUCTION

ESSENTIAL QUESTION: What are some milestones on the path to growing up?

LAUNCH TEXT
NONFICTION
NARRATIVE MODEL
Red Roses

WHOLE-CLASS LEARNING

ANCHOR TEXT: SHORT STORY
The Medicine Bag
Virginia Driving Hawk Sneve

COMPARE

MEDIA: VIDEO
Apache Girl's Rite of Passage
National Geographic

SMALL-GROUP LEARNING

LETTERS
You Are the Electric Boogaloo
Geoff Herbach

Just Be Yourself!
Stephanie Pellegrin

POETRY COLLECTION
Hanging Fire
Audre Lorde

Translating Grandfather's House
E. J. Vega

SHORT STORY
The Setting Sun and the Rolling World
Charles Mungoshi

▸ MEDIA CONNECTION: Stories of Zimbabwean Women

INDEPENDENT LEARNING

MEMOIR
Cub Pilot on the Mississippi
Mark Twain

AUTOBIOGRAPHY
from I Know Why the Caged Bird Sings
Maya Angelou

NEWS ARTICLE
Quinceañera Birthday Bash Preserves Tradition, Marks Passage to Womanhood
Natalie St. John

REFLECTIVE ESSAY
Childhood and Poetry
Pablo Neruda

SHORT STORY
The Winter Hibiscus
Minfong Ho

PERFORMANCE TASK
WRITING FOCUS:
Write a Nonfiction Narrative

PERFORMANCE TASK
SPEAKING AND LISTENING FOCUS:
Present Nonfiction Narratives

PERFORMANCE-BASED ASSESSMENT PREP
Review Evidence for a Nonfiction Narrative

PERFORMANCE-BASED ASSESSMENT

Narrative: Nonfiction Narrative and Oral Presentation
PROMPT: What rite of passage has held the most significance for you or for a person you know well?

What are some milestones on the path to growing up?

Introduce the Essential Question and point out that students will respond to related prompts.

- **Whole-Class Learning** What event changed your understanding of yourself, or that of someone you know?
- **Small-Group Learning** What defines an event or experience in a young person's life as a milestone or rite of passage?
- **Performance-Based Assessment** What rite of passage has held the most significance for you or for a person you know well?

Using Trade Books

Refer to the Teaching With Trade Books section in this book or online in the Interactive Teacher's Edition for suggestions on how to incorporate the following thematically related novels into this unit:

- *Rules of the Road* by Joan Bauer
- *The House on Mango Street* by Sandra Cisneros
- *All Quiet on the Western Front* by Erich Maria Remarque

Current Perspectives

To increase student engagement, search online for stories about the many experiences that pave the way to adulthood, and invite your students to recommend stories they find. Always preview content before sharing it with your class.

- **Article: Special Education Prom Is a "Rite of Passage" (Southbend Tribune)**
A community comes together to ensure that all students get to go to the prom.
- **Video: Karla's Quinceañera (BBC)**
Mexican teenage girl celebrates a coming-of-age ceremony.

Introduce Small-Group Learning

Letters: You Are the Electric Boogaloo • Just Be Yourself!

| 19 | 20 | 21 | 22 |

Poetry Collection: Hanging Fire • Translating Grandfather's House

| 23 | 24 | 25 | 26 |

The Setting Sun and the Rolling World

| 27 | 28 | 29 | 30 |

Performance Task

| 31 | 32 |

Introduce Independent Learning

Independent Learning

| 33 | 34 |

Performance-Based Assessment

| 35 | 36 |

Unit Introduction 3

INTRODUCTION

About the Unit Goals

These unit goals were backward designed from the Performance-Based Assessment at the end of the unit and the Whole-Class and Small-Group Performance Tasks. Students will practice and become proficient in many more standards over the course of this unit.

Unit Goals ▶

Review the goals with students and explain that as they read and discuss the selections in this unit, they will improve their skills in reading, writing, research, language, and speaking and listening.

- Have students watch the video on Goal Setting.
- A video on this topic is available online in the Professional Development Center.

Reading Goals Tell students they will read and evaluate nonfiction narratives. They will also read arguments, informative essays, and fictional narratives to study the ways writers express ideas.

Writing and Research Goals Tell students they will learn the elements of nonfiction narrative writing and write a nonfiction narrative. Students will write for a number of reasons, including to organize and share ideas, reflect on experiences, and gather evidence. They will research to clarify and explore ideas.

Language Goal Tell students they will study grammar, including moods of verbs. They will then practice demonstrating command of standard English grammar in their own writing.

Speaking and Listening Explain to students that they will work to build on one another's ideas, develop consensus, and communicate with one another.

HOME Connection ✉

A Home Connection letter to students' parents or guardians is available in myPerspectives+. The letter explains what students will be learning in this unit and how they will be assessed.

UNIT 1 INTRODUCTION

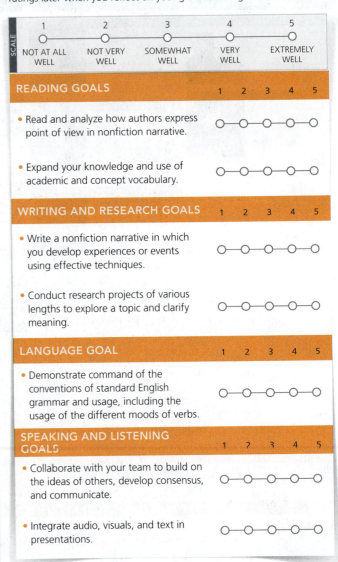

STANDARDS
Language
Acquire and use accurately grade-appropriate general academic and domain-specific words and phrases; gather vocabulary knowledge when considering a word or phrase important to comprehension or expression.

4 UNIT 1 • RITES OF PASSAGE

AUTHOR'S PERSPECTIVE: Ernest Morrell, Ph.D.

Why Goal Setting Matters Establishing goals helps students take responsibility for their own learning and become independent scholars and thinkers. One way to encourage students to set, follow, and achieve goals is to have them write their goals down. Students can use the following process for crafting well-defined and measurable goals:

- **Decide What You Want:** Have students skim the Unit 1 Table of Contents and decide what they most want to learn from the unit. Guide students to set specific, realistic goals, such as "learn and correctly use five new concept words from the unit."

- **Write the Goals Down:** Have students draft the goals in clear, precise language. Students should also include a way to measure results so they can assess their progress.

- **Set a Time Frame:** Have students include a realistic schedule for completion, using the length of the selections in Unit 1 as a guide. As necessary, have students break large goals into smaller ones to make the goal more likely to be completed.

When students take more responsibility for their learning, they may learn to rely more on themselves and take more interest in their success.

ESSENTIAL QUESTION: What are some milestones on the path to growing up?

Academic Vocabulary: Nonfiction Narrative

Academic terms appear in all subjects and can help you read, write, and discuss with more precision. Nonfiction narratives are based on true events and written in a story form to engage and keep readers' interest. Here are five academic words that will be useful to you in this unit as you analyze and write nonfiction narratives.

Complete the chart.

1. Review each word, its root, and the mentor sentences.
2. Use the information and your own knowledge to predict the meaning of each word.
3. For each word, list at least two related words.
4. Refer to the dictionary or other resources if needed.

TIP

FOLLOW THROUGH
Study the words in this chart, and mark them or their forms wherever they appear in the unit.

WORD	MENTOR SENTENCES	PREDICT MEANING	RELATED WORDS
attribute ROOT -trib- "give"	1. I *attribute* my success to hard work. 2. People *attribute* this song to Bill, but, actually, Shana wrote it.		contribute; tribute
gratifying ROOT -grat- "thankful" or "pleasing"	1. It was *gratifying* to get an A on the test after studying all week. 2. Getting praise from her co-workers for a job well done was *gratifying* to Lisa.		
persistent ROOT -sist- "stand"	1. The East Coast experienced *persistent* rain for days. 2. The dog's barking from inside the house was *persistent*.		
notable ROOT -not- "mark"	1. Mrs. Smith's garden was *notable* for its bright flowers. 2. The book club asked a *notable* writer to speak to their group about his achievements.		
inspire ROOT -spir- "breathe"	1. This poster will *inspire* people to vote. 2. If you want to *inspire* me, you'll have to say something positive about my work.		

Unit Introduction 5

INTRODUCTION

Purpose of the Launch Text
The Launch Text provides students with a common starting point to address the unit topic. After reading the Launch Text, all students will be able to participate in discussions about rites of passage.

Lexile: 560 The easier reading level of this selection makes it perfect to assign for homework. Students will need little or no support to understand it.

Additionally, "Red Roses" provides a writing model for the Performance-Based Assessment students will complete at the end of the unit.

Launch Text: Nonfiction Narrative Model
Have students pay attention to the way the narrator's attitude changes as the story goes on. What are her first reactions? What are her later responses? When does she begin to respond differently? Why does she change?

Also remind students to think about the descriptive details the author uses and the events the author describes to tell the story.

Encourage students to read this text on their own and annotate unfamiliar words and sections of text they think are particularly important.

🔊 AUDIO SUMMARIES
Audio summaries of "Red Roses" are available online in both English and Spanish in the Interactive Teacher's Edition or Unit Resources. Assigning these summaries before students read the Launch Text may help them build additional background knowledge and set a context for their reading.

UNIT 1 INTRODUCTION

LAUNCH TEXT | NONFICTION NARRATIVE

This text presents a **nonfiction narrative**, a type of writing in which an author explores an experience using descriptive details and events. This is the type of writing you will develop in the Performance-Based Assessment at the end of the unit.

As you read, look at the way the girl's reactions change as she understands the situation better.

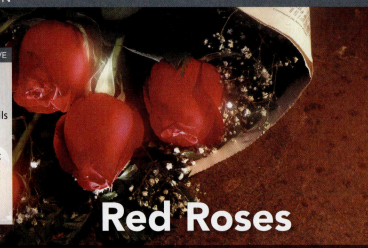

Red Roses

NOTES

1   When I was in middle school what I wanted most was to fit in. That's all anybody wants in middle school. In middle school, you're suspicious of anyone who stands out for any reason. Derek stood out. We all avoided him.

2   My mom had always told us never to make fun of people, so I never did. I can't say the same for my friends. Not that they were outright *mean* or anything, but they'd whisper behind their hands, and it was obvious who they were whispering about. I took no part in this, as I said, but I have to admit I steered clear of Derek like everyone else.

3   Despite my standoffishness, Derek started leaving me little gifts: every couple of days, something new—treasures out of a cereal box or a gum machine would turn up in my locker, in my desk, in the pocket of my jacket. I did not acknowledge these things, and immediately tossed them into the back of my closet when I got home. I guess I could have told my mother, but I didn't. Sometimes you have to figure things out for yourself.

4   The weeks passed. I continued to ignore Derek, and made sure to stay out of his way. Still, the presents continued, a different one each time. I resented the fact that he spent so much time thinking up ways to get my attention. Didn't he have better things to do?

5   My friends teased me. "Oooooh, Lila has a boyfriend! Lila has a boyfriend!" they sang out. It didn't seem fair. I'd tried so hard to fit in, to fade into the woodwork, but here I was, being teased, the butt of a joke. The center of attention.

6   One day Derek strode up to me in the lunchroom and presented me with a dozen roses—red, long-stemmed, in a fluted paper wrapper with a note tucked inside: *I know I'm not the coolest kid/But take these roses/You'll be glad you did.*

6 UNIT 1 • RITES OF PASSAGE

SCAN FOR MULTIMEDIA

CROSS-CURRICULAR PERSPECTIVES

Social Studies In some cultures, gift-giving and hospitality are extremely important. Have students research one of these cultures and report on it to the class. Discuss differences and similarities between these cultures and the social culture of the United States.

ESSENTIAL QUESTION: What are some milestones on the path to growing up?

7 I should have been flattered, but I was good and angry. The fact that he stood there grinning lopsidedly, roses in hand, with that hopeful look in his eyes, made me even angrier. I wanted to squash him like a bug.

8 "Leave me alone," I growled. "Don't you get it? GO AWAY!"

9 "Ooooooooooh!" sang the chorus of girls. I wanted to crawl under a rock. Derek looked as miserable as I did. And then—horrors!—I saw his bottom lip quiver. He looked like he was going to cry. He *couldn't* cry! If he cried they'd call him a crybaby. *Derek is a crybaby* would follow him around for the rest of his life!

10 I decided I would not, could not let that happen. No one was going to make me. Not even my friends!

11 I took the roses. I carried them around all day.

12 I never did talk to Derek after that. We nodded politely to each other in the hallway, but I never pretended to like him, and he never gave me another present. Somehow we'd worked it out. I lost track of Derek when his family moved away.

13 I guess you could say this was the first time I did something I didn't want to do just to protect someone else's feelings from getting hurt. Maybe you could call this growth or maturity, I honestly don't know.

14 Even though it happened a long time ago, I can picture myself on that day, striding through the corridor proudly, the dozen roses clenched tightly in my hand, walking tall, feeling like no one could touch me.

NOTES

WORD NETWORK FOR RITES OF PASSAGE

Vocabulary A Word Network is a collection of words related to a topic. As you read the selections in this unit, identify interesting words related to the idea of rites of passage and add them to your Word Network. For example, you might begin by adding words from the Launch Text, such as *acknowledge, attention* and *maturity*. Continue to add words as you complete this unit.

🔧 **Tool Kit**
Word Network Model

- acknowledge
- attention
- maturity

RITES OF PASSAGE

INTRODUCTION

Summary

Have students read the introductory paragraph. Provide them with tips for writing a summary:

- Write in the present tense.
- Make sure to include the title of the work.
- Be concise: a summary should not be equal in length to the original text.
- If you need to quote the words of the author, use quotation marks.
- Don't put your own opinions, ideas, or interpretations into the summary. The purpose of writing a summary is to accurately represent what the author says, not to provide a critique.

If necessary, students can refer to the Tool Kit for help in understanding the elements of a good summary.

See possible summary on student page.

Launch Activity

Explain to students that as they work on this unit, they will have many opportunities to focus on milestones and to discuss the topic of rites of passage. Remind students that they should participate in the discussion by referencing material they've read and viewed as well as their own experiences.

Encourage students to keep an open mind and really listen to their classmates.

UNIT 1 INTRODUCTION

Summary

Write a summary of "Red Roses." A **summary** is a concise, complete, and accurate overview of a text. It should not include a statement of your opinion or an analysis of the text.

> **Possible response:** In "Red Roses," Lila shares an experience from when she was a middle school student. She remembers a boy named Derek who seemed different from other students. She explains that she initially ignored him, but he began to leave gifts for her each day. Her friends teased her, and so the gifts annoyed her. One day, Derek presented Lila with a dozen roses. She got angry with him and told him to leave her alone, but then she noticed that he looked like he was going to cry. To protect him, she took the flowers and carried them all day in school. They never spoke again, but she counts this as an important day in her life. It was a day she did something she didn't want to do just to protect someone else.

Launch Activity

Create a Timeline Consider this statement: The journey into adulthood is marked by life-changing events and observations.

Work with your class to complete the following activity:

- With your classmates, brainstorm for and list milestones that many people experience. Milestones may include sports events, social or religious events, or academic or work-related events.
- After listing types of milestones, take turns with other students to put a star next to each of the five they deem most important.
- Work with the class to create a timeline of the chosen milestones. Are the milestones scattered, or do they seem to occur during a specific time of life?

VOCABULARY DEVELOPMENT

Academic Vocabulary Reinforcement Students will benefit from additional examples and practice with the academic vocabulary. Reinforce their comprehension with "show-you-know" sentences. The first part of the sentence uses the vocabulary word in an appropriate context. The second part of the sentence—the "show-you-know" part—clarifies the first. Model the strategy with this example for *attribute*:

Samuel would *attribute* his good grades to eating well and getting enough sleep; he thought his success was associated with his habits.

Then give students these sentence prompts and coach them in creating the clarification part:

1. Aisha found the letter of recommendation *gratifying*; _____.
   Possible response: she was glad to see her work recognized.

2. Jim was *persistent* in fixing the car; _____.
   Possible response: after hours he finally succeeded.

3. We developed a list of *notable* apps; _____.
   Possible response: every one was highly rated.

4. The teacher could *inspire* pride in her students; _____.
   Possible response: she made them proud of their work.

ESSENTIAL QUESTION: What are some milestones on the path to growing up?

DIGITAL PERSPECTIVES

QuickWrite

Consider class discussions, presentations, the video, and the Launch Text as you think about the prompt. Record your first thoughts here.

PROMPT: What rite of passage has held the most significance for you or for a person you know well?

Possible response: While I think that starting middle school is a rite of passage for a young person, I don't think it is the most important rite of passage. Starting middle school is a sign that a child is getting older. It might mean taking more interest in someone else's feelings over your own, as Lila does in the story "Red Roses."

Middle school is also an adjustment because it's organized differently. It's more like high school and college than grade school is, and you have more freedom. This is another sign that you're growing up, and another way that starting middle school is a rite of passage.

I think the most important rite of passage may be when a young person learns to drive a car. My brother just got his license and I see how much freedom his license gives him.

EVIDENCE LOG FOR RITES OF PASSAGE

Review your QuickWrite and summarize your ideas in one sentence to record in your Evidence Log. Then, record details from "Red Roses" that provide insights about rites of passage.

After each selection, use your Evidence Log to record the details you gather and the connections you make. This graphic shows what your Evidence Log looks like.

Title of Text:		Date: _____
CONNECTION TO PROMPT	TEXT EVIDENCE/DETAILS	ADDITIONAL NOTES/IDEAS

How does this text change or add to my thinking?   Date: _____

Tool Kit
Evidence Log Model

SCAN FOR MULTIMEDIA

Unit Introduction 9

QuickWrite

In this QuickWrite, students should present their own response to the prompt based on the material in the Unit Opener. This initial response will help inform their work when they complete the Performance-Based Assessment at the end of the unit. Students should make sure they present their ideas clearly and support them logically with relevant evidence and accurate details.

See possible QuickWrite on student page.

Evidence Log for Rites of Passage

Students should record their initial thinking in their Evidence Logs. Then, they should record details from "Red Roses" that reflect insight.

If you choose to print the Evidence Log, distribute it to students at this point so they can use it throughout the rest of the unit.

Performance-Based Assessment: Refining Your Thinking
- Have students watch the video on Refining Your Thinking
- A video on this topic is available online in the Professional Development Center.

WriteNow Express and Reflect

Analyze Have students write one or two sentences in which they answer the following questions: Why are rites of passage important? How might someone's life be changed after going through a rite of passage?

Red Roses 9

OVERVIEW

WHOLE-CLASS LEARNING

What are some milestones on the path to growing up?

The road to adulthood is often paved with memorable, and sometimes difficult, events. These events shape our lives and will eventually make us adults who are wiser for having had the experiences. During Whole-Class Learning, students will read selections about the triumphs and obstacles that lie between childhood and adulthood.

Whole-Class Learning Strategies

Review the Learning Strategies with students and explain that as they work through Whole-Class Learning, they will develop strategies to work in large-group environments.

- Have students watch the video on Whole-Class Learning Strategies
- A video on this topic is available in the Professional Development Center.

You may wish to discuss some action items to add to the chart as a class before students complete it on their own. For example, for "Listen actively," you might solicit the following from students:

- Take notes so that you can remember important details later.
- Ask questions afterwards so that anything that was unclear can be explained to you.

Block Scheduling

Each day in this Pacing Plan represents a 40- to 50-minute class period. Teachers using block scheduling may combine days to reflect their class schedule. In addition, teachers may revise pacing to differentiate and support core instruction by integrating components and resources as students require.

📅 **Pacing Plan**

OVERVIEW: WHOLE CLASS LEARNING

ESSENTIAL QUESTION:

What are some milestones on the path to growing up?

The path to growing up is lined with milestones; some are universal, but others are meaningful only to you. Often you don't recognize them as milestones until later, after you've passed them. As you read, you will work with your whole class to explore a wide range of milestones on the path to growing up.

Whole-Class Learning Strategies

Throughout your life, in school, in your community, and in your career, you will continue to learn and work in large-group environments.

Review these strategies and the actions you can take to practice them as you work with your whole class. Add ideas of your own for each category for each step. Get ready to use these strategies during Whole-Class Learning.

STRATEGY	ACTION PLAN
Listen actively	• Eliminate distractions. For example, put your cellphone away. • Keep your eyes on the speaker. •
Clarify by asking questions	• If you're confused, other people probably are, too. Ask a question to help your whole class. • If you see that you are guessing, ask a question instead. •
Monitor understanding	• Notice what information you already know and be ready to build on it. • Ask for help if you are struggling. •
Interact and share ideas	• Share your ideas and answer questions, even if you are unsure. • Build on the ideas of others by adding details or making a connection. •

SCAN FOR MULTIMEDIA

Pacing Plan

1 | 2 — Unit Introduction
3 — Introduce Whole-Class Learning
4–12 — The Medicine Bag
13–15 — Media: Apache Girl's Rite of Passage
16–18 — Performance Task

WHOLE-CLASS LEARNING

DIGITAL PERSPECTIVES

CONTENTS

ANCHOR TEXT: SHORT STORY

The Medicine Bag
Virginia Driving Hawk Sneve

An aging Lakota man passes on a mysterious gift to his grandchild.

COMPARE

MEDIA: VIDEO

Apache Girl's Rite of Passage
National Geographic

In preparation for womanhood, Apache girls undergo tests of strength and endurance.

PERFORMANCE TASK

WRITING FOCUS

Write a Nonfiction Narrative

The Whole-Class reading and video describe some traditional rites of passage. After reading and viewing, you will write a nonfiction narrative in which you relate an experience that you or someone you know had that might be considered a rite of passage.

Contents

Anchor Texts Preview the anchor text and media with students to generate interest. Encourage students to discuss other texts they may have read or movies or television shows they may have seen that deal with the issues of growing up.

You may wish to conduct a poll to determine which selection students think looks more interesting and discuss the reasons for their preference. Students can return to this poll after they have read and viewed the selections to see if their preference changed.

Performance Task

Write a Nonfiction Narrative Explain to students that after they have finished reading and viewing the selections, they will write a nonfiction narrative about events that change people's experiences as they grow up. To help them prepare, encourage students to think about the topic as they progress through the selections and as they participate in the Whole-Class Learning experience.

PLANNING

WHOLE-CLASS LEARNING • THE MEDICINE BAG

The Medicine Bag

AUDIO SUMMARIES
Audio summaries of "The Medicine Bag" are available in both English and Spanish and can be assigned to students in the Interactive Teacher's Edition or Unit Resources. Assigning these summaries prior to reading the selection may help students build additional background knowledge and set a context for their first read.

Summary
In "The Medicine Bag" by Virginia Driving Hawk Sneve, Martin's Lakota grandfather comes to live with his family. Martin is worried that, in person, his grandfather will not impress his friends as much as the stories he's told about him. He also doesn't feel ready for his grandfather to pass down a family tradition to him. But both his friends and his grandfather see more nuance than he expects.

Insight
"The Medicine Bag" is a thoughtful, humane story about cultural understanding. Martin's friends are impressed by his grandfather even though he doesn't look like TV images of Native Americans. His grandfather understands that it wouldn't be appropriate for Martin to wear the medicine bag everywhere. Indeed, the quest story his grandfather tells involves bringing Western things, symbolized by the piece of the iron pot, into Lakota tradition.

ESSENTIAL QUESTION:
What are some milestones on the path to growing up?

Connection to Essential Question
This story explores an important milestone in a young Native American boy's life. The passing of the medicine bag symbolizes maturity. Less concrete milestones in this story could include reconciling oneself to one's family history, and the loss of a beloved relative.

WHOLE-CLASS LEARNING PERFORMANCE TASK
What event changed your understanding of yourself, or that of someone you know?

Connection to Performance Tasks

Whole-Class Learning Performance Task This story may help students prepare for the performance task. Students may see that Martin's responses to the events in the story are critical to the way he understands himself.

UNIT PERFORMANCE-BASED ASSESSMENT
What rite of passage has held the most significance for you or for a person you know well?

Unit Performance-Based Assessment There are several events here that students may use as inspiration or reflection as they prepare to answer the prompt. This story includes the passing of an important family item, the grandfather's implied death, and the visit itself. This may spark student reflection on family items that are important to them.

DIGITAL PERSPECTIVES   Audio   Video   Document   Annotation Highlights   EL Highlights   Online Assessment

LESSON RESOURCES

	Making Meaning	Language Development	Effective Expression
Lesson	First Read Close Read Analyze the Text Analyze Craft and Structure	Concept Vocabulary Word Study Conventions	Writing to Sources Speaking and Listening
Instructional Standards	**RL.10** By the end of the year, read and comprehend literature . . . **RL.4** Determine the meaning of words and phrases as they are used in a text . . .	**L.4** Determine or clarify the meaning of unknown and multiple-meaning words or phrases . . . **L.4.c** Consult general and specialized reference materials . . . **L.4.d** Verify the preliminary determination . . . **L.3** Use knowledge of language . . . **L.3.a** Use verbs in the active and passive voice . . . **L.1** Demonstrate command of the conventions . . . **L.1.b** Form and use verbs . . .	**W.3** Write narratives . . . **W.3.a** Engage and orient the reader . . . **W.3.b** Use narrative techniques . . . **W.3.d** Use precise words and phrases . . . **W.3.e** Provide a conclusion . . . **SL.4** Present claims and findings . . .
STUDENT RESOURCES			
Available online in the Interactive Student Edition or Unit Resources	Selection Audio First-Read Guide: Fiction Close-Read Guide: Fiction	Word Network	Evidence Log
TEACHER RESOURCES			
Selection Resources Available online in the Interactive Teacher's Edition or Unit Resources	Audio Summaries Annotation Highlights EL Highlights English Language Support Lesson: Point of View Analyze Craft and Structure: Symbolism	Concept Vocabulary and Word Study Conventions: Verbs in Active and Passive Voice	Writing to Sources: Retelling Speaking and Listening: Monologue
Reteach/Practice (RP) Available online in the Interactive Teacher's Edition or Unit Resources	Analyze Craft and Structure: Symbolism (RP)	Word Study: Animal Words (RP) Conventions: Verbs in Active and Passive Voice (RP)	Writing to Sources: Retelling (RP) Speaking and Listening: Monologue (RP)
Assessment Available online in Assessments	Selection Test		
My Resources	A Unit 1 Answer Key is available online and in the Interactive Teacher's Edition.		

Whole-Class Learning 12B

PERSONALIZE FOR LEARNING
WHOLE-CLASS LEARNING • THE MEDICINE BAG

Reading Support

Text Complexity Rubric: The Medicine Bag

Quantitative Measures

Lexile: 920   Text Length: 3,516 words

Qualitative Measures

Knowledge Demands ①—②—③—**④**—⑤	This story explores several complex themes and experiences that are unfamiliar to many readers, including aging, cultural identity, Lakota cultural traditions, and generational ties.
Structure ①—**②**—③—④—⑤	Story is clear and chronological; story elements are interspersed with cultural background. Dialogue breaks up text, making story concrete and easier to read.
Language Conventionality and Clarity ①—**②**—③—④—⑤	Language is explicit, literal, and straightforward. Vocabulary is on-level, contemporary, and familiar. Sentences are mostly simple construction, though some are longer with multiple clauses.
Levels of Meaning/Purpose ①—②—③—**④**—⑤	Multiple levels of meaning; Themes of aging, cultural traditions, and different perceptions are subtle and revealed over the entirety of the text.

DECIDE AND PLAN

English Language Support
Provide English Learners with support for knowledge demands and meaning as they read the selection.

Knowledge Demands Talk about the word *indigenous*, a synonym of *native*. Point out that *Native American* and *indigenous people* are two other ways to describe *Indians*. The *Lakota* are one group of Indians. Preview the story: the family lives in a city, and the great-grandfather is Lakota and lives on the reservation. He is following the tradition of passing down a medicine bag to the oldest male child.

Meaning Help students to outline plot events. Have them complete sentences, for example *The grandfather lived _____ (on the reservation).* Then discuss the feelings and the more subtle meanings associated with these events: *When he visited, the grandson felt _____ (ashamed and embarrassed).*

Strategic Support
Provide students with strategic support to ensure that they can successfully read the text.

Knowledge Demands Find out what students know about any Native American groups. Use the background to review the name and location of the Lakota. Then discuss the information in the background and beginning of the story.

Meaning Ask about the basic plot elements of the story—for example, *Where did the grandfather come from? (the reservation). What did he want to give to the grandson? (the medicine bag).* Then point out the more subtle elements of the story—for example (paragraph 4): *How did the grandson feel when the grandfather came? (ashamed and embarrassed) Why? (He is embarrassed by the grandfather's appearance and behavior. He thinks others will make fun of him.)*

Challenge
Provide students who need to be challenged with ideas for how they can go beyond a simple interpretation of the text.

Text Analysis Discuss why the grandfather seems different because of his dress and behavior. Cite evidence that shows how the grandfather thinks and feels about getting older and examples of what his life was like living on the reservation. Describe why the narrator feels both embarrassment and pride in his grandfather at different points in the story.

Written Response Ask students to research and read more about the Lakota people and the tradition of the medicine bag. Ask them to find additional information about Lakota traditions and how they have changed over time. Have them write short essays on the most interesting information they find and to share their essays with the class.

TEACH

Read and Respond
Have students do their first read of the selection. Then, have them complete their close read. Finally, work with them on the Making Meaning, Language Development, and Effective Expression activities.

Standards Support Through Teaching and Learning Cycle

IDENTIFY NEEDS

Analyze results of the Beginning-of-Year Assessment, focusing on the items relating to Unit 1. Also take into consideration student performance to this point and your observations of where particular students struggle.

ANALYZE AND REVISE

- Analyze student work for evidence of student learning.
- Identify whether or not students have met the expectations in the standards.
- Identify implications for future instruction.

TEACH

Implement the planned lesson, and gather evidence of student learning.

DECIDE AND PLAN

- If students have performed poorly on items matching these standards, then provide selection scaffolds before assigning them the on-level lesson provided in the Student Edition.
- If students have done well on the Beginning-of-Year Assessment, then challenge them to keep progressing and learning by giving them opportunities to practice the skills in depth.
- Use the Selection Resources listed on the Planning pages for "The Medicine Bag" to help students continually improve their ability to master the standards.

Instructional Standards: The Medicine Bag

	Catching Up	This Year	Looking Forward
Reading	You may wish to administer the **Analyze Craft and Structure: Symbolism (RP)** worksheet to help students understand how to recognize the use of symbols in the story and to determine what the symbols mean.	**RL.4** Determine the meaning of words and phrases as they are used in a text . . .	Invite students to provide additional examples of symbolism. Have them evaluate how the use of the symbols enhances the narrative.
Writing	You may wish to administer the **Writing to Sources: Retelling (RP)** worksheet to help students retell the story from the grandfather's point of view.	**W.3.a** Engage and orient the reader by establishing a context and point of view . . . **W.3.b** Use narrative techniques, such as dialogue, pacing, description, and reflection . . .	Challenge students to review their narratives to make sure they have used vivid, descriptive words and phrases.
Speaking and Listening	You may wish to administer the **Speaking and Listening: Monologue (RP)** worksheet to help students plan and deliver their monologues.	**SL.4** Present claims and findings . . .	You may wish to challenge students to organize and present increasingly longer or more complex monologues.
Language	You may wish to administer the **Conventions: Verbs in Active and Passive Voice (RP)** worksheet to help students identify the use of active and passive voice in sentences. You may wish to administer the **Word Study: Animal Words (RP)** worksheet to help students understand how animal characteristics drive the meaning of some adjectives.	**L.3.a** Use verbs in the active and passive voice and in the conditional and subjunctive mood to achieve particular effects. **L.4** Determine or clarify the meaning of unknown and multiple-meaning words or phrases . . .	Challenge students to identify active and passive voice in their own writing. Have students rewrite passive sentences to use the active voice. Have students identify other adjectives that they know based on animals.

Whole-Class Learning **12D**

TEACHING

Jump Start

FIRST READ Prior to students' first read, engage them in a discussion about how older and younger generations, such as grandparents and grandchildren, interact to help them make connections between the text and their own experiences.

The Medicine Bag 🔊 📄

How does the narrator feel about his grandfather? How do the narrator and his sister feel about Grandpa's visit? How do you think Grandpa feels about this visit? Modeling questions such as these will help students connect to "The Medicine Bag" and to the Performance Task assignment. Selection audio and print capability for the selection are available in the Interactive Teacher's Edition.

Concept Vocabulary

Support students as they rank the words. Ask if they've ever heard, read, or used them. Reassure them that the definitions for these words are listed in the selection.

As they read, students should perform the steps of the first read:

NOTICE: You may want to encourage students to track the narrator's feelings about Grandpa and to note how they change during the story.

ANNOTATE: Remind students to mark passages they feel are particularly evocative or worthy of analysis in their close read. For example, students may want to focus on passages that explain why or how the narrator's feelings change.

CONNECT: Encourage students to go beyond the selection to make connections to additional texts and personal experiences. If they cannot make connections to their own lives or other texts, have them consider movies and TV shows as well.

RESPOND: Students will answer questions and write a summary to demonstrate understanding. Point out to students that while they will always complete the Respond step at the end of the first read, the other steps will probably happen somewhat concurrently. You may wish to print copies of the **First-Read Guide: Fiction** for students to use. 📄

Remind students that during their first read, they should not answer the close-read questions that appear in the selection.

MAKING MEANING

THE MEDICINE BAG

Comparing Text to Media
In this lesson, you will compare "The Medicine Bag" and "Apache Girl's Rite of Passage." First, you will complete the first-read and close-read activities for "The Medicine Bag."

APACHE GIRL'S RITE OF PASSAGE

About the Author

Virginia Driving Hawk Sneve (b. 1933) grew up on the Rosebud Reservation in South Dakota. Her grandmothers were storytellers, sharing traditional Sioux legends and folk tales that became an inspiration for Sneve's work. She realized that American Indians were often misrepresented in children's books, and she has worked throughout her writing career to portray American Indians realistically. In 2000, President Bill Clinton awarded Sneve a National Humanities Medal.

🔧 **Tool Kit**
First-Read Guide and Model Annotation

📋 **STANDARDS**
Reading Literature
By the end of the year, read and comprehend literature, including stories, dramas, and poems, at the high end of the grades 6–8 text complexity band independently and proficiently.

12 UNIT 1 • RITES OF PASSAGE

The Medicine Bag

Concept Vocabulary
You will encounter the following words as you read "The Medicine Bag." Before reading, note how familiar you are with each word. Then, rank the words in order from most familiar (1) to least familiar (5).

WORD	YOUR RANKING
wearily	
straggled	
fatigue	
frail	
sheepishly	

After completing the first read, come back to the concept vocabulary and review your rankings. Mark any changes to your original rankings.

First Read FICTION

Refer to the information below as you conduct your first read. You will have an opportunity to complete the close-read notes after your first read.

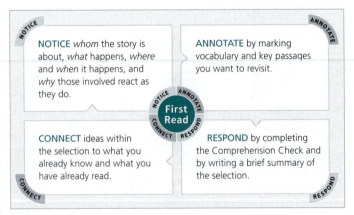

NOTICE whom the story is about, *what* happens, *where* and *when* it happens, and *why* those involved react as they do.

ANNOTATE by marking vocabulary and key passages you want to revisit.

CONNECT ideas within the selection to what you already know and what you have already read.

RESPOND by completing the Comprehension Check and by writing a brief summary of the selection.

AUTHOR'S PERSPECTIVE Kelly Gallagher, M.Ed.

Teacher as the Best Reader in the Class
Rather than being the wizard behind the curtain, use modeling to do the work of reading in front of students. When students see that even good readers wrestle with difficult text, they gain confidence. Use these methods:

- **Using Think-Aloud:** Choose a passage from this unit and model read alouds/think alouds to show students what effective readers do when they are confused. The *Annotate Question Conclude* feature and the teacher edition support highlight the importance of this work.

- **Marking the Text:** If students say they don't understand, have them use a yellow highlighter (or sticky notes) for parts they understand and a pink highlighter for those they don't.

ANCHOR TEXT | SHORT STORY

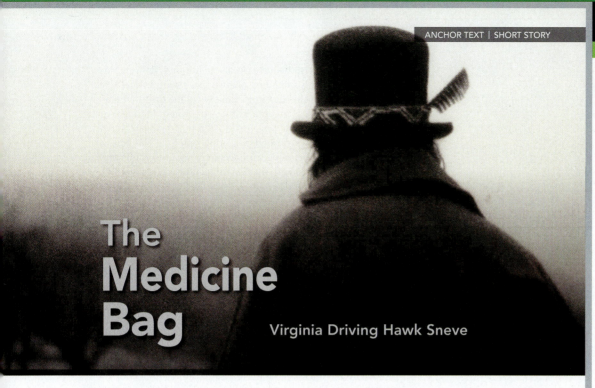

The Medicine Bag

Virginia Driving Hawk Sneve

BACKGROUND
The Lakota Indians are part of the Sioux Nation, an indigenous people of the Great Plains region of North America. Today there are about 170,000 Sioux Indians living in the United States. About one-fifth of the American Indian population live on *reservations,* which are designated pieces of land ruled by tribal law.

1 Grandpa wasn't tall and stately like TV Indians. His hair wasn't in braids; it hung in stringy, gray strands on his neck, and he was old. He was my great-grandfather, and he didn't live in a tipi[1]; he lived all by himself in a part log, part tar-paper shack on the Rosebud Reservation in South Dakota.

2 My kid sister, Cheryl, and I always bragged about our Lakota[2] grandpa, Joe Iron Shell. Our friends, who had always lived in the city and only knew about Indians from movies and TV, were impressed by our stories. Maybe we exaggerated and made Grandpa and the reservation sound glamorous, but when we returned home to Iowa after our yearly summer visit to Grandpa, we always had some exciting tale to tell.

3 We usually had some authentic Lakota article to show our listeners. One year Cheryl had new moccasins[3] that Grandpa had

---
1. **tipi** *n.* cone-shaped tent traditionally made of animal skins or bark.
2. **Lakota** *adj.* belonging to a Native American tribe from the Great Plains region (present-day North and South Dakota).
3. **moccasins** (MOK uh suhnz) *n.* soft shoes traditionally made from animal hide.

CLOSER LOOK

Analyze Characterization
Students may have marked paragraph 1 during their first read. Use this paragraph to help students understand how the narrator feels about Grandpa. Encourage them to talk about the annotations that they marked. You may want to model a close read with the class based on the highlights shown in the text.

ANNOTATE: Have students mark details in paragraph 1 that describe Grandpa's appearance, or have students participate while you highlight them.

QUESTION: Guide students to consider what these details might tell them. Ask what a reader can infer about Grandpa's appearance from these descriptions, and accept student responses.

Possible response: Grandpa doesn't look like the Indians that people see on TV. The TV Indians described in the selection are based on stereotypes which create distorted expectations for Native Americans.

CONCLUDE: Help students to formulate conclusions about the importance of these details in the text. Ask students why the author might have included these details at the beginning of the story.

Possible response: By including these details, the author is suggesting that the narrator might be embarrassed about Grandpa's appearance.

Remind students that there are two types of **characterization**. In **direct characterization,** the author directly states a character's traits. In **indirect characterization,** an author provides clues about a character by describing the character's appearance, actions, and feelings, as well as how other characters react to him or her.

- **Using Sentence Starters:** To identify where students are having comprehension problems, have them complete this sentence starter: "I don't understand…" Then, as a class, work to resolve the issues. Use these additional sentence starters: *I noticed…; I wonder…; I think…; I'm surprised that…; I realized…; I'm not sure…*

It is also important for students to know that applying tools like these doesn't always work: sometimes, readers decide to live with ambiguity.

CROSS-CURRICULAR PERSPECTIVES

Geography In paragraph 1, the narrator mentions that his grandfather's home is on the Rosebud Reservation in South Dakota. On a map of South Dakota, have students locate the Rosebud Reservation. Have them research which two groups of Lakota the reservation is home to and choose one of the two groups to learn about. As a class, discuss what the two groups' lives are like on the reservation.

TEACHING

NOTES

made. On another visit he gave me a small, round, flat rawhide drum decorated with a painting of a warrior riding a horse. He taught me a Lakota chant to sing while I beat the drum with a leather-covered stick that had a feather on the end. Man that really made an impression.

4   We never showed our friends Grandpa's picture. Not that we were ashamed of him but because we knew that the glamorous tales we told didn't go with the real thing. Our friends would have laughed, so when Grandpa came to visit us, I was so ashamed and embarrassed I could have died.

5   There are a lot of yippy poodles and other fancy little dogs in our neighborhood, but they usually barked singly at the mailman from the safety of their own yards. Now it sounded as if a whole pack of mutts were barking together in one place.

6   I walked to the curb to see what the commotion was. About a block away I saw a crowd of little kids yelling, with the dogs yipping and growling around someone who was walking down the middle of the street.

7   I watched the group as it slowly came closer and saw that in the center of the strange procession was a man wearing a tall black hat. He'd pause now and then to peer at something in his hand and then at the houses on either side of the street. I felt cold and hot at the same time. I recognized the man. "Oh, no!" I whispered, "It's Grandpa!"

8   I stood on the curb, unable to move even though I wanted to run and hide. Then I got mad when I saw how the yippy dogs were growling and nipping at the old man's baggy pant legs and how **wearily** he poked them away with his cane. "Stupid mutts," I said as I ran to rescue Grandpa.

wearily (WEER uh lee) *adv.* in a tired way

9   When I kicked and hollered at the dogs to get away, they put their tails between their legs and scattered. The kids ran to the curb where they watched me and the old man.

10   "Grandpa," I said and reached for his beat-up old tin suitcase tied shut with a rope. But he set it down right in the street and shook my hand.

11   "*Hau, Takoza,* Grandchild," he greeted me formally in Lakota.

12   All I could do was stand there with the whole neighborhood watching and shake the hand of the leather-brown old man. I saw how his gray hair **straggled** from under his big black hat, which had a drooping feather in its crown. His rumpled black suit hung like a sack over his stooped frame. As he shook my hand, his coat fell open to expose a bright red satin shirt with a beaded bolo tie under the collar. His getup wasn't out of place on the reservation, but it sure was here, and I wanted to sink right through the pavement.

straggled (STRAG uhld) *v.* hung in messy strands

💬 Additional **English Language Support** is available in the Interactive Teacher's Edition.

14   UNIT 1 • RITES OF PASSAGE

PERSONALIZE FOR LEARNING

English Language Support

Understand Connotations Explain to students that the word *mutts* in paragraph 8 refers to a dog that is a mixed breed. Because some people think that mixed-breed dogs are not as good as one-breed dogs, often called purebreds, sometimes the word *mutt* is used as an insult, as it is here. **ALL LEVELS**

13 "Hi," I muttered with my head down. I tried to pull my hand away when I felt his bony hand trembling and then looked up to see fatigue in his face. I felt like crying. I couldn't think of anything to say so I picked up Grandpa's suitcase, took his arm, and guided him up the driveway to our house.

14 Mom was standing on the steps. I don't know how long she'd been watching, but her hand was over her mouth and she looked as if she couldn't believe what she saw. Then she ran to us.

15 "Grandpa," she gasped. "How in the world did you get here?"

16 She checked her move to embrace Grandpa and I remembered that such a display of affection is unseemly to the Lakota and would have embarrassed him.

17 "*Hau*, Marie," he said as he shook Mom's hand. She smiled and took his other arm.

18 As we supported him up the steps, the door banged open and Cheryl came bursting out of the house. She was all smiles and was so obviously glad to see Grandpa that I was ashamed of how I felt.

19 "Grandpa!" she yelled happily. "You came to see us!"

20 Grandpa smiled, and Mom and I let go of him as he stretched out his arms to my ten-year-old sister, who was still young enough to be hugged.

21 "*Wicincila*, little girl," he greeted her and then collapsed.

22 He had fainted. Mom and I carried him into her sewing room, where we had a spare bed.

23 After we had Grandpa on the bed, Mom stood there patting his shoulder. "You make Grandpa comfortable, Martin," she decided, "while I call the doctor."

24 I reluctantly moved to the bed. I knew Grandpa wouldn't want to have Mom undress him, but I didn't want to either. He was so skinny and **frail** that his coat slipped off easily. When I loosened his tie and opened his shirt collar, I felt a small leather pouch that hung from a thong around his neck. I left it alone and moved to remove his boots. The scuffed old cowboy boots were tight, and he moaned as I put pressure on his legs to jerk them off.

25 I put the boots on the floor and saw why they fit so tight. Each one was stuffed with money. I looked at the bills that lined the boots and started to ask about them, but Grandpa's eyes were closed again.

26 Mom came back with a basin of water. "The doctor thinks Grandpa may be suffering from heat exhaustion," she explained as she bathed Grandpa's face. Mom gave a big sigh, "Oh *hinh*, Martin. How do you suppose he got here?"

27 We found out after the doctor's visit. Grandpa was angrily sitting up in bed while Mom tried to feed him some soup.

28 "Tonight you let Marie feed you, Grandpa," said my dad, who had gotten home from work. "You're not really sick," he said as

NOTES

fatigue (fuh TEEG) *n.* physical or mental exhaustion

CLOSE READ
ANNOTATE: Mark details in paragraphs 12–13 and 18–21 that show how the narrator and Cheryl each greet Grandpa.

QUESTION: Why are their greetings so different?

CONCLUDE: What can you conclude about Martin and his sister by the way they greet Grandpa?

frail (frayl) *adj.* delicate; weak

The Medicine Bag **15**

TEACHING

CLOSE READ

You may wish to model the Close Read using the following think-aloud format. Possible responses to questions on the student page are included.

ANNOTATE: As I read paragraphs 31–32, I notice that Grandpa traveled on buses for two and a half days. I also see text that tells me what happened to Grandpa after he arrived in the city and then what happened after he arrived in the narrator's neighborhood.

QUESTION: These details show me how hard it was for Grandpa to get here, and they show me that he is not that familiar with the city.

CONCLUDE: These details show me that Grandpa had a lot of courage to strike out on a new, completely unfamiliar course of action. He also had the persistence to see it through.

NOTES

sheepishly (SHEEP ihsh lee) *adv.* in an embarrassed way

CLOSE READ
ANNOTATE: Note the language the author uses in paragraphs 31–32 that shows the difficulty of Grandpa's journey.

QUESTION: Why does the author provide so much detail about the journey?

CONCLUDE: What can you conclude about Grandpa from the journey he took?

---

he gently pushed Grandpa back against the pillows. "The doctor thinks you just got too tired and hot after your long trip."

29 Grandpa relaxed, and between sips of soup, he told us of his journey. Soon after we visited him, Grandpa decided that he would like to see where his only living descendants lived and what our home was like. Besides, he admitted **sheepishly**, he was lonesome after we left.

30 I knew that everybody felt as guilty as I did—especially Mom. Mom was all Grandpa had left. So even after she married my dad, who's not an Indian, and after Cheryl and I were born, Mom made sure that every summer we spent a week with Grandpa.

31 I never thought that Grandpa would be lonely after our visits, and none of us noticed how old and weak he had become. But Grandpa knew, so he came to us. He had ridden on buses for two and a half days. When he arrived in the city, tired and stiff from sitting for so long, he set out walking to find us.

32 He had stopped to rest on the steps of some building downtown, and a policeman found him. The officer took Grandpa to the city bus stop, waited until the bus came, and then told the driver to let Grandpa out at Bell View Drive. After Grandpa got off the bus, he started walking again. But he couldn't see the house numbers on the other side when he walked on the sidewalk, so he walked in the middle of the street. That's when all the little kids and dogs followed him.

33 I knew everybody felt as bad as I did. Yet I was so proud of this eighty-six-year-old man who had never been away from the reservation but who had the courage to travel so far alone.

34 "You found the money in my boots?" he asked Mom.

35 "Martin did," she answered and then scolded, "Grandpa, you shouldn't have carried so much money. What if someone had stolen it from you?"

36 Grandpa laughed. "I would've known if anyone tried to take the boots off my feet. The money is what I've saved for a long time—a hundred dollars—for my funeral. But you take it now to buy groceries so that I won't be a burden to you while I am here."

37 "That won't be necessary, Grandpa," Dad said. "We are honored to have you with us, and you will never be a burden. I am only sorry that we never thought to bring you home with us this summer and spare you the discomfort of a long bus trip."

38 Grandpa was pleased. "Thank you," he answered. "But don't feel bad that you didn't bring me with you, for I would not have come then. It was not time." He said this in such a way that no one could argue with him. To Grandpa and the Lakota, he once told me, a thing would be done when it was the right time to do it, and that's the way it was.

16 UNIT 1 • RITES OF PASSAGE

VOCABULARY DEVELOPMENT

Multiple-Meaning Words Explain that the word *reservation* in paragraph 2 has more than one meaning. In the story it means "public land set aside for some special use." Other meanings include: 1) an arrangement to have something held for one's use, as in a restaurant reservation; 2) a limiting condition; doubt; misgiving, as in having reservations about a big purchase.

Provide the following sentences and ask students which meaning of *reservation* is correct in each:

I agree with your proposal, but I have a reservation about whether it will work.

We could not get a table at the popular restaurant without a reservation.

Hunting was prohibited on the wildlife reservation.

NOTES

39 "Also," Grandpa went on, looking at me. "I have come because it is soon time for Martin to have the medicine bag."

40 We all knew what that meant. Grandpa thought he was going to die, and he had to follow the tradition of his family to pass the medicine bag, along with its history, to the oldest male child.

41 "Even though the boy," he said, still looking at me, "doesn't have an Indian name, the medicine bag will be his."

42 I didn't know what to say. I had the same hot and cold feeling that I had when I first saw Grandpa in the street. The medicine bag was the dirty leather pouch I had found around his neck. "I could never wear it," I almost said aloud. I thought of having my friends see it in gym class or at the swimming pool and could imagine the smart things they would say. But I just swallowed hard and took a step toward the bed. I knew I would have to take it.

43 But Grandpa was tired. "Not now, Martin," he said waving his hand in dismissal. "It is not time. Now I will sleep."

44 So that's how Grandpa came to be with us for two months. My friends kept asking to come see the old man, but I put them off. I told myself that I didn't want them laughing at Grandpa. But even as I made excuses, I knew it wasn't Grandpa I was afraid they'd laugh at.

45 Nothing bothered Cheryl about bringing her friends to see Grandpa. Every day after school started, there'd be a crew of giggling little girls or round-eyed little boys crowded around the

The Medicine Bag 17

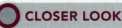

CLOSER LOOK

Analyze Character

Students may have marked paragraphs 41–42 during their first read. Encourage them to talk about the annotations they marked. You may want to model a close read with the class based on the highlights shown in the text.

ANNOTATE: Have students mark details in paragraphs 41–42 that describe how Martin feels about what Grandpa is going to do and that indicate why he feels this way, or have students participate while you highlight them.

QUESTION: Guide students to consider what these details reveal. Ask what a reader can infer from these details, and accept student responses.

Possible response: Martin is upset or unhappy about being given the medicine bag. He is especially unhappy about having to wear it because he is worried about what his friends will say if they see it.

CONCLUDE: Help students to formulate conclusions about the importance of these details. Ask students why the author might have included them.

Possible response: By including these details, the author is suggesting that Martin does not relate to his Indian heritage; he might be ashamed or embarrassed by it.

Remind students that a **character** is a person in a fictional story. In these details the author is directly stating that Martin is worried about what his friends will say if they see the medicine bag. The author is also suggesting that Martin does not relate to his Indian heritage and might be ashamed or embarrassed by it.

PERSONALIZE FOR LEARNING

English Language Support

Vocabulary Explain to students that the word *medicine* in paragraph 40 refers to an object considered, in traditional American Indian belief, to give control over natural or magical forces. Native Americans traditionally carry such objects in a small bag. For these people, something that is "strong medicine" has great power.

The word *medicine* also has other meanings, including: 1) a substance or preparation used to treat disease; 2) something that affects well-being; and 3) the science and art of maintaining health and preventing or curing disease. **ALL LEVELS**

TEACHING

● **CLOSE READ**

Remind students to look for details that indicate a change in characters or events. You may wish to model the Close Read using the following think-aloud format. Possible responses to questions on the student page are included.

ANNOTATE: As I read paragraphs 50 and 51, I notice these actions: his eyes twinkle, and he nods to Martin.

QUESTION: His actions show that he remembers what it's like to be a young man and that he understands that Martin may have been embarrassed about him.

CONCLUDE: Readers can identify with Martin's growing respect for his grandfather.

Additional **English Language Support** is available in the Interactive Teacher's Edition.

NOTES

CLOSE READ
ANNOTATE: Mark details in paragraphs 50 and 51 that describe Grandpa's actions.

QUESTION: What do these actions suggest about Grandpa's character?

CONCLUDE: What is the effect of readers learning more about Grandpa at the same time Martin does?

old man on the porch, where he'd gotten in the habit of sitting every afternoon.

46 Grandpa smiled in his gentle way and patiently answered their questions, or he'd tell them stories of brave warriors, ghosts, and animals, and the kids listened in awed silence. Those little guys thought Grandpa was great.

47 Finally, one day after school, my friends came home with me because nothing I said stopped them. "We're going to see the great Indian of Bell View Drive," said Hank, who was supposed to be my best friend. "My brother has seen him three times so he oughta be well enough to see us."

48 When we got to my house, Grandpa was sitting on the porch. He had on his red shirt, but today he also wore a fringed leather vest trimmed with beads. Instead of his usual cowboy boots, he had solidly beaded moccasins on his feet. Of course, he had his old black hat on—he was seldom without it. But it had been brushed, and the feather in the beaded headband was proudly erect, its tip a bright white. His hair lay in silver strands over the red shirt collar.

49 I stared just as my friends did, and I heard one of them murmur, "'Wow!'"

50 Grandpa looked up, and when his eyes met mine they twinkled as if he were laughing inside. He nodded to me, and my face got all hot. I could tell that he had known all along I was afraid he'd embarrass me in front of my friends.

51 "*Hau, hoksilas,* boys," he greeted and held out his hand.

52 My buddies passed in single file and shook his hand as I introduced them. They were so polite I almost laughed. "How, Grandpa," and even a "How . . . do . . . you . . . do, sir."

53 "You look fine, Grandpa," I said as the guys sat down.

54 "*Hanh,* yes," he agreed. "When I woke up this morning, it seemed the right time to dress in the good clothes. I knew that my grandson would be bringing his friends."

55 "You guys want a soda or . . . ?" I offered, but no one answered. They were listening to Grandpa as he told how he'd killed the deer from which his vest was made.

56 Grandpa did most of the talking. I was proud of him and amazed at how respectfully quiet my friends were. Mom had to chase them home at supper time. As they left, they shook Grandpa's hand again and said to me, "Can we come back?"

57 But after they left, Mom said, "no more visitors for a while, Martin. Grandpa won't admit it, but his strength hasn't returned. He likes having company, but it tires him."

18 UNIT 1 • RITES OF PASSAGE

WriteNow Analyze and Interpret

Paraphrase, Describe, and Speculate Have students review paragraph 48 to paraphrase how Grandpa is dressed when Martin's friends come to visit. Then, ask them to briefly describe the differences in Grandpa's appearance compared to the way he was described earlier in the story. Finally, ask them to write a few sentences to speculate about why Grandpa is dressed differently.

58 That evening Grandpa called me to his room before he went to sleep. "Tomorrow," he said, "when you come home, it will be time to give you the medicine bag."

59 I felt a hard squeeze from where my heart is supposed to be and was scared, but I answered, "OK, Grandpa."

60 All night I had weird dreams about thunder and lightning on a high hill. From a distance I heard the slow beat of a drum. When I woke up in the morning, I felt as if I hadn't slept at all. At school it seemed as if the day would never end, and when it finally did, I ran home.

61 Grandpa was in his room, sitting on the bed. The shades were down, and the place was dim and cool. I sat on the floor in front of Grandpa, but he didn't even look at me. After what seemed a long time, he spoke.

62 "I sent your mother and sister away. What you will hear today is only for your ears. What you will receive is only for your hands." He fell silent. I felt shivers down my back.

63 "My father in his early manhood," Grandpa began, "made a vision quest[4] to find a spirit guide for his life. You cannot understand how it was in that time, when the great Teton Lakota were first made to stay on the reservation. There was a strong need for guidance from *Wakantanka*,[5] the Great Spirit. But too many of the young men were filled with despair and hatred. They thought it was hopeless to search for a vision when the glorious life was gone and only the hated confines of a reservation lay ahead. But my father held to the old ways.

64 "He carefully prepared for his quest with a purifying sweat bath, and then he went alone to a high butte[6] top to fast and pray. After three days he received his sacred dream—in which he found, after long searching, the white man's iron. He did not understand his vision of finding something belonging to the white people, for in that time they were the enemy. When he came down from the butte to cleanse himself at the stream below, he found the remains of a campfire and broken shell of an iron kettle. This was a sign that reinforced his dream. He took a piece of the iron for his medicine bag, which he had made of elk skin years before, to prepare for his quest.

65 "He returned to his village, where he told his dream to the wise old men of the tribe. They gave him the name *Iron Shell*, but they did not understand the meaning of the dream either. At first Iron Shell kept the piece of iron with him at all times and believed it gave him protection from the evils of those unhappy days.

---

4. **vision quest** *n.* in Native American cultures, a difficult search for spiritual guidance.
5. **Wakantanka** (WAH kuhn tank uh) Lakota religion's most important spirit—the creator of the world.
6. **butte** (byoot) *n.* isolated mountaintop with steep sides.

NOTES

CLOSE READ

ANNOTATE: Mark the details in paragraphs 59 and 60 that show how Martin feels.

QUESTION: Why might the author have chosen to include this information?

CONCLUDE: What do these details suggest about Martin?

TEACHING

CLOSE READ

Remind students to look for details that reveal things about a character, even when someone may not be a main character in a story. You may wish to model the Close Read using the following think-aloud format. Possible responses to questions on the student page are included.

ANNOTATE: As I read paragraph 66, I notice words and details that tell me how Iron Shell felt at the boarding school. These details also show how he changed over time when he was at the school.

QUESTION: Grandpa tells Martin the story of Iron Shell to teach him the history of the medicine bag, help him understand what the medicine bag is, and connect Martin to his Native American heritage.

CONCLUDE: Grandpa believes that fate and destiny play a role in a person's life.

NOTES

CLOSE READ
ANNOTATE: Mark details the author uses in paragraph 66 that describe Iron Shell's experience.

QUESTION: What important information does this passage reveal?

CONCLUDE: What can you conclude about Grandpa's belief in fate and destiny?

---

66 "Then a terrible thing happened to Iron Shell. He and several other young men were taken from their homes by the soldiers and sent to a boarding school far from home. He was angry and lonesome for his parents and for the young girl he had wed before he was taken away. At first Iron Shell resisted the teachers' attempts to change him, and he did not try to learn. One day it was his turn to work in the school's blacksmith shop. As he walked into the place, he knew that his medicine had brought him there to learn and work with the white man's iron.

67 "Iron Shell became a blacksmith and worked at the trade when he returned to the reservation. All his life he treasured the medicine bag. When he was old and I was a man, he gave it to me."

68 Grandpa quit talking, and I stared in disbelief as he covered his face with his hands. His shoulders shook with quiet sobs. I looked away until he began to speak again.

69 "I kept the bag until my son, your mother's father, was a man and had to leave us to fight in the war across the ocean. I gave him the bag, for I believed it would protect him in battle, but he did not take it with him. He was afraid he would lose it. He died in a faraway land."

70 Again Grandpa was still, and I felt his grief around me.

71 "My son," he went on after clearing his throat, "had no sons, only one daughter, your mother. So the medicine bag must be passed to you."

72 He unbuttoned his shirt, pulled out the leather pouch, and lifted it over his head. He held it in his hand, turning it over and over as if memorizing how it looked.

73 "In the bag," he said, as he opened it and removed two objects, "is the broken shell of the iron kettle, a pebble from the butte, and a piece of the sacred sage.⁷" He held the pouch upside down and fine dust drifted out.

74 "After the bag is yours you must put a piece of prairie sage within and never open it again until you pass it on to your son." He replaced the pebble and the piece of iron and tied the bag.

75 I stood up, somehow knowing I should. Grandpa slowly rose from the bed and stood upright in front of me holding the bag before my face. I closed my eyes and waited for him to slip it over my head. But he spoke.

76 "No, you need not wear it." He placed the soft leather bag in my right hand and closed my other hand over it. "It would not be right to wear it in this time and place where no one will understand. Put it safely away until you are again on the reservation. Wear it then, when you replace the sacred sage."

77 Grandpa turned and sat again on the bed. Wearily he leaned his head against the pillow. "Go," he said. "I will sleep now."

---

7. **sage** (sayj) *n.* type of herb.

20 UNIT 1 • RITES OF PASSAGE

HOW LANGUAGE WORKS

Symbolism Remind students that a symbol is something that stands for or represents something else. Have students discuss paragraphs 73, 74, and 79. In the story, Martin is on the reservation putting sacred sage in his medicine bag. What does this action symbolize? Why? Have students write one or two sentences, in Martin's words, that express this symbolism and that could be added to the end of the story.

20 UNIT 1 • RITES OF PASSAGE

78 "Thank you, Grandpa," I said softly and left with the bag in my hands.

79 That night Mom and Dad took Grandpa to the hospital. Two weeks later I stood alone on the lonely prairie of the reservation and put the sacred sage in my medicine bag.

NOTES

Comprehension Check
Complete the following items after you finish your first read.

1. What makes Grandpa sound glamorous to the narrator's friends?

2. What happens when Grandpa arrives at Martin's house?

3. Why does Grandpa want Martin to have the medicine bag?

4. What is in the medicine bag, and what does Martin add to it at the end of the story?

Notebook Write a three-sentence summary of "The Medicine Bag."

RESEARCH

Research to Clarify Choose at least one unfamiliar detail from the text. Briefly research that detail. In what way does the information you learned shed light on an aspect of the story?

Research to Explore Choose something that interested you from the text and formulate a research question.

The Medicine Bag 21

DIGITAL PERSPECTIVES

Comprehension Check

Possible responses:

1. Grandpa sounds glamorous to the narrator's friends because they picture him as a character from television or the movies. The narrator also admits to exaggerating in the stories he told his friends about Grandpa and the reservation.
2. He faints because of heat exhaustion—getting too tired and hot.
3. It is passed down to the sons in the family. Grandpa got it from his father. Grandpa's son died with no sons, so now it will go to Martin—Grandpa's great-grandson.
4. The medicine bag holds a piece of iron from Grandpa's father, a pebble from the butte where he went for his vision quest, and a piece of sacred sage. At the end of the story, Martin adds more sacred sage from the reservation.

Summaries will vary; however, students should include details such as: Martin is initially embarrassed by Grandpa; Grandpa has come to give Martin his medicine bag; Martin doesn't want the medicine bag; Martin is given the medicine bag and comes to accept his Native American heritage.

Research

Research to Clarify If students struggle to decide on a detail to research, you may want to suggest that they focus on one of the following topics: Lakota Indians, Native American rituals, Native American reservations.

Research to Explore If students aren't sure how to go about formulating a research question, suggest that they use their findings from Research to Clarify as a starting point. For example, if students researched Lakota Indians, they might formulate a question such as *What is the history of the Lakota people?*

PERSONALIZE FOR LEARNING

Challenge
Research Encourage students to conduct research about sage and write brief reports on this plant. Reports should include information about the history of sage and its various uses, as well as images of sage. Have students present their reports to the class and discuss why sage might be part of a Native American's medicine bag.

TEACHING

Jump Start

CLOSE READ Have students close read the title, "The Medicine Bag." Point out that the author could have titled this story "Grandpa" or "Grandpa's Visit," but she deliberately chose this title. Ask students to suggest reasons why she picked this particular title and why the title is so appropriate for this story.

Close Read the Text

Walk students through the annotation model on the student page. Encourage them to complete items 2 and 3 on their own. Review and discuss the sections students have marked. If needed, continue to model close reading by using the Annotation Highlights in the Interactive Teacher's Edition.

Analyze the Text

Possible responses:
1. Grandpa did make the right decision to travel and visit his family because he knows he is going to die soon and he wants to give Martin the medicine bag. **DOK 3**
2. Responses will vary. Grandpa knows he is going to die soon. He wants Martin to understand the history and meaning of the medicine bag before giving it to him. (Paragraph 61) **DOK 2**
3. Grandpa dies; Martin returns to the Lakota reservation to help mourn him. Evidence: "That night Mom and Dad took Grandpa to the hospital. Two weeks later I stood alone on the lonely prairie of the reservation and put the sacred sage in my medicine bag." (Paragraph 77) **DOK 2**
4. Students may conclude that part of growing up often includes learning about and taking responsibility for the history of your family and culture. **DOK 3**

FORMATIVE ASSESSMENT

Analyze the Text

- If students **fail to cite evidence,** **then** remind them to support their ideas with specific information from the text.
- If students **fail to understand motivations and emotions indirectly stated in the text,** **then** remind them that authors include details about characters and their actions to show how they change.

MAKING MEANING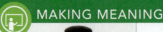

THE MEDICINE BAG

Close Read the Text

1. This model, from paragraph 37 of the text, shows two sample annotations, along with questions and conclusions. Close read the passage, and find another detail to annotate. Then, write a question and your conclusion.

> **ANNOTATE:** These details hint at Grandpa's personality.
> **QUESTION:** Why does the writer reveal two sides of Grandpa's personality?
> **CONCLUDE:** Creating a compassionate but firm character makes Grandpa seem real.
>
> "But **don't feel bad** that you didn't bring me with you, for I would not have come then. It was not time." He said this in such a way that **no one could argue with him**. To Grandpa and the Lakota, he once told me, a thing would be done when it was the right time to do it….
>
> **ANNOTATE:** The author repeats the word *time*.
> **QUESTION:** What effect does the repetition create?
> **CONCLUDE:** The repetition stresses the Lakota belief in doing things only when the time is right.

Tool Kit
Close-Read Guide and Model Annotation

2. For more practice, go back into the text and complete the close-read notes.

3. Revisit a section of the text you found important. Read this section closely and **annotate** what you notice. Ask yourself **questions** such as "Why did the author make this choice?" What can you **conclude**?

Analyze the Text

CITE TEXTUAL EVIDENCE to support your answers.

Notebook Respond to these questions.

1. **Evaluate** Do you think Grandpa made the right decision to travel and visit his family? Use details from the story to support your answer.
2. **Interpret** Summarize the story Grandpa tells about his father. Why do you think Grandpa tells Martin this story at this time?
3. **Draw Conclusions** What happens to Grandpa and to Martin at the end of the story? Cite story details to support your conclusion.
4. **Essential Question:** *What are some milestones on the path to growing up?* What have you learned about the path to growing up by reading this story?

STANDARDS
Reading Literature
Determine the meaning of words and phrases as they are used in a text, including figurative and connotative meanings; analyze the impact of specific word choices on meaning and tone, including analogies or allusions to other texts.

22 UNIT 1 • RITES OF PASSAGE

WriteNow Analyze and Interpret

Description Have students write a paragraph predicting Martin's behavior when he returns to Iowa after going to the reservation to mourn Grandpa. Use these questions to spark students' thinking: *What does he do with the medicine bag? Does he wear it or leave it at home? Does he show it to his friends? Why or why not? If he shows the medicine bag to his friends, how do they respond? Why?*

ESSENTIAL QUESTION: What are some milestones on the path to growing up?

DIGITAL PERSPECTIVES

Analyze Craft and Structure

Figurative Meaning: Symbolism A **symbol** is anything that stands for or represents something else. **Symbolism** is the use of symbols.

- Symbols are common in everyday life as well as in literature. For example, a dove with an olive branch in its beak is a symbol of peace.
- In literature, symbolism can highlight certain ideas the author wishes to emphasize.
- Symbolism can also add levels of meaning to a text.

Most Native American cultures show deep respect for nature, and the natural world is considered to have profound spiritual qualities. Symbols of nature play an important role in Native American traditions, especially religious ones. In "The Medicine Bag," the medicine bag is an important symbol. Think about other symbols connected with Grandpa in the story.

Practice

CITE TEXTUAL EVIDENCE to support your answers.

📓 **Notebook** Respond to these questions.

1. **(a)** What details in the story suggest that the medicine bag is a symbol and is important to Grandpa? **(b)** Why do you think the author wants readers to understand Grandpa's connection to the medicine bag?

2. **(a)** How does Martin's view of the medicine bag change? What changes his mind? **(b)** How do Martin's changing feelings about the medicine bag help show what it represents?

3. **(a)** The medicine bag is not the only symbol in the story. Record in the chart two other details from the story that serve as symbols and what each one represents. **(b)** What is the purpose of each symbol? Write your answers in the chart.

THE MEDICINE BAG: SYMBOLS		
SYMBOL	WHAT IT REPRESENTS	PURPOSE IN THE STORY
Grandpa's worn cowboy boots	Grandpa's long journey and long life	highlights how difficult Grandpa's life and trip have been
the medicine bag	Lakota tradition	adds depth to the idea that traditions are passed down through family

Analyze Craft and Structure

Figurative Meaning: Symbolism Discuss with students that when an author uses symbolism, a symbol might be obvious or suggested. An example of obvious symbolism would be the medicine bag and how it helps the narrator, Martin, connect to the great grandfather and understand why the great grandfather's past is important enough to carry into the future. An example of less obvious, or suggested, symbolism occurs when the narrator visits the reservation at the end of the story, which suggests the great grandfather has died. For more support, see **Analyze Craft and Structure: Symbolism.**

MAKE IT INTERACTIVE

Have students write a few sentences about someone at a turning point, using symbolism to convey an idea.

Practice

Possible responses:

1. (a) Grandpa wears the medicine bag on his neck. He never opens it. Before Grandpa had it, his father had it, and it has been passed down among the generations of the family. (b) The author wants readers to understand why Grandpa thinks it is important for the narrator to have the medicine bag, and why Martin finally puts it on at the end of the story.

2. (a) At first, Martin is embarrassed by the medicine bag. He can't imagine wearing it. After he hears Grandpa's story, Martin feels a connection to the history of the bag. (b) Martin's feelings about the medicine bag change when he learns about its role in his family history and in Lakota customs. This helps shows that the bag represents family and Lakota tradition.

3. See possible responses in chart on student page.

FORMATIVE ASSESSMENT

Analyze Craft and Structure

- **If** students have difficulty understanding symbols, **then** show them common symbols (an arrow, a stop sign, an image of an airplane) and ask students to explain in their own words what each means.

- **If** students fail to identify or understand the use of symbolism in the story, **then** review the symbols in the chart on the student page. Ask students to explain in their own words why they think the author included them in the story. For Reteach and Practice, see **Analyze Craft and Structure: Symbolism (RP).**

CROSS-CURRICULAR PERSPECTIVES

Science Native American medicines include plants and other natural substances that have been found to have effective medicinal properties. Challenge students to research Native American medicines and learn about these medicinal properties. Have students answer questions such as:

Which Native American medicines have proven medicinal properties?

What are these medicinal properties?

Are any of these medicines used today in mainstream medicine?

TEACHING

Concept Vocabulary
Why These Words?
Possible responses:
1. The concept vocabulary helps the reader to more clearly understand that Grandpa is old and has had a difficult journey to reach his family. The words describe where he lives, emphasize how tired and physically weak he seems, and provide details about how he behaves.
2. *collapsed* (paragraph 20); *heat exhaustion* (paragraph 25); *fringed leather vest* (paragraph 47)

Practice
Possible responses:
1. Many Native American people live on this *reservation*. After a long hike, we returned *wearily* to our cabins. The people at the end of the line *straggled* behind the group. At the end of the marathon, the runner felt *fatigue*. Older people often have *frail* bones. Adam admitted *sheepishly* that he had played a joke on his sister.
2. *wearily*: energetically; *frail*: strong; *sheepishly*: boldly. If Grandpa were described this way, he would seem stronger and less lost in a new place.

Word Network
Possible words: *tradition, history, embarrassed, proud*

Word Study
For more support, see **Concept Vocabulary and Word Study.**

Possible responses:
doggedly: persistent; *bullheaded*: stubborn; *lionize*: treat specially or treat as a celebrity; *elephantine*: large, clumsy, awkward

FORMATIVE ASSESSMENT
Word Study
If students have trouble identifying the meaning of the identified animal words, **then** have them list the characteristics normally associated with each animal. For Reteach and Practice, see **Word Study: Animal Words (RP).**

LANGUAGE DEVELOPMENT

THE MEDICINE BAG

Concept Vocabulary

| wearily | fatigue | sheepishly |
| straggled | frail | |

Why These Words? These concept vocabulary words show someone who is not at full strength or does not look his or her best. For example, Grandpa *wearily* pokes his cane at the dogs that are chasing him. When he arrives at the house, Martin can see the *fatigue* in his face. Notice that both words emphasize how tired Grandpa seems.

1. How does the concept vocabulary sharpen the reader's understanding of Grandpa's state of health and his appearance?

2. What other words in the selection connect to the concept of Grandpa's state of health and his appearance?

Practice
CITE TEXTUAL EVIDENCE to support your answers.

Notebook The concept words appear in "The Medicine Bag."

1. Use each concept word in a sentence that demonstrates your understanding of the word's meaning.
2. With a partner, come up with an **antonym**, a word with the opposite meaning, for each of the following words: *wearily, frail,* and *sheepishly*. How would Grandpa seem different if the author had used the antonyms to describe him instead of the original words?

Word Study

Animal Words In "The Medicine Bag," the narrator describes Grandpa as *sheepishly* admitting he was lonely after his family finished their visit and drove away from the reservation. Grandpa is acting like a sheep—suddenly bashful and shy—because he is embarrassed to admit his true feelings. Comparing him with a sheep presents a vivid image of Grandpa's behavior.

There are many words that acquire their meanings from the characteristics we associate with certain animals. Guess the meanings of each of the following words based on the characteristics of the animal: *doggedly, bullheaded, lionize, elephantine*. Then, verify their actual definitions using a dictionary or thesaurus.

WORD NETWORK
Add words related to the topic of rites of passage from the text to your Word Network.

STANDARDS
Language
Determine or clarify the meaning of unknown and multiple-meaning words or phrases based on *grade 8 reading and content,* choosing flexibly from a range of strategies.
  c. Consult general and specialized reference materials, both print and digital, to find the pronunciation of a word or determine or clarify its precise meaning or its part of speech.
  d. Verify the preliminary determination of the meaning of a word or phrase.

AUTHOR'S PERSPECTIVE | Elfrieda Hiebert, Ph.D.

Author's Word Choice In a text, authors may or may not explicitly state the underlying theme. When the theme is left unstated, readers will have to use clues in the text to infer it.

Teachers can show how word choices can be clues to theme by selecting a narrative from Unit 1 and guiding students to find words and phrases that are part of a network. The words should be related because of their denotations, connotations, or imagery. For example, if the passage describes cooking, students can select words from the passage such as *warm, clean, fragrant*, and *sweetness*. Be sure the list is narrowly focused and students can explain the relationship among the words and why they chose each word. Then have students explore how the words convey the author's theme.

ESSENTIAL QUESTION: What are some milestones on the path to growing up?

Conventions

Verbs in Active and Passive Voice It's important to learn and use active and passive voice of verbs in your writing. The **voice** of a verb shows whether the subject of the verb is performing the action or receiving it. A verb is in the **active voice** when its subject performs the action. A verb is in the **passive voice** when its subject receives the action.

A passive verb is a verb phrase made from a form of *be* with the past participle of an action verb, as shown in the chart:

ACTIVE VOICE	PASSIVE VOICE
We **filled** the bucket.	The bucket **was filled**. (**Filled** is the past participle of *fill*.)
Alison **is winning** the race.	The race **is being won** by Alison. (**Won** is the past participle of *win*.)

Generally, the active voice is considered a better choice for writers. The active voice communicates ideas in a more engaging, concise way. It also put the emphasis on the person performing the action.

Passive voice should be used when the performer of the action is unknown or when it is desirable to stress the action instead of its performer. In general, avoid passive voice to keep your writing from sounding vague.

Read It

1. Identify whether each sentence uses the active or the passive voice.
   a. Our friends were impressed by our stories about Grandpa.
   b. Grandpa taught me a Lakota chant to sing.
   c. Grandpa's old black hat had been brushed.
2. Reread paragraph 66 of "The Medicine Bag." Mark and then label one example of passive voice and one of active voice.

Write It

Revise each sentence to use the active voice, to stress the performer of each verb's action.

> EXAMPLE
> Grandpa was brought to Martin's neighborhood by the bus.
> **The bus brought Grandpa to Martin's neighborhood.**

1. Martin was embarrassed by the way Grandpa looked.

2. Grandpa's father was given the name Iron Shell by the wise old men.

3. The medicine bag was given to Martin by Grandpa.

STANDARDS
Language
• Demonstrate command of the conventions of standard English grammar and usage when writing or speaking.
  b. Form and use verbs in the active and passive voice.
• Use knowledge of language and its conventions when writing, speaking, reading, or listening.
  a. Use verbs in the active and passive voice and in the conditional and subjunctive mood to achieve particular effects.

DIGITAL PERSPECTIVES

Conventions

Verbs in Active and Passive Voice Discuss with students the difference between the active and passive voice. Review that a passive verb phrase consists of a form of *be* and the past participle of an action verb (*is given; was thrown*). For more support, see **Conventions: Verbs in Active and Passive Voice.**

MAKE IT INTERACTIVE
Have students write a sentence in the passive voice, and then write the same sentence in the active voice.
Possible responses:
Active: Jack read that book.
Passive: That book was read by Jack.

Read It
Possible responses:
1. a. passive voice; b. active voice; c. passive voice
2. Active voice: "Then a terrible thing happened..."; "At first Iron Shell resisted the teachers' attempts..." Passive voice: "He and several other young men were taken... and sent..."

Write It
Possible responses:
1. Grandpa's looks embarrassed Martin.
2. The wise old men gave Grandpa's father the name Iron Shell.
3. Grandpa gave the medicine bag to Martin.

HOW LANGUAGE WORKS

Active and Passive Voice If students struggle to understand the difference between the active and passive voice, assist them by giving them examples of both voices. Have students read the following sentences and identify the voice as active or passive.

Grandpa told Martin the story of the medicine bag. (active)
The story of the medicine bag was told to Martin by Grandpa. (passive)
Martin's friends visited Grandpa. (active)
Grandpa was visited by Martin's friends. (passive)

FORMATIVE ASSESSMENT
Conventions
- **If** students have trouble identifying the active voice, **then** review the sentence and ask who or what is *performing* the action.
- **If** students have trouble identifying the passive voice, **then** review the sentence and ask who or what is *receiving* the action. For Reteach and Practice, see **Conventions: Verbs in Active and Passive Voice (RP).**

TEACHING

Writing to Sources

Discuss with students the importance of point of view in narrative nonfiction. Point out that when a story is written from a particular character's point of view, everything is expressed and described as that character sees it. In "The Medicine Bag," the reader knows only what Martin sees and thinks. Remind students that when they rewrite the story from Grandpa's point of view, they will express and write about only what Grandpa sees and thinks. Encourage students to think about the events in the story from Grandpa's point of view before they start writing. For more support, see **Writing to Sources: Retelling a Story.**

Reflect on Your Writing

Possible responses:
1. Responses will vary. If students need support, ask them to consider the insights they gained from writing their narrative.
2. Responses will vary. Be sure that students make connections between the way the story was originally written and what they wrote in their narrative.
3. **Why These Words?** Responses will vary. Have students list specific examples of words they have chosen that add power to their narrative.

FORMATIVE ASSESSMENT

Writing to Sources

If students have trouble rewriting the story from Grandpa's point of view, **then** review key parts of the story and ask them to tell you what they think Grandpa feels or thinks at that moment in the story. For Reteach and Practice, see **Writing to Sources: Retelling a Story (RP).**

EFFECTIVE EXPRESSION

THE MEDICINE BAG

Writing to Sources

Short stories, like "The Medicine Bag," have a narrator—the character or voice that relates story events. **Point of view** is the perspective, or vantage point, from which a narrator tells a story. "The Medicine Bag" is told from Martin's point of view. How would the story be different if it were told from another character's point of view?

Assignment

Write a **retelling** of the story "The Medicine Bag" from Grandpa's point of view: Based on the details provided in the story, imagine Grandpa's journey to see his family. What are his impressions of Martin and his friends? How does he feel about giving the medicine bag to Martin to preserve a sacred Lakota tradition?

Draft your retelling of the story. Make sure to do the following:
- Make Grandpa the narrator, the character who tells the story using the pronoun "I."
- Include details, thoughts, feeling, and insights from Grandpa's point of view.

Vocabulary and Conventions Connection You may want to include several of the concept vocabulary words in your retelling. Also, remember to use the active voice to keep your sentences lively.

| wearily | fatigue | sheepishly |
| straggled | frail | |

STANDARDS

Writing
Write narratives to develop real or imagined experiences or events using effective technique, relevant descriptive details, and well-structured event sequences.

   a. Engage and orient the reader by establishing a context and point of view and introducing a narrator and/or characters; organize an event sequence that unfolds naturally and logically.
   b. Use narrative techniques, such as dialogue, pacing, description, and reflection, to develop experiences, events, and/or characters.
   d. Use precise words and phrases, relevant descriptive details, and sensory language to capture the action and convey experiences and events.
   e. Provide a conclusion that follows from and reflects on the narrated experiences or events.

Speaking and Listening
Present claims and findings, emphasizing salient points in a focused, coherent manner with relevant evidence, sound valid reasoning, and well-chosen details; use appropriate eye contact, adequate volume, and clear pronunciation.

Reflect on Your Writing

After you have written your retelling of the story, answer the following questions.

1. How well do you think your retelling expressed Grandpa's point of view?

2. What was the most challenging part of retelling the story from Grandpa's point of view?

3. **Why These Words?** The words you choose make a difference in your writing. Which words did you specifically choose to add power to your retelling?

PERSONALIZE FOR LEARNING

English Language Support

Considering Different Points of View Have pairs of students work together to make a list of traits or qualities that the reader learns about both Martin and his great grandfather in the story. Then have them discuss how the reader knows about these qualities. Guide the discussion to help students see that Martin's traits are stated in a more direct way and Grandpa's traits are stated indirectly. Ask: *How do you know that Grandpa has this trait?* **EMERGING**

Have students write a few sentences explaining which point of view they think is better for telling Martin's story. Ask them to include at least two reasons for their opinion. **EXPANDING**

Have students write a paragraph explaining which point of view they think is better for telling Martin's story. Do they think that the story would be more effective if it were written from the great grandfather's perspective? Why or why not? Ask them to include at least three reasons for their opinion. **BRIDGING**

An expanded **English Language Support Lesson** on Point of View is available in the Interactive Teacher's Edition.

ESSENTIAL QUESTION: What are some milestones on the path to growing up?

Speaking and Listening

Assignment

A **monologue** is a speech given by a character that expresses that character's point of view. Imagine you are the narrator of "The Medicine Bag." Write and present a monologue in which you reflect on how you came to understand the importance of the Lakota tradition of the medicine bag.

1. **Plan Your Interpretation** As you write your monologue, plan how you want to express the narrator's thoughts and feelings about the medicine bag. Answer the following questions to help guide your delivery.

    - How does the narrator think and feel about the medicine bag tradition when Grandpa first mentions it?
    - Did the narrator's thoughts and feelings change over the course of the story? How? What caused these changes?
    - What word choices can help you sound as if you are speaking from the narrator's point of view?

2. **Prepare Your Delivery** Practice reciting your monologue before you present it to your class. Include the following performance techniques to help you achieve the desired effect.

    - Use details from the story about the importance of the medicine bag.
    - Make appropriate eye contact with the audience.
    - Speak at adequate volume.
    - Pronounce each word clearly so your audience can easily understand what you are saying.

3. **Evaluate Presentations** As your classmates deliver their presentations, listen attentively. Use a presentation evaluation guide like the one shown to analyze their presentations.

PRESENTATION EVALUATION GUIDE

Rate each statement on a scale of 1 (not demonstrated) to 5 (demonstrated).

☐ The monologue reflects the narrator's voice and character.

☐ The details used convey insights about the importance of the Lakota tradition.

☐ The speaker made appropriate eye contact with the audience.

☐ The speaker spoke at an appropriate volume.

☐ The speaker's pronunciation was clear.

EVIDENCE LOG

Before moving on to a new selection, go to your Evidence Log and record what you learned from "The Medicine Bag."

DIGITAL PERSPECTIVES

Illuminating the Standard To help students understand how to perform a monologue, use search terms such as "performing monologues" and "monologues performed" to find video footage online showing monologues being performed. (Note: Be sure to preview any video before showing it to students.)

Have students discuss what they see and hear in the video and how this helps them understand and appreciate the art of performing a monologue. Then, have students write a paragraph explaining how the video helped them or how they think it will help them prepare and present their monologue.

DIGITAL PERSPECTIVES

Speaking and Listening

1. **Plan Your Interpretation** You may wish to guide students in choosing a narrator by asking them to consider whether the narrator is Native American, and if so, whether he or she is Lakota. You might also ask students to consider whether their narrator might have known Grandpa or his family.

2. **Prepare Your Delivery** Suggest to students that they rehearse several times before presenting their monologue so they are completely comfortable with it. Encourage them to practice any words or phrases they have difficulty pronouncing.

3. **Evaluate Presentations** Encourage students to make one supportive comment about each presentation. For more support, see **Speaking and Listening: Monologue.**

Evidence Log Support students in completing their Evidence Log. This paced activity will help prepare them for the Performance-Based Assessment at the end of the unit.

FORMATIVE ASSESSMENT

Speaking and Listening

- **If** students have trouble creating a narrator character, **then** discuss possible characters, such as someone who lives on Grandpa's reservation or someone whom Martin knows.

- **If** students have trouble delivering their monologue, **then** suggest that instead of "performing," they imagine they are telling this story to someone they know well and are comfortable with. For Reteach and Practice, see **Speaking and Listening: Monologue (RP).**

Selection Test

Administer the "The Medicine Bag" Selection Test, which is available in both print and digital formats online in Assessments.

PLANNING
WHOLE-CLASS LEARNING • APACHE GIRL'S RITE OF PASSAGE

Apache Girl's Rite of Passage

Summary
The video "Apache Girl's Rite of Passage" follows a group of Mescalero Apache girls going through a coming-of-age ceremony. It centers on a girl named Dashina. The rites stretch over four days, testing strength and endurance. The girls receive little food or sleep. They must be stoic and display tight control over their emotions. The ceremonies parallel both the Apache creation story and the Apache notion of four stages of progress to adulthood—infancy, childhood, adolescence, and womanhood. The rites culminate with over ten hours of dancing through the night. At the end of the ceremony, the girls receive their Apache women's names, signaling their move into adulthood.

> **Insight**
> Students may notice that this event happens in the American Southwest in the present day. The ceremony helps a culture preserve an ancient way of life.

AUDIO SUMMARIES
Audio summaries of "Apache Girl's Rite of Passage" are available in both English and Spanish and can be assigned to students in the Interactive Teacher's Edition or Unit Resources. Assigning these summaries prior to viewing the selection may help students build additional background knowledge and set a context for their first review.

ESSENTIAL QUESTION:
What are some milestones on the path to growing up?

Connection to Essential Question
Completing a difficult task in the company of peers and others in one's community is a common part of ceremonial milestones. This video models a ritual intended to showcase the kinds of challenges the girls will face as women.

WHOLE-CLASS LEARNING PERFORMANCE TASK
What event changed your understanding of yourself, or that of someone you know?

UNIT PERFORMANCE-BASED ASSESSMENT
What rite of passage has held the most significance for you or for a person you know well?

Connection to Performance Tasks
Whole-Class Learning Performance Task This is an excellent opportunity for students to consider how going through particular events not only can change how other people see young women but also may show how the rituals change the way the women experience the world.

Unit Performance-Based Assessment While most students probably haven't gone through the rite explored in this video, the content may serve as a springboard to help them make connections to their rites of passages and discuss the challenges in their own lives that made them who they are today.

DIGITAL PERSPECTIVES | Audio | Video | Document | Annotation Highlights | EL Highlights | Online Assessment

LESSON RESOURCES

	Making Meaning	**Effective Expression**
Lesson	First Review Close Review Analyze the Media Media Vocabulary	Writing to Compare
Instructional Standards	**RI.10** By the end of the year, read and comprehend literary nonfiction . . . **L.6** Acquire and use accurately grade-appropriate general academic and domain-specific words . . .	**SL.2** Analyze the purpose of information . . . **RI.7** Evaluate the advantages and disadvantages . . . **W.2** Write informative/explanatory texts . . . **W.2.a** Introduce a topic clearly . . .
STUDENT RESOURCES		
Available online in the Interactive Student Edition or Unit Resources	Selection Video First-Review Guide: Media: Video Close-Review Guide: Media: Video	Evidence Log
TEACHER RESOURCES		
Selection Resources Available online in the Interactive Teacher's Edition or Unit Resources	Audio Summaries Media Vocabulary	Writing to Compare: Compare-and-Contrast Essay
My Resources	A Unit 1 Answer Key is available online and in the Interactive Teacher's Edition.	

Media Complexity Rubric: Apache Girl's Rite of Passage

Quantitative Measures

Length and Format: Video of 4 minutes, 39 seconds

Qualitative Measures

Knowledge Demands ①—②—③—**④**—⑤	Video explores the Apache rite of passage. It is clearly explained, but the experience is uncommon to readers. Background knowledge about the Apache or other rites of passage is helpful.
Structure ①—**②**—③—④—⑤	Organization of content is clear and logical. There is a high correspondence between visuals and audio, making it easier to understand the content.
Language Conventionality and Clarity ①—②—**③**—④—⑤	Language is clear and explicit; sentences are short and a few are complex; speech is sufficiently slow and clearly enunciated; some vocabulary is subject-specific (*ritual, ceremony, ceremonial, symbol,* etc).
Levels of Meaning/Purpose ①—**②**—③—④—⑤	Purpose is explicitly stated, clear, concrete, and narrowly focused. Correspondence of visuals and audio make it easy to understand.

Whole-Class Learning

TEACHING

Jump Start

FIRST REVIEW Engage students in a discussion about how seeing and hearing something might be different from reading about the same thing. In "The Medicine Bag," students read about a character undergoing a Native American rite of passage. Now students will watch a video in which they'll see a girl undergoing a Native American rite of passage.

Apache Girl's Rite of Passage

What is it like to undergo a Native American rite of passage that lasts four days? Why do people undergo rituals like this one? Modeling the questions viewers might ask as they watch "Apache Girl's Rite of Passage" brings the video alive for students and connects it to the Whole-Class Performance Task assignment. Project the video in class, ask students to open the video in their interactive textbooks, or have students scan the Bounce Page icon with their phones to access the video.

Media Vocabulary

Encourage students to discuss the media vocabulary. Have they seen or used these terms or concepts before? Ask students to explain how narration might be used in a film.

FIRST REVIEW

Have students perform the steps of the first review independently.

WATCH: Students should pay attention to the topic of the video. Ask them to consider how music and the camera are used to bring the events in the video to life.

NOTE: Students should note the time stamp of any scenes or moments they find especially powerful or important.

CONNECT: Encourage students to increase their understanding by connecting the events and scenes in the video to other media they have seen or heard.

RESPOND: Students will answer questions and write a description to demonstrate understanding.

Point out to students that while they will complete the Respond step at the end of the first review, the other steps will probably happen somewhat concurrently. You may wish to print copies of the **First-Review Guide: Media: Video** for students to use.

MAKING MEANING

Comparing Text to Media

The video you will watch features an Apache girl participating in tests of strength and endurance. As you watch the selection, compare the public rite with the personal experience of the boy in "The Medicine Bag."

About National Geographic

The National Geographic Society was founded in 1888 and is one of the largest nonprofit scientific and educational institutions in the world. Its magazine *National Geographic* allows people to read about places and cultures that they might otherwise never experience. In addition to the magazine, the National Geographic Society produces films, videos, and television shows.

STANDARDS
Reading Informational Text
By the end of the year, read and comprehend literary nonfiction at the high end of the grades 6–8 text complexity band independently and proficiently.
Language
Acquire and use accurately grade-appropriate general academic and domain-specific words and phrases; gather vocabulary knowledge when considering a word or phrase important to comprehension or expression.

Apache Girl's Rite of Passage

Media Vocabulary

The following words or concepts will be useful to you as you analyze, discuss, and write about the video.

narration: commentary that accompanies a film	• The narration may clarify events or add background and further information.
audio: relating to the sound of a film	• Audio includes narration, music, and real-world sounds that are part of the video.
close-up: camera shot taken from a short distance	• Close-ups are used to show facial expressions and details.
contrast: amount of difference between bright and dark elements in filming and viewing	• The use of contrast can create atmosphere and change the mood.
pan: vertical or horizontal camera motion used to follow a subject	• A pan allows a cameraperson to follow action through a scene, or to show a wider or taller expanse on the screen.
synchronization (sync): coordination of motion and sound	• It's important that sounds and actions are in sync, as they would be in real life.

First Review MEDIA: VIDEO

Refer to the information below as you watch the video. As you watch, write down your observations and questions, noting time codes so you can revisit sections later.

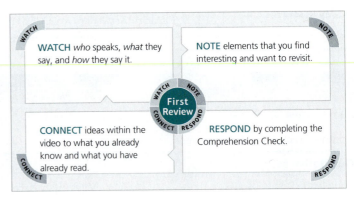

PERSONALIZE FOR LEARNING

English Language Support
Media Vocabulary Help students better understand media vocabulary words they might confuse with other, similar words.

- Explain how the media word *close-up* is different from the phrase *close up*, and point out how each is pronounced (CLOSE up vs. close UP).
- Explain how the media word *contrast* is different from *contrast* (as in compare and contrast), and point out how each is pronounced (CONtrast vs. conTRAST).
- Explain how the media vocabulary word *pan* has a different meaning from a pan used for cooking.
- Explain that the media vocabulary word *sync* is pronounced the same as a sink used for washing dishes. **ALL LEVELS**

ESSENTIAL QUESTION: What are some milestones on the path to growing up?

MEDIA: VIDEO

Apache Girl's Rite of Passage
National Geographic

BACKGROUND
For hundreds of years, the Mescalero Apaches were nomadic hunters and warriors who roamed throughout the American Southwest and northern Mexico. Today, this Native American tribe lives on a major reservation in New Mexico, in what was once the center of their homelands. The ceremony in this video is one of their most important and sacred traditions.

SCAN FOR MULTIMEDIA

NOTES

DIGITAL PERSPECTIVES

Closer Review

Analyze Expository Information

Students may have noted the section of the video from 1:10–1:58 during their first review. Use this segment to help students understand the experience of Dachina's public rite of passage. Encourage them to talk about what they noted. You may want to model a close review with the class.

NOTE: Have students note details in the video that outline the steps of the ceremony.

Possible response: It is a four-day ceremony; it moves through the stages of life, including infancy, childhood, and womanhood; it includes an all-night dance. It requires limited sleep and food, and the young women are expected to show little emotion.

QUESTION: Guide students to consider what these details might tell them. Ask what a viewer can infer from these details, and accept student responses.

Possible response: Dachina's rite of passage was more difficult than Martin's because she had to do things in front of people, and if she failed everyone would see it.

CONCLUDE: Help students to formulate conclusions about the importance of these details in the video. Ask students why the video might include these details.

Possible response: The video includes these details to give viewers a sense of what is to come in the rest of the video.

Remind students that **exposition** in a video helps to set up the action that is to follow. The rest of the video should show these stages and provide more detail. The exposition helps to ground viewers and provide a foundational understanding.

DIGITAL PERSPECTIVES

Enriching the Selection To help students understand Apache culture and traditions, use search terms such as "Apache Indians" and "Apache culture" to find video footage online. Be sure to preview any video before showing it to students.

Have students discuss what they see and hear in the video and how this helps them understand Apache culture. Then, have students write a paragraph discussing the similarities and differences they see between the video and "Apache Girl's Rite of Passage."

TEACHING

Comprehension Check

Possible Responses:

1. According to Apache tradition, the ritual makes her a woman.

2. Four days represent the four stages of life and the Apache creation story. Pollen represents fertility. White clay represents the goddess.

3. Much of the ceremony takes place inside a sacred teepee built by male relatives. Dachina meets with a medicine woman and learns about Apache women's traditions. She runs four circles around a basket full of special objects. She prays to the mountain spirits on top of a hill. On the last night of the ritual, Dachina must dance all night.

4. Dachina receives her Apache woman's name, Morning Star Feather.

Responses will vary; students should mention the setting (the Apache reservation in New Mexico), people (Dachina, her mother, the medicine woman, Dachina's family, members of the tribe); and events (preparing for the ritual; building the sacred teepee; Dachina in the sacred teepee; parts of the ritual; Dachina dancing all night; Dachina succeeding).

Comprehension Check

Complete the following items after you finish your first review of the video.

1. What is the purpose of Dachina's coming-of-age ritual?

2. What symbols are part of the ritual, and what does each represent?

3. What special places, events, and tasks are part of the ritual?

4. What happens to Dachina at the end of the four-day ritual?

Notebook Confirm your understanding of the video "Apache Girl's Rite of Passage" by writing a description of the setting, people, and events the video portrays.

30 UNIT 1 • RITES OF PASSAGE

PERSONALIZE FOR LEARNING

Challenge

Research Encourage students to conduct research and write brief reports about coming-of-age rituals in other Native American cultures. Reports should include information about the culture or tribe, a description of a ritual, and how it is similar to or different from the rituals in "The Medicine Bag" and "Apache Girl's Rite of Passage."

MAKING MEANING

Close Review

Watch the video again. Write down any new observations that seem important. What **questions** do you have? What can you **conclude**?

APACHE GIRL'S RITE OF PASSAGE

Analyze the Media

CITE TEXTUAL EVIDENCE to support your answers.

📓 **Notebook** Respond to these questions.

1. **(a) Analyze** In what order are the events presented in the video? **(b) Connect** What is the advantage of using this organizational structure for this piece?

2. **(a) Analyze** Who is narrating the video? **(b) Evaluate** Would the video have been more effective or less effective if the story had been told by Dachina? Explain.

3. **Essential Question:** *What are some milestones on the path to growing up?* How does Dachina's coming-of-age ritual symbolize the milestones she has reached on her path to adulthood? How do you think the ritual helps her achieve this goal? Support your response with evidence from the video.

LANGUAGE DEVELOPMENT

Media Vocabulary

| narration | close-up | pan |
| audio | contrast | synchronization |

Use the vocabulary words in your responses to the questions.

1. **(a)** How is the sequence of events conveyed in the video? **(b)** How is this different from the way the sequence of events is conveyed in the story "The Medicine Bag"?

2. **(a)** What tools does the video use to emphasize different parts of the ritual? **(b)** How does the video use each tool?

EVIDENCE LOG

Before moving on to a new selection, go to your Evidence Log and record what you learned from the "Apache Girl's Rite of Passage" video.

DIGITAL PERSPECTIVES

Jump Start

CLOSE REVIEW Discuss with students how family and friends can help someone undergo a rite of passage. Ask students to make connections to the contemporary rites of passage they know.

Close Review

If needed, model close reviewing by using the Closer Review notes in the Interactive Teacher's Edition.

Analyze the Media

1. (a) The video mostly follows chronological order except for a few moments when it provides deeper explanation or context.
   (b) Responses will vary but should be well supported by logic.

2. (a) The narrator is a person who describes the events but does not participate in them. He is probably not a member of the tribal community.
   (b) Responses will vary but should be supported by details from the video.

3. Dachina has passed through several life stages already: being a baby, a child, and an adolescent. She has learned from the medicine woman about how to be an Apache woman. Going through the ritual shows that Dachina is ready to face the demands of being an Apache woman. In the ritual, she faces challenges such as lack of sleep, lack of food, having to hide her emotions, and dancing for ten hours without stopping.

Media Vocabulary

For more support, see **Media Vocabulary**.

Possible Responses:

1. (a) Sequence is conveyed through audio narration in synchronization with the visual parts of the video. (b) In "The Medicine Bag," the main character tells what is happening. In the video, a narrator describes what the video shows.

2. (a) The video uses close-ups, contrast, and pans to emphasize different parts of the ritual. (b) The video uses close-ups to show Dachina and her family, contrast to emphasize the different times of day, and pans to show the location.

FORMATIVE ASSESSMENT

Analyze the Media
- **If** students struggle to understand the video, **then** ask them to identify three main ideas they take away from their viewing.

Media Vocabulary
- **If** students struggle to relate the media vocabulary to the video, **then** review relevant parts of the video and point out the use of the terms and concepts in the media vocabulary.

Evidence Log

Support students in completing their Evidence Log. This paced activity will help prepare them for the Performance-Based Assessment at the end of the unit.

TEACHING

Writing to Compare

As students prepare to compare the story by Virginia Driving Hawk Sneve and the National Geographic video, they will consider how these two types of media present similar material in different ways.

Prewriting

Gathering Evidence

See possible responses in the chart on the student page.

Possible responses:

1. (a) Each rite of passage involves a young person following a Native American tradition. The young person is supported by family members. (b) One rite of passage is for males, and the other is for females. The Apache rite of passage involves a group ceremony, and the Lakota rite of passage does not.

2. The video shows the girl's actions and comments as she undergoes the rite of passage. It also gives an idea of the physical effort that is required.

EFFECTIVE EXPRESSION

THE MEDICINE BAG

APACHE GIRL'S RITE OF PASSAGE

Writing to Compare

You have reviewed two selections about rites of passage for young Native Americans, a short story titled "The Medicine Bag" and a documentary video titled "Apache Girl's Rite of Passage." Now, deepen your analysis of the two selections, and express your observations in writing.

Assignment

Write a **comparison-and-contrast essay** in which you compare the rites of passage in the two selections about young Native Americans. Your essay should focus on the following:

- How the Lakota rite of passage and the Apache rite of passage are similar and different
- The advantages and disadvantages of text versus video for presenting the material

Prewriting

Gathering Evidence Use this chart to analyze how the text and the video each describe a young person's rite of passage. Think about the strengths and weaknesses of each medium.

	WHAT I LEARNED FROM THE SHORT STORY	WHAT I LEARNED FROM THE VIDEO	HOW TEXT COMPARES WITH VIDEO
Choice of narrator and impact on audience	Martin narrates, making the story more personal.	There is an outside narrator, creating a sense of distance from the ritual.	The personal narration in the story enables the audience to feel more connected to the experience.
Story details that are emphasized	Martin's adolescence and its conflicts; the changing way he views his grandfather; elements of Native American life.	Dachina's passage into adult responsibility as a powerful woman; elements of the Native American ritual, such as pollen and white clay	Dachina's rite of passage has more of a physical element than Martin's does.
How the young person feels about the rite of passage	Martin has mixed feelings, especially because he is initially embarrassed. But he grows to respect his heritage, and as his grandfather is dying, he accepts the rite.	Dachina is excited to become a woman and proud of her success in passing through the ritual.	There is more inherent conflict (and sadness) in Martin's experience.

Notebook Respond to these questions.

1. (a) In what ways are the two rites of passage most similar? (b) In what ways are they most different?
2. How does seeing the Apache rite of passage on video help you to understand it more fully?

STANDARDS
Speaking and Listening
Analyze the purpose of information presented in diverse media and formats and evaluate the motives behind its presentation.

CROSS-CURRICULAR PERSPECTIVES

Music Have students consider the role music plays in "Apache Girl's Rite of Passage" and answer questions such as:

What type of music is used in the video?

How does music help create the mood or set the scene?

How does music help viewers understand or better appreciate what they are seeing and hearing?

Would a different kind of music be appropriate for this video? Why or why not?

ESSENTIAL QUESTION: What are some milestones on the path to growing up?

Drafting

As you draft your essay, consider factors such as the presence of a narrator, as well as differences in how each medium shares the experience and shows the action. Then, evaluate the advantages and disadvantages of how each medium presents the ritual.

Structuring the Body of Your Essay You have two subtopics to write about in your essay. One involves similarities and differences. The other topic involves advantages and disadvantages. You may want to structure the body of your essay using this format.

I. Similarities and Differences

   A. Similarities between rites of passage

   B. Differences between rites of passage

II. Advantages and Disadvantages

   A. Advantages and Disadvantages of Text

   B. Advantages and Disadvantages of Video

Writing the Introduction The introduction of an essay should not only introduce your central idea but also engage the reader. Think of an image or a piece of information that you can work into your introduction to "hook" the reader's interest.

It is often a good idea to wait to write your introduction until after you have written the other parts of the essay. That way you will be able to clearly identify your central idea.

Review, Revise, and Edit

Once you have finished drafting, review your comparison-and-contrast essay.

- Ensure that your introduction and conclusion are closely related and that you have stated and supported your central idea.
- Add additional details, if needed, to support your statements.
- Add transitions to clearly indicate relationships among ideas.
- Proofread to ensure your essay is free from errors in spelling, punctuation, and grammar.

EVIDENCE LOG

Before moving on to a new selection, go to your Evidence Log and record what you learned from the "Apache Girl's Rite of Passage" video.

STANDARDS

Reading Informational Text
Evaluate the advantages and disadvantages of using different mediums to present a particular topic or idea.

Writing
Write informative/explanatory texts to examine a topic and convey ideas, concepts, and information through the selection, organization, and analysis of relevant content.

  a. Introduce a topic clearly, previewing what is to follow; organize ideas, concepts, and information into broader categories; include formatting, graphics, and multimedia when useful to aiding comprehension.

DIGITAL PERSPECTIVES

Drafting

Structuring the Body of Your Essay If students have trouble understanding the outline format, encourage them to list a few phrases under each section to show their main ideas.

Writing the Introduction Remind students not to overload their introduction with too much information. Introductions should focus on a thesis statement plus a few sentences outlining the support, as well as a "hook."

Review, Revise, and Edit As students revise, encourage them to review their draft to be sure they have explained their thinking clearly. Ask them to make sure they have organized their ideas into separate paragraphs. Finally, remind students to check for grammar, usage, and mechanics. For more support, see **Writing to Compare: Comparison-and-Contrast Essay.**

Evidence Log Support students in completing their Evidence Log. This paced activity will help prepare them for the Performance-Based Assessment at the end of the unit.

FORMATIVE ASSESSMENT

Writing to Compare

If students struggle to identify details in the video, **then** allow them to replay the video additional times, with headphones if they are available.

PERSONALIZE FOR LEARNING

English Language Support

Transitions Help students better understand how to express sequences of events by reviewing the uses and meanings of appropriate transition words and phrases such as:

- first, second, third
- earlier, later, finally, at last
- before, after, starts with, ends with
- then, after which

ALL LEVELS

TEACHING

Jump Start

Ask students to write two things they have learned about events that change people as they grow up as a result of reading "The Medicine Bag" and watching "Apache Girl's Rite of Passage." You might guide them with questions such as "What are some key events one experiences as he or she grows up? Why are these experiences important?" As students share, ask them to cite specific examples from the text or video to support their ideas.

Write a Nonfiction Narrative

Make sure students understand what they are being asked to do in the assignment. Explain that they will be describing an event that changed their ideas and feelings or an event that changed the life of someone they know. Students should complete the assignment using word processing software to take advantage of editing tools and features.

Elements of a Nonfiction Narrative

Remind students that a nonfiction narrative is a true story about a person's life experiences. It should have well-developed characters, descriptive details, a clear sequence of events, and a description of a change in the life, ideas, or feelings of the main character.

MAKE IT INTERACTIVE
Project "Red Roses" from the Interactive Teacher's Edition and have students identify the elements of a nonfiction narrative, such as dialogue, vivid, descriptive details, and a conclusion that reflects on the experiences in the narrative.

Academic Vocabulary

Ask students to suggest ways they might use the academic vocabulary in their narratives.

PERFORMANCE TASK: WRITING FOCUS

WRITING TO SOURCES
- THE MEDICINE BAG
- APACHE GIRL'S RITE OF PASSAGE

Tool Kit
Student Model of a Nonfiction Narrative

ACADEMIC VOCABULARY
As you craft your narrative, consider using some of the academic vocabulary you learned in the beginning of the unit.

attribute
gratifying
persistent
notable
inspire

STANDARDS
Writing
Write narratives to develop real or imagined experiences or events using effective technique, relevant descriptive details, and well-structured event sequences.

34 UNIT 1 • RITES OF PASSAGE

Write a Nonfiction Narrative

You have just read a text and watched a video about rites of passage. In the short story "The Medicine Bag," a boy learns about his great-great-grandfather's vision quest—and he himself takes on the responsibility of family and Lakota tradition. In the "Apache Girl's Rite of Passage" video, a young woman goes through a four-day coming-of-age ritual to become an Apache woman.

Assignment

You have learned about two people who experience changes, learn about their heritage, and begin to think differently. Think about an event that changed your ideas and feelings or an event that changed the life of someone you know. Write a **nonfiction narrative** that answers this question:

> What event changed your understanding of yourself, or that of someone you know?

Elements of a Nonfiction Narrative

A **nonfiction narrative** tells the true story of events the writer or someone else has experienced. Writers adopt the first-person point of view (using *I* and *me*) to tell about their own experience. Writers adopt the third-person point of view (using *he* and *him, she* and *her, they* and *them,* etc.) to tell someone else's experience.

An effective nonfiction narrative contains these elements:
- characterizations of people who play different roles in the event
- a description of the impact of the event on the different people involved
- a clear sequence of events that unfolds naturally and logically
- narrative techniques such as dialogue, description, and pacing that effectively build the action
- a variety of transitional words, phrases, and clauses
- precise words, well-chosen quotations, vivid descriptive details, and powerful sensory language
- a conclusion reflecting on the experiences in the narrative

Model Nonfiction Narrative For a model of a well-crafted nonfiction narrative, see the Launch Text, "Red Roses."

Challenge yourself to find all the elements of an effective nonfiction narrative in the text. You will have an opportunity to review these elements as you prepare to write your own.

AUTHOR'S PERSPECTIVE Kelly Gallagher, M.Ed.

Pump Up the Volume of Writing Spend some time talking to students about why they should write—not just how. Students should write more than the teacher can grade. To help students get the most from their writing, teachers can use techniques such as these:

- **Confer** Teachers can achieve more in a two-minute conference than they can by spending five to seven minutes writing comments on a paper. Developing writers need face time with the most experienced writer in the class—the teacher.

- **Model** Teachers can model how they write by frequently writing in front of students. Show students that effective writing extends far past correctness. Teachers can do this in short bursts, and model authentic writing, whether brainstorming a topic, working to add details, or revising to find the right word. Note: Other times the teacher can bring a model to class that has already been written for the students to study.

- **Share Models of Excellent Writing** Show students models from professional writers and

ESSENTIAL QUESTION: What are some milestones on the path to growing up?

Prewriting / Planning

Choose Your Topic Reread the assignment. Consider the person and event you would like to highlight in your narrative. State your main idea in a sentence.

_____ changed how
(event or experience)

_____ viewed or felt about
(person)

_____.
(something in life or the world)

Gather Evidence Evidence for a nonfiction narrative comes mainly from memories and experiences. A photo album or a conversation with a friend or relative may stimulate your memory and help you find a topic. There are many different types of evidence you can use to craft your nonfiction narrative.

TYPE OF EVIDENCE	EXPLANATION	YOUR EVIDENCE
anecdotes	brief stories that illustrate a point or key idea	
quotations	statements from personal interviews or conversations with the subjects of your narrative	
examples	facts, ideas, and events that support an idea or insight	

Connect Across Texts To effectively develop your nonfiction narrative, look again at the Launch Text and Anchor Texts. Understanding how an author uses narrative techniques will enable you to apply those techniques to your own writing. Ask yourself these questions and take notes on your findings:

- How does dialogue help you understand the people in the narrative better?

- How does the pacing of the story—how slowly or quickly it moves—add interest and convey the sequence of events?

- How does the author use description to help you appreciate what he or she experienced?

EVIDENCE LOG
Review your Evidence Log and identify key details you may want to cite in your nonfiction narrative.

STANDARDS
Writing
Write narratives to develop real or imagined experiences or events using effective technique, relevant descriptive details, and well-structured event sequences.
  a. Engage and orient the reader by establishing a context and point of view and introducing a narrator and/or characters; organize an event sequence that unfolds naturally and logically.
  b. Use narrative techniques, such as dialogue, pacing, description, and reflection, to develop experiences, events, and/or characters.

Performance Task: Write a Nonfiction Narrative 35

DIGITAL PERSPECTIVES

Prewriting/Planning

Choose Your Topic Suggest that students think about the person and event that they found most engaging.

Gather Evidence Suggest that students consider how well they remember the experience they are writing about. If they don't remember it well, or want to get another perspective on it, they might discuss this experience with others who were part of it. If they are writing about something that happened to someone else, they might talk to that person about what happened and how he or she felt about it.

Connect Across Texts Encourage students to review the text and video more than once before they begin writing to see if the experience they're writing about relates to the selections. During this process, students should take note of how the selections are similar to or different from the experience they plan to write about.

---

from other students. As they study mentor texts, students begin to see the moves a writer has made, and they can work to emulate those moves.

- **Use a Rubric** Experiment with changing the rubric. Encourage students to help you build it. This creates buy-in when the students see that each rubric is personalized to some degree to their needs.

PERSONALIZE FOR LEARNING

Strategic Support
Understanding Story Structure Help students understand narrative structure by reviewing the importance of having a beginning, a middle, and an end. Discuss how the beginning of a narrative sets up the situation and the characters. The middle introduces a problem or conflict and develops the characters by describing how they react.

The end may or may not resolve the conflict, describes what the characters may or may not have learned, and brings the narrative to a conclusion. Encourage students to think about the beginning, middle, and end of their narrative before they start writing.

Whole-Class Learning 35

TEACHING

Drafting

Organize a Sequence of Events Remind students to tell their story in chronological order, with one event logically proceeding to the next in the order they happened. Also remind students that creating a timeline before they write will help them organize their ideas and remember which events and ideas are important. If necessary, review how to create a simple timeline.

Write a First Draft with text that grabs the reader's attention, describes the characters and setting, and introduces the conflict. Students should follow their timeline when writing their narrative. Remind students to write an ending that reflects on the experiences.

PERFORMANCE TASK: WRITING FOCUS

Drafting

Organize a Sequence of Events In a nonfiction narrative, the writer often sequences events in **chronological order** so that one event proceeds to the next in the order in which they actually happened.

- Use a timeline to organize your narrative so that it flows in chronological order.
- Start by introducing important people, as well as the setting and the background of the story.
- Then, add details in the order in which they occur.

The timeline here shows key events in the Launch Text. Think about how each event supports the message of the narrative.

LAUNCH TEXT

MODEL: "Red Roses" Personal Narrative Timeline

INTRODUCTION
The narrator, Lila, remembers a boy named Derek that no one liked, herself included.

1. Lila finds little presents from Derek hidden in her locker, desk, and jacket pocket.
2. She is annoyed and ignores Derek.
3. Her friends tease her about having a "boyfriend."
4. Derek presents her with a dozen roses.
5. Lila snaps at him; then she sees that he's about to cry.

CONCLUSION
Lila accepts the flowers to protect Derek from being called a crybaby, and she feels good about it.

Nonfiction Narrative Timeline

INTRODUCTION
1.

2.

3.

4.

5.

CONCLUSION

STANDARDS
Writing
Write narratives to develop real or imagined experiences or events using effective technique, relevant descriptive details, and well-structured event sequences.
  a. Engage and orient the reader by establishing a context and point of view and introducing a narrator and/or characters; organize an event sequence that unfolds naturally and logically.
  c. Use a variety of transition words, phrases, and clauses to convey sequence, signal shifts from one time frame or setting to another, and show the relationships among experiences and events.

Write a First Draft Refer to your prewriting notes and timeline, and then begin drafting your narrative. As you draft, strive to engage your audience by:

- Beginning with an exciting detail that hints at the story's conclusion.
- Keeping your audience's interest by showing, not telling.
- Interspersing dialogue to bring people's personalities to life.
- Concluding with an original observation about the importance of the event.

AUTHOR'S PERSPECTIVE — Jim Cummins, Ph.D.

Writing Enhances Student Identity Writing is an expression of oneself, and writing projects that self into the new social spheres. However, students learning English are often defined by what they are missing rather than by what they possess. While teaching writing through the Performance Tasks in *my*Perspectives, you may want to supplement the writing instruction and practice for English Learners by using *identity texts*. These texts allow students to invest their identities into their writing. The results hold a mirror up to students and reflect their identities in a positive light. Teachers can use this process:

1. Encourage students to have a hand in picking the topic to ensure they are writing about something that reflects themselves or their identities. Have students write their drafts in English, illustrate them, and work with various sources, such as parents and older students fluent in their home language, to translate the drafts into their home language.

2. Publish these texts. Help students share identity texts with multiple audiences including peers, teachers, parents, grandparents, sister classes,

ESSENTIAL QUESTION: What are some milestones on the path to growing up?

LANGUAGE DEVELOPMENT: AUTHOR'S STYLE

Create Cohesion: Transitions

Transitions are words and phrases that connect and show relationships among events and ideas. Transitional words and phrases perform an essential function in a narrative. They help the writer guide the reader through the sequence of events and show the relationships among ideas.

Read It

These sentences from the Launch Text use transitions to show specific connections among ideas and events.

- *Despite* my standoffishness, Derek started leaving me little gifts. (shows contrast)
- *And then*—horrors!—I saw his bottom lip quiver. (shows time order)
- I *immediately* tossed them into the back of my closet when I got home. (emphasizes)

Write It

As you draft your nonfiction narrative, choose transitions that accurately show specific relationships among your ideas. Transitions are especially important when connecting one paragraph to the next.

If you want to . . .	consider using one of these transitions
list or add ideas	first of all, second, next, last, in addition
show time order	before, after, the next day, then
compare	also, equally, likewise
contrast	although, however, on the other hand, despite
emphasize	most of all, immediately, in fact
show effect	therefore, as a result, so, consequently
illustrate or show	for example, for instance, specifically

TIP

PUNCTUATION
Make sure to punctuate transitional expressions correctly.

- Some transitional expressions at the beginning of a sentence should be followed by a comma; e.g., *In addition, The next day, Most of all.*
- Some transitional expressions in the middle of a sentence should be preceded by a comma (or a semicolon) and followed by a comma; e.g., *however, therefore, for example.*

STANDARDS
Writing
Use a variety of transition words, phrases, and clauses to convey sequence, signal shifts from one time frame or setting to another, and show the relationships among experiences and events.

Performance Task: Write a Nonfiction Narrative 37

DIGITAL PERSPECTIVES

Create Cohesion: Transitions

Read It
Remind students that transitions strengthen a narrative because they can help the reader quickly "get" the story. For example, the phrase "even though" at the beginning of a sentence signals the reader that a contradiction is coming. The phrase "years later" signals the reader that there will be a lot of time between events in the narrative.

MAKE IT INTERACTIVE
Project "Red Roses" from the Interactive Teacher's Edition and ask students to identify additional examples of transitions.

- *Still*, the presents continued. *(shows contrast)*
- I never did talk to Derek *after that*. *(shows time order)*

Write It
As students revise their drafts they should think about the relationships between their ideas and use the suggested transitions to improve the clarity and cohesion of their narratives.

---

and the media. It is critical that students share their writing with broad audiences to build this positive experience. Students are likely to receive positive feedback and affirmation of self by providing true audiences with which to share their work.

Writing and publishing identity texts helps English Learners take active control and ownership of the learning process and invest their identities in their drafts.

PERSONALIZE FOR LEARNING

English Language Support
Using Transitions Help students better understand transition words and phrases by assisting them in writing sentences that compare (using *equally* or *also*); contrast (using *however* or *although*); emphasize (using *most of all*); show effect (using *as a result* or *so*); and illustrate (using *for example*). **ALL LEVELS**

Whole-Class Learning 37

TEACHING

Revising

Evaluating Your Draft
Before students begin revising their writing, they should evaluate their drafts. Each draft should contain all of the required elements, follow a logical organization, and adhere to the norms and conventions of a nonfiction narrative.

Revising for Focus and Organization
Clear Conclusion Students should check to see that their conclusions don't leave the reader with unanswered questions. The conclusion should provide readers with a feeling that the narrative is "finished." You may wish to explain that an author can choose to leave a narrative "unfinished," but it should be clear that this has been done deliberately. For example: "What did she mean by that? To this day, I don't know."

Precise Language Remind students that precise language and descriptive words help a narrative "come alive." Encourage students to look for flat descriptions and replace them with language that paints a picture for the reader. For example, "He was big" could be replaced with "He towered over me." "She was quiet" could be replaced with "She was silent as a shadow."

PERFORMANCE TASK: NONFICTION NARRATIVE

Revising

Evaluating Your Draft
Use the following checklist to evaluate the effectiveness of your first draft. Then, use your evaluation and the instructions on this page to guide your revision.

FOCUS AND ORGANIZATION	EVIDENCE AND ELABORATION	CONVENTIONS
☐ Describes a change in the life, ideas, or feelings of the writer or of another person.	☐ Develops the people in the narrative through dialogue and description.	☐ Attends to the norms and conventions of the discipline, especially the correct use and punctuation of transitions.
☐ Describes the experience that caused the writer's or another person's life, ideas, or feelings to change.	☐ Builds the action through dialogue, description, and pacing.	
☐ Has a clear sequence of events that unfolds naturally and logically.	☐ Captures the action and illustrates experiences and events using precise words, descriptive details, and sensory language.	
☐ Includes a conclusion that follows from and reflects on the experiences in the narrative.		

⛬ WORD NETWORK
Include interesting words from your Word Network in your narrative.

Revising for Focus and Organization
Clear Conclusion The conclusion of a nonfiction narrative clarifies the essay's overall message and provides readers with a sense of **resolution**, or completion. It resolves any conflicts or questions presented in the narrative. Reread the conclusion in the Launch Text, and then review your own conclusion. To increase clarity, begin by summarizing the relationship between the events and experiences that you present and the overall message that you would like to communicate. Strengthen your conclusion by reflecting on this relationship and sharing any insights you have gained from making these connections.

Revising for Evidence and Elaboration
Precise Language In order to craft a lively narrative that engages readers, avoid words and language that leave the reader with questions such as *What kind? How? In what way? How often?* and *To what extent?* As you review your draft, identify vague words that do not provide specific answers to those questions. As you revise, replace vague words with specific, precise words that convey your ideas more vividly and accurately. Here are some examples.

vague noun:	*stuff*	use	*souvenirs, gifts, photos*
vague verb:	*said*	use	*exclaimed, whispered, declared*
vague adjective:	*pretty*	use	*attractive, exquisite, adorable*
vague adverb:	*greatly*	use	*enormously, incredibly, remarkably*

≡ STANDARDS
Writing
Write narratives to develop real or imagined experiences or events using effective technique, relevant descriptive details, and well-structured event sequences.
  d. Use precise words and phrases, relevant descriptive details, and sensory language to capture the action and convey experiences and events.
  e. Provide a conclusion that follows from and reflects on the narrated experiences or events.

HOW LANGUAGE WORKS

Transitions As students move into the revision work on their narratives, remind them to pay attention to transitional words and phrases to connect and show the relationships among ideas. Review the types of transitions already discussed (list or add ideas; show time order; compare; contrast; emphasize; show effect; illustrate or show), and discuss how different transitional words and phrases express or clarify these ideas or relationships.

ESSENTIAL QUESTION: What are some milestones on the path to growing up?

PEER REVIEW

Exchange narratives with a classmate. Use the checklist to evaluate your classmate's nonfiction narrative and provide supportive feedback.

1. Is the point of view clear and are the people in the narrative well developed?
   ☐ yes ☐ no   If no, suggest how the writer might improve them.

2. Is there a clear sequence of events that unfolds chronologically and is clarified by transitions?
   ☐ yes ☐ no   If no, explain what confused you.

3. Does the narrative end with a conclusion that connects to and reflects on the events and experiences presented?
   ☐ yes ☐ no   If no, tell what you think might be missing.

4. What is the strongest part of your classmate's narrative? Why?

   _____

   _____

   _____

Editing and Proofreading

Edit for Conventions Reread your draft for accuracy and consistency. Correct errors in grammar and word usage. Be sure you have included a variety of transitions to make connections among events.

Proofread for Accuracy Read your draft carefully, looking for errors in spelling and punctuation. As you proofread, make sure that any **dialogue**—the actual words spoken by people—is enclosed in quotation marks. A split dialogue is a quotation that is interrupted by additional information, such as the identification of the speaker. Refer to the Launch Text for examples of each type of dialogue.

Publishing and Presenting

Create a final version of your narrative. Share it with a small group so that your classmates can read it and make comments. In turn, review and comment on your classmates' work. As a group, discuss what your narratives have in common and the ways in which they are different. Always maintain a polite and respectful tone when commenting.

Reflecting

Reflect on what you learned as you wrote your narrative. In what ways did writing about past experiences and events help to heighten your understanding of them?

STANDARDS

Writing
- Produce clear and coherent writing in which the development, organization, and style are appropriate to task, purpose, and audience.
- With some guidance and support from peers and adults, develop and strengthen writing as needed by planning, revising, editing, rewriting, or trying a new approach, focusing on how well purpose and audience have been addressed.

Performance Task: Write a Nonfiction Narrative 39

DIGITAL PERSPECTIVES

Peer Review
Before students begin their peer review, remind them that they are reviewing for clarity and completeness, not whether they like what the narrative is about or if they agree with the author's ideas. However, they might make helpful suggestions if they see something in the narrative that could be stronger.

Editing and Proofreading
Remind students to check for the proper formatting of dialogue. In a conversation, each time a different character speaks, the writer should start a new paragraph. This applies whether the character has many lines to say or just one word.

Publishing and Presenting
Before students review their classmates' narratives, remind them to:

- Be honest, but maintain a respectful tone in their comments.
- Use formal rather than informal language.
- Don't just agree with what people say; move the discussion forward by building on the ideas of others.
- Disagree respectfully. Different opinions are fine, but they should be expressed politely.

Reflecting
Remind students to reflect not only on their narrative and the process of writing it, but also on the comments they received.

PERSONALIZE FOR LEARNING

Challenge
Research Encourage students to conduct research about modern rituals that young people experience as they grow up. These can be formal rituals such as getting a driver's license, or informal rituals such as going from elementary school to middle school. Have students imagine they are taking part in one of the rituals they have learned, and write narratives to describe the experience.

Whole-Class Learning 39

OVERVIEW

SMALL-GROUP LEARNING

What are some milestones on the path to growing up?

Growing up is a process marked by many memorable experiences that, together, make us who we are as adults. Many of these experiences can be life changing. During Small-Group Learning, students will read selections that describe some of these events that define our childhoods.

Small-Group Learning Strategies 🔊

Review the Learning Strategies with students and explain that as they work through Small-Group Learning they will develop strategies to work in small-group environments.

- Have students watch the video on Small-Group Learning Strategies.
- A video on this topic is available online in the Professional Development Center.

You may wish to discuss some action items to add to the chart as a class before students complete it on their own. For example, for "Participate fully," you might solicit the following from students:

- Take notes so that you will remember the important details.
- Ask follow-up questions after the speaker has finished, so that you will be sure to fully understand the speaker's points.

Block Scheduling

Each day in this Pacing Plan represents a 40–50-minute class period. Teachers using block scheduling may combine days to reflect their class schedule. In addition, teachers may revise pacing to differentiate and support core instruction by integrating components and resources as students require.

📅 **Pacing Plan**

OVERVIEW: SMALL-GROUP LEARNING

ESSENTIAL QUESTION:

What are some milestones on the path to growing up?

Roads to adulthood may differ around the world, but they all have some recognizable landmarks in common. Learning about rites of passage in different cultures may echo your own experiences or may introduce you to a challenge you never considered. You will work in a group to continue your exploration of the experiences that change and define people as they grow up.

Small-Group Learning Strategies

Throughout your life, in school, in your community, in college, and in your career, you will continue to learn and work with others.

Look at these strategies and the actions you can take to practice them as you work in teams. Add ideas of your own for each step. Use these strategies during Small-Group Learning.

STRATEGY	ACTION PLAN
Prepare	• Complete your assignments so that you are prepared for group work. • Organize your thinking so you can contribute to your group's discussion. •
Participate fully	• Make eye contact to signal that you are listening and taking in what is being said. • Use text evidence when making a point. •
Support others	• Build off ideas from others in your group. • Invite others who have not yet spoken to do so. •
Clarify	• Paraphrase the ideas of others to ensure that your understanding is correct. • Ask follow-up questions. •

SCAN FOR MULTIMEDIA

Unit Introduction	Introduce Whole-Class Learning	The Medicine Bag	Media: Apache Girl's Rite of Passage	Performance Task
1 2	3	4 5 6 7 8 9 10 11 12	13 14 15	16 17 18

CONTENTS

LETTERS

You Are the Electric Boogaloo
Geoff Herbach

Just Be Yourself!
Stephanie Pellegrin

Two authors look back at their younger selves with amusement and encouragement.

POETRY COLLECTION

Hanging Fire
Audre Lorde

Translating Grandfather's House
E. J. Vega

What does it mean to be a "young adult"?

SHORT STORY

The Setting Sun and the Rolling World
Charles Mungoshi

Do you have to abandon the familiar to find yourself?

▶ MEDIA CONNECTION: Stories of Zimbabwean Women

PERFORMANCE TASK

SPEAKING AND LISTENING FOCUS

Present Nonfiction Narratives

After reading the selections, your group will plan and deliver a series of nonfiction narratives that explore the different rites of passage on the path to adulthood.

Contents

Selections Circulate among groups as they preview the selections. You might encourage groups to discuss any knowledge they already have about any of the selections or the situations and settings shown in the photographs. Students may wish to take a poll within their group to determine which selections look the most interesting.

Remind students that communicating and collaborating in groups is an important skill that they will use throughout their lives—in school, in their careers, and in their community.

Performance Task

Present a Nonfiction Narrative Give groups time to read about and briefly discuss the multimedia presentation they will create after reading. Encourage students to do some preliminary thinking about the types of media they may want to use. This may help focus their subsequent reading and group discussion.

OVERVIEW

SMALL-GROUP LEARNING

Working as a Team

1. **Discuss the Topic** Remind groups to let all members share their responses. You may wish to set a time limit for this discussion.
2. **List Your Rules** You may want to have groups share their lists of rules and consolidate them into a master list to be displayed and followed by all groups.
3. **Apply the Rules** As you circulate among the groups, ensure that students are staying on task. Consider a short time limit for this step.
4. **Name Your Group** This task can be creative and fun. If students have trouble coming up with a name, suggest that they think of something related to the unit topic. Encourage groups to share their names with the class.
5. **Create a Communication Plan** Encourage groups to include in their plans agreed-upon times during the day to share ideas. They should record and save their ideas.

Accountable Talk

Offer students these Accountable Talk suggestions:

Remember to . . .
Ask clarifying questions.

Which sounds like . . .
Would you say that again?
Can you give me an example?
I think you said _____. Did I understand you?

Remember to . . .
Explain your thinking.

Which sounds like . . .
I think this is true because _____.

Remember to . . .
Build on the ideas of others.

Which sounds like . . .
When _____ said _____, it made me think of _____.

OVERVIEW: SMALL-GROUP LEARNING

Working as a Team

1. **Discuss the Topic** In your group, discuss the following question:

   What defines an event in a young person's life as a milestone or rite of passage?

   As you take turns sharing your positions, be sure to provide examples for your choice. After all group members have shared, discuss the similarities and differences in your responses.

2. **List Your Rules** As a group, decide on the rules that you will follow as you work together. Two samples are provided. Add two more of your own. You may add or revise rules based on your experience together.

   - Everyone should participate in group discussions.
   - People should not interrupt.
   - _____
   - _____

3. **Apply the Rules** When you share what you have learned about growing up, make sure each person in the group contributes and follows the group's rules.

4. **Name Your Group** Choose a name that reflects the unit topic.

   Our group's name: _____

5. **Create a Communication Plan** Decide how you want to communicate with one another. For example, you might use online collaboration tools, email, or instant messaging.

   Our group's decision: _____

42 UNIT 1 • RITES OF PASSAGE

AUTHOR'S PERSPECTIVE — Kelly Gallagher, M.Ed.

- **Meaningful Talk** Instead of asking teacher-directed questions that lead students to see specific elements, give the power back to the students. Help them find their own big ideas and support them by building in talk opportunities. Use these three strategies to help students achieve deeper comprehension:

- **See the Relevance in Reading:** Teachers have students read great works of literature to give students an opportunity to think deeply about issues that will affect their lives. Asking students "What is worth talking about here?" helps them find themes and interpretations and get to the heart of the unit theme.

- **One Question, One Comment Strategy:** To get students to revisit a chapter or passage they find particularly challenging and generate an in-depth discussion of the text, teachers can ask students to come to class with one question and one comment generated from their reading assignment. During the class discussion, have the first

ESSENTIAL QUESTION: What are some milestones on the path to growing up?

Making a Schedule

First, find out the due dates for the Small-Group activities. Then, preview the texts and activities with your group and make a schedule for completing the tasks.

SELECTION	ACTIVITIES	DUE DATE
You Are the Electric Boogaloo Just Be Yourself!		
Hanging Fire Translating Grandfather's House		
The Setting Sun and the Rolling World		

Working on Group Projects

Different projects require different roles. As your group works together, you'll find it more effective if each person has a specific role. Before beginning a project, discuss the necessary roles and choose one for each group member. Here are some possible roles; add your own ideas.

Project Manager: monitors the schedule and keeps everyone on task
Researcher: organizes research activities
Recorder: takes notes during group meetings

_____
_____
_____
_____
_____
_____

 SCAN FOR MULTIMEDIA

Overview: Small-Group Learning 43

DIGITAL PERSPECTIVES

Making a Schedule

Encourage groups to preview the reading selections and to consider how long it will take them to complete the activities accompanying each selection. Point out that they can adjust the due dates for particular selections as needed as they work on their small-group projects; however, they must complete all assigned tasks before the group Performance Task is due. Encourage groups to review their schedules upon completing the activities for each selection to make sure they are on track to meet the final due date.

Working on Group Projects

Point out to groups that the roles they assign can also be changed later. Students might have to make changes based on who is best at doing what. Try to make sure that there is no favoritism, cliquishness, or stereotyping by gender or other means in the assignment of roles.

Also, you should review the roles each group assigns to its members. Based on your understanding of students' individual strengths, you might find it necessary to suggest some changes.

---

student share one comment or question. The next student can answer the question, respond to the comment, or build on the discussion with his or her own question or comment. Continue the process until everyone in class has participated.

- **Silent Talk:** Students write their thoughts quietly for four minutes and then rotate their papers to the next student. The next student then continues the "conversation."

Using these strategies will lessen student dependence on the teacher and so help build independence.

FACILITATING SMALL-GROUP CLOSE LEARNING

Forming Groups You may wish to form groups for Small-Group Learning so that each consists of students with different learning abilities. Some students may be adept at organizing information whereas others may have strengths related to generating or synthesizing information. A good mix of abilities can make the experience of Small-Group Learning dynamic and productive.

Small-Group Learning 43

PLANNING
SMALL-GROUP LEARNING • YOU ARE THE ELECTRIC BOOGALOO • JUST BE YOURSELF!

You Are the Electric Boogaloo • Just Be Yourself!

🔊 AUDIO SUMMARIES
Audio summaries of "You Are the Electric Boogaloo" and "Just Be Yourself!" are available in both English and Spanish and can be assigned to students in the Interactive Teacher's Edition or Unit Resources. Assigning these summaries prior to reading the selection may help students build additional background knowledge and set a context for their first read.

Summary
In the narrative "You Are the Electric Boogaloo," Geoff Herbach reminisces about breakdancing when he was younger. He talks about good moments, like hanging out with his friends, success, and the beauty of his efforts. Most of the selection is focused on an embarrassing moment when the author got stuck to the floor while dancing with his crew. Herbach points out that it wasn't winning that he remembers from his youth as clearly as he remembers losing. And the importance in losing was getting up and trying again.

Stephanie Pellegrin writes the narrative "Just Be Yourself!" as an address to her teenage self. In it, she admonishes herself for some past choices. Pellegrin believes that her younger self tried too hard to try to find a place where she fit in rather than searching for what she wanted from life more gradually and with less of a rush. Pellegrin makes the point that it's important to be yourself at any age.

> ### Insight
> These letters are ultimately optimistic. "You Are the Electric Boogaloo" sees a path through embarrassments to becoming a better person. In particular, it emphasizes learning not to be frustrated by failure. "Just Be Yourself!" suggests that things will work out even if you don't feel as if you're capable of doing enough.

ESSENTIAL QUESTION:
What are some milestones on the path to growing up?

Connection to Essential Question
Especially for teenagers, our culture talks a lot about "finding yourself." Developing a sense of your identity, the theme of "Just Be Yourself!" does matter! Similarly, in "You Are the Electric Boogaloo," the unpleasant experience Herbach went through ultimately made him who he is today. Recovering from a bad experience is a milestone everyone goes through.

SMALL-GROUP LEARNING PERFORMANCE TASK
What defines an event or experience in a young person's life as a milestone or rite of passage?

UNIT PERFORMANCE-BASED ASSESSMENT
What rite of passage has held the most significance for you or for a person you know well?

Connection to Performance Tasks
Small-Group Learning Task These texts help students to consider the types of experiences that students face—whether awkward, or full-of-doubt, these experiences help adolescents determine who they are.

Unit Performance-Based Assessment Small-scale, personal events can be important turning points for people. The topics of these texts can help students reflect on the informal rites of passages that have shaped their personalities and values.

DIGITAL PERSPECTIVES Audio Video Document Annotation Highlights EL Highlights Online Assessment

LESSON RESOURCES

Lesson	Making Meaning	Language Development	Effective Expression
	First Read Close Read Analyze the Text Analyze Craft and Structure	Concept Vocabulary Word Study Conventions	Speaking and Listening
Instructional Standards	**RI.10** By the end of the year, read and comprehend literary nonfiction . . . **L.4** Determine or clarify the meaning . . . **L.4.a** Use context as a clue . . . **L.5** Demonstrate understanding of figurative language . . . **L.5.c** Distinguish among the connotations of words . . .	**RI.4** Determine the meaning of words and phrases . . . **L.4** Determine or clarify the meaning of unknown and multiple-meaning words or phrases . . . **L.4.b** Use common, grade-appropriate Greek or Latin affixes and roots . . . **L.4.c** Consult general and specialized reference materials . . . **L.1** Demonstrate command of the conventions . . . **L.1.c** Form and use verbs . . . **L.1.d** Recognize and correct inappropriate shifts . . .	**W.7** Conduct short research projects . . . **SL.4** Present claims and findings . . . **SL.5** Integrate multimedia and visual displays . . .
▶ STUDENT RESOURCES			
Available online in the Interactive Student Edition or Unit Resources	🔊 Selection Audio 📄 First-Read Guide: Nonfiction 📄 Close-Read Guide: Nonfiction	📄 Word Network	📄 Evidence Log
▶ TEACHER RESOURCES			
Selection Resources Available online in the Interactive Teacher's Edition or Unit Resources	🔊 Audio Summaries ✏️ Annotation Highlights 💬 EL Highlights 📄 You Are the Electric Boogaloo • Just Be Yourself! Text Questions 📄 English Language Support Lesson: Connotations 📄 Analyze Craft and Structure: Tone	📄 Concept Vocabulary and Word Study 📄 Conventions: Verb Moods	📄 Speaking and Listening: Visual Presentation
Reteach/Practice (RP) Available online in the Interactive Teacher's Edition or Unit Resources	📄 Analyze Craft and Structure: Tone (RP)	📄 Word Study: Latin Suffix -ous (RP) 📄 Conventions: Verb Moods (RP)	📄 Speaking and Listening: Visual Presentation (RP)
Assessment Available online in Assessments	📄 ✓ Selection Test		
My Resources	📄 A Unit 1 Answer Key is available online and in the Interactive Teacher's Edition.		

Small-Group Learning 44B

PERSONALIZE FOR LEARNING

SMALL-GROUP LEARNING • YOU ARE THE ELECTRIC BOOGALOO • JUST BE YOURSELF!

Reading Support

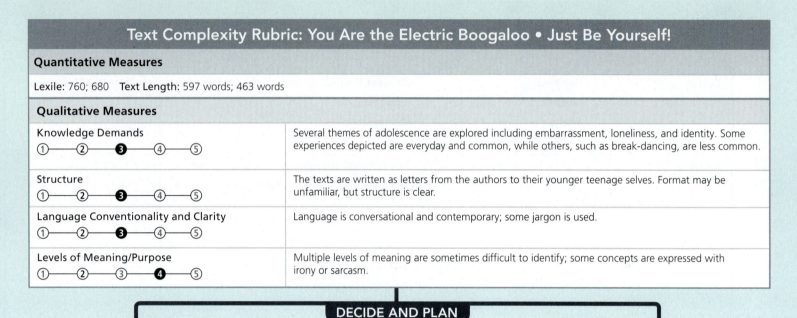

Text Complexity Rubric: You Are the Electric Boogaloo • Just Be Yourself!

Quantitative Measures

Lexile: 760; 680   Text Length: 597 words; 463 words

Qualitative Measures

Knowledge Demands (3 of 5)	Several themes of adolescence are explored including embarrassment, loneliness, and identity. Some experiences depicted are everyday and common, while others, such as break-dancing, are less common.
Structure (3 of 5)	The texts are written as letters from the authors to their younger teenage selves. Format may be unfamiliar, but structure is clear.
Language Conventionality and Clarity (3 of 5)	Language is conversational and contemporary; some jargon is used.
Levels of Meaning/Purpose (4 of 5)	Multiple levels of meaning are sometimes difficult to identify; some concepts are expressed with irony or sarcasm.

DECIDE AND PLAN

English Language Support

Provide English Learners with support for structure and meaning as they read the selection.

Structure Make sure students understand the basic structure: letters older people are writing about past experiences. Ask students to locate the pronouns *I, me, my,* and *I'm*. Ask them whom those refer to (the older self). Then ask them to locate *you, your,* or *you're* and ask whom those refer to (the younger self).

Meaning For "You Are the Electric Boogaloo," review that the text is about *breakdancing,* and that the words *pop, worm, spin,* and *windmill* describe breakdance moves. Ask students to read paragraph 7 and list the events that were embarrassing. Help students to see that the older self is comforting the younger self.

Strategic Support

Provide students with strategic support to ensure that they can successfully read the text.

Structure Ask questions to make sure students understand the format and structure. For example, *It starts "Dear Teen Me," so what is it? (a letter). Whom are the authors writing to? (their younger selves).* Point out the use of first person (*I, me, my, I'm*) and second person (*you, your, you're*). Ask whom those pronouns represent (first person: the older self; second person: the self as a teenager).

Meaning Confirm that students understand the meaning by having them tell what events happened in the past that the authors are writing to their younger selves. Together, make a list of the emotions that the younger selves may have been feeling at those times.

Challenge

Provide students who need to be challenged with ideas for how they can go beyond a simple interpretation of the text.

Text Analysis Pair students. Ask partners to choose one of the letters and write a summary in their own words. Summaries should reflect the personality of the younger self, the events that happened, and the feelings they were having. Have students trade summaries and add to each other's descriptions. Then have volunteers read the summaries to the class.

Written Response Ask each student to copy the style of one of the selections to write a letter to a younger self. Encourage them to pick an event in the past or a typical day in the past. For example, they might write to themselves at 5 or 10 years old on a difficult day they remember at school. Have students share their letters with the class.

TEACH

Read and Respond

Have the groups read the selection and complete the Making Meaning, Language Development, and Effective Expression activities.

Standards Support Through Teaching and Learning Cycle

IDENTIFY NEEDS

Analyze results of the Beginning-of-Year Assessment, focusing on the items relating to Unit 1. Also take into consideration student performance to this point and your observations of where particular students struggle.

ANALYZE AND REVISE

- Analyze student work for evidence of student learning.
- Identify whether students have met the expectations in the standards.
- Identify implications for future instruction.

TEACH

Implement the planned lesson, and gather evidence of student learning.

DECIDE AND PLAN

- If students have performed poorly on items matching these standards, then provide selection scaffolds before assigning them the on-level lesson provided in the Student Edition.
- If students have done well on the Beginning-of-Year Assessment, then challenge them to keep progressing and learning by giving them opportunities to practice the skills in depth.
- Use the Selection Resources listed on the Planning pages for "You Are the Electric Boogaloo" and "Just Be Yourself!" to help students continually improve their ability to master the standards.

Instructional Standards: You Are the Electric Boogaloo • Just Be Yourself!

	Catching Up	This Year	Looking Forward
Reading	You may wish to administer the **Analyze Craft and Structure: Tone (RP)** worksheet to help students understand how a writer uses tone to show his or her attitude toward the subject or audience.	**L.5** Demonstrate understanding of figurative language, word relationships, and nuances in word meaning.	Challenge students to analyze the tone in other selections, making note of words with strong connotations and the feelings they evoke.
Speaking and Listening	You may wish to administer the **Speaking and Listening: Visual Presentation (RP)** worksheet to help students organize their presentations.	**SL.5** Integrate multimedia and visual displays into presentations to clarify information, strengthen claims and evidence, and add interest.	Challenge students to incorporate visual media in their presentations to back up or enhance their ideas and to add interest.
Language	You may wish to administer the **Conventions: Verb Moods (RP)** worksheet to help students understand the different moods of verbs. You may wish to administer the **Word Study: Latin Suffix -ous (RP)** worksheet to help students recognize adjectives ending in -ous.	**L.1.b** Form and use verbs in the indicative, imperative, interrogative, conditional, and subjunctive mood. **L.4** Determine or clarify the meaning of unknown or multiple-meaning words and phrases based on *grade 8 reading and content,* choosing flexibly from a range of strategies.	Challenge students to write two sentences for each type of mood. Have students identify additional words with the suffix -ous.

Small-Group Learning 44D

FACILITATING

Jump Start

FIRST READ What makes an experience memorable? What makes it life changing? Engage students in a discussion about rites of passage that sets the context for reading "You Are the Electric Boogaloo" and "Just Be Yourself!" As students share their thoughts, guide them to identify the reasons that they hold their opinions.

Concept Vocabulary

Ask groups to look closely at the explanation of context clues and discuss how these types of clues can help unlock meaning. Have students discuss the examples and encourage groups to think of additional ones. Possibilities include using images surrounding the text.

FIRST READ

As they read, students should perform the steps of the first read:

NOTICE: You may want to encourage students to notice how the authors address their teen selves.

ANNOTATE: Remind students to mark passages that seem especially meaningful.

CONNECT: Have students compare the experiences of the two letter writers with their own experiences and with those you have read about.

RESPOND: Students will answer questions and write a summary to demonstrate understanding.

Point out to students that while they will always complete the Respond step at the end of the first read, the other steps will probably happen somewhat concurrently. You may wish to print copies of the **First-Read Guide: Nonfiction** for students to use.

MAKING MEANING

LETTERS

You Are the Electric Boogaloo
Just Be Yourself!

Concept Vocabulary

As you perform your first read of "You Are the Electric Boogaloo" and "Just Be Yourself!" you will encounter these words.

| immense | majestic | numerous |

Context Clues To find the meaning of unfamiliar words, look for clues in the context, which is made up of the words that surround the unknown word in a text. Consider the following examples.

> **Example:** They **emblazoned** the crew's name on the T-shirts.
>
> **Context clue:** To get the name on the T-shirt, they **emblazoned** it.
>
> **Possible meaning: Emblazoned** means "inscribed" or "displayed a name on something."
>
> **Example:** It's about finding out who you really are on your own **terms** and in your own way.
>
> **Context clue:** You do it on your own **terms** and in your own way.
>
> **Possible meaning: Terms** means "conditions."

Apply your knowledge of context clues and other vocabulary strategies to determine the meanings of unfamiliar words you encounter during your first read.

First Read NONFICTION

Apply these strategies as you conduct your first read. You will have an opportunity to complete a close read after your first read.

NOTICE the general ideas of the text. What is it about? Who is it about?

ANNOTATE by marking vocabulary and key passages you want to revisit.

CONNECT ideas within the selections to what you already know and what you have already read.

RESPOND by completing the Comprehension Check and by writing a brief summary of the selections.

STANDARDS

Reading Informational Text
By the end of the year, read and comprehend literary nonfiction at the high end of the grades 6–8 text complexity band independently and proficiently.

Language
Determine or clarify the meaning of unknown and multiple-meaning words or phrases based on *grade 8 reading and content*, choosing flexibly from a range of strategies.
 a. Use context as a clue to the meaning of a word or phrase.

AUTHOR'S PERSPECTIVE   Jim Cummins, Ph.D.

Literacy Engagement Academic language is found primarily in printed text rather than in everyday conversation. Thus, when students have abundant access to printed texts and engage actively with these texts, they have far greater opportunities to broaden their vocabulary knowledge and develop strong reading comprehension skills. Students' engagement will be enhanced when they discuss in small groups the texts they have read in *my*Perspectives as well as other selections of their choice. Teachers can help make texts more meaningful to students in the following ways:

- **Scaffold Meaning:** Visuals such as illustrations and graphic organizers in the text enhance students' understanding. Students who are learning English can also use electronic translators and bilingual dictionaries to gain access to the meaning of words or phrases.

- **Connect to Students' Lives:** It is important to activate students' pre-existing knowledge so that they can relate new information to what they already know. English Learners can use their first language as a resource to help them extend their

ESSENTIAL QUESTION: What are some milestones on the path to growing up?

DIGITAL PERSPECTIVES

Meet the Authors

Geoff Herbach is the author of the series *Stupid Fast* and other works of literature for young adults. His books have won the 2011 Cybils Award for best YA novel and the Minnesota Book Award. He lives in a log cabin in Minnesota and teaches creative writing.

Stephanie Pellegrin was in second grade when she wrote her first book. Pellegrin lives in Austin, Texas, and is involved with the Austin chapter of the Society of Children's Book Writers and Illustrators.

Backgrounds

You Are the Electric Boogaloo

Break dancing, or "breaking," is an athletic style of street dance that originated in New York City in the 1970s. Break dancing has continued to grow in popularity and is now performed in many different countries.

Just Be Yourself!

There is so much to learn, and no way to tell what the future will hold! This author writes a reassuring letter to her younger self saying that it will all work out in the end.

You Are the Electric Boogaloo • Just Be Yourself!

What kinds of experiences are especially important when you are a teenager? How might your view of those experiences change over time? Modeling questions such as these will help students connect to "You Are the Electric Boogaloo" and "Just Be Yourself!" and to the Small-Group Performance Task assignment. Selection audio and print capability for the selection are available in the Interactive Teacher's Edition.

English academic skills (e.g., by brainstorming in groups, writing in the first language as a stepping stone to writing in English, and carrying out Internet research in their first language).

- **Extend Language:** Teachers can extend students' academic language skills by consistently and explicitly drawing attention to new words, unusual syntax, and other textual features that are not found in everyday conversation.

FACILITATING

CLOSER LOOK

Analyze Word Choice

Circulate among groups as students conduct their close read. Suggest that groups close read paragraph 6. Encourage them to talk about the annotations they mark. If needed, provide the following support.

ANNOTATE: Have students mark details in paragraph 6 in which the writer describes his actions at the mall when he was a teenager, or work with small groups as you highlight them together.

QUESTION: Guide students to consider what these details might tell them. Ask them what impression the author creates with the details and his use of language, and accept student responses.

Possible response: By including these details, the author develops a vivid picture of a teenager exhibiting teenage behavior. The word choice is informal and slangy in the case of "went for broke."

CONCLUDE: Help students to formulate conclusions about the importance of these details in the text. Ask students why the author might have included these details.

Possible response: By carefully choosing words about the specific setting, how the boys danced, and what the dancers screamed, the writer creates a humorous picture of the boys' feelings of self-importance in the midst of a fairly ordinary place and situation.

Remind students that **diction,** an author's word choice, is especially important when writing **humor,** or writing that is intended to evoke laughter or entertain.

> Additional **English Language Support** is available in the Interactive Teacher's Edition.

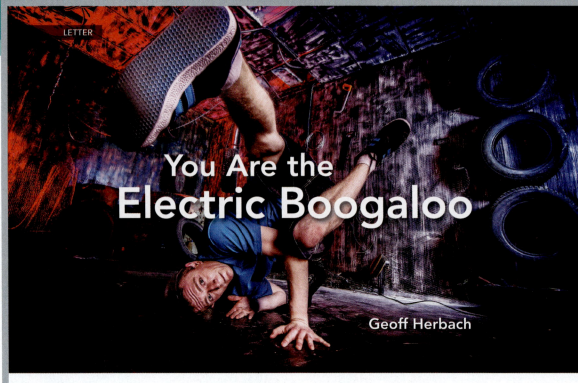

LETTER

You Are the Electric Boogaloo

Geoff Herbach

SCAN FOR MULTIMEDIA

NOTES

1 Dear Teen Me,

2 Humiliation and hilarity are closely linked, my little friend. Don't lie there in bed, your guts churning, as you replay the terrible scene. I'm *glad* your shirt stuck to the floor.

3 I love your break-dancing crew, okay? You and your friends from the rural Wisconsin hills have that K-Tel how-to album (including posters and diagrams). You pop. You worm. You spin on your backs. You windmill. In fact, you're not even that bad!

4 I love your silver "butterfly" pants (with forty-six zippers) that burst red fabric when you spin. Beautiful.

5 I love it when you take your giant piece of cardboard (mobile dance floor) down the corner of Kase Street and Highway 81 to dance for traffic. Maybe you're right. Maybe a talent scout will be driving between Stitzer and Hazel Green. Maybe you *will* be discovered . . . Keep at it!

6 I love it that you have the guts to go into Kennedy Mall in Dubuque, Iowa, to dance across from Hot Sam's Pretzels. You and your buddies go for broke in front of a small, glum crowd (who all eat Hot Sam's pretzels), and when security comes to escort you out, you scream, "Dancing is not a crime!" I love that.

46 UNIT 1 • RITES OF PASSAGE

FACILITATING SMALL-GROUP LEARNING

CLOSE READ: Letters As groups perform the close read, circulate and offer support as needed.

- Remind groups to pay attention to pronouns as they read each letter.
- Ask students to think about the intent of each letter and the message the writers convey to both their teenage selves and a general audience.
- Challenge groups to write a one-sentence summary of the author's advice.

7   I especially love what happened at Dubuque's Five Flags Center a few months later. You and your crew (Breakin Fixation) challenged Dubuque's 4+1 Crew to a dance-off. You practiced. You got T-shirts with your crew name emblazoned on them. You worked hard, and you daydreamed harder. You imagined the roaring crowd lifting you onto their shoulders. You didn't expect the Five Flags floor to be so sticky. You didn't expect to sweat through your new shirt. You didn't expect the flesh of your back to be gripped and twisted so that it felt like it was on fire. You didn't expect it, but that's how it was, and it hurt so bad that instead of spinning into a windmill—the main part of your routine—you just writhed on the floor, howling.

8   So okay, sure, people laughed at you—and you know why? Because you looked really funny.

9   Don't stay awake worrying about it, though. Don't wonder what you should have done differently. Don't beat yourself up, gut boiling with embarrassment. Don't imagine punching out the members of 4+1—you can't blame them for wearing slick Adidas tracksuits that didn't grip the floor. Just go to sleep, kid, and get ready for the next dance. It's all going to be great, okay?

10 How do I know?

11 Because now, so many years later, you can barely remember your victories (although there were some). What you think about now are the high-wire acts, the epic falls, and the punishing jeers of your classmates. You think about how excellent it is that you got up, dusted yourself off and, with utter seriousness of purpose, tried again.

12 Your *immense* dorkiness as a teen will be the center of your artistic life, the center of your sense of humor, the center of ongoing friendships with so many of the kids you knew back then. (You guys never discuss the relatively boring victories—you only talk about the grand, *majestic*, hilarious failures.)

13 What if you hit it big at that contest? Would you be a professional break-dancer now? Would success have gone to your head? Or would you be a rich banker? Or a lawyer? Terrible!

14 But instead, you stuck to that floor, with your back on fire with the pain, and you screamed.

15 Don't beat yourself up over it, okay? Just relax. Keep dancing by the highway, you splendid little dork.

NOTES

Mark context clues or indicate another strategy you used that helped you determine meaning.

immense (ih MEHNS) *adj.*
MEANING:

majestic (muh JEHS tihk) *adj.*
MEANING:

You Are the Electric Boogaloo 47

DIGITAL PERSPECTIVES

Concept Vocabulary

IMMENSE If groups are struggling to define the word *immense* in paragraph 12, point out that they should look for context clues to help determine meaning. Draw students' attention to the context clue *the center of your artistic life*. Point out that this shows that the author's "dorkiness" was important to his life. Have students use this context clue to define the word.

Possible response: In this context, *immense* means "huge."

MAJESTIC If groups are struggling to define the word *majestic* in paragraph 12, point out that they should look for context clues. Draw students' attention to the word *grand*. Point out that sometimes context clues are synonyms for an unfamiliar word. Have students use this context clue to define the word.

Possible response: In this context, *majestic* means "grand" or "impressive."

PERSONALIZE FOR LEARNING

Strategic Support
Review paragraphs 1–7 of the text. For students to understand the title of the selection and the references to break dancing, they should know that the Electric Boogaloos were a street dance crew in the 1970s and 1980s, and that "Electric Boogaloo" was a dance style made popular by the group. There was even a movie titled *Breakin 2: Electric Boogaloo*, which was a sequel to an earlier movie titled *Breakin*. Consider supporting students by sharing videos of street dancing. Preview all content before sharing with students. Have students discuss why the author uses the dance name in the title to the selection.

Small-Group Learning   47

FACILITATING

Concept Vocabulary

NUMEROUS If groups are struggling to define the word *numerous* in paragraph 4, encourage them to look for context clues in the surrounding words and sentences. Draw students' attention to the context clues from the beginning of the sentence: "I just counted and you're in eighteen…" Have students use this context clue to define the word. Students may also recognize the related word *number* in the word *numerous*.

Possible response: *Numerous* means "many."

LETTER

Just Be Yourself!
Stephanie Pellegrin

SCAN FOR MULTIMEDIA

NOTES

Mark context clues or indicate another strategy you used that helped you

numerous (NOO muhr uhs) *adj.*

MEANING:

1   Dear Teen Me,

2   Psst! Hey! You in the corner of the library with your nose stuck in a book. Yes, you. Don't recognize me without that awful perm, do you? (Remind me again why you thought that was a good idea?)

3   Anyway, I hope you don't mind if I sit with you for a minute, but we need to talk. Don't worry about the "no talking in the library" rule. I'm sure we'll be fine. Librarians aren't as bad as they seem.

4   Judging from the hair and braces I'd have to guess you're in your junior year. Yes? Thought so. I'd forgotten how many lonely lunch hours you spent in the school library. You have some friends in the cafeteria that you could sit with, but you don't feel like you really fit in, do you? That's why you joined every school club you could. I just counted and you're in eighteen, not to mention the **numerous** after-school activities you're involved in. I mean honestly, you joined the ROTC.[1] You don't even *like* ROTC! And I won't even bother bringing up that time you tried ballet. I'm still having nightmares about the fifth position!

5   Let me ask you, how's it all working out? Not very well, am I right? By spending so much time trying to *find* yourself, you're slowly *losing* yourself. We don't all have one single rock-star talent, and honestly, I think those of us who don't are the lucky ones. Life isn't about finding the one thing you're good at and never doing anything else; it's about exploring yourself and

1. **ROTC** *n.* abbreviation for Reserve Officers Training Corps, a college-based training program for the U.S. military.

PERSONALIZE FOR LEARNING

English Language Support

Idioms Explain to students that the title of the selection "Just Be Yourself!" is an idiom. Remind students that an idiom is a commonly used expression that is not meant literally. Explain that *just be yourself* means "try to act in your ordinary, natural way." There are other idioms in the selection, including "trying to find yourself" in paragraph 5. Point out that this idiom means "trying to discover your abilities and interests." Have students look at the second part of the sentence: "you're slowly *losing* yourself." Ask students to discuss what the author means by that phrase, using context clues to do so.   **ALL LEVELS**

finding out who you really are on your own terms and in your own way. You don't have to exhaust yourself to do that.

6 Oh, don't be so down in the dumps about it. You'll eventually find something you're good at, I promise. It's a long, winding road to get there, but you'll find it. Being able to spend all day doing what you love (or one of the things that you love) is the most amazing feeling in the world. And no, I won't tell you what it is, so don't even ask me. Just remember to always be yourself, because there's nobody else who can do it for you. I think E. E. Cummings put it best when he said, "It takes courage to grow up and become who you really are."

7 Looks like the bell is about to ring so I'll leave you to your book. What are you reading, anyway? Oh, *The Last Battle* by C. S. Lewis. I should have guessed. You should give those Harry Potter books a try. I saw you roll your eyes! I know they seem like just another fad, but trust me, they're better than you think. They've got a real future!

NOTES

Comprehension Check

Complete the following items after you finish your first read. Review and clarify details with your group.

YOU ARE THE ELECTRIC BOOGALOO

1. What activity does the author focus on in his letter to his teenage self?

2. What does the teen author scream when security comes to escort him out of the mall?

JUST BE YOURSELF!

3. Why did the author join so many clubs when she was a teenager?

4. What does the author tell her teen self is happening as a result of all the time she is spending trying to find herself?

5. **Notebook** Confirm your understanding by writing a short summary of each letter.

RESEARCH

Research to Clarify Choose at least one unfamiliar detail from one of the letters. Briefly research that detail. In what way does the information you learned shed light on an aspect of the letter?

You Are the Electric Boogaloo • Just Be Yourself! 49

PERSONALIZE FOR LEARNING

Challenge
Writing a Letter Invite students to write their own letter in which they give advice to their younger selves. Have them begin by thinking about an experience that was very important to them when they were younger. Tell them to think about how they handled the experience at the time, and ask them to think about whether they would handle it differently now. Remind students to address their younger selves as "you," and to use standard format for a friendly letter, including a greeting and closing.

DIGITAL PERSPECTIVES

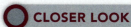

CLOSER LOOK

Analyze Allusions
Circulate among groups as students conduct their close read. Suggest that groups close read paragraphs 6 and 7. Encourage them to talk about the annotations they mark. If needed, provide the following support.

ANNOTATE: Have students mark the references to literature that the author includes, or work with small groups as you highlight them together.

QUESTION: Guide students to consider what they can infer from the quotation and the allusions.

Possible response: The author refers to what she probably read as a teenager and what she would suggest to that same teenager now. It shows that reading was and is important to her.

CONCLUDE: Help students explore why the author might have included these details.

Possible response: By including the poet's words and the references to two books, the author shows how important books and writing are to her. These may be a clue to how the author has been able to find what she loves.

Remind students that writers use **allusions**, or references to other literary works, in order to express important ideas. The book and book series that the author refers to both have to do with growing up and going through rites of passage. If readers recognize the allusion, the references can pack more information into text.

Comprehension Check

You Are the Electric Boogaloo
1. The author focuses on the activity of break dancing. They were breakdancers.
2. He screams, "Dancing is not a crime!"

Just Be Yourself!
3. The author was trying to find her talents and skills.
4. The author believes that in trying so hard to figure out who she is, her teenage self is actually losing herself.
5. Summaries will vary.

Research to Clarify If students struggle to come up with an unfamiliar detail, have them reread the letters and notice an idea that might be new to them, such as a K-Tel record or ROTC.

Small-Group Learning

FACILITATING

Jump Start

CLOSE READ Ask students to brainstorm about the events and activities that are important in their own lives. As students discuss in their groups, ask them to consider whether these events might be considered rites of passage and how they may view these activities and events in the future.

Close Read the Text

If needed, model close reading by using the Annotation Highlights in the Interactive Teacher's Edition.
Remind students to use Accountable Talk in their discussions and to support one another as they complete the close read.

Analyze the Text

1. **Possible response:** The author means that if he had won the breakdancing contest, he still probably would not be a successful breakdancer, and without the funny experience, he might be a more boring person.
2. **Passages will vary by group.** Remind students to explain why they chose the passage they present to the group members.
3. **Responses will vary by group.**

Concept Vocabulary

Why These Words? Possible response: The concept words all have to do with a sense of the extreme. Another word that fits the category is *epic* from "You Are the Electric Boogaloo."

Practice

Responses will vary.

Word Network

Possible responses: *jeers, teen, friendships, dork, courage, future*

Word Study

For more support, see **Concept Vocabulary and Word Study.**
Possible responses:
numerous: many, full of a number of items.
continuous: without interruption, continuing.
desirous: wanting, full of desire.
prosperous: wealthy, having full prosperity.

MAKING MEANING

YOU ARE THE ELECTRIC BOOGALOO | JUST BE YOURSELF!

TIP
GROUP DISCUSSION
As you discuss the letters, compare your own experiences with those of the authors.

WORD NETWORK
Add interesting words related to rites of passage from the text to your Word Network.

STANDARDS
Reading Informational Text
Determine the meaning of words and phrases as they are used in a text, including figurative, connotative, and technical meanings; analyze the impact of specific word choices on meaning and tone, including analogies or allusions to other texts.

Language
• Determine or clarify the meaning of unknown and multiple-meaning words or phrases based on *grade 8 reading and content*, choosing flexibly from a range of strategies.
 b. Use common, grade-appropriate Greek or Latin affixes and roots as clues to the meaning of a word.
 c. Consult general and specialized reference materials, both print and digital, to find the pronunciation of a word or determine or clarify its precise meaning or its part of speech.
• Demonstrate understanding of figurative language, word relationships, and nuances in word meanings.
 c. Distinguish among the connotations of words with similar denotations.

50 UNIT 1 • RITES OF PASSAGE

Close Read the Text

With your group, revisit sections of the text you marked during your First Read. **Annotate** what you notice. What **questions** do you have? What can you **conclude**?

Analyze the Text

CITE TEXTUAL EVIDENCE to support your answers.

Notebook Complete the activities.

1. **Review and Clarify** With your group, reread paragraph 13 of "You Are the Electric Boogaloo." What do you think the author means by asking these questions? What is he trying to say about the importance of failure?

2. **Present and Discuss** Now, work with your group to share the passages from the text that you found especially important. Take turns presenting your passages. Discuss what you noticed in the text, what questions you asked, and what conclusions you reached.

3. **Essential Question:** *What are some milestones on the path to growing up?* What kinds of milestones do the letters include? Why are they important? Discuss with your group.

LANGUAGE DEVELOPMENT

Concept Vocabulary

| immense | majestic | numerous |

Why These Words? The concept vocabulary words from the text are related. With your group, determine what the words have in common. Record your ideas, and add another word that fits the category.

Practice

Notebook Confirm your understanding of the concept vocabulary words by using each word in a sentence.

Word Study

Latin Suffix: -ous The Latin suffix *-ous* means "characterized by" or "full of" and often indicates that a word is an adjective. In "Just Be Yourself!," the author uses the word *numerous* to describe the after-school activities she was involved in as a teen. Based on your understanding of the suffix *-ous*, write a definition for the word *numerous*. Then, explain how the suffix contributes to the meanings of the following words: *continuous, desirous, prosperous*.

FORMATIVE ASSESSMENT

Analyze the Text
If students struggle to close read the text, **then** provide the You Are the Electric Boogaloo • Just Be Yourself!: Text Questions available online in the Interactive Teacher's Edition or Unit Resources. Answers and DOK levels are also available.

Concept Vocabulary
If students struggle to identify the concept, **then** have them use each word in a sentence and think about what is similar about the sentences.

Word Study
If students fail to locate the word that ends in *-ous*, **then** direct them to paragraph 12.
For Reteach and Practice, see **Word Study: Latin Suffix -ous (RP).**

ESSENTIAL QUESTION: What are some milestones on the path to growing up?

DIGITAL PERSPECTIVES

Analyze Craft and Structure

Author's Word Choice: Tone An author's **tone** is his or her attitude toward a subject or audience. An author's tone may be described using adjectives such as *serious, humorous, casual,* or *formal.* The tone of a literary work is often conveyed through the author's **word choice,** or the individual words as well as the phrases and expressions he or she uses.

To develop the tone of a literary work, an author considers the **connotations** of the words he or she uses, or the ideas and feelings associated with the words. Connotations often suggest meaning beyond the word's dictionary definition, or **denotation.** A word's connotations may be positive or negative. For example, the words *postpone* and *procrastinate* have similar denotations—"to put off until a later time." However, the word *postpone* has a more positive connotation that suggests that something is being rescheduled due to circumstances beyond one's control. In contrast, the word *procrastinate* has the negative connotation of putting something off because one doesn't feel like doing it.

> **TIP**
> **PROCESS**
> As you work with your group to analyze the authors' word choices, discuss any differences in the connotations you have for specific words.

Practice

> **CITE TEXTUAL EVIDENCE** to support your answers.

Work with your group to analyze the authors' word choices and how these choices work together to convey the tone of each letter. Use the charts to take notes as you review each letter. Consult a dictionary to determine the precise denotation of each word.

YOU ARE THE ELECTRIC BOOGALOO	
WORD AND ITS DENOTATION	CONNOTATIONS
butterfly	unusual style; funny
guts	courage; positive feeling
epic	amazing; good
dork	silly; funny

Writer's tone: The tone of the letter is humorous and light-hearted.

JUST BE YOURSELF!	
WORD AND ITS DENOTATION	CONNOTATIONS
nightmares	extremely bad dreams; negative
rock-star	unrealistic but positive
"down in the dumps"	mildly unhappy; not a serious problem
exploring	positive search

Writer's tone: The tonze of the letter is compassionate and light-hearted.

You Are the Electric Boogaloo • Just Be Yourself! 51

Analyze Craft and Structure

Author's Word Choice: Tone Students may need examples to understand how words with strong connotation affect tone. As they fill out the chart, have them suggest words with similar meanings that have different connotations. Ask them to note the change in tone. For more support, see **Analyze Craft and Structure: Tone.**

Practice

See possible responses in the charts on the student page.

FORMATIVE ASSESSMENT

Analyze Craft and Structure

If students are unable to identify words with strong connotations, **then** review the second paragraph of "You Are the Electric Boogaloo" together. Have them rewrite the first two sentences in their own words and then note how that changes the tone. Have students identify which of the author's words grabbed their attention and affected the tone. For Reteach and Practice, see **Analyze Craft and Structure: Tone (RP).**

PERSONALIZE FOR LEARNING

English Language Support

Using Connotative Language Ask students to list three words that have connotative meanings. Then have them write a literal meaning and the implied, connotative meaning. **EMERGING**

Have students write a paragraph on a topic of their choice using language with strong connotations. Encourage students to include at least three words with an implied meaning, and remind them that the connotation should be clear in the context of the paragraph. **EXPANDING**

Have students write a paragraph on a topic of their choice using language with strong connotations. Encourage students to include at least three words with an implied meaning. Then have them trade paragraphs with a partner and point out the connotative words and whether their implied meaning is positive or negative. **BRIDGING**

An expanded **English Language Support Lesson** on Connotations is available in the Interactive Teacher's Edition.

Small-Group Learning 51

FACILITATING

Conventions

Verb Moods As you review the moods of the verbs in the selection with students, point out to them that a verb's mood is different from its tense. While a mood expresses an attitude or intent, a tense expresses a time or condition. Tense and mood are independent, and changing one does not require changing the other. Tense changes based on *when* or *whether* something happens, while mood changes based on the purpose of the sentence. A few tenses and moods cannot be combined, such as the imperative mood and the past tense. For more support, see **Conventions: Verb Moods.**

Read It

Possible responses:
Indicative: paragraph 2, "Humiliation and hilarity are closely linked, my little friend." Interrogative: paragraph 13, "Would success have gone to your head?" Imperative: paragraph 15, "Just relax."

Write It

Possible responses:
1. Dancers should try to perform in public. They should wear colorful costumes.
2. Authors may write about themselves, and they should use what they know.

FORMATIVE ASSESSMENT

Conventions

If students are unable to identify specific textual examples, **then** point out that they should use the end punctuation as a clue. Verbs in the interrogative mood are in sentences that end in a question mark. Verbs in the imperative mood are in sentences that end in periods or exclamation marks. Verbs in the indicative mood are in sentences that end in periods. Verbs in the exclamatory mood are in sentences that end in exclamation marks. For Reteach and Practice, see **Conventions: Verb Moods (RP).**

LANGUAGE DEVELOPMENT

YOU ARE THE ELECTRIC BOOGALOO | JUST BE YOURSELF!

Conventions

Verb Moods Verbs can express different **moods**. Speakers and writers express their attitudes through the verbs they use, as Geoff Herbach shows in "You Are the Electric Boogaloo."

- Verbs in the **indicative mood** state facts and opinions.
- Verbs in the **imperative mood** issue commands or make requests. This mood can also be used to give a strong suggestion or advice.
- Verbs in the **interrogative mood** pose, or ask, questions.

Types of Verb Moods Use the chart to review three types of verb moods.

INDICATIVE	IMPERATIVE	INTERROGATIVE
States, or declares, an idea	Gives a command or direction	Asks a question
Librarians aren't as bad as they seem.	Just be yourself!	What are you reading, anyway?

STANDARDS

Writing
Conduct short research projects to answer a question, drawing on several sources and generating additional related, focused questions that allow for multiple avenues of exploration.

Speaking and Listening
- Present claims and findings, emphasizing salient points in a focused, coherent manner with relevant evidence, sound valid reasoning, and well-chosen details; use appropriate eye contact, adequate volume, and clear pronunciation.
- Integrate multimedia and visual displays into presentations to clarify information, strengthen claims and evidence, and add interest.

Language
Demonstrate command of the conventions of standard English grammar and usage while writing or speaking.
  c. Form and use verbs in the indicative, imperative, interrogative, conditional, and subjunctive mood.
  d. Recognize and correct inappropriate shifts in verb voice and mood.

Read It

Work individually. Find an example of one sentence in the indicative, one in the interrogative, and one in the imperative mood in "You Are the Electric Boogaloo."

Write It

Sometimes writers and speakers shift between indicative and imperative moods in a jarring or confusing way. Review the example below, and then correct the improper mood shift in the following sentences.

> EXAMPLE
>
> Students should come to class prepared. Arrive on time. *[improper shift to imperative]*
>
> Students should come to class prepared. They should arrive on time.

1. Dancers should try to perform in public. Wear colorful costumes!

2. Authors may write about themselves, and use what you know.

PERSONALIZE FOR LEARNING

Strategic Support

Verb Moods Some students may require additional support as they work on verb moods. Explain to students that if they see question words, such as *why, where, what, when, how,* and *who* at the beginning of a sentence, then the verb in that sentence is interrogative. Have students work in pairs to locate more examples of each type of verb mood in the selections.

EFFECTIVE EXPRESSION

Speaking and Listening

Assignment

Work with your group to conduct research for a **visual presentation** on one of the following topics:

☐ Write and present **illustrated instructions** in which you explain how to perform one of the break-dancing steps mentioned in "You Are the Electric Boogaloo."

☐ Write and deliver an **illustrated informational report** on the history and culture of break-dancing.

Project Plan Make a list of tasks that your group will need to perform. Decide which group members will carry out each task. Use this chart to organize your plans.

TASK	WHO	PART IN PRESENTATION

Conduct Research As you conduct research, be sure to use a variety of reliable print and digital sources. Remember to find useful visual aids that will help your audience understand and visualize the information in your presentation.

Present and Evaluate After you have rehearsed your presentation, deliver it to the class. Remember to speak clearly and make eye contact with your audience regularly. After your presentation, evaluate your performance as well as the performances of other groups.

EVIDENCE LOG

Before moving on to a new selection, go to your Evidence Log, and record what you learned from "You Are the Electric Boogaloo" and "Just Be Yourself!"

DIGITAL PERSPECTIVES

Enriching the Text Once students have chosen one of the three assignments, encourage them to find examples of presentations online. For example, for "Dance Instructions," students might look at videos on YouTube or scenes from movies that feature break-dancing.

DIGITAL PERSPECTIVES

Speaking and Listening

If groups have difficulty in deciding which option to choose, encourage them to consider what individual strengths the members of the group have. For example, if someone in the group is a trained dancer, the first option might be a good choice. If group members excel at research, the second option might be a good choice. Remind them, however, that all of the options will require them to conduct research and find visuals.

Project Plan Remind students to consult the schedule for Small-Group Activities as they create their Project Plan. Check to make sure each group has made assignments and that the work is divded evenly among group members. For more support, see **Speaking and Listening: Visual Presentation.**

Conduct Research If necessary, work with students to find appropriate images using targeted search words and reliable search engines. Encourage students to choose images that are appropriate to the task and audience.

Present and Evaluate Encourage students to practice their presentations so they feel confident.

Evidence Log Support students in completing their Evidence Log. This paced activity will help prepare them for the Performance-Based Assessment at the end of the unit.

FORMATIVE ASSESSMENT

Speaking and Listening

If students have difficulty creating a meaningful visual presentation, **then** have them first outline what exactly they want to communicate. After they create the outline, they can develop the script for the presentation and choose appropriate images for each section. For Reteach and Practice, see **Speaking and Listening: Visual Presentation (RP).**

Selection Test

Administer the "You Are the Electric Boogaloo"/"Just Be Yourself!" Selection Test, which is available in both print and digital formats online in Assessments.

/ PLANNING / SMALL-GROUP LEARNING • HANGING FIRE • TRANSLATING GRANDFATHER'S HOUSE

Hanging Fire • Translating Grandfather's House

🔊 **AUDIO SUMMARIES**
Audio summaries of "Hanging Fire" and "Translating Grandfather's House" are available in both English and Spanish and can be assigned to students in the Interactive Teacher's Edition or Unit Resources. Assigning these summaries prior to reading the selections may help students build additional background knowledge and set a context for their first read.

Summary

Audre Lorde's poem "Hanging Fire" is an account of adolescence told from the point of view of a fourteen-year-old girl. The speaker runs through a long list of anxieties—about her body, about the people around her, about what she needs to get done, and about her own mortality.

In E. J. Vega's poem "Translating Grandfather's House," the young speaker describes the experience of a drawing assignment in school. He draws his grandfather's house in a rural setting. His teacher says it looks like a movie, and she doesn't seem happy with his drawing. When he draws a city house like those of his classmates, she gives him an A+.

Insight

"Hanging Fire" emphasizes the stress over worries large and small that so many experience growing up.

"Translating Grandfather's House" provides insight into how people's assumptions can mislead them. The poem shows the ways that people can make incorrect assumptions about others.

ESSENTIAL QUESTION:
What are some milestones on the path to growing up?

Connection to Essential Question

The process of growing up can be challenging as young people struggle with identity and what is important to them. In "Hanging Fire," the speaker may feel alone as she travels her adolescent path. In "Translating Grandfather's House," the student seems to downplay what he or she believes about his or her family to smooth things over with the teacher.

SMALL-GROUP LEARNING PERFORMANCE TASK
What defines an event or experience in a young person's life as a milestone or rite of passage?

UNIT PERFORMANCE-BASED ASSESSMENT
What rite of passage has held the most significance for you or for a person you know well?

Connection to Performance Tasks

Small-Group Learning Task Each of these poems describes the anxiety of learning to fit in. Both large and small problems can loom over someone. Even seemingly "minor" choices, such as choosing not to say something, can have a great effect as one reflects on the consequences of doing so. These texts will help students prepare to address the prompt.

Unit Performance-Based Assessment While it's easy to say "be yourself," sometimes other people don't want adolescents to follow this advice. These poems ask students to consider whether learning how to manage in a world where fitting in is difficult is part of the path to adulthood. Each speaker's experience may help students to consider the challenges of growing up and consider the experiences in their own lives that help them address the prompt.

DIGITAL PERSPECTIVES

 Audio Video Document Annotation Highlights EL Highlights Online Assessment

LESSON RESOURCES

	Making Meaning	Language Development	Effective Expression
Lesson	First Read Close Read Analyze the Text Analyze Craft and Structure	Concept Vocabulary Word Study Author's Style	Speaking and Listening
Instructional Standards	**RL.10** By the end of the year, read and comprehend literature . . . **L.4** Determine or clarify the meaning of unknown and multiple-meaning words or phrases . . . **RL.2** Determine a theme or central idea of a text . . . **RL.5** Compare and contrast the structure of two or more texts . . .	**L.4** Determine or clarify the meaning of unknown and multiple-meaning words or phrases . . . **L.4.b** Use common, grade-appropriate Greek or Latin affixes and roots . . .	**SL.1** Engage effectively in a range of collaborative discussions . . . **SL.1.a** Come to discussions prepared . . . **SL.1.c** Pose questions . . . **SL.1.d** Acknowledge new information . . .
STUDENT RESOURCES Available online in the Interactive Student Edition or Unit Resources	Selection Audio First-Read Guide: Poetry Close-Read Guide: Poetry	Word Network	Evidence Log
TEACHER RESOURCES **Selection Resources** Available online in the Interactive Teacher's Edition or Unit Resources	Audio Summaries Annotation Highlights EL Highlights Poetry Collection: Text Questions English Language Support Lesson: Verb Moods Analyze Craft and Structure: Forms of Poetry	Concept Vocabulary and Word Study Author's Style: Word Choice	Speaking and Listening: Group Discussion
Reteach/Practice (RP) Available online in the Interactive Teacher's Edition or Unit Resources	Analyze Craft and Structure: Forms of Poetry (RP)	Word Study: Etymology (RP) Author's Style: Word Choice (RP)	Speaking and Listening: Group Discussion (RP)
Assessment Available online in Assessments	Selection Test		
My Resources	A Unit 1 Answer Key is available online and in the Interactive Teacher's Edition.		

Small-Group Learning 54B

PERSONALIZE FOR LEARNING

SMALL-GROUP LEARNING • HANGING FIRE • TRANSLATING GRANDFATHER'S HOUSE

Reading Support

Text Complexity Rubric: Hanging Fire • Translating Grandfather's House

Quantitative Measures

Lexile: NP Text Length: 35 lines; 35 lines

Qualitative Measures

Knowledge Demands ①—②—③—**④**—⑤	Multiple themes are explored in both poems, including teenage worries, fear of death, and teacher authority.
Structure ①—②—**③**—④—⑤	Both poems are in free verse; in "Hanging Fire" stanzas have multiple ideas in stream of consciousness, with no separation; each stanza has a repeating refrain. The second poem has no repetition.
Language Conventionality and Clarity ①—**②**—③—④—⑤	"Hanging Fire" language is straightforward, with short lines; vocabulary and style of a fourteen-year-old; mostly literal, with some figurative phrases. "Translating…" has descriptive, abstract language.
Levels of Meaning/Purpose ①—②—③—**④**—⑤	Poems have multiple levels of meaning that are not easy to identify and interpret; some lines have subtle or ambiguous meaning.

DECIDE AND PLAN

English Language Support

Provide English Learners with support for knowledge demands and meaning as they read the selection.

Knowledge Demands With students' help, list some issues that a fourteen-year-old faces: physical changes, falling in love, school pressures, home pressures. For each item on the list, ask students to find words in "Hanging Fire" that relate to that issue. For example, for physical changes, they might highlight lines with *my skin, my knees*. Read the lines together.

Meaning For each of the issues and lines from "Hanging Fire" that students located, confirm that students understand the meaning. Explain words or rephrase as necessary. For example, say (line 6–7) " *my knees are always so ashy*" means they are dry and flaky. *Is she happy or unhappy with her appearance?* (unhappy).

Strategic Support

Provide students with strategic support to ensure that they can successfully read the text.

Knowledge Demands Ask students to name issues a fourteen-year-old deals with, such as changes of appearance and growth, identity, love interests, academic pressures, social pressures, and relationships with family and teachers. Have them reread the poems, making notes of lines relating to these issues.

Meaning Discuss lines of the poems, asking questions to help with meaning of words or phrases. Then discuss the feelings that are expressed. For "Hanging Fire," discuss how the girl feels when "momma's in the bedroom with the door closed." For "Translating…," discuss how the boy feels when the teacher doesn't believe the house is real.

Challenge

Provide students who need to be challenged with ideas for how they can go beyond a simple interpretation of the text.

Text Analysis Ask students to describe the feelings the girl in "Hanging Fire" has about her appearance, her social inadequacies, and her anxieties about death. Ask what the refrain about momma expresses about the girl's feelings.

For "Translating…," ask students to describe the boy's feelings about the house and how he feels when the teacher won't believe him, and ask students to interpret the last two lines of the text.

Written Response Ask students to write what they think are the biggest challenges, pressures, or emotional upsets facing teenagers. They may use examples from their own lives or write their observations in general terms.

TEACH

Read and Respond

Have the groups read the selection and complete the Making Meaning, Language Development, and Effective Expression activities.

Standards Support Through Teaching and Learning Cycle

IDENTIFY NEEDS

Analyze results of the Beginning-of-Year Assessment, focusing on the items relating to Unit 1. Also take into consideration student performance to this point and your observations of where particular students struggle.

ANALYZE AND REVISE

- Analyze student work for evidence of student learning.
- Identify whether students have met the expectations in the standards.
- Identify implications for future instruction.

TEACH

Implement the planned lesson, and gather evidence of student learning.

DECIDE AND PLAN

- If students have performed poorly on items matching these standards, then provide selection scaffolds before assigning them the on-level lesson provided in the Student Edition.
- If students have done well on the Beginning-of-Year Assessment, then challenge them to keep progressing and learning by giving them opportunities to practice the skills in depth.
- Use the Selection Resources listed on the Planning pages for "Hanging Fire" and "Translating Grandfather's House."

Instructional Standards: Hanging Fire • Translating Grandfather's House

	Catching Up	This Year	Looking Forward
Reading	You may wish to administer the **Analyze Craft and Structure: Forms of Poetry (RP)** worksheet to help students understand the main elements of lyric and narrative poems.	**RL.5** Compare and contrast the structure of two or more texts and analyze how the differing structure of each text contributes to its meaning and style.	Challenge students to read and analyze other lyric and narrative poems. Then have students discuss the elements of each with a partner. What overall impression does each poem leave?
Speaking and Listening	You may wish to administer the **Speaking and Listening: Group Discussion (RP)** worksheet to help students prepare to discuss the poems.	**SL.1** Engage effectively in a range of collaborative discussions with diverse partners on *grade 8 topics, texts, and issues,* building on others' ideas and expressing their own clearly.	Challenge students to select a favorite poem to share in a small group discussion. Have students discuss the main elements of the poem.
Language	You may wish to administer the **Author's Style Word Choice (RP)** worksheet to help students understand word choice. You may wish to administer the **Word Study: Etymology (RP)** worksheet to help students understand the word origins and the way to study words from this angle.	**L.1** Demonstrate command of the conventions of standard English grammar and usage when writing or speaking. **L.4** Determine or clarify the meaning of unknown and multiple-meaning words and phrases based on *grade 8 reading and content,* choosing flexibly from a range of strategies.	Challenge students to write two sentences using each type of verb mood. Challenge students to find the etymology of several other words.

Small-Group Learning 54D

FACILITATING

Jump Start

FIRST READ How can poets describe important rites of passage? Can poetry help us understand what it means to grow up? Engage students in a discussion about why poetry can sometimes express important incidents and events better than other genres.

Concept Vocabulary

Encourage groups to discuss the three concept vocabulary words. Have they seen the words in selections or used these words in their speech and writing?

Ask groups to look closely at the examples of context clues. Explain that by looking for familiar words or phrases surrounding the unfamiliar word, students may begin to understand more about the context. Discuss with students other types of context clues that they might find, including synonyms, antonyms, and restatement.

FIRST READ

As they read, students should perform the steps of the first read:

NOTICE: Students should focus on the basic elements of the poem to ensure they understand the message that the author is conveying.

ANNOTATE: Students should mark passages that show how the author uses poetic devices, such as alliteration and repetition, to create rhythm and emphasize important images.

CONNECT: Have students compare the experiences of the poems' speakers with their own experiences and with the experiences of other teenagers in fiction and in real life.

RESPOND: Students will answer questions and write a summary to demonstrate understanding.

Point out to students that while they will always complete the Respond step at the end of the first read, the other steps will probably happen somewhat concurrently. You may wish to print copies of the **First-Read Guide: Poetry** for students to use.

54 UNIT 1 • RITES OF PASSAGE

MAKING MEANING

POETRY COLLECTION

Hanging Fire
Translating Grandfather's House

Concept Vocabulary

As you perform your first read of "Hanging Fire" and "Translating Grandfather's House," you will encounter these words.

| horizon | awakenings | beaming |

Context Clues If these words are unfamiliar to you, try using context clues—other words and phrases that appear in a text—to help you determine their meanings. Here are three types of context clues that might help you as you read.

> **Synonym** Gregory has one **sibling**, his <u>brother</u> Anthony.
>
> **Contrast of Ideas:** The winner was **elated**, but the loser was <u>filled with sadness.</u>
>
> **Explanation:** The **cupola** on the roof looked like a <u>little dog house</u>.

Apply your knowledge of context clues and other vocabulary strategies to determine the meanings of unfamiliar words you encounter during your first read.

First Read POETRY

Apply these strategies as you conduct your first read. You will have an opportunity to complete a close read after your first read.

NOTICE who or what is "speaking" in each poem and whether the poem tells a story or describes a single moment.

ANNOTATE by marking vocabulary and key passages you want to revisit.

CONNECT ideas within the selection to what you already know and what you have already read.

RESPOND by completing the Comprehension Check and by writing a brief summary of each poem.

STANDARDS

Reading Literature
By the end of the year, read and comprehend literature, including stories, dramas, and poems, at the high end of grades 6–8 text complexity band independently and proficiently.

Language
Determine or clarify the meaning of unknown and multiple-meaning words or phrases based on *grade 8 reading and content*, choosing flexibly from a range of strategies.
a. Use context as a clue to the meaning of a word or phrase.

54 UNIT 1 • RITES OF PASSAGE

ESSENTIAL QUESTION: What are some milestones on the path to growing up?

Meet the Poets

Audre Lorde (1934–1992) was a Caribbean American poet and civil rights activist. Her poetry and writing addresses social prejudices and injustices. She was the Poet Laureate of New York from 1991 until her death.

E.J. Vega (b. 1961) is an award-winning poet, novelist, and journalist. He was born in Cuba and worked as a sailor on tugboats and ocean barges. He has degrees in writing, literature, and journalism from Brooklyn College and Columbia University. He lives in New York City.

Backgrounds

Hanging Fire

Adolescence can be a challenging stage of life, with childhood left behind but adulthood not yet achieved. In "Hanging Fire," Audre Lorde explores the frustrating feelings that can arise from the contradictions of being a "young adult."

Translating Grandfather's House

In the poem, E.J. Vega mentions Zorro, a popular fictional character, originally created in 1919 by writer Johnston McCulley. In McCulley's novel, Zorro is a heroic outlaw and a skilled sword fighter who wears a mask to hide his true identity—he is actually a wealthy noble named Diego de la Vega.

DIGITAL PERSPECTIVES

Hanging Fire • Translating Grandfather's House

What problems does the speaker describe? What problems might seem more or less important if the poem's speaker were older? Modeling questions such as these will help students connect to "Hanging Fire" and "Translating Grandfather's House" and to the Small-Group Performance Task assignment. Selection audio and print capability for the selections are available in the Interactive Teacher's Edition.

👥 FACILITATING SMALL-GROUP CLOSE READING

CLOSE READ: Poetry As groups perform the close read, circulate and offer support as needed.

- Remind groups that when they read poetry, they should pay attention to line breaks as they may be important in the rhythm of the poem and in interpreting its meaning.
- If a group is confused about a poem's meaning, suggest that they reread the text to find whether it is telling a story or conveying one speaker's thoughts.
- Encourage students to look at the poet's word choice so that they can identify the poem's overall emotional tone.

FACILITATING

POETRY COLLECTION

Hanging Fire

Audre Lorde

56 UNIT 1 • RITES OF PASSAGE

PERSONALIZE FOR LEARNING

English Language Support

Idioms Tell students that the title *Hanging Fire* is an idiom. Remind students that an idiom is a commonly used expression that is not meant literally.

Explain that the expression "hang fire" originally referred to an unexpected pause that occurred between pulling a gun's trigger and having the propellant move. Later, the term was used metaphorically to mean waiting before taking action. Have students think about why the poem might have this title, and what that might mean about the speaker's state of mind. **ALL LEVELS**

SCAN FOR
MULTIMEDIA

NOTES

I am fourteen
and my skin has betrayed me
the boy I cannot live without
still sucks his thumb
5   in secret
how come my knees are
always so ashy
what if I die
before morning
10 and momma's in the bedroom
with the door closed.

I have to learn how to dance
in time for the next party
my room is too small for me
15 suppose I die before graduation
they will sing sad melodies
but finally
tell the truth about me
There is nothing I want to do
20 and too much
that has to be done
and momma's in the bedroom
with the door closed.

Nobody even stops to think
25 about my side of it
I should have been on Math Team
my marks were better than his
why do I have to be
the one
30 wearing braces
I have nothing to wear tomorrow
will I live long enough
to grow up
and momma's in the bedroom
35 with the door closed.

Hanging Fire 57

DIGITAL PERSPECTIVES

CLOSER LOOK

Analyze Tone

Circulate among groups as students conduct their close read. Encourage them to talk about the annotations they mark in lines 1–11. If needed, provide the following support.

ANNOTATE: Have students mark details in the first stanza that help establish the writer's attitude to the subject matter, or work with small groups as you highlight them together.

QUESTION: Guide students to consider what these details might tell them. Ask what a reader can infer from the poet's choice of words, and accept student responses.

Possible response: The speaker seems to have big concerns and worries, and she uses strong language to describe her concerns.

CONCLUDE: Help students to formulate conclusions about the importance of these details in the text. Ask students why the author might have included these details.

Possible response: The highlighted words show how strongly the speaker feels about things, from a boy she says she cannot live without to her concerns about dying. The fact that her mother is closed away from her means that she is worrying alone. The poem conveys an anxious feeling.

Remind students that the **tone** of a poem is the writer's feeling toward a subject. It is impacted by the author's word choice but is also affected by line length, structure, and repetition. Have students take note of the repetition of "momma's in the bedroom with the door closed" as they further examine the tone and meaning of the poem.

Additional **English Language Support** is available in the Interactive Teacher's Edition.

CROSS-CURRICULAR PERSPECTIVES

Math In lines 24–27 of "Hanging Fire," the speaker complains about not being placed on Math Team even though her marks were better than the boy who did get on the team. Have students share what they know about the kinds of questions that eighth grade math teams would have to solve in a contest. Then challenge each group to find or write three questions and trade their questions with another group. Ask students who are involved in math competitions to describe the activity.

Small-Group Learning 57

FACILITATING

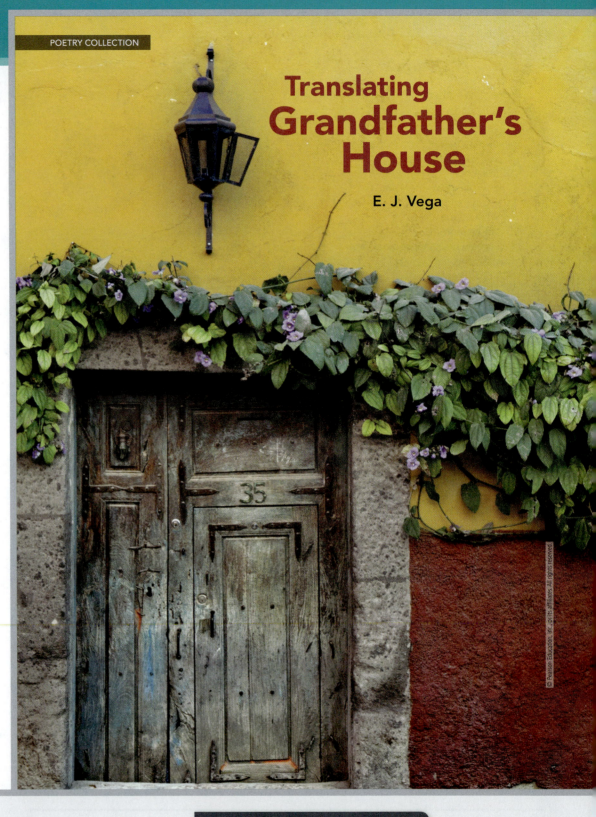

POETRY COLLECTION

Translating Grandfather's House

E. J. Vega

PERSONALIZE FOR LEARNING

Challenge

Drawing a Picture Review lines 1–8 of "Translating Grandfather's House." Point out to students that the speaker describes drawing his grandfather's house in school. Ask students to draw the home of someone in their family. Students should try to draw the home exactly as they remember it. Then, to make connections with the poem, have students discuss how they would feel if someone questioned their memories or the images they have drawn.

According to my sketch,
Rows of lemon & mango
Trees frame the courtyard
Of Grandfather's stone
5   And clapboard home;
The shadow of a palomino[1]
Gallops on the lip
Of the horizon.

The teacher says
10 The house is from
Some Zorro
Movie I've seen.

"Ask my mom," I protest.
"She was born there—
15 Right there on the second floor!"

Crossing her arms she moves on.

Memories once certain as rivets
Become confused as awakenings
In strange places and I question
20 The house, the horse, the wrens
Perched on the slate roof—
The roof Oscar Jartín
Tumbled from one hot Tuesday,
Installing a new weather vane;
25 (He broke a shin and two fingers).
Classmates finish drawings of New York City
Housing projects[2] on Navy Street.
I draw one too, with wildgrass
Rising from sidewalk cracks like widows.
30 In big round letters I title it:

GRANDFATHER'S HOUSE

Beaming, the teacher scrawls
An A+ in the corner and tapes
It to the green blackboard.

To the green blackboard.

---

1. **palomino** (pal uh MEE noh) *n.* horse with a light golden coat and a white mane and tail.
2. **housing projects** *n.* apartment buildings subsidized by the government, usually for low-income households.

NOTES

Mark context clues or indicate another strategy you used that helped you determine meaning.

horizon (huh RY zuhn) *n.*
MEANING:

awakenings (uh WAY kuhn ihngz) *n.*
MEANING:

beaming (BEEM ihng) *v.*
MEANING:

FACILITATING

Comprehension Check

Possible responses:

Hanging Fire

1. She is unhappy about her skin and her ashy knees.
2. Momma is in the bedroom with the door closed.
3. She has to learn how to dance.

Translating Grandfather's House

4. The first drawing is the speaker's grandfather's home. It a stone and clapboard home with a courtyard. Lots of lemon and mango trees are close by, and a horse is running.
5. The teacher questions what the speaker has drawn. She thinks that he got the idea from a movie.

Comprehension Check

Complete the following items after you finish your first read. Review and clarify details with your group.

HANGING FIRE

1. In the first stanza, what is the speaker unhappy about?

2. Where is momma in the poem?

3. What does the speaker have to learn before the next party?

TRANSLATING GRANDFATHER'S HOUSE

4. What is the subject of the speaker's first drawing?

5. What is the teacher's reaction to the speaker's first drawing?

60 UNIT 1 • RITES OF PASSAGE

PERSONALIZE FOR LEARNING

Strategic Support

Poetic Structure Students may require support to understand the story in the narrative poem "Translating Grandfather's House." Point out to students that the title refers to the sketch the boy is making of his grandfather's house. Have them review the poem, and ask them to paraphrase what the speaker is saying in their own words. When they are finished, have them discuss why the teacher did not believe that the speaker's sketch of his grandfather's house was accurate, and how the speaker "translated" his sketch so that the teacher would approve.

6. What grade does the speaker receive on the second drawing?

7. 📓 **Notebook** Confirm your understanding by writing a short summary of each poem.

RESEARCH

Research to Clarify Choose one unfamiliar detail from one of the poems. Briefly research that detail. In what way does the information you learned shed light on an aspect of the poem?

Research to Explore Choose something that interests you from the texts, and perform research on it. Share your findings with your group.

DIGITAL PERSPECTIVES

Comprehension Check

6. He gets an A+.
7. Summaries will vary but should include that both poems are told about the experiences of a young person and their struggles as they grow.

Research

Research to Clarify If students struggle to come up with an unfamiliar detail, have them reread the poems and notice an idea or concept that might be new to them, such as a math team, a Zorro movie, or housing projects in New York City.

Research to Explore Encourage students to make connections so they conduct research that will engage them.

PERSONALIZE FOR LEARNING

Challenge
Write a Poem Have interested students write their own poem about a significant experience. Students might write a lyric poem in the style of "Hanging Fire," in which they create a vivid impression by using musical effects while sharing the thoughts and feelings of a single speaker. Alternatively, they may write a narrative poem in the style of "Translating Grandfather's House," in which they tell a story. As students share their poems, guide listeners to identify the words that contribute to the poem's tone.

FACILITATING

Jump Start

CLOSE READ Engage students in a discussion about what makes poetry an important way to address issues of growing up. *What can poetry distill about rites of passage for the reader? How is poetry different from nonfiction and fiction, and does that difference make it especially effective for conveying certain ideas and emotions?*

Close Read the Text

If needed, model close reading by using the Annotation Highlights in the Interactive Teacher's Edition.

Remind students to use Accountable Talk in their discussions and to support one another as they complete the close read.

Analyze the Text

1. **Possible response:** The repeated line is "Momma's in the bedroom with the door closed." This suggests that the speaker does not have an open relationship with her mother.
2. **Passages will vary by group.** Remind students to explain why they chose the passage they present to the group
3. Responses will vary by group.

Concept Vocabulary

Why These Words? Possible response: The concept words seem to suggest a positive change. Another word that fits the category is *graduation*.

Practice

Responses will vary.

Word Network

Possible words: *momma, graduation, awakenings*

Word Study

For more support, see **Concept Vocabulary and Word Study.**

Possible responses:
Horizon describes a visual line in the distance. Knowing that horizon means boundary may help students see that the *horizon* is at the boundary of their sight.

POETRY COLLECTION

TIP
GROUP DISCUSSION Allow each member of the group to share reactions to the poems. Discuss the similarities and differences in group members' reactions.

WORD NETWORK
Add interesting words related to rites of passage from the text to your Word Network.

MAKING MEANING

Close Read the Text

With your group, revisit sections of the text you marked during your first read. **Annotate** what you notice. What **questions** do you have? What can you **conclude**?

Analyze the Text

CITE TEXTUAL EVIDENCE to support your answers.

Notebook Complete the activities.

1. **Review and Clarify** With your group, reread "Hanging Fire." Identify the lines that are repeated throughout the poem. What does this repetition suggest about the relationship between the speaker and the mother?

2. **Present and Discuss** Now, work with your group to share the passages from the poems that you found especially important. Take turns presenting your passages. Discuss what you noticed in the text, what questions you asked, and what conclusions you reached.

3. **Essential Question:** *What are some milestones on the path to growing up?* What have you learned about growing up by reading these poems? Discuss with your group.

LANGUAGE DEVELOPMENT

Concept Vocabulary

horizon   awakenings   beaming

Why These Words? The concept vocabulary words from the text are related. With your group, determine what the words have in common. Write your ideas, and add another word that fits the category.

Practice

Notebook Confirm your understanding of these words from the text by using them in sentences. Provide context clues for each word.

Word Study

Etymology: *horizon* In "Translating Grandfather's House," the author uses the word *horizon*. The etymology, or word origin, of *horizon* can be traced back to the Greek word *horos*, meaning "boundary marker." The related Greek word *horizon* means "limiting" or "creating a boundary." How does understanding the origin of the word horizon help you to better understand its meaning? How does this knowledge enhance your appreciation of the poem?

62 UNIT 1 • RITES OF PASSAGE

FORMATIVE ASSESSMENT

Analyze the Text
If students struggle to close read the text, **then** provide the **Poetry Collection: Text Questions** available online in the Interactive Teacher's Edition or Unit Resources. Answers and DOK levels are also available.

Concept Vocabulary
If students struggle to identify the concept, **then** discuss the words in more detail, encouraging students to think of the words the way a poet might.

Word Study
If students failed to identify other words, **then** suggest they use a dictionary to find out whether words they might choose have multiple meanings. For Reteach and Practice, see **Word Study: Etymology (RP).**

ESSENTIAL QUESTION: What are some milestones on the path to growing up?

Analyze Craft and Structure

Forms of Poetry Two major **forms of poetry** are lyric poetry and narrative poetry. Understanding a poem's structure and style will help you to analyze the meaning of a poem and identify a **theme,** or insight about life that it conveys.

- The purpose of **lyric poetry** is to create a single, vivid impression of an object, person, or moment in time. Lyric poems are generally short. They may be rhymed or unrhymed, but most lyric poems contain musical qualities that help to convey meaning. These musical effects are created through the repetition of words and sounds as well as the rhythm created by the strong and weak stresses a reader naturally places on words.

- A **narrative poem** tells a story and includes the main elements of a short story—characters, setting, conflict, and plot. A narrative poem may also include musical effects, but generally not to the same degree that a lyric poem does.

Practice

CITE TEXTUAL EVIDENCE to support your answers.

Analyze the poems and fill in the charts with your findings. Then, answer the questions that follow. Share your responses with your group.

HANGING FIRE	
ELEMENTS OF LYRIC POETRY	EXAMPLES/EVIDENCE
musical effects (repetition of words and sounds; rhythms)	repetition of "and momma's in the bedroom/with the door closed" Stanza 1: alliteration: still sucks his thumb in secret
expresses thoughts and feelings	stanza 2: "suppose I die before graduation…" "There is nothing I want to do/and too much/that has to be done" stanza 3: "will I live long enough/to grow up"
details create a single, vivid impression	details show speaker's age: Line 2: "my skin has betrayed me"; Lines 6-7: "my knees are / always so ashy"; Line 14: "my room is too small for me"

TRANSLATING GRANDFATHER'S HOUSE	
ELEMENTS OF NARRATIVE POETRY	EXAMPLES/EVIDENCE
characters	speaker, teacher, Oscar Jartín, classmates
setting	classroom
conflict	teacher does not believe that speaker's drawing really shows speaker's grandfather's home

1. **(a)** What overall impression does "Hanging Fire" create? **(b)** What theme is conveyed by the poem?

2. **(a)** How is the conflict resolved in "Translating Grandfather's House"? **(b)** What theme does the poem suggest?

Poetry Collection 63

DIGITAL PERSPECTIVES

Analyze Craft and Structure

Forms of Poetry Point out that lyric poems express emotion, the way that songs do. In addition, lyric poems include musical devices. Explain that narrative poems may also use musical effects, such as repetition and alliteration. In addition, they use the elements of story telling.

Explain to students that a writer's tone is conveyed through the words he or she uses. Encourage students to pay special attention to attention-grabbing words in each poem. For more support, see **Analyze Craft and Structure: Forms of Poetry.**

Hanging Fire
See possible responses in the chart on the student page.

1. (a) This leaves me with the impression that the fourteen-year-old is very anxious and unsure about her future. She wishes she could go to her mother, who is shut away. (b) Life has many challenges, and sometimes one has to wait for them to be resolved.

Translating Grandfather's House
See possible responses in the chart on the student page.

2. (a) There is a conflict between the truth of the speaker's experience and how it is seen in the outside world. (b) One of the challenges of life is growing up and being different in a world where everyone else is the same.

FORMATIVE ASSESSMENT

Analyze Craft and Structure: Forms of Poetry

If students have difficulty in identifying examples from the poetry, **then** review each element of poetry with them (e.g., musical effects, expresses thoughts and feelings). For Reteach and Practice, see **Analyze Craft and Structure: Forms of Poetry (RP).**

PERSONALIZE FOR LEARNING

English Language Support
Musical Effects Have students review the types of musical effects that a writer might use in a poem, including *alliteration* and *repetition*. Encourage them to review the poem "Hanging Fire" to replace words that create alliteration. (For example, instead of "still sucks his thumb in secret", they might write, "keeps sucking his thumb in private.") Have students discuss what effect is lost when the alliteration is replaced with less musical wording. **ALL LEVELS**

Small-Group Learning

FACILITATING

Author's Style

Word Choice Suggest to students that they explore alternatives to some of the words chosen in the poetry they have read. Encourage them to think about how the alternatives would, or would not, improve the poetry.

For more support, see **Author's Style: Word Choice**.

Read It
See chart on student page for possible responses.

Write It
Students' responses will vary but should offer a different speaker's perspective and personality.

FORMATIVE ASSESSMENT

Author's Style
If students have difficulty evaluating word choice, **then** have them review each text for words that are unique. Ask students to replace those words with synonyms and decide if the meaning or feeling of the text changes.

For Reteach and Practice, see **Author's Style: Word Choice (RP)**.

POETRY COLLECTION

LANGUAGE DEVELOPMENT

Author's Style

Word Choice Writers carefully choose words to create meaning. The poems you have just read are carefully crafted to convey each speaker's personality, situation, and attitude. When you analyze poetry, pay attention to word choice and ask the following:

- Has the poet used figurative language, like similes or metaphors, or more straightforward descriptions?
- Has the poet used slang, informal language, or formal language?
- Has the poet repeated ideas, words, or phrases?

Once you have examined the word choices, draw conclusions about how the word choices help to build the speaker's character and enhance the overall meaning of the poem.

Read It
In the chart, mark words from each passage that are descriptive or interesting in some way. Describe how the word choice helps reveal the speaker's personality and situation. Then, find one more passage from each poem that reveals something about the speaker, and share it with your group.

PASSAGE FROM THE TEXT	WHAT WORD CHOICE REVEALS ABOUT THE SPEAKER
I am fourteen / and my skin has betrayed me / the boy I cannot live without / still sucks his thumb / in secret . . . ("Hanging Fire," lines 1–5)	speaker is anxious but thoughtful
Memories once certain as rivets / Become confused as awakenings / In strange places and I question / The house, the horse, the wrens / Perched on the slate roof— . . . ("Translating Grandfather's House," lines 17–21)	speaker becomes skeptical of memories

Write It
Choose one stanza from either "Hanging Fire" or "Translating Grandfather's House." Rewrite the stanza as if it were spoken by a different speaker. Choose words that help to reveal your speaker's distinct personality. Then, share your stanzas with the group, and discuss how your versions create a new tone that fits the speakers you created.

STANDARDS
Reading Literature
Determine the meaning of words and phrases as they are used in a text, including figurative and connotative meanings; analyze the impact of specific word choices on meaning and tone, including analogies or allusions to other texts.

Speaking and Listening
Engage effectively in a range of collaborative discussions with diverse partners on grade 8 topics, texts, and issues, building on others' ideas and expressing their own clearly.
  a. Come to discussions prepared, having read or researched material under study; explicitly draw on that preparation by referring to evidence on the topic, text, or issue to probe and reflect on ideas under discussion.
  c. Pose questions that connect the ideas of several speakers and respond to others' questions and comments with relevant evidence, observations, and ideas.
  d. Acknowledge new information expressed by others, and, when warranted, qualify or justify their own views in light of the evidence presented.

PERSONALIZE FOR LEARNING

English Language Support
Word Choice Remind students that word choice, like a decision about what to wear, is a way for writers to present themselves and their unique style to the world. Use these selected lines from the poetry to support students as they examine each author's word choice.

Ask students what contradiction they see in the last line of "Translating Grandfather's House." What other words could the poet have chosen? **EMERGING**

Ask students to consider alternate words for "protest" in line 13 of "Translating Grandfather's House." What is the value of that word over "said" or "mumble"? **EXPANDING**

Ask students to look for words they consider difficult in "Hanging Fire." Discuss the impact of the word choice in the poem in helping them understand the speaker. **BRIDGING**

An expanded **English Language Support Lesson** on Word Choice is available in the Interactive Teacher's Edition.

EFFECTIVE EXPRESSION

Speaking and Listening

Assignment

Conduct a **group discussion** about "Hanging Fire" and "Translating Grandfather's House." Draw on the texts to explore and reflect on ideas. Choose one of the following topics.

☐ Explore the **aspects of growing up** that are described in each poem. Are these experiences specific to the speakers or more universal in nature? Support your ideas with details from the poems as well as your own experiences.

☐ **Compare and contrast the speakers** in the two poems. In what ways are they similar? How do they differ? Would the two become friends if they were to meet? Use details from the poems to support your analysis.

Discussion Preparation Identify examples from the text that support your ideas. Record the examples in the chart, and write notes and ideas related to the discussion topic. Then, join with others in your group and compare notes:

HANGING FIRE	TRANSLATING GRANDFATHER'S HOUSE

EVIDENCE LOG

Before moving on to a new selection, record what you learned from "Hanging Fire" and "Translating Grandfather's House" in your Evidence Log.

Holding the Discussion As your group discusses the information in the chart, take turns asking each other questions. Look for connections among the various ideas. Listen carefully to other group members and clarify anything you do not understand. Be open to changing your opinions, and at all times be respectful of others' ideas.

Poetry Collection 65

WriteNow Analyze and Interpret

Analysis Students have reviewed the tone of both "Hanging Fire" and "Translating Grandfather's House." Have students choose one of the poems and write a one-page analysis about whether the meaning of each of the poems would change if its tone were different. Suggest these prompts to support students:

- If "Hanging Fire" had a light-hearted tone instead of an anxious tone, would it have the same meaning?
- Do you think the melodramatic aspects of the speaker's reactions to her situation would be emphasized for a humorous effect? How would that affect readers' responses to the poem? Would readers be as concerned about the speaker?

DIGITAL PERSPECTIVES

Speaking and Listening

If students have difficulty choosing a discussion topic, point out that, while both topics require that students use evidence from the text, the first is about the substance of the poems, and the second is about the form.

Discussion Preparation If students are working on "Aspects of Growing Up," they will need to review each poem to find details to connect to a larger idea about growing up. For example, in "Hanging Fire," the speaker says, "why do I have to be/the one/wearing braces/" showing that she cares about how she looks. She also feels singled out. These are common parts of growing up. Students might note their own feelings as they prepare for the discussion.

If students are working on "Compare and Contrast Speakers," they will need to look for evidence of word choice that reveals the poet's attitudes. For example, in "Translating Grandfather's House," the speaker reveals his negative attitude toward the teacher by using words like "scrawls" to describe her actions. Have students think about questions such as: *Am I more interested in a poem that has a serious tone? How does a poem's tone draw us into its meaning?* In both poems, the speaker feels alienated. It's possible that the speakers would therefore be able to relate to each other.

Holding the Discussion As students conduct their discussions, circulate to observe each group. Ask them to provide notes that they can use to summarize their discussion for the rest of the class.

For more support, see **Speaking and Listening: Group Discussion.**

Evidence Log Support students in completing their Evidence Log. This paced activity will help prepare them to for the Performance-Based Assessment at the end of the unit.

FORMATIVE ASSESSMENT

Speaking and Listening

If groups struggle to get all members to take part in the group discussion, **then** encourage quiet members to speak up by asking for their ideas. For Reteach and Practice, see **Speaking and Listening: Group Discussion (RP).**

Selection Test

Administer the "Poetry Collection" Selection Test, which is available in both print and digital formats online in Assessments.

Small-Group Learning 65

PLANNING

SMALL-GROUP LEARNING • THE SETTING SUN AND THE ROLLING WORLD

The Setting Sun and the Rolling World

🔊 **AUDIO SUMMARIES**
Audio summaries of "The Setting Sun and the Rolling World" are available in both English and Spanish and can be assigned to students in the Interactive Teacher's Edition or Unit Resources. Assigning these summaries prior to reading the selection may help students build additional background knowledge and set a context for their first read.

Summary

In "The Setting Sun and the Rolling World," a short story by Charles Mungoshi, an old father and his son argue about the future. Old Musoni has been a farmer in rural Zimbabwe his whole life, and the land is very difficult to manage. His son Nhamo wants to leave home and pursue a new life. The father and son argue about this decision, and the father begs his son not to leave. Old Musoni fears that his son will face danger and death. Nhamo believes that his education has prepared him for new things. In the end, the father understands the son will leave. Nhamo agrees to visit a man in town who will bless him and give him charms, but he knows those charms and what they represent are meaningless to him.

Insight

Some of the most painful decisions to make are those where children disagree with their parents. Nearly everyone wants something at least a little different from what their family wants from them. These can be some of the biggest decisions in young adulthood.

ESSENTIAL QUESTION:
What are some milestones on the path to growing up?

Connection to Essential Question

This story will help students see that leaving a parent—both literally and in following a different path than a parent expected—is an important event that most people go through as part of their path to adulthood.

SMALL-GROUP LEARNING PERFORMANCE TASK
What defines an event or experience in a young person's life as a milestone or rite of passage?

Connection to Performance Tasks

Small-Group Learning Performance Task Moving out of the family home is a milestone that most Americans have to manage. It's worth noting that in the story, Nhomo moves out before knowing exactly how he'll work and support himself. Students should recognize that leaving the family home is a significant and common event in a young person's life, but the separation described here is extreme. Students should consider whether this is a step that they would take.

UNIT PERFORMANCE-BASED ASSESSMENT
What rite of passage has held the most significance for you or for a person you know well?

Unit Performance-Based Assessment This story will help students to consider a major turning point in a young person's life. Nhamo and his father argue about his future, and the young man must ultimately decide who is in charge of his future. The events in this story may encourage students to prepare for the prompt by considering rites of passage in their own lives.

DIGITAL PERSPECTIVES Audio Video Document Annotation Highlights EL Highlights Online Assessment

LESSON RESOURCES

	Making Meaning	Language Development	Effective Expression
Lesson	First Read Close Read Analyze the Text Analyze Craft and Structure	Concept Vocabulary Word Study Conventions	Research
Instructional Standards			
STUDENT RESOURCES Available online in the Interactive Student Edition or Unit Resources	🔊 Selection Audio 📄 First-Read Guide: Fiction 📄 Close-Read Guide: Fiction	📄 Word Network	📄 Evidence Log
TEACHER RESOURCES **Selection Resources** Available online in the Interactive Teacher's Edition or Unit Resources	🔊 Audio Summaries ✏️ Annotation Highlights 💬 EL Highlights 📄 The Setting Sun and the Rolling World: Text Questions 📄 English Language Support Lesson: Theme 📄 Analyze Craft and Structure: Point of View in Fiction	📄 Concept Vocabulary and Word Study 📄 Conventions: Verb Moods	📄 Research: Informational Report
Reteach/Practice (RP) Available online in the Interactive Teacher's Edition or Unit Resources	📄 Analyze Craft and Structure: Point of View in Fiction (RP)	📄 Word Study: Greek Root -*psych*- (RP) 📄 Conventions: Verb Moods (RP)	📄 Research: Informational Report (RP)
Assessment Available online in Assessments	📄 ✅ Selection Test		
My Resources	📄 A Unit 1 Answer Key is available online and in the Interactive Teacher's Edition.		

Small-Group Learning 66B

PERSONALIZE FOR LEARNING

SMALL-GROUP LEARNING • THE SETTING SUN AND THE ROLLING WORLD

Reading Support

Text Complexity Rubric: The Setting Sun and the Rolling World

Quantitative Measures

Lexile: 800   Text Length: 1,726 words

Qualitative Measures

Knowledge Demands ①—②—③—●—⑤	To fully understand the text, reader needs knowledge of African cultural background, including farming culture and Zimbabwe.
Structure ①—②—❸—④—⑤	Story is structured around dialogue of two characters, interspersed with thoughts, memories, and reflections. Situations are not explicitly stated. Names are not identified in dialogue, which may make it harder for some students to follow.
Language Conventionality and Clarity ①—②—③—●—⑤	Story has a lot of flowery, descriptive, and complex language; there is metaphorical language that is often abstract and/or ironic. There is some difficult vocabulary.
Levels of Meaning/Purpose ①—②—③—●—⑤	Story explores complex and sophisticated themes about tradition, generations, identity, perseverance, and self-determination.

DECIDE AND PLAN

English Language Support

Provide English Learners with support for knowledge demands and structure as they read the selection.

Knowledge Demands Preview key elements of the story: Ask students to locate the two characters' names. Direct them to the end of paragraph 1 to find the relationship (father and son). Help them to locate the text (paragraph 10) that explains the situation: *If his son was going away, he must not be angry.* Check for understanding by asking *Who are the characters?* (a father and son) *Who wants to go away?* (the son)

Structure Help students to navigate the structure of the story. Ask them to mark lines spoken by each character and to identify whose thoughts are shown at different paragraphs in the text.

Strategic Support

Provide students with strategic support to ensure that they can successfully read the text.

Knowledge Demands Preview the story. Have students read the background to understand the cultural context. Discuss that the story is a dialogue between two characters. Their words are given in the dialogue, but their thoughts are also described. As students read, ask them to keep a list of situations and feelings described by the dialogue.

Meaning Break the text into sections. As a group, have students take turns reading aloud, with two students acting as father and son. After each section that you read, confirm understanding by asking students to tell what the character feels. Together, write a chart summarizing the characters' intentions and feelings.

Challenge

Provide students who need to be challenged with ideas for how they can go beyond a simple interpretation of the text

Text Analysis Pair students. Ask one to be the son and the other to be the father and do a dramatic reading of sections of the dialogue. Then ask students each to write a description of their character's intentions and feelings in their own words. Ask for volunteers to do the dramatic reading in front of the class and then to explain the characters' feelings.

Written Response Ask students to write several paragraphs of dialogue of conflict between two modern-day characters—a mother or father who wants a teenager to stay close to home to go to college and a teenager who wants to travel to a school far away.

TEACH

Read and Respond

Have the groups read the selection and complete the Making Meaning, Language Development, and Effective Expression activities.

Standards Support Through Teaching and Learning Cycle

IDENTIFY NEEDS

Analyze results of the Beginning-of-Year Assessment, focusing on the items relating to Unit 1. Also take into consideration student performance to this point and your observations of where particular students struggle.

ANALYZE AND REVISE

- Analyze student work for evidence of student learning.
- Identify whether students have met the expectations in the standards.
- Identify implications for future instruction.

TEACH

Implement the planned lesson, and gather evidence of student learning.

DECIDE AND PLAN

- If students have performed poorly on items matching these standards, then provide selection scaffolds before assigning them the on-level lesson provided in the Student Edition.
- If students have done well on the Beginning-of-Year Assessment, then challenge them to keep progressing and learning by giving them opportunities to practice the skills in depth.
- Use the Selection Resources listed on the Planning pages for "The Setting Sun and the Rolling World" to help students continually improve their ability to master the standards.

Instructional Standards: The Setting Sun and the Rolling World

	Catching Up	This Year	Looking Forward
Reading	You may wish to administer the **Analyze Craft and Structure: Point of View in Fiction (RP)** worksheet to help students consider the way a text's point of view controls the type of information provided.	**RL.6** Analyze how differences in the points of view of the characters and the audience or reader create such effects as suspense or humor.	Ask students to write a section of this story from the point of view of one of the characters and to identify the differences in the two versions.
Writing	You may wish to administer the **Research: Informational Report (RP)** worksheet to help students organize their informational reports.	**W.2** Write informative/explanatory texts to examine a topic and convey ideas, concepts, and information through the selection, organization, and analysis of relevant content.	Ask students to write an informational report about a custom that is important in their own lives. Encourage students to share their reports in small groups.
Language	You may wish to administer the **Conventions: Verb Moods (RP)** worksheet to help students understand verb moods. You may wish to administer the **Word Study: Greek Root -psych- (RP)** worksheet to help students understand words with the root.	**L.1.c** Form and use verbs in the indicative, imperative, interrogative, conditional, and subjunctive mood. **L.4.b** Use common, grade-appropriate Greek or Latin affixes and roots as clues to the meaning of a word.	Challenge students to identify verb moods in increasingly difficult selections. Have students identify and define other words that have the Greek root –psych–.

FACILITATING

Jump Start

FIRST READ *How is leaving home a rite of passage? How might this milestone look different to the person leaving than to the person who is staying home?* Engage students in a discussion about leaving home that sets the context for reading "The Setting Sun and the Rolling World."

The Setting Sun and the Rolling World

Do staying home and leaving home both pose dangerous risks? Is it important for young people to leave home to fully mature? Modeling questions such as this will help students connect to "The Setting Sun and the Rolling World" and to the Small-Group Performance Task assignment. Selection audio and print capability for the selection are available in the Interactive Teacher's Edition.

Concept Vocabulary

Ask students to preview the concept vocabulary words. Encourage them to look at the three types of context clues—synonyms, restatement of an idea, and contrast of ideas and topics. Discuss how these context clues can help clarify meaning. Encourage groups to think of one other type of context clue that they might find in a text. Possibilities include antonyms, definitions, and examples.

FIRST READ

As they read, students should perform the steps of the first read:

NOTICE: You may want to encourage students to notice how the two main characters—Old Musoni and Nhamo—are portrayed.

ANNOTATE: Remind students to mark passages that will help them to determine the theme of the selection when they come back for a close read.

CONNECT: Ask students to think of other stories or real-life experiences that help them relate to this text.

RESPOND: Students will answer questions and write a summary to demonstrate understanding.

Point out to students that while they will always complete the Respond step at the end of the first read, the other steps will probably happen somewhat concurrently. You may wish to print copies of the **First-Read Guide: Fiction** for students to use.

66 UNIT 1 • RITES OF PASSAGE

MAKING MEANING

About the Author

Charles Mungoshi (b. 1947) is a Zimbabwean writer. He grew up working on his father's farm, where the time he spent alone inspired him to start creating stories. He writes in both English and Shona, one of the main languages spoken in Zimbabwe. His works have won the International PEN Award and the Commonwealth Writers Prize.

The Setting Sun and the Rolling World

Concept Vocabulary

As you perform your first read of "The Setting Sun and the Rolling World," you will encounter these words.

| patronized | obligations | psychological |

Base Words If these words are unfamiliar to you, analyze each one to see if it contains a base word, or "inside" word, you know. Then, use your knowledge of the "inside" word, to determine the meaning of the unfamiliar word. Here is an example of how to apply this strategy.

> **Unfamiliar Word:** murkiness
>
> **Familiar "Inside" Word:** murky
>
> **Context:** But just as dust quickly settles over a glittering pebble revealed by a hoe, so a **murkiness** hid the gleam . . .
>
> **Conclusion:** The word **murkiness** must mean something dusty or cloudy that makes it hard to see.

Apply your knowledge of base words and other vocabulary strategies to determine the meanings of unfamiliar words you encounter during your first read of "The Setting Sun and the Rolling World."

First Read FICTION

Apply these strategies as you conduct your first read. You will have an opportunity to complete a close read after your first read.

NOTICE whom the *story* is about, *what* happens, *where* and *when* it happens, and *why* those involved react as they do.

ANNOTATE by marking vocabulary and key passages you want to revisit.

CONNECT ideas within the selection to what you already know and what you have already read.

RESPOND by completing the Comprehension Check and by writing a brief summary of the selection.

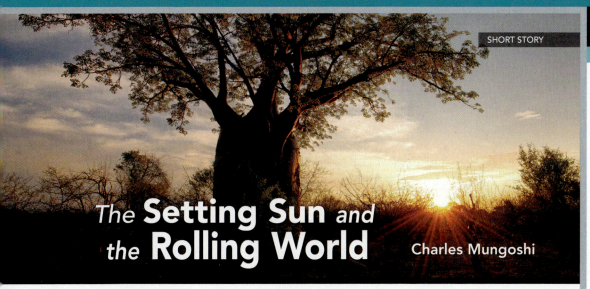

SHORT STORY

The Setting Sun and the Rolling World

Charles Mungoshi

BACKGROUND
Zimbabwe is a landlocked country in Africa. Traditionally, many Zimbabweans have made a living farming the land. When farming goes well, food is plentiful, but farmers are always at the mercy of unpredictable rainfall and weather.

1   Old Musoni raised his dusty eyes from his hoe and the unchanging stony earth he had been tilling and peered into the sky. The white speck whose sound had disturbed his work and thoughts was far out at the edge of the yellow sky, near the horizon. Then it disappeared quickly over the southern rim of the sky and he shook his head. He looked to the west. Soon the sun would go down. He looked over the sunblasted land and saw the shadows creeping east, blearier and taller with every moment that the sun shed each of its rays. Unconsciously wishing for rain and relief, he bent down again to his work and did not see his son, Nhamo, approaching.

2   Nhamo crouched in the dust near his father and greeted him. The old man half raised his back, leaning against his hoe, and said what had been bothering him all day long.

3   "You haven't changed your mind?"

4   "No, father."

5   There was a moment of silence. Old Musoni scraped earth off his hoe.

6   "Have you thought about this, son?"

7   "For weeks, father."

8   "And you think that's the only way?"

9   "There is no other way."

10   The old man felt himself getting angry again. But this would be the last day he would talk to his son. If his son was going away, he must not be angry. It would be equal to a curse. He himself

FACILITATING

Concept Vocabulary

PATRONIZED If groups are struggling to define the word *patronized* in paragraph 16, point out to students that they can use context clues to help determine the word's meaning. Point out that the sentence also includes the words *son* and *hampered*. In addition, ask students to think about the dialogue and how the son might feel.

Possible response: *Patronized* means "to be undercut or talked down to by a person in authority."

OBLIGATIONS If groups are struggling to define the word *obligations* in paragraph 17, remind them to point out that students may look for a contrast of ideas and topics. Point out that the sentence also includes the words *Release me*. Have these students use the context clues to define the word.

Possible response: *Obligations* means "ties and responsibilities."

NOTES

had taken chances before, in his own time, but he felt too much of a father. He had worked and slaved for his family and the land had not betrayed him. He saw nothing now but disaster and death for his son out there in the world. Lions had long since vanished but he knew of worse animals of prey, animals that wore redder claws than the lion's, beasts that would not leave an unprotected homeless boy alone. He thought of the white metal bird and he felt remorse.

11 "Think again. You will end dead. Think again, of us, of your family. We have a home, poor though it is, but can you think of a day you have gone without?"

12 "I have thought everything over, father, I am convinced this is the only way out."

13 "There is no only way out in the world. Except the way of the land, the way of the family."

14 "The land is overworked and gives nothing now, father. And the family is almost broken up."

15 The old man got angry. Yes, the land is useless. True, the family tree is uprooted and it dries in the sun. True, many things are happening that haven't happened before, that we did not think would happen, ever. But nothing is more certain to hold you together than the land and a home, a family. And where do you think you are going, a mere beardless kid with the milk not yet dry on your baby nose? What do you think you will do in the great treacherous world where men twice your age have gone and returned with their backs broken—if they returned at all? What do you know of life? What do you know of the false honey bird that leads you the whole day through the forest to a snake's nest? But all he said was: "Look. What have you asked me and I have denied you? What, that I have, have I not given you for the asking?"

16 "All. You have given me all, father." And here, too, the son felt hampered, **patronized** and his pent-up fury rolled through him. It showed on his face but stayed under control. You have given me damn all and nothing. You have sent me to school and told me the importance of education, and now you ask me to throw it on the rubbish heap and scrape for a living on this tired cold shell of the moon. You ask me to forget it and muck around in this slow dance of death with you. I have this one chance of making my own life, once in all eternity, and now you are jealous. You are afraid of your own death. It is, after all, your own death. I shall be around a while yet. I will make my way home if a home is what I need. I am armed more than you think and wiser than you can dream of. But all he said, too, was:

17 "Really, father, have no fear for me. I will be all right. Give me this chance. Release me from all **obligations** and pray for me."

Mark base words or indicate another strategy you used that helped you determine meaning.

patronized (PAY truh nyzd) *v.*
MEANING:

obligations (ob lih GAY shuhnz) *n.*
MEANING:

FACILITATING SMALL-GROUP READING

CLOSE READ: Fiction As groups perform the close read, circulate and offer support as needed.

- Remind groups that as they read fiction, they should be sure to identify the main characters and the plot.
- If a group is confused about why particular events are important, remind them to think about the cultural experiences reflected in the selection.
- Challenge groups to determine the theme of the text.

18 There was a spark in the old man's eyes at these words of his son. But just as dust quickly settles over a glittering pebble revealed by the hoe, so a murkiness hid the gleam in the old man's eye. Words are handles made to the smith's[1] fancy and are liable to break under stress. They are too much fat on the hard unbreaking sinews of life.

19 "Do you know what you are doing, son?"

20 "Yes."

21 "Do you know what you will be a day after you leave home?"

22 "Yes, father."

23 "A homeless, nameless vagabond living on dust and rat's droppings, living on thank-yous, sleeping up a tree or down a ditch, in the rain, in the sun, in the cold, with nobody to see you, nobody to talk to, nobody at all to tell your dreams to. Do you know what it is to see your hopes come crashing down like an old house out of season and your dreams turning to ash and dung without a tang of salt in your skull? Do you know what it is to live without a single hope of ever seeing good in your own lifetime?" And to himself: Do you know, young bright ambitious son of my loins, the ruins of time and the pains of old age? Do you know how to live beyond a dream, a hope, a faith? Have you seen black despair, my son?

24 "I know it, father. I know enough to start on. The rest I shall learn as I go on. Maybe I shall learn to come back."

25 The old man looked at him and felt: Come back where? Nobody comes back to ruins. You will go on, son. Something you don't know will drive you on along deserted plains, past ruins and more ruins, on and on until there is only one ruin left: yourself. You will break down, without tears, son. You are human, too. Learn to the *haya*—the rain bird, and heed its warning of coming storm: plow no more, it says. And what happens if the storm catches you far, far out on the treeless plain? What, then, my son?

26 But he was tired. They had taken over two months discussing all this. Going over the same ground like animals at a drinking place until, like animals, they had driven the water far deep into the stony earth, until they had sapped all the blood out of life and turned it into a grim skeleton, and now they were creating a stampede on the dust, groveling for water. Mere thoughts. Mere words. And what are words? Trying to grow a fruit tree in the wilderness.

27 "Go son, with my blessings. I give you nothing. And when you remember what I am saying you will come back. The land is still yours. As long as I am alive you will find a home waiting for you."

28 "Thank you, father."

1. **smith** *n.* blacksmith; artisan who creates objects out of iron.

FACILITATING

Concept Vocabulary

PSYCHOLOGICAL If groups are struggling to define the word *psychological* in paragraph 32, point out to students that they may contrast the meaning of the word *psychological* with the word *biological* in the same sentence. Have students use the context clues to determine the word's meaning.

Possible response: *Psychological* means "having to do with the mind, as opposed to the body."

NOTES

Mark base words or indicate another strategy you used that helped you determine meaning.

psychological (sy kuh LAHJ ih kuhl) *adj.*
MEANING:

---

29 "Before you go, see Chiremba. You are going out into the world. You need something to strengthen yourself. Tell him I shall pay him. Have a good journey, son."

30 "Thank you, father."

31 Nhamo smiled and felt a great love for his father. But there were things that belonged to his old world that were just lots of humbug[2] on the mind, empty load, useless scrap. He would go to Chiremba but he would burn the charms as soon as he was away from home and its sickening environment. A man stands on his feet and guts. Charms were for you—so was God, though much later. But for us now the world is godless, no charms will work. All that is just the opium you take in the dark in the hope of a light. You don't need that now. You strike a match for a light. Nhamo laughed.

32 He could be so easily light-hearted. Now his brain worked with a fury only known to visionaries. The **psychological** ties were now broken, only the biological tied him to his father. He was free. He too remembered the aeroplane which his father had seen just before their talk. Space had no bounds and no ties. Floating laws ruled the darkness and he would float with the fiery balls. He was the sun, burning itself out every second and shedding tons of energy which it held in its power, giving it the thrust to drag its brood wherever it wanted to. This was the law that held him. The mystery that his father and ancestors had failed to grasp and which had caused their being wiped off the face of the earth. This thinking reached such a pitch that he began to sing, imitating as intimately as he could Satchmo's[3] voice: "What a wonderful world." It was Satchmo's voice that he turned to when he felt buoyant.

33 Old Musoni did not look at his son as he left him. Already, his mind was trying to focus at some point in the dark unforeseeable future. Many things could happen and while he still breathed he would see that nothing terribly painful happened to his family, especially to his stubborn last born, Nhamo. Tomorrow, before sunrise, he would go to see Chiremba and ask him to throw bones over the future of his son. And if there were a couple of ancestors who needed appeasement, he would do it while he was still around.

34 He noticed that the sun was going down and he scraped the earth off his hoe.

35 The sun was sinking slowly, bloody red, blunting and blurring all the objects that had looked sharp in the light of day. Soon a chilly wind would blow over the land and the cold cloudless sky would send down beads of frost like white ants over the unprotected land. 🌿

---

2. **humbug** *n.* nonsense.
3. **Satchmo** nickname for famous American jazz musician Louis Armstrong (1901–1971).

VOCABULARY DEVELOPMENT

Graphic Organizer Give students more practice with the word *psychological*, which appears in paragraph 32. Have students analyze the word *psychological* using a Four-Square Diagram. If necessary, guide students as they complete the diagram.

Definition	Synonyms
Having to do with the mind	mental, emotional
Example sentence	**Related forms**
Her *psychological* ties to her family were strong.	psychology, psychologically

MEDIA CONNECTION

STORIES OF ZIMBABWEAN WOMEN

🗨 **Discuss It** How does this video help you understand more about life in a rural village like the one where Nhamo lived?

Write your response before sharing your ideas.

SCAN FOR MULTIMEDIA

Comprehension Check

Complete the following items after you finish your first read. Review and clarify details with your group.

1. Why does Nhamo want to leave his family?

2. Why does Old Musoni want him to stay?

3. How does Nhamo feel about getting charms from Chiremba?

4. 📓 **Notebook** Confirm your understanding of the story by writing a short summary.

RESEARCH

Research to Clarify Choose at least one unfamiliar detail from the story. Briefly research that detail. How does the information you learned shed light on an aspect of the story?

The Setting Sun and the Rolling World 71

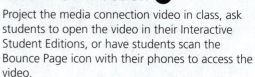

Media Connection ▶

Project the media connection video in class, ask students to open the video in their Interactive Student Editions, or have students scan the Bounce Page icon with their phones to access the video.

Discuss It

Possible response: The woman featured in the video lives a very hard life without the comforts of western countries. She breaks rocks for a living and is paid very little. She can't afford to send her children to school. In the video, children stand by, watching her work. Nhamo, the young man in the story, wants to leave his father in a rural area and make a life for himself. This video shows that his life may be vastly different from whathe knows.

Comprehension Check

Possible responses:

1. Nhamo wants to leave his family to travel to the city and find a new life.
2. Old Musoni wants him to stay because he is afraid his son will not find success.
3. Nhamo will get the charms for his father's sake, but he thinks they are useless.
4. Summaries will vary; however, students should include the main plot points and the different views of Musoni and Nhamo.

Research to Clarify

If students struggle to come up with a detail to research, you may want to suggest that they focus on one of the following topics: rural farming in Africa, village life in Africa, rural-urban migration in Africa, medicine men, and charms.

PERSONALIZE FOR LEARNING

Challenge

Research Encourage interested students to conduct research about challenges facing people in Zimbabwe today, including drought, poverty, educational challenges, and health issues. Ask them to write a brief informational article about the obstacles facing the country and its people.

FACILITATING

Jump Start

CLOSE READ Have students close read "The Setting Sun and Rolling World." Ask students to think about the title of the story and how it relates to the content of the story. Explain that when trying to determine theme, sometimes looking at the title can be helpful. Ask students what they think "the setting sun" and "rolling world" might suggest.

Close Read the Text

If needed, model close reading by using the Annotation Highlights in the Interactive Teacher's Edition.

Remind groups to use Accountable Talk in their discussions and to support one another as they complete the close read.

Analyze the Text

Possible responses:
1. The father has taken some chances but is too worried about his son to want him to take chances. The "animals of prey" could be actual animals or could be people who will try to take advantage of a young rural man who is alone.
2. Passages will vary by group. Remind students to explain why they chose their passage.
3. Responses will vary by group.

Concept Vocabulary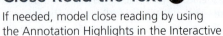

Why These Words? Possible response: The concept words all have to do with Nhamo's relationship to his father. Another word from the selection that fits is *hampered*.

Practice

Responses will vary.

Word Network

Possible words: *remorse, convinced, hampered, free*

Word Study

For more support, see **Concept Vocabulary and Word Study.**

Possible responses:
psychiatrist: a doctor who specializes in treating and preventing mental illness
psychology: the science of the mind and behavior
psychopath: a person who is severely mentally ill
psychic: a person who is believed to have special powers including mind-reading

---

MAKING MEANING

THE SETTING SUN AND THE ROLLING WORLD

TIP
GROUP DISCUSSION
As you discuss the story, build on the comments of others and refer to the text to support your ideas.

WORD NETWORK
Add interesting words about growing up from the text to your Word Network.

STANDARDS
Reading Literature
Analyze how differences in the points of view of the characters and the audience or reader create such effects as suspense or humor.
Language
Determine or clarify the meaning of unknown and multiple-meaning words or phrases based on *grade 8 reading and content,* choosing flexibly from a range of strategies.
  b. Use common, grade-appropriate Greek or Latin affixes and roots as clues to the meaning of a word.
  c. Consult general and specialized reference materials, both print and digital, to find the pronunciation of a word or determine or clarify its precise meaning or its part of speech.

Close Read the Text

With your group, revisit sections of the text you marked during your First Read. **Annotate** what you notice. What **questions** do you have? What can you **conclude**?

Analyze the Text

CITE TEXTUAL EVIDENCE to support your answers.

📓 **Notebook** Complete the activities.

1. **Review and Clarify** With your group, reread paragraph 10 of "The Setting Sun and the Rolling World." What does the author mean when he says that Musoni "felt too much of a father"? What "animals of prey" do you think the father worries about?

2. **Present and Discuss** Now, work with your group to share the passages from the text that you found especially important. Take turns presenting your passages. Discuss what you noticed in the text, what questions you asked, and what conclusions you reached.

3. **Essential Question:** *What are some milestones on the path to growing up?* What kind of milestone does the story explore? Why is it important? Discuss with your group.

LANGUAGE DEVELOPMENT

Concept Vocabulary

| patronized | obligations | psychological |

Why These Words? The concept vocabulary words from the text are related. With your group, determine what the words have in common. Write your ideas, and add another word that fits the category.

Practice

📓 **Notebook** Confirm your understanding of these words from the text by using each in a sentence. Provide context clues for the words.

Word Study

Greek Root: *-psych-* In "The Setting Sun and the Rolling World," the narrator observes that the "psychological ties" with his father were broken. The word *psychological* contains the Greek root *-psych-* which means "mind" or "spirit." Use a dictionary or thesaurus to identify several other words that have the same root. Write the words and their meanings.

FORMATIVE ASSESSMENT

Analyze the Text
If students struggle to close read the text, **then** provide The Setting Sun and the Rolling World: Text Questions available online in the Interactive Teacher's Edition or Unit Resources. Answers and DOK levels are also available.

Concept Vocabulary
If students struggle to identify the concept that connects the words, **then** suggest that they reread the context clues for these words that they highlighted during the first read.

Word Study
If students have difficulty identifying other words with the root *-psych-*, **then** encourage them to use a dictionary to find other words. For Reteach and Practice, see **Word Study: Greek Root *-psych-* (RP).**

ESSENTIAL QUESTION: What are some milestones on the path to growing up?

Analyze Craft and Structure

Point of View in Fiction The perspective from which a story is told is its **point of view.** Using point of view, authors can control the information readers receive. Most stories are told from the first-person or third-person point of view.

- **First-person point of view** presents the story from the perspective of a character in the story. This character is the narrator and participates in the story's action. The narrator uses the pronouns *I*, *me*, and *my* to communicate what he or she sees, knows, thinks, or feels.
- **Third-person point of view** tells the story from the perspective of a narrator outside the story. The narrator uses pronouns such as *he*, *she*, and *they* to refer to the characters in the story. An **omniscient** third-person narrator knows everything that happens and reveals what each character thinks and feels. A **limited** third-person narrator reveals only the thoughts and feelings of a single character.

Notebook Work with your group to identify the point of view the author uses in "The Setting Sun and the Rolling World." Then, use a chart like the one shown to compare and contrast the points of view of Old Musoni and his son Nhamo. In the chart, note key passages from the story that show each character's thoughts and feelings. Then, answer the questions that follow.

OLD MUSONI'S POINT OF VIEW	NHAMO'S POINT OF VIEW
a. See possible responses in Teacher's Edition	b.
c.	d.

1. (a) Use the details in your chart to identify key differences in the points of view of Old Musoni and Nhamo. (b) How do these differences develop the plot?

2. How would the story be different if it were told from a different point of view?

TIP

GROUP DISCUSSION
As you analyze a story, discuss the ways in which the story would change if it were told from a different point of view. How would these changes impact readers' understanding?

The Setting Sun and the Rolling World 73

Analyze Craft and Structure

Explain to students that a story's point of view is critical to the story as it controls the type of information that the reader gets about the situation. For more support, see **Analyze Craft and Structure: Point of View in Fiction.**

Possible responses:

a. Old Musoni feels the world will not welcome his son.

b. Nhamo feels he needs to go out into the world and make a way for himself.

c. Old Musoni thinks that charms from a villager will protect his son.

d. Nhamo does not have faith in these rituals and beliefs

1. (a) Musoni is living a traditional farming life and his son wants to have a different life. (b)These differences drive the conflict of the plot.

2. If the story were told from one of the characters' point of view, it might express more emotion.

FORMATIVE ASSESSMENT

Analyze Craft and Structure: Theme
If students have difficulty in identifying theme, **then** have them review Old Musoni's insights throughout the story. For Reteach and Practice, see **Analyze Craft and Structure: Point of View in Fiction (RP).**

PERSONALIZE FOR LEARNING

English Language Support

Analyzing Point of View in Fiction Have students consider the way that a story's point of view can change the information that a writer includes.

Have pairs of students tell a story about two people with a conflict. Ask them to list the details that each person would include in story and to compare the information each version would include. **EMERGING**

Have pairs of students write a paragraph about a conflict between two people. Ask students to highlight the details in the paragraph that show the paragraph's point of view. **EXPANDING**

Have pairs of students write two versions of a paragraph about a conflict between two people. Each version should reflect one character's point of view. Ask students to highlight the details in each paragraph that show the different information that the unique point of view provides. **BRIDGING**

An expanded **English Language Support Lesson** on Point of View in Fiction is available in the Interactive Teacher's Edition.

Small-Group Learning 73

FACILITATING

Conventions

Verb Moods Discuss with students that a verb's mood indicates a state of being, including whether something has happened. You may want to devote special emphasis to the subjunctive verb mood, since students may be least familiar with it. Explain the times when a speaker might use the subjunctive. For example, a speaker might say, "Chiremba is powerful." But in the story, Nhamo does not believe Chiremba is powerful. In Nhamo's case, he might say, "If Chiremba *were* powerful, he could protect me in my travels." Here, because Nhamo is expressing a condition that is contrary to fact—he does not believe Chiremba is powerful—he uses *were* instead of *was*. For more support see **Conventions: Verb Moods.**

MAKE IT INTERACTIVE
Have students think of an activity that interests them, and direct them to write a paragraph about it in which they use each of the five verb moods shown in the chart. Have students use a different color marker to highlight or label each verb mood in their writing. Ask volunteers to share their work with the class.

Read It
Possible responses:
- Interrogative verb mood: "Have you thought about this, son?" (paragraph 6)
- Imperative verb mood: "Think again." (paragraph 11)
- Conditional verb mood: "He would go to Chiremba but he would burn the charms as soon as he was away from home and its sickening environment." (paragraph 31)
- Subjunctive verb mood: "And if there were a couple of ancestors who needed appeasement, he would do it while he was still around." (paragraph 33)

Write It
1. If Musoni were younger, he would understand Nhamo better.
2. Sons should listen to their fathers and should not talk back!

FORMATIVE ASSESSMENT
Conventions
If students are unable to identify verb moods, **then** have students work with a partner who can help them to find more examples of each verb mood in the text. For Reteach and Practice, see **Conventions: Verb Moods (RP).**

LANGUAGE DEVELOPMENT

THE SETTING SUN AND THE ROLLING WORLD

Conventions

Verb Moods To write effectively and precisely, writers use a variety of **verb moods.**

VERB MOOD	WRITERS USE IT TO	EXAMPLE
Interrogative	ask a question	*Is* Nhamo happy about leaving?
Imperative	give a command	*Do not* leave!
Indicative	declare a fact or opinion	The land *is* dry.
Conditional	refer to something that may or may not happen	I *could* go see Chiremba.
	express uncertainty	I *might* travel by plane.
Subjunctive	express a wish, a hope, or a statement contrary to fact	If Musoni *were* traveling, he would walk.
	express a request, demand, or proposal	Musoni asks that Nhamo *be* cautious.

Read It
Work individually to find in the text an example of an interrogative verb, an imperative verb, a conditional verb, and a subjunctive verb. When you have finished, compare your findings with the group.

Write It
Writers sometimes use verb moods incorrectly. For example, writers may shift improperly between the **indicative** and the **imperative**.

> **Incorrect:** Travelers <u>must be</u> cautious and <u>don't get</u> lost!
> **Correct:** Travelers <u>must be</u> cautious and <u>not get</u> lost.

Writers sometimes use **indicative** when they should use **subjunctive**.

> **Incorrect:** If I <u>was</u> Nhamo, I would be sad.
> **Correct:** If I <u>were</u> Nhamo, I would be sad.

Work with your group to rewrite each sentence correctly.

1. If Musoni was younger, he **would understand Nhamo better**.

2. Sons should listen to their fathers and don't talk back!

74 UNIT 1 • RITES OF PASSAGE

PERSONALIZE FOR LEARNING

English Language Support
Verb Moods Have English Learners identify and use verb moods in their speaking and writing. When students find models of the verbs, have them read the sentences aloud to hear how each one sounds.

Ask student pairs to work together to find examples of each verb mood type in "The Setting Sun and the Rolling World." **EMERGING**

Ask students to use the different verb moods to describe the plot of the text. **EXPANDING**

Ask students to consider how Old Musoni and Nhamo each feels about home and the wider world. Then ask students to write a comparison of their views using the different verb moods. They may use sentences from the text as necessary. **BRIDGING**

EFFECTIVE EXPRESSION

Research

Assignment

Deepen your understanding of the story by conducting research on Zimbabwean culture and writing an **informational report**. With your group, choose one of the following topics.

☐ In the story, Old Musoni tells his son to see Chiremba, a traditional Zimbabwean healer. Conduct research, and write an informational report about **Zimbabwean healers.** Conclude your report by explaining whether you think Nhamo's rejection of this traditional aspect of his culture is justified.

☐ Conduct research to learn more about **traditional family life in Zimbabwe.** Then, write an informational report in which you describe the customs and traditions. Conclude your report by explaining the ways in which your research increased your understanding of the perspectives of Old Musoni and Nhamo.

Project Plan Using effective search terms, find multiple print and digital sources of information for your report. Make sure to evaluate each of your sources for credibility and accuracy. With your group, use the following checklist to evaluate your sources.

Does the source go into enough depth to cover the subject?	☐ yes	☐ no
Does the publisher have a good reputation?	☐ yes	☐ no
Is the author an authority on the subject?	☐ yes	☐ no
Do at least two other sources agree with this source?	☐ yes	☐ no
Is the information current? (Check publication date or date it was posted.)	☐ yes	☐ no

📝 **EVIDENCE LOG**

Before moving on to a new selection, go to your Evidence Log, and record what you learned from "The Setting Sun and the Rolling World."

Once you have found valid sources, use the facts they provide to develop your report. Paraphrase information and properly credit your sources to avoid plagiarism. Follow a standard format to cite your sources.

Work with your group to organize the information you have found and to create a final draft of your informational report.

DIGITAL PERSPECTIVES

Research

Point out to students that as they begin to conduct their research, they may start with a background source, such as an encyclopedia article, to get an overview of the topic. As they continue, they will want to use a variety of other sources. Remind students that primary sources are first-hand original accounts such as interview transcripts or letters. Secondary resources are accounts that analyze events.

Project Plan Remind groups to consult the schedule for Small-Group Activities as they create their Project Plan. Students should make sure each group member has made assignments, and that the work is divided evenly among group members.

The chart will help groups evaluate their possible sources. Point out that groups will have a stronger presentation if they use sources that are clearly credible. For more support, see **Research: Informational Report.**

Evidence Log Support students in completing their Evidence Log. This paced activity will help prepare them for the Performance-Based Assessment at the end of the unit.

FORMATIVE ASSESSMENT

Research

If students have difficulty researching a topic, **then** have them work with their group to review effective search terms. For Reteach and Practice, see **Research: Informational Report (RP).**

Selection Test

Administer the "The Setting Sun and Rolling World" Selection Test, which is available in both print and digital formats online in Assessments.

PERSONALIZE FOR LEARNING

Strategic Support

Informational Report Help students find trustworthy online sources for their research by pointing out the following information about the last three letters of an Internet URL, which identify the domain of the site.

- **.gov:** Government sites are sponsored by a branch of the United States federal government and are considered reliable.
- **.edu:** Information from an educational research center or department is likely to be carefully checked but may also include student pages that are not edited or monitored.
- **.org:** Groups with organization domains are nonprofit groups. Nonprofit groups usually maintain a high standard of credibility, but their content may reflect strong biases.
- **.com:** Commercial sites exist to make a profit. Information might be biased. The purpose of a commercial site may not align with a student's research purpose, either. For example, a site may provide parody or satire, or it might aim to sell a product or service.

FACILITATING

Present a Nonfiction Narrative

Before groups begin work on their projects, have them clearly differentiate the role each group member will play. Remind groups to consult the schedule for Small-Group Learning to guide their work during the Performance Task.

Students should complete the assignment using presentation software to take advantage of text, graphics, and sound features.

Plan With Your Group

Analyze the Texts Remind students that they are not limited by the rites of passage featured in the selections. If students are having trouble identifying rites of passage that they have experienced, have them brainstorm for ideas, thinking about responsibilities and new experiences children and teenagers may have, such as baby sitting, caring for a family pet, enduring the death of a family member, learning to ride a bike, or starting middle school. Students can use this list as a jumping-off point for thinking about their own rites of passage.

Gather Evidence and Media Examples Suggest that groups brainstorm not only for the types of visuals to use but also for ideas about *where* to find these visuals. If students have trouble identifying potential sources of visuals, suggest possibilities such as stock image search engines, magazines, and their own personal photo collections.

PERFORMANCE TASK: SPEAKING AND LISTENING FOCUS

SOURCES
- YOU ARE THE ELECTRIC BOOGALOO
- JUST BE YOURSELF!
- HANGING FIRE
- TRANSLATING GRANDFATHER'S HOUSE
- THE SETTING SUN AND THE ROLLING WORLD

Present Nonfiction Narratives

Assignment
You have read about characters facing different milestones on the path to growing up. Work with your group to create a **series of nonfiction narratives** about rites of passage to present to the class. Use the following prompt to guide you as you develop your presentation:

> What defines an event or experience in a young person's life as a milestone or rite of passage?

Plan With Your Group

Analyze the Texts With your group, discuss the various milestones that characters in the selections face. Use the chart to list your ideas. For each selection, identify the rite of passage that the main character undergoes and why it is important to the character's growth. Talk more generally about rites of passage that you or people you know have undergone, and identify how the event or experience has helped each person on the road to maturity. Then, have each group member select a different type of rite of passage, such as a journey or ritual, to focus on in the presentation. You may choose a rite of passage explored in one of the selections or one from a different experience.

TITLE	RITE OF PASSAGE
You Are the Electric Boogaloo	
Just Be Yourself!	
Hanging Fire	
Translating Grandfather's House	
The Setting Sun and the Rolling World	
Your Rite of Passage:	

Gather Evidence and Media Examples Review the selections and your notes to determine what information is relevant to your presentation. Then, discuss multimedia, such as illustrations and audio, that you can use to enhance your presentation.

STANDARDS
Speaking and Listening
- Present claims and findings, emphasizing salient points in a focused, coherent manner with relevant evidence, sound valid reasoning, and well-chosen details; use appropriate eye contact, adequate volume, and clear pronunciation.
- Integrate multimedia and visual displays into presentations to clarify information, strengthen claims and evidence, and add interest.

AUTHOR'S PERSPECTIVE — Ernest Morrell, Ph.D.

How to Package a Speech/Oral Presentation The small-group speaking and listening activity will help students learn how to engage an audience during a presentation. This is important for students as they prepare for careers, public service, and higher education. Help students learn to become better speakers by reminding them to ask themselves these questions as they practice and rehearse their speeches and oral presentation:

- **Posture:** Does my posture convey authority and ease? Do I look relaxed and comfortable as I'm presenting?
- **Body Language:** How do I connect physically with my audience? For instance, do I make eye contact, lean forward at key points to show emphasis, and use appropriate gestures?
- **Voice:** Am I changing my voice by varying my pitch and volume to show emotion and convey meaning? Does my voice project to the back rows?
- **Humor:** How do I add humor when it suits my audience and purpose? Do I tell jokes or anecdotes, for instance?
- **Tone:** Do I speak with passion to engage my audience? Remind students that the way they present their information is often just as important as what they are saying.

ESSENTIAL QUESTION: What are some milestones on the path to growing up?

Draft and Organize Work individually to craft a brief nonfiction narrative for the rite of passage you chose. Make sure that your narrative has an introduction, a clear sequence of events, and a meaningful conclusion. Then, work as a group to sequence your individual narratives into a cohesive whole for your presentation. Finally, add multimedia to highlight important points and add interest.

Rehearse With Your Group

Practice With Your Group As you prepare to deliver your presentation, use this checklist to evaluate the effectiveness of your group's rehearsal. Then, use your evaluation and the instructions here to guide your revision.

CONTENT	USE OF MEDIA	PRESENTATION TECHNIQUES
☐ Each narrative has an introduction, a clear sequence of events, and a meaningful conclusion.	☐ Multimedia highlights the main points in the presentation.	☐ The speaker makes eye contact and speaks clearly.
☐ Individual narratives are sequenced to create a cohesive presentation.	☐ Multimedia adds interest to the presentation.	

Fine-Tune the Content To make your narrative stronger, you may need to work on the sequence of events to make sure that the importance of your rite of passage is clear. Work as a group to identify ideas that may be unclear, and revise these sections by rewording them or adding clarifying information.

Improve Your Use of Media Double-check that your multimedia elements are effective and that they add to the narrative. If any element is not helpful to your presentation, work to replace it with a more useful item.

Brush Up on Your Presentation Techniques Practice a few times with your group before you deliver your narratives to a wider audience. Make sure that you make eye contact and pronounce words correctly.

Present and Evaluate

When you present as a group, be sure that each member has taken into account each of the checklist items. As you watch other groups, evaluate how well their presentations meet the checklist criteria.

Performance Task: Present Nonfiction Narratives 77

PERSONALIZE FOR LEARNING

Strategic Support
Order of Events If some students have trouble organizing the events in their narrative sequentially, have pairs of students work together to support each other. One student can retell his or her narrative, and the second student can ask about the order of events. For example, pairs can work on asking each other what happened *first, next, later, last,* and so on. Students can write down each other's answers. Then, the pairs can use these notes and work together to build a timeline of the events in their narratives.

DIGITAL PERSPECTIVES

Draft and Organize Encourage students to develop their own portion of the presentation and then support groups as they prepare a full presentation. Students may want to consider the best order of the individual narratives, building from formal to informal, moving humorous to more serious, or following another organizational path that makes sense.

Encourage students to think about formal rites of passage that they know about from their own, or someone else's culture.

Rehearse With Your Group

Practice With Your Group Emphasize to students the importance of practicing presentations ahead of time. Rehearsing will help with the timing and flow of the presentation, and it will give students an opportunity to receive and incorporate feedback from their peers. It can also reveal any technical problems that may need to be resolved.

Fine-Tune the Content Suggest that students go point by point for clarity.

Improve Your Use of Media Suggest that students return to their original notes if they need to replace any of their visuals. They may find that one of their original ideas will work better.

Brush Up on Your Presentation Techniques Suggest that pairs record each other's presentations and then watch the recordings together as a way of rehearsing and then identifying problem areas.

Present and Evaluate

Before beginning the presentations, set the expectations for the audience. You may wish to have students consider these questions as speakers present.

- What was the speaker's rite of passage?
- What did the speaker learn from his or her rite of passage?
- How did the speaker connect his or her rite of passage with ideas from the texts?
- How did the speaker's use of media support his or her message?
- What presentation skills did the speaker use?

Small-Group Learning 77

OVERVIEW

INDEPENDENT LEARNING

What are some milestones on the path to growing up?

Encourage students to think carefully about what they have already learned and what more they want to know about the unit topic of rites of passage. This is a key first step to previewing and selecting the text they will read in Independent Learning.

Independent Learning Strategies

Review the Learning Strategies with students and explain that as they work through Independent Learning, they will develop strategies to work on their own.

- Have students watch the video on Independent Learning Strategies.
- A video on this topic is available online in the Professional Development Center.

Students should include any favorite strategies that they might have devised on their own during Whole-Class and Small-Group Learning. For example, for the strategy "Take notes," students might include:

- When reviewing your notes as a study strategy, use highlighters or colored pencils to categorize information.
- If you are unsure about the meaning of something, ask questions to clarify.

Block Scheduling

Each day in this Pacing Plan represents a 40- to 50-minute class period. Teachers using block scheduling may combine days to reflect their class schedule. In addition, teachers may revise pacing to differentiate and support core instruction by integrating components and resources as students require.

Pacing Plan

OVERVIEW: INDEPENDENT LEARNING

ESSENTIAL QUESTION:

What are some milestones on the path to growing up?

There are many different kinds of events and experiences in a young person's life that can be thought of as milestones. What makes an event or experience a milestone? Why are milestones important in our lives? In this section, you will complete your study of major events on the path to adulthood by exploring an additional selection related to the topic. You'll then share what you learn with classmates. To choose a text, follow these steps.

Look Back Think about the selections you have already read. What more do you want to know about the topic of rites of passage?

Look Ahead Preview the selections by reading the descriptions. Which one seems most interesting and appealing to you?

Look Inside Take a few minutes to scan through the text you chose. Make another selection if this text doesn't meet your needs.

Independent Learning Strategies

Throughout your life, in school, in your community, and in your career, you will need to rely on yourself to learn and work on your own. Review these strategies and the actions you can take to practice them during Independent Learning. Add ideas of your own for each category.

STRATEGY	ACTION PLAN
Create a schedule	• Understand your goals and deadlines. • Make a plan for what to do each day. •
Practice what you've learned	• Use first-read and close-read strategies to deepen your understanding. • Evaluate the usefulness of the evidence to help you understand the topic. • Consider the quality and reliability of the source. •
Take notes	• Record important ideas and information. • Review your notes before preparing to share with a group. •

SCAN FOR MULTIMEDIA

78 UNIT 1 • RITES OF PASSAGE

Choose one selection. Selections are available online only.

CONTENTS

MEMOIR

Cub Pilot on the Mississippi
Mark Twain

Tempers flare between sailors on the Mississippi River.

AUTOBIOGRAPHY

from I Know Why the Caged Bird Sings
Maya Angelou

When someone recognizes the potential in an ordinary girl, she begins to see things, and herself, differently.

NEWS ARTICLE

Quinceañera Birthday Bash Preserves Tradition, Marks Passage to Womanhood
Natalie St. John

For a Latina girl, her Quinceañera is a celebration to anticipate and treasure.

REFLECTIVE ESSAY

Childhood and Poetry
Pablo Neruda

A mysterious exchange of toys connects two children.

SHORT STORY

The Winter Hibiscus
Minfong Ho

Passing the driver's test is a daunting task for any teenager. For Saeng, it's a chance to turn her life around.

PERFORMANCE-BASED ASSESSMENT PREP

Review Evidence for a Nonfiction Narrative
Complete your Evidence Log for the unit by evaluating what you have learned and synthesizing the information you have recorded.

SCAN FOR MULTIMEDIA

Overview: Independent Learning 79

DIGITAL PERSPECTIVES

Contents

Selections Encourage students to scan and preview the selections before choosing the one they would like to read. Suggest that they consider the genre and subject matter of each one before making their decision. You can use the information on the following planning pages to advise students in making their choice.

> Remind students that the selections for Independent Learning are only available in the Interactive Student Edition of *my*Perspectives. Allow students who do not have digital access at home to preview the digital selections using classroom or computer lab technology. Then either have students print the selection they choose or provide a printout for them.

Performance Based-Assessment Prep
Review Evidence for a Nonfiction Narrative Point out to students that collecting evidence during Independent Learning is the last step in completing their Evidence Log. After they finish their independent reading, they will synthesize all the evidence they have compiled in the unit.

The evidence students collect will serve as the primary source of information they will use to complete the writing and oral presentation for the Performance-Based Assessment at the end of the unit.

Independent Learning 79

PLANNING   INDEPENDENT LEARNING

SELECTION RESOURCES
- First-Read Guide: Nonfiction
- Close-Read Guide: Nonfiction
- Cub Pilot on the Mississippi: Text Questions
- Audio Summaries
- Selection Audio
- Selection Test

Cub Pilot on the Mississippi

Summary
In this memoir excerpt, "Cub Pilot on the Mississippi," Mark Twain recalls his time on a steamboat crew. He remembers his time as a great source of life experience despite its difficulties. In this part of the memoir, Twain has to deal with a superior named Brown, who treated the young Twain badly. He gets used to Brown's unfair treatment but ultimately ends up hitting him in anger. This was an immensely foolish and risky thing to do. Could he escape the consequences?

Insight
Violence in the workplace is an extremely bad idea, and that's even more true today than it was in Twain's time. Yet more abstractly, it's very tempting to rebel against unfair treatment. Twain ultimately doesn't end up in trouble because Brown is so disliked among the rest of the crew.

Connection to Essential Question
This text can help students answer the Essential Question, *What are some milestones on the path to growing up?* Young Twain has a common experience when he struggles to learn how to get along with a powerful boss.

Connection to Performance-Based Assessment
In this unit, students consider this prompt: "Drawing on your own experiences, what do you think is the most important rite of passage in a young person's life?" This text might encourage students an opportunity to think about similar challenges in their own life, and ask: *When do you take a risk and stand up for yourself?*

Text Complexity Rubric: Cub Pilot on the Mississippi

Quantitative Measures

Lexile: 890   Text Length: 3,192 words

Qualitative Measures

Knowledge Demands ①—②—③—**④**—⑤	Text explores sophisticated themes. Experiences depicted involve steamboat piloting before the Civil War—this may require background knowledge for most readers.
Structure ①—②—③—**④**—⑤	First person narrative. Story is told chronologically but has intricate storyline, detail, and dense text; dialogue breaks up text at various points in story.
Language Conventionality and Clarity ①—②—③—**④**—⑤	Language is nonconventional, with much archaic and unfamiliar syntax and vocabulary. Dialogue has slang and incorrect grammar as part of style.
Levels of Meaning/Purpose ①—②—③—**④**—⑤	Multiple ambiguous levels of meaning revealed throughout the text.

80A   UNIT 1 • RITES OF PASSAGE

DIGITAL PERSPECTIVES

Audio | Video | Document | Annotation Highlights | EL Highlights | Online Assessment

from *I Know Why the Caged Bird Sings*

Summary

This is an excerpt from a memoir, *I Know Why the Caged Bird Sings*, written by Maya Angelou in 1969. In this chapter, she talks about her childhood around a store her family owned. An important turning point in young Angelou's life was a visit with Mrs. Flowers, a local lady who frequented the store. Mrs. Flowers encouraged her to read, asked her to memorize a poem, and gave her excellent life advice.

Insight

Angelou receives advice from an unexpected source, and this has a big impact on her future life. Her closing note reminds readers that being respected for herself rather than for her family ties made a great difference to her.

Connection to Essential Question

It is clear that Angelou was shaped both by her life around the store and by her visit with Mrs. Flowers. Having someone take an interest can be a very important moment in a young person's life. The memoir provides students with several answers to the Essential Question: *What are some milestones on the path to growing up?*

Connection to Performance-Based Assessment

The prompt for this unit is "Drawing on your own experiences, what do you think is the most important rite of passage in a young person's life?" The text might help students see that spending time with a mentor can be a great moment in a young life. While Mrs. Flowers helps Angelou seemingly spontaneously, the courage to seek out someone for advice can be enormously helpful.

SELECTION RESOURCES

- First-Read Guide: Nonfiction
- Close-Read Guide: Nonfiction
- I Know Why the Caged Bird Sings: Text Questions
- Audio Summaries
- Selection Audio
- Selection Test

Text Complexity Rubric: *from I Know Why the Caged Bird Sings*

Quantitative Measures

Lexile: 1030   Text Length: 2,301 words

Qualitative Measures

Knowledge Demands ①—②—③—**④**—⑤	Memoir depicts experiences that may not be common to some readers. Text may require background knowledge about rural life in the segregated South in the 1930s.
Structure ①—②—**③**—④—⑤	Personal narrative structure. Story is told chronologically, but storyline has plot with character description and reflection. Text includes some dialogue.
Language Conventionality and Clarity ①—②—**③**—④—⑤	Language is descriptive, poetic, and sometimes figurative; some sentences are complex with multiple clauses. Vocabulary is contemporary and familiar.
Levels of Meaning/Purpose ①—②—**③**—④—⑤	Multiple levels of meaning are revealed over entirety of the text; reader needs to infer meaning based on characters' interactions.

Independent Learning   80B

PLANNING   INDEPENDENT LEARNING

SELECTION RESOURCES

- First-Read Guide: Nonfiction
- Close-Read Guide: Nonfiction
- Quinceañera Birthday Bash Preserves Tradition: Text Questions
- Audio Summaries
- Selection Audio
- Selection Test

Quinceañera Birthday Bash Preserves Tradition, Marks Passage to Womanhood

Summary

In the news article "Quinceañera Birthday Bash Preserves Tradition, Marks Passage to Womanhood," reporter Natalie St. John describes both the quinceañera of one girl in her community and the quinceañera tradition more generally. This fifteenth birthday celebration is a combination of a spiritual milestone and a public party. It is particularly important in Hispanic communities, both in the U.S. and in Latin America. Often an expensive event, the quinceañera marks the passage from youth to adulthood. The party isn't only about the girl celebrating. It can also mark the whole family's progress and show that they can afford an extravagant party.

Insight

This article will help students gain insight into an important cultural practice, as seen from an outsider's perspective. The article may seem to laud the high spending that sometimes happens. However, the event is important in its symbolism around growing up.

Connection to Essential Question

This article provides a cultural response to the Essential Question *What are some milestones on the path to growing up?* Students should be able to make a connection to similar ceremonies popular in other cultures.

Connection to Performance-Based Assessment

The prompt for this unit is "Drawing on your own experiences, what do you think is the most important rite of passage in a young person's life?" The text might help students see that culturally recognized rites of passage have meaning to the adolescent, the family, and the community.

Text Complexity Rubric: Quinceañera Birthday Bash Preserves Tradition, Marks Passage to Womanhood

Quantitative Measures

Lexile: 1290   Text Length: 1,273 words

Qualitative Measures

Knowledge Demands ①—②—❸—④—⑤	Readers from Mexican or Latin American backgrounds or those who know families from these places may be more familiar with the traditions of the quinceañera.
Structure ①—②—❸—④—⑤	Selection alternates between general information about quinceañeras and description of a specific event. Information is presently clearly and logically.
Language Conventionality and Clarity ①—②—③—❹—⑤	Language is clear, written in a journalistic style, but many sentences have complex constructions and multiple clauses. Vocabulary is mostly on-level, with some more difficult words.
Levels of Meaning/Purpose ①—②—❸—④—⑤	The article explores the tradition of the quinceañera. Purpose is clear and easy to identify based on the descriptions and context.

UNIT 1 • RITES OF PASSAGE

| DIGITAL PERSPECTIVES | Audio | Video | Document | Annotation Highlights | EL Highlights | Online Assessment |

Childhood and Poetry

Summary

"Childhood and Poetry," an excerpt from Pablo Neruda's autobiography, describes an incident from his childhood in Chile that leads him to reflect on its long-term power. As a child, he explores the backyard of his house, and through a hole in a fence, he sees the hand of a boy his own age. He is handed a small toy sheep, and he in return hands the unknown child a pinecone. He never saw the boy again, but he made an important realization. The gift let him see a connection among the people of the world. In his adult life, his poems became the gifts he shared with others.

Insight

Neruda's deeply humane poetry—and his life in politics—can be seen as outgrowths from this simple act of sharing. Reading this selection will help students gain insight into how small acts of compassion can lead to larger ones.

SELECTION RESOURCES

- First-Read Guide: Nonfiction
- Close-Read Guide: Nonfiction
- Childhood and Poetry: Text Questions
- Audio Summaries
- Selection Audio
- Selection Test

Connection to Essential Question

This incident is a charming example of an event that changed a young life. It gives a sweet and personal example of what the Essential Question—*What are some milestones on the path to growing up?*—asks us to consider.

Connection to Performance-Based Assessment

The prompt for this unit is "Drawing on your own experiences, what do you think is the most important rite of passage in a young person's life?" The event described in Neruda's text is unique and personal. Students may consider whether events like this or events everyone goes through have a greater impact on the adults young children become.

Text Complexity Rubric: Childhood and Poetry

Quantitative Measures

Lexile: 910   Text Length: 491 words

Qualitative Measures

Knowledge Demands (4 of 5)	Text explores themes of humanity, communication, and intimacy among people. Concepts are sophisticated and ideas are abstract.
Structure (3 of 5)	Text is a first-person narrative. It is a reflection of a past event mixed with reflections on its meaning.
Language Conventionality and Clarity (4 of 5)	Language is fairly complex and has some poetic, descriptive, and figurative phrases. Some vocabulary may be difficult; some sentences are simple, but others are complex with multiple clauses.
Levels of Meaning/Purpose (4 of 5)	Narrative is reflective and requires readers to understand the writer's generalizations, which spring from a single incident.

Independent Learning   80D

PLANNING   INDEPENDENT LEARNING

SELECTION RESOURCES

- First-Read Guide: Fiction
- Close-Read Guide: Fiction
- The Winter Hibiscus: Text Questions
- Audio Summaries
- Selection Audio
- Selection Test

The Winter Hibiscus

Summary
"The Winter Hibiscus," a short story by Minfong Ho, tells the story of an important day in the life of a teenage girl named Saeng. She is an immigrant from Laos whose family has made many sacrifices to get to America. On this day, Saeng prepares to take her driving test. David, the American son of a family friend, drives her to the test. To thank him, her mother had given her money to take him out for a burger later. When she fails the test, David drops her off before she can invite him for a meal. On her way home, she stops in a flower shop and spends the money on a plant that reminds her of her home in Laos. At home, her mother is at first surprised by the purchase, but she helps her plant it, and they look forward to the spring.

Insight
Though Saeng fails the test and doesn't use the money as her mother asks, her mother understands and supports her need to comfort herself by buying the plant. Readers may see the winter hibiscus itself as a symbol: it reminds Saeng of her childhood but is adapted to the cold of her new home. She plants it in American soil in much the same way she'd like to become better-rooted in America.

Connection to Essential Question
The Essential Question for this unit is *What are some milestones on the path to growing up?* The driving test is an obvious one, but it is not the only milestone in this story. Saeng also struggles to fit in and feel confident in her transplanted life.

Connection to Performance-Based Assessment
The prompt for this unit is "Drawing on your own experiences, what do you think is the most important rite of passage in a young person's life?" Saeng's high school experiences, full of tests and the challenge of making friends and fitting in, are typical of many young people's experiences.

Text Complexity Rubric: The Winter Hibiscus

Quantitative Measures

Lexile: 990   Text Length: 5,744 words

Qualitative Measures

Knowledge Demands ①—②—**③**—④—⑤	Specific references to Laotian culture and adjustment to the United States may not be common, but story reflects adolescent anxieties that will be common to students.
Structure ①—②—**③**—④—⑤	Story is told chronologically, with some event plots mixed with reflections and memory. Dialogue is used in many places and breaks up text.
Language Conventionality and Clarity ①—②—**③**—④—⑤	Rich, descriptive, poetic language includes some lengthy, complex sentences. Vocabulary is mostly on-level. Some Laotian is included, which can be mostly understood from context of dialogue.
Levels of Meaning/Purpose ①—②—**③**—④—⑤	Multiple levels of meaning are clear and easy to identify, but meaning sometimes needs to be inferred by characters' actions and dialogue. Symbolism is used throughout.

DIGITAL PERSPECTIVES

Audio Video Document Annotation Highlights EL Highlights Online Assessment

MY NOTES

ADVISING

You may wish to direct students to use the generic **First-Read** and **Close-Read Guides** in the Print Student Edition. Alternatively, you may wish to print copies of the genre-specific **First-Read** and **Close-Read Guides** for students. These are available online in the Interactive Student Edition or Unit Resources.

FIRST READ

Students should perform the steps of the first read independently:

NOTICE: Students should focus on the basic elements of the text to ensure they understand what is happening.

ANNOTATE: Students should mark any passages they wish to revisit during their close read.

CONNECT: Students should increase their understanding by connecting what they've read to other texts or personal experiences.

RESPOND: Students will write a summary to demonstrate their understanding.

Point out to students that while they will always complete the Respond step at the end of the first read, the other steps will probably happen somewhat concurrently. Remind students that they will revisit their first-read annotations during the close read.

After students have completed the First-Read Guide, you may wish to assign the Text Questions for the selection that are available in the Interactive Teacher's Edition.

Anchor Standards

In the first two sections of the unit, students worked with the whole class and in small groups to gain topical knowledge and greater understanding of the skills required by the anchor standards. In this section, they are asked to work independently, applying what they have learned and demonstrating increased readiness for college and career.

INDEPENDENT LEARNING

First-Read Guide

 Tool Kit
First-Read Guide and Model Annotation

Use this page to record your first-read ideas.

Selection Title: _____

NOTICE new information or ideas you learned about the unit topic as you first read this text.

ANNOTATE by marking vocabulary and key passages you want to revisit.

CONNECT ideas within the selection to other knowledge and the selections you have read.

RESPOND by writing a brief summary of the selection.

STANDARD
Reading Read and comprehend complex literary and informational texts independently and proficiently.

PERSONALIZE FOR LEARNING

English Language Support
Skim, Predict, and Use KWL Chart Use the Text Complexity Rubrics to help individual students select a text appropriate for their English proficiency level.

Help students identify the genre of the selection they chose. Then have them skim the selection to notice text features, such as headings or visuals. They can also look for quotation marks and words that stand out to them. Explain to students that when they skim, they should focus on understanding the general idea and should not stop to figure out unfamiliar words.

Next, have students work with a partner to predict what their selection will be about. Instruct them to ask and answer *Wh-* questions. Provide sample question frames such as *What _____? Who _____? How _____?* Finally, help partners complete a KWL chart to note what they already know about the topic and what they want to learn, and then after their first read, what they learned. Use these heads in a three-column chart:

Know   Want to Know   Learned
ALL LEVELS

ESSENTIAL QUESTION: What are some milestones on the path to growing up?

Close-Read Guide

Use this page to record your close-read ideas.

🔧 **Tool Kit**
Close-Read Guide and Model Annotation

Selection Title: _____

Close Read the Text

Revisit sections of the text you marked during your first read. Read these sections closely and **annotate** what you notice. Ask yourself **questions** about the text. What can you **conclude**? Write down your ideas.

Analyze the Text

Think about the author's choices of patterns, structure, techniques, and ideas included in the text. Select one, and record your thoughts about what this choice conveys.

QuickWrite

Pick a paragraph from the text that grabbed your interest. Explain the power of this passage.

▦ **STANDARD**
Reading Read and comprehend complex literary and informational texts independently and proficiently.

Independent Learning **81**

DIGITAL PERSPECTIVES

🔴 CLOSE READ

Students should begin their close read by revisiting the annotations they made during their first read. Then, students should analyze one of the author's choices regarding the following elements:

- **patterns,** such as repetition or parallelism
- **structure,** such as cause-and-effect or problem-solution
- **techniques,** such as description or dialogue
- **ideas,** such as the author's main idea or claim

MAKE IT INTERACTIVE
Group students according to the selection they have chosen. Then, have students meet to discuss the selection in depth. Their discussions should be guided by their insights and questions.

PERSONALIZE FOR LEARNING

English Language Support
Read Aloud and Confirm Predictions Pair students or put them in groups so they can take turns reading aloud to one another. Each student can read one paragraph, or you can split up the text in any other way that makes sense. For example, for a short story, you may wish to assign different characters and the role of the narrator to individual students to take turns reading aloud.

Have students make predictions as they listen, and then have partners or groups discuss, compare, and confirm the predictions they made. Ask: *Did anything surprise you? Were any predictions correct? Which ones?* Finally, have partners or groups work together to add more details about what they learned to the Close Read the Text box on their Close-Read Guide. **ALL LEVELS**

Independent Learning **81**

ADVISING

Share Your Independent Learning

Prepare to Share
Explain to students that sharing what they learned from their Independent Learning selection provides classmates who read a different selection with an opportunity to consider the text as a source of evidence during the Performance-Based Assessment. As students prepare to share, remind them to highlight how their selection contributed to their knowledge of the concept of rites of passage as well as how the selection connects to the question *What are some milestones on the path to growing up?*

Learn From Your Classmates
As students discuss the Independent Learning selections, direct them to take particular note of how their classmates' chosen selections align with their current position on the Performance-Based Assessment question.

Reflect
Students may want to add their reflection to their Evidence Log, particularly if their insight relates to a specific selection from the unit.

MAKE IT INTERACTIVE
Have groups of students discuss and share their reflections. Challenge each group to try to come up with a general insight—one that covers or includes the main insight of each student. Then have a representative from each group present the group's insight to the class. Can students think of an even more general insight, one that encompasses what each group shared?

INDEPENDENT LEARNING

EVIDENCE LOG
Go to your Evidence Log and record what you learned from the text you read.

Share Your Independent Learning

Prepare to Share
What are some milestones on the path to growing up?

Even when you read something independently, your understanding continues to grow by sharing what you've learned with others. Reflect on the text you explored independently and write notes about its connection to the unit. In your notes, consider why this text belongs in this unit.

Learn From Your Classmates
Discuss It Share your ideas about the text you explored on your own. As you talk with others in your class, jot down ideas that you learn from them.

Reflect
Review your notes, and underline the most important insight you gained from these writing and discussion activities. Explain how this idea adds to your understanding of the topic.

STANDARDS
Speaking and Listening
Engage effectively in a range of collaborative discussions with diverse partners on *grade 8 topics, texts, and issues*, building on others' ideas and expressing their own clearly.

AUTHOR'S PERSPECTIVE — Ernest Morrell, Ph.D.

Learning From Others Independent Learning helps students build vocabulary, background knowledge, and fluency. Teach students how to learn from each other by modeling how to ask clarifying questions when other students are sharing their experiences. Questions like these can guide the discussion:

- Why did you choose this text? For example, did the topic interest you? Have you heard of the author or read anything else by the author?
- For narrative text: What is the problem in the story? When and where does the story take place? Why?
- For nonfiction text: How is the information organized? What is the most interesting thing you've learned so far?
- What parts of the text do you think were most important? Why?
- Did the text meet your expectations? Why or why not? Would you recommend this text to a classmate? Explain your answer.
- How does the text relate to other texts you have read on this subject? How does it relate to your life?

PERFORMANCE-BASED ASSESSMENT PREP

Review Evidence for a Nonfiction Narrative

At the beginning of this unit you identified evidence and examples to support the following question:

> What rite of passage has held the most significance for you or for a person you know well?

EVIDENCE LOG

Review your Evidence Log and your QuickWrite from the beginning of the unit. Did you learn anything new?

NOTES

Identify three details that most interested you about rites of passage in a young person's life.

1.

2.

3.

Identify a real-life experience that illustrates one of your ideas about a life-changing rite of passage you experienced or know about.

_____

Develop your thoughts into an introduction for a nonfiction narrative. Complete this sentence starter:
An example of a life-changing milestone or rite of passage in a person's life is

_____

_____

Evaluate the Strength of Your Evidence Consider your point of view. How did the texts you read impact your point of view?

STANDARDS
Writing
Write narratives to develop real or imagined experiences or events using effective technique, relevant descriptive details, and well-structured event sequences.

DIGITAL PERSPECTIVES

Review Evidence for a Nonfiction Narrative

Evidence Log Students should focus on a rite of passage that is especially important to them or to someone else.

Evaluate the Strength of Your Evidence
Remind students that there are many kinds of evidence they can use to support their points of view, including:
- personal and family experience
- anecdotes
- nonfiction texts and media
- fiction texts and media

Students should be able to evaluate the reliability of their evidence. Discuss the characteristics of credible evidence:
- personal memories confirmed by others
- credibility of references
- expert background or experience of authors

ASSESSING

Writing to Sources: Nonfiction Narrative

Students should complete the Performance-Based Assessment independently, with little to no input or feedback during the process. Students should use word processing software to take advantage of editing tools and features.

Prior to beginning the assessment, ask students to think about the various characters and people they have read about and how those experiences may relate to their own experience (or that of someone else). Have them reflect on which ones underwent true rites of passage and how these experiences affected each one.

Reread the Assignment Encourage students to make sure they are clear about what is being asked of them.

Review the Elements of Nonfiction Narrative Students can review the work they did earlier in the unit as they complete the Performance-Based Assessment. They may also consult other resources such as:

- the elements of an effective nonfiction narrative, including characters, a sequence of events, narrative techniques, transitions, precise words, and a satisfying conclusion, as well as how to organize a nonfiction narrative, available in Whole-Class Learning
- their Evidence Log
- their Word Network

PERFORMANCE-BASED ASSESSMENT

SOURCES
- WHOLE-CLASS SELECTIONS
- SMALL-GROUP SELECTIONS
- INDEPENDENT-LEARNING SELECTION

WORD NETWORK
As you write and revise your nonfiction narrative, use your Word Network to help vary your word choices.

STANDARDS

Writing
- Write narratives to develop real or imagined experiences or events using effective technique, relevant descriptive details, and well-structured event sequences.
- Produce clear and coherent writing in which the development, organization, and style are appropriate to task, purpose, and audience.
- Write routinely over extended time frames and shorter time frames for a range of discipline-specific tasks, purposes, and audiences.

PART 1
Writing to Sources: Nonfiction Narrative

In this unit, you read about various fictional characters and real-life people and their rites of passage. Some went through experiences that were confusing and difficult, while others felt joy at the changes in their lives.

> **Assignment**
> Write a **nonfiction narrative** in which you respond to the following prompt:
>
> What rite of passage has held the most significance for you or for a person you know well?
>
> Narrate the events leading up to and following the rite of passage. If writing about yourself, use the first-person point of view. If writing about someone else, use the third-person. Use transition words to make your narrative easy to follow, and use sensory language to convey notable experiences. Conclude with a reflection that inspires readers and shares what you have learned about rites of passage.

Reread the Assignment Review the assignment to be sure you fully understand it. The assignment may reference some of the academic words presented at the beginning of the unit. Be sure you understand each of the words here in order to complete the assignment correctly.

Academic Vocabulary

attribute	persistent	inspire
gratifying	notable	

Review the Elements of Nonfiction Narrative Before you begin writing, read the Nonfiction Narrative Rubric. Once you have completed your first draft, check it against the rubric. If one or more of the elements are missing or not as strong as they could be, revise your essay to add or strengthen those components.

AUTHOR'S PERSPECTIVE Kelly Gallagher, M. Ed.

Building a Writing Portfolio with Students Teachers can create a portfolio that enables students to demonstrate the variety of writing they complete over the year. There are three elements of keeping a portfolio: collection of all the writing a student has done, selection of the best pieces, and reflection to evaluate growth.

Teachers can set the criteria using such categories as *Best Argument, Best Narrative Piece, Best Informative Piece, Best On-Demand Writing, Best Poetry, Best Blended Genre, Best Writing from Another Class, Best Model of Revision,* and *Best Single Line You Wrote This Year.* Students should also include a reflective letter at the end of the year.

To help them learn to reflect, use questions like these throughout the year:
- Where does your writing still need improvement? How will you improve?
- Reflect on a struggle you faced during this unit. How did you overcome it?
- Discuss a specific writing strategy you used and how it worked for you.

ESSENTIAL QUESTION: What are some milestones on the path to growing up?

Nonfiction Narrative Rubric

	Focus and Organization	Evidence and Elaboration	Conventions
4	The introduction is engaging and introduces the characters and situation in a way that appeals to readers. Events in the narrative progress in logical order and are linked by clear transitions. The conclusion follows from and reflects on what is related in the rest of the narrative.	The narrative includes techniques such as dialogue and description to add interest and to develop the characters and events. The narrative includes vivid adjectives, verbs, and sensory language to convey the experiences and to help the reader imagine the characters and scenes.	The narrative consistently uses standard English conventions of usage and mechanics.
3	The introduction is somewhat engaging and clearly introduces the characters and situation. Events in the narrative progress logically and are frequently linked by transition words. The conclusion follows from the rest of the narrative and provides some reflection on the experiences related in the narrative.	The narrative includes some dialogue and description to add interest and develop experiences and events. The narrative includes precise words and some sensory language to convey experiences and to describe the characters and scenes.	The narrative demonstrates accuracy in standard English conventions of usage and mechanics.
2	The introduction is not engaging but introduces the characters and situation. Events in the narrative progress somewhat logically and are sometimes linked by transition words. The conclusion adds very little to the narrative and does not provide reflection on the experiences related in the narrative.	The narrative includes some dialogue and descriptions. The words in the narrative vary between vague and precise, and some sensory language is included.	The narrative demonstrates some accuracy in standard English conventions of usage and mechanics.
1	The introduction does not introduce characters and a situation, or there is no clear introduction. The events in the narrative do not progress logically. The ideas seem disconnected and the sentences are not linked by transitional words and phrases. The conclusion does not connect to the narrative, or there is no conclusion.	Dialogue and descriptions are not included in the narrative. The narrative does not incorporate sensory language or precise words to convey experiences and to develop characters.	The narrative contains mistakes in standard English conventions of usage and mechanics.

DIGITAL PERSPECTIVES

Nonfiction Narrative Rubric

As you review the Nonfiction Narrative Rubric with students, remind them that the rubric is a resource that can guide their revisions. Students should pay particular attention to the differences between a nonfiction narrative that contains all of the required elements (a score of 3) and one that is engaging, introduces the characters and situation in a way that appeals to the readers, and includes a conclusion that reflects on and is related to the rest of the narrative (a score of 4).

- What strengths have you developed as a writer? Where are those strengths found in this portfolio?
- Where can you demonstrate in this portfolio that you have improved as a reader and as a writer?

At the end of the year, students can review these pieces to see their growth as writers.

PERSONALIZE FOR LEARNING

Strategic Support
Have students review elements of a nonfiction narrative to help them understand that the genre describes and explains real events. Guide them to understand that nonfiction narratives often are written in a sequence, or the order the events occurred. Help students craft a short nonfiction narrative that includes time-order words that describe when each event happened, such as *first, next, then,* and *finally*. Afterward, instruct them to make changes as needed as they work on their revisions.

ASSESSING

Speaking and Listening: Oral Presentation

Students should annotate their written nonfiction narrative in preparation for the oral presentation, marking the important elements (compelling introduction, characters, sequence of events, satisfying conclusion) as well as quotations and details from the selections.

Remind students that the effectiveness of an oral narrative relies on how the speaker establishes credibility with his or her audience. If a speaker comes across as confident and lively, it will be easier to engage in the audience and sustain their interest.

Review the Rubric As you review the Oral Presentation Rubric with students, remind them that it is a valuable tool that can help them plan their presentation. They should strive to include all of the criteria required to achieve a score of 3. Draw their attention to some of the subtle differences between scores of 2 and 3.

PERFORMANCE-BASED ASSESSMENT

PART 2
Speaking and Listening: Oral Presentation

Assignment
After completing the final draft of your nonfiction narrative, use it as the foundation for a brief **oral presentation**.

Do not simply read your narrative aloud. Take the following steps to make your presentation lively and engaging.

- Review your narrative, and annotate the main parts of the story and the parts that provide reflection on the experiences you are describing.
- Refer to the annotations to guide your presentation.
- Choose visuals that add interest to your presentation.
- Maintain eye contact with your audience. Make sure to speak loud enough for people to hear you, and pronounce words clearly.

Review the Rubric The criteria by which your nonfiction narrative will be evaluated appear in the rubric. Review these criteria before presenting to ensure that you are prepared.

STANDARDS
Speaking and Listening
- Present claims and findings, emphasizing salient points in a focused, coherent manner with relevant evidence, sound valid reasoning, and well-chosen details; use appropriate eye contact, adequate volume, and clear pronunciation.
- Integrate multimedia and visual displays into presentations to clarify information, strengthen claims and evidence, and add interest.

	Content	Use of Media	Presentation Techniques
3	The presentation has an engaging introduction, a logical sequence of events, and a meaningful conclusion. The presentation includes narrative techniques and a variety of transitions for clarity. The presentation includes descriptive details relevant to the story.	The images in the presentation connect well to all parts of the narrative. The images enhance and add interest to the narrative. The timing of the images matches the timing of the narrative.	The speaker maintains effective eye contact and speaks clearly and with adequate volume. The speaker varies tone and volume to create an engaging presentation.
2	The presentation has an introduction, a somewhat logical sequence of events, and a conclusion. The presentation includes some narrative techniques and some transitions for clarity. The presentation includes some descriptive details.	The images in the presentation connect to some parts of the narrative. The images somewhat enhance and add interest to the narrative. The timing of the images somewhat matches the timing of the narrative.	The speaker sometimes maintains effective eye contact and speaks somewhat clearly and with adequate volume. The speaker sometimes varies tone and emphasis to create an engaging presentation.
1	The presentation does not have a logical sequence of events, and lacks an introduction or conclusion. The presentation does not include narrative techniques and transitions. The presentation does not include descriptive details.	The images in the presentation do not connect to the narrative. The images do not enhance and add interest to the narrative. The timing of the images does not match the timing of the narrative.	The speaker does not maintain effective eye contact or speak clearly with adequate volume. The speaker does not vary tone and emphasis to create an engaging presentation.

DIGITAL PERSPECTIVES

Preparing for the Assignment To help students understand what an effective nonfiction narrative looks and sounds like, find examples on the Internet of students or adults presenting nonfiction narratives. Project the examples for the class, and have students note the techniques that make each speaker successful—inflection, pacing, and gestures. Suggest that students record themselves presenting their nonfiction narratives prior to presenting to the class so that they can practice incorporating some of the elements in the examples you showed them.

UNIT 1 REFLECTION

Reflect on the Unit

Now that you've completed the unit, take a few moments to reflect on your learning.

Reflect on the Unit Goals

Look back at the goals at the beginning of the unit. Use a different colored pen to rate yourself again. Think about readings and activities that contributed the most to the growth of your understanding. Record your thoughts.

Reflect on the Learning Strategies

Discuss It Write a reflection on whether you were able to improve your learning based on your Action Plans. Think about what worked, what didn't, and what you might do to keep working on these strategies. Record your ideas before a class discussion.

Reflect on the Text

Choose a selection that you found challenging and explain what made it difficult.

Explain something that surprised you about a text in the unit.

Which activity taught you the most about childhood? What did you learn?

SCAN FOR MULTIMEDIA

DIGITAL PERSPECTIVES

Reflect on the Unit

- Have students watch the video on Reflecting on Your Learning.
- A video on this topic is available online in the Professional Development Center.

Reflect on the Unit Goals

Students should re-evaluate how well they met the unit goals now that they have completed the unit. You might ask them to provide a written commentary on the goal they made the most progress with as well as the goal they feel warrants continued focus.

Reflect on the Learning Strategies

Discuss It If you want to make this a digital activity, go online and navigate to the Discussion Board. Alternatively, students can share their learning strategies reflections in a class discussion.

Reflect on the Text

Consider having students share their text reflections with one another.

MAKE IT INTERACTIVE

Have students prepare one slide using presentation software that summarizes their reflection.

Collate student slides into a presentation that can be viewed by the class. Students should be prepared to give a 30-second oral summary for their slide.

Unit Test and Remediation

After students have completed the Performance-Based Assessment, administer the Unit Test. Based on students' performance on the test, assign the resources as indicated on the Interpretation Guide to remediate. Students who take the test online will be automatically assigned remediation, as warranted by test results.

The Holocaust

UNIT 2

INTRODUCTION

> ### Jump Start
> Ask students why they think people still care about things that happened long ago. What do they think we can learn by looking at and remembering history?

The Holocaust
Ask students what they know about the Holocaust. Point out that as they work through this unit, they will read many texts relating to the Holocaust.

Video ▶
Project the introduction video in class, ask students to open the video in their digital textbooks, or have students scan the BouncePage icon with their phones to access the video.

Discuss It If you want to make this a digital activity, go online and navigate to the Discussion Board. Alternatively, students can share their responses in a class discussion.

> ### Block Scheduling
> Each day in this pacing calendar represents a 40–50 minute class period. Teachers using block scheduling may combine days to reflect their class schedule. In addition, teachers may revise pacing to differentiate and support core instruction by integrating components and resources as students require.

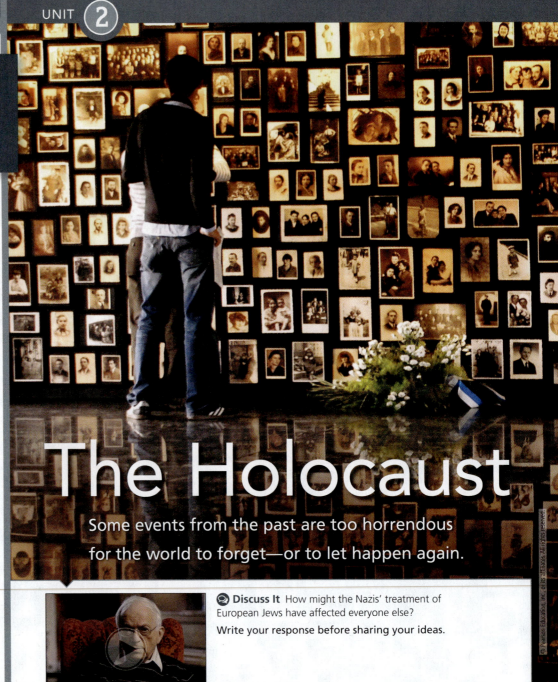

UNIT 2

The Holocaust

Some events from the past are too horrendous for the world to forget—or to let happen again.

The Holocaust

💬 **Discuss It** How might the Nazis' treatment of European Jews have affected everyone else?

Write your response before sharing your ideas.

SCAN FOR MULTIMEDIA

88

📅 Pacing Plan

Unit Introduction		Introduce Whole-Class Learning	The Diary of Anne Frank, Act I					The Diary of Anne Frank, Act II					Media: Frank Family and World War II Timelines		Performance Task		
1	2	3	4	5	6	7	8	9	10	11	12	13	14	15	16	17	18

DIGITAL PERSPECTIVES

Audio | Video | Document | Annotation Highlights | EL Highlights | Online Assessment

UNIT 2

UNIT INTRODUCTION

ESSENTIAL QUESTION:

How do we remember the past?

LAUNCH TEXT
EXPLANATORY MODEL
The Grand Mosque of Paris

WHOLE-CLASS LEARNING

ANCHOR TEXT: DRAMA
The Diary of Anne Frank, Act I
Frances Goodrich and Albert Hackett

COMPARE

ANCHOR TEXT: DRAMA
The Diary of Anne Frank, Act II
Frances Goodrich and Albert Hackett

MEDIA: TIMELINE
Frank Family and World War II Timeline

SMALL-GROUP LEARNING

DIARY ENTRIES
from Anne Frank: The Diary of a Young Girl
Anne Frank

SPEECH
Acceptance Speech for the Nobel Peace Prize
Elie Wiesel

MEDIA: GRAPHIC NOVEL
from Maus
Art Spiegelman

INDEPENDENT LEARNING

TELEVISION TRANSCRIPT
Saving the Children
Bob Simon

REFLECTIVE ESSAY
A Great Adventure in the Shadow of War
Mary Helen Dirkx

INFORMATIVE ARTICLE
Irena Sendler: Rescuer of the Children of Warsaw
Chana Kroll

HISTORICAL WRITING
Quiet Resistance
from Courageous Teen Resisters
Ann Byers

NEWS ARTICLE
Remembering a Devoted Keeper of Anne Frank's Legacy
Moni Basu

FIRST-PERSON ACCOUNT
I'll Go Fetch Her Tomorrow
from Hidden Like Anne Frank
Bloeme Emden with Marcel Prins

PERFORMANCE TASK
WRITING FOCUS:
Write an Explanatory Essay

PERFORMANCE TASK
SPEAKING AND LISTENING FOCUS:
Deliver a Multimedia Presentation

PERFORMANCE-BASED ASSESSMENT PREP
Review Evidence for an Explanatory Essay

PERFORMANCE-BASED ASSESSMENT

Explanatory Text: Essay and Oral Presentation

PROMPT:
How can literature help us remember and honor the victims of the Holocaust?

How do we remember the past?

Introduce the Essential Question and point out that students will respond to related prompts.

- **Whole-Class Learning** How are historical events reflected in the play *The Diary of Anne Frank*?
- **Small-Group Learning** How do the selections contribute to your understanding of the Holocaust and the ways in which we remember the past?
- **Performance-Based Assessment** How can literature help us remember and honor the victims of the Holocaust?

Using Trade Books

Refer to the Teaching with Trade Books section for suggestions on how to incorporate the following thematically-related titles into this unit:

- *The Devil's Arithmetic* by Jane Yolen
- *The Boy in the Striped Pajamas* by John Boyne
- *Night* by Elie Wiesel

Current Perspectives

To increase student engagement, search online for stories about the horrible atrocities of the Holocaust and the people who managed to survive, and invite your students to recommend stories they find. Always preview content before sharing it with your class.

- **Article: Holocaust survivors demand Israel help refugees** An article by Oren Liebermann (CNN, 9/10/15) about calls by several Holocaust survivors for Israel to shelter Middle Eastern refugees
- **Video: Why we remember the Holocaust** A video (The U.S. Holocaust Memorial Museum, 4/21/10) that explains why it is so important to remember the Holocaust

---

Introduce Small-Group Learning

from Anne Frank: The Diary of a Young Girl — 19, 20, 21, 22, 23, 24

Acceptance Speech for the Nobel Peace Prize — 25, 26

Media: *from* Maus — 27, 28, 29, 30

Performance Task — 31, 32

Introduce Independent Learning — 33

Independent Learning — 34

Performance-Based Assessment — 35, 36

Unit Introduction

INTRODUCTION

About the Unit Goals
These unit goals were backward designed from the Performance-Based Assessment at the end of the unit and the Whole-Class and Small-Group Performance Tasks. Students will practice and become proficient in many more standards over the course of this unit.

Unit Goals
Review the goals with students and explain that as they read the selections in this unit, they will improve in reading, writing, research, language, and speaking and listening.

Reading Goals Tell students they will read and evaluate informative essays. They will also read nonfiction narratives and arguments to better understand the ways writers express ideas.

Writing and Research Goals Tell students that they will learn the elements of writing an informative essay. Students will write for a number of reasons, including reflecting on experiences and gathering evidence. They will conduct research to clarify and explore ideas.

Language Goal Tell students that they will develop understanding of the conventions of standard English grammar and usage. They will practice usage of verbs and conjunctions here in their own writing.

Speaking and Listening Explain to students that they will work together to build on one another's ideas, and communicate with one another. They will also learn to incorporate audio, visuals, and text in presentations.

HOME Connection
A Home Connection letter to students' parents or guardians is available in the Interactive Teacher's Edition. The letter explains what students will be learning in this unit and how they will be assessed.

UNIT 2 INTRODUCTION

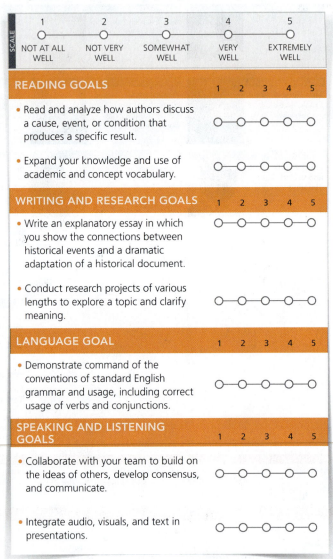

STANDARDS
Language
Acquire and use accurately grade-appropriate general academic and domain-specific words and phrases; gather vocabulary knowledge when considering a word or phrase important to comprehension or expression.

90 UNIT 2 • THE HOLOCAUST

AUTHOR'S PERSPECTIVE Ernest Morrell, Ph.D.

Self-Assessing Progress The Unit Goals will help students share responsibility for their learning. This is an important ownership for students as they prepare for life in higher education, in their professional career, and as leaders in their families and communities. One way to encourage students to practice monitoring their own learning is to give them guiding questions like these to help them assess their progress as they work through the unit. Remind students to ask themselves such questions as they complete each selection or activity in the unit so they can track their progress.

- Do I have a better understanding of the parts of an explanatory essay and how to recognize them when reading and using them when writing?
- Do I have a better understanding of the differences between academic and concept vocabulary?
- Am I demonstrating command of the conventions of standard English grammar and usage?
- Am I effective when I collaborate with others?

ESSENTIAL QUESTION: How do we remember the past?

DIGITAL PERSPECTIVES

Academic Vocabulary: Explanatory Text

Academic terms appear in all subjects and can help you read, write, and discuss with more precision. Explanatory writing relies on facts to inform or explain. Here are five academic words that will be useful to you in this unit as you analyze and write explanatory texts.

Complete the chart.

1. Review each word, its root, and the mentor sentences.
2. Use the information and your own knowledge to predict the meaning of each word.
3. For each word, list at least two related words.
4. Refer to the dictionary or other resources if needed.

TIP

FOLLOW THROUGH
Study the words in this chart, and mark them or their forms wherever they appear in the unit.

WORD	MENTOR SENTENCES	PREDICT MEANING	RELATED WORDS
theorize ROOT: -theo-/-thea- "view"; "consider"	1. When you *theorize*, you think of possible explanations for an idea or fact. 2. Since they could not agree on the true cause, doctors could only *theorize* about the illness.		theory; theoretical
sustain ROOT: -tain- "hold"	1. It is difficult to *sustain* a pose long enough for an artist to paint your portrait. 2. Those sandwiches will *sustain* us until dinner.		
declaration ROOT: -clar- "clear"	1. The country's *declaration* of peace made all the citizens happy that the war was finally over. 2. Congress issued a *declaration* in which the new election laws were explained.		
pronounce ROOT: -nounc-/-nunc- "declare"; "report"	1. If you don't *pronounce* your words clearly, people might not be able to understand your ideas. 2. "I now *pronounce* this game officially over," said the referee.		
enumerate ROOT: -numer- "number"	1. I have created a list in which I *enumerate* the tasks that should be completed. 2. In her book, the author tries to *enumerate* all the possible explanations for the conflict.		

Unit Introduction 91

Academic Vocabulary: Explanatory Text

Introduce the blue academic vocabulary words in the chart on the student page. Point out that the root of each word provides a clue to its meaning. Discuss the mentor sentences to ensure students understand each word's usage. Students should also use the mentor sentences as context to help them predict the meaning of each word. Check that students are able to fill the chart in correctly. Complete pronunciations, parts of speech, and definitions are provided for you. Students are only expected to provide the definition.

Possible responses:

theorize *v.* (THEE uh ryz)
Meaning: to form an explanation based on observation and reasoning; speculate
Related words: theoretical, theory
Additional words related to the root *-theo-/-thea-* theater, theatrical

sustain *v.* (suh STAYN)
Meaning: to maintain or keep up
Related words: sustainable, sustainability, sustained
Additional words related to the root *-tain-*: abstain, detain, maintain, retain

declaration *v.* (dehk luh RAY shuhn)
Meaning: announcement; formal statement
Related words: declarative, declare
Additional words related to the root *-clar-*: clarification, clarify, clarity

pronounce *v.* (pruh NOWNS)
Meaning: to say a word in the correct way; to officially announce
Related words: pronouncer, pronunciation
Additional words related to the root *-nounc-/-nunc-*: announce, denunciation, enunciation

enumerate *v.* (ih NOO muh rayt)
Meaning: to specify as in a list; to count
Related words: enumerator, enumeration
Additional words related to the root *-numer-*: number, numeral, numerical

---

PERSONALIZE FOR LEARNING

English Language Support
Cognates Many of the academic words have Spanish cognates. Use these cognates with students whose home language is Spanish.
ALL LEVELS

theorize – teorizar   pronounce – pronunciar

sustain – sostener   enumerate – enumerar

declaration – declaración

Unit Introduction 91

INTRODUCTION

Purpose of the Launch Text

The Launch Text provides students with a common starting point to address the unit topic. After reading the Launch Text, all students will be able to participate in discussions about the Holocaust.

Lexile: 990 The easier reading level of this selection makes it perfect to assign for homework. Students will need little or no support to understand it.

Additionally, "The Grand Mosque of Paris" provides a writing model for the Performance-Based Assessment students will complete at the end of the unit.

Launch Text: Explanatory Essay

Remind students that the purpose of an explanatory text is to provide the reader with facts and details about a subject. It does not offer opinions or points of view.

Have students read the title of the text and ask what they think the text will be about. Have them read the first paragraph and ask: *Based on this paragraph, what point in history is this text going to be about?* Instruct students to read paragraph 2. Ask: *What is the main idea of this paragraph? What fact do we learn about the Muslims in Paris at this point in history?* As they read, have students make note of important details that will help them to summarize the text.

Encourage students to read this text on their own and annotate unfamiliar words and sections of text they think are particularly important.

🔊 **AUDIO SUMMARIES**

Audio summaries of "The Grand Mosque of Paris" are available in both English and Spanish in the Interactive Teacher's Edition or Unit Resources. Assigning these summaries before students read the Launch Text may help them build additional background knowledge and set a context for their reading.

UNIT 2 INTRODUCTION

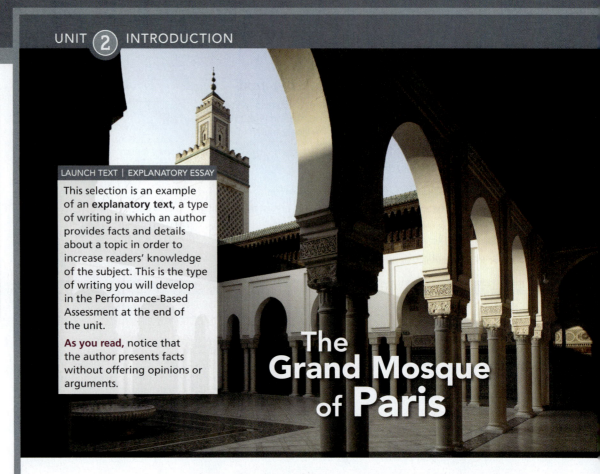

LAUNCH TEXT | EXPLANATORY ESSAY

This selection is an example of an **explanatory text**, a type of writing in which an author provides facts and details about a topic in order to increase readers' knowledge of the subject. This is the type of writing you will develop in the Performance-Based Assessment at the end of the unit.

As you read, notice that the author presents facts without offering opinions or arguments.

The Grand Mosque of Paris

NOTES

1 After the Nazis conquered France in 1940, the country fell under the control of the Vichy government. This regime supported Hitler's plan to rid the world of Jews and other "undesirables."

2 In Paris, it was a terrifying time. No Jew was safe from arrest and deportation. Few Parisians were willing to come to their aid, as there was too much risk involved. Despite the deadly campaign, many Jewish children living in Paris at the time survived. Some of those children found refuge in the Grand Mosque of Paris, where heroic Muslims saved Jews from the Nazis.

3 The Grand Mosque of Paris is a fortress-like structure the size of a city block. It was built in 1926 as an expression of France's thanks to the many North African Muslims who fought with the French during World War I. In 1940, it provided an ideal hiding place and escape route for Jews on the run.

4 The rescue involved an extensive network of men and women of all religions and political persuasions. Rescuers took the children from detention centers or homes. They got them false

SCAN FOR MULTIMEDIA

92 UNIT 2 • THE HOLOCAUST

CROSS-CURRICULAR PERSPECTIVES

Social Studies In difficult times, there are always stories to be found about everyday heroes—ordinary people who have risked their own lives and safety to help others. The Holocaust was no exception. Have students research a story about an everyday hero from the time of the Holocaust and have them share the stories with the class, either orally or through a project. Ask students to discuss: *What is inspiring about an everyday hero from the Holocaust that you read about?*

papers, found them temporary shelter in safe houses, and raised funds to pay for their care.

5   Rescuers kept records of the children's real names and fake names, as well as their hiding places. They escorted the children to these locations in small groups. Many who participated were themselves arrested and deported.

6   The Grand Mosque was the perfect cover. Not just a place of worship, it was a community center. Visitors could walk through its doors without attracting a lot of attention. Under these conditions, it was possible for a Jew to pass as a Muslim.

7   Directly beneath the mosque's grounds lay the sewer system of Paris. This complicated web of underground passages now served as a hiding place and escape route. It also reached the Seine. From there, barges were used to smuggle human cargo to ports in the South of France and then to Algeria or Spain.

8   Many believe that the "soul" of the rescue effort was the mosque's rector, Si Kaddour Benghabrit. Benghabrit wrote out false birth certificates for Jewish children, claiming they were Muslim. He is thought to have set up an alarm system warning fugitives to run into the women's section of the prayer room, where men were normally not allowed.

9   Other Muslims also took a stand against the Nazi oppressors by refusing to reveal the whereabouts of fugitives. Some helped Jews avoid detection by coaching them to speak and act like Arabs. Albert Assouline, a North African Jew who found refuge at the Paris mosque, wrote that in life and death situations, there are always people who can be counted on to do the right thing. There may not be a better way to describe the heroic actions of Paris's Muslim community during a horrific time in world history.

NOTES

WORD NETWORK FOR THE HOLOCAUST

Vocabulary A Word Network is a collection of words related to a topic. As you read the selections in this unit, identify words related to the Holocaust, and add them to your Word Network. For example, you might begin by adding words from the Launch Text, such as *deportation*, *detention*, and *fugitive*. Continue to add words as you complete this unit.

Tool Kit
Word Network Model

- deportation
- detention
- fugitive

THE HOLOCAUST

DIGITAL PERSPECTIVES

Word Network for The Holocaust

Tell students that they can fill in the Word Network as they read texts in the unit, or they can record the words elsewhere and add them later. Point out to students that people may have personal associations with some words. A word that one student thinks is related to the Holocaust might not be a word another student would pick. However, students should feel free to add any word they personally think is relevant to their Word Network. Each person's Word Network will be unique. If you choose to print the Word Network, distribute it to students at this point so they can use it throughout the rest of the unit.

AUTHOR'S PERSPECTIVE: Elfrieda Hiebert, Ph.D.

Generative Vocabulary Rare words are the words that typically account for only 10 percent of all the words in a text, compared to the more common vocabulary words that students know better. Generative vocabulary strategies can help students build their rare vocabulary.

Generative refers to the way students can apply knowledge of how words work—morphologically and conceptually—when encountering new words. Building off of a big idea like this unit's Holocaust, words can be taught as networks of ideas rather than as single, unrelated but grade-appropriate words. Studying words in conceptual groupings enables students to learn more words while reading.

Although some "Holocaust" words may be unfamiliar to students, the overarching concept will not be. Students may not know every word related to the idea of the Holocaust, but the concept of connections between "our past and ourselves" should be familiar to them. Word Networks help students build vocabulary as they see a wide variety of words can relate to one concept.

INTRODUCTION

Summary

Have students read the introductory paragraph. Provide them with tips for writing a summary:
- Write in the present tense.
- Make sure to include the title of the work.
- Be concise: a summary should not be equal in length to the original text.
- If you need to quote the words of the author, use quotation marks.
- Don't put your own opinions, ideas, or interpretations into the summary. The purpose of writing a summary is to accurately represent what the author says, not to provide a critique.

If necessary, students can refer to the Tool Kit for help in understanding the elements of a good summary.

See possible Summary on student page.

Launch Activity

Explain to students that as they work on this unit, they will have many opportunities to discuss moments when people have done the right thing. Point out that in this story, people risked their lives to save others. Ask students if they know of other stories like this. Remind students that doing the right thing happens every day. Ask students to give everyday examples of doing the right thing. Ask students to share moments in their lives when they have done the right thing.

UNIT 2 INTRODUCTION

Summary

Write a summary of "The Grand Mosque of Paris." A **summary** is a concise, complete, and accurate overview of a text. It should not include a statement of your opinion or an analysis.

Possible response: "The Grande Mosque of Paris" is an explanatory text that describes how during World War II, Paris's Muslim population helped save Jewish children from the Nazis. Very few people in the city were willing to help Jewish people because of the risk. However, a network of people (of many religions) realized that they could safely smuggle people out through the Grand Mosque. Visitors got little attention from the occupiers, and underground tunnels beneath the mosque were an excellent way to sneak away to reach a ship out of France. This network saved many lives.

Launch Activity

Conduct a Discussion Consider this statement: There are always people who can be counted on to do the right thing.
- Write what you think about the question. Briefly explain your thinking.

- Get together with a small group of students, and discuss your responses. Support your ideas with examples from stories you have heard or read, including the Launch Text. Consider how your ideas are similar and different.
- After your discussion, choose someone from your group to present a summary of your conversation.
- After all the groups have shared their ideas, discuss as a class similarities and differences among the views presented.

ESSENTIAL QUESTION: How do we remember the past?

DIGITAL PERSPECTIVES

QuickWrite

Consider class discussions, the video, and the Launch Text as you think about the prompt. Record your first thoughts here.

PROMPT: How can literature help us remember and honor the victims of the Holocaust?

Possible response: Literature can help us remember and honor the victims of the Holocaust by teaching people about this horrible event in the past. It is important to continue teaching young people about what happened so that they can learn about how evil can take over a country, a region, or even the world. True stories about people who helped or people who lost their lives can help others learn about this tragic eent in human history.

EVIDENCE LOG FOR THE HOLOCAUST

Review your QuickWrite. Summarize your thoughts in one sentence to record in your Evidence Log. Then, record textual details and evidence from "The Grand Mosque of Paris" that support your thinking.

Prepare for the Performance-Based Assessment at the end of the unit by completing the Evidence Log after each selection.

Tool Kit
Evidence Log Model

Title of Text: _____		Date: _____
CONNECTION TO PROMPT	TEXT EVIDENCE/DETAILS	ADDITIONAL NOTES/IDEAS

How does this text change or add to my thinking? _____ Date: _____

SCAN FOR MULTIMEDIA

Unit Introduction 95

QuickWrite

In this QuickWrite, students should present their own response to the prompt based on the material they have read and viewed in the Unit Overview and Introduction. This initial response will help inform their work when they complete the Performance-Based Assessment at the end of the unit. Students should make sure to refer to details from the text, class discussion, and presentations to support their writing.

See possible QuickWrite on student page.

Evidence Log for The Holocaust

Students should record their initial thoughts in their Evidence Logs along with evidence from "The Grand Mosque of Paris" that support their thoughts.

If you choose to print the Evidence Log, distribute it to students at this point so they can use it throughout the rest of the unit.

Performance-Based Assessment: Refining Your Thinking

- Have students watch the video on Refining Your Thinking.
- A video on this topic is available online in the Professional Development Center.

The Grand Mosque of Paris 95

OVERVIEW

WHOLE-CLASS LEARNING

How do we remember the past?

Engage students in a discussion about the Holocaust and what we know about it from the sources during that time. Through literature, film, and from talking to those who witnessed history firsthand, we record history to remember and learn from it. During Whole-Class Learning, students will read a play about Anne Frank and her family during the Holocaust.

Whole-Class Learning Strategies

Review the Learning Strategies with students and explain that as they work through Whole-Class Learning they will develop strategies to work in large-group environments.

- Have students watch the video on Whole-Class Learning Strategies.
- A video on this topic is available online in the Professional Development Center.

You may wish to discuss some action items to add to the chart as a class before students complete it on their own. For example, for "Interact and share ideas," you might solicit the following from students:

- Ask questions if you need something clarified.
- Share and compare notes with classmates.

Block Scheduling

Each day in this Pacing Plan represents a 40–50 minute class period. Teachers using block scheduling may combine days to reflect their class schedule. In addition, teachers may revise pacing to differentiate and support core instruction by integrating components and resources as students require.

Pacing Plan

OVERVIEW: WHOLE-CLASS LEARNING

ESSENTIAL QUESTION:

How do we remember the past?

There are many ways to remember the past: We can honor it, study it, analyze it, and learn from it. In the case of the Holocaust, we can work to make sure it never happens again. As you read, you will work with your whole class to explore some of the ways we remember the past.

Whole-Class Learning Strategies

Throughout your life, in school, in your community, and in your career, you will continue to learn and work in large-group environments.

Review these strategies and the actions you can take to practice them as you work with your whole class. Add ideas of your own for each step. Get ready to use these strategies during Whole-Class Learning.

STRATEGY	ACTION PLAN
Listen actively	• Eliminate distractions. For example, put your cellphone away. • Keep your eyes on the speaker. •
Clarify by asking questions	• If you're confused, other people probably are, too. Ask a question to help your whole class. • If you see that you are guessing, ask a question instead. •
Monitor understanding	• Notice what information you already know and be ready to build on it. • Ask for help if you are struggling. •
Interact and share ideas	• Share your ideas and answer questions, even if you are unsure. • Build on the ideas of others by adding details or making a connection. •

SCAN FOR MULTIMEDIA

Pacing Plan:
- 1, 2: Unit Introduction
- 3: Introduce Whole-Class Learning
- 4, 5, 6, 7, 8: The Diary of Anne Frank, Act I
- 9, 10, 11, 12, 13: The Diary of Anne Frank, Act II
- 14, 15: Media: Frank Family and World War II Timeline
- 16, 17, 18: Performance Task

WHOLE-CLASS LEARNING

CONTENTS

ANCHOR TEXT: DRAMA

The Diary of Anne Frank, Act I
Frances Goodrich and Albert Hackett

This play tells the true story of a young Jewish girl and her family who hide from the Nazis.

COMPARE

ANCHOR TEXT: DRAMA

The Diary of Anne Frank, Act II
Frances Goodrich and Albert Hackett

In the second part of the play, the characters struggle to maintain their humanity as their situation worsens.

MEDIA: TIMELINE

Frank Family and World War II Timeline

This timeline shows events in Anne Frank's life set against the backdrop of cataclysmic world events.

PERFORMANCE TASK

WRITING FOCUS

Write an Explanatory Essay

The Whole-Class readings focus on the events in history that are collectively known as the Holocaust. After reading, you will write an explanatory essay in which you discuss the ways in which the events of World War II are reflected in the drama *The Diary of Anne Frank*.

DIGITAL PERSPECTIVES

Contents

Anchor Texts Preview the anchor texts and media with students to generate interest. Encourage students to discuss other texts they may have read or movies or television shows they may have seen that deal with the issues of the Holocaust.

You may wish to conduct a poll to determine which selection students want to learn more about and discuss the reasons for their preference. Students can return to this poll after they have read the selections to discuss which provoked the most questions and interests.

Performance Task

Explanatory Essay Explain to students that after reading the selections, they will write an explanatory essay that shows how outside historical events affected the lives of the two families living in the Secret Annex. To help them prepare, encourage students to think about the topic as they progress through the selections and as they participate in the Whole-Class Learning experience.

PLANNING
WHOLE-CLASS LEARNING • THE DIARY OF ANNE FRANK, ACT I

The Diary of Anne Frank, Act I

🔊 **AUDIO SUMMARIES**
Audio summaries of *The Diary of Anne Frank*, Act I are available online in both English and Spanish in the Interactive Teacher's Edition or Unit Resources. Assigning these summaries prior to reading the selection may help students build additional background knowledge and set a context for their first read.

Summary
In the drama *The Diary of Anne Frank* by Frances Goodrich and Albert Hackett, Act I begins after the war with Mr. Frank returning to his pre-war office in the Netherlands. After he begins reading his daughter's diary, the play goes back in time. It shows how the Frank family first went into hiding and the stresses and arguments that came with their situation. There is little food, little privacy, and great danger; any self-expression is a risk. Yet there are joys as well, such as celebrating Hannukah while in hiding. The act concludes with a scene of mingled joy and fear.

Insight
This selection provides a wide, multi-perspective view of events to set the scene for students, before getting into the intensely personal view from Anne Frank's diary itself. It captures the tension and lack of privacy that families in hiding faced.

ESSENTIAL QUESTION:
How do we remember the past?

Connection to Essential Question
This act interweaves scenes seen from Mr. Frank's perspective and from Anne's perspective. Reading her diary prompts him to remember past events, but we also see events that she remembered and wrote down.

WHOLE-CLASS LEARNING PERFORMANCE TASK
How are historical events reflected in the play *The Diary of Anne Frank*?

Connection to Performance Tasks

Whole-Class Learning Performance Task Early in the play, we see how the increasingly strict laws drive the family to realize they will be in great danger if they don't go into hiding. For this performance task, students will need to track the ways that historical events are expressed an illustrated in the play.

UNIT PERFORMANCE-BASED ASSESSMENT
How can literature help us remember and honor the victims of the Holocaust?

Unit Performance-Based Assessment Mr. Frank doesn't want to think about the past at all; he wants to burn everything that would remind him of life during the war. However, he decides to save the diary, which ends up being published in many languages and read all over the world for years to come. The diary serves readers as a source of inspiration about the human spirit, as well as a reminder of the appalling events that occurred. Learning about how these horrific events unfolded can help people to try to prevent such things from ever occurring again.

DIGITAL PERSPECTIVES | Audio | Video | Document | Annotation Highlights  | EL Highlights | Online Assessment

LESSON RESOURCES

	Making Meaning	**Language Development**
Lesson	First Read Close Read Analyze the Text Analyze Craft and Structure	Concept Vocabulary Word Study Conventions
Instructional Standards	**RL.10** By the end of the year, read and comprehend literature . . . **RL.3** Analyze how particular lines of dialogue . . . **RL.6** Analyze how differences in the points of view . . .	**L.1** Demonstrate command of the conventions . . . **L.4** Determine or clarify the meaning of unknown and multiple-meaning words and phrases . . . **L.4.b** Use common, grade-appropriate Greek or Latin affixes and roots . . . **L.5** Demonstrate understanding of figurative language . . . **L.5.b** Use the relationship between particular words . . .
STUDENT RESOURCES Available online in the Interactive Student Edition or Unit Resources	Selection Audio First-Read Guide: Fiction Close-Read Guide: Fiction	Word Network
TEACHER RESOURCES **Selection Resources** Available online in the Interactive Teacher's Edition or Unit Resources	Audio Summaries Annotation Highlights EL Highlights English Language Support Lesson: Dialogue Analyze Craft and Structure: Text Structures in Drama	Concept Vocabulary and Word Study Conventions: Principal Parts of Verbs
Reteach/Practice (RP) Available online in the Interactive Teacher's Edition or Unit Resources	Analyze Craft and Structure: Text Structures in Drama (RP)	Word Study: Latin Suffix -ion (RP) Conventions: Principal Parts of Verbs (RP)
Assessment Available online in Assessments	Selection Test	
My Resources	A Unit 2 Answer Key is available online and in the Interactive Teacher's Edition.	

Whole-Class Learning   98B

PERSONALIZE FOR LEARNING
WHOLE-CLASS LEARNING • *THE DIARY OF ANNE FRANK*, ACT I

Reading Support

Text Complexity Rubric: *The Diary of Anne Frank*, Act I

Quantitative Measures

Lexile: NP   Text Length: 16,792

Qualitative Measures

Knowledge Demands ①—②—**③**—④—⑤	The selection relies on knowledge of the Nazi occupation and the Holocaust. Students have been exposed to the subject, but the experiences portrayed are outside their personal experience.
Structure ①—**②**—③—④—⑤	Setting and background are clearly described, and characters listed; some time shifts occur, but are labeled (begins 1945, then 1942); reader needs to infer the change of situation from the change in set (room appearance).
Language Conventionality and Clarity ①—**②**—③—④—⑤	Set descriptions have concrete, descriptive language; play has mix of spoken dialogue and written words from a diary in first person. Dialogue is conversational, with short sentences that are easily understood.
Levels of Meaning/Purpose ①—②—**③**—④—⑤	The situation is not immediately revealed, but can be inferred if reader has enough background knowledge; reader must infer meaning and feelings of characters based on dialogue.

DECIDE AND PLAN

English Language Support
Provide English learners with support for knowledge demands and structure as they read the selection.

Knowledge Demands List some words and names students will need to know about the selection. For example, write *Nazi occupation, Amsterdam, Anne Frank, diary*. With students, go through the list and discuss word meanings and basic information about each one.

Structure Help students to locate and write notes on information about the setting and situation. For example, have students read the first few paragraphs and write *Setting: a building in Amsterdam, Holland. Date: November 1945*. Ask them to find the year of the next scene (1942, three years earlier). Have them find sections with dialogue and those with the written diary (labeled "Anne's Voice").

Strategic Support
Provide students with strategic support to ensure that they can successfully read the text.

Knowledge Demands Make a list of words and names students will need to know about the selection, for example: *Nazi occupation, Holocaust, Amsterdam, Anne Frank*. For each item on the list, ask students to say what they know about the item. Fill in basic information as needed.

Meaning As a group, have students take turns reading aloud sections of the stage directions at the beginning of Scene i. For the dialogue, have students take turns being different characters and reading their parts aloud. Stop periodically to discuss the meaning. If necessary, point out clues to the situation. For example, in paragraph 17, they find out the war is over. In paragraph 25, the father is given the diary.

Challenge
Provide students who need to be challenged with ideas for how they can go beyond a simple interpretation of the text.

Text Analysis Have two volunteers read aloud the dialogue between Anne and Mr. Dussel beginning at paragraph 335 in Act I, Scene 3, and a third volunteer read Anne's diary entry in paragraph 365 of Act I, Scene 3. As a group, discuss the stresses a family could have sharing a tight space in that situation. Ask students to comment on Anne's attitude toward Dussel at first (generous, helpful, kind), and the difficulties she has afterward.

Dramatic Reading Have students form groups. Ask them to choose characters and practice a dramatic reading of a section of the play. They may read from the page or memorize lines. Then have them perform for the class. Ask other students to comment on the performance.

TEACH

Read and Respond
Have students do their first read of the selection. Then have them complete their close read. Finally, work with them on the Making Meaning and Language Development activities.

Standards Support Through Teaching and Learning Cycle

IDENTIFY NEEDS

Analyze results of the Beginning-of-Year Assessment, focusing on the items relating to Unit 2. Also take into consideration student performance to this point and your observations of where particular students struggle.

DECIDE AND PLAN

- If students have performed poorly on items matching these standards, then provide selection scaffolds before assigning them the on-level lesson provided in the Student Edition.
- If students have done well on the Beginning-of-Year Assessment, then challenge them to keep progressing and learning by giving them opportunities to practice the skills in depth.
- Use the Selection Resources listed on the Planning pages for *The Diary of Anne Frank,* Act I, to help students continually improve their ability to master the standards.

Instructional Standards: *The Diary of Anne Frank*, Act I

	Catching Up	This Year	Looking Forward
Reading	You may wish to administer the **Analyze Craft and Structure: Text Structures in Drama (RP)** worksheet to help students understand how dialogue develops character, establishes tone and meaning, and propels the plot.	**RL.3** Analyze how particular lines of dialogue or incidents in a story or drama propel the action, reveal aspects of a character, or provoke a decision.	Challenge students to practice the dialogue in a small group, using clues from the worksheet to determine how they think the characters would sound and interact.
Language	You may wish to administer the **Word Study: Latin suffix *-ion* (RP)** worksheet to help students understand the meanings of words with the *-ion* suffix. You may wish to administer the **Conventions: Principal Parts of Verbs (RP)** worksheet to help students understand the four principal parts or forms of verbs.	**L.4.b** Use common, grade-appropriate Greek or Latin affixes and roots as clues to the meaning of a word. **L.5.b** Use the relationship between particular words to better understand each of the words.	Challenge students to find three words with the *-ion* suffix. Have students use each word in a sentence that includes context clues.

ANALYZE AND REVISE

- Analyze student work for evidence of student learning.
- Identify whether or not students have met the expectations in the standards.
- Identify implications for future instruction.

TEACH

Implement the planned lesson, and gather evidence of student learning.

TEACHING

HISTORICAL PERSPECTIVES

The Holocaust

This section covers some of the key events of the twentieth century: how the end of World War I planted the seeds for World War II, the rise of the Nazis in Germany, and the German campaign to annihilate Jewish populations during World War II. Have students connect these events with the Essential Question: How do we remember the past?

The Nazi Rise to Power

Point out to students that World War I devastated large parts of Europe, severely damaging the economies of victors and vanquished. The reparation payments that the Germans had to make to the Allied victors had an additional consequence: instead of rebuilding its own economy, Germany found itself paying for the rebuilding efforts of countries like France, Belgium, and Holland. Then, with the collapse of the world economy in the Great Depression, these reparation payments became increasingly difficult for the German government. Lead a discussion about how a country's economy might affect its people. Ask students to consider the following prompts: *What kinds of situations make people want a drastic change? Why might it be easier to influence desperate people than people who are content?*

Nazi Ideology

Tell students that Nazi ideology on race was not unique. Many races have, in the past, considered themselves superior to others. Point out that the Nazis used their ideology to create scapegoats—people (in this case, the Jews) who could be unjustifiably blamed for the situation Germany found itself in.

HISTORICAL PERSPECTIVES

The Holocaust

The Nazi Rise to Power

In 1918, the First World War came to an end and Germany was defeated. The Treaty of Versailles set harsh terms for Germany's surrender—the country had to make huge payments, give up territory, and severely limit the size of its armed forces.

One of the surviving soldiers was a man named Adolf Hitler, who was outraged by the terms of the treaty and determined that they should be overturned. In 1921, Hitler became the leader of a small political party, the National Socialist German Workers Party, also known as the Nazi Party. At first, the party had little influence, but it quickly gained support as the Great Depression of 1929 began to devastate the German economy and impoverish German citizens. Many Germans were desperate for change, and Hitler was a charismatic speaker who promised to make Germany prosperous and powerful again.

In 1933, Hitler became chancellor—head of the government. From the very beginning, Nazis made it their goal to control all aspects of German life. All newspapers and radio stations that did not support the party were censored, bookstores and libraries were raided, and thousands of books were burned. All other political parties and social organizations except the Nazi Party and Hitler Youth were banned, and Hitler's opponents were arrested or killed. This all happened within the first few months of 1933.

Nazi Ideology

Nazis believed in the superiority of the "Aryan" race—an invented category of "pure" Germans that excluded Jews, gypsies, and the

▲ Adolf Hitler was in firm control of Nazi Germany from 1933 until his suicide in 1945. His actions and ideas led to the deaths of an estimated 40 million people.

▽ Throughout the late 1930s, German power was on display at massive rallies, such as this Nazi rally at Nuremberg.

98 UNIT 2 • THE HOLOCAUST

CROSS-CURRICULAR PERSPECTIVES

Social Studies Have students research the socialist element of the National Socialist German Workers Party. *What was the situation of working-class Germans during the 1920s and 1930s? Were their fortunes rising or falling? What kind of economic policies did the Nazis promise working-class Germans?* When students have completed their research, have them present their findings to the class.

ESSENTIAL QUESTION: How do we remember the past?

DIGITAL PERSPECTIVES

Hungarian Jewish prisoners arrive at Auschwitz-Birkenau, the largest of the extermination camps. About one million Jews were killed there.

descendants of immigrants from Eastern Europe. They targeted German Jews in particular for violence and persecution. Nazis forced Germans to boycott Jewish-run businesses, banned Jews from many professions, and prevented Jews from marrying those they considered Aryan or "pure" Germans. Schools taught that Jews were "polluting" German society and culture.

In 1938, the Nazis organized a rampage, "The Night of Broken Glass," against German Jews, destroying homes, businesses, and synagogues. More than 90 Jews were killed, and 30,000 were imprisoned in concentration camps. The message to German Jews was clear—leave everything behind and flee Germany, or face persecution.

The Final Solution

In 1939, Germany invaded Poland, starting World War II. As the Nazis overran much of Europe, their plans for Jews became increasingly extreme. They rounded them up and relocated them to sealed ghettos, in which overcrowding and starvation were common.

Even treatment this harsh rapidly intensified, as German plans grew more organized and deadly. In 1942, the Nazis began to transport millions of Jews from all across Europe to forced labor camps and extermination camps they had established. In two camps in Poland, perhaps a quarter of the prisoners were worked to death. The rest were sent immediately to gas chambers to be killed. In the other four camps, all of the prisoners were gassed as soon as they arrived.

When the Allied forces finally occupied Germany and Poland in 1945, the camps were liberated, and the Nazis' horrific plans were stopped. But the "Final Solution" had already resulted in the deaths of about six million Jews—two-thirds of Europe's prewar Jewish population.

The words *Arbeit Macht Frei*—"work makes you free"—appeared at the entrance to every concentration camp. Meant to give false hope, the slogan became a cruel joke in camps where prisoners were gassed, starved, or worked to death.

Historical Perspectives 99

The Final Solution

Have students read this section of the Historical Perspective. Then ask them if what they have read supports what they already knew about the Holocaust. If the "Final Solution" was not one of Hitler's original goals, why might the idea have gradually evolved?

After the discussion, ask students to attempt to quantify the number *six million* in terms that they can understand. *What cities or nations have a population of that number? What other referents can students find?* You might suggest that students attempt to estimate the number of people they see in one day, and then to see how many days it would take to see six million people. (If they saw 300 different people each and every day, it would take more than 50 years to see 6 million people.)

PERSONALIZE FOR LEARNING

English Language Support

Multiple-Meaning Words English learners may have difficulty with the term *concentration camp*. Explain that the word *concentration* has several meanings, each related to the verb *concentrate*.

- *The chess players' concentration was unbroken by the television cameras.* (the act of focusing one's attention on something)
- *Ocean currents create great concentrations of plastic debris far from shore.* (the state of being gathered together)
- *The concentration of lead in the city's water supply exceeded state limits.* (the amount of something in a given body or volume)

Point out that *concentration camp* is a compound noun, and ask students which meaning of *concentration* pertains here. **ALL LEVELS**

Whole-Class Learning 99

TEACHING

Jump Start

FIRST READ Prior to students' first read, engage them in a discussion about what it would be like to leave your home and all you know to go into hiding in hopes of saving your life.

The Diary of Anne Frank, Act I

Who is Anne Frank? Why is she important? Why is the family hiding? Modeling questions such as these will help students connect to *The Diary of Anne Frank*, Act I, and to the Whole-Class Performance Task assignment. Selection audio and print capability for the selection are available in the Interactive Teacher's Edition.

Concept Vocabulary

Support students as they rank their words. Reassure them that the definitions for these words are listed in the selection.

As they read, students should perform the steps of the first read:

NOTICE: You may want to encourage students to notice how the characters in the play interact with each other.

ANNOTATE: Remind students to mark passages that they feel help build the drama of the play, including dialogue as well as stage direction.

CONNECT: Encourage students to go beyond the text to make connections to their own lives. Have students connect to other stories about the time, as well as plays and movies they may have seen.

RESPOND: Students will answer questions and write a summary to demonstrate understanding.

Point out to students that while they will always complete the Respond step at the end of the first read, the other steps will probably happen somewhat concurrently. You may wish to print copies of the **First-Read Guide: Fiction** for students to use.

MAKING MEANING

About the Playwrights

Frances Goodrich (1890–1984) and **Albert Hackett** (1900–1995) began working together in 1927 and were married in 1931. The couple's writings include screenplays for such classic films as *The Thin Man* (1934), *It's a Wonderful Life* (1946), and *Father of the Bride* (1950). Goodrich and Hackett spent two years writing *The Diary of Anne Frank*, which went on to win many awards, including the Pulitzer Prize for Drama.

🔧 **Tool Kit**
First-Read Guide and Model Annotation

STANDARDS
Reading Literature
By the end of the year, read and comprehend literature, including stories, dramas, and poems, at the high end of grades 6–8 text complexity band independently and proficiently.

100 UNIT 2 • THE HOLOCAUST

The Diary of Anne Frank, Act I

Concept Vocabulary

As you conduct your first read of *The Diary of Anne Frank*, Act I, you will encounter these words. Before reading, note how familiar you are with each word. Then rank the words in order from most familiar (1) to least familiar (6).

WORD	YOUR RANKING
anxiously	
tension	
restraining	
quarrels	
bickering	
hysterically	

After completing the first read, come back to the concept vocabulary and review your rankings. Mark changes to your original rankings as needed.

First Read DRAMA

Apply these strategies as you conduct your first read. You will have an opportunity to complete the close-read notes after your first read.

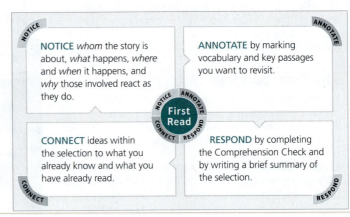

NOTICE whom the story is about, what happens, where and when it happens, and why those involved react as they do.

ANNOTATE by marking vocabulary and key passages you want to revisit.

CONNECT ideas within the selection to what you already know and what you have already read.

RESPOND by completing the Comprehension Check and by writing a brief summary of the selection.

AUTHOR'S PERSPECTIVE Kelly Gallagher, M.Ed.

First-Read Strategies As students encounter unfamiliar and challenging text for the first time, some may hit a frustration point early. Students often think that if they don't understand something on the first try that they will never understand. Comprehension when reading is not an all-or-nothing situation. Share these strategies for getting through the gray areas:

- **Read on with Uncertainty** Students who are "a little bit lost" may be able to read a little further to resolve confusion. Demonstrate that many questions arise at the beginning as readers place themselves in the world the writer has created.

- **Monitor Comprehension** To make their comprehension more concrete for students, have them use two different colors to mark the text: one color for text they understand, and another color to highlight the text that is challenging to them.

- **Apply Fix-It Strategies** Students who are struggling with comprehension may start by rereading at the word level and decoding words they don't know. They can then move to the sentence level to make sure that they are following the text. When students have the tools to monitor their comprehension, they can get past the literal interpretation of text. Then they can uncover deeper meaning.

ANCHOR TEXT | DRAMA

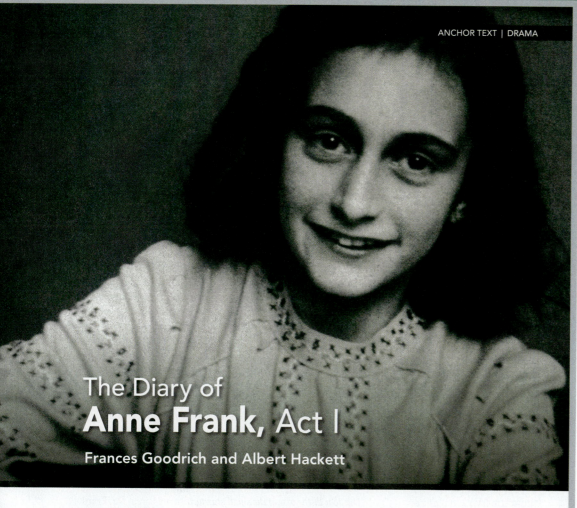

The Diary of Anne Frank, Act I

Frances Goodrich and Albert Hackett

BACKGROUND

Anne Frank was a young Jewish girl living in Amsterdam during the Nazi occupation of the Netherlands in World War II. Fearing for their lives, the Frank family was forced into hiding. The diary that Anne kept during their time in hiding is one of the most famous and heartbreaking pieces of literature from the Holocaust. Anne's diary gained recognition both for its historical significance and for her incredible talent as a writer and storyteller. Tragically, Anne died in a concentration camp just weeks before it was liberated by British soldiers. The play you will read was based on her life and diary.

Characters
Anne Frank	Miep Gies	Mrs. Van Daan
Otto Frank	Mr. Kraler	Mr. Van Daan
Edith Frank	Mr. Dussel	
Margot Frank	Peter Van Daan	

CROSS-CURRICULAR PERSPECTIVES

Social Studies Show a map of Europe during World War II. Point out the location of Germany, France, and The Netherlands. Ask students what they notice about the locations of these two countries and Germany. Explain that the Nazis occupied many countries during the war. Use the map to demonstrate the wide reach of the Nazis during World War II.

TEACHING

CLOSE READ

As students look for descriptive details, remind them to find words that tell what something looks like. You may wish to model the close read using the following think-aloud format. Possible responses to questions on the student page are included. You may also want to print copies of the **Close-Read Guide: Fiction** for students to use.

ANNOTATE: As I read paragraphs 1–5, I notice and annotate details that describe the sizes of the rooms.

QUESTION: I think that these details help readers and people involved in staging the play understand how cramped the quarters were.

CONCLUDE: The description of the rooms supports the idea that the people who lived there must have struggled during the war.

NOTES

1. **carillon** (KAR uh lon) *n.* set of bells, each producing one note of the scale.

2. **blackout curtains** dark curtains that conceal all lights that might be visible to bombers from the air.

CLOSE READ
ANNOTATE: Mark details in paragraphs 1–5 that describe the dimensions, or sizes, of the various rooms.

QUESTION: Why do the playwrights note these details of the setting?

CONCLUDE: What is the effect of these details?

3. **barrel organ** mechanical musical instrument often played by street musicians in past decades.

Act I

Scene 1

1 [*The scene remains the same throughout the play. It is the top floor of a warehouse and office building in Amsterdam, Holland. The sharply peaked roof of the building is outlined against a sea of other rooftops, stretching away into the distance. Nearby is the belfry of a church tower, the Westertoren, whose carillon[1] rings out the hours. Occasionally faint sounds float up from below: the voices of children playing in the street, the tramp of marching feet, a boat whistle from the canal.*

2 *The three rooms of the top floor and a small attic space above are exposed to our view. The largest of the rooms is in the center, with two small rooms, slightly raised, on either side. On the right is a bathroom, out of sight. A narrow steep flight of stairs at the back leads up to the attic. The rooms are sparsely furnished with a few chairs, cots, a table or two. The windows are painted over, or covered with makeshift blackout curtains.[2] In the main room there is a sink, a gas ring for cooking and a woodburning stove for warmth.*

3 *The room on the left is hardly more than a closet. There is a skylight in the sloping ceiling. Directly under this room is a small steep stairwell, with steps leading down to a door. This is the only entrance from the building below. When the door is opened we see that it has been concealed on the outer side by a bookcase attached to it.*

4 *The curtain rises on an empty stage. It is late afternoon, November 1945.*

5 *The rooms are dusty, the curtains in rags. Chairs and tables are overturned.*

6 *The door at the foot of the small stairwell swings open.* **Mr. Frank** *comes up the steps into view. He is a gentle, cultured European in his middle years. There is still a trace of a German accent in his speech.*

7 *He stands looking slowly around, making a supreme effort at self-control. He is weak, ill. His clothes are threadbare.*

8 *After a second he drops his rucksack on the couch and moves slowly about. He opens the door to one of the smaller rooms, and then abruptly closes it again, turning away. He goes to the window at the back, looking off at the Westertoren as its carillon strikes the hour of six, then he moves restlessly on.*

9 *From the street below we hear the sound of a barrel organ[3] and children's voices at play. There is a many-colored scarf hanging from a nail.* **Mr. Frank** *takes it, putting it around his neck. As he starts back for his rucksack, his eye is caught by something lying on the floor. It is a woman's white glove. He holds it in his hand and suddenly all of his self-control is gone. He breaks down, crying.*

10 *We hear footsteps on the stairs.* Miep Gies *comes up, looking for Mr. Frank. Miep is a Dutch girl of about twenty-two. She wears a coat and hat, ready to go home. She is pregnant. Her attitude toward Mr. Frank is protective, compassionate.*

11 **Miep.** Are you all right, Mr. Frank?

12 **Mr. Frank.** [*Quickly controlling himself*] Yes, Miep, yes.

13 **Miep.** Everyone in the office has gone home . . . It's after six. [*Then pleading*] Don't stay up here, Mr. Frank. What's the use of torturing yourself like this?

14 **Mr. Frank.** I've come to say good-bye . . . I'm leaving here, Miep.

15 **Miep.** What do you mean? Where are you going? Where?

16 **Mr. Frank.** I don't know yet. I haven't decided.

17 **Miep.** Mr. Frank, you can't leave here! This is your home! Amsterdam is your home. Your business is here, waiting for you . . . You're needed here . . . Now that the war is over, there are things that . . .

18 **Mr. Frank.** I can't stay in Amsterdam, Miep. It has too many memories for me. Everywhere there's something . . . the house we lived in . . . the school . . . that street organ playing out there . . . I'm not the person you used to know, Miep. I'm a bitter old man. [*Breaking off*] Forgive me. I shouldn't speak to you like this . . . after all that you did for us . . . the suffering . . .

19 **Miep.** No. No. It wasn't suffering. You can't say we suffered. [*As she speaks, she straightens a chair which is overturned.*]

20 **Mr. Frank.** I know what you went through, you and Mr. Kraler. I'll remember it as long as I live. [*He gives one last look around.*] Come, Miep. [*He starts for the steps, then remembers his rucksack, going back to get it.*]

21 **Miep.** [*Hurrying up to a cupboard*] Mr. Frank, did you see? There are some of your papers here. [*She brings a bundle of papers to him.*] We found them in a heap of rubbish on the floor after . . . after you left.

22 **Mr. Frank.** Burn them. [*He opens his rucksack to put the glove in it.*]

23 **Miep.** But, Mr. Frank, there are letters, notes . . .

24 **Mr. Frank.** Burn them. All of them.

25 **Miep.** Burn *this*? [*She hands him a paperbound notebook.*]

26 **Mr. Frank.** [*Quietly*] Anne's diary. [*He opens the diary and begins to read.*] "Monday, the sixth of July, nineteen forty-two." [*To Miep*] Nineteen forty-two. Is it possible, Miep? . . . Only three years ago. [*As he continues his reading, he sits down*

NOTES

The Diary of Anne Frank, Act I 103

PERSONALIZE FOR LEARNING

Strategic Support

Timeline Ask the students which characters are in this scene. (Mr. Frank and Miep) Point out that this dialogue is taking place after Anne is gone. Explain that the playwrights are bringing you to the end of the story first. Ask: Why do you think the playwrights do this? Point out the following text in paragraph 26: "Nineteen forty-two. Is it possible Miep?. . . Only three years ago."

Whole-Class Learning 103

TEACHING

NOTES

4. **capitulation** (kuh pihch uh LAY shuhn) *n.* surrender.

5. **yellow stars** Stars of David, the six-pointed stars that are symbols of Judaism. The Nazis ordered all Jews to wear them on their clothing.

6. **portly** (PAWRT lee) *adj.* large and heavy.

on the couch.] "Dear Diary, since you and I are going to be great friends, I will start by telling you about myself. My name is Anne Frank. I am thirteen years old. I was born in Germany the twelfth of June, nineteen twenty-nine. As my family is Jewish, we emigrated to Holland when Hitler came to power."

27 [*As* Mr. Frank *reads on, another voice joins his, as if coming from the air. It is* Anne's Voice.]

28 **Mr. Frank and Anne.** "My father started a business, importing spice and herbs. Things went well for us until nineteen forty. Then the war came, and the Dutch capitulation,[4] followed by the arrival of the Germans. Then things got very bad for the Jews."

29 [Mr. Frank's Voice *dies out.* Anne's Voice *continues alone. The lights dim slowly to darkness. The curtain falls on the scene.*]

30 **Anne's Voice.** You could not do this and you could not do that. They forced Father out of his business. We had to wear yellow stars.[5] I had to turn in my bike. I couldn't go to a Dutch school any more. I couldn't go to the movies, or ride in an automobile, or even on a streetcar, and a million other things. But somehow we children still managed to have fun. Yesterday Father told me we were going into hiding. Where, he wouldn't say. At five o'clock this morning Mother woke me and told me to hurry and get dressed. I was to put on as many clothes as I could. It would look too suspicious if we walked along carrying suitcases. It wasn't until we were on our way that I learned where we were going. Our hiding place was to be upstairs in the building where Father used to have his business. Three other people were coming in with us . . . the Van Daans and their son Peter . . . Father knew the Van Daans but we had never met them . . .

31 [*During the last lines the curtain rises on the scene. The lights dim on.* Anne's Voice *fades out.*]

⌘ ⌘ ⌘

Scene 2

1 [*It is early morning, July 1942. The rooms are bare, as before, but they are now clean and orderly.*

2 Mr. Van Daan, *a tall portly[6] man in his late forties, is in the main room, pacing up and down, nervously smoking a cigarette. His clothes and overcoat are expensive and well cut.*

WriteNow Inform and Explain

Description Have students reread paragraph 30 of Scene 1. Explain that Anne is providing a description of her experiences before she went into hiding. Ask students to write a brief description of how life had changed for Anne under the Nazis. What could she no longer do? What was her father asking her to do?

3   **Mrs. Van Daan** *sits on the couch, clutching her possessions, a hatbox, bags, etc. She is a pretty woman in her early forties. She wears a fur coat over her other clothes.*

4   **Peter Van Daan** *is standing at the window of the room on the right, looking down at the street below. He is a shy, awkward boy of sixteen. He wears a cap, a raincoat, and long Dutch trousers, like "plus fours."*[7] *At his feet is a black case, a carrier for his cat.*

5   *The yellow Star of David is conspicuous on all of their clothes.*]

6   **Mrs. Van Daan.** [*Rising, nervous, excited*] Something's happened to them! I know it!

7   **Mr. Van Daan.** Now, Kerli!

8   **Mrs. Van Daan.** Mr. Frank said they'd be here at seven o'clock. He said . . .

9   **Mr. Van Daan.** They have two miles to walk. You can't expect . . .

10 **Mrs. Van Daan.** They've been picked up. That's what's happened. They've been taken . . .

11 [**Mr. Van Daan** *indicates that he hears someone coming.*]

12 **Mr. Van Daan.** You see?

13 [**Peter** *takes up his carrier and his schoolbag, etc., and goes into the main room as* **Mr. Frank** *comes up the stairwell from below.* **Mr. Frank** *looks much younger now. His movements are brisk, his manner confident. He wears an overcoat and carries his hat and a small cardboard box. He crosses to the* **Van Daans,** *shaking hands with each of them.*]

NOTES

7. **plus fours** *n.* short pants worn for active sports.

CLOSE READ

ANNOTATE: In paragraphs 6–10, mark punctuation that suggests the characters are anxious or being interrupted.

QUESTION: Why might the playwrights have used these punctuation marks?

CONCLUDE: What **mood**, or feeling, does this punctuation help convey?

Anne in happier times, out for a stroll with her family and friends.

DIGITAL PERSPECTIVES

CLOSE READ

In a play, the playwright uses dialogue and stage direction to provide the reader with the details of the story. The playwright can also use punctuation in dialogue, such as the ellipses and exclamation points in paragraphs 6–10, to enhance the mood or meaning of the character's lines. You may wish to model the close read using the following think-aloud format. Possible responses to questions on the student page are included.

ANNOTATE: As I read paragraphs 6–10, I mark the punctuation that helps express emotion.

QUESTION: I feel the playwrights used this punctuation to provide cues to actors (and to readers) about the pacing and emphasis they intend in the dialogue.

CONCLUDE: The exclamation marks indicate alarm and extreme worry, which shows the Van Daans' fear and concern. The ellipses indicate pauses in the dialogue, as if the speakers are being interrupted. The punctuation works together to help show how frightened and worried the characters are, almost as if they are afraid to speak the full thoughts in their minds.

TEACHING

NOTES

8. **Green Police** Dutch Gestapo, or Nazi police, who wore green uniforms and were known for their brutality. Those in danger of being arrested or deported feared the Gestapo, especially because of their practice of raiding houses to round up victims in the middle of the night—when people are most confused and vulnerable.

9. **mercurial** (muhr KYUR ee uhl) *adj.* quick or changeable in behavior.

10. **ration books** books of stamps given to ensure the equal distribution of scarce items, such as meat or gasoline, in times of shortage.

---

14 **Mr. Frank.** Mrs. Van Daan, Mr. Van Daan, Peter. [*Then, in explanation of their lateness*] There were too many of the Green Police[8] on the streets . . . we had to take the long way around.

15 [*Up the steps come* Margot Frank, Mrs. Frank, Miep (*not pregnant now*) *and* Mr. Kraler. *All of them carry bags, packages, and so forth. The Star of David is conspicuous on all of the* Franks' *clothing.* Margot *is eighteen, beautiful, quiet, shy.* Mrs. Frank *is a young mother, gently bred, reserved. She, like* Mr. Frank, *has a slight German accent.* Mr. Kraler *is a Dutchman, dependable, kindly.*]

16 *As* Mr. Kraler *and* Miep *go upstage to put down their parcels,* Mrs. Frank *turns back to call* Anne.]

17 **Mrs. Frank.** Anne?

18 [Anne *comes running up the stairs. She is thirteen, quick in her movements, interested in everything, mercurial*[9] *in her emotions. She wears a cape, long wool socks and carries a schoolbag.*]

19 **Mr. Frank.** [*Introducing them*] My wife, Edith. Mr. and Mrs. Van Daan [Mrs. Frank *hurries over, shaking hands with them.*] . . . their son, Peter . . . my daughters, Margot and Anne.

20 [Anne *gives a polite little curtsy as she shakes* Mr. Van Daan's *hand. Then she immediately starts off on a tour of investigation of her new home, going upstairs to the attic room.*]

21 Miep *and* Mr. Kraler *are putting the various things they have brought on the shelves.*]

22 **Mr. Kraler.** I'm sorry there is still so much confusion.

23 **Mr. Frank.** Please. Don't think of it. After all, we'll have plenty of leisure to arrange everything ourselves.

24 **Miep.** [*To* Mrs. Frank] We put the stores of food you sent in here. Your drugs are here . . . soap, linen here.

25 **Mrs. Frank.** Thank you, Miep.

26 **Miep.** I made up the beds . . . the way Mr. Frank and Mr. Kraler said. [*She starts out.*] Forgive me. I have to hurry. I've got to go to the other side of town to get some ration books[10] for you.

27 **Mrs. Van Daan.** Ration books? If they see our names on ration books, they'll know we're here.

28 **Mr. Kraler.** There isn't anything . . .

29 **Miep.** Don't worry. Your names won't be on them. [*As she hurries out*] I'll be up later.

30 **Mr. Frank.** Thank you, Miep.

PERSONALIZE FOR LEARNING

Challenge

Wartime Review paragraphs 25–28 and help students identify details related to wartime. The story of Anne Frank took place many years ago. Items and concepts that were common during her time may not be familiar now. Explain that during times of war, many everyday items, like food and clothing, were not easy to get. Tell students that governments attempted to make sure that people got the same amounts of needed items by rationing them, or by giving each person a set amount. Ask students to think about the story and to consider why ration books had names on them. Possible response: It was how the government kept track of the rations, or items to be given out.

31 **Mrs. Frank.** [*To* Mr. Kraler] It's illegal, then, the ration books? We've never done anything illegal.

32 **Mr. Frank.** We won't be living here exactly according to regulations.

33 [*As* Mr. Kraler *reassures* Mrs. Frank, *he takes various small things, such as matches, soap, etc., from his pockets, handing them to her.*]

34 **Mr. Kraler.** This isn't the black market,[11] Mrs. Frank. This is what we call the white market . . . helping all of the hundreds and hundreds who are hiding out in Amsterdam.

35 [*The carillon is heard playing the quarter-hour before eight.* Mr. Kraler *looks at his watch.* Anne *stops at the window as she comes down the stairs.*]

36 **Anne.** It's the Westertoren!

37 **Mr. Kraler.** I must go. I must be out of here and downstairs in the office before the workmen get here. [*He starts for the stairs leading out.*] Miep or I, or both of us, will be up each day to bring you food and news and find out what your needs are. Tomorrow I'll get you a better bolt for the door at the foot of the stairs. It needs a bolt that you can throw yourself and open only at our signal. [*To* Mr. Frank] Oh . . . You'll tell them about the noise?

38 **Mr. Frank.** I'll tell them.

39 **Mr. Kraler.** Good-bye then for the moment. I'll come up again, after the workmen leave.

40 **Mr. Frank.** Good-bye, Mr. Kraler.

41 **Mrs. Frank.** [*Shaking his hand*] How can we thank you?

42 [*The others murmur their good-byes.*]

43 **Mr. Kraler.** I never thought I'd live to see the day when a man like Mr. Frank would have to go into hiding. When you think—

44 [*He breaks off, going out.* Mr. Frank *follows him down the steps, bolting the door after him. In the interval before he returns,* Peter *goes over to* Margot, *shaking hands with her. As* Mr. Frank *comes back up the steps,* Mrs. Frank *questions him* anxiously.]

45 **Mrs. Frank.** What did he mean, about the noise?

46 **Mr. Frank.** First let us take off some of these clothes.

47 [*They all start to take off garment after garment. On each of their coats, sweaters, blouses, suits, dresses, is another yellow Star of David.* Mr. *and* Mrs. Frank *are underdressed quite simply.*]

NOTES

11. **black market** illegal way of buying scarce items.

anxiously (ANGK shuhs lee) *adv.* in a nervous or worried way

TEACHING

● CLOSE READ

Stage directions in a play include directions for the set design, props, and character blocking, as well as sound effects, such as the sound described in paragraph 54 stage directions. You may wish to model the close read using the following think-aloud format. Possible responses to questions on the student page are included.

ANNOTATE: As I read paragraph 54, I notice the stage direction calling for the sound of marching feet on the street outside the building.

QUESTION: I think the playwrights included this detail to give evidence of the types of threats that faced the Jews of Amsterdam during the war. Just the sound of soldiers marching causes them all to think that they are about to be arrested.

CONCLUDE: The sound effect has the effect of reminding us that, while the characters may be in relative safety while they are in hiding, they are still in great danger, and any unlucky mistake could alert the Nazis to their presence.

Additional **English Language Support** is available in the Interactive Teacher's Edition.

NOTES

CLOSE READ
ANNOTATE: In paragraph 54, mark the sound that causes the characters to feel afraid.

QUESTION: Why do the playwrights include this detail?

CONCLUDE: How does this detail clarify the characters' situation?

12. **w.c.** water closet; bathroom.

tension (TEHN shuhn)
n. nervous, worried, or excited condition that makes relaxation impossible

---

The others wear several things: sweaters, extra dresses, bathrobes, aprons, nightgowns, etc.]

48 **Mr. Van Daan.** It's a wonder we weren't arrested, walking along the streets . . . Petronella with a fur coat in July . . . and that cat of Peter's crying all the way.

49 **Anne.** [*As she is removing a pair of panties*] A cat?

50 **Mrs. Frank.** [*Shocked*] Anne, please!

51 **Anne.** It's alright. I've got on three more.

52 [*She pulls off two more. Finally, as they have all removed their surplus clothes, they look to* Mr. Frank, *waiting for him to speak.*]

53 **Mr. Frank.** Now. About the noise. While the men are in the building below, we must have complete quiet. Every sound can be heard down there, not only in the workrooms, but in the offices too. The men come at about eight-thirty, and leave at about five-thirty. So, to be perfectly safe, from eight in the morning until six in the evening we must move only when it is necessary, and then in stockinged feet. We must not speak above a whisper. We must not run any water. We cannot use the sink, or even, forgive me, the w.c.[12] The pipes go down through the workrooms. It would be heard. No trash . . .

54 [Mr. Frank *stops abruptly as he hears the sound of marching feet from the street below. Everyone is motionless, paralyzed with fear.* Mr. Frank *goes quietly into the room on the right to look down out of the window.* Anne *runs after him, peering out with him. The tramping feet pass without stopping. The tension is relieved.* Mr. Frank, *followed by* Anne, *returns to the main room and resumes his instructions to the group.*] . . . No trash must ever be thrown out which might reveal that someone is living up here . . . not even a potato paring. We must burn everything in the stove at night. This is the way we must live until it is over, if we are to survive.

55 [*There is silence for a second.*]

56 **Mrs. Frank.** Until it is over.

57 **Mr. Frank.** [*Reassuringly*] After six we can move about . . . we can talk and laugh and have our supper and read and play games . . . just as we would at home. [*He looks at his watch.*] And now I think it would be wise if we all went to our rooms, and were settled before eight o'clock. Mrs. Van Daan, you and your husband will be upstairs. I regret that there's no place up there for Peter. But he will be here, near us. This will be our common room, where we'll meet to talk and eat and read, like one family.

58 **Mr. Van Daan.** And where do you and Mrs. Frank sleep?

59 **Mr. Frank.** This room is also our bedroom.

60 [*Together*] { **Mrs. Van Daan.** That isn't right. We'll sleep here and you take the room upstairs.
Mr. Van Daan. It's your place.

61 **Mr. Frank.** Please. I've thought this out for weeks. It's the best arrangement. The only arrangement.

62 **Mrs. Van Daan.** [*To* Mr. Frank] Never, never can we thank you. [*Then to* Mrs. Frank] I don't know what would have happened to us, if it hadn't been for Mr. Frank.

63 **Mr. Frank.** You don't know how your husband helped me when I came to this country . . . knowing no one . . . not able to speak the language. I can never repay him for that. [*Going to* Mr. Van Daan] May I help you with your things?

64 **Mr. Van Daan.** No. No. [*To* Mrs. Van Daan] Come along, *liefje*.[13]

65 **Mrs. Van Daan.** You'll be all right, Peter? You're not afraid?

66 **Peter.** [*Embarrassed*] Please, Mother.

67 [*They start up the stairs to the attic room above.* Mr. Frank *turns to* Mrs. Frank.]

68 **Mr. Frank.** You too must have some rest, Edith. You didn't close your eyes last night. Nor you, Margot.

69 **Anne.** I slept, Father. Wasn't that funny? I knew it was the last night in my own bed, and yet I slept soundly.

70 **Mr. Frank.** I'm glad, Anne. Now you'll be able to help me straighten things in here. [*To* Mrs. Frank *and* Margot] Come with me . . . You and Margot rest in this room for the time being.

71 [*He picks up their clothes, starting for the room on the right.*]

72 **Mrs. Frank.** You're sure . . . ? I could help . . . And Anne hasn't had her milk . . .

73 **Mr. Frank.** I'll give it to her. [*To* Anne *and* Peter] Anne, Peter . . . it's best that you take off your shoes now, before you forget.

74 [*He leads the way to the room, followed by* Margot.]

75 **Mrs. Frank.** You're sure you're not tired, Anne?

76 **Anne.** I feel fine. I'm going to help Father.

77 **Mrs. Frank.** Peter, I'm glad you are to be with us.

78 **Peter.** Yes, Mrs. Frank.

13. *liefje* (LEEF yuh) Dutch for "little love."

TEACHING

Jews were regularly rounded up and forced to leave their homes without notice.

NOTES

79 [*Mrs. Frank goes to join Mr. Frank and Margot.*]

80 [*During the following scene Mr. Frank helps Margot and Mrs. Frank to hang up their clothes. Then he persuades them both to lie down and rest. The Van Daans in their room above settle themselves. In the main room Anne and Peter remove their shoes. Peter takes his cat out of the carrier.*]

81 **Anne.** What's your cat's name?

82 **Peter.** Mouschi.

83 **Anne.** Mouschi! Mouschi! Mouschi! [*She picks up the cat, walking away with it. To* Peter] I love cats. I have one . . . a darling little cat. But they made me leave her behind. I left some food and a note for the neighbors to take care of her . . . I'm going to miss her terribly. What is yours? A him or a her?

84 **Peter.** He's a tom. He doesn't like strangers. [*He takes the cat from her, putting it back in its carrier.*]

85 **Anne.** [*Unabashed*] Then I'll have to stop being a stranger, won't I? Is he fixed?

86 **Peter.** [*Startled*] Huh?

87 **Anne.** Did you have him fixed?

88 **Peter.** No.

89 **Anne.** Oh, you ought to have him fixed—to keep him from— you know, fighting. Where did you go to school?

90 **Peter.** Jewish Secondary.

91 **Anne.** But that's where Margot and I go! I never saw you around.

92 **Peter.** I used to see you . . . sometimes . . .

93 **Anne.** You did?

94 **Peter.** . . . In the school yard. You were always in the middle of a bunch of kids. [*He takes a penknife from his pocket.*]

95 **Anne.** Why didn't you ever come over?

96 **Peter.** I'm sort of a lone wolf. [*He starts to rip off his Star of David.*]

97 **Anne.** What are you doing?

98 **Peter.** Taking it off.

99 **Anne.** But you can't do that. They'll arrest you if you go out without your star.

100 [*He tosses his knife on the table.*]

110 UNIT 2 • THE HOLOCAUST

CROSS-CURRICULAR PERSPECTIVES

Art The writer uses dialogue and stage direction to create a picture for the reader of what the characters experienced. By talking about what the characters wore and what they carried, we can visualize them on stage. Have students look at the photograph of Jews leaving their homes. Ask them to describe the details they see. They may notice that it is black and white, the stars on the clothing, or the small packages the people carry. They may notice that the people are going somewhere. Ask students to imagine the story behind this picture. Ask students to tell the story they see. Have students respond to each other's stories in discussion.

101 **Peter.** Who's going out?

102 **Anne.** Why, of course! You're right! Of course we don't need them any more. [*She picks up his knife and starts to take her star off.*] I wonder what our friends will think when we don't show up today?

103 **Peter.** I didn't have any dates with anyone.

104 **Anne.** Oh, I did. I had a date with Jopie to go and play ping-pong at her house. Do you know Jopie de Waal?

105 **Peter.** No.

106 **Anne.** Jopie's my best friend. I wonder what she'll think when she telephones and there's no answer? . . . Probably she'll go over to the house . . . I wonder what she'll think . . . we left everything as if we'd suddenly been called away . . . breakfast dishes in the sink . . . beds not made . . . [*As she pulls off her star, the cloth underneath shows clearly the color and form of the star.*] Look! It's still there! [*Peter goes over to the stove with his star.*] What're you going to do with yours?

107 **Peter.** Burn it.

108 **Anne.** [*She starts to throw hers in, and cannot.*] It's funny, I can't throw mine away. I don't know why.

109 **Peter.** You can't throw . . . ? Something they branded you with . . . ? That they made you wear so they could spit on you?

110 **Anne.** I know. I know. But after all, it *is* the Star of David, isn't it?

111 [*In the bedroom, right,* Margot *and* Mrs. Frank *are lying down.* Mr. Frank *starts quietly out.*]

112 **Peter.** Maybe it's different for a girl.

113 [Mr. Frank *comes into the main room.*]

114 **Mr. Frank.** Forgive me, Peter. Now let me see. We must find a bed for your cat. [*He goes to a cupboard.*] I'm glad you brought your cat. Anne was feeling so badly about hers. [*Getting a used small washtub*] Here we are. Will it be comfortable in that?

115 **Peter.** [*Gathering up his things*] Thanks.

116 **Mr. Frank.** [*Opening the door of the room on the left*] And here is your room. But I warn you, Peter, you can't grow any more. Not an inch, or you'll have to sleep with your feet out of the skylight. Are you hungry?

117 **Peter.** No.

118 **Mr. Frank.** We have some bread and butter.

NOTES

CLOSE READ
ANNOTATE: In paragraphs 94–107, mark details that show what Peter is doing and why.

QUESTION: Think about what the yellow star represents during World War II. Why do the playwrights include the details of Peter's actions?

CONCLUDE: What do Peter's actions show about his character?

Characters' actions in a play both advance the plot and also reveal the values and nature of the characters, such as the sequence in which Peter tears off his yellow star and burns it in paragraphs 94–107. You may wish to model the close read using the following think-aloud format. Possible responses to questions on the student page are included.

ANNOTATE: As I read paragraphs 94–107, I notice stage directions and dialogue explaining what Peter is doing and what it means.

QUESTION: I know that the Star of David is an important symbol for the Jewish people and in Nazi-occupied Netherlands, Jews were forced to identify themselves by wearing yellow Jewish stars on their clothing. The playwrights must have included this detail to reinforce the time and place of the story, and the plight of the characters.

CONCLUDE: By ripping off his star, Peter is showing his anger at the degradation forced upon the Jews by the Nazis and his desire to see the Nazis defeated. He is also communicating that he is not as powerless as he felt when forced to wear the star. Including these details in the stage directions and the dialogue helps the playwrights demonstrate aspects of Peter's character we have not yet seen.

TEACHING

● CLOSE READ

Stage directions affect the meaning of the dialogue and of the story as a whole. In both Anne's dialogue and in the stage directions, readers see in paragraphs 129–135 how her mood changes from happiness to resignation. You may wish to model the close read using the following think-aloud format. Possible responses to questions on the student page are included.

ANNOTATE: As I read paragraphs 129–135, I notice stage directions and dialogue showing Anne's mood changing dramatically.

QUESTION: I notice that these details show how Anne's mood changes when her joy over receiving a gift is interrupted by her father's harsh reminder of the real danger in which they are living.

CONCLUDE: These details show readers that the realities of going into hiding are so grim that even Anne, who is always trying to make the best of things, is sobered by the dangers still threatening them.

NOTES

14. **Annele** (AHN eh leh) nickname for "Anne."

15. **Queen Wilhelmina** (vihl hehl MEE nah) Queen of the Netherlands from 1890 to 1948.

CLOSE READ
ANNOTATE: In paragraphs 129–135, mark details that show the changes in Anne's mood.

QUESTION: Why do the playwrights include these details?

CONCLUDE: How do these details help readers appreciate the extreme nature of the Franks' situation?

16. **Anneke** (AHN eh keh) another nickname for "Anne."

---

119 **Peter.** No, thank you.

120 **Mr. Frank.** You can have it for luncheon then. And tonight we will have a real supper . . . our first supper together.

121 **Peter.** Thanks. Thanks. [*He goes into his room. During the following scene he arranges his possessions in his new room.*]

122 **Mr. Frank.** That's a nice boy, Peter.

123 **Anne.** He's awfully shy, isn't he?

124 **Mr. Frank.** You'll like him, I know.

125 **Anne.** I certainly hope so, since he's the only boy I'm likely to see for months and months.

126 [*Mr. Frank sits down, taking off his shoes.*]

127 **Mr. Frank.** Annele,[14] there's a box there. Will you open it?

128 [*He indicates a carton on the couch. Anne brings it to the center table. In the street below there is the sound of children playing.*]

129 **Anne.** [*As she opens the carton*] You know the way I'm going to think of it here? I'm going to think of it as a boarding house. A very peculiar summer boarding house, like the one that we—[*She breaks off as she pulls out some photographs.*] Father! My movie stars! I was wondering where they were! I was looking for them this morning . . . and Queen Wilhelmina![15] How wonderful!

130 **Mr. Frank.** There's something more. Go on. Look further. [*He goes over to the sink, pouring a glass of milk from a thermos bottle.*]

131 **Anne.** [*Pulling out a pasteboard-bound book*] A diary! [*She throws her arms around her father.*] I've never had a diary. And I've always longed for one. [*She looks around the room.*] Pencil, pencil, pencil, pencil. [*She starts down the stairs.*] I'm going down to the office to get a pencil.

132 **Mr. Frank.** Anne! No! [*He goes after her, catching her by the arm and pulling her back.*]

133 **Anne.** [*Startled*] But there's no one in the building now.

134 **Mr. Frank.** It doesn't matter. I don't want you ever to go beyond that door.

135 **Anne.** [*Sobered*] Never . . . ? Not even at nighttime, when everyone is gone? Or on Sundays? Can't I go down to listen to the radio?

136 **Mr. Frank.** Never. I am sorry, Anneke.[16] It isn't safe. No, you must never go beyond that door.

137 [*For the first time Anne realizes what "going into hiding" means.*]

138 **Anne.** I see.

139 **Mr. Frank.** It'll be hard, I know. But always remember this, Anneke. There are no walls, there are no bolts, no locks that anyone can put on your mind. Miep will bring us books. We will read history, poetry, mythology. [*He gives her the glass of milk.*] Here's your milk. [*With his arm about her, they go over to the couch, sitting down side by side.*] As a matter of fact, between us, Anne, being here has certain advantages for you. For instance, you remember the battle you had with your mother the other day on the subject of overshoes? You said you'd rather die than wear overshoes? But in the end you had to wear them? Well now, you see, for as long as we are here you will never have to wear overshoes! Isn't that good? And the coat that you inherited from Margot, you won't have to wear that any more. And the piano! You won't have to practice on the piano. I tell you, this is going to be a fine life for you!

140 [*Anne's panic is gone.* Peter *appears in the doorway of his room, with a saucer in his hand. He is carrying his cat.*]

141 **Peter.** I . . . I . . . I thought I'd better get some water for Mouschi before . . .

142 **Mr. Frank.** Of course.

143 [*As he starts toward the sink the carillon begins to chime the hour of eight. He tiptoes to the window at the back and looks down at the street below. He turns to* Peter, *indicating in pantomime that it is too late.* Peter *starts back for his room. He steps on a creaking board. The three of them are frozen for a minute in fear. As* Peter *starts away again,* Anne *tiptoes over to him and pours some of the milk from her glass into the saucer for the cat.* Peter *squats on the floor, putting the milk before the cat.* Mr. Frank *gives* Anne *his fountain pen, and then goes into the room at the right. For a second* Anne *watches the cat, then she goes over to the center table, and opens her diary.*]

144 *In the room at the right,* Mrs. Frank *has sat up quickly at the sound of the carillon.* Mr. Frank *comes in and sits down beside her on the settee, his arm comfortingly around her.*

145 *Upstairs, in the attic room,* Mr. *and* Mrs. Van Daan *have hung their clothes in the closet and are now seated on the iron bed.* Mrs. Van Daan *leans back exhausted.* Mr. Van Daan *fans her with a newspaper.*

146 Anne *starts to write in her diary. The lights dim out, the curtain falls.*

147 *In the darkness* Anne's Voice *comes to us again, faintly at first, and then with growing strength.*]

The Diary of Anne Frank, Act I

DIGITAL PERSPECTIVES

Illuminating the Text In paragraphs 143–145, a lot of action takes place in silence and pantomime. Ask students to consider why there is no talking here and why a creaky floorboard was so important. Possible response: People are now coming to work and if they hear noise from upstairs, they may call the authorities. To help students visualize the tension the playwrights are trying to convey, share a video of this scene from a professional performance. Ask students how the actors show how the characters felt in that moment.

TEACHING

CLOSE READ

Remind students that stage directions are purposeful. You may wish to model the close read using the following think-aloud format. Possible responses to questions on the student page are included.

ANNOTATE: As I read these paragraphs, I notice and mark the text that refers to silence and stillness.

QUESTION: I think that the playwrights want the audience to understand what it may be like to endure forced quiet;

CONCLUDE: These details help me see that the character's daily lives are very quiet. I imagine being quiet all day must be very difficult. There is also the added pressure for the reason for silence—the family does not want to be found and captured.

NOTES

148 **Anne's Voice.** I expect I should be describing what it feels like to go into hiding. But I really don't know yet myself. I only know it's funny never to be able to go outdoors . . . never to breathe fresh air . . . never to run and shout and jump. It's the silence in the nights that frightens me most. Every time I hear a creak in the house, or a step on the street outside, I'm sure they're coming for us. The days aren't so bad. At least we know that Miep and Mr. Kraler are down there below us in the office. Our protectors, we call them. I asked Father what would happen to them if the Nazis found out they were hiding us. Pim said that they would suffer the same fate that we would . . . Imagine! They know this, and yet when they come up here, they're always cheerful and gay as if there were nothing in the world to bother them . . . Friday, the twenty-first of August, nineteen forty-two. Today I'm going to tell you our general news. Mother is unbearable. She insists on treating me like a baby, which I loathe. Otherwise things are going better. The weather is . . .

149 [*As Anne's Voice is fading out, the curtain rises on the scene.*]

✣ ✣ ✣

Scene 3

1 [*It is a little after six o'clock in the evening, two months later.*]

2 *Margot is in the bedroom at the right, studying. Mr. Van Daan is lying down in the attic room above.*

3 *The rest of the "family" is in the main room. Anne and Peter sit opposite each other at the center table, where they have been doing their lessons. Mrs. Frank is on the couch. Mrs. Van Daan is seated with her fur coat, on which she has been sewing, in her lap. None of them are wearing their shoes.*

CLOSE READ

ANNOTATE: In paragraphs 4–8, mark details that relate to quiet or confinement. Mark other details that relate to being free or letting go.

QUESTION: Why do the playwrights go into such detail about this moment?

CONCLUDE: What do these details suggest about the characters' daily lives?

4 *Their eyes are on Mr. Frank, waiting for him to give them the signal which will release them from their day-long quiet.* Mr. Frank, *his shoes in his hand, stands looking down out of the window at the back, watching to be sure that all of the workmen have left the building below.*

5 *After a few seconds of motionless silence,* Mr. Frank *turns from the window.*]

6 **Mrs. Frank.** [*Quietly, to the group*] It's safe now. The last workman has left.

7 [*There is an immediate stir of relief.*]

8 **Anne.** [*Her pent-up energy explodes.*] WHEE!

114 UNIT 2 • THE HOLOCAUST

9 **Mr. Frank.** [*Startled, amused*] Anne!

10 **Mrs. Van Daan.** I'm first for the w.c.

11 [*She hurries off to the bathroom.* Mrs. Frank *puts on her shoes and starts up to the sink to prepare supper.* Anne *sneaks* Peter's *shoes from under the table and hides them behind her back.* Mr. Frank *goes in to* Margot's *room.*]

12 **Mr. Frank.** [*To* Margot] Six o'clock. School's over.

13 [Margot *gets up, stretching.* Mr. Frank *sits down to put on his shoes. In the main room* Peter *tries to find his.*]

14 **Peter.** [*To* Anne] Have you seen my shoes?

15 **Anne.** [*Innocently*] Your shoes?

16 **Peter.** You've taken them, haven't you?

17 **Anne.** I don't know what you're talking about.

18 **Peter.** You're going to be sorry!

19 **Anne.** Am I?

20 [Peter *goes after her.* Anne, *with his shoes in her hand, runs from him, dodging behind her mother.*]

21 **Mrs. Frank.** [*Protesting*] Anne, dear!

22 **Peter.** Wait till I get you!

23 **Anne.** I'm waiting! [Peter *makes a lunge for her. They both fall to the floor.* Peter *pins her down, wrestling with her to get the shoes.*] Don't! Don't! Peter, stop it. Ouch!

24 **Mrs. Frank.** Anne! . . . Peter!

25 [*Suddenly* Peter *becomes self-conscious. He grabs his shoes roughly and starts for his room.*]

26 **Anne.** [*Following him*] Peter, where are you going? Come dance with me.

27 **Peter.** I tell you I don't know how.

28 **Anne.** I'll teach you.

29 **Peter.** I'm going to give Mouschi his dinner.

30 **Anne.** Can I watch?

31 **Peter.** He doesn't like people around while he eats.

32 **Anne.** Peter, please.

33 **Peter.** No! [*He goes into his room.* Anne *slams his door after him.*]

34 **Mrs. Frank.** Anne, dear, I think you shouldn't play like that with Peter. It's not dignified.

35 **Anne.** Who cares if it's dignified? I don't want to be dignified.

NOTES

36 [*Mr. Frank and Margot come from the room on the right. Margot goes to help her mother. Mr. Frank starts for the center table to correct Margot's school papers.*]

37 **Mrs. Frank.** [*To Anne*] You complain that I don't treat you like a grownup. But when I do, you resent it.

38 **Anne.** I only want some fun . . . someone to laugh and clown with . . . After you've sat still all day and hardly moved, you've got to have some fun. I don't know what's the matter with that boy.

39 **Mr. Frank.** He isn't used to girls. Give him a little time.

40 **Anne.** Time? Isn't two months time? I could cry. [*Catching hold of Margot*] Come on, Margot . . . dance with me. Come on, please.

41 **Margot.** I have to help with supper.

42 **Anne.** You know we're going to forget how to dance . . . When we get out we won't remember a thing.

43 [*She starts to sing and dance by herself. Mr. Frank takes her in his arms, waltzing with her. Mrs. Van Daan comes in from the bathroom.*]

44 **Mrs. Van Daan.** Next? [*She looks around as she starts putting on her shoes.*] Where's Peter?

45 **Anne.** [*As they are dancing*] Where would he be!

46 **Mrs. Van Daan.** He hasn't finished his lessons, has he? His father'll kill him if he catches him in there with that cat and his work not done. [*Mr. Frank and Anne finish their dance. They bow to each other with extravagant formality.*] Anne, get him out of there, will you?

47 **Anne.** [*At Peter's door*] Peter? Peter?

48 **Peter.** [*Opening the door a crack*] What is it?

49 **Anne.** Your mother says to come out.

50 **Peter.** I'm giving Mouschi his dinner.

51 **Mrs. Van Daan.** You know what your father says. [*She sits on the couch, sewing on the lining of her fur coat.*]

52 **Peter.** For heaven's sake, I haven't even looked at him since lunch.

53 **Mrs. Van Daan.** I'm just telling you, that's all.

54 **Anne.** I'll feed him.

55 **Peter.** I don't want you in there.

116 UNIT 2 • THE HOLOCAUST

CROSS-CURRICULAR PERSPECTIVES

Music In paragraphs 40–46, Anne is trying to get others to dance a waltz with her. The dance she chooses is formal and there are many customs associated with it, including a curtsy. It involves partners and has specific steps. Find a video example of a waltz and share it with the class. Explain that even though this dancing style was more popular in the past, people still learn how to waltz. Ask students to compare this to other, more popular ways we dance today.

56 **Mrs. Van Daan.** Peter!

57 **Peter.** [*To* Anne] Then give him his dinner and come right out, you hear?

58 [*He comes back to the table.* Anne *shuts the door of* Peter's *room after her and disappears behind the curtain covering his closet.*]

59 **Mrs. Van Daan.** [*To* Peter] Now is that any way to talk to your little girl friend?

60 **Peter.** Mother . . . for heaven's sake . . . will you please stop saying that?

61 **Mrs. Van Daan.** Look at him blush! Look at him!

62 **Peter.** Please! I'm not . . . anyway . . . let me alone, will you?

63 **Mrs. Van Daan.** He acts like it was something to be ashamed of. It's nothing to be ashamed of, to have a little girl friend.

64 **Peter.** You're crazy. She's only thirteen.

65 **Mrs. Van Daan.** So what? And you're sixteen. Just perfect. Your father's ten years older than I am. [*To* Mr. Frank] I warn you, Mr. Frank, if this war lasts much longer, we're going to be related and then . . .

66 **Mr. Frank.** *Mazel tov!*[17]

67 **Mrs. Frank.** [*Deliberately changing the conversation*] I wonder where Miep is. She's usually so prompt.

68 [*Suddenly everything else is forgotten as they hear the sound of an automobile coming to a screeching stop in the street below. They are tense, motionless in their terror. The car starts away. A wave of relief sweeps over them. They pick up their occupations again.* Anne *flings open the door of* Peter's *room, making a dramatic entrance. She is dressed in* Peter's *clothes.* Peter *looks at her in fury. The others are amused.*]

69 **Anne.** Good evening, everyone. Forgive me if I don't stay. [*She jumps up on a chair.*] I have a friend waiting for me in there. My friend Tom. Tom Cat. Some people say that we look alike. But Tom has the most beautiful whiskers, and I have only a little fuzz. I am hoping . . . in time . . .

70 **Peter.** All right, Mrs. Quack Quack!

71 **Anne.** [*Outraged—jumping down*] Peter!

72 **Peter.** I heard about you . . . How you talked so much in class they called you Mrs. Quack Quack. How Mr. Smitter made you write a composition . . . "'Quack, Quack,' said Mrs. Quack Quack."

NOTES

17. **Mazel tov** (MAH zuhl tohv) "good luck" in Hebrew and Yiddish; a phrase used to offer congratulations.

73 **Anne.** Well, go on. Tell them the rest. How it was so good he read it out loud to the class and then read it to all his other classes!

74 **Peter.** Quack! Quack! Quack . . . Quack . . . Quack . . .

75 [*Anne pulls off the coat and trousers.*]

76 **Anne.** You are the most intolerable, insufferable boy I've ever met!

77 [*She throws the clothes down the stairwell. Peter goes down . . . after them.*]

78 **Peter.** Quack, quack, quack!

79 **Mrs. Van Daan.** [*To* Anne] That's right, Anneke! Give it to him!

80 **Anne.** With all the boys in the world . . . Why I had to get locked up with one like you!

81 **Peter.** Quack, quack, quack, and from now on stay out of my room!

82 [*As* Peter *passes her,* Anne *puts out her foot, tripping him. He picks himself up, and goes on into his room.*]

83 **Mrs. Frank.** [*Quietly*] Anne, dear . . . your hair. [*She feels* Anne's *forehead.*] You're warm. Are you feeling all right?

84 **Anne.** Please, Mother. [*She goes over to the center table, slipping into her shoes.*]

85 **Mrs. Frank.** [*Following her*] You haven't a fever, have you?

86 **Anne.** [*Pulling away*] No. No.

87 **Mrs. Frank.** You know we can't call a doctor here, ever. There's only one thing to do . . . watch carefully. Prevent an illness before it comes. Let me see your tongue.

88 **Anne.** Mother, this is perfectly absurd.

89 **Mrs. Frank.** Anne, dear, don't be such a baby. Let me see your tongue. [*As* Anne *refuses,* Mrs. Frank *appeals to* Mr. Frank] Otto . . . ?

90 **Mr. Frank.** You hear your mother, Anne.

91 [Anne *flicks out her tongue for a second, then turns away.*]

92 **Mrs. Frank.** Come on—open up! [*As* Anne *opens her mouth very wide*] You seem all right . . . but perhaps an aspirin . . .

93 **Mrs. Van Daan.** For heaven's sake, don't give that child any pills. I waited for fifteen minutes this morning for her to come out of the w.c.

94 **Anne.** I was washing my hair!

PERSONALIZE FOR LEARNING

Strategic Support
Have students reread paragraph 76. Point out the words *intolerable* and *insufferable*. Tell students that Anne uses these two words to describe Peter. Point out to students that they can use context clues to figure out what these words mean and what message Anne is sending to Peter here. Assign roles to students and have them read aloud paragraphs 74–81. Ask: What is Peter doing here?

Possible response: He is teasing Anne. How is Anne feeling? Possible response: She's feeling frustrated. Point out that paragraphs 82 and 83 support this idea. Given these clues, ask students to guess what the words *intolerable* and *insufferable* mean. Point out that the prefix *in-* is negative. After they guess, ask students to use a dictionary to verify the meanings of these words.

95 **Mr. Frank.** I think there's nothing the matter with our Anne that a ride on her bike, or a visit with her friend Jopie de Waal wouldn't cure. Isn't that so, Anne?

96 [*Mr. Van Daan comes down into the room. From outside we hear faint sounds of bombers going over and a burst of ack-ack.*[18]]

97 **Mr. Van Daan.** Miep not come yet?

98 **Mrs. Van Daan.** The workmen just left, a little while ago.

99 **Mr. Van Daan.** What's for dinner tonight?

100 **Mrs. Van Daan.** Beans.

101 **Mr. Van Daan.** Not again!

102 **Mrs. Van Daan.** Poor Putti! I know. But what can we do? That's all that Miep brought us.

103 [*Mr. Van Daan starts to pace, his hands behind his back. Anne follows behind him, imitating him.*]

104 **Anne.** We are now in what is known as the "bean cycle." Beans boiled, beans en casserole, beans with strings, beans without strings . . .

105 [*Peter has come out of his room. He slides into his place at the table, becoming immediately absorbed in his studies.*]

106 **Mr. Van Daan.** [*To Peter*] I saw you . . . in there, playing with your cat.

107 **Mrs. Van Daan.** He just went in for a second, putting his coat away. He's been out here all the time, doing his lessons.

108 **Mr. Frank.** [*Looking up from the papers*] Anne, you got an excellent in your history paper today . . . and very good in Latin.

109 **Anne.** [*Sitting beside him*] How about algebra?

110 **Mr. Frank.** I'll have to make a confession. Up until now I've managed to stay ahead of you in algebra. Today you caught up with me. We'll leave it to Margot to correct.

111 **Anne.** Isn't algebra *vile*, Pim!

112 **Mr. Frank.** Vile!

113 **Margot.** [*To Mr. Frank*] How did I do?

114 **Anne.** [*Getting up*] Excellent, excellent, excellent, excellent!

115 **Mr. Frank.** [*To Margot*] You should have used the subjunctive[19] here . . .

This photo shows the front of the building that held the Secret Annex.

NOTES

18. **ack-ack** (AK AK) *n.* slang for an anti-aircraft gun's fire.

19. **subjunctive** (suhb JUHNGK tihv) *n.* form of a verb that is used to express doubt or uncertainty.

The Diary of Anne Frank, Act I **119**

TEACHING

CLOSE READ

A character's dialogue reveals much about his or her character, as do other characters' reactions to the character. In paragraphs 123–135, Mrs. Van Daan reveals a lot about her personality, and the reader's inferences are supported by the other characters' reactions to her behavior. You may wish to model the close read using the following think-aloud format. Possible responses to questions on the student page are included.

ANNOTATE: As I read paragraphs 123–133, I notice dialogue and stage directions that show Mrs. Van Daan's words and actions.

QUESTION: I notice that Mrs. Van Daan is a bold person who doesn't follow normal social etiquette and seems to enjoy embarrassing other people. She also seems quite self-absorbed, talking about herself possibly too much.

CONCLUDE: Mrs. Van Daan embarrasses Peter and angers Mr. Van Daan. We can see they are uncomfortable with her behavior and with what she is saying. From their reactions, we can also infer that she frequently behaves like this, so they are not entirely surprised.

NOTES

116 **Margot.** Should I? . . . I thought . . . look here . . . I didn't use it here . . .

117 [*The two become absorbed in the papers.*]

118 **Anne.** Mrs. Van Daan, may I try on your coat?

119 **Mrs. Frank.** No, Anne.

120 **Mrs. Van Daan.** [*Giving it to* Anne] It's all right . . . but careful with it. [Anne *puts it on and struts with it.*] My father gave me that the year before he died. He always bought the best that money could buy.

121 **Anne.** Mrs. Van Daan, did you have a lot of boy friends before you were married?

122 **Mrs. Frank.** Anne, that's a personal question. It's not courteous to ask personal questions.

CLOSE READ
ANNOTATE: In paragraphs 123–133, mark words and phrases that show Mrs. Van Daan's words and actions.

QUESTION: What do these words and phrases reveal about her personality?

CONCLUDE: How do Mrs. Van Daan's actions affect Peter and Mr. Van Daan?

123 **Mrs. Van Daan.** Oh I don't mind. [*To Anne*] Our house was always swarming with boys. When I was a girl we had . . .

124 **Mr. Van Daan.** Oh, God. Not again!

125 **Mrs. Van Daan.** [*Good-humored*] Shut up! [*Without a pause, to* Anne, Mr. Van Daan *mimics* Mrs. Van Daan, *speaking the first few words in unison with her.*] One summer we had a big house in Hilversum. The boys came buzzing round like bees around a jam pot. And when I was sixteen! . . . We were wearing our skirts very short those days and I had good-looking legs. [*She pulls up her skirt, going to* Mr. Frank.] I still have 'em. I may not be as pretty as I used to be, but I still have my legs. How about it, Mr. Frank?

126 **Mr. Van Daan.** All right. All right. We see them.

127 **Mrs. Van Daan.** I'm not asking you. I'm asking Mr. Frank.

128 **Peter.** Mother, for heaven's sake.

129 **Mrs. Van Daan.** Oh, I embarrass you, do I? Well, I just hope the girl you marry has as good. [*Then to* Anne] My father used to worry about me, with so many boys hanging round. He told me, if any of them gets fresh, you say to him . . . "Remember, Mr. So-and-So, remember I'm a lady."

130 **Anne.** "Remember, Mr. So-and-So, remember I'm a lady."

131 [*She gives* Mrs. Van Daan *her coat.*]

132 **Mr. Van Daan.** Look at you, talking that way in front of her! Don't you know she puts it all down in that diary?

133 **Mrs. Van Daan.** So, if she does? I'm only telling the truth!

134 [Anne *stretches out, putting her ear to the floor, listening to what is going on below. The sound of the bombers fades away.*]

WriteNow Express and Reflect

Narrative In paragraphs 120–133, the playwrights let readers know a little bit about Mrs. Van Daan's past. Ask students to reread this page and write a brief narrative about a young Mrs. Van Daan based on the information in her dialogue. Have them write the story in the third person and remind them that it should reflect what they have learned here. Have several students share their narratives. Ask students to reflect on how their narratives compare to the dialogue and stage direction in the play.

135 **Mrs. Frank.** [*Setting the table*] Would you mind, Peter, if I moved you over to the couch?

136 **Anne.** [*Listening*] Miep must have the radio on.

137 [Peter *picks up his papers, going over to the couch beside* Mrs. Van Daan.]

138 **Mr. Van Daan.** [*Accusingly, to* Peter] Haven't you finished yet?

139 **Peter.** No.

140 **Mr. Van Daan.** You ought to be ashamed of yourself.

141 **Peter.** All right. All right. I'm a dunce. I'm a hopeless case. Why do I go on?

142 **Mrs. Van Daan.** You're not hopeless. Don't talk that way. It's just that you haven't anyone to help you, like the girls have. [*To* Mr. Frank] Maybe you could help him, Mr. Frank?

143 **Mr. Frank.** I'm sure that his father . . . ?

144 **Mr. Van Daan.** Not me. I can't do anything with him. He won't listen to me. You go ahead . . . if you want.

145 **Mr. Frank.** [*Going to* Peter] What about it, Peter? Shall we make our school coeducational?

146 **Mrs. Van Daan.** [*Kissing* Mr. Frank] You're an angel, Mr. Frank. An angel. I don't know why I didn't meet you before I met that one there. Here, sit down, Mr. Frank . . . [*She forces him down on the couch beside* Peter.] Now, Peter, you listen to Mr. Frank.

147 **Mr. Frank.** It might be better for us to go into Peter's room.

148 [Peter *jumps up eagerly, leading the way.*]

149 **Mrs. Van Daan.** That's right. You go in there, Peter. You listen to Mr. Frank. Mr. Frank is a highly educated man.

150 [*As* Mr. Frank *is about to follow Peter into his room,* Mrs. Frank *stops him and wipes the lipstick from his lips. Then she closes the door after them.*]

151 **Anne.** [*On the floor, listening*] Shh! I can hear a man's voice talking.

152 **Mr. Van Daan.** [*To* Anne] Isn't it bad enough here without your sprawling all over the place?

153 [Anne *sits up.*]

154 **Mrs. Van Daan.** [*To* Mr. Van Daan] If you didn't smoke so much, you wouldn't be so bad-tempered.

155 **Mr. Van Daan.** Am I smoking? Do you see me smoking?

NOTES

CLOSE READ

ANNOTATE: In paragraphs 138–148, mark words and phrases that suggest disappointment, anger, and blame.

QUESTION: Why do the playwrights include these details?

CONCLUDE: What is the effect of these details, especially in making Peter and Mr. Van Daan's relationship clearer?

CLOSE READ

As the play progresses and social niceties fade, ongoing family tensions come to the surface, and conflicts are intensified by the close presence of the other family. In paragraphs 138–148, the playwrights show the very different approaches to parenting by Mr. Van Daan and Mr. Frank. You may wish to model the close read using the following think-aloud format. Possible responses to questions on the student page are included.

ANNOTATE: As I read paragraphs 138–148, I notice language that shows disappointment, anger, and blame.

QUESTION: The playwrights include these details to show the relationship between Peter and his father.

CONCLUDE: I can conclude that there is a lot of tension between Peter and his father. Mr. Van Daan treats Peter with scorn and indifference, and Peter is frustrated and angry that his father doesn't seem to understand him or take his needs seriously.

TEACHING

156 **Mrs. Van Daan.** Don't tell me you've used up all those cigarettes.

157 **Mr. Van Daan.** One package. Miep only brought me one package.

158 **Mrs. Van Daan.** It's a filthy habit anyway. It's a good time to break yourself.

159 **Mr. Van Daan.** Oh, stop it, please.

160 **Mrs. Van Daan.** You're smoking up all our money. You know that, don't you?

161 **Mr. Van Daan.** Will you shut up?

162 [*During this,* Mrs. Frank *and* Margot *have studiously kept their eyes down. But* Anne, *seated on the floor, has been following the discussion interestedly.* Mr. Van Daan *turns to see her staring up at him.*] And what are you staring at?

163 **Anne.** I never heard grownups quarrel before. I thought only children quarreled.

164 **Mr. Van Daan.** This isn't a quarrel! It's a discussion. And I never heard children so rude before.

165 **Anne.** [*Rising, indignantly*] I, rude!

166 **Mr. Van Daan.** Yes!

167 **Mrs. Frank.** [*Quickly*] Anne, will you get me my knitting? [Anne *goes to get it.*] I must remember, when Miep comes, to ask her to bring me some more wool.

168 **Margot.** [*Going to her room*] I need some hairpins and some soap. I made a list. [*She goes into her bedroom to get the list.*]

169 **Mrs. Frank.** [*To* Anne] Have you some library books for Miep when she comes?

170 **Anne.** It's a wonder that Miep has a life of her own, the way we make her run errands for us. Please, Miep, get me some starch. Please take my hair out and have it cut. Tell me all the latest news, Miep. [*She goes over, kneeling on the couch beside* Mrs. Van Daan] Did you know she was engaged? His name is Dirk, and Miep's afraid the Nazis will ship him off to Germany to work in one of their war plants. That's what they're doing with some of the young Dutchmen . . . they pick them up off the streets—

171 **Mr. Van Daan.** [*Interrupting*] Don't you ever get tired of talking? Suppose you try keeping still for five minutes. Just five minutes.

172 [*He starts to pace again. Again* Anne *follows him, mimicking him.* Mrs. Frank *jumps up and takes her by the arm up to the sink, and gives her a glass of milk.*]

HOW LANGUAGE WORKS

Verbs To support an in-text lesson on verbs, call student attention to paragraphs 151–161. There are regular verbs and irregular verbs. There are four principle parts, or forms, of verbs: present, present participle, past, past participle. Ask students to identify a few examples of verbs in the text. Create a list. Ask students to sort the list into two categories, past and present. Next, call their attention to paragraph 156. Highlight the words *you've used* and write: You have used. Explain that when you have a form of the word *have* before a verb, it is called a participle. When the verb is in the past tense, it is a past participle. Ask students to come up with an example of a past participle and share it with the class, including using it in a sentence.

173 **Mrs. Frank.** Come here, Anne. It's time for your glass of milk.

174 **Mr. Van Daan.** Talk, talk, talk. I never heard such a child. Where is my . . . ? Every evening it's the same talk, talk, talk. [*He looks around.*] Where is my . . . ?

175 **Mrs. Van Daan.** What're you looking for?

176 **Mr. Van Daan.** My pipe. Have you seen my pipe?

177 **Mrs. Van Daan.** What good's a pipe? You haven't got any tobacco.

178 **Mr. Van Daan.** At least I'll have something to hold in my mouth! [*Opening* Margot's *bedroom door*] Margot, have you seen my pipe?

179 **Margot.** It was on the table last night.

180 [Anne *puts her glass of milk on the table and picks up his pipe, hiding it behind her back.*]

181 **Mr. Van Daan.** I know. I know. Anne, did you see my pipe? . . . Anne!

182 **Mrs. Frank.** Anne, Mr. Van Daan is speaking to you.

183 **Anne.** Am I allowed to talk now?

184 **Mr. Van Daan.** You're the most aggravating . . . The trouble with you is, you've been spoiled. What you need is a good old-fashioned spanking.

185 **Anne.** [*Mimicking* Mrs. Van Daan] "Remember, Mr. So-and-So, remember I'm a lady." [*She thrusts the pipe into his mouth, then picks up her glass of milk.*]

186 **Mr. Van Daan.** [*Restraining himself with difficulty*] Why aren't you nice and quiet like your sister Margot? Why do you have to show off all the time? Let me give you a little advice, young lady. Men don't like that kind of thing in a girl. You know that? A man likes a girl who'll listen to him once in a while . . . a domestic girl, who'll keep her house shining for her husband . . . who loves to cook and sew and . . .

187 **Anne.** I'd cut my throat first! I'd open my veins! I'm going to be remarkable! I'm going to Paris . . .

188 **Mr. Van Daan.** [*Scoffingly*] Paris!

189 **Anne.** . . . to study music and art.

190 **Mr. Van Daan.** Yeah! Yeah!

191 **Anne.** I'm going to be a famous dancer or singer . . . or something wonderful.

192 [*She makes a wide gesture, spilling the glass of milk on the fur coat in* Mrs. Van Daan's *lap.* Margot *rushes quickly over with a towel.* Anne *tries to brush the milk off with her skirt.*]

NOTES

restraining (rih STRAY nihng) *v.* holding back; controlling one's emotions

CLOSER LOOK

Analyzing Cultural Context

Students may have marked paragraph 186 during their first read. Use this paragraph to help students analyze the cultural beliefs at play during the historic period. You may want to model a close read with the class based on the highlights shown in the text.

ANNOTATE: Have students highlight language in paragraph 186 that shows Mr. Van Daan's attitude about women in society.

QUESTION: Guide students to consider what these details might tell them. Ask what a reader can infer from what was marked, and accept student responses.

Possible response: These details show that Mr. Van Daan has a very traditional view of how women should behave; a very narrow view of a woman's role in society. He thinks women should be satisfied with homemaking.

CONCLUDE: Help students to formulate conclusions about the importance of the details in the text. Ask students why the author might have included these details.

Possible responses: Anne's reaction shows her rebellious spirit and her desire to do more with her life than the confines of such a traditional view would allow. It reveals her passionate feelings for a more progressive role for women in society.

TEACHING

● **CLOSE READ**

You may wish to model the close read using the following think-aloud format. Possible responses to questions on the student page are included.

ANNOTATE: As I read paragraphs 202–207, I notice words and phrases related to control and calm.

QUESTION: The contrasts set up the tension between how Anne behaves and the way her mother wants her to behave.

CONCLUDE: The dialogue reveals the tension in this mother-daughter relationship. It reveals a conflict, or struggle, that is common in mother-daughter relationships during teenage years but is made more difficult by the circumstances in which the Franks must live. It also shows how Margot's behavior contrasts with Anne's.

NOTES

193 **Mrs. Van Daan.** Now look what you've done . . . you clumsy little fool! My beautiful fur coat my father gave me . . .

194 **Anne.** I'm so sorry.

195 **Mrs. Van Daan.** What do you care? It isn't yours . . . So go on, ruin it! Do you know what that coat cost? Do you? And now look at it! Look at it!

196 **Anne.** I'm very, very sorry.

197 **Mrs. Van Daan.** I could kill you for this. I could just kill you!

198 [Mrs. Van Daan *goes up the stairs, clutching the coat*. Mr. Van Daan *starts after her*.]

199 **Mr. Van Daan.** Petronella . . . *Liefje! Liefje!* . . . Come back . . . the supper . . . come back!

200 **Mrs. Frank.** Anne, you must not behave in that way.

201 **Anne.** It was an accident. Anyone can have an accident.

CLOSE READ
ANNOTATE: In paragraphs 202–207, mark details related to control and calm. Mark other details related to lack of control or strong emotions.

QUESTION: Why do the playwrights use these contrasting details?

CONCLUDE: What is the effect of these details, especially in portraying Anne's character and relationships with her family?

202 **Mrs. Frank.** I don't mean that. I mean the answering back. You must not answer back. They are our guests. We must always show the greatest courtesy to them. We're all living under terrible tension. [*She stops as* Margot *indicates that* Mr. Van Daan *can hear. When he is gone, she continues*.] That's why we must control ourselves . . . You don't hear Margot getting into arguments with them, do you? Watch Margot. She's always courteous with them. Never familiar. She keeps her distance. And they respect her for it. Try to be like Margot.

203 **Anne.** And have them walk all over me, the way they do her? No, thanks!

204 **Mrs. Frank.** I'm not afraid that anyone is going to walk all over you, Anne. I'm afraid for other people, that you'll walk on them. I don't know what happens to you, Anne. You are wild, self-willed. If I had ever talked to my mother as you talk to me . . .

205 **Anne.** Things have changed. People aren't like that any more. "Yes, Mother." "No, Mother." "Anything you say, Mother." I've got to fight things out for myself! Make something of myself!

206 **Mrs. Frank.** It isn't necessary to fight to do it. Margot doesn't fight, and isn't she . . . ?

207 **Anne.** [*Violently rebellious*] Margot! Margot! Margot! That's all I hear from everyone . . . how wonderful Margot is . . . "Why aren't you like Margot?"

208 **Margot.** [*Protesting*] Oh, come on, Anne, don't be so . . .

209 **Anne.** [*Paying no attention*] Everything she does is right, and everything I do is wrong! I'm the goat around here! . . . You're all against me! . . . And you worst of all!

210 [*She rushes off into her room and throws herself down on the settee, stifling her sobs.* Mrs. Frank *sighs and starts toward the stove.*]

211 **Mrs. Frank.** [*To* Margot] Let's put the soup on the stove . . . if there's anyone who cares to eat. Margot, will you take the bread out? [Margot *gets the bread from the cupboard.*] I don't know how we can go on living this way . . . I can't say a word to Anne . . . she flies at me . . .

212 **Margot.** You know Anne. In half an hour she'll be out here, laughing and joking.

213 **Mrs. Frank.** And . . . [*She makes a motion upwards, indicating the* Van Daans.] . . . I told your father it wouldn't work . . . but no . . . no . . . he had to ask them, he said . . . he owed it to him, he said. Well, he knows now that I was right! These **quarrels**! . . . This **bickering**!

214 **Margot.** [*With a warning look*] Shush. Shush.

215 [*The buzzer for the door sounds.* Mrs. Frank *gasps, startled.*]

216 **Mrs. Frank.** Every time I hear that sound, my heart stops!

217 **Margot.** [*Starting for* Peter's *door*] It's Miep. [*She knocks at the door.*] Father?

218 [Mr. Frank *comes quickly from* Peter's *room.*]

219 **Mr. Frank.** Thank you, Margot. [*As he goes down the steps to open the outer door*] Has everyone his list?

220 **Margot.** I'll get my books. [*Giving her mother a list*] Here's your list. [Margot *goes into her and* Anne's *bedroom on the right.* Anne *sits up, hiding her tears, as* Margot *comes in.*] Miep's here. [Margot *picks up her books and goes back.* Anne *hurries over to the mirror, smoothing her hair.*]

221 **Mr. Van Daan.** [*Coming down the stairs*] Is it Miep?

222 **Margot.** Yes. Father's gone down to let her in.

223 **Mr. Van Daan.** At last I'll have some cigarettes!

224 **Mrs. Frank.** [*To* Mr. Van Daan] I can't tell you how unhappy I am about Mrs. Van Daan's coat. Anne should never have touched it.

225 **Mr. Van Daan.** She'll be all right.

226 **Mrs. Frank.** Is there anything I can do?

227 **Mr. Van Daan.** Don't worry.

NOTES

quarrels (KWAWR uhlz) *n.* arguments; disagreements

bickering (BIHK uhr ihng) *n.* arguing over unimportant things

---

PERSONALIZE FOR LEARNING

English Language Support
Plot As you review paragraphs 203–210, tell students that a reader must be able to identify moments of change, or turning points, in the plot. Not all turning points involve big scene changes or dramatic events. Read aloud or have students take parts and read aloud paragraphs 203–210. Ask students to describe the mood of the scene. (Possible response: It's tense or angry.)

Then read paragraphs 217–223. Guide students to describe what happens. (Possible response: Miep arrives.) Read the rest of the page. Ask students to describe the mood in these lines. (Possible response: There is a lot of excitement and anticipation. The anger seems to have gone away.) Point out the words, "It's Miep."

TEACHING

NOTES

228 [*He turns to meet* Miep. *But it is not* Miep *who comes up the steps. It is* Mr. Kraler, *followed by* Mr. Frank. *Their faces are grave.* Anne *comes from the bedroom.* Peter *comes from his room.*]

229 **Mrs. Frank.** Mr. Kraler!

230 **Mr. Van Daan.** How are you, Mr. Kraler?

231 **Margot.** This is a surprise.

232 **Mrs. Frank.** When Mr. Kraler comes, the sun begins to shine.

233 **Mr. Van Daan.** Miep is coming?

234 **Mr. Kraler.** Not tonight.

235 [Mr. Kraler *goes to* Margot *and* Mrs. Frank *and* Anne, *shaking hands with them.*]

236 **Mrs. Frank.** Wouldn't you like a cup of coffee? . . . Or, better still, will you have supper with us?

237 **Mr. Frank.** Mr. Kraler has something to talk over with us. Something has happened, he says, which demands an immediate decision.

238 **Mrs. Frank.** [*Fearful*] What is it?

239 [Mr. Kraler *sits down on the couch. As he talks he takes bread, cabbages, milk, etc., from his briefcase, giving them to* Margot *and* Anne *to put away.*]

240 **Mr. Kraler.** Usually, when I come up here, I try to bring you some bit of good news. What's the use of telling you the bad news when there's nothing that you can do about it? But today something has happened . . . Dirk . . . Miep's Dirk, you know, came to me just now. He tells me that he has a Jewish friend living near him. A dentist. He says he's in trouble. He begged me, could I do anything for this man? Could I find him a hiding place? . . . So I've come to you . . . I know it's a terrible thing to ask of you, living as you are, but would you take him in with you?

241 **Mr. Frank.** Of course we will.

242 **Mr. Kraler.** [*Rising*] It'll be just for a night or two . . . until I find some other place. This happened so suddenly that I didn't know where to turn.

243 **Mr. Frank.** Where is he?

244 **Mr. Kraler.** Downstairs in the office.

245 **Mr. Frank.** Good. Bring him up.

246 **Mr. Kraler.** His name is Dussel . . . Jan Dussel.

247 **Mr. Frank.** Dussel . . . I think I know him.

248 **Mr. Kraler.** I'll get him.

126 UNIT 2 • THE HOLOCAUST

PERSONALIZE FOR LEARNING

Challenge

Research In paragraph 240, Mr. Kraler presents everyone with a serious situation. There is somebody new who needs a place to hide and he needs them to take him in. Mr. Frank says, "Of course, we will." Have students consider why they might have said no. (Possible response: not enough space, not enough food, one more person that might make noise and alert the authorities) Then have them consider why Mr. Frank said yes with no hesitation. (Possible response: Mr. Frank knew how dangerous it was for Jews to be out in the open. He knew that he was safe because others helped him and he was doing the same.) There are many stories of everyday heroes during the Holocaust. Have students extend their thinking on this topic by doing research about people who risked their lives to save others during this time.

249 [*He goes quickly down the steps and out. Mr. Frank suddenly becomes conscious of the others.*]

250 **Mr. Frank.** Forgive me. I spoke without consulting you. But I knew you'd feel as I do.

251 **Mr. Van Daan.** There's no reason for you to consult anyone. This is your place. You have a right to do exactly as you please. The only thing I feel . . . there's so little food as it is . . . and to take in another person . . .

252 [*Peter turns away, ashamed of his father.*]

253 **Mr. Frank.** We can stretch the food a little. It's only for a few days.

254 **Mr. Van Daan.** You want to make a bet?

255 **Mrs. Frank.** I think it's fine to have him. But, Otto, where are you going to put him? Where?

256 **Peter.** He can have my bed. I can sleep on the floor. I wouldn't mind.

257 **Mr. Frank.** That's good of you, Peter. But your room's too small . . . even for *you*.

258 **Anne.** I have a much better idea. I'll come in here with you and Mother, and Margot can take Peter's room and Peter can go in our room with Mr. Dussel.

259 **Margot.** That's right. We could do that.

260 **Mr. Frank.** No, Margot. You mustn't sleep in that room . . . neither you nor Anne. Mouschi has caught some rats in there. Peter's brave. He doesn't mind.

261 **Anne.** Then how about *this*? I'll come in here with you and Mother, and Mr. Dussel can have my bed.

262 **Mrs. Frank.** *No. No. No!* Margot will come in here with us and he can have her bed. It's the only way. Margot, bring your things in here. Help her, Anne.

263 [*Margot hurries into her room to get her things.*]

264 **Anne.** [*To her mother*] Why Margot? Why can't I come in here?

265 **Mrs. Frank.** Because it wouldn't be proper for Margot to sleep with a . . . Please, Anne. Don't argue. Please.

266 [*Anne starts slowly away.*]

This photograph shows the stairway to the Secret Annex that was hidden behind a swinging bookcase.

NOTES

TEACHING

NOTES

267 **Mr. Frank.** [*To* Anne] You don't mind sharing your room with Mr. Dussel, do you, Anne?

268 **Anne.** No. No, of course not.

269 **Mr. Frank.** Good. [Anne *goes off into her bedroom, helping* Margot. Mr. Frank *starts to search in the cupboards.*] Where's the cognac?

270 **Mrs. Frank.** It's there. But, Otto, I was saving it in case of illness.

271 **Mr. Frank.** I think we couldn't find a better time to use it. Peter, will you get five glasses for me?

272 [Peter *goes for the glasses.* Margot *comes out of her bedroom, carrying her possessions, which she hangs behind a curtain in the main room.* Mr. Frank *finds the cognac and pours it into the five glasses that* Peter *brings him.* Mr. Van Daan *stands looking on sourly.* Mrs. Van Daan *comes downstairs and looks around at all the bustle.*]

273 **Mrs. Van Daan.** What's happening? What's going on?

274 **Mr. Van Daan.** Someone's moving in with us.

275 **Mrs. Van Daan.** In here? You're joking.

276 **Margot.** It's only for a night or two . . . until Mr. Kraler finds him another place.

277 **Mr. Van Daan.** Yeah! Yeah!

278 [Mr. Frank *hurries over as* Mr. Kraler *and* Dussel *come up.* Dussel *is a man in his late fifties, meticulous, finicky . . . bewildered now. He wears a raincoat. He carries a briefcase, stuffed full, and a small medicine case.*]

279 **Mr. Frank.** Come in, Mr. Dussel.

280 **Mr. Kraler.** This is Mr. Frank.

281 **Dussel.** Mr. Otto Frank?

282 **Mr. Frank.** Yes. Let me take your things. [*He takes the hat and briefcase, but* Dussel *clings to his medicine case.*] This is my wife, Edith . . . Mr. and Mrs. Van Daan . . . their son, Peter . . . and my daughters, Margot and Anne.

283 [Dussel *shakes hands with everyone.*]

284 **Mr. Kraler.** Thank you, Mr. Frank. Thank you all. Mr. Dussel, I leave you in good hands. Oh . . . Dirk's coat.

285 [Dussel *hurriedly takes off the raincoat, giving it to* Mr. Kraler. *Underneath is his white dentist's jacket, with a yellow Star of David on it.*]

286 **Dussel.** [*To* Mr. Kraler] What can I say to thank you . . . ?

128 UNIT 2 • THE HOLOCAUST

CROSS-CURRICULAR PERSPECTIVES

Social Studies How did the Netherlands become part of World War II and the Holocaust? Often, when discussing the Holocaust, students think of Germany. It is important to understand the history of Dutch participation in the war and in resisting Adolf Hitler. Have students research Internet resources to familiarize themselves with how people like the Franks and the Van Daans ended up where they did. Ask students to share what they have learned with the class. Discuss the findings to be sure that students understand the history behind the play. **(Research to Inform)**

287 **Mrs. Frank.** [*To* Dussel] Mr. Kraler and Miep . . . They're our life line. Without them we couldn't live.

288 **Mr. Kraler.** Please. Please. You make us seem very heroic. It isn't that at all. We simply don't like the Nazis. [*To* Mr. Frank, *who offers him a drink*] No, thanks. [*Then going on*] We don't like their methods. We don't like . . .

289 **Mr. Frank.** [*Smiling*] I know. I know. "No one's going to tell us Dutchmen what to do with our damn Jews!"

290 **Mr. Kraler.** [*To* Dussel] Pay no attention to Mr. Frank. I'll be up tomorrow to see that they're treating you right. [*To* Mr. Frank] Don't trouble to come down again. Peter will bolt the door after me, won't you, Peter?

291 **Peter.** Yes, sir.

292 **Mr. Frank.** Thank you, Peter. I'll do it.

293 **Mr. Kraler.** Good night. Good night.

294 **Group.** Good night, Mr. Kraler. We'll see you tomorrow, etc., etc.

295 [Mr. Kraler *goes out with* Mr. Frank. Mrs. Frank *gives each one of the "grownups" a glass of cognac.*]

296 **Mrs. Frank.** Please, Mr. Dussel, sit down.

297 [Mr. Dussel *sinks into a chair.* Mrs. Frank *gives him a glass of cognac.*]

298 **Dussel.** I'm dreaming. I know it. I can't believe my eyes. Mr. Otto Frank here! [*To* Mrs. Frank] You're not in Switzerland then? A woman told me . . . She said she'd gone to your house . . . the door was open, everything was in disorder, dishes in the sink. She said she found a piece of paper in the wastebasket with an address scribbled on it . . . an address in Zurich. She said you must have escaped to Zurich.

299 **Anne.** Father put that there purposely . . . just so people would think that very thing!

300 **Dussel.** And you've been *here* all the time?

301 **Mrs. Frank.** All the time . . . ever since July.

302 [Anne *speaks to her father as he comes back*]

303 **Anne.** It worked, Pim . . . the address you left! Mr. Dussel says that people believe we escaped to Switzerland.

304 **Mr. Frank.** I'm glad . . . And now let's have a little drink to welcome Mr. Dussel.

305 [*Before they can drink,* Mr. Dussel *bolts his drink.* Mr. Frank *smiles and raises his glass.*]

NOTES

CLOSER LOOK

Analyze Dialogue

Dialogue in a play can be used to express a character's motivation. We understand why the people in the attic are hiding there. They are trying to survive. But why are Mr. Kraler and Miep risking their own safety for the Jews? Students may have marked paragraph 288 during their first read. Encourage them to talk about the annotations that they marked. You may want to model a close read with the class based on the highlights shown in the text.

ANNOTATE: Have students mark details in paragraph 288 that show why Mr. Kraler was helping them, or have students participate while you highlight them.

QUESTION: Guide students to consider what these details might tell them. Ask what a reader can infer about Mr. Kraler from his answers, and accept student responses.

Possible response: He is humble and moral. He does not agree with the Nazis.

CONCLUDE: Help students to formulate conclusions about the importance of these details in the text. Ask students why the playwrights might have included these details.

Possible response: The playwrights want the reader to know that there were people in Amsterdam who not only disagreed with the Nazis, but they were willing to risk their own lives and well-being to stand up to them in their own way.

Remind students that **dialogue** is an indirect way of revealing what a character is like. Expand on the conversation about characters' motivations by reading Mr. Frank's response to Mr. Kraler. Point out the comment, "No one's going to tell us Dutchmen what to do with our damn Jews!" Note the stage direction—*smiling*. This line of dialogue indicates that Mr. Frank respects Miep and Mr. Kraler. It also shows that he still has his sense of humor.

TEACHING

CLOSE READ

The arrival of a new character can create a number of types of changes, including tone, conflict, plot, and the development of other characters. In paragraphs 312–322, Mr. Dussel relates details of how Jews are being treated in Amsterdam that shocks the characters with a deepening awareness about their situation. You may wish to model the close read using the following think-aloud format. Possible responses to questions on the student page are included.

ANNOTATE: As I read paragraphs 312–322, I notice details that show how the characters react to Dussel's news.

QUESTION: The playwrights include these details to show the horrible, shocking nature of the developments Dussel describes.

CONCLUDE: The characters' reactions emphasize their isolation and their lack of contact with people in the outside world.

NOTES

CLOSE READ
ANNOTATE: Mark details in paragraphs 312–322 that show how the characters react to Dussel's news of the outside world.

QUESTION: Why do the playwrights include these details?

CONCLUDE: What is the effect of these details?

20. **Mauthausen** (MOW tow zuhn) village in Austria that was the site of a Nazi concentration camp.

---

306 To Mr. Dussel. Welcome. We're very honored to have you with us.

307 **Mrs. Frank.** To Mr. Dussel, welcome.

308 [*The* Van Daans *murmur a welcome. The "grownups" drink.*]

309 **Mrs. Van Daan.** Um. That was good.

310 **Mr. Van Daan.** Did Mr. Kraler warn you that you won't get much to eat here? You can imagine . . . three ration books among the seven of us . . . and now you make eight.

311 [Peter *walks away, humiliated. Outside a street organ is heard dimly.*]

312 **Dussel.** [*Rising*] Mr. Van Daan, you don't realize what is happening outside that you should warn me of a thing like that. You don't realize what's going on . . . [*As* Mr. Van Daan *starts his characteristic pacing,* Dussel *turns to speak to the others.*] Right here in Amsterdam every day hundreds of Jews disappear . . . They surround a block and search house by house. Children come home from school to find their parents gone. Hundreds are being deported . . . people that you and I know . . . the Hallensteins . . . the Wessels . . .

313 **Mrs. Frank.** [*In tears*] Oh, no. No!

314 **Dussel.** They get their call-up notice . . . come to the Jewish theater on such and such a day and hour . . . bring only what you can carry in a rucksack. And if you refuse the call-up notice, then they come and drag you from your home and ship you off to Mauthausen.[20] The death camp!

315 **Mrs. Frank.** We didn't know that things had got so much worse.

316 **Dussel.** Forgive me for speaking so.

317 **Anne.** [*Coming to* Dussel] Do you know the de Waals? . . . What's become of them? Their daughter Jopie and I are in the same class. Jopie's my best friend.

318 **Dussel.** They are gone.

319 **Anne.** Gone?

320 **Dussel.** With all the others.

321 **Anne.** Oh, no. Not Jopie!

322 [*She turns away, in tears.* Mrs. Frank *motions to* Margot *to comfort her.* Margot *goes to* Anne, *putting her arms comfortingly around her.*]

323 **Mrs. Van Daan.** There were some people called Wagner. They lived near us . . . ?

324 **Mr. Frank.** [*Interrupting, with a glance at* Anne] I think we should put this off until later. We all have many questions we want to ask . . . But I'm sure that Mr. Dussel would like to get settled before supper.

325 **Dussel.** Thank you. I would. I brought very little with me.

326 **Mr. Frank.** [*Giving him his hat and briefcase*] I'm sorry we can't give you a room alone. But I hope you won't be too uncomfortable. We've had to make strict rules here . . . a schedule of hours . . . We'll tell you after supper. Anne, would you like to take Mr. Dussel to his room?

327 **Anne.** [*Controlling her tears*] If you'll come with me, Mr. Dussel? [*She starts for her room.*]

328 **Dussel.** [*Shaking hands with each in turn*] Forgive me if I haven't really expressed my gratitude to all of you. This has been such a shock to me. I'd always thought of myself as Dutch. I was born in Holland. My father was born in Holland, and my grandfather. And now . . . after all these years . . . [*He breaks off.*] If you'll excuse me.

329 [Dussel *gives a little bow and hurries off after* Anne. Mr. Frank *and the others are subdued.*]

330 **Anne.** [*Turning on the light*] Well, here we are.

331 [Dussel *looks around the room. In the main room* Margot *speaks to her mother.*]

332 **Margot.** The news sounds pretty bad, doesn't it? It's so different from what Mr. Kraler tells us. Mr. Kraler says things are improving.

333 **Mr. Van Daan.** I like it better the way Kraler tells it.

334 [*They resume their occupations, quietly.* Peter *goes off into his room. In* Anne's *room,* Anne *turns to* Dussel.]

335 **Anne.** You're going to share the room with me.

336 **Dussel.** I'm a man who's always lived alone. I haven't had to adjust myself to others. I hope you'll bear with me until I learn.

337 **Anne.** Let me help you. [*She takes his briefcase.*] Do you always live all alone? Have you no family at all?

338 **Dussel.** No one. [*He opens his medicine case and spreads his bottles on the dressing table.*]

339 **Anne.** How dreadful. You must be terribly lonely.

340 **Dussel.** I'm used to it.

341 **Anne.** I don't think I could ever get used to it. Didn't you even have a pet? A cat, or a dog?

NOTES

PERSONALIZE FOR LEARNING

Strategic Support

Dramatic Pauses Read aloud Mr. Dussel's speech in paragraph 328. Point out the ellipses in this line: "And now...after all these years..." Remind students that the ellipses here are dramatic pauses in his speech. Ask students to consider what Mr. Dussel is trying to tell us here when he describes who he has always believed himself to be. Discuss what has changed. Possible response: While he considered himself Dutch, that has been taken away from him. He is no longer welcome in his own home country.

DIGITAL PERSPECTIVES

TEACHING

CLOSER LOOK

Analyze Structure

The use of stage directions as structure in a play helps the reader and the actors to better understand characters and what motivates them. Students may have marked paragraphs 348–350 during their first read. Use these lines to help students understand how a simple descriptive word lets the reader understand more about the characters. Encourage them to talk about the annotations that they marked. You may want to model a close read with the class based on the highlights shown in the text.

ANNOTATE: Have students mark details in paragraphs 348–350 that describe Mr. Dussel's actions, or have students participate while you highlight them.

QUESTION: Guide students to consider what these details might tell them. Ask what a reader can infer from the adverbs used to describe Mr. Dussel's speech in these paragraphs, and accept student responses.

Possible response: Mr. Dussel is impatient with Anne already. He is also uncomfortable.

CONCLUDE: Help students to formulate conclusions about the importance of these details in the text. Ask students why the playwrights might have included these details.

Possible response: The playwrights may have included these details to let the reader know that Mr. Dussel is not comfortable with the living arrangement or with Anne's social nature.

Playwrights can use stage directions as part of the **structure**, or organization, of the drama. *Interrupting* and *stiffly* in the stage directions in this example show how Mr. Dussel interacts with Anne. The simplicity of the stage directions here replaces the need for complex dialogue to give us Mr. Dussel's personality traits.

NOTES

342 **Dussel.** I have an allergy for fur-bearing animals. They give me asthma.

343 **Anne.** Oh, dear. Peter has a cat.

344 **Dussel.** Here? He has it here?

345 **Anne.** Yes. But we hardly ever see it. He keeps it in his room all the time. I'm sure it will be all right.

346 **Dussel.** Let us hope so. [*He takes some pills to fortify himself.*]

347 **Anne.** That's Margot's bed, where you're going to sleep. I sleep on the sofa there. [*Indicating the clothes hooks on the wall*] We cleared these off for your things. [*She goes over to the window.*] The best part about this room . . . you can look down and see a bit of the street and the canal. There's a houseboat . . . you can see the end of it . . . a bargeman lives there with his family . . . They have a baby and he's just beginning to walk and I'm so afraid he's going to fall into the canal some day. I watch him . . .

348 **Dussel.** [*Interrupting*] Your father spoke of a schedule.

349 **Anne.** [*Coming away from the window*] Oh, yes. It's mostly about the times we have to be quiet. And times for the w.c. You can use it now if you like.

350 **Dussel.** [*Stiffly*] No, thank you.

351 **Anne.** I suppose you think it's awful, my talking about a thing like that. But you don't know how important it can get to be, especially when you're frightened . . . About this room, the way Margot and I did . . . she had it to herself in the afternoons for studying, reading . . . lessons, you know . . . and I took the mornings. Would that be all right with you?

352 **Dussel.** I'm not at my best in the morning.

353 **Anne.** You stay here in the mornings then. I'll take the room in the afternoons.

354 **Dussel.** Tell me, when you're in here, what happens to me? Where am I spending my time? In there, with all the people?

355 **Anne.** Yes.

356 **Dussel.** I see. I see.

357 **Anne.** We have supper at half past six.

358 **Dussel.** [*Going over to the sofa*] Then, if you don't mind . . . I like to lie down quietly for ten minutes before eating. I find it helps the digestion.

359 **Anne.** Of course. I hope I'm not going to be too much of a bother to you. I seem to be able to get everyone's back up.

360 [*Dussel lies down on the sofa, curled up, his back to her.*]

361 **Dussel.** I always get along very well with children. My patients all bring their children to me, because they know I get on well with them. So don't you worry about that.

362 [*Anne leans over him, taking his hand and shaking it gratefully.*]

363 **Anne.** Thank you. Thank you, Mr. Dussel.

364 [*The lights dim to darkness. The curtain falls on the scene.* Anne's Voice *comes to us faintly at first, and then with increasing power.*]

365 **Anne's Voice.** . . . And yesterday I finished Cissy Van Marxvelt's latest book. I think she is a first-class writer. I shall definitely let my children read her. Monday the twenty-first of September, nineteen forty-two. Mr. Dussel and I had another battle yesterday. Yes, Mr. Dussel! According to him, nothing, I repeat . . . nothing, is right about me . . . my appearance, my character, my manners. While he was going on at me I thought . . . sometime I'll give you such a smack that you'll fly right up to the ceiling! Why is it that every grownup thinks he knows the way to bring up children? Particularly the grownups that never had any. I keep wishing that Peter was a girl instead of a boy. Then I would have someone to talk to. Margot's a darling, but she takes everything too seriously. To pause for a moment on the subject of Mrs. Van Daan. I must tell you that her attempts to flirt with Father are getting her nowhere. Pim, thank goodness, won't play.

366 [*As she is saying the last lines, the curtain rises on the darkened scene.* Anne's Voice *fades out.*]

⌘ ⌘ ⌘

Scene 4

1 [*It is the middle of the night, several months later. The stage is dark except for a little light which comes through the skylight in* Peter's *room.*

2 *Everyone is in bed.* Mr. *and* Mrs. Frank *lie on the couch in the main room, which has been pulled out to serve as a makeshift double bed.*

3 Margot *is sleeping on a mattress on the floor in the main room, behind a curtain stretched across for privacy. The others are all in their accustomed rooms.*

4 *From outside we hear two drunken soldiers singing "Lili Marlene." A girl's high giggle is heard. The sound of running feet is heard*

NOTES

CLOSE READ
ANNOTATE: In paragraph 361, mark details that relate to Dussel's feelings toward children. Mark details in paragraph 365 that refer to his feelings toward Anne.

QUESTION: Why do the playwrights include these contrasting details?

CONCLUDE: What do these details show about Mr. Dussel's character and conflicts that arise as the story continues?

The Diary of Anne Frank, Act I 133

DIGITAL PERSPECTIVES

CLOSE READ

One tool playwrights use in developing characters is to create dialogue spoken by a character that contradicts the character's behavior. You may wish to model the close read using the following think-aloud format. Possible responses to questions on the student page are included.

ANNOTATE: As I read paragraph 361, I notice words and phrases that show Mr. Dussel's attitude toward children. As I read paragraph 365, I notice language that indicates his attitude toward Anne.

QUESTION: These details show the contrast between what Mr. Dussel says and how he actually behaves.

CONCLUDE: These details show that, even though Mr. Dussel likes to think of himself as agreeable, he is actually very impatient and argumentative.

DIGITAL PERSPECTIVES

Enriching the Text Have students read aloud paragraph 365. While stage directions are an effective way to set mood and give insight into characters, watching the play acted out can help readers more fully understand a scene. Provide a video clip of a film or stage performance of this scene for students. Ask them to compare the written text with the video. Have them note the dramatic effect of lighting and Anne's voice in the movie. Discuss the first three lines of the text and what they tell the reader or the audience about Anne. Possible response: She has hope because she is talking about her children. Be sure to preview all video clips before presenting them to students.

TEACHING

CLOSER LOOK

Identifying Foreshadowing

Students may have marked paragraphs 8–13 during their first read. Use these paragraphs to help students analyze foreshadowing in the play. You may want to model a close read with the class based on the highlights shown in the text.

ANNOTATE: Have students highlight language in paragraphs 8–13 that show Anne's nightmare.

QUESTION: Guide students to consider what these details might tell them. Ask what a reader can infer from what was marked, and accept student responses.

Possible responses: The fact that Anne is having a nightmare in which she is being captured foreshadows the Nazis capturing Anne.

CONCLUDE: Help students to formulate conclusions about the importance of the details in the text. Ask students why the author might have included these details.

Possible responses: This frightening scene serves to hint at what is to come. Readers and audiences know of Anne Frank's tragic fate based on the first scene of the play. This scene returns the focus to her future doom, adding a sense of dread as the play progresses.

Remind students that **foreshadowing** is a literary technique that authors use to hint at events to come in the plot.

NOTES

Anne's Dutch passport and samples of her writing.

coming closer and then fading in the distance. Throughout the scene there is the distant sound of airplanes passing overhead.

5 *A match suddenly flares up in the attic. We dimly see* Mr. Van Daan. *He is getting his bearings. He comes quickly down the stairs, and goes to the cupboard where the food is stored. Again the match flares up, and is as quickly blown out.*

6 *The dim figure is seen to steal back up the stairs.*

7 *There is quiet for a second or two, broken only by the sound of airplanes, and running feet on the street below.*

8 *Suddenly, out of the silence and the dark, we hear* Anne *scream.*]

9 **Anne.** [*Screaming*] No! No! Don't . . . don't take me!

10 [*She moans, tossing and crying in her sleep. The other people wake, terrified.* Dussel *sits up in bed, furious.*]

11 **Dussel.** Shush! Anne! Anne, for God's sake, shush!

12 **Anne.** [*Still in her nightmare*] Save me! Save me!

13 [*She screams and screams.* Dussel *gets out of bed, going over to her, trying to wake her.*]

14 **Dussel.** For God's sake! Quiet! Quiet! You want someone to hear?

15 [*In the main room* Mrs. Frank *grabs a shawl and pulls it around her. She rushes in to* Anne, *taking her in her arms.* Mr. Frank *hurriedly gets up, putting on his overcoat.* Margot *sits up, terrified.* Peter's *light goes on in his room.*]

16 **Mrs. Frank.** [*To* Anne, *in her room*] Hush, darling, hush. It's all right. It's all right. [*Over her shoulder to* Dussel] Will you be kind enough to turn on the light, Mr. Dussel? [*Back to* Anne] It's nothing, my darling. It was just a dream.

134 UNIT 2 • THE HOLOCAUST

17 [*Dussel turns on the light in the bedroom. Mrs. Frank holds Anne in her arms. Gradually Anne comes out of her nightmare still trembling with horror. Mr. Frank comes into the room, and goes quickly to the window, looking out to be sure that no one outside has heard Anne's screams. Mrs. Frank holds Anne, talking softly to her. In the main room Margot stands on a chair, turning on the center hanging lamp. A light goes on in the Van Daans' room overhead. Peter puts his robe on, coming out of his room.*]

18 **Dussel.** [*To Mrs. Frank, blowing his nose*] Something must be done about that child, Mrs. Frank. Yelling like that! Who knows but there's somebody on the streets? She's endangering all our lives.

19 **Mrs. Frank.** Anne, darling.

20 **Dussel.** Every night she twists and turns. I don't sleep. I spend half my night shushing her. And now it's nightmares!

21 [*Margot comes to the door of Anne's room, followed by Peter. Mr. Frank goes to them, indicating that everything is all right. Peter takes Margot back.*]

22 **Mrs. Frank.** [*To Anne*] You're here, safe, you see? Nothing has happened. [*To Dussel*] Please, Mr. Dussel, go back to bed. She'll be herself in a minute or two. Won't you, Anne?

23 **Dussel.** [*Picking up a book and a pillow*] Thank you, but I'm going to the w.c. The one place where there's peace!

24 [*He stalks out. Mr. Van Daan, in underwear and trousers, comes down the stairs.*]

25 **Mr. Van Daan.** [*To Dussel*] What is it? What happened?

26 **Dussel.** A nightmare. She was having a nightmare!

27 **Mr. Van Daan.** I thought someone was murdering her.

28 **Dussel.** Unfortunately, no.

29 [*He goes into the bathroom. Mr. Van Daan goes back up the stairs. Mr. Frank, in the main room, sends Peter back to his own bedroom.*]

30 **Mr. Frank.** Thank you, Peter. Go back to bed.

31 [*Peter goes back to his room. Mr. Frank follows him, turning out the light and looking out the window. Then he goes back to the main room, and gets up on a chair, turning out the center hanging lamp.*]

32 **Mrs. Frank.** [*To Anne*] Would you like some water? [*Anne shakes her head.*] Was it a very bad dream? Perhaps if you told me . . . ?

33 **Anne.** I'd rather not talk about it.

NOTES

The Diary of Anne Frank, Act I 135

VOCABULARY DEVELOPMENT

Word Analysis Understanding the parts of a word will help students when they come upon an unfamiliar word. In paragraph 28 of the text, Mr. Dussel says, "Unfortunately, no." Point out the word *unfortunately*. Underline the prefix *un-* and ask the students to tell you if it is positive or negative. (Possible response: It is negative). Ask the students to tell you if the word *fortunately* is positive or negative. (Possible response: It is positive). Now ask what happens when you put the two together. (Possible response: The word is negative). Read Mr. Van Daan's line and then Mr. Dussel's line twice. The first time, replace unfortunately with fortunately. The second time, read it as it is written. Guide students to understand that taken literally, the phrase means Mr. Dussel is sorry that no one was murdering Anne. However, he is exaggerating.

Whole-Class Learning 135

TEACHING

NOTES

34 **Mrs. Frank.** Poor darling. Try to sleep then. I'll sit right here beside you until you fall asleep. [*She brings a stool over, sitting there.*]

35 **Anne.** You don't have to.

36 **Mrs. Frank.** But I'd like to stay with you . . . very much. Really.

37 **Anne.** I'd rather you didn't.

38 **Mrs. Frank.** Good night, then. [*She leans down to kiss* Anne. Anne *throws her arm up over her face, turning away.* Mrs. Frank, *hiding her hurt, kisses* Anne's *arm.*] You'll be all right? There's nothing that you want?

39 **Anne.** Will you please ask Father to come.

40 **Mrs. Frank.** [*After a second*] Of course, Anne dear. [*She hurries out into the other room.* Mr. Frank *comes to her as she comes in.*] *Sie verlangt nach Dir!*[21]

41 **Mr. Frank.** [*Sensing her hurt*] Edith, *Liebe, schau*[22] . . .

42 **Mrs. Frank.** *Es macht nichts! Ich danke dem lieben Herrgott, dass sie sich wenigstens an Dich wendet, wenn sie Trost braucht! Geh hinein, Otto, sie ist ganz hysterisch vor Angst.*[23] [*As* Mr. Frank *hesitates*] *Geh zu ihr.*[24] [*He looks at her for a second and then goes to get a cup of water for* Anne. Mrs. Frank *sinks down on the bed, her face in her hands, trying to keep from sobbing aloud.* Margot *comes over to her, putting her arms around her.*] She wants nothing of me. She pulled away when I leaned down to kiss her.

43 **Margot.** It's a phase . . . You heard Father . . . Most girls go through it . . . they turn to their fathers at this age . . . they give all their love to their fathers.

44 **Mrs. Frank.** You weren't like this. You didn't shut me out.

45 **Margot.** She'll get over it . . .

46 [*She smooths the bed for* Mrs. Frank *and sits beside her a moment as* Mrs. Frank *lies down. In* Anne's *room* Mr. Frank *comes in, sitting down by* Anne. Anne *flings her arms around him, clinging to him. In the distance we hear the sound of ack-ack.*]

47 **Anne.** Oh, Pim. I dreamed that they came to get us! The Green Police! They broke down the door and grabbed me and started to drag me out the way they did Jopie.

48 **Mr. Frank.** I want you to take this pill.

49 **Anne.** What is it?

50 **Mr. Frank.** Something to quiet you.

---

21. *Sie verlangt nach Dir* (zee FER langt nokh DIHR) German for "She is asking for you."
22. *Liebe, schau* (LEE buh SHOW) German for "Dear, look."
23. *Es macht . . . vor Angst* German for "It's all right. I thank dear God that at least she turns to you when she needs comfort. Go in, Otto, she is hysterical because of fear."
24. *Geh zu ihr* (GAY tsoo eer) German for "Go to her."

PERSONALIZE FOR LEARNING

English Language Support

Translations Call attention to paragraph 40. Some of the dialogue on this page is in German, such as Mrs. Frank's lines in paragraph 40. This may present a challenge for a wide range of readers. Point out the translations provided in the side column. Assign roles and have students read the text aloud, replacing the German with the translation and discuss what the characters are saying to each other. Once students understand what the characters have said to each other, remind students that the real people who the characters represent would not have been speaking to each other in English. The English is for the audience. Initiate a class discussion about why the playwrights chose to put the German dialogue here. Possible response: They wanted to create an emotional moment between a husband and wife.

51 [*She takes it and drinks the water. In the main room* Margot *turns out the light and goes back to her bed.*]

52 **Mr. Frank.** [*To* Anne] Do you want me to read to you for a while?

53 **Anne.** No. Just sit with me for a minute. Was I awful? Did I yell terribly loud? Do you think anyone outside could have heard?

54 **Mr. Frank.** No. No. Lie quietly now. Try to sleep.

55 **Anne.** I'm a terrible coward. I'm so disappointed in myself. I think I've conquered my fear . . . I think I'm really grownup . . . and then something happens . . . and I run to you like a baby . . . I love you, Father. I don't love anyone but you.

56 **Mr. Frank.** [*Reproachfully*] Annele!

57 **Anne.** It's true. I've been thinking about it for a long time. You're the only one I love.

58 **Mr. Frank.** It's fine to hear you tell me that you love me. But I'd be happier if you said you loved your mother as well . . . She needs your help so much . . . your love . . .

59 **Anne.** We have nothing in common. She doesn't understand me. Whenever I try to explain my views on life to her she asks me if I'm constipated.

60 **Mr. Frank.** You hurt her very much just now. She's crying. She's in there crying.

61 **Anne.** I can't help it. I only told the truth. I didn't want her here . . . [*Then, with sudden change*] Oh, Pim, I was horrible, wasn't I? And the worst of it is, I can stand off and look at myself doing it and know it's cruel and yet I can't stop doing it. What's the matter with me? Tell me. Don't say it's just a phase! Help me.

62 **Mr. Frank.** There is so little that we parents can do to help our children. We can only try to set a good example . . . point the way. The rest you must do yourself. You must build your own character.

63 **Anne.** I'm trying. Really I am. Every night I think back over all of the things I did that day that were wrong . . . like putting the wet mop in Mr. Dussel's bed . . . and this thing now with Mother. I say to myself, that was wrong. I make up my mind, I'm never going to do that again. Never! Of course I may do something worse . . . but at least I'll never do *that* again! . . . I have a nicer side, Father . . . a sweeter, nicer side. But I'm scared to show it. I'm afraid that people are going to laugh at me if I'm serious. So the mean Anne comes to the

NOTES

CLOSE READ
ANNOTATE: In paragraph 63, mark the detail that suggest the kinds of mischief Anne carries out against adults in the Annex.

QUESTION: Why might the playwrights have chosen to include this detail—but no others—about Anne's bad behavior?

CONCLUDE: What does this detail reveal about Anne's character?

The Diary of Anne Frank, Act I **137**

CLOSE READ

You may wish to model the close read using the following think-aloud format.

ANNOTATE: As I read 63, I notice and highlight text that shows Anne's mischievous character.

QUESTION: The playwrights may have included this information to help reader's understand Anne's difficulty in behaving well under the circumstances.

CONCLUDE: These details reveal that Anne is a searching, growing, and learning person. She is genuinely trying to improve herself and to please her father, showing her emerging maturity and self-awareness. She is struggling to be good. These qualities make her a very sympathetic character.

Whole-Class Learning **137**

TEACHING

CLOSER LOOK

Infer Key Ideas

Students may have marked paragraph 65 during their first read. Use this paragraph to help students understand that when playwrights provide dialogue, they are not just giving you the characters' words, they are letting you into the characters' worlds. When reading dialogue, the reader can infer important ideas about the characters. Encourage students to talk about the annotations that they marked. You may want to model a close read with the class based on the highlights shown in the text.

ANNOTATE: Have students mark details in paragraph 65 that show what Anne longs to do after the war, or have students participate while you highlight them.

QUESTION: Guide students to consider what these details might tell them. Ask what a reader can infer about Anne from the list of things Anne would like to do after the war, and accept student responses.

Possible response: She longs to do ordinary things, things people do every day.

CONCLUDE: Help students to formulate conclusions about the importance of these details in the text. Ask students what Anne's list reveals about her.

Possible response: Anne longs to have a normal life. She misses the things she may have taken for granted in the past.

Remind students that **key ideas** in a play can be communicated through dialogue. The playwrights had Anne list everybody's wishes in her monologue. When Anne finally reached her own wishes, the playwrights used ellipses to separate each mundane activity. Point out this use of ellipses to the class and discuss their use here. Explain that when she is discussing her own wishes, it is more personal, and the ellipses emphasize her longing for each of these activities.

NOTES

outside and the good Anne stays on the inside, and I keep on trying to switch them around and have the good Anne outside and the bad Anne inside and be what I'd like to be . . . and might be . . . if only . . . only . . .

64 [*She is asleep.* Mr. Frank *watches her for a moment and then turns off the light, and starts out. The lights dim out. The curtain falls on the scene.* Anne's Voice *is heard dimly at first, and then with growing strength.*]

65 **Anne's Voice** . . . The air raids are getting worse. They come over day and night. The noise is terrifying. Pim says it should be music to our ears. The more planes, the sooner will come the end of the war. Mrs. Van Daan pretends to be a fatalist. What will be, will be. But when the planes come over, who is the most frightened? No one else but Petronella! . . . Monday, the ninth of November, nineteen forty-two. Wonderful news! The Allies have landed in Africa. Pim says that we can look for an early finish to the war. Just for fun he asked each of us what was the first thing we wanted to do when we got out of here. Mrs. Van Daan longs to be home with her own things, her needlepoint chairs, the Beckstein piano her father gave her . . . the best that money could buy. Peter would like to go to a movie. Mr. Dussel wants to get back to his dentist's drill. He's afraid he is losing his touch. For myself, there are so many things . . . to ride a bike again . . . to laugh till my belly aches . . . to have new clothes from the skin out . . . to have a hot tub filled to overflowing and wallow in it for hours . . . to be back in school with my friends . . .

66 [*As the last lines are being said, the curtain rises on the scene. The lights dim on as* Anne's Voice *fades away.*]

❋ ❋ ❋

Scene 5

1 [*It is the first night of the Hanukkah*[25] *celebration.* Mr. Frank *is standing at the head of the table on which is the Menorah.*[26] *He lights the Shamos,*[27] *or servant candle, and holds it as he says the blessing. Seated listening is all of the "family," dressed in their best. The men wear hats,* Peter *wears his cap.*]

2 **Mr. Frank.** [*Reading from a prayer book*] "Praised be Thou, oh Lord our God, Ruler of the universe, who has sanctified us with Thy commandments and bidden us kindle the Hanukkah lights. Praised be Thou, oh Lord our God, Ruler of

25. **Hanukkah** (HAH nu kah) Jewish celebration that lasts eight days.

26. **Menorah** (muh NAWR uh) *n.* candleholder with nine candles, used during Hanukkah.

27. **Shamos** (SHAH muhs) *n.* candle used to light the others in a menorah.

This still image from a film version of the play shows the Hanukkah scene.

the universe, who has wrought wondrous deliverances for our fathers in days of old. Praised be Thou, oh Lord our God, Ruler of the universe, that Thou has given us life and sustenance and brought us to this happy season." [Mr. Frank *lights the one candle of the Menorah as he continues.*] "We kindle this Hanukkah light to celebrate the great and wonderful deeds wrought through the zeal with which God filled the hearts of the heroic Maccabees, two thousand years ago. They fought against indifference, against tyranny and oppression, and they restored our Temple to us. May these lights remind us that we should ever look to God, whence cometh our help." Amen.

3 **All.** Amen.

4 [Mr. Frank *hands* Mrs. Frank *the prayer book.*]

5 **Mrs. Frank.** [*Reading*] "I lift up mine eyes unto the mountains, from whence cometh my help. My help cometh from the Lord who made heaven and earth. He will not suffer thy foot to be moved. He that keepeth thee will not slumber. He that keepeth Israel doth neither slumber nor sleep. The Lord is thy keeper. The Lord is thy shade upon thy right hand. The sun shall not smite thee by day, nor the moon by night. The Lord shall keep thee from all evil. He shall keep thy soul. The Lord shall guard thy going out and thy coming in, from this time forth and forevermore." Amen.

NOTES

CLOSE READ
ANNOTATE: In paragraph 2, mark the sentences that explain why the Hanukkah candles are lit.

QUESTION: Why might the playwrights have included this explanation of the Hanukkah story?

CONCLUDE: What is the effect of this explanation?

The Diary of Anne Frank, Act I **139**

DIGITAL PERSPECTIVES

CLOSE READ

For much of the play, the characters have been developed by how they behave in relation to each other. In paragraph 2, the playwrights provide more context to other sides of the characters, such as their religious identity. You may wish to model the close read using the following think-aloud format. Possible responses to questions on the student page are included.

ANNOTATE: As I read paragraph 2, I notice the sentences in Mr. Frank's dialogue in which he explains why they are lighting Hanukkah candles.

QUESTION: The playwrights probably included this explanation to create a connection between the Jewish legend of the past with their struggle in the present.

CONCLUDE: The Hanukkah story reflects the Jews' current plight because the ancient Jews struggled heroically against a tyrannical rulers. The story gives the families hope that they might some day win back their freedom.

PERSONALIZE FOR LEARNING

English Language Support
Archaic Words Paragraphs 2–5 contain several prayers connected to the holiday of Hanukkah. The language of the prayers is archaic and might be difficult for developing readers. Read this page to the class. Ask students to point out unfamiliar words or words that they feel are not used today. (*thou, cometh, keepeth*) Ask students if they can use context clues to figure out what *thou* means. (you) Use the same approach for *cometh* and *keepeth*. After students present their ideas, point out that by removing *–eth* from each word, students should find familiar words.

Whole-Class Learning **139**

TEACHING

NOTES

6 **All.** Amen.

7 [*Mrs. Frank puts down the prayer book and goes to get the food and wine. Margot helps her. Mr. Frank takes the men's hats and puts them aside.*]

8 **Dussel.** [*Rising*] That was very moving.

9 **Anne.** [*Pulling him back*] It isn't over yet!

10 **Mrs. Van Daan.** Sit down! Sit down!

11 **Anne.** There's a lot more, songs and presents.

12 **Dussel.** Presents?

13 **Mrs. Frank.** Not this year, unfortunately.

14 **Mrs. Van Daan.** But always on Hanukkah everyone gives presents . . . everyone!

15 **Dussel.** Like our St. Nicholas's Day.[28]

16 [*There is a chorus of "no's" from the group.*]

17 **Mrs. Van Daan.** No! Not like St. Nicholas! What kind of a Jew are you that you don't know Hanukkah?

18 **Mrs. Frank.** [*As she brings the food*] I remember particularly the candles . . . First one, as we have tonight. Then the second night you light two candles, the next night three . . . and so on until you have eight candles burning. When there are eight candles it is truly beautiful.

19 **Mrs. Van Daan.** And the potato pancakes.

20 **Mr. Van Daan.** Don't talk about them!

21 **Mrs. Van Daan.** I make the best *latkes* you ever tasted!

22 **Mrs. Frank.** Invite us all next year . . . in your own home.

23 **Mr. Frank.** God willing!

24 **Mrs. Van Daan.** God willing.

25 **Margot.** What I remember best is the presents we used to get when we were little . . . eight days of presents . . . and each day they got better and better.

26 **Mrs. Frank.** [*Sitting down*] We are all here, alive. That is present enough.

27 **Anne.** No, it isn't. I've got something . . . [*She rushes into her room, hurriedly puts on a little hat improvised from the lamp shade, grabs a satchel bulging with parcels and comes running back.*]

28 **Mrs. Frank.** What is it?

29 **Anne.** Presents!

30 **Mrs. Van Daan.** Presents!

31 **Dussel.** Look!

28. **St. Nicholas' Day** December 6, the day Christian children in the Netherlands receive gifts.

CROSS-CURRICULAR PERSPECTIVES

Social Studies Two winter holidays are mentioned in paragraphs 14 and 15, Hanukkah and St. Nicholas' Day. Both are part of the cultural experiences of the characters in the play. Provide a research opportunity for students to learn more about each holiday and share what they have learned with the class. Create a chart that includes the traditions of both holidays. Discuss why the playwrights might have felt it was important to include this scene in the play. Possible response: It shows the passage of time. It gives the characters an opportunity to be normal, but also highlights how they cannot be normal.

32 **Mr. Van Daan.** What's she got on her head?

33 **Peter.** A lamp shade!

34 **Anne.** [*She picks out one at random.*] This is for Margot. [*She hands it to* Margot, *pulling her to her feet.*] Read it out loud.

35 **Margot.** [*Reading*]
"You have never lost your temper.
You never will, I fear,
You are so good.
But if you should,
Put all your cross words here."

36 [*She tears open the package.*] A new crossword puzzle book! Where did you get it?

37 **Anne.** It isn't new. It's one that you've done. But I rubbed it all out, and if you wait a little and forget, you can do it all over again.

38 **Margot.** [*Sitting*] It's wonderful, Anne. Thank you. You'd never know it wasn't new.

39 [*From outside we hear the sound of a streetcar passing.*]

40 **Anne.** [*With another gift*] Mrs. Van Daan.

41 **Mrs. Van Daan.** [*Taking it*] This is awful . . . I haven't anything for anyone . . . I never thought . . .

42 **Mr. Frank.** This is all Anne's idea.

43 **Mrs. Van Daan.** [*Holding up a bottle*] What is it?

44 **Anne.** It's hair shampoo. I took all the odds and ends of soap and mixed them with the last of my toilet water.

45 **Mrs. Van Daan.** Oh, Anneke!

46 **Anne.** I wanted to write a poem for all of them, but I didn't have time. [*Offering a large box to* Mr. Van Daan] Yours, Mr. Van Daan, is really something . . . something you want more than anything. [*As she waits for him to open it*] Look! Cigarettes!

47 **Mr. Van Daan.** Cigarettes!

48 **Anne.** Two of them! Pim found some old pipe tobacco in the pocket lining of his coat . . . and we made them . . . or rather, Pim did.

49 **Mrs. Van Daan.** Let me see . . . Well, look at that! Light it, Putti! Light it.

50 [Mr. Van Daan *hesitates.*]

51 **Anne.** It's tobacco, really it is! There's a little fluff in it, but not much.

TEACHING

CLOSE READ

As the play progresses, the playwrights expose the readers to many facets of the characters and their relationships with each other, which builds complexity and credibility. You may wish to model the close read using the following think-aloud format. Possible responses to questions on the student page are included.

ANNOTATE: As I read paragraphs 57–63, I notice details that show Mrs. Frank's reaction to Anne's gift.

QUESTION: These details show readers and audiences that Mrs. Frank is deeply moved and appreciative of Anne's gift, emphasizing how deeply she loves her daughter and how appreciative she is that Anne is making a gesture to overcome their differences.

CONCLUDE: Anne's gift is another example of Anne's maturity, her self-awareness, and her desire to resolve differences with the people she loves.

NOTES

CLOSE READ
ANNOTATE: Mark details in paragraphs 57–63 that show Mrs. Frank's reaction to Anne's gift.

QUESTION: Why do the playwrights include these details?

CONCLUDE: What is the effect of this scene, especially in showing growth in Anne's character?

52 [*Everyone watches intently as Mr. Van Daan cautiously lights it. The cigarette flares up. Everyone laughs.*]

53 **Peter.** It works!

54 **Mrs. Van Daan.** Look at him.

55 **Mr. Van Daan.** [*Spluttering*] Thank you, Anne. Thank you.

56 [*Anne rushes back to her satchel for another present.*]

57 **Anne.** [*Handing her mother a piece of paper*] For Mother, Hanukkah greeting.

58 [*She pulls her mother to her feet.*]

59 **Mrs. Frank.** [*She reads*] "Here's an I.O.U. that I promise to pay. Ten hours of doing whatever you say. Signed, Anne Frank." [*Mrs. Frank, touched, takes Anne in her arms, holding her close.*]

60 **Dussel.** [*To Anne*] Ten hours of doing what you're told? Anything you're told?

61 **Anne.** That's right.

62 **Dussel.** You wouldn't want to sell that, Mrs. Frank?

63 **Mrs. Frank.** Never! This is the most precious gift I've ever had!

64 [*She sits, showing her present to the others. Anne hurries back to the satchel and pulls out a scarf, the scarf that Mr. Frank found in the first scene.*]

65 **Anne.** [*Offering it to her father*] For Pim.

66 **Mr. Frank.** Anneke . . . I wasn't supposed to have a present!

67 [*He takes it, unfolding it and showing it to the others.*]

68 **Anne.** It's a muffler . . . to put round your neck . . . like an ascot, you know. I made it myself out of odds and ends . . . I knitted it in the dark each night, after I'd gone to bed. I'm afraid it looks better in the dark!

69 **Mr. Frank.** [*Putting it on*] It's fine. It fits me perfectly. Thank you, Annele.

70 [*Anne hands Peter a ball of paper with a string attached to it.*]

71 **Anne.** That's for Mouschi.

72 **Peter.** [*Rising to bow*] On behalf of Mouschi, I thank you.

73 **Anne.** [*Hesitant, handing him a gift*] And . . . this is yours . . . from Mrs. Quack Quack. [*As he holds it gingerly in his hands*] Well . . . open it . . . Aren't you going to open it?

74 **Peter.** I'm scared to. I know something's going to jump out and hit me.

75 **Anne.** No. It's nothing like that, really.

76 **Mrs. Van Daan.** [*As he is opening it*] What is it, Peter? Go on. Show it.

77 **Anne.** [*Excitedly*] It's a safety razor!

78 **Dussel.** A what?

79 **Anne.** A razor!

80 **Mrs. Van Daan.** [*Looking at it*] You didn't make that out of odds and ends.

81 **Anne.** [*To* Peter] Miep got it for me. It's not new. It's secondhand. But you really do need a razor now.

82 **Dussel.** For what?

83 **Anne.** Look on his upper lip . . . you can see the beginning of a mustache.

84 **Dussel.** He wants to get rid of that? Put a little milk on it and let the cat lick it off.

85 **Peter.** [*Starting for his room*] Think you're funny, don't you.

86 **Dussel.** Look! He can't wait! He's going in to try it!

87 **Peter.** I'm going to give Mouschi his present!

88 [*He goes into his room, slamming the door behind him.*]

89 **Mr. Van Daan.** [*Disgustedly*] Mouschi, Mouschi, Mouschi.

90 [*In the distance we hear a dog persistently barking.* Anne *brings a gift to* Dussel.]

91 **Anne.** And last but never least, my roommate, Mr. Dussel.

92 **Dussel.** For me? You have something for me?

93 [*He opens the small box she gives him.*]

94 **Anne.** I made them myself.

95 **Dussel.** [*Puzzled*] Capsules! Two capsules!

96 **Anne.** They're ear-plugs!

97 **Dussel.** Ear-plugs?

98 **Anne.** To put in your ears so you won't hear me when I thrash around at night. I saw them advertised in a magazine. They're not real ones . . . I made them out of cotton and

NOTES

DIGITAL PERSPECTIVES

Illuminating the Text Have students perform a dramatic reading of the gift-giving scene, paragraphs 26–103. Next, play a video of the same scene for the class. Ask students to take note of how the actors show their emotions in the scene. Ask students to note the mood shifts within the scene. Possible response: Mrs. Van Daan's embarrassment, everybody's excitement, Peter's frustration and then a return to excitement. Ask students to discuss how the emotions were conveyed to the audience in the video version. Ask them to consider if the video version matches their expectations of what this scene might have looked like. Ask students to consider which version is more authentic. Possible response: They are both authentic. When a play is performed, there is a certain amount of interpretation by the actors to be expected.

candle wax. Try them . . . See if they don't work . . . see if you can hear me talk . . .

99 **Dussel.** [*Putting them in his ears*] Wait now until I get them in . . . so.

100 **Anne.** Are you ready?

101 **Dussel.** Huh?

102 **Anne.** Are you ready?

103 **Dussel.** Good God! They've gone inside! I can't get them out! [*They laugh as Mr. Dussel jumps about, trying to shake the plugs out of his ears. Finally he gets them out. Putting them away*] Thank you, Anne! Thank you!

104 [*Together*]
- **Mr. Van Daan.** A real Hanukkah!
- **Mrs. Van Daan.** Wasn't it cute of her?
- **Mrs. Frank.** I don't know when she did it.
- **Margot.** I love my present.

105 **Anne.** [*Sitting at the table*] And now let's have the song, Father . . . please . . . [*To Dussel*] Have you heard the Hanukkah song, Mr. Dussel? The song is the whole thing! [*She sings.*] "Oh, Hanukkah! Oh, Hanukkah! The sweet celebration . . ."

106 **Mr. Frank.** [*Quieting her*] I'm afraid, Anne, we shouldn't sing that song tonight. [*To Dussel*] It's a song of jubilation, of rejoicing. One is apt to become too enthusiastic.

107 **Anne.** Oh, please, please. Let's sing the song. I promise not to shout!

108 **Mr. Frank.** Very well. But quietly now . . . I'll keep an eye on you and when . . .

109 [*As Anne starts to sing, she is interrupted by Dussel, who is snorting and wheezing.*]

110 **Dussel.** [*Pointing to Peter*] You . . . You! [*Peter is coming from his bedroom, ostentatiously holding a bulge in his coat as if he were holding his cat, and dangling Anne's present before it.*] How many times . . . I told you . . . Out! Out!

111 **Mr. Van Daan.** [*Going to Peter*] What's the matter with you? Haven't you any sense? Get that cat out of here.

112 **Peter.** [*Innocently*] Cat?

In this photograph, the common room of the Secret Annex appears much as it did when Anne Frank lived there.

NOTES

113 **Mr. Van Daan.** You heard me. Get it out of here!

114 **Peter.** I have no cat. [*Delighted with his joke, he opens his coat and pulls out a bath towel. The group at the table laugh, enjoying the joke.*]

115 **Dussel.** [*Still wheezing*] It doesn't need to be the cat, his clothes are enough . . . when he comes out of that room . . .

116 **Mr. Van Daan.** Don't worry. You won't be bothered any more. We're getting rid of it.

117 **Dussel.** At last you listen to me. [*He goes off into his bedroom.*]

118 **Mr. Van Daan.** [*Calling after him*] I'm not doing it for you. That's all in your mind . . . all of it! [*He starts back to his place at the table.*] I'm doing it because I'm sick of seeing that cat eat all our food.

119 **Peter.** That's not true! I only give him bones . . . scraps . . .

120 **Mr. Van Daan.** Don't tell me! He gets fatter every day! Damn cat looks better than any of us. Out he goes tonight!

121 **Peter.** No! No!

122 **Anne.** Mr. Van Daan, you can't do that! That's Peter's cat. Peter loves that cat.

123 **Mrs. Frank.** [*Quietly*] Anne.

124 **Peter.** [*To Mr. Van Daan*] If he goes, I go.

The Diary of Anne Frank, Act I 145

TEACHING

● **CLOSE READ**

Use these paragraphs to help students see and discuss the effect of sentence length. You may wish to model the close read using the following think-aloud format. Possible responses to questions on the student page are included.

ANNOTATE: As I read paragraphs 133–140, I notice sentence lengths and mark the sentences that are four words or less.

QUESTION: I think the characters are afraid and trying to limit what they say so they can stay quiet.

CONCLUDE: These sentences establish the fear of the scene and increase the pacing to build suspense.

NOTES

125 **Mr. Van Daan.** Go! Go!

126 **Mrs. Van Daan.** You're not going and the cat's not going! Now please . . . this is Hanukkah . . . Hanukkah . . . this is the time to celebrate . . . What's the matter with all of you? Come on, Anne. Let's have the song.

127 **Anne.** [*Singing*]
"Oh, Hanukkah! Oh, Hanukkah! The sweet celebration."

128 **Mr. Frank.** [*Rising*] I think we should first blow out the candle . . . then we'll have something for tomorrow night.

129 **Margot.** But, Father, you're supposed to let it burn itself out.

130 **Mr. Frank.** I'm sure that God understands shortages. [*Before blowing it out*] "Praised be Thou, oh Lord our God, who hast sustained us and permitted us to celebrate this joyous festival."

131 [*He is about to blow out the candle when suddenly there is a crash of something falling below. They all freeze in horror, motionless. For a few seconds there is complete silence.* Mr. Frank *slips off his shoes. The others noiselessly follow his example.* Mr. Frank *turns out a light near him. He motions to* Peter *to turn off the center lamp.* Peter *tries to reach it, realizes he cannot and gets up on a chair. Just as he is touching the lamp he loses his balance. The chair goes out from under him. He falls. The iron lamp shade crashes to the floor. There is a sound of feet below, running down the stairs.*]

132 **Mr. Van Daan.** [*Under his breath*] God Almighty! [*The only light left comes from the Hanukkah candle.* Dussel *comes from his room.* Mr. Frank *creeps over to the stairwell and stands listening. The dog is heard barking excitedly.*] Do you hear anything?

133 **Mr. Frank.** [*In a whisper*] No. I think they've gone.

134 **Mrs. Van Daan.** It's the Green Police. They've found us.

135 **Mr. Frank.** If they had, they wouldn't have left. They'd be up here by now.

136 **Mrs. Van Daan.** I know it's the Green Police. They've gone to get help. That's all. They'll be back!

137 **Mr. Van Daan.** Or it may have been the Gestapo,[29] looking for papers . . .

138 **Mr. Frank.** [*Interrupting*] Or a thief, looking for money.

139 **Mrs. Van Daan.** We've got to do something . . . Quick! Quick! Before they come back.

140 **Mr. Van Daan.** There isn't anything to do. Just wait.

CLOSE READ

ANNOTATE: In paragraphs 133–140, mark sentences of four words or less.

QUESTION: Why do the characters speak in a series of short sentences during this scene?

CONCLUDE: How does the series of short sentences add to the scene's tension?

29. **Gestapo** (guh STAH poh) *n.* secret police force of Nazi Germany, known for its brutality.

PERSONALIZE FOR LEARNING

Strategic Support

Role Playing Direct students to the stage directions in paragraph 131. Point out that this set of directions contains an entire scene without words. Discuss why there are no words in this scene. Ask them to consider whether or not they agree with the playwrights' decision to show us what was happening here, rather than tell us. Possible response: Yes, because they needed to be silent, fearing that they would be caught. Divide students into groups and have each group prepare the scene and perform it for the rest of the class. In preparing their scenes, remind groups that they will have to decide details like facial expressions, which are also a form of communication. Discuss the challenges they experienced in preparing acting out this scene.

141 [Mr. Frank *holds up his hand for them to be quiet. He is listening intently. There is complete silence as they all strain to hear any sound from below. Suddenly* Anne *begins to sway. With a low cry she falls to the floor in a faint.* Mrs. Frank *goes to her quickly, sitting beside her on the floor and taking her in her arms.*]

142 **Mrs. Frank.** Get some water, please! Get some water!

143 [Margot *starts for the sink.*]

144 **Mr. Van Daan.** [*Grabbing* Margot] No! No! No one's going to run water!

145 **Mr. Frank.** If they've found us, they've found us. Get the water. [Margot *starts again for the sink.* Mr. Frank, *getting a flashlight*] I'm going down.

146 [Margot *rushes to him, clinging to him.* Anne *struggles to consciousness.*]

147 **Margot.** No, Father, no! There may be someone there, waiting . . . It may be a trap!

148 **Mr. Frank.** This is Saturday. There is no way for us to know what has happened until Miep or Mr. Kraler comes on Monday morning. We cannot live with this uncertainty.

149 **Margot.** Don't go, Father!

150 **Mrs. Frank.** Hush, darling, hush. [Mr. Frank *slips quietly out, down the steps and out through the door below.*] Margot! Stay close to me. [Margot *goes to her mother.*]

151 **Mr. Van Daan.** Shush! Shush!

152 [Mrs. Frank *whispers to* Margot *to get the water.* Margot *goes for it.*]

153 **Mrs. Van Daan.** Putti, where's our money? Get our money. I hear you can buy the Green Police off, so much a head. Go upstairs quick! Get the money!

154 **Mr. Van Daan.** Keep still!

155 **Mrs. Van Daan.** [*Kneeling before him, pleading*] Do you want to be dragged off to a concentration camp? Are you going to stand there and wait for them to come up and get you? Do something, I tell you!

156 **Mr. Van Daan.** [*Pushing her aside*] Will you keep still!

157 [*He goes over to the stairwell to listen.* Peter *goes to his mother, helping her up onto the sofa. There is a second of silence, then* Anne *can stand it no longer.*]

158 **Anne.** Someone go after Father! Make Father come back!

159 **Peter.** [*Starting for the door*] I'll go.

160 **Mr. Van Daan.** Haven't you done enough?

161 [*He pushes* Peter *roughly away. In his anger against his father* Peter *grabs a chair as if to hit him with it, then puts it down, burying his face in his hands.* Mrs. Frank *begins to pray softly.*]

162 **Anne.** Please, please, Mr. Van Daan. Get Father.

163 **Mr. Van Daan.** Quiet! Quiet!

164 [Anne *is shocked into silence.* Mrs. Frank *pulls her closer, holding her protectively in her arms.*]

165 **Mrs. Frank.** [*Softly, praying*] "I lift up mine eyes unto the mountains, from whence cometh my help. My help cometh from the Lord who made heaven and earth. He will not suffer thy foot to be moved . . . He that keepeth thee will not slumber . . ."

166 [*She stops as she hears someone coming. They all watch the door tensely.* Mr. Frank *comes quietly in.* Anne *rushes to him, holding him tight.*]

167 **Mr. Frank.** It was a thief. That noise must have scared him away.

168 **Mrs. Van Daan.** Thank God.

169 **Mr. Frank.** He took the cash box. And the radio. He ran away in such a hurry that he didn't stop to shut the street door. It was swinging wide open. [*A breath of relief sweeps over them.*] I think it would be good to have some light.

170 **Margot.** Are you sure it's all right?

171 **Mr. Frank.** The danger has passed. [Margot *goes to light the small lamp.*] Don't be so terrified, Anne. We're safe.

172 **Dussel.** Who says the danger has passed? Don't you realize we are in greater danger than ever?

173 **Mr. Frank.** Mr. Dussel, will you be still!

174 [Mr. Frank *takes* Anne *back to the table, making her sit down with him, trying to calm her.*]

175 **Dussel.** [*Pointing to* Peter] Thanks to this clumsy fool, there's someone now who knows we're up here! Someone now knows we're up here, hiding!

176 **Mrs. Van Daan.** [*Going to* Dussel] Someone knows we're here, yes. But who is the someone? A thief! A thief! You think

a thief is going to go to the Green Police and say . . . I was robbing a place the other night and I heard a noise up over my head? You think a thief is going to do that?

177 **Dussel.** Yes. I think he will.

178 **Mrs. Van Daan.** [*Hysterically*] You're crazy!

179 [*She stumbles back to her seat at the table.* Peter *follows protectively, pushing* Dussel *aside.*]

180 **Dussel.** I think some day he'll be caught and then he'll make a bargain with the Green Police . . . If they'll let him off, he'll tell them where some Jews are hiding!

181 [*He goes off into the bedroom. There is a second of appalled silence.*]

182 **Mr. Van Daan.** He's right.

183 **Anne.** Father, let's get out of here! We can't stay here now . . . Let's go . . .

184 **Mr. Van Daan.** Go! Where?

185 **Mrs. Frank.** [*Sinking into her chair at the table*] Yes. Where?

186 **Mr. Frank.** [*Rising, to them all*] Have we lost all faith? All courage? A moment ago we thought that they'd come for us. We were sure it was the end. But it wasn't the end. We're alive, safe. [*Mr. Van Daan goes to the table and sits.* Mr. Frank *prays.*]

187 "We thank Thee, oh Lord our God, that in Thy infinite mercy Thou hast again seen fit to spare us." [*He blows out the candle, then turns to* Anne.] Come on, Anne. The song! Let's have the song!

188 [*He starts to sing.* Anne *finally starts falteringly to sing, as* Mr. Frank *urges her on. Her voice is hardly audible at first.*]

189 **Anne.** [*Singing*]
"Oh, Hanukkah! Oh, Hanukkah! The sweet . . . celebration . . ."

190 [*As she goes on singing, the others gradually join in, their voices still shaking with fear.* Mrs. Van Daan *sobs as she sings.*]

191 **Group.** Around the feast . . . we . . . gather
In complete . . . jubilation . . .
Happiest of sea . . . sons
Now is here.
Many are the reasons for good cheer.

192 [Dussel *comes from the bedroom. He comes over to the table, standing beside* Margot, *listening to them as they sing.*]

NOTES

hysterically (hihs TEHR ihk lee) *adv.* in a way that shows uncontrolled emotion

The Diary of Anne Frank, Act I **149**

TEACHING

CLOSE READ

The staging of a play has an important role in conveying emotion to an audience. You may wish to model the close read using the following think-aloud format. Possible responses to questions on the student page are included.

ANNOTATE: As I read paragraphs 194 and 198, I mark the details that relate to the characters' singing and to the stage lights.

QUESTION: I think the playwrights might want to show the contrast between the characters' courage and their situation. They are effectively singing in the dark.

CONCLUDE: This scene leaves readers and audiences with the image of the people singing despite the darkness. It shows the strength of the human spirit, as they are singing despite the dismal scene.

NOTES

CLOSE READ
ANNOTATE: In paragraphs 194 and 198, mark details related to the characters' singing and the stage lights.

QUESTION: Why do the playwrights set up a contrast between the singing and the lights?

CONCLUDE: What is the effect of this final scene of Act I?

193 "Together
We'll weather
Whatever tomorrow may bring."

194 [*As they sing on with growing courage, the lights start to dim.*]

195 "So hear us rejoicing
And merrily voicing
The Hanukkah song that we sing.
Hoy!"

196 [*The lights are out. The curtain starts slowly to fall.*]

197 "Hear us rejoicing
And merrily voicing
The Hanukkah song that we sing."

198 [*They are still singing, as the curtain falls.*]

This photo of Anne Frank was taken before she and her family went into hiding.

150 UNIT 2 • THE HOLOCAUST

Comprehension Check

Complete the following items after you finish your first read.

1. In Scene 1, what year is it?

2. How does the time period change in Scene 2?

3. Why must the Franks and the Van Daans be quiet during the day?

4. Why does Mr. Dussel join the group in the attic?

5. What happens to interrupt the Hanukkah celebration?

6. 📓 **Notebook** Write a summary of *The Diary of Anne Frank,* Act I.

RESEARCH

Research to Clarify Choose at least one unfamiliar detail from the text. Briefly research that detail. In what way does the information you learned shed light on an aspect of the play?

Research to Explore Choose something that interested you from the text, and formulate a research question.

The Diary of Anne Frank, Act I **151**

DIGITAL PERSPECTIVES

Comprehension Check

Possible responses:

1. It is 1945.
2. Scene 2 begins a flashback to 1942, three years earlier.
3. They are hiding above a work space, and they must keep their presence a secret from the workers below.
4. He is Jewish and needs a place to hide, so Mr. Frank agrees that he can stay in the attic.
5. A thief breaks into the office below, frightening the group and making them think that the Green Police have found them.
6. Summaries will vary, but should demonstrate an understanding of the content in a concise fashion.

Research

Research to Clarify If students struggle to select a detail, suggest they use the foreign terms noted in the side columns and learn more about them. They might choose the Green Police or the Gestapo. They might also choose to research the Dutch involvement in World War II.

Research to Explore Guide students to select topics that sparked their interest while reading. If students struggle, you can brainstorm a list of ideas as a class and have each student select a topic from the list to form research questions.

PERSONALIZE FOR LEARNING

Challenge The descriptions of the characters come from the words they speak and their actions. Select a character and write a character sketch. Based on what students have learned here and information they have found elsewhere, have them write a paragraph that describes who that character is. If students use additional sources, remind them to cite their sources. Have students share their paragraphs with the class and compare each perspective on the various characters.

Whole-Class Learning **151**

TEACHING

Jump Start

CLOSE READ Tell students that they can learn a lot about characters in plays from their words and from the stage directions provided. Ask students to consider examples in Act I of *The Diary of Anne Frank*.

Close Read the Text

Walk students through the annotation model on the student page. Encourage them to complete items 2 and 3 on their own. Review and discuss the sections students have marked. If needed, continue to model close reading by using the Annotation Highlights in the Interactive Teacher's Edition.

Analyze the Text

Possible responses:

1. Anne responds with excitement and a sense of adventure in contrast to Margot, who is calm and quiet. **DOK 2**

2. Students might say it is fair because she does not seem to exhibit self-control. Some might say it is not fair because she is a child and is behaving as such. **DOK 3**

3. During a crisis, people want to hang on to memories and practices that help them feel as normal as possible. **DOK 3**

4. Because the play is based on real people and events, it provides a way of remembering the people who were tragic victims of the Holocaust. The play opens with Mr. Frank discovering Anne's diary, which opens the door for him to begin remembering and celebrating the lives of the members of his family who had died. I understand that perhaps the only way Mr. Frank might find peace is to remember his family in this way and that these memories have healing powers for a person who has suffered and survived. **DOK 3**

FORMATIVE ASSESSMENT

Analyze the Text

- **If** students fail to cite evidence, **then** remind them to support their ideas with specific information.

- **If** students struggle to analyze how fear causes conflict in the play, **then** remind students that conflict is demonstrated throughout the play both through dialogue and stage direction.

152 UNIT 2 • THE HOLOCAUST

MAKING MEANING

THE DIARY OF ANNE FRANK, ACT I

Close Read the Text

1. The model—from Act I, Scene 1, paragraph 18—shows two sample annotations, along with questions and conclusions. Close read the passage, and find another detail to annotate. Then, write a question and your conclusion.

> **ANNOTATE:** These details show why Mr. Frank feels he must leave Amsterdam.
> **QUESTION:** Why might the playwrights have included these details?
> **CONCLUDE:** These details show what Mr. Frank has lost, and why he feels that he is a different person.

> **Mr. Frank.** I can't stay in Amsterdam, Miep. It has too many memories for me. Everywhere there's something ... the house we lived in ... the school ... that street organ playing out there ... I'm not the person you used to know, Miep. I'm a bitter old man. [*Breaking off*] Forgive me. I shouldn't speak to you like this ... after all that you did for us ... the suffering ...

> **ANNOTATE:** The playwrights use many ellipses in this dialogue.
> **QUESTION:** Why have the playwrights punctuated the dialogue in this way?
> **CONCLUDE:** The ellipses show hesitation and the difficulty of speaking. They hint at Mr. Frank's sorrow and pain.

Tool Kit
Close-Read Guide and Model Annotation

2. For more practice, go back into the text, and complete the close-read notes.

3. Revisit a section of the text you found important during your first read. Read this section closely, and **annotate** what you notice. Ask yourself **questions** such as "Why did the author make this choice?" What can you **conclude**?

Analyze the Text
CITE TEXTUAL EVIDENCE to support your answers.

Notebook Respond to these questions.

1. **Compare and Contrast** How is Anne's response to her confinement different from her sister's?

2. **Make a Judgment** Many of the adults in the play become frustrated with Anne's behavior. Do you think they are being unfair? Explain.

3. **(a) Draw Conclusions** What insights does the Hanukkah scene suggest about the different ways in which people deal with crisis?

4. **Essential Question:** *How do we remember the past?* What has this selection taught you about how people remember the past?

STANDARDS
Reading Literature
• Analyze how particular lines of dialogue or incidents in a story or drama propel the action, reveal aspects of a character, or provoke a decision.
• Analyze how differences in the points of view of the characters and the audience or reader create such effects as suspense or humor.

152 UNIT 2 • THE HOLOCAUST

WriteNow Analyze and Interpret

QuickWrite In the first act of the play, the reader learns that the overarching emotion in the Secret Annex is fear. Have students reflect on how the various characters manage their fears of being caught. You can create a list as a class, or have students do this independently. Then have students write a paragraph reflecting on a character and how that character showed and managed fear in Act I.

ESSENTIAL QUESTION: How do we remember the past?

Analyze Craft and Structure

Text Structures in Drama **Dialogue** is the conversation between or among characters. In a play, dialogue serves three main functions:

- helping readers learn about the characters, their relationships, and their goals
- setting the **mood** or emotional quality, of a scene in order to prompt the desired feeling or response in readers
- developing the plot and subplots—**Conflicts**, or problems and struggles, come to life as characters confide in friends, argue with enemies, and plan their actions.

Dialogue also helps playwrights create **dramatic irony,** a situation in which the audience knows more than the characters do. For example, in a play based on tragic historical events, such as *The Diary of Anne Frank*, the audience knows the characters' fates. That knowledge contributes to the suspense and tension of the story.

Practice

CITE TEXTUAL EVIDENCE to support your answers.

Notebook Review *The Diary of Anne Frank,* Act I. For each item in the chart, identify passages of dialogue that serve that purpose. Explain each choice.

PURPOSE OF DIALOGUE	EXAMPLES FROM ACT I	EXPLANATION
shows what characters are like and what they want	Scene 4, paragraphs 42–48 Scene 5, paragraphs 94–99	
sets the mood	Scene 2, paragraphs 37–43	
shows conflicts and action, moving the plot forward	Scene 5, paragraphs 133–140	

1. Reread Scene 2, paragraph 139. What does Mr. Frank mean when he says, "There are . . . no locks that anyone can put on your mind"? What does this dialogue show about Mr. Frank as a father and as the leader of the group in hiding?
2. Reread Scene 3, paragraphs 40–45. What subplot, or secondary conflict, does this dialogue develop?
3. Review the Background for Act I, and consider what you know about Anne's fate. How does this knowledge add dramatic irony to the end of Act I?

The Diary of Anne Frank, Act I **153**

DIGITAL PERSPECTIVES

Analyze Craft and Structure

Text Structures in Drama Dialogue provides insight into what characters in a play are thinking and how they are feeling. Dialogue is more than just the words characters say, but also how they say them. Punctuation and stage directions help bring dialogue to life and help the words the characters say set the mood and tone for the play. Remind students to take note of punctuation as they read dialogue and understand how it sets the tone. Read the same line with different punctuation to demonstrate this concept. For more support, see **Analyze Craft and Structure: Text Structures in Drama.**

MAKE IT INTERACTIVE
Ask students to work in pairs to present a piece of dialogue from Act I. Decide how much dialogue you would like each group to present. They may select the dialogue that is most meaningful to them and present it to the class. Have partners explain why they chose their dialogue before they present it.

Practice
Possible responses:
See possible responses on chart on student page.

1. Students may say that Mr. Frank is a good father who is trying to encourage his daughters. He is a good leader who is trying to keep people calm.
2. The dialogue develops the subplot of Anne's frustration in her relationship with Peter. Peter is the only person present in Anne's age group, and she is growing impatient in her attempts to develop a relationship with him.
3. Knowing that Anne and the others are eventually caught and deported to death camps adds dramatic irony to their singing of the Hanukkah song at the end of Act I. The song speaks of jubilation and having many reasons for good cheer. The characters are trying to be hopeful, but this is in stark contrast with their fate.

PERSONALIZE FOR LEARNING

English Language Support
Using Dialogue and Stage Directions Have students look at the examples of dialogue and stage directions from Scene 5, paragraphs 34–35, 113–115, and 131–132.

Have small groups work together to identify the stage directions and/or dialogue as examples of character development, plot development, and/or external conflict (war) and tell why they think so. **EMERGING**

Have partners take turns sharing how each develops character, advances the plot, and/or suggests the external conflict (war). **EXPANDING**

Have partners take turns identifying each example as to which element of the play it develops (character, plot, conflict) and tell how **effective** it is. **BRIDGING**

An expanded **English Language Support Lesson** on Dialogue is available in the Interactive Teacher's Edition.

FORMATIVE ASSESSMENT
Analyze Craft and Structure

- **If** students struggle to see how dialogue provides plot and subplot, **then** have students summarize the plot and cite evidence.
- **If** students struggle to understand dialogue, **then** have students perform dramatic readings of the dialogue.

For Reteach and Practice, see **Analyze Craft and Structure: Text Structures in Drama (RP).**

Whole-Class Learning **153**

TEACHING

Concept Vocabulary

Why These Words?
Possible responses:
1. The concept words all relate to stress and the tension that results from living in confinement and fear.
2. *battle, unbearable, bad-tempered, aggravating, tense, terror*

Practice
Possible responses:
1. Responses will vary.
2. anxiously: nervously, calmly

   tension: stress, relaxation

   restraining: holding back, releasing

   quarrels: arguments, harmony

   bickering: fighting, agreeing

   hysterically: uncontrollably, calmly

Word Network
Possible words: *unbearable, aggravating, terror*

Word Study

For more support, see **Concept Vocabulary and Word Study.**

Possible responses:
1. The suffix *-ion* means "act or condition of," *tension* is an emotional state of being tense or anxious.
2. *aggression:* the condition of being aggressive by attacking or confronting *confusion:* the condition of being confused; the condition of being unable to think clearly *possession:* the condition of possessing or owning

FORMATIVE ASSESSMENT

Concept Vocabulary
If students do not understand how these words relate to the mood of the play, **then** review the dialogue that includes them.

Word Study
If the student does not understand the impact the suffix *-ion* has on the meaning of a word, **then** review the meaning and example of words ending in the suffix. For Reteach and Practice, see **Word Study: Latin Suffix *-ion* (RP).**

154 UNIT 2 • THE HOLOCAUST

LANGUAGE DEVELOPMENT

THE DIARY OF ANNE FRANK, ACT I

Concept Vocabulary

| anxiously | restraining | bickering |
| tension | quarrels | hysterically |

Why These Words? These concept vocabulary words are used to describe feelings of stress and conflict. For example, the *bickering* between Mr. and Mrs. Van Daan shows how small issues can expand into heated *quarrels* for people experiencing extreme *tension*.

1. How does the concept vocabulary help the reader understand the experiences of the characters?

2. What other words in the selection connect to this concept?

Practice

Notebook The six concept vocabulary words appear in Act I of *The Diary of Anne Frank*.

1. Write a paragraph about this part of the play, using as many of the concept words as possible.

2. Work with a partner. Take turns listing **synonyms**, or words with similar meanings, for each concept word. When you have finished, take turns listing **antonyms**, or words with opposite meanings, for each concept word.

Word Study

Latin Suffix: *–ion* The Latin suffix *-ion* means "act or condition of." In the play *The Diary of Anne Frank*, the characters feel *tension* when they hear noise outside.

1. Using your knowledge of the suffix *-ion*, write a definition of the word *tension*.

2. Use your understanding of the suffix *-ion*, to write definitions for the following words: *aggression, confusion, possession*. Then, use a dictionary to verify your definitions.

WORD NETWORK
Add words related to the Holocaust from the text to your Word Network.

STANDARDS
Language
- Demonstrate command of the conventions of standard English grammar and usage when writing or speaking.
- Determine or clarify the meaning of unknown and multiple-meaning words or phrases based on *grade 8 reading and content*, choosing flexibly from a range of strategies.
  b. Use common, grade-appropriate Greek or Latin affixes and roots as clues to the meaning of a word.
  d. Verify the preliminary determination of the meaning of a word or phrase.
- Demonstrate understanding of figurative language, word relationships, and nuances in word meanings.
  b. Use the relationship between particular words to better understand each of the words.

154 UNIT 2 • THE HOLOCAUST

AUTHOR'S PERSPECTIVE — Elfrieda Hiebert, Ph.D.

Collecting Sentences To help students become more adept with words, give them the experience of working with them. By studying sentences that use new vocabulary well, students can build their vocabulary strength. Encourage students to collect model sentences using two strategies:

- **Find sentences in the text.** Help students locate sentences that use new vocabulary, or have students identify sentences where word choice truly packs power into the text. Discuss how the words are used, and have students emulate the writer by writing similar sentences.

- **Find sentences in online vocabulary resources.** When students are learning new words, it is useful to see the word used correctly in a variety of contexts. Many online dictionaries provide contemporary and cross-

ESSENTIAL QUESTION: How do we remember the past?

Conventions

Principal Parts of Verbs A **verb** is a word that expresses an action or state of being. All verbs have four **principal parts,** or forms. Most verbs are **regular,** but some common verbs are **irregular**—their past and past participle do not follow a single predictable pattern.

The chart below shows the four principal parts of one regular verb, *ask*, and one irregular verb, *write*.

PRINCIPAL PART	HOW TO FORM	EXAMPLES
Present	Basic form. Add *-s* or *-es* for third-person singular.	Peter asks her to be quiet. Anne writes in her diary each night.
Present Participle	Add *-ing*. Use after a form of *be* (*is, are, was, were, will be*, etc.).	They are asking if there is more food. She was writing about her experiences.
Past	REGULAR: Add *-d* or *-ed*. IRREGULAR: No one predictable pattern.	Mr. Dussel asked to be left alone. Mr. Frank wrote a list of items.
Past Participle	REGULAR: Add *-d* or *-ed*. Use after a form of *have* (*have, has, had*). IRREGULAR: No one predictable pattern. Use after a form of *have*.	Mrs. Van Daan has asked for her coat. Margot had written in her book.

Read It

1. Mark the verb form in each sentence. Then, label it present, present participle, past, or past participle.

   a. Yesterday, I finished her latest book.

   b. Margot is sleeping on a mattress on the floor.

   c. Nothing has happened.

2. Read the stage directions at the beginning of Scene 5. Mark the verb form in each sentence. Then, label each one present or present participle.

Write It

Notebook Reread the stage directions at the beginning of Scene 5. Then, rewrite them using the past and past participle.

The Diary of Anne Frank, Act I 155

DIGITAL PERSPECTIVES

Conventions

Principal Parts of Verbs Have students practice finding and using the four principal parts of regular verbs, such as *walk* and *rain*. Then have them practice finding and using the four parts of irregular verbs, such as *think* and *eat*. For more support, see **Conventions: Principal Parts of Verbs.**

Read It
Possible responses:
1. a. finished: past
   b. is sleeping: present participle
   c. has happened: past participle
2. It is [present] *the first night of the Hanukkah celebration.* Mr. Frank is standing [present participle] *at the head of the table on which* is [present] *the Menorah. He* lights [present] *the Shamos, or servant candle, and* holds [present] *it as he* says [present] *the blessing. Seated* listening is [present participle] *all of the "family," dressed in their best. The men* wear [present] *hats,* Peter wears [present] *his cap.*

Write It
Possible responses:
[*It was the first night of the Hanukkah celebration.* Mr. Frank *was standing at the head of the table on which was the Menorah. He* lit *the Shamos, or servant candle, and* held *it as he* said *the blessing. Seated listening was all of the "family," dressed in their best. The men* wore *hats,* Peter wore *his cap.*]

FORMATIVE ASSESSMENT

Conventions
If students cannot identify principal parts of verbs, **then** review the chart on the student page and provide more examples. For Reteach and Practice, see **Conventions: Principal Parts of Verbs (RP).**

---

curricular examples to help learners see the words in action.

There are several benefits of this approach. First, a study of words and the way they are used can help students appreciate and understand writers. Second, looking closely at vocabulary and the spectrum of related words can help students improve their own writing.

Whole-Class Learning

PLANNING

WHOLE-CLASS LEARNING • *THE DIARY OF ANNE FRANK*, ACT II

The Diary of Anne Frank, Act II

AUDIO SUMMARIES
Audio summaries of *The Diary of Anne Frank*, Act II, are available online in both English and Spanish in the Interactive Teacher's Edition or Unit Resources. Assigning these summaries prior to reading the selection may help students build additional background knowledge and set a context for their first read.

Summary

This is the second act of the drama *The Diary of Anne Frank* by Frances Goodrich and Albert Hackett. The family has been in hiding for a year and a half. Miep comes to visit, and the Van Daans fall into an argument. Anne, Margot, and Peter sort through their relationships. Later, Dussel and Mr. Van Daan get into a fight over food. Good news comes as they hear about the Allied invasion. But their good fortune eventually ends, as the conclusion that was foreshadowed at the beginning of Act I plays out.

Insight

The Diary of Anne Frank is one of the finest examples of how people can endure the worst of experiences. Even though most of the people in the Secret Annex lost their lives, their stories live on in Anne's words.

ESSENTIAL QUESTION:
How do we remember the past?

Connection to Essential Question

Mr. Frank and Miep share their recollections. Much of what Mr. Frank recalls in the last scene is scattered and fragmentary, as if he can only bring himself to remember the most important points.

WHOLE-CLASS LEARNING PERFORMANCE TASK
How are historical events reflected in the play *The Diary of Anne Frank*?

Connection to Performance Tasks

Whole-Class Learning Performance Task As students read the second act of the play, historical details come into focus. For example, stricter law enforcement presents more danger and the limited availability of ration books makes life more difficult.

UNIT PERFORMANCE-BASED ASSESSMENT
How can literature help us remember and honor the victims of the Holocaust?

Unit Performance-Based Assessment Mr. Frank recalls how Anne stayed optimistic in spite of all the challenges she faced. The diary has been shared for so many years and in so many countries that it has become both a source of inspiration and information, helping people to use events of the past to understand cultural behavior and to try to prevent horrific events from ever occurring again.

156A UNIT 2 • THE HOLOCAUST

DIGITAL PERSPECTIVES Audio Video Document Annotation Highlights EL Highlights Online Assessment

LESSON RESOURCES

	Making Meaning	Language Development	Effective Expression
Lesson	First Read Close Read Analyze the Text Analyze Craft and Structure	Concept Vocabulary Word Study Conventions	Writing to Sources Speaking and Listening
Instructional Standards	**RL.10** By the end of the year, read and comprehend literature . . . **RL.1** Cite the textual evidence . . . **RL.3** Analyze how particular lines of dialogue . . .	**L.1** Demonstrate command of the conventions . . . **L.3** Use knowledge of language and its conventions . . . **L.4.b** Use common, grade-appropriate Greek or Latin affixes and roots as clues . . . **L.4** Determine or clarify the meaning of unknown and multiple-meaning words or phrases . . . **L.4.c** Consult general and specialized reference materials . . . **L.4.d** Verify the preliminary determination . . .	**SL.1** Engage effectively in a range of collaborative discussions . . . **SL.1.a** Come to discussions prepared . . . **SL.4** Present claims and findings . . . **SL.1.b** Follow rules for collegial discussions . . . **RL.7** Analyze the extent to which a filmed or live production . . . **W.2** Write informative/explanatory texts . . . **W.2.b** Develop the topic with relevant, well-chosen facts . . . **W.2.f** Provide a concluding statement . . .
STUDENT RESOURCES			
Available online in the Interactive Student Edition or Unit Resources	Selection Audio First-Read Guide: Fiction Close-Read Guide: Fiction	Word Network	Evidence Log
TEACHER RESOURCES			
Selection Resources Available online in the Interactive Teacher's Edition or Unit Resources	Audio Summaries Annotation Highlights EL Highlights English Language Support Lesson: Character Motivation Analyze Craft and Structure: Character Motivation	Concept Vocabulary and Word Study Conventions: Simple Tenses of Verbs	Writing to Sources: Drama Review Speaking and Listening: Dramatic Reading
Reteach/Practice (RP) Available online in the Interactive Teacher's Edition or Unit Resources	Analyze Craft and Structure: Character Motivation (RP)	Word Study: Latin Suffix -*ent* (RP) Conventions: Simple Tenses of Verbs (RP)	Writing to Sources: Drama Review (RP) Speaking and Listening: Dramatic Reading (RP)
Assessment Available online in Assessments	Selection Test		
My Resources	A Unit 2 Answer Key is available online and in the Interactive Teacher's Edition.		

Whole-Class Learning 156B

PERSONALIZE FOR LEARNING
WHOLE-CLASS LEARNING • *THE DIARY OF ANNE FRANK,* ACT II

Reading Support

Text Complexity Rubric: *The Diary of Anne Frank,* Act II

Quantitative Measures

Lexile NP   Text Length 11,129

Qualitative Measures

Knowledge Demands (3 of 5)	As a continuation of the previous selection, knowledge of Act I is assumed, but not essential; Act II also relies on knowledge of the Nazi occupation and conditions while in hiding.
Structure (2 of 5)	Setting and background are described, but not fully, as some information is given only in Act I and not repeated in Act II. Scenes are chronological, with shifts forward in time.
Language Conventionality and Clarity (2 of 5)	As in Act I, play has mix of background information and direction, spoken dialogue and written words from diary in first person. Dialogue is conversational, with short sentences that are easily understood.
Levels of Meaning/Purpose (3 of 5)	Situations are presented explicitly through Anne's diary, but for the sections of dialogue, reader must infer meaning and feelings of characters based on actions and stage directions.

DECIDE AND PLAN

English Language Support
Provide English Learners with support for knowledge demands and language as they read the selection.

Knowledge Demands Before students read, review the list you made for Act I of background information (see Act I, English Language Support). Then review what happened in Act I. Ask students to recall the setting and characters, looking back to Act I if necessary for character lists and descriptions.

Language Point out the changes in voice and pronouns that are used in different parts of the text. For example, the sections of Anne's diary are written in first person (I, me, my, mine). The stage directions are in third person (she, he, her, him, they), and the dialogue has both of those, plus second person (you, your, we, our).

Strategic Support
Provide students with strategic support to ensure that they can successfully read the text.

Knowledge Demands As a group, review what students remember from Act I about the background information and the events described in the play. Ask volunteers to describe the situation of the characters, where they live, and why they are in hiding.

Meaning Review sections of dialogue with students, asking questions to confirm that they understand the meaning behind characters' actions or words. For example, (Scene 1, paragraphs 74–77) *Why is Mrs. Van Daan so upset about the coat?* (she doesn't want to sell it) *What do you think it represents to her that makes her this upset?* (their lifestyle before being in hiding)

Challenge
Provide students who need to be challenged with ideas for how they can go beyond a simple interpretation of the text.

Text Analysis Have four volunteers act out the section from Scene 1, paragraphs 116–128. (Three students read character parts and the fourth reads the stage directions). As a group, discuss Anne's words about holding onto ideals rather than focusing on the horrors of the world. Ask students to give their opinions about some ways to deal with terrible realities in the world.

Written Response The play deals with material that can strongly affect students emotionally. Ask students to write about some of the feelings that the play evokes in them in different sections. In a group, ask for volunteers to share some of these feelings and reactions.

TEACH

Read and Respond
Have students do their first read of the selection. Then have them complete their close read. Finally, work with them on the Making Meaning, Language Development, and Effective Expression activities.

Standards Support Through Teaching and Learning Cycle

IDENTIFY NEEDS

Analyze results of the Beginning-of-Year Assessment, focusing on the items relating to Unit 2. Also take into consideration student performance to this point and your observations of where particular students struggle.

ANALYZE AND REVISE

- Analyze student work for evidence of student learning.
- Identify whether or not students have met the expectations in the standards.
- Identify implications for future instruction.

TEACH

Implement the planned lesson, and gather evidence of student learning.

DECIDE AND PLAN

- If students have performed poorly on items matching these standards, then provide selection scaffolds before assigning them the on-level lesson provided in the Student Edition.
- If students have done well on the Beginning-of-Year Assessment, then challenge them to keep progressing and learning by giving them opportunities to practice the skills in depth.
- Use the Selection Resources listed on the Planning pages for *The Diary of Anne Frank,* Act II, to help students continually improve their ability to master the standards.

Instructional Standards: *The Diary of Anne Frank,* Act II

	Catching Up	This Year	Looking Forward
Reading	You may wish to administer the **Analyze Craft and Structure: Character Motivation (RP)** worksheet to help students analyze the actions of the characters in the selection.	**RL.3** Analyze how particular lines of dialogue or incidents in a story or drama propel the action, reveal aspects of a character, or provoke a decision.	Ask students to write an overview that describes each character's personality and traits. Have them use text evidence to develop each overview. Then have students share their analysis with a partner.
Writing	You may wish to administer the **Writing to Sources: Drama Review (RP)** worksheet to help students write a drama review.	**W.2.b** Develop the topic with relevant, well-chosen facts, definitions, concrete details, quotations, or other information and examples.	Work with students to review their writing and add text evidence to bolster their writing, including quotations and details.
Speaking and Listening	You may wish to administer the **Speaking and Listening: Dramatic Reading (RP)** worksheet to help students prepare a dramatic reading.	**SL.4** Present claims and findings, emphasizing salient points in a focused, coherent manner with relevant evidence, sound valid reasoning, and well-chosen details; use appropriate eye contact, adequate volume, and clear pronunciation.	Allow students to practice their dramatic reading with a peer. Have students use the evaluation guide to give very specific feedback to their classmate.
Language	You may wish to administer the **Word Study: Latin Suffix -ent (RP)** worksheet to help students understand the meanings of words with the -ent suffix. You may wish to administer the **Conventions: Simple Tenses of Verbs (RP)** worksheet to help students understand the three principal tenses of verbs.	**L.4.b** Use common, grade-appropriate Greek or Latin affixes and roots as clues to the meaning of a word. **L.3** Use knowledge of language and its conventions when writing, speaking, reading, or listening.	Challenge students to find three words with the -ent suffix. Have students use each word in a sentence that includes context clues. Have students write a short paragraph in which they use the three tenses to show shifts in time.

TEACHING

Jump Start

FIRST READ Ask students to consider a moment in their lives when they felt brave. Then, ask them to imagine what it must have felt like for the families in the Secret Annex when they defiantly sang a Hanukkah song at the end of Act I.

The Diary of Anne Frank, Act II

Who was in the office? Will Miep and Mr. Kraler be found out? Will everyone remain in the annex? Will they be discovered? Modeling the questions readers might ask as they read *The Diary of Anne Frank*, Act II, brings the text alive for students and connects it to the Performance Task assignment. Selection audio and print capability for the selection are available in the Interactive Teacher's Edition.

Concept Vocabulary

Support students as they rank their words. Ask if they've ever heard, read, or used them. Reassure them that the definitions for these words are listed in the selection.

FIRST READ

As they read, students should perform the steps of the first read:

NOTICE: You may want to encourage students to notice how the mood in the Secret Annex changes throughout Act II.

ANNOTATE: Remind students to mark dialogue and stage direction that give them insight into how the characters are surviving this ordeal.

CONNECT: Encourage students to go beyond the text to make connections. Have them consider challenges in their own lives, as well as current events and other stories from the time of the Holocaust.

RESPOND: Students will answer questions and write a summary to demonstrate understanding. Point out to students that while they will always complete the Respond step at the end of the first read, the other steps will probably happen somewhat concurrently. You may wish to print copies of the **First-Read Guide: Fiction** for students to use.

Remind students that during their first read, they should not answer the close-read questions that appear in the selection.

UNIT 2 • THE HOLOCAUST

MAKING MEANING

Playwrights

Frances Goodrich and Albert Hackett

The Diary of Anne Frank, Act II

Concept Vocabulary

As you conduct your first read of *The Diary of Anne Frank*, Act II, you will encounter these words. Before reading, note how familiar you are with each word. Then, rank the words in order from most familiar (1) to least familiar (6).

WORD	YOUR RANKING
foreboding	
apprehension	
intuition	
mounting	
rigid	
insistent	

After completing the first read, come back to the concept vocabulary and review your rankings. Mark changes to your original rankings as needed.

First Read DRAMA

Apply these strategies as you conduct your first read. You will have an opportunity to complete the close-read notes after your first read.

NOTICE whom the story is about, *what* happens, *where* and *when* it happens, and *why* those involved react as they do.

ANNOTATE by marking vocabulary and key passages you want to revisit.

CONNECT ideas within the selection to what you already know and what you have already read.

RESPOND by completing the Comprehension Check and by writing a brief summary of the selection.

Tool Kit
First-Read Guide and Model Annotation

STANDARDS
Reading Literature
By the end of the year, read and comprehend literature, including stories, dramas, and poems, at the high end of grades 6–8 text complexity band independently and proficiently.

156 UNIT 2 • THE HOLOCAUST

PERSONALIZE FOR LEARNING

Strategic Support
Story Map Create a story map to review what has happened so far. As a class, students will contribute to the map as a form of review and preparation for the next act. Ask students to select important moments to include. Decide as a class if the moments suggested should be included. You may choose to begin the chart like this:

| Mr. Frank returns to the annex and finds Anne's diary. | → | |

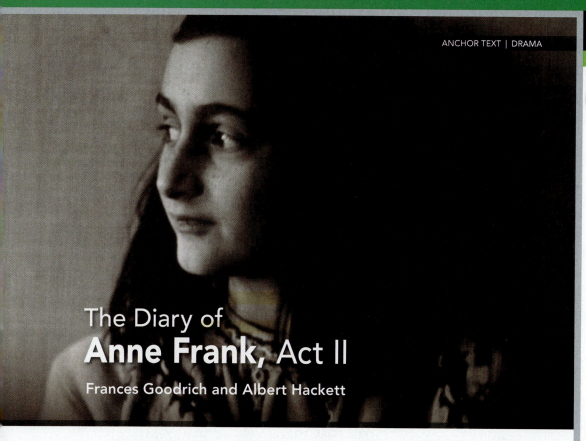

ANCHOR TEXT | DRAMA

The Diary of Anne Frank, Act II

Frances Goodrich and Albert Hackett

BACKGROUND

In Act I, Anne Frank's father visits the attic where his family and four others hid from the Nazis during World War II. As he holds his daughter's diary, Anne's offstage voice draws him into the past as the families begin their new life in hiding. As the months drag on, fear and lack of privacy in the attic rooms contribute to increasing tension among the family members.

Scene 1

1 [*In the darkness we hear Anne's Voice, again reading from the diary.*]

2 **Anne's Voice.** Saturday, the first of January, nineteen forty-four. Another new year has begun and we find ourselves still in our hiding place. We have been here now for one year, five months and twenty-five days. It seems that our life is at a standstill.

3 [*The curtain rises on the scene. It is late afternoon. Everyone is bundled up against the cold. In the main room* Mrs. Frank *is taking down the laundry which is hung across the back.* Mr. Frank

NOTES

CLOSE READ
ANNOTATE: In paragraph 2, mark words that refer to date and time.

QUESTION: Why do the playwrights include these details?

CONCLUDE: What is the effect of these details?

sits in the chair down left, reading. Margot is lying on the couch with a blanket over her and the many-colored knitted scarf around her throat. Anne is seated at the center table, writing in her diary. Peter, Mr. and Mrs. Van Daan and Dussel are all in their own rooms, reading or lying down.

4 As the lights dim on, Anne's Voice continues, without a break.]

5 **Anne's Voice.** We are all a little thinner. The Van Daans' "discussions" are as violent as ever. Mother still does not understand me. But then I don't understand her either. There is one great change, however. A change in myself. I read somewhere that girls of my age don't feel quite certain of themselves. That they become quiet within and begin to think of the miracle that is taking place in their bodies. I think that what is happening to me is so wonderful . . . not only what can be seen, but what is taking place inside. Each time it has happened I have a feeling that I have a sweet secret.

6 [We hear the chimes and then a hymn being played on the carillon outside. The buzzer of the door below suddenly sounds. Everyone is startled. Mr. Frank tiptoes cautiously to the top of the steps and listens. Again the buzzer sounds, in Miep's V-for-Victory signal.[1]]

7 **Mr. Frank.** It's Miep!

8 [He goes quickly down the steps to unbolt the door. Mrs. Frank calls upstairs to the Van Daans and then to Peter.]

9 **Mrs. Frank.** Wake up, everyone! Miep is here!
[Anne quickly puts her diary away. Margot sits up, pulling the blanket around her shoulders. Mr. Dussel sits on the edge of his bed, listening, disgruntled. Miep comes up the steps, followed by Mr. Kraler. They bring flowers, books, newspapers, etc. Anne rushes to Miep, throwing her arms affectionately around her.]
Miep . . . and Mr. Kraler . . . What a delightful surprise!

10 **Mr. Kraler.** We came to bring you New Year's greetings.

11 **Mrs. Frank.** You shouldn't . . . you should have at least one day to yourselves. [She goes quickly to the stove and brings down teacups and tea for all of them.]

12 **Anne.** Don't say that, it's so wonderful to see them! [Sniffing at Miep's coat] I can smell the wind and the cold on your clothes.

13 **Miep.** [Giving her the flowers] There you are. [Then to Margot, feeling her forehead] How are you, Margot? . . . Feeling any better?

14 **Margot.** I'm all right.

15 **Anne.** We filled her full of every kind of pill so she won't cough and make a noise. [She runs into her room to put the

1. **V-for-Victory signal** three short rings and one long one (the letter V in Morse code).

flowers in water. Mr. and Mrs. Van Daan come from upstairs. Outside there is the sound of a band playing.]

16 **Mrs. Van Daan.** Well, hello, Miep. Mr. Kraler.

17 **Mr. Kraler.** [*Giving a bouquet of flowers to* Mrs. Van Daan] With my hope for peace in the New Year.

18 **Peter.** [*Anxiously*] Miep, have you seen Mouschi? Have you seen him anywhere around?

19 **Miep.** I'm sorry, Peter. I asked everyone in the neighborhood had they seen a gray cat. But they said no.

20 [Mrs. Frank *gives* Miep *a cup of tea.* Mr. Frank *comes up the steps, carrying a small cake on a plate.*]

21 **Mr. Frank.** Look what Miep's brought for us!

22 **Mrs. Frank.** [*Taking it*] A cake!

23 **Mr. Van Daan.** A cake! [*He pinches* Miep's *cheeks gaily and hurries up to the cupboard.*] I'll get some plates.

24 [Dussel, *in his room, hastily puts a coat on and starts out to join the others.*]

25 **Mrs. Frank.** Thank you, Miepia. You shouldn't have done it. You must have used all of your sugar ration for weeks. [*Giving it to* Mrs. Van Daan] It's beautiful, isn't it?

26 **Mrs. Van Daan.** It's been ages since I even saw a cake. Not since you brought us one last year. [*Without looking at the cake, to* Miep] Remember? Don't you remember, you gave us one on New Year's Day? Just this time last year? I'll never forget it because you had "Peace in nineteen forty-three" on it. [*She looks at the cake and reads*] "Peace in nineteen forty-four!"

27 **Miep.** Well, it has to come sometime, you know. [*As* Dussel *comes from his room*] Hello, Mr. Dussel.

28 **Mr. Kraler.** How are you?

29 **Mr. Van Daan.** [*Bringing plates and a knife*] Here's the knife, *liefje*. Now, how many of us are there?

30 **Miep.** None for me, thank you.

31 **Mr. Frank.** Oh, please. You must.

32 **Miep.** I couldn't.

33 **Mr. Van Daan.** Good! That leaves one . . . two . . . three . . . seven of us.

34 **Dussel.** Eight! Eight! It's the same number as it always is!

35 **Mr. Van Daan.** I left Margot out. I take it for granted Margot won't eat any.

CLOSE READ
ANNOTATE: In paragraph 26, mark details that show what Miep wrote on two cakes she brought to the Secret Annex.

QUESTION: Why do the playwrights include these details?

CONCLUDE: What do these details show about the war, the characters' situation, and Miep's character?

36 **Anne.** Why wouldn't she!

37 **Mrs. Frank.** I think it won't harm her.

38 **Mr. Van Daan.** All right! All right! I just didn't want her to start coughing again, that's all.

39 **Dussel.** And please, Mrs. Frank should cut the cake.

40 [*Together*] {
Mr. Van Daan. What's the difference?
Mrs. Van Daan. It's not Mrs. Frank's cake, is it, Miep? It's for all of us.
}

41 **Dussel.** Mrs. Frank divides things better.

42 [*Together*] {
Mrs. Van Daan. [*Going to* Dussel] What are you trying to say?
Mr. Van Daan. Oh, come on! Stop wasting time!
}

43 **Mrs. Van Daan.** [*To* Dussel] Don't I always give everybody exactly the same? Don't I?

44 **Mr. Van Daan.** Forget it, Kerli.

45 **Mrs. Van Daan.** No. I want an answer! Don't I?

46 **Dussel.** Yes. Yes. Everybody gets exactly the same . . . except Mr. Van Daan always gets a little bit more.

47 [Mr. Van Daan *advances on* Dussel, *the knife still in his hand*.]

48 **Mr. Van Daan.** That's a lie!

49 [Dussel *retreats before the onslaught of the* Van Daans.]

50 **Mr. Frank.** Please, please! [*Then to* Miep] You see what a little sugar cake does to us? It goes right to our heads!

51 **Mr. Van Daan.** [*Handing* Mrs. Frank *the knife*] Here you are, Mrs. Frank.

52 **Mrs. Frank.** Thank you. [*Then to* Miep *as she goes to the table to cut the cake*] Are you sure you won't have some?

53 **Miep.** [*Drinking her tea*] No, really, I have to go in a minute.

54 [*The sound of the band fades out in the distance.*]

55 **Peter.** [*To* Miep] Maybe Mouschi went back to our house . . . they say that cats . . . Do you ever get over there . . . ? I mean . . . do you suppose you could . . . ?

56 **Miep.** I'll try, Peter. The first minute I get I'll try. But I'm afraid, with him gone a week . . .

Ration cards, the kind Miep Gies might have used to get food for the Franks.

57 **Dussel.** Make up your mind, already someone has had a nice big dinner from that cat!

58 [*Peter is furious, inarticulate. He starts toward* Dussel, *as if to hit him.* Mr. Frank *stops him.* Mrs. Frank *speaks quickly to ease the situation.*]

59 **Mrs. Frank.** [*To* Miep] This is delicious, Miep!

60 **Mrs. Van Daan.** [*Eating hers*] Delicious!

61 **Mr. Van Daan.** [*Finishing it in one gulp*] Dirk's in luck to get a girl who can bake like this!

62 **Miep.** [*Putting down her empty teacup*] I have to run. Dirk's taking me to a party tonight.

63 **Anne.** How heavenly! Remember now what everyone is wearing, and what you have to eat and everything, so you can tell us tomorrow.

64 **Miep.** I'll give you a full report! Good-bye, everyone!

65 **Mr. Van Daan.** [*To* Miep] Just a minute. There's something I'd like you to do for me.

66 [*He hurries off up the stairs to his room.*]

67 **Mrs. Van Daan.** [*Sharply*] Putti, where are you going? [*She rushes up the stairs after him, calling hysterically.*] What do you want? Putti, what are you going to do?

68 **Miep.** [*To* Peter] What's wrong?

69 **Peter.** [*His sympathy is with his mother.*] Father says he's going to sell her fur coat. She's crazy about that old fur coat.

70 **Dussel.** Is it possible? Is it possible that anyone is so silly as to worry about a fur coat in times like this?

71 **Peter.** It's none of your darn business . . . and if you say one more thing . . . I'll, I'll take you and I'll . . . I mean it . . . I'll . . .

72 [*There is a piercing scream from* Mrs. Van Daan *above. She grabs at the fur coat as* Mr. Van Daan *is starting downstairs with it.*]

73 **Mrs. Van Daan.** No! No! No! Don't you dare take that! You hear? It's mine! [*Downstairs* Peter *turns away, embarrassed, miserable.*] My father gave me that! You didn't give it to me. You have no right. Let go of it . . . you hear?

74 [Mr. Van Daan *pulls the coat from her hands and hurries downstairs.* Mrs. Van Daan *sinks to the floor, sobbing. As* Mr. Van Daan *comes into the main room the others look away, embarrassed for him.*]

75 **Mr. Van Daan.** [*To* Mr. Kraler] Just a little—discussion over the advisability of selling this coat. As I have often reminded Mrs. Van Daan, it's very selfish of her to keep it when people

NOTES

CLOSE READ
ANNOTATE: Mark words and phrases in paragraphs 67–74 that show Mrs. Van Daan's reaction to her husband's decision to sell her coat.

QUESTION: Why do the playwrights include these details?

CONCLUDE: What conflicts do these details reveal?

The Diary of Anne Frank, Act II **161**

DIGITAL PERSPECTIVES

CLOSE READ

Playwrights assign symbolic meaning and emotional importance to objects, allowing characters to reveal themselves in their reactions to those objects. You may wish to model the close read using the following think-aloud format. Possible responses to questions on the student page are included.

ANNOTATE: As I read lines 67–74, I notice Mrs. Van Daan's reactions to her husband's decision to sell her coat.

QUESTION: The playwrights present Mrs. Van Daan's reaction to convey not only that the coat is expensive, but that is has sentimental value.

CONCLUDE: The details show that Mrs. Van Daan is losing things that are important to her. The coat symbolizes one of Mrs. Van Daan's last connections to her former life of freedom and happiness, as well as to her extended family, all of whom have likely perished in the war.

PERSONALIZE FOR LEARNING

English Language Support

Stage Directions In paragraph 69, the playwrights provide a piece of stage direction that might be overlooked by English learners because it does not clearly define an action or a tone. The directions say: "*His sympathy is with his mother.*" This note impacts how the reader understands Peter. Discuss this direction with students. Explain what sympathy is. What does it mean here?

Possible answer: He feels sorry for his mother. Have students read paragraph 69 twice, the first time without this stage direction and the second time with it. How does this direction change how Peter's words are read? Extend the conversation by initiating a discussion considering why Peter might feel sympathy for his mother here. **ALL LEVELS**

Whole-Class Learning **161**

TEACHING

NOTES

outside are in such desperate need of clothing . . . [*He gives the coat to* Miep.] So if you will please to sell it for us? It should fetch a good price. And by the way, will you get me cigarettes. I don't care what kind they are . . . get all you can.

76 **Miep.** It's terribly difficult to get them, Mr. Van Daan. But I'll try. Good-bye.

77 [*She goes.* Mr. Frank *follows her down the steps to bolt the door after her.* Mrs. Frank *gives* Mr. Kraler *a cup of tea.*]

78 **Mrs. Frank.** Are you sure you won't have some cake, Mr. Kraler?

79 **Mr. Kraler.** I'd better not.

80 **Mr. Van Daan.** You're still feeling badly? What does your doctor say?

81 **Mr. Kraler.** I haven't been to him.

82 **Mrs. Frank.** Now, Mr. Kraler! . . .

83 **Mr. Kraler.** [*Sitting at the table*] Oh, I tried. But you can't get near a doctor these days . . . they're so busy. After weeks I finally managed to get one on the telephone. I told him I'd like an appointment . . . I wasn't feeling very well. You know what he answers . . . over the telephone . . . Stick out your tongue! [*They laugh. He turns to* Mr. Frank *as* Mr. Frank *comes back.*] I have some contracts here . . . I wonder if you'd look over them with me . . .

84 **Mr. Frank.** [*Putting out his hand*] Of course.

85 **Mr. Kraler.** [*He rises*] If we could go downstairs . . . [Mr. Frank *starts ahead;* Mr. Kraler *speaks to the others.*] Will you forgive us? I won't keep him but a minute. [*He starts to follow* Mr. Frank *down the steps.*]

foreboding (fawr BOH dihng) *n.* sudden feeling that something bad is going to happen

86 **Margot.** [*With sudden* foreboding] What's happened? Something's happened! Hasn't it, Mr. Kraler?

87 [Mr. Kraler *stops and comes back, trying to reassure* Margot *with a pretense of casualness.*]

88 **Mr. Kraler.** No, really. I want your father's advice . . .

89 **Margot.** Something's gone wrong! I know it!

90 **Mr. Frank.** [*Coming back, to* Mr. Kraler] If it's something that concerns us here, it's better that we all hear it.

91 **Mr. Kraler.** [*Turning to him, quietly*] But . . . the children . . . ?

92 **Mr. Frank.** What they'd imagine would be worse than any reality.

apprehension (ap rih HEHN shuhn) *n.* fearful feeling about what will happen next

93 [*As* Mr. Kraler *speaks, they all listen with intense* apprehension. Mrs. Van Daan *comes down the stairs and sits on the bottom step.*]

162 UNIT 2 • THE HOLOCAUST

VOCABULARY DEVELOPMENT

Concept Vocabulary Reinforcement
Paragraph 86 contains the concept vocabulary word *foreboding*, and the stage direction in paragraph 93 contains the word *apprehension*. Review the definitions provided for each of these words. Point out that context clues might help students to better understand the new words. Create a chart to complete with class.

	Definition	Context clues	Sentence
foreboding	Anxiety or worry	Something's gone wrong! I know it!	When Mr. Frank was asked to go downstairs, Margot had a sense of foreboding. She was worried that something was wrong.
apprehension	Nervousness or worry	What they'd imagine would be worse than any reality.	They listened with apprehension. They were nervous that the news would be bad.

94 **Mr. Kraler.** It's a man in the storeroom . . . I don't know whether or not you remember him . . . Carl, about fifty, heavy-set, nearsighted . . . He came with us just before you left.

95 **Mr. Frank.** He was from Utrecht?

96 **Mr. Kraler.** That's the man. A couple of weeks ago, when I was in the storeroom, he closed the door and asked me . . . how's Mr. Frank? What do you hear from Mr. Frank? I told him I only knew there was a rumor that you were in Switzerland. He said he'd heard that rumor too, but he thought I might know something more. I didn't pay any attention to it . . . but then a thing happened yesterday . . . He'd brought some invoices to the office for me to sign. As I was going through them, I looked up. He was standing staring at the bookcase . . . your bookcase. He said he thought he remembered a door there . . . Wasn't there a door there that used to go up to the loft? Then he told me he wanted more money. Twenty guilders[2] more a week.

97 **Mr. Van Daan.** Blackmail!

98 **Mr. Frank.** Twenty guilders? Very modest blackmail.

99 **Mr. Van Daan.** That's just the beginning.

100 **Dussel.** [*Coming to* Mr. Frank] You know what I think? He was the thief who was down there that night. That's how he knows we're here.

101 **Mr. Frank.** [*To* Mr. Kraler] How was it left? What did you tell him?

102 **Mr. Kraler.** I said I had to think about it. What shall I do? Pay him the money? . . . Take a chance on firing him . . . or what? I don't know.

103 **Dussel.** [*Frantic*] Don't fire him! Pay him what he asks . . . keep him here where you can have your eye on him.

104 **Mr. Frank.** Is it so much that he's asking? What are they paying nowadays?

105 **Mr. Kraler.** He could get it in a war plant. But this isn't a war plant. Mind you. I don't know if he really knows . . . or if he doesn't know.

106 **Mr. Frank.** Offer him half. Then we'll soon find out if it's blackmail or not.

107 **Dussel.** And if it is? We've got to pay it, haven't we? Anything he asks we've got to pay!

108 **Mr. Frank.** Let's decide that when the time comes.

109 **Mr. Kraler.** This may be all my imagination. You get to a point, these days, where you suspect everyone and

NOTES

2. **guilders** (GIHL duhrz) *n.* monetary unit of the Netherlands at the time.

CLOSE READ
ANNOTATE: In paragraphs 97–109, mark details that show the characters' responses to Mr. Kraler's news.

QUESTION: Why do the playwrights include this range of reactions?

CONCLUDE: How does this passage increase suspense for readers?

everything. Again and again . . . on some simple look or word, I've found myself . . .

110 [*The telephone rings in the office below.*]

111 **Mrs. Van Daan.** [*Hurrying to* Mr. Kraler] There's the telephone! What does that mean, the telephone ringing on a holiday?

112 **Mr. Kraler.** That's my wife. I told her I had to go over some papers in my office . . . to call me there when she got out of church. [*He starts out.*] I'll offer him half then. Goodbye . . . we'll hope for the best!

113 [*The group calls their good-byes halfheartedly.* Mr. Frank *follows* Mr. Kraler *to bolt the door below. During the following scene,* Mr. Frank *comes back up and stands listening, disturbed.*]

114 **Dussel.** [*To* Mr. Van Daan] You can thank your son for this . . . smashing the light! I tell you, it's just a question of time now.

115 [*He goes to the window at the back and stands looking out.*]

116 **Margot.** Sometimes I wish the end would come . . . whatever it is.

117 **Mrs. Frank.** [*Shocked*] Margot!

118 [Anne *goes to* Margot, *sitting beside her on the couch with her arms around her.*]

119 **Margot.** Then at least we'd know where we were.

120 **Mrs. Frank.** You should be ashamed of yourself! Talking that way! Think how lucky we are! Think of the thousands dying in the war, every day. Think of the people in concentration camps.

121 **Anne.** [*Interrupting*] What's the good of that? What's the good of thinking of misery when you're already miserable? That's stupid!

122 **Mrs. Frank.** Anne!

123 [*As* Anne *goes on raging at her mother,* Mrs. Frank *tries to break in, in an effort to quiet her.*]

124 **Anne.** We're young, Margot and Peter and I! You grownups have had your chance! But look at us . . . If we begin thinking of all the horror in the world, we're lost! We're trying to hold onto some kind of ideals . . . when everything . . . ideals, hopes . . . everything, are being destroyed! It isn't our fault that the world is in such a mess! We weren't around when all this started! So don't try to take it out on us! [*She rushes off to her room, slamming the door after her. She picks up a brush from the chest and hurls it to the floor. Then she sits on the settee, trying to control her anger.*]

125 **Mr. Van Daan.** She talks as if we started the war! Did we start the war?

126 [*He spots* Anne's *cake. As he starts to take it,* Peter *anticipates him.*]

127 **Peter.** She left her cake. [*He starts for* Anne's *room with the cake. There is silence in the main room.* Mrs. Van Daan *goes up to her room, followed by* Mr. Van Daan. Dussel *stays looking out the window.* Mr. Frank *brings* Mrs. Frank *her cake. She eats it slowly, without relish.* Mr. Frank *takes his cake to* Margot *and sits quietly on the sofa beside her.* Peter *stands in the doorway of* Anne's *darkened room, looking at her, then makes a little movement to let her know he is there.* Anne *sits up, quickly, trying to hide the signs of her tears.* Peter *holds out the cake to her.*] You left this.

128 **Anne.** [*Dully*] Thanks.

129 [Peter *starts to go out, then comes back.*]

130 **Peter.** I thought you were fine just now. You know just how to talk to them. You know just how to say it. I'm no good . . . I never can think . . . especially when I'm mad . . . That Dussel . . . when he said that about Mouschi . . . someone eating him . . . all I could think is . . . I wanted to hit him. I wanted to give him such a . . . a . . . that he'd . . . That's what I used to do when there was an argument at school . . . That's the way I . . . but here . . . And an old man like that . . . it wouldn't be so good.

131 **Anne.** You're making a big mistake about me. I do it all wrong. I say too much. I go too far. I hurt people's feelings . . .

132 [Dussel *leaves the window, going to his room.*]

133 **Peter.** I think you're just fine . . . What I want to say . . . if it wasn't for you around here, I don't know. What I mean . . .

134 [Peter *is interrupted by* Dussel's *turning on the light.* Dussel *stands in the doorway, startled to see* Peter. Peter *advances toward him forbiddingly.* Dussel *backs out of the room.* Peter *closes the door on him.*]

135 **Anne.** Do you mean it, Peter? Do you really mean it?

136 **Peter.** I said it, didn't I?

137 **Anne.** Thank you, Peter!

138 [*In the main room* Mr. *and* Mrs. Frank *collect the dishes and take them to the sink, washing them.* Margot *lies down again on the couch.* Dussel, *lost, wanders into* Peter's *room and takes up a book, starting to read.*]

139 **Peter.** [*Looking at the photographs on the wall*] You've got quite a collection.

NOTES

CLOSE READ
ANNOTATE: In paragraphs 127–135, mark details that relate to Peter's struggle to express himself in words. Mark other details that show what he does—his actions.

QUESTION: Why have the playwrights included these details?

CONCLUDE: What is the effect of these details, especially in showing how Peter has changed?

The Diary of Anne Frank, Act II **165**

DIGITAL PERSPECTIVES

CLOSE READ

As a play progresses, readers will notice how characters transform and how relationships change, as in the exchange between Peter and Anne in paragraphs 127–135. You may wish to model the close read using the following think-aloud format. Possible responses to questions on the student page are included.

ANNOTATE: As I read paragraphs 127–135, I notice words and phrases that show Peter's struggle to express himself.

QUESTION: I think the playwrights included these details to demonstrate how Peter supports Anne's feeling.

CONCLUDE: Peter has learned to control his anger, but he struggles to communicate. The stress of the Secret Annex adds an extra challenge. Peter has realized the characteristics he admires in Anne and has worked up the courage to tell her about it.

HOW LANGUAGE WORKS

Simple Tenses of Verbs Review verb tenses with students by studying paragraph 127. When using verbs in writing, it is important to make sure that the tenses are the same. The simple tenses are *past, present,* and *future*. In paragraph 127, when Peter takes Anne her cake, the text includes many stage directions. Ask students: In what tense are these directions written? (present) Have students read the following sentence:

Mr. Frank *takes his cake to* Margot *and sits quietly on the sofa beside her.*

Ask students to identify the verbs. (takes, sits) Ask them to change this sentence to past tense and then to future tense. (took, sat; will take, will sit)

Display the following sentence: *Mr. Frank took his cake and sits quietly on the sofa beside her.*

Ask students to identify the error in this sentence. (The verb tenses do not match.) Have the students correct the sentence.

Whole-Class Learning

NOTES

140 **Anne.** Wouldn't you like some in your room? I could give you some. Heaven knows you spend enough time in there . . . doing heaven knows what . . .

141 **Peter.** It's easier. A fight starts, or an argument . . . I duck in there.

142 **Anne.** You're lucky, having a room to go to. His lordship is always here . . . I hardly ever get a minute alone. When they start in on me, I can't duck away. I have to stand there and take it.

143 **Peter.** You gave some of it back just now.

144 **Anne.** I get so mad. They've formed their opinions . . . about everything . . . but we . . . we're still trying to find out . . . We have problems here that no other people our age have ever had. And just as you think you've solved them, something comes along and bang! You have to start all over again.

145 **Peter.** At least you've got someone you can talk to.

146 **Anne.** Not really. Mother . . . I never discuss anything serious with her. She doesn't understand. Father's all right. We can talk about everything . . . everything but one thing. Mother. He simply won't talk about her. I don't think you can be really intimate with anyone if he holds something back, do you?

147 **Peter.** I think your father's fine.

148 **Anne.** Oh, he is, Peter! He is! He's the only one who's ever given me the feeling that I have any sense. But anyway, nothing can take the place of school and play and friends of your own age . . . or near your age . . . can it?

149 **Peter.** I suppose you miss your friends and all.

150 **Anne.** It isn't just . . . [*She breaks off, staring up at him for a second.*] Isn't it funny, you and I? Here we've been seeing each other every minute for almost a year and a half, and this is the first time we've ever really talked. It helps a lot to have someone to talk to, don't you think? It helps you to let off steam.

151 **Peter.** [*Going to the door*] Well, any time you want to let off steam, you can come into my room.

152 **Anne.** [*Following him*] I can get up an awful lot of steam. You'll have to be careful how you say that.

153 **Peter.** It's all right with me.

154 **Anne.** Do you mean it?

155 **Peter.** I said it, didn't I?

156 [*He goes out.* Anne *stands in her doorway looking after him. As* Peter *gets to his door he stands for a minute looking back at her. Then he goes into his room.* Dussel *rises as he comes in, and quickly passes him, going out. He starts across for his room.* Anne *sees him coming, and pulls her door shut.* Dussel *turns back toward* Peter's *room.* Peter *pulls his door shut.* Dussel *stands there, bewildered, forlorn.*]

157 [*The scene slowly dims out. The curtain falls on the scene.* Anne's Voice *comes over in the darkness . . . faintly at first, and then with growing strength.*]

158 **Anne's Voice.** We've had bad news. The people from whom Miep got our ration books have been arrested. So we have had to cut down on our food. Our stomachs are so empty that they rumble and make strange noises, all in different keys. Mr. Van Daan's is deep and low, like a bass fiddle. Mine is high, whistling like a flute. As we all sit around waiting for supper, it's like an orchestra tuning up. It only needs Toscanini[3] to raise his baton and we'd be off in the Ride of the Valkyries.[4] Monday, the sixth of March, nineteen forty-four. Mr. Kraler is in the hospital. It seems he has ulcers. Pim says we are his ulcers. Miep has to run the business and us too. The Americans have landed on the southern tip of Italy. Father looks for a quick finish to the war. Mr. Dussel is waiting every day for the warehouse man to demand more money. Have I been skipping too much from one subject to another? I can't help it. I feel that spring is coming. I feel it in my whole body and soul. I feel utterly confused. I am longing . . . so longing . . . for everything . . . for friends . . . for someone to talk to . . . someone who understands . . . someone young, who feels as I do . . .

159 [*As these last lines are being said, the curtain rises on the scene. The lights dim on.* Anne's Voice *fades out.*]

⌘ ⌘ ⌘

Scene 2

1 [*It is evening, after supper. From outside we hear the sound of children playing. The "grownups," with the exception of* Mr. Van Daan, *are all in the main room.* Mrs. Frank *is doing some mending.* Mrs. Van Daan *is reading a fashion magazine.* Mr. Frank *is going over business accounts.*]

NOTES

CLOSE READ
ANNOTATE: A **soliloquy** is a speech in which a character, usually alone on stage, expresses his or her private thoughts or feelings aloud. In paragraphs 157–159, mark words that indicate how the stage should look and sound during Anne's soliloquy.

QUESTION: Why might the playwrights have included these details?

CONCLUDE: What mood do these stage directions create?

3. **Toscanini** (TOS kuh NEE nee) Arturo Toscanini, a famous Italian orchestra conductor.

4. **Ride of the Valkyries** (VAL kih reez) stirring selection from an opera by Richard Wagner, a German composer.

The Diary of Anne Frank, Act II **167**

DIGITAL PERSPECTIVES

CLOSE READ

Throughout the play, Anne has several soliloquys in which she reads aloud from her diary, and stage directions indicate differences to enhance the change in dialogue style. You may wish to model the close read using the following think-aloud format. Possible responses to questions on the student page are included.

ANNOTATE: As I read paragraphs 157–159, I notice stage directions that indicate how the stage should look during Anne's soliloquy.

QUESTION: I think the playwrights chose these stage directions to help emphasize the difference between ordinary dialogue between characters and Anne's soliloquy, in which she is reciting her inner thoughts.

CONCLUDE: The effect of these stage directions is to bring the reader closer to Anne's perspective and to sympathize with her even more. Readers might feel more strongly that they are experiencing the story through her eyes.

PERSONALIZE FOR LEARNING

English Language Support
Figurative Language Writers use figurative language to help the reader picture the image they are trying to convey. In Anne's dialogue in paragraph 158, she uses **metaphors** and **similes**. A metaphor is a comparison of two things without the words *like* or *as*. A simile compares two things using the words *like* or *as*. These types of figurative language can be difficult for English learners to understand. Point out the following pieces of Anne's dialogue. Help students to identify the metaphor and similes and to explain what they mean here.

Mr. Van Daan's is deep and low, like a bass fiddle. Mine is high, whistling like a flute.
Mr. Kraler is in the hospital. It seems he has ulcers. Pim says we are his ulcers.

ALL LEVELS

Whole-Class Learning **167**

TEACHING

NOTES

2 Dussel, *in his dentist's jacket, is pacing up and down, impatient to get into his bedroom.* Mr. Van Daan *is upstairs working on a piece of embroidery in an embroidery frame.*

3 *In his room* Peter *is sitting before the mirror, smoothing his hair. As the scene goes on, he puts on his tie, brushes his coat and puts it on, preparing himself meticulously for a visit from* Anne. *On his wall are now hung some of* Anne's *motion picture stars.*

4 *In her room* Anne *too is getting dressed. She stands before the mirror in her slip, trying various ways of dressing her hair.* Margot *is seated on the sofa, hemming a skirt for* Anne *to wear.*

5 *In the main room* Dussel *can stand it no longer. He comes over, rapping sharply on the door of his and* Anne's *bedroom.*]

6 **Anne.** [*Calling to him*] No, no, Mr. Dussel! I am not dressed yet. [Dussel *walks away, furious, sitting down and burying his head in his hands.* Anne *turns to* Margot.] How is that? How does that look?

7 **Margot.** [*Glancing at her briefly*] Fine.

8 **Anne.** You didn't even look.

9 **Margot.** Of course I did. It's fine.

10 **Anne.** Margot, tell me, am I terribly ugly?

11 **Margot.** Oh, stop fishing.

12 **Anne.** No. No. Tell me.

13 **Margot.** Of course you're not. You've got nice eyes . . . and a lot of animation, and . . .

14 **Anne.** A little vague, aren't you?

15 [*She reaches over and takes a brassiere out of* Margot's *sewing basket. She holds it up to herself, studying the effect in the mirror. Outside,* Mrs. Frank, *feeling sorry for* Dussel, *comes over, knocking at the girls' door.*]

16 **Mrs. Frank.** [*Outside*] May I come in?

17 **Margot.** Come in, Mother.

18 **Mrs. Frank.** [*Shutting the door behind her*] Mr. Dussel's impatient to get in here.

19 **Anne.** [*Still with the brassiere*] Heavens, he takes the room for himself the entire day.

20 **Mrs. Frank.** [*Gently*] Anne, dear, you're not going in again tonight to see Peter?

21 **Anne.** [*Dignified*] That is my intention.

22 **Mrs. Frank.** But you've already spent a great deal of time in there today.

DIGITAL PERSPECTIVES

Illuminating the Text The stage directions in paragraphs 1–5 present several scenes taking place at the same time. When reading about several different scenes taking place simultaneously, it can be difficult for the reader to picture and appreciate the scene. First, read the stage directions as written. Next, assign roles and locations based on this text. Ask each student cast in a role to consider how they would act out the stage directions and dialogue on this page. Have the students act out this page. Ask the audience if they were able to follow everything taking place in the scene. Next, show a video of this scene performed by professional actors. Have students compare all three experiences.

This photo shows a re-creation of the room Anne shared with Mr. Dussel.

NOTES

23 **Anne.** I was in there exactly twice. Once to get the dictionary, and then three-quarters of an hour before supper.

24 **Mrs. Frank.** Aren't you afraid you're disturbing him?

25 **Anne.** Mother, I have some **intuition**.

26 **Mrs. Frank.** Then may I ask you this much, Anne. Please don't shut the door when you go in.

27 **Anne.** You sound like Mrs. Van Daan! [*She throws the brassiere back in* Margot's *sewing basket and picks up her blouse, putting it on.*]

28 **Mrs. Frank.** No. No. I don't mean to suggest anything wrong. I only wish that you wouldn't expose yourself to criticism . . . that you wouldn't give Mrs. Van Daan the opportunity to be unpleasant.

29 **Anne.** Mrs. Van Daan doesn't need an opportunity to be unpleasant!

30 **Mrs. Frank.** Everyone's on edge, worried about Mr. Kraler. This is one more thing . . .

31 **Anne.** I'm sorry, Mother. I'm going to Peter's room. I'm not going to let Petronella Van Daan spoil our friendship.

32 [Mrs. Frank *hesitates for a second, then goes out, closing the door after her. She gets a pack of playing cards and sits at the center table, playing solitaire. In* Anne's *room* Margot *hands the finished skirt to* Anne. *As* Anne *is putting it on,* Margot *takes off her high-heeled shoes and stuffs paper in the toes so that* Anne *can wear them.*]

intuition (ihn too IHSH uhn) *n.* ability to see the truth of something immediately without reasoning

The Diary of Anne Frank, Act II **169**

TEACHING

NOTES

33 **Margot.** [*To* Anne] Why don't you two talk in the main room? It'd save a lot of trouble. It's hard on Mother, having to listen to those remarks from Mrs. Van Daan and not say a word.

34 **Anne.** Why doesn't she say a word? I think it's ridiculous to take it and take it.

35 **Margot.** You don't understand Mother at all, do you? She can't talk back. She's not like you. It's just not in her nature to fight back.

36 **Anne.** Anyway . . . the only one I worry about is you. I feel awfully guilty about you. [*She sits on the stool near* Margot, *putting on* Margot's *high-heeled shoes.*]

37 **Margot.** What about?

38 **Anne.** I mean, every time I go into Peter's room, I have a feeling I may be hurting you. [Margot *shakes her head.*] I know if it were me, I'd be wild. I'd be desperately jealous, if it were me.

39 **Margot.** Well, I'm not.

40 **Anne.** You don't feel badly? Really? Truly? You're not jealous?

41 **Margot.** Of course I'm jealous . . . jealous that you've got something to get up in the morning for . . . But jealous of you and Peter? No.

42 [Anne *goes back to the mirror.*]

43 **Anne.** Maybe there's nothing to be jealous of. Maybe he doesn't really like me. Maybe I'm just taking the place of his cat . . . [*She picks up a pair of short white gloves, putting them on.*] Wouldn't you like to come in with us?

44 **Margot.** I have a book.

45 [*The sound of the children playing outside fades out. In the main room* Dussel *can stand it no longer. He jumps up, going to the bedroom door and knocking sharply.*]

46 **Dussel.** Will you please let me in my room!

47 **Anne.** Just a minute, dear, dear Mr. Dussel. [*She picks up her mother's pink stole and adjusts it elegantly over her shoulders, then gives a last look in the mirror.*] Well, here I go . . . to run the gauntlet.[5]

48 [*She starts out, followed by* Margot.]

49 **Dussel.** [*As she appears—sarcastic*] Thank you so much.

50 [Dussel *goes into his room.* Anne *goes toward* Peter's *room, passing* Mrs. Van Daan *and her parents at the center table.*]

5. **run the gauntlet** (GAWNT liht) literally, to pass between two rows of men who struck at the offender with clubs as he passed; here, a series of troubles or difficulties.

170 UNIT 2 • THE HOLOCAUST

PERSONALIZE FOR LEARNING

Strategic Support

Mood Call student attention to paragraphs 33–44 and ask them to consider the mood of these lines. Throughout the play, the use of punctuation and short sentences serve to set the mood of the scene. Reading a play aloud gives students an opportunity to refine their reading skills, as well as their oral presentation skills.

Dramatic readings also allow the audience to better appreciate the mood the playwright is trying to create. Prepare a dramatic reading of the exchange between Anne and Margot in paragraphs 33–44. Have students work with partners to prepare this scene. Ask volunteers to perform their reading for the class.

51 **Mrs. Van Daan.** My God, look at her! [Anne *pays no attention. She knocks at* Peter's *door.*] I don't know what good it is to have a son. I never see him. He wouldn't care if I killed myself. [Peter *opens the door and stands aside for* Anne *to come in.*] Just a minute, Anne. [*She goes to them at the door.*] I'd like to say a few words to my son. Do you mind? [Peter *and* Anne *stand waiting.*] Peter, I don't want you staying up till all hours tonight. You've got to have your sleep. You're a growing boy. You hear?

52 **Mrs. Frank.** Anne won't stay late. She's going to bed promptly at nine. Aren't you, Anne?

53 **Anne.** Yes, Mother . . . [*To* Mrs. Van Daan] May we go now?

54 **Mrs. Van Daan.** Are you asking me? I didn't know I had anything to say about it.

55 **Mrs. Frank.** Listen for the chimes, Anne dear.

56 [*The two young people go off into* Peter's *room, shutting the door after them.*]

57 **Mrs. Van Daan.** [*To* Mrs. Frank] In my day it was the boys who called on the girls. Not the girls on the boys.

58 **Mrs. Frank.** You know how young people like to feel that they have secrets. Peter's room is the only place where they can talk.

59 **Mrs. Van Daan.** Talk! That's not what they called it when I was young.

60 [Mrs. Van Daan *goes off to the bathroom.* Margot *settles down to read her book.* Mr. Frank *puts his papers away and brings a chess game to the center table. He and* Mrs. Frank *start to play. In* Peter's *room,* Anne *speaks to* Peter, *indignant, humiliated.*]

61 **Anne.** Aren't they awful? Aren't they impossible? Treating us as if we were still in the nursery.

62 [*She sits on the cot.* Peter *gets a bottle of pop and two glasses.*]

63 **Peter.** Don't let it bother you. It doesn't bother me.

64 **Anne.** I suppose you can't really blame them . . . they think back to what *they* were like at our age. They don't realize how much more advanced we are . . . When you think what wonderful discussions we've had! . . . Oh, I forgot. I was going to bring you some more pictures.

65 **Peter.** Oh, these are fine, thanks.

66 **Anne.** Don't you want some more? Miep just brought me some new ones.

67 **Peter.** Maybe later. [*He gives her a glass of pop and, taking some for himself, sits down facing her.*]

TEACHING

● **CLOSE READ**

Characters have several manners of revealing themselves in dialogue, through internal monologue or soliloquy, through dialogue with others in which they reveal part of the truth or intentionally mask the truth, and through dialogue with others in which they state their honest feelings. You may wish to model the close read using the following think-aloud format. Possible responses to questions on the student page are included.

ANNOTATE: As I read paragraph 68, I notice Anne's dialogue that reveals her thoughts about how she has changed and her attitude toward the future.

QUESTION: It's possible that Anne's perspective has changed because she has encountered grim, life-and-death circumstances while in hiding. She realizes she has become more serious and no longer feels she would be satisfied with frivolous activies.

CONCLUDE: Anne talks of what she would like to be when she grows up, demonstrating an attitude of hope for the future in spite of her grim circumstances.

NOTES

CLOSE READ
ANNOTATE: In paragraph 68, mark the details that reveal Anne's self-described change in perspective as well as her attitude toward the future.

QUESTION: Why might Anne's perspective have changed?

CONCLUDE: What does Anne's attitude toward the future reveal about her character?

---

68 **Anne.** [*Looking up at one of the photographs.*] I remember when I got that . . . I won it. I bet Jopie that I could eat five ice-cream cones. We'd all been playing ping-pong . . . We used to have heavenly times . . . we'd finish up with ice cream at the Delphi, or the Oasis, where Jews were allowed . . . there'd always be a lot of boys . . . we'd laugh and joke . . . I'd like to go back to it for a few days or a week. But after that I know I'd be bored to death. I think more seriously about life now. I want to be a journalist . . . or something. I love to write. What do you want to do?

69 **Peter.** I thought I might go off some place . . . work on a farm or something . . . some job that doesn't take much brains.

70 **Anne.** You shouldn't talk that way. You've got the most awful inferiority complex.

71 **Peter.** I know I'm not smart.

72 **Anne.** That isn't true. You're much better than I am in dozens of things . . . arithmetic and algebra and . . . well, you're a million times better than I am in algebra. [*With sudden directness*] You like Margot, don't you? Right from the start you liked her, liked her much better than me.

73 **Peter.** [*Uncomfortably*] Oh, I don't know.

74 [*In the main room* Mrs. Van Daan *comes from the bathroom and goes over to the sink, polishing a coffee pot.*]

75 **Anne.** It's all right. Everyone feels that way. Margot's so good. She's sweet and bright and beautiful and I'm not.

76 **Peter.** I wouldn't say that.

77 **Anne.** Oh, no, I'm not. I know that. I know quite well that I'm not a beauty. I never have been and never shall be.

78 **Peter.** I don't agree at all. I think you're pretty.

79 **Anne.** That's not true!

80 **Peter.** And another thing. You've changed . . . from at first, I mean.

81 **Anne.** I have?

82 **Peter.** I used to think you were awful noisy.

83 **Anne.** And what do you think now, Peter? How have I changed?

84 **Peter.** Well . . . er . . . you're . . . quieter.

85 [*In his room* Dussel *takes his pajamas and toilet articles and goes into the bathroom to change.*]

86 **Anne.** I'm glad you don't just hate me.

87 **Peter.** I never said that.

172 UNIT 2 • THE HOLOCAUST

CROSS-CURRICULAR PERSPECTIVES

Social Studies In paragraph 68, Anne says: ". . . we'd finish up with ice cream at the Delphi, or the Oasis, where Jews were allowed. . . " This tells the reader that before they reached the point of having to go into hiding to save their lives, the Dutch Jews already faced laws restricting what they could do and where they could go. They had to wear yellow stars to identify themselves as Jews. Have students research when in Dutch history these laws came to be. Have students answer the following questions: When did the Nazis take over Holland? When were laws against Jews enacted there? What were those laws? How long was it from when these laws were enforced to when authorities deported Dutch Jews to concentration camps?

88 **Anne.** I bet when you get out of here you'll never think of me again.

89 **Peter.** That's crazy.

90 **Anne.** When you get back with all of your friends, you're going to say . . . now what did I ever see in that Mrs. Quack Quack.

91 **Peter.** I haven't got any friends.

92 **Anne.** Oh, Peter, of course you have. Everyone has friends.

93 **Peter.** Not me. I don't want any. I get along all right without them.

94 **Anne.** Does that mean you can get along without me? I think of myself as your friend.

95 **Peter.** No. If they were all like you, it'd be different.

96 [*He takes the glasses and the bottle and puts them away. There is a second's silence and then* Anne *speaks, hesitantly, shyly.*]

97 **Anne.** Peter, did you ever kiss a girl?

98 **Peter.** Yes. Once.

99 **Anne.** [*To cover her feelings*] That picture's crooked. [*Peter goes over, straightening the photograph.*] Was she pretty?

100 **Peter.** Huh?

101 **Anne.** The girl that you kissed.

102 **Peter.** I don't know. I was blindfolded. [*He comes back and sits down again.*] It was at a party. One of those kissing games.

103 **Anne.** [*Relieved*] Oh. I don't suppose that really counts, does it?

104 **Peter.** It didn't with me.

105 **Anne.** I've been kissed twice. Once a man I'd never seen before kissed me on the cheek when he picked me up off the ice and I was crying. And the other was Mr. Koophuis, a friend of Father's who kissed my hand. You wouldn't say those counted, would you?

106 **Peter.** I wouldn't say so.

107 **Anne.** I know almost for certain that Margot would never kiss anyone unless she was engaged to them. And I'm sure too that Mother never touched a man before Pim. But I don't know . . . things are so different now . . . What do you think? Do you think a girl shouldn't kiss anyone except if she's engaged or something? It's so hard to try to think what to do, when here we are with the whole world falling around our ears and you think . . . well . . . you don't know what's going to happen tomorrow and . . . What do you think?

The Diary of Anne Frank, Act II **173**

CLOSER LOOK

Infer from Dialogue

Students may have marked paragraphs 96–105 during their first read. Use this dialogue to help students understand how Anne is changing. Encourage them to talk about the annotations that they marked. You may want to model a close read with the class based on the highlights shown in the text.

ANNOTATE: Have students mark details in paragraphs 96–105 that show the questions Anne is asking Peter, or have students participate while you highlight them.

QUESTION: Guide students to consider what these details might tell them. Ask what a reader can infer from the questions Anne is asking Peter, and accept student responses.

Possible response: Anne is asking if Peter has ever really kissed a girl and she wants him to know she has never kissed a boy.

CONCLUDE: Help students to formulate conclusions about the importance of these details in the text. Ask students why the playwrights might have included these details.

Possible response: It shows that she wants to be liked, that she seeks approval, and that she likes Peter.

Discuss with students that making **inferences** about characters from their dialogue helps readers to understand how characters change and grow as a play proceeds.

TEACHING

● **CLOSE READ**

Stage directions without dialogue indicate important moments in a play when the action on stage is meant to advance plot or express meaning without the reader or audience having direct access to the character's thoughts. You may wish to model the close read using the following think-aloud format. Possible responses to questions on the student page are included.

ANNOTATE: As I read paragraph 119, I mark details in the stage directions that show what Anne and Peter are doing.

QUESTION: The playwrights describe these actions in the stage directions so people reading the drama will know what is happening. The incident could not be expressed through dialogue. The stage directions also tell actors how to perform the scene.

CONCLUDE: The inclusion of this sequence suggests to readers that, although Anne and Peter are living in unusual, extremely difficult circumstances, they are still teenagers and they still can have normal teenage experiences.

NOTES

108 **Peter.** I suppose it'd depend on the girl. Some girls, anything they do's wrong. But others . . . well . . . it wouldn't necessarily be wrong with them. [*The carillon starts to strike nine o'clock.*] I've always thought that when two people . . .

109 **Anne.** Nine o'clock. I have to go.

110 **Peter.** That's right.

111 **Anne.** [*Without moving*] Good night.

112 [*There is a second's pause, then* Peter *gets up and moves toward the door.*]

113 **Peter.** You won't let them stop you coming?

114 **Anne.** No. [*She rises and starts for the door.*] Sometimes I might bring my diary. There are so many things in it that I want to talk over with you. There's a lot about you.

115 **Peter.** What kind of things?

116 **Anne.** I wouldn't want you to see some of it. I thought you were a nothing, just the way you thought about me.

117 **Peter.** Did you change your mind, the way I changed my mind about you?

118 **Anne.** Well . . . You'll see . . .

CLOSE READ
ANNOTATE: In paragraph 119, mark details that relate to feelings. Mark other details that relate to silence or quiet.

QUESTION: Why do the playwrights present this incident in stage directions rather than in dialogue?

CONCLUDE: What is the effect of these details?

119 [*For a second* Anne *stands looking up at* Peter, *longing for him to kiss her. As he makes no move she turns away. Then suddenly* Peter *grabs her awkwardly in his arms, kissing her on the cheek.* Anne *walks out dazed. She stands for a minute, her back to the people in the main room. As she regains her poise she goes to her mother and father and* Margot, *silently kissing them. They murmur their good nights to her. As she is about to open her bedroom door, she catches sight of* Mrs. Van Daan. *She goes quickly to her, taking her face in her hands and kissing her first on one cheek and then on the other. Then she hurries off into her room.* Mrs. Van Daan *looks after her, and then looks over at* Peter's *room. Her suspicions are confirmed.*]

120 **Mrs. Van Daan.** [*She knows.*] Ah hah!

121 [*The lights dim out. The curtain falls on the scene. In the darkness* Anne's Voice *comes faintly at first and then with growing strength.*]

122 **Anne's Voice.** By this time we all know each other so well that if anyone starts to tell a story, the rest can finish it for him. We're having to cut down still further on our meals. What makes it worse, the rats have been at work again. They've carried off some of our precious food. Even

174 UNIT 2 • THE HOLOCAUST

WriteNow Analyze and Interpret

Reflection Have students read the stage directions in paragraph 119. Point out Mrs. Van Daan's simple direction in paragraph 120: [*She knows.*] Ah hah!
 Discuss what she knows and how she knows it. Possible response: Anne's behavior here gives her away. Ask: Does Mrs. Van Daan know for sure or is she inferring something from Anne's behavior? Have students write a diary entry that Mrs. Van Daan might have written about this moment. What details would she include? How would she analyze the moment?

Mr. Dussel wishes now that Mouschi was here. Thursday, the twentieth of April, nineteen forty-four. Invasion fever is mounting every day. Miep tells us that people outside talk of nothing else. For myself, life has become much more pleasant. I often go to Peter's room after supper. Oh, don't think I'm in love, because I'm not. But it does make life more bearable to have someone with whom you can exchange views. No more tonight. P.S. . . . I must be honest. I must confess that I actually live for the next meeting. Is there anything lovelier than to sit under the skylight and feel the sun on your cheeks and have a darling boy in your arms? I admit now that I'm glad the Van Daans had a son and not a daughter. I've outgrown another dress. That's the third. I'm having to wear Margot's clothes after all. I'm working hard on my French and am now reading *La Belle Nivernaise*.

123 [*As she is saying the last lines—the curtain rises on the scene. The lights dim on, as Anne's Voice fades out.*]

⌘ ⌘ ⌘

Scene 3

1 [*It is night, a few weeks later. Everyone is in bed. There is complete quiet. In the* Van Daans' *room a match flares up for a moment and then is quickly put out.* Mr. Van Daan, *in bare feet, dressed in underwear and trousers, is dimly seen coming stealthily down the stairs and into the main room, where* Mr. *and* Mrs. Frank *and* Margot *are sleeping. He goes to the food safe and again lights a match. Then he cautiously opens the safe, taking out a half-loaf of bread. As he closes the safe, it creaks. He stands rigid.* Mrs. Frank *sits up in bed. She sees him.*]

2 **Mrs. Frank.** [*Screaming.*] Otto! Otto! *Komme schnell!*[6]

3 [*The rest of the people wake, hurriedly getting up.*]

4 **Mr. Frank.** *Was ist los? Was ist passiert?*[7]

5 [Dussel, *followed by* Anne, *comes from his room.*]

6 **Mrs. Frank.** [*As she rushes over to* Mr. Van Daan] *Er stiehlt das Essen!*[8]

7 **Dussel.** [*Grabbing* Mr. Van Daan] You! You! Give me that.

8 **Mrs. Van Daan.** [*Coming down the stairs*] Putti . . . Putti . . . what is it?

9 **Dussel.** [*His hands on* Van Daan's *neck*] You dirty thief . . . stealing food . . . you good-for-nothing . . .

NOTES

mounting (MOWN tihng) *adj.* increasing gradually; building up

rigid (RIHJ ihd) *adj.* stiff and unbending

6. *Komme schnell!* (KOHM uh SHNEHL) German for "Come quick!"

7. *Was ist los? Was ist passiert?* (VAHS ihst LOS VAHS ihst PAHS eert) German for "What's the matter? What happened?"

8. *Er stiehlt das Essen!* (ehr SHTEELT dahs EHS uhn) German for "He steals food!"

CLOSER LOOK

Analyze Motivation

Students may have marked paragraph 1 of Scene 3 during their first read. Use these lines to help students understand Mr. Van Daan's motivation. Encourage them to talk about the annotations that they marked. You may want to model a close read with the class based on the highlights shown in the text.

ANNOTATE: Have students mark details in paragraph 1 that demonstrate how Mr. Van Daan moves in this scene.

QUESTION: Guide students to consider what these details might tell them. Ask why Mr. Van Daan is being cautious about making noise, and accept student responses.

Possible response: Mr. Van Daan does not want anyone to wake up and see him stealing food.

CONCLUDE: Help students to formulate conclusions about the importance of these details in the text. Ask students why the playwrights might have included these details.

Possible Response: Mr. Van Daan's caution shows that he knows that he is doing something wrong.

Remind students that **motivation** is the reason or reasons for a character's actions. Most characters' motives are a combination of internal and external factors, such as fear in response to danger or ambition in response to poverty—or perhaps even ambition in response to shame in response to poverty.

TEACHING

NOTES

10 **Mr. Frank.** Mr. Dussel! For God's sake! Help me, Peter!

11 [*Peter comes over, trying, with* Mr. Frank, *to separate the two struggling men.*]

12 **Peter.** Let him go! Let go!

13 [*Dussel drops* Mr. Van Daan, *pushing him away. He shows them the end of a loaf of bread that he has taken from* Van Daan.]

14 **Dussel.** You greedy, selfish . . . !

15 [*Margot turns on the lights.*]

16 **Mrs. Van Daan.** Putti . . . what is it?

17 [*All of* Mrs. Frank's *gentleness, her self-control, is gone. She is outraged, in a frenzy of indignation.*]

18 **Mrs. Frank.** The bread! He was stealing the bread!

19 **Dussel.** It was you, and all the time we thought it was the rats!

20 **Mr. Frank.** Mr. Van Daan, how could you!

21 **Mr. Van Daan.** I'm hungry.

22 **Mrs. Frank.** We're all of us hungry! I see the children getting thinner and thinner. Your own son Peter . . . I've heard him moan in his sleep, he's so hungry. And you come in the night and steal food that should go to them . . . to the children!

23 **Mrs. Van Daan.** [*Going to* Mr. Van Daan *protectively*] He needs more food than the rest of us. He's used to more. He's a big man.

24 [Mr. Van Daan *breaks away, going over and sitting on the couch.*]

25 **Mrs. Frank.** [*Turning on* Mrs. Van Daan] And you . . . you're worse than he is! You're a mother, and yet you sacrifice your child to this man . . . this . . . this . . .

26 **Mr. Frank.** Edith! Edith!

27 [*Margot picks up the pink woolen stole, putting it over her mother's shoulders.*]

28 **Mrs. Frank.** [*Paying no attention, going on to* Mrs. Van Daan] Don't think I haven't seen you! Always saving the choicest bits for him! I've watched you day after day and I've held my tongue. But not any longer! Not after this! Now I want him to go! I want him to get out of here!

29 [*Together*] { **Mr. Frank.** Edith!
Mr. Van Daan. Get out of here?
Mrs. Van Daan. What do you mean? }

176 UNIT 2 • THE HOLOCAUST

PERSONALIZE FOR LEARNING

Time Line In paragraphs 25–28, the reader sees a change in Mrs. Frank. Ask students to create a timeline that shows the evolution of Mrs. Frank's character. Have them cite text evidence for their analyses of her character. Students' analyses should include at least three distinct points from the play. Ask students to consider, at each point of change, what caused the change.

30 **Mrs. Frank.** Just that! Take your things and get out!

31 **Mr. Frank.** [*To* Mrs. Frank] You're speaking in anger. You cannot mean what you are saying.

32 **Mrs. Frank.** I mean exactly that!

33 [Mrs. Van Daan *takes a cover from the Franks' bed, pulling it about her.*]

34 **Mr. Frank.** For two long years we have lived here, side by side. We have respected each other's rights . . . we have managed to live in peace. Are we now going to throw it all away? I know this will never happen again, will it, Mr. Van Daan?

35 **Mr. Van Daan.** No. No.

36 **Mrs. Frank.** He steals once! He'll steal again!

37 [Mr. Van Daan, *holding his stomach, starts for the bathroom.* Anne *puts her arms around him, helping him up the step.*]

38 **Mr. Frank.** Edith, please. Let us be calm. We'll all go to our rooms . . . and afterwards we'll sit down quietly and talk this out . . . we'll find some way . . .

39 **Mrs. Frank.** No! No! No more talk! I want them to leave!

40 **Mrs. Van Daan.** You'd put us out, on the streets?

41 **Mrs. Frank.** There are other hiding places.

42 **Mrs. Van Daan.** A cellar . . . a closet. I know. And we have no money left even to pay for that.

43 **Mrs. Frank.** I'll give you money. Out of my own pocket I'll give it gladly. [*She gets her purse from a shelf and comes back with it.*]

44 **Mrs. Van Daan.** Mr. Frank, you told Putti you'd never forget what he'd done for you when you came to Amsterdam. You said you could never repay him, that you . . .

45 **Mrs. Frank.** [*Counting out money.*] If my husband had any obligation to you, he's paid it, over and over.

46 **Mr. Frank.** Edith, I've never seen you like this before. I don't know you.

47 **Mrs. Frank.** I should have spoken out long ago.

48 **Dussel.** You can't be nice to some people.

Anne Frank [R] with her sister, Margot [L].

NOTES

The Diary of Anne Frank, Act II 177

CLOSER LOOK

Analyze Characters in Conflict

Students may have marked paragraphs 26–46 during their first read. Use these paragraphs to help students notice how characters can change as a result of the events of a play. You may want to model a close read with the class based on the highlights shown in the text.

ANNOTATE: Have students highlight language in paragraphs 26–46 that shows the contrasting reactions of Mr. Frank and Mrs. Frank to Mr. Van Daan's theft.

QUESTION: Guide students to consider what these details might tell them. Ask what a reader can infer from what was marked, and accept student responses.

Possible responses: Mrs. Frank has always been demanding of Anne but always polite and conciliatory toward the Van Daans. Suddenly, her reaction to the accusation against Mr. Van Daan is extremely bitter and angry, perhaps revealing resentments she has kept inside, or they are feelings she has just formed.

CONCLUDE: Help students to formulate conclusions about the importance of the details in the text. Ask students why the author might have included these details.

Possible responses: Mr. Frank attempts to find a way of resolving the situation without expelling Mr. Van Daan from the annex. His reaction mirrors all his other relationships, especially his relationship with Anne, in which he is often a peace maker.

Remind students that—just as it does in life—the **conflict** in literature sometimes brings out the worst and best in the characters. In this scene, the theft forces anger and resentment, but it also allows the playwrights to showcase Mr. Frank's patience.

Whole-Class Learning 177

TEACHING

NOTES

49 **Mrs. Van Daan.** [*Turning on* Dussel] There would have been plenty for all of us, if *you* hadn't come in here!

50 **Mr. Frank.** We don't need the Nazis to destroy us. We're destroying ourselves.

51 [*He sits down, with his head in his hands.* Mrs. Frank *goes to* Mrs. Van Daan.]

52 **Mrs. Frank.** [*Giving* Mrs. Van Daan *some money*] Give this to Miep. She'll find you a place.

53 **Anne.** Mother, you're not putting Peter out. Peter hasn't done anything.

54 **Mrs. Frank.** He'll stay, of course. When I say I must protect the children, I mean Peter too.

55 [Peter *rises from the steps where he has been sitting.*]

56 **Peter.** I'd have to go if Father goes.

57 [Mr. Van Daan *comes from the bathroom.* Mrs. Van Daan *hurries to him and takes him to the couch. Then she gets water from the sink to bathe his face.*]

58 **Mrs. Frank.** [*While this is going on*] He's no father to you . . . that man! He doesn't know what it is to be a father!

59 **Peter.** [*Starting for his room*] I wouldn't feel right. I couldn't stay.

60 **Mrs. Frank.** Very well, then. I'm sorry.

61 **Anne.** [*Rushing over to* Peter] No. Peter! No! [Peter *goes into his room, closing the door after him.* Anne *turns back to her mother, crying.*] I don't care about the food. They can have mine! I don't want it! Only don't send them away. It'll be daylight soon. They'll be caught . . .

62 **Margot.** [*Putting her arms comfortingly around* Anne] Please, Mother!

63 **Mrs. Frank.** They're not going now. They'll stay here until Miep finds them a place. [*To* Mrs. Van Daan] But one thing I insist on! He must never come down here again! He must never come to this room where the food is stored! We'll divide what we have . . . an equal share for each! [Dussel *hurries over to get a sack of potatoes from the food safe.* Mrs. Frank *goes on, to* Mrs. Van Daan] You can cook it here and take it up to him.

64 [Dussel *brings the sack of potatoes back to the center table.*]

65 **Margot.** Oh, no. No. We haven't sunk so far that we're going to fight over a handful of rotten potatoes.

178 UNIT 2 • THE HOLOCAUST

HOW LANGUAGE WORKS

Contractions and Verb Tenses Verbs can be past, present, or future tense. The same is true for contractions. Have students find contractions in paragraphs 49–63 and list each one in a chart. They should then write the words that make up the contractions as well as the tense of each contraction.

Contraction	Words	Tense
don't	do not	present
hadn't	had not	past
she'll	she will	future
you're	you are	present

66 **Dussel.** [*Dividing the potatoes into piles*] Mrs. Frank, Mr. Frank, Margot, Anne, Peter, Mrs. Van Daan, Mr. Van Daan, myself . . . Mrs. Frank . . .

67 [*The buzzer sounds in* Miep's *signal.*]

68 **Mr. Frank.** It's Miep! [*He hurries over, getting his overcoat and putting it on.*]

69 **Margot.** At this hour?

70 **Mrs. Frank.** It is trouble.

71 **Mr. Frank.** [*As he starts down to unbolt the door*] I beg you, don't let her see a thing like this!

72 **Mr. Dussel.** [*Counting without stopping*] . . . Anne, Peter, Mrs. Van Daan, Mr. Van Daan, myself . . .

73 **Margot.** [*To* Dussel] Stop it! Stop it!

74 **Dussel.** . . . Mr. Frank, Margot, Anne, Peter, Mrs. Van Daan, Mr. Van Daan, myself, Mrs. Frank . . .

75 **Mrs. Van Daan.** You're keeping the big ones for yourself! All the big ones . . . Look at the size of that! . . . And that! . . .

76 [*Dussel continues on with his dividing.* Peter, *with his shirt and trousers on, comes from his room.*]

77 **Margot.** Stop it! Stop it!

78 [*We hear* Miep's *excited voice speaking to* Mr. Frank *below.*]

79 **Miep.** Mr. Frank . . . the most wonderful news! . . . The invasion has begun!

80 **Mr. Frank.** Go on, tell them! Tell them!

81 [Miep *comes running up the steps ahead of* Mr. Frank. *She has a man's raincoat on over her nightclothes and a bunch of orange-colored flowers in her hand.*]

82 **Miep.** Did you hear that, everybody? Did you hear what I said? The invasion has begun! The invasion!

83 [*They all stare at* Miep, *unable to grasp what she is telling them.* Peter *is the first to recover his wits.*]

84 **Peter.** Where?

85 **Mrs. Van Daan.** When? When, Miep?

86 **Miep.** It began early this morning . . .

87 [*As she talks on, the realization of what she has said begins to dawn on them. Everyone goes crazy. A wild demonstration takes place.* Mrs. Frank *hugs* Mr. Van Daan.]

88 **Mrs. Frank.** Oh, Mr. Van Daan, did you hear that?

NOTES

CLOSE READ
ANNOTATE: Mark details in paragraph 81 that describe Miep's appearance.

QUESTION: Why do the playwrights include these specific details?

CONCLUDE: What is the effect of these details?

The Diary of Anne Frank, Act II

DIGITAL PERSPECTIVES

CLOSE READ

You may wish to model the close read using the following think-aloud format. Possible responses to questions on the student page are included.

ANNOTATE: As I read paragraph 81, I notice words and phrases that describe Miep's appearance.

QUESTION: Miep's clothes suggest that she was at home and maybe sleeping. She did not take time to get dressed before she came to the Secret Annex.

CONCLUDE: These details tell us that the news she has to share is so important that it can't wait.

TEACHING

NOTES

89 [*Dussel embraces* Mrs. Van Daan. Peter *grabs a frying pan and parades around the room, beating on it, singing the Dutch National Anthem.* Anne *and* Margot *follow him, singing, weaving in and out among the excited grown-ups.* Margot *breaks away to take the flowers from* Miep *and distribute them to everyone. While this pandemonium is going on* Mrs. Frank *tries to make herself heard above the excitement.*]

90 **Mrs. Frank.** [*To* Miep] How do you know?

91 **Miep.** The radio . . . The B.B.C.!⁹ They said they landed on the coast of Normandy!

9. **B.B.C.** British Broadcasting Corporation.

92 **Peter.** The British?

93 **Miep.** British, Americans, French, Dutch, Poles, Norwegians . . . all of them! More than four thousand ships! Churchill spoke, and General Eisenhower! D-Day they call it!

94 **Mr. Frank.** Thank God, it's come!

95 **Mrs. Van Daan.** At last!

96 **Miep.** [*Starting out*] I'm going to tell Mr. Kraler. This'll be better than any blood transfusion.

97 **Mr. Frank.** [*Stopping her*] What part of Normandy did they land, did they say?

98 **Miep.** Normandy . . . that's all I know now . . . I'll be up the minute I hear some more! [*She goes hurriedly out.*]

99 **Mr. Frank.** [*To* Mrs. Frank] What did I tell you? What did I tell you?

100 [Mr. Frank *indicates that he has forgotten to bolt the door after* Miep. *He hurries down the steps.* Mr. Van Daan, *sitting on the couch, suddenly breaks into a convulsive*¹⁰ *sob. Everybody looks at him, bewildered.*]

10. **convulsive** (kuhn VUHL sihv) *adj.* having an uncontrolled muscular spasm; shuddering.

101 **Mrs. Van Daan.** [*Hurrying to him*] Putti! Putti! What is it? What happened?

102 **Mr. Van Daan.** Please, I'm so ashamed.

103 [Mr. Frank *comes back up the steps.*]

104 **Dussel.** Oh, for God's sake!

105 **Mrs. Van Daan.** Don't, Putti.

106 **Margot.** It doesn't matter now!

107 **Mr. Frank.** [*Going to* Mr. Van Daan] Didn't you hear what Miep said? The invasion has come! We're going to be liberated! This is a time to celebrate! [*He embraces* Mrs. Frank *and then hurries to the cupboard and gets the cognac and a glass.*]

108 **Mr. Van Daan.** To steal bread from children!

180 UNIT 2 • THE HOLOCAUST

> Additional **English Language Support** is available in the Interactive Teacher's Edition.

DIGITAL PERSPECTIVES

Enriching the Text In paragraph 91, Miep refers to the Allied landing at Normandy, which she learned about from the BBC. Provide students with background of this event. Find an audio recording of the BBC broadcast. Alternatively, find newsreel video from this event. Providing these materials will allow the students to get a feel for how people at the time experienced the news. You might also want to gather or task students to gather images of newspaper headlines from this period. Remind students that there was no Internet at the time, so news did not travel quite as rapidly.

109 **Mrs. Frank.** We've all done things that we're ashamed of.

110 **Anne.** Look at me, the way I've treated Mother . . . so mean and horrid to her.

111 **Mrs. Frank.** No, Anneke, no.

112 [Anne *runs to her mother, putting her arms around her.*]

113 **Anne.** Oh, Mother, I was. I was awful.

114 **Mr. Van Daan.** Not like me. No one is as bad as me!

115 **Dussel.** [*To* Mr. Van Daan] Stop it now! Let's be happy!

116 **Mr. Frank.** [*Giving* Mr. Van Daan *a glass of cognac*] Here! Here! Schnapps! L'chaim![11]

117 [Van Daan *takes the cognac. They all watch him. He gives them a feeble smile.* Anne *puts up her fingers in a V-for-Victory sign. As* Van Daan *gives an answering V-sign, they are startled to hear a loud sob from behind them. It is* Mrs. Frank, *stricken with remorse. She is sitting on the other side of the room.*]

118 **Mrs. Frank.** [*Through her sobs*] When I think of the terrible things I said . . .

119 [Mr. Frank, Anne *and* Margot *hurry to her, trying to comfort her.* Mr. Van Daan *brings her his glass of cognac.*]

120 **Mr. Van Daan.** No! No! You were right!

121 **Mrs. Frank.** That I should speak that way to you! . . . Our friends! . . . Our guests! [*She starts to cry again.*]

122 **Dussel.** Stop it, you're spoiling the whole invasion!

123 [*As they are comforting her, the lights dim out. The curtain falls.*]

124 **Anne's Voice.** [*Faintly at first and then with growing strength*] We're all in much better spirits these days. There's still excellent news of the invasion. The best part about it is that I have a feeling that friends are coming. Who knows? Maybe I'll be back in school by fall. Ha, ha! The joke is on us! The warehouse man doesn't know a thing and we are paying him all that money! . . . Wednesday, the second of July, nineteen forty-four. The invasion seems temporarily to be bogged down. Mr. Kraler has to have an operation, which looks bad. The Gestapo have found the radio that was stolen. Mr. Dussel says they'll trace it back and back to the thief, and then, it's just a matter of time till they get to us. Everyone is low. Even poor Pim can't raise their spirits. I have often been downcast myself . . . but never in despair. I can shake off everything if I write. But . . . and that is the great question . . . will I ever be able to write well? I want to so much. I want to go on living even after my death. Another birthday has gone by, so now I

NOTES

11. **Schnapps!** (SHNAHPS) German for "a drink." **L'chaim!** (luh KHAH yihm) Hebrew toast meaning "To life!"

The Diary of Anne Frank, Act II **181**

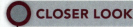

CLOSER LOOK

Analyze Character

Students may have marked paragraphs 109–113 during their first read. Use these lines to help students understand how characters have evolved through the play. Encourage them to talk about the annotations that they marked. You may want to model a close read with the class based on the highlights shown in the text.

ANNOTATE: Have students mark details in paragraphs 109–113 that show how Anne treated her mother, or have students participate while you highlight them.

QUESTION: Guide students to consider what these details might tell them. Ask what a reader can infer from Anne deciding to admit this about her behavior, and accept student responses.
Possible response: She is trying to comfort Mr. Van Daan and she is becoming aware of her behavior toward her mother.

CONCLUDE: Help students to formulate conclusions about the importance of these details in the text. Ask students why the playwrights might have included these details.
Possible response: These details show that Anne has changed over the time she has spent in the annex. She has matured and developed empathy.

Discuss with students that playwrights use dialogue and stage direction to show the evolution of the **characters**. None of the characters are the same as when they arrived in the annex. Setting aside what was happening in the world, the dynamics established by being together without a break for two years had an impact on all of them. Earlier in this scene, characters achieved both their low points and their high points (the food and the invasion). It is worth noting that rather than being the agitator, Anne is now the comforter.

Whole-Class Learning **181**

TEACHING

NOTES

am fifteen. Already I know what I want. I have a goal, an opinion.

125 [*As this is being said—the curtain rises on the scene, the lights dim on, and* Anne's Voice *fades out.*]

✶ ✶ ✶

Scene 4

1 [*It is an afternoon a few weeks later . . . Everyone but* Margot *is in the main room. There is a sense of great tension.*

2 *Both* Mrs. Frank *and* Mr. Van Daan *are nervously pacing back and forth,* Dussel *is standing at the window, looking down fixedly at the street below.* Peter *is at the center table, trying to do his lessons.* Anne *sits opposite him, writing in her diary.* Mrs. Van Daan *is seated on the couch, her eyes on* Mr. Frank *as he sits reading.*

3 *The sound of a telephone ringing comes from the office below. They all are* rigid, *listening tensely.* Dussel *rushes down to* Mr. Frank.]

4 **Dussel.** There it goes again, the telephone! Mr. Frank, do you hear?

5 **Mr. Frank.** [*Quietly*] Yes. I hear.

insistent (ihn SIHS tuhnt) *adj.* demanding that something should happen

6 **Dussel.** [*Pleading, insistent*] But this is the third time, Mr. Frank! The third time in quick succession! It's a signal! I tell you it's Miep, trying to get us! For some reason she can't come to us and she's trying to warn us of something!

7 **Mr. Frank.** Please. Please.

8 **Mr. Van Daan.** [*To* Dussel] You're wasting your breath.

9 **Dussel.** Something has happened, Mr. Frank. For three days now Miep hasn't been to see us! And today not a man has come to work. There hasn't been a sound in the building!

10 **Mrs. Frank.** Perhaps it's Sunday. We may have lost track of the days.

11 **Mr. Van Daan.** [*To* Anne] You with the diary there. What day is it?

12 **Dussel.** [*Going to* Mrs. Frank] I don't lose track of the days! I know exactly what day it is! It's Friday, the fourth of August. Friday, and not a man at work. [*He rushes back to* Mr. Frank. *Pleading with him, almost in tears.*] I tell you Mr. Kraler's dead. That's the only explanation. He's dead and they've closed down the building, and Miep's trying to tell us!

182 UNIT 2 • THE HOLOCAUST

VOCABULARY DEVELOPMENT

Word Forms Remind students that the concept vocabulary word *insistent* (paragraph 6) is an adjective. This word is connected to other words with the same root. Have students look up the word *insistent* in the dictionary and find other words that share the same root. Have them create a chart with those new words.

Word	Definition
insistent (adj.)	demanding that something happen
insistently (adv.)	in a demanding way
insist (v.)	demand

13 **Mr. Frank.** She'd never telephone us.

14 **Dussel.** [*Frantic*] Mr. Frank, answer that! I beg you, answer it!

15 **Mr. Frank.** No.

16 **Mr. Van Daan.** Just pick it up and listen. You don't have to speak. Just listen and see if it's Miep.

17 **Dussel.** [*Speaking at the same time*] For God's sake . . . I ask you.

18 **Mr. Frank.** No. I've told you, no. I'll do nothing that might let anyone know we're in the building.

19 **Peter.** Mr. Frank's right.

20 **Mr. Van Daan.** There's no need to tell us what side you're on.

21 **Mr. Frank.** If we wait patiently, quietly, I believe that help will come.

22 [*There is silence for a minute as they all listen to the telephone ringing.*]

23 **Dussel.** I'm going down. [*He rushes down the steps.* Mr. Frank *tries ineffectually to hold him.* Dussel *runs to the lower door, unbolting it. The telephone stops ringing.* Dussel *bolts the door and comes slowly back up the steps.*] Too late. [Mr. Frank *goes to* Margot *in Anne's bedroom.*]

24 **Mr. Van Daan.** So we just wait here until we die.

25 **Mrs. Van Daan.** [*Hysterically*] I can't stand it! I'll kill myself! I'll kill myself!

26 **Mr. Van Daan.** For God's sake, stop it!

27 [*In the distance, a German military band is heard playing a Viennese waltz.*]

28 **Mrs. Van Daan.** I think you'd be glad if I did! I think you want me to die!

29 **Mr. Van Daan.** Whose fault is it we're here? [Mrs. Van Daan *starts for her room. He follows, talking at her.*] We could've been safe somewhere . . . in America or Switzerland. But no! No! You wouldn't leave when I wanted to. You couldn't leave your things. You couldn't leave your precious furniture.

30 **Mrs. Van Daan.** Don't touch me!

31 [*She hurries up the stairs, followed by* Mr. Van Daan. Peter, *unable to bear it, goes to his room.* Anne *looks after him, deeply concerned.* Dussel *returns to his post at the window.* Mr. Frank *comes back into the main room and takes a book, trying to read.* Mrs. Frank *sits near the sink, starting to peel some potatoes.* Anne *quietly goes to* Peter's *room closing the door after her.* Peter *is lying face down on the cot.* Anne *leans over him, holding him in her arms, trying to bring him out of his despair.*]

TEACHING

● **CLOSE READ**

You may wish to model the close read using the following think-aloud format. Possible responses to questions on the student page are included.

ANNOTATE: As I read paragraph 32, I notice and highlight words related to the senses.

QUESTION: The playwrights probably included these lines to remind readers of everything Anne has missed for the time she was in hiding. These details also reinforce the idea that Anne's optimism and hope have not been squelched.

CONCLUDE: These details remind readers and audiences about Anne's optimistic attitude at this point in the play. Despite all of her difficulties, she has retained her sense of hope for the future.

NOTES

CLOSE READ
ANNOTATE: In paragraph 32, mark sensory details—words and phrases related to sight, hearing, touch, smell, or taste.

QUESTION: Why might the playwrights have included these details?

CONCLUDE: What is the effect of these details? What do they show about Anne's character?

12. **Orthodox** (AWR thuh doks) *adj.* strictly observing the rites and traditions of Judaism.
13. **purgatory** (PUR guh tawr ee) *n.* state or place of temporary punishment.

32 **Anne.** Look, Peter, the sky. [*She looks up through the skylight.*] What a lovely, lovely day! Aren't the clouds beautiful? You know what I do when it seems as if I couldn't stand being cooped up for one more minute? I *think* myself out. I think myself on a walk in the park where I used to go with Pim. Where the jonquils and the crocus and the violets grow down the slopes. You know the most wonderful part about *thinking* yourself out? You can have it any way you like. You can have roses and violets and chrysanthemums all blooming at the same time . . . It's funny . . . I used to take it all for granted . . . and now I've gone crazy about everything to do with nature. Haven't you?

33 **Peter.** I've just gone crazy. I think if something doesn't happen soon . . . if we don't get out of here . . . I can't stand much more of it!

34 **Anne.** [*Softly*] I wish you had a religion, Peter.

35 **Peter.** No, thanks! Not me!

36 **Anne.** Oh, I don't mean you have to be Orthodox[12] . . . or believe in heaven and hell and purgatory[13] and things . . . I just mean some religion . . . it doesn't matter what. Just to believe in something! When I think of all that's out there . . . the trees . . . and flowers . . . and seagulls . . . when I think of the dearness of you, Peter . . . and the goodness of the people we know . . . Mr. Kraler, Miep, Dirk, the vegetable man, all risking their lives for us every day. . . When I think of these good things, I'm not afraid any more . . . I find myself, and God, and I . . .

37 [*Peter interrupts, getting up and walking away.*]

38 **Peter.** That's fine! But when I begin to think, I get mad! Look at us, hiding out for two years. Not able to move! Caught here like . . . waiting for them to come and get us . . . and all for what?

39 **Anne.** We're not the only people that've had to suffer. There've always been people that've had to . . . sometimes one race . . . sometimes another . . . and yet . . .

40 **Peter.** That doesn't make me feel any better!

41 **Anne.** [*Going to him*] I know it's terrible, trying to have any faith . . . when people are doing such horrible . . . But you know what I sometimes think? I think the world may be going through a phase, the way I was with Mother. It'll pass, maybe not for hundreds of years, but some day . . . I still believe, in spite of everything, that people are really good at heart.

42 **Peter.** I want to see something now . . . Not a thousand years from now! [*He goes over, sitting down again on the cot.*]

43 **Anne.** But, Peter, if you'd only look at it as part of a great pattern . . . that we're just a little minute in the life . . . [*She breaks off.*] Listen to us, going at each other like a couple of stupid grownups! Look at the sky now. Isn't it lovely? [*She holds out her hand to him. Peter takes it and rises, standing with her at the window looking out, his arms around her.*] Some day, when we're outside again, I'm going to . . .

44 [*She breaks off as she hears the sound of a car, its brakes squealing as it comes to a sudden stop. The people in the other rooms also become aware of the sound. They listen tensely. Another car roars up to a screeching stop.* Anne *and* Peter *come from* Peter's *room.* Mr. *and* Mrs. Van Daan *creep down the stairs.* Dussel *comes out from his room. Everyone is listening, hardly breathing. A doorbell clangs again and again in the building below.* Mr. Frank *starts quietly down the steps to the door.* Dussel *and* Peter *follow him. The others stand rigid, waiting, terrified.*]

45 [*In a few seconds* Dussel *comes stumbling back up the steps. He shakes off* Peter's *help and goes to his room.* Mr. Frank *bolts the door below, and comes slowly back up the steps. Their eyes are all on him as he stands there for a minute. They realize that what they feared has happened.* Mrs. Van Daan *starts to whimper.* Mr. Van Daan *puts her gently in a chair; and then hurries off up the stairs to their room to collect their things.* Peter *goes to comfort his mother. There is a sound of violent pounding on a door below.*]

46 **Mr. Frank.** [*Quietly*] For the past two years we have lived in fear. Now we can live in hope.

47 [*The pounding below becomes more insistent. There are muffled sounds of voices, shouting commands.*]

48 **Men's Voices.** *Auf machen! Da drinnen! Auf machen! Schnell! Schnell! Schnell!*[14] etc., etc.

49 [*The street door below is forced open. We hear the heavy tread of footsteps coming up.* Mr. Frank *gets two school bags from the shelves, and gives one to* Anne *and the other to* Margot. *He goes to get a bag for* Mrs. Frank. *The sound of feet coming up grows louder.* Peter *comes to* Anne, *kissing her good-bye, then he goes to his room to collect his things. The buzzer of their door starts to ring.* Mr. Frank *brings* Mrs. Frank *a bag. They stand together, waiting. We hear the thud of gun butts on the door, trying to break it down.*]

NOTES

14. *Auf machen!. . . Schnell!* German for "Open up, you in there, open up, quick, quick, quick!"

The Diary of Anne Frank, Act II **185**

DIGITAL PERSPECTIVES

CLOSER LOOK

Most characters are introduced and developed through the course of a play. In some cases, a playwright might introduce characters with a very small amount of dialogue and late in a play, yet those characters can still have a major impact. The sudden appearance of offstage German dialogue in paragraph 48 introduces new characters who bring a climax to the play. You may wish to model the close read using the following think-aloud format. Possible responses to questions on the student page are included.

ANNOTATE: As I read paragraph 48, I notice and highlight German words spoken by characters who are offstage.

QUESTION: After the words are spoken, the characters in the annex calmly go through the process of preparing to depart, and Peter kisses Anne goodbye.

CONCLUDE: By having German soldiers appear with this dialogue, the playwrights create a sudden, dramatic awareness that all the hopes of the people in the annex are lost. With the use of offstage voices, the reader realizes in a moment that the Franks and their friends have been discovered and that their hope is gone.

WriteNow

Express and Reflect One of the most famous, most quoted sentences from *The Diary of Anne Frank* can be found here. In the last three lines of paragraph 41 Anne says, "I still believe, in spite of everything, that people are really good at heart." Have students reread the entire paragraph. Ask them to read the rest of the play and consult other sources to learn what happened to the Franks and what happened in the world. Have students write a reflection based on the famous quote. Students can write about World War II or apply Anne's idea to another difficult period.

Whole-Class Learning **185**

50 Anne *stands, holding her school satchel, looking over at her father and mother with a soft, reassuring smile. She is no longer a child, but a woman with courage to meet whatever lies ahead.*

51 *The lights dim out. The curtain falls on the scene. We hear a mighty crash as the door is shattered. After a second* Anne's Voice *is heard.*]

52 **Anne's Voice.** And so it seems our stay here is over. They are waiting for us now. They've allowed us five minutes to get our things. We can each take a bag and whatever it will hold of clothing. Nothing else. So, dear Diary, that means I must leave you behind. Good-bye for a while. P.S. Please, please, Miep, or Mr. Kraler, or anyone else. If you should find this diary, will you please keep it safe for me, because some day I hope . . .

53 [*Her voice stops abruptly. There is silence. After a second the curtain rises.*]

⌘ ⌘ ⌘

Scene 5

1 [*It is again the afternoon in November, 1945. The rooms are as we saw them in the first scene. Mr. Kraler has joined* Miep *and* Mr. Frank. *There are coffee cups on the table. We see a great change in Mr. Frank. He is calm now. His bitterness is gone. He slowly turns a few pages of the diary. They are blank.*]

2 **Mr. Frank.** No more. [*He closes the diary and puts it down on the couch beside him.*]

3 **Miep.** I'd gone to the country to find food. When I got back the block was surrounded by police . . .

4 **Mr. Kraler.** We made it our business to learn how they knew. It was the thief . . . the thief who told them.

5 [Miep *goes up to the gas burner, bringing back a pot of coffee.*]

6 **Mr. Frank.** [*After a pause*] It seems strange to say this, that anyone could be happy in a concentration camp. But Anne was happy in the camp in Holland where they first took us. After two years of being shut up in these rooms, she could be out . . . out in the sunshine and the fresh air that she loved.

7 **Miep.** [*Offering the coffee to* Mr. Frank] A little more?

8 **Mr. Frank.** [*Holding out his cup to her*] The news of the war was good. The British and Americans were sweeping through France. We felt sure that they would get to us in time. In

September we were told that we were to be shipped to Poland . . . The men to one camp. The women to another. I was sent to Auschwitz.[15] They went to Belsen.[16] In January we were freed, the few of us who were left. The war wasn't yet over, so it took us a long time to get home. We'd be sent here and there behind the lines where we'd be safe. Each time our train would stop . . . at a siding, or a crossing . . . we'd all get out and go from group to group . . . Where were you? Were you at Belsen? At Buchenwald?[17] At Mauthausen? Is it possible that you knew my wife? Did you ever see my husband? My son? My daughter? That's how I found out about my wife's death . . . of Margot, the Van Daans . . . Dussel. But Anne . . . I still hoped . . . Yesterday I went to Rotterdam. I'd heard of a woman there . . . She'd been in Belsen with Anne . . . I know now.

9 [*He picks up the diary again, and turns the pages back to find a certain passage. As he finds it we hear* Anne's Voice.]

10 **Anne's Voice.** In spite of everything, I still believe that people are really good at heart. [Mr. Frank *slowly closes the diary.*]

11 **Mr. Frank.** She puts me to shame.

12 [*They are silent.*]

NOTES

15. **Auschwitz** (OWSH vihts) Nazi concentration camp in Poland at which approximately 1.1 million Jews were murdered.
16. **Belsen** (BEL zuhn) village in Germany that, with the village of Bergen, was the site of Bergen-Belsen, a Nazi concentration camp; another name for this camp.
17. **Buchenwald** (BOO kuhn wawld) Nazi concentration camp in central Germany.

Comprehension Check
Complete the following items after you finish your first read.

> **Notebook** Respond to the questions.
>
> 1. How long have the characters been in hiding at the beginning of Act II?
> 2. What happens to Mr. Kraler that prevents him from coming to the attic?
> 3. What does Anne give Peter to decorate his room?
> 4. What does Mr. Van Daan do that upsets the others?
> 5. At the end of the war, what happened to all the members of the Frank family except Mr. Frank?
> 6. Write a summary of *The Diary of Anne Frank*, Act II.
>
> ### RESEARCH
>
> **Research to Clarify** Choose at least one unfamiliar detail from the text. Briefly research that detail. In what way does the information you learned shed light on an aspect of the play?
>
> **Research to Explore** Choose something that interested you from the text, and formulate a research question you might use to learn more about it.

The Diary of Anne Frank, Act II **187**

DIGITAL PERSPECTIVES

Comprehension Check

Possible responses:
1. They have been in hiding for about a year and a half.
2. He is hospitalized for ulcers.
3. She offers to give him some of her photographs.
4. They discover that Mr. Van Daan has been stealing food.
5. She and the others were sent to a concentration camp in Holland. Anne was later sent to Bergen-Belsen.
6. The family celebrates 1944 with a cake. Peter and Anne begin to talk. Mr. Kraler is sick with worry. Mrs. Frank grows concerned with Anne and Peter's relationship while Mrs. Van Daan grows suspicious. Peter and Anne kiss. Mrs. Frank catches Mr. Van Daan stealing food. She warns him that she'll throw him out, but Peter says he will also leave. News arrives that the Allies' invasion of Europe has begun. Phone calls make the family suspicious. Mr. Van Daan blames Mrs. Van Daan for refusing to leave Europe years earlier. They are found by the green police. The act closes with Mr. Frank reading Anne's diary after the war and stating that she was braver than him.

Research

Research to Clarify If students struggle to decide on a detail to research, you may want to suggest that they focus on one of the following topics: The anti-Jewish laws, the German invasion of Holland, a specific concentration camp, the Gestapo, the green police, the Allied invasion.

Research to Explore If students aren't sure how to go about formulating a research question, suggest that they use their findings from Research to Clarify as a starting point. For example, if students researched the Allied invasion, they might formulate a question such as *What happened when the Allies reached Normandy?*

CROSS-CURRICULAR PERSPECTIVES

Social Studies Understanding what happened afterward to the Franks, Van Daans, and Mr. Dussel is an important part of understanding how their stories fit into the story of the Holocaust. In Scene 5, Mr. Frank lists some of the many concentration camps from the Holocaust where millions were murdered: Auschwitz, Bergen-Belsen, Buchenwald, Mauthausen. Have students select one of the camps listed here and prepare a presentation for the class. The presentation can include pictures and facts about the camp.

Whole-Class Learning **187**

TEACHING

Jump Start

CLOSE READ Throughout *The Diary of Anne Frank*, the characters evolve. Discuss with students how playwrights show the reader, rather than tell the reader, how characters change over time. Sometimes the change is subtle and sometimes it is not. It can come in their words, their movements, or in how they say their dialogue.

Close Read the Text

Walk students through the annotation model on the student page. Encourage them to complete items 2 and 3 on their own. Review and discuss the sections students have marked. If needed, continue to model close reading by using the Annotation Highlights in the Interactive Teacher's Edition.

Analyze the Text

Possible responses:

1. (a) A worker in the office below the annex demanded more money and was staring at the bookcase. **DOK 1** (b) This incident foreshadows the thief who robbed the office and eventually told the police about the people hiding there. **DOK 2**

2. Anne was able to preserve her sense of optimism and her belief in the goodness of human nature. And she attempted to inspire the others in the annex to share her sense of hope. **DOK 2**

3. Answers will vary. Sample answer: The play has taught me that we remember the past by learning about what happened and why it happened. These memories are important to keep alive so we do not repeat past mistakes and allow events like the Holocaust to happen again. **DOK 3**

FORMATIVE ASSESSMENT

Analyze the Text

- **If** students fail to cite evidence, **then** remind them to support their ideas with specific information.
- **If** students struggle to analyze character growth, **then** discuss how a specific character has changed throughout the play, and illustrate with examples.

188   UNIT 2 • THE HOLOCAUST

MAKING MEANING

THE DIARY OF ANNE FRANK, ACT II

Tool Kit
Close-Read Guide and Model Annotation

STANDARDS
Reading Literature
• Cite the textual evidence that most strongly supports an analysis of what the text says explicitly as well as inferences drawn from the text.
• Analyze how particular lines of dialogue or incidents in a story or drama propel the action, reveal aspects of a character, or provoke a decision.

Close Read the Text

1. The model—from Act II, Scene 4, paragraph 44—shows two sample annotations, along with questions and conclusions. Close read the passage, and find another detail to annotate. Then, write a question and your conclusion.

> **ANNOTATE:** These details identify sounds coming from outside the Secret Annex.
> **QUESTION:** Why do the playwrights include these details in the stage directions?
> **CONCLUDE:** These details build suspense as readers' wonder what the sounds imply about future events.

> **ANNOTATE:** These sentences describe characters' reactions to the alarming noises.
> **QUESTION:** Why do the playwrights include these descriptions?
> **CONCLUDE:** These details convey the characters' sense of dread.

[*She breaks off as she hears* the sound of a car, its brakes squealing as it comes to a sudden stop. *The people in the other rooms also become aware of the sound.* They listen tensely. Another car roars up to a screeching stop.... *Everyone is listening, hardly breathing.* A doorbell clangs again and again *in the building below.*]

2. For more practice, go back into the text, and complete the close-read notes.

3. Revisit a section of the text you found important during your first read. Read this section closely, and **annotate** what you notice. Ask yourself **questions** such as "Why did the author make this choice?" What can you **conclude**?

Analyze the Text

CITE TEXTUAL EVIDENCE to support your answers.

Notebook Respond to these questions.

1. **(a)** What disturbing news does Mr. Kraler bring on New Year's Day? **(b) Connect** What hint does this news give about the play's ending?

2. **Analyze** How is Anne able to preserve her dignity and hope despite her suffering?

3. **Essential Question:** *How do we remember the past?* What has the play taught you about how we remember the past?

188   UNIT 2 • THE HOLOCAUST

PERSONALIZE FOR LEARNING

English Language Support

Identifying Character Motivation Point out that character's actions are driven by a character's motivations, values, or beliefs. Guide students to recall these incidents from Act II:

SCENE 1: Cutting the Cake / Selling Mrs. Van Daan's Fur Coat / Blackmail
SCENE 2: Anne and Peter's "Date"
SCENE 3: Stolen Bread / Miep's Good News
SCENE 4: The Army Comes to Take Them

SCENE 5: Miep and Mr. Frank Discuss the Past

Ask partners to choose a scene and a character and write a couple of sentences about how that character reacted to the incident. Have all share and compare. **EMERGING**

Ask partners to choose a character and write a few sentences about how that character reacted

ESSENTIAL QUESTION: How do we remember the past?

Analyze Craft and Structure

Characters' Motivations A character's motivation is the reason he or she takes a particular action. The reason may be internal, external, or a combination of the two.

- **Internal motivations** include emotions, such as jealousy or loneliness.
- **External motivations** include factors in the setting or situation, such as war or poverty.

Playwrights reveal characters' motivation through their dialogue and actions, as well as by including revealing details in the stage directions. To identify characters' motivations in a drama, make **inferences,** or educated guesses, about their behavior. Consider what characters say and how they say it. Take note of what they do, and what their attitudes are toward their actions. Also, think about descriptive details or explanations that are given in stage directions.

Practice

CITE TEXTUAL EVIDENCE to support your answers.

Notebook Analyze the characters' motivations in Act II. Use the chart to gather your observations. Then, respond to the questions.

ACTION	MOTIVATION	INTERNAL OR EXTERNAL?
Mr. Kraler tells those in hiding about Carl.	He is seeking advice from Mr. Frank on how to respond to Carl's demand for money.	external
Mr. Van Daan steals bread.	He is hungry and thinks little of others.	internal and external
Peter offers to leave.	He is expressing his devotion to his family.	internal

1. (a) What is Anne's motivation for keeping a diary? (b) Cite at least two details from the play that support your inference.
2. What can you infer from details in Act II about why an informer might be motivated to tell authorities about a family in hiding?
3. Identify at least three ways in which the setting contributes the characters' motivations. For each item, cite specific details from the text that support your thinking.

The Diary of Anne Frank, Act II 189

Analyze Craft and Structure

Characters' Motivations A play is intended to be a visual medium. We learn a character's motivation by what we see them do and what we hear them say. The audience or reader will interpret what the character's motivation is by watching or visualizing a scene on a stage and making inferences about what is presented. For more support, see **Analyze Craft and Structure: Character Motivation.**

MAKE IT INTERACTIVE

Have students present pieces of scenes from Act II. After each presentation, have students make inferences about character motivation in that scene.

Practice

Possible responses:

1. (a) Anne's motivation for keeping a diary is to provide herself with a private, serious outlet to express her deepest thoughts and emotions. (b) She makes several references for her need to have someone to talk to who understands her and she tells Peter that she thinks "more seriously" about life and that she loves to write and wants to become a journalist. From these details, the reader can infer that she uses her diary writing to sort out her most serious thoughts.
2. From the stories Mr. Kraler and Miep relate about the difficult conditions for people in Amsterdam, one can infer that people would be motivated to be in good favor with the authorities. Turning in a family of Jews in hiding would be considered such a favor, and a person might be rewarded for it.
3. Answers will vary. Students should note that the cramped quarters, the loss of freedom, and the need for silence impact the characters in different ways.

---

to incidents from two scenes. Have all share and compare. **EXPANDING**

Have partners choose an incident and write about it from the perspective of several characters. Have all share and compare. **BRIDGING**

An expanded **English Language Support Lesson** on Character Motivation is available in the Interactive Teacher's Edition.

FORMATIVE ASSESSMENT

Analyze Craft and Structure

- **If** students struggle to see the impact of environment on character motivation, **then** play a video of a scene to illustrate the concept.
- **If** students struggle to make inferences about character motivation, **then** select a moment in the play and guide students to make inferences.

For Reteach and Practice, see **Analyze Craft and Structure: Character Motivation (RP).**

Whole-Class Learning 189

TEACHING

Concept Vocabulary

Why These Words? Possible responses:
1. The words relate directly to the characters' anxiety about what might happen as well as to their hopes that they will soon be free.
2. bewildered, miserable, longing

Practice
Responses will vary but should show an understanding of each word's meaning.

Word Network
Possible words: *concentration camps, destroy, Gestapo, Nazis, sacrifice*

Word Study
For more support, see **Concept Vocabulary and Word Study.**

Possible responses:
1. Our teacher was quite insistent that all students bring no notes into the room during our final exam.
2. adherent: a person who follows rules (noun); dependent: relying on something or someone (adjective); excellent: possessing outstanding quality (adjective); intelligent: smart, having a good understanding (adjective)

FORMATIVE ASSESSMENT

Concept Vocabulary
If students struggle to understand the concept vocabulary and how the words relate to the story, **then** review the concept vocabulary in context.

Word Study
If students struggle to understand the suffix *-ent*, **then** review more words with this construct. For Reteach and Practice, see **Word Study: Latin Suffix -ent (RP).**

LANGUAGE DEVELOPMENT

THE DIARY OF ANNE FRANK, ACT II

Concept Vocabulary

| foreboding | intuition | rigid |
| apprehension | mounting | insistent |

Why These Words? These concept words are used to reveal feelings about the future—hopes, fears, and a sense of anticipation. For example, when Mr. Kraler comes to tell Mr. Frank about Carl, Margot can sense his *apprehension* about telling the group. As a result, she experiences a sense of *foreboding*. Notice that both of these words relate to the characters' feelings of fear and anxiety about the future.

1. How does the concept vocabulary help the reader understand the characters' experiences?

2. What other words in the selection connect to this concept?

Practice

Notebook The first word in each pair is a concept vocabulary word. For each pair, write a sentence in which you correctly use both words.

1. *apprehension,* unknown
2. *mounting,* future
3. *insistent,* voice
4. *foreboding,* tension
5. *intuition,* guess
6. *rigid,* movement

Word Study

Latin Suffix: *-ent* The Latin suffix *-ent* can make a verb or a noun into an adjective. Adding the suffix *-ent* to the verb *insist* changes the verb into the adjective *insistent*. In Act II, Scene 4, Mr. Dussel's pleading with Mr. Frank to investigate the ringing telephone downstairs is described as *insistent*.

1. Write a sentence in which you correctly use the adjective *insistent*.

2. Based on your understanding of the suffix *-ent*, write a definition for each of the following words: *adherent, dependent, excellent, intelligent*. Then, identify the part of speech for each word. Use a dictionary to verify each word's part of speech and definition.

WORD NETWORK
Add words related to the Holocaust from the text to your Word Network.

STANDARDS
Language
- Demonstrate command of the conventions of standard English grammar and usage when writing or speaking.
- Determine or clarify the meaning of unknown and multiple-meaning words or phrases based on *grade 8 reading and content*, choosing flexibly from a range of strategies.
  b. Use common, grade-appropriate Greek or Latin affixes and roots as clues to the meaning of a word.
  c. Consult general and specialized reference materials, both print and digital, to find the pronunciation of a word or determine or clarify its precise meaning or its part of speech.
  d. Verify the preliminary determination of the meaning of a word or phrase.
- Use knowledge of language and its conventions when writing, speaking, reading, or listening.

VOCABULARY DEVELOPMENT

Concept Vocabulary Reinforcement Review the Concept Vocabulary words for comprehension. Have students create "show-you-know" sentences with each word. Provide examples of both successful and unsuccessful sentences.

Unsuccessful: Anne was filled with *apprehension*. She went to Peter's room.

Successful: Anne was filled with *apprehension*. She was afraid that Peter did not feel about her the way she felt about him.

Point out that the first example does not show what the word *apprehension* means, but the second does. Have students share their sentences with the class.

ESSENTIAL QUESTION: How do we remember the past?

Conventions

Simple Tenses of Verbs The **tense** of a verb shows the time of an action or a condition. Writers need verb tenses to tell when the events they write about took place. There are three **simple tenses** of verbs: *past*, *present*, and *future*.

The chart below shows how to form these tenses. Note that the past and future forms are the same for all persons.

PRESENT TENSE	PAST TENSE	FUTURE TENSE
Use the base form; add -s or -es for the third person.	For regular verbs, add -d or -ed to base form. For irregular verbs, there is no predictable pattern, so you need to memorize their forms.	Use *will* before base form.
I *wait* You *wait* He, she, it *waits* We *wait* They *wait*	REGULAR: I *waited* IRREGULAR: I *ran*, you *came*, we *went*	I *will wait* You *will wait* He, she, it *will wait* We *will wait* They *will wait*

When telling a sequence of events, do not shift tense unnecessarily.
   Incorrect: I *walked* to the door and *open* it.
   Correct: I *walked* to the door and *opened* it.

In some cases, however, it is necessary to shift tense to show the order of events.
   Incorrect: Because I *run* yesterday, I *ache* today.
   Correct: Because I *ran* yesterday, I *ache* today.

Read It

1. Label the underlined verb in each sentence from the selection *past*, *present*, or *future*.
   a. We <u>came</u> to bring you New Year's greetings.
   b. If we wait patiently, quietly, I believe that help <u>will come</u>.
   c. Mr. Van Daan always <u>gets</u> a little bit more.
2. Rewrite the underlined verb in each sentence using the correct tense.
   a. They <u>ate</u> dinner together tomorrow night.
   b. The war <u>happens</u> decades ago, but for some, it could have been yesterday.

Write It

Reread the stage directions at the end of Scene 1. Rewrite the stage directions so that they are in the simple past tense.

The Diary of Anne Frank, Act II

Conventions

Simple Tenses of Verbs Take this opportunity to review verb tenses with students. Point out that it is important in writing to make sure that verb tenses within a sentence or paragraph match. Give examples and ask students to determine if the example is correct or incorrect. If it is incorrect, have them correct it. Possible example: *Incorrect:* =I ran to the store yesterday and will buy milk. *Corrected:* I ran to the store yesterday and bought milk. (Or, I will run to the store tomorrow and will buy milk.) For more support, see **Conventions: Simple Tenses of Verbs.**

Read It
Possible responses:
1. a. past
   b. future
   c. present
2. a. will eat
   b. happened

Write It
Possible responses:
As these last lines were said, the curtain rose on the scene. The lights dimmed. Anne's Voice *faded out*.

FORMATIVE ASSESSMENT
Conventions
If students struggle to understand simple verb tenses, **then** review more examples of past, present, and future tense within the text and from other sources. For Reteach and Practice, see **Conventions: Simple Tenses of Verbs (RP).**

WriteNow Inform and Explain

Past and Future Interest Paragraph Now that students have reviewed verb tenses, have students write about the past and future using the different verb tenses. You can suggest that they choose topics that appeal to them. Students might select hobbies as their topic. They can write about a past hobby, a present one, and one they might take up in the future. Example: When I was younger, I collected stuffed animals. Now, I build models. Someday I will create my own video games.

TEACHING

Speaking and Listening

Choose a Scene and a Character As students review the play to choose a scene, they should think about all of the characters and how they evolve.

Rehearse Ask students to consider characters' roles in their scenes and to discuss how they think characters would be feeling at the moment. Ask them to use adjectives to describe their characters in the moment of each scene. For more support, see **Speaking and Listening: Dramatic Reading.**

Evaluate Presentations As students review the work of classmates, encourage them to share at least one positive comment with each group.

FORMATIVE ASSESSMENT

Speaking and Listening

- **If** students struggle to read their lines clearly, **then** have students spend more time practicing.
- **If** students struggle to convey the emotions of the characters in the scene, **then** have students review the stage directions as well as the preceding scene.

For Reteach and Practice, see **Speaking and Listening: Dramatic Reading (RP).**

EFFECTIVE EXPRESSION

THE DIARY OF ANNE FRANK, ACT II

Speaking and Listening

Assignment
With a partner, deliver a **dramatic reading** of a scene from *The Diary of Anne Frank*. As you perform, use your voice as well as gestures and movements to accurately re-create the scene and convey meaning.

1. **Choose a Scene and a Character** With a partner, choose a scene from either Act I or Act II of the play. Then, decide who will portray each character. If you choose a scene with more than two characters, decide how you will make the shifts from one character to another clear for your audience.

2. **Analyze the Scene** Analyze the scene you chose, considering how each character contributes to the emotions and actions. Use this analysis to decide how to perform the scene. Think about the following questions:
   - How does the scene fit into the play as a whole?
   - What does the scene reveal about the characters' perspectives, personalities, and motivations?

3. **Rehearse** As you practice your performance, use these guidelines to make your delivery effective:
   - Speak the dialogue as it is written. Adjust your tone according to the instructions provided in the stage directions.
   - Use your voice, gestures, and movements to portray your character accurately and to show your interpretation of the playwrights' intentions.

4. **Evaluate Presentations** As your classmates deliver their scenes, listen and watch attentively. Use an evaluation guide like the one shown to evaluate their dramatic readings. You will use this evaluation to write a drama review during the Writing to Sources activity.

STANDARDS
Speaking and Listening
- Engage effectively in a range of collaborative discussions with diverse partners on *grade 8 topics, texts, and issues,* building on others' ideas and expressing their own clearly.
   a. Come to discussions prepared, having read or researched materials under study; explicitly draw on that preparation by referring to evidence on the topic, text, or issue to probe and reflect on issues under discussion.
   b. Follow rules for collegial discussions and decision-making, track progress toward specific goals and deadlines, and define individual roles as needed.
- Present claims and findings, emphasizing salient points in a focused, coherent manner with relevant evidence, sound valid reasoning, and well-chosen details; use appropriate eye contact, adequate volume, and clear pronunciation.

DRAMATIC READING EVALUATION GUIDE

Rate each statement on a scale of 1 (not demonstrated) to 5 (demonstrated).

- ☐ The actors spoke the lines clearly.
- ☐ The actors spoke in a way that captured the characters' personalities.
- ☐ The actors interacted in a way that was believable and true to the play's meaning.
- ☐ The actors used gestures and movements effectively.

DIGITAL PERSPECTIVES

Illuminating the Text Present a movie version of *The Diary of Anne Frank*. Watch the movie in its entirety. Upon completion, have each student write a review of the performance. Discuss the reviews as a whole class. Use these questions to help students write their reviews: How did the performance compare to the reading? Which reviews were most effective? Why?

ESSENTIAL QUESTION: How do we remember the past?

Writing to Sources

A **drama review** is an evaluation of a dramatic performance. In a review, a writer describes a performance and evaluates its quality. The writer states an opinion and then supports it with specific details. For example, it is not enough to say that an actor did a good job portraying a character. The reviewer must explain what, specifically, made the actor's portrayal successful.

Assignment

During the Speaking and Listening activity, classmates delivered dramatic readings of scenes from the play, and you evaluated those performances. Now, write a **drama review** of one of the performances. Prepare to write your review by considering these questions:

- How did watching the performance differ from reading the text?
- Did the actors make effective choices that captured the emotions, personalities, and motivations of the characters?
- Was the performance faithful to the text?
- Did the performance reveal something about the text that was new or surprising?

Draft a review in which you analyze the similarities and differences between the written text and the dramatic reading. In your conclusion, explain whether the dramatic reading effectively captured the written version of the scene. Be sure to support your analysis and evaluation with relevant details from both the text and the performance.

📝 EVIDENCE LOG

Before moving on to a new selection, go to your Evidence Log and record what you learned from *The Diary of Anne Frank*.

≡ STANDARDS

Reading Literature
Analyze the extent to which a filmed or live production of a story or drama stays faithful to or departs from the text or script, evaluating the choices made by the director or actors.

Writing
Write informative/explanatory texts to examine a topic and convey ideas, concepts, and information through the selection, organization, and analysis of relevant content.
 b. Develop the topic with relevant, well-chosen facts, definitions, concrete details, quotations, or other information and examples.
 f. Provide a concluding statement or section that follows from and supports the information or explanation presented.

DIGITAL PERSPECTIVES

Writing to Sources

This assignment gives students the opportunity to write about the performances they saw in class. As they consider the way the performances brought the text to life, remind students to provide evidence for their evaluations. For more support, see **Writing to Sources: Drama Review.**

Reflect on Your Writing

1. Responses will vary. If students need support, then have them consider where in the process they were bogged down or could not decide what to write.
2. Responses will vary. Students might consider revising to improve the clarity of their language, to add evidence, or to eliminate unnecessary details.
3. **Why These Words?** Responses will vary. Have students list specific examples of words they have chosen that will help them convey their ideas.

Evidence Log Support students in completing their Evidence Log. This paced activity will help prepare them for the Performance-Based Assessment at the end of the unit.

FORMATIVE ASSESSMENT

Writing to Sources

If students struggle to understand how to write an effective drama review, **then** provide more outside examples, including a review of a performance of this play. For Reteach and Practice, see **Writing to Sources: Drama Review (RP).**

Selection Test

Administer *The Diary of Anne Frank*, Act II Selection Test, which is available in both print and digital formats online in Assessments.

PERSONALIZE FOR LEARNING

English Language Support

Providing Support When writing an opinion piece, writers are sharing their thoughts and ideas. What separates a substantive opinion piece from just an opinion is support or evidence. Remind students that for every opinion that they share in their writing, they need to back it up with evidence. Strong arguments and opinions always rely on evidence. Provide examples of sentence starters like: I believe . . . because . . . or I think . . . as demonstrated by . . .
ALL LEVELS

PLANNING
WHOLE-CLASS LEARNING • FRANK FAMILY AND WORLD WAR II TIMELINE

Frank Family and World War II Timeline

Summary

The "Frank Family and World War II Timeline" illustrates important events during the war itself and during the lives of the Frank family. Otto Frank took steps to bring his family to safety, moving it out of Germany to the Netherlands after Hitler came to power. Unfortunately, seven years later the Nazis invaded the Netherlands. Two years after the invasion, the Nazis sent an order telling Margot Frank to go to a labor camp, so the family went into hiding and was later joined by others. Two years later—mere months after the Allies invaded Europe to throw out the Nazis—the family was discovered, arrested, and sent to concentration camps. World War II ended the following year. After the war, Anne's diary was published and Adolf Eichmann was tried for war crimes.

> ### Insight
> This selection gives students an overview of World War II. It also shows how events during the war did and did not affect one family involved in it. Positive large-scale events, like the Allied invasion, can fail to help many individuals.

🔊 AUDIO SUMMARIES
Audio summaries of "Frank Family and World War II Timeline" are available online in both English and Spanish in the Interactive Teacher's Edition or Unit Resources. Assigning these summaries prior to reviewing the selection may help students build additional background knowledge and set a context for their first review.

ESSENTIAL QUESTION:
How do we remember the past?

Connection to Essential Question

This selection shows a chronological summary of the past. The timeline describe events, but these straightforward descriptions might not be what individuals remember about the past. For example, people such as the Franks might have remembered how it felt to be arrested, but that memory of an event would not appear in a timeline.

Connection to Performance Tasks

Whole-Class Learning Performance Task This timeline allows students to see key historical events related to World War II. It is an important resource for students as they prepare for the Performance Task.

Unit Performance-Based Assessment This selection shows the terrible tragedies that happened, both on a personal scale and in their full scope. It also shows that the Nazis were ultimately defeated and prevented from doing any more harm.

WHOLE-CLASS LEARNING PERFORMANCE TASK
How are historical events reflected in the play *The Diary of Anne Frank?*

UNIT PERFORMANCE-BASED ASSESSMENT
How can literature help us remember and honor the victims of the Holocaust?

DIGITAL PERSPECTIVES Audio Video Document Annotation Highlights EL Highlights Online Assessment

LESSON RESOURCES

	Making Meaning	Language Development	Effective Expression
Lesson	First Review Close Review Analyze the Media	Media Vocabulary	Writing to Compare
Instructional Standards	**RI.10** By the end of the year, read and comprehend literary nonfiction . . .		**RI.7** Evaluate the advantages and disadvantages . . . **W.2** Write informative/explanatory texts . . . **W.2.a** Introduce a topic... **W.2.b** Develop the topic . . .
STUDENT RESOURCES Available online in the Interactive Student Edition or Unit Resources	🔊 Selection Audio 📄 First-Review Guide: Media–Art and Photography 📄 Close-Review Guide: Media–Art and Photography	📄 Word Network	📄 Evidence Log
TEACHER RESOURCES Selection Resources Available online in the Interactive Teacher's Edition or Unit Resources	🔊 Audio Summaries	📄 Media Vocabulary	📄 Writing to Compare: Comparison-and-Contrast Essay
Assessment Available online in Assessments	📄 ✓ Selection Test		
My Resources	📄 A Unit 2 Answer Key is available online and in the Interactive Teacher's Edition.		

Media Support: Frank Family and World War II Timeline

Quantitative Measures

Format and Length: Timeline with graphics and text

Qualitative Measures

Knowledge Demands ①—②—**③**—④—⑤	Individual events are clearly explained, but reader needs prior knowledge about Anne Frank and the Holocaust from earlier in the unit in order to understand the context and details.
Structure ①—**②**—③—④—⑤	Information is presented in short paragraphs of text with dates and pointers to the timeline, making it easy to find information and follow the events chronologically.
Language Conventionality and Clarity ①—**②**—③—④—⑤	Language is clear and explicit, with straightforward reporting of events; present tense is used to describe events; sentences are mostly simple; vocabulary is on-level.
Levels of Meaning/Purpose ①—**②**—③—④—⑤	Purpose is explicit, clear; the timeline shows the connection between events during the Holocaust and in Anne Frank's life. The chronology covers many detailed events.

TEACHING

Jump Start

FIRST READ The Franks were locked away from the world—cut off from what was happening. Ask students to consider how it would feel to be cut off from the world.

Frank Family and World War II Timeline 🔊 📄

What was happing in the world while the Franks hid? How did what was happening impact their lives, even if they did not know about it? Modeling the questions readers might ask as they review "Frank Family and World War II Timeline" brings the timeline alive for students and connects them to the Performance Task assignment. Selection audio is available in the Interactive Teacher's Edition.

Media Vocabulary

Encourage students to discuss the media vocabulary. Have they seen the terms in texts before? Do they use any of them in their speech and writing?

FIRST READ

As they read students should perform the steps of the first read.

NOTICE: Remind students to notice the events above and below the timelines. Remind them to also look at the photos.

ANNOTATE: Encourage students to notice how the events above the timelines connect to the events below them.

CONNECT: Encourage students to make connections to other information they have learned or research they have done about the Holocaust. If they cannot make connections to their own lives, have them consider reading articles or watching documentaries about the Holocaust.

RESPOND: Students will answer questions and write a summary to demonstrate understanding.

Point out to students that while they will always complete the Respond step at the end of the first read, the other steps will probably happen somewhat concurrently. You may wish to print copies of the **First-Read Guide: Nonfiction** for students to use. 📄

194 UNIT 2 • THE HOLOCAUST

MAKING MEANING

Comparing Text to Media

In this lesson, you will examine a timeline showing how events in the Frank family correspond to events in history. You will then compare the information in the timeline and the play *The Diary of Anne Frank*.

THE DIARY OF ANNE FRANK

FRANK FAMILY AND WORLD WAR II TIMELINE

About the Frank Family

Otto and Edith Frank were born in Germany, where they were married and had two daughters—Margot in 1926 and Anne in 1929. The Franks began to worry about the increasing persecution of the Jews under the Nazis. In 1930, when Anne was four, the family emigrated to the Netherlands. There, at least for a while, they felt safe and free. On May 10, 1940, Germany invaded the Netherlands, and the Franks—along with all the other Jews of Holland—were in danger once more.

Frank Family and World War II Timeline

Media Vocabulary

The following words or concepts will be useful to you as you analyze, discuss, and write about timelines.

annotated: containing explanatory notes	• An annotated timeline lists events and the dates on which they occurred. • It may also include brief descriptions or explanations.
chronological: arranged in a sequence that follows the time order of events	The events in a timeline appear in chronological order, with the earliest events on the left and more recent events on the right.
parallel: similar and happening at the same time	Parallel timelines show events that are related to each other and happen during the same time period.

First Read NONFICTION

Apply these strategies as you conduct your first read. You will have an opportunity to complete a close read after your first read.

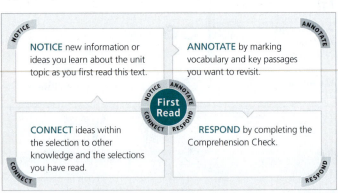

📋 STANDARDS
Reading Informational Text
By the end of the year, read and comprehend literary nonfiction at the high end of the grades 6–8 text complexity band independently and proficiently.

194 UNIT 2 • THE HOLOCAUST

PERSONALIZE FOR LEARNING

English Language Support

Media Vocabulary The media vocabulary on this page may be difficult for English learners. Ask students to read the terms aloud and discuss the concepts. Have them use the terms in sentences.

Have students who are unsure of their use ask clarifying questions, while other students answer with complete sentences. **ALL LEVELS**

MEDIA | TIMELINE

Frank Family and World War II Timeline

BACKGROUND

When you study historical events, it is important to consult a wide variety of text types. There are two broad categories of text type: primary sources and secondary sources.

A **primary source** offers a firsthand, eyewitness view of an event. Primary sources include a wide variety of text types, such as diaries, speeches, and official records. Photographs, maps, and artifacts are also types of primary sources.

- A **secondary source** interprets or analyzes a primary source. Secondary sources are one or more steps removed from an event. Such sources include textbooks, commentaries, encyclopedias, and histories. Interestingly, the play *The Diary of Anne Frank* is a secondary source. However, it is based closely on a primary source—Anne Frank's actual diary.

The annotated timeline on these pages is a secondary source because it pulls together and interprets other texts and images. Some of those texts and images are primary sources. As you read the annotations and look at the images, consider how the various types of texts help you build a deeper understanding of the Frank family, World War II, and the Holocaust. Think about how the events depicted here continue to shape the world today. Use the Notes boxes to make connections and to capture your observations.

NOTES

CROSS-CURRICULAR PERSPECTIVES

Social Studies Before the Jews were taken to concentration camps, they were taken from their homes and communities and put into ghettos. Provide students with background information about one of the most famous ghettos, the Warsaw Ghetto. Use this as an opportunity to discuss Jewish resistance. After discussing the history of the ghetto, explain the Warsaw Ghetto uprising. Ask students to consider this question: Given all they have learned, does this act of defiance surprise them?

TEACHING

Frank Family and World War II Timeline

TIMELINE OF THE FRANK FAMILY

1929: Anne Frank is born in Frankfurt, Germany.

Summer 1933: Alarmed by Nazi actions in Germany, Otto Frank begins the process of moving his family to safety in the Netherlands.

1934: Anne starts kindergarten at the Montessori school in Amsterdam.

1941: Growing Nazi restrictions on the daily lives of Dutch Jews force the Frank girls to attend an all-Jewish school.

June 12, 1942: Otto gives Anne a diary for her thirteenth birthday.

July 6, 1942: The Franks go into hiding after receiving an order for Margot to report to a forced labor camp. They hide in the attic rooms above Mr. Frank's workplace with the help of close friends. Another family, the Van Pels (called the "Van Daans" in her diary), joins them, followed by Fritz Pfeffer ("Dussel"), months later.

1930 — 1935 — 1940

TIMELINE OF WORLD WAR II EVENTS

January 1933: Adolf Hitler comes to power in Germany. Over the next few months, all political parties, except the Nazi Party, are banned. Jews are dismissed from medical, legal, government, and teaching positions.

1935: The Nuremberg Laws are passed in Germany, stripping Jews of their rights as German citizens. Laws passed over the next several years further isolate Jews, including the requirement to wear a yellow Star of David.

September 1, 1939: Germany invades Poland, triggering the beginning of World War II.

May 1940: The Nazis invade the Netherlands. Once in control, they set up a brutal police force, the Gestapo, to administer laws to isolate Dutch Jews from the rest of the Dutch population.

NOTES

196 UNIT 2 • THE HOLOCAUST

DIGITAL PERSPECTIVES

Enriching the Media Collect newsreels from the period and share them with the class to give students a better feel for how people understood what was happening. Point out that people did not see newsreels at home. They were played in movie theaters at the beginning of feature films, the way previews are played today. Include examples of Hitler speaking, the Allied newsreels, and the concentration camp liberations.
(Research to Explore)

August 4, 1944: The hiding place of the Franks is discovered and the families are arrested.

September 3, 1944: All eight of those who hid in the attic are deported from the Netherlands to Auschwitz death camp.

March 1945:* Anne and Margo die of the disease typhus in the Bergan-Belsen concentration camp.

1947: Anne's diary is published in Dutch. Over the next few years it is translated and published in France, Germany, the United States, Japan, and Great Britain.

1960: The hiding place of the Franks is converted into a permanent museum that tells the story of Anne and those who hid with her.

| 1945 | 1950 | 1955 | 1960 |

May 1945: The Allies win as the war in Europe ends.

1960: Adolf Eichmann, one of the last major Nazi figures to be tried, is captured and put on trial in Israel. He is convicted and executed for his role in arranging the transport of Jews to concentration camps and ghettoes, where an estimated six million Jews died.

January 1943: The Battle of Stalingrad marks the turning of the tide against the Nazis.

June 1944: The Allies carry out a successful invasion of France. Their success gives many who live under Nazi occupation hope that the end of the war is near.

NOTES

Frank Family and World War II Timeline

DIGITAL PERSPECTIVES

● CLOSE READ

Reflect on Chronology

Students may have noted key dates and events on the timelines during their first read. Use the timelines to help students understand what was happening in the world while the Franks were hiding. Encourage them to talk about what they noted. You may want to model a close read with the class based on the notes below.

NOTE: Have students note specific events that took place toward the end of World War II or have students participate while you note them.

QUESTION: Guide students to consider what these details might tell them. Ask students what specific events took place, and accept student responses.

Possible response: The Allies invade France a few months before the Franks' hiding place is discovered.

CONCLUDE: Help students to formulate conclusions about the importance of these details in the timelines. Ask students why the writer might have included these details.

Possible response: The writer included these details to help the reader understand the final tragedy of the Franks' experience.

TEACHING

Comprehension Check

Possible responses:

1. The Jews were being dismissed from medical, legal, government, and teaching positions.
2. They lose their rights as German citizens.
3. They received an order for Margot to report to a forced labor camp.
4. conditions in the concentration camps
5. Although the timelines do not say when Anne died, it does tell that the war ended in May 1945, which was about 8 months after the Franks were arrested.
6. The Gestapo administered laws to isolate Dutch Jews from the rest of the Dutch population.

Research

Research to Clarify If students struggle to decide on a detail to research, you may want to suggest that they focus on one of the following topics: the Nuremberg Laws, the German invasion of Poland, the German invasion of the Netherlands, or the Eichmann trial.

Research to Explore If students aren't sure how to go about formulating a research question, suggest that they use their findings from Research to Clarify as a starting point. For example, if students researched the Nuremberg Laws, they might formulate a question such as, *What impact did the Nuremberg Laws have on the Jews of Germany?*

Comprehension Check

Complete the following items after you finish your first read.

1. What was happening to Jews in Germany around the time the Frank family fled to the Netherlands?

2. What happens to Jews when the Nuremberg Laws are passed in 1935?

3. What event prompted the Franks to go into hiding in 1942?

4. What was the cause of death of Anne and her sister Margot?

5. How long after Anne's death did the war in Europe end?

6. 📓 **Notebook** Describe the situation for Dutch Jews at the time the Frank family went into hiding.

RESEARCH

Research to Clarify Choose at least one unfamiliar detail from the timeline. Briefly research that detail. In what way does the information you learned shed light on an aspect of the Holocaust?

Research to Explore Choose something that interested you from the timeline, and formulate a research question you might use to find out more about it.

198 UNIT 2 • THE HOLOCAUST

PERSONALIZE FOR LEARNING

Challenge

Research Have students select an event from the timelines. Have students research the selected topics and create a presentation for the class. The presentation should include at least five points about the event, as well as either charts or photographs from the event. Students should share their presentations with the class and be prepared to answer questions about their topics.

MAKING MEANING

Close Read
Read the timeline again. Write down any new observations that seem important. What **questions** do you have? What can you **conclude**?

Analyze the Media

CITE TEXTUAL EVIDENCE to support your answers.

Notebook Respond to these questions.

1. **(a)** What events in the lives of Anne and her family are recorded in the timeline? **(b) Connect** How do these events relate to the World War II events in the timeline?

2. **Analyze** Describe the organization of the timeline.

3. The timeline entry for July 6, 1942, notes that Anne Frank changed the names of the Van Daans and Dussel in her diary. Why might she have made this choice? Explain your thinking.

4. **Essential Question:** *How do we remember the past?* Consider the two timeline entries from 1960. What do these two events suggest about the ways in which we remember the past?

LANGUAGE DEVELOPMENT

Media Vocabulary

| annotated | chronological | parallel |

1. Choose one of the timeline entries with an illustration. How do the text and illustration combine to express the significance of the entry?

2. **(a)** Which timeline entries identify the beginning of the end for the Nazi war effort? **(b)** What is happening to the Frank family around the same time?

3. Choose a year that is represented with an entry in both timelines. What do the entries suggest about the relationship between the experiences of the Frank family and the events of World War II?

FRANK FAMILY AND WORLD WAR II TIMELINE

WORD NETWORK
Add words related to the Holocaust from the timeline to your Word Network.

Frank Family and World War II Timeline 199

PERSONALIZE FOR LEARNING

English Language Support
Timelines Following information on a timeline can be difficult for students. If students are struggling, break the timelines into smaller periods. Focus on the years 1925 through 1933. There are only three events listed here. Ask students what the first event is. Then have them identify the second and third. Both of these events fall on the same spot on the timelines.

Students will have to look for additional clues to determine which came next. The clues can be found in the event descriptions, such as January of 1933 and Summer of 1933. Ask students how event number 2 caused event number 3. Breaking the timelines down into smaller pieces may make it easier for students to absorb. **ALL LEVELS**

DIGITAL PERSPECTIVES

Jump Start

CLOSE READ Timelines are helpful tools in understanding how events unfolded. They also provide background information and context. Assign two students to read the first several entries on the timeline. One student will read the Frank side and one the World War II side. Have them read the events in the order in which they occurred to help bring to life how these events were related and took place simultaneously.

Close Read
If needed, model close reading by using the Close Read note in the Interactive Teacher's Edition.
Remind groups to use Accountable Talk in their discussions and to support one another as they complete the close review.

Analyze the Media
Possible responses:
1. (a) birth dates, when they moved to the Netherlands, when Anne started school, when she started a Jewish school, when she got her diary, when they went into hiding, when they are discovered and deported, and when Anne's diary was published. **DOK 1** (b) The war events often cause the events that happen to Anne. **DOK 2**
2. They are organized in chronological order from left to right. **DOK 2**
3. Anne may have changed their names to protect their true identities.
4. One of the entries shows how we honor people who have suffered; the other shows how we work to punish those responsible for evil.

Media Vocabulary
1. Responses will vary.
2. (a) The 1943 Battle of Stalingrad and the Allies conducting a successful invasion of France show the weakening of Nazi power. (b) During this time, the Franks are captured, arrested, and sent to concentration camps.
3. Responses will vary.

For more support, see **Media Vocabulary**.

FORMATIVE ASSESSMENT
Analyze the Media
If students struggle to interpret how events in the Franks' lives parallel those of World War II, **then** have them find an event from the Frank Family timeline and read the events from the WWII timeline that preceded and succeeded it.

Whole-Class Learning 199

TEACHING

Writing to Compare

As students prepare to compare the play with the timeline, they will consider what each medium offers for those who want to learn about the time period.

Planning and Prewriting
Compare Play and Timeline Techniques
Remind students that when they evaluate each medium, they aren't necessarily determining whether the medium is right or wrong. Guide students to look for evidence that shows strong or weak expression of the topics listed in the chart.

Responses may vary.

Possible responses:

As students complete the chart, they will see that the play includes the personal and emotional experiences of a family against a backdrop of the war. The timeline provides the bigger picture of events without much support or elaboration.

Possible responses:

1. Responses may vary, but students should describe which medium helped them better understand and relate to the historical details.

2. Responses may vary. Students may say that the timeline is better at explaining the military motivations related to World War II, but the play is better at explaining the personal motivations related to the hiding and capture of Jews in Amsterdam during the period.

EFFECTIVE EXPRESSION

THE DIARY OF ANNE FRANK

FRANK FAMILY AND WORLD WAR II TIMELINE

Writing to Compare

Both the play *The Diary of Anne Frank* and the Frank Family and World War II Timeline describe aspects of the same topic, the Holocaust. Deepen your understanding of the topic by comparing what you learn from literature with what you learn from factual information and pictures.

Assignment
Goodrich and Hackett's play *The Diary of Anne Frank* is a dramatic adaptation of the events described in Anne Frank's real-life diary. The play and the timeline use different strategies to combine information about historical events and personal family issues. Write a **comparison-and-contrast essay** in which you explain similar and different information you learned from the two texts. Explain how each text might be useful for different reading purposes.

Planning and Prewriting

Compare Play and Timeline Techniques Think about the kinds of information you learned from reading the play and from reading and looking at the timeline. Use the chart to capture your thoughts.

WHAT I LEARNED ABOUT...	FROM THE PLAY	FROM THE TIMELINE
Historical Events	a. See possible responses in Teacher's Edition.	
Causes of Events		
Effects of Events		

Notebook Respond to these questions.

1. Which medium presents historical details more accurately and effectively? Explain.

2. Which medium is better at revealing **motivations,** the reasons for people's actions? Explain.

PERSONALIZE FOR LEARNING

Strategic Support
1944–1945 Some students may struggle to complete the chart. Encourage them to select the events that took place from 1944 to 1945 and add them to the chart. Focus on Anne being discovered and World War II ending. Work with students to complete the chart using the play and the timelines.

ESSENTIAL QUESTION: How do we remember the past?

Drafting

Outline Decide the order in which you will present details in your essay. Block organization will work well for this task, allowing you to explain what you learned and did not learn from one text and then the other. Complete the outline to organize your ideas.

I. Introduction State your central idea and the two works you will compare.
   _____

II. Play: *The Diary of Anne Frank*
   A. What I learned from the play _____
      _____
   B. What I did or could not learn from the play _____
      _____

III. Timeline: Frank Family and World War II Timeline
   A. What I learned from the timeline _____
      _____
   B. What I did or could not learn from the timeline _____
      _____

IV. Conclusion Explain how each type of text offers information that is useful in different ways.
   _____

Choose Strong Examples Scan or reread both sources to make sure you have chosen passages and details that clearly support your ideas. You should have at least one strong supporting detail for every point you make.

Support Your Conclusion In the final paragraph, present a broad statement about the advantages and disadvantages of using different types of texts for different purposes.

Reviewing and Revising After drafting your essay, review the assignment, and then reread your essay. Make sure you have met the requirements of the assignment. Ask yourself the following questions:

- Do I clearly explain what I learned from each text?
- Do I present information in a clear and logical order?
- Do I clearly explain how the two types of texts are useful in different ways?

EVIDENCE LOG

Before moving on to a new selection, go to your Evidence Log and record what you have learned from the play *The Diary of Anne Frank* and the Frank Family and World War II Timeline.

STANDARDS

Reading Informational Text
Evaluate the advantages and disadvantages of using different mediums to present a particular topic or idea.

Writing
Write informative/explanatory texts to examine a topic and convey ideas, concepts, and information through the selection, organization, and analysis of relevant content.
a. Introduce a topic clearly, previewing what is to follow; organize ideas, concepts, and information into broader categories; include formatting, graphics, and multimedia when useful to aiding comprehension.
b. Develop the topic with relevant, well-chosen facts, definitions, concrete details, quotations, or other information and examples.

DIGITAL PERSPECTIVES

Drafting

Outline Encourage students to use the charts they created during Prewriting to help them formulate a central idea. Explain that they need to find additional information in the text as they develop their ideas during drafting.

Choose Strong Examples Suggest that students focus on those parts of the play that are related to the information in the timelines. Otherwise, students may be overwhelmed by the amount of information in the play.

Support Your Conclusion Make clear to students that they need to the value of each medium.

Reviewing and Revising

As students revise, encourage them to review their draft to be sure they have explained their thinking clearly. Ask them to make sure they have supported their ideas with evidence from both texts. Finally, remind students to check for grammar, usage, and mechanics.

For more support, see **Writing to Compare: Comparison-Contrast Essay.**

Evidence Log Support students in completing their Evidence Log. This paced activity will help prepare them for the Performance-Based Assessment at the end of the unit.

FORMATIVE ASSESSMENT

Writing to Compare
- **If** students struggle to compare and contrast the play and the timeline, **then** ask them to make a Venn diagram showing the similarities and differenced between each medium.

PERSONALIZE FOR LEARNING

Challenge

Graphic Organizers Review what graphic organizers are and how they help writers. Throughout this unit, students used charts and webs to help organize their thoughts. Have students return to these graphic organizers to help complete their assignments. Draw students' attention to the chart on the previous page. Ask students to suggest how they can turn information in the chart into sentences in their essays.

TEACHING

Jump Start

Changes happen over time. This is true of all of history, and the Holocaust is no exception. Remind students that millions of people, including Anne Frank, died in concentration camps during World War II. Ask students to consider this: when Hitler came to power, his first act was not to send the Jews to concentration camps. This evolved out of policies that first placed restrictions on what Jews could do and grew from there.

Write an Explanatory Essay

Review the writing assignment with the class. Make sure students understand how it connects to the story of Anne Frank and to the events laid out on the timeline.

Students should complete the assignment using word processing software to take advantage of editing tools and features.

Elements of an Explanatory Essay

Remind students that an explanatory essay is a true story and it explains a piece of information. A successful explanatory essay shares information with the reader in a clear, concise, and cohesive fashion. It provides evidence to back up claims and educates the reader about a topic.

MAKE IT INTERACTIVE

Project "The Grand Mosque of Paris" from the Interactive Teacher's Edition for the class. Refer students to the list of elements of an Explanatory Essay on this page. As a group, identify examples of these elements in the projected essay.

Academic Vocabulary

Ask students to use academic vocabulary words in sentences that they might use in their essays.

PERFORMANCE TASK: WRITING FOCUS

WRITING TO SOURCES
- THE DIARY OF ANNE FRANK
- FRANK FAMILY AND WORLD WAR II TIMELINE

Write an Explanatory Essay

The characters in the play *The Diary of Anne Frank* are based on real people who faced the terrifying threat of discovery, arrest, persecution, and death. In this unit, background information about the time period and a timeline of historical events provide context for the action of the play.

Assignment

Drawing on information from the Historical Perspectives feature and the Frank Family and World War II Timeline, write an **explanatory essay** addressing the following question:

> How are historical events reflected in the play *The Diary of Anne Frank*?

Cite specific historical events, and explain how the playwrights choose to filter them through the action in key scenes of the play. Explain how outside events affected the moods of the residents of the Secret Annex and their relationships with one another. Conclude your essay with a judgment about how well the playwrights capture the relationship between the outside world of the war and the inside world of the attic.

Tool Kit
Student Model of an Explanatory Text

ACADEMIC VOCABULARY
As you craft your explanatory essay, consider using some of the academic vocabulary you learned in the beginning of the unit.

theorize
sustain
declaration
pronounce
enumerate

Elements of an Explanatory Essay

An **explanatory essay** provides information about a subject. A well-written essay is organized so that the controlling idea is supported by reasons, facts, and examples.

An effective explanatory essay contains these elements:

- an introduction with a clear thesis statement
- a logical organization and effective conclusion
- valid reasoning and evidence, including relevant facts, details, and examples that support the thesis
- appropriate transitions to clarify relationships among ideas
- precise language and vocabulary
- formal language
- varied sentences that include accurate punctuation

STANDARDS
Writing
• Write informative/explanatory texts to examine a topic and convey ideas, concepts, and information through the selection, organization, and analysis of relevant content.
• Write routinely over extended time frames and shorter time frames for a range of discipline-specific tasks, purposes, and audiences.

Model Explanatory Essay For a model of a well-crafted explanatory essay, see the Launch Text, "The Grand Mosque of Paris."

Challenge yourself to find all of the elements of an explanatory essay in the text. You will have an opportunity to review these elements as you prepare to write your own essay.

202 UNIT 2 • THE HOLOCAUST

AUTHOR'S PERSPECTIVE Kelly Gallagher, M.Ed.

The Best Writer in the Room Intensive modeling is one of the most effective ways to improve writing instruction. When teachers model at every stage of the writing process, they stop *assigning* writing and start *teaching* it. While you are teaching writing through this Performance Task, show your students how you attack these parts of the assignment:

Prewriting Brainstorm counterclaims and ask students to add their own ideas to your list. List types of evidence you could use.

Drafting Outline the argument and draft alongside students.

Revising Use your model or a student model as an example.

Do this work in front of students each time. While it may seem more efficient to follow the same steps with each class or show a perfectly polished essay, don't take this path. If you authentically model the work of writing, students may be more open to the work of writing. It is important for the students to see the teacher struggle a bit with the work.

ESSENTIAL QUESTION: How do we remember the past?

DIGITAL PERSPECTIVES

Prewriting / Planning

Draft a Working Thesis A strong thesis does more that just state the topic of an essay—it introduces a controlling idea that sparks readers' curiosity. Notice how the opening paragraphs of the Launch Text build to an effective thesis:

> *Some of those children found refuge in the Grand Mosque of Paris, where heroic Muslims saved Jews from the Nazis.*
> —"The Grand Mosque of Paris"

After reading this thesis, readers might ask themselves, "What is the Grand Mosque of Paris?" or "How did Muslims save Jews?" The rest of the essay provides the answers.

Drafting a working thesis can help you develop ideas and choose supporting evidence from the selections. You will take a position on how well the playwrights of *The Diary of Anne Frank* capture the influence of historical events on the families hidden in the attic, as well as explaining what that relationship was. As you continue to write your essay, you may revise your thesis or even change it entirely.

Working Thesis: _____
_____.

Gather Evidence from Sources Your essay will explain how historical events are reflected in the play *The Diary of Anne Frank*. Review the sources to find evidence that supports your thesis. A chart can help you identify useful evidence and make connections among the background information, timeline, and play.

FACTS AND DETAILS Events described in Historical Perspectives and the Timeline	EXAMPLES Characters' actions, descriptions of the setting, and other details from the play that reflect each event

Take Accurate Notes While you collect evidence for your essay, think about how you might use each detail you find. Use these strategies to cite evidence you collect:

- **Exact quotations:** If the precise words from the source are important, use exact quotations. Use quotation marks in your notes, and identify the source.
- **Paraphrase:** Restate ideas in your own words to clarify.

EVIDENCE LOG
Review your Evidence Log and identify key details you may want to cite in your explanatory essay.

STANDARDS
Writing
Write informative/explanatory texts to examine a topic and convey ideas, concepts, and information through the selection, organization, and analysis of relevant content.

a. Introduce a topic clearly, previewing what is to follow; organize ideas, concepts, and information into broader categories; include formatting, graphics, and multimedia when useful to aiding comprehension.

b. Develop the topic with relevant, well-chosen facts, definitions, concrete details, quotations, or other information and examples.

Prewriting/Planning

Draft a Working Thesis Guide students to understand how to construct a thesis statement. Explain that the thesis statement is what their essay is about—what point they are trying to get across. Provide an example, such as: Increasingly strict laws targeting Jews led to the Holocaust; by beginning with minor restrictions, each increase in severity seemed to be a logical step toward the ultimate horror.

Gather Evidence From Sources Reinforce for students that while *The Diary of Anne Frank* is based on real events, it is a fictionalized version of history and of real people's lives. Some of the facts in the play may be related from characters' perspectives and are therefore not entirely trustworthy or accurate. Students' observations of these differences are useful points to note for use in their essays.

Take Accurate Notes Review with students to make sure they are accurately connecting facts from the historical sources to examples from the play. Guide students to resist the urge to quote excessively from the sources and to balance quoting with paraphrasing. Guide students in careful, complete, and accurate paraphrasing.

PERSONALIZE FOR LEARNING

Strategic Support

Evidence Explain to students that when gathering information, they should distinguish between information that they knew before, or background knowledge, and information they have gathered through this unit. Background information provides a strong basis for understanding a topic and it is vital for comprehending world events. When writing an essay, background information may support the writer's understanding, but the writer must be able to cite evidence to support the essay. Remind students that this evidence comes from the text.

TEACHING

Drafting

Evaluate Your Evidence After students review the evidence they have, encourage them to gather more information if necessary.

Choose a Logical Organization Students may want build an outline to help them see the structure that works best for the details they have gathered. If students use word-processing software, they can copy and paste paragraph main ideas until they find an organization that suits their goals.

Build to a Strong Conclusion The final part of each student's outline should be the conclusion which restates their main idea. Encourage students to make sure that the conclusion follows clearly from the details in the body of their essay.

Write a First Draft For many students, the most important part of writing a first draft is simply getting their ideas on paper. Tell them that many writers don't worry too much about spelling, grammar, or cohesion in their first drafts. Instead they write down their important ideas, knowing that they come back later to improve organization, correct grammar, and add details.

PERFORMANCE TASK: WRITING FOCUS

Drafting

Evaluate Your Evidence Take time to consider the strength of the evidence you collect. Ask yourself these questions:

- Do I have enough evidence? _____

- Which evidence provides the strongest support for my thesis? Why? _____

- Will I be able to answer most of the questions my readers are likely to have? If not, what other information do I need? _____

- Did I find any evidence that contradicts, or goes against, my thesis? If so, should I revise my thesis? If so, how? _____

Choose a Logical Organization Use an organizational structure that makes sense for your essay. You might consider one of the following structures:

- **Chronology:** Explain events in the order in which they happened. Your essay might begin by explaining how historical events that took place before the beginning of the play are reflected in the opening scene. Then, continue to write about events following time order.

- **Subject:** You might organize your essay by general topics. For example, you might begin by explaining how historical events are reflected in the play's setting. In the next sections of your essay, you might talk about the play's characters and their actions.

After choosing your organization, create an outline to follow as you write.

Build to a Strong Conclusion The assignment contains specific requirements for writing an effective conclusion. It asks you to make a judgment about how well Frances Goodrich and Albert Hackett, the authors of the play, show the influence of large historical events in the outside world on the interior world of the attic. Be sure that your conclusion follows logically from the evidence you present in the body of your essay.

Write a First Draft Use your outline to guide your first draft. While writing, you may think of additional ideas to include, but be sure they are relevant and are clearly connected to the topic. Finally, end your draft with a strong conclusion.

STANDARDS
Writing
Write informative/explanatory texts to examine a topic and convey ideas, concepts, and information through the selection, organization, and analysis of relevant content.
  b. Develop the topic with relevant, well-chosen facts, definitions, concrete details, quotations, or other information and examples.
  f. Provide a concluding statement or section that follows from and supports the information or explanation presented.

AUTHOR'S PERSPECTIVE — Jim Cummins, Ph.D.

Sentence Frames Students learning English may be challenged by a blank page. Support them with scaffolding to help them organize their explanatory essays and flesh out their outlines. They may benefit from using sentence frames like the following to help them map out their writing.

Introduction: Laws targeting Jewish people would eventually lead to the Holocaust in several ways: _____.

Evidence from the text: My point of view is supported by the fact that _____.

Counterclaim: Others may not say that laws targeting Jewish people led to the Holocaust because _____, but this view is problematic because _____.

Remind students that the writing process is recursive, and they will be able to refine their outlines and sentence frames as they draft. These are simply tools to help them organize their thoughts before they begin writing.

ESSENTIAL QUESTION: How do we remember the past?

DIGITAL PERSPECTIVES

LANGUAGE DEVELOPMENT: AUTHOR'S STYLE

Revising Sentences by Combining With Conjunctions

Compound sentences are made up of two or more independent clauses, which—if separated—could each form a complete sentence.

Coordinating conjunctions are words that can join independent clauses into a compound sentence. The conjunctions *and, but, or, nor, so, yet,* and *for* can help make your writing smoother by connecting too closely related ideas. You can also use coordinating conjunctions to revise run-on sentences or to improve two short, choppy sentences.

Read It

These sentences based on *The Diary of Anne Frank* show coordinating conjunctions used to join closely related independent clauses.

- The residents of the Secret Annex must remain silent, <u>or</u> the Gestapo will discover them (shows alternatives)
- Anne constantly annoys Dussel, <u>yet</u> they manage to live together. (shows contrast)
- Mrs. Frank nearly evicts the Van Daans, <u>for</u> Mr. Van Daan has been stealing food. (shows cause)

Write It

As you draft your essay, choose coordinating conjunctions that help you connect important ideas and make your writing smoother.

ORIGINAL	COORDINATING CONJUNCTION	REVISION
In 1933, Germany stopped Jewish involvement in the medical profession. Jewish doctors lost their jobs.	*so* (shows effect)	In 1933, Germany stopped Jewish involvement in the medical profession, <u>so</u> Jewish doctors lost their jobs.
Nuremburg Laws were targeted at Jews. Even Christians with Jewish grandparents were considered Jews.	*but* (shows contrast)	Nuremburg Laws were targeted at Jews, <u>but</u> even Christians with Jewish grandparents were considered Jews.
In 1938, Jews were excluded from public schools. They were barred from cinemas and theaters.	*and* (shows addition)	In 1938, Jews were excluded from public schools, *and* they were barred from cinemas and theaters.

TIP

PUNCTUATION
Make sure to correctly punctuate sentences with coordinating conjunctions.

- Use a comma before a coordinating conjunction in a compound sentence.
- If the clauses are very short, the comma that precedes the coordinating conjunction may be omitted.

STANDARDS
Language
- Demonstrate command of the conventions of standard English grammar and usage when writing or speaking.
- Demonstrate command of the conventions of standard English capitalization, punctuation, and spelling when writing.
- Use knowledge of language and its conventions when writing, speaking, reading, or listening.

Revising Sentences by Combining with Conjunctions

Read It
Explain to students that they should use conjunctions to connect their ideas and make their writing flow better. Point out to students that they use conjunctions in their everyday speech and writing, probably without thinking about it. For example, "I would hand in my homework, but I left it at home." "She wanted to get a better grade, so she spent extra time studying." Have students suggest their own sentences that could be revised with a coordinating conjunction.

Write It
As students prepare to revise their draft, they should have an opportunity to practice using coordinating conjunctions. Give students a topic. Ask two students to provide short sentences about the topic. Next, ask a volunteer to use a conjunction to combine the two sentences. Through serious or humorous topics, students will practice this skill. For example, for the topic pets, "I like dogs. I do not like cats." Combined: "I like dogs, but I do not like cats."

PERSONALIZE FOR LEARNING

English Language Support
Read Aloud To emphasize the importance of conjunctions, use the sentences in the chart to reinforce the benefit of conjunctions in constructing sentences. Read each short sentence aloud. Then read the new sentence with the conjunction, emphasizing the conjunction as you say it. Have students share their opinions about the differences. **ALL LEVELS**

TEACHING

Revising

Evaluating Your Draft
Self-editing is one of the great challenges of writing. Remind students that good writers always revise their work. Have students use the checklist as a starting point.

Revising for Focus and Organization
Logical Organization Suggest that students use highlighters to underline the main idea of each paragraph. This will help them track the organization of their draft. Looking at this outline version of their text will allow them to see where they may need to reorder paragraphs or add transitions to help readers follow their ideas.

Revising for Evidence and Elaboration
Depth of Support If students decide they need to elaborate on their main points, encourage them to go back to the selections to find more information.

Revising for Word Choice and Style
Formal Style Encourage students to strengthen the formal tone of their drafts by replacing any slang or informal language. Students should also confirm that all their sentences express complete ideas, as sentence fragments can add an informality to a piece of writing.

PERFORMANCE TASK: WRITING FOCUS

Revising

Evaluating Your Draft
Use this checklist to evaluate the effectiveness of your first draft. Then, use your evaluation and the instruction on this page to guide your revision.

FOCUS AND ORGANIZATION	EVIDENCE AND ELABORATION	CONVENTIONS
☐ Begins with an introduction that presents a clear thesis.	☐ Supports the thesis and makes clear connections among ideas.	☐ Attends to the norms and conventions of the discipline, especially the correct use and punctuation of transitions.
☐ Includes valid reasoning and evidence, including relevant facts and details.	☐ Provides adequate support for all of the main points in the essay.	☐ Uses coordinating conjunctions to ensure smooth sentences and connections between important ideas.
☐ Provides a concluding section that logically completes the essay.	☐ Explains ideas clearly and completely.	
☐ Follows a logical and effective organization.	☐ Uses vocabulary that clearly informs and explains.	
☐ Uses transitions to show the connections between ideas.	☐ Establishes and maintains a formal style.	

🔠 WORD NETWORK
Include words from your Word Network in your explanatory essay.

Revising for Focus and Organization
Logical Organization Reread your draft, paying attention to the organization of ideas. Is each main point stated clearly? Does each point connect to the thesis? Do any ideas or evidence seem out of place? If so, do they belong in another section or should they be deleted?

Transitions When you transition from one idea to the next, do you use words and phrases such as *therefore, on the other hand, in contrast, similarly,* and *next* to show the relationship between ideas? If not, revise to make it easier on your readers to follow the path of your ideas.

Revising for Evidence and Elaboration
Depth of Support Review your draft. Identify your main points by underlining them. Then, read the information that follows. Have you provided at least one strong detail to support your point? Have you provided at least one example from the selections? If not, add support.

Revising for Word Choice and Style
Formal Style An explanatory essay is a formal piece of writing. To write formally, avoid slang words, imprecise words, and contractions. Use precise words that are appropriate for the topic. Consider these examples:

Informal and Imprecise: *A lot of important things went down during World War II.*

Formal and Precise: *Many significant events happened during World War II.*

📋 STANDARDS
Writing
Write informative/explanatory texts to examine a topic and convey ideas, concepts, and information through the selection, organization, and analysis of relevant content.
  c. Use appropriate and varied transitions to create cohesion and clarify the relationships among ideas and concepts.
  d. Use precise language and domain-specific vocabulary to inform about or explain the topic.
  e. Establish and maintain a formal style.

HOW LANGUAGE WORKS

Verb Tenses When writing an essay, it is important to maintain consistent verb tense. When writing about history, writers should always use the past tense. Ask students to consider why this is the case. Then ask students to consider when they would write in the present tense. Have students provide examples. Finally, have students provide examples of when they would use the future tense in their writing. Have students return to their essays and check to make sure they used the past tense for all of their verbs.

ESSENTIAL QUESTION: How do we remember the past?

DIGITAL PERSPECTIVES

PEER REVIEW

Exchange essays with a classmate. Use the checklist to evaluate your classmate's explanatory essay and provide supportive feedback.

1. Does the thesis state a controlling idea and make readers curious about the subject?

   ☐ yes   ☐ no   If no, explain what element the thesis is missing.

2. Are ideas clearly stated and supported by facts and examples?

   ☐ yes   ☐ no   If no, point out which ideas need more support.

3. Does the conclusion logically wrap up the essay?

   ☐ yes   ☐ no   If no, tell why the conclusion needs improvement.

4. What is the strongest part of your classmate's essay?

   _____

Editing and Proofreading

Edit for Conventions Reread your draft for accuracy and consistency. Correct errors in grammar and word usage. Then, check to make sure that commas precede coordinating conjunctions linking independent clauses.

Proofread for Accuracy Read your draft carefully, looking for errors in spelling and punctuation. Check quotations to be sure you have used quotation marks around the exact words from the original source. Review spellings of proper nouns, including the names of people and places.

Publishing and Presenting

Create a final version of your essay. Trade essays with a partner and read each other's work. Review and comment on your partner's essay, maintaining a polite and respectful tone. Discuss your thesis statements and the evidence you each used to support your points.

Reflecting

Think about what you learned by writing your essay and what you learned by reading your partner's essay. What could you do differently the next time you need to write an explanatory essay?

STANDARDS
Writing
With some guidance and support from peers and adults, develop and strengthen writing as needed by planning, revising, editing, rewriting, or trying a new approach, focusing on how well purpose and audience have been addressed.

Peer Review

Peer review is a helpful tool in the editing process. Writers often see their own writing as they imagine it to be, as opposed to what is actually written on the paper. Having peers review each other's work will likely shed light on mistakes they made or important information they overlooked. Remind students to use the checklist to maintain their focus when they do peer review.

Publishing and Presenting

Remind students that this is an opportunity to clarify and fine-tune their thoughts before they turn in and present their essays. As students review their classmates' essays, remind them to:

- Keep comments positive.
- Offer helpful suggestions for revision.
- Use formal rather than informal language.

PERSONALIZE FOR LEARNING

English Language Support

Punctuation One of the great challenges of completing a piece of writing is the editing for punctuation. As English learners saw in *The Diary of Anne Frank,* punctuation is a powerful tool for conveying a message. Review punctuation conventions with students.

Write the following sentences on the board and have students supply the correct punctuation:

- Which group helped save Jews from the Nazis (question mark)
- No Jew was safe from arrest or deportation (period)
- In Paris it was a terrifying time (comma after Paris, period at end of sentence) Ask: Do your sentences end with the proper punctuation? Do they contain the proper punctuation within themselves? Focusing on punctuation in the review process will help students in their editing. **ALL LEVELS**

OVERVIEW

SMALL-GROUP LEARNING

How do we remember the past?

By recording their experiences, Holocaust survivors ensured that their powerful stories would always be known to future generations. During Small-Group Learning, students will read selections that tell the stories of some of the people who lived through the Holocaust.

Small-Group Learning Strategies ▶

Review the Learning Strategies with students and explain that as they work through Small-Group Learning they will develop strategies to work in small-group environments.

- Have students watch the video on Small-Group Learning Strategies.
- A video on this topic is available online in the Professional Development Center.

You may wish to discuss some action items to add to the chart as a class before students complete it on their own. For example, for "Participate fully," you might solicit the following from students:

- Ask questions.
- Offer suggestions to help create your group's presentation.

Block Scheduling

Each day in this Pacing Plan represents a 40–50 minute class period. Teachers using block scheduling may combine days to reflect their class schedule. In addition, teachers may revise pacing to differentiate and support core instruction by integrating components and resources as students require.

Pacing Plan

OVERVIEW: SMALL-GROUP LEARNING

ESSENTIAL QUESTION:

How do we remember the past?

Much of what we know about the Holocaust comes from the writings and recollections of those who experienced the events firsthand. You will work in a group to continue your explorations into this time in history, focusing on the important role of personal accounts.

Small-Group Learning Strategies

Throughout your life, in school, in your community, and in your career, you will continue to learn and work with others.

Review these strategies and the actions you can take to practice them. Add ideas of your own for each step. Use these strategies during Small-Group Learning.

STRATEGY	ACTION PLAN
Prepare	• Complete your assignments so that you are prepared for group work. • Organize your thinking so you can contribute to your group's discussion. •
Participate fully	• Make eye contact to signal that you are listening and taking in what is being said. • Use text evidence when making a point. •
Support others	• Build on ideas from others in your group. • Invite others who have not yet spoken to do so. •
Clarify	• Paraphrase the ideas of others to ensure that your understanding is correct. • Ask follow-up questions. •

208 UNIT 2 • THE HOLOCAUST

SCAN FOR MULTIMEDIA

Pacing Plan:

Unit Introduction (1, 2) — Introduce Whole-Class Learning (3) — *The Diary of Anne Frank*, Act I (4, 5, 6, 7, 8) — *The Diary of Anne Frank*, Act II (9, 10, 11, 12, 13) — Media: Frank Family and World War II Timelines (14, 15) — Performance Task (16, 17, 18)

CONTENTS

DIARY ENTRIES

from Anne Frank: The Diary of a Young Girl
Anne Frank

Anne Frank's diary is both a first-person account of a family in hiding and the coming-of-age story of a young girl trying to live a normal life in a world gone mad.

SPEECH

Acceptance Speech for the Nobel Peace Prize
Elie Wiesel

Wiesel's acceptance speech is as much about safeguarding the future as it is about remembering the past.

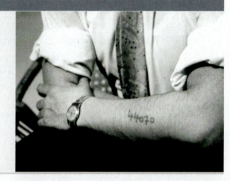

MEDIA: GRAPHIC NOVEL

from Maus
Art Spiegelman

In this graphic novel, the author tells the story of his father's experiences as a Polish Jew living under Nazi occupation.

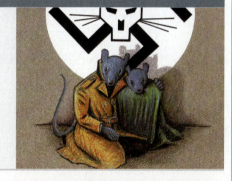

PERFORMANCE TASK

SPEAKING AND LISTENING FOCUS

Deliver a Multimedia Presentation

After reading, your group will plan and deliver an explanatory multimedia presentation based on the selections in this section and your own research.

Overview: Small-Group Learning 209

DIGITAL PERSPECTIVES

Contents

Selections Circulate among groups as they preview the selections. You might encourage groups to discuss any knowledge they already have about any of the selections or the situations and settings shown in the photographs. Students may wish to take a poll within their group to determine which selections students have heard of before.

Remind students that communicating and collaborating in groups is an important skill that they will use throughout their lives—in school, in their careers, and in their community.

Performance Task

Deliver a Multimedia Presentation Give groups time to read about and briefly discuss the multimedia presentation they will create after reading. Encourage students to do some preliminary thinking about the types of media they may want to use. This may help focus their subsequent reading and group discussion.

OVERVIEW

SMALL-GROUP LEARNING

Working as a Team

1. **Discuss the Topic** Remind groups to let all members share their responses. You may wish to set a time limit for this discussion.

2. **List Your Rules** You may want to have groups share their lists of rules and consolidate them into a master list to be displayed and followed by all groups.

3. **Apply the Rules** As you circulate among the groups, ensure that students are staying on task. Consider a short time limit for this step.

4. **Name Your Group** This task can be creative and fun. If students have trouble coming up with a name, suggest that they think of something related to the unit topic. Encourage groups to share their names with the class.

5. **Create a Communication Plan** Encourage groups to include in their plans agreed-upon times during the day to share ideas. They should also devise a method for recording and saving their communications.

Accountable Talk

Remind students that groups should communicate politely. You can post these Accountable Talk suggestions and encourage students to add their own. Students should:

Remember to . . .
Ask clarifying questions.

Which sounds like . . .
Can you please repeat what you said?
Would you give me an example?
I think you said _____. Did I understand you correctly?

Remember to . . .
Explain your thinking.

Which sounds like . . .
I believe _____ is true because _____.
I feel _____ because _____.

Remember to . . .
Build on the ideas of others.

Which sounds like . . .
When _____ said _____, it made me think of _____.

OVERVIEW: SMALL-GROUP LEARNING

Working as a Team

1. **Discuss the Topic** In your group, discuss the following question:

   What do you think you can learn about the Holocaust from diaries, interviews, and personal accounts?

   As you take turns sharing your positions, be sure to provide reasons for your choice. After all group members have shared, discuss some of the strengths and weaknesses of information from these types of accounts.

2. **List Your Rules** As a group, decide on the rules that you will follow as you work together. Two samples are provided. Add two more of your own. You may add or revise rules based on your experience together.

   - Everyone should participate in group discussions.
   - People should not interrupt.
   - _____
   - _____

3. **Apply the Rules** Practice working as a group. Share what you have learned about the Holocaust. Make sure each person in the group contributes. Take notes on and be prepared to share one thing you learned from another member of your group.

4. **Name Your Group** Choose a name that reflects the unit topic.

   Our group's name: _____

5. **Create a Communication Plan** Decide how you want to communicate with one another. For example, you might use online collaboration tools, email, or instant messaging.

   Our group's decision: _____

FACILITATING SMALL-GROUP LEARNING

Forming Groups You may wish to form groups for Small-Group Learning so that each consists of students with different learning abilities. Some students may be adept at organizing information whereas others may have strengths related to generating or synthesizing information. A good mix of abilities can make the experience of Small-Group Learning dynamic and productive.

ESSENTIAL QUESTION: How do we remember the past?

Making a Schedule

First, find out the due dates for the Small-Group activities. Then, preview the texts and activities with your group and make a schedule for completing the tasks.

SELECTION	ACTIVITIES	DUE DATE
from Anne Frank: The Diary of a Young Girl		
Acceptance Speech for the Nobel Peace Prize		
from Maus		

Working on Group Projects

As your group works together, you'll find it more effective if each person has a specific role. Different projects require different roles. Before beginning a project, discuss the necessary roles, and choose one for each group member. Some possible roles are listed here. Add your own ideas to the list.

Project Manager: monitors the schedule and keeps everyone on task

Researcher: organizes research activities

Recorder: takes notes during group meetings

_____

_____

_____

_____

SCAN FOR MULTIMEDIA

Overview: Small-Group Learning **211**

DIGITAL PERSPECTIVES

Making a Schedule

Encourage groups to preview the reading selections and to consider how long it will take them to complete the activities accompanying each selection. Point out that they can adjust the due dates for particular selections as needed as they work on their small-group projects; however, they must complete all assigned tasks before the group Performance Task is due. Encourage groups to review their schedules upon completing the activities for each selection to make sure they are on track to meet the final due date.

Working on Group Projects

Point out to groups that the roles they assign can also be changed later. Students might have to make changes based on who is best at doing what. Try to make sure that there is no favoritism, cliquishness, or stereotyping by gender or other means in the assignment of roles.

Also, you should review the roles each group assigns to its members. Based on your understanding of students' individual strengths, you might find it necessary to suggest some changes.

AUTHOR'S PERSPECTIVE — Ernest Morrell, Ph.D.

Supporting Small-Group Learning Because the dominant mode of discourse in classrooms has historically been teacher-led, many students may not be immediately comfortable discussing and collaborating in groups. The first few times students meet in their groups, you may need to provide additional support by setting expectations for collaborative behavior and discussions.

Remind students that it is important for all group members to contribute to discussion, but that no one member of the group should monopolize discussion. Whether students are speaking or listening, they should be active participants. Visit groups to explain that even when students aren't speaking, they should be listening to other group members and noting important points that they would like to build upon when it is their turn to speak.

Small-Group Learning **211**

PLANNING

SMALL-GROUP LEARNING • *from* ANNE FRANK: THE DIARY OF A YOUNG GIRL

from Anne Frank: The Diary of a Young Girl

AUDIO SUMMARIES
Audio summaries of "*from* Anne Frank: The Diary of a Young Girl" are available online in both English and Spanish in the Interactive Teacher's Edition or Unit Resources. Assigning these summaries prior to reading the selection may help students build additional background knowledge and set a context for their first read.

Summary
This excerpt from Anne Frank's diary includes two entries. The first is from June 1942, just before the Franks went into hiding from the Nazis, and the second is from November 1942, after the Franks had been in hiding for several months. In the first entry, Anne provides details about the Nazi occupation of the Netherlands and the many restrictions placed on Jews. She talks about friends and family and her desire for deeper relationships. In the second entry, Anne talks about Dussel, the new person with whom she shares her room in the Secret Annex, and how the Nazis continue daily round-ups of the Jews. She grows increasingly worried about the state of the outside world and feels guilty that she may be safer than many.

Insight
This selection provides a first-person look at the danger and dread of this dark time. It is psychologically nuanced, showing issues like survivor's guilt and loneliness despite close contact; Anne Frank's writing is very relatable.

ESSENTIAL QUESTION:
How do we remember the past?

Connection to Essential Question
The excerpts from Anne Frank's diary provide a clear connection to the Essential Question, "How do we remember the past?" Because Anne wrote down what went on in her life and the lives of the others in the Secret Annex, readers are able to gain a deeper understanding of the horrors of that time.

SMALL-GROUP LEARNING PERFORMANCE TASK
How do the selections contribute to your understanding of the Holocaust and the ways in which we remember the past?

UNIT PERFORMANCE-BASED ASSESSMENT
How can literature help us remember and honor the victims of the Holocaust?

Connection to Performance Tasks

Small-Group Learning Performance Task In this Performance Task, students will develop a multimedia presentation that addresses the prompt. This selection provides students with insight into the lives of Jews who went into hiding to escape Nazi persecution.

Unit Performance-Based Assessment While the events in these diary entries were in the present for Anne Frank, they are in the past for today's readers. They provide an opportunity for us to develop a deeper understanding of the horrors of those years and to make sure it never happens again.

DIGITAL PERSPECTIVES

 Audio   Video   Document   Annotation Highlights   EL Highlights   Online Assessment

LESSON RESOURCES

Lesson	Making Meaning	Language Development	Effective Expression
	First Read Close Read Analyze the Text Analyze Craft and Structure	Concept Vocabulary Word Study Author's Style	Speaking and Listening
Instructional Standards	**RI.10** By the end of the year, read and comprehend literary nonfiction . . . **L.4** Determine or clarify the meaning of unknown and multiple-meaning words or phrases . . . **L.4.a** Use context as a clue . . . **RI.2** Determine a central idea of a text . . . **RI.1** Cite the textual evidence **RI.5** Analyze in detail the structure of a specific paragraph in a text . . .	**L.4** Determine or clarify the meaning of unknown and multiple-meaning words or phrases . . . **L.4.b** Use common, grade-appropriate Greek or Latin affixes and roots . . . **L.4.d** Verify the preliminary determination . . . **RI.4** Determine the meaning of words and phrases . . .	**SL.1** Engage effectively in a range of collaborative discussions . . . **SL.1.a** Come to discussions prepared . . . **SL.1.c** Pose questions . . . **SL.1.d** Acknowledge new information . . .
STUDENT RESOURCES Available online in the Interactive Student Edition or Unit Resources	Selection Audio First-Read Guide: Nonfiction Close-Read Guide: Nonfiction	Word Network	Evidence Log
TEACHER RESOURCES **Selection Resources** Available online in the Interactive Teacher's Edition or Unit Resources	Audio Summaries Annotation Highlights EL Highlights from Anne Frank: The Diary of a Young Girl: Text Questions Analyze Craft and Structure: Central Idea and Supporting Details	Concept Vocabulary and Word Study Author's Style: Word Choice English Language Support Lesson: Word Choices	Speaking and Listening: Group Discussion
Reteach/Practice (RP) Available online in the Interactive Teacher's Edition or Unit Resources	Analyze Craft and Structure: Central Idea and Supporting Details (RP)	Word Study: Latin Root *-strict-* (RP) Author's Style: Word Choice (RP)	Speaking and Listening: Group Discussion (RP)
Assessment Available online in Assessments	Selection Test		
My Resources	A Unit 2 Answer Key is available online and in the Interactive Teacher's Edition.		

Small-Group Learning 212B

PERSONALIZE FOR LEARNING

SMALL-GROUP LEARNING • from ANNE FRANK: THE DIARY OF A YOUNG GIRL

Reading Support

Text Complexity Rubric: from Anne Frank: The Diary of a Young Girl

Quantitative Measures

Lexile: 1010   Text Length: 1,317 words

Qualitative Measures

Measure	Rating	Description
Knowledge Demands	3	Content about the Nazi occupation, Hitler, concentration camps, and anti-Jewish sentiments and laws may not be familiar to readers, though these topics are clearly explained.
Structure	2	Letter-writing structure in diary breaks up text; labels of dates for each letter in the diary help reader identify the time frame of the excerpts.
Language Conventionality and Clarity	3	The writing is conversational. But the diary was translated from the Dutch in the 1940s, so it has an older, formal style. There is some difficult vocabulary and figurative language.
Levels of Meaning/Purpose	3	Some concepts are sophisticated, but concepts and situations are clearly explained, as are Anne's feelings, attitudes, and opinions about the larger significance of the conditions.

DECIDE AND PLAN

English Language Support

Provide English Learners with support for knowledge demands and language as they read the selection.

Knowledge Demands Review the background information that students discussed when they read the play based on Anne Frank's diary. (See English Language Support, Acts I and II of *The Diary of Anne Frank* in Whole-Class Learning.)

Language Point out phrasing or sentences that may be unfamiliar because of the time they were written or the style of writing. For example, the expression *there is no doubt* (paragraph 1) gives emphasis or shows agreement. The phrase *failing that* (paragraph 2) means "if it doesn't happen." The phrase *enhance in my mind's eye* (paragraph 3) is a poetic way of talking about what she is imagining.

Strategic Support

Provide students with strategic support to ensure that they can successfully read the text.

Language Discuss the saying *Paper is more patient than man.* (paragraph 1) Remind students that Anne Frank is referring to her diary. Ask students what they think this means about writing and how Anne feels when she writes.

Ask students to list unfamiliar phrases or words (see English Language support for examples) and explain as needed.

Meaning Discuss the events, for example, the family's emigration to Holland in 1933 or the arrival of the Germans in 1940. Then, with students, list some of the feelings and attitudes. For example, in the last paragraphs, Anne describes a range of emotions: fortunate, sad, "wicked" (guilty), and frightened.

Challenge

Provide students who need to be challenged with ideas for how they can go beyond a simple interpretation of the text.

Text Analysis Have students work in pairs. Ask them to reread the last few paragraphs, focusing on the range of emotions Anne describes, for example, scared, fortunate, sad, or guilty. Ask them to write examples from the text. Discuss as a group. Then talk about other feelings people could have in this situation, such as anger, frustration, or despair.

Written Response Have students work in pairs to discuss and list their responses to the text. As a group, have partners share. Then ask volunteers to say positive things they can find in Anne Frank's attitudes, or positive things people can do to respond to a horrific event such as this one.

TEACH

Read and Respond

Have the groups do their first read of the selection. Then have them complete their close read. Finally, work with them on the Making Meaning, Language Development, and Effective Expression activities.

Standards Support Through Teaching and Learning Cycle

IDENTIFY NEEDS

Analyze results of the Beginning-of-Year Assessment, focusing on the items relating to Unit 2. Also take into consideration student performance to this point and your observations of where particular students struggle.

ANALYZE AND REVISE

- Analyze student work for evidence of student learning.
- Identify whether or not students have met the expectations in the standards.
- Identify implications for future instruction.

TEACH

Implement the planned lesson, and gather evidence of student learning.

DECIDE AND PLAN

- If students have performed poorly on items matching these standards, then provide selection scaffolds before assigning them the on-level lesson provided in the Student Edition.
- If students have done well on the Beginning-of-Year Assessment, then challenge them to keep progressing and learning by giving them opportunities to practice the skills in depth.
- Use the Selection Resources listed on the Planning pages for *Anne Frank: The Diary of a Young Girl* to help students continually improve their ability to master the standards.

Instructional Standards: *from* **Anne Frank: The Diary of a Young Girl**

Reading	You may wish to administer the **Analyze Craft and Structure: Central Idea and Supporting Details (RP)** worksheet to help students recognize and understand a text's central idea and supporting details. You may wish to administer the **Author's Style: Word Choice (RP)** worksheet to help students consider the way a wirter's word choices impact style and meaning.	**RI.2** Determine a central idea of a text and analyze its development over the course of the text, including its relationship to supporting ideas; provide an objective summary of the text. **RI.4** Determine the meaning of words and phrases as they are used in a text, including figurative, connotative, and technical meanings; analyze the impact of specific word choices on meaning and tone, including analogies or allusions to other texts.	Ask students to read a nonfiction text of their own choosing. Have them write a sentence or two telling the selection's central idea. Then have them give two or three examples of evidence from the text that supports this central idea. Challenge students to find another text with a more formal diction and have them compare the effect of word choice on the reader.
Language	You may wish to administer the **Word Study: Latin Root -strict- (RP)** worksheet to help students identify and understand words with the *-tion* suffix.	**L.4.b** Use common, grade-appropriate Greek or Latin affixes and roots as clues to the meaning of a word.	Work with students to find three verbs that they can turn into nouns by adding *-tion*. Have them use each of the words in a sentence that includes context clues.
Speaking and Listening	You may wish to administer the **Speaking and Listening: Group Discussion (RP)** worksheet to help students get the most out of group discussions.	**SL.1** Engage effectively in a range of collaborative discussions with diverse partners on *grade 8 topics, texts, and issues,* building on others' ideas and expressing their own clearly.	Work with students to drive group discussions that support new topics.

FACILITATING

Jump Start

FIRST READ *How can someone get used to living in hiding with others? What can people do to stay strong?* Engage students in a discussion about ways of coping with extremely dangerous situations that sets the context for reading the excerpt from *Anne Frank: The Diary of a Young Girl*.

from Anne Frank: The Diary of a Young Girl

How did people try to survive, even during Hitler's rule? Modeling questions such as this will help students connect to the excerpt from *Anne Frank: The Diary of a Young Girl* and to the Small-Group Performance Task assignment. Selection audio and print capability for the selection are available in the Interactive Teacher's Edition.

Concept Vocabulary

Ask groups to look closely at the information about context clues and discuss how these types of clues can help clarify a word's meaning. Have students discuss the examples and encourage groups to use context clues as they come across additional unfamiliar words.

FIRST READ

Have students perform the steps of the first read independently:

NOTICE: You may want to encourage students to notice key events that Anne relates.

ANNOTATE: Remind students to mark passages that include the main ideas and details in the diary.

CONNECT: Have students compare Anne Frank's diary with the play about her life, and with the writings of other young people.

RESPOND: Students will answer questions and write a summary to demonstrate understanding.

Point out to students that while they will always complete the Respond step at the end of the first read, the other steps will probably happen somewhat concurrently. You may wish to print copies of the **First-Read Guide: Nonfiction** for students to use.

212   UNIT 2 • THE HOLOCAUST

MAKING MEANING

About the Author

Anne Frank (1929–1945) was a young girl who lived in Amsterdam with her family during World War II. Fleeing Nazi persecution of Jews, the Franks went into hiding, where Anne began writing her thoughts, experiences, and observations in a diary. She was 15 when the family was found and sent to the concentration camps. Anne and her sister died at Bergen-Belsen, just weeks before the camp was liberated.

Tool Kit
First-Read Guide and Model Annotation

STANDARDS

Reading Informational Text
By the end of the year, read and comprehend literary nonfiction at the high end of the grades 6–8 text complexity band independently and proficiently.

Language
Determine or clarify the meaning of unknown and multiple-meaning words or phrases based on *grade 8 reading and content*, choosing flexibly from a range of strategies.
  a. Use context as a clue to the meaning of a word or phrase.

212 UNIT 2 • THE HOLOCAUST

from Anne Frank: The Diary of a Young Girl

Concept Vocabulary

You will encounter the following words as you read the excerpt from *Anne Frank: The Diary of a Young Girl*.

| forbidden | restrictions | sacrifices |

Context Clues If these words are unfamiliar to you, try using **context clues**—other words and phrases that appear nearby in the text—to help you determine their meanings. There are various types of context clues that may help you unlock word meanings.

> **Synonyms:** The **bifurcated** tree branch looked remarkably similar to a snake's forked tongue.
>
> **Restatement:** A healthful breakfast can **invigorate** you, giving you the energy you need to get through your morning.
>
> **Contrast of Ideas:** The first crate looked **cumbersome**, so I grabbed the second one, which was small and easy to handle.

Apply your knowledge of context clues and other vocabulary strategies to determine the meanings of unfamiliar words you encounter during your first read.

First Read NONFICTION

Apply these strategies as you conduct your first read. You will have an opportunity to complete a close read after your first read.

> **NOTICE** the general ideas of the text. *What* is it about? *Who* is involved?
>
> **ANNOTATE** by marking vocabulary and key passages you want to revisit.
>
> **CONNECT** ideas within the selection to what you already know and what you have already read.
>
> **RESPOND** by completing the Comprehension Check and by writing a brief summary of the selection.

AUTHOR'S PERSPECTIVE   Jim Cummins, Ph.D.

Importance of Background Knowledge It is important for all students, and especially for English learners, to learn to tap into their background knowledge when they read a text. Teachers can help students access this knowledge and integrate it with new textual information. One way to do this is to encourage groups to share what they know about the topic of the text before they begin reading. For example, some students may have prior knowledge about the Holocaust, which can help scaffold understanding of *Anne Frank: The Diary of a Young Girl*. On a deeper level, more students may be able to relate to the idea of writing their most personal thoughts in a diary. After students have completed their first read, have them discuss how their background knowledge helped them understand the text.

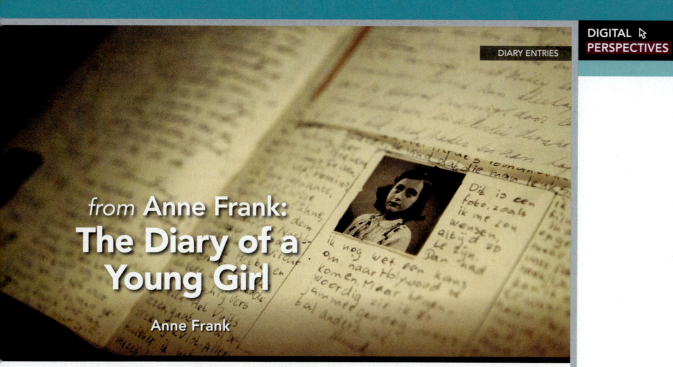

DIARY ENTRIES

from Anne Frank: The Diary of a Young Girl

Anne Frank

BACKGROUND

Otto Frank was the only member of the Frank family to survive the concentration camps. He discovered that his daughter Anne's diary had been salvaged by Miep Gies, a close friend who had been a great help to the family during their time in hiding. He decided to publish Anne's diary as a way to honor her memory and share her story with the world.

SCAN FOR MULTIMEDIA

Saturday, 20 June, 1942

1   . . . There is a saying that "paper is more patient than man"; it came back to me on one of my slightly melancholy days, while I sat chin in hand, feeling too bored and limp even to make up my mind whether to go out or stay at home. Yes, there is no doubt that paper is patient and as I don't intend to show this cardboard-covered notebook, bearing the proud name of "diary," to anyone, unless I find a real friend, boy or girl, probably nobody cares. And now I come to the root of the matter, the reason for my starting a diary: it is that I have no such real friend.

2   Let me put it more clearly, since no one will believe that a girl of thirteen feels herself quite alone in the world, nor is it so. I have darling parents and a sister of sixteen. I know about thirty people whom one might call friends—I have strings of boy friends, anxious to catch a glimpse of me and who, failing that, peep at me through mirrors in class. I have relations, aunts and uncles, who are darlings too, a good home, no—I don't seem to lack anything. But it's the same with all my friends, just fun and

FACILITATING

Concept Vocabulary

FORBIDDEN If groups are struggling to define the word *forbidden* in paragraph 5, point out they can use context clues to find its meaning. In this case, students can read the rest of the sentence in which the word is highlighted to find the synonym *banned*. Have them use *banned* to define the word.

Possible response: The word *forbidden* means "not allowed."

RESTRICTIONS If groups are struggling to define the word *restrictions* in paragraph 5, point out that they should look for context clues to find its meaning. Have students read the sentences near the word: "Swimming baths, tennis courts, hockey fields, and other sports grounds are all prohibited to them. Jews may not visit Christians. Jews must go to Jewish schools, and many more *restrictions* of a similar kind." Have them use the surrounding sentences to define the word.

Possible response: The word *restrictions* means "limits."

NOTES

joking, nothing more. I can never bring myself to talk of anything outside the common round. We don't seem to be able to get any closer, that is the root of the trouble. Perhaps I lack confidence, but anyway, there it is, a stubborn fact and I don't seem to be able to do anything about it.

3   Hence, this diary. In order to enhance in my mind's eye the picture of the friend for whom I have waited so long, I don't want to set down a series of bald facts in a diary like most people do, but I want this diary itself to be my friend, and I shall call my friend Kitty. No one will grasp what I'm talking about if I begin my letters to Kitty just out of the blue, so, albeit[1] unwillingly, I will start by sketching in brief the story of my life.

4   My father was thirty-six when he married my mother, who was then twenty-five. My sister Margot was born in 1926 in Frankfort-on-Main, I followed on June 12, 1929, and, as we are Jewish, we emigrated to Holland in 1933, where my father was appointed Managing Director of Travies N.V. This firm is in close relationship with the firm of Kolen & Co. in the same building, of which my father is a partner.

5   The rest of our family, however, felt the full impact of Hitler's anti-Jewish laws, so life was filled with anxiety. In 1938 after the pogroms,[2] my two uncles (my mother's brothers) escaped to the U.S.A. My old grandmother came to us, she was then seventy-three. After May 1940 good times rapidly fled: first the war, then the capitulation,[3] followed by the arrival of the Germans, which is when the sufferings of us Jews really began. Anti-Jewish decrees followed each other in quick succession. Jews must wear a yellow star, Jews must hand in their bicycles, Jews are banned from trains and are **forbidden** to drive. Jews are only allowed to do their shopping between three and five o'clock and then only in shops which bear the placard "Jewish shop." Jews must be indoors by eight o'clock and cannot even sit in their own gardens after that hour. Jews are forbidden to visit theaters, cinemas, and other places of entertainment. Jews may not take part in public sports. Swimming baths, tennis courts, hockey fields, and other sports grounds are all prohibited to them. Jews may not visit Christians. Jews must go to Jewish schools, and many more **restrictions** of a similar kind.

Mark context clues or indicate another strategy you used that helped you determine meaning.

forbidden (fuhr BIHD uhn) *v.*
MEANING:

restrictions (rih STRIHK shuhnz) *n.*
MEANING:

---

1. **albeit** (awl BEE iht) *conj.* although.
2. **pogroms** (POH gruhmz) *n.* organized killings and other persecution of Jews.
3. **capitulation** (kuh pihch uh LAY shuhn) *n.* act of surrendering.

VOCABULARY DEVELOPMENT

Concept Vocabulary Reinforcement To increase familiarity with the concept vocabulary, ask students to use each of the paragraph 5 vocabulary words in a sentence. Encourage students to include context clues in their own sentences to demonstrate their knowledge of the word. If students are still struggling with the words, encourage them to identify the base word in each term, look up the base word in a dictionary (*forbid* and *restrict*), and then use the definition to come up with the meaning of the concept vocabulary word.

6   So we could not do this and were forbidden to do that. But life went on in spite of it all. Jopie[4] used to say to me, "You're scared to do anything, because it may be forbidden." Our freedom was strictly limited. Yet things were still bearable.

7   Granny died in January 1942; no one will ever know how much she is present in my thoughts and how much I love her still.

8   In 1934 I went to school at the Montessori Kindergarten and continued there. It was at the end of the school year, I was in form 6B, when I had to say good-by to Mrs. K. We both wept, it was very sad. In 1941 I went, with my sister Margot, to the Jewish Secondary School, she into the fourth form[5] and I into the first.

9   So far everything is all right with the four of us and here I come to the present day.

Thursday, 19 November, 1942

10 Dear Kitty,

11 Dussel is a very nice man, just as we had all imagined. Of course he thought it was all right to share my little room.

12 Quite honestly I'm not so keen that a stranger should use my things, but one must be prepared to make some **sacrifices** for a good cause, so I shall make my little offering with a good will. "If we can save someone, then everything else is of secondary importance," says Daddy, and he's absolutely right.

13 The first day that Dussel was here, he immediately asked me all sorts of questions: When does the charwoman[6] come? When can one use the bathroom? When is one allowed to use the lavatory?[7] You may laugh, but these things are not so simple in a hiding place. During the day we mustn't make any noise that might be heard downstairs; and if there is some stranger—such as the charwoman for example—then we have to be extra careful. I explained all this carefully to Dussel. But one thing amazed me: he is very slow on the uptake. He asks everything twice over and still doesn't seem to remember. Perhaps that will wear off in time, and it's only that he's thoroughly upset by the sudden change.

14 Apart from that, all goes well. Dussel has told us a lot about the outside world, which we have missed for so long now. He had very sad news. Countless friends and acquaintances have gone to a terrible fate. Evening after evening the green and gray army

---
4. **Jopie** (YOH pee) Jacqueline van Maarsen, Anne's best friend.
5. **fourth form** here, a grade in secondary school.
6. **charwoman** *n.* cleaning woman.
7. **lavatory** *n.* toilet.

NOTES

Mark context clues or indicate another strategy you used that helped you determine meaning.

sacrifices (SAK ruh fys ihz) *n.*
MEANING:

from Anne Frank: The Diary of a Young Girl

FACILITATING

CLOSER LOOK

Analyze Sensory Language

Circulate among groups as students close read. Suggest that groups close read paragraph 14. Encourage them to talk about the annotations they mark. If needed, provide the following support.

ANNOTATE: Have students mark details in paragraph 14 that describe the Jewish people being led away on the streets. You may also work with small groups as you highlight them together.

QUESTION: Guide students to consider what these details might tell them. Ask what a reader can infer from the descriptions of the crying children and exhausted families, as well as the phrase "the march of death," and accept student responses.
Possible response: The people are suffering even as they leave their homes. The children don't want to go, and the Germans treat the children and the adults very roughly. Also, the phrase "march of death" shows that Anne Frank knows that many will not survive.

CONCLUDE: Help students to formulate conclusions about the importance of these details in the text. Ask students why the author might have included these details.
Possible response: The details show that Anne Frank understood what was happening around her. By describing how people looked and sounded, she also helps us understand.

Remind students that writers use **sensory language**, or language that appeals to one or more of the five senses, to describe how things or people look, feel, or sound. The language can help readers better imagine the experience that the author describes.

NOTES

lorries trundle past.[8] The Germans ring at every front door to inquire if there are any Jews living in the house. If there are, then the whole family has to go at once. If they don't find any, they go on to the next house. No one has a chance of evading them unless one goes into hiding. Often they go around with lists, and only ring when they know they can get a good haul. Sometimes they let them off for cash—so much per head. It seems like the slave hunts of olden times. But it's certainly no joke; it's much too tragic for that. In the evenings when it's dark, I often see rows of good, innocent people accompanied by crying children, walking on and on, in charge of a couple of these chaps, bullied and knocked about until they almost drop. No one is spared—old people, babies, expectant mothers, the sick—each and all join in the march of death.

15   How fortunate we are here, so well cared for and undisturbed. We wouldn't have to worry about all this misery were it not that we are so anxious about all those dear to us whom we can no longer help.

16   I feel wicked sleeping in a warm bed, while my dearest friends have been knocked down or have fallen into a gutter somewhere out in the cold night. I get frightened when I think of close friends who have now been delivered into the hands of the cruelest brutes that walk the earth. And all because they are Jews!

17   Yours, Anne

---
8. **lorries trundle past** trucks move along.

PERSONALIZE FOR LEARNING

Strategic Support
First-Read Support If students struggle to comprehend the text during the first read, have a partner conduct a think aloud to explain the thought process as he or she works through the ANNOTATE, QUESTION, and CONCLUDE steps. For example, the student can isolate details as suggested, and explain what they reveal.

Comprehension Check

Complete the following items after you finish your first read. Review and clarify details with your group.

1. What does the author say is her reason for starting a diary?

2. Why does Anne start her diary entries with the words *Dear Kitty*?

3. How old were Anne's parents when they got married?

4. In the beginning of her entry from November 1942, how does Anne describe Dussel?

5. 📓 **Notebook** Confirm your understanding of the text by writing a summary of the diary excerpt.

RESEARCH

Research to Clarify Choose at least one unfamiliar historical detail from the text. Briefly research that detail. In what way does the information you learned shed light on an aspect of the diary entries?

Research to Explore These diary entries may inspire you to learn more about young people affected by war. Formulate a research question about the subject, and briefly research it. Share what you discover with your group.

from Anne Frank: The Diary of a Young Girl 217

DIGITAL PERSPECTIVES

Comprehension Check

Possible responses:

1. The author says she is starting a diary because she has no real friend.
2. The author wants the diary to be her friend, so she gives it a name, *Kitty*.
3. Her father was 36, and her mother was 25.
4. She describes him as a "very nice man."
5. Summaries will vary. Students should include Anne's reason for writing the diary, the situation faced by Jewish people at the time, the fact that Anne and her family are in hiding, and a description of what Anne thinks about as the situation for Jewish people worsens.

Research

Research to Clarify Students will be unfamiliar with many relevant historical details. If they do not know what to research, you may want to suggest the following details: the pogroms in Germany in 1938 or the capitulation of the Netherlands in 1940.

Research to Explore If groups struggle to focus their research question, you may want to suggest that they narrow the focus to one of the following topics: How were young Jewish people in the Netherlands during World War II affected by war? How are young people in war-torn countries today affected by war? How does experiencing the trauma of war when you are young affect you later in life?

PERSONALIZE FOR LEARNING

Challenge

Research Have students research information about other diaries that have gained an international audience. Ask them to consider what makes the diaries important, and what, if anything, these diaries have in common with *Anne Frank: The Diary of a Young Girl*. Possible subjects include *Zlata's Diary: A Child's Life in Wartime Sarajevo*, which was written by a young girl in the former Yugoslavia during the early 1990s, or *A Diary of Darkness: The Wartime Diary of Kiyosawa Kiyoshi*, written by a journalist in Japan during World War II.

Small-Group Learning

FACILITATING

Jump Start

CLOSE READ *Why do you think Anne Frank's diary speaks to people today?* As students discuss this with their groups, ask them to consider what Anne Frank chose to include in her diary and how she confided her thoughts and feelings.

Close Read the Text

If needed, model close reading by using the Annotation Highlights in the Interactive Teacher's Edition.

Remind students to use Accountable Talk in their discussions and to support one another as they complete the close read.

Analyze the Text

1. **Responses will vary by group.** Students should identify the main idea that the situation was becoming increasingly worse for Jewish people in the Netherlands and provide details to support that.
2. **Passages will vary by group.** Remind students to explain why they chose the passage they presented to group members.
3. **Responses will vary by group.**

Concept Vocabulary

Why These Words? Possible response: The words all describe limits and loss experienced by Jewish people during the Holocaust. Other possible words are *banned* and *suffering*.

Practice

Responses will vary by group, but should show that students understand the meaning of each word.

Word Network

Possible responses: *banned, sufferings, prohibited*

Word Study

For more support, see **Concept Vocabulary and Word Study.**

Possible responses:
district: a limited area;
constrict: to make narrower by tightening.

from ANNE FRANK: THE DIARY OF A YOUNG GIRL

MAKING MEANING

Close Read the Text

With your group, revisit sections of the text you marked during your first read. **Annotate** what you notice. What **questions** do you have? What can you **conclude**?

Analyze the Text

CITE TEXTUAL EVIDENCE to support your answers.

Notebook Complete the activities.

1. **Review and Clarify** With your group, review the diary entries. Though Anne died during the Holocaust, do you think she lives on through her diary? Explain.
2. **Present and Discuss** Now, work with your group to share the passages from the text that you found especially important. Take turns presenting your passages. Discuss what you noticed in the text, what questions you asked, and what conclusions you reached.
3. **Essential Question:** *How do we remember the past?* What has this diary excerpt taught you about how we remember the past? Discuss your thoughts with your group.

TIP
FOR GROUP DISCUSSION
When you work in your group to answer the Analyze the Text questions, be sure to support your opinions and ideas with evidence from the text.

WORD NETWORK
Add words related to the Holocaust from the text to your Word Network.

STANDARDS
Reading Informational Text
• Cite the textual evidence that most strongly supports an analysis of what the text says explicitly as well as inferences drawn from the text.
• Determine a central idea of a text and analyze its development over the course of the text, including its relationship to supporting ideas; provide an objective summary of the text.
• Analyze in detail the structure of a specific paragraph in a text, including the role of particular sentences in developing and refining a key concept.
Language
Determine or clarify the meaning of unknown and multiple-meaning words or phrases based on *grade 8 reading and content*, choosing flexibly from a range of strategies.
  b. Use common, grade-appropriate Greek or Latin affixes and roots as clues to the meaning of a word.
  d. Verify the preliminary determination of the meaning of a word or phrase.

218 UNIT 2 • THE HOLOCAUST

LANGUAGE DEVELOPMENT

Concept Vocabulary

| forbidden | restrictions | sacrifices |

Why These Words? The concept vocabulary words from the text are related. With your group, determine what the words have in common. Record your ideas, and add another word that fits the category.

Practice

Notebook Confirm your understanding of the vocabulary words by using a dictionary to verify the meaning of each word.

Word Study

Latin Root: *-strict-* In her diary entry for Saturday, June 20, Anne Frank mentions the many *restrictions* Jewish people were subjected to. The word *restriction* includes the Latin root *-strict-*, which means "draw tight." Find another word that contains the root *-strict-*, and explain how the root contributes to the meaning of the word.

FORMATIVE ASSESSMENT

Analyze the Text
If students struggle to close read the text, **then** provide the *from* **Anne Frank: The Diary of a Young Girl: Text Questions** available online in the Interactive Teacher's Edition or Unit Resources. Answers and DOK levels are also available.

Concept Vocabulary
If students fail to see the connection among the words, **then** have them use each word in a sentence and think about what is similar about the sentences.

Word Study
If students are unable to identify the meaning and part of speech for *restriction*, **then** have them reread paragraph 5. For Reteach and Practice, see **Word Study: Latin Root *-strict-* (RP).**

218 UNIT 2 • THE HOLOCAUST

ESSENTIAL QUESTION: How do we remember the past?

Analyze Craft and Structure

Central Idea and Supporting Details Informational texts are often organized according to a central idea and supporting details. The **central idea** is the most important idea about the topic that a paragraph or an entire selection conveys. The central idea may either be directly stated or implied using the details provided.

- To find a **stated central idea** in a paragraph or section of text, identify the **topic,** or what it is about. Then, look for the **topic sentence**—the sentence that states the author's central idea about the topic. Often, the first sentence of a paragraph expresses its central idea.
- To determine an **implied central idea** in a paragraph or section of text, make an inference based on details in the text. An **inference** is an educated guess that you reach by analyzing the details in the text and making connections among them. For example, if someone walks into a room with a wet umbrella, you can infer that it is raining outside without needing the person with the umbrella to tell you that directly.

Practice

CITE TEXTUAL EVIDENCE to support your answers.

📓 **Notebook** Work individually to fill in this chart for paragraph 5 of the excerpt from *Anne Frank: The Diary of a Young Girl*.

PARAGRAPH 5	
Topic:	what has happened to Anne's family since 1938
Central Idea:	Things are getting increasingly worse for Anne's family and other Jewish people in the Netherlands.
Supporting Detail:	Her two uncles escaped to the U.S.A.
Supporting Detail:	Grandmother came to live with the family.
Supporting Detail:	Germans arrive in the Netherlands.
Supporting Detail:	Anti-Jewish decrees are enacted.
Supporting Detail:	Jews must wear a yellow star.
Supporting Detail:	Jews cannot ride a bicycle, ride the train, or drive.

When you have finished, share your completed chart with your group, and come to a consensus about the topic, central idea, and supporting details.

DIGITAL PERSPECTIVES

Analyze Craft and Structure

Central Idea and Supporting Details You may point out to students that the central idea of a paragraph may not be the same as the central idea of an entire selection. This is especially true since they are reading an excerpt from a longer work. For more support, see **Analyze Craft and Structure: Central Idea and Supporting Details**.

See possible responses in chart on student page.

MAKE IT INTERACTIVE
Project the Interactive Teacher's Edition for this selection. Then choose a paragraph and model how to determine the main idea and how to find text details that support the main idea.

FORMATIVE ASSESSMENT

Central Idea and Supporting Details
If students are struggling to identify the central idea, **then** have them review each detail they have identified and look for connections among them. For Reteach and Practice, see **Analyze Craft and Structure: Central Idea and Supporting Details (RP)**.

PERSONALIZE FOR LEARNING

Strategic Support

Central Ideas and Supporting Details Some students may not understand the difference between a detail and a central idea. Pair students, and have them discuss what the topic of paragraph 5 is and what seems to be happening to Jewish people in the Netherlands in general. Once they have identified that life is getting worse and more limited for Jewish people, have them look for the details that support that idea.

FACILITATING

Author's Style

Word Choice Discuss with students that the words an author chooses help establish the tone—the author's attitude toward a topic or audience. The conversational style of a diary might convey a friendly attitude toward the diary itself and to other possible readers. For more support, see **Author's Style: Word Choice.**

Read It
See possible responses in chart on student page.

Write It
Diary entries will vary. Entries should have an informal, friendly style.

FORMATIVE ASSESSMENT

Author's Style
If students have difficulty in understanding the difference between an informal and formal writing style, **then** have them work with a partner to state a piece of news about the class. Have them first use an informal style, so that it sounds as if they were talking to a friend. Then have them use a formal style, such as something that would be heard in a news report. For Reteach and Practice, see **Author's Style: Word Choice (RP).**

LANGUAGE DEVELOPMENT

from ANNE FRANK: THE DIARY OF A YOUNG GIRL

Author's Style

Word Choice An author's **style** is his or her way of using language. Style includes a writer's **word choice**, or **diction**, and sentence structure. The author of a diary often uses an informal, conversational style. Anne Frank is no exception. In her diary, her style is conversational and even intimate, as if she were speaking to a trusted friend. In fact, she even gives this friend a name—Kitty. Notice the unique qualities of her style in the passages from her diary shown here:

> **Passage 1:** Notice her use of a contraction, as well as plain, straightforward words.
> *I don't want to set down a series of bald facts in a diary like most people do, but I want this diary itself to be my friend, and I shall call my friend Kitty.*
>
> **Passage 2** Notice how her sentence has a natural flow rather than a stiff formality.
> *Perhaps I lack confidence, but anyway, there it is, a stubborn fact and I don't seem to be able to do anything about it.*

Read It
Work with your group to identify two additional examples of Anne Frank's style. Explain specific ways in which her diction and syntax create an informal, conversational style. Use the chart to record your notes.

PASSAGE FROM THE DIARY	DICTION AND/OR SYNTAX
Paragraph 2: "But it's the same with all my friends, just fun and joking, nothing more."	The writing is informal and upbeat.
Paragraph 13: "But one thing amazed me: he is very slow on the uptake."	The writing is conversational but she uses punctuation to draw connections. It shows that Anne is a keen observer of human nature.

STANDARDS
Reading Informational Text
Determine the meaning of words and phrases as they are used in a text, including figurative, connotative, and technical meanings; analyze the impact of specific word choices on meaning and tone, including analogies or allusions to other texts.

Write It

Notebook Write a diary entry in which you use diction and syntax to create an informal, friendly style. Your diary entry can simply be about your day or about an interesting event in your life. Avoid any personal subjects that you do not want to share with a wider audience.

220 UNIT 2 • THE HOLOCAUST

PERSONALIZE FOR LEARNING

English Language Support
Recognizing Word Choice Have all students read the following diary entries:
And now I come to the root of the matter, *the reason for my starting a diary: it is that I have no such real friend.* (1)
We don't seem to be able to get any closer, that is the root of the trouble. (2)
So far everything is all right with the four of us *and here I come to* the present day. (9)

Apart from that, *all goes well.* (14)
How fortunate we are here, *so well cared for and undisturbed.* (15)

Have students pick a sentence or idea and paraphrase it in their own words. Ask them to explain how effective the idea is as a diary entry. **EMERGING**

Have students write a short paragraph commenting on Anne's choice of words, sentence structure, and informal style. **EXPANDING**

Have students identify the tone Anne created with her word choice. Then have them write a short paragraph on how the diary entries convey Anne's range of feelings. **BRIDGING**

An expanded **English Language Support Lesson** on Word Choices is available in the Interactive Teacher's Edition.

EFFECTIVE EXPRESSION

Speaking and Listening

> **Assignment**
> Reread the excerpt from *Anne Frank: The Diary of a Young Girl*. Then, engage in a **collaborative group discussion** in which you discuss what you learned from Anne Frank's diary entries.

Prepare for the Discussion To prepare for your group discussion, reread the diary entries. Then, briefly respond to the following questions:

- What does Anne mean when she says "I have no such real friend"?

- How might learning Anne's thoughts add to readers' understanding of the horror of the Holocaust?

- Otto Frank decided to publish his daughter's private thoughts and feelings. Was that the right thing to do?

During the Discussion Use the questions and your responses to guide your group discussion. During the discussion, follow these guidelines:

- Ask questions of other group members. For example, you may ask someone to elaborate on an idea, or explain it more thoroughly. You may also ask someone to clarify a point.

- Respond to other group members' questions with relevant observations and new ideas.

- Think about new ideas or information expressed by others, and consider the ways in which these ideas and information confirm your views or change your perspective.

- Use evidence from Anne Frank's diary entries to support your ideas during the discussion.

EVIDENCE LOG
Before moving on to a new selection, go to your Evidence Log and record what you learned from the excerpt from *Anne Frank: The Diary of a Young Girl*.

STANDARDS
Speaking and Listening
Engage effectively in a range of collaborative discussions with diverse partners on *grade 8 topics, texts, and issues*, building on others' ideas and expressing their own clearly.
  a. Come to discussions prepared, having read or researched material under study; explicitly draw on that preparation by referring to evidence on the topic, text, or issue to probe and reflect on ideas under discussion.
  c. Pose questions that connect the ideas of several speakers and respond to others' questions and comments with relevant evidence, observations, and ideas.
  d. Acknowledge new information expressed by others, and, when warranted, qualify or justify their own views in light of the evidence presented.

DIGITAL PERSPECTIVES

Speaking and Listening

Guide students to draft questions for their group discussions about which they do not necessarily have firm opinions. Remind them that the purpose of the discussion is as much to learn from others as it is to contribute one's own ideas.

For more support, see **Speaking and Listening: Group Discussion.**

Evidence Log Support students in completing their Evidence Log. This paced activity will help prepare them for the Performance-Based Assessment at the end of the unit.

FORMATIVE ASSESSMENT

Speaking and Listening

If students have difficulty evaluating Otto Frank's decision to publish Anne's diary, **then** ask them to consider the pros and cons of the two alternatives: maintaining his daughter's privacy even in death or helping the world learn about important events by sharing a detailed first-hand account. For Reteach and Practice, see **Speaking and Listening: Group Discussion (RP).**

Selection Test

Administer the *from* Anne Frank: The Diary of a Young Girl Selection Test, which is available in both print and digital formats online in Assessments.

PLANNING
SMALL-GROUP LEARNING • ACCEPTANCE SPEECH FOR THE NOBEL PEACE PRIZE

Acceptance Speech for the Nobel Peace Prize

🔊 **AUDIO SUMMARIES**
Audio summaries of "Acceptance Speech for the Nobel Peace Prize" are available online in both English and Spanish in the Interactive Teacher's Edition or Unit Resources. Assigning these summaries prior to reading the selection may help students build additional background knowledge and set a context for their first read.

Summary
Elie Wiesel's Nobel Prize acceptance speech recounts some of the terror Wiesel and his father went through in the Nazi concentration camps during World War II and what he learned from those experiences. Wiesel passionately calls for direct action against oppression, arguing that silence and neutrality necessarily benefit the oppressor and harm the oppressed. He calls for an end to injustice throughout the world. Wiesel concludes by saying he still has faith and that action can remedy the indifference that allows terrible abuses to occur.

Insight
Wiesel's message of hope and concern for justice, in the face of the tragedies he lived through and the ones that continue, is inspiring and important.

ESSENTIAL QUESTION:
How do we remember the past?

Connection to Essential Question
"Acceptance Speech for the Nobel Peace Prize" provides a strong connection to the Essential Question, "How do we remember the past?" Elie Wiesel does not shrink from discussing the horrors he survived. He uses them as a jumping-off point to discuss current injustice and suffering. He uses them as a reminder to us all of the importance of working together to end persecution.

SMALL-GROUP LEARNING PERFORMANCE TASK
How do the selections contribute to your understanding of the Holocaust and the ways in which we remember the past?

UNIT PERFORMANCE-BASED ASSESSMENT
How can literature help us remember and honor the victims of the Holocaust?

Connection to Performance Tasks

Small-Group Learning Performance Task In this Performance Task, students will develop a multimedia presentation about the Holocaust. This selection provides students with firsthand information from a Holocaust survivor whose message is that remembering past events is a crucial part motivating people to fighting against similar events from recurring today.

Unit Performance-Based Assessment Wiesel takes this question on explicitly; he says that striving to keep the memory alive and fight those who would forget is the best response. In addition to the more recent injustices that Wiesel points to in his speech, students should also consider events that have happened in the years since Wiesel was awarded the Nobel Prize.

DIGITAL PERSPECTIVES Audio Video Document Annotation Highlights EL Highlights Online Assessment

LESSON RESOURCES

	Making Meaning	Language Development	Effective Expression
Lesson	First Read Close Read Analyze the Text Analyze Craft and Structure	Concept Vocabulary Word Study Conventions	Speaking and Listening
Instructional Standards	**RI.10** By the end of the year, read and comprehend literary nonfiction . . . **L.4** Determine or clarify the meaning of unknown and multiple-meaning words or phrases . . . **L.4.c** Consult general and specialized reference materials . . . **L.4.d** Verify the preliminary determination . . . **RI.1** Cite the textual evidence . . . **RI.6** Determine an author's point of view . . .	**RI.4** Determine the meaning of words and phrases as they are used in a text . . . **L.4** Determine or clarify the meaning of unknown and multiple-meaning words or phrases . . . **L.4.b** Use common, grade-appropriate Greek or Latin affixes and roots . . . **L.1** Demonstrate command of the conventions . . .	**SL.1** Engage effectively in a range of collaborative discussions . . . **SL.1.a** Come to discussions prepared . . . **SL.1.b** Follow rules for collegial discussions . . .
▶ **STUDENT RESOURCES**			
Available online in the Interactive Student Edition or Unit Resources	🔊 Selection Audio 📄 First-Read Guide: Nonfiction 📄 Close-Read Guide: Nonfiction	📄 Word Network	📄 Evidence Log
▶ **TEACHER RESOURCES**			
Selection Resources Available online in the Interactive Teacher's Edition or Unit Resource	🔊 Audio Summaries ✏️ Annotation Highlights 💬 EL Highlights 📄 English Language Support Lesson: Group Discussion 📄 Acceptance Speech for the Nobel Peace Prize: Text Questions 📄 Analyze Craft and Structure: Author's Purpose and Point of View	📄 Concept Vocabulary and Word Study 📄 Conventions: Perfect Tenses of Verbs	📄 Speaking and Listening: Group Discussion
Reteach/Practice (RP) Available online in the Interactive Teacher's Edition or Unit Resources	📄 Analyze Craft and Structure: Author's Purpose and Point of View (RP)	📄 Word Study: Word Families (RP) 📄 Conventions: Perfect Tenses of Verbs (RP)	📄 Speaking and Listening: Group Discussion (RP)
Assessment Available online in Assessments	📄 ✓ Selection Test		
My Resources	📄 A Unit 2 Answer Key is available online and in the Interactive Teacher's Edition.		

Small-Group Learning   222B

PERSONALIZE FOR LEARNING

SMALL-GROUP LEARNING • ACCEPTANCE SPEECH FOR THE NOBEL PEACE PRIZE

Reading Support

Text Complexity Rubric: Acceptance Speech for the Nobel Peace Prize

Quantitative Measures

Lexile: 770   Text Length: 893 words

Qualitative Measures

Knowledge Demands ①—②—③—**④**—⑤	Knowledge of the Holocaust is assumed; multiple references are made to people or events. Footnotes clarify most text references to people and events.
Structure ①—②—**③**—④—⑤	Structure is a combination of narrative and argument based on Wiesel's experiences; the organization of ideas is fluid and not always explicit or predictable.
Language Conventionality and Clarity ①—②—③—**④**—⑤	Language is formal, complex, and sometimes abstract, with rhetorical questions and sentence fragments used for emphasis; author talks to his child self and refers to that child in the third person.
Levels of Meaning/Purpose ①—②—③—**④**—⑤	Purpose is explicit, but there are multiple ideas expressed, some of which are abstract, complex, and may not be easy to identify.

DECIDE AND PLAN

English Language Support

Provide English learners with support for knowledge demands and language as they read the selection.

Knowledge Demands Review background information, defining terms if necessary. Check that students are familiar with the Nobel Peace Prize. Review some of the basic terms and meanings, such as the Holocaust, Nazis, and concentration camps.

Language Students may be confused by the use of third person that Wiesel uses to talk about himself as a young boy. Ask a volunteer to read aloud the first three sentences of paragraph 4. Explain that the "young Jewish boy" is Wiesel as a child. Then have volunteers read aloud paragraphs 5, 6, and 7. Point out the use of first person (*I, me, my*) for Wiesel in the present, and third person (*he, his, him*) for Wiesel as a young boy.

Strategic Support

Provide students with strategic support to ensure that they can successfully read the text.

Language Ask questions about the text to confirm that students understand how Wiesel uses point of view—the use of first person (*I, me, my*) for himself now, and third person (*he, him, his*) for himself as a young boy. For example, ask *Who is the young Jewish boy?* (paragraph 4) Ask *Who does he refer to?* (Wiesel as a young boy)

Meaning Ask students to copy these lines: (paragraph 7) *If we forget, we are guilty.* (paragraph 8) *I swore never to be silent,* and (paragraph 12) *one person can make a difference.* Discuss each one, making abstractions more concrete. For example, *What is Wiesel saying we should not forget?* (the Holocaust, the suffering)

Challenge

Provide students who need to be challenged with ideas for how they can go beyond a simple interpretation of the text.

Text Analysis Discuss Wiesel's pledge in paragraph 8 never to be silent when people are suffering, and his claim in paragraph 12 that one person can make a difference. Ask students to work in pairs to list ways that individuals or nations can speak up or make a difference in situations as horrific as the Holocaust, and in instances of personal humiliation or discrimination in daily life. Ask pairs to share their ideas with the class.

Written Response Ask students to write about instances of discrimination they have experienced or witnessed in their lives, or that they have read or heard about from people they know. Ask volunteers to share their work.

TEACH

Read and Respond

Have groups read the selection and then complete the Making Meaning, Language Development, and Effective Expression activities.

Standards Support Through Teaching and Learning Cycle

IDENTIFY NEEDS

Analyze results of the Beginning-of-Year Assessment, focusing on the items relating to Unit 2. Also take into consideration student performance to this point and your observations of where particular students struggle.

ANALYZE AND REVISE

- Analyze student work for evidence of student learning.
- Identify whether or not students have met the expectations in the standards.
- Identify implications for future instruction.

TEACH

Implement the planned lesson, and gather evidence of student learning.

DECIDE AND PLAN

- If students have performed poorly on items matching these standards, then provide selection scaffolds before assigning them the on-level lesson provided in the Student Edition.
- If students have done well on the Beginning-of-Year Assessment, then challenge them to keep progressing and learning by giving them opportunities to practice the skills in depth.
- Use the Selection Resources listed on the Planning pages for "Acceptance Speech for the Nobel Peace Prize" to help students continually improve their ability to master the standards.

Instructional Standards: Acceptance Speech for the Nobel Peace Prize

	Catching Up	This Year	Looking Forward
Reading	You may wish to administer the **Analyze Craft and Structure: Author's Purpose and Point of View (RP)** worksheet to help students identify the author's purpose and point of view in the selection.	**RI.6** Determine an author's point of view or purpose in a text and analyze how the author acknowledges and responds to conflicting evidence or viewpoints.	Ask students to create a list of words with strong connotations. Have them discuss their lists with a partner. How do these words help to figure out the author's feelings or point of view?
Speaking and Listening	You may wish to administer the **Speaking and Listening: Group Discussion (RP)** worksheet to help students plan and practice for the group discussion.	**SL.1** Engage effectively in a range of collaborative discussions with diverse partners on *grade 8 topics, texts, and issues,* building on others' ideas and expressing their own clearly.	Have students discuss their ideas for the group discussion with a peer. Challenge students to acknowledge the other person's ideas and follow up with questions to help clarify the ideas.
Language	You may wish to administer the **Conventions: Perfect Tenses of Verbs (RP)** worksheet to help students understand and form the perfect tenses of verbs. You may wish to administer the **Word Study: Word Families (RP)** worksheet to help students understand word families.	**L.1** Demonstrate command of the conventions of standard English grammar and usage when writing or speaking. **L.4.b** Use common, grade-appropriate Greek or Latin affixes and roots as clues to the meaning of a word.	Challenge students to use the perfect tenses of verbs in their own writing. Tell students to write three words that can be formed from the word *oppress*. Have them use each word in a sentence.

FACILITATING

Jump Start

FIRST READ Why is remembering the past important? Engage students in a discussion about the value of remembering the past to set the context for reading "Acceptance Speech for the Nobel Peace Prize." As students share their thoughts, have them explain the factors that influence their opinions.

Acceptance Speech for the Nobel Peace Prize 🔊 📄

How can remembering horrific events serve a purpose? Modeling questions such as this will help students connect to "Acceptance Speech for the Nobel Peace Prize" and to the Small-Group Performance Task assignment. Selection audio and print capability for the selection are available in the Interactive Teacher's Edition.

Concept Vocabulary

Ask groups to study the information about using a dictionary and thesaurus, and discuss how they can be useful. Encourage groups to think about different situations when they would use a dictionary and when they would use a thesaurus.

● FIRST READ

As they read, students should perform the steps of the first read:

NOTICE: You may want to encourage students to notice the problems the author calls out and what his main point is.

ANNOTATE: Remind students to mark passages that support the author's main point.

CONNECT: Encourage students to think about why it might be important to remember the Holocaust and other events of the past. Point out that they may find some similarities to situations in the news.

RESPOND: Students will answer questions and write a summary to demonstrate understanding.

Point out to students that while they will always complete the Respond step at the end of the first read, the other steps will probably happen somewhat concurrently. You may wish to print copies of the **First-Read Guide: Nonfiction** for students to use. 📄

MAKING MEANING

About the Author

Elie Wiesel (1928–2016) was a Nobel Prize–winning writer, activist, orator, and teacher, best known for his internationally acclaimed memoir *Night*, in which he recounts his experiences surviving the Holocaust. Wiesel became a revered figure of peace over the years, speaking out against persecution and injustice all across the globe.

🔧 Tool Kit
First-Read Guide and Model Annotation

≡ STANDARDS

Reading Informational Text
By the end of the year, read and comprehend literary nonfiction at the high end of the grades 6–8 text complexity band independently and proficiently.

Language
Determine or clarify the meaning of unknown and multiple-meaning words or phrases *based on grade 8 reading and content,* choosing flexibly from a range of strategies.
  c. Consult general and specialized reference materials, both print and digital, to find the pronunciation of a word or determine or clarify its precise meaning or its part of speech.
  d. Verify the preliminary determination of the meaning of a word or phrase.

222 UNIT 2 • THE HOLOCAUST

Acceptance Speech for the Nobel Peace Prize

Concept Vocabulary

As you read Elie Wiesel's Nobel Peace Prize acceptance speech, you will encounter these words.

| humiliation | persecuted | traumatized |

Using a Dictionary and Thesaurus When you come across an unfamiliar word and cannot determine its meaning from context clues alone, it's a good idea to look up the word in a **dictionary** or **thesaurus.**

When you look up a word in a dictionary, you will find its meaning, part of speech, and pronunciation. In a thesaurus, you will find **synonyms** for a word, or words with similar meaning. A thesaurus can be helpful when you're looking to vary your word choices in your writing.

Compare these two entries for the word *verdict*:

Dictionary

ver•dict (VUR dihkt) *n.*
1. decision arrived at by a jury at the end of a trial
2. any decision or judgment

Thesaurus

verdict *n.* judgment, finding, decision, answer, opinion, sentence, determination

Notice that a thesaurus does not provide definitions. Before you use a word you find in a thesaurus, check a dictionary to verify its meaning.

First Read NONFICTION

Apply these strategies as you conduct your first read. You will have an opportunity to complete a close read after your first read.

NOTICE the general ideas of the text. *What* is it about? *Who* is involved?

ANNOTATE by marking vocabulary and key passages you want to revisit.

CONNECT ideas within the selection to what you already know and what you have already read.

RESPOND by completing the Comprehension Check and by writing a brief summary of the selection.

AUTHOR'S PERSPECTIVE — Kelly Gallagher, M.Ed.

First-Read Strategies As students encounter unfamiliar and challenging text for the first time, some may hit a frustration point early. Students often think that if they don't understand something on the first try that they will never understand. Comprehension when reading is not an all-or-nothing situation. Share these strategies for getting through the gray areas:

• **Read on with Uncertainty** Students who are "a little bit lost" may be able to read a little further to resolve confusion. Model this with the opening paragraphs of a novel or long work. Read the text, and show students what questions you already have. Demonstrate that many questions arise at the beginning as readers place themselves in the world the writer has created. Good readers can live with

SPEECH

Acceptance Speech for the Nobel Peace Prize
Elie Wiesel

BACKGROUND
Elie Wiesel wrote more than sixty books, many of which are about his experiences in the Buchenwald and Auschwitz concentration camps. He was honored with a Nobel Peace Prize in 1986 for his commitment to serving people around the world who have been persecuted or currently face persecution.

1 It is with a profound sense of humility that I accept the honor you have chosen to bestow upon me. I know: Your choice transcends me. This both frightens and pleases me.

2 It frightens me because I wonder: Do I have the right to represent the multitudes who have perished? Do I have the right to accept this great honor on their behalf? . . . I do not. That would be presumptuous. No one may speak for the dead, no one may interpret their mutilated dreams and visions.

3 It pleases me because I may say that this honor belongs to all the survivors and their children, and through us, to the Jewish people with whose destiny I have always identified.

4 I remember: It happened yesterday or eternities ago. A young Jewish boy discovered the kingdom of night. I remember his bewilderment, I remember his anguish. It all happened so fast. The ghetto. The deportation. The sealed cattle car. The fiery altar upon which the history of our people and the future of mankind were meant to be sacrificed.

5 I remember: He asked his father, "Can this be true?" This is the twentieth century, not the Middle Ages. Who would allow such crimes to be committed? How could the world remain silent?

6 And now the boy is turning to me: "Tell me," he asks. "What have you done with my future? What have you done with your life?"

7 And I tell him that I have tried. That I have tried to keep memory alive, that I have tried to fight those who would forget. Because if we forget, we are guilty, we are accomplices.

FACILITATING

Concept Vocabulary

HUMILIATION If groups are struggling to define the word *humiliation* in paragraph 8, point out that after trying to find the meaning of the word through context, they may want to use a dictionary. Explain that they can use a thesaurus to find synonyms for the word. Have students guess the meaning of *humiliation* through context, and then check their guesses using the dictionary.

Possible response: *Humiliation* means "loss of dignity."

PERSECUTED If groups are struggling to define the word *persecuted* in paragraph 8, point out that after trying to find the meaning of the word through context, they may want to use a dictionary. Explain that they can use a thesaurus to find synonyms for the word. Have students guess the meaning of *persecuted* through context, and then check their guesses using the dictionary.

Possible response: *Persecuted* means "oppressed."

TRAUMATIZED If groups are struggling to define the word *traumatized* in paragraph 9, suggest that after trying to find the meaning of the word through context, they may want to use a dictionary. Explain that they can use a thesaurus to find synonyms for the word. Have students guess the meaning of *traumatized* through context, and then check their guesses using the dictionary.

Possible response: *Traumatized* means "injured" or "devastated."

 Additional **English Language Support** is available in the Interactive Teacher's Edition.

NOTES

Use a dictionary or thesaurus or indicate another strategy you used that helped you determine meaning.

humiliation (hyoo mihl ee AY shuhn) *n.*
MEANING:

persecuted (PUR suh kyoo tihd) *v.*
MEANING:

traumatized (TRAW muh tyzd) *adj.*
MEANING:

---

8 And then I explained to him how naive we were, that the world did know and remain silent. And that is why I swore never to be silent whenever and wherever human beings endure suffering and **humiliation**. We must always take sides. Neutrality helps the oppressor, never the victim. Silence encourages the tormentor, never the tormented. Sometimes we must interfere. When human lives are endangered, when human dignity is in jeopardy, national borders and sensitivities become irrelevant. Wherever men or women are **persecuted** because of their race, religion, or political views, that place must—at that moment—become the center of the universe.

9 Of course, since I am a Jew profoundly rooted in my people's memory and tradition, my first response is to Jewish fears, Jewish needs, Jewish crises. For I belong to a **traumatized** generation, one that experienced the abandonment and solitude of our people. It would be unnatural for me not to make Jewish priorities my own: Israel, Soviet Jewry, Jews in Arab lands . . . But there are others as important to me. Apartheid[1] is, in my view, as abhorrent as anti-Semitism. To me, Andrei Sakharov's[2] isolation is as much of a disgrace as Josef Biegun's[3] imprisonment. As is the denial of Solidarity and its leader Lech Wałęsa's[4] right to dissent. And Nelson Mandela's[5] interminable imprisonment.

10 There is so much injustice and suffering crying out for our attention: victims of hunger, of racism, and political persecution, writers and poets, prisoners in so many lands governed by the Left and by the Right. Human rights are being violated on every continent. More people are oppressed than free. And then, too, there are the Palestinians[6] to whose plight I am sensitive but whose methods I deplore. Violence and terrorism are not the answer. Something must be done about their suffering, and soon. I trust Israel, for I have faith in the Jewish people. Let Israel be given a chance, let hatred and danger be removed from her horizons, and there will be peace in and around the Holy Land.

11 Yes, I have faith. Faith in God and even in His creation. Without it no action would be possible. And action is the only remedy to indifference: the most insidious danger of all. Isn't this the meaning of Alfred Nobel's legacy? Wasn't his fear of war a shield against war?

---

1. **Apartheid** *n.* social policy in South Africa from 1950 to 1994 that separated the country's white and nonwhite populations, creating discrimination against the nonwhites.
2. **Andrei Sakharov** (1921–1989) nuclear physicist and human-rights activist who was banished from the Soviet Union for criticizing the government.
3. **Josef Biegun** Jewish man who was imprisoned and murdered during the Holocaust.
4. **Lech Wałęsa** (b. 1943) labor activist who helped form and led Poland's first independent trade union, Solidarity, despite opposition from the Polish government.
5. **Nelson Mandela** (1918–2013) leader of the struggle to end apartheid in South Africa; he had been sentenced to life in prison at the time this speech.
6. **Palestinians** reference to the violent conflict between Palestinian Arabs and Israeli Jews, who have been fighting to claim the same territory.

FACILITATING SMALL-GROUP CLOSE READING

CLOSE READ: SPEECH As groups perform the close read, circulate and offer support as needed.

- Remind groups that when they read a speech, they should be sure to identify the author's purpose for making the speech.
- If a group is confused about what the author's purpose is, remind them to look at the title of the speech, and the occasion on which it was given. They should also review the main points the speaker makes.
- Challenge groups to determine the author's point of view in the text and identify specific details that they used to infer the author's point of view.

12   There is much to be done, there is much that can be done. One person—a Raoul Wallenberg,[7] an Albert Schweitzer,[8] one person of integrity—can make a difference, a difference of life and death. As long as one dissident[9] is in prison, our freedom will not be true. As long as one child is hungry, our lives will be filled with anguish and shame. What all these victims need above all is to know that they are not alone; that we are not forgetting them, that when their voices are stifled we shall lend them ours, that while their freedom depends on ours, the quality of our freedom depends on theirs.

13   This is what I say to the young Jewish boy wondering what I have done with his years. It is in his name that I speak to you and that I express to you my deepest gratitude. No one is as capable of gratitude as one who has emerged from the kingdom of night. We know that every moment is a moment of grace, every hour an offering; not to share them would mean to betray them. Our lives no longer belong to us alone; they belong to all those who need us desperately.

14   Thank you, Chairman Aarvik. Thank you, members of the Nobel Committee. Thank you, people of Norway, for declaring on this singular occasion that our survival has meaning for mankind.

---

7. **Raoul Wallenberg** (1912–1947?) Swedish diplomat in Hungary who saved tens of thousands of Jews during the Holocaust by issuing passports and providing shelter.
8. **Albert Schweitzer** (1875–1965) Alsatian doctor known for his important contributions in many fields, such as philosophy, religion, music, and medicine.
9. **dissident** *n.* person who disagrees with an official religious or political system.

Comprehension Check

Complete the following items after you finish your first read. Review and clarify details with your group.

Notebook Respond to the questions.

1. Upon accepting the honor of the Nobel Peace Prize, what two emotions does Elie Wiesel have?

2. According to Weisel, what is the biggest threat to freedom?

3. Confirm your understanding of the speech by writing a summary of the author's main points.

RESEARCH

Research to Explore Choose one historical figure mentioned in the speech whom you would like to know more about. Briefly research that person. How does knowing more about this person help you better understand the points Wiesel makes?

Acceptance Speech for the Nobel Peace Prize **225**

Comprehension Check

Possible responses:

1. He is both frightened and pleased.
2. Possible response: According to Wiesel, the biggest threat to freedom is indifference, inaction, and silence in the face of oppression and evil.
3. Summaries will vary. However, students should include the reason that Wiesel is giving the speech, the subject of his writing, and his main point—that we must all pay attention to and fight oppression and persecution.

Research

Research to Explore If students have difficulty researching one of the famous leaders that Wiesel mentions in his speech, encourage them to use an encyclopedia to get an overview of the person's life. With that to guide them, they can look for information that tells more about the specifics of the injustice and oppression that the person fought.

PERSONALIZE FOR LEARNING

English Language Support
Domain-Specific Vocabulary Review paragraphs 8–10 and call out any new vocabulary for students. The domain-specific vocabulary that appears in this selection may present challenges to English learners. Review the following terms with them:

- **neutrality** (paragraph 8) the policy of a nation that does not take sides in a conflict between other nations.
- **national borders** (paragraph 8) the lines that separate geographic areas and serve as political boundaries.
- **the Left** (paragraph 10) internationally, those whose political views are anywhere from liberal to socialist.
- **the Right** (paragraph 10) internationally, those who support conservative positions and whose political views are anywhere from conservative to fascist.

Have students use each of the terms in a sentence to show their understanding. **ALL LEVELS**

FACILITATING

Jump Start

CLOSE READ How did having lived through the Holocaust affect Elie Wiesel's thinking about the world? As students discuss the question in their groups, ask them to consider how the experience of enormous trauma may affect people in different ways.

Close Read the Text

If needed, model close reading by using the Annotation Highlights in the Interactive Teacher's Edition.

Remind students to use Accountable Talk in their discussions and to support one another as they complete the close read.

Analyze the Text

Possible responses:
1. The boy is Elie Wiesel himself in the past. The boy symbolizes all the innocent Jewish children full of promise and hope who were exposed to evils of humanity in the Holocaust. Wiesel may have chosen to portray this boy as a symbol because he describes how the boy speaks to him in the present, challenging him to make meaning out of his life. This image is very compelling when related as a boy speaking from the past.
2. Passages will vary by group. Remind students to explain why they chose the passage they present to the group members.
3. Responses will vary by group.

Concept Vocabulary

Why These Words? Possible response:
The words all have to do with suffering and oppression. Another word that fits the category is *mutilated*.

Practice

Discussions will vary among groups.

Word Network

Possible words: *anguish, tormented, endangered*

Word Study

For more support, see **Concept Vocabulary and Word Study.**

Possible responses: *captivity, captivating; humiliating, humiliation; injury, injurious*

ACCEPTANCE SPEECH FOR THE NOBEL PEACE PRIZE

TIP

GROUP DISCUSSION
When you work in your group to answer the Analyze the Text questions, be sure to support your opinions and ideas with evidence from the text.

WORD NETWORK

Add words related to the Holocaust from the text to your Word Network.

STANDARDS

Reading Informational Text
- Cite the textual evidence that most strongly supports an analysis of what the text says explicitly as well as inferences drawn from the text.
- Determine the meaning of words and phrases as they are used in a text, including figurative, connotative, and technical meanings; analyze the impact of specific word choices on meaning and tone, including analogies or allusions to other texts.
- Determine an author's point of view or purpose in a text and analyze how the author acknowledges and responds to conflicting evidence or viewpoints.

Language
Determine or clarify the meaning of unknown and multiple-meaning words or phrases based on *grade 8 reading and content,* choosing flexibly from a range of strategies.
  b. Use common, grade-appropriate Greek or Latin affixes and roots as clues to the meaning of a word.

226 UNIT 2 • THE HOLOCAUST

MAKING MEANING

Close Read the Text

With your group, revisit sections of the text you marked during your first read. **Annotate** what you notice. What **questions** do you have? What can you **conclude**?

Analyze the Text

CITE TEXTUAL EVIDENCE to support your answers.

Notebook Complete the activities.

1. **Review and Clarify** With your group, reread paragraphs 4–7 of the selection. Discuss the young Jewish boy to whom the author refers. Whom or what does this boy **symbolize,** or represent? Why might Wiesel have chosen to convey his point through symbolism?

2. **Present and Discuss** Now, work with your group to share the passages from the text that you found especially important. Take turns presenting your passages. Discuss what you noticed in the text, what questions you asked, and what conclusions you reached.

3. **Essential Question:** *How do we remember the past?* What has this speech taught you about how we remember the past? Discuss.

LANGUAGE DEVELOPMENT

Concept Vocabulary

| humiliation | persecution | traumatized |

Why These Words? The concept vocabulary words from the text are related. With your group, determine what the words have in common. Write your ideas and add another word that fits the category.

Practice

Notebook Confirm your understanding of the concept vocabulary words by correctly using each one in a sentence.

Word Study

Notebook **Word Families** The noun *trauma* is the base word for a word family, or group of related words, that includes the verb *traumatize,* the adjective *traumatic,* and the adverb *traumatically.* For each of the following words, identify at least two words that are part of its word family: *captive; humility; injure.*

FORMATIVE ASSESSMENT

Analyze the Text

If students struggle to close read the text, **then** provide the **Acceptance Speech for the Nobel Peace Prize: Text Questions** available online in the Interactive Teacher's Edition or Unit Resources. Answers and DOK levels are also available.

Concept Vocabulary

If students struggle to identify the concept, **then** have them use each word in a sentence and think about what is similar about the sentences.

Word Study

If students fail to identify other words, **then** suggest that they use a dictionary to browse for words related to *captive, humility* and *injure.* For Reteach and Practice, see **Word Study: Word Families (RP).**

226 UNIT 2 • THE HOLOCAUST

ESSENTIAL QUESTION: How do we remember the past?

Analyze Craft and Structure

Author's Purpose and Point of View An **author's purpose** is his or her reason for writing. In a broad sense, a writer's purpose may be to inform or explain, to persuade, or to entertain. Usually, an author's purpose is some mixture of all of those things. No matter what an author's purpose, his or her point of view will influence the writing.

An **author's point of view** is his or her perspective on a topic. It is shaped by the author's knowledge, beliefs, and experiences. Sometimes, an author states his or her point of view directly. Often, however, readers must use evidence in the text to make **inferences,** or educated guesses, to determine the author's point of view.

When you analyze author's purpose and point of view, focus on how the author acknowledges and responds to conflicting evidence or viewpoints. Doing so will reveal telling details about an author's position—how the author distinguishes his or her perspective from those who may disagree.

Practice

CITE TEXTUAL EVIDENCE to support your answers.

Notebook Reread Elie Wiesel's Acceptance Speech for the Nobel Peace Prize. Work with your group to analyze the speech, and determine Wiesel's purposes and point of view. Use the chart to record your ideas. Then, answer the questions that follow.

PURPOSE AND POINT OF VIEW	EVIDENCE THAT SUPPORTS MY INFERENCE
Purpose #1: a. See answers in Teacher's Edition.	b.
Purpose #2: c.	d.
Point of View: e.	f.

1. (a) In paragraph 7, Wiesel claims, "Because if we forget, we are guilty, we are accomplices." What do you think he means by this statement? (b) What does this statement reveal about his point of view?

2. What is Wiesel's point of view, or perspective, on the individual's responsibility to end human suffering? Identify a quotation from the text that supports your response.

3. Review paragraphs 9–11 of the speech. (a) How does Wiesel acknowledge and respond to other viewpoints on contemporary political conflicts? (b) What aspects of his unique point of view does he use to distinguish, or differentiate, his viewpoint from others?

Acceptance Speech for the Nobel Peace Prize **227**

VOCABULARY DEVELOPMENT

Concept Vocabulary Reinforcement Provide additional practice with the concept vocabulary by using "show-you-know" sentences. The first clause uses the word in an appropriate context. The second clause clarifies the first. Model the strategy with this example for *humiliation*:

The bullied teenager felt a deep *humiliation*; she felt a loss of dignity.

Then give students these sentence prompts and coach them in creating the clarification part:

1. Jewish people in Germany during World War II faced *persecution*;_____
   Possible response: they were singled out for abuse.
2. The soldier was *traumatized* by the war; _____.
   Possible response: he went through an emotional shock.

DIGITAL PERSPECTIVES

Analyze Craft and Structure

Author's Purpose and Point of View Discuss with students how a person's point of view, or perspective, about something will depend on his or her experiences. For example, if you have witnessed an event, you will have a different perspective on it than if you have merely read about it.

As students review the speech, direct their attention to phrases like "crying out for our attention" in paragraph 10 and "our lives will be filled with anguish and shame." What do the connotations of the language suggest about Wiesel's point of view? For more support, see **Analyze Craft and Structure: Author's Purpose and Point of View.**

Possible responses:

a. to accept the Nobel Peace Prize; b. from the title of the speech and the first paragraph; c. to persuade listeners to act to end injustice and suffering wherever it exists; d. Paragraph 8: "Wherever men and women are persecuted . . . that place must—at that moment—become the center of the universe." Paragraph 10: "There is so much injustice and suffering crying out for our attention . . ."; e. One person can make a difference and it is each person's responsibility to try to end suffering.; f. Paragraph 12: "There is much to be done, there is much that can be done. One person . . . can make a difference, a difference of life and death."

1. (a) It is every human's responsibility to fight against injustice, and by forgetting past injustices, we are contributing to the same crimes recurring in the present. (b) His point of view is that of someone who has devoted his life to keeping the memory of the Holocaust alive.

2. His perspective is that each individual has a responsibility to fight against human suffering. He says, "Our lives no longer belong to us alone; they belong to all those who need us desperately."

3. (a) Wiesel acknowledges the suffering of many people, including the Palestinian Arabs, whose plight he supports but whose methods he condemns. (b) He points out that based on his experience and heritage, he is naturally most closely aligned with issues of Jewish freedom, but this does not diminish his sensitivity to many other groups of people who are victims of persecution.

FORMATIVE ASSESSMENT

Analyze Craft and Structure

If students struggle to identify the author's purpose, **then** have them review the speech, looking at whether the speaker is primarily trying to entertain, inform, or persuade. For Reteach and Practice, see **Analyze Craft and Structure: Author's Purpose and Point of View (RP).**

Small-Group Learning **227**

FACILITATING

Conventions

Perfect Tenses of Verbs Point out to students that one way to understand perfect tenses is to use them in a story. For example, one might say, "Andrea is thirteen years old and *has lived* in Houston for nine years." This sentence uses the present perfect. Then, one might say, "Andrea *will have lived* there for ten years in May." This sentence uses the future perfect. Finally, one might say, "Andrea's parents *had considered* moving to Chicago last year, but decided to stay." That sentence uses the past perfect. For more support, see **Conventions: Perfect Tenses of Verbs.**

Read It

MAKE IT INTERACTIVE
Project the digital version of "Acceptance Speech for the Nobel Peace Prize" and read paragraph 7. Model how to locate an example of present perfect ("And I tell him that I *have tried*.") and discuss its significance to help students understand what they have to do to complete the chart correctly.

See possible responses in chart on student page.

Write It
Possible responses:
Paragraphs will vary, but make sure that students use the present perfect tense at least twice to indicate something that they have been doing and continue to do.

FORMATIVE ASSESSMENT
Conventions
If students struggle to identify the present perfect tense, **then** remind them to look for a form of the verb *have* linked to a past participle of a main verb (for example, *have tried*). For Reteach and Practice, see **Conventions: Perfect Tenses of Verbs (RP).**

LANGUAGE DEVELOPMENT

ACCEPTANCE SPEECH FOR THE NOBEL PEACE PRIZE

Conventions

Perfect Tenses of Verbs The **tense** of a verb shows the time of an action or a condition. Each of the **perfect tenses** describes an action or a condition that was or will be completed before a certain time, or a past action or condition that continues into the present.

Perfect tenses are formed by adding a form of the verb *have* to the past participle of the main verb.

VERB TENSE	EXAMPLE
present perfect: action in the past that continues into the present	I <u>have tried</u> to call you five times.
past perfect: action in the past that ended before another past action	I <u>had tried</u> to text but got no reply.
future perfect: action in the future that will have ended before a certain point in time	If I call again, I <u>will have tried</u> to contact you six times.

Read It

Work with your group to identify examples of the use of the present perfect tense in Elie Wiesel's Nobel Peace Prize acceptance speech. Then, discuss as a group the significance of Wiesel's use of the present perfect tense.

EXAMPLE	SIGNIFICANCE
paragraph 7; "And I tell him that I <u>have tried</u>."	It shows that Wiesel has tried in the past and continues until the present.
paragraph 7: "That I <u>have tried</u> to keep memory alive,…"	It shows that Wiesel has continually worked to keep people from forgetting about the Holocaust.
paragraph 13: "No one is as capable of gratitude as one who <u>has emerged</u> from the kingdom of night."	It shows that Wiesel's emergence from "the night," or the horror of the Holocaust, is ongoing.

STANDARDS
Language
Demonstrate command of the conventions of standard English grammar and usage when writing or speaking.

Write It

Notebook Write a paragraph about something that you have been doing for some time and continue to do. Use the present perfect tense at least twice in your paragraph, marking each use.

228 UNIT 2 • THE HOLOCAUST

PERSONALIZE FOR LEARNING

English Language Support
Perfect Tenses of Verbs Some English learners may require additional support in using the present perfect tense correctly in their writing. Have pairs interview each other, using questions such as:

How long have you lived in your current home? How long have you been attending this school?

Students should then answer using the perfect tense, and use these answers in their paragraphs. Have partners check each other's work.

EFFECTIVE EXPRESSION

Speaking and Listening

Assignment

With your group, conduct a **discussion** on one of the following quotations from Elie Wiesel's speech.

- ☐ "We must always take sides. Neutrality helps the oppressor, never the victim. Silence encourages the tormentor, never the tormented. Sometimes we must interfere." *(paragraph 8)*

- ☐ "What all these victims need above all is to know that they are not alone; that we are not forgetting them, that when their voices are stifled we shall lend them ours, that while their freedom depends on ours, the quality of our freedom depends on theirs." *(paragraph 12)*

Prepare for the Discussion Prior to the discussion, review the speech individually and briefly respond to the following questions:

- What does the quotation mean? What larger idea is Wiesel trying to communicate?

- How does Wiesel develop and support the ideas expressed in the quotation throughout his speech?

Use your responses to these questions to guide your group discussion.

During the Discussion Before you begin your discussion, assign roles for each member of your group. Roles may include a group leader, who keeps the discussion on topic; a timekeeper, who makes sure the discussion stays within the timeframe designated by your teacher; and a note-taker to record the group's ideas. Use these guidelines to ensure a productive group discussion:

- Draw on the speech to explore and develop your ideas. Be sure to refer to specific passages to support your opinions.
- Take turns speaking, and listen attentively as other group members express their thoughts and opinions.
- Be respectful of others' ideas and opinions. If you disagree with a speaker, express your difference of opinion respectfully and politely.

EVIDENCE LOG

Before moving on to a new selection, go to your Evidence Log and record what you learned from Elie Wiesel's Nobel Peace Prize acceptance speech.

STANDARDS

Speaking and Listening
Engage effectively in a range of collaborative discussions with diverse partners on *grade 8 topics, texts, and issues*, building on others' ideas and expressing their own clearly.

a. Come to discussions prepared, having read or researched material under study; explicitly draw on that preparation by referring to evidence on the topic, text, or issue to probe and reflect on ideas under discussion.

b. Follow rules for collegial discussions and decision-making, track progress toward specific goals and deadlines, and define individual roles as needed.

PERSONALIZE FOR LEARNING

English Language Support

Taking Part in Discussion Have all students read each point from Wiesel's acceptance speech and think about the meaning of his speech, in view of his experiences during the Holocaust.

Have students choose one statement from the speech to discuss. Tell them to write questions about the statement and try to answer their questions themselves. (e.g., *What is an accomplice? Why does he say that if we forget, we are all accomplices?*) **EMERGING**

Have students paraphrase two or three ideas or statements and write them down. **EXPANDING**

Have students select three ideas, write what they think each means, and give examples. **BRIDGING**

An expanded **English Language Support Lesson** on Group Discussion is available in the Interactive Teacher's Edition.

DIGITAL PERSPECTIVES

Speaking and Listening

Once students have chosen an assignment, point out that they will need to prepare for their discussions. If students are discussing the first option, they may want to take some time to review current events and their understanding of a group's oppression. If they are discussing the second option, they will want to review the speech to find evidence to support their points about Wiesel's positions.

Prepare for the Discussion Students may want to appoint a moderator to keep the discussion on track. Remind groups to consult the schedule for Small-Group Activities as they create their Project Plan. Check to make sure each group has made assignments, and that the work is divided evenly among group members.

During the Discussion Explain to students that when they use evidence from the text or elsewhere, they should mention the source. Point out that in the discussion, they should not repeat each other's ideas, but instead build support for an idea by adding examples or evidence. Emphasize that students should not seek to dominate the discussion by talking the longest or by dismissing the ideas of others. For more support, see **Speaking and Listening: Group Discussion.**

Evidence Log Support students in completing the Evidence Log. This paced activity will help prepare them for the Performance-Based Assessment at the end of the unit.

FORMATIVE ASSESSMENT

Speaking and Listening

If groups struggle to plan their discussions, **then** work with them to write questions that apply to the topic they have chosen. For Reteach and Practice, see **Speaking and Listening: Group Discussion (RP).**

Selection Test

Administer the "Acceptance Speech for the Nobel Peace Prize" Selection Test, which is available in both print and digital formats online in Assessments.

PLANNING

INDEPENDENT LEARNING • *from* MAUS

from Maus

Summary

This excerpt comes from the graphic novel *Maus*. Author Art Spiegelman uses images and text to recount his father's experiences during the Holocaust. The graphic novel depicts different groups of people as different types of animals. As the excerpt begins, Spiegelman's father, Vladek, is in hiding in Poland. He and several other Jewish people who are also in hiding attempt to find a way to flee to Hungary. His friend's nephew, Abraham, escapes first. Vladek receives a letter that appears to be from Abraham that says he made it out safely, so Vladek and his wife pay a group of smugglers and begin their escape. Soon after their train journey begins, however, the smugglers betray the Jews to the Nazis.

> **Insight**
>
> This excerpt shows the paranoia and terrible conditions in which many in hiding had to live. It also hints at the far worse dangers faced by those who were caught.

AUDIO SUMMARIES
Audio summaries of this excerpt from *Maus* are available online in both English and Spanish in the Interactive Teacher's Edition or Unit Resources. Assigning these summaries prior to reading the selection may help students build additional background knowledge and set a context for their first read.

ESSENTIAL QUESTION:
How do we remember the past?

Connection to Essential Question

Because it is a retelling of a true story from the author's father, *Maus* provides a unique perspective on the Essential Question, "How do we remember the past?"

SMALL-GROUP LEARNING PERFORMANCE TASK
What were some of the ways people fought back against Nazi rule?

UNIT PERFORMANCE-BASED ASSESSMENT
How can literature help us remember and honor the victims of the Holocaust?

Connection to Performance Tasks

Small-Group Learning Performance Task By describing the characters' attempts to hide from the Nazis and to flee, *Maus* provides vivid information about the many ways in which people fought for their survival during the Holocaust. As such, the text should be useful to students as they develop their explanatory essay.

Unit Performance-Based Assessment In *Maus*, students learn about the terrible consequences suffered by people who were captured trying to escape Nazi-controlled countries. Students could use such details from the graphic novel as vivid supporting evidence for the explanatory essay they will write.

DIGITAL PERSPECTIVES   Audio   Video   Document   Annotation Highlights   EL Highlights   Online Assessment

LESSON RESOURCES

Lesson	Making Meaning	Language Development	Effective Expression
	First Review Analyze the Media Close Review	Media Vocabulary	Research
Instructional Standards	**RL.10** By the end of the year, read and comprehend literature . . . **L.6** Acquire and use accurately grade-appropriate general academic and domain-specific words and phrases . . . **SL.2** Analyze the purpose of information presented in diverse media and formats . . .	**L.6** Acquire and use accurately grade-appropriate general academic and domain-specific words and phrases . . .	**W.2** Write informative/explanatory texts . . . **W.2.a** Introduce a topic clearly . . . **W.2.b** Develop the topic . . . **W.2.d** Use precise language . . . **W.7** Conduct short research projects . . . **W.8** Gather relevant information . . .
STUDENT RESOURCES Available online in the Interactive Student Edition or Unit Resources	Selection Audio First-Review Guide: Media–Art and Photography Close-Review Guide: Media–Art and Photography	Word Network	Evidence Log
TEACHER RESOURCES **Selection Resources** Available online in the Interactive Teacher's Edition or Unit Resources	Audio Summaries from *Maus*: Media Questions	Media Vocabulary	Research: Informative Report

Media Complexity Rubric: *from* Maus

Quantitative Measures

Format and Length: graphic novel, 7 pages

Qualitative Measures

Knowledge Demands ①—②—③—❹—⑤	Selection relies on knowledge of the Holocaust, with specific references to Nazi concentration camps and smugglers trying to aid in escape. Situations portrayed are outside readers' experience.
Structure ①—②—③—❹—⑤	Graphic novel has high correspondence between text and illustrations. Reader must follow plot by simultaneously interpreting narration, dialogue, and illustrations.
Language Conventionality and Clarity ①—②—❸—④—⑤	Language is conversational and not complex, but has some unfamiliar syntax (imperfect English of non-native speaker); use of tense alternates (narration in past, dialogue with a mix of tenses).
Levels of Meaning/Purpose ①—②—❸—④—⑤	Narration and dialogue are concrete and explicit. However, reader must navigate structure and have enough background knowledge in order to understand meaning.

Small-Group Learning   230B

FACILITATING

Jump Start

FIRST REVIEW If you were living in danger, would you try to run far away or hide where you are? How would you make the decision? Engage students in a discussion about trying to escape from oppression that sets the context for reading this excerpt from *Maus*.

from Maus

What does it mean to have Jews drawn as mice? Who are the cats? What do other animals represent? Modeling the questions a reader might ask as they review *Maus* brings the graphic novel alive for students and connects it to the Small-Group Performance Task assignment. Selection audio is available in the Interactive Teacher's Edition.

Media Vocabulary

Encourage groups to discuss the media vocabulary. Have they seen the terms in texts before? Do they use any of them in their speech and writing?

Ask students to find whether the words have a different meaning outside of the context of a graphic novel. For example, outside of the graphic novel context, a *panel* is a flat rectangular part. Once they have found the meanings of each word, have students discuss why that word makes sense for graphic novels. (For example, *panels* in graphic novels are flat and rectangular.)

FIRST REVIEW

As they review, students should perform the steps of the first review:

LOOK: Remind students to look closely at how each character is drawn and what the drawings convey about them.

NOTE: Encourage students to pay attention to any panels that intrigue or confuse them, so that they can reread that part of the selection.

CONNECT: Encourage students to make connections with what they already know about the Holocaust from books or from their classes.

RESPOND: Students will answer questions and create a storyboard to demonstrate understanding.

Point out to students that while they will always complete the Respond step at the end of the first read, the other steps will probably happen somewhat concurrently. You may wish to print copies of the **First-Review Guide: Media–Art and Photography** for students to use.

230 UNIT 2 • THE HOLOCAUST

MAKING MEANING

About the Author

Art Spiegelman (b. 1948) is an American author and illustrator whose Holocaust narratives—*Maus* (1986) and *Maus II* (1991)—helped to establish the graphic novel as a sophisticated literary form. *Maus* was serialized from 1980 to 1991, and it depicts Spiegelman interviewing his father about his experiences as a Polish Jew and Holocaust survivor.

STANDARDS

Reading Literature
By the end of the year, read and comprehend literature, including stories, dramas, and poems, at the high end of grades 6–8 text complexity band independently and proficiently.

Language
Acquire and use accurately grade-appropriate general academic and domain-specific words and phrases; gather vocabulary knowledge when considering a word or phrase important to comprehension or expression.

from Maus

Media Vocabulary

The following words will be useful to you as you analyze, discuss, and write about graphic novels.

panel: individual frame of a graphic novel depicting a single moment	• The panels work together to tell a story. • The panels cannot show everything that happens, so readers must use their imaginations to fill in the blanks.
encapsulation: choice of which scenes to capture, or display, in panels	• The layout and choice of the scenes drives the readers' interpretations. • Graphic novelists can use different sizes and shapes to give more or less weight to scenes.
speech balloon: display of what a character is speaking or thinking	• The size, shape, and color of the speech balloon can show the emotion of the speaker. • Speech balloons can also show emotion through the use of punctuation marks and musical symbols.

First Review MEDIA: GRAPHIC NOVEL

Apply these strategies as you conduct your first review. You will have an opportunity to a close review after your first review.

LOOK at each image and determine *whom* or *what* it portrays.

NOTE elements in each image that you find interesting and want to revisit.

CONNECT details in the images to other media you've experienced, texts you've read, or images you've seen.

RESPOND by completing the Comprehension Check.

PERSONALIZE FOR LEARNING

Strategic Support

Magnify It To help students who are visually impaired, project the pages from the graphic novel on a screen to enlarge the images. As necessary, zoom in on a particular panel to help students view the details, especially those that tell about the characters.

MEDIA | GRAPHIC NOVEL

art spiegelman
MAUS
A SURVIVOR'S TALE
I MY FATHER BLEEDS HISTORY

BACKGROUND
In *Maus*, Art Spiegelman tells the story of his parents, Vladek and Anja Spiegelman, who survived the Holocaust. At the start of this excerpt, Vladek and Anja are living in hiding with Mrs. Motonowa, whose husband does not know she is hiding Jews. They arrange a meeting with smugglers at the house of a woman named Mrs. Kawka to discuss plans to be smuggled out of Poland.

SCAN FOR MULTIMEDIA

from Maus 231

👥 FACILITATING SMALL-GROUP CLOSE REVIEW

CLOSE REVIEW: Graphic Novel As groups perform the close review, circulate and offer support as needed.

- Remind groups that when they view the panels, they should be sure to note the characters and their situation. Point out that they should use both pictures and text to do so.

- If a group is confused about what is happening in any single panel, have them review the panels immediately before and after so that they can determine meaning from context.

- Challenge students to choose a panel and write a few sentences explaining who is in the panel, what is happening, and what they are saying.

Small-Group Learning 231

FACILITATING

● **CLOSER REVIEW**

Analyzing Visual Metaphors

Circulate among groups as students conduct their first review. Suggest that groups close review panels 1 and 2. Encourage them to talk about the notes they make. If needed, provide the following support.

NOTE: Have students note the details in the drawings that show which animals are representing which people, or work with small groups to have students participate while you note them together.

QUESTION: Guide students to consider what these details might tell them. Ask why some of the characters are drawn as mice and others are drawn as pigs, and accept student responses.

Possible response: Some characters might be mice because they are meek and hated. Some might be pigs because they are prosperous and greedy.

CONCLUDE: Help students to formulate conclusions about the importance of these details in the drawings. Ask students why the artist might have included these details.

Possible response: By drawing his father and other Jewish characters as mice, the author associates them with animals that some want eliminated. By drawing the other characters as pigs, the author associates them with materialistic, greedy behavior.

Point out that in a graphic novel, authors can use **visual metaphors** to convey their ideas. Remind students that a metaphor works by pointing out the similarity between two things.

PERSONALIZE FOR LEARNING

English Language Support

Syntax English learners may struggle with the syntax that the narrator, Vladek, uses in some parts of the excerpt. For example, in panel 8, the narrator says: "If it came a good letter, we'll go." Explain that Vladek's first language is not English, and that fact is purposely represented in the word choice for the character. Encourage students to use the images and surrounding text as context to determine the meaning of unknown or unclear words and sentence structure. In the example above, the narrator means "If he (Mandelbaum) sent good news in a letter, we would also leave." **ALL LEVELS**

from Maus 233

VOCABULARY DEVELOPMENT

Media Vocabulary Reinforcement Students will benefit from additional examples and practice with the media vocabulary. Reinforce their comprehension with "show-you-know" sentences. The first part of the sentence uses the vocabulary word in an appropriate context. The second part of the sentence—the "show-you-know" part—clarifies the first. Model the strategy with this example:

The artist fit so much into one *panel*, with the characters, the setting, and their situation all clear in just one box.

Then give students these sentence prompts and coach them to create the clarification part in reference to panels 9–16:

The *encapsulation* of the discussion between Vladek, Anja, and the man who is hiding them reveals the tension between them, and _____.

Possible response: compresses the talk into a strong image.

Vladek's *speech balloons* are the largest because _____.

Possible response: he says the most words and the artist wanted to draw attention to his speech.

FACILITATING

● CLOSER REVIEW

Analyzing Art

Circulate among groups as students conduct their first review. Suggest that groups close review panel 19. Encourage them to talk about the notes they make. If needed, provide the following support.

NOTE: Have students note the details in panel 19 that show Vladek, Miloch, and Miloch's hiding place, or work with small groups to have students participate while you note them together.

QUESTION: Guide students to consider what these details might tell them. Ask why Vladek is wearing a mask and why Miloch is living in a garbage hole, and accept student responses.

Possible response: Vladek is wearing a mask so that he will appear to be a pig, not a mouse, and hide his identity. Miloch is using the garbage hole as his hiding place.

CONCLUDE: Help students to formulate conclusions about the importance of these details in the drawings. Ask students why the artist might have included these details.

Possible response: The artist included these details to show how extreme and dangerous the situation had become for Jewish people in Poland at this point in the war.

Remind students that in a graphic novel, the **artwork** is just as important as the text. Artists can include details in the drawings to communicate ideas.

234 UNIT 2 • THE HOLOCAUST

PERSONALIZE FOR LEARNING

English Language Support

Syntax Review panel 18 with students. English learners may continue to struggle with the syntax that the narrator, Vladek, uses in some parts of the excerpt. If they are confused, remind them to use the images and surrounding text as context clues. Review the following sentence from panel 18 with students: "The conditions how Miloch was living—you couldn't believe." Encourage students to paraphrase the sentence in their own words. (Possible response: You couldn't believe the conditions in which Miloch was living.) Then encourage students to paraphrase this sentence from the last panel on the page: "Nobody made me any questions going back to Szopienice." (Possible response: Nobody asked me any questions when I went back to Szopienice.) **ALL LEVELS**

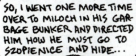
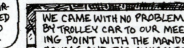

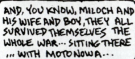

from *Maus* 235

PERSONALIZE FOR LEARNING

Challenge

Research Review panels 24–30. The letter from Mandelbaum's nephew is in Yiddish, which seems to show that it is genuine. Have students research the history of the Yiddish language, which is the language Vladek and his family spoke. Encourage them to report on the roots of the Yiddish language, the time period when Yiddish was most widely spoken, and what caused a decline in the number of speakers.

FACILITATING

● **CLOSER REVIEW**

Analyzing Art

Circulate among groups as students conduct their first review. Suggest that groups close review panels 35–37. Encourage them to talk about the notes they make. If needed, provide the following support.

NOTE: Have students note the details in the artwork that show what happens to change Vladek and Anja's situation, or work with small groups to have students participate while you note them together.

QUESTION: Guide students to consider what these details tell them. Ask how the artist shows the dramatic changes to their situation, and accept student responses.

Possible response: The artist shows Gestapo coming onto the train, and he shows Vladek having his mask removed. He also shows Vladek and Anja in silhouette being marched through the city.

CONCLUDE: Help students to formulate conclusions about the importance of these details in the graphic novel. Ask students why the artist might have included these details.

Possible response: The artist depicts the dramatic situation by showing the Gestapo removing the pig masks, which reveals that Vladek is a mouse, or Jew. This emphasizes Vladek's vulnerability. In the last panel, the artist shows Vladek, Anja, and the Mandelbaums being marched through the city by the Gestapo. The black silhouette emphasizes the darkness of their situation.

Remind students that in a graphic novel, the author depicts an event both through text and **pictures**. Encourage students to discuss what the images add to their understanding of the text.

236 UNIT 2 • THE HOLOCAUST

PERSONALIZE FOR LEARNING

English Language Support

Syntax Review panel 37. English learners may continue to struggle with the syntax that the narrator, Vladek, uses in some parts of the excerpt. Encourage them to use the images and surrounding text as context clues. Review the following sentence from the bottom panel with students: "We passed by the factory what once I owned." Encourage students to reword the sentence. (Possible response: We passed by the factory that I once owned.) Then encourage students to reword this sentence: "We passed the market where we always bought to eat and passed even the street where we used to live, and we came 'til the prison, and there they put us." (Possible response: We passed the market where we always bought food and even passed the street where we used to live. Then we got to the prison, where they put us.) **ALL LEVELS**

from Maus 237

DIGITAL PERSPECTIVES

Enriching the Text To help students understand the excerpt from the graphic novel *Maus*, have them view a video in which Art Spiegelman is interviewed about the book. For example, students might watch "The Holocaust Through the Eyes of a Maus" (Art Spiegelman), an interview recorded in 1991. After students have viewed the video, encourage them to discuss what Spiegelman's own words added to their understanding of the excerpt they read. **(Research to Explore)**

Small-Group Learning 237

FACILITATING

CROSS-CURRICULAR PERSPECTIVES

Social Studies Review panel 52. The excerpt from *Maus* ends as Vladek and Anja are entering Auschwitz in a Nazi truck. Vladek says, "We knew the stories—that they will gas us and throw us in the ovens. This was 1944... We knew everything. And here we were." Have students research the concentration camp called Auschwitz. Encourage them to present information they find through a visual presentation. Students may use charts, graphs, and images to support their informational presentation. Instruct students to be sensitive to the feelings of others when choosing the visuals and information they will present to others.

Comprehension Check

Complete the following items after you finish your first read. Review and clarify details with your group.

1. Why does Vladek Spiegelman want to go to Hungary?

2. What does Anja Spiegelman feel about the smuggling idea?

3. Once the Spiegelmans are on the train, whom do the smugglers say they're calling? Whom do they actually call?

4. Why does Vladek Spiegelman wear a pig mask in some of the panels of the graphic novel?

5. **Notebook** Confirm your understanding of the excerpt by writing a summary..

RESEARCH

Research to Clarify Choose at least one unfamiliar historical detail in the graphic novel. Briefly research that detail. In what way does the historical information shed light on the story?

Research to Explore The excerpt from the graphic novel may inspire you to learn more about the plight of European Jews under the Nazis. Formulate a research question about the subject, and briefly research it. Share your findings with your group.

DIGITAL PERSPECTIVES

Comprehension Check

Possible responses:

1. He wants to go to Hungary to escape danger from the Germans. He thinks if he and his family can get to Hungary, they will be safe.

2. Anja thinks it is too dangerous. She believes they are safe where they are.

3. They say they are calling the men they'll meet at the border to help them; however, they call the Gestapo. He and his family were planning to go to Hungary by train, being escorted by smugglers.

4. He wears a pig mask because he is pretending to be Polish. The non-Jewish Polish characters in the book are drawn as pigs, while the Jewish people are drawn as mice. Vladek is trying to hide his Jewishness.

5. Summaries will vary. However, students should include:
   - Vladek arguing about escape with Anja
   - Vladek visiting his cousin in the garbage hole
   - Vladek meeting with Mandelbaum and the others and deciding to escape
   - Vladek and Anja leaving on a train
   - Vladek and Anja being caught by the Gestapo

Research

Research to Clarify If students struggle to identify a topic to research, suggest that they research the Gestapo or the role of smugglers in helping and hurting Jewish people in Poland. Encourage students to share their findings with others and to discuss how the information sheds light on the story.

Research to Explore Research questions will vary. If students have difficulty forming research questions, direct them to certain topics, such as "What happened to the Jewish population in Poland during and after World War II?" or "How many prisoners of concentration camps survived?" Encourage students to share their findings.

FACILITATING

Jump Start

CLOSE REVIEW Ask students to consider the following question: *How do Vladek, Anja, Mr. Mandelbaum, and Miloch each decide to try to survive the Holocaust?* Encourage students to note the precautions each character takes and what happens to them, according to the excerpt.

Close Review

If needed, model close reviewing by using the Closer Review notes in the Interactive Teacher's Edition.

Remind students to use Accountable Talk in their discussions and to support one another as they complete the close review.

Analyze the Media

1. **Possible response:** Miloch and his family are living in a garbage hole, underground in the cold. They are there because they are hiding from the Nazis. The graphics show what the garbage hole looked like, how garbage was poured into it, and how a stench surrounded it. These details help us understand how awful their situation is.

2. Panel choices will vary by group. Remind students to explain why they chose the panels they presented to group members.

3. Responses will vary by group but should explain what was learned about remembering the past.

Media Vocabulary

Possible responses:

1. The author places a character's words in *speech balloons* to show that he or she is speaking.

2. In some cases, the author makes the *speech balloons* and words within the balloon larger to show how important the exchange is. He also makes some whole *panels* larger, as in the last panel, when the truck carrying the characters enters Auschwitz. This is part of the *encapsulation* of events, which is how a graphic novelist presents scenes through text and art in panels.

3. The first-person narration shows readers that the narrator, Vladek, is remembering events from his own past. The first-person narration helps us understand his experience and his feelings.

Word Network

Possible words: *smugglers, Gestapo, prison, concentration camp, Auschwitz, gas*

MAKING MEANING

from MAUS

Close Review

With your group, revisit sections of the graphic novel you marked during your first read. What do you notice? What **questions** do you have? What can you **conclude**?

Analyze the Media

CITE TEXTUAL EVIDENCE to support your answers.

Notebook Complete the activities.

1. **Review and Clarify** With your group, review the panels that focus on Miloch and his family. Where are they living? What are they doing there? How do the graphics help you understand their situation?

2. **Present and Discuss** Now, work with your group to share the panels that you found especially significant or moving. Take turns presenting your panels. Discuss what you noticed, what questions you asked, and what conclusions you reached.

3. **Essential Question:** *How do we remember the past?* What has this graphic novel taught you about how we remember the past? Discuss with your group.

LANGUAGE DEVELOPMENT

Media Vocabulary

| panel | encapsulation | speech balloon |

Use these vocabulary words in your responses to the following questions.

1. What technique does the author use to show that a character is speaking?

2. How does the author give special emphasis to important scenes, lines of dialogue, or exchanges between characters?

3. How does the author help readers interpret the story in a graphic novel?

WORD NETWORK

Add words related to the Holocaust from the text to your Word Network.

STANDARDS

Speaking and Listening
Analyze the purpose of information presented in diverse media and formats and evaluate the motives behind its presentation.

Language
Acquire and use accurately grade-appropriate general academic and domain-specific words and phrases; gather vocabulary knowledge when considering a word or phrase important to comprehension or expression.

240 UNIT 2 • THE HOLOCAUST

FORMATIVE ASSESSMENT

Analyze the Media

If students struggle to close review the graphic novel, **then** provide the *from Maus: Media Questions* available online in the Interactive Teacher's Edition or Unit Resources. Answers and DOK levels are also available.

Media Vocabulary

If students struggle to identify how the author emphasizes scenes and dialogue, **then** have them review the meaning of the word *encapsulation* and look for examples of the way the author encapsulates important events.

EFFECTIVE EXPRESSION

Research

Assignment
Work with your group to research Art Spiegelman, the author of *Maus*. Then, write a brief **informative report** in which you discuss the ways in which Spiegelman's personal experiences are reflected in his graphic novel.

Conduct Research Work with your group to find the information you will need to write your report. Consult multiple print and digital sources, and evaluate the credibility of each one. *Credibility* refers to the believability of a source. A credible source can be trusted to provide accurate, unbiased information. To evaluate the credibility of sources you might use, answer the following questions. If you check "no" for any source, do not plan to use it.

- **Does the information come from a reliable publication?** ☐ Yes ☐ No
  A reliable print publication may be a respected newspaper, a scholarly journal, or a textbook. A reliable web site may be managed by the government (.gov), a museum or other nonprofit (.org), or a college or university (.edu).

- **Does the author have a good reputation?** ☐ Yes ☐ No
  Find out if the author is connected to a university or other reliable institution. Consider what else the author has written.

- **Does the text show bias or prejudice?** ☐ Yes ☐ No
  Bias can sometimes be hidden. Be on the alert for statements that are not supported with evidence, or opinions masquerading as facts.

For each source you plan to use, collect the information you will need to create a **Works-Cited list,** or **bibliography.** To avoid plagiarism, or presenting someone else's ideas as your own, be sure to credit all the sources you use in your report.

Organize Your Ideas After you have finished your research, discuss how events and experiences in Spiegelman's life are reflected in the excerpt from *Maus*. With your group, determine two or three key points on which to focus in your report.

Clarify and Support Your Ideas As you draft, be sure to make clear connections that show how Spiegelman's events and experiences are reflected in *Maus*. Use details from the graphic novel and your research to support and elaborate on your main points.

Use Domain-Specific Vocabulary As you write your report, use specific vocabulary to relate the story and other information presented in *Maus*. Using the media vocabulary words provided and other media-specific words will help you describe your subject clearly and precisely. In your report, be sure to define or explain any terms with which your audience may be unfamiliar.

EVIDENCE LOG
Before moving on to a new selection, go to your Evidence Log and record what you learned from the excerpt from *Maus*.

STANDARDS
Writing
- Write informative/explanatory texts to examine a topic and convey ideas, concepts, and information through the selection, organization, and analysis of relevant content.
  a. Introduce a topic clearly, previewing what is to follow; organize ideas, concepts, and information into broader categories; include formatting, graphics, and multimedia when useful to aiding comprehension.
  b. Develop the topic with relevant, well-chosen facts, definitions, concrete details, quotations, or other information and examples.
  d. Use precise language and domain-specific vocabulary to inform about or explain the topic.
- Conduct short research projects to answer a question, drawing on several sources and generating additional related, focused questions that allow for multiple avenues of exploration.
- Gather relevant information from multiple print and digital sources, using search terms effectively; assess the credibility and accuracy of each source; and quote or paraphrase the data and conclusions of others while avoiding plagiarism and following a standard format for citation.

DIGITAL PERSPECTIVES

Research

Conduct Research Point out to students that there are many excellent sources of information about Art Spiegelman online and in the library. He has been profiled in news and media sources (newspapers, magazines, websites), and biographies of him are also available. Many of these sources detail his life history and that of his family. Students may want to search for additional information on Spiegelman in reference sources about cartoonists and graphic novels and Holocaust history.

Organize Your Ideas Encourage students to list all ideas as they conduct their research. As they organize their ideas, they can decide which are most important to include. They should also organize them into an appropriate order.

Clarify and Support Your Ideas Remind students that their ideas must be supported by evidence both from *Maus* and from outside sources about Spiegelman's life. In doing so, students should make sure they fully understand the source material and that the examples they cite truly support their ideas.

Using Domain-Specific Vocabulary Remind students that when they use technical or domain-specific terminology, they must demonstrate their understanding of the terms in relation to the context of their topic. For example, for the term *fascism,* students would need to go beyond a dictionary definition of the term and demonstrate which group in the war was fascist and how elements of *fascism* are evident in *Maus*. For more support, see **Research: Informative Report**

Evidence Log Support students in completing their Evidence Log. This paced activity will help prepare them for the Performance-Based Assessment at the end of the unit.

PERSONALIZE FOR LEARNING

Strategic Support

Research If students are conducting research on the Internet, discuss the importance of search terms. Have them ask what specific information they need to complete the assignment. For example, searching "Art Spiegelman" will result in a large number of links, but it may be hard to find the information needed for the project. A more specific search term, such as "Art Spiegelman biographical information" will provide a more focused list of links. Have students try more than one term in their search and evaluate the results.

FORMATIVE ASSESSMENT

Research

If students have trouble compiling their information to make a well-ordered presentation, **then** encourage them to choose an organizational structure, such as presenting information in chronological order or by topic. For Reteach and Practice, see **Research: Informative Report (RP).**

FACILITATING

Deliver a Multimedia Presentation

Assignment Before groups begin work on their projects, have them clearly differentiate the role each group member will play. Remind groups to consult the schedule for Small-Group Learning to guide their work during the Performance Task.

Students should complete the assignment using presentation software to take advantage of text, graphics, and sound features.

Plan With Your Group

Analyze the Texts Discuss with students that remembering the past is both an objective and subjective activity, and when we discuss the importance of remembering past events such as the Holocaust, no two people share the identical impressions or attitudes about the events we remember. It is important for students to understand that the texts they are analyzing portray historical events, but each text is, to varying degrees, subjective. Part of the students' analysis of the texts can involve an examination of how these texts interpret history, and the effect this can have on readers.

Gather Evidence and Media Examples After students have analyzed the text to fill in the chart, have them discuss the last column of the chart, which will help them answer the prompt.

PERFORMANCE TASK: SPEAKING AND LISTENING FOCUS

SOURCES
- from ANNE FRANK: THE DIARY OF A YOUNG GIRL
- ACCEPTANCE SPEECH FOR THE NOBEL PEACE PRIZE
- from MAUS

Deliver a Multimedia Presentation

Assignment
Create and present an **explanatory multimedia presentation** in response to the following prompt:

> How do the selections contribute to your understanding of the Holocaust and the ways in which we remember the past?

Plan With Your Group

Analyze the Texts With your group, analyze how each selection contributes to your understanding of the Holocaust. Use this chart to organize your ideas.

SELECTION	PLACES AND PEOPLE AFFECTED	HISTORICAL EVENTS	HOW REMEMBERED TODAY
from Anne Frank: The Diary of a Young Girl			
Acceptance Speech for the Nobel Peace Prize			
from Maus			

Gather Evidence and Media Examples Each group member should choose one selection on which to focus. Work individually to gather important details and information. Next, organize the ideas, and draft a brief explanatory essay for your section of the presentation. Then, conduct additional research to find relevant media to include in the presentation.

Organize Your Ideas As a group, organize the sections of the presentation, and decide how to transition smoothly from one section and speaker to the next. Be sure you tie all the ideas and information together at the end of your presentation.

AUTHOR'S PERSPECTIVE | Ernest Morrell, Ph.D.

Strategic Use of Media Media is becoming more important as a communication tool, but teachers need to guide students to understand media's value. As groups plan their presentation, remind them that it is important to use media and visuals strategically so that they support the presentation but don't dominate it. Share these suggestions:

- Students should ensure that each piece of media has a specific purpose and is not mere "filler."
- Encourage students to let the content of their presentation drive their decisions about which media support to include, rather than finding appealing media and trying to force fit into a presentation where it might not work.
- Remind groups that although media and visuals can enhance a presentation, the content of what students say during the presentation is what is most important.
- Ultimately, the presentation should be able to stand alone without media support and still make sense.

ESSENTIAL QUESTION: How do we remember the past?

Rehearse With Your Group

Practice With Your Group As you deliver your portion of the presentation, use this checklist to evaluate the effectiveness of your group's rehearsal. Then, use your evaluation and the instruction here to guide your revisions to the presentation.

CONTENT	USE OF MEDIA	PRESENTATION TECHNIQUES
☐ The presentation clearly responds to the prompt.	☐ The use of photographs, illustrations, and other still images supports the presentation.	☐ Each member uses a formal tone, appropriate eye contact, adequate volume, and clear pronunciation.
☐ The presentation includes information from the texts and from additional research that supports the main idea.	☐ Videos, recorded interviews, and other multimedia enhance and clarify the presentation.	☐ The pacing of the presentation is measured and helps the audience comprehend the information.
☐ The presentation includes a strong conclusion.		

Fine-Tune the Content Be sure you are clearly explaining the events of the Holocaust and the ways in which we remember the past. Use specific details from the text as well as outside research.

Improve Your Use of Media Check that images and multimedia are presented in context. Each piece of multimedia should relate directly to a key point and should help the audience better understand the information.

Brush-Up on Your Presentation Techniques As you rehearse, point out where group members should vary their pacing and tone to emphasize certain parts of the presentation. Be sure everyone uses formal English when speaking.

Present and Evaluate

Give members of your group and members of other groups your full support and attention when they are presenting. As you listen to other groups, consider their content, use of media, and presentation techniques. Think about the ways in which other groups' presentations deepened your understanding of the Holocaust and the ways in which we remember the past. Be ready to ask questions.

STANDARDS
Speaking and Listening
• Present claims and findings, emphasizing salient points in a focused, coherent manner with relevant evidence, sound valid reasoning, and well-chosen details; use appropriate eye contact, adequate volume, and clear pronunciation.
• Integrate multimedia and visual displays into presentations to clarify information, strengthen claims and evidence, and add interest.
• Adapt speech to a variety of contexts and tasks, demonstrating command of formal English when indicated or appropriate.

DIGITAL PERSPECTIVES

Rehearse With Your Group

Practice With Your Group Encourage groups to pair up to practice their presentations before giving their presentations in front of the whole class. While one group presents, the other can note areas that could be improved. Make sure that groups include any multimedia that will be used in the final presentation in this first run-through.

Fine-Tune the Content Have students review the material in the presentation to make sure that it addresses the prompt. Point out that multimedia or text that does not directly address the main point of their presentation should be removed. Have students make sure that transitions are included to help listeners follow the flow of ideas.

Improve Your Use of Media For the topic of the Holocaust, students may want to consider whether some images or videos are too upsetting to be used in a classroom presentation. Encourage them to avoid using media for shock value, but instead use images that support their main ideas.

Present and Evaluate

Before beginning the presentations, set the expectations for the audience. You may wish to have students consider these questions as groups present:

- What information does the group present that tells how people fought back against Nazi rule?
- What are some of the group's main points?
- What multimedia does the group use to illustrate its points?
- Which multimedia is most effective at illustrating a certain point?
- What presentation skills does this group excel at?

PERSONALIZE FOR LEARNING

Strategic Support

Media Sources While students may find a wealth of information about the Holocaust on the Internet, they may be unclear about which websites are credible. As they conduct research, have them try to assess the purpose of each website. For example, some websites exist that have the purpose of denying the existence of the Holocaust. These should not be considered credible sources. Remind students that well-known institutions such as the United States Memorial Holocaust Museum are likely to be trustworthy. They may also find images through respected newspapers and magazines, such as *The Atlantic* or the *New York Times*.

OVERVIEW

INDEPENDENT LEARNING

How do we remember the past?

Encourage students to think carefully about what they have already learned and what more they want to know about the unit topic of the Holocaust. This is a key first step to previewing and selecting the text they will read in Independent Learning.

Independent Learning Strategies ▶

Review the Learning Strategies with students and explain that as they work through Independent Learning they will develop strategies to work on their own.

- Have students watch the video on Independent Learning Strategies.
- A video on this topic is available online in the Professional Development Center.

Students should include any favorite strategies that they might have devised on their own during Whole-Class and Small-Group Learning. For example, for the strategy "Apply strategies" students might include:

- Make an outline of everything I want to discuss.
- Divide available time to make sure that there is enough time to cover everything.

Block Scheduling

Each day in this Pacing Plan represents a 40–50 minute class period. Teachers using block scheduling may combine days to reflect their class schedule. In addition, teachers may revise pacing to differentiate and support core instruction by integrating components and resources as students require.

📅 **Pacing Plan**

OVERVIEW: INDEPENDENT LEARNING

ESSENTIAL QUESTION:

How do we remember the past?

There are many ways to remember, and all of them can add to our understanding of the past. In this section, you will choose one additional selection about the Holocaust for your final reading experience in this unit. You'll then share what you learn with classmates. To choose a text, follow these steps.

Look Back Think about the selections you have already read. What more do you want to know about the Holocaust?

Look Ahead Preview the selections by reading the descriptions. Which one seems most interesting and appealing to you?

Look Inside Take a few minutes to scan through the text you chose. Make another selection if this text doesn't meet your needs.

Independent Learning Strategies

Throughout your life, in school, in your community, and in your career, you will need to rely on yourself to learn and work on your own. Review these strategies and the actions you can take to practice them during Independent Learning. Add ideas of your own for each category.

STRATEGY	ACTION PLAN
Apply strategies	• Understand your goals and deadlines. • Make a plan for what to do each day. •
Practice what you have learned	• Use first-read and close-read strategies to deepen your understanding. • After you read, evaluate the usefulness of the evidence to help you understand the topic. • Consider the quality and reliability of the source. •
Take notes	• Record important ideas and information. • Review your notes before preparing to share with a group. •

SCAN FOR MULTIMEDIA

244 UNIT 2 • THE HOLOCAUST

Pacing Plan:

- Unit Introduction (1, 2)
- Introduce Whole-Class Learning (3)
- *The Diary of Anne Frank*, Act I (4, 5, 6, 7, 8)
- *The Diary of Anne Frank*, Act II (9, 10, 11, 12, 13)
- Media: Frank Family and World War II Timelines (14, 15)
- Performance Task (16, 17, 18)

CONTENTS

Choose one selection. Selections are available online only.

TELEVISION TRANSCRIPT

Saving the Children Bob Simon

In an interview, a Londoner who helped save hundreds of Czechoslovakian children from the Nazis relates his experiences.

REFLECTIVE ESSAY

A Great Adventure in the Shadow of War
Mary Helen Dirkx

An American girl growing up in postwar Germany sees a country desperate to repair itself.

INFORMATIVE ARTICLE

Irena Sendler: Rescuer of the Children of Warsaw Chana Kroll

This article tells the true-life story of a courageous woman who smuggled thousands of children out of the Warsaw Ghetto.

HISTORICAL WRITING

Quiet Resistance
from **Courageous Teen Resisters** Ann Byers

In their own words, people tell about their lives as Jewish teenagers under Nazi oppression.

NEWS ARTICLE

Remembering a Devoted Keeper of Anne Frank's Legacy Moni Basu

An article about Buddy Elias, a cousin of Anne Frank, who devoted his life to keeping Anne's memory alive.

FIRST-PERSON ACCOUNT

I'll Go Fetch Her Tomorrow
from **Hidden Like Anne Frank** Bloeme Emden with Marcel Prins

A harrowing first-person account of what it was like to go into hiding as a child in the Netherlands during World War II.

PERFORMANCE-BASED ASSESSMENT PREP

Review Evidence for an Explanatory Essay

Complete your Evidence Log for the unit by evaluating what you've learned and synthesizing the information you've recorded.

SCAN FOR MULTIMEDIA

DIGITAL PERSPECTIVES

Contents

Selections Encourage students to scan and preview the selections before choosing the one they would like to read. Suggest that they consider the genre and subject matter of each one before making their decision. You can use the information on the following Planning pages to advise students in making their choice.

> Remind students that the selections for Independent Learning are only available in the Interactive Student Edition. Allow students who do not have digital access at home to preview the selection(s) using classroom or computer lab technology. Then either have students print the selection they choose or provide a printout for them.

Performance Based-Assessment Prep
Review Evidence for an Explanatory Essay Point out to students that collecting evidence during Independent Learning is the last step in completing their Evidence Log. After they finish their independent reading, they will synthesize all the evidence they have compiled in the unit.

The evidence students collect will serve as the primary source of information they will use to complete the writing and oral presentation for the Performance-Based Assessment at the end of the unit.

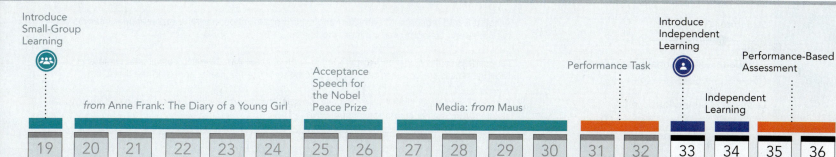

PLANNING INDEPENDENT LEARNING

Saving the Children

Summary
In this television transcript of a report called "Saving the Children," Bob Simon recounts the story of Nicholas Winton. This young man saved the lives of hundreds of children during World War II. Winton followed the news and knew how much danger refugees trying to flee the Nazis were in. He went to Czechoslovakia in 1938 to help. Later that year, the Nazis invaded Czechoslovakia. Though Winton had no experience, he managed to set up an organization and sneak more than 600 children out to England. For decades after the war, few knew what he did. He was very humble and never talked about it. In 1998, the BBC introduced him to many people he had saved.

Insight
This piece shows how anyone, with goodwill and intent, can do a tremendous amount of good. It also illustrates how immensely rewarding helping others feels.

SELECTION RESOURCES
- First-Read Guide: Nonfiction
- Close-Read Guide: Nonfiction
- Saving the Children: Text Questions
- Audio Summaries
- Selection Audio
- Selection Test

Connection to Essential Question
This report sheds light on a positive action in a dark time, helping students to consider the Essential Question, "How do we remember the past?" Winton's memories of that short time are vivid and positive; he only wishes he could have done more.

Connection to Performance-Based Assessment
Students may consider this man's story as they answer the Performance-Based Assessment Prompt, "What is the best way to cope with disturbing events of the past?" Later in his life, Winton chose not to speak of the era; he was very focused on the present, and on what other humanitarian work he could do as his work went on.

Text Complexity Rubric: Saving the Children

Quantitative Measures

Lexile: 740   Text Length: 1,925 words

Qualitative Measures

Knowledge Demands ①—②—**❸**—④—⑤	Selection relies on understanding of Holocaust, including details of the Munich Agreement, Polish Transports, and Auschwitz. Although these events may be unfamiliar, they are clearly explained.
Structure ①—**❷**—③—④—⑤	Account is told sequentially, with clear and explicit organization; narrative explanation is interspersed with interview dialogue, making it easy to follow.
Language Conventionality and Clarity ①—②—**❸**—④—⑤	Language is conventional and contemporary, with a mix of narration and conversation in interview. Most sentences are simple in structure, but some sentence fragments appear in the transcript.
Levels of Meaning/Purpose ①—**❷**—③—④—⑤	Purpose is explicit, concrete, and narrowly focused. This report tells the story of one man's quest to save children from the concentration camps.

A Great Adventure in the Shadow of War

Summary

In "A Great Adventure in the Shadow of War," a reflective essay, Mary Helen Dirkx talks about a piece of her childhood when she lived as an American teenager in Germany. During this time, the criminals responsible for the atrocities at Auschwitz were on trial. Dirkx and her friends spent much of their time exploring buildings abandoned during the war, with little thought for what had happened. She describes the trial and the way that news of the murders at Auschwitz horrified the world. She realized that her German friends were no different than she—and yet, hearing about the Nuremberg trials let her know that human beings, just like her, had chosen to do terrible things. She hoped that her generation would do better.

Insight

There are several life lessons one can extract from this piece, but perhaps the most important is the insight into how evil happens. Normal people can choose to ignore things they know, and enable terrible things. The final paragraph, on her fears that her own generation didn't do enough, is especially important.

SELECTION RESOURCES

- First-Read Guide: Nonfiction
- Close-Read Guide: Nonfiction
- A Great Adventure in the Shadow of War: Text Questions
- Audio Summaries
- Selection Audio
- Selection Test

Connection to Essential Question

This essay provides a first-person response to the Essential Question: "How do we remember the past?" Dirkx remembers both how she felt at the time, and what she learned on reflection years later. The essay also stresses that the court system worked to place accountability.

Connection to Performance-Based Assessment

Students may choose to consider this essay as they prepare for the Performance-Based Assessment prompt, which asks "What is the best way to cope with disturbing events of the past?" The text calls for acknowledging accountability for past crimes and trying to create a better future. However, in the end Dirkx makes it clear that simply hoping to do better is not enough.

Reading Support: A Great Adventure in the Shadow of War

Quantitative Measures

Lexile: 1260   Text Length: 821 words

Qualitative Measures

Knowledge Demands ①—②—③—❹—⑤	Basic knowledge is needed of the Holocaust and details such as use of poison gas in Auschwitz; references to other global events, such as Rwanda's Tutsi genocide, and the Bosnian Srebrenica massacre, may be unfamiliar.
Structure ①—②—❸—④—⑤	Narrative structure is used in this first-person account. Selection presents a range of events and ideas that are mostly explained in a straightforward way. Some connections between ideas are not immediately apparent.
Language Conventionality and Clarity ①—②—❸—④—⑤	Language is somewhat complex and highly descriptive; there are many complex, lengthy sentences with multiple clauses and above-level vocabulary.
Levels of Meaning/Purpose ①—②—❸—④—⑤	The text presents a view of the Auschwitz trial from the point of view of a 14-year-old girl. However, some concepts and reactions of the girl are sophisticated or subtle. Rhetorical questions are used to state ideas.

Independent Learning   246B

PLANNING   INDEPENDENT LEARNING

SELECTION RESOURCES

- First-Read Guide: Nonfiction
- Close-Read Guide: Nonfiction
- Irena Sendler: Rescuer of the Children of Warsaw
- Audio Summaries
- Selection Audio
- Selection Test

Irena Sendler: Rescuer of the Children of Warsaw

Summary

"Irena Sendler: Rescuer of the Children of Warsaw" is a news article by Chana Kroll. It tells the story of a woman who saved 2,500 children from the Warsaw Ghetto during World War II. The Warsaw Ghetto was a closed district where Jews in Poland were forced to live, and where many were eventually killed. Sendler spent the whole war helping in the ways she could, from forging documents that would keep people safe to providing food. Later she literally carried children to freedom, hiding them in a sack to get them to a safe place, then coaching them on how to avoid being detected. She made sure to keep contact information so that after the war, children and their parents could be reunited. She was caught and tortured, but didn't give anyone up. After the war, she continued helping people. Sendler's work came to light in 1999, when high school students in Kansas began a research project. They learned about her life, wrote a play, won contests, and ultimately had the chance to meet Sendler. The play became a key influencer on the way the Holocaust is taught in Poland, and led to an exchange program that helps students in both the United States and Poland.

Insight

The compassion and cleverness Sendler displayed set an excellent example. Students may be amazed to see the power of high school research. Sendler was still alive when the Kansas students began their research and they had the opportunity to meet her. The article also goes into the value she has provided as a role model to others in her country.

Connection to Essential Question

This text sheds an interesting light on the Essential Question: "How do we remember the past?" Sendler would have been forgotten if not for a few written records, but the Kansas class brought her the acclaim she had earned.

Connection to Performance-Based Assessment

The prompt is "What is the best way to cope with disturbing events of the past?" Sendler felt it was less important for her own work to be recognized and more important that the work of her organization, Zegota, be honored. Students may see that Sendler's interest in keeping her fellow rescuers in mind—focusing on those who helped others, and on those she saved—can help us cope with the past.

Text Complexity Rubric: Irena Sendler: Rescuer of the Children of Warsaw

Quantitative Measures

Lexile: 1130   Text Length: 2,589 words

Qualitative Measures

Knowledge Demands ①—②—❸—④—⑤	Selection relies on knowledge about the Holocaust, specifically the Warsaw Ghetto and the practice of rescuing children by smuggling. Events are not in the realm of students' experience, but are clearly explained.
Structure ①—②—❸—④—⑤	Text is dense, with many details, and is not broken up by many quotations or dialogue. However, the account is sequentially organized, clear, and straightforward.
Language Conventionality and Clarity ①—②—❸—④—⑤	Language is conventional and contemporary, but somewhat complex; many sentences are long and complex, with multiple clauses. Vocabulary is mostly on-level.
Levels of Meaning/Purpose ①—②—❸—④—⑤	Article describes two stories—Sendler's experiences during World War II and the Kansas students who researched her many decades later.

Quiet Resistance

Summary

This selection, compiled from primary sources by Ann Byers, describes Jewish life in Poland under the Nazi occupation. The Germans forced the Jewish population into the Warsaw Ghetto a cramped section of the capital city. Little food was available, and disease spread in the poor conditions. Oppression was thorough and made it very difficult to resist. The article includes diary entries and first-person accounts that detail people's experiences. Some young people found ways to break out of confinement to bring food or information back from outside the ghetto walls. They took enormous risks to help their families and friends, and some paid with their lives.

Insight

This selection focuses on the fear and discrimination that Jews experienced during the Holocaust. Through the words of people who were forced to live in the ghetto, the writer shows the bravery and self-control necessary to stay hidden under conditions of great danger. The text also demonstrates the lifelong pain that even survival can cause.

SELECTION RESOURCES

- First-Read Guide: Nonfiction
- Close-Read Guide: Nonfiction
- Quiet Resistance: Text Questions
- Audio Summaries
- Selection Audio
- Selection Test

Connection to Essential Question

In this text, those who lived through a difficult time can help students consider the Essential Question: "How do we remember the past?" One survivor, Leah Hammerstein, recalls how harrowing it was to hide her identity, and how lonely it made her feel.

Connection to Performance-Based Assessment

The prompt is "What is the best way to cope with disturbing events of the past?" This article discusses the techniques young people used to resist discrimination and oppression. Students may see that writing about their experiences helps to validate what happened and to educate others.

Text Complexity Rubric: Quiet Resistance

Quantitative Measures

Lexile: 910   Text Length: 2,012 words

Qualitative Measures

Knowledge Demands (3 of 5)	Background about Holocaust is needed to fully understand the selection, but events are clearly described and will be familiar from studying this unit. Firsthand accounts make information accessible.
Structure (2 of 5)	Text is dense, but two sections are labeled; multiple quotations break up density of the text and make it easier to understand; organization of ideas within sections is clear and logical.
Language Conventionality and Clarity (3 of 5)	Narration has clear and simple language, but there are multiple quotations from different people with a variety of complexity and language styles; some rhetorical and figurative language is used.
Levels of Meaning/Purpose (2 of 5)	Text is a collection of firsthand experiences of Nazi occupation. Overall purpose of text is clear and explicit; both events and feelings are clearly stated.

Independent Learning   246D

PLANNING   INDEPENDENT LEARNING

Remembering a Devoted Keeper of Anne Frank's Legacy

SELECTION RESOURCES

- First-Read Guide: Nonfiction
- Close-Read Guide: Nonfiction
- Remembering a Devoted Keeper of Anne Frank's Legacy: Text Questions
- Audio Summaries
- Selection Audio
- Selection Test

Summary

"Remembering a Devoted Keeper of Anne Frank's Legacy" is an article by Moni Basu. It was written when Buddy Elias, a cousin of Anne Frank, died at the age of 80. Basu fondly remembers a time when she met Elias when he was on a book tour in America. Elias and Frank were cousins and childhood friends, but lost touch as the war began. After the war was over, Anne's father Otto published her diary and helped to get a play written. Elias waited until the book was translated into German, but he learned a great deal about his cousin, and mourned her loss. From then on, he was dedicated to keeping her legacy alive.

Insight

The article emphasizes a family tradition of kindness and intellectual pursuit in contrast with the cruelty of the Nazi regime. It reminds readers of what was lost—and what can be done to rebuild from what remains.

Connection to Essential Question

Elias's life and passion provide a strong response to the Essential Question: "How do we remember the past?" Buddy Elias worked to preserve the past by spreading knowledge of Anne Frank's life as widely as he could.

Connection to Performance-Based Assessment

Students may choose to consider Elias's approach to life as they consider the Performance-Based Assessment prompt: "What is the best way to cope with disturbing events of the past?" He seemed to concentrate on the good of those who were lost, and made sure they were not forgotten.

Text Complexity Rubric: Remembering a Devoted Keeper of Anne Frank's Legacy

Quantitative Measures

Lexile: 950   Text Length: 800 words

Qualitative Measures

Knowledge Demands (3)	Article assumes knowledge of Anne Frank and the Holocaust. Students will have this knowledge from this unit, and content is clearly explained.
Structure (2)	Information is straightforward and clear, with short paragraphs to separate ideas. At times organization is not predictable. Some quotations make text easier to understand.
Language Conventionality and Clarity (2)	Language is concrete and clear; sentence structure is easy to understand, with only some complex sentences with multiple clauses; vocabulary is on-level.
Levels of Meaning/Purpose (2)	Purpose of text is clear and explicit: writer provides a remembrance of Buddy Elias and his work on keeping Anne Frank's memory alive.

DIGITAL PERSPECTIVES | Audio | Video | Document | Annotation Highlights | EL Highlights | Online Assessment

I'll Go Fetch Her Tomorrow

SELECTION RESOURCES

- First-Read Guide: Nonfiction
- Close-Read Guide: Nonfiction
- I'll Go Fetch Her Tomorrow: Text Questions
- Audio Summaries
- Selection Audio
- Selection Test

Summary

In this first-person account entitled "I'll Go Fetch Her Tomorrow," Bloeme Emden talks about returning home from the concentration camp after the war, and about what happened earlier in the war. As the occupation began, she was scheduled to be sent to a labor camp during her high school exams. She arranged to take all her exams on the same day so she could get her diploma before having to go to the camp. Like so many others, she had been tricked into thinking there was no danger as long as she followed the rules and went to the camp. Fortunately, she managed to avoid deportation and she moved among hiding places for most of the war. She received news that her family had been taken, and she lived in fear. Before the end of the war, she was captured and put in prison. Finally she was sent to a camp.

Insight

This memoir provides insight into the ways that people worked to evade deportation during the Nazi occupation. Often, they had to leave their families and deny their identities.

Connection to Essential Question

This memoir provides a survivor's take on the Essential Question: "How do we remember the past?" Bloeme Emden recalls the specific ways she hid and the emotions provoked by the trials she went through.

Connection to Performance-Based Assessment

Students may find Bloeme Emden's coping processes to be useful as they prepare to respond to the Performance-Based Assessment prompt: "What is the best way to cope with disturbing events of the past?" She ultimately breaks up with her boyfriend because his attempts to keep track of her reminded her too much of being imprisoned.

Text Complexity Rubric: I'll Go Fetch Her Tomorrow

Quantitative Measures

Lexile: 800   Text Length: 4,095 words

Qualitative Measures

Knowledge Demands ①—②—❸—④—⑤	Selection relies on knowledge of the Holocaust. All events and background are explained fully and in first person, making content accessible.
Structure ①—②—❸—④—⑤	After an early time shift near the beginning of the text, organization is chronological and logical. Text is dense, with many details and little dialogue.
Language Conventionality and Clarity ①—❷—③—④—⑤	Events are narrated in first person, in clear and accessible language. Sentence structure is mostly simple, with a few compound sentences or multiple clauses. Vocabulary is on-level.
Levels of Meaning/Purpose ①—❷—③—④—⑤	Purpose is clear and narrowly focused. Detailed account of author's experience is told clearly and explicitly, with plot events and feelings explained fully.

Independent Learning   246F

ADVISING

You may wish to direct students to use the generic First-Read and Close-Read Guides in the Print Student Edition. Alternatively, you may wish to print copies of the genre-specific First-Read and Close-Read Guides for students. These are available online in the Interactive Student Edition or Unit Resources.

FIRST READ

Students should perform the steps of the first read independently.

NOTICE: Students should focus on the basic elements of the text to ensure they understand what is happening.

ANNOTATE: Students should mark any passages they wish to revisit during their close read.

CONNECT: Students should increase their understanding by connecting what they've read to other texts or personal experiences.

RESPOND: Students will write a summary to demonstrate their understanding.

Point out to students that while they will always complete the Respond step at the end of the first read, the other steps will probably happen somewhat concurrently. Remind students that they will revisit their first-read annotations during the close read. You may wish to print copies of the First-Read Guide for students to use.

> After students have completed the First-Read Guide, you may wish to assign the Text Questions for the selection that are available in the Interactive Teacher's Edition.

Anchor Standards

In the first two sections of the unit, students worked with the whole class and in small groups to gain topical knowledge and greater understanding of the skills required by the anchor standards. In this section, they are asked to work independently, applying what they have learned and demonstrating increased readiness for college and career.

INDEPENDENT LEARNING

First-Read Guide

Use this page to record your first-read ideas.

Selection Title: _____

 Tool Kit
First-Read Guide and Model Annotation

NOTICE new information or ideas you learn about the unit topic as you first read this text.

ANNOTATE by marking vocabulary and key passages you want to revisit.

CONNECT ideas within the selection to other knowledge and the selections you have read.

RESPOND by writing a brief summary of the selection.

STANDARD
Reading Read and comprehend complex literary and informational texts independently and proficiently.

246 UNIT 2 • THE HOLOCAUST

PERSONALIZE FOR LEARNING

Strategic Support

Text Preview Remind students who struggle with independent reading to preview the text by looking at the title along with visuals, captions, and headings. Ask them to track their ideas about the topic or genre of the text, along with their thoughts about the author's purpose for writing. Encourage students to consider what they already know about the topic and to share their observations about the text they will read.

During the first read, students should annotate words that are unfamiliar or stand out to them as possible clues to the meaning of the text.

When First- and Close-Read Guide entries are completed by students independently, and students learn the meaning of all their annotated words, encourage students to compile the vocabulary words into a class dictionary that everyone can consult.

ESSENTIAL QUESTION: How do we remember the past?

Close-Read Guide

Use this page to record your close-read ideas.

🔧 **Tool Kit**
Close-Read Guide and Model Annotation

Selection Title: _____

Close Read the Text

Revisit sections of the text you marked during your first read. Read these sections closely and **annotate** what you notice. Ask yourself **questions** about the text. What can you **conclude**? Write down your ideas.

Analyze the Text

Think about the author's choices of patterns, structure, techniques, and ideas included in the text. Select one, and record your thoughts about what this choice conveys.

QuickWrite

Pick a paragraph from the text that grabbed your interest. Explain the power of this passage.

STANDARD
Reading Read and comprehend complex literary and informational texts independently and proficiently.

Overview: Independent Learning 247

DIGITAL PERSPECTIVES

CLOSE READ

Students should begin their close read by revisiting the annotations they made during their first read. Then students should analyze one of the author's choices regarding the following elements:

- **patterns**, such as repetition or parallelism
- **structure**, such as cause-and-effect or problem-solution
- **techniques**, such as description or dialogue
- **ideas**, such as the author's main idea or claim

MAKE IT INTERACTIVE
Group students according to the selection they have chosen. Then have students meet to discuss the selection in depth. Their discussions should be guided by their insights and questions.

PERSONALIZE FOR LEARNING

Strategic Support
Annotations Reinforce the strategies of close reading for students who struggle with its benefits. After they complete the Close-Read Guide, review the experience. Have students choose a first-read annotation that helped them understand the text more deeply during the close read.

Discuss the following questions with students:
- How did a revisit of the first-read annotation help you better understand the text during your close read?
- What did you learn about that passage during the close read? What strategies did you use to study the passage you marked?
- What can you conclude about the text, based on the passage you selected?

Ask for student volunteers to discuss how using the First-Read and Close-Read Guides helped them understand the text better.

Independent Learning 247

ADVISING

Share Your Independent Learning

Prepare to Share
Explain to students that sharing what they learned from their Independent Learning selection provides classmates who read a different selection with an opportunity to consider the text as a source of evidence during the Performance-Based Assessment. As students prepare to share, remind them to highlight how their selection contributed to their knowledge of the concept of the Holocaust, as well as how the selection connects to the question: *How do we remember the past?*

Learn from Your Classmates
As students discuss the Independent Learning selections, direct them to take particular note of how their classmates' chosen selections align with their current position on the Performance-Based Assessment question.

Reflect
Students may want to add their reflection to their Evidence Log, particularly if their insight relates to a specific selection from the unit.

MAKE IT INTERACTIVE
Assemble an "expert panel" so students can share what they have learned from their selections with students who chose another selection. Have students who read each of the selections submit two or three questions for the panel to answer. Appoint a moderator and provide her or him with the questions that have been submitted. The moderator will ask panel members questions based on the selection each read. Sample questions might include:

What is this selection mostly about? What details provided more information about the main idea? What have you learned from this selection about remembering the past?

Evidence Log Support students in completing their Evidence Log. This paced activity will help prepare them for the Performance-Based Assessment at the end of the unit.

INDEPENDENT LEARNING

EVIDENCE LOG
Go to your Evidence Log and record what you learned from the text you read.

Share Your Independent Learning
Prepare to Share
How do we remember the past?

Even when you read something independently, you can continue to grow by sharing what you have learned with others. Reflect on the text you explored independently, and write notes about its connection to the unit. In your notes, consider why this text belongs in this unit.

Learn from Your Classmates
Discuss It Share your ideas about the text you explored on your own. As you talk with others in your class, jot down ideas that you learn from them.

Reflect
Review your notes, and mark the most important insight you gained from these writing and discussion activities. Explain how this idea adds to your understanding of the Holocaust.

STANDARDS
Speaking and Listening
Engage effectively in a range of collaborative discussions with diverse partners on *grade 8 topics, texts, and issues*, building on others' ideas and expressing their own clearly.

AUTHOR'S PERSPECTIVE — Ernest Morrell, Ph.D.

Active Listening and Learning It's important to support students as they learn and develop the skills of participating in small-group discussions. As students discuss their Independent Learning selection with classmates, remind them that it is important to be an active, but not dominant, participant. Explain that an active participant is one who speaks confidently, but also listens carefully to others, while a dominant participant is one who takes over and does not allow others to contribute. Remind students that being an active listener involves these strategies:

- **Taking notes** Students who take useful notes capture the speaker's main points and note ideas to contribute once the speaker is done talking.

- **Restating others' ideas to show understanding** Encourage students to use such language as "This is what I heard you saying . . ." and "I think this is what you meant when you said . . ."

- **Asking clarifying questions** When they don't understand, or if they want to move the conversation forward, students might ask peers questions like, "Could you explain what you meant when you said . . ."

PERFORMANCE-BASED ASSESSMENT PREP

Review Evidence for an Explanatory Essay

At the beginning of this unit, you took a position on the following statement:

> How can literature help us remember and honor the victims of the Holocaust?

EVIDENCE LOG

Review your Evidence Log and your QuickWrite from the beginning of the unit. Did you learn anything new?

NOTES

Identify at least three pieces of evidence that suggest the role literature can play in honoring and remembering Holocaust victims.

1.

2.

3.

Identify one or two key quotations from the evidence you listed:

_____
_____

Develop your thoughts into a topic sentence for an explanatory essay. Clarify your thinking by completing these sentence starters:

In honoring and remembering victims of the Holocaust, we face these challenges:

_____
_____

Literature can help us overcome these challenges by

_____
_____

STANDARDS

Writing
Write informative/explanatory texts to examine a topic and convey ideas, concepts, and information through the selection, organization, and analysis of relevant content.
  b. Develop the topic with relevant, well-chosen facts, definitions, concrete details, quotations, or other information and examples.

DIGITAL PERSPECTIVES

Review Evidence for an Explanatory Essay

Evidence Log Students should understand that their position on an issue could evolve as they learn more about the subject and are exposed to additional points of view. Point out that just because they took an initial position on the question *How can literature help us remember and honor the victims of the Holocaust?* doesn't mean that their position can't change after careful consideration of their learning and evidence.

Encourage students to use the sentence starters provided to help them express their thoughts. Once they have a statement, students may find details in their evidence logs to support their ideas.

ASSESSING

Writing to Sources: Explanatory Essay

Students should complete the Performance-Based Assessment independently, with little to no input or feedback during the process. Students should use word processing software to take advantage of editing tools and features.

Prior to beginning the Assessment, have students discuss the different ways that the real people in the selections who survived the Holocaust have coped with the trauma. Then discuss how people not directly affected by the Holocaust have tried to understand and deal with the enormity of the events.

Review the Elements of Effective Explanatory Essays Students can review the work they did earlier in the unit as they complete the Performance-Based Assessment. They may also consult other resources such as:

- the elements of an explanatory essay, including an introduction with a controlling idea, a logical organization, valid reasoning and evidence, and a formal and objective tone, available in Whole-Class Learning
- their Evidence Log
- their Word Network

Although students will use evidence from unit selections for their explanatory essay, they may need to collect additional evidence, including facts, statistics, anecdotes, quotations from authorities, or examples.

PERFORMANCE-BASED ASSESSMENT

SOURCES
- WHOLE-CLASS SELECTIONS
- SMALL-GROUP SELECTIONS
- INDEPENDENT-LEARNING SELECTION

PART 1
Writing to Sources: Explanatory Essay

In this unit, you have read a variety of selections that are related to the historical events known as the Holocaust. These selections are all examples of literature that addresses one of the most terrible periods in human history.

> **Assignment**
> Write an **explanatory essay** in response to the following question:
>
> How can literature help us remember and honor the victims of the Holocaust?
>
> Use your analysis of the selections in this unit to enumerate the ways in which literature can help us remember and honor victims of the Holocaust. Consider how the various texts in the unit illuminate the experiences of different types of people in a wide variety of places. Support your explanation with relevant details, quotations, and examples from the texts.

Reread the Assignment Review the assignment to be sure you fully understand it. The assignment may reference some of the academic words presented at the beginning of the unit. Be sure you understand each of the words given below in order to complete the assignment correctly.

Academic Vocabulary

| theorize | sustain | declaration |
| pronounce | enumerate | |

WORD NETWORK

As you write and revise your explanatory essay, use your Word Network to help vary your word choices.

Review the Elements of Effective Explanatory Essays Before you begin writing, read the Explanatory Essay Rubric. Once you have completed your first draft, check it against the rubric. If one or more of the elements is missing or not as strong as it could be, revise your essay to add or strengthen that component.

STANDARDS
Writing
- Write informative/explanatory texts to examine a topic and convey ideas, concepts, and information through the selection, organization, and analysis of relevant content.
- Write routinely over extended time frames and shorter time frames for a range of discipline-specific tasks, purposes, and audiences.

ESSENTIAL QUESTION: How do we remember the past?

DIGITAL PERSPECTIVES

Explanatory Essay Rubric

	Focus and Organization	Evidence and Elaboration	Language Conventions
4	The introduction is clear and engaging and establishes the topic in a compelling way. Ideas are well organized and progress logically. A variety of transitions are included to create cohesion and show the relationships among ideas. The conclusion follows from and supports the information in the essay.	The topic is developed with relevant and well-chosen facts, definitions, details, quotations, and other examples. The tone of the essay is formal. The vocabulary is precise and relevant to the topic, audience, and purpose.	The essay intentionally uses standard English conventions of usage and mechanics.
3	The introduction is clear and engaging in a way that grabs readers' attention. Ideas are well organized. Transitions are included to show the relationships among ideas. The conclusion mostly follows from the information in the essay.	The topic is developed with some relevant facts, definitions, details, quotations, and other examples. The tone of the essay is mostly formal. The vocabulary is generally appropriate for the topic, audience, and purpose.	The essay demonstrates accuracy in standard English conventions of usage and mechanics.
2	The introduction establishes the topic. Ideas are somewhat organized. A few transitions are included that show the relationships among ideas. The conclusion is related to the topic of the essay.	The topic is developed with a few facts, definitions, details, quotations, or other examples. The tone of the essay is occasionally formal. The vocabulary is somewhat appropriate for the topic, audience, and purpose.	The essay demonstrates some accuracy in standard English conventions of usage and mechanics.
1	The topic is not clearly stated. Ideas are disorganized and do not follow a logical sequence. Transitions are not included. The conclusion is not related to the essay topic, or is nonexistent.	The topic is not developed with relevant evidence. The tone is informal. The vocabulary is limited or inappropriate.	The essay contains mistakes in standard English conventions of usage and mechanics.

Performance-Based Assessment **251**

Explanatory Essay Rubric

As you review the Explanatory Essay Rubric with students, remind them that the rubric is a resource that can guide their revisions. Students should pay particular attention to the differences between an essay that contains all of the required elements (a score of 3) and one that is engaging, has a logical progression of ideas, and uses well-chosen facts and examples (a score of 4).

PERSONALIZE FOR LEARNING

English Language Support
Define Key Terms Ask students to review key terms used in the lesson, for example, *explanatory*, *essay*, and *thesis*. Then have them find or review the definitions for the terms: *explanatory*—used to describe something that informs or explains; *essay*—a short nonfiction work on a particular subject; *thesis*—the central claim. Discuss aspects of the words that will help students understand their meanings, for example, *explanatory* is related to *explain*. After reviewing the terms, students should have a better understanding of what they are required to do for their project. **ALL LEVELS**

ASSESSING

Speaking and Listening: Oral Presentation

Students should annotate their written explanatory essay in preparation for the oral presentation, marking the important elements such as the thesis or controlling idea, transitions that show the relationship between ideas, and a concluding statement that logically completes the essay, as well as relevant facts, details, and examples.

Remind students that the effectiveness of an oral presentation relies on how the speaker establishes credibility with his or her audience. If a speaker comes across as confident and authoritative, it will be easier for the audience to give credence to the speaker's presentation.

Review the Oral Presentation Rubric As you review the Oral Presentation Rubric with students, remind them that it is a valuable tool that can help them plan their presentation. They should strive to include all of the criteria required to achieve a score of 3. Draw their attention to some of the subtle differences between scores of 2 and 3.

PERFORMANCE-BASED ASSESSMENT

PART 2
Speaking and Listening: Oral Presentation

Assignment
After completing the final draft of your essay, use it as the foundation for a brief **oral presentation**.

Do not simply read your essay aloud. Instead, take the following steps to make your presentation lively and engaging.

- Go back to your essay and annotate the most important ideas and supporting details from your introduction, body paragraphs, and conclusion.
- Refer to your annotated text to guide your presentation and keep it focused.
- Speak clearly and make eye contact with the audience.

Review the Rubric The criteria by which your oral presentation will be evaluated appears in the rubric. Review these criteria before presenting to ensure that you are prepared.

STANDARDS
Speaking and Listening
Present claims and findings, emphasizing salient points in a focused, coherent manner with relevant evidence, sound valid reasoning, and well-chosen details; use appropriate eye contact, adequate volume, and clear pronunciation.

	Content	Organization	Presentation Technique
3	The introduction is engaging and clearly establishes the topic in a compelling way.	The presentation uses time effectively, devoting the right amount of time to each idea.	The speaker speaks clearly and loudly enough for the audience to hear.
	The speaker points to key details and evidence to support his or her ideas.	Ideas progress logically and are presented in a focused, coherent manner. Listeners can follow presentation.	The speaker maintains eye contact.
	The conclusion is clear and reflects the information presented.		
2	The introduction clearly establishes the topic.	The presentation mostly uses time effectively, but may spend too much or too little time on some parts.	The speaker speaks clearly.
	The speaker uses some evidence to support his or her ideas.		The speaker makes some eye contact.
	The conclusion reflects the information presented.	Ideas progress somewhat logically. Listeners can mostly follow presentation.	
1	The introduction does not establish the topic.	The presentation does not use time effectively.	The speaker speaks too quickly or slowly or mumbles.
	The speaker does not support his or her ideas with evidence.	Ideas do not progress logically. Listeners have difficulty following presentation.	The speaker does not make eye contact with the audience.
	The conclusion is not related to the topic.		

DIGITAL PERSPECTIVES

Preparing for the Assignment To help students understand what an effective explanatory essay looks like, find examples on the Internet of essays presented by students or adults. Project the examples for the class, and have students note the elements that make each presentation successful (that is, an engaging introduction, appropriate pacing and gestures, and an effective speaking style). Suggest that students record themselves presenting their essays before they present them to the class so that they can practice incorporating some of the elements from the examples they have seen.

UNIT 2 REFLECTION

Reflect on the Unit
Now that you've completed the unit, take a few moments to reflect on your learning.

Reflect on the Unit Goals
Look back at the goals at the beginning of the unit. Use a different colored pen to rate yourself again. Then, think about readings and activities that contributed the most to the growth of your understanding. Record your thoughts.

Reflect on the Learning Strategies
Discuss It Write a reflection on whether you were able to improve your learning based on your Action Plans. Think about what worked, what didn't, and what you might do to keep working on these strategies. Record your ideas before joining a class discussion.

Reflect on the Text
Choose a selection that you found challenging, and explain what made it difficult.

Describe something that surprised you about a text in the unit.

Which activity taught you the most about the Holocaust? What did you learn?

SCAN FOR MULTIMEDIA

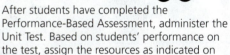

Reflect on the Unit
- Have students watch the video on Reflecting on Your Learning.
- A video on this topic is available online in the Professional Development Center.

Reflect on the Unit Goals
Students should reevaluate how well they met the unit goals now that they have completed the unit. You might ask them to provide a written commentary on the goal they made the most progress with as well as the goal they feel warrants continued focus.

Reflect on the Learning Strategies
Discuss It If you want to make this a digital activity, go online and navigate to the Discussion Board. Alternatively, students can share their learning strategies reflections in a class discussion.

Reflect on the Text
Consider having students share their text reflections with one another.

MAKE IT INTERACTIVE
Have students prepare one slide using presentation software that summarizes their reflection.

Collate student slides into a slideshow that can be viewed by the class. Students should be prepared to give a 30-second oral presentation of their slide.

Unit Test and Remediation

After students have completed the Performance-Based Assessment, administer the Unit Test. Based on students' performance on the test, assign the resources as indicated on the Interpretation Guide to remediate. Students who take the test online will be automatically assigned remediation, as warranted by test results.

What Matters

UNIT 3

INTRODUCTION

Jump Start

Ask students to think about something in their lives that really matters to them. It may be something they are willing to work hard for and never give up on. What would they be willing to do to achieve it? Have several volunteers briefly share their responses. Then engage the class in a discussion of whether people should expect to make sacrifices to achieve what matters most to them.

What Matters

Ask students what the phrase *what matters* suggests to them. Point out that as they work through this unit, they will read about what matters to many people.

Video

Project the introduction video in class, ask students to open the video in their interactive textbooks, or have students scan the BouncePage icon with their phones to access the video.

Discuss It If you want to make this a digital activity, go online and navigate to the Discussion Board. Alternatively, students can share their responses in a class discussion.

Block Scheduling

Each day in this Pacing Plan represents a 40–50-minute class period. Teachers using block scheduling may combine days to reflect their class schedule. In addition, teachers may revise pacing to differentiate and support core instruction by integrating components and resources as students require.

Pacing Plan

UNIT 3

What Matters

Sometimes standing up means refusing to back down.

Philippe Petit

Discuss It Why is volunteering, engaging in sports and hobbies, and pursing personal dreams so fulfilling?

Write your response before sharing your ideas.

SCAN FOR MULTIMEDIA

Pacing Plan:

Unit Introduction	Introduce Whole-Class Learning	Barrington Irving, Pilot and Educator	Three Cheers for the Nanny State	Ban the Ban! • Soda's a Problem but...	Performance Task
1 2	3	4 5 6 7 8	9 10 11 12 13	14 15	16 17 18

254 UNIT 3 • WHAT MATTERS

DIGITAL PERSPECTIVES

 Audio Video Document Annotation Highlights EL Highlights Online Assessment

UNIT 3

UNIT INTRODUCTION

ESSENTIAL QUESTION:
When is it right to take a stand?

LAUNCH TEXT ARGUMENT MODEL
Freedom of the Press?

WHOLE-CLASS LEARNING

ANCHOR TEXT: MAGAZINE ARTICLE
Barrington Irving, Pilot and Educator
National Geographic

▸ MEDIA CONNECTION: Barrington Irving: Got 30 Dollars in My Pocket

ANCHOR TEXT: OPINION PIECE
Three Cheers for the Nanny State
Sarah Conly

COMPARE

ANCHOR TEXTS: OPINION PIECES
Ban the Ban!
SidneyAnne Stone

Soda's a Problem but . . .
Karin Klein

PERFORMANCE TASK
WRITING FOCUS:
Write an Argument

SMALL-GROUP LEARNING

PERSUASIVE SPEECH
Words Do Not Pay
Chief Joseph

NONFICTION NARRATIVE
from Follow the Rabbit-Proof Fence
Doris Pilkington

MEDIA: VIDEO
The Moth Presents: Aleeza Kazmi

PERFORMANCE TASK
SPEAKING AND LISTENING FOCUS:
Deliver an Oral Presentation

INDEPENDENT LEARNING

MEMOIR
from Through My Eyes
Ruby Bridges

POETRY
The Unknown Citizen
W. H. Auden

BIOGRAPHY
Harriet Tubman: Conductor on the Underground Railroad
Ann Petry

PERFORMANCE-BASED ASSESSMENT PREP
Review Evidence for an Argument

PERFORMANCE-BASED ASSESSMENT

Argument: Essay and Oral Presentation

PROMPT:
Is it important for people to make their own choices in life?

When is it right to take a stand?

Introduce the Essential Question and point out that students will respond to related prompts.

- **Whole-Class Learning** *What is a problem you think needs to be solved? How would you solve it?*
- **Small-Group Learning** *When you take a stand, how much does winning matter?*
- **Performance-Based Assessment** *Is it important for people to make their own choices in life?*

Using Trade Books

Refer to the Teaching with Trade Books section for suggestions on how to incorporate the following thematically related titles into this unit:

- *Roll of Thunder, Hear My Cry* by Mildred Taylor
- *Does My Head Look Big in This?* by Randa Abdel-Fattah
- *Farewell to Manzanar* by Jeanne Wakatsuki Houston

Current Perspectives

To increase student engagement, search online for stories about the kinds of things that matter to people. Always preview content before sharing it with your class.

- **Video: Severn Suzuki at Rio Summit (We Canada)** Twelve-year-old Severn Suzuki silences the United Nations assembly in Brazil.
- **Video: Michael Garcia, Waiter Who Defended Boy With Special Needs, Gives Donations Away (Huffington Post)** Michael Garcia stands up for a five-year-old with Down Syndrome.

Introduce Small-Group Learning

Words Do Not Pay — 19 20 21 22 23 24

from Follow the Rabbit-Proof Fence — 25 26 27 28

Media: The Moth Presents: Aleeza Kazmi — 29 30

Performance Task — 31 32

Introduce Independent Learning — 33

Independent Learning — 34

Performance-Based Assessment — 35 36

Unit Introduction 255

INTRODUCTION

About the Unit Goals
These unit goals were backward designed from the Performance-Based Assessment at the end of the unit and the Whole-Class and Small-Group Performance Tasks. Students will practice and become proficient in many more standards over the course of this unit.

Unit Goals
Review the goals with students and explain that as they read the selections in this unit, they will improve their reading, writing, research, language, and speaking and listening.

- Have students watch the video on Goal Setting.
- A video on this topic is available online in the Professional Development Center.

Reading Goals Tell students they will read and evaluate an argument. They will also read a news article, a memoir, poetry, and a biography to better understand how writers express ideas.

Writing and Research Goals Tell students that they will learn the elements of argumentative writing. Students will write for a number of reasons, including reflecting on experiences and gathering evidence. They will conduct research to clarify and explore ideas.

Language Goal Tell students that they will develop understanding of conventions of standard English grammar and usage. They will then practice this usage.

Speaking and Listening Explain to students that they will work together to build on one another's ideas and communicate with one another. They will also learn to incorporate audio, visuals, and text in presentations.

HOME Connection
A Home Connection letter to students' parents or guardians is available in the Interactive Teacher's Edition. The letter explains what students will be learning in this unit and how they will be assessed.

UNIT 3 INTRODUCTION

Unit Goals
Throughout this unit, you will deepen your perspective about what it means to stand up for things that matter, by reading, writing, speaking, listening, and presenting. These goals will help you succeed on the Unit Performance-Based Assessment.

Rate how well you meet these goals right now. You will revisit your ratings later when you reflect on your growth during this unit.

1 NOT AT ALL WELL
2 NOT VERY WELL
3 SOMEWHAT WELL
4 VERY WELL
5 EXTREMELY WELL

READING GOALS
- Evaluate written arguments by analyzing how authors state and support their claims.
- Expand your knowledge and use of academic and concept vocabulary.

WRITING AND RESEARCH GOALS
- Write an argumentative essay in which you effectively incorporate the key elements of an argument.
- Conduct research projects of various lengths to explore a topic and clarify meaning.

LANGUAGE GOAL
- Demonstrate command of the conventions of standard English grammar and usage, including correct usage of nouns, pronouns, adjectives, adverbs, clauses, and sentence structure.

SPEAKING AND LISTENING GOALS
- Collaborate with your team to build on the ideas of others, develop consensus, and communicate.
- Integrate audio, visuals, and text in presentations.

STANDARDS
Language
Acquire and use accurately grade-appropriate general academic and domain-specific words and phrases; gather vocabulary knowledge when considering a word or phrase important to comprehension or expression.

AUTHOR'S PERSPECTIVE — Ernest Morrell, Ph.D.

Goals and Identity Setting and meeting goals is closely linked to our sense of self, so it is important to help students learn to think of themselves as powerful readers, writers, and speakers. Introduce goal setting by comparing it to the actions of outstanding high school athletes. How do these athletes excel? They continue to improve by establishing and working to reach challenging new goals.

Then ask students: "What goals do you need to set in order to continue to develop as a powerful reader? As a skilled writer? As an effective speaker?" Have students decide on their own goals and write them down. As they work through this unit, direct students to refer back to their goals to assess how successfully they have achieved them. Guide students to develop reasonable benchmarks for assessment. Possibilities include increased reading fluency, greater comprehension, improved grades on essays, and more comfort speaking up in groups. Then have students set goals for developing these skills.

ESSENTIAL QUESTION: When is it right to take a stand?

DIGITAL PERSPECTIVES

Academic Vocabulary: Argument

Academic terms appear in all subjects and can help you read, write, and discuss with more precision. Here are five academic words that will be useful to you in this unit as you analyze and write arguments.

Complete the chart.

1. Review each word, its root, and the mentor sentences.
2. Use the information and your own knowledge to predict the meaning of each word.
3. For each word, list at least two related words.
4. Refer to the dictionary or other resources if needed.

TIP

FOLLOW THROUGH
Study the words in this chart, and mark them or their forms wherever they appear in the unit.

WORD	MENTOR SENTENCES	PREDICT MEANING	RELATED WORDS
retort ROOT: **-tort-** "twist"	1. His grumpy *retort* made me sorry I had asked the question. 2. I fired off a *retort* so clever she couldn't think of anything to add.		contort; torture
candid ROOT: **-cand-** "shine"; "white"	1. Take a *candid* photo of us so that we look like we do in real life. 2. I wish she were more *candid* with me; I never know what she means.		
rectify ROOT: **-rect-** "straight"	1. I will try to *rectify* the situation, but I think things are beyond fixing. 2. Don't worry, I will *rectify* the problem as soon as I get to the office.		
speculate ROOT: **-spec-** "look"	1. The police did not want to *speculate* as to what motivated the crime. 2. When I'm reading a really good book, it is hard not to *speculate* on how it is going to end.		
verify ROOT: **-ver-** "truth"	1. Can you please *verify* that your name is correct on this form? 2. The claim isn't valid because no one can *verify* the source of the information on which it is based.		

Unit Introduction 257

Academic Vocabulary: Argument

Introduce the blue academic vocabulary words in the chart on the student page. Point out that the root of each word provides a clue to its meaning. Discuss the mentor sentences to ensure students understand each word's usage. Students should also use the mentor sentences as context to help them predict the meaning of each word. Check that students are able to fill the chart in correctly. Complete pronunciations, parts of speech, and definitions are provided for you. Students are only expected to provide the definition.

Possible responses:

retort and *n.* (rih TAWRT)
Meaning: *v.* to reply quickly, sharply; *n.* a witty, sharp reply
Related words: retorter, retortion
Additional words related to root -*tort*-: contort, torture, torsion, tortuous

candid *adj.* (KAN dihd)
Meaning: very honest; informal, unposed
Related words: candidly, candidness
Additional words related to root -*cand*-: candle, candor, incandescent

rectify *v.* (REHK tuh fy)
Meaning: to correct; to set right
Related words: rectification, rectifiable
Additional words related to root -*rect*-: rectangle, direction, incorrect

speculate *v.* (SPEHK yoo layt)
Meaning: to guess without evidence
Related words: speculation, unspeculating
Additional words related to root -*spec*-: specific, specify, especially

verify *v.* (VEHR uh fy)
Meaning: to prove to be true
Related words: verification, verifiable
Additional words related to root -*ver*-: very, veritable, verdict

---

PERSONALIZE FOR LEARNING

English Language Support
Cognates Many of the academic vocabulary words have Spanish cognates. Use these cognates with students whose home language is Spanish. **ALL LEVELS**

verify – verificar

inspect – inspeccionar

rectify – rectificar

INTRODUCTION

Purpose of the Launch Text
The Launch Text provides students with a common starting point to address the unit topic. After reading the Launch Text, all students will be able to participate in discussions about what matters.

Lexile: 1000 The easier reading level of this selection makes it perfect to assign for homework. Students will need little or no support to understand it.

Additionally, "Freedom of the Press?" provides a writing model for the Performance-Based Assessment students complete at the end of the unit.

Launch Text: Argument Model
Point out that the writer of "Freedom of the Press?" is making an argument. As they read, students should determine what the argument is. They should identify the writer's claim and whether there is an opposing claim acknowledged. As the writer makes points throughout the article, students should identify the evidence given as support. Identifying all of these features will help prepare students for making arguments of their own.

Encourage students to read this text on their own and annotate unfamiliar words and sections of text they think are particularly important.

🔊 AUDIO SUMMARIES
Audio summaries of "Freedom of the Press?" are available in both English and Spanish in the Interactive Teacher's Edition or Unit Resources. Assigning these summaries before students read the Launch Text may help them build additional background knowledge and set a context for their reading.

UNIT 3 INTRODUCTION

LAUNCH TEXT | ARGUMENT MODEL

This selection is an example of an **argument**, a type of writing in which an author states and defends a position on a topic. This is the type of writing you will develop in the Performance-Based Assessment at the end of the unit.

As you read, look at the way the writer builds a case. Mark the text to answer this question: What is the writer's position, and how does he or she support it?

Freedom of the Press?

NOTES

1 The First Amendment of the U.S. Constitution gives newspapers, magazines, and other publications the right to print whatever they see fit, without interference from the government. The framers of the Constitution felt that a free press is vital to a democratic society.

2 This important idea breaks down when schools are involved. As it turns out, there is a difference between "free press" and high school newspapers.

3 The difference is technical. The First Amendment prevents the government from censoring the press. However, private publishers can censor whatever they want. Since schools and school districts pay the student newspaper's publication costs, they are private publishers. This means that they can edit information as they see fit. They can even refuse to publish some articles.

4 This is a tough lesson for budding journalists, some of whom have challenged the restrictions. One case even made it to the Supreme Court, in *Hazelwood School District v. Kuhlmeier*.

5 Here are the facts. In 1983, students at Hazelwood High, a public high school near St. Louis, Missouri, saw two pages missing from their school newspaper, *The Spectrum*. They found out that the principal, Robert Reynolds, had removed two of the articles after finding them unfit for publication. One article, about teen pregnancy, contained interviews with pregnant students whose names were changed; the other article dealt with divorce.

6 Principal Reynolds said the pregnancy article was not appropriate for a high school audience. He was also concerned

SCAN FOR MULTIMEDIA

CROSS-CURRICULAR PERSPECTIVES

Social Studies What is "free press" as it is used in paragraph 2? Share the First Amendment with the class. Initiate a discussion about why the founders included this in the Constitution and why it is still important today.

Congress shall make no law respecting an establishment of religion, or prohibiting the free exercise thereof; or abridging the freedom of speech, or of the press; or the right of the people peaceably to assemble, and to petition the government for a redress of grievances.

AUTHOR'S PERSPECTIVE: Elfrieda Hiebert, Ph.D.

Word Networks Vary by Word Type Concept maps—the graphic organizers that help students understand the essential attributes, qualities, or characteristics of a word's meaning—vary depending on the type of word noted.

In concept maps related to physical phenomenon, the words are typically not synonyms. They are connected by topic. For example, for *press*, the words *magazine, newspaper, newscast,* and *podcast* have different meanings but each could be used.

that the girls' identities would have been revealed eventually in such a small school. His problem with the divorce article was that it was not "fair and balanced." He felt it criticized parents without providing their side of the story.

7   Some students were outraged and sued the school. They argued that the issue was not the content of the articles, but whether or not the school had the right to suppress them.

8   In 1988, the Supreme Court ruled 5–3 in favor of the school. The ruling said that while students "do not shed their first amendment rights at the schoolhouse gate," no school should tolerate activities "inconsistent with its basic educational mission." In other words, when student expression is school-sponsored, it can be censored—as long as those doing the censoring have valid educational reasons. The law now varies from state to state. States that disagree with parts of the ruling have their own laws that govern students' freedom of expression.

9   We are now left with these critical questions: Is it fair for some students to have greater freedom of speech in their high school newspapers when others are subjected to censorship? What does this situation say about us as a society and a nation?

10   The framers of the Constitution believed that if governments could censor opinions they did not like, the public would be less educated. Given that schools are places of education, it seems counterproductive to limit students' free speech. The more opinions students are exposed to, the better equipped they will be to handle the issues they will face later in life.

WORD NETWORK FOR TAKING A STAND

Vocabulary A Word Network is a collection of words related to a topic. As you read the selections in this unit, identify words related to the idea of taking a stand and add them to your Word Network. For example, you might begin by adding words from the Launch Text, such as *counterproductive*, *democratic*, and *censored*. Continue to add words as you complete this unit.

- counterproductive
- democratic
- censored

TAKING A STAND

Tool Kit
Word Network Model

Freedom of the Press? **259**

INTRODUCTION

Summary

Have students read the introductory paragraph. Provide them with tips for writing a summary:

- Write in the present tense.
- Make sure to include the title of the work.
- Be concise: a summary should not be equal in length to the original text.
- If you need to quote the words of the author, use quotation marks.
- Don't put your own opinions, ideas, or interpretations into the summary. The purpose of writing a summary is to accurately represent what the author says, not to provide a critique.

If necessary, students can refer to the Tool Kit for help in understanding the elements of a good summary.

See possible summary on the student page.

Launch Activity

Explain to students that as they work on this unit, they will have many opportunities to discuss how people determine what matters to them and how they make their own choices in life. Remind students that solid arguments contain facts and evidence. Throughout the unit, students will have opportunities to consider arguments made by others and determine if they agree or disagree. This will help them in formulating their own arguments. Remind students to listen to each other and respect each other's opinions.

UNIT 3 INTRODUCTION

Summary

Write a summary of "Freedom of the Press?" A **summary** is a concise, complete, and accurate overview of a text. It should not include a statement of your opinion or an analysis.

Possible responses: The argument that the author makes in "Freedom of the Press?" hinges upon a detail of the law that surprises many young people. The first amendment guarantees freedom of the press. But that means freedom from government censorship; a private publisher can do whatever it wants with what its writers provide. In 1983, students sued their school for refusing to print certain articles they had written for the school newspaper. The Supreme Court ruled that the school could refuse to print things when it had a valid educational reason not to. The author argues that the court shouldn't have, and that students should be able to publish and read materials that the school does not support or advocate.

Launch Activity

Class Statement Think about this question: How do people determine what matters to them and make their own choices in life? Consider your response by completing this statement:
Some things people should bear in mind when making important decisions are _____

- On a sticky note, record a brief phrase to complete the statement.
- Place all sticky notes with suggestions on the board; and then read the suggestions aloud. Work together to group ideas that are related.
- As a class, decide which phrase or phrases best complete the statement. Students may vote for one, two, or three phrases.
- Place a tally mark on the notes that indicate your choices.
- Use the tally results to create and edit a class thesis statement.

ESSENTIAL QUESTION: When is it right to take a stand?

DIGITAL PERSPECTIVES

QuickWrite

Consider class discussions, the video, and the Launch Text as you think about the prompt. Record your first thoughts here.

PROMPT: **Is it important for people to make their own choices in life?**

> Possible response:
> I believe that it is important for people to make many of their own choices in life. I will want to choose my career, my friends, and my activities. I will want to pursue my own interests. I think that making your own choices allows you to follow your own ideas and interests. For example, I enjoy music and not football. I have joined many school music ensembles and they have helped me grow as a student. Even though I have an athlete's build, I do not want to play competitive sports, and I am glad I have that choice. There may be things that I will require support on because I am not an expert. For example, I believe that people should not have the choice to drive a car before they reach a certain age and pass a road test. There are some laws that protect us. It may be that the line of protection vs. personal freedoms can blur, and I am interested in thinking more about those types of situations.

📝 EVIDENCE LOG FOR TAKING A STAND

Review your QuickWrite. Summarize your point of view in one sentence to record in your Evidence Log. Then, record evidence from "Freedom of the Press?" that supports your point of view.

Prepare for the Performance-Based Assessment at the end of the unit by completing the Evidence Log after each selection.

🔧 **Tool Kit**
Evidence Log Model

Title of Text: _____		Date: _____
CONNECTION TO PROMPT	TEXT EVIDENCE/DETAILS	ADDITIONAL NOTES/IDEAS

How does this text change or add to my thinking?   Date: _____

SCAN FOR MULTIMEDIA

Unit Introduction 261

QuickWrite

In this QuickWrite, students should present their own response to the prompt based on the material in the Unit Overview. This initial response will help inform their work when they complete the Performance-Based Assessment at the end of the unit. Students should think about how they clearly state a claim and support it with reasons and evidence. Have them consider all of the places where they find information and guidance for decision-making.

See possible QuickWrite on the student page.

Evidence Log for What Matters 📄

Students should record their initial position in their Evidence Logs along with evidence from "Freedom of the Press?" that support this position.

If you choose to print the Evidence Log, distribute it to students at this point so they can use it throughout the rest of the unit.

Performance-Based Assessment: Refining Your Thinking 📄

- Have students watch the video on Refining Your Thinking.
- A video on this topic is available online in the Professional Development Center.

VOCABULARY DEVELOPMENT

Academic Vocabulary Reinforcement Students will benefit from additional examples and practice with the academic vocabulary. Reinforce their comprehension with "show-you-know" sentences. The first part of the sentence uses the vocabulary word in an appropriate context. The second part of the sentences—the "show-you-know" part—clarifies the first. Model the strategy with this example for *retort*:

My mother gave a witty retort; my dad had made a joke at her expense.

Then give students these sentence prompts and coach them in creating the clarification part:

1. We had a candid conversation; _____.
   Possible response: everyone explained what they felt.
2. Gerardo can rectify the problem; _____.
   Possible response: he knows what went wrong.

Unit Introduction 261

OVERVIEW

WHOLE-CLASS LEARNING

When is it right to take a stand?

A person may be willing to work very hard and even sacrifice for something that is really important to him or her. During Whole-Class Learning, students will read selections about people who faced challenges and overcame obstacles because something mattered so much to them that they could not give up until they had achieved it.

Whole-Class Learning Strategies

Review the Learning Strategies with students and explain that as they work through Whole-Class Learning they will develop strategies to work in large-group environments.

- Have students watch the video on Whole-Class Learning Strategies.
- A video on this topic is available online in the Professional Development Center.

You may wish to discuss some action items to add to the chart as a class before students complete it on their own. For example, for "Monitor understanding," you might solicit the following from students:

- Be able to summarize what you have read.
- Reread anything that doesn't make sense.

Block Scheduling

Each day in this Pacing Plan represents a 40–50-minute class period. Teachers using block scheduling may combine days to reflect their class schedule. In addition, teachers may revise pacing to differentiate and support core instruction by integrating components and resources as students require.

Pacing Plan

Unit Introduction	Introduce Whole-Class Learning	Barrington Irving, Pilot and Educator	Three Cheers for the Nanny State	Ban the Ban! • Soda's a Problem but…	Performance Task
1 2	3	4 5 6 7 8	9 10 11 12 13	14 15	16 17 18

WHOLE-CLASS LEARNING

OVERVIEW: WHOLE-CLASS LEARNING

ESSENTIAL QUESTION:

When is it right to take a stand?

What issues are worth defending? In today's complex world, it's important to get our priorities straight. Each of us must decide for ourselves what matters most—a principle, another human being, or the right to express ourselves. As you read, you will work with your whole class to explore some of the issues that have caused people to take a stand.

Whole-Class Learning Strategies

Throughout your life, in school, in your community, and in your career, you will continue to learn and work in large-group environments.

Review these strategies and the actions you can take to practice them as you work with your whole class. Add ideas of your own for each step. Get ready to use these strategies during Whole-Class Learning.

STRATEGY	ACTION PLAN
Listen actively	• Eliminate distractions. For example, put your cellphone away. • Keep your eyes on the speaker. •
Clarify by asking questions	• If you're confused, other people probably are, too. Ask a question to help your whole class. • If you see that you are guessing, ask a question instead. •
Monitor understanding	• Notice what information you already know and be ready to build on it. • Ask for help if you are struggling. •
Interact and share ideas	• Share your ideas and answer questions, even if you are unsure. • Build on the ideas of others by adding details or making a connection. •

SCAN FOR MULTIMEDIA

CONTENTS

ANCHOR TEXT: MAGAZINE ARTICLE

Barrington Irving, Pilot and Educator
National Geographic

When a poor kid from Miami learns to fly, his life really takes off.

▶ MEDIA CONNECTION: Barrington Irving: Got 30 Dollars in My Pocket

COMPARE

ANCHOR TEXT: OPINION PIECE

Three Cheers for the Nanny State
Sarah Conly

Is being told what to do actually in our interests?

ANCHOR TEXTS: OPINION PIECES

Ban the Ban!
SidneyAnne Stone

Soda's a Problem but. . .
Karin Klein

When food choices are regulated, we stop thinking for ourselves.

PERFORMANCE TASK

WRITING FOCUS

Write an Argument

The Whole-Class readings focus on people who have taken a stand for or against something they felt strongly about. After reading, you will write an essay in which you make an argument about a problem you think is worth solving and how to solve it.

Overview: Whole-Class Learning 263

DIGITAL PERSPECTIVES

Contents

Anchor Texts Preview the anchor texts with students to generate interest. Encourage students to discuss other texts they may have read or movies or television shows they may have seen that deal with the issues of people standing up for what matters to them.

You may wish to conduct a poll to determine which selection students think looks more interesting, and discuss the reasons for their preference. Students can return to this poll after they have read the selections to see if their preference changed.

Performance Task

Write an Argument Explain to students that after they have finished reading the selections, they will write problem-and-solution essay about a problem they think is worth solving. To help them prepare, encourage students to think about the topic as they progress through the selections and as they participate in the Whole-Class Learning experience.

Introduce Small-Group Learning | Words Do Not Pay | from Follow the Rabbit-Proof Fence | Media: The Moth Presents: Aleeza Kazmi | Performance Task | Introduce Independent Learning | Independent Learning | Performance-Based Assessment

19 20 21 22 23 24 25 26 27 28 29 30 31 32 33 34 35 36

Whole-Class Learning 263

PLANNING

WHOLE-CLASS LEARNING • BARRINGTON IRVING, PILOT AND EDUCATOR

Barrington Irving, Pilot and Educator

🔊 **AUDIO SUMMARIES**
Audio summaries of "Barrington Irving, Pilot and Educator" are available in both English and Spanish in the Interactive Teacher's Edition or Unit Resources. Assigning these summaries prior to reading the selection may help students build additional background knowledge and set a context for their first read.

Summary
This magazine article from *National Geographic* is about an impressive man named Barrington Irving. Despite his difficult upbringing, he became an expert on aviation. At age 23 he became the youngest person—and only African American—ever to fly solo around the world. Irving recommends determination above all; if you confidently pursue what you want, you can probably do more than you think you're capable of. He now runs a nonprofit group to help more kids get into aviation, and the math and science that relates to it.

Insight
Barrington Irving's life story helps show that no matter what your background, you are capable of doing great things when you put your heart into them.

ESSENTIAL QUESTION
When is it right to take a stand?

Connection to Essential Question
Irving stood up and pursued his goals, even when people didn't think he could achieve them. Through careful, diligent work, he achieved his goals.

WHOLE-CLASS LEARNING PERFORMANCE TASK
What is a problem you think needs to be solved? How would you solve it?

Connection to Performance Tasks

Whole-Class Learning Performance Task This selection addresses individuals and small organizations finding solutions to problems they felt were worth solving.

UNIT PERFORMANCE-BASED ASSESSMENT
Is it important for people to make their own choices in life?

Unit Performance-Based Assessment Irving realized what he wanted to pursue when he had a chance to sit in a plane's cockpit. Students may decide that this selection supports the idea that self-determination is key. They may argue that seeing something that you could do in the future is immensely motivating.

DIGITAL PERSPECTIVES   Audio   Video   Document   Annotation Highlights EL Highlights   Online Assessment

LESSON RESOURCES

Lesson	Making Meaning	Language Development	Effective Expression
	First Read Close Read Analyze the Text Analyze Craft and Structure	Concept Vocabulary Word Study Conventions	Writing to Sources Speaking and Listening
Instructional Standards	**RI.10** By the end of the year, read and comprehend literary nonfiction . . . **RI.1** Cite the textual evidence that most strongly supports an analysis . . . **RI.3** Analyze how a text makes connections . . .	**L.1** Demonstrate command of the conventions of standard English grammar . . . **L.2** Demonstrate command of the conventions of standard English capitalization . . . **L.2.c** Spell correctly . . . **L.4** Determine or clarify the meaning of unknown and multiple-meaning words and phrases . . . **L.5** Demonstrate understanding of figurative language . . . **L.5.b** Use the relationship between particular words . . .	**W.1** Write arguments to support claims . . . **W.1.a** Introduce claim(s) . . . **W.1.b** Support claim(s) . . . **W.1.e** Provide a concluding statement . . . **W.7** Conduct short research projects . . . **SL.3** Delineate a speaker's argument and specific claims . . . **SL.4** Present claims and findings . . .

STUDENT RESOURCES

Available online in the Interactive Student Edition or Unit Resources	Selection Audio First-Read Guide: Nonfiction Close-Read Guide: Nonfiction	Word Network	Evidence Log

TEACHER RESOURCES

Selection Resources Available online in the Interactive Teacher's Edition or Unit Resources	Audio Summaries Annotation Highlights EL Highlights Analyze Craft and Structure: Characterization in Nonfiction	Concept Vocabulary and Word Study Conventions: Nouns and Pronouns English Language Support Lesson: Nouns and Pronouns	Writing to Sources: Argumentative Essay Speaking and Listening: Persuasive Presentation
Reteach/Practice (RP) Available online in the Interactive Teacher's Edition or Unit Resources	Analyze Craft and Structure: Characterization in Nonfiction (RP)	Word Study: Old English Suffix -ful (RP) Conventions: Nouns and Pronouns (RP)	Writing to Sources: Argumentative Essay (RP) Speaking and Listening: Persuasive Presentation (RP)
Assessment Available online in Assessments	Selection Test		
My Resources	A Unit 3 Answer Key is available online and in the Interactive Teacher's Edition.		

Whole-Class Learning 264B

PERSONALIZE FOR LEARNING
WHOLE-CLASS LEARNING • BARRINGTON IRVING, PILOT AND EDUCATOR

Reading Support

Text Complexity Rubric: Barrington Irving, Pilot and Educator

Quantitative Measures

Lexile: 1110   Text Length: 935 words

Qualitative Measures

Measure	Rating	Description
Knowledge Demands	3 (of 5)	Students may have little knowledge about the central content, but clear explanations are given. Some references (universities, organizations, and locations) may be unfamiliar.
Structure	2 (of 5)	Organization of text is clear and explicit, with clear connections between ideas. Text explains Irving's history and then his current projects and plans. Quotations break up text.
Language Conventionality and Clarity	2 (of 5)	Language is explicit and easy to understand. Vocabulary is familiar and contemporary; most sentences are not overly complex, though some are longer or more complex.
Levels of Meaning/Purpose	2 (of 5)	Purpose of text is clear and explicit (inspiring readers by describing Irving's experiences). Irving's life is summarized in beginning and his message to kids is stated early in text.

DECIDE AND PLAN

English Language Support

Provide English Learners with support for knowledge demands and structure as they read the selection.

Knowledge Demands Write or say sentences and ask students in a group to help you complete them. For example, *Irving was the only African American pilot who _____ (flew solo around the world).*

Structure Point out to students that there are three main kinds of information in the text: Irving's life experiences, his message to kids, and his current projects and plans. Together, discuss information about each area. For example, for Irving's message, write the words *determination, hard work, passion, having a dream.* Discuss the meaning of each one, explaining words if needed: *If you are determined, you never give up.*

Strategic Support

Provide students with strategic support to ensure that they can successfully read the text.

Knowledge Demands After students read the background information, ask questions to help them summarize what they learned, for example, *How old do you have to be to get a pilot's license? What are some things a pilot needs to be able to do? (communicate, solve problems, observe and react quickly).*

Structure Write these three words: *experience, message, plans.* Have students copy them. Tell students that as they read they will find information about Irving's life, his message to kids, and his plans. Ask students to take notes about two things they learned for each item. For example, under *experience,* they could write *flew solo around the world.*

Challenge

Provide students who need to be challenged with ideas for how they can go beyond a simple interpretation of the text.

Text Analysis Ask students to work in pairs. Ask them to read the section about Irving's message to kids (paragraph 2) and to list qualities Irving says kids need in order to achieve great things. Then have them find examples of how Irving showed these qualities in his life. For example, he showed determination by continuing to look for sponsorship for his solo flight, even when faced with many rejections.

Written Response Ask students to write about something in their own life (or the life of a close friend or family member) that shows determination or passion, or that requires hard work in order to pursue a dream.

TEACH

Read and Respond

Have students do their first read of the selection. Then have them complete their close read. Finally, work with them on the Making Meaning, Language Development, and Effective Expression activities.

Standards Support Through Teaching and Learning Cycle

IDENTIFY NEEDS

Analyze results of the Beginning-of-Year Assessment, focusing on the items relating to Unit 3. Also take into consideration student performance to this point and your observations of where particular students struggle.

ANALYZE AND REVISE

- Analyze student work for evidence of student learning.
- Identify whether students have met the expectations in the standards.
- Identify implications for future instruction.

TEACH

Implement the planned lesson, and gather evidence of student learning.

DECIDE AND PLAN

- If students have performed poorly on items matching these standards, then provide selection scaffolds before assigning them the on-level lesson provided in the Student Edition.
- If students have done well on the Beginning-of-Year Assessment, then challenge them to keep progressing and learning by giving them opportunities to practice the skills in depth.
- Use the Selection Resources listed on the Planning pages for "Barrington Irving, Pilot and Educator" to help students continually improve their ability to master the standards.

Instructional Standards: Barrington Irving, Pilot and Educator

	Catching Up	This Year	Looking Forward
Reading	You may wish to administer the **Analyze Craft and Structure: Characterization in Nonfiction (RP)** worksheet to help students understand how to infer meaning as they read.	**RI.1** Cite the textual evidence that most strongly supports an analysis of what the text says explicitly as well as inferences drawn from the text.	Challenge students to work with partners to analyze the selection for text evidence that supports their inferences. Have students take turns sharing their ideas.
Writing	You may wish to administer the **Writing to Sources: Argumentative Essay (RP)** worksheet to help students organize their arguments.	**W.1** Write arguments to support claims with clear reasons and relevant evidence.	Have students review each of the claims in their argument and make sure they have supported each claim clearly and with evidence that is logical.
Speaking and Listening	You may wish to administer the **Speaking and Listening: Class Presentation (RP)** worksheet to help students prepare to argue their positions.	**SL.4** Present claims and findings, emphasizing salient points in a focused, coherent manner with relevant evidence, sound valid reasoning, and well-chosen details; use appropriate eye contact, adequate volume, and clear pronunciation.	Have students work with a partner to practice their presentations. Then have them use the Presentation Evaluation Guide to provide feedback to their partners prior to presenting to the class.
Language	You may wish to administer the **Word Study: Old English Suffix -ful (RP)** worksheet to help students understand the meanings of words with these roots. You may wish to administer the **Conventions: Nouns and Pronouns (RP)** worksheet to help students recognize different kinds of nouns and pronouns.	**L.4** Determine or clarify the meaning of unknown and multiple-meaning words and phrases based on *grade 8 reading and content*, choosing flexibly from a range of strategies. **L.1** Demonstrate command of the conventions of standard English grammar and usage when writing or speaking.	Work with students to find three words with the suffix *-ful*. Then have them use each word in a sentence. Have students analyze the use of proper nouns, personal pronouns, and possessive pronouns in different contexts.

TEACHING

Jump Start

FIRST READ Has anyone ever told you that you can't do something? Sometimes all it takes is one person to tell you to believe in yourself. Have students think about dreams they have and how they can work toward achieving them.

Barrington Irving, Pilot and Educator 🔊 📄

Who is Barrington Irving? What did he do that was important? Modeling questions such as these will help students connect to "Barrington Irving, Pilot and Educator" and to the Performance Task assignment. Selection audio and print capability for the selection are available in the Interactive Teacher's Edition.

Concept Vocabulary

Support students as they rank their words. Ask if they've ever heard, read, or used them. Reassure them that the definitions for these words are listed in the selection.

⬤ FIRST READ

Students should perform the steps of the first read independently.

NOTICE: You may want to encourage students to notice who this article is about and what he has done.

ANNOTATE: Remind students to mark passages that provide evidence to support the idea that Barrington Irving is a noteworthy individual.

CONNECT: Encourage students to go beyond the text to make connections to their own lives. Have students consider what influence caused Irving to believe in himself and how they could apply that idea to their own dreams.

RESPOND: Students will answer questions to demonstrate understanding.

Point out to students that while they will always complete the Respond step at the end of the first read, the other steps will probably happen somewhat concurrently. You may wish to print copies of the **First-Read Guide: Nonfiction** for students to use. 📄

MAKING MEANING

About the Publication
National Geographic (originally named *The National Geographic Magazine*) has been published continuously for more than 125 years. It is famous for its articles on history, geography, and culture around the world. Early in its life, the magazine became equally celebrated for the quality and content of its photography, which has remained a standard that many other publications try to match.

🔧 **Tool Kit**
First-Read Guide and Model Annotation

STANDARDS
Reading Informational Text
By the end of the year, read and comprehend literary nonfiction at the high end of the grades 6–8 text complexity band independently and proficiently.

264 UNIT 3 • WHAT MATTERS

Barrington Irving, Pilot and Educator

Concept Vocabulary

As you conduct your first read of "Barrington Irving, Pilot and Educator," you will encounter these words. Before reading, note how familiar you are with each word. Then, rank the words in order from most familiar (1) to least familiar (6).

WORD	YOUR RANKING
determination	
achieve	
pursue	
tackling	
accomplish	
purposeful	

After completing your first read, review your original rankings. Mark changes to your original rankings as needed.

First Read NONFICTION

Apply these strategies as you conduct your first read. You will have an opportunity to complete the close-read notes after your first read.

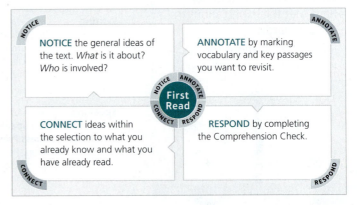

NOTICE the general ideas of the text. *What* is it about? *Who* is involved?

ANNOTATE by marking vocabulary and key passages you want to revisit.

CONNECT ideas within the selection to what you already know and what you have already read.

RESPOND by completing the Comprehension Check.

AUTHOR'S PERSPECTIVE Kelly Gallagher, M.Ed.

The Value of Rereading To get the most out of a text, it is important for students to move beyond surface-level comprehension into deeper, inferential meaning that yields insights and understanding. Give students rereading strategies that allow them to break free from the habit of complaining, "I read it, but I don't get it" by having them ask themselves the following four questions, in order, as they read:

1. What does it say?
2. What does it mean?
3. How is it said?
4. Why does it matter?

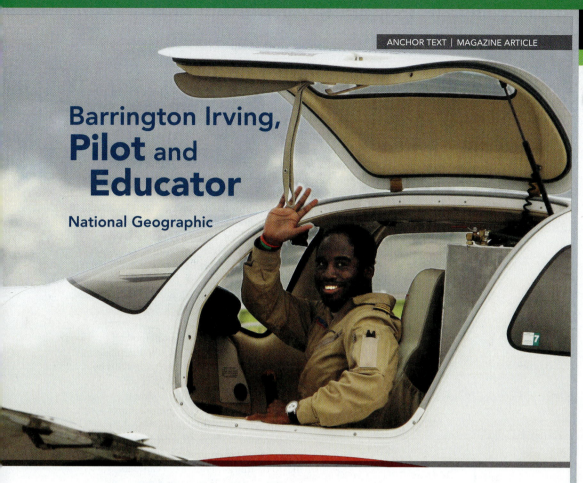

ANCHOR TEXT | MAGAZINE ARTICLE

Barrington Irving, Pilot and Educator

National Geographic

BACKGROUND

One way to travel around the world is to become a pilot. In order to get a professional pilot's license, a person must be at least eighteen years old, pass a written exam, and practice flying for more than 1,000 hours. Pilots need to be able to communicate clearly, solve problems, observe and react quickly, and know how to use aircraft computer and navigation systems.

1 Barrington Irving is very good at rising above obstacles. Literally. Raised in Miami's inner city, surrounded by crime, poverty, and failing schools, he beat the odds to become the youngest person and only African American ever to fly solo around the world. He built a plane himself, made his historic flight, graduated magna cum laude[1] from an aeronautical science program, and founded a dynamic educational nonprofit. Then he turned 28.

---

1. **magna cum laude** (MAG nuh kum LOW duh) with high honors, from Latin.

TEACHING

NOTES

determination (dih TUR muh NAY shuhn) *n.* quality of pursuing a goal even when it is difficult

achieve (uh CHEEV) *v.* succeed in doing something you want to do

pursue (puhr SOO) *v.* continue doing an activity over a period of time

2   His message for kids: "The only thing that separates you from CEOs in corner offices or scientists in labs is **determination**, hard work, and a passion for what you want to **achieve**. The only person who can stop you from doing something great is you. Even if no one believes in your dream, you have to **pursue** it." The secret, he believes, is having a dream in the first place, and that starts with powerful learning experiences that inspire kids to pursue careers—particularly in science, technology, engineering, and math.

3   The moment of inspiration for Irving came at age 15 while he was working in his parents' bookstore. One of their customers, a Jamaican-born professional pilot, asked Irving if he'd ever thought about becoming a pilot. "I told him I didn't think I was smart enough; but the next day he gave me the chance to sit in the cockpit of the commercial airplane he flew, and just like that I was hooked. There are probably millions of kids out there like me who find science and exploration amazing, but lack the confidence or opportunity to take the next step."

4   To follow his dream, Irving turned down a full football scholarship to the University of Florida. He washed airplanes to earn money for flight school and increased his flying skills by practicing at home on a $40 flight simulator video game.

5   Then another dream took hold: flying solo around the world. He faced more than 50 rejections for sponsorship before convincing several manufacturers to donate individual aircraft components. He took off with no weather radar, no de-icing system, and just $30 in his pocket. "I like to do things people say I can't do."

> "The only person who can stop you from doing something great is you."

6   After 97 days, 26 stops, and dozens of thunderstorms, monsoons, snowstorms, and sandstorms, he touched down to a roaring crowd in Miami. "Stepping from the plane, it wasn't all the fanfare that changed my life. It was seeing so many young people watching and listening. I had no money, but I was determined to give back with my time, knowledge, and experience." He's been doing it ever since.

7   Irving's nonprofit organization,[2] Experience Aviation, aims to boost the numbers of youth in aviation and other science- and math-related careers. Middle and high school students attend

---

2. **nonprofit organization** company formed to provide a benefit to the community rather than to make money for its own gain.

PERSONALIZE FOR LEARNING

English Language Support

Structure Review paragraphs 2 and 3 with students and ask them to consider the purpose of this text. "Barrington Irving, Pilot and Educator" is an article. Point out to students that its purpose is not just to inform them about Irving's life, but to inspire them. Tell them that the author uses different tools to convey that message. One such tool that may be confusing is the use of quotations. In paragraphs 2 and 3, Irving is speaking directly to the reader. Ask students to consider how they can figure out that Irving is speaking to them. Point out the choice of pronouns in the quotation. The word *you* is the hint that he is speaking to the reader. Guide students to discuss the message that Irving is sending to the reader. **ALL LEVELS**

summer and after-school programs **tackling** hands-on robotics projects, flight simulator challenges, and field trips to major industries and corporations. In his Build and Soar program, 60 students from failing schools built an airplane from scratch in just ten weeks and then watched Irving pilot it into the clouds.

8   "We want to create a one-of-a-kind opportunity for students to take ownership and **accomplish** something amazing," he notes. "Meaningful, real-world learning experiences fire up the neurons in kids' minds. If you don't do that, you've lost them. **Purposeful**, inspiring activities increase the chance they'll stay on that learning and career path. We've had one young lady receive a full scholarship to Duke University as a math major, and several young men are now pilots, engineers, and aircraft mechanics."

9   "It's great to reach a few hundred kids every year," he says, "but I also wanted to find a way to inspire on a larger scale." How about millions of kids? Irving's next endeavor will transform a jet into a flying classroom that will circle the globe sharing science, technology, engineering, math, geography, culture, and history. "This isn't just an aircraft; it's an exploration vehicle for learning that will teach millions of kids in ways they've never been taught before—making them part of the expedition and research."

10   A web-based experience will make it easy for kids to participate at home and school, voting on everything from where Irving should make a fuel stop to what local food he should sample. He plans to call classrooms from the cockpit; broadcast live video from 45,000 feet; blog with students; collect atmospheric data; communicate with the International Space Station; and wear a NASA[3] body suit that transmits his heart rate, blood pressure, and other vital signs.

11   Along the way, kids will have a virtual window on about 75 ground expeditions, including Machu Picchu, the Galápagos Islands, the Pyramids, the Serengeti Plains, the Roman Coliseum, the Taj Mahal, and the Great Wall of China. Cameras will provide 360-degree panoramic views of destinations from ancient archeological sites to Hong Kong skyscrapers. Apps will track adventures such as shark tagging, giving students ongoing location and water temperature data.

12   A steady stream of challenges will let kids compete to solve problems ranging from evacuating populations after tsunamis to collecting trash in space. "We also want to create a forum where

---

3. **NASA** *abbr.* National Aeronautics and Space Administration.

NOTES

tackling (TAK lihng) *v.* dealing with or handling a problem or situation

accomplish (uh KOM plish) *v.* carry out; finish or complete

purposeful (PUR puhs fuhl) *adj.* having a clear aim or goal

CLOSE READ
ANNOTATE: Mark details in paragraph 11 that describe the "virtual window."

QUESTION: Why do you think the writer has listed so many details?

CONCLUDE: What do these details lead you to conclude about the scope of Irving's project?

DIGITAL PERSPECTIVES

CLOSE READ

As students are reading paragraph 11, remind them to focus on names of locations and how those details add to the text. You may wish to model the close read using the following think-aloud format. Possible responses to questions on the student page are included.

ANNOTATE: As I read paragraph 11, I notice and mark details about the "virtual window."

QUESTION: I think the author included details about these locations because they are exotic, exciting places that people might never get to visit except through the "virtual window."

CONCLUDE: Because these locations are so far away and also so different from each other, readers will understand that the scope of the project is huge; these locations are only some of the 75 that are mentioned.

TEACHING

Media Connection ▶

Project the media connection video in class, ask students to open the video in their interactive textbooks, or have students scan the Bounce Page icon with their phones to access the video.

Discuss It

Possible response: I think it's interesting to see Barrington Irving talk about his life because I can see—and feel—his passion. Watching him talk and gesture helps me understand him better because I can tell what he's excited about and what he's proud of.

NOTES

kids, parents, and teachers can speak to astronauts, scientists, and other specialists."

13   This "Journey for Knowledge" flight is scheduled to depart in 2013 and will make Irving the youngest person ever to fly to all seven continents.

14   Perhaps Irving's most compelling educational tool is the example his own life provides. After landing his record-breaking flight at age 23, he smiled out at the airfield crowd and said, "Everyone told me what I couldn't do. They said I was too young, that I didn't have enough money, experience, strength, or knowledge. They told me it would take forever and I'd never come home. Well . . . guess what?"

MEDIA CONNECTION

Barrington Irving: Got 30 Dollars in My Pocket

💬 **Discuss It** How does viewing this video add to your appreciation of Barrington Irving's personal accomplishments?

Write your response before sharing your ideas.

SCAN FOR MULTIMEDIA

268 UNIT 3 • WHAT MATTERS

DIGITAL PERSPECTIVES

Illuminating the Text Show students the media connection video interview with Barrington Irving. Ask students to discuss their impressions of him from the interview and how those impressions compare with the article. Point out that when reading a story about a person and even when reading that person's own words, we get a limited picture of who that person is. Ask students what feelings about Irving they took away from the video that they did not get from reading the article.

268 UNIT 3 • WHAT MATTERS

Comprehension Check

Complete the following items after you finish your first read.

1. Name two obstacles Barrington Irving had to overcome in order to achieve his dream.

2. What were two of Irving's first big dreams?

3. How did Irving increase his flying skills at home?

4. What is Experience Aviation?

5. **Notebook** Write a timeline of events in the life of Barrington Irving.

RESEARCH

Research to Clarify Choose at least one unfamiliar detail from the text. Briefly research that detail. In what way does the information you learned shed light on an aspect of the article?

Research to Explore Choose something that interested you from the text, and use it to formulate a research question.

Barrington Irving, Pilot and Educator **269**

DIGITAL PERSPECTIVES

Comprehension Check

Possible responses:

1. He had to overcome his surroundings of crime, poverty, and failing schools, as well as his own lack of confidence in his abilities.
2. Barrington Irving dreamed of being a pilot and of flying solo around the world.
3. Irving practiced at home by playing a flight simulator video game.
4. Experience Aviation is Irving's nonprofit organization.
5. Timelines will vary but should include some of the following events: Worked in his parents' bookstore, got a scholarship to University of Florida but went to flight school instead, flew around the world, started a nonprofit, created the "Journey for Knowledge" flying classroom.

Research

Research to Clarify If students struggle to decide on a detail to research, you may want to suggest that they focus on one of the following topics: life of Barrington Irving, aeronautical engineering, flying a plane, building a plane, Experience Aviation.

Research to Explore If students aren't sure how to go about formulating a research question, suggest that they use their findings from Research to Clarify as a starting point. For example, if students researched Experience Aviation, they might formulate a question such as *What impact has Experience Aviation had on young people?*

PERSONALIZE FOR LEARNING

Challenge

Research Have students select a topic related to the article and do research to learn more about it. Students will prepare a brief presentation using information and images to teach the class about what they have learned. Remind students that selecting a broad topic, such as "All About Airplanes," will make it difficult to provide a brief presentation. A topic like "the importance of the jet engine for flight" would be specific. Remind students to be respectful of each others' presentations.

TEACHING

Jump Start

CLOSE READ Barrington Irving had big plans. He was going to fly around the world. Imagine the preparation such a trip would take! Think about everything you would need to be successful. If you did not know that Irving made it, would you think his decisions were wise?

Close Read the Text

Walk students through the annotation model on the student page. Encourage them to complete items 2 and 3 on their own. Review and discuss the sections students have marked. If needed, continue to model close reading by using the Annotation Highlights in the Interactive Teacher's Edition.

Analyze the Text

Possible responses:

1. Irving became inspired to follow his dream when a professional pilot encouraged him and gave him a hands-on experience with his plane. **DOK 1**

2. Students may say that Irving's life shows young people that they can overcome obstacles—including poverty, failing schools, and lack of support—to successfully reach their dreams. **DOK 2**

3. It is important to take a stand and work to achieve your own dreams, and to help others achieve their dreams. **DOK 4**

FORMATIVE ASSESSMENT

Analyze the Text

- **If** students fail to cite evidence, **then** remind them to support their ideas with specific information.
- **If** students struggle to paraphrase how Irving became inspired to follow his dream, **then** review the steps needs to paraphrase a text and provide examples.

MAKING MEANING

BARRINGTON IRVING, PILOT AND EDUCATOR

Close Read the Text

1. The model, from paragraph 5, shows two sample annotations, along with questions and conclusions. Close read the passage, and find another detail to annotate. Then, write a question and your conclusion.

> **ANNOTATE:** These details relate to Irving's pursuit of his next dream.
> **QUESTION:** Why might the author have included these details?
> **CONCLUDE:** These details show Irving's ambition, the obstacles he faced, and his attitude toward those obstacles.

Then another dream took hold: flying solo around the world. **He faced more than 50 rejections** for sponsorship before convincing several manufacturers to donate individual aircraft components. He took off with **no weather radar, no de-icing system, and just $30 in his pocket.** "I like to do things people say I can't do."

> **ANNOTATE:** The author includes details about what Irving *did not* have on his solo flight.
> **QUESTION:** Why might the author have included these details?
> **CONCLUDE:** These details show the challenges Irving faced and overcame.

2. For more practice, go back into the text and complete the close-read notes.

3. Revisit a section of the text you found important during your first read. Read this section closely, and **annotate** what you notice. Ask yourself **questions** such as "Why did the author make this choice?" What can you **conclude**?

🔧 Tool Kit
Close-Read Guide and Model Annotation

≡ STANDARDS
Reading Informational Text
- Cite the textual evidence that most strongly supports an analysis of what the text says explicitly as well as inferences drawn from the text.
- Analyze how a text makes connections among and distinctions between individuals, ideas, or events.

Analyze the Text
CITE TEXTUAL EVIDENCE to support your answers.

📓 **Notebook** Respond to these questions.

1. **Paraphrase** A **paraphrase** is a restatement of another person's ideas in your own words. Reread paragraph 3. Then, paraphrase how Barrington Irving discovered his life's calling.

2. **Make a Judgment** The author states that Irving's life is his "most compelling educational tool." Do you agree? Explain your thinking.

3. **Essential Question:** *When is it right to take a stand?* What have you learned about when and how to take action from reading this article?

270 UNIT 3 • WHAT MATTERS

PERSONALIZE FOR LEARNING

English Language Support

Interpret In this article, the author tells the reader what Barrington Irving did. It is up to the reader to interpret why he did things the way he did and whether they agree with how he got where he did. It might be surprising for students to realize that Irving's flight around the world involved some decisions that put his safety at risk. Ask students to identify these decisions. Ask them to consider why he chose to go forward in spite of the risks. **ALL LEVELS**

ESSENTIAL QUESTION: When is it right to take a stand?

DIGITAL PERSPECTIVES

Analyze Craft and Structure

Characterization in Nonfiction Nonfiction writers often adapt techniques typically used by fiction writers to vividly portray the real-life people who are the subjects of their works. Taken together, the techniques writers use to portray characters are called **characterization**. There are two types of characterization:

- With **direct characterization,** the author simply tells the reader what a person is like. For example, the author might say a person is *stubborn, generous, shy,* or *brave.*

- With **indirect characterization,** the author reveals a subject's personality by including his or her words and describing his or her actions, appearance, and behavior. The author may also show how other people feel about the person.

When an author uses indirect characterization, the reader must make **inferences,** or educated guesses, to determine what the person is like. To make inferences, connect details in the text to your own background knowledge. For example, if an author describes someone who arrives as arriving late and out of breath, you might infer that the person had been running. Practice making an inference by reading this passage and marking details about Irving. Then, note an inference you can make based on those details.

PASSAGE FROM THE TEXT	MY INFERENCE
A web-based experience will make it easy for kids to participate at home and school, voting on everything from where Irving should make a fuel stop to what local food he should sample. He plans to call classrooms from the cockpit; broadcast live video from 45,000 feet; blog with students; collect atmospheric data; communicate with the International Space Station; and wear a NASA3 body suit that transmits his heart rate, blood pressure, and other vital signs. (paragraph 10)	Irving is very capable; he will be able to do these things which seem challenging for a young person who is also piloting the plane.

Practice

CITE TEXTUAL EVIDENCE to support your answers.

Notebook Respond to these questions.

1. (a) Identify an example of direct characterization in paragraph 1. (b) What clues in the text indicate that this is direct characterization?

2. (a) Reread paragraph 6 of the article. What type of characterization does the author use in this paragraph? (b) What does the information in this paragraph reveal about Irving's character?

3. In paragraph 9, the author uses direct quotations, or Irving's exact words, to reveal Irving's goals for the future. What can you infer about Irving based on the quotations in this paragraph?

4. Reread paragraph 14. (a) How many examples of characterization appear in that passage? (b) Which detail do you find most revealing? Explain.

TEACHING

Concept Vocabulary
Why These Words?
Possible responses:
1. The vocabulary words send a message to kids that they can be successful and achieve their goals and dreams through hard work and determination, no matter what their circumstances.
2. *practicing; aims; endeavor*

Practice
Possible responses:
1. Responses will vary but students should state their goals and list a few things needed to achieve those goals.
2. determination: boldness, dedication, grit, persistence; pursue: go after, seek, chase, follow; accomplish: reach, attain, finish, pull off; achieve: complete, carry out, reach a goal; tackling: trying, attempting, undertaking; purposeful: deliberate, determined, persistent

Word Study
For more support, see **Concept Vocabulary and Word Study**

Possible responses:
1. *Meaningful* means full of or possessing meaning.
2. Resourceful, successful, helpful

Word Network
Possible words: *passion; inspiration; convincing*

FORMATIVE ASSESSMENT

Concept Vocabulary
If students struggle to understand the relevance of these words to the story, **then** revisit the vocabulary within the text.

Word Study
If students struggle to understand the Old English suffix -*ful*, **then** identify other words that use this suffix, what these words mean, and how they are connected to the suffix. For Reteach and Practice, see **Word Study: Old English Suffix: -*ful* (RP).**

LANGUAGE DEVELOPMENT

BARRINGTON IRVING, PILOT AND EDUCATOR

Concept Vocabulary

| determination | pursue | accomplish |
| achieve | tackling | purposeful |

Why These Words? The concept vocabulary words all relate to the effort an individual puts forth in order to succeed. For example, according to Irving, *determination* is a key factor in a person's success.

1. How does the concept vocabulary help the reader understand the reasons for Barrington's Irving's success?

2. What other words in the selection relate to success?

Practice
Notebook Complete the following activities.

1. What goals do you have and what will you need to *achieve* them? Use concept vocabulary words in your response.

2. With a partner, take turns listing as many **synonyms,** or words with similar meanings, as you can for each concept vocabulary word.

Word Study
Old English Suffix: -*ful* The Old English suffix -*ful* means "full of" or "having qualities of." In the article, Irving says that he thinks *purposeful* activities, or activities that are goal-oriented, are most likely to inspire kids.

1. Irving says, "Meaningful, real-world learning experiences fire up the neurons in kids' minds." Based on this sentence and on what you know about the suffix -*ful*, define *meaningful*.

2. What other words containing the suffix -*ful* can you use to describe Barrington Irving?

WORD NETWORK
Add words related to taking a stand from the text to your Word Network.

STANDARDS
Language
• Demonstrate command of the conventions of standard English grammar and usage when writing or speaking.
• Demonstrate command of the conventions of standard English capitalization, punctuation, and spelling when writing.
  c. Spell correctly.
• Determine or clarify the meaning of unknown and multiple-meaning words or phrases based on *grade 8 reading and content*, choosing flexibly from a range of strategies.
• Demonstrate understanding of figurative language, word relationships, and nuances in word meanings.
  b. Use the relationship between particular words to better understand each of the words.

AUTHOR'S PERSPECTIVE Elfrieda Hiebert, Ph.D.

Frequency of Concepts in Narrative Texts In describing character traits or problems, skilled authors rarely repeat the same word, other than to achieve unity through repetition. Instead, authors use different words to create an interesting style. For instance, authors use a variety of words to describe setting, such as *lagoon, swales, bog*. Specifically, in *The Wizard of Oz*, L. Frank Baum describes what Dorothy and her companions see on arriving in the Emerald City with these words: *brilliance, dazzled, glittering*. Word variety also helps authors build characterization in jobs (*actor, lawyer, expert*) and roles (*adult, relative, female, male*). Especially in stories, the concepts represented by rare words are often known by common words that most students understand, such as *down* and *blah* for the rare words *lethargic, listless, slothful*, and *sluggish*. However, the more complex the text, the rarer the words that describe a particular concept will be. For instance, in a complex text, rather than describing a character as *calm*, the author might use *phlegmatic*. However, be sure that students understand that words such as these in a concept network have subtle differences in meaning and cannot necessarily be substituted for one another.

ESSENTIAL QUESTION: When is it right to take a stand?

Conventions

Nouns and Pronouns Correct capitalization and spelling of nouns and pronouns are key to clear writing. A **noun** is used to name a person, place, or thing. A **pronoun** is used to replace a noun in a sentence. There are different kinds of nouns and pronouns, such as the ones listed here:

- **Proper nouns** name specific persons, places, or things, such as *Barrington Irving*. Proper nouns begin with capital letters.
- **Possessive nouns** such as *Miami's* show ownership.
- **Personal pronouns** such as *I, you,* and *they* refer to persons or things. The personal pronoun *I* is always capitalized.
- **Possessive pronouns** such as *my, your, its,* and *their* replace possessive nouns and also show ownership.

Be sure not to confuse possessive pronouns with words that sound the same: *Your* is a possessive pronoun, while *you're* is a contraction that stands for "you are." *Its* is a possessive pronoun, while *it's* is a contraction that stands for "it is." *Their* is a possessive pronoun, while *they're* is a contraction that stands for "they are."

TIP

Pay attention to capitalization and spelling when you use nouns and pronouns. Remember, all proper nouns and the personal pronoun I are capitalized.

Read It

1. Identify the proper nouns, personal pronouns, possessive nouns, and possessive pronouns in the following sentences from the selection.
   a. To follow his dream, Irving turned down a full football scholarship to the University of Florida.
   b. Irving's nonprofit organization, Experience Aviation, aims to boost the numbers of youth in aviation and other science- and math-related careers.

2. Reread paragraph 10 of "Barrington Irving, Pilot and Educator." Mark and then label at least one example of each of the following: proper noun, personal pronoun, and possessive pronoun.

Write It

Notebook Revise the paragraph below. Make sure that proper nouns and pronouns are capitalized correctly and that possessive pronouns are spelled correctly.

When barrington irving was a young man, no one encouraged him to pursue his dreams. In fact, he said, "Everyone told me what i couldn't do." Irving started a nonprofit organization. It's goal is to help kids achieve they're dreams in science and aviation.

DIGITAL PERSPECTIVES

Conventions

Nouns and Pronouns Review the various noun and pronoun forms with students. Use an example like the following sentence, which contains all four types of nouns and pronouns in this lesson, to practice identifying nouns and pronouns.

Poppy loves her popping popcorn, which is called Poppy's Popping Popcorn Delight, a treat she invented on her own. For more support, see **Conventions: Nouns and Pronouns.**

MAKE IT INTERACTIVE
Ask students to come up with two sentences that contain all four types of nouns and pronouns mentioned in this lesson. Have students present their sentences and have other students identify the types of nouns and pronouns in the sentences.

Read It

1. a. proper nouns: Irving, University of Florida; possessive pronoun: his
   b. proper noun: 2 Experience Aviation; possessive noun: Irving's

2. Proper nouns: Irving, International Space Station, NASA; personal pronoun: he; possessive pronoun: his

Write It
Possible responses:
When **Barrington Irving** was a young man, no one encouraged him to pursue his dreams. In fact, he said, "Everyone told me what **I** couldn't do." Irving started a nonprofit organization. **Its** goal is to help kids achieve **their** dreams in science and aviation.

FORMATIVE ASSESSMENT
Conventions
If students struggle to identify the different types of nouns and pronouns, **then** provide examples of each type. For Reteach and Practice, see **Conventions: Nouns and Pronouns (RP).**

PERSONALIZE FOR LEARNING

English Language Support
Practicing with Nouns and Pronouns
Have students write about the lessons that they learned from the selection. Ask them to make two columns after they finish writing—one that lists the nouns that they used and one that lists the pronouns that they used.

Ask students to write three sentences about what they learned from Barrington Irving's story. **EMERGING**

Ask students to write a paragraph about what they learned from Barrington Irving's story. In the pronoun column of their chart, have them write the nouns that each of the pronouns refers to. **EXPANDING**

Ask students to write a paragraph about what they learned from Barrington Irving's story. Have them list which nouns the pronouns refer to. Then ask them to read the paragraph to a partner without using the pronouns and discuss how it is different from their original. **BRIDGING**
An expanded **English Language Support Lesson** on Nouns and Pronouns is available in the Interactive Teacher's Edition.

TEACHING

Writing to Sources

Remind students that when they write an argumentative essay, it is not enough to simply make a claim. A claim without any support is not a strong claim and can be easily discounted. A successful argument contains evidence to support the claim and perhaps to discount any counterclaims, which are claims that disagree with your claim. For more support, see **Writing to Sources: Argumentative Essay.**

Vocabulary and Conventions Connection

Remind students that they should make sure to proofread for any spelling, grammar, or capitalization errors. Encourage students to include concept vocabulary words in their writing where appropriate.

Reflect on Your Writing

1. **Responses will vary.** Make sure students are able to tell how their evidence supports their claim.
2. **Responses will vary.** Suggest students present their evidence in a different way if the writing is not persuasive.
3. **Why These Words?** Responses will vary.

FORMATIVE ASSESSMENT

Writing to Sources

If students struggle to compose a claim and find text support for it, **then** review examples of claims and supports. For Reteach and Practice, see **Writing to Sources: Argumentative Essay (RP).**

BARRINGTON IRVING, PILOT AND EDUCATOR

STANDARDS

Writing
• Write arguments to support claims with clear reasons and relevant evidence.
  a. Introduce claim(s), acknowledge and distinguish the claim(s) from alternate or opposing claims, and organize the reasons and evidence logically.
  b. Support claim(s) with logical reasoning and relevant evidence, using accurate, credible sources and demonstrating an understanding of the topic or text.
  e. Provide a concluding statement or section that follows from and supports the argument presented.
• Conduct short research projects to answer a question, drawing on several sources and generating additional related, focused questions that allow for multiple avenues of exploration.

Speaking and Listening
• Delineate a speaker's argument and specific claims, evaluating the soundness of the reasoning and relevance and sufficiency of the evidence and identifying when irrelevant evidence is introduced.
• Present claims and findings, emphasizing salient points in a focused, coherent manner with relevant evidence, sound valid reasoning, and well-chosen details; use appropriate eye contact, adequate volume, and clear pronunciation.

274 UNIT 3 • WHAT MATTERS

EFFECTIVE EXPRESSION

Writing to Sources

In an argumentative essay, a writer states a claim, or position, on a subject. He or she then explains reasons for that position, and uses evidence to show why the reasons makes sense.

> **Assignment**
> Write an **argumentative essay** in which you state a claim in response to the following statement:
>
> > Having passion for a subject is more important than having knowledge about it.
>
> Be sure each piece of evidence you use to support your claim clearly relates to the reasons you provide. Begin your essay with a clear introduction in which you state your claim. Then, explain your reasons and give evidence that supports them. Finally, end with a conclusion that states your claim in a different way. Try to make that conclusion memorable for readers.

Vocabulary and Conventions Connection Consider including several of the concept vocabulary words in your essay. Also, remember to proofread your draft to correct any errors in the spelling and capitalization of nouns and pronouns.

determination	achieve	pursue
tackling	accomplish	purposeful

Reflect on Your Writing

After you have written your argument, answer the following questions.

1. How do you think your evidence helps support your claim?

2. How might you revise the way you present your evidence so that it supports the claim more persuasively?

3. **Why These Words?** The words you choose make a difference in your writing. Which words did you specifically choose to clearly convey your ideas?

VOCABULARY DEVELOPMENT

Concept Vocabulary Reinforcement Have students review the concept vocabulary words for this lesson. For each word, review what it means and why it is important for understanding the article about Barrington Irving. Ask students to suggest how each word could support an argument relevant to the assignment. Have students construct sentences that use the concept vocabulary words to support the claim: *Barrington Irving has achieved success by recognizing problems and finding ways to solve them.* Remind students that they can use these examples to guide their own writing.

ESSENTIAL QUESTION: When is it right to take a stand?

Speaking and Listening

> **Assignment**
> Work with a partner to conduct research on one of the educational nonprofit organizations or programs mentioned in the article. Use the information you gather to develop and deliver a **persuasive presentation** that highlights the benefits of the organization or program. Show why the organization deserves support, or why its programs provide valuable experiences.

1. **Evaluate Your Evidence** As you prepare your presentation, make sure you have supported your claims about the program or organization. Answer the following questions to determine whether you need more supporting evidence:
   - Have you described the features of the organization or program clearly and accurately?
   - Do you explain why each feature is beneficial or exciting?
   - Did you include evidence to show the organization or program and its features are successful?

2. **Prepare Your Presentation** Practice your presentation before you deliver it to the class. Use the following techniques in your delivery:
   - Speak loudly enough to be heard by the entire class.
   - Maintain eye contact with your audience as you present.

3. **Evaluate Presentations** As your classmates deliver their presentations, listen attentively. Then, evaluate the presentations to decide which one you felt was most convincing. Consider the reasoning and evidence and the speakers' presentation skills. Use a presentation evaluation guide like the one shown to analyze classmates' presentations.

> **EVIDENCE LOG**
> Before moving on to a new selection, go to your Evidence Log and record what you learned from "Barrington Irving, Pilot and Educator."

EVALUATION GUIDE

Rate each statement on a scale of 1 (not demonstrated) to 5 (demonstrated).

☐ The presentation was persuasive and supported by relevant evidence.

☐ The speaker clearly explained his or her reasons.

☐ The speaker spoke at an appropriate volume and maintained eye contact.

DIGITAL PERSPECTIVES

Speaking and Listening

Remind students that as they conduct their research, they should make sure to focus on only one of the organizations or programs mentioned in the article. They should be sure to include details about the program and the reason for their choice.

1. **Evaluate Your Evidence** Encourage students to ask themselves, "Does this piece of evidence support my presentation? How?"

2. **Prepare Your Presentation** As they are practicing their presentations, remind students to speak at a volume loud enough for the audience to hear and not read directly from their writing or notes. Remind students that the object of the presentation is to persuade, so they should remember to include clear reasons why they chose this specific organization or program.

3. **Evaluate Presentations** Tell students that by carefully and fairly evaluating others' presentations, they can think about what they found convincing and determine how they might strengthen their own presentations. For more support, see **Speaking and Listening: Persuasive Presentation.**

Evidence Log Support students in completing their Evidence Log. This paced activity will help prepare them for the Performance-Based Assessment at the end of the unit.

FORMATIVE ASSESSMENT

Speaking and Listening

- **If** students are not providing relevant evidence, **then** review what makes a piece of evidence strong in supporting an argument.
- **If** students are unable to present in a clear fashion, **then** review oral presentation skills.

For Reteach and Practice, see **Speaking and Listening: Persuasive Presentation (RP).**

Selection Test

Administer the "Barrington Irving, Pilot and Educator" Selection Test, which is available in both print and digital formats online in Assessments.

PERSONALIZE FOR LEARNING

Strategic Support

Presentations As students are preparing their presentations for the assignment, explain the importance of expressing their ideas clearly and using valid evidence to support their claims. Display a sentence that might interest students, such as: *The school is considering extending winter break.* Explain to students that this topic could have arguments for or against it. As practice for their assignment, ask students to present a claim for or against extending winter break, and remind them to support their claims with a few examples of evidence. As students share, remind them to speak clearly and at an appropriate pace.

PLANNING
WHOLE-CLASS LEARNING • THREE CHEERS FOR THE NANNY STATE

Three Cheers for the Nanny State

🔊 **AUDIO SUMMARIES**
Audio summaries of "Three Cheers for the Nanny State" are available in both English and Spanish in the Interactive Teacher's Edition or Unit Resources. Assigning these summaries prior to reading the selection may help students build additional background knowledge and set a context for their first read.

Summary
In the opinion piece "Three Cheers for the Nanny State," Sarah Conly argues in favor of government interventions that encourage people to be healthier. She argues that, as much as we would like to think we are totally rational and know what is best for us, we do not. People predictably and routinely make mistakes that prevent them from getting what they want. Therefore, making it harder for people to buy large sodas will help them be healthier.

Insight
This opinion piece makes a case that this type of social health policy is helpful. These policies arguably reduce freedom, but their benefits are greater than the freedom they cost.

ESSENTIAL QUESTION
When is it right to take a stand?

Connection to Essential Question
Conly argues that, though controversial, the ban on large-size soda in New York City is truly a health benefit. Her main claim is that the law stands to make a meaningful change to many people's health, so it is worth asking everyone to give up a small amount of freedom.

WHOLE-CLASS LEARNING PERFORMANCE TASK
What is a problem you think needs to be solved? How would you solve it?

UNIT PERFORMANCE-BASED ASSESSMENT
Is it important for people to make their own choices in life?

Connection to Performance Tasks
Whole-Class Learning Performance Task This opinion piece notes that government interventions, such as laws that require people to drink sugary drinks from smaller containers, can help people avoid eating too much.

Unit Performance-Based Assessment The author argues that people are subject to cognitive biases and may have trouble believing bad things will really happen to them. In the case of New York City's ban on large-size sodas, she argues that it is in people's best interest for the government to promote public health and ban the largest containers. She argues that people should not make their own choices in some cases.

DIGITAL PERSPECTIVES

 Audio Video Document Annotation Highlights EL Highlights Online Assessment

LESSON RESOURCES

	Making Meaning	Language Development
Lesson	First Read Close Read the Text Analyze the Text Analyze Craft and Structure	Concept Vocabulary Word Study Conventions
Instructional Standards	**RI.10** By the end of the year, read and comprehend literary nonfiction . . . **RI.6** Determine an author's point of view or purpose. . . **RI.8** Delineate and evaluate the argument and specific claims in a text . . .	**L.1** Demonstrate command of the conventions of standard English grammar . . . **L.2** Demonstrate command of the conventions of standard English capitalization . . . **L.4** Determine or clarify the meaning of unknown and multiple-meaning words and phrases . . . **L.4.b** Use common, grade-appropriate Greek or Latin affixes and roots . . . **L.5** Demonstrate understanding of figurative language . . . **L.5.b** Use the relationship between particular words . . .
▶ STUDENT RESOURCES		
Available online in the Interactive Student Edition or Unit Resources	🔊 Selection Audio 📄 First-Read Guide: Nonfiction 📄 Close-Read Guide: Nonfiction	📄 Word Network
▶ TEACHER RESOURCES		
Selection Resources Available online in the Interactive Teacher's Edition or Unit Resources	🔊 Audio Summaries ✏️ Annotation Highlights 💬 EL Highlights 📄 Analyze Craft and Structure: Argument	📄 Concept Vocabulary and Word Study 📄 Conventions: Clauses 📄 English Language Support Lesson: Clauses
Reteach/Practice (RP) Available online in the Interactive Teacher's Edition or Unit Resources	📄 Analyze Craft and Structure: Author's Argument (RP)	📄 Word Study: Latin root *-just-* (RP) 📄 Conventions: Clauses (RP)
Assessment Available online in Assessments	📄 ✅ Selection Test	
My Resources	📄 A Unit 3 Answer Key is available online and in the Interactive Teacher's Edition.	

Whole-Class Learning **276B**

PERSONALIZE FOR LEARNING

WHOLE-CLASS LEARNING • THREE CHEERS FOR THE NANNY STATE

Reading Support

Text Complexity Rubric: Three Cheers for the Nanny State

Quantitative Measures

Lexile: 1180   Text Length: 1,233 words

Qualitative Measures

Knowledge Demands ①—②—**❸**—④—⑤	Selection has a mix of practical knowledge and some specific content knowledge; there are many references (philosophical principles, behavioral psychology), but most are explained in text or footnotes.
Structure ①—②—**❸**—④—⑤	Opinion piece poses questions and presents ideas, but it doesn't clearly state author's conclusion until the end of the piece. Organization is not always apparent, as ideas flow from one to next.
Language Conventionality and Clarity ①—②—**❸**—④—⑤	Language is conventional and contemporary but sometimes abstract; some sentences have complex phrases and academic vocabulary; some have unclear referents (referring back to previous paragraphs).
Levels of Meaning/Purpose ①—②—**❸**—④—⑤	Author poses questions that are not immediately answered; there is a lot of generalizing from individual situations to more abstract theories or ideas.

DECIDE AND PLAN

English Language Support

Provide English Learners with support for language and meaning as they read the selection.

Language List and discuss terms in the text or footnotes that are essential to the content. Some words include *ban, prohibit, controversial, restrictions, bias, cognitive, psychological, behavioral*. In addition, clarify referents (what words refer to) if needed. For example, *almost* in paragraph 6 refers to the sentence with *almost* in the previous paragraph.

Meaning Summarize main concepts or questions, rephrasing if necessary. Ask students to help fill in information. For example, *The article is about the soda ban in New York City in 2013. The soda ban prohibited _____ (containers larger than 16 oz). In paragraph 19, the author gives her opinion—does she think the ban is a good idea?*

Strategic Support

Provide students with strategic support to ensure that they can successfully read the text.

Knowledge Demands Before students read, preview some concepts that they should look for in the text. For example, tell students that the author is going to discuss some ideas about people's freedom and whether the government should interfere in order to prevent harm.

Meaning Ask questions about the main concepts to confirm that students understand the meaning. For example, (paragraph 8–10) *The author discusses some examples of "cognitive bias." What is an "optimism bias"? (Bad things will happen, but not to us.) What about a "status quo" bias? (We value what we have already.)*

Challenge

Provide students who need to be challenged with ideas for how they can go beyond a simple interpretation of the text.

Text Analysis Ask students to work in pairs. Have each pair prepare a written summary in their own words of one part of the text. For example, have one pair summarize the "present bias" and another pair summarize the "optimism bias." Ask them to give their own examples of these ideas. Reform a group and ask each pair to read aloud their summaries and examples.

Written Response Ask students to each write an example of a situation in which a person does not act in her or his own best interests, and write about a law that might be needed to protect people from their own negative behaviors.

TEACH

Read and Respond

Have students do their first read of the selection. Then have them complete their close read. Finally, work with them on the Making Meaning and Language Development activities.

Standards Support Through Teaching and Learning Cycle

IDENTIFY NEEDS

Analyze results of the Beginning-of-Year Assessment, focusing on the items relating to Unit 3. Also take into consideration student performance to this point and your observations of where particular students struggle.

ANALYZE AND REVISE

- Analyze student work for evidence of student learning.
- Identify whether students have met the expectations in the standards.
- Identify implications for future instruction.

TEACH

Implement the planned lesson, and gather evidence of student learning.

DECIDE AND PLAN

- If students have performed poorly on items matching these standards, then provide selection scaffolds before assigning them the on-level lesson provided in the Student Edition.
- If students have done well on the Beginning-of-Year Assessment, then challenge them to keep progressing and learning by giving them opportunities to practice the skills in depth.
- Use the Selection Resources listed on the Planning pages for "Three Cheers for the Nanny State" to help students continually improve their ability to master the standards.

Instructional Standards: Three Cheers for the Nanny State

	Catching Up	This Year	Looking Forward
Reading	You may wish to administer the **Analyze Craft and Structure: Author's Argument (RP)** worksheet to help students identify and analyze an author's perspective and purpose.	**RI.6** Determine an author's point of view or purpose in a text and analyze how the author acknowledges and responds to conflicting evidence or viewpoints.	Have students work with a partner and discuss the author's perspective. Challenge students to assess the author's reasoning to determine if it is sound. Do they agree with the author's perspective? Why or why not?
Language	You may wish to administer the **Conventions: Clauses (RP)** worksheet to help students understand how to identify and write different kinds of clauses. You may wish to administer the **Word Study: Latin root -just- (RP)** worksheet to help students understand how the root contributes meaning to various English words.	**L.1** Demonstrate command of the conventions of standard English grammar and usage when writing or speaking. **L.2** Demonstrate command of the conventions of standard English capitalization, punctuation, and spelling when writing. **L.4** Determine or clarify the meaning of unknown and multiple-meaning words and phrases based on *grade 8 reading and content*, choosing flexibly from a range of strategies.	You may wish to challenge students to use increasingly complex clauses in their writing. Challenge students to identify other words formed from the Latin root *-just-*.

TEACHING

Jump Start

FIRST READ Imagine it is against the law for anybody under the age of 18 to purchase candy without an adult's permission. Children, it has been decided, are not capable of making sound decisions when it comes to sugar. Suppose this idea became a possibility where you live. How would you respond?

Three Cheers for the Nanny State

Why have some local governments tried to implement bans on large-size sodas? Why are so many opposed to these bans? What is the real issue here? Modeling questions such as these will help students connect to "Three Cheers for the Nanny State" and to the Performance Task assignment. Selection audio and print capability for the selection are available in the Interactive Teacher's Edition.

Concept Vocabulary

Support students as they rank their words. Ask if they've ever heard, read, or used these words. Reassure them that the definitions for these words are listed in the selection.

FIRST READ

Students should perform the steps of the first read independently.

NOTICE: You may want to encourage students to notice the writer's key arguments and the way she supports them.

ANNOTATE: Remind students to mark passages that include evidence and details to support a claim.

CONNECT: Encourage students to connect the argument in this article to their own lives. The concept discussed here is something students should be able to relate to on a basic level.

RESPOND: Students will answer questions and write a summary to demonstrate understanding.

Point out to students that while they will always complete the Respond step at the end of the first read, the other steps will probably happen somewhat concurrently. You may wish to print copies of the **First-Read Guide: Nonfiction** for students to use.

Remind students that during their first read, they should not answer the close-read questions that appear in the selection.

276   UNIT 3 • WHAT MATTERS

MAKING MEANING

THREE CHEERS FOR THE NANNY STATE

• BAN THE BAN!
• SODA'S A PROBLEM BUT...

Comparing Texts

In this lesson, you will read and compare two selections that present different arguments about the same issue. First, you will complete the first read and close read activities for "Three Cheers for the Nanny State."

About the Author

Sarah Conly holds the title of Associate Professor of Philosphy at Bowdoin College in Brunswick, Maine. She is the author of numerous essays, journal articles, and opinion pieces focusing on issues of personal choice and public policy.

🛠 **Tool Kit**
First-Read Guide and Model Annotation

Three Cheers for the Nanny State

Concept Vocabulary

As you conduct your first read of "Three Cheers for the Nanny State," you will encounter these words. Before you read, rate how familiar you are with each word. Then, rank the words in order from most familiar (1) to least familiar (5).

WORD	YOUR RANKING
impose	
rational	
justifiable	
principle	
status quo	

After completing your first read, come back to the selection vocabulary and review your ratings. Mark changes to your original rankings as needed.

First Read NONFICTION

Apply these strategies as you conduct your first read. You will have an opportunity to complete a close read after your first read.

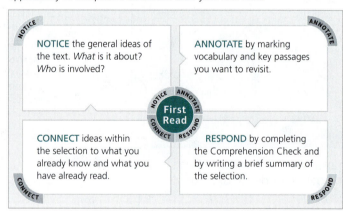

NOTICE the general ideas of the text. *What* is it about? *Who* is involved?

ANNOTATE by marking vocabulary and key passages you want to revisit.

CONNECT ideas within the selection to what you already know and what you have already read.

RESPOND by completing the Comprehension Check and by writing a brief summary of the selection.

📋 **STANDARDS**
Reading Informational Text
By the end of the year, read and comprehend literary nonfiction at the high end of the grades 6–8 text complexity band independently and proficiently.

276   UNIT 3 • WHAT MATTERS

VOCABULARY DEVELOPMENT

Concept Vocabulary Reinforcement When a reader encounters a new or unfamiliar word, one useful strategy is to look for a familiar word within the new word. Point out the word *justifiable*. Ask students to list words that sound like this word. They may come up with *justify*, *just*, and *justice*. Discuss how these words are all connected. Then, select the word *impose* and repeat the process. Explain that looking for the familiar in an unfamiliar word can help a reader understand the new word.

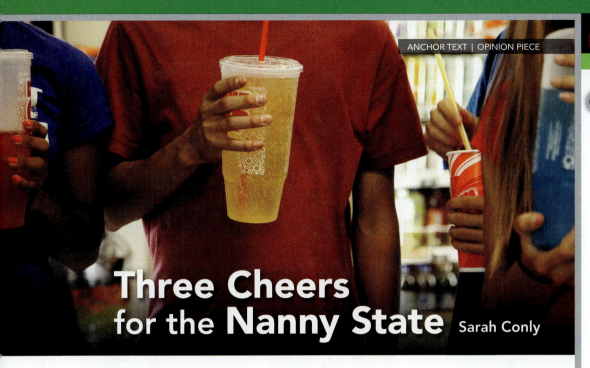

ANCHOR TEXT | OPINION PIECE

Three Cheers for the Nanny State

Sarah Conly

BACKGROUND

The term "nanny state" is a negative nickname for a welfare state, which is a model of government that takes direct responsibility for the protection and well-being of its citizens. Welfare states offers basic social support, such as free health care or low-income housing, but also create laws and policies that attempt to control or influence how people behave.

1   Why has there been so much fuss about New York City's attempt to **impose** a soda ban,[1] or more precisely, a ban on large-size "sugary drinks"? After all, people can still get as much soda as they want. This isn't Prohibition. It's just that getting it would take slightly more effort. So, why is this such a big deal?

2   Obviously, it's not about soda. It's because such a ban suggests that sometimes we need to be stopped from doing foolish stuff, and this has become, in contemporary American politics, highly controversial, no matter how trivial the particular issue. (Large cups of soda as symbols of human dignity? Really?)

3   Americans, even those who generally support government intervention in our daily lives, have a reflexive response to being told what to do, and it's not a positive one. It's this common desire to be left alone that prompted the Mississippi Legislature earlier this month to pass a ban on bans—a law that forbids municipalities to place local restrictions on food or drink.

---

1. **soda ban** In 2013, New York City passed a law prohibiting soda containers larger than 16 ounces in volume. The New York State Court of Appeals later overturned the law.

NOTES

impose (im POHZ) *v.* force a law, idea, or belief on someone by using authority

CLOSE READ

ANNOTATE: In paragraph 1, mark the questions that the author does not answer.

QUESTION: Why might the author have begun the article with several unanswered questions?

CONCLUDE: What effect do these questions have on the reader?

DIGITAL PERSPECTIVES

CLOSE READ

Some writers use questions as a way of drawing readers in and engaging them in a topic. As students read paragraph 1, remind them to focus on questions the author asks. You may wish to model the close read using the following think-aloud format. Possible responses to questions on the student page are included. You may also want to print copies of the **Close-Read Guide: Nonfiction** for students to use.

ANNOTATE: As I read paragraph 1, I notice and mark questions that are not answered by the author.

QUESTION: The author might have left the questions unanswered so that the reader would answer for himself or herself.

CONCLUDE: I think the questions are meant to make the reader agree with the author, that this ban should not be as big a deal as people are making it out to be.

CROSS-CURRICULAR PERSPECTIVES

Social Studies The author mentions Prohibition in paragraph 1. Prohibition was a constitutional amendment banning alcohol. Have students research or provide them with resources about Prohibition. Divide students into presentation groups. Have different groups present on the following topics: What events led up to Prohibition? How did it become law? What did people do to get around this law? How did it cause the rise of organized crime? Why and how was it repealed? Have students present what they have learned in chronological order. **(Research to Explore)**

TEACHING

● CLOSE READ

As they read paragraphs 8–10, remind students to focus on the different types of bias the author describes. You may wish to model the close read using the following think-aloud format. Possible responses to questions on the student page are included.

ANNOTATE: As I read paragraphs 8–10, I notice and highlight the details that explain the types of "bias" the author is referring to.

QUESTION: I see that the author explains different biases here. I think the purpose is to explain why we do what we do.

CONCLUDE: I think the writer included this information to help make a strong argument. By giving research-based evidence, she makes her argument stronger.

> Additional **English Language Support** is available in the Interactive Teacher's Edition.

NOTES

rational (RASH uh nuhl) *adj.* able to make decisions based on reason rather than emotion; sensible

justifiable (juhs tuh FY uh buhl) *adj.* able to be defended as correct; reasonable and logical

principle (PRIHN suh puhl) *n.* moral rule or set of ideas about right or wrong that influences individuals to behave in a certain way

CLOSE READ
ANNOTATE: In paragraphs 8–10, mark the types of **bias**, or judgments and prejudices, the author describes.

QUESTION: Why does the author include these explanations of different biases?

CONCLUDE: How does this information affect the persuasiveness of her argument?

status quo (STAT uhs kwoh) *n.* existing state or condition at a particular time

---

4 We have a vision of ourselves as free, **rational** beings who are totally capable of making all the decisions we need to in order to create a good life. Give us complete liberty, and, barring natural disasters, we'll end up where we want to be. It's a nice vision, one that makes us feel proud of ourselves. But it's false.

5 John Stuart Mill[2] wrote in 1859 that the only **justifiable** reason for interfering in someone's freedom of action was to prevent harm to others. According to Mill's "harm **principle**," we should almost never stop people from behavior that affects only themselves, because people know best what they themselves want.

6 That "almost," though, is important. It's fair to stop us, Mill argued, when we are acting out of ignorance and doing something we'll pretty definitely regret. You can stop someone from crossing a bridge that is broken, he said, because you can be sure no one wants to plummet into the river. Mill just didn't think this would happen very often.

7 Mill was wrong about that, though. A lot of times we have a good idea of where we want to go, but a really terrible idea of how to get there. It's well established by now that we often don't think very clearly when it comes to choosing the best means to attain our ends. We make errors. This has been the object of an enormous amount of study over the past few decades, and what has been discovered is that we are all prone to identifiable and predictable miscalculations.

8 Research by psychologists and behavioral economists, including the Nobel Prize-winner Daniel Kahneman and his research partner Amos Tversky, identified a number of areas in which we fairly dependably fail. They call such a tendency a "**cognitive**[3] **bias**," and there are many of them—a lot of ways in which our own minds trip us up.

9 For example, we suffer from an **optimism bias**, that is we tend to think that however likely a bad thing is to happen to most people in our situation, it's less likely to happen to us—not for any particular reason, but because we're irrationally optimistic. Because of our "**present bias**," when we need to take a small, easy step to bring about some future good, we fail to do it, not because we've decided it's a bad idea, but because we procrastinate.

10 We also suffer from a **status quo bias**, which makes us value what we've already got over the alternatives, just because we've already got it—which might, of course, make us react badly to

---

2. **John Stuart Mill** (1806–1873) British philosopher.
3. **cognitive** (KOG nih tihv) *adj.* related to thinking.

278 UNIT 3 • WHAT MATTERS

PERSONALIZE FOR LEARNING

English Language Support
Difficult Concepts The writer refers to the idea of cognitive bias in paragraph 8. Point out that the term *cognitive* is defined in the footnote as "related to thinking." Then explain that the term *bias* means "a feeling or opinion that is not justified." When you put the two terms together, the phrase means "thinking in a way that is not justified." With a cognitive bias, there is no evidence to support the argument. It is just the way somebody feels about the issue. **ALL LEVELS**

new laws, even when they are really an improvement over what we've got. And there are more.

11   The crucial point is that in some situations it's just difficult for us to take in the relevant information and choose accordingly. It's not quite the simple ignorance Mill was talking about, but it turns out that our minds are more complicated than Mill imagined. Like the guy about to step through the hole in the bridge, we need help.

12   Is it always a mistake when someone does something imprudent, when, in this case, a person chooses to chug 32 ounces of soda? No. For some people, that's the right choice. They don't care that much about their health, or they won't drink too many big sodas, or they just really love having a lot of soda at once.

13   But laws have to be sensitive to the needs of the majority. That doesn't mean laws should trample the rights of the minority, but that public benefit is a legitimate concern, even when that may inconvenience some.

14   So do these laws mean that some people will be kept from doing what they really want to do? Probably—and yes, in many ways it hurts to be part of a society governed by laws, given that laws aren't designed for each one of us individually. Some of us can drive safely at 90 miles per hour, but we're bound by the same laws as the people who can't, because individual speeding laws aren't practical. Giving up a little liberty is something we agree to when we agree to live in a democratic society that is governed by laws.

15   The freedom to buy a really large soda, all in one cup, is something we stand to lose here. For most people, given their desire for health, that results in a net gain. For some people, yes, it's an absolute loss. It's just not much of a loss.

16   Of course, what people fear is that this is just the beginning: today it's soda, tomorrow it's the guy standing behind you making you eat your broccoli, floss your teeth, and watch *PBS NewsHour*[4] every day. What this ignores is that successful paternalistic[5] laws are done on the basis of a cost-benefit analysis: if it's too painful, it's not a good law. Making these analyses is something the government has the resources to do, just as now it sets automobile construction standards while considering both the need for affordability and the desire for safety.

17   Do we care so much about our health that we want to be forced to go to aerobics every day and give up all meat, sugar and salt?

---

4. **PBS NewsHour** television news program in the United States.
5. **paternalistic** (puh tuhr nuh LIHS tihk) *adj.* protective, but controlling; in the manner of a parent.

NOTES

CLOSE READ
ANNOTATE: In paragraph 14, mark the example the author uses to support her claim.

QUESTION: Why might the author have chosen this specific example as support?

CONCLUDE: How does the inclusion of this example affect the author's argument?

TEACHING

NOTES

No. But in this case, it's some extra soda. Banning a law on the grounds that it might lead to worse laws would mean we could have no laws whatsoever.

18   In the old days we used to blame people for acting imprudently, and say that since their bad choices were their own fault, they deserved to suffer the consequences. Now we see that these errors aren't a function of bad character, but of our shared cognitive inheritance. The proper reaction is not blame, but an impulse to help one another.

19   That's what the government is supposed to do, help us get where we want to go. It's not always worth it to intervene, but sometimes, where the costs are small and the benefit is large, it is. That's why we have prescriptions for medicine. And that's why, as irritating as it may initially feel, the soda regulation is a good idea. It's hard to give up the idea of ourselves as completely rational. We feel as if we lose some dignity. But that's the way it is, and there's no dignity in clinging to an illusion.

PERSONALIZE FOR LEARNING

Strategic Support

Unfamiliar Words In paragraph 18, students will read the word *imprudently*. This word is likely unfamiliar, but it is important in understanding this paragraph. Point out the word. Ask students to try to use context to infer its meaning. Next, direct them to context clues, such as *bad choices*, *own fault*, and *suffer the consequences*. All of these clues imply that *imprudently* is a negative word. Next, have students look *imprudently* up in the dictionary and define it.

Comprehension Check

Complete the following items after you finish your first read.

1. What new law was proposed in New York City?

2. What is a "cognitive bias"?

3. According to the author, what do people fear they will lose as a result of the new law?

4. According to the author, what will most people gain from the soda ban?

5. **Notebook** Write a summary of "Three Cheers for the Nanny State."

RESEARCH

Research to Clarify Choose at least one unfamiliar detail from the text. Briefly research that detail. In what way does the information you learned shed light on an aspect of the text?

Research to Explore Write a research question that you might use to find out more about the concept of the "nanny state."

DIGITAL PERSPECTIVES

Comprehension Check

Possible responses:

1. New York City proposed a ban on large-size sodas, or sugary drinks.
2. A cognitive bias is an unjustified conclusion people come to as a result of their personal experiences or their emotions.
3. People fear that they will lose other freedoms and lose the ability to make other decisions.
4. The author believes most people will gain better health by not buying and drinking large amounts of soda.
5. The summary should point out that the writer agrees with laws like the soda ban and should include evidence from the article to support that position.

Research

Research to Clarify If students struggle to decide on a detail to research, you may want to suggest that they focus on one of the following topics: the New York City soda ban, obesity in America, laws that restrict citizens' choices.

Research to Explore If students aren't sure how to go about formulating a research question, suggest that they use their findings from Research to Clarify as a starting point. For example, if students researched the New York City soda ban, they might formulate a question such as *Was the soda ban effective?*

PERSONALIZE FOR LEARNING

Challenge

Have students analyze the New York City soda ban in greater depth. Create a two-column chart, with one column labeled *Pros* and the other *Cons*. Guide students to work in groups. Have one group research support for the ban and the other, opposition to the ban. Have students create bullet points supporting their sides. Come together as a class and fill in the chart. Discuss how students feel about the idea after the chart is complete. Remind students to be respectful of each other's opinions.

TEACHING

Jump Start

CLOSE READ *No, you can't! Yes, I can!* This might sound like a kids' argument, but it is a common feature of many arguments. Guide students to discuss how it relates to official rules and laws.

Close Read the Text

Walk students through the Annotation Model on the student page. Encourage them to complete items 2 and 3 on their own. Review and discuss the sections students have marked. If needed, continue to model close reading by using the Annotation Highlights in the Interactive Teacher's Edition.

Analyze the Text

Possible responses:

1. (a) The author's tone seems to suggest that she realizes most people are capable of making good decisions, but that sometimes people need to be saved from themselves (from drinking too much soda and suffering bad health, specifically). She does not think the soda ban is necessarily a terrible idea, but people think that this ban will lead to other restrictions on their freedom. (b) "...we often don't think very clearly...," "...it's just difficult for us to...choose accordingly." "...what people fear is that this is just the beginning..." **DOK 2**

2. (a) The larger issue is that laws are intended to stop people from harming themselves, not just in the case of drinking too much soda. (b) The author probably used the soda-ban debate because it's a relatively easy subject to relate to. **DOK 2**

3. It may be right to take a stand to help people achieve goals and avoid harm when they cannot easily do so on their own. **DOK 4**

FORMATIVE ASSESSMENT

Analyze the Text

- **If** students fail to cite evidence, **then** remind them to support their ideas with specific information.
- **If** students struggle to evaluate the author's argument, **then** review the evidence provided by the author to support the argument.

MAKING MEANING

THREE CHEERS FOR THE NANNY STATE

Close Read the Text

1. The model, from paragraph 16, shows two sample annotations, along with questions and conclusions. Close read the passage, and find another detail to annotate. Then, write a question and your conclusion.

> **ANNOTATE:** The author begins the paragraph with the transition phrase *Of course.*
> **QUESTION:** Why might the author have chosen this specific transition?
> **CONCLUDE:** The author uses this phrase to show that she recognizes and, to some degree, understands opposing views.

ANNOTATE: The author lists activities.
QUESTION: Why does the author list these activities?
CONCLUDE: Each activity is considered "good" for people, and is something we usually do at home. The list exaggerates the idea of government control of our behavior.

> Of course, what people fear is that this is just the beginning: today it's soda, tomorrow it's the guy standing behind you making you eat your broccoli, floss your teeth, and watch *PBS NewsHour* every day.

Tool Kit
Close-Read Guide and Model Annotation

2. For more practice, go back into the text and complete the close-read notes.

3. Revisit a section of the text you found important during your first read. Read this section closely, and **annotate** what you notice. Ask yourself **questions** such as "Why did the author make this choice?" What can you **conclude**?

Analyze the Text

CITE TEXTUAL EVIDENCE to support your answers.

Notebook Respond to these questions.

1. **(a) Distinguish** What is the author's **tone**, or attitude toward her subject and audience? **(b) Support** What words and phrases does the author use that create that tone?

2. **(a) Deduce** What is the larger issue that the author is addressing in this opinion piece? **(b) Interpret** Why do you think the author uses the soda-ban debate as a catalyst, or motivating force, for addressing this issue?

3. **Essential Question:** *When is it right to take a stand?* What have you learned from this text about when it is right to take a stand?

STANDARDS

Reading Informational Text
- Determine an author's point of view or purpose in a text and analyze how the author acknowledges and responds to conflicting evidence or viewpoints.
- Delineate and evaluate the argument and specific claims in a text, assessing whether the reasoning is sound and the evidence is relevant and sufficient; recognize when irrelevant evidence is introduced.

282 UNIT 3 • WHAT MATTERS

PERSONALIZE FOR LEARNING

Strategic Support

Evidence When evaluating an argument, exploring evidence is vital. There is a lot of information in the text to support the author's argument, but some of it may be confusing. Create an evidence chart. Place the argument at the top and have students summarize support for the argument found in the article. Add these pieces of evidence as bullet points on the chart.

ESSENTIAL QUESTION: When is it right to take a stand?

DIGITAL PERSPECTIVES

Analyze Craft and Structure

Author's Argument An **author's argument** is his or her position on a controversial or debatable topic or issue. In an argument, the author makes a **claim,** or statement of a specific position. The author's reason for writing is to convince readers to share that position. To do so, the author gives reasons for taking the position, and provides supporting evidence that is **relevant**, or related, to it. The most basic forms of evidence are facts and opinions:

- A **fact** is something that can be proved.
- An **opinion** is a person's judgment or belief. It may be supported by facts, but it cannot be proved.

A successful persuasive argument relies on factual evidence. It also uses **logical reasoning,** or clear thinking, that shows how an author has arrived at his or her position.

An author's argument and choices of supporting evidence can be influenced by various factors, including his or her perspective. An **author's perspective,** which can also be called **point of view,** includes his or her attitudes, beliefs, and feelings. If an author's personal beliefs, attitudes, or feelings are too prominent, an argument may seem less convincing. In extreme cases, it may even be read as **bias,** which is an unfair preference either for or against an idea, person, or group.

Practice

CITE TEXTUAL EVIDENCE to support your answers.

Notebook Use the chart to identify at least four facts the author uses to support her argument. Then, answer the questions that follow.

FACTS	HOW THEY SUPPORT THE ARGUMENT

1. (a) What **generalizations,** or broad statements, does the author make about Americans? (b) What reasons does the author give for these generalizations? (c) Are the reasons based on facts or opinions?
2. (a) Do you think the author's argument will benefit the health of most people? Why or why not? (b) What evidence from the text supports your opinion?
3. Based on your evaluation, did you find the author's argument convincing and persuasive? Why or why not?

Three Cheers for the Nanny State **283**

PERSONALIZE FOR LEARNING

English Language Support

Important Terms When reading an opinion piece, there are terms that can be generally applied. Understanding these terms will help students understand the author's point and construct meaningful responses. Review the following terms with students: *argument, fact, opinion, valid, relevant.* **ALL LEVELS**

Analyze Craft and Structure

Author's Argument

When reading an argument, the author's claim is usually easy to determine. Have students consider why this is true. Point out that if the author's purpose is to convince the reader his or her claim is correct, then the reader needs to know what that claim is. A successful argument should be clear and supported by valid and compelling evidence. For more support, see **Analyze Craft and Structure: Author's Argument.**

Practice

Possible responses for chart on student page:
FACT: Mississippi passed a law against local food/drink restrictions. SUPPORT: We don't like being told what to do.

FACT: Cognitive biases exist. SUPPORT: Our minds can make us make bad choices.

Have students use the information they noted in their chart to answer the questions.

Possible responses:
1. (a) The author assumes that in general, Americans do not want the government telling us what to do, but the author thinks we are often wrong about what is best for us. (b) The author's reasons are that we as Americans can decide for ourselves what is best for us, even if we make errors or bad things sometimes happen. (c) The author's reasons seem to be based on her opinions, but she does support her generalizations with evidence and examples.

2. (a) I don't think the author's argument will benefit the health of most people, because there are certain things people will do whether there is a ban or not. People know that drinking a lot of soda is bad for them, but they still do it. The argument might benefit some people, but not most. (b) The author says it's not "always a mistake when someone does something imprudent," and I think that people might have to have a personal bad experience for them to change their habits.

3. I found the author's argument to be convincing and persuasive only because she included examples not related to the soda ban of laws that help people more than they interfere with people's freedom.

FORMATIVE ASSESSMENT

Analyze Craft and Structure

- **If** students are unable to determine the author's perspective, **then** have them reread the article.
- **If** students are unable to identify evidence, **then** point out several examples of evidence from the article.

For Reteach and Practice, see **Analyze Craft and Structure: Author's Argument (RP).**

Whole-Class Learning **283**

TEACHING

Concept Vocabulary
Why These Words?
Possible responses:
1. The author says that people are upset about New York City's attempt to *impose* a ban on soda. The author argues that there are *rational* and *justifiable* reasons for the new law, and that it is based on a sound *principle*. Still, many people prefer the *status quo* to new changes.
2. *Ban, intervention, Legislature, liberty, society, paternalistic, government*

Practice
Possible responses:
My brother was angry about the rules our parents tried to *impose* on him.; I felt like I made a *rational* decision to stay home instead of go for a walk when the huge storm blew through our neighborhood.; Some people think restrictions on junk food at school are *justifiable* because kids need to have good nutrition.; The basic *principle* of the volunteer work was not for recognition but for helping others.; My sister has always been happy with the *status quo* because she fears change.
impose: synonym: *enforce*
rational: synonym: *logical*
justifiable: synonym: *defensible*
principle: synonym: *basis, foundation*
status quo: synonym: *current situation*

Word Network
Possible words: *bias, irrationally, imprudently*

Word Study
Possible responses:
1. Cheating on a test is never *justifiable;* there is never a good reason that you could have for not studying or doing your own work.
2. The root contributes to the three words in similar ways: *adjust* means "to make right," *justice* has the quality of being right or lawful, and *justification* is the state of being right, or *justified.*

For more support, see **Concept Vocabulary and Word Study.**

FORMATIVE ASSESSMENT
Concept Vocabulary
If students struggle to properly use concept vocabulary, **then** review the meanings of concept vocabulary words and use them in sentences.

Word Study
If students struggle to understand the morphology, **then** provide more examples. For Reteach and Practice, see **Word Study: Latin Root -*just*- (RP).**

284 UNIT 3 • WHAT MATTERS

LANGUAGE DEVELOPMENT

THREE CHEERS FOR THE NANNY STATE

Concept Vocabulary

| impose | justifiable | status quo |
| rational | principle | |

Why These Words? These concept words help the author discuss rules and laws. For example, part of deciding whether a law is *justifiable*, or defensible, is to see if it is *rational*, or reasonable. Rules are often based on a *principle*, or idea, about cooperation or safety.

1. How is each concept vocabulary word related to the author's argument about the new law in New York?

2. What other words in the selection connect to rules or laws?

Practice
Notebook The concept vocabulary words appear in "Three Cheers for the Nanny State." First, use each concept vocabulary word in a sentence that shows your understanding of the word's meaning. Then, find a **synonym**, or word with a similar meaning, for each vocabulary word. Confirm your understanding of each synonym by checking the meanings in a dictionary.

Word Study

Latin Root: *-just-* The Latin root *-just-* means "law" or "fair and right." In "Three Cheers for the Nanny State," the author refers to John Stuart Mill's idea that preventing harm to others is the only *justifiable* reason for interfering with a person's freedom. Mill felt that this was the only "fair and right" reason to interfere.

1. Think about how the root *-just-* contributes to the meaning of the concept vocabulary word *justifiable*. Then, write a sentence in which you correctly use *justifiable*. Remember to include context clues that show the relationship between the root *-just-* and the word's meaning.

2. Using your knowledge of the Latin root *-just-*, explain how the root contributes to the meaning of the following words: *adjust, justice, justification.*

WORD NETWORK
Add words related to taking a stand from the text to your Word Network.

STANDARDS
Language
- Demonstrate command of the conventions of standard English grammar and usage when writing or speaking.
- Demonstrate command of the conventions of standard English capitalization, punctuation, and spelling when writing.
- Determine or clarify the meaning of unknown and multiple-meaning words or phrases based on *grade 8 reading and content*, choosing flexibly from a range of strategies.
   b. Use common, grade-appropriate Greek or Latin affixes and roots as clues to the meaning of a word.
   d. Verify the preliminary determination of the meaning of a word or phrase.
- Demonstrate understanding of figurative language, word relationships, and nuances in word meanings.
   b. Use the relationship between particular words to better understand each of the words.

284 UNIT 3 • WHAT MATTERS

ESSENTIAL QUESTION: When is it right to take a stand?

Conventions

Clauses A **clause** is a group of words that has both a subject and a verb. An **independent clause** has a subject and a verb, and it can stand by itself as a sentence. A **dependent**, or **subordinate**, **clause** has a subject and a verb, but it cannot stand alone as a complete sentence.

Subordinate clauses are classified according to their function in a sentence. The three kinds are **adverb clauses, relative clauses** (also called **adjective clauses**), and **noun clauses.**

CLAUSE	DESCRIPTION	EXAMPLE
Independent clause	• Can stand by itself as a sentence	Although many people oppose the new law, the author supports it.
Adverb clause	• Acts as an adverb • Begins with a subordinating conjunction such as *if, although, when,* or *because*	Although many people oppose the new law, the author supports it.
Relative clause	• Acts as an adjective • Usually begins with a relative pronoun: *who, whom, whose, which,* or *that*	The author supports a law that bans large-size sugary drinks.
Noun clause	• Acts as a noun • Begins with a word such as *what, whatever, when, where, why,* or *how*	The author explains how the new law will work.

In a sentence with two or more clauses, you may need a comma between the clauses. For example, you usually need a comma between an adverb clause and an independent clause.

Read It

1. Identify whether each clause is an independent clause or a dependent clause. If it is a dependent clause, tell which kind.
   a. People suffer from "cognitive bias"
   b. Which makes us value what we already have
   c. Because we procrastinate
   d. Some new laws are really an improvement

2. Reread paragraph 5 of "Three Cheers for the Nanny State." Mark and then label one example of an independent clause and one example of a dependent clause.

Write It

Notebook Write a brief paragraph about the goals of the new law in New York. Make sure to use at least two independent clauses and two dependent clauses in your paragraph. Then, identify each type of clause in your writing.

EVIDENCE LOG

Before moving on to a new selection, go to your Evidence Log and record what you have learned from "Three Cheers for the Nanny State."

Three Cheers for the Nanny State **285**

PERSONALIZE FOR LEARNING

English Language Development

Using Independent and Dependent Clauses Ask students to write a brief summary of the selection. Have students include at least two dependent clauses in at least three sentences. **EMERGING**

Have students use at least three dependent clauses, and encourage them to use at least one noun clause. Remind them that these clauses typically begin with *what, whatever, when, where, why,* or *how.* **EXPANDING**

Ask students to write about the central idea of the selection and include three supporting details. Tell them to include at least three dependent clauses, and encourage them to include an adverb clause in their writing. **BRIDGING**

An expanded **English Language Support Lesson** on Clauses is available in the Interactive Teacher's Edition.

DIGITAL PERSPECTIVES

Conventions

Clauses Understanding sentence structure will help students to become better writers. Explain that clauses help writers to create more complex sentences. Complex sentences make writing more interesting and help a writer to express an idea in a more sophisticated, interesting way. For more support, see **Conventions: Clauses.**

MAKE IT INTERACTIVE
Provide students with examples of short sentences, and have them combine those sentences to create more compelling ideas. Have them refer to the chart of clauses to understand sentence structures. Example: *Many people oppose the new law. The author supports it.* Combined sentence: *Although many people oppose the new law, the author supports it.* Students can suggest examples connected to the article topic or to their own lives.

Read It

Possible responses:

1. a. independent clause; b. dependent clause, noun clause; c. dependent clause, adverb clause d. independent clause

2. independent clauses: John Stuart Mill wrote in 1859; we should almost never stop people from behavior; dependent clauses: that the only justifiable reason for interfering in someone's freedom of action was to prevent harm to others; that affects only themselves; because people know best; what they themselves want

Write It

Responses will vary but should include an example of each type of clause.

Evidence Log Support students in completing their Evidence Logs. This paced activity will help prepare them for the Performance-Based Assessment at the end of the unit.

FORMATIVE ASSESSMENT

Conventions

If students struggle to understand independent and dependent clauses, **then** review examples of each. For Reteach and Practice, see **Conventions: Clauses (RP).**

Selection Test

Administer the "Three Cheers for the Nanny State" Selection Test, which is available in both print and digital formats online in Assessments.

Whole-Class Learning **285**

PLANNING
WHOLE-CLASS LEARNING • BAN THE BAN! • SODA'S A PROBLEM BUT...

Ban the Ban! • Soda's a Problem but...

🔊 **AUDIO SUMMARIES**
Audio summaries of "Ban the Ban!" and "Soda's a Problem but..." are available in both English and Spanish in the Interactive Teacher's Edition or Unit Resources. Assigning these summaries prior to reading the selection may help students build additional background knowledge and set a context for their first read.

Summary

"Ban the Ban" is an article by SidneyAnne Stone. The writer argues that New York City Mayor Michael Bloomberg's laws around soda portion control impact her civil liberties. The writer begins by discussing some of the other laws that Bloomberg has made to control behavior. For example, there are laws that limit where people can smoke and laws that require restaurants to post calorie information. These laws made sense to Stone, but the soda ban does not. She says that the soda ban limits her options and her rights. She argues that government should not be allowed to make these kinds of decisions for citizens. She warns that these limits may start with soda but move into other kinds of food bans. Ultimately, this may impact future freedoms. Stone encourages readers to fight back for their freedom.

"Soda's a problem but Bloomberg doesn't have the solution" is an article by Karin Klein. She argues that New York City Mayor Michael Bloomberg does not have the right to make a law that regulates the size of soda a person can drink. Klein says that soda is not healthy, especially in large portions. However, she says that Bloomberg's law crosses the line by interfering with people's personal choices. Klein points out that the law was developed without following a collaborative process. Instead, she says Bloomberg made the decision himself. Klein questions whether government should be able to dictate what people eat. She argues that people should be able to make their own choices, and she suggests that people nationally are beginning to learn about the dangers of too much soda.

Insight
These opinion pieces argue that free choice is more important than promoting health.

ESSENTIAL QUESTION:
When is it right to take a stand?

Connection to Essential Question
The authors argue that Bloomberg's soda ban interferes with people's freedom to make their own choices and that the government should not be able to make these types of decisions for us.

WHOLE-CLASS LEARNING PERFORMANCE TASK
What is a problem you think needs to be solved? How would you solve it?

UNIT PERFORMANCE-BASED ASSESSMENT
Is it important for people to make their own choices in life?

Connection to Performance Tasks

Whole-Class Learning Performance Task The authors argue that people should be free to make their own choices even about something that could impact their health in a negative way. Students should see these texts as examples of people trying to find solutions to problems they feel are important.

Unit Performance-Based Assessment Both authors argue that people should take control of their own decisions and choices. Students will use examples from these two selections and the others in this unit to explore this question about determining what matters and making choices.

DIGITAL PERSPECTIVES Audio Video Document Annotation Highlights EL Highlights Online Assessment

LESSON RESOURCES

Lesson	Making Meaning	Language Development	Effective Expression
	First Read Close Read Analyze the Text Analyze Craft and Structure	Concept Vocabulary Word Study Conventions	Writing to Compare
Instructional Standards	**RI.10** By the end of the year, read and comprehend literary nonfiction . . . **RI.1** Cite the textual evidence that most strongly supports an analysis . . . **RI.8** Delineate and evaluate the argument and specific claims in a text . . . **RI.9** Analyze a case in which two or more texts provide conflicting information . . .	**L.2** Demonstrate command of the conventions . . . **L.3** Use knowledge of language and its conventions . . . **L.4** Determine or clarify the meaning of unknown and multiple-meaning words and phrases . . . **L.4.b** Use common, grade-appropriate Greek or Latin affixes and roots . . . **L.5** Demonstrate understanding of figurative language . . . **L.5.b** Use the relationship between particular words . . .	**RI.9** Analyze a case in which two or more texts provide conflicting information . . . **W.1** Write arguments to support claims . . . **W.9** Draw evidence from literary or informational texts . . . **W.9.b** Apply *grade 8 reading standards* . . . **W.1.b** Support claim(s) . . . **W.1.c** Use words, phrases, and clauses . . . **W.4** Produce clear and coherent writing . . .

STUDENT RESOURCES

Available online in the Interactive Student Edition or Unit Resources	First-Read Guide: Nonfiction Close-Read Guide: Nonfiction		Evidence Log

TEACHER RESOURCES

Selection Resources Available online in the Interactive Teacher's Edition or Unit Resources	Audio Summaries Annotation Highlights EL Highlights Analyze Craft and Structure: Conflicting Arguments	Concept Vocabulary and Word Study Conventions: Basic Sentence Structures English Language Support Lesson: Compound and Complex Sentences	Writing to Compare: Argumentative Essay
Reteach/Practice (RP) Available online in the Interactive Teacher's Edition or Unit Resources	Analyze Craft and Structure: Conflicting Arguments (RP)	Word Study: Latin prefix *ex-* (RP) Conventions: Basic Sentence Structures (RP)	
Assessment Available online in Assessments	Selection Test		
My Resources	A Unit 3 Answer Key is available online and in the Interactive Teacher's Edition.		

Whole-Class Learning

PERSONALIZE FOR LEARNING
WHOLE-CLASS LEARNING • BAN THE BAN! • SODA'S A PROBLEM BUT...

Reading Support

Text Complexity Rubric: Ban the Ban! • Soda's a Problem but...

Quantitative Measures

Lexile: 930, 1250   Text Length: 570 words, 641 words

Qualitative Measures

Knowledge Demands ①—②—❸—④—⑤	Each text relies on an understanding of the 2013 NYC soda ban and the idea of personal freedom vs. government rules.
Structure ①—②—❸—④—⑤	Each argument is brief and well-organized.
Language Conventionality and Clarity ①—②—❸—④—⑤	"Ban the Ban" is written in a conversational tone. "Soda's a Problem but..." contains more formal language and above-level vocabulary.
Levels of Meaning/Purpose ①—②—❸—④—⑤	Each article presents an argument against the soda ban. Each article aims to call readers to action.

DECIDE AND PLAN

English Language Support
Provide English Learners with support for knowledge demands and language as they read the selection.

Knowledge Demands Before students read, review the meaning of the soda ban. Point out that these articles were written in response to the soda ban.

Language These texts include language that reinforces the idea of government and legislation. Review the following vocabulary with students: *dictate, initiative, legal, illegal, exemption, administration*. As students read the text, ask them how the use of these words and others like them helps the writers make their arguments.

Strategic Support
Provide students with strategic support to ensure that they can successfully read the text.

Knowledge Demands Before reading, preview some of the ideas that are in the selection: the NYC soda ban of 2013, America's obesity epidemic, the connection to health problems, the 1964 surgeon general's report on smoking, and the 2008 ban on trans fat.

Meaning Help students locate the parts of the articles that express each author's viewpoints most clearly. For example, in "Ban the Ban," the writer uses paragraph 3 to move from the specific discussion of a soda ban into a broader discussion of personal rights. In paragraph 4, the writer argues that people should push back to keep their freedoms. Ask students to look for evidence of the author's viewpoint in "Soda's a Problem but..."

Challenge
Provide students who need to be challenged with ideas for how they can go beyond a simple interpretation of the text.

Text Analysis Ask students to review each text to locate especially powerful language that helps each writer make a point. For example, students may see that "Ban the Ban" uses strong language like *big brother, spread throughout the nation,* and *land of the free and the home of the brave* to provoke readers' fear and spark them to action.

Written Response Ask students to write a summary of the pros and cons of the soda ban based on the selections they have read. Then have them write their opinion about whether there should be laws like this to regulate people's health.

TEACH

Read and Respond
Have students do their first read of the selection. Then have them complete their close read. Finally, work with them on the Making Meaning, Language Development, and Effective Expression activities.

Standards Support Through Teaching and Learning Cycle

IDENTIFY NEEDS

Analyze results of the Beginning-of-Year Assessment, focusing on the items relating to Unit 3. Also take into consideration student performance to this point and your observations of where particular students struggle.

DECIDE AND PLAN

- If students have performed poorly on items matching these standards, then provide selection scaffolds before assigning them the on-level lesson provided in the Student Edition.
- If students have done well on the Beginning-of-Year Assessment, then challenge them to keep progressing and learning by giving them opportunities to practice the skills in depth.
- Use the Selection Resources listed on the Planning pages for "Ban the Ban!" and "Soda's a Problem but…" to help students continually improve their ability to master the standards.

Instructional Standards: Ban the Ban! • Soda's a Problem but...

	Catching Up	This Year	Looking Forward
Reading	You may wish to administer the **Analyze Craft and Structure: Conflicting Arguments (RP)** worksheet to help students find strategies for analyzing arguments.	**RI.8** Delineate and evaluate the argument and specific claims in a text, assessing whether the reasoning is sound and the evidence is relevant and sufficient; recognize when irrelevant evidence is introduced.	Challenge students to work with a partner to find other editorials or opinion pieces and to summarize the writer's arguments.
Language	You may wish to administer the **Conventions: Basic Sentence Structures (RP)** worksheet to help students understand the four basic sentence structures. You may wish to administer the **Word Study: Latin Prefix ex- (RP)** worksheet to help students understand they can use Greek and Latin prefixes to infer the meanings of words.	**L.2** Demonstrate command of the conventions of standard English capitalization, punctuation, and spelling when writing. **L.4.b** Use common, grade-appropriate Greek or Latin affixes and roots as clues to the meaning of a word.	Ask students to write one of each type of sentence. Work with students to find three words from the selections that begin with Greek or Latin prefixes and use each word in a sentence that includes context clues.

ANALYZE AND REVISE

- Analyze student work for evidence of student learning.
- Identify whether students have met the expectations in the standards.
- Identify implications for future instruction.

TEACH

Implement the planned lesson, and gather evidence of student learning.

TEACHING

Jump Start

FIRST READ Who decides what you get to do? How fast can drivers drive? Have students discuss whether making choices, healthy or unhealthy, is a normal part of life and whether government should play a role.

Ban the Ban! • Soda's a Problem but... 🔊 📄

Why did Mayor Bloomberg push for the soda ban? Is it fair? Will it work? What is the best approach to the problem? Modeling questions such as these will help students connect to the selections "Ban the Ban!" and "Soda's a Problem but..." and to the Performance Task assignment. Selection audio and print capability for the selections are available in the Interactive Teacher's Edition.

Concept Vocabulary

Support students as they rank the words. Ask if they've ever heard, read, or used them. Reassure them that the definitions for these words are listed in the selection.

● FIRST READ

As they read, students should perform the steps of the first read:

NOTICE: You may want to encourage students to notice the writers' arguments and evidence used to support those arguments.

ANNOTATE: Remind students to mark passages that show the writers' opinions and the support they use to back up their point of view.

CONNECT: Encourage students to go beyond the text to make connections. Have them consider healthy and unhealthy choices they make in their lives and how they make those choices.

RESPOND: Students will answer questions and write a summary to demonstrate understanding.

Point out to students that while they will always complete the Respond step at the end of the first read, the other steps will probably happen somewhat concurrently. You may wish to print copies of the **First-Read Guide: Nonfiction** for students to use. 📄

Remind students that during their first read, they should not answer the close-read questions that appear in the selection.

286 UNIT 3 • WHAT MATTERS

MAKING MEANING

Comparing Texts

You will now read "Ban the Ban!" and "Soda's a Problem but...." First, complete the first-read and close-read activities. Then, compare the arguments in these opinion pieces with the argument in "Three Cheers for the Nanny State."

• THREE CHEERS FOR THE NANNY STATE

• BAN THE BAN!
• SODA'S A PROBLEM BUT...

About the Authors
SidneyAnne Stone is a freelance writer, entrepreneur, marathoner, breast cancer survivor, and activist. She is currently working on her first novel and documentary.

Karin Klein has won awards for her editorial and environmental writing. She attended Wellesley College and the University of California—Berkeley, and she is now an adjunct professor at Chapman University in Orange, California.

🔧 **Tool Kit**
First-Read Guide and Model Annotation

📋 STANDARDS
Reading Informational Text
By the end of the year, read and comprehend literary nonfiction at the high end of the grades 6–8 text complexity band independently and proficiently.

286 UNIT 3 • WHAT MATTERS

Ban the Ban!
Soda's a Problem but...

Concept Vocabulary

You will encounter these words as you read. Before reading, note how familiar you are with each word. Then, rank the words from most familiar (1) to least familiar (6).

WORD	YOUR RANKING
implemented	
mandates	
intervene	
intentions	
dictate	
exemption	

After completing the first read, come back to the concept vocabulary and review your rankings. Mark changes to your original rankings as needed.

First Read NONFICTION

Apply these strategies as you conduct your first read. You will have an opportunity to complete the close-read notes after your first read.

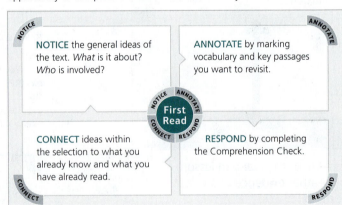

NOTICE the general ideas of the text. *What* is it about? *Who* is involved?

ANNOTATE by marking vocabulary and key passages you want to revisit.

CONNECT ideas within the selection to what you already know and what you have already read.

RESPOND by completing the Comprehension Check.

VOCABULARY DEVELOPMENT

Concept Vocabulary Reinforcement Have students select the concept vocabulary connected to government and legislation. These are *mandates, dictate,* and *exemption*. Have students discuss what they know about each of these terms. Review their definitions. Have students use each in a sentence. Next, have students consider how these terms are related to each other. Ask a volunteer to make a meaningful sentence that contains all three terms.

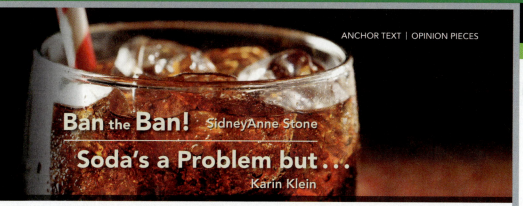

ANCHOR TEXT | OPINION PIECES

Ban the Ban!
SidneyAnne Stone

Soda's a Problem but . . .
Karin Klein

BACKGROUND In 2012, New York City's Mayor Bloomberg pushed for a law limiting soft-drink sizes as part of his focus on public health. The law won the approval of the city's Board of Health, but industry groups claimed it was illegal because it interfered with consumers' choices. A judge ruled against the law because it excluded certain businesses and did not apply to all beverages.

SCAN FOR MULTIMEDIA

Ban the Ban!

1 When Mayor Bloomberg **implemented** laws banning smoking in bars, parks and restaurants, that made sense. Whether or not I agreed, I understood the rationale because other people's health would inadvertently be impacted by the smoke. When he insisted on calorie counts being posted, I think many of us cringed but, again, it made sense. If you want to know how many calories something is before you indulge, it is now spelled out for you. On days when you feel like being especially naughty, you just don't look and order it anyway! That's what life is all about, isn't it? Choices. Informed decisions. I respect being given information that enables me to make an informed decision. What I do not respect is having my civil liberties stripped away.

2 When you take away the option to order a soda over a certain size, you have now removed my options. I no longer have a choice. That is not what this country is all about. I agree wholeheartedly that obesity is an issue that needs to be addressed. It is one that needs to be addressed with education, compassion and support, not government **mandates**. If, despite all those efforts, someone chooses to have a sugary drink anyway, that is their choice and their right. If they know all the facts and they do it anyway, that is a personal choice. It is not the place of our elected officials to **intervene**.

3 We cannot allow our government to make these kinds of decisions for us. I have said it before and I will say it again, once you allow the government to make choices on your behalf, it becomes a very slippery slope. I, personally, feel that it goes against everything this country stands for—we are a country built on freedom. That includes basic freedoms like what you are going to drink while watching a movie, and eating what will soon be un-buttered and un-salted popcorn, according to Mayor Bloomberg. Remember the days when New York was a really cool and fun place

NOTES

implemented (IHM pluh mehnt ihd) *v.* carried out; put into effect

mandates (MAN dayts) *n.* orders or commands

intervene (ihn tuhr VEEN) *v.* interfere with; take action to try to stop a dispute or conflict

TEACHING

CLOSE READ

As students read paragraph 4, remind them to focus on words that the author repeats. You may wish to model the close read using the following think-aloud format. Possible responses to questions on the student page are included. You may also want to print copies of the **Close-Read Guide: Nonfiction** for students to use.

ANNOTATE: As I read paragraph 4, I notice that the author repeats the term "freedom."

QUESTION: I think the author is trying to emphasize the importance of the word. She is trying to tap into each reader's ideas of this word.

CONCLUDE: The use of this word connects the soda ban to the larger issue of limiting personal freedoms.

NOTES

CLOSE READ
ANNOTATE: Mark the term in the fourth sentence of paragraph 4 that the author repeats.

QUESTION: Why do you think the author repeats this term?

CONCLUDE: What effect does this repetition have on the reader?

intentions (ihn TEHN shuhnz) *n.* purposes for or goals of one's actions

dictate (DIHK tayt) *v.* give orders to control or influence something

exemption (ehg ZEHMP shuhn) *n.* permission not to do or pay for something that others are required to do or pay

to live? Me too. Now a simple thing like going to the movies has even lost its "flavor."

4   The people of New York need to show our mayor that money can't buy him everything. He says he's going to "fight back" to get this pushed through. Well, it is our responsibility to fight back too. People might think it is not important because it is just soda but it is so much more than that—it is about freedom and the freedom to make your own decisions about what you do and what you put into your bodies. It started with soda and he has already moved on to salt. What is going to be next? If you're reading this and you are not a New Yorker, don't think you are not going to be affected. You will! It starts here and it will spread throughout the nation. I hope you will all start to speak up about this issue or, before you know it, it won't be the "land of the free and home of the brave" anymore. One day in the not too distant future we are all going to wake up in the land of "Big Brother"[1] with a list of things we can and cannot do, eat, drink, say, and so on, and we'll be wondering how we got there. Well, this is how.

Soda's a Problem but . . .

1   The **intentions** of New York Mayor Michael R. Bloomberg may be laudable, but it's wrong for one man, even an elected official and even a well-meaning one at that, to **dictate** to people how big a cup of sugary soda they're allowed.

2   Not that I have tremendous regard for soda. It's bad for you, especially in large quantities. The evidence against it mounts on a semi-regular basis. But the mayor's initiative goes further than something like a soda tax, which might aim to discourage people from purchasing something by making it cost a bit more but leaves the decision in their hands. Bloomberg is playing nanny in the worst sort of way by interfering in a basic, private transaction involving a perfectly legal substance. In restaurants and other establishments overseen by the city's health inspectors, it would have been illegal to sell a serving of most sugary drinks (except fruit juice; I always wonder about that **exemption**, considering the sugar calories in apple juice) that's more than 16 ounces.

3   Convenience stores such as 7-Eleven are overseen by the state and would be exempt, but a Burger King across the street would be restricted. A pizza restaurant would not be able to sell a 2-liter bottle of soda that would be shared out among the children at a birthday party. But they could all have a 16-ounce cup. The inherent contradictions that make it easy to sneer at such rules have been well-reported and were a good part of why earlier this week a judge stopped the new rules from being implemented. But he also pointed out a deeper problem: Bloomberg essentially made this decision himself. It was approved by the Board of Health, but that's a board of the administration, appointed by the mayor. That was

---

1. **the land of "Big Brother"** place in which the government or another organization exercises total control over people's lives; the term *Big Brother* was coined by George Orwell in his famous dystopian novel, *1984*.

an overreach that thwarted the system of checks and balances, according to the judge: The separately elected City Council would have to approve the law.

4 That still leaves the question of whether governments or their leaders can begin dictating the look of an individual's meal, the portion sizes for each aspect. There are times when government has to step in on obviously dangerous situations—especially those, such as smoking, that affect people other than the person whose behavior would be curbed—but it's my belief that we want to scrutinize them carefully and keep them to a minimum. For that matter, it's not as though the mayor is moving to limit sales of tobacco to two cigarettes per transaction.

5 Not that government has to aid and abet the situation. Schools don't have to sell junk foods, and, thankfully, after years of sacrificing their students' health to their desire to raise more money, most of them have stopped allowing vending machines stocked with sodas. Governments are under no obligation to sell such stuff in park or pool vending machines or in their offices. In such cases, government is simply the vendor making a decision about what it wants to sell.

6 I don't buy the argument that people are helpless in the face of sugar and that it's better to have the government rather than the corporations dictate their behaviors. If people are so helpless against soda, the mayor's edict would be even more meaningless because people would simply buy two 16-ounce cups. But people are not helpless, and it's worrisome to promote a philosophy that infantilizes the individual. The public is simply ill-informed. It takes a while for people to become aware, but they do and they react. Soda consumption already is slipping nationwide.

7 Let's not forget that scientists and even governments have at times pushed people—with better intentions than food corporations, certainly—into eating high levels of refined carbohydrates and sugars by sending out word that the only thing that really matters when it comes to obesity is to eat a very low-fat diet.

NOTES

CLOSE READ
ANNOTATE: Mark the text in paragraph 4 in which the author makes exceptions to her claims.

QUESTION: Why might the author have chosen to include this information, which does not support her argument?

CONCLUDE: What effect does the author's inclusion of this information have on the reader?

Comprehension Check

Complete the following items after you finish your first review.

1. Who is Michael Bloomberg?

2. According to the author of "Ban the Ban!," what is "life all about"?

3. What does the author of "Soda's a Problem but..." think of the argument that "people are helpless in the face of sugar"?

RESEARCH

Research to Explore
Formulate a research question that you might use to find out more about other issues that relate to the concept of the "nanny state."

Ban the Ban! • Soda's a Problem but... 289

PERSONALIZE FOR LEARNING

Challenge

Research Related Topics Issues of public health are an important part of the American conversation. Explain to students that public health crises pose many challenges and lead to higher health care costs. Ask students to select a public health crisis in the United States. Have them create posters to increase awareness of the crisis. The posters should include at least three facts about the crisis. Display the posters.

DIGITAL PERSPECTIVES

CLOSE READ

As they read paragraph 4, remind students to look for text that shows the author making an exception to her claims.

ANNOTATE: As I read paragraph 4, I notice and mark the second sentence.

QUESTION: I notice that the author is pointing out a situation that might need the government to step in when other people's health could be at risk.

CONCLUDE: I think that the reader might agree that sometimes intervention can be good, even when it means taking away people's choices.

Comprehension Check

Possible responses:
1. Michael Bloomberg was the mayor of New York City at the time these selections were written.
2. According to "Ban the Ban!," life is all about freedom to make your own choices.
3. The author of "Soda's a Problem but..." thinks that the argument is worrisome. She thinks people just need to be better informed.

Research

Research to Explore If students have trouble formulating a research question, suggest that they focus on one of these topics: obesity in America, government mandates, Big Brother.

Whole-Class Learning 289

TEACHING

Jump Start

CLOSE READ Use the following prompt to engage students in a class discussion: *Do you agree that it is a good idea for the government to make laws that protect us from ourselves, or do you think people should get to decide for themselves, even if they make poor decisions?*

Close Read the Text

Walk students through the Annotation Model on the student page. Encourage them to complete items 2 and 3 on their own. Review and discuss the sections students have marked. If needed, continue to model close reading by using the Annotation Highlights in the Interactive Teacher's Edition.

Analyze the Text

Possible responses:

1. (a) The author means that if we let the government decide how much soda we are allowed to have, then they will surely start taking away other personal choices, like what we are allowed to eat. **DOK 2** (b) The author talks about our "basic freedoms" and believes that if we are told how much soda we're allowed to drink, then we'll soon be told what kind of popcorn we can have at the movies. **DOK 3**

2. (a) The judge stopped the new rules from being put into effect partly because it would be hard to enforce the rules the same way in different places. Another reason is because the law was not approved by everyone that needed to approve it. **DOK 2** (b) The author believes that because the rules for selling soda would not be the same in all places, the law would not be effective. **DOK 4**

3. (a) The author views the public as ill-informed, but not helpless. **DOK 2** (b) I don't really agree with her views that the public is ill-informed, but I do think that not everyone seeks out the information available to them. **DOK 4**

4. Responses will vary. **DOK 4**

FORMATIVE ASSESSMENT

Analyze the Text

- **If** students fail to cite evidence, **then** remind them to support their ideas with specific information.
- **If** students struggle to understand the author's argument, **then** discuss point of view, and illustrate with examples.

290 UNIT 3 • WHAT MATTERS

MAKING MEANING

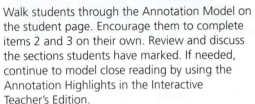

BAN THE BAN! | SODA'S A PROBLEM BUT . . .

Tool Kit
Close-Read Guide and Model Annotation

STANDARDS
Reading Informational Text
• Cite the textual evidence that most strongly supports an analysis of what the text says explicitly as well as inferences drawn from the text.
• Delineate and evaluate the argument and specific claims in a text, assessing whether the reasoning is sound and the evidence is relevant and sufficient; recognize when irrelevant evidence is introduced.
• Analyze a case in which two or more texts provide conflicting information on the same topic and identify where the texts disagree on matters of fact or interpretation.

290 UNIT 3 • WHAT MATTERS

Close Read the Text

1. This model from paragraph 6 of "Soda's a Problem but..." shows two sample annotations along with questions and conclusions. Close read the passage, and find another detail to annotate. Then, write a question and your conclusion.

> **ANNOTATE:** The author repeats the word *helpless*. She also uses a negative word that suggests people are being treated like babies (infants).
> **QUESTION:** Why does the author stress the idea of helplessness?
> **CONCLUDE:** She stresses this idea to engage readers' emotions. Adults do not want to be treated like helpless infants.

> If people are so helpless against soda, the mayor's edict would be even more meaningless because people would simply buy two 16-ounce cups. But people are not helpless, and it's worrisome to promote a philosophy that infantilizes the individual.

> **ANNOTATE:** The author considers a premise, but then rejects it.
> **QUESTION:** Why does the author structure her idea in this way?
> **CONCLUDE:** This structure shows that the author considered another point of view, but found it unconvincing.

2. For more practice, go back into the text, and complete the close-read notes.

3. Revisit a section of the text you found important during your first read. Read this section closely, and **annotate** what you notice. Ask yourself **questions** such as "Why did the author make this choice?" What can you **conclude**?

Analyze the Text

CITE TEXTUAL EVIDENCE to support your answers.

Notebook Respond to these questions.

1. (a) **Make Inferences** In paragraph 3 of "Ban the Ban!," what does the author mean by the phrase "a very slippery slope"? (b) **Support** Which details in the text support your thinking?

2. (a) According to the author of "Soda's a Problem but...," why did the judge stop the soda ban from being put into effect? (b) **Connect** What "inherent contradictions" in the soda ban does the author believe the judge's opinion reflects?

3. (a) How does the author of "Soda's a Problem but..." view the public? (b) **Make a Judgment** Do you agree with her assessment of "the public"? Why or why not?

4. **Essential Question:** *When is it right to take a stand?* What have you learned about taking a stand from reading these opinion pieces?

PERSONALIZE FOR LEARNING

English Language Support

Idioms Have students revisit this sentence from paragraph 6 of "Soda's a Problem but...":

I don't buy the argument that people are helpless in the face of sugar and that it's better to have the government rather than the corporations dictate their behavior.

The idiom *in the face of* might present challenges for English learners. Have students discuss this sentence and guess what the idiom might mean. To check their understanding, ask students to come up with other sentences using *in the face of* in the same way it is used in the text. **ALL LEVELS**

ESSENTIAL QUESTION: When is it right to take a stand?

DIGITAL PERSPECTIVES

Analyze Craft and Structure

Conflicting Arguments In an **argument,** an author presents a **claim,** or position, about a debatable topic. He or she then explains reasons for taking that position, and uses evidence to show why the reasons are sound. Strong arguments rely on facts. Weak arguments may express the author's opinions but not use facts to support them. Weak arguments may also have poor reasoning or rely too heavily on exciting readers' emotions. Some types of poor reasoning or over-reliance on emotions are called **logical fallacies.** Common logical fallacies include the following:

- An **overgeneralization** is a conclusion that overstates the facts. A statement that includes words such as *always, never, everything,* or *only* may be an overgeneralization.
- A **slippery slope** assumes that if A happens then B, C, D,…X, Y, Z are inevitable. This fallacy says that event A, which might be minor, is the same as event Z, which might be terrible. If you do not want Z to occur, you must prevent A from occurring, too. The idea that such a chain of events will definitely happen may simply be untrue.

Although two authors might express the same position, they may not present it in the same way. Authors arguing similar positions may offer different reasons and evidence. One may use facts and sound reasoning, whereas another may use few or no facts and logical fallacies.

Practice

CITE TEXTUAL EVIDENCE to support your answers.

Notebook Answer the following questions.

1. What position on the question of the soda ban do both authors express?
2. (a) Identify one fact about Mayor Bloomberg and the soda ban that both authors cite. (b) Note one fact that appears in one piece, but not in the other.
3. Consider this statement from paragraph 3 of "Ban the Ban!": "Remember the days when New York was a really cool and fun place to live? Me too. Now a simple thing like going to the movies has even lost its 'flavor.'" In what ways is this statement an example of overgeneralization?
4. In the last paragraph of "Ban the Ban!" explain how the sentence "What is going to be next?" introduces the logical fallacy of slippery slope.
5. Which author presents a more convincing argument? Explain your thinking.

Ban the Ban! • Soda's a Problem but . . . **291**

WriteNow Express and Reflect

Opinion Piece Based on all that they have read so far, ask students to write a brief opinion piece on the following subject: Should sugary snacks or drinks be banned? Students should make sure to include a main idea, which states their opinions. They should also include at least two supporting details based on their reading and their background knowledge.

Analyze Craft and Structure

Conflicting Arguments When writing an argument, an author is trying to convince the reader that his or her argument is the correct one. The way an argument is presented can differ by author but must always be based on facts, valid evidence, and reasons in order to be effective. Arguments can have errors in reasoning, or logical fallacies, when an author bases the argument more on emotional appeals than on facts. Readers might encounter common logical fallacies such as *overgeneralization, slippery slope,* or *ad populum* in emotional arguments, none of which is clearly connected to the facts. For more support, see **Analyze Craft and Structure: Conflicting Arguments**

Practice

Possible responses:
1. Both authors argue that the soda ban should not be put into law.
2. (a) Both articles cite the actual ban of soda in a cup larger than 16 ounces. (b) Stone's article includes information about other rules Bloomberg has enforced, such as smoking in parks.
3. The statement suggests that New York is no longer fun—a broad generalization.
4. The statement includes the "slippery slope" fallacy by suggesting that soda bans will lead to many other restrictions on people's lives.
5. Answers will vary. Students should defend their positions.

FORMATIVE ASSESSMENT

Analyze Craft and Structure

- **If** students struggle to identify logical fallacies in the articles, **then** review the types of logical fallacies they should look for in the texts.
- **If** students struggle to identify claims, **then** revisit the articles and to help them to identify the claims each author makes.

For Reteach and Practice, see **Analyze Craft and Structure: Conflicting Arguments (RP).**

Whole-Class Learning **291**

TEACHING

Concept Vocabulary
Why These Words?
Possible responses:
1. The vocabulary words draw attention to health problems related to obesity and poor diet choices, and to how the government is attempting to address these concerns.
2. *Freedom, "Big Brother," initiative, interfering, decision, dictating*

Practice
1. *intentions*
2. *implemented*
3. *exemption*
4. *mandates*
5. *intervene*
6. *dictate*

Word Network
Possible words: *choices, respect, decisions, liberties, individual*

Word Study
For more support, see **Concept Vocabulary and Word Study.**

Possible responses:
The prefix *ex-*, meaning "out," contributes to the meaning of these words in this way: *exhale* means to breathe out; *explore* can mean to venture out; *exceptional* can mean out of the ordinary; "ex" in *excommunicate* means cut off from.

FORMATIVE ASSESSMENT
Concept Vocabulary
If students struggle to understand concept vocabulary, **then** review concept vocabulary and its use in the text.

Word Study
If students do not understand how the prefix *ex-* lends itself to the meaning of the words given, **then** help them use the words in sentences. For Reteach and Practice, see **Word Study: Latin Prefix *ex-* (RP).**

292   UNIT 3 • WHAT MATTERS

LANGUAGE DEVELOPMENT

BAN THE BAN! | SODA'S A PROBLEM BUT . . .

Concept Vocabulary

| implemented | mandates | intervene |
| intentions | dictate | exemption |

Why These Words? The concept vocabulary words help the authors discuss the rules, laws, and regulations involved in the soda-ban debate. In "Ban the Ban!," the author feels that it is not the government's place to *intervene* with an individual's personal choice. In other words, she feels that elected officials should not make laws that interfere with an individual's right to make his or her own decisions.

1. How does the concept vocabulary clarify your understanding of the issues presented in the opinion pieces?

2. What other words in the opinion pieces connect to the concept of rules, laws, and regulations?

WORD NETWORK
Add words related to taking a stand from the text to your Word Network.

Practice
Correctly complete the following sentences using a concept vocabulary word.

1. Roberto's repeated efforts to help shows that he has good _____.
2. My school _____ a new dress code this year that requires all students to wear uniforms.
3. Some large companies receive a tax _____ when they move to a rural area in the hope that they will improve the local economy.
4. New local _____ require that all dogs be on leashes in public places.
5. The doctor felt it was necessary to _____ when he saw a patient being given the wrong treatment.
6. The new community council will _____ the terms and conditions of the new development.

STANDARDS
Language
- Demonstrate command of the conventions of standard English capitalization, punctuation, and spelling when writing.
- Use knowledge of language and its conventions when writing, speaking, reading, or listening.
- Determine or clarify the meaning of unknown and multiple-meaning words or phrases based on *grade 8 reading and content*, choosing flexibly from a range of strategies.
  b. Use common, grade-appropriate Greek or Latin affixes and roots as clues to the meaning of a word.
- Demonstrate understanding of figurative language, word relationships, and nuances in word meanings.
  b. Use the relationship between particular words to better understand each of the words.

Word Study
Notebook Latin Prefix: *ex-* The Latin prefix *ex-* means "out" or "out from within." In "Soda's a Problem but...," the author is curious about the reasons sales of fruit juices are given an *exemption* from the 16-ounce cap on soda sizes. Sellers of juice receive an *exemption* because the new rules do not apply to them—they are left "out" of the new laws. Explain how the prefix *ex-* contributes to the meaning of each of the following words: *exhale, explore, exceptional, excommunicate*.

ESSENTIAL QUESTION: When is it right to take a stand?

Conventions

Basic Sentence Structures Good writers use a variety of sentence structures to make their writing smoother and more interesting to the reader. **Sentence structure** is defined by the types of **clauses** in a sentence. An **independent clause** forms a complete thought or a stand-alone sentence. A **dependent clause** is an incomplete thought. The four basic sentence structures are shown in the chart. Independent clauses are shown in bold. Dependent clauses are underlined.

SENTENCE STRUCTURE	EXAMPLE
A **simple sentence** has a single independent clause with at least one subject and verb.	**The author opposes the new law.**
A **compound sentence** consists of two or more independent clauses joined either by a comma and a conjunction or by a semicolon.	**The author opposes the new law,** but **many people support it.**
A **complex sentence** consists of an independent clause and one or more dependent clauses.	**The author opposes the new law,** which bans sales of large-size sweet drinks.
A **compound-complex sentence** consists of two or more independent clauses and one or more dependent clauses.	**The author opposes the new law,** which bans sales of large-size sweet drinks, but **many people support it.**

Read It

1. Identify the type of sentence represented in each lettered item.
   a. If you want to know how many calories something is before you indulge, it is now spelled out for you.
   b. Soda consumption already is slipping nationwide.
   c. It takes a while for people to become aware, but they do and they react.
2. Reread the first four sentences in paragraph 1 of "Ban the Ban!" Identify the type of sentence each one represents.

Write It

Notebook Add one or more clauses to this simple sentence to form the type of sentence indicated in each numbered item: *Sugary drinks are unhealthy.*

1. Compound sentence
2. Complex sentence
3. Compound-complex sentence

Ban the Ban! • Soda's a Problem but . . . 293

Conventions

Basic Sentence Structures Review with students the components of a complete sentence. A sentence can be as simple as a noun and a verb that make a complete thought. Remind them that this is an independent clause. It stands on its own. Point out that as we add clauses to our sentences, they transform into different types of sentences. For more support, see **Conventions: Basic Sentence Structures.**

MAKE IT INTERACTIVE
Ask students to suggest examples of sentences. Display the examples for the class. Have the class determine if the sentences are simple, compound, complex, or compound-complex.

Read It
Possible responses:
1. a. complex sentence, b. simple sentence
   c. compound sentence
2. sentence 1: complex; sentence 2: compound-complex

Write It
Possible responses:
1. Sugary drinks are unhealthy, so some people want to ban larger-size drinks.
2. Although they taste delicious, sugary drinks are unhealthy.
3. Although they taste delicious, sugary drinks are unhealthy, so some people want to ban larger-size drinks.

FORMATIVE ASSESSMENT
Conventions
If students struggle to understand basic sentence structure, **then** review examples of different types of sentences. For Reteach and Practice, see **Conventions: Basic Sentence Structures (RP).**

PERSONALIZE FOR LEARNING

English Language Support
Creating Compound and Complex Sentences Tell students to write their opinion about the selection. Their writing should feature compound and complex sentences. Then have partners or small groups discuss their opinions and have all participants ask and answer questions. Have students write two or three sentences that express their opinion. **EMERGING**

Have students write a paragraph that expresses their opinion and support it with evidence from the text. **EXPANDING**

Have students write a brief persuasive essay that expresses their opinion and support it with evidence from the text and their background knowledge. **BRIDGING**

An expanded **English Language Support Lesson** on Compound and Complex Sentences is available in the Interactive Teacher's Edition.

TEACHING

Writing to Compare
As students prepare to compare arguments regarding soda bans, they will consider which essay was most compelling to them.

Planning and Prewriting
Analyze the Text Encourage students to carefully analyze and classify the arguments. Remind students that argument is a logical presentation of a claim. Have students consider the issue and their planned claims from the perspectives of a supporting, an opposing, and an undecided reader.

Possible responses for chart on student page:

a. Details about the ban; details about human biases

b. Good idea, but this is not about soda.

c. This is not such a big deal.

d. Details about the ban; details about other Bloomberg initiatives

e. Don't take away civil rights; beware a slippery slope.

f. Obesity is a problem; New York will be less fun.

g. Details about ban and exemption

h. Bloomberg doesn't have this right; he shouldn't treat people like babies.

i. Soda is bad for you; schools don't have to enable obesity.

Possible Responses:

1. Responses will vary but may include that the authors disagree on the facts; they disagree on whether individuals are responsible enough to cut down on soda without government intervention.
2. Responses will vary.
3. Responses will vary; ask students to defend their ideas.

EFFECTIVE EXPRESSION

THREE CHEERS FOR THE NANNY STATE

BAN THE BAN! | SODA'S A PROBLEM BUT . . .

Writing to Compare
You have studied opinion pieces that present arguments on the same topic—the soda ban in New York City and the larger question of how much the government should be involved in personal decisions. Deepen your analysis by comparing and contrasting the arguments presented in the pro-soda ban opinion piece, "Three Cheers for the Nanny State," and the anti-soda ban opinion pieces, "Ban the Ban!" and "Soda's a Problem but. . . ."

Assignment
Write an **argumentative essay** in which you state a claim about which of the three arguments you found most convincing. To support your claim, analyze the facts and other information the three authors include. Consider these questions:

- What facts do all three authors include?
- Do they use any conflicting information—facts that are not the same? If so, what are they and why are they conflicting?
- Is one author's conclusion or interpretation of the facts more convincing than the others? If so, why?

Include evidence from all three opinion pieces to support your ideas.

STANDARDS
Reading Informational Text
Analyze a case in which two or more texts provide conflicting information on the same topic and identify where the texts disagree on matters of fact or interpretation.

Writing
Draw evidence from literary or informational texts to support analysis, reflection, and research.
  b. Apply *grade 8 Reading standards* to literary nonfiction.

Planning and Prewriting
Analyzing the Texts Review the texts and identify facts each author uses, conclusions each author draws, and personal opinions each author expresses. Use the chart to capture your observations.

	THREE CHEERS FOR THE NANNY STATE	BAN THE BAN!	SODA'S A PROBLEM BUT...
facts included	a. See possible responses in Teacher's Edition.	d.	g.
conclusion or interpretation based on facts	b.	e.	h.
author's personal opinions (if any)	c.	f.	i.

Notebook Respond to these questions.

1. Do the authors disagree on the facts or is it just their interpretation of those facts that differs?
2. Are there any weaknesses in any author's reasoning? Explain.
3. Which argument is strongest? Explain your thinking.

294 UNIT 3 • WHAT MATTERS

PERSONALIZE FOR LEARNING

English Language Support
Organization In making an informed decision, organizing one's thoughts is of vital importance. It can also be a challenge. Have students consider choices they have had to make in their lives. They can be serious choices, like life decisions, or simple choices, like what to make for lunch. Have students create a chart to compare the two sides of their choices and the evidence available to support each side.
ALL LEVELS

ESSENTIAL QUESTION: When is it right to take a stand?

DIGITAL PERSPECTIVES

Drafting

Write a Strong Claim A strong, specific claim is the basis for a strong argument. A narrower claim is usually more effective because it focuses your argument and makes it more manageable. Consider using words and phrases that limit the scope of your claim. These types of words and phrases include *generally, for the most part,* and *on average.* Consider the following examples:

> **Broad Claim:** Laws governing food safety do a good job of protecting public health.
>
> **Narrower Claim:** In general, laws governing food safety do a reasonably good job of protecting public health.

Use the space to write a working claim. As you draft your essay, you may refocus your claim as necessary.

_____

_____

_____

Review, Revise, and Edit

Revising for Clarity and Cohesion Precise word choices can clarify and strengthen your argument. Review your draft, and look for places in which you have not clearly connected your claim, reasons, and evidence. Ask yourself questions such as: *How does this fact support my reasoning? How does the fact in combination with my reasons support my claim?* Consider the following examples:

> **Unclear Connection:** Our town should invest in computers. Libraries that have computers are more useful.
>
> **Clear Connection:** There are many reasons why our town should invest in computers for the library. First, libraries that have computers provide a wider range of service. Second, libraries with computers are used more often by the community.

In the first example, the relationship between the ideas is not clear or specific. In the second example, the relationship is clear. "Many reasons" is followed by two specific examples that are set up in order of importance.

Edit for Word Choice and Conventions Reread your essay to identify any words that are vague or do not mean exactly what you want to say. If necessary, consult a thesaurus or other resource to find other words that are more accurate. Make sure you are sure of a word's meaning before you use it. Then, reread your essay again, identifying errors in grammar, spelling, or punctuation. Fix any errors you find.

EVIDENCE LOG

Before moving on to a new selection, go to your Evidence Log and record what you learned from "Ban the Ban!," and "Soda's a Problem but...."

STANDARDS

Writing
- Write arguments to support claims with clear reasons and relevant evidence.
  b. Support claim(s) with logical reasoning and relevant evidence, using accurate, credible sources and demonstrating an understanding of the topic or text.
  c. Use words, phrases, and clauses to create cohesion and clarify the relationships among claim(s), counterclaims, reasons, and evidence.
- Produce clear and coherent writing in which the development, organization, and style are appropriate to task, purpose, and audience.

Drafting

Encourage students to review the selections before writing their drafts. They should make sure their claim is strong and narrow.

Review, Revise, and Edit

As students revise, encourage them to review their evidence and reasons. Ask them to review their word choice. Finally, remind students to check for grammar, usage, and mechanics.

For more support, see **Writing to Compare: Argumentative Essay.**

Evidence Log Support students in completing their Evidence Log. This paced activity will help prepare them for the Performance-Based Assessment at the end of the unit.

FORMATIVE ASSESSMENT

Writing to Compare

If students struggle to gather evidence, **then** ask them to sort claims based on logic vs. emotion, fact vs. opinion, or subjective vs. objective.

Selection Test

Administer the "Ban the Ban!; Soda's a Problem but . . ." Selection Test, which is available in both print and digital formats online in Assessments.

PERSONALIZE FOR LEARNING

Strategic Support

Composing an Argument If students struggle to compose their argumentative essays, have them revisit the charts they made. Remind students that when there are two different points of view, both may be valid. Arguments do not have to have one solution. Have students decide which argument is more convincing. Have a few students explain to the rest of the class which argument they agree with and why. After several have offered their thoughts, have the class complete the writing assignment.

TEACHING

Jump Start

Poor eating habits are a serious issue in this country. Ask students to write on a slip of paper whether they think society should help solve the problem. Then poll the class and have students give a one-sentence reason for their position.

Write an Argument

Review the writing assignment with the class. Make sure students understand that they are writing an argument. They need to consider how a city, school, or local organization should help solve a problem. Remind students to keep in mind what they learned in the selections they read.

Students should complete the assignment using word processing software to take advantage of editing tools and features.

Elements of an Argument

Remind students that an effective argument such as "Freedom of the Press?" includes the listed required elements, flows well, and is organized clearly.

MAKE IT INTERACTIVE

Project "Freedom of the Press?" and have students identify the elements of an argument, such as claim, counterclaim, reason, evidence, and conclusion.

Academic Vocabulary

Verbally, prompt students to correctly use each academic vocabulary word in a sentence to demonstrate understanding before beginning the writing task.

PERFORMANCE TASK: WRITING FOCUS

WRITING TO SOURCES
- BARRINGTON IRVING, PILOT AND EDUCATOR
- THREE CHEERS FOR THE NANNY STATE
- BAN THE BAN! | SODA'S A PROBLEM BUT . . .

Tool Kit
Student Model of an Argument

ACADEMIC VOCABULARY
As you craft your argument, consider using some of the academic vocabulary you learned in the beginning of the unit.

retort
candid
rectify
speculate
verify

STANDARDS
Writing
Write arguments to support claims with clear reasons and relevant evidence.

296 UNIT 3 • WHAT MATTERS

Write an Argument

The texts in Whole-Class reading focus on problems and solutions. For example, Barrington Irving found solutions to the obstacles he faced as he pursued his dream of becoming a pilot. In the opinion pieces about the New York City soda ban, authors discuss their responses to a proposed solution for a public health problem. Now you will have a chance to write about a problem you think is important and propose a solution you think will help.

> **Assignment**
> Write a **problem-and-solution essay** on these questions:
>
> What is a problem you think needs to be solved? How would you solve it?
>
> Base your essay on your own observations and experiences, and conduct research as needed. In your essay, define the problem, explain the importance of solving it, and propose a specific solution in a persuasive way.

Elements of an Argument

A **problem-and-solution essay** is a type of argument in which a writer identifies a problem and proposes at least one way to solve it. Both elements—the problem and the solution— require the building of an argument. The writer must convince readers that a situation is actually a problem, and that a proposed solution will make things better. An effective problem-and-solution essay contains these elements:

- a central claim about the importance of a problem and the effectiveness of a particular solution
- reasons, evidence, and examples that support the claim
- a clear and logical organization
- consideration of opposing positions, or counterclaims
- a formal style that conveys ideas in a serious way
- a conclusion that follows from and supports the claim

Model Argument For a model of a well-crafted argument, see the Launch Text, "Freedom of the Press?"

Challenge yourself to find all of the elements of an effective argument in the text. You will have an opportunity to review these elements as you prepare to write your own argument.

AUTHOR'S PERSPECTIVE Kelly Gallagher, M.Ed.

Revision E.B. White once said, "The best writing is rewriting." Unfortunately, many students come to us with the "I wrote it once; I'm done" philosophy. Demonstrate the importance of *revision*—making writing better by looking at it again—through teacher modeling. First, write with the class for eight minutes on a specific topic. Then, complete the activity with the class.

1. Display your first draft on the screen. Use think alouds as you use RADaR strategies for revision: REPLACE; ADD; DELETE; REORDER. For each change you implement, mark the type of change you made.
2. Have students use the same process on their first drafts. Remind students that they will work on making their papers *correct* later; for now, they are to revise with the goal of being able to point out places where their second draft is better than their first.
3. Last, have students hold their two drafts side-by-side as you modeled, and indicate which RADaR strategies they used to revise their first drafts.

296 UNIT 3 • WHAT MATTERS

ESSENTIAL QUESTION: When is it right to take a stand?

Prewriting / Planning

Choose a Focus Reread the prompt. Then, decide what problem you will explain and what solution you can offer. This will be the starting point for your claim. Write your ideas here: State your claim in a sentence:

Problem: An important problem that demands a solution is _____
_____

Solution: The most effective solution to this problem would be _____

Consider Possible Counterclaims A strong argument does not just present a claim. It also considers opposing positions, or counterclaims. Think about reasons people might *not* agree that the situation you describe is a problem, or that your proposed solution will be effective. List possible counterclaims in the chart. Then, decide how you will address and refute, or disprove, each one. Will be you able to provide specific details or examples? Will you need to do some research?

COUNTERCLAIM	STRATEGY ADDRESS IT

Gather Evidence From Sources While some of your evidence can come from your own experience and knowledge, you will probably need to do some research to find specific information that supports your position. Consult a variety of reliable sources—both print and digital—to find facts, data, or expert opinions.

Reliable sources are up-to-date and free from bias. The information provided in a reliable source can be confirmed in other sources. If you see a ".gov" or a ".edu" on the end of a Web address, that means the information comes from a governmental or educational institution. These types of web sites are often more trustworthy than those managed by private individuals or businesses.

Using evidence from a variety of sources can make your argument stronger. Study the Launch Text to identify the different types of evidence the author uses to develop the argument.

Connect Across Texts To see how a problem can be identified and solved creatively, consider how Barrington Irving devised ways to help young people learn about aviation, the larger world, and their own futures.

To consider how to deal effectively with counterclaims, review the articles on New York City's soda ban. For example, you might consider how the authors of "Ban the Ban!" and "Soda's a Problem but. . ." answer the counterclaim that there are already widely accepted bans in place for other unhealthy activities, such as smoking. The authors simply point out how cigarettes are different from soda. The harmful effects of smoking are not limited to the smoker—other people are affected. By contrast, the drinking of large amounts of soda affects only the health of the drinker.

EVIDENCE LOG
Review your Evidence Log and identify key details you may want to cite in your argument.

STANDARDS
Writing
Write arguments to support claims with clear reasons and relevant evidence.
a. Introduce claim(s), acknowledge and distinguish the claim(s) from alternate or opposing claims, and organize the reasons and evidence logically.
b. Support claim(s) with logical reasoning and relevant evidence, using accurate, credible sources and demonstrating an understanding of the topic or text.

Performance Task: Write an Argument 297

DIGITAL PERSPECTIVES

Prewriting/Planning

Write a Claim

Choose a Focus Encourage students to discuss issues that they might like to discuss in their essays. You may want to have a brainstorming activity and ask each student to suggest at least one problem.

Gather Evidence From Sources What counts as evidence? While the writer's background knowledge and experiences count, it is always good to support an argument with documented facts from reliable sources. Take this opportunity to remind students that not all websites are reliable. Point them in the direction of acceptable online resources.

Connect Across Texts Students can use Barrington Irving's experience as an example of how a person can make change happen. The article about his life should serve to inspire their arguments. The other articles are a point and counter-point. All of the articles are example of successful argument pieces. Students can refer to them for writing style. How did the writers use evidence as well as writing conventions to make their pieces more effective?

PERSONALIZE FOR LEARNING

Strategic Support
Graphic Organizer Have students organize their thoughts in a chart before they begin to write. This will help them to make sure they have included all of the components of a good argument.

Argument	
Claim	Evidence
Claim	Evidence
Counterclaim	Evidence
Counterclaim	Evidence
Conclusion	

Whole-Class Learning 297

TEACHING

Drafting

Organize Ideas and Evidence How does a writer decide the order of the evidence presented? In the end, the goal is to create the most convincing argument possible. Point out to students that as they think about how to organize the information in their evidence, they need to ask themselves how their evidence can have the greatest impact. Suggest that students begin by identifying their strongest, most compelling piece of evidence. Then, they can add the supporting details and work on logical order of other evidence and details they wish to present.

Write a First Draft Encourage students to write freely in their first draft. The goal should be to get their ideas down on paper, incorporating all the elements of an argument. Later they can concentrate on organizing their ideas and editing their language.

PERFORMANCE TASK: WRITING FOCUS

STANDARDS

Writing
Write arguments to support claims with clear reasons and relevant evidence

a. Introduce claim(s), acknowledge and distinguish the claim(s) from alternate or opposing claims, and organize the reasons and evidence logically.
c. Use words, phrases, and clauses to create cohesion and clarify the relationships among claim(s), counterclaims, reasons, and evidence.
e. Provide a concluding statement or section that follows from and supports the argument presented.

Drafting

Organize Ideas and Evidence A logical organization can make your ideas easier for readers to follow. Some arguments present the strongest ideas and supporting evidence first. Others go from weakest to strongest. Create an outline to plan a sequence for your ideas and supporting evidence.

- Start by introducing your problem and solution.
- Add supporting reasons and evidence in a logical order.
- Use transitional words and phrases such as *furthermore, additionally,* and *on the other hand,* to make clear connections from your claim, to your reasons, to the evidence. Work to guide your readers through your ideas.
- Finish with a conclusion that restates your claim.

The outline here shows how the Launch Text is organized.

LAUNCH TEXT

Model: "Freedom of the Press?" Argument Outline

INTRODUCTION
The claim is introduced: *Freedom of the press does not apply to school newspapers.*

BODY
- High-school journalists have challenged efforts to limit their freedom of expression.
- Counterclaim: The Supreme Court ruled in the school's favor, because the censorship was for "valid educational reasons."
- "Valid educational reasons" is not a clear standard.
- Freedom of expression is an important part of becoming educated.

CONCLUSION
Schools should not limit students' free speech.

Argument Outline

INTRODUCTION

BODY
-
-
-
-

CONCLUSION

Write a First Draft Follow the order of ideas and evidence you planned in your outline. As you write, you may see a better way to sequence your ideas. Allow yourself to make adjustments that will improve the flow of your essay.

As you write, use a formal, academic style. Avoid slang or expressions that sound as though you are simply talking to someone. Instead, choose words that convey your ideas accurately. Define terms and explain situations that may be unfamiliar to your audience. Make sure to include transitional words and phrases that show how your ideas and evidence connect.

298 UNIT 3 • WHAT MATTERS

AUTHOR'S PERSPECTIVE Jim Cummins, Ph.D.

The Importance of Frequent Writing Writing develops a different awareness from reading. Second-language learners need abundant opportunities to write for varied audiences and purposes to determine what they do and do not know. Frequent writing can be accomplished through a combination of low-stakes (informal, ungraded) and high-stakes (formal, revised, graded) writing. Using this approach allows the teacher to nurture writing without needing to grade everything. Here are some suggestions for fostering regular writing:

- Do QuickWrites daily to review lessons and learning.
- Assign public writing, aimed at real audiences.

ESSENTIAL QUESTION: When is it right to take a stand?

DIGITAL PERSPECTIVES

LANGUAGE DEVELOPMENT: CONVENTIONS

Revising for Pronoun-Antecedent Agreement

A **pronoun** is a word that takes the place of a noun or another pronoun. An **antecedent** is the word or group of words to which a pronoun refers. Pronouns should agree with their antecedents in number and person. *Number* refers to whether a pronoun is singular or plural. *Person* tells to whom a pronoun refers—the one(s) speaking, the one(s) spoken to, or the one(s) spoken about.

Read It

These Launch Text sentences contain pronouns and their antecedents.

- *His problem with **the divorce article** was that **it** was not "fair and balanced."* **(third person singular)**
- *He felt it criticized **parents** without providing **their** side of the story.* **(third person plural)**

Write It

As you draft your problem-and-solution essay, make sure your pronouns agree with their antecedents in person and number. This chart may help you.

PERSON	NUMBER	PRONOUNS
First—the one speaking	Singular	I, me, my, mine
First—the ones speaking	Plural	we, us, our, ours
Second—the one spoken to	Singular	you, your, yours
Second—the ones spoken to	Plural	you, your, yours
Third—the one spoken about	Singular	he, she, it, his, her, hers, its
Third—the ones spoken about	Plural	they, them, their, theirs

Some **indefinite** pronouns—words that take the place of non-specific nouns or pronouns—can cause agreement problems.

- If the antecedent is a singular indefinite pronoun, use a singular personal pronoun to refer back to it. These indefinite pronouns are always singular: *another, anyone, anything, each, everybody, everything, little, much, nobody, nothing, one, other, someone, something.*
- If the antecedent is a plural indefinite pronoun, use a plural personal pronoun to refer back to it. These indefinite pronouns are always plural: *both, few, many, others, several.*
- If the antecedent can be either singular or plural, match the antecedent of the indefinite pronoun. These indefinite pronouns can be either singular or plural: *all, any, most, none, some.*

TIP

SPELLING
Make sure to spell pronouns correctly. Some are easily confused with other words or forms.

- *Your* refers to something that belongs to you. *You're* is a contraction for "you are."
- *Their* refers to something that belongs to them. *There* refers to a place.
- *Its* refers to something that belongs to it. *It's* is a contraction for "it is." There is no correct use of *its'*.

STANDARDS

Language
- Demonstrate command of the conventions of standard English grammar and usage when writing or speaking.
- Demonstrate command of the conventions of standard English capitalization, punctuation, and spelling when writing.
  c. Spell correctly.

Performance Task: Write an Argument 299

Revising for Pronoun-Antecedent Agreement

Read It

Why do pronouns and antecedents need to match? In order for a reader to follow the writer's meaning, the relationship between the pronoun and the thing to which it refers must be easily identified. Provide an example of a sentence in which the pronoun and antecedent do not match. Ask students to identify and fix the mistake. Ask: *Why is this sentence incorrect?* Possible response: It is incorrect because the reader is led to believe that the parts of the sentence refer to different things.

Write It

Indefinite pronouns are pronouns that are not specific as to which noun they replace. They may be singular or plural and must agree with their antecedents in number.

Indefinite pronouns can refer to nonspecific nouns, such as *anything, no one, anybody, someone,* or *something.* For example, *I hear someone talking* does not specifically identify the person *someone* refers to.

An indefinite pronoun can also refer back to a specific noun that appears in a sentence or in text. Some of these indefinite pronouns are *all, each, neither,* and *several.* For example: *Did he eat all of that cake?* (*all* refers to cake); *The class is going to have a party, and everyone is invited.* (*everyone* refers to the class)

Indefinite pronoun agreement can appear complex. Provide students with sample sentences using indefinite pronouns as antecedents, to clarify the concept.

Singular indefinite: It is always the same; **nothing** is new here.

Plural indefinite: **They** are big fans of football because **both** played as children.

An antecedent that can be either singular or plural: You can choose **any** flavor, and **it** will be delicious. Or, I will watch **any** of those movies, because **all** of them are excellent.

- Include personal writing, such as journals and diaries.
- Have students write reactions in response to their readings. Students can upload their reviews to class or school webpages.
- Have students write across genres. Try each one, having students pay attention to the conventions of each genre, such as stage directions in drama and dialogue in fiction. All genres have value; for example, poetry is powerful and likely easier for ESL students because of its condensed vocabulary. These assignments can be linked to word networks, too.

Whole-Class Learning 299

TEACHING

Revising

Evaluating Your Draft
Maintain Formal Style Have students suggest examples of informal language that might not help support their arguments. Remind students that examples should be appropriate for the classroom and for the type of writing they are doing. Then work with the group to revise the examples, making them more formal and appropriate for academic writing.

Revising for Evidence and Elaboration
Use Relevant, Logical Evidence How do you determine if evidence is relevant? Students might find it helpful to work with a peer to decide which pieces of their evidence best support their argument and are most relevant to their claim. Remind students to show respect for each other's ideas and provide constructive feedback.

 PERFORMANCE TASK: WRITING FOCUS

Revising

Evaluating Your Draft
Use the following checklist to evaluate the effectiveness of your first draft. Then, use your evaluation and the instruction on this page to guide your revision.

FOCUS AND ORGANIZATION	EVIDENCE AND ELABORATION	CONVENTIONS
☐ Presents a clearly stated claim about a problem and proposed solution.	☐ Uses relevant, logical evidence and reasons to support the main claim.	☐ Attends to the norms and conventions of the discipline, especially correct pronoun-antecedent agreement.
☐ Organizes supporting reasons, evidence, and examples in a logical way.	☐ Addresses and refutes possible counterclaims.	
☐ Presents ideas in a clear and formal style.	☐ Includes language that clarifies how claims, counterclaims, and supporting details are related.	
☐ Includes a conclusion that supports the main argument.		

🔠 WORD NETWORK
Include words from your Word Network in your argument.

Revising for Focus and Organization
Maintain Formal Style Writers that propose solutions to important problems make sure that their **tone**—their attitude toward their subject—is earnest and serious. Their goal is to persuade readers that theirs is the best solution. Review your essay, and make sure your style and tone are formal and serious.

- Avoid informal expressions and slang words.
- Use precise words to help your readers grasp your ideas easily.
- Use humor sparingly. Overall, your style and tone should be serious.

Revising for Evidence and Elaboration
Use Relevant, Logical Evidence Make sure all of your reasons and evidence directly support your main claim.

To do so, review your essay and mark your claim. Then, mark each supporting reason for your claim. Finally, mark each piece of evidence that supports your reasons. Look at your marked-up essay to determine if some points need additional support. Consider eliminating any details that do not support your main claim or reasons.

📋 STANDARDS
Writing
Write arguments to support claims with clear reasons and relevant evidence.
  b. Support claim(s) with logical reasoning and relevant evidence, using accurate, credible sources and demonstrating an understanding of the topic or text.
  d. Establish and maintain a formal style.

HOW LANGUAGE WORKS
Pronoun-Antecedent Agreement As students revise their arguments, remind them of the importance of pronoun-antecedent agreement in their writing. This convention makes a sentence coherent. When pronouns and antecedents do not agree, it is difficult for the reader to fully understand what the writer is trying to convey. Suggest that students review each other's writing for examples of pronoun-antecedent agreement. Have students mark examples of success and point out errors in agreement. Have partners explain to each other what they have noticed.

ESSENTIAL QUESTION: When is it right to take a stand?

DIGITAL PERSPECTIVES

PEER REVIEW

Exchange essays with a classmate. Use the checklist to evaluate your classmate's problem-and-solution essays and provide supportive feedback.

1. Is the claim clearly stated, and does it propose a solution to a problem?
   ☐ yes   ☐ no   If no, suggest how the writer might improve it.

2. Are the reasons and evidence logical and relevant?
   ☐ yes   ☐ no   If no, explain what the author might add or remove.

3. Does the argument address counterclaims?
   ☐ yes   ☐ no   If no, tell what you think might be missing.

4. What is the strongest part of your classmate's essay? Why?

_____

Peer Review
Support students in conducting helpful peer reviews. Remind them that giving and receiving feedback on what works well is as important or more important than feedback on areas that need improvement. As students identify strengths in each other's arguments, guide them to articulate what makes a particular phrase or section convincing.

Editing and Proofreading

Edit for Conventions Reread your draft for accuracy and consistency. Correct errors in grammar and word usage. Make sure all the pronouns you use agree in person and number with their antecedents.

Proofread for Accuracy Read your draft carefully, looking for errors in spelling and punctuation. As you proofread, watch out for **homophones**. A homophone is a word that sounds the same as another word but is spelled differently, such as *your* and *you're*, *there* and *their*, and *its* and *it's*.

Publishing and Presenting

Create a final version of your essay. Consider one of the following ways to share your essay:

- Post your essay online or on a bulletin board, along with the essays written by other class members. Read and comment on the essays of other class members, and respond to comments on your own essay.
- Ask your city, your school, or another local organization to help implement the solution to the problem suggested in your essay. Note any action taken and how well it worked.

Reflecting

Reflect on what you learned as you wrote your argument. What was the most challenging aspect of composing your argument? What did you learn from reviewing the work of others and discussing your argument with your classmates that might inform your writing process in the future?

STANDARDS

Writing
- Produce clear and coherent writing in which the development, organization, and style are appropriate to task, purpose, and audience.
- With some guidance and support from peers and adults, develop and strengthen writing as needed by planning, revising, editing, rewriting, or trying a new approach, focusing on how well purpose and audience have been addressed.
- Use technology, including the Internet, to produce and publish writing and present the relationships between information and ideas efficiently as well as to interact and collaborate with others.

Language
Demonstrate command of the conventions of standard English capitalization, punctuation, and spelling when writing.
   c. Spell correctly.

Performance Task: Write an Argument 301

Editing and Proofreading
Remind students that editing and proofreading one's own work can be difficult. Often, a writer sees the piece of writing the way it was meant to be written, rather than the way it was actually written. Provide strategies for overcoming this, such as reading a sentence backwards to check for spelling errors. Ask students to share some of their strategies. Compile a list and post it in the classroom.

Reflecting
Students should reflect not only on their argument and the process of writing it, but also on the comments they received from their peers.

PERSONALIZE FOR LEARNING

Challenge

Make Connections Have students consider the arguments they made in their essays. Are there steps they can suggest to help bring about a positive change in the school? Have students think about an action plan to implement some of the ideas raised through this exercise. Are there simple ideas that would be easily accepted? Are there small ways to make an impact? Have a class discussion. Remind students of Barrington Irving's example and how he took it upon himself to make things happen.

Whole-Class Learning 301

OVERVIEW

SMALL-GROUP LEARNING

When is it right to take a stand?

Point out that a person may be willing to go to great lengths for a principle he or she feels should be upheld. On behalf of others as well as themselves, individuals have braved discrimination and danger to obtain rights and opportunities. During Small-Group Learning, students will read selections that describe people who are willing to face and meet any challenge to realize their dreams.

Small-Group Learning Strategies ▶

Review the Learning Strategies with students and explain that as they work through Small-Group Learning, they will develop strategies to work in small-group environments.

- Have students watch the video on Small-Group Learning Strategies.
- A video on this topic is available online in the Professional Development Center.

You may wish to discuss some action items to add to the chart as a class before students complete it on their own. For example, for "Participate fully," you might solicit the following from students:

- Wait for others to finish speaking; do not interrupt.
- Eliminate distractions so you are present in discussions.

> ### Block Scheduling
> Each day in this Pacing Plan represents a 40–50-minute class period. Teachers using block scheduling may combine days to reflect their class schedule. In addition, teachers may revise pacing to differentiate and support core instruction by integrating components and resources as students require.

📅 **Pacing Plan**

OVERVIEW: SMALL-GROUP LEARNING

ESSENTIAL QUESTION:

When is it right to take a stand?

What issues matter to you? Maybe they matter to other people, too. When you stand up for what you believe in, you may find that your action inspires others to act as well. In this section, you will work with your group to learn about individuals who took a stand in an effort to promote the greater good.

Small-Group Learning Strategies

Throughout your life, in school, in your community, and in your career, you will continue to learn and work with others.

Review these strategies and the actions you can take to practice them as you work in teams. Add ideas of your own for each step. Use these strategies during Small-Group Learning.

STRATEGY	ACTION PLAN
Prepare	• Complete your assignments so that you are prepared for group work. • Organize your thinking so you can contribute to your group's discussion. •
Participate fully	• Make eye contact to signal that you are listening and taking in what is being said. • Use text evidence when making a point. •
Support others	• Build on ideas from others in your group. • Invite others who have not yet spoken to do so. •
Clarify	• Paraphrase the ideas of others to ensure that your understanding is correct. • Ask follow-up questions. •

302 UNIT 3 • WHAT MATTERS

SCAN FOR MULTIMEDIA

Pacing Plan:

| 1 | 2 | 3 | 4 | 5 | 6 | 7 | 8 | 9 | 10 | 11 | 12 | 13 | 14 | 15 | 16 | 17 | 18 |

- Unit Introduction (1–2)
- Introduce Whole-Class Learning (3)
- Barrington Irving, Pilot and Educator (4–8)
- Three Cheers for the Nanny State (9–13)
- Ban the Ban! • Soda's a Problem but... (14–15)
- Performance Task (16–18)

CONTENTS

PERSUASIVE SPEECH

Words Do Not Pay
Chief Joseph

What meaning do words have if they are not followed by actions?

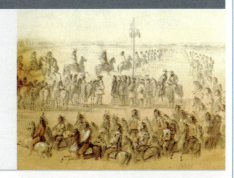

NONFICTION NARRATIVE

from Follow the Rabbit-Proof Fence
Doris Pilkington

Three girls risk everything to find their way home.

MEDIA: VIDEO

The Moth Presents: Aleeza Kazmi

A high-school student relates her ongoing struggle for a way to describe herself.

PERFORMANCE TASK

SPEAKING AND LISTENING FOCUS

Present an Argument

The Small-Group readings focus on real people who took a stand in words, deeds, or both. After reading, your group will plan and deliver an oral presentation about whether winning or losing matters when you take a stand.

DIGITAL PERSPECTIVES

Contents

Selections Circulate among groups as they preview the selections. You might encourage groups to discuss any knowledge they already have about any of the selections or the situations and settings shown in the photographs. Students may wish to take a poll within their group to determine which selections look the most interesting.

Remind students that communicating and collaborating in groups is an important skill that they will use throughout their lives—in school, in their careers, and in their community.

Performance Task

Deliver an Oral Presentation Give groups time to read about and briefly discuss the Oral Presentation they will create after reading. Encourage students to do some preliminary thinking about the types of media they may want to use. This may help focus their subsequent reading and group discussion.

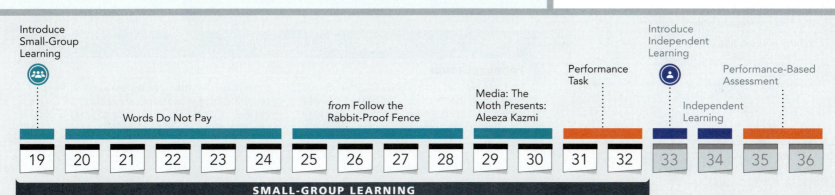

OVERVIEW

SMALL-GROUP LEARNING

Working as a Team

1. **Take a Position** Remind groups to let all members share their responses. You may wish to set a time limit for this discussion.

2. **List Your Rules** You may want to have groups share their lists of rules and consolidate them into a master list to be displayed and followed by all groups.

3. **Apply the Rules** As you circulate among the groups, ensure that students are staying on task. Consider a short time limit for this step.

4. **Name Your Group** This task can be creative and fun. If students have trouble coming up with a name, suggest that they think of something related to the unit topic. Encourage groups to share their names with the class.

5. **Create a Communication Plan** Encourage groups to include in their plans agreed-upon times during the day to share ideas. They should also devise a method for recording and saving their communications.

Accountable Talk

Remind students that groups should communicate politely. You can post these Accountable Talk suggestions and encourage students to add their own. Students should:

Remember to . . .
Ask clarifying questions.

Which sounds like . . .
Can you please repeat what you said?
Would you give me an example?
I think you said _____. Did I understand you correctly?

Remember to . . .
Explain your thinking.

Which sounds like . . .
I believe _____ is true because _____.
I feel _____ because _____.

Remember to . . .
Build on the ideas of others.

Which sounds like . . .
When _____ said _____, it made me think of _____.

OVERVIEW: SMALL-GROUP LEARNING

Working as a Team

1. **Take a Position** In your group, discuss the following question:

   What are some character traits of people who stand up for their beliefs?

   As you take turns sharing your thoughts, be sure to provide examples. After all group members have shared, discuss the ways in which these character traits are demonstrated in the actions of those who stand up for their beliefs.

2. **List Your Rules** As a group, decide on the rules that you will follow as you work together. Two samples are provided; add two more of your own. You may add or revise rules based on your experience together.

   - Everyone should participate in group discussions.
   - People should not interrupt.
   - _____
   - _____

3. **Apply the Rules** Share what you have learned about taking a stand. Make sure each person in the group contributes. Take notes and be prepared to share with the class one thing that you heard from another member of your group.

4. **Name Your Group** Choose a name that reflects the unit topic.

   Our group's name: _____

5. **Create a Communication Plan** Decide how you want to communicate with one another. For example, you might use online collaboration tools, email, or instant messaging.

   Our group's decision: _____

304 UNIT 3 • WHAT MATTERS

FACILITATING SMALL-GROUP LEARNING

Forming Groups

You may wish to form groups for Small-Group Learning so that each consists of students with different learning abilities. Some students may be adept at organizing information whereas other may have strengths related to generating or synthesizing information. A good mix of abilities can make the experience of Small-Group Learning dynamic and productive.

ESSENTIAL QUESTION: When is it right to take a stand?

Making a Schedule

First, find out the due dates for the small-group activities. Then, preview the texts and activities with your group and make a schedule for completing the tasks.

SELECTION	ACTIVITIES	DUE DATE
Words Do Not Pay		
from Follow the Rabbit-Proof Fence		
The Moth Presents: Aleeza Kazmi		

Working on Group Projects

As your group works together, you'll find it more effective if each person has a specific role. Different projects require different roles. Before beginning a project, discuss the necessary roles and choose one for each group member. Here are some possible roles; add your own ideas.

Project Manager: monitors the schedule and keeps everyone on task

Researcher: organizes research activities

Recorder: takes notes during group meetings

_____
_____
_____
_____
_____
_____

SCAN FOR MULTIMEDIA

DIGITAL PERSPECTIVES

Making a Schedule

Encourage groups to preview the reading selections and to consider how long it will take them to complete the activities accompanying each selection. Point out that they can adjust the due dates for particular selections as needed as they work on their small-group projects; however, they must complete all assigned tasks before the group Performance Task is due. Encourage groups to review their schedules upon completing the activities for each selection to make sure they are on track to meet the final due date.

Working on Group Projects

Point out to groups that the roles they assign can also be changed later. Students might have to make changes based on who is best at doing what. Try to make sure that there is no favoritism, cliquishness, or stereotyping by gender or other means in the assignment of roles.

Also, you should review the roles each group assigns to its members. Based on your understanding of students' individual strengths, you might find it necessary to suggest some changes.

AUTHOR'S PERSPECTIVE Kelly Gallagher, M.Ed.

The Teacher's Role After the ability to read and write with fluency, the skill that employers value most is the ability to collaborate successfully. Talking with other people can help us all learn more, change our opinions, and make us more thoughtful because we are exposed to ideas that we may not have previously considered. Student collaboration also serves as a useful formative assessment tool. An effective strategy for identifying what students are thinking about and for pinpointing the information they're missing about a text is to ask, "What is worth talking about?" Hearing what students get and what they've missed informs further instruction. Here are some additional strategies for encouraging effective collaboration:

- *Flow in and out of groups* as students work. Circulate from group to group, modeling and encouraging meaningful talk, a lifelong literacy skill.
- *Take notes* on what is being said outright and what is being implied. See what prior knowledge and background individuals contribute.
- *Plan pathways for subsequent lessons* from what you've heard and observed.

PLANNING

SMALL-GROUP LEARNING • WORDS DO NOT PAY

Words Do Not Pay

AUDIO SUMMARIES
Audio summaries of "Words Do Not Pay" are available in both English and Spanish in the Interactive Teacher's Edition or Unit Resources. Assigning these summaries prior to reading the selection may help students build additional background knowledge and set a context for their first read.

Summary
In his speech "Words Do Not Pay," Chief Joseph protests unkept promises. He lists harms inflicted on his people that words cannot compensate for: deaths, a damaged grave, seizures of domestic animals, and broken promises. Chief Joseph calls for equal treatment and law. According to Chief Joseph, the lack of peace and equal rights has done tremendous harm, and this ultimately stems from a mix of misunderstandings and lies. In his view, simple freedom under the law is better than the arrangements the U.S. military tried to make with his people.

Insight
This speech teaches students about the deceptive promises the United States made to many Native American groups. Chief Joseph's speech also emphasizes the value of action, and of freedom.

ESSENTIAL QUESTION:
When is it right to take a stand?

Connection to Essential Question
In his speech, Chief Joseph lists the many harms that came to his people. His speech is a strong protest and a stand against further mistreatment of his tribe by federal authorities.

SMALL-GROUP LEARNING PERFORMANCE TASK
When you take a stand, how much does winning matter?

Connection to Performance Tasks

Small-Group Learning Performance Task In addition to the safety of people and possessions, Chief Joseph calls for freedom of movement, trade, religion, and speech. Students should consider how much value he places in the importance of winning. He suggests this is a matter of life and death for his people.

UNIT PERFORMANCE-BASED ASSESSMENT
Is it important for people to make their own choices in life?

Unit Performance-Based Assessment Chief Joseph protests against the way the United States has treated and communicated with the Nez Percé. He believes that its lies have caused his people to make bad choices about what matters to them. Students may use this text as evidence to help them answer the prompt.

DIGITAL PERSPECTIVES

 Audio Video Document Annotation Highlights EL Highlights Online Assessment

LESSON RESOURCES

Lesson	Making Meaning	Language Development	Effective Expression
	First Read Close Read Analyze the Text Analyze Craft and Structure	Concept Vocabulary Word Study Author's Style	Research
Instructional Standards	**RI.10** By the end of the year, read and comprehend literary nonfiction . . . **L.4** Determine or clarify the meaning of unknown and multiple-meaning words or phrases . . . **L.4.a** Use context as a clue . . . **L.4.d** Verify the preliminary determination . . . **RI.4** Determine the meaning of words and phrases . . . **L.5** Demonstrate understanding of figurative language . . . **L.5.c** Distinguish among the connotations . . .	**L.4** Determine or clarify the meaning . . . **L.1** Demonstrate command of the conventions . . . **L.3** Use knowledge of language	**W.2** Write informative/explanatory texts . . . **W.2.a** Introduce a topic . . . **W.2.b** Develop the topic . . . **W.2.f** Provide a concluding statement . . . **W.7** Conduct short research projects . . . **W.8** Gather relevant information . . .

STUDENT RESOURCES

Available online in the Interactive Student Edition or Unit Resources	Selection Audio First-Read Guide: Nonfiction Close-Read Guide: Nonfiction	Word Network	Evidence Log

TEACHER RESOURCES

Selection Resources Available online in the Interactive Teacher's Edition or Unit Resources	Audio Summaries Annotation Highlights EL Highlights English Language Support Lesson: Parallelism Words Do Not Pay: Text Questions Analyze Craft and Structure: Persuasive Techniques and Word Choice	Concept Vocabulary and Word Study Author's Style: Rhetorical Devices	Research: Research Report
Reteach/Practice (RP) Available online in the Interactive Teacher's Edition or Unit Resources	Analyze Craft and Structure: Persuasive Techniques and Word Choice (RP)	Word Study: Old English Prefix *mis-* (RP) Author's Style: Rhetorical Devices (RP)	Research: Research Report (RP)
Assessment Available online in Assessments	Selection Test		
My Resources	A Unit 3 Answer Key is available online and in the Interactive Teacher's Edition.		

PERSONALIZE FOR LEARNING
SMALL-GROUP LEARNING • WORDS DO NOT PAY

Reading Support

Text Complexity Rubric: Words Do Not Pay

Quantitative Measures

Lexile: 830   Text Length: 347 words

Qualitative Measures

Knowledge Demands (3 of 5)	Selection relies on knowledge that is not explained in the text; however, the situation is explained in the background paragraph about the Nez Percé.
Structure (2 of 5)	Speech has repetitive phrases followed by different verbs, which makes it predictable and easier to read.
Language Conventionality and Clarity (2 of 5)	Selection is a written version of a speech, so it has the style of spoken language. Sentences are generally short and simple, with repetitive phrases, and on-level vocabulary.
Levels of Meaning/Purpose (3 of 5)	Purpose of selection is clear and explicit; Chief Joseph's sentiments are expressed clearly in the speech, with some use of figurative language for emphasis.

DECIDE AND PLAN

English Language Support
Provide English Learners with support for structure and meaning as they read the selection.

Structure With students, make a list of some of the phrases in the text that are repeated. For example, in paragraph 1 students may identify the phrases "words do not pay . . . they do not protect," "Good words will not give," and "I will not make . . . will not get." Point out that the same structure repeats with different verbs. Ask students to list the verbs and to circle phrases that center around each repetitive phrase. Then have them reread the sections aloud.

Meaning Make sure students understand why Chief Joseph says "[Good words] do not pay." Point out that Chief Joseph is saying that it's not enough to talk or promise without taking action.

Strategic Support
Provide students with strategic support to ensure that they can successfully read the text.

Structure Ask students to take turns reading aloud, each student reading several sentences. Have other students identify the repetitive phrases, such as "words do not last long" and "[words] do not pay." Ask students to list the phrases. Then have them reread.

Meaning Discuss figurative phrases such as "You might as well expect the rivers to run backward" (paragraph 1). Point out that this phrase helps Chief Joseph emphasize his point about freedom. Just as a river cannot run backward, a free man could never be happy without freedom.

Challenge
Provide students who need to be challenged with ideas for how they can go beyond a simple interpretation of the text.

Text Analysis Ask students to explain in their own words why Chief Joseph uses the idea that good words do not pay, protect, or give people health. Then ask them to describe the emotions Chief Joseph is communicating in his speech about this situation.

Written Response Have students research the Nez Percé tribe to find out how they live today. Have students find information about their location, customs, and lifestyle. Ask students each to write a paragraph about the information they found most interesting and to share it with the class.

TEACH

Read and Respond
Have groups do their first read of the selection. Then have them complete their close read. Finally, work with them on the Making Meaning, Language Development, and Effective Expression activities.

Standards Support Through Teaching and Learning Cycle

IDENTIFY NEEDS

Analyze results of the Beginning-of-Year Assessment, focusing on the items relating to Unit 3. Also take into consideration student performance to this point and your observations of where particular students struggle.

DECIDE AND PLAN

- If students have performed poorly on items matching these standards, then provide selection scaffolds before assigning them the on-level lesson provided in the Student Edition.
- If students have done well on the Beginning-of-Year Assessment, then challenge them to keep progressing and learning by giving them opportunities to practice the skills in depth.
- Use the Selection Resources listed on the Planning pages for "Words Do Not Pay" to help students continually improve their ability to master the standards.

Instructional Standards: Words Do Not Pay

	Catching Up	This Year	Looking Forward
Reading	You may wish to administer the **Analyze Craft and Structure: Persuasive Techniques and Word Choice (RP)** worksheet to help students identify and understand persuasive techniques used in the selection.	**RI.4** Determine the meaning of words and phrases as they are used in a text, including figurative, connotative, and technical meanings; analyze the impact of specific word choices on meaning and tone, including analogies or allusions to other texts.	Have students look at the words in the chart that have negative connotations. Challenge students to work in small groups to analyze the impact of these words. What words might the writer have used that would have been less effective?
Writing	You may wish to administer the **Research: Research Report (RP)** worksheet to help students organize and plan their research projects.	**W.7** Conduct short research projects to answer a question, drawing on several sources and generating additional related focused questions that allow for multiple avenues of exploration. **W.8** Gather relevant information from multiple print and digital sources, using search terms effectively; assess the credibility and accuracy of each source; and quote or paraphrase the data and conclusions of others while avoiding plagiarism and following a standard format for citation.	Challenge students to review their drafts and identify and replace words that are vague or imprecise. Also, have students look for words that are repeated throughout their draft and replace overused words with synonyms. Have students review their sources and evidence to make sure they are using relevant information.
Language	You may wish to administer the **Author's Style: Rhetorical Devices (RP)** worksheet to help students understand how parallelism adds rhythm and balance to writing and strengthens the connections among an author's ideas.	**L.1** Demonstrate command of the conventions of standard English grammar and usage when writing or speaking.	Encourage students to read their writing out loud to get a better sense of the rhythm and balance of words.

ANALYZE AND REVISE

- Analyze student work for evidence of student learning.
- Identify whether students have met the expectations in the standards.
- Identify implications for future instruction.

TEACH

Implement the planned lesson, and gather evidence of student learning.

Small-Group Learning 306D

FACILITATING

Jump Start

FIRST READ Political leaders must take a stand when necessary. What can a leader do when a treaty with another government gets broken? What if other political leaders go back on their word? Engage students in a discussion about political leadership that sets the context for reading "Words Do Not Pay."

Words Do Not Pay

What does Chief Joseph mean by the phrase "good words"? Has he suffered the consequences of bad words? Modeling questions such as these will help students connect "Words Do Not Pay" to the Small-Group Performance Task assignment. Selection audio and print capability for the selection are available in the Interactive Teacher's Edition.

Concept Vocabulary

Ask groups to explain how different types of context clues work. Remind them that they can use a dictionary, if necessary.

FIRST READ

Have students perform the steps of the first read independently:

NOTICE: You may want to encourage students to notice the main ideas of the speech.

ANNOTATE: Remind students to mark passages that show Chief Joseph's attitude toward those he is speaking to.

CONNECT: Have students compare Chief Joseph's speech to other speeches or words of protest from other oppressed groups.

RESPOND: Students will answer questions and write a summary to demonstrate understanding.

Point out to students that while they will always complete the Respond step at the end of the first read, the other steps will probably happen somewhat concurrently. You may wish to print copies of the **First-Read Guide: Nonfiction** for students to use.

MAKING MEANING

About the Author

Chief Joseph was a famous leader of the Nez Percé tribe. He was known by his people as Hin-mah-too-yah-lat-kekt, or Thunder Rolling Down the Mountain. He was born in Wallowa Valley in 1840, in what is now Oregon. In 1877, when the U.S. government threatened to forcefully move the Nez Percé to a reservation, Chief Joseph refused, choosing instead to lead leading his people north toward Canada. Chief Joseph died in 1904, never having returned to the land he had fought so hard to keep for his tribe. His doctor said he died "of a broken heart."

STANDARDS

Reading Informational Text
By the end of the year, read and comprehend literary nonfiction at the high end of the grades 6–8 text complexity band independently and proficiently.

Language
Determine or clarify the meaning of unknown and multiple-meaning words or phrases based on *grade 8 reading and content*, choosing flexibly from a range of strategies.
a. Use context as a clue to the meaning of a word or phrase.
d. Verify the preliminary determination of the meaning of a word or phrase.

306 UNIT 3 • WHAT MATTERS

Words Do Not Pay

Concept Vocabulary

You will encounter the following words as you read "Words Do Not Pay."

| misrepresentations | misunderstandings |

Context Clues To find the meaning of an unfamiliar word, look for clues in the context, which consists of the other words that surround the unknown word in a text. If you are still unsure of the meaning, look up the word in a dictionary. Consider this example of how to apply the strategy.

> **Example:** Good words will neither return our land nor restore our way of life.
>
> **Analysis of Clues in the Text:** Good words will not return or *restore* something that has been taken.
>
> **Possible Meaning:** *Restore* means "to return or give back."

Apply your knowledge of context clues and other vocabulary strategies to determine the meanings of unfamiliar words you encounter during your first read of "Words Do Not Pay."

First Read NONFICTION

Apply these strategies as you conduct your first read. You will have an opportunity to complete a close read after your first read.

NOTICE the general idea of the speech. *What* is it about? *Who* is involved?

ANNOTATE by marking vocabulary and key passages you want to revisit.

CONNECT ideas within the selection to what you already know and what you have already read.

RESPOND by completing the Comprehension Check and by writing a brief summary of the speech.

AUTHOR'S PERSPECTIVE Jim Cummins, Ph.D.

Critical Literacies Recent research shows that even early-stage English learners can use higher-order thinking skills and engage with complex social issues with the appropriate instructional support. The following questions illustrate how teachers can support the development of critical thinking:

Step 1: Textual Dimension: In order to help students read deeply to understand how the language and multimodal dimensions of the text construct meaning, ask, "When, where, and how did it happen?" and "Who did it? Why?"

Step 2: Personal Dimension: Encourage students to reflect critically on the text in relation to their experiences and emotions. Ask, "Have you ever seen, felt, or experienced something like this?" or "Have you ever wanted something similar?"

Step 3: Critical Dimension: Engage students in critical analysis of issues in the text by asking questions such as: "Is what this person said valid? Always? Under what conditions? Are there any alternatives to this situation?"

PERSUASIVE SPEECH

Words Do Not Pay

Chief Joseph

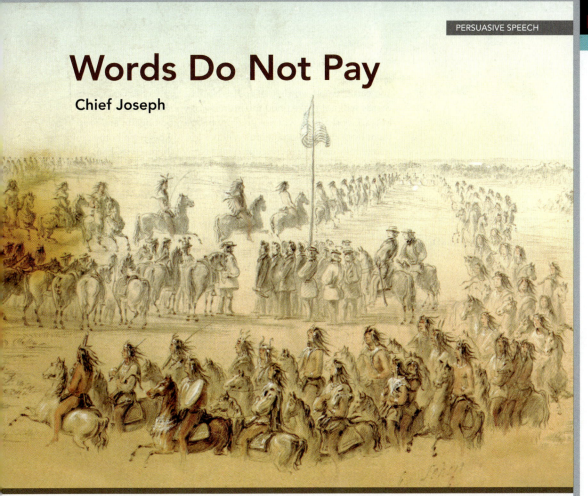

BACKGROUND

In 1863, the Nez Percé tribe refused to sign a treaty that would make them move from their ancestral land in Oregon to a much smaller reservation in Idaho. Despite the refusal, the United States government sent in federal troops to force the Nez Percé off their land. In response, Chief Joseph led his people toward Canada in a three-month, 1600-mile flight across the Rocky Mountains. He eventually surrendered to General Miles in 1877, under the terms that his tribe could return to their homeland. Instead, the Nez Percé were sent to Oklahoma, and half of them died during the trip. In one of many appeals to Congress on behalf of his people, Chief Joseph made this speech in 1879 in Washington D.C.

SCAN FOR MULTIMEDIA

1   I do not understand why nothing is done for my people. I have heard talk and talk, but nothing is done. Good words do not last long unless they amount to something. Words do not pay for my dead people. They

FACILITATING

Concept Vocabulary

MISREPRESENTATIONS If groups are struggling to define the word *misrepresentations* in paragraph 1, point out that they can use context clues to infer the meaning. Draw their attention to the context clue "talking by men who had no right to talk" in a nearby sentence. Have students use this context clue to define the word.

Possible response: In this context, *misrepresentations* means "a false account."

MISUNDERSTANDINGS If groups are struggling to define the word *misunderstandings* in paragraph 1, point out that they can break down the word to find familiar word parts. Have students use their knowledge of the word *understanding* and the prefix *mis-* to help them define the word.

Possible response: *Misunderstandings* means "a fight or argument based on miscommunication."

> Additional **English Language Support** is available in the Interactive Teacher's Edition.

NOTES

Mark context clues or indicate another strategy that helped you determine meaning.

misrepresentations (mihs rehp rih zehn TAY shuhnz) *n.*
MEANING:

misunderstandings (mihs uhn duhr STAND ihngz) *n.*
MEANING:

---

do not pay for my country, now overrun by white men. They do not protect my father's grave. They do not pay for all my horses and cattle. Good words will not give me back my children. Good words will not make good the promise of your war chief General Miles. Good words will not give my people good health and stop them from dying. Good words will not get my people a home where they can live in peace and take care of themselves. I am tired of talk that comes to nothing. It makes my heart sick when I remember all the good words and all the broken promises. There has been too much talking by men who had no right to talk. Too many **misrepresentations** have been made, too many **misunderstandings** have come up between the white men about the Indians. If the white man wants to live in peace with the Indian he can live in peace. There need be no trouble. Treat all men alike. Give them all the same law. Give them all an even chance to live and grow. All men were made by the same Great Spirit Chief. They are all brothers. The earth is the mother of all people, and all people should have equal rights upon it. You might as well expect the rivers to run backward as that any man who was born a free man should be contented when penned up and denied liberty to go where he pleases. . . .

2 Let me be a free man—free to travel, free to stop, free to work, free to trade where I choose, free to choose my own teachers, free to follow the religion of my fathers, free to think and talk and act for myself—and I will obey every law, or submit to the penalty.

👥 FACILITATING SMALL-GROUP CLOSE READING

CLOSE READ: Argument As groups perform the close read, circulate and offer support as needed.

- Point out that Chief Joseph is making an argument in his speech.
- Remind students that when they read an argument, they should look at what the speaker wants and how he or she builds a case.
- If the group is confused about what Chief Joseph is arguing for, point out that they may not find it at the beginning of the speech. Challenge them to find where Chief Joseph states what he wants. (One possible response: paragraph 1: "Treat all men alike. Give them all the same law....")
- Challenge groups to find all the types of evidence that Chief Joseph uses (facts, anecdotes, or examples).

Comprehension Check

Complete these items after you finish your first read. Review and clarify details with your group.

1. What is one problem that Chief Joseph has with the "good words" of others?

2. According to Chief Joseph, what is one thing the white man needs to do to live in peace with the Indian?

3. According to Chief Joseph, what is one thing all men have in common?

4. What activities does Chief Joseph associate with being a "free man"?

5. **Notebook** Confirm your understanding of the speech by writing a summary.

RESEARCH

Research to Clarify Choose at least one unfamiliar detail from the speech. Briefly research that detail. In what way does the information you learned shed light on an aspect of the speech?

Words Do Not Pay 309

Comprehension Check

Possible responses:

1. They do not help his people.
2. Treat all people the same way.
3. According to Chief Joseph, all men were made by the same god and should have equal rights to the Earth. Also, all men who are born free desire to stay free.
4. A free man can travel and work where he chooses and can follow the religion he chooses.
5. Summaries will vary; however, students should include the following points in their summary:
   - the reasons that Chief Joseph wants change
   - the change that Chief Joseph asks for

Research

Research to Clarify If groups struggle to find a research topic, you may want to suggest that they focus on one of the following topics: previous agreements between the Nez Percé and the U.S. government; how the Nez Percé used horses and cattle for their livelihood; or what the Nez Percé believed about the Great Spirit Chief.

PERSONALIZE FOR LEARNING

Challenge Have students find and examine Chief Joseph's famous speech, "I Will Fight No More Forever," in which he surrenders to U.S. forces. Have students compare the word choice and tone of "Words Do Not Pay" and "I Will Fight No More Forever." Students may also be interested in comparing the circumstances surrounding each speech.

Small-Group Learning 309

FACILITATING

Jump Start

CLOSE READ Is making a speech an effective way of taking a stand? Ask students to compare speakers and listeners with writers and readers: Are the relationships the same? How are they different? How does a speaker use language to make a case?

Close Read the Text

If needed, model close reading by using the Annotation Highlights in the Interactive Teacher's Edition.

Remind students to use Accountable Talk in their discussions and to support one another as they complete the close read.

Analyze the Text

1. **Possible response:** Chief Joseph means that good words cannot make up for what his people have lost. He references the loss of horses and cattle and the illnesses of his people.
2. Passages will vary by group. Remind students to explain why they chose the passage they shared with the group members.
3. Responses will vary by group.

Concept Vocabulary

Why These Words? Possible response: The concept words all have to do with the hardships and misery that Chief Joseph and his people endured. These words enhance the impact of the text by helping the reader to understand Chief Joseph's argument that his people had been wronged and that all people should be treated equally.

Practice

Sample response: Luis thought there had been many *misrepresentations* of what the campground was like, both in the travel brochure and the online review site he'd visited. Their were many others at the campground who had similar *misunderstandings* about the facilities.

Word Network

Possible words: *equal, contented, rights*

Word Study

For more support, see **Concept Vocabulary and Word Study.**

Possible responses: You would show up to meet your friend too early or too late.

The food could turn out to be salty, undercooked, or too bland.

310   UNIT 3 • WHAT MATTERS

MAKING MEANING

WORDS DO NOT PAY

Close Read the Text

With your group, revisit sections of the text you marked during your first read. **Annotate** details that you notice. What **questions** do you have? What can you **conclude**?

Analyze the Text

CITE TEXTUAL EVIDENCE to support your answers.

Notebook Complete the activities.

1. **Review and Clarify** With your group, reread the speech. What do you think the author means when he claims that "words do not pay"? How does he use examples to support his claim?

2. **Present and Discuss** Share the passages from the text that you found important. Discuss what you noticed in the text, what questions you asked, and what conclusions you reached.

3. **Essential Question:** *When is it right to take a stand?* How is Chief Joseph taking a stand? Do you think his reasons for doing so are legitimate? Discuss with your group.

TIP

GROUP DISCUSSION
As you discuss the speech, make sure that everyone listens respectfully to each other's ideas.

WORD NETWORK

Add words related to taking a stand from the text to your Word Network.

STANDARDS

Reading Informational Text
Determine the meaning of words and phrases as they are used in a text, including figurative, connotative, and technical meanings; analyze the impact of specific word choices on meaning and tone, including analogies or allusions to other texts.

Language
• Determine or clarify the meaning of unknown and multiple-meaning words or phrases based on *grade 8 reading and content*, choosing flexibly from a range of strategies.
• Demonstrate understanding of figurative language, word relationships, and nuances in word meanings.
   c. Distinguish among the connotations of words with similar denotations.

LANGUAGE DEVELOPMENT

Concept Vocabulary

misrepresentations   misunderstandings

Why These Words? The two concept vocabulary words from the text are related. With your group, discuss the words and identify a concept they have in common. How do these words enhance the impact of the text?

Practice

Notebook Confirm your understanding of the concept vocabulary words by using each one in a sentence.

Word Study

Notebook Old English Prefix: *mis-* The Old English prefix *mis-* means "opposite," "badly," or "wrongly." When added to a word, it creates an opposing or contrasting meaning. In his speech, Chief Joseph refers to "misrepresentations," or wrong representations, of Indians. Using your knowledge of the prefix *mis-*, answer the following questions.

• What might happen if you have a *miscommunication* as to the time you are meeting a friend?
• What can happen if you *misread* the instructions for a recipe?

FORMATIVE ASSESSMENT

Analyze the Text

If students struggle to close read the text, **then** provide the **Words Do Not Pay: Text Questions** available online in the Interactive Teacher's Edition or Unit Resources. Answers and DOK levels are also available.

Concept Vocabulary

If students struggle to identify the concept, **then** discuss the words in more detail, looking back at how they are used in the speech.

Word Study

If students struggle to answer the questions, **then** review the prefix *mis-* again, and discuss the words *mistake* and *misread*. For Reteach and Practice, see **Word Study: Old English Prefix: *mis-* (RP).**

ESSENTIAL QUESTION: When is it right to take a stand?

Analyze Craft and Structure

Persuasive Techniques and Word Choice Writers use persuasive techniques in an argument to lead an audience to agree with them. These are some of the persuasive techniques that writers use:

- **Repetition** consists of saying something repeatedly for effect.
- **Appeals to reason** invite the audience to use logic as they draw conclusions from the evidence presented by the writer.
- **Appeals to emotions** attempt to persuade readers by triggering their feelings about a subject.
- **Appeals to authority** are references to expert opinions.

A writer's **word choice** includes not only individual words but also the phrases and expressions the writer uses. Word choice can convey **tone**—the writer's attitude toward the topic or audience. These factors influence word choice:

- the writer's intended audience and purpose
- the **denotations** of words, or their dictionary definitions
- the **connotations** of words, or their negative or positive associations (For example, *assertive* and *pushy* have similar denotations but different connotations.)

A writer's word choice and tone can contribute to the power of the argument he or she presents. The denotations and connotations of the words a writer chooses as well as the phrases and expressions he or she includes in an argument can impact the effectiveness of persuasive techniques. For example, a writer may choose to create repetition in an argument using words with specific connotations in order to appeal to a specific audience.

TIP

CLARIFICATION
Consulting a dictionary for a word's denotation will help you grasp the difference between a word's precise meaning and the meaning suggested by its connotations.

Practice

CITE TEXTUAL EVIDENCE to support your answers.

📓 **Notebook** Use a chart like this one to analyze Chief Joseph's persuasive techniques. Then, share your chart with your group, and discuss any different examples you have noted.

WORDS DO NOT PAY	
PERSUASIVE TECHNIQUE	EXAMPLES
repetition	a. See possible responses in Teacher's Edition sidebar
appeal to reason	b.
appeal to emotion	c.
appeal to authority	d.

Now, work as a group to identify words, phrases, and expressions in the examples that contribute to Chief Joseph's word choice and convey his tone. Then, discuss whether Chief Joseph's word choice and tone are effective and persuasive.

DIGITAL PERSPECTIVES

Analyze Craft and Structure

Persuasive Techniques and Word Choice Discuss with students the persuasive techniques that they have experienced in their own lives. Talk about whether they use these techniques when they argue for something. Point out that they may identify these techniques in advertisements for products or for political candidates. Remind students that persuasive appeals will not always be obvious. For more support, see **Analyze Craft and Structure: Persuasive Techniques and Word Choice.**

Encourage students to name words or phrases with strong positive and negative connotations. For example, in the text, the words *peace* and *free* have strong positive connotations. The phrase *makes my heart sick* and the word *overrun* have negative connotations.

Possible responses:

a. Words <u>do not pay</u> for my dead people. They <u>do not pay</u> for my country, now overrun by white men. . . . They <u>do not pay</u> for all my horses and cattle.
b. There need be no trouble. Treat all men alike. Give them the same law. Give them all an even chance to live and grow.
c. I am tired of talk that comes to nothing. It makes my heart sick when I remember all the good words and all the broken promises.
d. All men were made by the same Great Spirit Chief.

FORMATIVE ASSESSMENT

Analyze Craft and Structure

If students have difficulty recognizing persuasive techniques, **then** review more examples of each in "Words Do Not Pay." For Reteach and Practice, see **Analyze Craft and Structure: Persuasive Techniques and Word Choice (RP).**

WriteNow Inform and Explain

Speech Chief Joseph uses persuasive techniques to make the case that his people should be better treated by the U.S. government. Have students use similar techniques in a speech in which they build a case for something they want for their school, city, or country. Have them include repetition, appeals to reason, appeals to emotion, and appeals to authority as they build their case with evidence, facts, statistics, and anecdotes.

FACILITATING

Author's Style

Rhetorical Devices Point out to students that when authors use parallelism, they may repeat a word or some words of a phrase, as in Dickens' famous opening in *A Tale of Two Cities*, "It was the best of times, it was the worst of times." However, authors may simply repeat the pattern of parts of speech. Point out the examples of nouns on the chart, and discuss this form of phrasing: *adjective noun, adjective noun, adjective noun*. If the author did not use parallel construction, it might read: "bright eyes, large hands, and fingers that were strong." Review the rest of the chart, pointing out the pattern of parts of speech for each. For more support, see **Author's Style: Rhetorical Devices**.

Read It

Possible responses:

Paragraph 1, beginning at line 3: Words do not pay for my dead people. They do not pay for my country, now overrun by white men. They do not protect my father's grave. They do not pay for all my horses and cattle.

Paragraph 1, beginning at line 6: Good words will not give me back my children. Good words will not make good the promise of your war chief General Miles. Good words will not give my people good health and stop them from dying. Good words will not get my people a home where they can live in peace and take care of themselves.

Paragraph 1, beginning at line 14: Too many misrepresentations have been made, too many misunderstandings have come up between the white men about the Indians.

Paragraph 1, beginning at line 18: Give them all the same law. Give them all an even chance to live and grow.

Paragraph 2, beginning at line 1: . . . free to travel, free to stop, free to work, free to trade where I choose, free to choose my own teachers, free to follow the religion of my fathers, free to think and talk and act for myself . . .

Yes, I think his argument is stronger and more persuasive, because the use of parallelism strongly emphasizes his ideas.

Write It

Responses will vary. Be sure that students include parallelism in their three sentences.

FORMATIVE ASSESSMENT

Author's Style

If students have difficulty identifying examples of parallelism in the speech, **then** review the first few examples with them, pointing out how the speaker uses the same structure to make his points. For Reteach and Practice, see **Author's Style: Rhetorical Devices (RP)**.

312 UNIT 3 • WHAT MATTERS

LANGUAGE DEVELOPMENT

WORDS DO NOT PAY

Author's Style

Rhetorical Devices Parallelism is the use of similar grammatical forms or patterns to express similar ideas within a sentence. Parallelism adds rhythm and balance to writing and strengthens the connections among an author's ideas.

Writing without parallelism produces awkward, distracting shifts for readers. By contrast, parallel constructions place ideas of equal weight in words, phrases, or clauses of similar types.

Nonparallel: Dress codes are less restrictive, less costly, and are not a controversial system.

Parallel: Dress codes are less restrictive, less costly, and less controversial.

SAMPLE PARALLEL FORMS	
modified nouns	bright eyes, large hands, strong fingers
verb forms	to ask, to learn, to share
phrases	under a gray sky, near an icy river
adverb clauses	when I am happy, when I am peaceful
adjective clauses	who read with care, who act with concern

Read It

Work with your group to identify examples of parallelism in Chief Joseph's speech "Words Do Not Pay." Underline the parallel constructions of words, phrases, and clauses throughout the speech. Then, discuss with your group the ways in which Chief Joseph's use of parallelism creates rhythm and balance in the speech. How do his parallel constructions strengthen the connections between his ideas? Does the use of parallelism make his argument stronger and more persuasive?

Write It

Write three sentences about the speech in which you correctly use parallelism.

STANDARDS

Writing
• Write informative/explanatory texts to examine a topic and convey ideas, concepts, and information through the selection, organization, and analysis of relevant content.
  a. Introduce a topic clearly, previewing what is to follow; organize ideas, concepts, and information into broader categories; include formatting, graphics, and multimedia when useful to aiding comprehension.
  b. Develop the topic with relevant, well-chosen facts, definitions, concrete details, quotations, or other information and examples.
  f. Provide a concluding statement or section that follows from and supports the information or explanation presented.
• Conduct short research projects to answer a question, drawing on several sources and generating additional related, focused questions that allow for multiple avenues of exploration.
• Gather relevant information from multiple print and digital sources, using search terms effectively; assess the credibility and accuracy of each source; and quote or paraphrase the data and conclusions of others while avoiding plagiarism and following a standard format for citation.

Language
• Demonstrate command of the conventions of standard English grammar and usage when writing or speaking.
• Use knowledge of language and its conventions when writing, speaking, reading, or listening.

312 UNIT 3 • WHAT MATTERS

PERSONALIZE FOR LEARNING

English Language Support

Justifying an Opinion Using Parallelism Have students write their opinion about what happened to Chief Joseph and his people. Tell them to use parallelism in their writing to emphasize the most important points.

Ask students to write two or three sentences and then share them with a partner. **EMERGING**

Have students write a paragraph and then share it with the class. Have students discuss the writer's opinion. **BRIDGING**

Ask students to write a persuasive speech about their opinion and then deliver the speech for the class. **EXPANDING**

An expanded **English Language Support Lesson** on Parallelism is available in the Interactive Teacher's Edition.

EFFECTIVE EXPRESSION

Research

Assignment

Work with your group to create a **research report** about Chief Joseph or the Nez Percé people. In your report, analyze the ways in which the topic your group chooses contributes to your understanding of Chief Joseph's argument. Choose one of the following topics:

- [ ] a **historical report** on the history of the Nez Percé tribe, including information about their beliefs and culture
- [ ] a **biographical report** on the life of Chief Joseph, including his upbringing and influences

Assign Tasks Use the chart to assign tasks for each group member.

TASK	GROUP MEMBER(S)	COMPLETED
Search for and take notes on reliable sources.		
Organize the information.		
Write the report.		
Proofread and edit the report.		

Conduct Research As you conduct research, follow these guidelines:

- When researching online, choose search terms that are specific and unique to your topic. General terms may have more than one meaning, and therefore may produce unhelpful results.
- Make sure the sources you find are relevant and reliable, and take detailed notes to use in your bibliography or Works Cited page.
- Include information from several different sources. Do not rely solely on one source, even if it is a credible one.
- **Paraphrase,** or restate, information from sources, and note **direct quotations,** that are particularly powerful. Remember to put direct quotations in quotation marks to indicate that they are the exact words of another writer.

Organize Your Report Organize the information from your research logically. For example, in a historical or biographical report, you may choose to present information about events and experiences in **chronological order,** or the order in which the events happened. Conclude your report by reflecting on the ways in which the knowledge you gained from your research helped you to better understand the Chief Joseph's speech.

EVIDENCE LOG
Before moving on to a new selection, go to your Evidence Log, and record what you learned from "Words Do Not Pay."

DIGITAL PERSPECTIVES

Research
If students have difficulty in choosing a topic, point out that if they choose the first option, they may research how the Nez Percé have lived through the centuries. Students may want to narrow the topic to focus on a specific time period or cultural aspect. If students are more interested in biography or how one leader took a stand, they will prefer the second option.

Assign Tasks Encourage students to use the chart to plan and keep track of their work. Remind groups to consult the schedule for Small-Group Activities as they create their Project Plan. Check to make sure each group has made assignments and that the work is divided evenly among group members. For more support, see **Research: Research Report.**

Evidence Log Support students in completing their Evidence Log. This paced activity will help prepare them for the Performance-Based Assessment at the end of the unit.

FORMATIVE ASSESSMENT
Research
If students have difficulty conducting research, **then** review search terms and point out how students can improve them. Also, point out that students may use books and journals in their research report. For Reteach and Practice, see **Research: Research Report (RP).**

Selection Test
Administer the "Words Do Not Pay" Selection Test, which is available in both print and digital formats online in Assessments.

PERSONALIZE FOR LEARNING

Strategic Support

Timeline As students research their topic, have them create a timeline of events. For the first option, students would create a timeline of major events for the Nez Percé. For the second option, students would create a timeline of major events in Chief Joseph's life. Creating a timeline will help students organize events for their paper and will help them understand the sequence of major events.

PLANNING

SMALL-GROUP LEARNING • *from* FOLLOW THE RABBIT-PROOF FENCE

from Follow the Rabbit-Proof Fence

AUDIO SUMMARIES
Audio summaries of the excerpt from *Follow the Rabbit-Proof Fence* are available online in both English and Spanish in the Interactive Teacher's Edition or Unit Resources. Assigning these summaries prior to reading the selection may help students build additional background knowledge and set a context for their first read.

Summary
In this excerpt from the nonfiction narrative *Follow the Rabbit-Proof Fence* by Doris Pilkington, three sisters decide to run away from the settlement where they have been forced to live. They want to find their way back to their home village. The oldest of the girls decides that they can follow the rabbit-proof fence, an obvious and large structure, to get all the way home. The sisters gather their few possessions, a little food, and get ready to run. After fleeing from the camp, they find a way to cross a dangerous river.

Insight
This nonfiction narrative illustrates how children separated from their families bravely resist the unjust treatment that many Australian Aboriginal people received.

ESSENTIAL QUESTION:
When is it right to take a stand?

Connection to Essential Question
This selection illustrates how a person might be easily compelled to act when subjected to cruelty. In this case, Molly and her sisters have been unjustly separated from their family, and she is willing to take great risks to return home.

SMALL-GROUP LEARNING PERFORMANCE TASK
When you take a stand, how much does winning matter?

UNIT PERFORMANCE-BASED ASSESSMENT
Is it important for people to make their own choices in life?

Connection to Performance Tasks
Small-Group Learning Performance Task This selection provides students with an example of a simple but significant issue—an individual's right to live where he or she chooses. Students should notice how important winning seems to Molly.

Unit Performance-Based Assessment In this selection, Molly's decision to run away from the settlement and travel a long distance to return to Jigalong seems to come from a strong connection to her home. Students may apply Molly's experiences and beliefs to their responses to the prompt.

DIGITAL PERSPECTIVES Audio Video Document Annotation Highlights EL Highlights ✓ Online Assessment

LESSON RESOURCES

Lesson	Making Meaning	Language Development	Effective Expression
	First Read Close Read Analyze the Text Analyze Craft and Structure	Concept Vocabulary Word Study Conventions	Writing to Sources
Instructional Standards	**RI.10** By the end of the year, read and comprehend literary nonfiction . . . **L.4** Determine or clarify the meaning of unknown and multiple-meaning words and phrases . . . **L.4.c** Consult general and specialized reference materials . . . **RI.4** Determine the meaning of words and phrases . . . **RI.5** Analyze in detail the structure . . . **RI.6** Determine an author's point of view . . . **L.5** Demonstrate understanding of figurative language . . .	**L.1** Demonstrate command of the conventions . . .	**W.3** Write narratives . . . **W.3.a** Engage and orient the reader . . . **W.3.b** Use narrative techniques . . . **W.3.d** Use precise words and phrases . . . **W.5** With some guidance and support from peers and adults, develop and strengthen writing . . . **W.7** Conduct short research projects . . .
🖱 **STUDENT RESOURCES** Available online in the Interactive Student Edition or Unit Resources	🔊 Selection Audio 📄 First-Read Guide: Nonfiction 📄 Close-Read Guide: Nonfiction	📄 Word Network	📄 Evidence Log
🖱 **TEACHER RESOURCES** **Selection Resources** Available online in the Interactive Teacher's Edition or Unit Resources	🔊 Audio Summaries ✏️ Annotation Highlights 💬 EL Highlights 📄 English Language Support Lesson: Sensory Details 📄 from Follow the Rabbit-Proof Fence: Text Questions 📄 Analyze Craft and Structure: Descriptive Writing	📄 Concept Vocabulary and Word Study 📄 Conventions: Adjectives and Adverbs	📄 Writing to Sources: First-Person Account
Reteach/Practice (RP) Available online in the Interactive Teacher's Edition or Unit Resources	📄 Analyze Craft and Structure: Descriptive Writing (RP)	📄 Word Study: Old English Suffix -ly (RP) 📄 Conventions: Adjectives and Adverbs (RP)	📄 Writing to Sources: First-Person Account (RP)
Assessment Available online in Assessments	📄 ✓ Selection Test		
My Resources	📄 A Unit 3 Answer Key is available online and in the Interactive Teacher's Edition.		

PERSONALIZE FOR LEARNING
SMALL-GROUP LEARNING • *from* FOLLOW THE RABBIT-PROOF FENCE

Reading Support

Text Complexity Rubric: *from* Follow the Rabbit-Proof Fence

Quantitative Measures

Lexile: 1160   Text Length: 1,789 words

Qualitative Measures

Knowledge Demands ①—②—③—**④**—⑤	Selection relies on knowledge that will be unfamiliar to students (the experiences of Australian Aboriginal children during the 1930s).
Structure ①—②—**③**—④—⑤	Structure is straightforward, with clear organization. Story is told sequentially; plot elements are interspersed with descriptions of locations and daily life in those places.
Language Conventionality and Clarity ①—②—**③**—④—⑤	Tense shifts can be confusing (for descriptions of immediate plot events, past events, or usual habits). Text has a lot of descriptive vocabulary. Some Aboriginal words are included (translated in footnotes).
Levels of Meaning/Purpose ①—②—**③**—④—⑤	There is one level of meaning, but the situation is not revealed right away; characters' feelings are sometimes communicated through word choice.

DECIDE AND PLAN

English Language Support

Provide English Learners with support for language and meaning as they read the selection.

Language Draw attention to the way sentences are written to describe events in the immediate plot and descriptions of common activities (using *would*). For example, *she started to run* (paragraph 25) describes what just happened, but *they would give the signal* (paragraph 26) describes a common activity.

Meaning Draw attention to some of the word choices that the author makes to convey information. For example, the author uses *grabbed* (paragraph 22) to tell how Molly picked up the bucket because it shows that she was in a hurry.

Strategic Support

Provide students with strategic support to ensure that they can successfully read the text.

Knowledge Demands Have a group of students read aloud the first few paragraphs. Stop frequently to check for understanding of the situation, referring to the background information. For example, after paragraphs 8–10, make sure students understand that Molly is telling the two girls that they will be escaping, and ask students to recall why they need to escape.

Meaning Have students read selected paragraphs aloud. Point out that we can learn how characters are feeling from the direct description and the author's word choice. For example, *Daisy and Gracie were stunned and stood staring* (paragraph 8).

Challenge

Provide students who need to be challenged with ideas for how they can go beyond a simple interpretation of the text.

Text Analysis Ask students to work in pairs. Have them go through the text and list aspects of the setting or the character's situation that are different from their own lives. For example, paragraph 4 describes having to empty a toilet bucket. Ask students to share their findings with the class.

Response Have a group of students practice and perform a dramatic reading, with several narrators (rotating) and several students playing each of the characters. Encourage students to convey the feelings of the characters. Ask other students to share their reactions to each reading and to tell what they found interesting in the story.

TEACH

Read and Respond

Have the groups read the selection and complete the Making Meaning, Language Development, and Effective Expression activities.

Standards Support Through Teaching and Learning Cycle

IDENTIFY NEEDS

Analyze results of the Beginning-of-Year Assessment, focusing on the items relating to Unit 3. Also take into consideration student performance to this point and your observations of where particular students struggle.

ANALYZE AND REVISE

- Analyze student work for evidence of student learning.
- Identify whether students have met the expectations in the standards.
- Identify implications for future instruction.

TEACH

Implement the planned lesson, and gather evidence of student learning.

DECIDE AND PLAN

- If students have performed poorly on items matching these standards, then provide selection scaffolds before assigning them the on-level lesson provided in the Student Edition.
- If students have done well on the Beginning-of-Year Assessment, then challenge them to keep progressing and learning by giving them opportunities to practice the skills in depth.
- Use the Selection Resources listed on the Planning pages for the excerpt from *Follow the Rabbit-Proof Fence* to help students continually improve their ability to master the standards.

Instructional Standards: *from* **Follow the Rabbit-Proof Fence**

	Catching Up	This Year	Looking Forward
Reading	You may wish to administer the **Analyze Craft and Structure: Descriptive Writing (RP)** worksheet to help students identify and understand the impact of descriptive writing in the selection.	**RI.4** Determine the meaning of words and phrases as they are used in a text, including figurative and connotative meanings; analyze the impact of specific word choices on meaning and tone, including analogies or allusions to other texts.	Challenge students to write a descriptive paragraph about a place that is important to them. Have students share their writing in small groups.
Writing	You may wish to administer the **Writing to Sources: First-Person Account (RP)** worksheet to help students understand how to organize and plan their first-person accounts.	**W.3** Write narratives to develop real or imagined experiences or events using effective technique, relevant descriptive details, and well-structured event sequences.	Challenge students to peer review a partner's account and offer specific suggestions to clarify ideas.
Language	You may wish to administer the **Conventions: Adjectives and Adverbs (RP)** worksheet to help students identify and understand the use of adjectives and adverbs.	**L.1** Demonstrate command of the conventions of standard English grammar and usage when writing or speaking.	Challenge students to use increasingly complex examples of adjectives and adverbs in their speaking and writing.

FACILITATING

Jump Start

FIRST READ *What would you do if you were removed from your parents and your home? How would you take a stand?* Engaging students in a discussion about young people taking a stand sets the context for reading the excerpt from *Follow the Rabbit-Proof Fence*. As students share their thoughts, have them explain the factors that influence their opinion.

from Follow the Rabbit-Proof Fence

Why does Molly want to leave the settlement? Why do the other girls agree to go with her? Modeling questions readers might ask as they read the excerpt from *Follow the Rabbit-Proof Fence* brings the text alive for students and connects it to the Small-Group Performance Task assignment. Selection audio and print capability for the selection are available in the Interactive Teacher's Edition.

Concept Vocabulary

Ask groups to study the information about using a dictionary and thesaurus, and discuss how they can be useful. Encourage groups to consider how differences in the girls' personalities can be emphasized with specific word choices.

FIRST READ

Students should perform the steps of the first read independently.

NOTICE: Encourage students to notice differences in the girls' personalities.

ANNOTATE: Remind students to mark passages that include descriptive language.

CONNECT: Encourage students to think of other stories they have read in which people escape from somewhere or take a long journey.

RESPOND: Students will answer questions to demonstrate understanding.

Point out to students that while they will always complete the Respond step at the end of the first read, the other steps will probably happen somewhat concurrently. You may wish to print copies of the **First-Read Guide: Nonfiction** for students to use.

314   UNIT 3 • WHAT MATTERS

MAKING MEANING

About the Author

Doris Pilkington (1937–2014) was an Aboriginal author best known for her nonfiction narrative *Follow the Rabbit-Proof Fence*, based on her mother's 1931 escape from the Moore River Mission. Under the Aborigines Act (1906–1954), approximately 100,000 children were removed from their tribal lands and placed in the care of the state. In 1940, when she was three-and-a-half years old, Doris became one of these children.

STANDARDS

Reading Informational Text
By the end of the year, read and comprehend literary nonfiction at the high end of the grades 6–8 text complexity band independently and proficiently.

Language
Determine or clarify the meaning of unknown and multiple-meaning words or phrases based on *grade 8 reading and content*, choosing flexibly from a range of strategies.

c. Consult general and specialized reference materials, both print and digital, to find the pronunciation of a word or determine or clarify its precise meaning or its part of speech.

from Follow the Rabbit-Proof Fence

Concept Vocabulary

As you conduct your first read of the excerpt from *Follow the Rabbit-Proof Fence,* you will encounter these words.

| urgently | nervously | confidently | cautiously |

Using a Dictionary and Thesaurus If a word is unfamiliar to you and you cannot understand the meaning from the context, look up the word in a dictionary or thesaurus. Most **dictionaries**, whether print or online, will provide the meaning of the word, its part of speech, its pronunciation, and its etymology. A **thesaurus**, on the other hand, will not provide definitions but will include synonyms of the word, or words with similar meanings. For instance, compare these two entries for the word *crimson*.

Dictionary
crim•son (KRIHM zuhn) *adj.* red in color

Thesaurus
crimson *adj.* dark red, bloody, cherry, scarlet, rosy, cardinal, ruby

Apply your knowledge of using a dictionary and thesaurus as well as other vocabulary strategies to determine the meanings of unfamiliar words you encounter during your first read.

First Read NONFICTION

Apply these strategies as you conduct your first read. You will have an opportunity to complete a close read after your first read.

NOTICE the general ideas of the text. *What* is it about? *Who* is involved?

ANNOTATE by marking vocabulary and key passages you want to revisit.

CONNECT ideas within the selection to what you already know and what you have already read.

RESPOND by completing the Comprehension Check and by creating a storyboard of the events in the excerpt.

VOCABULARY DEVELOPMENT

Word Analysis The concept vocabulary words *urgently, nervously, confidently,* and *cautiously* end with the suffix *-ly*. When this suffix is added to a verb, it creates an adverb that tells more information about the verb. Adverbs often end in the suffix *-ly*, which tells in what manner the action was performed. Have students name other adverbs that contain the suffix *-ly* and ask them to practice using those words in sentences.

NONFICTION NARRATIVE

from Follow the Rabbit-Proof Fence

Doris Pilkington

BACKGROUND

Aboriginal Australians are the native people of the Australian continent. From 1910 to 1970, many children of mixed Aboriginal and white descent were taken from their families by the government in an effort to train them to fit into white Australian culture. *Follow the Rabbit-Proof Fence* is a nonfiction narrative account of three Mardu Aboriginal girls who escaped a government settlement in 1931 to return home. The Mardu are the indigenous, or native, people of the Australian desert.

1 The other girls were now getting ready for school, and the three watched quietly amidst all the activity. Bossing and bullying was everywhere around them and there were cries and squeals of, "Don't, you're hurting my head," as the tangled knots were combed out with tiny, fragile combs.

2 "Oh, Mummy, Daddy, Mummy, Daddy, my head," yelled a young girl, who stamped her feet and tried to pull away from her torturer, an older, well-built girl who seemed to have adopted the girl as her baby sister. They performed this ritual together every morning before school.

3 "Come on, you girls," ordered Martha Jones as she passed by their bed. "The school bell's gone. Don't be late on your first day."

4 "Alright, we're coming as soon as we empty the toilet bucket," answered Molly softly.

5 "I'll wait for you then," said Martha.

6 "No, don't wait we'll follow you, we know where the school is."

7 "Alright then, we'll go along. Come on, Rosie," she said as she rushed out of the door into the cold, drizzly morning.

8 As soon as the other girls left the dormitory, Molly beckoned her two sisters to come closer to her, then she whispered **urgently**, "We're not going to school, so grab your bags. We're not staying here." Daisy and Gracie were stunned and stood staring at her.

9 "What did you say?" asked Gracie.

10 "I said, we're not staying here at the settlement, because we're going home to Jigalong."[1]

---

1. **Jigalong** *n.* region in Western Australia where the Mardu Aboriginal people live.

NOTES

Use a dictionary or a thesaurus or indicate another strategy you used to help you determine meaning.

urgently (UR juhnt lee) *adv.*
MEANING:

FACILITATING

CLOSER LOOK

Analyze Character

Circulate among groups as students conduct their close read. Suggest that groups close read paragraph 17. Encourage them to talk about the annotations that they mark. If needed, provide the following support.

ANNOTATE: Have students mark details in paragraph 17 that tell about Molly, or work with small groups to have students participate while you highlight them together.

QUESTION: Guide students to consider what these details might tell them. Ask what a reader can infer from the details, and accept student responses.

Possible response: Molly knows things about the country and takes charge.

CONCLUDE: Help students to formulate conclusions about the importance of these details in the text. Ask students why the author might have included these details.

Possible response: These details are important because they help show why Molly believed she was capable of getting them back and home and why her sisters trusted her.

Explain that authors help readers understand **characters** by giving information about them, by showing how they talk and behave, and by showing how others react to them. Point out that the author of *Follow the Rabbit-Proof Fence* uses several techniques to develop Molly's character.

NOTES

Use a dictionary or a thesaurus or indicate another strategy you used to help you determine meaning.

nervously (NUR vuhs lee) *adv.*
MEANING:

confidently (KON fuh dehnt lee) *adv.*
MEANING:

---

11 Gracie and Daisy weren't sure whether they were hearing correctly or not.

12 "Move quickly," Molly ordered her sisters. She wanted to be miles away before their absence was discovered. Time was of the essence.

13 Her two young sisters faced each other, both looking very scared and confused. Daisy turned to Molly and said **nervously**, "We're frightened, Dgudu.[2] How are we going to find our way back home to Jigalong? It's a long way from home."

14 Molly leaned against the wall and said **confidently**, "I know it's a long way to go but it's easy. We'll find the rabbit-proof fence[3] and follow that all the way home."

15 "We gunna walk all the way?" asked Daisy.

16 "Yeah," replied Molly, getting really impatient now. "So don't waste time."

17 The task of finding the rabbit-proof fence seemed like a simple solution for a teenager whose father was an inspector who traveled up and down the fences, and whose grandfather had worked with him. Thomas Craig told her often enough that the fence stretched from coast to coast, south to north across the country. It was just a matter of locating a stretch of it then following it to Jigalong. The two youngsters trusted their big sister because she was not only the eldest but she had always been the bossy one who made all the decisions at home. So they did the normal thing and said, "Alright, Dgudu, we'll run away with you."

18 They snatched up their meager possessions and put them into calico bags and pulled the long drawstrings and slung them around their necks. Each one put on two dresses, two pairs of calico bloomers, and a coat.

19 Gracie and Daisy were about to leave when Molly told them to, "Wait. Take those coats off. Leave them here."

20 "Why?" asked Gracie.

21 "Because they're too heavy to carry."

22 The three sisters checked to make sure they hadn't missed anything then, when they were absolutely satisfied, Molly grabbed the galvanized bucket and ordered Gracie to get hold of the other side and walk quickly trying not to spill the contents as they made their way to the lavatories. Daisy waited under the large pine tree near the stables. She reached up and broke a small twig that was hanging down low and was examining it closely when the other two joined her.

---

2. **Dgudu** older sister in Mardudjara, the Mardu Aborigines' native language.
3. **the rabbit-proof fence** fence that ran from the north coast of Australia to the south coast to deter pests such as rabbits.

FACILITATING SMALL-GROUP CLOSE READING

CLOSE READ: Nonfiction Narrative As groups perform the close read, circulate and offer support as needed.

- Remind groups that as they read the selection, they should look for the main events of the story.
- If groups are confused about what events are important, remind them to think about which events they would include in a summary if they were telling someone else what happened. Have them note how these events fit into the theme of taking a stand for what matters.
- Challenge groups to determine the main idea of the selection and the specific details that support the main idea.

23 "Look, Dgudu, like grass indi?[4]" asked Daisy, passing the twig to Molly to feel.

24 "Youay,"[5] she said, as she gave it to Gracie who crushed the green pine needles into her small hands and sniffed them. She liked the smell and was about to give her opinion when Molly reminded them that they didn't have time to stand around examining pine needles.

25 "Come on, run, you two," she said sharply as she started to run towards the river.

26 Many young people had stood under the same big pine tree and waited while someone went into the stable or the garage to distract Maitland, the caretaker and stableman. Then they would give the signal that the coast was clear and everyone would dash into the grainary and fill their empty fruit tins with wheat from one of the opened bags at the back of the shed. Some of it was roasted on flat tins over the hot coals, the rest was saved to fill initials that had been dug into the sloping embankment of firm yellow sand along the cliffs. These were left until the first rain came, then all the inmates would rush down to inspect the cliffs. This grass graffiti revealed the new summer romances between the older boys and girls. But these three girls from the East Pilbara had no intention of participating, they had a more important task ahead of them.

27 On they went, dashing down the sandy slope of the cliffs, dodging the small shrubs on the way and following the narrow path to the flooded river. They slowed down only when they reached the bottom. Molly paused briefly, glancing at the pumping shed on their right where they had been the day before. Turning towards it she said to Gracie and Daisy, "This way." She ran for about 25 meters, crashing into the thick paperbark trees and the branches of the river gums that blocked their path.

28 Molly strode on as best as she could along the muddy banks, pausing only to urge her young sisters to hurry up and try to keep up with her. She kept up that pace until she saw what she thought to be a likely spot to cross the swift flowing river.

29 The three girls watched the swirling currents and the white and brown frothy foam that clung to the trunks of the young river gums and clumps of tea-trees. They didn't know that this became one of the most popular spots during the hot summer days. This was the local swimming pool that would be filled with naked or semi-naked brown bodies, laughing, splashing, swimming and diving into the cool brown water during the long summer afternoons. Every now and then, the swimmers would sit on the coarse river sand and yank ugly, brown, slimy leeches off

---

4. **indi?** "isn't it?" (Mardudjara).
5. **Youay** "Yes" (Mardudjara).

from Follow the Rabbit-Proof Fence

PERSONALIZE FOR LEARNING

English Language Support

Idioms Tell students that the expression *the coast was clear* in paragraph 26 is an idiom. Remind them that an idiom is a commonly used expression that is not meant literally.

Explain that *the coast is clear* means that people are not in danger. Have students review how the idiom is used in the selection. What do the young people mean specifically when they signal that *the coast was clear*? (Maitland, the caretaker, is not at the grainary.) Have students think of a time when they might use the idiom.

ALL LEVELS

FACILITATING

their bodies and impale them on sticks and turn them inside out and plunge them into the hot burning mud. The next day the swimmers would pull the sticks out of the sand and gloat at the shriveled dry skins that once were horrible little creatures, ready to suck all the blood from their bodies—or so the young people were led to believe.

30 "The river is too deep and fast here, let's try up further," Molly said, leading the way through the thick young suckers and washed-up logs. They continued along the bank making slow progress through the obstacles that nature had left in their path. At last they came to a section in the river that seemed narrow enough to cross.

31 "We'll try here," said Molly as she bent down to pick up a long stick. She slid down the bank into the river and began measuring its depth just as she had seen Edna Green do the previous afternoon, while Daisy and Gracie watched patiently on the bank.

32 "Nah, too deep," Molly said in disgust. "Not here."

33 "Gulu,[6] Dgudu," cried the youngsters as they ran to follow her through the wet foliage.

34 The three girls walked along the muddy banks for another 25 meters when they came to a clearing, devoid of any shrubs or young suckers, where the floods had receded.

35 ==In a couple of weeks' time, this place would become a muddy skating rink where the girls of the settlement would spend hours having fun skating up and down the slippery mud. The idea to skate by placing one foot in front of the other and maintain your balance for a couple of meters at least. The boys had their own skating area further up in a more secluded place amongst the thick tea-tree shrub. Peeping toms never existed in those days. Each group respected each other's privacy. Nearby, a huge fire would be lit and kept stoked. When everyone had finished skating in the slippery mud they would dive into the icy cold river to wash off the mud, then dry themselves by the roaring fire, dress, and return to the compound.==

36 Molly decided to follow the paths made by the cattle. Another attempt was made to cross the river but once again proved unsuccessful. She walked on angrily, pushing the thick growth of eucalyptus suckers roughly aside, at the same time urging Daisy and Gracie to walk faster. But they decided that it was much safer at a distance and they followed her muddy footprints in silence without any questions, trusting her leadership totally.

37 They were still fighting their way through the tea-trees for almost an hour when they heard Molly call out to them somewhere down the track. "Yardini! Bukala! Bukala!"[7]

---

6. **Gulu** "wait" (Mardudjara).
7. **Yardini! Bukala! Bukala!** "Come here! Hurry! Hurry!" (Mardudjara).

318 UNIT 3 • WHAT MATTERS

> Additional **English Language Support** is available in the Interactive Teacher's Edition.

HOW LANGUAGE WORKS

Adjectives and Adverbs Draw students' attention to paragraph 34. Remind students that an adjective modifies a noun or pronoun and that an adverb modifies a verb, an adjective, or another adverb. If students struggle to comprehend the difference between an adjective and an adverb, help them by giving examples of each. Have students complete the following sentences and identify the words they add as adjectives or adverbs.

- The girls walked along the _____ bank. [adjective; tells about the bank]
- The girls walked _____ along the bank. [adverb; tells about how the girls walked]

38   Daisy and Gracie ran as fast as they could along the muddy path until they reached her. Molly was standing near a large river gum. As they stood gasping for wind she said, "We gunna cross here."

39   As three pairs of eager eyes examined it closely, they knew that they had found the perfect place to cross the flooded river. A tree leaned over the water creating a natural bridge for them to cross safely to the other side.

40   The girls scraped mud from their feet then climbed onto the trunk and walked cautiously to the end then swung down off the limb onto the slippery, muddy bank on the other side. They sloshed through the wet, chocolate-colored banks for at least another two hours, then decided to rest amongst the thick reeds behind the tall river gums.

41   A few minutes later, Molly stood up and told her young sisters to get up. "We go kyalie[8] now all the way." They obeyed without any protests. Ducking under the hanging branches of the paperbark trees they hurried as best they could, stomping on the reeds and bull rushes that covered the banks of the fast flowing river. The only sounds that could be heard were the startled birds fluttering above as they left their nests in fright, and the *slish, slosh* of the girls' feet as they trampled over the bull rushes.

8. **kyalie** "north" (Mardudjara).

NOTES

Use a dictionary or a thesaurus or indicate another strategy you used to help you determine meaning.

cautiously (KAW shuhs lee) *adv.*
MEANING:

Comprehension Check

Complete the following items after you finish your first read. Review and clarify details with your group.

1. At the beginning of the excerpt, where are the three sisters living?

2. Where does Molly want to go?

3. How does Molly know about the rabbit-proof fence?

4. What does Molly try to avoid when looking for a place to cross the river?

5. **Notebook** Confirm your understanding of the excerpt by creating a storyboard of events.

RESEARCH

Research to Clarify Choose at least one unfamiliar detail in the text. Briefly research that detail. In what way does the information you learned shed light on an aspect of the narrative?

from Follow the Rabbit-Proof Fence

PERSONALIZE FOR LEARNING

Challenge In the excerpt from *Follow the Rabbit-Proof Fence*, the author describes in great detail the area in western Australia where the girls make their journey. Encourage students to research the plant and animal life of the region, including the eucalyptus and gum trees. Have them use what they learn in their research, along with the details in the selection, to draw an illustration of the area where the girls travel.

DIGITAL PERSPECTIVES

CLOSER LOOK

Analyze Descriptive Language

Circulate among groups as students conduct their close read. Suggest that groups close read paragraph 40. Encourage them to talk about the annotations that they mark. If needed, provide the following support.

ANNOTATE: Have students mark details in paragraph 40 that include descriptive language, or work with small groups to have students participate while you highlight them together.

QUESTION: Guide students to consider what these details might tell them. Ask what a reader can infer from the details, and accept student responses.

Possible response: Walking along the riverbank is messy and difficult.

CONCLUDE: Help students to formulate conclusions about the importance of these details in the text. Ask students why the author might have included these details.

Possible response: The details help better describe their experience traveling on foot.

Remind students that authors use **descriptive language** to help readers visualize events, characters, and settings.

Comprehension Check

Possible responses:

1. They are living at a settlement.
2. Molly wants to go home to Jigalong.
3. Her father was an inspector who traveled along the fences.
4. She tries to avoid crossing where the river is too deep.
5. Storyboards will vary. However, students should include that the girls escape from a settlement to follow the rabbit-proof fence home and successfully cross a river.

Research

Research to Clarify If groups struggle to identify a detail to research, you may want to suggest they focus on one of the following topics: settlements or the rabbit-proof fence.

FACILITATING

Jump Start

CLOSE READ Ask groups to consider the prompt: *How do the girls stand up for themselves by running away?* As students discuss in their groups, ask them to consider the reasons Molly was willing to embark on such a difficult journey.

Close Read the Text

If needed, model close reading by using the Annotation Highlights in the Interactive Teacher's Edition.

Remind students to use Accountable Talk in their discussions and to support one another as they complete the close read.

Analyze the Text

1. **Possible response:** Paragraph 17 conveys that Molly is bossy and that her sisters listen to her.
2. **Passages will vary by group.** Remind students to explain why they chose the passage they presented to group members.

Concept Vocabulary

Why These Words?
Possible response: The concept words relate to the girls' journey on foot along the rabbit-proof fence. The words explain how the girls were feeling, and walking, on their journey.

Practice

Possible response: When I realized I was late, I ran **urgently** to the bus stop.; The bus hadn't come yet, so I **nervously** tapped my foot, worrying.; Knowing he would do well on his essay, the student **confidently** started writing.; When the dog started growling at me, I walked **cautiously** past it.

Word Network

Possible words: *escaped, decisions, bullying, leadership*

Word Study

For more support, see **Concept Vocabulary and Word Study.**

Possible responses:
nervously: done in an uneasy or apprehensive way; **confidently:** done in a confident or self-assured way; **cautiously:** done with caution or in a cautious way

---

MAKING MEANING

from FOLLOW THE RABBIT-PROOF FENCE

TIP

GROUP DISCUSSION
As you discuss the nonfiction narrative, ask questions that help other group members elaborate on their ideas.

WORD NETWORK

Add words related to taking a stand from the text to your Word Network.

STANDARDS

Reading Informational Text
• Determine the meaning of words and phrases as they are used in a text, including figurative, connotative, and technical meanings; analyze the impact of specific word choices on meaning and tone, including analogies or allusions to other texts.
• Analyze in detail the structure of a specific paragraph in a text, including the role of particular sentences in developing and refining a key concept.
• Determine an author's point of view or purpose in a text and analyze how the author acknowledges and responds to conflicting evidence or viewpoints.

Language
Demonstrate understanding of figurative language, word relationships, and nuances in word meanings.

320 UNIT 3 • WHAT MATTERS

Close Read the Text

With your group, revisit sections of the text you marked during your first read. **Annotate** details that you noticed. What **questions** do you have? What can you **conclude**?

Analyze the Text

CITE TEXTUAL EVIDENCE to support your answers.

📓 **Notebook** Complete the activities.

1. **Review and Clarify** With your group, reread paragraph 17 of the selection. What important information about the three girls is conveyed? What is the author saying about the way the girls relate to one another?

2. **Present and Discuss** Now, work with your group to share the passages from the text that you found especially important. Take turns presenting your passages. Discuss what you noticed in the text, what questions you asked, and what conclusions you reached.

LANGUAGE DEVELOPMENT

Concept Vocabulary

| urgently | nervously | confidently | cautiously |

Why These Words? The concept vocabulary words from the text are related. With your group, determine what the words have in common. How do these words enhance the impact of the text?

Practice

📓 **Notebook** Confirm your understanding of the vocabulary words by using them in sentences.

Word Study

Old English Suffix: -ly The Old English suffix *-ly* is often used to make an adjective into an **adverb,** or a word that describes how, when, or how often something is done. For example, adding the suffix *-ly* to the adjective *urgent* creates the adverb *urgently*. In the excerpt, Molly whispers *urgently* to the other girls because the situation requires immediate action. Use a dictionary to find the precise meanings of the other three concept vocabulary words, which all end with the suffix *-ly*. Then, write a sentence or two explaining how the suffix *-ly* contributes to the meaning of each vocabulary word.

FORMATIVE ASSESSMENT

Analyze the Text

If students struggle to close read the text, **then** provide the *from Follow the Rabbit-Proof Fence: Text Questions* available online in the Interactive Teacher's Edition or Unit Resources. Answers and DOK levels are also available.

Concept Vocabulary

If students struggle to identify the concept, **then** have them reread the paragraphs in which the words appear and think about how they are related.

Word Study

If students are unable to explain how the suffix *-ly* contributes to the meaning of the vocabulary words, **then** review the suffix by giving students additional examples of words and sentences. For Reteach and Practice, see **Word Study: Old English Suffix -ly (RP).**

ESSENTIAL QUESTION: When is it right to take a stand?

Analyze Craft and Structure

Descriptive Writing A **description** is a portrait in words of a person, place, or thing. Descriptive writing uses **sensory details,** or language that appeals to the senses: sight, hearing, taste, smell, and touch. Effective description helps readers visualize settings, events, and characters clearly. It also helps convey emotions and ideas. Authors use description to emphasize a point of view and to create mood in a literary work.

- An author's **point of view** is his or her perspective or unique way of viewing a topic. Point of view is shaped by the author's knowledge, beliefs, and experiences. Description helps to convey that point of view because it shows more than just what a subject looks like. It reveals *how* the author sees the subject.
- **Mood** is the overall feeling created in a reader by a literary work. The mood of a work can typically be described using emotion words, such as *joyous, gloomy, peaceful,* or *frightening*. Some literary works convey a single mood. In other works, the mood changes within the selection.

TIP
CLARIFICATION
As you analyze descriptive writing, consider the ways in which an author's descriptions contribute to the development of his or her ideas.

Practice

CITE TEXTUAL EVIDENCE to support your answers.

Analyze how the author's use of description reveals his or her point of view and creates a specific mood, or emotional atmosphere, in the excerpt. Note words and phrases from the text that support your analysis. Use the chart to capture your observations.

PASSAGE	POINT OF VIEW	MOOD
a. Paragraph 29	b. The author's point of view shows admiration of the swimmers' freedom, physicality, and connection to nature.	c. The mood in this passage seems thoughtful.
a. See possible responses in the Teacher's Edition.	b.	c.
d.	c.	d.

from Follow the Rabbit-Proof Fence **321**

PERSONALIZE FOR LEARNING

English Language Support

Sensory Details Have students choose an excerpt from the text that makes use of sensory details and ask them to write about what senses are being appealed to and the kind of scene that the description creates. Ask students to write three sentences that describe their excerpt. **EMERGING**

Have students write a paragraph that describes their excerpt and then with a partner, share their opinions about why the author chose to use sensory details in the excerpt. **EXPANDING**

Have students write a few paragraphs that describe their excerpt and then discuss why they think the author describes events as she does. Ask students to present their essay to the class. **BRIDGING**

An expanded **English Language Support Lesson** on Sensory Details is available in the Interactive Teacher's Edition.

DIGITAL PERSPECTIVES

Analyze Craft and Structure

Descriptive Writing Discuss with students that sensory details, point of view, and mood are all important elements of descriptive writing that help readers more deeply understand what an experience was like for the people in a story. Effective descriptive writing helps readers visualize the story and also conveys point of view and mood. For more support, see **Analyze Craft and Structure: Descriptive Writing.**

MAKE IT INTERACTIVE
Have students think of a recent event in their lives that they found interesting or exciting. Next, have them write a few sentences about the event in a matter-of-fact way and then with descriptive, lively words.

Practice

Possible responses:

Row 2: a. Paragraphs 37–38; b. In these paragraphs, the author's point of view is showing the girls' determination and urgency; c. The passage creates a mood of excitement.

Row 3: a. Paragraph 41; b. The author's point of view here conveys the girls' vulnerability while making their long journey.; c. The last part of the selection has a mood of uncertainty.

FORMATIVE ASSESSMENT

Analyze Craft and Structure

If students struggle to identify descriptive writing, **then** review examples from the selection. For Reteach and Practice, see **Analyze Craft and Structure: Descriptive Writing (RP).**

Small-Group Learning

FACILITATING

Conventions

Adjectives and Adverbs Explain to students that when trying to identify an adverb that modifies a verb, they should first identify the verb in a sentence. If they find a word that tells more about the verb, then that is the adverb. Use the following sentence as an example: *Molly always bosses her sisters*. Have students name the verb (*bosses*). Then have students name the word that tells more about the verb (*always*). The adverb *always* tells when Molly bosses her sisters. For more support, see **Conventions: Adjectives and Adverbs**.

Read It

1. a. They did the <u>normal</u> thing.
   b. They dashed <u>down</u> the <u>sandy</u> slopes.
2. a. Molly spoke softly.
   b. Daisy tried to walk slowly.

Write It

Responses will vary, but make sure that students include at least two adjectives and two adverbs in their paragraphs.

FORMATIVE ASSESSMENT
Conventions

If students have trouble distinguishing between adjectives and adverbs, **then** have them list words that describe objects in the classroom (adjectives). Review with them that adverbs modify verbs, adjectives, and other adverbs. For Reteach and Practice, see **Conventions: Adjectives and Adverbs (RP)**.

LANGUAGE DEVELOPMENT

from FOLLOW THE RABBIT-PROOF FENCE

Conventions

Adjectives and Adverbs Authors use **adjectives** and **adverbs** to tell more about the nouns and verbs in their sentences. An adjective modifies, or adds meaning to, a noun or a pronoun. An adverb modifies a verb, an adjective, or another adverb.

An adjective gives more information about a noun. For example, in the sentence *It's a long way from home*, the adjective *long* modifies the noun *way*. It answers the question *What kind (of way)?* Look at the chart to see examples of questions that adjectives answer.

What kind?	cold, long, easy, muddy, simple
Which one?	that, this, those
How many?	two, many, three
How much?	most, some, meager, huge
Whose?	her, their, my, your

An adverb gives more information about a verb, adjective, or another adverb. For example, in the sentence *She whispered urgently*, the adverb *urgently* modifies the verb *whispered*, answering the question *In what manner (did she whisper)?* Look at the chart to see examples of questions that adverbs answer. Note that adverbs often end in the suffix *-ly*.

When?	now, before, yesterday
Where?	everywhere, here, ahead
In what manner?	quietly, playfully, correctly, well
To what extent?	too, absolutely, totally

Be careful not to use adjectives in place of adverbs, as shown in this example: **Incorrect:** Move <u>quick</u>. **Correct:** Move <u>quickly</u>.

Read It

1. Work individually. Underline the adjective in each sentence.
   a. They did the normal thing.
   b. They dashed down the sandy slopes.
2. Correct each sentence by replacing the adjective with an adverb.
   a. Molly spoke soft.
   b. Daisy tried to walk careful.

STANDARDS
Language
Demonstrate command of the conventions of standard English grammar and usage when writing or speaking.

Write It

Notebook Write a short paragraph about the excerpt. Use at least two adjectives and two adverbs in your paragraph.

PERSONALIZE FOR LEARNING

English Language Support

Adjectives and Adverbs Review the definitions of adjectives and adverbs. Have students identify two examples of each, and use their examples in sentences. Support students in completing as many of these steps as they can. **ALL LEVELS**

EFFECTIVE EXPRESSION

Writing to Sources

Assignment

Work individually to write a **fictional retelling** of the excerpt from *Follow the Rabbit-Proof Fence* from the perspective of Molly, Daisy, or Gracie. If needed, conduct research to find out more information to help you create a vivid picture for your readers. Choose from the following topics:

- [ ] Write a **journal entry** from the perspective of the character you chose. Include the events and experiences detailed in the excerpt as well as your reflections on these events and experiences—were you afraid? frustrated? sad?

- [ ] Write a **letter** to one of the girls still living at the government settlement. Use details from the excerpt to describe how you escaped, the challenges of doing so, and the obstacles you encountered on your journey. Also, include your reflections on these events and experiences—were you nervous? confident? happy?

Establish Your Point of View Decide from which character's point of view you will write. Then, use the **first-person point of view** to retell the story. This means that your character participates in the story, relates events from her perspective, and uses the first-person pronouns *I, me, us,* and *we.* Draw on details from the text to represent your narrator vividly and accurately.

Conduct Additional Research To make the events and experiences in your retelling come alive for readers, briefly research topics that will help you better understand the setting and characters. For example, conduct research on life in the Australian Outback, the natural environment and wildlife of Australia, and techniques people use to survive in the wilderness.

Compare Your Retellings Once you have completed drafting, share your retelling with your group. Compare the ways in which your retellings are similar and different. Are you surprised at the way other members portrayed certain characters? Comment on each other's retellings, and offer ideas that will help others to improve their narratives:

- Did the character's actions and reactions make sense to you based on the details in the excerpt?
- Are there things that you found confusing or that did not align with your understanding of the excerpt?

Use the feedback from your group members to revise your retelling before handing it in to your teacher.

EVIDENCE LOG

Before moving on to a new selection, go to your Evidence Log, and record what you learned from *Follow the Rabbit-Proof Fence.*

STANDARDS

Writing

- Write narratives to develop real or imagined experiences or events using effective techniques, relevant descriptive details, and well-structured event sequences.
  a. Engage and orient the reader by establishing a context and point of view and introducing a narrator and/or characters; organize an event sequence that unfolds naturally and logically.
  b. Use narrative techniques, such as dialogue, pacing, description, and reflection, to develop experiences, events, and/or characters.
  d. Use precise words and phrases, relevant descriptive details, and sensory language to capture the action and convey experiences and events.
- With some guidance and support from peers and adults, develop and strengthen writing as needed by planning, revising, editing, rewriting, or trying a new approach, focusing on how well purpose and audience have been addressed.
- Conduct short research projects to answer a question, drawing on several sources and generating additional related, focused questions that allow for multiple avenues of exploration.

from Follow the Rabbit-Proof Fence **323**

PERSONALIZE FOR LEARNING

Strategic Support

Planning Some students may have trouble choosing the character whose perspective they find most inviting or may struggle to develop that character in an imaginative way. Invite such students to scan the selection and write any details that help them understand each sister. They should identify each girl's approximate age, the things she seems to want or be interested in, and the ways she relates to her sisters. Have students consider their lists of details and choose the character they find most appealing or feel they could develop most effectively in their own narrative.

DIGITAL PERSPECTIVES

Writing to Sources

For groups that choose the first option, review the usual elements of a journal entry, including the date, a description of recent events, and the writer's thoughts and feelings about those events. Point out that some writers include lots of personal information in their journals and that others are more reserved.

For groups that choose the second option, review the format of a letter, including the date and greeting, details of the escape from the settlement, and their reflections on what happened. Have members of the group discuss whether the girl left behind at the settlement is a friend or family member and what they want to communicate before they begin to write. For more support, see **Writing to Sources: First-Person Account.**

Establish Your Point of View Remind students that they must write their retelling from the first person point of view, writing as the character they chose but making sure to use the pronoun "I."

Conduct Additional Research Have students make notes of details they encounter during their research. They might think about including vivid descriptions of the landscape of the Australian Outback, or use some words, phrases, or expressions that would be unique to the place their character comes from.

Compare Your Retellings Encourage students to offer helpful and constructive comments when others in their group are sharing their retellings. Have students clarify anything that was unclear and use feedback they received to strengthen their writing as they revise.

Evidence Log Support students in completing their Evidence Log. This paced activity will help prepare them for the Performance-Based Assessment at the end of the unit.

FORMATIVE ASSESSMENT

Writing to Sources

If students have difficulty retelling events in their personal accounts, **then** encourage them to skim the excerpt from *Follow the Rabbit-Proof Fence* for ideas. For Reteach and Practice, see **Writing to Sources: First-Person Account (RP).**

Selection Test

Administer the *"from* Follow the Rabbit-Proof Fence" Selection Test, which is available in both print and digital formats online in Assessments.

PLANNING
SMALL-GROUP LEARNING • THE MOTH PRESENTS: ALEEZA KAZMI

The Moth Presents: Aleeza Kazmi

AUDIO SUMMARIES
Audio summaries of "The Moth Presents: Aleeza Kazmi" are available online in both English and Spanish in the Interactive Teacher's Edition or Unit Resources. Assigning these summaries prior to reading the selection may help students build additional background knowledge and set a context for their first read.

Summary
In the video "The Moth Presents: Aleeza Kazmi," Aleeza Kazmi tells a story about how she came to stand up for her identity. When she was six years old, she had a project to draw a self-portrait in school. She describes looking forward to coloring with oil pastels and used the same peach color that her friends used. Her teacher told her that peach was not "her color" and insisted that Kazmi color her portrait over with a brown crayon. As a result, the portrait looked worse and Kazmi felt terrible. Years later, in sixth grade, an incident reminded her of that portrait day, and she used the memory of disappointment to inspire her to stand up for herself.

Insight
This video illustrates how people come to understand the social construct of race. The content may be sensitive to students who have grappled with their racial identities or had them challenged by others.

ESSENTIAL QUESTION:
When is it right to take a stand?

Connection to Essential Question
Aleeza Kazmi stands up to a boy who tells her that she cannot call herself "brown." She has a right to determine her own identity, so he cannot tell her who she is.

SMALL-GROUP LEARNING PERFORMANCE TASK
When you take a stand, how much does winning matter?

Connection to Performance Tasks
Small-Group Learning Performance Task Aleeza Kazmi's interaction with the sixth-grade boy reminds her of her first-grade portrait day and the anger she felt when Miss Harrington imposed an identity on her. As she confronts the boy, Kazmi realizes that determining her own identity is something that is important to her. In that moment, as a sixth grader, she makes the choice to ensure a win as she defines her identity in her own terms.

UNIT PERFORMANCE-BASED ASSESSMENT
Is it important for people to make their own choices in life?

Unit Performance-Based Assessment This selection supports the idea that people should make their own choices. Students may use Kazmi's experiences to help them address the prompt.

DIGITAL PERSPECTIVES | Audio | Video | Document | Annotation Highlights | EL Highlights | Online Assessment

LESSON RESOURCES

	Making Meaning	Language Development	Effective Expression
Lesson	First Review Close Review Analyze the Media	Media Vocabulary	Speaking and Listening
Instructional Standards	**RI.10** By the end of the year, read and comprehend literary nonfiction . . . **L.6** Acquire and use accurately grade-appropriate general academic and domain-specific words and phrases . . . **SL.2** Analyze the purpose of information . . .		**SL.1** Engage effectively in a range of collaborative discussions . . . **SL.1.a** Come to discussions prepared . . . **SL.1.c** Pose questions . . . **SL.1.d** Acknowledge new information . . . **SL.2** Analyze the purpose of information . . .
STUDENT RESOURCES Available online in the Interactive Student Edition or Unit Resources	🔊 Selection Audio 📄 First-Review Guide: Media: Video 📄 Close-Review Guide: Media: Video	📄 Word Meaning	📄 Evidence Log
TEACHER RESOURCES **Selection Resources** Available online in the Interactive Teacher's Edition or Unit Resources	🔊 Audio Summaries	📄 Media Vocabulary	📄 Speaking and Listening: Group Discussion

Media Complexity Rubric: The Moth Presents: Aleeza Kazmi

Quantitative Measures

Format and Length: Video, 6:04 minutes

Qualitative Measures

Knowledge Demands ①—**②**—③—④—⑤	The story is mostly based on practical knowledge and experiences that students will find familiar and understandable.
Structure ①—②—**③**—④—⑤	The video shows a speaker telling a story, but there are no visual clues aside from some facial expressions. Rate of speaking is fast, but diction is clear, so the story is understandable.
Language Conventionality and Clarity ①—②—**③**—④—⑤	The language is conversational and contemporary. The speaker is telling about past events, but sometimes switches between past and present tense for effect. The speaker uses some lengthy or run-on sentences.
Levels of Meaning/Purpose ①—②—**③**—④—⑤	Plot events have a greater significance that is not fully revealed until the end of the story, but viewers can infer meaning throughout by interpreting feelings and relating to the speaker's experience.

FACILITATING

Jump Start

FIRST REVIEW Ask students to think about when it is important for people to speak up for themselves. How are people silenced? What does it mean to find a voice? Engage students in a discussion about how storytelling can provide a means to finding one's voice.

The Moth Presents: Aleeza Kazmi

Is it right to question somebody else's sense of identity? What if the person is six years old? Modeling questions such as this will help students connect "The Moth Presents: Aleeza Kazmi" to the Small-Group Performance Task assignment. Selection audio for the selection is available in the Interactive Teacher's Edition.

Media Vocabulary

Encourage students to discuss the media vocabulary. Have they seen or used these words or concepts before? Do they use them in their speech or writing? Have students brainstorm three examples of performances and share with the class.

FIRST REVIEW

Have students perform the steps of the first review independently:

WATCH: Remind students to watch how the speaker uses gestures and inflection as she speaks.

NOTE: Encourage students to listen to the speaker to note key ideas.

CONNECT: Encourage students to make connections beyond the video. If they cannot make connections to their own lives, have them consider other similar examples on television or in film.

RESPOND: Students will answer questions to demonstrate understanding.

Point out to students that while they will always complete the Respond step at the end of the first viewing, the other steps will probably happen somewhat concurrently. You may wish to print copies of the **First-Review Guide: Media-Video** for students to use.

MAKING MEANING

About the Speaker

Aleeza Kazmi is a student who attended the Beacon School in New York City. She intends to major in Journalism and Political Science. In her spare time, Aleeza can be found with her friends or in her backyard with her dogs.

STANDARDS

Reading Informational Text
By the end of the year, read and comprehend literary nonfiction at the high end of the grades 6–8 text complexity band independently and proficiently.

Language
Acquire and use accurately grade-appropriate general academic and domain-specific words and phrases; gather vocabulary knowledge when considering a word or phrase important to comprehension or expression.

The Moth Presents: Aleeza Kazmi

Media Vocabulary

These words will be useful to you as you analyze, discuss, and write about the video.

performance: entertainment presented before an audience, such as music or a drama	• Storytelling is the oldest form of performance art. • A storyteller can perform live or on a recording, from notes or without notes. • Stories can be rehearsed or improvised.
personal account: account of a personal experience, told from the first-person point of view	• A personal account can be written, performed live, or recorded. • When telling about a personal experience in front of a live audience, the storyteller (and audience) can get caught up in emotion.
volume and pacing: softness or loudness of one's voice and the rate at which one speaks (e.g., quickly or slowly)	• A speaker may vary the volume of his or her voice to convey emotion and to keep the audience's attention. • During a performance, a speaker may change his or her pacing by pausing, speeding up, or slowing down to emphasize ideas or express emotion.

First Review MEDIA: VIDEO

Apply these strategies as you conduct your first review. You will have an opportunity to complete a close review after your first review.

WATCH who speaks, *what* they say, and *how* they say it.

NOTE elements in the video that you find interesting and want to revisit.

CONNECT ideas in the video to other media you've experienced, texts you've read, or images you've seen.

RESPOND by completing the Comprehension Check at the end.

PERSONALIZE FOR LEARNING

English Language Support

Taking Notes Support students as they watch the video. Form groups and have them watch the video in roughly 60-second segments. After each segment plays, have students take notes on key ideas and details. Ask students to compare their notes. Then go on to the next segment, repeating the process until students have watched the entire video. **ALL LEVELS**

DIGITAL PERSPECTIVES

MEDIA | VIDEO

The Moth Presents: Aleeza Kazmi

BACKGROUND

The Moth is a nonprofit organization devoted to the art and craft of storytelling. Established in 1997, The Moth has featured thousands of stories that showcase a wide range of human experiences. The Moth's storytellers present their narratives live and without notes to standing-room-only crowds throughout the world. Each of The Moth's shows centers around a different theme, which the featured storytellers explore in distinct, and often unexpected, ways. Some of the storytellers are experienced in the art and craft of narration, whereas others have never told a story in performance before. The stories featured in The Moth's shows are recorded for broadcast and can be heard on many National Public Radio radio stations.

SCAN FOR MULTIMEDIA

NOTES

● CLOSER REVIEW

Circulate among groups as students conduct their close review. Suggest that groups close review 4:50–5:55 in the video. Encourage them to talk about what they note. If needed, provide the following support.

NOTE: Have students note details in the video that explain how and why Aleeza Kazmi takes a stand, or work with small groups to have students participate while you note them together.

Possible response: Aleeza describes her interaction with a boy in a new school. She says she screams at him.

QUESTION: Guide students to consider what these details might tell them. Ask what a viewer can infer from the details, and accept student responses.

Possible response: Aleeza mentions that her six-year-old self is screaming, which shows that the earlier experience has shaped her response to the boy's question. She also mentions that she herself is screaming at the boy who questions her race, from which we can infer that she is angry that anyone is questioning her view of herself.

CONCLUDE: Help students to formulate conclusions about the importance of these details in the video. Ask students why the storyteller might have included these details.

Possible response: The detail about Aleeza's six-year-old self screaming is important because it shows that she has stayed angry at the experience of having someone doubt her own sense of identity. She screams at the boy because he questions her racial identity, causing her to remember the earlier experience. This shows that she now can stand up for her own sense of identity.

PERSONALIZE FOR LEARNING

Challenge

Storytelling Encourage students to have their own storytelling series inspired by The Moth, using the theme "Taking a Stand." With Aleeza Kazmi's story as inspiration, have them tell a three-to five-minute story about an incident in their own lives where they stood up for themselves. Remind them to prepare the story in advance and to use sensory details that bring the story to life. Invite other classes to the storytelling session.

FACILITATING

Comprehension Check

Possible responses:

1. Aleeza is excited about the self-portrait project because she feels like she has become a good artist and she wants to show off her new skills.
2. Aleeza thinks peach is a good color because all of her friends use peach and she thinks they are all the same.
3. Miss Harrington tells Aleeza that she has used the wrong color and has her "fix" the drawing by coloring the skin with a brown crayon. Miss Harrington also hangs up the picture, which Aleeza is no longer proud of.
4. Aleeza takes a stand when a boy asks her what her race is. At first, she answers that she is brown. When the boy tells her that brown is not a race, Aleeza tells him that he cannot tell her what she is.

Close Review

If needed, model close reviewing by using the Close Review Notes in the Interactive Teacher's Edition.

Remind students to use Accountable Talk in their discussions and to support one another as they complete the close review.

Analyze the Media

1. **Responses will vary by group.** Remind students to explain why they chose the section they presented to the group members.
2. **Possible response:** I think Aleeza told the story both to entertain and to express her point of view. Her sincerity and personal account help viewers understand her viewpoint because without knowing how Aleeza felt as a six-year-old forced to change her self-portrait, people might not understand why she does not want anyone to try to define her race or color.
3. **Responses will vary by group.** Groups should support their answers with evidence from the video.

Media Vocabulary

For more support, see **Media Vocabulary**.

Word Network

Possible words: *self-portrait, identity, race*

MAKING MEANING

Comprehension Check

Complete the following items after you finish your first review. Review and clarify details with your group.

1. Why was Aleeza excited about the self-portrait project?

2. Why did she think peach was a good color to use?

3. What did Miss Harrington do that upset Aleeza?

4. How does Aleeza finally take a stand?

MEDIA VOCABULARY

Use these words as you discuss and write about the video.

performance
personal account
volume and pacing

WORD NETWORK

Add interesting words related to taking a stand from the text to your Word Network.

Close Review

Watch the video, or parts of it, again. Write down any new observations that seem important. What **questions** do you have? What can you **conclude**?

Analyze the Media

📓 **Notebook** Complete the activities.

1. **Present and Discuss** Choose the section of the video you found most interesting or powerful. Explain what you noticed in the section, what questions it raised for you, and what conclusions you reached about it.

2. **Review and Synthesize** With your group, review the video. What do you think Aleeza's purpose was in telling her story? How does Aleeza's sincerity in her storytelling help viewers understand her perspective and her experience?

3. **Essential Question:** *When is it right to take a stand?* What has this video taught you about taking a stand? Discuss with your group.

STANDARDS
Speaking and Listening
Analyze the purpose of information presented in diverse media and formats and evaluate the motives behind its presentation.

326 UNIT 3 • WHAT MATTERS

FORMATIVE ASSESSMENT

Analyze the Media

If students struggle to close review the video, **then** provide the **The Moth Presents: Aleeza Kazmi: Media Questions** available online in the Interactive Teacher's Edition or Unit Resources. Answers and DOK levels are also available.

Media Vocabulary

If students struggle to understand the term *personal account*, **then** have them review the definition and ask them to explain whether Aleeza Kazmi's story is personal account.

326 UNIT 3 • WHAT MATTERS

EFFECTIVE EXPRESSION

Speaking and Listening

Assignment
Take part in a **group discussion** about Aleeza Kazmi's story. Choose from the following topics:

☐ How does Kazmi's story support the idea that it is important to stand up for yourself and your beliefs?

☐ How does Kazmi's story support the idea that each person should be able to determine her or his own identity?

Prepare for the Discussion To prepare for the discussion, review the video and take notes on the following aspects:

- sections of the video in which Kazmi discusses specific central ideas that are relevant to your discussion topic
- ideas that Kazmi **implies**, or suggests, but does not state directly
- descriptive details that Kazmi uses to develop her story and capture her audience's attention
- **direct quotations**, or Kazmi's exact words, that are related to your discussion topic
- the ways in which Kazmi delivers her story—changes in her tone that indicate emotion, emphasis she places on specific words or phrases, key points she repeats for emphasis

Review your notes and consider the ways in which Kazmi deals will both the internal and external conflicts created by her experience. An **internal conflict** takes place in a person's mind, as when he or she is struggling with opposing feelings. An **external conflict** takes place between a person and an outside force, such as another person or the environment with which they are surrounded. Consider how Kazmi's conflicts and the ways in which she resolves them relate to your discussion topic.

During the Discussion Listen to the ideas of other members of your group and consider the ways in which they are similar to and different from your own. To connect your own ideas with the ideas of other group members, ask questions that help to clarify the relationship between the different ideas expressed. Use your notes to support your ideas when responding to questions from other group members. Don't be afraid to change your ideas or views if another group member offers new thoughts or information that you agree with, provided that the ideas are well supported with evidence.

THE MOTH PRESENTS: ALEEZA KAZMI

EVIDENCE LOG
Before moving on to a new selection, go to your Evidence Log, and record what you learned from "The Moth Presents: Aleeza Kazmi."

STANDARDS
Speaking and Listening
- Engage effectively in a range of collaborative discussions with diverse partners on *grade 8 topics, texts, and issues,* building on others' ideas and expressing their own clearly.
  a. Come to discussions prepared, having read or researched material under study; explicitly draw on that preparation by referring to evidence on the topic, text, or issue to probe and reflect on ideas under discussion.
  c. Pose questions that connect the ideas of several speakers and respond to others' questions and comments with relevant evidence, observations, and ideas.
  d. Acknowledge new information expressed by others, and, when warranted, qualify or justify their own views in light of the evidence presented.
- Analyze the purpose of information presented in diverse media and formats and evaluate the motives behind its presentation.

DIGITAL PERSPECTIVES

Speaking and Listening

If students are having difficulty choosing the discussion topic, point out that both topics require that students use evidence from the video to support their main points. Explain that the first topic relates to standing up for oneself generally and the second topic relates to identity. Students who are uncomfortable discussing issues of identity and determining one's own identity may prefer to discuss the first topic. Students who are interested in questions of identity, including race, may be more interested in the second topic.

Prepare for the Discussion Have students use the bulleted list to help them take notes as they view the video again. Remind them to keep their assignment prompt in mind as they look for evidence. Students should write down Aleeza Kazmi's exact words as they watch the video so that they can use direct quotations in the discussion. They should also note how she uses gestures, pauses, inflection, and volume as she tells the story, and how her speaking skills help to make her points.

During the Discussion When students hold the discussion, have them use the notes that they have taken so that they can support their points with evidence from the video. As they pose questions to each other about different points, encourage them to try to stay on topic, always keeping the discussion prompt in mind. For more support, see **Speaking and Listening: Group Discussion.**

Evidence Log Support students in completing their Evidence Log. This paced activity will help prepare them for the Performance-Based Assessment at the end of the unit.

FORMATIVE ASSESSMENT
Speaking and Listening

If one or two students are dominating the group discussion, **then** remind students to take turns during the discussion so that each member has a chance to speak.

FACILITATING

Deliver an Oral Presentation

Explain to students that for the argument skit, each group member will help to consider the conflicts in each text and prepare an oral presentation. Before groups begin work on their projects, have them clearly differentiate the role each group member will play. Remind groups to consult the schedule for Small-Group Learning to guide their work during the Performance Task.

Students should complete the assignment using presentation software to take advantage of text, graphics, and sound features.

Plan With Your Group

Analyze the Text Students should link each issue they identify to the author's or speaker's purpose. Suggest that they analyze details in each selection to identify the topic about which each person feels most strongly as well as his or her claim or central idea.

Gather Evidence and Media Examples After groups fill in the chart, have them return to the selections to choose details that relate strongly to the prompt for the presentation. Encourage groups to assemble and review a list of these details to help them craft a group position statement. The statement will help guide them as they assign roles and draft a script.

PERFORMANCE TASK: SPEAKING AND LISTENING FOCUS

SOURCES
- WORDS DO NOT PAY
- from FOLLOW THE RABBIT-PROOF FENCE
- THE MOTH PRESENTS: ALEEZA KAZMI

STANDARDS
Speaking and Listening
Engage effectively in a range of collaborative discussions with diverse partners on *grade 8 topics, texts, and issues*, building on others' ideas and expressing their own clearly.
a. Come to discussions prepared, having read or researched material under study; explicitly draw on that preparation by referring to evidence on the topic, text, or issue to probe and reflect on ideas under discussion.

Deliver an Oral Presentation

Assignment
The selections in this section present people who took a stand, often against hopeless odds. Each one demonstrates courage and determination. Their efforts, however, are not always successful. They raise questions about ideas of winning and losing when one acts on principle. Work with your group to prepare and deliver an **oral presentation** in response to this question:

> When you take a stand, how much does winning matter?

Plan With Your Group

Analyze the Texts All of the people featured in the Small-Group readings took a stand in words, actions, or both. In each case, the people or group they opposed were powerful, and the odds of success in opposing them were low. Review the texts and think about what was at stake for Chief Joseph, the three Mardu sisters, and Aleeza Kami. Consider how these people or groups probably viewed their chances of success and why they chose to take a stand. With your group, discuss your observations and ideas, and note them in the chart.

TITLE	WHOM/WHAT THEY OPPOSED AND CHANCES OF SUCCESS
Words Do Not Pay	
from Follow the Rabbit-Proof Fence	
The Moth Presents: Aleeza Kazmi	

Determine Your Position and Gather Evidence As you discuss the texts, work toward a consensus about the position you will present. Will you argue that taking a stand is valuable, even if the result is failure? Or will you argue that people should measure the possibility of success before taking a stand against something? Use evidence from the texts to support your claims. Identify passages to quote directly, details to paraphrase, and situations to summarize and use as examples.

AUTHOR'S PERSPECTIVE — Ernest Morrell, Ph.D.

Mastering Classroom Talk Complex texts can be intimidating and alien to some students, especially those who have had limited exposure to such texts. However, these same students often show deep critical and analytical skills when considering popular culture. Teachers can use their students' background knowledge of popular culture and their enthusiasm for it to increase motivation and classroom talk, especially debate skills, small-group work, and formal public presentations. Start by incorporating elements of popular culture such as rap and hip-hop, movies, or sports into a traditional unit of study. Place popular culture alongside the other historical/literacy periods covered in the unit so students can use their knowledge of the familiar works as a lens through which to evaluate the new ones. Second, have students evaluate one literary work in the program, such as a poem, alongside a contemporary reference of their choice. This approach helps students gain the understanding and confidence they need to discuss classroom texts and enhance their critical perspectives.

ESSENTIAL QUESTION: When is it right to take a stand?

DIGITAL PERSPECTIVES

Organize Your Ideas. As a group, organize the script for your skit. Each member of the group should play a character who expresses his or her ideas in response to the question "What can you learn from people who have chosen to take a stand?" Each character should present evidence from the text to support his or her points.

TASK	ASSIGNED TO

Rehearse With Your Group

Practice With Your Group Practice delivering your oral presentation. Then, use this checklist to evaluate the effectiveness of your first run-through. If you need to improve the content, rewrite or reorganize the material. If you need to improve the delivery, practice again, speaking clearly and with energy and expression.

CONTENT	PRESENTATION TECHNIQUES
☐ Claims and evidence are presented clearly and in a logical order.	☐ Each speaker presents with energy, enthusiasm, and expression.
☐ Claims and reasons are effectively supported with textual evidence.	☐ Speakers do not rush through the presentation, nor do they speak too slowly.
☐ The content engages viewers' interest from start to finish.	☐ Speakers behave with an appropriate level of formality.
☐ Transitions from section to section are smooth.	

Fine-Tune the Content To make your oral presentation stronger, you may need to reorder ideas, add or change supporting reasons, or replace evidence. Review the presentation, adding material or finding better ways to phrase your ideas.

Improve Use of Media If you have included images or other media, make sure they are necessary and effective. If any media choices are not directly related to your claims and evidence, or are simply distracting, take them out of the presentation.

Brush Up on Your Presentation Techniques Practice your oral presentation before you present it to the class. Pay attention to all aspects of your delivery, including how you use your voice and how you conduct yourself in front of the class.

Present and Evaluate

When you deliver your oral presentation, make sure that all of you have considered each of the checklist items. As you listen to other groups' presentations, consider their claims and reasoning as you evaluate how well they meet the requirements.

STANDARDS
Speaking and Listening
Present claims and findings, emphasizing salient points in a focused, coherent manner with relevant evidence, sound valid reasoning, and well-chosen details; use appropriate eye contact, adequate volume, and clear pronunciation.

Performance Task: Deliver an Oral Presentation **329**

Organize Your Ideas As group members work on the script, remind them that, once they have outlined the key argument for each character from the selections, they should work to make sure that the characters talk to each other, addressing each other's points.

Rehearse With Your Group

Practice With Your Group Make sure that groups include visuals they plan to use in the final presentation in this first run-through.

Fine-Tune the Content Have groups make sure their presentations address the prompt.

Improve Your Use of Media Remind groups to revisit the group's consensus or position statement and revise if necessary.

Brush Up on Your Presentation Techniques Point out to students that since they are acting out a skit, their characters need to address each other, speaking loudly enough for the audience to hear.

Present and Evaluate

Before beginning the presentations, set the expectations for the audience. You may wish to have students consider these questions as groups present:

- What is each character's claim?
- What were some of their supporting ideas?
- Which visuals best illustrated their claims?
- What presentation skills did this group excel at?

After the presenting group listens to student feedback, encourage members to take notes so that they can incorporate useful ideas into their next presentation.

PERSONALIZE FOR LEARNING

Strategic Support

Dialogue If students have difficulty turning their arguments into dialogue, encourage them to review the main claim for each character. Then have students improvise in character. Explain that when they improvise, they will each speak in character about why a specific issue is important enough to fight for. Characters should try to convince one another that their issues are worthwhile. After improvising, have students take notes for their scripts.

Small-Group Learning **329**

OVERVIEW

INDEPENDENT LEARNING

When is it right to take a stand?

Encourage students to think carefully about what they have already learned and what more they want to know about the unit topic of what matters to people and why some issues are worth fighting for. This is a key first step to previewing and selecting the text or media they will read or review in Independent Learning.

Independent Learning Strategies ▶

Review the Learning Strategies with students and explain that as they work through Independent Learning they will develop strategies to work on their own.

- Have students watch the video on Independent Learning Strategies.
- A video on this topic is available online in the Professional Development Center.

Students should include any favorite strategies that they might have devised on their own during Whole-Class and Small-Group Learning. For example, for the strategy "Create a schedule," students might include:

- Understand the goals and deadlines.
- Make a schedule for what to do each day.

Block Scheduling

Each day in this Pacing Plan represents a 40–50-minute class period. Teachers using block scheduling may combine days to reflect their class schedule. In addition, teachers may revise pacing to differentiate and support core instruction by integrating components and resources as students require.

📅 **Pacing Plan**

OVERVIEW: INDEPENDENT LEARNING

ESSENTIAL QUESTION:

When is it right to take a stand?

As you have learned from the selections you have read so far, "taking a stand" can be defined in many ways—it can be small or large, personal or political, for the benefit of an individual or an entire community. In this section, you will choose one additional selection about this topic for your final reading experience in this unit. Follow these steps to help you choose.

Look Back Think about the selections you have already read. What more do you want to know about taking a stand?

Look Ahead Preview the selections by reading the descriptions. Which one seems most interesting and appealing to you?

Look Inside Take a few minutes to scan through the text you chose. Choose a different one if this text doesn't meet your needs.

Independent Learning Strategies

Throughout your life, in school, in your community, and in your career, you will need to rely on yourself to learn and work on your own. Review these strategies and the actions you can take to practice them during Independent Learning. Add ideas of your own for each category.

STRATEGY	ACTION PLAN
Create a schedule	• Understand your goals and deadlines. • Make a plan for what to do each day. •
Practice what you have learned	• Use first-read and close-read strategies to deepen your understanding. • After you read, evaluate usefulness of the evidence to help you understand the topic. • Consider the quality and reliability of the source. •
Take notes	• Record important ideas and information. • Review your notes before sharing with the group. •

330 UNIT 3 • WHAT MATTERS

SCAN FOR MULTIMEDIA

Pacing Plan:

1 | 2 | 3 Introduce Whole-Class Learning | 4 | 5 | 6 | 7 | 8 Barrington Irving, Pilot and Educator | 9 | 10 | 11 | 12 | 13 Three Cheers for the Nanny State | 14 | 15 Ban the Ban! • Soda's a Problem but... | 16 | 17 | 18 Performance Task

Unit Introduction

Choose one selection. Selections are available online only.

CONTENTS

MEMOIR

from Through My Eyes
Ruby Bridges

A young girl's story about breaking the segregation barrier takes place in the context of one of the most important historical events of our time.

POETRY

The Unknown Citizen
W. H. Auden

A renowned poet criticizes a society that no longer values individuals and their emotions and beliefs.

BIOGRAPHY

Harriet Tubman: Conductor on the Underground Railroad
Ann Petry

An escaped slave risks her freedom and her life to lead others to safety.

PERFORMANCE-BASED ASSESSMENT PREP

Review Evidence for an Argument
Complete your Evidence Log for the unit by evaluating what you have learned and synthesizing the information you have recorded.

SCAN FOR MULTIMEDIA

Overview: Independent Learning **331**

DIGITAL PERSPECTIVES

Contents

Selections Encourage students to scan and preview the selections before choosing the one they would like to read or review. Suggest that they consider the genre and subject matter of each one before making their decision. You can use the information on the following Planning pages to advise students in making their choice.

Remind students that the selections for Independent Learning are only available in the Interactive Student Edition. Allow students who do not have digital access at home to preview the selections or review the media selection(s) using classroom or computer lab technology. Then either have students print the selection they choose or provide a printout for them.

Performance Based-Assessment Prep
Review Evidence for an Argument Point out to students that collecting evidence during Independent Learning is the last step in completing their Evidence Log. After they finish their independent reading, they will synthesize all the evidence they have compiled in the unit.

The evidence students collect will serve as the primary source of information they will use to complete the writing and oral presentation for the Performance-Based Assessment at the end of the unit.

PLANNING INDEPENDENT LEARNING

Through My Eyes

Summary

Through My Eyes is a memoir by Ruby Bridges. She grew up in New Orleans, and she was one of the first black children in the city who went from a segregated school to an integrated one. As part of the integration process, black children were given a very difficult test. Five-year-old Ruby did very well on it; she was one of the few who could choose to switch schools. The NAACP and her mother wanted Ruby to go to the integrated school, though her father feared that she would be in danger if she did. Ruby did not understand the historical value of the day. There was a large crowd of segregationist protestors, and police and her mother protected her on her way. At the time, she didn't realize this was anything out of the ordinary for a big school.

Insight

This selection shows what the early days of integration were like from a child's perspective. It also shows how some people, like Ruby's father, were worried about the outcome.

SELECTION RESOURCES

- First-Read Guide: Nonfiction
- Close-Read Guide: Nonfiction
- Through My Eyes: Text Questions
- Audio Summaries
- Selection Audio
- Selection Test

Connection to Essential Question

The Essential Question is *When is it right to take a stand?* This memoir provides a first-person account of a child who lived in a moment in history when people decided the risks of integration were worth the rewards.

Connection to Performance-Based Assessment

Ruby Bridges's story provides students a strong angle on the prompt "Is it important for people to make their own choices in life?" Ruby's mother decided that the opportunity to get a better education for her daughter, and thus better opportunities in later life, was worth it.

Text Complexity Rubric: Through My Eyes

Quantitative Measures

Lexile: 920 Text Length: 1,213 words

Qualitative Measures

Knowledge Demands ①—**②**—③—④—⑤	Some knowledge of segregation in the south in 1960s is helpful, and the experiences are not common to readers, but the content is clearly explained from the view of the child.
Structure ①—**②**—③—④—⑤	Story is told chronologically and in straightforward way, with all of the events and details clearly explained. Subheadings divide text into sections, making it easy to navigate.
Language Conventionality and Clarity ①—**②**—③—④—⑤	Language is clear and straightforward, with no figurative language. Sentences are mostly simple.
Levels of Meaning/Purpose ①—**②**—③—④—⑤	Purpose of autobiographic story is revealed early and is clearly explained. The young girl's memories and feelings are mostly explicit.

332A UNIT 3 • WHAT MATTERS

The Unknown Citizen

Summary

"The Unknown Citizen," a poem by W. H. Auden, details the life of a man through the details that are available in public reports. He had a job. He belonged to the union. He was for peace during peacetime but went to war when war was being fought. The speaker includes details of hospital records and of the man's family. The speaker concludes that the man was normal, and that he must have been happy because there is no record that he wasn't.

Insight

This poem critiques centralized control and monitoring of people's lives and implies that a "normal" life is not necessarily a good one. It also shows what cannot be captured in data.

Connection to Essential Question

As students read this poem, they may question the quality of the unknown citizen's life, based on the data provided. The Essential Question is *When is it right to take a stand?* Students may determine that the poet was challenging a state where statistics like these would be collected by the government.

Connection to Performance-Based Assessment

This poem may support students as they respond to the Performance-Based Assessment prompt: "Is it important for people to make their own choices in life?" The speaker implies that tracking people and imposing narrow expectations on them stops people from making their own choices.

SELECTION RESOURCES

- First-Read Guide: Poetry
- Close-Read Guide: Poetry
- The Unknown Citizen: Text Questions
- Audio Summaries
- Selection Audio
- Selection Test

Text Complexity Rubric: The Unknown Citizen

Quantitative Measures

Lexile: NP   Text Length: 29 lines

Qualitative Measures

Knowledge Demands (4 of 5)	The poem's meaning is based on themes of individuality and attitudes toward government control, which may not be familiar to all readers.
Structure (3 of 5)	Poem contains some rhyming couplets; rhyme scheme changes several times, so it is not always predictable; poem is not divided into stanzas, which may make pacing a little harder for readers.
Language Conventionality and Clarity (3 of 5)	Language has somewhat formal style, with a mix of full sentences and phrases. Some vocabulary or phrasing is complex and above level.
Levels of Meaning/Purpose (4 of 5)	Poem contains multiple levels of meaning, with twist of irony in ending, and subtle humor throughout the poem that may not be immediately obvious to readers.

Independent Learning   332B

PLANNING   INDEPENDENT LEARNING

SELECTION RESOURCES

- First-Read Guide: Nonfiction
- Close-Read Guide: Nonfiction
- Harriet Tubman: Text Questions
- Audio Summaries
- Selection Audio
- Selection Test

Harriet Tubman: Conductor on the Underground Railroad

Summary

In the biography *Harriet Tubman: Conductor on the Underground Railroad,* author Ann Petry describes how Harriet Tubman helped over 300 slaves escape to freedom. Harriet Tubman was herself born into slavery, but as a young woman escaped to the North and became a free person. After gaining her own freedom, Tubman began helping other enslaved people escape. One trip she took was particularly difficult. Laws in the United States had become more strict, and she decided to go to Canada. She led eleven people further north than she had ever gone. She was unable to use a trusted Underground Railroad stop for food and shelter, and the group had to keep up an exhausting pace. Along the way, she told stories of others who had made the journey, and who could help.

Insight

This selection describes the danger and difficulty that people escaping to freedom faced, and the courage that saw them through.

Connection to Essential Question

Harriet Tubman's work modeled one woman's answer to the Essential Question: *"Is it important for people to make their own choices in life?"* Her bravery and knowledge kept people motivated to live freely rather than live as slaves. It's hard to think of a practice that deserved protest and resistance more than slavery did.

Connection to Performance-Based Assessment

The prompt is "How can people determine what matters to them and make their own choices in life?" The journey to freedom was very hard, and life in the free north wasn't easy. Tubman and those who helped the travelers along the way knew it was worth the struggle.

Text Complexity Rubric: Harriet Tubman: Conductor on the Underground Railroad

Quantitative Measures

Lexile: 1000   Text Length: 3,581 words

Qualitative Measures

Knowledge Demands ①—②—**❸**—④—⑤	Some prior knowledge is needed about slavery, the Underground Railroad, and Harriet Tubman; references are made to multiple locations and names of those who helped escaped slaves.
Structure ①—②—**❸**—④—⑤	Text is dense and lengthy, but story is told chronologically and with straightforward organization. Connection between events is clear and logical.
Language Conventionality and Clarity ①—②—**❸**—④—⑤	Language is concrete and descriptive; many sentences are lengthy, with complex syntax and multiple clauses; there is some difficult vocabulary.
Levels of Meaning/Purpose ①—**❷**—③—④—⑤	Purpose is explicit and narrowly focused; there are many details, but relationship of details to main events is clear.

332C UNIT 3 • WHAT MATTERS

MY NOTES

ADVISING

You may wish to direct students to use the generic **First-Read** and **Close-Read Guides** in the Print Student Edition. Alternatively, you may wish to print copies of the genre-specific **First-Read** and **Close-Read Guides** for students. These are available online in the Interactive Student Edition or Unit Resources.

FIRST READ

Students should perform the steps of the first read independently:

NOTICE: Students should focus on the basic elements of the text to ensure they understand what is happening.

ANNOTATE: Students should mark any passages they wish to revisit during their close read.

CONNECT: Students should increase their understanding by connecting what they've read to other texts or personal experiences.

RESPOND: Students will write a summary to demonstrate their understanding.

Point out to students that while they will always complete the Respond step at the end of the first read, the other steps will probably happen somewhat concurrently. Remind students that they will revisit their first-read annotations during the close read.

> After students have completed the First-Read Guide, you may wish to assign the Comprehension Check and Analyze the Text questions for the selection that are available in the Interactive Teacher's Edition.

Anchor Standards

In the first two sections of the unit, students worked with the whole class and in small groups to gain topical knowledge and greater understanding of the skills required by the anchor standards. In this section, they are asked to work independently, applying what they have learned and demonstrating increased readiness for college and career.

INDEPENDENT LEARNING

First-Read Guide

Use this page to record your first-read ideas.

Selection Title: _____

Tool Kit
First-Read Guide and Model Annotation

NOTICE new information or ideas you learn about the unit topic as you first read this text.

ANNOTATE by marking vocabulary and key passages you want to revisit.

CONNECT ideas within the selection to other knowledge and the selections you have read.

RESPOND by writing a brief summary of the selection.

STANDARD
Reading Read and comprehend complex literary and informational texts independently and proficiently.

332 UNIT 3 • WHAT MATTERS

PERSONALIZE FOR LEARNING

Strategic Support

Text Connections To help students make connections to the text, remind them that ideas in a text may spark memories in readers. The memories may be connected to real-life experiences or something the student previously read or discovered through media. Point out that these connections tap into what students already know. They make a text interesting and often help readers better understand what the text means.

To pursue and support the text connections approach, ask students to annotate passages that trigger memories and connections for them. Students can organize their ideas in a chart. One column ("The Text") should show annotated passages, enclosed in quotation marks. In the other column ("My Connection"), students can use their own words to describe the connection they made to the text. Students can then use this chart to complete the First-Read Guide.

ESSENTIAL QUESTION: When is it right to take a stand?

Close-Read Guide

Use this page to record your close-read ideas.

🔧 **Tool Kit**
Close-Read Guide and Model Annotation

Selection Title: _____

Close Read the Text

Revisit sections of the text you marked during your first read. Read these sections closely and **annotate** what you notice. Ask yourself **questions** about the text. What can you **conclude**? Write down your ideas.

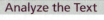

Analyze the Text

Think about the author's choices of patterns, structure, techniques, and ideas included in the text. Select one, and record your thoughts about what this choice conveys.

QuickWrite

Pick a paragraph from the text that grabbed your interest. Explain the power of this passage.

▬ **STANDARD**
Reading Read and comprehend complex literary and informational texts independently and proficiently.

ADVISING

Share Your Independent Learning

Prepare to Share
Explain to students that sharing what they learned from their Independent Learning selection provides classmates who read a different selection with an opportunity to consider the text as a source of evidence during the Performance-Based Assessment. As students prepare to share, remind them to highlight how their selection contributed to their knowledge of the concept of what matters to people as well as how the selection connects to the question *Is it important for people to make their own choices in life?*

Learn From Your Classmates
As students discuss the Independent Learning selections, direct them to take particular note of how their classmates' chosen selections align with their current position on the Performance-Based Assessment question.

Reflect
Students may want to add their reflection to their Evidence Log, particularly if their insight relates to a specific selection from the unit.

MAKE IT INTERACTIVE
Have students participate in a fishbowl or panel discussion. Group students who read the same selection and have them field questions from the rest of the class. Guide students to rephrase questions in their answers, and use specific examples from the text to support their responses. Some questions students might ask and answer are *Did your ideas about what matters change as you read the selection? Why or why not? Which passages struck you as being particularly relevant to the question* How can people determine what matters to them and make their own choices in life?

Evidence Log Support students in completing their Evidence Log. This paced activity will help prepare them for the Performance-Based Assessment at the end of the unit.

INDEPENDENT LEARNING

EVIDENCE LOG
Go to your Evidence Log, and record what you learned from the text you read.

Share Your Independent Learning

Prepare to Share
When is it right to take a stand?

Even when you read something independently, you can continue to grow by sharing what you have learned with others. Reflect on the text you explored independently, and take notes about its connection to the unit. As you take notes, consider why this text belongs in this unit.

Learn From Your Classmates
Discuss It Share your ideas about the text you explored on your own. As you talk with your classmates, jot down ideas that you learn from them.

Reflect
Mark the most important insight you gained from these writing and discussion activities. Explain how this idea adds to your understanding of the topic.

STANDARDS
Speaking and Listening
Engage effectively in a range of collaborative discussions with diverse partners on *grade 8 topics, texts, and issues,* building on others' ideas and expressing their own clearly.

AUTHOR'S PERSPECTIVE — Ernest Morrell, Ph.D.

Preparing Students to Be Powerful Speakers Use these suggestions to help students develop the ability to speak confidently in large discussions or presentations:

1. To help students overcome their fear of public speaking, have them visualize success, practice and get feedback on their speech, and exercise briefly before the speech to release stress.
2. Emphasize the importance of speaking loudly and clearly when presenting to the class. The farther away a listener is, the louder a speaker must talk to be heard clearly. Also have students practice speaking with clarity and articulation, paying special attention to not slurring contractions, reversing sounds, omitting letters, and adding letters.
3. As students share in whole groups, remind them to listen carefully and fully before responding, take notes while listening so they can respond on point, and speak with courtesy and

PERFORMANCE-BASED ASSESSMENT PREP

Review Evidence for an Argument

At the beginning of this unit you took a position on the following question:

Is it important for people to make their own choices in life?

✎ EVIDENCE LOG

Review your Evidence Log and your QuickWrite from the beginning of the unit. Has your position changed?

☐ YES	☐ NO
Identify at least three pieces of evidence that convinced you to change your mind.	Identify at least three new pieces of evidence that reinforced your initial position.
1.	1.
2.	2.
3.	3.

State your position: _____

_____

_____

Identify a possible counterclaim, or opposing position: _____

_____

_____

Evaluate the Strength of Your Evidence Consider your argument. Do you have enough evidence to support your claim? Do you have enough evidence to refute a counterclaim? If not, make a plan.

☐ Do more research   ☐ Talk with my classmates

☐ Reread a selection   ☐ Ask an expert

☐ Other: _____

⋮≡ STANDARDS

Writing
Write arguments to support claims with clear reasons and relevant evidence.
  a. Introduce claim(s), acknowledge and distinguish the claim(s) from alternate or opposing claims, and organize the reasons and evidence logically.
  b. Support claim(s) with logical reasoning and relevant evidence, using accurate, credible sources and demonstrating an understanding of the topic or text.

DIGITAL PERSPECTIVES

Review Evidence for an Argument

Evidence Log Students should understand that their position on an issue can evolve as they learn more about the subject and are exposed to additional points of view. Point out that just because they took an initial position on the question *Is it important for people to make their own choices in life?* doesn't mean that their position can't change after careful consideration of their learning and evidence.

Evaluate the Strength of Your Evidence Remind students that a strong argument is composed of a claim supported by logical reasoning and relevant evidence. Writers should ask themselves *What evidence could be used to support a counterclaim? Am I prepared to address that evidence and refute it with additional evidence supporting my own claim? Does my evidence come from credible sources? Is it correctly attributed? Have I made the connections between my quotations or paraphrases and my own ideas obvious to the reader?* Guide students to return to the selections or do additional research as needed.

---

respect. They may also wish to draft points for a response quickly before speaking.

4. To field questions, tell students to repeat the question before answering it, as this allows a few seconds to think about a response as well as make sure that everyone hears the question.

ASSESSING

Writing to Sources: Argument

Students should complete the Performance-Based Assessment independently, with little to no input or feedback during the process. Students should use word processing software to take advantage of editing tools and features.

Prior to beginning the assignment, ask students to think about the various characters in the selections they have read who have tried to make their own choices about what matters to them. Encourage them to discuss the obstacles characters had to overcome to make these choices.

Review the Elements of Effective Argument Students can review the work they did earlier in the unit as they complete the Performance-Based Assessment. They may also consult other resources such as:

- the elements of an effective argument, including a clear claim, relevant evidence, possible counterclaims, and a strong conclusion, available in Whole-Class Learning
- their Evidence Log
- their Word Network

Although students will use evidence from the unit selections for their argument, they may need to collect additional evidence, including facts, statistics, anecdotes, quotations from authorities, or examples that support their position.

PERFORMANCE-BASED ASSESSMENT

SOURCES
- WHOLE-CLASS SELECTIONS
- SMALL-GROUP SELECTIONS
- INDEPENDENT-LEARNING SELECTION

WORD NETWORK
As you write and revise your argument, use your Word Network to help vary your word choices.

STANDARDS
Writing
- Write arguments to support claims with clear reasons and relevant evidence.
- Draw evidence from literary or informational texts to support analysis, reflection, and research.
- Write routinely over extended time frames and shorter time frames for a range of discipline-specific tasks, purposes, and audiences.

PART 1
Writing to Sources: Argument

In this unit, you read about various people who take a stand for what matters. In some cases, they are the authors themselves, writing to convince others to adopt their point of view. In others, the authors or their subjects are discovering what matters to them.

> **Assignment**
> Write an **argument** in which you state and defend a claim in response to the following question:
>
> > Is it important for people to make their own choices in life?
>
> Use examples from the selections you read, viewed, and researched in this unit to support and verify your claim. Organize your ideas so that they flow logically and are easy for readers to follow. Use a formal style and tone.

Reread the Assignment Review the assignment to be sure you fully understand it. The task may reference some of the academic words presented at the beginning of the unit. Be sure you understand each of the words in order to complete the assignment correctly. Also, consider using the academic vocabulary words in your argument. These words may help you to clarify your claims.

Academic Vocabulary

verify	speculate	rectify
candid	retort	

Review the Elements of Effective Argument Before you begin writing, read the Argument Rubric. Once you have completed your first draft, check it against the rubric. If one or more of the elements is missing or not as strong as it could be, revise your argument to add or strengthen that component.

ESSENTIAL QUESTION: When is it right to take a stand?

DIGITAL PERSPECTIVES

Argument Rubric

	Focus and Organization	Evidence and Elaboration	Language Conventions
4	The introduction engages the reader and establishes the claim in a compelling way. The claim is supported by logical reasons and relevant evidence, and opposing claims are addressed. The reasons and evidence are organized logically so that the argument is easy to follow. Clearly shows the relationships among claims, counterclaims, reasoning, and relevant evidence. The conclusion supports the argument presented and provides a new insight that follows from the information in the argument.	The sources of evidence are relevant and credible. Logical reasoning is used to connect specific supporting evidence to specific claims. The tone and style of the argument is formal and objective. Words are carefully chosen and suited to the audience and purpose.	The argument intentionally uses standard English conventions of usage and mechanics. The argument intentionally uses transitions to create cohesion.
3	The introduction is somewhat engaging and states the claim clearly. The claim is supported by reasons and evidence, and opposing claims are acknowledged. Reasons and evidence are organized so that the argument can be followed. Shows the relationships among claims, counterclaims, reasoning, and relevant evidence. The conclusion restates the claim and supports the argument.	The sources are relevant. Logical reasoning is used to connect supporting evidence to claims. The tone and style of the argument is mostly formal and objective. Words are generally suited to the audience and purpose.	The argument demonstrates general accuracy in standard English conventions of usage and mechanics. The argument uses transitions to create cohesion.
2	The introduction states the claim. The claim is supported by some reasons and evidence, and opposing claims may be briefly acknowledged. Reasons and evidence are organized somewhat logically. The conclusion relates to the claim.	Some sources are relevant. Logical reasoning is sometimes used to connect supporting evidence to claims. The tone and style of the argument is occasionally formal and objective. Words are somewhat suited to the audience and purpose.	The argument demonstrates some accuracy as well as minor mistakes in standard English conventions of usage and mechanics. The argument sometimes uses transitions to create cohesion.
1	The claim is not clearly stated. The claim is not supported by reasons and evidence, and opposing claims are not addressed. Reasons and evidence are disorganized and the argument is difficult to follow. The conclusion does not relate to the argument presented.	Reliable and relevant evidence is not included. The tone and style of the argument is informal. Vague words are used and word choices are not appropriate to the audience or purpose.	The argument contains many mistakes in standard English conventions of usage and mechanics. The argument does not use transitions to create cohesion.

Argument Rubric

As you review the Argument Rubric with students, remind them that the rubric is a resource that can guide their revisions. Students should pay particular attention to the differences between an argument that contains all of the required elements (a score of 3) and one that is engaging and compelling and offers fresh insight (a score of 4).

PERSONALIZE FOR LEARNING

English Language Support

Writing a Claim Support students as they write a claim for their argument. Have students review the definition of *argument*. Then offer the following sentence frames: People can determine what matters to them by _____. I know this because _____. People can make their own choices in life if they _____. I know this because _____. **ALL LEVELS**

ASSESSING

Speaking and Listening: Oral Presentation

Students should annotate their written arguments by marking the essential elements (claims, reasons, evidence, and counterclaims) as well as facts and anecdotes.

Remind students that the effectiveness of an oral argument rests on how the speaker establishes credibility with his or her audience. If a speaker comes across as confident and authoritative, it will be easier for the audience to give credence to the speaker's presentation.

Review the Oral Presentation Rubric As you review the Oral Presentation Rubric with students, remind them that it is a valuable tool that can help them plan their presentation. They should strive to include all of the criteria required to achieve a score of 3. Draw their attention to some of the subtle differences between scores of 2 and 3.

 PERFORMANCE-BASED ASSESSMENT

PART 2
Speaking and Listening: Oral Presentation

Assignment
After completing the final draft of your argument, use it as the foundation for a short **oral presentation**.

Instead of reading your argument aloud, take the following steps to make your oral presentation lively and engaging.

- In your argument, annotate the most important claims and supporting details from the introduction, body paragraphs, and conclusion.
- Include visuals or other media that add interest to your presentation.
- Refer to your annotated text to keep your presentation focused.
- Deliver your argument with confidence. Look up from your annotated text frequently, and make eye contact with listeners.

Review the Oral Presentation Rubric Before you deliver your presentation, check your plans against this rubric. If elements are missing or not as strong as they could be, revise your presentation.

STANDARDS
Speaking and Listening
- Present claims and findings, emphasizing salient points in a focused, coherent manner with relevant evidence, sound valid reasoning, and well-chosen details; use appropriate eye contact, adequate volume, and clear pronunciation.
- Integrate multimedia and visual displays into presentations to clarify information, strengthen claims and evidence, and add interest.

	Content	Organization	Presentation Techniques
3	The introduction engages the reader and establishes a claim in a compelling way. The presentation has valid reasons and evidence for support and answers counterclaims. The conclusion offers fresh insight into the claim.	The speaker uses a variety of media effectively to support the claim. Ideas progress logically, with clear transitions so that listeners can easily follow the argument. The speaker uses time effectively by spending the right amount of time on each part.	The speaker maintains appropriate eye contact and speaks clearly and with adequate volume. The speaker presents with strong confidence and energy.
2	The introduction establishes the claim. The presentation includes some valid reasons and evidence to support the claim and acknowledges counterclaims. The conclusion offers some insight into the claim and restates important information.	The speaker uses some media to support the claim. Ideas progress somewhat logically, with transitions among ideas so that listeners can follow the argument. The speaker mostly uses time effectively by spending almost the right amount of time on each part.	The speaker sometimes maintains appropriate eye contact and speaks somewhat clearly and with adequate volume. The speaker presents with some confidence and energy.
1	The introduction does not clearly state the claim. The presentation does not include reasons or evidence to support the claim or acknowledge counterclaims. The conclusion does not restate information about the claim.	The speaker doesn't use media to support the claim. Ideas do not progress logically. Listeners have difficulty following. The speaker does not use time effectively, spending too much time on some parts of the presentation, and too little on others.	The speaker does not maintain appropriate eye contact or speak clearly with adequate volume. The speaker presents without confidence or energy.

DIGITAL PERSPECTIVES

Preparing for the Assignment To help students understand what an effective oral presentation looks and sounds like, find examples on the Internet of students or adults presenting arguments. Project the examples for the class, and have them note the techniques that make each speaker successful (that is, varying inflection, speaking with adequate volume and energy, making gestures, and so on). Suggest that students videotape themselves presenting their arguments prior to presenting to the class so that they can practice incorporating some of the techniques from the examples they viewed.

UNIT 3 REFLECTION

Reflect on the Unit
Now that you've completed the unit, take a few moments to reflect on your learning.

Reflect on the Unit Goals
Look back at the goals at the beginning of the unit. Use a different colored pen to rate yourself again. Then, think about readings and activities that contributed the most to the growth of your understanding. Record your thoughts.

Reflect on the Learning Strategies
Discuss It Write a reflection on whether you were able to improve your learning based on your Action Plans. Think about what worked, what didn't, and what you might do to keep working on these strategies. Record your ideas before joining a class discussion.

Reflect on the Text
Choose a selection that you found challenging and explain what made it difficult.

Explain something that surprised you about a text in the unit.

Which activity taught you the most about standing up for what matters? What did you learn?

DIGITAL PERSPECTIVES

Reflect on the Unit
- Have students watch the video on Reflecting on Your Learning.
- A video on this topic is available online in the Professional Development Center.

Reflect on the Unit Goals
Students should re-evaluate how well they met the unit goals now that they have completed the unit. You might ask them to provide a written commentary on the goal they made the most progress with as well as the goal they feel warrants continued focus.

Reflect on the Learning Strategies
Discuss It If you want to make this a digital activity, go online and navigate to the Discussion Board. Alternatively, students can share their learning strategies reflections in a class discussion.

Reflect on the Text
Consider having students share their text reflections with one another.

MAKE IT INTERACTIVE
Have students prepare one slide using presentation software that summarizes their reflection.

Collate student slides into a presentation that can be viewed by the class. Students should be prepared to give a 30-second oral summary for their slide.

> **Unit Test and Remediation**
> After students have completed the Performance-Based Assessment, administer the Unit Test. Based on students' performance on the test, assign the resources as indicated on the Interpretation Guide to remediate. Students who take the test online will be automatically assigned remediation, as warranted by test results.

Human Intelligence

UNIT 4

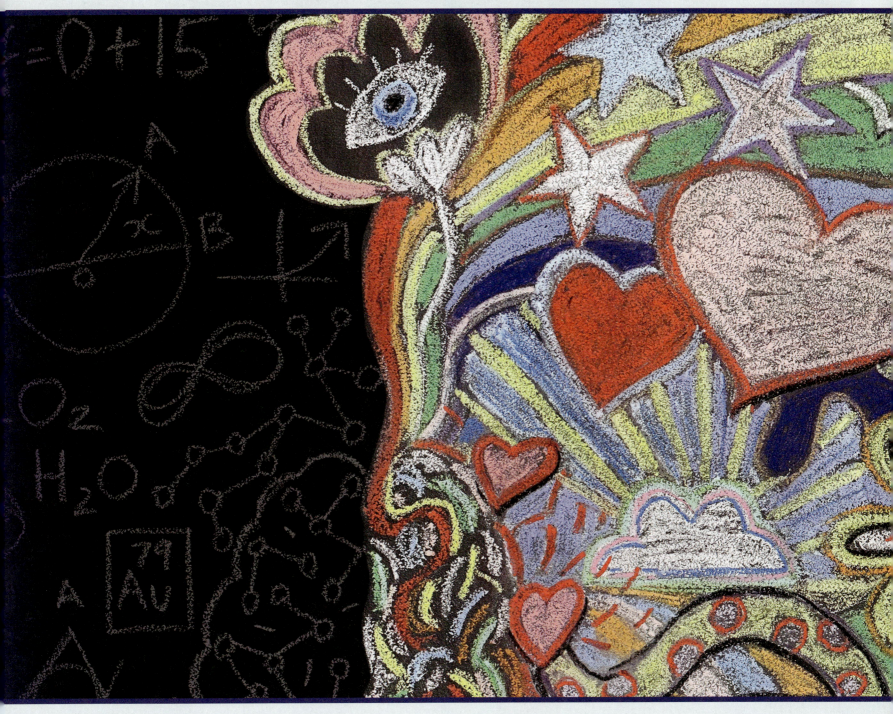

INTRODUCTION

Jump Start

Engage students in a discussion about human intelligence by prompting them with questions such as the following:

If a person can speak five languages, do complex math problems without a calculator, recite entire plays from Shakespeare from memory, would you think that he or she is smart? What does it mean to be intelligent?

Have students jot down what they think makes a person "smart," and ask volunteers to share their responses. Then discuss what it means to have wisdom through life experience, and what it means to have practical knowledge.

Human Intelligence

Ask students what the phrase *human intelligence* suggests to them. Point out that they will read many examples of the different ways that people display intelligence.

Video

Project the introduction video in class, ask students to open the video in their interactive textbooks, or have students scan the BouncePage icon with their phones to access the video.

Discuss It If you want to make this a digital activity, go online to the Discussion Board.

Block Scheduling

Each day in this pacing calendar represents a 40–50 minute class period. Teachers using block scheduling may combine days to reflect their class schedule. In addition, teachers may revise pacing to differentiate and support core instruction by integrating components and resources as students require.

Pacing Plan

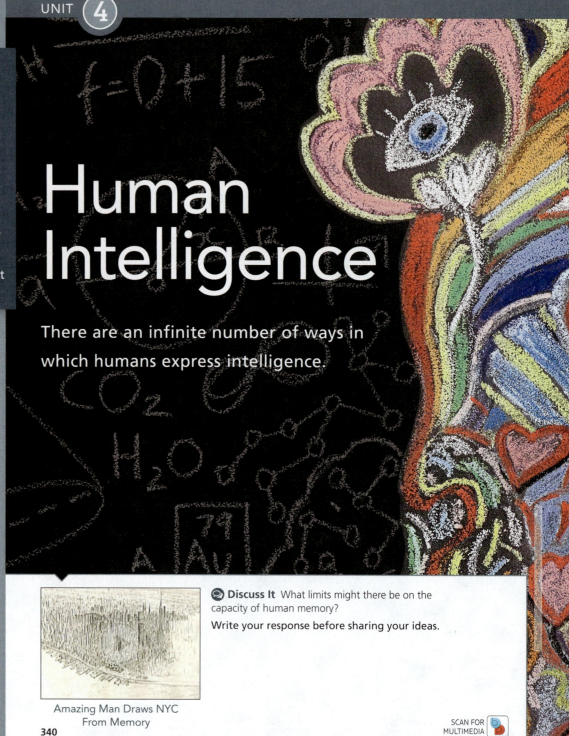

UNIT 4

Human Intelligence

There are an infinite number of ways in which humans express intelligence.

Amazing Man Draws NYC From Memory

Discuss It What limits might there be on the capacity of human memory?

Write your response before sharing your ideas.

SCAN FOR MULTIMEDIA

Unit Introduction	Introduce Whole-Class Learning		Flowers for Algernon										Script: from Flowers for Algernon		Performance Task		
1	2	3	4	5	6	7	8	9	10	11	12	13	14	15	16	17	18

UNIT 4

DIGITAL PERSPECTIVES — Audio · Video · Document · Annotation Highlights · EL Highlights · Online Assessment

UNIT INTRODUCTION

ESSENTIAL QUESTION: In what different ways can people be intelligent?

LAUNCH TEXT / INFORMATIVE MODEL: The Human Brain

WHOLE-CLASS LEARNING

ANCHOR TEXT: SHORT STORY
Flowers for Algernon
Daniel Keyes
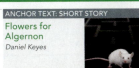

COMPARE

SCRIPT
from Flowers for Algernon
David Rogers

SMALL-GROUP LEARNING

MEMOIR
from Blue Nines and Red Words
from Born on a Blue Day
Daniel Tammet

MEDIA: INFOGRAPHIC
The Theory of Multiple Intelligences Infographic
Howard Gardner

POETRY COLLECTION
Retort
Paul Laurence Dunbar

from The People, Yes
Carl Sandburg

INDEPENDENT LEARNING

ARGUMENT
Is Personal Intelligence Important?
John D. Mayer, Ph.D.

BLOG POST
Why Is Emotional Intelligence Important for Teens?
Divya Parekh

EXPLANATORY ESSAY
The More You Know, the Smarter You Are?
Jim Vega

EXPOSITORY NONFICTION
from The Future of the Mind
Michio Kaku

PERFORMANCE TASK
WRITING FOCUS:
Write an Informative Speech

PERFORMANCE TASK
SPEAKING AND LISTENING FOCUS:
Deliver a Multimedia Presentation

PERFORMANCE-BASED ASSESSMENT PREP
Review Evidence for an Informative Essay

PERFORMANCE-BASED ASSESSMENT

Informative Text: Essay and Speech

PROMPT:
In what different ways can people be intelligent?

In what different ways can people be intelligent?

Introduce the Essential Question and point out that students will respond to related prompts.

- **Whole-Class Learning** What has happened to you so far as a result of the experiment, and what do you predict will happen to you as time progresses?
- **Small-Group Learning** How does each selection highlight a different way to be intelligent?
- **Performance-Based Assessment** In what different ways can people be intelligent?

Using Trade Books

Refer to the Teaching with Trade Books section for suggestions on how to incorporate the following thematically-related titles into this unit:

- *Ender's Game* by Orson Scott Card
- *Mango-Shaped Space* by Wendy Mass
- *Queen's Own Fool* by Jane Yolen

Current Perspectives

To increase student engagement, search online for stories about the different ways that people display intelligence, and invite your students to recommend stories they find. Always preview content before sharing it with your class.

- **News Story: Kid Who Got Into All 8 Ivy League Schools Explains Why He Chose Harvard Over Stanford** (*Business Insider*) A high school senior was accepted by all eight Ivy League colleges.
- **Video: How Einstein's Brain Is Different Than Yours** (*DNews*) How does Albert Einstein's brain differ from a normal brain?

Introduce Small-Group Learning		from Blue Nines and Red Words					Media: The Theory of Multiple Intelligences Infographic	• Retort • from The People, Yes			Performance Task		Introduce Independent Learning	Independent Learning		Performance-Based Assessment
19	20	21	22	23	24	25	26	27	28	29	30	31	32	33	34	35	36

Unit Introduction   341

INTRODUCTION

About the Unit Goals
These unit goals were backward designed from the Performance-Based Assessment at the end of the unit and the Whole-Class and Small-Group Performance Tasks. Students will practice and become proficient in many more standards over the course of this unit.

Unit Goals ▶
Review the goals with students and explain that as they read and discuss the selections in this unit, they will improve their skills in reading, writing, research, language, and speaking and listening.

- Have students watch the video on Goal Setting.
- A video on this topic is available online in the Professional Development Center.

Reading Goals Tell students they will read a variety of text types. They will also read nonfiction, fiction, and poetry to better understand the ways writers express ideas.

Writing and Research Goals Tell students that they will learn the elements of informative texts. They will also write their own informative speech. Students will write for a number of reasons, including organizing and sharing ideas, reflecting on experiences, and gathering evidence. They will conduct research to clarify and explore ideas.

Language Goal Tell students that they will develop a deeper understanding of the conventions of standard English grammar and usage. They will then practice conventions of standard English grammar in their own writing.

Speaking and Listening Goals Explain to students that they will work together to build on one another's ideas, develop consensus, and communicate with one another. They will also learn to incorporate audio, visuals, and text in presentations.

HOME Connection ✉
A Home Connection letter to students' parents or guardians is available in the Interactive Teacher's Edition. The letter explains what students will be learning in this unit and how they will be assessed.

342 UNIT 4 • HUMAN INTELLIGENCE

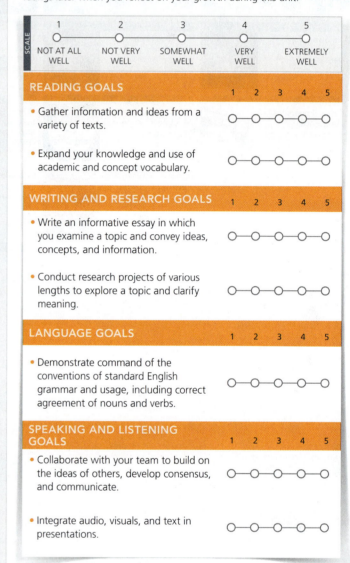

UNIT 4 INTRODUCTION

Unit Goals
Throughout this unit, you will deepen your perspective about human intelligence by reading, writing, speaking, listening, and presenting. These goals will help you succeed on the Unit Performance-Based Assessment.

Rate how well you meet these goals right now. You will revisit your ratings later when you reflect on your growth during this unit.

SCALE: 1 NOT AT ALL WELL — 2 NOT VERY WELL — 3 SOMEWHAT WELL — 4 VERY WELL — 5 EXTREMELY WELL

READING GOALS
- Gather information and ideas from a variety of texts.
- Expand your knowledge and use of academic and concept vocabulary.

WRITING AND RESEARCH GOALS
- Write an informative essay in which you examine a topic and convey ideas, concepts, and information.
- Conduct research projects of various lengths to explore a topic and clarify meaning.

LANGUAGE GOALS
- Demonstrate command of the conventions of standard English grammar and usage, including correct agreement of nouns and verbs.

SPEAKING AND LISTENING GOALS
- Collaborate with your team to build on the ideas of others, develop consensus, and communicate.
- Integrate audio, visuals, and text in presentations.

STANDARDS
Language
Acquire and use accurately grade-appropriate general academic and domain-specific words and phrases; gather vocabulary knowledge when considering a word or phrase important to comprehension or expression.

342 UNIT 4 • HUMAN INTELLIGENCE

SCAN FOR MULTIMEDIA

PERSONALIZE FOR LEARNING

English Language Support
Cognates Many of the academic words have Spanish cognates. Use these cognates with students whose home language is Spanish.
ALL LEVELS

assimilate – asimilar citation – citación
tendency – tendencia document – documento
integrate – integrar

ESSENTIAL QUESTION: In what different ways can people be intelligent?

DIGITAL PERSPECTIVES

Academic Vocabulary: Informative Texts

Academic terms appear in all subjects and can help you read, write, and discuss with more precision. Informative writing relies on facts to inform or explain. Here are five academic words that will be useful to you in this unit as you analyze and write informative texts.

Complete the chart.

1. Review each word, its root, and the mentor sentences.
2. Use the information and your own knowledge to predict the meaning of each word.
3. For each word, list at least two related words.
4. Refer to the dictionary or other resources if needed.

TIP

FOLLOW THROUGH
Study the words in this chart, and mark them or their forms wherever they appear in the unit.

WORD	MENTOR SENTENCES	PREDICT MEANING	RELATED WORDS
assimilate ROOT: -sim- "like"	1. Once I *assimilate* all the information, I will start the project. 2. The body can *assimilate* nutrients and use them for energy.		similar; simile
tendency ROOT: -ten- "stretch"	1. People have a *tendency* to believe good things about friends. 2. My *tendency* is to avoid trouble rather than risk a fight.		
integrate ROOT: -teg- "touch"	1. We will *integrate* this new activity into the lesson. 2. The new student should *integrate* into our school very quickly.		
observation ROOT: -serv- "watch over"	1. My findings are based on close *observation* over many weeks. 2. Ed went to the hospital for *observation* after he fainted.		
documentation ROOT: -doc- "show"	1. The *documentation* explains how to use the software. 2. They found *documentation* from the 1800s that proved the family owned the land.		

Academic Vocabulary: Informative Texts

Introduce the blue academic vocabulary words in the chart on the student page. Point out that the root of each word provides a clue to its meaning. Discuss the mentor sentences to ensure students understand each word's usage. Students should also use the mentor sentences as context to help them predict the meaning of each word. Check that students are able to fill the chart in correctly. Complete pronunciations, parts of speech, and definitions are provided for you. Students are only expected to provide the definition.

Possible responses:

assimilate v. (uh SIHM uh layt)
Meaning: to absorb a culture or ideas
Related words: assimilated, assimilation, assimilator
Additional words related to root -sim-: similar, simile

tendency n. (TEHN duhn see)
Meaning: an inclination; a movement toward
Related words: tend, tended
Additional words related to root -ten-: tension, tense

integrate v. (IHN tuh grayt)
Meaning: to abolish segregation; to bring together different parts
Related words: integrated, integration
Additional words related to root -integ-: integrity, disintegrate, integral

observation (ahb zur VAY shuhn)
Meaning: an act of noticing or watching
Related words: observe, observation, observatory
Additional words related to root –serv-: conserve, reserve, preserve, serve

documentation n. (dok yuh muhn TAY shuhn)
Meaning: printed information; proof
Related words: documentary, document, documented
Additional words related to root -doc-: docile, doctor, doctrine

---

AUTHOR'S PERSPECTIVE Ernest Morrell, Ph.D.

Taking Responsibility for Learning Teachers can talk to students about becoming motivated learners. Start by having students reflect on things they are good at outside of class, such as sports, music, and video games. Then have students think about how they take responsibility for their own achievement in these areas, such as having the discipline to practice. Help students further understand the value of becoming independent learners by providing tips on how to do so, such as these:

1. **Be self-motivated and persistent.** Don't be discouraged when faced with minor setbacks.
2. **Develop effective time management skills.** Track assignments and deadlines.
3. **Seek help when necessary.** Don't be afraid to get assistance when you need it.
4. **Set realistic goals.** Then plan ways to achieve your goals.
5. **Believe in yourself.** Visualize success. Recognize that you have the ability to soar.

Encourage students to add to this list to help them focus on strategies for taking ownership of their learning.

INTRODUCTION

Purpose of the Launch Text

The Launch Text provides students with a common starting point to address the unit topic. After reading the Launch Text, all students will be able to participate in discussions about human intelligence.

Lexile: 1120 The easier reading level of this selection makes it perfect to assign for homework. Students will need little or no support to understand it.

Additionally, "The Human Brain" provides a writing model for the Performance-Based Assessment students complete at the end of the unit.

Launch Text: Informative Text Model

Remind students that the purpose of an informative essay is to inform, or give facts. This essay will teach them about the brain. As with other types of essays, it begins with a thesis. The paragraphs that follow give the reader details about the brain and how it works.

Encourage students to read this text on their own and annotate unfamiliar words and sections of text they think are particularly important.

🔊 AUDIO SUMMARIES

Audio summaries of "The Human Brain" are available in both English and Spanish in the Interactive Teacher's Edition or Unit Resources. Assigning these summaries before students read the Launch Text may help them build additional background knowledge and set a context for their reading.

UNIT 4 INTRODUCTION

The Human Brain

LAUNCH TEXT | INFORMATIVE MODEL

This selection is an example of an **informative text**, a type of writing in which an author presents facts and details. This is the type of writing you will develop in the Performance-Based Assessment at the end of the unit.

As you read, look at the way the ideas are introduced and facts and details are presented. Mark the text to help you determine key ideas and details.

NOTES

1 The famous scientist James Watson summarized it this way: The brain boggles the mind! The human brain is truly impressive: It weighs only about three pounds but controls everything a person does, ever has done, and ever will do—physically, intellectually, and emotionally. No computer even comes close to having the brain's abilities. The brain controls a person's actions, reactions, and survival functions, such as breathing. It also has the ability to think, remember, process information, and learn new things.

2 The brain is one part of the central nervous system—the system that controls all of the body's activities. The central nervous system is made up of the brain and the spinal cord. The brain is protected by the skull, and the spinal cord runs through vertebrae of the back—the bones that make up the spine. The spinal cord transmits messages between the brain and other parts of the body through nerve cells called neurons. If a person decides to pick up a book from the shelf—a voluntary action—the brain sends that message to the arm and hand through the spinal cord. And if a person touches a hot surface and burns his or her hand—an involuntary action—the nerve cells in the hand send a pain message to the brain through the spinal cord.

344 UNIT 4 • HUMAN INTELLIGENCE

SCAN FOR MULTIMEDIA

CROSS-CURRICULAR PERSPECTIVES

Science The human brain is like a control panel. Have students research what different parts of the brain control. Have them use their research to create diagrams of the brain. Ask them to label the control centers and be prepared to share their diagrams with the class. **(Research to Explore)**

ESSENTIAL QUESTION: In what different ways can people be intelligent?

3   A constant stream of messages travels through the neurons in the spinal cord, at speeds of more than 150 miles per hour. The human brain never stops working, even when a person is asleep. As well as transmitting messages through the spinal cord, neurons transmit messages from one part of the brain to another. There are approximately 85 billion of these cells in the brain alone. Neurons send messages through tiny branch-like structures that connect to other neurons in different parts of the brain, as well as other parts of the body. The points where neurons meet and transmit information to each other are called synapses. Each neuron may be connected to as many as 10,000 other neurons, resulting in more than 100 trillion synapses in a single brain.

4   Although a person cannot increase the amount of neurons in his or her brain, learning new things increases the number of synapse connections between them. Learning and education actually change the structure of the human brain. That structure changes every time a person learns, and every time that person has a new thought or memory. The more a person learns the more there is to think about. And the more there is to think about, the more there is to remember. As a result, the connections between neurons get stronger, and the brain is able to function more effectively. It processes, thinks, analyzes, and stores information more quickly and productively than it did before these connections were made. Neurons are just cells, and everything a person knows is the result of the connections between them.

5   Scientists have gained a wealth of knowledge about the human brain, but there is a lot they do not yet understand. The neurologist Santiago Ramón y Cajal, for example, compares the brain to a world of unexplored continents with great stretches of unknown territory. Even so, new discoveries continually increase our knowledge of how the brain functions and how people learn.

NOTES

WORD NETWORK FOR HUMAN INTELLIGENCE

Vocabulary A Word Network is a collection of words related to a topic. As you read the selections in this unit, identify interesting words related to human intelligence, and add them to your Word Network. For example, you might begin by adding words from the Launch Text, such as *spinal cord*, *neuron*, and *synapse*.

Tool Kit
Word Network Model

(Word Network diagram with HUMAN INTELLIGENCE at center, connected to: spinal cord, neuron, synapse, and blank boxes)

The Human Brain **345**

DIGITAL PERSPECTIVES

Word Network for Human Intelligence

Tell students that they can fill in the Word Network as they read texts in the unit, or they can record the words elsewhere and add them later. Point out to students that people may have personal associations with some words. A word that one student relates to human intelligence might not be a word another student would pick. However, students should feel free to add any word they personally think is relevant to their Word Network. Each person's Word Network will be unique. If you choose to print the Word Network, distribute it to students at this point so they can use it throughout the rest of the unit.

AUTHOR'S PERSPECTIVE Elfrieda Hiebert, Ph.D.

Words in Complex Texts Reassure students that complex texts will always have some words that they haven't encountered before. This point needs to be reviewed year after year because the texts always get harder, and with harder texts come more complex words. Share these ideas with students:

- Many words will be familiar, but they may be used in a different way with new topics and meanings.
- Authors choose the more complex words (the rare words) for deliberate effect—not serendipitously—to describe characters and contexts, to develop obstacles or problems, to show ways of solving problems.

Making and reviewing word networks helps students develop multiple words related to a concept, and the multiple meanings or concept applications for words. Also encourage students to study the words in context. Students may wish to use digital tools as they do so.

The Human Brain **345**

INTRODUCTION

Summary

Have students read the introductory paragraph. Provide them with tips for writing a summary:

- Write in the present tense.
- Make sure to include the title of the work.
- Be concise: a summary should not be equal in length to the original text.
- If you need to quote the words of the author, use quotation marks.
- Don't put your own opinions, ideas, or interpretations into the summary. The purpose of writing a summary is to accurately represent what the author says, not to provide a critique.

If necessary, students can refer to the Tool Kit for help in understanding the elements of a good summary.

See a possible Summary on the student page.

Launch Activity

Explain to students that as they work on this unit, they will have many opportunities to discuss where human intelligence comes from. Preparing for research will help students notice possible sources and supporting evidence in the selections they read and view.

UNIT 4 INTRODUCTION

Summary

Write a summary of "The Human Brain." A **summary** is a concise, complete, and accurate overview of a text. It should not include a statement of your opinion or an analysis.

> **Possible response:** The informative essay "The Human Brain" explains just how incredible the brain is and gives a brief overview of how it works. You *are* your brain; the brain is how you control everything you do, think, remember old information, and learn new information. When you decide to move your arm, your brain sends a signal down through your spine and into your arm. And messages—like "I'm touching something hot"—can come from your arm back up the spine and into the brain. Your brain is made mainly of cells called *neurons*, which pass information between each other and between nerve cells in the rest of the body. Every time you learn something new, the connections between neurons get stronger; that's what learning is!

Launch Activity

Draft a Research Plan Think about this question: **In what different ways can people be intelligent?** Consider your response by completing this statement: *I can find more information about human intelligence by . . .*

- On a sticky note, record a brief phrase to complete the statement.
- Place all sticky notes on the board, and then read the suggestions aloud. Work together to group ideas that are the same or closely related.
- As a class, decide on the order in which the suggested research strategies should be pursued. Vote on which suggestion should be done first.
- Place a tally mark on the note or notes that list your choice or choices.
- Use the tally results to create a class research plan.

ESSENTIAL QUESTION: In what different ways can people be intelligent?

DIGITAL PERSPECTIVES

QuickWrite

Consider class discussions, the video, and the Launch Text as you think about the prompt. Record your first thoughts here.

PROMPT: In what different ways can people be intelligent?

> There are countless ways in which the brain controls our bodies and our thinking, so there are many different ways we can be intelligent. Intelligence doesn't come just from reading facts in books. Our minds store our memories so we can refer back to past experience, so there is learned intelligence. Our bodies learn through action and repetition, so there is body intelligence. We come up with new ideas and invent things, so there is creative intelligence. As we go through life, we interact with many different people and learn how to relate to them, so there is social intelligence. We develop beliefs and emotions that guide our actions, so there is personal intelligence. In school, we learn many different subjects, and each requires a different kind of intelligence. There's an endless list of different ways we learn, and so there is probably just as long a list of different kinds of intelligence.

✏️ EVIDENCE LOG FOR HUMAN INTELLIGENCE

Review your QuickWrite. Summarize your point of view in one sentence to record in your Evidence Log. Then, record evidence from "The Human Brain" that supports your point of view.

After each selection, you will continue to use your Evidence Log to record the evidence you gather and the connections you make. This graphic shows what your Evidence Log looks like.

🔧 **Tool Kit**
Evidence Log Model

Title of Text: _____ Date: _____

CONNECTION TO PROMPT	TEXT EVIDENCE/DETAILS	ADDITIONAL NOTES/IDEAS

How does this text change or add to my thinking?   Date: _____

SCAN FOR MULTIMEDIA

Unit Introduction 347

QuickWrite

In this QuickWrite, students should present their own response to the prompt based on the material they have read and viewed in the Unit Overview and Introduction. This initial response will help inform their work when they complete the Performance-Based Assessment at the end of the unit. Students should think about what they have read and what they already know about where human intelligence comes from.

See a possible QuickWrite on the student page.

Evidence Log for Human Intelligence 📄

Students should record their initial thinking in their Evidence Logs along with evidence from "The Human Brain" that supports this thinking.

If you choose to print the Evidence Log, distribute it to students at this point so they can use it throughout the rest of the unit.

> **Performance-Based Assessment: Refining Your Thinking ▶**
>
> - Have students watch the video on Refining Your Thinking.
> - A video on this topic is available online in the Professional Development Center.

PERSONALIZE FOR LEARNING

English Language Support
Background Knowledge When reading from sources about the human brain, students will encounter many unfamiliar and complex scientific words. It is likely that many of the same words will come up over and over again. To aid students' comprehension, create an unfamiliar terms chart with a column for terms and a column for explanations and hang it in the classroom. Model selecting a term from the Launch Text and adding it to the chart. Then have students select another term from the Launch Text to add. Finally, tell students that when they come across other brain-related terms, they should add them to the chart. **ALL LEVELS**

The Human Brain 347

OVERVIEW

WHOLE-CLASS LEARNING

In what different ways can people be intelligent?

Explain to students that different people have different ideas about what being intelligent means. Point out that a person's age, culture, and personal beliefs can affect how he or she views and measures intelligence. Even the historical period in which a person lives can have an effect. And, while there are tests to measure intelligence, there is no definitive gauge. During Whole-Class Learning, students will read selections that grapple with what it means to be intelligent.

Whole-Class Learning Strategies

Review the Learning Strategies with students and explain that as they work through Whole-Class Learning they will develop strategies to work in large-group environments.

- Have students watch the video on Whole-Class Learning Strategies.
- A video on this topic is available online in the Professional Development Center.

You may wish to discuss some action items to add to the chart as a class before students complete it on their own. For example, for "Interact and share ideas," you might solicit the following from students:

- Ask for opinions and feedback on your work.
- Be positive and supportive, especially when offering feedback.

Block Scheduling

Each day in this Pacing Plan represents a 40–50 minute class period. Teachers using block scheduling may combine days to reflect their class schedule. In addition, teachers may revise pacing to differentiate and support core instruction by integrating components and resources as students require.

Pacing Plan

OVERVIEW: WHOLE-CLASS LEARNING

ESSENTIAL QUESTION:

In what different ways can people be intelligent?

Intelligence shows itself in many ways—sometimes in ways that do not overlap. A master painter may be terrible at mathematics; a bestselling author may have no sense of direction. Where one person excels, another may fail—and it's often impossible to make a judgment about which of the two people is smarter. As you read, you will work with your whole class to explore some of the ways in which people are intelligent.

Whole-Class Learning Strategies

Throughout your life, in school, in your community, and in your career, you'll continue to learn in large-group environments.

Review these strategies and the actions you can take to practice them as you work with your whole class. Add ideas of your own for each step. Get ready to use these strategies during Whole-Class Learning.

STRATEGY	ACTION PLAN
Listen actively	• Eliminate distractions. For example, put your cellphone away. • Keep your eyes on the speaker. •
Clarify by asking questions	• If you're confused, other people probably are, too. Ask a question to help your whole class. • If you see that you are guessing, ask a question instead. •
Monitor understanding	• Notice what information you already know, and be ready to build on it. • Ask for help if you are struggling. •
Interact and share ideas	• Share your ideas and answer questions, even if you are unsure. • Build on the ideas of others by adding details or making a connection. •

348 UNIT 4 • HUMAN INTELLIGENCE

SCAN FOR MULTIMEDIA

CONTENTS

ANCHOR TEXT | SHORT STORY

Flowers for Algernon
Daniel Keyes

This short story examines the relationship between a character's intelligence and his personality.

COMPARE

ANCHOR TEXT | SCRIPT

from Flowers for Algernon
by David Rogers

A man's life changes drastically—but what does he think of who he used to be?

PERFORMANCE TASK

WRITING FOCUS

Write an Informative Speech
The Whole-Class selections focus on a fictional story about a character named Charlie whose level of intelligence is transformed dramatically by an experimental treatment. After reading the texts, you will write an informative speech from Charlie's point of view.

Overview: Whole-Class Learning 349

DIGITAL PERSPECTIVES

Contents

Anchor Texts Preview the anchor texts with students to generate interest. Encourage students to discuss other texts they may have read or movies or television shows they may have seen that deal with the issue of understanding human intelligence.

You may wish to invite students to create an encyclopedia article or wiki in which they combine their background knowledge on the topic of human intelligence. Ask students to summarize and paraphrase sources with which they are familiar. Students can return to this shared text after they have compared the selections, then add to it or make edits to reflect their new understandings.

Performance Task

Write an Informative Speech Explain to students that after they have read the texts, they will write an informative speech about the nature of intelligence. To help them prepare, encourage students to think about the topic as they progress through the selections and as they participate in the Whole-Class Learning experience.

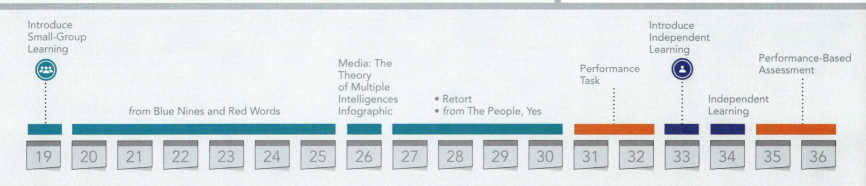

Whole-Class Learning 349

PLANNING
WHOLE-CLASS LEARNING • FLOWERS FOR ALGERNON

Flowers for Algernon

AUDIO SUMMARIES
Audio summaries of "Flowers for Algernon" are available online in both English and Spanish in the Interactive Teacher's Edition or Unit Resources. Assigning these summaries prior to reading the selection may help students build additional background knowledge and set a context for their first read.

Summary
The short story "Flowers for Algernon" by Daniel Keyes is told from the perspective of a man named Charlie. Charlie has a disability that affects his intelligence, and he has an operation intended to make him smarter. He takes a series of tests first. Afterward, he rapidly gets smarter. He spends time playing with an unusually smart mouse called Algernon, who had the same operation Charlie did. Charlie's new intelligence brings him rewards, but it also damages his relationships with people as he equals and then exceeds their abilities. And the change may not last.

Insight
This classic science fiction story is about education and disability. It emphasizes the humanity of the developmentally disabled. It also touches on the theme that intelligence and knowledge are very valuable, but they can separate you from other people.

ESSENTIAL QUESTION:
In what different ways can people be intelligent?

Connection to Essential Question
In the May 15 entry, Charlie writes about how Dr. Nemur and Dr. Strauss are both intelligent, though in different ways. Charlie's boosted intelligence seems to be all-encompassing—from math and languages to literature and science. However, he struggles to communicate and understand human behavior, which is a kind of knowledge he cannot gain from reading a book.

Connection to Performance Tasks

WHOLE-CLASS LEARNING PERFORMANCE TASK
What has happened to you so far as a result of the experiment, and what do you predict will happen to you as time progresses?

Whole-Class Learning Performance Task The assignment asks students to take on the perspective of Charlie at the beginning of June. At this point, Charlie has become highly intelligent, and seeks to find out why Algernon's behavior has changed. Charlie surely suspects he is in danger of a similar change.

UNIT PERFORMANCE-BASED ASSESSMENT
In what different ways can people be intelligent?

Unit Performance-Based Assessment In this story, intelligence is partly a capacity to learn quickly and partly the knowledge that one learns. Charlie gets most of his knowledge by reading, but we see that there are other ways of being intelligent.

DIGITAL PERSPECTIVES Audio Video Document Annotation Highlights EL Highlights Online Assessment

LESSON RESOURCES

	Making Meaning	**Language Development**
Lesson	First Read Close Read the Text Analyze the Text Analyze Craft and Structure	Concept Vocabulary Word Study Conventions
Instructional Standards	**RL.10** By the end of the year, read and comprehend literature . . . **RL.1** Cite the textual evidence . . . **RL.2** Determine a theme or central idea of a text . . . **RL.6** Analyze how differences in the points of view . . . **RL.9** Analyze how a modern work of fiction . . .	**L.1** Demonstrate command of the conventions . . . **L.4.b** Use common, grade-appropriate Greek or Latin affixes and roots . . . **L.5** Demonstrate understanding of figurative language . . . **L.6** Acquire and use accurately grade-appropriate general academic and domain-specific words and phrases . . .
STUDENT RESOURCES Available online in the Interactive Student Edition or Unit Resources	Selection Audio First-Read Guide: Fiction Close-Read Guide: Fiction	Word Network
TEACHER RESOURCES **Selection Resources** Available online in the Interactive Teacher's Edition or Unit Resources	Audio Summaries Annotation Highlights EL Highlights English Language Support Lesson: Direct and Indirect Objects Analyze Craft and Structure: Development of Themes	Concept Vocabulary and Word Study Conventions: Direct and Indirect Objects
Reteach/Practice (RP) Available online in the Interactive Teacher's Edition or Unit Resources	Analyze Craft and Structure: Development of Themes (RP)	Word Study: Latin Prefix *sub-* (RP) Conventions: Direct and Indirect Objects (RP)
Assessment Available online in Assessments	Selection Test	
My Resources	A Unit 4 Answer Key is available online and in the Interactive Teacher's Edition	

Whole-Class Learning

PERSONALIZE FOR LEARNING
WHOLE-CLASS LEARNING • FLOWERS FOR ALGERNON

Reading Support

Text Complexity Rubric: Flowers for Algernon

Quantitative Measures

Lexile: 830   Text Length: 11,949 words

Qualitative Measures

Measure	Rating	Description
Knowledge Demands	4 (of 5)	Situations and experiences of science fiction story are unfamiliar, but told in everyday terms. Story addresses multiple sophisticated themes (identity and self-acceptance, mistreatment of mentally disabled, ethics in experimentation, types of intelligence).
Structure	3 (of 5)	Text has unconventional structure of progress report/diary entries by the main character, each dated to show the passage of time. Progressive reports show a decrease in misspelled words to show changing cognitive ability.
Language Conventionality and Clarity	4 (of 5)	Language is conversational, with some complex sentences and challenging vocabulary. Misspelled words show a lack of writing and cognitive abilities, and an increase and decrease in these abilities.
Levels of Meaning/Purpose	4 (of 5)	Multiple meanings occur throughout story. Based on character's thoughts and actions, reader can interpret multiple sophisticated themes.

DECIDE AND PLAN

English Language Support
Provide English Learners with support for language and meaning as they read the selection.

Language Students may be confused by the misspellings and run-on sentences. Explain that there will be many misspelled words and some improper grammar to indicate Charlie's lack of spelling ability. Pair students and ask them to list and correct misspelled words.

Meaning Ask questions at various points in the text to encourage students to think about the meaning of the story. For example, ask *Why does Charlie make fewer spelling errors in the later progress reports? How does he feel about his increasing abilities?*

Strategic Support
Provide students with strategic support to ensure that they can successfully read the text.

Knowledge Demands Before reading, list some themes that students may notice as they read. For example, ask them to look for Charlie's thoughts about his own identity, or how much he accepts himself the way he is, or how he accepts others who are the way he used to be. After students read, discuss what they noticed about that theme.

Language Ask students to notice Charlie's spelling and grammar. Then have volunteers read aloud some of the entries. Discuss how the spelling changes in the story to show Charlie's changing abilities.

Challenge
Provide students who need to be challenged with ideas for how they can go beyond a simple interpretation of the text.

Text Analysis Ask students how Charlie's language changes throughout the story and is used to reflect intelligence. Then ask students to find indications in the story of how Charlie feels about himself during different points in the story, and how he feels about others with lesser abilities.

Written Response Ask students to give their opinion on whether language is the best indicator of intelligence. Ask them to write their opinion on how important it is to increase the abilities of someone with a handicap.

TEACH

Read and Respond
Have students do their first read of the selection. Then have them complete their close read. Finally, work with them on the Making Meaning, Language Development, and Effective Expression activities.

Standards Support Through Teaching and Learning Cycle

IDENTIFY NEEDS

Analyze results of the Beginning-of-Year Assessment, focusing on the items relating to Unit 4. Also take into consideration student performance to this point and your observations of where particular students struggle.

ANALYZE AND REVISE

- Analyze student work for evidence of student learning.
- Identify whether or not students have met the expectations in the standards.
- Identify implications for future instruction.

TEACH

Implement the planned lesson, and gather evidence of student learning.

DECIDE AND PLAN

- If students have performed poorly on items matching these standards, then provide selection scaffolds before assigning them the on-level lesson provided in the Student Edition.
- If students have done well on the Beginning-of-Year Assessment, then challenge them to keep progressing and learning by giving them opportunities to practice the skills in depth.
- Use the Selection Resources listed on the Planning pages for "Flowers for Algernon" to help students continually improve their ability to master the standards.

Instructional Standards: Flowers for Algernon			
	Catching Up	This Year	Looking Forward
Reading	You may wish to administer the **Analyze Craft and Structure: Development of Themes (RP)** worksheet to help students better determine themes in a work of literature.	**RL.2** Determine a theme or central idea of a text and analyze its development over the course of the text, including its relationship to the characters, setting, and plot; provide an objective summary of the text.	Challenge students to summarize the text, its theme, and how the theme is introduced, shaped, and refined over the course of the text.
Language	Review the **Conventions: Direct and Indirect Objects (RP)** worksheet to help students understand the difference between direct and indirect objects. Review the **Word Study: Latin Prefix sub- (RP)** worksheet to help students understand that sub- means "beneath" or "under."	**L.1** Demonstrate command of the conventions of standard English grammar and usage when writing or speaking. **L.4.b** Use common, grade-appropriate Greek or Latin affixes and roots as clues to the meaning of a word.	Have students find a short article online and identify the subjects, verbs, direct and indirect objects of the sentences in one paragraph. Have students identify other words in the selection that contain prefixes they recognize.

TEACHING

Jump Start

FIRST READ *What does it mean to be intelligent?* Have students discuss their understandings of intelligence.

Flowers for Algernon

Who is Charlie Gordon? Modeling the questions readers might ask as they read "Flowers for Algernon" for the first time brings the text alive for students and connects it to the Performance Task assignment. Selection audio and print capability for the selection are available in the Interactive Teacher's Edition.

Concept Vocabulary

Support students as they rank their words. Ask if they've ever heard, read, or used them. Reassure them that the definitions for these words are listed in the selection.

FIRST READ

Students should perform the steps of the first read independently.

NOTICE: Encourage students to notice that the author chose to write this story from Charlie's perspective.

ANNOTATE: Remind students to mark passages that demonstrate Charlie's character development.

CONNECT: Encourage students to go beyond the text to make connections with what they have learned about the brain and what they know about learning from their own experiences.

RESPOND: Students will answer questions and write a summary to demonstrate understanding.

Point out to students that while they will always complete the Respond step at the end of the first read, the other steps will probably happen somewhat concurrently. You may wish to print copies of the **First-Read Guide: Fiction** for students to use.

About the Author

Raised in Brooklyn, New York, writer and teacher **Daniel Keyes** (1927–2014) was also a photographer, a merchant seaman, and an editor. Keyes was fascinated by unusual psychological conditions. A meeting with a man with a mental disability gave Keyes the idea for "Flowers for Algernon." After winning the Hugo Award for the story in 1959, Keyes expanded "Flowers for Algernon" into a novel. The story also inspired the award-winning movie adaptation *Charly,* released in 1968.

Tool Kit
First-Read Guide and Model Annotation

STANDARDS
Reading Literature
By the end of the year, read and comprehend literature, including stories, dramas, and poems, at the high end of grades 6–8 text complexity band independently and proficiently.

MAKING MEANING

Comparing Texts

In this lesson, you will read the short story "Flowers for Algernon." You will then read an excerpt from the script for a film adaptation of the story. Finally, you will compare the short story and the script.

FLOWERS FOR ALGERNON (short story)

from FLOWERS FOR ALGERNON (script)

Flowers for Algernon

Concept Vocabulary

As you conduct your first read of "Flowers for Algernon," you will encounter these words. Before reading, note how familiar you are with each word. Then, rank the words in order from most familiar (1) to least familiar (6).

WORD	YOUR RANKING
subconscious	
suspicion	
despised	
deterioration	
introspective	
regression	

First Read FICTION

Apply these strategies as you conduct your first read. You will have an opportunity to complete the close-read notes after your first read.

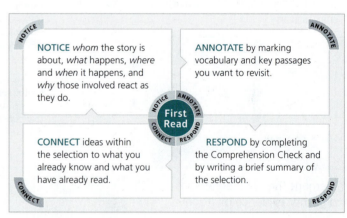

NOTICE *whom* the story is about, *what* happens, *where* and *when* it happens, and *why* those involved react as they do.

ANNOTATE by marking vocabulary and key passages you want to revisit.

CONNECT ideas within the selection to what you already know and what you have already read.

RESPOND by completing the Comprehension Check and by writing a brief summary of the selection.

350 UNIT 4 • HUMAN INTELLIGENCE

AUTHOR'S PERSPECTIVE Kelly Gallagher, M.Ed.

Deep Reading *Deep reading* means taking the time to consider more than just what the text says by making inferences, seeing, and thinking about information not literally on the page. Teachers can use the following techniques to model how to make inferences:

- **Study Photographs:** Have students study a photo and describe what might have happened in it. Discuss their responses, encouraging students to support their ideas.

- **Complete a Says/Doesn't Say T-chart:** Draw a T-chart on the board. On the left, have students write what the passage says (literal comprehension). On the right, have them record what the passage doesn't say. This helps students get at author's inference.

- **Use Positive-Negative Chart:** Have students chart a character's good and bad behavior, positive and negative influence, or the highest and lowest point in a story. This technique is an excellent way to have students track specific literary elements in a novel or a play.

- **Play Literary Dominoes:** Start with the resolution of a narrative and have students work backwards, recording the events that led to it. This creates a chain of key events.

350 UNIT 4 • HUMAN INTELLIGENCE

ANCHOR TEXT | SHORT STORY

Flowers for Algernon

Daniel Keyes

BACKGROUND
Charlie Gordon, the main character in "Flowers for Algernon," undergoes surgery to increase his intelligence. In the story, doctors measure his progress with IQ, or intelligence quotient, tests. These tests were once widely used to measure intelligence and learning ability. Researchers now recognize that one test cannot accurately measure the wide range of intellectual abilities.

SCAN FOR MULTIMEDIA

progris riport 1—martch 5 1965

1   Dr. Strauss says I shud rite down what I think and evrey thing that happins to me from now on. I dont know why but he says its importint so they will see if they will use me. I hope they use me. Miss Kinnian says maybe they can make me smart. I want to be smart. My name is Charlie Gordon. I am 37 years old and 2 weeks ago was my brithday. I have nuthing more to rite now so I will close for today.

progris riport 2—martch 6

2   I had a test today. I think I faled it. and I think that maybe now they wont use me. What happind is a nice young man was in the room and he had some white cards with ink spilled all over them. He sed Charlie what do you see on this card. I was very skared even tho I had my rabits foot in my pockit because when I was a kid I always faled tests in school and I spillled ink to.

3   I told him I saw a inkblot. He said yes and it made me feel good. I thot that was all but when I got up to go he stopped me.

NOTES

TEACHING

● CLOSE READ

As students read paragraph 8, explain that writers sometimes choose to ignore conventions such as spelling, but they do it with a purpose in mind—creating perspective. You may wish to model the close read using the following think-aloud format. Possible responses to questions on the student page are included.

ANNOTATE: As I read paragraph 8, I mark all the misspelled words.

QUESTION: There are many misspelled words.

CONCLUDE: Because there are so many misspelled words, I can conclude that the person writing these diary entries has trouble with spelling, and perhaps he has a learning disability.

NOTES

He said now sit down Charlie we are not thru yet. Then I dont remember so good but he wantid me to say what was in the ink. I dint see nuthing in the ink but he said there was picturs there other pepul saw some picturs. I coudnt see any picturs. I reely tryed to see. I held the card close up and then far away. Then I said if I had my glases I coud see better I usually only ware my glases in the movies or TV but I said they are in the closit in the hall. I got them. Then I said let me see that card agen I bet Ill find it now.

4   I tryed hard but I still coudnt find the picturs I only saw the ink. I told him maybe I need new glases. He rote something down on a paper and I got skared of faling the test. I told him it was a very nice inkblot with littel points all around the eges. He looked very sad so that wasnt it. I said please let me try agen. Ill get it in a few minits becaus Im not so fast somtimes. Im a slow reeder too in Miss Kinnians class for slow adults but I'm trying very hard.

5   He gave me a chance with another card that had 2 kinds of ink spilled on it red and blue.

6   He was very nice and talked slow like Miss Kinnian does and he explained it to me that it was a *raw shok*.[1] He said pepul see things in the ink. I said show me where. He said think. I told him I think a inkblot but that wasnt rite eather. He said what does it remind you—pretend somthing. I closd my eyes for a long time to pretend. I told him I pretned a fowntan pen with ink leeking all over a table cloth. Then he got up and went out.

7   I dont think I passd the *raw shok* test.

progris riport 3—martch 7

8   Dr Strauss and Dr Nemur say it dont matter about the inkblots. I told them I dint spill the ink on the cards and I coudnt see anything in the ink. They said that maybe they will still use me. I said Miss Kinnian never gave me tests like that one only spelling and reading. They said Miss Kinnian told that I was her bestist pupil in the adult nite scool because I tryed the hardist and I reely wantid to lern. They said how come you went to the adult nite scool all by yourself Charlie. How did you find it. I said I askd pepul and sumbody told me where I shud go to lern to read and spell good. They said why did you want to. I told them becaus all my life I wantid to be smart and not dumb. But its very hard to be smart. They said you know it will probly be tempirery. I said yes. Miss Kinnian told me. I dont care if it herts.

9   Later I had more crazy tests today. The nice lady who gave it me told me the name and I asked her how do you spellit so I can rite it in my progris riport. THEMATIC APPERCEPTION TEST.[2]

CLOSE READ
ANNOTATE: In paragraph 8, mark every misspelled word you see.

QUESTION: Looking over the marked words, would you describe the number of spelling errors as a few, some, or many?

CONCLUDE: What does the number of spelling errors suggest about the person writing these diary entries?

---

1. *raw shok* misspelling of Rorschach (RAWR shok) test, a psychological test that requires a subject to describe the images suggested by inkblots.
2. **THEMATIC** (thee MAT ihk) **APPERCEPTION** (ap uhr SEHP shuhn) **TEST** personality test in which the subject makes up stories about a series of pictures.

I dont know the frist 2 words but I know what *test* means. You got to pass it or you get bad marks. This test lookd easy becaus I coud see the picturs. Only this time she dint want me to tell her the picturs. That mixd me up. I said the man yesterday said I shoud tell him what I saw in the ink she said that dont make no difrence. She said make up storys about the pepul in the picturs.

10   I told her how can you tell storys about pepul you never met. I said why shud I make up lies. I never tell lies any more becaus I always get caut.

11   She told me this test and the other one the raw-shok was for getting personalty. I laffed so hard. I said how can you get that thing from inkblots and fotos. She got sore and put her picturs away. I dont care. It was sily. I gess I faled that test too.

12   Later some men in white coats took me to a difernt part of the hospitil and gave me a game to play. It was like a race with a white mouse. They called the mouse Algernon. Algernon was in a box with a lot of twists and turns like all kinds of walls and they gave me a pencil and a paper with lines and lots of boxes. On one side it said START and on the other end it said FINISH. They said it was *amazed*[3] and that Algernon and me had the same *amazed* to do. I dint see how we could have the same *amazed* if Algernon had a box and I had a paper but I dint say nothing. Anyway there wasnt time because the race started.

13   One of the men had a watch he was trying to hide so I woudnt see it so I tryed not to look and that made me nervus.

14   Anyway that test made me feel worser than all the others because they did it over 10 times with difernt *amazeds* and Algernon won every time. I dint know that mice were so smart. Maybe thats because Algernon is a white mouse. Maybe white mice are smarter than other mice.

progris riport 4—Mar 8

15   Their going to use me! Im so exited I can hardly write. Dr Nemur and Dr Strauss had a argument about it first. Dr Nemur was in the office when Dr Strauss brot me in. Dr Nemur was worryed about using me but Dr Strauss told him Miss Kinnian rekemmended me the best from all the pepul who she was teaching. I like Miss Kinnian becaus shes a very smart teacher. And she said Charlie your going to have a second chance. If you volenteer for this experament you mite get smart. They dont know if it will be perminint but theirs a chance. Thats why I said ok even when I was scared because she said it was an operashun. She said dont be scared Charlie you done so much with so little I think you deserv it most of all.

---

3. **amazed** Charlie means "a maze," or a confusing series of paths. Often, the intelligence of animals is assessed by how fast they go through a maze.

TEACHING

Charlie—as portrayed by Cliff Robinson in the 1968 film adaptation—with scientists and Algernon

NOTES

16 So I got scaird when Dr Nemur and Dr Strauss argud about it. Dr Strauss said I had something that was very good. He said I had a good *motor-vation*.[4] I never even knew I had that. I felt proud when he said that not every body with an eye-q[5] of 68 had that thing. I dont know what it is or where I got it but he said Algernon had it too. Algernons *motor-vation* is the cheese they put in his box. But it cant be that because I didnt eat any cheese this week.

17 Then he told Dr Nemur something I dint understand so while they were talking I wrote down some of the words.

18 He said Dr Nemur I know Charlie is not what you had in mind as the first of your new brede of intelek** (coudnt get the word) superman. But most people of his low ment** are host** and uncoop** they are usualy dull apath** and hard to reach. He has a good natcher hes intristed and eager to please.

19 Dr Nemur said remember he will be the first human beeng ever to have his intelijence trippled by surgicle meens.

20 Dr Strauss said exakly. Look at how well hes lerned to read and write for his low mentel age its as grate an acheve** as you and I lerning einstines therey of **vity without help. That shows the intenss motor-vation. Its comparat** a tremen** achev** I say we use Charlie.

---

4. ***motor-vation*** motivation, or desire to work hard and achieve a goal.
5. ***eye-q*** IQ, or intelligence quotient—a way of measuring human intelligence.

PERSONALIZE FOR LEARNING

Strategic Support

Text Clues Point out the use of asterisks and Charlie's parenthetical comment in paragraph 18. Ask students to discuss what the author is doing here. Point out that Charlie is reporting in his journal things he heard, but does not remember well or understand. He is using the asterisks to tell the reader that he is unsure of these words. He is explaining this to the reader through the use of a parenthetical comment. Ask students to think about what this says about Charlie.

21   I dint get all the words and they were talking to fast but it sounded like Dr Strauss was on my side and like the other one wasnt.

22   Then Dr Nemur nodded he said all right maybe your right. We will use Charlie. When he said that I got so exited I jumped up and shook his hand for being so good to me. I told him thank you doc you wont be sorry for giving me a second chance. And I mean it like I told him. After the operashun Im gonna try to be smart. Im gonna try awful hard.

progris ript 5—Mar 10

23   Im skared. Lots of people who work here and the nurses and the people who gave me the tests came to bring me candy and wish me luck. I hope I have luck. I got my rabits foot and my lucky penny and my horse shoe. Only a black cat crossed me when I was comming to the hospitil. Dr Strauss says don't be supersitis Charlie this is sience. Anyway Im keeping my rabits foot with me.

24   I asked Dr Strauss if Ill beat Algernon in the race after the operashun and he said maybe. If the operashun works Ill show that mouse I can be as smart as he is. Maybe smarter. Then Ill be abel to read better and spell the words good and know lots of things and be like other people. I want to be smart like other people. If it works perminint they will make everybody smart all over the wurld.

25   They dint give me anything to eat this morning. I dont know what that eating has to do with getting smart. Im very hungry and Dr Nemur took away my box of candy. That Dr Nemur is a grouch. Dr Strauss says I can have it back after the operashun. You cant eat befor a operashun . . .

Progress Report 6—Mar 15

26   The operashun dint hurt. He did it while I was sleeping. They took off the bandijis from my eyes and my head today so I can make a PROGRESS REPORT. Dr Nemur who looked at some of my other ones says I spell PROGRESS wrong and he told me how to spell it and REPORT too. I got to try and remember that.

27   I have a very bad memary for spelling. Dr Strauss says its ok to tell about all the things that happin to me but he says I shoud tell more about what I feel and what I think. When I told him I dont know how to think he said try. All the time when the bandijis were on my eyes I tryed to think. Nothing happened. I dont know what to think about. Maybe if I ask him he will tell me how I can think now that Im suppose to get smart. What do smart people think about. Fancy things I suppose. I wish I knew some fancy things alredy.

NOTES

CLOSE READ
ANNOTATE: Mark the sentences in the March 10 entry that set out Charlie's goals.

QUESTION: What do you notice about these goals and the way that Charlie writes about them?

CONCLUDE: How do Charlie's goals and the way he states them make you feel sympathetic toward him?

TEACHING

Progress Report 7—Mar 19

28 Nothing is happining. I had lots of tests and different kinds of races with Algernon. I hate that mouse. He always beats me. Dr Strauss said I got to play those games. And he said some time I got to take those tests over again. Thse inkblots are stupid. And those pictures are stupid too. I like to draw a picture of a man and a woman but I wont make up lies about people.

29 I got a headache from trying to think so much. I thot Dr Strauss was my frend but he dont help me. He dont tell me what to think or when Ill get smart. Miss Kinnian dint come to see me. I think writing these progress reports are stupid too.

Progress Report 8—Mar 23

30 Im going back to work at the factery. They said it was better I shud go back to work but I cant tell anyone what the operashun was for and I have to come to the hospitil for an hour evry night after work. They are gonna pay me mony every month for lerning to be smart.

31 Im glad Im going back to work because I miss my job and all my frends and all the fun we have there.

32 Dr Strauss says I shud keep writing things down but I don't have to do it every day just when I think of something or something speshul happins. He says dont get discoridged because it takes time and it happins slow. He says it took a long time with Algernon before he got 3 times smarter then he was before. Thats why Algernon beats me all the time because he had that operashun too. That makes me feel better. I coud probly do that *amazed* faster than a reglar mouse. Maybe some day Ill beat Algernon. Boy that would be something. So far Algernon looks like he mite be smart perminent.

Mar 25

33 (I dont have to write PROGRESS REPORT on top any more just when I hand it in once a week for Dr Nemur to read. I just have to put the date on. That saves time)

34 We had a lot of fun at the factery today. Joe Carp said hey look where Charlie had his operashun what did they do Charlie put some brains in. I was going to tell him but I remembered Dr Strauss said no. Then Frank Reilly said what did you do Charlie forget your key and open your door the hard way. That made me laff. Their really my friends and they like me.

35 Sometimes somebody will say hey look at Joe or Frank or George he really pulled a Charlie Gordon. I dont know why they say that but they always laff. This morning Amos Borg who is the 4 man at Donnegans used my name when he shouted at Ernie the

356 UNIT 4 • HUMAN INTELLIGENCE

PERSONALIZE FOR LEARNING

Strategic Support

Read Aloud Call student attention to paragraphs 28 and 29, The spelling and grammar mistakes within Charlie's journal can make it a challenge to read and understand. Have a volunteer read aloud these paragraphs. Ask students what Charlie is talking about here. Was it easy to understand when they listened to it? How did hearing the text differ from reading it? Guide students to discuss whether the text would have the same impact, or if they would have the same understanding of Charlie, if they had only heard the text and not seen the way he wrote it.

office boy. Ernie lost a packige. He said Ernie what are you trying to be a Charlie Gordon. I don't understand why he said that. I never lost any packiges.

Mar 28

36 Dr Straus came to my room tonight to see why I dint come in like I was suppose to. I told him I dont like to race with Algernon any more. He said I dont have to for a while but I shud come in. He had a present for me only it wasnt a present but just for lend. I thot it was a little television but it wasnt. He said I got to turn it on when I go to sleep. I said your kidding why shud I turn it on when Im going to sleep. Who ever herd of a thing like that. But he said if I want to get smart I got to do what he says. I told him I dint think I was going to get smart and he put his hand on my sholder and said Charlie you dont know it yet but your getting smarter all the time. You wont notice for a while. I think he was just being nice to make me feel good because I don't look any smarter.

37 Oh yes I almost forgot. I asked him when I can go back to the class at Miss Kinnians school. He said I wont go their. He said that soon Miss Kinnian will come to the hospital to start and teach me speshul. I was mad at her for not comming to see me when I got the operashun but I like her so maybe we will be frends again.

Mar 29

38 That crazy TV kept me up all night. How can I sleep with something yelling crazy things all night in my ears. And the nutty pictures. Wow. I dont know what it says when Im up so how am I going to know when Im sleeping.

39 Dr Strauss says its ok. He says my brains are lerning when I sleep and that will help me when Miss Kinnian starts my lessons in the hospitl (only I found out it isnt a hospitil its a labatory. I think its all crazy. If you can get smart when your sleeping why do people go to school. That thing I dont think will work. I use to watch the late show and the late late show on TV all the time and it never made me smart. Maybe you have to sleep while you watch it.

Progress Report 9—APRIL 3

40 Dr Strauss showed me how to keep the TV turned low so now I can sleep. I don't hear a thing. And I still dont understand what it says. A few times I play it over in the morning to find out what I lerned when I was sleeping and I dont think so. Miss Kinnian says Maybe its another langwidge or something. But most times it sounds american. It talks so fast faster then even Miss Gold who was my teacher in 6 grade and I remember she talked so fast I coudnt understand her.

NOTES

subconscious (suhb KON shuhs) *n.* mental activity that occurs without someone's being aware of it

41   I told Dr Strauss what good is it to get smart in my sleep. I want to be smart when Im awake. He says its the same thing and I have two minds. Theres the *subconscious* and the *conscious* (thats how you spell it). And one dont tell the other one what its doing. They dont even talk to each other. Thats why I dream. And boy have I been having crazy dreams. Wow. Ever since that night TV. The late late late late late show.

42   I forgot to ask him if it was only me or if everybody had those two minds.

43   (I just looked up the word in the dictionary Dr Strauss gave me. The word is *subconscious*. adj. *Of the nature of mental operations yet not present in consciousness; as, subconscious conflict of desires.*) There's more but I still dont know what it means. This isnt a very good dictionary for dumb people like me.

44   Anyway the headache is from the party. My frends from the factery Joe Carp and Frank Reilly invited me to go with them to Muggsys Saloon for some drinks. I dont like to drink but they said we will have lots of fun. I had a good time.

45   Joe Carp said I shoud show the girls how I mop out the toilet in the factory and he got me a mop. I showed them and everyone laffed when I told that Mr Donnegan said I was the best janiter he ever had because I like my job and do it good and never come late or miss a day except for my operashun.

46   I said Miss Kinnian always said Charlie be proud of your job because you do it good.

47   Everybody laffed and we had a good time and they gave me lots of drinks and Joe said Charlie is a card when hes potted. I dont know what that means but everybody likes me and we have fun. I cant wait to be smart like my best frends Joe Carp and Frank Reilly.

48   I dont remember how the party was over but I think I went out to buy a newspaper and coffe for Joe and Frank and when I came back there was no one their. I looked for them all over till late. Then I dont remember so good but I think I got sleepy or sick. A nice cop brot me back home. Thats what my landlady Mrs Flynn says.

49   But I got a headache and a big lump on my head and black and blue all over. I think maybe I fell. Anyway I got a bad headache and Im sick and hurt all over. I dont think Ill drink anymore.

April 6

50   I beat Algernon! I dint even know I beat him until Burt the tester told me. Then the second time I lost because I got so exited I fell off the chair before I finished. But after that I beat him 8 more times. I must be getting smart to beat a smart mouse like Algernon. But I dont *feel* smarter.

PERSONALIZE FOR LEARNING

Challenge

Analyze Have students reread paragraph 45. Explain that although Charlie is telling us exactly what he remembers, the reader can analyze what he is saying and make inferences about Charlie and the people he went out with. Have students write a paragraph analyzing what Charlie is telling the reader here. Have them consider the people Charlie spent the evening with, how they acted toward Charlie, and what they might think of him. Remind students to cite text evidence to support their theories.

Charlie with Miss Kinnian—as portrayed by Claire Bloom

51   I wanted to race Algernon some more but Burt said that's enough for one day. They let me hold him for a minit. Hes not so bad. Hes soft like a ball of cotton. He blinks and when he opens his eyes their black and pink on the eges.

52   I said can I feed him because I felt bad to beat him and I wanted to be nice and make frends. Burt said no Algernon is a very specshul mouse with an operashun like mine, and he was the first of all the animals to stay smart so long. He told me Algernon is so smart that every day he has to solve a test to get his food. Its a thing like a lock on a door that changes every time Algernon goes in to eat so he has to lern something new to get his food. That made me sad because if he coudnt lern he woud be hungry.

53   I dont think its right to make you pass a test to eat. How woud Dr Nemur like it to have to pass a test every time he wants to eat. I think Ill be frends with Algernon.

April 9

54   Tonight after work Miss Kinnian was at the laboratory. She looked like she was glad to see me but scared. I told her dont worry Miss Kinnian Im not smart yet and she laffed. She said I have confidence in you Charlie the way you struggled so hard to read and right better than all the others. At werst you will have it for a littel wile and your doing something for sience.

55   We are reading a very hard book. I never read such a hard book before. Its called *Robinson Crusoe*[6] about a man who gets merooned on a dessert Iland. Hes smart and figers out all kinds of things so

---

6. **Robinson Crusoe** (KROO soh) 1719 novel written by Daniel Defoe, a British author.

TEACHING

CLOSE READ

As Charlie's transformation continues, readers can infer these changes based on changes in the writing in his diary entries, such as the one for April 15 (paragraph 58). You may wish to model the close read using the following think-aloud format. Possible responses to questions on the student page are included.

ANNOTATE: As I read the April 15 entry, I mark the words that are misspelled.

QUESTION: I notice that there are not as many errors compared with the March 7 entry, and the errors are mostly mistakes in using apostrophes.

CONCLUDE: I can conclude that the operation has had the effect of improving Charlie's intelligence. His spelling is improving.

NOTES

he can have a house and food and hes a good swimmer. Only I feel sorry because hes all alone and has no frends. But I think their must be somebody else on the iland because theres a picture with his funny umbrella looking at footprints. I hope he gets a frend and not be lonly.

April 10

56   Miss Kinnian teaches me to spell better. She says look at a word and close your eyes and say it over and over until you remember. I have lots of truble with *through* that you say *threw* and *enough* and *tough* that you dont say *enew* and *tew*. You got to say *enuff* and *tuff*. Thats how I use to write it before I started to get smart. Im confused but Miss Kinnian says theres no reason in spelling.

April 14

57   Finished Robinson Crusoe. I want to find out more about what happens to him but Miss Kinnian says thats all there is. *Why*

April 15

58   Miss Kinnian says Im lerning fast. She read some of the Progress Reports and she looked at me kind of funny. She says Im a fine person and Ill show them all. I asked her why. She said never mind but I shoudnt feel bad if I find out that everybody isnt nice like I think. She said for a person who god gave so little to you done more then a lot of people with brains they never even used. I said all my frends are smart people but there good. They like me and they never did anything that wasnt nice. Then she got something in her eye and she had to run out to the ladys room.

April 16

59   Today, I lerned, the comma, this is a comma (,) a period, with a tail, Miss Kinnian, says its important, because, it makes writing, better, she said, somebody, coud lose, a lot of money, if a comma, isnt, in the, right place, I dont have, any money, and I dont see, how a comma, keeps you, from losing it,

60   But she says, everybody, uses commas, so Ill use, them too,

April 17

61   I used the comma wrong. Its punctuation. Miss Kinnian told me to look up long words in the dictionary to lern to spell them. I said whats the difference if you can read it anyway. She said its part of your education so now on Ill look up all the words Im not sure how to spell. It takes a long time to write that way but I think Im remembering. I only have to look up once and after that I get it right. Anyway thats how come I got the word *punctuation* right. (Its that way in the dictionary). Miss Kinnian says a period is punctuation too, and there are lots of other marks to lern. I told her I thot all the periods had to have tails but she said no.

CLOSE READ
ANNOTATE: Mark the spelling errors you find in Charlie's April 15 entry.

QUESTION: What do you notice about the number of errors, as compared to the total you marked in the March 7 entry?

QUESTION: What does this reveal about the effect of the operation on Charlie's ability to think and write?

VOCABULARY DEVELOPMENT

Word Analysis

Direct students to paragraph 56. Highlight the italicized words. Charlie points out words that end in *-ough*. Ask students what they think about his analysis of these words and their pronunciations. Create a class chart of words that end in *-ough*. Have them add familiar words to the chart.

-ough	
Pronounced "ew"	Pronounced "uff"

62   You got to mix them up, she showed? me" how. to mix! them(up,. and now; I can! mix up all kinds" of punctuation, in! my writing? There, are lots! of rules? to lern; but Im gettin'g them in my head.

63   One thing I? like about, Dear Miss Kinnian: (thats the way it goes in a business letter if I ever go into business) is she, always gives me' a reason" when—I ask. She's a gen'ius! I wish! I cou'd be smart" like, her;

64   (Punctuation, is; fun!)

April 18

65   What a dope I am! I didn't even understand what she was talking about. I read the grammar book last night and it explanes the whole thing. Then I saw it was the same way as Miss Kinnian was trying to tell me, but I didn't get it. I got up in the middle of the night, and the whole thing straightened out in my mind.

66   Miss Kinnian said that the TV working in my sleep helped out. She said I reached a plateau. Thats like the flat top of a hill.

67   After I figgered out how punctuation worked, I read over all my old Progress Reports from the beginning. Boy, did I have crazy spelling and punctuation! I told Miss Kinnian I ought to go over the pages and fix all the mistakes but she said, "No. Charlie, Dr. Nemur wants them just as they are. That's why he let you keep them after they were photostated, to see your own progress. You're coming along fast, Charlie."

68   That made me feel good. After the lesson I went down and played with Algernon. We don't race any more.

April 20

69   I feel sick inside. Not sick like for a doctor, but inside my chest it feels empty like getting punched and a heartburn at the same time.

70   I wasn't going to write about it, but I guess I got to, because its important. Today was the first time I ever stayed home from work.

71   Last night Joe Carp and Frank Reilly invited me to a party. There were lots of girls and some men from the factory. I remembered how sick I got last time I drank too much, so I told Joe I didn't want anything to drink. He gave me a plain coke instead. It tasted funny, but I thought it was just a bad taste in my mouth.

72   We had a lot of fun for a while. Joe said I should dance with Ellen and she would teach me the steps. I fell a few times and I couldn't understand why because no one else was dancing besides Ellen and me. And all the time I was tripping because somebody's foot was always sticking out.

TEACHING

NOTES

73 Then when I got up I saw the look on Joe's face and it gave me a funny feeling in my stomach. "He's a scream," one of the girls said. Everybody was laughing.

74 Frank said, "I ain't laughed so much since we sent him off for the newspaper that night at Muggsy's and ditched him."

75 "Look at him. His face is red."

76 "He's blushing. Charlie is blushing."

77 "Hey, Ellen, what'd you do to Charlie? I never saw him act like that before."

78 I didn't know what to do or where to turn. Everyone was looking at me and laughing and I felt naked. I wanted to hide myself. I ran out into the street and I threw up. Then I walked home. It's a funny thing I never knew that Joe and Frank and the others liked to have me around all the time to make fun of me.

79 Now I know what it means when they say "to pull a Charlie Gordon."

80 I'm ashamed.

Progress Report 11—April 21

81 Still didn't go into the factory. I told Mrs. Flynn my landlady to call and tell Mr. Donnegan I was sick. Mrs. Flynn looks at me very funny lately like she's scared of me.

82 I think it's a good thing about finding out how everybody laughs at me. I thought about it a lot. It's because I'm so dumb and I don't even know when I'm doing something dumb. People think it's funny when a dumb person can't do things the same way they can.

83 Anyway, now I know I'm getting smarter every day. I know punctuation and I can spell good. I like to look up all the hard words in the dictionary and I remember them. I'm reading a lot now, and Miss Kinnian says I read very fast. Sometimes I even understand what I'm reading about, and it stays in my mind. There are times when I can close my eyes and think of a page and it all comes back like a picture.

84 Besides history, geography and arithmetic, Miss Kinnian said I should start to learn a few foreign languages. Dr. Strauss gave me some more tapes to play while I sleep. I still don't understand how that conscious and unconscious mind works, but Dr. Strauss says not to worry yet. He asked me to promise that when I start learning college subjects next week I wouldn't read any books on psychology—that is, until he gives me permission.

85 I feel a lot better today, but I guess I'm still a little angry that all the time people were laughing and making fun of me because I wasn't so smart. When I become intelligent like Dr. Strauss says, with three times my I.Q. of 68, then maybe I'll be like everyone else and people will like me and be friendly.

> I didn't know what to do or where to turn. Everyone was looking at me and laughing and I felt naked.

WriteNow Express and Reflect

Analysis In paragraph 78, Charlie uses a figure of speech. He says, "I felt naked." Remind students that he was not actually naked, but he is trying to tell the reader something important here. Have students reread paragraphs 78–80 and write a few sentences about what Charlie means when he says, "I felt naked." Next, have students analyze how this comment marks a change for Charlie and how he sees himself and others.

86 I'm not sure what an I.Q. is. Dr. Nemur said it was something that measured how intelligent you were—like a scale in the drugstore weighs pounds. But Dr. Strauss had a big arguement with him and said an I.Q. didn't weigh intelligence at all. He said an I.Q. showed how much intelligence you could get, like the numbers on the outside of a measuring cup. You still had to fill the cup up with stuff.

87 Then when I asked Burt, who gives me my intelligence tests and works with Algernon, he said that both of them were wrong (only I had to promise not to tell them he said so). Burt says that the I.Q. measures a lot of different things including some of the things you learned already, and it really isn't any good at all.

88 So I still don't know what I.Q. is except that mine is going to be over 200 soon. I didn't want to say anything, but I don't see how if they don't know *what* it is, or *where* it is—I don't see how they know *how much* of it you've got.

89 Dr. Nemur says I have to take a *Rorshach Test* tomorrow. I wonder what *that* is.

April 22

90 I found out what a *Rorshach* is. It's the test I took before the operation—the one with the inkblots on the pieces of cardboard. The man who gave me the test was the same one.

91 I was scared to death of those inkblots. I knew he was going to ask me to find the pictures and I knew I wouldn't be able to. I was thinking to myself, if only there was some way of knowing what kind of pictures were hidden there. Maybe there weren't any pictures at all. Maybe it was just a trick to see if I was dumb enough too look for something that wasn't there. Just thinking about that made me sore at him.

92 "All right, Charlie," he said, "you've seen these cards before, remember?"

93 "Of course I remember."

94 The way I said it, he knew I was angry, and he looked surprised. "Yes, of course. Now I want you to look at this one. What might this be? What do you see on this card? People see all sorts of things in these inkblots. Tell me what it might be for you—what it makes you think of."

95 I was shocked. That wasn't what I had expected him to say at all. "You mean there are no pictures hidden in those inkblots?"

96 He frowned and took off his glasses. "What?"

97 "Pictures. Hidden in the inkblots. Last time you told me that everyone could see them and you wanted me to find them too."

98 He explained to me that the last time he had used almost the exact same words he was using now. I didn't believe it, and I still have the **suspicion** that he misled me at the time just for the

NOTES

CLOSE READ
ANNOTATE: Mark the sentences in paragraph 91 that begin in similar ways.

QUESTION: What emotions are emphasized by the repetition?

CONCLUDE: What is the author showing about Charlie's state of mind by writing the paragraph in this way?

suspicion (suh SPIHSH uhn) *n.* feeling of doubt or mistrust

Flowers for Algernon 363

fun of it. Unless—I don't know any more—could I have been *that* feeble-minded?

99   We went through the cards slowly. One of them looked like a pair of bats tugging at some thing. Another one looked like two men fencing with swords. I imagined all sorts of things. I guess I got carried away. But I didn't trust him any more, and I kept turning them around and even looking on the back to see if there was anything there I was supposed to catch. While he was making his notes, I peeked out of the corner of my eye to read it. But it was all in code that looked like this:

$$WF + A\ DdF\text{-}Ad\ orig.\ WF\text{-}A$$
$$SF + obj$$

100   The test still doesn't make sense to me. It seems to me that anyone could make up lies about things that they didn't really see. How could he know I wasn't making a fool of him by mentioning things that I didn't really imagine? Maybe I'll understand it when Dr. Strauss lets me read up on psychology.

April 25

101   I figured out a new way to line up the machines in the factory, and Mr. Donnegan says it will save him ten thousand dollars a year in labor and increased production. He gave me a $25 bonus.

102   I wanted to take Joe Carp and Frank Reilly out to lunch to celebrate, but Joe said he had to buy some things for his wife, and Frank said he was meeting his cousin for lunch. I guess it'll take a little time for them to get used to the changes in me. Everybody seems to be frightened of me. When I went over to Amos Borg and tapped him on the shoulder, he jumped up in the air.

103   People don't talk to me much any more or kid around the way they used to. It makes the job kind of lonely.

April 27

104   I got up the nerve today to ask Miss Kinnian to have dinner with me tomorrow night to celebrate my bonus.

105   At first she wasn't sure it was right, but I asked Dr. Strauss and he said it was okay. Dr. Strauss and Dr. Nemur don't seem to be getting along so well. They're arguing all the time. This evening when I came in to ask Dr. Strauss about having dinner with Miss Kinnian, I heard them shouting. Dr. Nemur was saying that it was *his* experiment and *his* research, and Dr. Strauss was shouting back that he contributed just as much, because he found me through Miss Kinnian and he performed the operation. Dr. Strauss said that someday thousands of neurosurgeons[7] might be using his technique all over the world.

---

7. **neurosurgeons** (NUR oh sur juhnz) *n.* doctors who operate on the nervous system, including the brain and spine.

PERSONALIZE FOR LEARNING

Strategic Support

Identify Details Ask a student to read aloud paragraph 101. Ask students what they notice about this paragraph. They should notice the success Charlie had and how he uses spelling and grammar. Then ask a student to read paragraph 1 aloud. Ask students to create a comparison chart of what they notice in the two paragraphs. Ask students to draw conclusions about the changes that have taken place in Charlie.

106 Dr. Nemur wanted to publish the results of the experiment at the end of this month. Dr. Strauss wanted to wait a while longer to be sure. Dr. Strauss said that Dr. Nemur was more interested in the Chair[8] of Psychology at Princeton than he was in the experiment. Dr. Nemur said that Dr. Strauss was nothing but an opportunist who was trying to ride to glory on *his* coattails.

107 When I left afterwards, I found myself trembling. I don't know why for sure, but it was as if I'd seen both men clearly for the first time. I remember hearing Burt say that Dr. Nemur had a shrew of a wife who was pushing him all the time to get things published so that he could become famous. Burt said that the dream of her life was to have a big shot husband.

108 Was Dr. Strauss really trying to ride on his coattails?

April 28

109 I don't understand why I never noticed how beautiful Miss Kinnian really is. She has brown eyes and feathery brown hair that comes to the top of her neck. She's only thirty-four!

110 I think from the beginning I had the feeling that she was an unreachable genius—and very, very old. Now, every time I see her she grows younger and more lovely.

111 We had dinner and a long talk. When she said that I was coming along so fast that soon I'd be leaving her behind, I laughed.

112 "It's true, Charlie. You're already a better reader than I am. You can read a whole page at a glance while I can take in only a few lines at a time. And you remember every single thing you read. I'm lucky if I can recall the main thoughts and the general meaning."

113 "I don't feel intelligent. There are so many things I don't understand."

114 "You've got to be a *little* patient. You're accomplishing in days and weeks what it takes normal people to do in half a lifetime. That's what makes it so amazing. You're like a giant sponge now, soaking things in. Facts, figures, general knowledge. And soon you'll begin to connect them, too. You'll see how the different branches of learning are related. There are many levels, Charlie, like steps on a giant ladder that take you up higher and higher to see more and more of the world around you."

115 "I can see only a little bit of that, Charlie, and I won't go much higher than I am now, but you'll keep climbing up and up, and see more and more, and each step will open new worlds that you never even knew existed." She frowned. "I hope . . . I just hope to God—"

116 "What?"

---

8. **Chair** *n.* professorship.

TEACHING

○ **CLOSER LOOK**

Analyze Analogy

Students may have marked paragraph 119 during their first read. In this paragraph, the author uses an analogy, a comparison that points out the similarities between two things. Encourage them to talk about the annotations that they marked. You may want to model a close read with the class based on the highlights shown in the text.

ANNOTATE: Have students mark details in paragraph 119 that show the author's use of an analogy, or have students participate while you highlight them.

QUESTION: Guide students to consider what these details might tell them. Ask what a reader can infer from Charlie's comparison of himself to elderly people, and accept student responses.

Possible response: The comparison implies that what Charlie believes Miss Kinnian is thinking about is something that will not make him happy.

CONCLUDE: Help students to formulate conclusions about the importance of these details in the text. Ask students why the author might have included these details.

Possible response: The writer is showing us how Charlie feels here. Instead of stating that he is concerned, the author brought in figurative language. It also shows that Charlie is thinking and communicating at a higher level than he did earlier in the story.

Remind students that an **analogy** is essentially an explanation of how two things are similar, usually with the aim of making it easier to understand one of those things.

Charlie and Miss Kinnian walking in the park

NOTES

117 "Never mind, Charles. I just hope I wasn't wrong to advise you to go into this in the first place."

118 I laughed. "How could that be? It worked, didn't it? Even Algernon is still smart."

119 We sat there silently for a while and I knew what she was thinking about as she watched me toying with the chain of my rabbit's foot and my keys. I didn't want to think of that possibility any more than elderly people want to think of death. I *knew* that this was only the beginning. I knew what she meant about levels because I'd seen some of them already. The thought of leaving her behind made me sad.

120 I'm in love with Miss Kinnian.

Progress Report 12—April 30

121 I've quit my job with Donnegan's Plastic Box Company. Mr. Donnegan insisted that it would be better for all concerned if I left. What did I do to make them hate me so?

122 The first I knew of it was when Mr. Donnegan showed me the petition. Eight hundred and forty names, everyone connected with the factory, except Fanny Girden. Scanning the list quickly, I saw at once that hers was the only missing name. All the rest demanded that I be fired.

123 Joe Carp and Frank Reilly wouldn't talk to me about it. No one else would either, except Fanny. She was one of the few people I'd known who set her mind to something and believed it no matter

what the rest of the world proved, said or did—and Fanny did not believe that I should have been fired. She had been against the petition on principle and despite the pressure and threats she'd held out.

124 "Which don't mean to say," she remarked, "that I don't think there's something mighty strange about you. Charlie. Them changes. I don't know. You used to be a good, dependable, ordinary man—not too bright maybe, but honest. Who knows what you done to yourself to get so smart all of a sudden. Like everybody around here's been saying, Charlie, it's not right."

125 "But how can you say that, Fanny? What's wrong with a man becoming intelligent and wanting to acquire knowledge and understanding of the world around him?"

126 She stared down at her work, and I turned to leave. Without looking at me, she said: "It was evil when Eve listened to the snake and ate from the tree of knowledge. It was evil when she saw that she was naked. If not for that none of us would ever have to grow old and sick, and die."

127 Once again now I have the feeling of shame burning inside me. This intelligence has driven a wedge between me and all the people I once knew and loved. Before, they laughed at me and **despised** me for my ignorance and dullness; now, they hate me for my knowledge and understanding. What do they want of me?

128 They've driven me out of the factory. Now I'm more alone than ever before . . .

despised (dih SPYZD) *v.* hated; scorned

May 15

129 Dr. Strauss is very angry at me for not having written any progress reports in two weeks. He's justified because the lab is now paying me a regular salary. I told him I was too busy thinking and reading. When I pointed out that writing was such a slow process that it made me impatient with my poor handwriting, he suggested that I learn to type. It's much easier to write now because I can type nearly seventy-five words a minute. Dr. Strauss continually reminds me of the need to speak and write simply so that people will be able to understand me.

130 I'll try to review all the things that happened to me during the last two weeks. Algernon and I were presented to the American Psychological Association sitting in convention with the World Psychological Association last Tuesday. We created quite a sensation. Dr. Nemur and Dr. Strauss were proud of us.

131 I suspect that Dr. Nemur, who is sixty—ten years older than Dr. Strauss—finds it necessary to see tangible[9] results of his work. Undoubtedly the result of pressure by Mrs. Nemur.

---

9. **tangible** (TAN juh buhl) *adj.* able to be felt or perceived; substantial.

DIGITAL PERSPECTIVES

Enriching the Text Ask students to reread paragraph 121–128, Charlie's journal entry for April 30. He quotes what Fanny says to him and then expresses his feelings about his life. Have students discuss how Charlie was feeling after his encounter with Fanny. Share a video clip that shows the exchange between Fanny and Charlie on April 30.

How do the actors show the emotions seen in the text? Have students compare the way the characters are portrayed in the video and in the text.

TEACHING

Remind students to focus on the author's word choice as they read paragraphs 134–138, and to mark any technical phrases or terms they notice. You may wish to model the close read using the following think-aloud format. Possible responses to questions on the student page are included.

ANNOTATE: As I read paragraphs 134–138, I notice and highlight academic phrases and specialized terms.

QUESTION: It's clear that Charlie has risen to a higher intellectual level than most people.

CONCLUDE: I can conclude that Charlie is aware he can make people feel uncomfortable and possibly ruin relationships if he makes himself appear more intelligent than others.

NOTES

CLOSE READ
ANNOTATE: Mark the specialized academic terms that Charlie uses in paragraphs 134–138.

QUESTION: From the use of this language, what is apparent about Charlie's level of intelligence compared to that of the people around him?

CONCLUDE: What potential problems could result from Charlie's use of language such as this?

132   Contrary to my earlier impressions of him, I realize that Dr. Nemur is not at all a genius. He has a very good mind, but it struggles under the specter of self-doubt. He wants people to take him for a genius. Therefore, it is important for him to feel that his work is accepted by the world. I believe that Dr. Nemur was afraid of further delay because he worried that someone else might make a discovery along these lines and take the credit from him.

133   Dr. Strauss on the other hand might be called a genius, although I feel that his areas of knowledge are too limited. He was educated in the tradition of narrow specialization; the broader aspects of background were neglected far more than necessary—even for a neurosurgeon.

134   I was shocked to learn that the only ancient languages he could read were Latin, Greek and Hebrew, and that he knows almost nothing of mathematics beyond the elementary levels of the calculus of variations. When he admitted this to me, I found myself almost annoyed. It was as if he'd hidden this part of himself in order to deceive me, pretending—as do many people I've discovered—to be what he is not. No one I've ever known is what he appears to be on the surface.

135   Dr. Nemur appears to be uncomfortable around me. Sometimes when I try to talk to him, he just looks at me strangely and turns away. I was angry at first when Dr. Strauss told me I was giving Dr. Nemur an inferiority complex. I thought he was mocking me and I'm oversensitive at being made fun of.

136   How was I to know that a highly respected psycho-experimentalist like Nemur was unacquainted with Hindustani[10] and Chinese? It's absurd when you consider the work that is being done in India and China today in the very field of his study.

137   I asked Dr. Strauss how Nemur could refute Rahajamati's attack on his method and results if Nemur couldn't even read them in the first place. That strange look on Dr. Strauss' face can mean only one of two things. Either he doesn't want to tell Nemur what they're saying in India, or else—and this worries me—Dr. Strauss doesn't know either. I must be careful to speak and write clearly and simply so that people won't laugh.

May 18

138   I am very disturbed. I saw Miss Kinnian last night for the first time in over a week. I tried to avoid all discussions of intellectual concepts and to keep the conversation on a simple, everyday level, but she just stared at me blankly and asked me what I meant about the mathematical variance equivalent in Dorbermann's *Fifth Concerto*.

---

10. **Hindustani** (hihn du STAH nee) *n.* a language of northern India.

139   When I tried to explain she stopped me and laughed. I guess I got angry, but I suspect I'm approaching her on the wrong level. No matter what I try to discuss with her, I am unable to communicate. I must review Vrostadt's equations on *Levels of Semantic Progression*. I find that I don't communicate with people much any more. Thank God for books and music and things I can think about. I am alone in my apartment at Mrs. Flynn's boarding house most of the time and seldom speak to anyone.

May 20

140   I would not have noticed the new dishwasher, a boy of about sixteen, at the corner diner where I take my evening meals if not for the incident of the broken dishes.

141   They crashed to the floor, shattering and sending bits of white china under the tables. The boy stood there, dazed and frightened, holding the empty tray in his hand. The whistles and catcalls from the customers (the cries of "hey, there go the profits!" . . . "*Mazeltov*!" . . . and "well, he didn't work here very long . . . " which invariably seems to follow the breaking of glass or dishware in a public restaurant) all seemed to confuse him.

142   When the owner came to see what the excitement was about, the boy cowered as if he expected to be struck and threw up his arms as if to ward off the blow.

143   "All right! All right, you dope," shouted the owner, "don't just stand there! Get the broom and sweep that mess up. A broom . . . a broom, you idiot! It's in the kitchen. Sweep up all the pieces."

144   The boy saw that he was not going to be punished. His frightened expression disappeared and he smiled and hummed as he came back with the broom to sweep the floor. A few of the rowdier customers kept up the remarks, amusing themselves at his expense.

145   "Here, sonny, over here there's a nice piece behind you . . ."

146   "C'mon, do it again . . ."

147   "He's not so dumb. It's easier to break 'em than to wash 'em . . ."

148   As his vacant eyes moved across the crowd of amused onlookers, he slowly mirrored their smiles and finally broke into an uncertain grin at the joke which he obviously did not understand.

149   I felt sick inside as I looked at his dull, vacuous smile, the wide, bright eyes of a child, uncertain but eager to please. They were laughing at him because he was mentally retarded.

150   And I had been laughing at him too.

151   Suddenly, I was furious at myself and all those who were smirking at him. I jumped up and shouted, "Shut up! Leave him

> . . . he slowly mirrored their smiles and finally broke into an uncertain grin at the joke which he obviously did not understand.

Flowers for Algernon **369**

NOTES

alone! It's not his fault he can't understand! He can't help what he is! But . . . he's still a human being!"

152 The room grew silent. I cursed myself for losing control and creating a scene. I tried not to look at the boy as I paid my check and walked out without touching my food. I felt ashamed for both of us.

153 How strange it is that people of honest feelings and sensibility, who would not take advantage of a man born without arms or legs or eyes—how such people think nothing of abusing a man born with low intelligence. It infuriated me to think that not too long ago I, like this boy, had foolishly played the clown.

154 And I had almost forgotten.

155 I'd hidden the picture of the old Charlie Gordon from myself because now that I was intelligent it was something that had to be pushed out of my mind. But today in looking at that boy, for the first time I saw what I had been. *I was just like him*!

156 Only a short time ago, I learned that people laughed at me. Now I can see that unknowingly l joined with them in laughing at myself. That hurts most of all.

157 I have often reread my progress reports and seen the illiteracy, the childish naivete, the mind of low intelligence peering from a dark room, through the keyhole, at the dazzling light outside. I see that even in my dullness I knew that I was inferior, and that other people had something I lacked—something denied me. In my mental blindness, I thought that it was somehow connected with the ability to read and write, and I was sure that if I could get those skills I would automatically have intelligence too.

158 Even a feeble-minded man wants to be like other men.

159 A child may not know how to feed itself, or what to eat, yet it knows of hunger.

160 This then is what I was like. I never knew. Even with my gift of intellectual awareness, I never really knew.

161 This day was good for me. Seeing the past more clearly, I have decided to use my knowledge and skills to work in the field of increasing human intelligence levels. Who is better equipped for this work? Who else has lived in both worlds? These are my people. Let me use my gift to do something for them.

162 Tomorrow, I will discuss with Dr. Strauss the manner in which I can work in this area. I may be able to help him work out the problems of widespread use of the technique which was used on me. I have several good ideas of my own.

163 There is so much that might be done with this technique. If I could be made into a genius, what about thousands of others like myself? What fantastic levels might be achieved by using this technique on normal people? On *geniuses*?

164 There are so many doors to open. I am impatient to begin.

CROSS-CURRICULAR PERSPECTIVES

Science What is the science of genius? In paragraph 163, Charlie talks about being a genius. In everyday life, the term *genius* is used freely, but what does it really mean? Ask students to explain what a genius is. Then have students do research about what science says a genius really is. What are the measures? Are there tests? What scientific evidence is needed to prove someone is a genius? Can someone be a genius in some intellectual areas and not in others?

PROGRESS REPORT 13—May 23

165   It happened today. Algernon bit me. I visited the lab to see him as I do occasionally, and when I took him out of his cage, he snapped at my hand. I put him back and watched him for a while. He was unusually disturbed and vicious.

May 24

166   Burt, who is in charge of the experimental animals, tells me that Algernon is changing. He is less cooperative; he refuses to run the maze any more; general motivation has decreased. And he hasn't been eating. Everyone is upset about what this may mean.

May 25

167   They've been feeding Algernon, who now refuses to work the shifting-lock problem. Everyone identifies me with Algernon. In a way we're both the first of our kind. They're all pretending that Algernon's behavior is not necessarily significant for me. But it's hard to hide the fact that some of the other animals who were used in this experiment are showing strange behavior.

168   Dr. Strauss and Dr. Nemur have asked me not to come to the lab any more. I know what they're thinking but I can't accept it. I am going ahead with my plans to carry their research forward. With all due respect to both of these fine scientists, I am well aware of their limitations. If there is an answer, I'll have to find it out for myself. Suddenly, time has become very important to me.

May 29

169   I have been given a lab of my own and permission to go ahead with the research. I'm on to something. Working day and night. I've had a cot moved into the lab. Most of my writing time is spent on the notes which I keep in a separate folder, but from time to time I feel it necessary to put down my moods and my thoughts out of sheer habit.

170   I find the *calculus of intelligence* to be a fascinating study. Here is the place for the application of all the knowledge I have acquired. In a sense it's the problem I've been concerned with all my life.

May 31

171   Dr. Strauss thinks I'm working too hard. Dr. Nemur says I'm trying to cram a lifetime of research and thought into a few weeks. I know I should rest, but I'm driven on by something inside that won't let me stop. I've got to find the reason for the sharp **regression** in Algernon. I've got to know *if* and *when* it will happen to me.

NOTES

CLOSE READ
ANNOTATE: In paragraph 169, mark the two shortest sentences.

QUESTION: What can you tell about Charlie's state of mind from the short sentences?

CONCLUDE: Why has the author made this choice?

regression (ri GREHSH uhn)
n. return to a previous, less advanced state

TEACHING

June 4

Letter to Dr. Strauss (copy)

Dear Dr. Strauss:

Under separate cover I am sending you a copy of my report entitled, "The Algernon-Gordon Effect: A Study of Structure and Function of Increased Intelligence," which I would like to have you read and have published.

As you see, my experiments are completed. I have included in my report all of my formulae, as well as mathematical analysis in the appendix. Of course, these should be verified.

Because of its importance to both you and Dr. Nemur (and need I say to myself, too?) I have checked and rechecked my results a dozen times in the hope of finding an error. I am sorry to say the results must stand. Yet for the sake of science, I am grateful for the little bit that I here add to the knowledge of the function of the human mind and of the laws governing the artificial increase of human intelligence.

I recall your once saying to me that an experimental *failure* or the *disproving* of a theory was as important to the advancement of learning as a success would be. I know now that this is true. I am sorry, however, that my own contribution to the field must rest upon the ashes of the work of two men I regard so highly.

Yours Truly,
Charles Gordon

encl.: rept.

June 5

I must not become emotional. The facts and the results of my experiments are clear, and the more sensational aspects of my own rapid climb cannot obscure the fact that the tripling of intelligence by the surgical technique developed by Drs. Strauss and Nemur must be viewed as having little or no practical applicability (at the present time) to the increase of human intelligence.

As I review the records and data on Algernon, I see that although he is still in his physical infancy, he has regressed mentally. Motor activity[11] is impaired; there is a general reduction of glandular activity; there is an accelerated loss of coordination.

There are also strong indications of progressive amnesia.

As will be seen by my report, these and other physical and mental **deterioration** syndromes[12] can be predicted with statistically significant results by the application of my formula.

The surgical stimulus to which we were both subjected has resulted in an intensification and acceleration of all mental processes. The unforeseen development, which I have taken the

deterioration (dih tihr ee uh RAY shuhn) *n.* process of becoming worse

---

11. **Motor activity** movement; physical coordination.
12. **syndromes** (SIHN drohmz) *n.* a number of symptoms occurring together and characterizing a specific disease or condition.

VOCABULARY DEVELOPMENT

Concept Vocabulary Reinforcement In paragraph 183, the concept vocabulary word *deterioration* appears in the text. Point out that the word *deteriorate* means "to get worse," so *deterioration* is the process of becoming worse. While this paragraph does not provide concrete clues to the meaning of this word, paragraph 181 does. Point out the words *regressed, impaired, reduction,* and *loss*. All of these words provide clues to the meaning of *deterioration*. Ask students to use the word *deterioration* in a sentence to show they know its meaning. Have them include one of the clue words from paragraph 181 in the sentence.

Charlie, months into the experiment

liberty of calling the "Algernon-Gordon Effect," is the logical extension of the entire intelligence speedup. The hypothesis here proven may be described simply in the following terms: Artificially increased intelligence deteriorates at a rate of time directly proportional to the quantity of the increase.

185   I feel that this, in itself, is an important discovery.

186   As long as I am able to write, I will continue to record my thoughts in these progress reports. It is one of my few pleasures. However, by all indications, my own mental deterioration will be very rapid.

187   I have already begun to notice signs of emotional instability and forgetfulness, the first symptoms of the burnout.

June 10

188   Deterioration progressing. I have become absent-minded. Algernon died two days ago. Dissection shows my predictions were right. His brain had decreased in weight and there was a general smoothing out of cerebral convolutions as well as a deepening and broadening of brain fissures.

189   I guess the same thing is or will soon be happening to me. Now that it's definite, I don't want it to happen.

CLOSE READ

ANNOTATE: Mark the choppy sentences that appear at the beginning of paragraph 188.

QUESTION: What does this change in writing style suggest?

CONCLUDE: What effect does knowing what is happening to Charlie have on the reader?

NOTES

190   I put Algernon's body in a cheese box and buried him in the back yard. I cried.

June 15

191   Dr. Strauss came to see me again. I wouldn't open the door and I told him to go away. I want to be left to myself. I have become touchy and irritable. I feel the darkness closing in. I keep telling myself how important this *introspective* journal will be.

192   It's a strange sensation to pick up a book that you've read and enjoyed just a few months ago and discover that you don't remember it. I remembered how great I thought John Milton[13] was, but when I picked up *Paradise Lost* I couldn't understand it at all. I got so angry I threw the book across the room.

193   I've got to try to hold on to some of it. Some of the things I've learned. Oh, God, please don't take it all away.

June 19

194   Sometimes, at night, I go out for a walk. Last night I couldn't remember where I lived. A policeman took me home. I have the strange feeling that this has all happened to me before—a long time ago. I keep telling myself I'm the only person in the world who can describe what's happening to me.

June 21

195   Why can't I remember? I've got to fight. I lie in bed for days and I don't know who or where I am. Then it all comes back to me in a flash. Fugues of amnesia.[14] Symptoms of senility—second childhood. I can watch them coming on. It's so cruelly logical. I learned so much and so fast. Now my mind is deteriorating rapidly. I won't let it happen. I'll fight it. I can't help thinking of the boy in the restaurant, the blank expression, the silly smile, the people laughing at him. No—please—not that again . . .

June 22

196   I'm forgetting things that I learned recently. It seems to be following the classic pattern—the last things learned are the first things forgotten. Or is that the pattern? I'd better look it up again . . .

197   I reread my paper on the "Algernon-Gordon Effect" and I get the strange feeling that it was written by someone else. There are parts I don't even understand.

198   Motor activity impaired. I keep tripping over things, and it becomes increasingly difficult to type.

June 23

199   I've given up using the typewriter completely. My coordination is bad. I feel that I'm moving slower and slower. Had a terrible

introspective (ihn truh SPEHK tihv) *adj.* thoughtful; inward-looking

---

13. **John Milton** British poet (1608–1674) who wrote *Paradise Lost*.
14. **Fugues** (fyoogz) **of amnesia** (am NEE zhuh) periods of memory loss.

shock today. I picked up a copy of an article I used in my research, Krueger's "Uber psychische Ganzheit," to see if it would help me understand what I had done. First I thought there was something wrong with my eyes. Then I realized I could no longer read German. I tested myself in other languages. All gone.

June 30

200 A week since I dared to write again. It's slipping away like sand through my fingers. Most of the books I have are too hard for me now. I get angry with them because I know that I read and understood them just a few weeks ago.

201 I keep telling myself I must keep writing these reports so that somebody will know what is happening to me. But it gets harder to form the words and remember spellings. I have to look up even simple words in the dictionary now and it makes me impatient with myself.

202 Dr. Strauss comes around almost every day, but I told him I wouldn't see or speak to anybody. He feels guilty. They all do. But I don't blame anyone. I knew what might happen. But how it hurts.

July 7

203 I don't know where the week went. Todays Sunday I know because I can see through my window people going to church. I think I stayed in bed all week but I remember Mrs. Flynn bringing food to me a few times. I keep saying over and over Ive got to do something but then I forget or maybe its just easier not to do what I say Im going to do.

204 I think of my mother and father a lot these days. I found a picture of them with me taken at a beach. My father has a big ball under his arm and my mother is holding me by the hand. I dont remember them the way they are in the picture. All I remember is my father arguing with mom about money.

205 He never shaved much and he used to scratch my face when he hugged me. He said he was going to take me to see cows on a farm once but he never did. He never kept his promises . . .

July 10

206 My landlady Mrs Flynn is very worried about me. She said she doesnt like loafers. If Im sick its one thing, but if Im a loafer thats another thing and she wont have it. I told her I think Im sick.

207 I try to read a little bit every day, mostly stories, but sometimes I have to read the same thing over and over again because I dont know what it means. And its hard to write. I know I should look up all the words in the dictionary but its so hard and Im so tired all the time.

NOTES

CLOSE READ
ANNOTATE: In paragraph 203, mark errors in Charlie's punctuation.

QUESTION: Why are these errors both familiar and alarming?

CONCLUDE: What effect do these errors have on the reader?

TEACHING

NOTES

208   Then I got the idea that I would only use the easy words instead of the long hard ones. That saves time. I put flowers on Algernon s grave about once a week. Mrs. Flynn thinks Im crazy to put flowers on a mouses grave but I told her that Algernon was special.

July 14

209   Its sunday again. I dont have anything to do to keep me busy now because my television set is broke and I dont have any money to get it fixed. (I think I lost this months check from the lab. I dont remember)

210   I get awful headaches and asperin doesnt help me much. Mrs. Flynn knows Im really sick and she feels very sorry for me. Shes a wonderful woman whenever someone is sick.

July 22

211   Mrs. Flynn called a strange doctor to see me. She was afraid I was going to die. I told the doctor I wasnt too sick and that I only forget sometimes. He asked me did I have any friends or relatives and I said no I dont have any. I told him I had a friend called Algernon once but he was a mouse and we used to run races together. He looked at me kind of funny like he thought I was crazy.

212   He smiled when I told him I used to be a genius. He talked to me like I was a baby and he winked at Mrs Flynn. I got mad and chased him out because he was making fun of me the way they all used to.

July 24

213   I have no more money and Mrs Flynn says I got to go to work somewhere and pay the rent because I havent paid for over two months. I dont know any work but the job I used to have at Donnegans Plastic Box Company. I dont want to go back there because they all knew me when I was smart and maybe they'll laugh at me. But I dont know what else to do to get money.

July 25

214   I was looking at some of my old progress reports and its very funny but I cant read what I wrote. I can make out some of the words but they dont make sense.

215   Miss Kinnian came to the door but I said go away I dont want to see you. She cried and I cried too but I wouldnt let her in because I didnt want her to laugh at me. I told her I didn't like her any more. I told her I didn't want to be smart any more. Thats not true. I still love her and I still want to be smart but I had to say that so shed go away. She gave Mrs. Flynn money to pay the rent. I dont want that. I got to get a job.

PERSONALIZE FOR LEARNING

English Language Support

Contractions Call student attention to paragraph 213. Remind students that contractions are made up of two words that are combined. They include an apostrophe. When they are spelled correctly, a reader who is familiar with the concept can easily identify them. As Charlie deteriorates, he continues to use contractions in his writing, but seldom uses the apostrophe. This can present a challenge for the reader. Have students review paragraph 213. Have them create a list of all of the misspelled contractions. Have them correct the contractions. (*haven't, don't*) Ask students to select another paragraph close to 213 and identify the misspelled contractions in it.

216   Please . . . please let me not forget how to read and write . . .

July 27

217   Mr. Donnegan was very nice when I came back and asked him for my old job of janitor. First he was very suspicious but I told him what happened to me then he looked very sad and put his hand on my shoulder and said Charlie Gordon you got guts.

218   Everybody looked at me when I came downstairs and started working in the toilet sweeping it out like I used to. I told myself Charlie if they make fun of you dont get sore because you remember their not so smart as you once thot they were. And besides they were once your friends and if they laughed at you that doesnt mean anything because they liked you too.

219   One of the new men who came to work there after I went away made a nasty crack he said hey Charlie I hear you're a very smart fella a real quiz kid. Say something intelligent. I felt bad but Joe Carp came over and grabbed him by the shirt and said leave him alone or Ill break your neck. I didn't expect Joe to take my part so **I guess hes really my friend.**

220   Later Frank Reilly came over and said Charlie if anybody bothers you or trys to take advantage you call me or Joe and we will set em straight. I said thanks Frank and I got choked up so I had to turn around and go into the supply room so he wouldnt see me cry. Its good to have friends.

July 28

221   I did a dumb thing today I forgot I wasnt in Miss Kinnians class at the adult center any more like I use to be. I went in and sat down in my old seat in the back of the room and she looked at me funny and she said Charles. I dint remember she ever called me that before only Charlie so I said hello Miss Kinnian Im ready for my lesin today only I lost my reader that we was using. She startid to cry and run out of the room and everybody looked at me and I saw they wasnt the same pepul who use to be in my class.

222   Then all of a suddin I rememberd some things about the operashun and me getting smart and I said holy smoke I reely pulled a Charlie Gordon that time. I went away before she come back to the room.

223   Thats why Im going away from New York for good. I don't want to do nothing like that agen. I dont want Miss Kinnian to feel sorry for me. Evry body feels sorry at the factery and I dont want that eather so Im going someplace where nobody knows that Charlie Gordon was once a genus and now he cant even reed a book or rite good.

> . . . Im going someplace where nobody knows that Charlie Gordon was once a genus and now he cant even reed a book or rite good.

NOTES

CLOSE READ
ANNOTATE: In paragraph 219, mark the conclusion that Charlie reaches about Joe Carp.

QUESTION: How is the situation not really as simple as Charlie describes?

CONCLUDE: What does the inclusion of this dialogue help the author show about Charlie?

224 Im taking a cuple of books along and even if I cant reed them Ill practise hard and maybe I wont forget every thing I lerned. If I try reel hard maybe Ill be a littel bit smarter then I was before the operashun. I got my rabits foot and my luky penny and maybe they will help me.

225 If you ever reed this Miss Kinnian dont be sorry for me Im glad I got a second chanse to be smart becaus I lerned a lot of things that I never even new were in this world and Im grateful that I saw it all for a littel bit. l dont know why Im dumb agen or what I did wrong maybe its becaus I dint try hard enuff. But if I try and practis very hard maybe Ill get a littl smarter and kow what all the words are. I remember a littel bit how nice I had a feeling with the blue book that has the torn cover when I reit. Thats why Im gonna keep trying to get smart so I can have that feeling agen. Its a good feeling to know things and be smart. I wish I had it rite now if I did I woud sit down and reed all the time. Anyway I bet Im the first dumb person in the world who ever found out something importent for sience. I remember I did somthing but I don't remember what. So I gess its like I did it for all the dumb pepul like me.

226 Goodbye Miss Kinnian and Dr Strauss and evreybody. And P.S. please tell Dr Nemur not to be such a grouch when pepul laff at him and he woud have more frends. Its easy to make frends if you let pepul laff at you. Im going to have lots of frends where I go.

227 P.P.S. Please if you get a chanse put some flowrs on Algernons grave in the bak yard . . .

Comprehension Check

Complete the following items after you finish your first read.

1. Who is Algernon, and why is he important?

2. What is the goal of the operation Dr. Strauss performs on Charlie?

3. What are three ways the operation changes Charlie's life?

4. What happens to Algernon in May and June?

5. What happens to Charlie at the end of the story?

6. **Notebook** Write a summary of "Flowers for Algernon."

RESEARCH

Research to Clarify Choose at least one unfamiliar detail from the text. Briefly research that detail. In what way does the information you learned shed light on an aspect of the story?

Research to Explore Choose something that interested you from the text, and formulate a research question.

DIGITAL PERSPECTIVES

Comprehension Check

Possible responses:
1. Algernon is a lab mouse. He is important because Dr. Strauss and Dr. Nemur experimented with surgery on Algernon before performing a similar operation on Charlie.
2. The goal of the operation is to triple Charlie's IQ, making him much more intelligent.
3. Charlie becomes able to learn many new subjects, including spelling, punctuation, foreign languages, and advanced math. Charlie becomes more aware of his emotions and the actions of people around him, from his teacher to his co-workers. Charlie becomes a talented researcher; he realizes and explains why the effects of his operation cannot last.
4. Algernon becomes hostile, and his brain deteriorates. Finally, he dies.
5. Charlie loses the extra intelligence he had gained through the operation.
6. Charlie is intellectually challenged. He has surgery and becomes a genius. Over time, he deteriorates and returns to his previous intellectual level.

Research

Research to Clarify If students struggle to decide on a detail to research, you may want to suggest that they focus on one of the following topics: IQ, the brain, genius, or brain trauma.

Research to Explore If students aren't sure how to go about formulating a research question, suggest that they use their findings from Research to Clarify as a starting point. For example, if students researched IQ, they might formulate a question such as, *How is IQ measured?*

PERSONALIZE FOR LEARNING

Challenge

Character Analysis Was it worth it? Charlie went through a tremendous change and went on a voyage of self-discovery. It seemed from his journals that with intelligence came a self-awareness he never had before. He understood how others were treating him. He became aware of not just matters of intellectual understanding but of emotional understanding. In the end, it all went away. If Charlie were able to talk to you about his experience, would he tell you it was worth it? Have students write a paragraph explaining their thoughts.

TEACHING

Jump Start

CLOSE READ Charlie had no idea how his life would change. For him, everything was simple. He got up each day, went to work, spent time with the people he thought were his friends, and did the same thing the next day. A doctor entered his world and suddenly, his life changed. Ask students: *How would you feel if everything about your life changed?*

Close Read the Text

Walk students through the annotation model on the student page. Encourage them to complete items 2 and 3 on their own. Review and discuss the sections students have marked. If needed, continue to model close reading by using the Annotation Highlights in the Interactive Teacher's Edition.

Analyze the Text

Possible responses:
1. By the end of the story, Charlie has lost much of the intelligence he gained through the experiment and is returning to the level of intelligence he had at the beginning. He is different because he has had the experience of being extremely intelligent. **DOK 2**
2. His diary shows how his mental and emotional capabilities are changing. First, they get stronger, and then he relapses to his former mental state. **DOK 2**
3. Through this experience, he has gained a better understanding of himself and the people around him. **DOK 2**
4. Charlie's relationships become more complicated. **DOK 2**
5. **Answers will vary.** Students may say that changes in the human brain can impact the way that people understand the world and communicate.

FORMATIVE ASSESSMENT

Analyze the Text

- **If** students fail to cite evidence, **then** remind them to support their ideas with specific information.
- **If** students struggle to form an opinion about Charlie's choice, **then** review the pros and cons of the choice.

380 UNIT 4 • HUMAN INTELLIGENCE

MAKING MEANING

FLOWERS FOR ALGERNON

Close Read the Text

1. This model, from paragraphs 149–150 of the text, shows two sample annotations, along with questions and conclusions. Close read the passage, and find another detail to annotate. Then, write a question and a conclusion.

> **ANNOTATE:** This sentence contains many descriptive adjectives.
> **QUESTION:** What purpose do these adjectives serve?
> **CONCLUDE:** The author is showing that Charlie has become quite perceptive about human behavior.
>
> I felt **sick** inside as I looked at his **dull, vacuous** smile, the **wide, bright** eyes of a child, **uncertain** but **eager** to please. They were laughing at him because he was mentally retarded.
> And I had been laughing at him too.
>
> **ANNOTATE:** This paragraph consists of a single sentence.
> **QUESTION:** What is the purpose of a single-sentence paragraph?
> **CONCLUDE:** The author is showing that this idea is important enough to stand alone.

🛠 Tool Kit
Close-Read Guide and Model Annotation

📋 STANDARDS
Reading Literature
- Cite the textual evidence that most strongly supports an analysis of what the text says explicitly as well as inferences drawn from the text.
- Determine a theme or central idea of a text and analyze its development over the course of the text, including its relationship to the characters, setting, and plot; provide an objective summary of the text.
- Analyze how differences in the points of view of the characters and the audience or reader create such effects as suspense or humor.
- Analyze how a modern work of fiction draws on themes, patterns of events, or character types from myths, traditional stories, or religious works such as the Bible, including describing how the material is rendered new.

2. For more practice, go back into the text, and complete the close-read notes.
3. Revisit a section of the text you found important during your first read. Read this section closely, and **annotate** what you notice. Ask yourself **questions** such as "Why did the author make this choice?" What can you **conclude**?

Analyze the Text

CITE TEXTUAL EVIDENCE to support your answers.

📓 **Notebook** Respond to these questions.

1. **Compare and Contrast** In what sense is Charlie the same at the end of the story as he is at the beginning? In what sense is he different?
2. **Analyze** How does Charlie's diary reveal his changing mental state?
3. **Draw Conclusions** Review the journal entry for July 28. What has Charlie gained through his experience?
4. **Analyze** In what ways does Charlie's operation affect his relationships with the people around him?
5. **Essential Question:** *In what different ways can people be intelligent?* What have you learned about human intelligence from reading this story?

380 UNIT 4 • HUMAN INTELLIGENCE

PERSONALIZE FOR LEARNING

English Language Support

Organization Have students review the story. Create a chart with three columns. Have students note events in the story and place them in the proper column. Ask students to explain why each event belongs in its column based on Charlie's behavior and intellect. After completing the chart, discuss why the order of events matters in composing a story. **ALL LEVELS**

Before Surgery	After Surgery	After Algernon Dies

ESSENTIAL QUESTION: In what different ways can people be intelligent?

Analyze Craft and Structure

Development of Theme The **theme** of a literary work is the central message about life that it conveys. In some works, the author expresses the theme by stating it directly. More often, however, the author implies or suggests the theme. To identify an implied theme, the reader analyzes the elements of the story, such as the setting, characters, and plot. The reader also considers the author's choices about how to structure the story and how to present details.

The **point of view,** or perspective from which a story is told, can provide clues to the theme.

- In **first-person point of view,** the narrator is a participant in the events of the story and uses first-person pronouns, such as *I, me,* and *my.* The narrator can tell only what he or she sees, knows, thinks, and feels. In **first-person naive point of view,** the narrator does not fully understand what is happening—for example, because he or she is a child or is traveling in an unfamiliar place.
- In **third-person point of view,** the narrator is not part of the story's events. Such a narrator uses only third-person pronouns, such as *he, she,* and *they.*

Authors may also provide clues to the theme by using allusions. An **allusion** is an unexplained reference to a well-known person, place, event, literary work, or work of art. For instance, an author may make an allusion to Greek or Roman mythology or to the Bible.

Practice

CITE TEXTUAL EVIDENCE to support your answers.

Notebook Answer the following questions.

1. (a) Who is the narrator of this story? (b) What point of view does this narrator use? Explain.
2. (a) At the beginning of the story, what does Charlie know and not know about himself and others? (b) How does his understanding change as the story progresses?
3. Cite specific ways in which the narrative point of view affects what readers learn about all the characters, especially their feelings and thoughts. Explain.
4. (a) Is Charlie's life better or worse at the end of the story than it was at the beginning? (b) What possible theme is suggested by Charlie's experience?
5. In paragraph 126, Fanny makes an allusion to a biblical story. If this story is unfamiliar to you, briefly research it. (a) How does this story relate to Charlie's experiences? (b) What theme does the author's use of this allusion help him develop? (c) In what ways is Charlie's experience different—a fresh take on the biblical story?

Flowers for Algernon 381

DIGITAL PERSPECTIVES

Analyze Craft and Structure

Development of Theme Explain to students that the theme of a piece of literature is not the same as its topic. The topic of this story could be stated as "the effect of artificially increased intelligence and its loss." The theme, however, is what the author has to say about that topic. A theme involves insights and ideas. For more support, see **Analyze Craft and Structure: Development of Themes.**

Practice
Possible responses:
1. (a) Charlie narrates the story through his journal entries. (b) The story is told in first-person naive point of view because Charlie doesn't often understand how people around him think about him.
2. (a) At the beginning, Charlie does not know why the scientists are interested in him. (b) He begins to see the way others treated him and he begins to understand that some people make fun of him.
3. Charlie can only describe what he understands. For example, he says they have fun at the factory, but he later learns that the men there mock him.
4. (a) Responses may vary. (b) Response may vary. Some students may suggest that science should not interfere with human intelligence. Some may say that gaining knowledge has risks and rewards.
5. (a) Charlie gets involved with something that many people believe should not be pursued. (b) Some students may say that this story develops a theme around the limits of scientific research. (c) Charlie's story may be different because Charlie does not make an informed decision to participate in the study.

PERSONALIZE FOR LEARNING

Strategic Support
Point of View Explain to students that the point of view from which a story is told affects how the reader experiences the characters and the plot. For example, in this story, the reader gets to understand and feel everything Charlie describes about his journey. Ask students to describe how the story would be different if it were told from the point of view of another character, or from a narrator who is outside the story. Guide students to explain their thinking.

FORMATIVE ASSESSMENT

Analyze Craft and Structure

- **If** students struggle to identify the theme, **then** review what a theme is and discuss the possible themes for this story.
- **If** students struggle to identify point of view, **then** review who is telling the story and how the different points of view are defined.

For Reteach and Practice, see **Analyze Craft and Structure: Development of Themes (RP).**

Whole-Class Learning 381

TEACHING

Concept Vocabulary

Why These Words?
Possible responses:
1. The concept vocabulary allows the reader to understand what Charlie went through.
2. *inkblot, Rorschach, laboratory, IQ, intelligence, genius, neurosurgeon, sensibility, limitations*

Practice
1. Answers will vary.
2. Possible response: *subconscious, subconsciously; despised, despicable; introspective, introspectively; suspicion, suspicious; deterioration, deteriorate; regression, regress*

Word Network
Possible words: *motivation, intellect, unconscious, inferior, impaired*

Word Study

For more support, see **Concept Vocabulary and Word Study.**

Possible responses:
1. A topic would be more important because a subtopic would come under a topic.
2. *Sub-* means "under," which helps explain that a submarine travels under the water.

FORMATIVE ASSESSMENT

Concept Vocabulary
If students struggle to understand the concept vocabulary and how the words relate to each other, **then** review the concept vocabulary words and their meanings.

Word Study
If students struggle to understand the meaning of the prefix *sub-* and its impact on the meaning of words, **then** review the prefix and other words that begin with it. For more support, see **Word Study: Latin Prefix *sub-* (RP).**

LANGUAGE DEVELOPMENT

FLOWERS FOR ALGERNON

Concept Vocabulary

| subconscious | despised | introspective |
| suspicion | deterioration | regression |

Why These Words? These concept vocabulary words are related to emotional and psychological states. Charlie experiences a range of these states. For example, the experiment makes him aware that his co-workers laughed at him and *despised* him. The experiment also changes Charlie's personality as his *suspicion* of everyone grows and he becomes more *introspective*.

1. How does the concept vocabulary sharpen the reader's understanding of the experiment Charlie undergoes?

2. What other words in the story connect to Charlie's experience?

Practice

Notebook The concept vocabulary words appear in "Flowers for Algernon."

1. Suppose you were a psychology researcher. Write a paragraph about an experiment you would like to design. Use at least four of the concept vocabulary words in your paragraph.

2. With a partner, see if you can match each concept word to a related word in the same word family.

Word Study

Latin Prefix: *sub-* You can use the Latin prefix *sub-*, which means "under" or "beneath," to help you determine the meaning of an unfamiliar word. In "Flowers for Algernon," Charlie learns that his *subconscious* is responsible for producing dreams and helping him learn. His subconscious thoughts, or the ones of which he is unaware, sit below his conscious thoughts, or the ones he knows he is having.

1. Which would you expect to be a more important part of an outline, a *topic* or a *subtopic*? Why?

2. How does the definition of *sub-* help you determine where you might find a *submarine*?

WORD NETWORK
Add words related to human intelligence from the text to your Word Network.

STANDARDS
Language
- Demonstrate command of the conventions of standard English grammar and usage when writing or speaking.
- Use common, grade-appropriate Greek or Latin affixes and roots as clues to the meaning of a word.
- Demonstrate understanding of figurative language, word relationships, and nuances in word meanings.
- Acquire and use accurately grade-appropriate general academic and domain-specific words and phrases; gather vocabulary knowledge when considering a word or phrase important to comprehension or expression.

AUTHOR'S PERSPECTIVE Elfrieda Hiebert, Ph.D.

Concept Vocabulary Teachers can help students expand their word networks by using morphemes and cognates.

- **Morphemes** are the smallest grammatical unit of a language that cannot be subdivided into further such elements. Tell students that morphemes can be words or parts of words, such as the words *as, the, write,* or the *–ed* in *stayed*. Many new words are members of morphological families of three-five words. For example, words that come from the Anglo-Saxon layer of English use inflected endings (such as *-s/-es, -ed, -ing*) and *-er* and *-est* for comparisons (such as *big, bigger, biggest*).

- **Cognates** are words that are descended from the same language, such as the English word *family*, the Spanish *familia*, the French *famille*, the Italian *famiglia*, and the German *familie*. Explain to students that knowing cognates can help build language by introducing multiple words and ways to decode unfamiliar words.

ESSENTIAL QUESTION: In what different ways can people be intelligent?

Conventions

Direct and Indirect Objects Writers use objects to show whom or what is affected by a verb's action. A **direct object** is a noun or pronoun that receives the action of the verb. A direct object answers the question *Whom?* or *What?* after an action verb.

An **indirect object** is a noun or pronoun that comes after an action verb and names the person or thing to which or for which something is done. To find the indirect object, first find the direct object of the verb. Then, ask: *To whom? For whom? To what?* or *For what?* The indirect object will almost always come between the verb and the direct object.

DIRECT OBJECT	INDIRECT OBJECT
S V DO **Sentence:** Bill baked some cookies. **Baked what?** cookies	S V IO DO **Sentence:** Bill baked Marissa some cookies. **Baked for whom?** Marissa

Read It

1. In each sentence, identify the subject, the verb, the direct object, and the indirect object. Some sentences do not include indirect objects.
   a. In their first race, Algernon beats Charlie.
   b. Miss Kinnian teaches Charlie reading and writing.
   c. Charlie trusts the doctors.
2. Reread the first clause of paragraph 174 of "Flowers for Algernon." Mark the subject, the verb, the direct object, and the indirect object.

Write It

Notebook In each sentence, identify the subject, the verb, the direct object, and the indirect object (if there is one). Then, rewrite the sentence with a different direct or indirect object. Your revisions do not have to stay true to the events of the story.

EXAMPLE
In his progress reports, Charlie expresses his feelings.

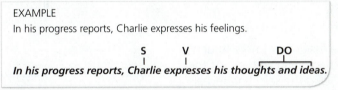

In his progress reports, Charlie expresses his thoughts and ideas.

1. The doctors give Charlie many tests.
2. Charlie's co-workers often trick him.
3. Charlie greatly admires Miss Kinnian.
4. Charlie brings Algernon flowers.

Flowers for Algernon 383

DIGITAL PERSPECTIVES

Conventions

Direct and Indirect Objects Identifying direct and indirect objects can be tricky. Point out that you cannot have an indirect object without having a direct object because the indirect object gives you more information about the direct object. Find the direct object first. If there is no direct object, there will be no indirect object. For more support, see **Conventions: Direct and Indirect Objects.**

MAKE IT INTERACTIVE
Review the example about Bill's cookies. Have students work with partners to create their own examples of sentences with only a direct object and sentences with a direct and indirect object. Have students be prepared to share their examples and identify their direct and indirect objects.

Read It
Possible responses:

1. (a) S: Algernon, V: beats, DO: Charlie
   (b) S: Miss Kinnian, V: teaches, DO: reading and writing, IO: Charlie (c) S: Charlie, V: trusts, DO: the doctors
2. S: I; V: am sending, DO copy; IO you

Write It
Possible responses:

1. S: doctors, V: give, DO: tests, IO: Charlie; The doctors give Charlie many opportunities.
2. S: co-workers, V: trick, DO: him; Charlie's co-workers often trick people who are less intelligent.
3. S: Charlie, V: admires, DO: Miss Kinnian; Charlie greatly admires Dr. Nemur and Dr. Strauss's work.
4. S: Charlie, V: brings, DO: flowers, IO: Algernon; Charlie brings Algernon food.

PERSONALIZE FOR LEARNING

English Language Support
Identifying and Using Direct and Indirect Objects
Display the following sentences: *I write the students a letter. Felipe bought Sonia a gift.*

Have students identify the direct and indirect object in each sentence (direct object: *a letter/a gift*; indirect object: *students/Sonia*) **EMERGING**

Have students explain how they can identify the direct and indirect object in each sentence. (Possible response: The direct object answers the question *whom* or *what*. The indirect object tells *to whom* or *what,* or *for whom* or *what.*) **EXPANDING**

Have students write two sentences each with a direct and indirect object. Then ask them to identify the direct and indirect object in each sentence. **BRIDGING**

An expanded **English Language Support Lesson** on Direct and Indirect Objects is available in the Interactive Teacher's Edition.

FORMATIVE ASSESSMENT

Conventions
If students struggle to understand direct and indirect objects, **then** provide more examples and practice opportunities. For Reteach and Practice, see **Conventions: Direct and Indirect Objects (RP).**

Selection Test
Administer the "Flowers for Algernon" Selection Test, which is available in both print and digital formats online in Assessments.

Whole-Class Learning 383

PLANNING

WHOLE-CLASS LEARNING • *from* FLOWERS FOR ALGERNON

from Flowers for Algernon

AUDIO SUMMARIES
Audio summaries of this excerpt from the play *Flowers for Algernon* are available online in both English and Spanish in the Interactive Teacher's Edition or Unit Resources. Assigning these summaries prior to reading the selection may help students build additional background knowledge and set a context for their first review.

Summary
This selection is an excerpt from a dramatic adaptation of the novel *Flowers for Algernon*. The scene involves two characters, Dr. Strauss and Burt, discussing Charlie, who is off-stage. They discuss how stenographers have been hired to transcribe Charlie's tape-recorded diary entries and how more stenographers are needed, given the unexpected number of recordings. The characters then express their disbelief over Charlie's incredible progress and their concerns for the future of the experiment and Charlie.

Insight
This excerpt reveals the reactions of others to Charlie, and the reaction is surprisingly mixed. The characters are amazed by Charlie's transformation, but they express a sense of foreboding about the experiment itself.

ESSENTIAL QUESTION:
In what different ways can people be intelligent?

Connection to Essential Question
The selection focuses on consequences of extraordinary intelligence rather than on different ways to be intelligent. By revealing the awe, disbelief, ambivalence, weariness, and perhaps even jealousy of the creators of the experiment, the selection provides an opportunity to consider unintended consequences of achieving extraordinary intelligence.

WHOLE-CLASS LEARNING PERFORMANCE TASK
What has happened to you so far as a result of the experiment, and what do you predict will happen to you as time progresses?

Connection to Performance Tasks
Whole-Class Learning Performance Task The assignment asks students to take on the perspective of Charlie at the beginning of June. At this point, Charlie has become highly intelligent, and the selection reveals the reactions of others when he is not present. This information will enrich students' work on the performance task by exposing them to others' perspectives.

UNIT PERFORMANCE-BASED ASSESSMENT
In what different ways can people be intelligent?

Unit Performance-Based Assessment Charlie deeply wanted to learn, even before the operation. His final intelligence seems to come partly from the resources available to him (including the operation) and partly from his willingness to spend lots of time learning.

DIGITAL PERSPECTIVES Audio Video Document Annotation Highlights EL Highlights Online Assessment

LESSON RESOURCES

	Making Meaning	Language Development	Effective Expression
Lesson	First Read Close Read Analyze the Text	Concept Vocabulary	Writing to Compare
Instructional Standards	**RL.10** By the end of the year, read and comprehend literature . . . **RL.7** Analyze the extent to which a filmed or live production of a story or drama . . .		**RL.5** Compare and contrast the structure of two or more texts . . . **W.2** Write informative/explanatory texts . . . **W.2.a** Introduce a topic . . . **W.2.b** Develop the topic . . . **W.2.f** Provide a concluding statement . . . **W.9.a** Apply *grade 8 Reading standards* . . .
STUDENT RESOURCES			
Available online in the Interactive Student Edition or Unit Resources	Selection Audio First-Read Guide: Fiction Close-Read Guide: Fiction		Evidence Log
TEACHER RESOURCES			
Selection Resources Available online in the Interactive Teacher's Edition or Unit Resources	Audio Summaries	Concept Vocabulary	Writing to Compare: Comparison-and-Contrast Essay
Available online in Assessments	Selection Test		
My Resources	A Unit 4 Answer Key is available online and in the Interactive Teacher's Edition.		

Text Complexity Rubric: *from* Flowers for Algernon

Quantitative Measures

Lexile: NP **Word Count:** 300 words

Qualitative Measures

Knowledge Demands ①—②—③—●—⑤	As the text is an excerpt, familiarity with the story is somewhat necessary, as the plot is not easy to understand from the events shown.
Structure ①—●—③—④—⑤	Scene from a drama script with conventional stage direction and dialogue that will be familiar to students.
Language Conventionality and Clarity ①—●—③—④—⑤	The dialogue and speech shown have clear, straightforward, and conventional language.
Levels of Meaning/Purpose ①—②—●—④—⑤	Based on the situations, students will need to infer the meaning and purpose of the scene.

Whole-Class Learning 384B

TEACHING

Jump Start

FIRST READ Reading a person's journal can give the reader great insight into who the person is. Turning the journal into a stage play creates both challenges and opportunities for a playwright. How can you maintain the depth of knowledge of a character when you add different points of view and show what happened rather than tell?

from Flowers for Algernon

How does the script differ from the story you read? Does your opinion about Charlie or any of the other characters change after reading this scene? Was the script effective at portraying Charlie's story? Modeling questions such as these will help students connect to *Flowers for Algernon* and to the Performance Task assignment. Selection audio for the selection is available in the Interactive Teacher's Edition.

Concept Vocabulary

Encourage students to discuss the concept vocabulary. Have they seen the terms in texts before? Do they use any of them in their speech and writing? For more support, see **Concept Vocabulary.**

FIRST READ

Students should perform the steps of the first read independently.

NOTICE: Remind students to pay attention to how all of the characters are portrayed in this scene.

ANNOTATE: Encourage students to notice if the script stays true to the way events are portrayed in Charlie's journal.

CONNECT: Encourage students to make connections beyond the text. If they cannot make connections to their own lives, have them consider examples of books written in journal format.

RESPOND: Students will answer questions to demonstrate understanding.

Point out to students that while they will always complete the Respond step at the end of the first read, the other steps will probably happen somewhat concurrently. You may wish to print copies of the **First-Read Guide: Fiction** for students to use.

MAKING MEANING

FLOWERS FOR ALGERNON (short story)

Comparing Texts

The script you are about to read is based on the novel version of *Flowers for Algernon*. After you read the script, you will perform the scene with a group and then analyze your classmates' performances. The work you do will help prepare you for the final comparing task.

from FLOWERS FOR ALGERNON (script)

About the Playwright
David Rogers (1927–2013) was an author, playwright, and actor. He was born in New York City and fell in love with the theater at an early age. In time, he became an actor himself, appearing on Broadway in a production of William Shakespeare's *As You Like It*. During his remarkable career, Rogers was a writer for the *Jackie Gleason Show* and the *Carol Burnett Show*; he also wrote an award-winning opera for New York City's Lincoln Center and numerous adaptations of literary works for the stage.

from Flowers for Algernon

Concept Vocabulary

You will encounter the following words as you read the excerpt from the script for *Flowers for Algernon*. Before reading, note how familiar you are with each word. Then, rank the words in order from most familiar (1) to least familiar (3).

WORD	YOUR RANKING
clarity	
peak	
unleashed	

After completing the first read, come back to the concept vocabulary and review your rankings. Mark changes to your original rankings as needed.

First Read DRAMA

Apply these strategies as you conduct your first read. You will have an opportunity to complete a close read after your first read.

STANDARDS
Reading
By the end of the year, read and comprehend literature, including stories, dramas, and poems, at the high end of the grades 6–8 text complexity band independently and proficiently.

384 UNIT 4 • HUMAN INTELLIGENCE

VOCABULARY DEVELOPMENT

Concept Vocabulary Reinforcement
Review the words *clarity, peak,* and *unleashed.* Have students use each word in a show-you-know sentence set.

You may choose to get students started by providing a sample, such as the following:

After reading a biography of the scientist, I understood her work with remarkable **clarity.** *It was the explicit description of her genetic research that contributed to this sense of* **clarity.**

ANCHOR TEXT | SCRIPT

from Flowers for Algernon

A play by David Rogers, based on the novel by Daniel Keyes

BACKGROUND

This script is based on Daniel Keyes's novel *Flowers for Algernon,* an expanded version of the short story you've just read. This particular scene is a dramatic expansion of the progress report dated May 31. The characters Doctor Strauss, Burt, and Charlie—or at least his voice—from the short story are present in this scene.

SCAN FOR MULTIMEDIA

1 [*Lights come up on* Strauss *in his office.* Burt *is just entering, carrying a huge pile of typed sheets which he puts on* Strauss' *desk.*]

2 **Strauss.** What's that?

3 **Burt.** More of Charlie's notes.

4 **Strauss.** How many days' work is that?

5 **Burt.** Two.

6 **Strauss.** Dear heaven.

7 **Burt.** I've got three stenographers[1] working. I had to call in extra help.

8 **Strauss.** Don't tell me. I'm here every night till one listening to his tapes. [*He pushes the play button of his tape recorder and they listen to:*]

9 **Charlie's Voice.** July eighteenth. They all think I'm killing myself at this pace. But they don't understand I'm living at a peak of clarity and beauty I never knew existed. It's as if all the knowledge I've soaked in during the past months has lifted me to a peak of light and understanding. This is beauty,

NOTES

peak (peek) *n.* highest level
clarity (KLAR uh tee) *n.* state of thinking clearly

---
1. **stenographers** (stuh NOG ruh fuhrz) *n.* office workers who transcribe speech into typed notes.

from Flowers for Algernon (script) **385**

TEACHING

Comprehension Check

Possible responses:

1. This scene takes place during the middle of the experiment. I can tell because the characters are amazed by Charlie's level of intelligence, which is highest during the middle phase.
2. They are astonished by Charlie's progress, almost as if they cannot believe it.
3. They have begun to understand that Charlie's new level of intelligence has exceeded what they thought was possible. They seem almost afraid of where the experiment might lead.
4. Charlie reveals that Algernon is going to deteriorate.

NOTES

love, and truth all rolled into one. This is joy. And now that I've found it, how can I give it up? [Strauss *snaps off the machine and inserts new tape as he speaks.*]

10 **Strauss.** It's incredible. I can't even believe any human being can work at this level . . . at this pace.

11 **Burt.** Doctor. I've read some of this . . . of course, I don't understand it, but . . . is this work as brilliant as it seems?

12 **Strauss.** What are you asking me for? It may take science forty years to understand what Charlie's telling us this month.

unleashed (uhn LEESHD) *v.* released; set loose on the world

13 **Burt.** What have we **unleashed**, Doctor? What do we do?

14 **Strauss.** We hire another stenographer . . . and make sure she gets it all down correctly. [Burt *exits right.* Strauss *pushes the play button.*]

15 **Charlie's Voice.** July twenty-fifth. Algernon became lost in the maze today. He threw himself against the walls . . .

CITE TEXTUAL EVIDENCE
to support your answers.

Comprehension Check

Complete the following items after you finish your first read.

1. What phase of the experiment does this scene depict? How can you tell?

2. Why are Dr. Strauss and Burt reacting to Charlie in this way?

3. How has the position of the other men changed in reference to Charlie?

4. What important information does Charlie reveal about Algernon?

MAKING MEANING

Close Read the Text

Reread the script. As you read, imagine how each line would be delivered on stage. What tones of voice would convey the amazement the characters feel about Charlie's progress?

from FLOWERS FOR ALGERNON (script)

Analyze the Text

CITE TEXTUAL EVIDENCE to support your answers.

Complete the activities.

1. **Prepare the Scene** Form groups of three. With your group, prepare to perform the scene in front of the class. First, reread the script. Next, discuss how you want to portray each character—his movements, gestures, voice inflections, and so on. Then, rehearse the scene several times. After each run-through, discuss ways to improve your performance. You may even consider changing the exact words of the script to better reflect your own interpretations of the story. Finally, when your group is ready to perform, rejoin the whole class.

2. **Perform the Scene** As a class, decide the order in which the groups will present their scenes. When it is your group's turn, perform the scene for the class. As other groups perform, take notes about the choices they have made. If they have decided to depart from the exact words of the script, jot down your ideas about the effectiveness of their choices.

3. **Analyze the Scene** As a class, analyze each group's performance. First, discuss the choices the actors made about how to portray the characters. Then, identify the extent to which they chose to depart from the exact words of the script. Cite specific examples. Finally, evaluate the effects and effectiveness of those choices.

Add words related to human intelligence from the text to your Word Network.

LANGUAGE DEVELOPMENT

Concept Vocabulary

| peak | clarity | unleashed |

Why These Words? The three concept vocabulary words are used to describe someone who is performing at the highest level—in this case, Charlie. For example, the experiment has *unleashed* his full potential. Identify two other words from the selection that relate to great intelligence or emotion.

Practice

Notebook Write a paragraph from the perspective of a high-performing athlete who is competing against other high-performing athletes. Use each of the vocabulary words correctly in the paragraph.

STANDARDS
Reading Literature
Analyze the extent to which a filmed or live production of a story or drama stays faithful to or departs from the text or script, evaluating the choices made by the director or actors.

DIGITAL PERSPECTIVES

CLOSE READ

Model how to read closely by using the Closer Look note for the script. Remind students to clarify anything they did not understand during their first review. You may wish to print the **Close-Read Guide: Fiction** for students to use.

Analyze the Text

1. **Prepare the Scene** Encourage students to mark the words in dialogue they want to stress. Students may want to experiment with different deliveries.

2. **Perform the Scene** As students perform, encourage students to be aware of differences in performances.

3. **Analyze the Scene** Encourage students to discuss the variations among the performances. Ask students to think about how these actor's choices affected the way the ideas were expressed.

Why These Words?
Possible Response: *joy, brilliant*

Practice
Responses will vary but should demonstrate an understanding of the meanings of the concept vocabulary words.

FORMATIVE ASSESSMENT

Analyze the Text

- **If** students fail to cite evidence, **then** remind them to support their ideas with specific details from both texts.

- **If** students struggle to compare the two texts, **then** discuss comparing and contrasting, and illustrate with examples.

TEACHING

Writing to Compare
As students prepare to compare the short story "Flowers for Algernon" and the excerpt from a script based on the novel, they will consider the characteristics of each genre form.

Planning and Prewriting
Clarify for students that the events depicted in the script excerpt do not appear in the short story. The writer of the script has taken "dramatic license." The scriptwriter has created a scene that is not found in the short story but that is loyal to the spirit of the story's content. Note that the scene in the script excerpt would take place roughly at the time of paragraph 171 of the story.

See possible response in chart on student page.

Possible responses
1. Visualization is more important when reading the short story, because in some sections Charlie provides little description. The script uses stage directions to help the reader visualize the action.
2. Students may say that the script provides multiple points of view, whereas the short story is told through the changing lens of Charlie's capabilities. Students may say that the short story forces readers to make more inferences as Charlie is not always a reliable narrator.

STANDARDS
Reading Literature
Compare and contrast the structure of two or more texts and analyze how the differing structure of each text contributes to its meaning and style.
Writing
• Write informative/explanatory texts to examine a topic and convey ideas, concepts, and information through the selection, organization, and analysis of relevant content.
  a. Introduce a topic clearly, previewing what is to follow; organize ideas, concepts, and information into broader categories; include formatting, graphics, and multimedia when useful to aiding comprehension.
  b. Develop the topic with relevant, well-chosen facts, definitions, concrete details, quotations, or other information and examples.
  f. Provide a concluding statement or section that follows from and supports the information or explanation presented.
• Apply *grade 8 Reading standards* to literature.

EFFECTIVE EXPRESSION

FLOWERS FOR ALGERNON
(short story)

from FLOWERS FOR ALGERNON
(script)

Writing to Compare
Daniel Keyes, the author of the short story "Flowers for Algernon," and David Rogers, the playwright behind the dramatic adaptation, use different techniques to tell the same story. The specific features of a writing form have a strong influence on a writer's choices. Now, deepen your understanding of those choices by comparing and contrasting them.

Assignment
Using information from class discussion, as well as details from the selections, write an explanatory **comparison-and-contrast essay** in which you identify the unique characteristics of a short story and a script and explain how those characteristics influence the ways in which a writer tells a story.

Planning and Prewriting
Compare Techniques Discuss the techniques used by the writers of the short story and the script to present the same topic. Use the chart below to note advantages and disadvantages of each medium.

	SHORT STORY	SCRIPT
Point of View From what point of view, or perspective, is the story told?	first person, from Charlie's point of view	third person, each character speaks, telling the story.
Characterization How do readers find out what characters are like?	From Charlie, who at first is positive about most characters but then turns negative about some	From dialogue, and also possibly from stage directions earlier in the script
Conflict How does the writer depict the conflicts characters face?	Charlie describes the conflicts; his analysis of the conflicts changes as his level of intelligence changes.	From dialogue, and from the stage direction that indicates that Burt has brought in a pile of work

Notebook Respond to these questions.

1. Visualization, or forming an image in your mind, can help you read both a short story and a script. Is visualization more important when reading one of these forms than when reading the other? Why or why not?

2. A story and a script usually reflect one point of view, or perspective, on events. Is one point of view more objective or reliable? Does one point of view force readers to make more inferences about what is *really* happening? Explain.

388 UNIT 4 • HUMAN INTELLIGENCE

ESSENTIAL QUESTION: In what different ways can people be intelligent?

Drafting

Outline Decide the order in which you will present details in your essay. If you use block organization, you will explain all of the techniques used in one form and then discuss all of the techniques used in the other. If you use point-by-point organization, you will choose important topics, or points, and explain the techniques used in both forms to present one topic, then another topic, and so on. Use the models below to help you complete an outline for your essay.

Block Organization	Point-by-Point Organization
I. Introduction	I. Introduction
II. Short Story	II. Point of View
A. Point of View	A. Short Story
B. Characterization	B. Script
C. Conflict	III. Characterization
III. Script	A. Short Story
A. Point of View	B. Script
B. Characterization	IV. Conflict
C. Conflict	A. Short Story
IV. Conclusion	B. Script
	V. Conclusion

Draft a Strong Introduction and Conclusion Planning your introduction and conclusion before you draft can help you write a satisfying essay. Follow these planning steps:

- **Write an introduction.** Begin with an introductory thesis statement that clearly identifies the forms you will be comparing and summarizes your main findings. Identify and mark key words in the assignment prompt, and consider using those words or synonyms in your introduction.

    Thesis Statement: _____
    _____

- **Write a concluding thought.** After presenting evidence in the body of your essay, your conclusion will restate your main points. End with a final statement that leaves readers with an interesting or challenging idea about the two forms you compared.

    Concluding Thought: _____
    _____

Reviewing, Revising, and Editing

After drafting your essay, review the assignment to make sure your writing fulfills your goals. Ask yourself:

- Have I compared and contrasted techniques used in both forms?
- Does the information provided follow a clear and logical organization?
- Are the introduction and conclusion effective?
- Is my essay free from errors in spelling, punctuation, and grammar?

EVIDENCE LOG

Before moving on to a new selection, go to your Evidence Log and record what you learned from the short story "Flowers for Algernon" and the scene from the script of the dramatic adaptation.

DIGITAL PERSPECTIVES

Drafting

Outline Clarify for students that block organization involves discussing each selection in separate sections of the paper. It can be effective to save comparisons for the section about the script, since the short story will have already been discussed in the previous section.

Draft a Strong Introduction and Conclusion Explain that the conclusion should not just restate information in the introduction. The conclusion should restate main ideas in a way that leads naturally to an interesting or challenging idea.

Reviewing, Revising, and Editing As students revise, have them review their draft to be sure they have explained their thinking clearly. Ask them to make sure they have identified how the two forms affect the way the writers tell the story. Finally, remind students to check for grammar, usage, and mechanics.

For more support, see **Writing to Compare: Comparison-and-Contrast Essay.**

Evidence Log Support students in completing their Evidence Log. This paced activity will help prepare them for the Performance-Based Assessment at the end of the unit.

FORMATIVE ASSESSMENT

Writing to Compare

If students struggle to identify the differences between the two forms, **then** review the definitions of fiction and drama and discuss the differences.

TEACHING

Jump Start
Charlie Gordon underwent a radical experiment and became a remarkably intelligent and insightful human. The thoughts recorded in his diary entries reveal an impressive and articulate observer of life. Now, the class will have the chance to try to live up to Charlie's example.

Write an Informative Speech
Students are being asked to write in someone else's voice, from someone else's point of view. Review point of view with students. Ask them what the difficulties might be in separating what they think from what Charlie might think. Point out that he used evidence to support how he felt.

Students should complete the assignment using word processing software to take advantage of editing tools and features.

Elements of an Informative Speech
Although a speech contains formal style and academic vocabulary, it is meant to be read aloud. Guide students to take into consideration such elements as sentence length and complexity. Provide models such as an address by the president to demonstrate how formal style can incorporate natural-sounding phrasing.

MAKE IT INTERACTIVE
Project "The Human Brain" from the Interactive Teacher's Edition and have students identify the elements of an informative speech such as a clear topic, multimedia elements, formal style, transitions, and concluding statement.

Academic Vocabulary
Review the academic vocabulary found in the Unit Opener. Point out that the words *assimilate, tendency, integrate, observation,* and *documentation* can all be used in their speeches. Have students suggest possible sentences that use some of these words.

PERFORMANCE TASK: WRITING FOCUS

WRITING TO SOURCES
- FLOWERS FOR ALGERNON (short story)
- from FLOWERS FOR ALGERNON (script)

🔧 **Tool Kit**
Student Model of an Informative Text

ACADEMIC VOCABULARY
As you craft your essay, consider using some of the academic vocabulary you learned in the beginning of the unit.

assimilate
tendency
integrate
observation
documentation

STANDARDS
Writing
• Write informative/explanatory texts to examine a topic and convey ideas, concepts, and information through the selection, organization, and analysis of relevant content.
• Write routinely over extended time frames and shorter time frames for a range of discipline-specific tasks, purposes, and audiences.

Write an Informative Speech
You have just read a short story and an excerpt from a script about a character whose intelligence transforms dramatically. Now, you will use your knowledge of these texts to write an informative speech from Charlie's point of view. Your speech should authentically portray Charlie's character, as well as his knowledge and ideas, based on details from the short story and script.

> **Assignment**
> You have read about Charlie's intellectual transformation, the research he is a part of, and the knowledge he gains from his experience. Imagine yourself as Charlie at the beginning of June, ten weeks after the experimental surgery. Write an **informative speech** on this question:
>
> What has happened to you so far as a result of the experiment, and what do you predict will happen to you as time progresses?

Elements of an Informative Speech
An informative text or speech provides facts and details about a topic. Your assignment—writing as Charlie—is to recount the results of the experiment you have undergone and predict what will happen to you as time progresses.

An effective informative text or speech does the following:
- introduces the topic clearly and organizes it in a way that an audience can easily understand
- uses headings, charts, tables, other graphics, or multimedia elements to help illustrate ideas related to the topic
- develops the topic with facts, definitions, concrete details, and quotations as needed
- uses a variety of transitions to make relationships among ideas clear
- demonstrates a formal style and precise word choices
- provides a concluding statement or section that supports or extends the information provided

Model Informative Text For a model of a well-crafted informative text, see the Launch Text, "The Human Brain."

Challenge yourself to find all of the elements of an effective informative text. You will have an opportunity to review these elements as you prepare to write your own informative speech.

| AUTHOR'S PERSPECTIVE | Kelly Gallagher, M.Ed. |

Purposeful Editing Many students resist editing because they don't see its value. Explain that **editing**, the process of making things correct, adds power to writing. Teachers can model the process by using the Sentence of the Week (SoW) strategy. Before students enter the classroom each Monday, write three sentences with the same structural, grammatical, or style feature on the board. For example:

1. John, 14, is too young to drive.
2. My girlfriend, who is afraid of snakes, refuses to go to the zoo.
3. The player, exhausted from the long game, collapsed.

Students copy the sentences. Below the sentences, write "What do I notice?" Students might write:
- All the sentences have interruptions.

- All have two commas.
- A comma goes before and after the interruption.
- If you take out the commas, the sentences still make sense.

Teaching editing skills through sentence study helps students to generate the grammar rules organically.

ESSENTIAL QUESTION: In what different ways can people be intelligent?

DIGITAL PERSPECTIVES

Prewriting / Planning

Focus on Giving Information Reread the assignment. Remember, an informative speech focuses on giving information about a topic, rather than simply telling a story. State your topic in a sentence:

This speech is meant to give information about _____.

Consider Central Ideas An informative speech presents details about key ideas on the topic. Determining your central ideas will keep your speech focused. What three ideas do you want your audience to walk away with?

1. _____
2. _____
3. _____

Gather Evidence To develop your topic, you will need to add relevant facts, details, and definitions. Start with information from the short story. You may wish to research information on related topics. Because the story and experiment are fictional, you may also invent details. Make sure, however, that the details are believable, based on information in the story, and that they make sense in the context of the story. Explain why or how each piece of evidence relates to your topic. Study the Launch Text to see how the writer uses different types of evidence to develop a topic.

📝 **EVIDENCE LOG**

Review your Evidence Log and identify key details you may want to cite in your informative speech.

EVIDENCE	SOURCE	WHY OR HOW EVIDENCE IS IMPORTANT

Connect Across Texts To connect your speech with the Anchor Texts, look for details that show the moment Charlie knows his intelligence has increased. How can you show this realization in your speech? In addition, consider how the script and the short story show Charlie's personality. Use this information to help write a speech in the character's voice.

▣ **STANDARDS**

Writing
Write informative/explanatory texts to examine a topic and convey ideas, concepts, and information through the selection, organization, and analysis of relevant content.
   a. Introduce a topic clearly, previewing what is to follow; organize ideas, concepts, and information into broader categories; include formatting, graphics, and multimedia when useful to aiding comprehension.
   b. Develop the topic with relevant, well-chosen facts, definitions, concrete details, quotations, or other information and examples.

Performance Task: Write an Informative Speech 391

Prewriting/Planning

Consider Central Ideas Remind students that some of their listed central ideas might be similar to each other. This is an indication they might combine two items to be one, more comprehensive idea. Also remind them to make sure supporting details or minor ideas are not on their lists. Students might want to keep track of supporting details on a separate piece of paper so they can use them in the drafting phase.

Gather Evidence A point of confusion in writing this speech might be that students are writing about a fictional character and a fictional event, yet they are being asked to cite evidence to support their speeches. Point out that while the evidence they provide should remain true to the story, they are allowed to be creative. If their evidence makes sense with the story, then they can incorporate it. This would not be the case if they were being asked to write a nonfiction speech.

Connect Across Texts The short story and the script show two different perspectives of the same story. In the short story, there is a first-person narrator, but the script has a third-person point of view. This gives students a wider perspective on who Charlie is and how he thinks. Have students consider both as they write.

TEACHING

Drafting

Choose an Effective Organization Explain that in writing a good speech, as with writing a good essay, the writer needs to create a sandwich, with an introduction and conclusion as the bread and the body as the filling. Have students review the different organization types listed here. Ask for volunteers for each type of organization to explain to the class why that type of organization would be an effective tool for their speeches. Point out that each one is useful and relevant here. The choice is based on personal preference. As long as the speech is well-constructed, any choice can work.

Write a First Draft As students write their first draft, suggest they work to include information about science and Charlie's experiences as well as focus on communicating Charlie's point of view. Stress the need for clarity in presenting information and some vivid details for describing how Charlie may present this speech.

PERFORMANCE TASK: WRITING FOCUS

Drafting

Choose an Effective Organization Keep in mind that the purpose of your informative speech is to help your audience understand the intellectual transformation Charlie undergoes. Put your details in an order that walks the audience through the experiment, the changes it causes, and Charlie's predictions of what will happen to him later. Consider organizing your speech in one of these ways:

- In **cause-and-effect organization,** you examine the relationships between or among events, explaining how one event or situation (the cause) leads to a certain effect, result, or outcome. For instance, the experiment can be the cause, and the effects can be the changes Charlie experiences.

- In **comparison-and-contrast organization,** you analyze the similarities and differences between or among two or more things. For example, you can explain the process by comparing and contrasting Charlie at various points in time.

- In **problem-and-solution organization,** you describe a problem, offer at least one solution, and lay out steps to achieve this solution. Similar to cause-and-effect organization, this organization presents the cause as the problem. Remember that you are writing from Charlie's point of view. What would Charlie describe as the problem—his intellect or the experiment? What would he list as possible solutions?

No matter which structure you choose, your informative speech should feature a clear introduction, body, and conclusion, and include supporting information and examples. The graphic organizer here shows how the Launch Text is organized.

STANDARDS
Writing
Write informative/explanatory texts to examine a topic and convey ideas, concepts, and information through the selection, organization, and analysis of relevant content.
a. Introduce a topic clearly, previewing what is to follow; organize ideas, concepts, and information into broader categories; include formatting, graphics, and multimedia when useful to aiding comprehension.

LAUNCH TEXT

MODEL: "The Human Brain"

INTRODUCTION
The human brain can do amazing things.

BODY ORGANIZATION
The author mostly uses cause-and-effect organization in describing how the brain works.

CONCLUSION
Scientists are still learning more about the human brain.

Charlie's Informative Speech

INTRODUCTION

BODY ORGANIZATION

CONCLUSION

Write a First Draft Use the information in your graphic organizer and the text structure you have chosen to write a first draft of your speech. Remember to use supporting evidence and examples to clarify your ideas.

392 UNIT 4 • HUMAN INTELLIGENCE

AUTHOR'S PERSPECTIVE Jim Cummins, Ph.D.

Transfer of First Language English learners' home languages are valuable cognitive tools that can be tapped to help them improve the quality of their first drafts. Having students write in their home language often produces higher quality writing than when students write only in English because it helps them capture, express, and organize their ideas. Translation software can be useful as a starting point to help students move from their home language draft to an English draft. Obviously, the machine-translated draft will require editing but this can be done collaboratively with help from the teacher and/or the students' classmates. After students have produced their initial drafts in English, teachers can work with them on the revision process, focusing on such key areas as organization, paragraph formation, and coherence. As students revise with teacher input, teachers should encourage them to pay special attention to cognates and genre rules.

ESSENTIAL QUESTION: In what different ways can people be intelligent?

DIGITAL PERSPECTIVES

LANGUAGE DEVELOPMENT: CONVENTIONS

Subject-Verb Agreement

A verb must agree with its subject in number. The number of a noun or pronoun may be **singular** (indicating *one*) or **plural** (indicating *more than one*).

- Here are examples of nouns and pronouns used as singular subjects: *bus, goose, I, you, Seth or Mia*
- Here are examples of nouns and pronouns used as plural subjects: *buses, geese, we, you, Seth and Mia*

Most verbs have the same singular and plural form, except that in the present tense they add *-s* or *-es* for the third-person singular form. For example, Sam *runs*; Trudy *goes*.

Like all verbs, the verb *be* must agree with its subject in person and number. It takes the form *am* or *was* with the subject *I*, *is* or *was* with third-person singular subjects (such as *she* or *Alex*), and *are* or *were* with the subject *you* and all third-person plural subjects (such as *they* or *children*).

Read It

These sentences from the Launch Text show subject-verb agreement.

- **The brain controls** a person's actions, reactions, and survival functions, such as breathing. (singular)
- **Neurons send** messages through tiny branch-like structures that connect to other neurons in different parts of the brain, as well as other parts of the body. (plural)

Write It

As you draft your speech, make sure your subjects and verbs agree. This chart may help you.

SUBJECT-VERB AGREEMENT	
SINGULAR	PLURAL
I *am* busy.	We *are* busy.
He *runs*.	They *run*.
The child *goes* to sleep.	The children *go* to sleep.
Seth *agrees*.	Seth and Mia *agree*.

TIP

CLARIFICATION
Make sure that every verb you use, whether in the **active voice** or the **passive voice,** agrees with its subject.

- In the **active voice**, a verb's subject performs the action—for example, *Amanda wrote the speech.*
- In the **passive voice**, the verb's subject receives the action—for example, *The speech was written by Amanda.*

Use mainly active verbs in your writing to emphasize the actor, not the action, of a sentence. Active voice makes writing livelier, more precise, and more dynamic.

STANDARDS
Language
Demonstrate command of the conventions of standard English grammar and usage when writing or speaking.
  b. Form and use verbs in the active and passive voice.

Performance Task: Write an Informative Speech 393

Subject-Verb Agreement

Read It
When determining whether or not they have proper subject-verb agreement, students should first identify if their subject is singular or plural. Once they have established that, they should look at the verb. Is it singular or plural? Remind the class that agreement comes when they are either both singular or both plural.

Write It
Point out that in the examples, the singular verbs end with an *s*, while the plural do not. This might be counter to what they expected. With nouns, we generally think of words ending with an *s* as plural. This is not the case with the verbs. While students use correct subject/verb agreement as a matter of everyday speech for these simple sentences, they may not have considered this pattern.

Consider reviewing additional examples of subject-verb agreement. For example, share these sentences with singular subjects:

The brain boggles the mind!

The brain controls a person's actions.

A person touches a hot surface.

A constant stream of messages travels.

Ask students to convert the sentences, using plural subjects and modifying the verbs accordingly. Responses: Brains boggle. Brains control. People touch. Streams travel.

PERSONALIZE FOR LEARNING

English Language Support

Subject-Verb Agreement Provide more practice with subject-verb agreement. Have students identify and explain the errors and then correct the following sentences. Provide more examples if more practice is needed.

Algernon were a nice mouse.

Charlie go to the lab.

The people likes Charlie's video.

Dr. Strauss study Charlie's progress. **ALL LEVELS**

TEACHING

Revising
Evaluating Your Draft
Before students begin revising their writing, they should first evaluate their draft to determine if it contains all the required elements, is organized well, and adheres to the norms and conventions of an informative speech.

Revising for Focus and Organization
Choose Precise, Formal Words If students struggle to recall the formal scientific words Charlie used, recommend that they review their notes on the text and video. Have students consider incorporating the concept vocabulary, as well as any related words they discovered. Finally, remind students that informative texts often provide definitions at point of use, through context clues, restatement, or other strategies.

Revising for Evidence and Elaboration
Use Transitions Remind students how important it is for them to use transitions that connect Charlie's thinking to the information they want to communicate. Transitions are especially helpful in cause-and-effect explanations as well as in comparisons and contrasts.

PERFORMANCE TASK: WRITING FOCUS

Revising
Evaluating Your Draft
Use the following checklist to evaluate the effectiveness of your first draft. Then, use your evaluation and the instruction on this page to guide your revision.

FOCUS AND ORGANIZATION	EVIDENCE AND ELABORATION	CONVENTIONS
☐ Introduces the topic clearly.	☐ Uses facts, definitions, concrete details, and quotations to develop the topic.	☐ Attends to the norms and conventions of the discipline, especially correct subject-verb agreement.
☐ Organizes supporting information and explanations in a way that is easy to understand, possibly including graphical or multimedia elements.	☐ Uses transitions to make relationships between ideas clear.	
☐ Presents ideas in a formal style using precise words.		
☐ Provides a conclusion that supports the information provided.		

🗂 WORD NETWORK
You may want to include interesting words from your Word Network in your informative speech.

≡ STANDARDS
Writing
Write informative/explanatory texts to examine a topic and convey ideas, concepts, and information through the selection, organization, and analysis of relevant content.
 a. Introduce a topic clearly, previewing what is to follow; organize ideas, concepts, and information into broader categories; include formatting, graphics, and multimedia when useful to aiding comprehension.
 c. Use appropriate and varied transitions to create cohesion and clarify the relationships among ideas and concepts.
 d. Use precise language and domain-specific vocabulary to inform about or explain the topic.
 e. Establish and maintain a formal style.

Revising for Focus and Organization
Choose Precise, Formal Words Choose words that capture your meaning precisely. For example, the term *IQ* might express your meaning more clearly than *smarts*. Since this is a speech about a scientific experiment, some technical language is appropriate. Avoid slang terms. Using words correctly will reflect Charlie's extended vocabulary at this point in the story. Remember to use complete sentences, correct grammar, and clear language to explain information.

Provide a Strong Introductory Statement
Strong informative speeches grab the audience's attention right away and hold it throughout the speech.

In your introduction, present your topic in a way that emphasizes its importance. Consider using a quotation from one of the texts, a personal anecdote, or another memorable statement to begin your speech. Remember that you are writing in Charlie's voice. Make sure that you choose details that Charlie might have chosen at the beginning of June.

Revising for Evidence and Elaboration
Use Transitions Transitions are words and phrases that connect and show relationships among ideas. In an informative text, transitions show readers or listeners how ideas or pieces of information are related.
- Words such as *likewise, similarly,* and *conversely* indicate a comparison or contrast.
- Words such as *first, next,* and *later* tell the order in which events occurred.
- Words such as *thus* and *consequently* signal causes and effects.

ESSENTIAL QUESTION: In what different ways can people be intelligent?

PEER REVIEW

Exchange speeches with a classmate. Use the checklist to evaluate your classmate's informative speech and provide supportive feedback.

1. Is the topic clearly introduced and organized in a way that is easy to understand?
   ☐ yes   ☐ no   If no, suggest how the writer might improve it.

2. Is the topic developed with facts, definitions, concrete details, and quotations as needed?
   ☐ yes   ☐ no   If no, explain what the author might add or remove.

3. Does the speech use formal, precise language?
   ☐ yes   ☐ no   If no, tell what you think might be missing.

4. What is the strongest part of your classmate's speech? Explain.

Editing and Proofreading

Edit for Conventions Reread your draft for accuracy and consistency. Correct errors in grammar and word usage. Make sure all your subjects and verbs agree in number.

Proofread for Accuracy Read your draft carefully, looking for errors in spelling and punctuation. Use a dictionary to check the spelling of all key terms. In addition, check your spelling of commonly confused words, such as *affect* (usually a verb) and *effect* (usually a noun). Finally, check your spelling of homonyms—words that sound the same but have different meanings and usually spellings, such as *their, they're,* and *there*.

Publishing and Presenting

Create a final version of your speech. Hold a class conference in which you present your speech to a small panel of your classmates. Discuss ways in which your speeches are similar and different. Did you include any of the same information? Did you connect your information in the same ways? Is the content similar but the style different? Share your thoughts with the class. Discuss what comparing the speeches taught you about developing a topic.

Reflecting

Reflect on what you learned as you wrote your informative speech. What did you learn about different ways to be intelligent? What was the most challenging aspect of writing your informative speech? Did you learn something from the review process that might inform your writing process in the future?

STANDARDS

Writing
- Produce clear and coherent writing in which the development, organization, and style are appropriate to task, purpose, and audience.
- With some guidance and support from peers and adults, develop and strengthen writing as needed by planning, revising, editing, rewriting, or trying a new approach, focusing on how well purpose and audience have been addressed.

Performance Task: Write an Informative Speech **395**

DIGITAL PERSPECTIVES

Peer Review
Point out to students that when they read each other's speeches, they are reading something meant to be read out loud, with the appropriate tone and pace. While they are focusing on the content and style, this aspect might get lost. Give students the opportunity to read the speeches aloud and listen to themselves, or use text recognition software and hear the speech read aloud.

Publishing and Presenting
Remind students that all of their speeches are meant to be written in the same voice: Charlie's voice. Have groups consider which speeches effectively portrayed Charlie. Ask students to find a moment in each of their peer's speeches that made them most feel like they were listening to Charlie give a speech. Have them explain why they felt that way.

Reflecting
As students reflect on their own speeches, encourage them to jot down ideas they observed in other students' speeches. Also, remind students to take into account comments they received and what they learned from peer editors.

PERSONALIZE FOR LEARNING

Challenge
Write a Letter Have students write follow-up or response letters from the points of view of different characters from Flowers for Algernon. Ask each student to imagine that Charlie Gordon has just given the speech he or she wrote in the Performance Task. How might Miss Kinnian react to what Charlie had to say? Would she agree with him? Have students write a letter from Miss Kinnian to Charlie Gordon, supporting her ideas and point of view with information from the story and film. Alternatively, students may write a letter from Dr. Strauss's point of view.

Whole-Class Learning **395**

OVERVIEW

SMALL-GROUP LEARNING

In what different ways can people be intelligent?

Explain to students that intelligence can manifest itself in many different ways, and there is no one correct definition for what it means to be intelligent. People process information in different ways, and the result may be an expression of intelligence through language, math, or art. During Small-Group Learning, students will read selections that explore different ways of expressing intelligence.

Small-Group Learning Strategies ▶

Review the Learning Strategies with students and explain that as they work through Small-Group Learning they will develop strategies to work in small-group environments.

- Have students watch the video on Small-Group Learning Strategies.
- A video on this topic is available online in the Professional Development Center.

You may wish to discuss some action items to add to the chart as a class before students complete it on their own. For example, for "Participate fully," you might solicit the following action from students:

- Offer feedback to classmates in a constructive, respectful way.
- Challenge yourself to offer an idea in every discussion.

> ### Block Scheduling
> Each day in this Pacing Plan represents a 40–50 minute class period. Teachers using block scheduling may combine days to reflect their class schedule. In addition, teachers may revise pacing to differentiate and support core instruction by integrating components and resources as students require.

Pacing Plan

OVERVIEW: SMALL-GROUP LEARNING

ESSENTIAL QUESTION:

In what different ways can people be intelligent?

Throughout history, the topic of human intelligence has been a subject of much debate. Scientists, writers, artists, and scholars have all reflected on the concept of human intelligence and the factors that define it. Work with your group to explore the ideas about different types of intelligence that are presented in the selections in this section.

Small-Group Learning Strategies

Throughout your life, in school, in your community, and in your career, you will continue to learn and work with others.

Review these strategies and the actions you can take to practice them as you work in teams. Add ideas of your own for each step. Use these strategies during Small-Group Learning.

STRATEGY	ACTION PLAN
Prepare	• Complete your assignments so that you are prepared for group work. • Organize your thinking so you can contribute to your group's discussion. •
Participate fully	• Make eye contact to signal that you are listening and taking in what is being said. • Use text evidence when making a point. •
Support others	• Build on ideas from others in your group. • Invite others who have not yet spoken to do so. •
Clarify	• Paraphrase the ideas of others to ensure that your understanding is correct. • Ask follow-up questions. •

SCAN FOR MULTIMEDIA

CONTENTS

MEMOIR

from Blue Nines and Red Words

from Born on a Blue Day
Daniel Tammet

A man who has an amazing memory and who can speak ten languages sees and feels numbers as shapes, colors, and textures.

MEDIA: INFOGRAPHIC

The Theory of Multiple Intelligences Infographic
Howard Gardner

A professor of psychology shows how people have recognizably different ways of learning, processing information, and being intelligent.

POETRY COLLECTION

Retort   Paul Laurence Dunbar

from The People, Yes   Carl Sandburg

Two poets explore distinctly different ways of thinking about the concept of intelligence.

PERFORMANCE TASK

SPEAKING AND LISTENING FOCUS

Deliver a Multimedia Presentation

The Small-Group readings explore the diversity of human intelligence. After reading, your group will plan and deliver a multimedia presentation showing how each selection in this section highlights different aspects of human intelligence.

Overview: Small-Group Learning **397**

DIGITAL PERSPECTIVES

Contents

Selections Circulate among groups as they preview the selections. You might encourage groups to discuss any knowledge they already have about any of the selections or the situations and settings shown in the photographs. Students may wish to take a poll within their group to determine which selections look the most interesting.

Remind students that communicating and collaborating in groups is an important skill that they will use throughout their lives—in school, in their careers, and in their community.

Performance Task

Deliver a Multimedia Presentation Give groups time to read about and briefly discuss the multimedia presentation they will create after reading. Encourage students to do some preliminary thinking about the types of media they may want to use. This may help focus their subsequent reading and group discussion.

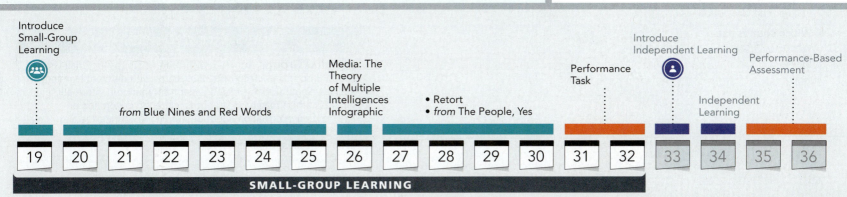

Small-Group Learning **397**

OVERVIEW

SMALL-GROUP LEARNING

Working as a Team

1. **Discuss the Topic** Remind groups to let all members share their responses. You may wish to set a time limit for this discussion.

2. **List Your Rules** You may want to have groups share their lists of rules and consolidate them into a master list to be displayed and followed by all groups.

3. **Apply the Rules** As you circulate among the groups, ensure that students are staying on task. Consider a short time limit for this step.

4. **Name Your Group** This task can be creative and fun. If students have trouble coming up with a name, suggest that they think of something related to the unit topic. Encourage groups to share their names with the class.

5. **Create a Communication Plan** Encourage groups to include in their plans agreed-upon times during the day to share ideas. They should also devise a method for recording and saving their communications.

Accountable Talk

Remind students that groups should communicate politely. You can post these Accountable Talk suggestions and encourage students to add their own. Students should:

Remember to . . .
Ask clarifying questions.

Which sounds like . . .
Can you please repeat what you said?
Would you give me an example?
I think you said _____. Did I understand you correctly?

Remember to . . .
Explain your thinking.

Which sounds like . . .
I believe _____ is true because _____.

Remember to . . .
Build on the ideas of others.

Which sounds like . . .
When _____ said _____, it made me think of _____.

OVERVIEW: SMALL-GROUP LEARNING

Working as a Team

1. **Discuss the Topic** In your group, discuss the following question:

   What are some ways in which intelligence can be obvious yet unconventional?

   As you take turns sharing your thoughts, be sure to provide examples and reasons for your responses. After all group members have shared, discuss some of the character traits associated with the ways of being intelligent that you identified.

2. **List Your Rules** As a group, decide on the rules that you will follow as you work together. Two samples are provided; add two more of your own. You may add or revise rules based on your experience together.

   - Everyone should participate in group discussions.
   - People should not interrupt.
   - _____
   - _____

3. **Apply the Rules** Share what you have learned about intelligence. Make sure each person in the group contributes. Take notes and be prepared to share with the class one thing that you heard from another member of your group.

4. **Name Your Group** Choose a name that reflects the unit topic.

   Our group's name: _____

5. **Create a Communication Plan** Decide how you want to communicate with one another. For example, you might use online collaboration tools, email, or instant messaging.

   Our group's decision: _____

FACILITATING SMALL-GROUP LEARNING

Forming Groups You may wish to form groups for Small-Group Learning so that each consists of students with different learning abilities. Some students may be adept at organizing information whereas others may have strengths related to generating or synthesizing information about different kinds of intelligences. A good mix of abilities can make the experience of Small-Group Learning dynamic and productive.

ESSENTIAL QUESTION: In what different ways can people be intelligent?

Making a Schedule

First, find out the due dates for the small-group activities. Then, preview the texts and activities with your group and make a schedule for completing the tasks.

SELECTION	ACTIVITIES	DUE DATE
from Blue Nines and Red Words		
The Theory of Multiple Intelligences Infographic		
Retort from The People, Yes		

Working on Group Projects

As your group works together, you'll find it more effective if each person has a specific role. Different projects require different roles. Before beginning a project, discuss the necessary roles, and choose one for each group member. Here are some possible roles; add your own ideas to the list.

Project Manager: monitors the schedule and keeps everyone on task
Researcher: organizes research activities
Recorder: takes notes during group meetings

_____
_____
_____
_____

SCAN FOR MULTIMEDIA

DIGITAL PERSPECTIVES

Making a Schedule

Encourage groups to preview the reading selections and to consider how long it will take them to complete the activities accompanying each selection. Point out that they can adjust the due dates for particular selections as needed as they work on their small-group projects. However, they must complete all assigned tasks before the group Performance Task is due. Encourage groups to review their schedules upon completing the activities for each selection to make sure they are on track to meet the final due date.

Working on Group Projects

Point out to groups that the roles they assign can also be changed later. Students might have to make changes based on who is best at doing what. Try to make sure that there is no favoritism, cliquishness, or stereotyping by gender or other means in the assignment of roles.

Also, you should review the roles each group assigns to its members. Based on your understanding of students' individual strengths, you might find it necessary to suggest some changes. Caution students to be mindful of their tone and aware of possible academic preferences in speaking about different intelligences. Encourage them to show respect for all kinds of intelligence.

AUTHOR'S PERSPECTIVE Ernest Morrell, Ph.D.

Small Group Learning in Higher Education College classrooms are becoming shared discussion spaces, marked by less lecturing and more small groups. That's because college professors increasingly realize that having students work in small groups helps develop higher-level learning and problem-solving skills, increases the success of computer-based instruction, and increases retention rates. As a result, more and more college professors now have small groups lead a portion of class by sharing/presenting what the group has learned. These professors focus on the importance of each group becoming expert at something that it must teach the class. Teachers can point out to students that the project-based small group learning in colleges is increasingly common in the workplace as well, as collective production is becoming a new norm. Teachers can encourage students to collaborate and develop rubrics to assess how well students are able to work together.

PLANNING

SMALL-GROUP LEARNING • *from* BLUE NINES AND RED WORDS

from Blue Nines and Red Words

AUDIO SUMMARIES
Audio summaries of the excerpt from "Blue Nines and Red Words" are available online in both English and Spanish in the Interactive Teacher's Edition or Unit Resources. Assigning these summaries prior to reading the selection may help students build additional background knowledge and set a context for their first read.

Summary

In this excerpt from a chapter of his memoir *Born on a Blue Day,* Daniel Tammet describes how he thinks. Tammet has a condition called savant syndrome, which allows him to easily do calculations with large numbers. Tammet can do complex math in part because of his synthesia, a neurological condition that causes a mixing of sensory input. When Tammet sees a number, he also sees specific colors, textures, and hears certain sounds. Tammet also explains that he has Asperger's syndrome, a mild form of autism. This condition makes it difficult for Tammet to understand emotions. Tammet illustrates how he uses numbers and his synthesia to help him understand how other people are feeling.

Insight

In this memoir, Tammet uses specific, vivid examples to help readers visualize what he sees in his mind. By illuminating his personal experience and using examples of similar people, Tammet introduces readers to other ways of experiencing the world.

ESSENTIAL QUESTION:
In what different ways can people be intelligent?

Connection to Essential Question
Intelligence can mean having a good memory, having the ability to calculate quickly, or having emotional skills.

SMALL-GROUP LEARNING PERFORMANCE TASK
How does each selection highlight a different way to be intelligent?

Connection to Performance Tasks

Small-Group Learning Performance Task Tammet emphasizes how his synesthesia helps him calculate. Interestingly, he also describes how he applies it to problems that come less naturally to him, such as envisioning a number that he associates with dark hollowness to help him understand depression.

UNIT PERFORMANCE-BASED ASSESSMENT
In what different ways can people be intelligent?

Unit Performance-Based Assessment Tammet demonstrates how challenges that we might think of as disabilities can be pathways to forms of intelligence.

DIGITAL PERSPECTIVES Audio Video Document Annotation Highlights EL Highlights Online Assessment

LESSON RESOURCES

	Making Meaning	Language Development	Effective Expression
Lesson	First Read Close Read Analyze the Text Analyze Craft and Structure	Concept Vocabulary Word Study Conventions	Research
Instructional Standards	**RI.10** By the end of the year, read and comprehend literary nonfiction . . . **L.4** Determine or clarify the meaning of unknown and multiple-meaning words or phrases . . . between particular words . . . **RI.2** Determine a central idea of a text . . . **RI.3** Analyze how a text makes connections . . . **RI.5** Analyze in detail the structure of a specific paragraph in a text . . . **RI.6** Determine an author's point of view or purpose . . .	**L.1** Demonstrate command of the conventions . . .	**W.2** Write informative/explanatory texts . . **W.2.b** Develop the topic. . . **W.2.d** Use precise language . . . **W.7** Conduct short research projects . . . **W.8** Gather relevant information . . .
▶ **STUDENT RESOURCES** Available online in the Interactive Student Edition or Unit Resources	Selection Audio First-Read Guide: Nonfiction Close-Read Guide: Nonfiction	Word Network	Evidence Log
▶ **TEACHER RESOURCES** **Selection Resources** Available online in the Interactive Teacher's Edition or Unit Resources	Audio Summaries Annotation Highlights EL Highlights from Blue Nines and Red Words: Text Questions Analyze Craft and Structure: Memoir and Reflective Writing	Concept Vocabulary and Word Study Conventions: Pronoun Case	Research: Informational Report English Language Support Lesson: Informational Report
Reteach/Practice (RP) Available online in the Interactive Teacher's Edition or Unit Resources	Analyze Craft and Structure: Memoir and Reflective Writing (RP)	Word Study: Latin Suffix -ical (RP) Conventions: Pronoun Case (RP)	Research: Informational Report (RP)
Assessment Available online in Assessments	Selection Test		
My Resources	A Unit 4 Answer Key is available online and in the Interactive Teacher's Edition.		

PERSONALIZE FOR LEARNING
SMALL-GROUP LEARNING • *from* BLUE NINES AND RED WORDS

Reading Support

Text Complexity Rubric: *from* Blue Nines and Red Words

Quantitative Measures

Lexile: 1200   Text Length: 2,391 words

Qualitative Measures

Knowledge Demands ①—②—❸—④—⑤	Selection is centered around content and concepts that may be unfamiliar, such as mathematical concepts, synesthesia, and savant syndrome. There are references to movies and books that may or may not be familiar to readers.
Structure ①—②—❸—④—⑤	Structure is straightforward, with clear progression and organization of ideas. Numerous examples of experiences are given that cover a wide range of ideas and details.
Language Conventionality and Clarity ①—②—❸—④—⑤	Language is clear, explicit, and descriptive, with use of many adjectives to describe sense experiences. Technical terms are defined in context; some figurative language is used.
Levels of Meaning/Purpose ①—②—③—❹—⑤	Ideas are explicitly stated, but the selection addresses challenging concepts, such as the author's unique perspective and how this impacts his daily interactions. The reader also needs to synthesize meaning based on multiple descriptions and details.

DECIDE AND PLAN

English Language Support
Provide English Learners with support for knowledge demands and language as they read the selection.

Knowledge Demands Use the background information to discuss synesthesia and give examples of what it means to describe one sense using terms from another. Ask students to name the senses as you list them. Then with students' help, list examples of terms associated with each sense, for example *taste: sweet, salty; sight: beautiful, ugly.*

Language Discuss the idioms in the background information. First, discuss the literal meaning. For example, ask *What is actually thick enough to cut with a knife?* (Possible responses: bread, pie). Discuss that idioms are *figurative* uses of the language but that people with synesthesia actually perceive the senses differently.

Strategic Support
Provide students with strategic support to ensure that they can successfully read the text.

Knowledge Demands Have students read the background information. Then determine what knowledge they have of some conditions described in the selection, such as autism and Asperger's syndrome. Discuss that these conditions sometimes give people special abilities, not just disabilities. The selection is written from the point of view of someone with special abilities.

Meaning If students have difficulty understanding Tammet's unique perspective, have them record examples of what he sees or experiences when he encounters different numbers, people, places, problems, and emotions. Have them identify patterns in his perceptions.

Challenge
Provide students who need to be challenged with ideas for how they can go beyond a simple interpretation of the text.

Text Analysis Ask students to examine how the author's unique perspective impacts his daily experiences and interactions. Ask them to cite examples from the text and to talk about both advantages and disadvantages of his condition.

Written Response Ask students to write about the advantages and disadvantages of having a special skill or trait. Have them use examples from the selection and also their own experiences or about themselves or others in their lives. Have them also comment on why it is important to look at what a person can do and not just what they are unable to do.

TEACH

Read and Respond
Have groups read the selection and complete the Making Meaning, Language Development, and Effective Expression activities.

Standards Support Through Teaching and Learning Cycle

IDENTIFY NEEDS

Analyze results of the Beginning-of-Year Assessment, focusing on the items relating to Unit 4. Also take into consideration student performance to this point and your observations of where particular students struggle.

ANALYZE AND REVISE

- Analyze student work for evidence of student learning.
- Identify whether or not students have met the expectations in the standards.
- Identify implications for future instruction.

TEACH

Implement the planned lesson, and gather evidence of student learning.

DECIDE AND PLAN

- If students have performed poorly on items matching these standards, then provide selection scaffolds before assigning them the on-level lesson provided in the Student Edition.
- If students have done well on the Beginning-of-Year Assessment, then challenge them to keep progressing and learning by giving them opportunities to practice the skills in depth.
- Use the Selection Resources listed on the Planning pages for the excerpt *from* Blue Nines and Red Words to help students continually improve their ability to master the standards.

Instructional Standards: *from* Blue Nines and Red Words

	Catching Up	This Year	Looking Forward
Reading	You may wish to administer the **Analyze Craft and Structure: Memoir and Reflective Writing (RP)** worksheet to familiarize students with this form of autobiographical writing.	**RI.3** Analyze how a text makes connections among and distinctions between individuals, ideas, or events.	Challenge students to analyze how the author unfolds the ideas and events in his memoir.
Writing	You may wish to administer the **Research: Informational Report (RP)** worksheet to help students better determine themes in a work of literature.	**W.7** Conduct short research projects to answer a question, drawing on several sources and generating additional related, focused questions that allow for multiple avenues of exploration.	Work with students to take their research into more depth, familiarizing them with the subject well enough to become "mini-experts," enabling them to field impromptu questions.
Language	Review **Conventions: Pronoun Case (RP)** to help students understand the three cases of pronouns. Review **Word Study: Latin Suffix -ical (RP)** to help students understand that *-ical* means "having to do with" or "made of."	**L.1** Demonstrate command of the conventions of standard English grammar and usage when writing or speaking. **L.4.b** Use common, grade-appropriate Greek or Latin affixes and roots as clues to the meaning of a word.	Ask students to find a short article online and identify the nominative, objective, and possessive cases of pronouns. Have students identify other words in the selection that contain suffixes they recognize.

Small-Group Learning 400D

FACILITATING

Jump Start

FIRST READ Ask students to consider the following questions: *What would it be like to see numbers as colors? How might seeing numbers in color affect a person's ability to calculate?* Engage students in a discussion about numbers and math that sets the context for reading this excerpt from "Blue Nines and Red Words."

from Blue Nines and Red Words

How can numbers have colors and shapes? How is it possible to do difficult mathematical calculations without having to think? Modeling questions such as these will help students connect the excerpt from "Blue Nines and Red Words" to the Small-Group Performance Task assignment. Selection audio and print capability for the selection are available in the Interactive Teacher's Edition.

Concept Vocabulary

Ask groups to look closely at the example of a base word and discuss how this type of clue can help clarify meaning. Encourage groups to think of more examples of words with familiar base words that they might encounter.

Students should perform the steps of the first read independently.

NOTICE: Encourage students to notice how the author's experience of numbers and words are unique.

ANNOTATE: Remind students to mark passages that include the author's reflections about his condition.

CONNECT: Have students compare the author's experiences with numbers and calculations to their own.

RESPOND: Students will answer questions and write a summary to demonstrate understanding.

Point out to students that while they will always complete the Respond step at the end of the first read, the other steps will probably happen somewhat concurrently. You may wish to print copies of the **First-Read Guide: Nonfiction** for students to use.

400   UNIT 4 • HUMAN INTELLIGENCE

MAKING MEANING

About the Author

Daniel Tammet (b. 1979) grew up in a working-class suburb of London, England, and is the eldest of nine children. In 2004, when he was 25, Tammet was diagnosed with "high-functioning autistic savant syndrome," a form of autism. In 2005, he was the subject of a documentary film entitled *Extraordinary People: The Boy With the Incredible Brain*, first broadcast on British television. Tammet's four books, the last of which was published in 2016, have been translated into 20 languages.

STANDARDS

Reading Informational Text
By the end of the year, read and comprehend literary nonfiction at the high end of the grades 6–8 text complexity band independently and proficiently.

Language
Determine or clarify the meaning of unknown and multiple-meaning words or phrases based on *grade 8 reading and content*, choosing flexibly from a range of strategies.

from Blue Nines and Red Words

Concept Vocabulary

As you perform your first read of the excerpt from "Blue Nines and Red Words," you will encounter the following words.

| symmetrical | spiral | aesthetic |

Base Words If these words are unfamilar to you, analyze each one to see whether it contains a base word you know. Then, use your knowledge of the base word, or "inside" word, along with context, to determine the meaning of the concept word. Here is an example of how to apply the strategy.

> **Unfamiliar Word:** *skillful*
>
> **Familiar "Inside" Word:** *skill*, with meanings including "expertise" and "learned power"
>
> **Context:** I was astonished at the professor's *skillful* ability to pass along complicated information.
>
> **Conclusion:** The narrator is impressed with someone's abililty, so *skillful* might mean "with skill," or "showing expertise."

Apply your knowledge of base words and other vocabulary strategies to determine the meanings of unfamiliar words you encounter during your first read.

First Read NONFICTION

Apply these strategies as you conduct your first read. You will have an opportunity to complete a close read after your first read.

NOTICE the general ideas of the text. *What is it about? Who is involved?*

ANNOTATE by marking vocabulary and key passages you want to revisit.

CONNECT ideas within the selection to what you already know and what you have already read.

RESPOND by completing the Comprehension Check and by writing a brief summary of the selection.

400   UNIT 4 • HUMAN INTELLIGENCE

AUTHOR'S PERSPECTIVE   Jim Cummins, Ph.D.

How Language Works Briefly explaining the origins of the English language will help demystify the difference between conversational and academic language. Today's English is a hybrid language, formed from a merger of Anglo-Saxon spoken in Britain from about 400–1000 and French brought by the Norman invaders in 1066. Students can see this merger in synonyms of words derived from Anglo-Saxon and Latin/Greek sources: *meet/encounter, ask/inquire, come/arrive*. The Anglo-Saxon words were used by peasants who generally didn't have much education; in contrast, Greek/Latin vocabulary was used by more educated and high-status people and became the language of written text. Today, words with Anglo-Saxon roots are short

MEMOIR

from Blue Nines and Red Words

from Born on a Blue Day

Daniel Tammet

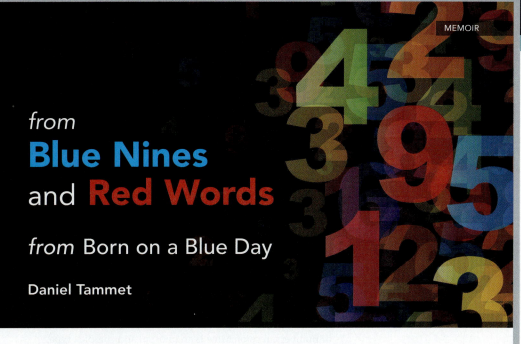

BACKGROUND

Although *synesthesia*, the topic of this memoir excerpt, is a neurological condition, it also refers to a figure of speech. In synesthesia, one sense is described using terms typically used to describe another. Many common idioms are examples of synesthesia, such as "I smell trouble" and "The air was so thick you could cut it with a knife."

1   I was born on January 31, 1979—a Wednesday. I know it was a Wednesday, because the date is blue in my mind and Wednesdays are always blue, like the number 9 or the sound of loud voices arguing. I like my birth date, because of the way I'm able to visualize most of the numbers in it as smooth and round shapes, similar to pebbles on a beach. That's because they are prime numbers: 31, 19, 197, 97, 79, and 1979 are all divisible only by themselves and 1. I can recognize every prime up to 9,973 by their "pebble-like" quality. It's just the way my brain works.

2   I have a rare condition known as savant syndrome, little known before its portrayal by actor Dustin Hoffman in the Oscar-winning 1988 film *Rain Man*. Like Hoffman's character, Raymond Babbitt, I have an almost obsessive need for order and routine which affects virtually every aspect of my life. For example, I eat exactly 45 grams of porridge for breakfast each morning: I weigh the bowl with an electronic scale to make sure. Then I count the number of items of clothing I'm wearing before I leave my house. I get anxious if I can't drink my cups of tea at the same time each day. Whenever I become too stressed and I can't breathe properly,

NOTES

FACILITATING

● CLOSER LOOK

Analyze Informative Texts

Circulate among groups as students conduct their close read. Suggest that groups close read paragraph 3. Encourage them to talk about the annotations they mark. If needed, provide the following support.

ANNOTATE: Have students mark details in paragraph 3 that tell how the author feels about certain numbers, or work with small groups as you highlight them together.

QUESTION: Guide students to consider what these details might tell them. Ask what a reader can infer from the way that the author describes his feelings about numbers, and accept student responses.

Possible response: The reader can infer that numbers are very important to the author.

CONCLUDE: Help students to formulate conclusions about the importance of these details in the text. Ask students why the author might have included these details.

Possible response: The details are important because they help the reader understand the author's condition and his feelings about it. By including reflections on his emotional response to numbers, the author encourages readers to compare their own thoughts and feelings about numbers and friends.

Explain to students that an **informative text** that provides information on a topic can also include reflection, in which the author offers insights into the meaning of his or her personal experience.

NOTES

I close my eyes and count. Thinking of numbers helps me to become calm again.

3   Numbers are my friends, and they are always around me. Each one is unique and has its own personality. The number 11 is friendly and 5 is loud, whereas 4 is both shy and quiet—it's my favorite number, perhaps because it reminds me of myself. Some are big—23, 667, 1,179—while others are small: 6, 13, 581. Some are beautiful, like 333, and some are ugly, like 289. To me, every number is special.

4   No matter where I go or what I'm doing, numbers are never far from my thoughts. In an interview with talk-show host David Letterman in New York, I told David he looked like the number 117—tall and lanky. Later outside, in the appropriately numerically named Times Square, I gazed up at the towering skyscrapers and felt surrounded by 9s—the number I most associate with feelings of immensity.

5   Scientists call my visual, emotional experience of numbers *synesthesia*, a rare neurological[1] mixing of the senses, which most commonly results in the ability to see alphabetical letters and/or numbers in color. Mine is an unusual and complex type, through which I see numbers as shapes, colors, textures, and motions. The number 1, for example, is a brilliant and bright white, like someone shining a flashlight into my eyes. Five is a clap of thunder or the sound of waves crashing against rocks. Thirty-seven is lumpy like porridge, while 89 reminds me of falling snow.

6   Probably the most famous case of synesthesia was the one written up over a period of thirty years from the 1920s by the Russian psychologist A. R. Luria of a journalist called Shereshevsky with a prodigious memory. "S," as Luria called him in his notes for the book *The Mind of a Mnemonist*, had a highly visual memory which allowed him to "see" words and numbers as different shapes and colors. "S" was able to remember a matrix of 50 digits after studying it for three minutes, both immediately afterwards and many years later. Luria credited Shereshevsky's synesthetic experiences as the basis for his remarkable short- and long-term memory.

7   Using my own synesthetic experiences since early childhood, I have grown up with the ability to handle and calculate huge numbers in my head without any conscious effort, just like the Raymond Babbitt character. In fact, this is a talent common to

---

1. **neurological** (nur uh LOJ uh kuhl) *adj.* occurring in the brain.

👥 FACILITATING SMALL-GROUP CLOSE READING

CLOSE READ: Informational Texts As groups conduct the close read, circulate and offer support as needed.

- Remind students that when they read nonfiction, they should look for sentences that clearly identify the topic. They should then look for the ways that the author develops the topic throughout the piece.

- Have groups identify and discuss different ways in which the author supports and develops the topic. These might include personal experience, anecdotes, examples from other literature, and reflection.

several other real-life savants (sometimes referred to as "lightning calculators"). Dr. Darold Treffert, a Wisconsin physician and the leading researcher in the study of savant syndrome, gives one example, of a blind man with "a faculty of calculating to a degree little short of marvelous" in his book *Extraordinary People*:

8   When he was asked how many grains of corn there would be in any one of 64 boxes, with 1 in the first, 2 in the second, 4 in the third, 8 in the fourth, and so on, he gave answers for the fourteenth (8,192), for the eighteenth (131,072) and the twenty-fourth (8,388,608) instantaneously, and he gave the figures for the forty-eighth box (140,737,488,355,328) in six seconds. He also gave the total in all 64 boxes correctly (18,446,744,073,709,551,616) in forty-five seconds.

9   My favorite kind of calculation is power multiplication, which means multiplying a number by itself a specified number of times. Multiplying a number by itself is called squaring; for example, the square of 72 is 72 × 72 = 5,184. Squares are always **symmetrical** shapes in my mind, which makes them especially beautiful to me. Multiplying the same number three times over is called cubing or "raising" to the third power. The cube, or third power, of 51 is equivalent to 51 × 51 × 51 = 132,651. I see each result of a power multiplication as a distinctive visual pattern in my head. As the sums and their results grow, so the mental shapes and colors I experience become increasingly more complex. I see 37's fifth power—37 × 37 × 37 × 37 × 37 = 69,343,957—as a large circle composed of smaller circles running clockwise from the top around.

10   When I divide one number by another, in my head I see a **spiral** rotating downwards in larger and larger loops, which seem to warp and curve. Different divisions produce different sizes of spirals with varying curves. From my mental imagery I'm able to calculate a sum like 13 ÷ 97 (0.1340206 . . .) to almost a hundred decimal places.

11   I never write anything down when I'm calculating, because I've always been able to do the sums in my head, and it's much easier for me to visualize the answer using my synesthetic shapes than to try to follow the "carry the one" techniques taught in the textbooks we are given at school. When multiplying, I see the two numbers as distinct shapes. The image changes and a third shape emerges—the correct answer. The process takes a matter of seconds and happens spontaneously. It's like doing math without having to think.

NOTES

Mark base words or indicate another strategy you used to help you determine meaning.

symmetrical (sih MEH trih kuhl) *adj.*
MEANING:

spiral (SPY ruhl) *n.*
MEANING:

from Blue Nines and Red Words   403

DIGITAL PERSPECTIVES

Concept Vocabulary

SYMMETRICAL If groups are struggling to define the word *symmetrical* in paragraph 9, point out that they can look for a base word that they know. In this case, the base word is *symmetry*. Help them identify that the context for the word is "Squares are always *symmetrical* shapes in my head . . . "
Have students use the base word, along with the context, as they try to define the word *symmetrical*.

Possible response: *Symmetrical* means "having balanced proportions."

SPIRAL If groups are struggling to define the word *spiral* in paragraph 10, point out that in this case there is not a more familiar related base word. Help them identify the context for the word ("rotating downwards in larger and larger loops"). Have students use the context as they try to define the word *spiral*.

Possible response: *Spiral* means "a shape like a coil."

HOW LANGUAGE WORKS

Spiral and Spire Point out to students that in some cases, words may seem to be related, as in the case of the word *spiral* in paragraph 10, which means "a shape like a coil," and *spire*, which means "a narrow, tapering structure on top of a building." Because English has developed from many languages, words that appear to be in the same family can have very different histories. Explain to students that *spiral* comes from the Latin *spira*, which means "coil." *Spire*, on the other hand, comes from Old English, and means "a stalk of grass." Challenge students to find other words that seem to be from the same family but that have different etymologies.

FACILITATING

Concept Vocabulary

AESTHETIC If groups are struggling to define the word *aesthetic* in paragraph 14, point out that they can try looking for a context clue. Then help them identify the context for *aesthetic*, contained in the next sentence. ("If I see a number I experience as particularly beautiful on a shop sign or a car license plate, there's a shiver of excitement and pleasure.") Have students use the base word, along with context, to define the word *aesthetic*.

Possible response: *Aesthetic* means "relating to the experience of beauty."

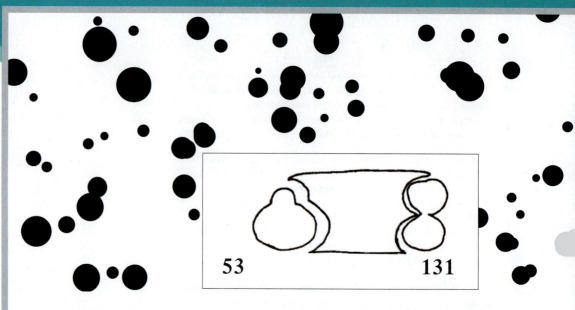

NOTES

Mark base words or indicate another strategy you used to help you determine meaning.

aesthetic (ehs THEHT ihk) *adj.*
MEANING:

12   In the illustration above I'm multiplying 53 by 131. I see both numbers as a unique shape and locate each spatially opposite the other. The space created between the two shapes creates a third, which I perceive as a new number: 6,943, the solution to the sum.

13   Different tasks involve different shapes, and I also have various sensations or emotions for certain numbers. Whenever I multiply with 11 I always experience a feeling of the digits tumbling downwards in my head. I find 6s hardest to remember of all the numbers, because I experience them as tiny black dots, without any distinctive shape or texture. I would describe them as like little gaps or holes. I have visual and sometimes emotional responses to every number up to 10,000, like having my own visual, numerical vocabulary. And just like a poet's choice of words, I find some combinations of numbers more beautiful than others: ones go well with darker numbers like 8s and 9s, but not so well with 6s. A telephone number with the sequence 189 is much more beautiful to me than one with a sequence like 116.

14   This **aesthetic** dimension to my synesthesia is something that has its ups and downs. If I see a number I experience as particularly beautiful on a shop sign or a car license plate, there's a shiver of excitement and pleasure. On the other hand, if the numbers don't match my experience of them—if, for example, a shop sign's price has "99 pence" in red or green (instead of blue)—then I find that uncomfortable and irritating.

15   It is not known how many savants have synesthetic experiences to help them in the areas they excel in. One reason for this is that, like Raymond Babbitt, many suffer profound disability, preventing them from explaining to others how they do the things that they do. I am fortunate not to suffer from any of the most severe impairments that often come with abilities such as mine.

404   UNIT 4 • HUMAN INTELLIGENCE

VOCABULARY DEVELOPMENT

Graphic Organizer Have students fill out a word map for the word *aesthetic*, which appears in paragraph 14.

Definition in your own words.		Synonyms
	Aesthetic	
Use it in a sentence.		Antonyms

16 Like most individuals with savant syndrome, I am also on the autistic spectrum. I have Asperger's syndrome, a relatively mild and high-functioning form of autism that affects around 1 in every 300 people in the United Kingdom. According to a 2001 study by the U.K.'s National Autistic Society, nearly half of all adults with Asperger's syndrome are not diagnosed until after the age of sixteen. I was finally diagnosed at age twenty-five following tests and an interview at the Autism Research Centre in Cambridge.

17 Autism, including Asperger's syndrome, is defined by the presence of impairments affecting social interaction, communication, and imagination (problems with abstract or flexible thought and empathy, for example). Diagnosis is not easy and cannot be made by a blood test or brain scan; doctors have to observe behavior and study the individual's developmental history from infancy.

18 People with Asperger's often have good language skills and are able to lead relatively normal lives. Many have above-average IQs and excel in areas that involve logical or visual thinking. Like other forms of autism, Asperger's is a condition affecting many more men than women (around 80 percent of autistics and 90 percent of those diagnosed with Asperger's are men). Single-mindedness is a defining characteristic, as is a strong drive to analyze detail and identify rules and patterns in systems. Specialized skills involving memory, numbers, and mathematics are common. It is not known for certain what causes someone to have Asperger's, though it is something you are born with.

19 For as long as I can remember, I have experienced numbers in the visual, synesthetic way that I do. Numbers are my first language, one I often think and feel in. Emotions can be hard for me to understand or know how to react to, so I often use numbers to help me. If a friend says they feel sad or depressed, I picture myself sitting in the dark hollowness of number 6 to help me experience the same sort of feeling and understand it. If I read in an article that a person felt intimidated by something, I imagine myself standing next to the number 9. Whenever someone describes visiting a beautiful place, I recall my numerical landscapes and how happy they make me feel inside. By doing this, numbers actually help me get closer to understanding other people.

20 Sometimes people I meet for the first time remind me of a particular number and this helps me to be comfortable around them. They might be very tall and remind me of the number 9, or round and remind me of the number 3. If I feel unhappy or anxious or in a situation I have no previous experience of (when I'm much more likely to feel stressed and uncomfortable), I count to myself. When I count, the numbers form pictures and patterns in my mind that are consistent and reassuring to me. Then I can relax and interact with whatever situation I'm in.

from Blue Nines and Red Words

FACILITATING

NOTES

21 Thinking of calendars always makes me feel good, all those numbers and patterns in one place. Different days of the week elicit different colors and emotions in my head: Tuesdays are a warm color while Thursdays are fuzzy. Calendrical calculation—the ability to tell what day of the week a particular date fell or will fall on—is common to many savants. I think this is probably due to the fact that the numbers in calendars are predictable and form patterns between the different days and months. For example, the thirteenth day in a month is always two days before whatever day the first falls on, excepting leap years, while several of the months mimic the behavior of others, like January and October, September and December, and February and March (the first day of February is the same as the first day of March). So if the first of February is a fuzzy texture in my mind (Thursday) for a given year, the thirteenth of March will be a warm color (Tuesday).

22 In his book *The Man Who Mistook His Wife for a Hat*, writer and neurologist Oliver Sacks mentions the case of severely autistic twins John and Michael as an example of how far some savants are able to take calendrical calculations. Though unable to care for themselves (they had been in various institutions since the age of seven), the twins were capable of calculating the day of the week for any date over a 40,000-year span.

23 Sacks also describes John and Michael as playing a game that involved swapping prime numbers with each other for hours at a time. Like the twins, I have always been fascinated by prime numbers. I see each prime as a smooth-textured shape, distinct from composite numbers (non-primes) that are grittier and less distinctive. Whenever I identify a number as prime, I get a rush of feeling in my head (in the front center) which is hard to put into words. It's a special feeling, like the sudden sensation of pins and needles.

24 Sometimes I close my eyes and imagine the first thirty, fifty, hundred numbers as I experience them spatially, synesthetically. Then I can see in my mind's eye just how beautiful and special the primes are by the way they stand out so sharply from the other number shapes. It's exactly for this reason that I look and look and look at them; each one is so different from the one before and the one after. Their loneliness among the other numbers makes them so conspicuous and interesting to me.

25 There are moments, as I'm falling into sleep at night, that my mind fills suddenly with bright light and all I can see are numbers—hundreds, thousands of them—swimming rapidly over my eyes. The experience is beautiful and soothing to me. Some nights, when I'm having difficulty falling asleep, I imagine myself walking around my numerical landscapes. Then I feel safe and happy. I never feel lost, because the prime number shapes act as signposts.

PERSONALIZE FOR LEARNING

English Language Support
Domain-Specific Vocabulary and Word Families Review paragraphs 21 and 22 with students. The domain-specific vocabulary that appears in the excerpt from *Blue Nines and Red Words* may present a challenge to English learners. Support them in finding familiar base words, familiar related words, or words that have already been defined in the story. For example, if students recognize that *calendrical* (paragraph 21) is related to the familiar word *calendar*, they can probably figure out that *calendrical* means "having to do with calendars." Similarly, when students see the word *neurologist* (paragraph 22), they will have an easier time defining it if they recognize that it is related to the word *neurology*.
ALL LEVELS

Comprehension Check

Complete the following items after you finish your first read. Review and clarify details with your group.

1. Why does Tammet call his birth date blue?

2. What is one way in which the author says he demonstrates savant syndrome?

3. How does the author compare his experience with numbers to a poet's choice of words?

4. What is the author's favorite type of calculation?

5. **Notebook** Confirm your understanding of the text by writing a short summary.

RESEARCH

Research to Clarify Choose at least one unfamiliar point that Daniel Tammet makes about intelligence. Briefly research that detail. In what way does the information you learned shed light on an aspect of the memoir?

from Blue Nines and Red Words

Comprehension Check

Possible responses:

1. Tammet was born on a Wednesday, and he sees Wednesdays as blue in his mind.
2. He can calculate huge numbers in his head without effort.
3. He thinks some combinations of numbers are beautiful and some are not, like a poet associating words.
4. His favorite type of calculation is power multiplication, or multiplying a number by itself a specified number of times.
5. Summaries will differ. However, summaries should include that Tammet is a savant, that he has synesthesia, and that he has Asperger's syndrome. Summaries should also include that numbers help Tammet understand others' emotions.

Research

Research to Clarify If groups struggle to identify their research topic, you may want to suggest that they focus on one of the following points that Tammet makes about intelligence: the benefits of a highly visual memory, the benefits of synesthesia, the IQ of people with Asperger's, or savant syndrome.

DIGITAL PERSPECTIVES

Enriching the Text To learn more about Daniel Tammet and savant syndrome, students can watch Tammet's TED talk, "Different Ways of Knowing." In the video, Tammet shows his own drawings that depict how he envisions numbers and words, in shapes and colors. He also shows how shapes help him do mental math. Additionally, he speculates on how the sounds of words are associated with their meaning. After students view the video, have them write a paragraph explaining how it enhances their understanding of synesthesia and the human brain.

FACILITATING

Jump Start

CLOSE READ Ask groups to consider the following prompt: *What can we learn about human intelligence by understanding the mind of someone with savant syndrome?* As students discuss in their groups, ask them to note that people with savant syndrome usually are on the autistic spectrum.

Close Read the Text

If needed, model close reading by using the Annotation Highlights in the Interactive Teacher's Edition.

Remind students to use Accountable Talk in their discussions and to support one another as they complete the close read.

Analyze the Text

1. **Possible response:** Tammet's experiences of numbers are an example of a kind of intelligence because they allow him to do complicated calculations in his head.
2. **Passages will vary by group.** Remind students to explain why they chose the passage they presented to group members.
3. **Responses will vary by group.**

Concept Vocabulary

Why These Words? **Possible response:** The concept words all have to do with Tammet's perceptions of numbers. Another word that has to do with this concept is *immensity*.

Practice

Possible responses:
- The butterfly's wings are *symmetrical*.
- The tornado was a *spiral* of winds.
- The gallery has a strong *aesthetic* appeal.

Word Network

Possible responses: *savant, synesthesia, memory, IQ*

Word Study

For more support, see **Concept Vocabulary and Word Study.**

Possible responses:
Other words from the selection are *numerical* and *neurological*. *Numerical* means "having to do with numbers." *Neurological* means "having to do with the study of the nervous system."

408   UNIT 4 • HUMAN INTELLIGENCE

from BLUE NINES AND RED WORDS

TIP

GROUP DISCUSSION
Listen carefully to others as they state their ideas. Try not to repeat an idea that someone has already stated. Instead, try to make a new point or add a new example to support points already made.

WORD NETWORK

Add words related to human intelligence from the text to your Word Network.

STANDARDS

Reading Informational Text
• Determine a central idea of a text and analyze its development over the course of the text, including its relationship to supporting ideas; provide an objective summary of the text.
• Analyze how a text makes connections among and distinctions between individuals, ideas, or events.
• Determine an author's point of view or purpose in a text and analyze how the author acknowledges and responds to conflicting evidence or viewpoints.

408 UNIT 4 • HUMAN INTELLIGENCE

MAKING MEANING

Close Read the Text

With your group, revisit sections of the text you marked during your first read. **Annotate** what you notice. What **questions** do you have? What can you **conclude**?

Analyze the Text

CITE TEXTUAL EVIDENCE to support your answers.

Notebook Complete the activities.

1. **Review and Clarify** With your group, reread paragraphs 9–12. Discuss the author's descriptions of his experiences with numbers. How are his experiences of numbers an example of a kind of intelligence?

2. **Present and Discuss** Now, work with your group to share the passages from the text that you found especially important. Take turns presenting your passages. Discuss what you noticed in the text, what questions you asked, and what conclusions you reached.

3. **Essential Question:** *In what different ways can people be intelligent?* What has this memoir taught you about the different ways people can be intelligent? Discuss with your group.

LANGUAGE DEVELOPMENT

Concept Vocabulary

symmetrical   spiral   aesthetic

Why These Words? The concept vocabulary words from the text are related. With your group, determine what the words have in common. Write your ideas, and add another word that fits the category.

Practice

Notebook Confirm your understanding of the concept vocabulary words by using each one in a sentence. In each sentence, provide context clues for the vocabulary word to demonstrate your understanding of the word's meaning.

Word Study

Latin Suffix: -ical In "Blue Nines and Red Words," Daniel Tammet uses the word *symmetrical* to describe how he envisions squared numbers. The word *symmetrical* ends with the Latin suffix *-ical*, which means "having to do with," "made of," or "characterized by." Find other words in the selection that have this suffix. Use a dictionary to verify the precise meanings of these words.

FORMATIVE ASSESSMENT

Analyze the Text

If students struggle to close read the text, **then** provide the *from* Blue Nines and Red Words: Text Questions available online in the Interactive Teacher's Edition or Unit Resources. Answers and DOK levels are also available.

Concept Vocabulary

If students struggle to identify what the concept words have in common, **then** have them use each word in a sentence and see what the sentences have in common.

Word Study

If students struggle to find other words in the selection ending with *-ical*, **then** have them name other words they know that end in *-ical*. For Reteach and Practice, see **Word Study: Latin Suffix: -ical (RP).**

ESSENTIAL QUESTION: In what different ways can people be intelligent?

Analyze Craft and Structure

Memoir and Reflective Writing An **autobiography** is a true account of events and experiences written by the person who directly experienced them. A **memoir** is a type of autobiography that focuses on a specific period in the author's life or an experience that holds particular significance for the author. For example, in the excerpt from "Blue Nines and Red Words," Daniel Tammet explores his experience with savant syndrome.

In a memoir, an author will often use **reflective writing** to communicate his or her thoughts and feelings—or reflections—about an event, experience, or idea. The purpose of reflective writing is to communicate these reflections in a way that inspires readers to respond with their own reflections. Reflective writing can reveal a variety of insights:

- what the author learned from the event or experience
- what the experience revealed about the author's personality
- how the author feels about other people in his or her life
- how the author relates to his or her environment and the world
- how the author responds to the conflicts, or struggles, with which he or she is faced

These insights help develop and reveal the author's **central ideas,** or main points, in a memoir. The ways in which the author structures and connects his or her experiences and insights in a reflective piece enable the author to achieve his or her purpose, or reason for writing.

TIP

CLARIFICATION
As you read a reflective piece, pay attention to the comparisons and contrasts an author makes to connect people, ideas, and events.

Practice

CITE TEXTUAL EVIDENCE to support your answers.

📓 **Notebook** Work individually to analyze Tammet's use of reflective writing in "Blue Nines and Red Words," using a chart like the one shown. After you have completed the chart, compare charts with your group members. Then, as a group, determine the central ideas that are revealed through your analysis.

TAMMET'S EXPERIENCES	TAMMET'S REFLECTIONS	CLUES ABOUT CENTRAL IDEA
has savant syndrome	numbers are friends	Answers will vary but may include his unique ability to perceive numbers in this way.
has synesthesia	has emotional and aesthetic responses to numbers	Answers will vary but may include having similar reactions to other things but not numbers.
is on the autism spectrum	numbers help understanding of other people	Answers will vary but may include his specialized skills involving memory, numbers, and mathematics being Asperger's characteristics.

from Blue Nines and Red Words

Analyze Craft and Structure

Memoir and Reflective Writing Point out to students that informational texts should inform the reader about something. In a memoir, the author tells about something specific in his or her life. Reflective writing offers the author's insights about his or her experiences. Not all informative texts include the author's reflections, but memoirs often do. For more support, see **Analyze Craft and Structure: Memoir and Reflective Writing.**

See possible responses in chart on student page.

FORMATIVE ASSESSMENT

Analyze Craft and Structure

If students have difficulty identifying Tammet's experiences, **then** point out that in this case, experiences can mean his neurological conditions affect the way he experiences the world. For Reteach and Practice, see **Analyze Craft and Structure: Memoir and Reflective Writing (RP).**

WriteNow Inform and Explain

Memoir In *Blue Nines and Red Words,* Daniel Tammet explains how it feels to have synesthesia and savant syndrome. He does this by using descriptive writing to explain how numbers look and feel to him. He also includes references to certain events, such as appearing on a television show (paragraph 4). Have students choose an event in their own life, and write one page about it, as if it were part of a larger memoir. Remind students that Daniel Tammet includes his own reflections in his memoir, and encourage them to do so, too.

DIGITAL PERSPECTIVES

FACILITATING

Conventions

Pronoun Case Point out to students that when they are trying to identify a pronoun case in a sentence, they can ask themselves whether the person the pronoun represents is doing something or receiving an action. For example, if Daniel Tammet gave books to his business partners, we would say, *He gave books to them.* In the sentence, there are two pronouns—*He* and *them*. Since David Tammet did the action of giving, *he* is the subject of the verb *gave*. Identifying the subject should tell students that the pronoun *he* is in the subjective case. Tammet's business partners will receive the books he gave to them, so in the sentence, *them* is the indirect object. Knowing that a pronoun is the object of a verb should tell students that it is in the objective case. Point out to students that if they continued by talking about who owns, or possesses, the books, they might write *The books will be the business partners'* or *They will be theirs.* That means that *theirs* tells who owns the books, and is in the possessive case. For more support, see **Conventions: Pronoun Case.**

Read It
1. he (nominative)
2. them (objective)
3. he (nominative) / them (objective)
4. his (possessive)

Write It
Possible response:
Daniel Tammet has Asperger's syndrome, and <u>he</u> uses numbers to help <u>him</u> relate to other peo<u>ple</u>. Numbers are friends to <u>him</u>. <u>His</u> abilities with numbers are rare.

FORMATIVE ASSESSMENT
Conventions

If students have difficulty in identify pronoun cases, **then** have students review whether the person or thing the pronoun represents is doing an action (subjective), receiving an action (objective), or is in possession of something (possessive). For Reteach and Practice, see **Conventions: Pronoun Case (RP).**

LANGUAGE DEVELOPMENT

from BLUE NINES AND RED WORDS

TIP
COLLABORATION
Discuss the definitions and examples of these pronoun cases as a group. If you have a good grasp of the concepts, explain them to others. If your group is still having difficulty, consult with your teacher.

Conventions

Pronoun Case English has three **cases**, or forms, of pronouns. Writers use pronoun cases according to a pronoun's function in a sentence.

- **nominative case:** used for the subjects of verbs and for predicate pronouns; also known as the **subjective case**
- **objective case:** used for direct and indirect objects and for objects of prepositions
- **possessive case:** used to show ownership

The chart below shows the three categories for personal pronouns.

CASE	PRONOUNS	FUNCTION IN A SENTENCE
nominative (subject)	I, we, you, he, she, it, they	subject of a verb ("*She* read the book.")
		predicate pronoun ("The book reader was *she*.")
objective (object)	me, us, you, him, her, it, them	direct object ("Daniel said *it* to Mia.")
		indirect object ("Daniel told *her* his idea.")
		object of a preposition ("Daniel told the idea to *her*.")
possessive	my, mine, our, ours, your, yours, his, her, hers, its, their, theirs	to show ownership ("Daniel told *his* idea to Mia.")

Read It
Work individually to choose the correct pronouns and give their cases.

1. When Daniel Tammet thinks of numbers, (he/his) sees colors.
2. Prime numbers look like pebbles, and Daniel likes (they/them).
3. When (he/him) adds or multiplies numbers, Daniel does not write (they/them) down.
4. Daniel Tammet sees (he/his) own birthday as blue.

STANDARDS
Language
Demonstrate command of the conventions of standard English grammar and usage when writing or speaking.

Write It
Notebook Write three sentences about the selection. Use all three pronoun cases at least once.

410 UNIT 4 • HUMAN INTELLIGENCE

PERSONALIZE FOR LEARNING

English Language Support

Pronoun Case Review the definitions of the pronoun cases referenced in this lesson (subjective, objective, possessive). Have students identify an example of each, and use their examples in sentences. Support students in completing as many of these steps themselves as they can. **ALL LEVELS**

EFFECTIVE EXPRESSION

Research

Assignment

With your group, write a brief **informational report.** Choose from the following options:

☐ Conduct research to learn more about the condition known as *synesthesia*. Then, write a report in which you explain the ways in which Daniel Tammet's experience serves as an example of this condition.

☐ Conduct research to learn more about a well-known savant in a specific field, such as mathematics, music, language, or memory. Then, write a report in which you compare the experience of the savant you chose to Tammet's experience.

Gather Evidence Gather a variety of evidence from relevant, reliable sources. Use the chart to guide your research and note important information.

QUESTION	EVIDENCE
What is the condition or ability, and what makes it extraordinary?	
How has the condition or ability shaped the person's life?	
In what ways does Tammet's experience reflect the condition or ability?	

Explain Technical Vocabulary In "Blue Nines and Red Words," you may have noticed scientific terms such as *autistic spectrum* and *Asperger's syndrome*. As you conduct research, you will encounter various other technical terms. It is important to understand what these words mean so that you can use and explain them in your report. The following strategies will help you clarify technical terms for readers who might not be familiar with them:

- Summarize or paraphrase the term's meaning by putting it into your own words.
- Provide examples of a complicated idea or process so readers can connect it with something familiar.

EVIDENCE LOG

Before moving on to a new selection, go to your Evidence Log, and record what you learned from the excerpt from "Blue Nines and Red Words."

STANDARDS

Writing
- Write informative/explanatory texts to examine a topic and convey ideas, concepts, and information through the selection, organization, and analysis of relevant content.
  b. Develop the topic with relevant, well-chosen facts, definitions, concrete details, quotations, or other information and examples.
  d. Use precise language and domain-specific vocabulary to inform about or explain the topic.
- Conduct short research projects to answer a question, drawing on several sources and generating additional related, focused questions that allow for multiple avenues of exploration.
- Gather relevant information from multiple print and digital sources, using search terms effectively; assess the credibility and accuracy of each source; and quote or paraphrase the data and conclusions of others while avoiding plagiarism and following a standard format for citation.

DIGITAL PERSPECTIVES

Research

If students have difficulty in choosing between the two options, point out that they may use their own interests as a guide. The first topic (synesthesia) will lead them to learn more about a neurological condition, and they will use what they learn to write an essay. The second option will focus on biographical research about a savant. In doing this research, they may read about a number of people before choosing their subject.

Gather Evidence As students research evidence, have them carefully note their sources, including paragraph numbers from the selection. Once they have gathered information, point out that an effective informational report includes a thesis statement that clearly expresses the group's claim.

Explain Technical Vocabulary Due to the extent of the technical vocabulary in the selection, guide students to allocate appropriate time to gain a full understanding of the technical vocabulary. They should gain an understanding of the terms that goes deeper than repeating definitions. Check to make sure each group has made assignments and that the work is divided evenly among group members. For more support, see **Research: Informational Report.**

Evidence Log Support students in completing their Evidence Log. This paced activity will help prepare them for the Performance-Based Assessment at the end of the unit.

FORMATIVE ASSESSMENT

Research

If students struggle with locating information, **then** have them refine their search terms to better target appropriate evidence. For Reteach and Practice, see **Research: Informational Report (RP).**

Selection Test

Administer the *Blue Nines and Red Words* Selection Test, which is available in both print and digital formats online in Assessments.

PERSONALIZE FOR LEARNING

English Language Support

Identifying Reliable Sources Display the following sources: a student blog about mathematics; an online mathematics book; a magazine article by a well-known mathematician.

Have students identify the least reliable source and explain why. **EMERGING**

Have students explain which source or sources they would choose to write an informational report about a mathematical topic. **EXPANDING**

Ask students to write a short paragraph describing the steps for locating reliable sources in order to write an informational report about a mathematical topic. Have a volunteer share their writing with the class. **BRIDGING**

An expanded **English Language Support Lesson** on Informational Report is available in the Interactive Teacher's Edition.

PLANNING

SMALL-GROUP LEARNING • THE THEORY OF MULTIPLE INTELLIGENCES INFOGRAPHIC

The Theory of Multiple Intelligences Infographic

AUDIO SUMMARIES
Audio summaries of "The Theory of Multiple Intelligences Infographic" are available online in both English and Spanish in the Interactive Teacher's Edition or Unit Resources. Assigning these summaries prior to reviewing the selection may help students build additional background knowledge and set a context for their first review.

Summary

This infographic illustrates Howard Gardner's theory of multiple intelligences. Gardner argues that "intelligence" is often thought of too narrowly. He argues that certain traits that are often called skills should be considered types of intelligence. The full list includes traits we often associate with socially talented people (e.g., intra-personal, interpersonal, and linguistic intelligence) or athletic people (e.g., spatial and bodily-kinesthetic intelligence), in addition to traits more traditionally thought of as intelligence.

Insight
This selection illustrates a variety of kinds of intelligence in a straightforward and engaging way.

ESSENTIAL QUESTION:
In what different ways can people be intelligent?

Connection to Essential Question
The infographic lists nine kinds of intelligence: naturalist, musical, logical-mathematical, existential, interpersonal, bodily-kinesthetic, linguistic, intra-personal, and spatial.

SMALL-GROUP LEARNING PERFORMANCE TASK
How does each selection highlight a different way to be intelligent?

Connection to Performance Tasks

Small-Group Learning Performance Task This selection discusses many ways to be intelligent, though the text around it particularly mentions linguistic, interpersonal, and math skills.

UNIT PERFORMANCE-BASED ASSESSMENT
In what different ways can people be intelligent?

Unit Performance-Based Assessment According to this selection, the essence of intelligence is understanding the world. Different types of intelligence describe different ways of understanding the world.

DIGITAL PERSPECTIVES Audio Video Document Annotation Highlights EL Highlights Online Assessment

LESSON RESOURCES

	Making Meaning	Language Development	Effective Expression
Lesson	First Review Close Review Analyze the Media	Media Vocabulary	Speaking and Listening
Instructional Standards	**RI.10** By the end of the year, read and comprehend literary nonfiction . . . **L.6** Acquire and use accurately grade-appropriate general academic and domain-specific words and phrases . . . **RI.7** Evaluate the advantages and disadvantages . . .		**SL.1** Engage effectively in a range of collaborative discussions . . . **SL.1.a** Come to discussions prepared . . . **SL.1.b** Follow rules for collegial discussions . . . **SL.1.c** Pose questions . . . **SL.1.d** Acknowledge new information . . .
STUDENT RESOURCES			
Available online in the Interactive Student Edition or Unit Resources	Selection Audio First-Read Guide: Nonfiction First-Read Guide: Nonfiction	Word Network	Evidence Log
TEACHER RESOURCES			
Selection Resources Available online in the Interactive Teacher's Edition or Unit Resources	Audio Summaries The Theory of Multiple Intelligences Infographic: Media Questions	Media Vocabulary	Speaking and Listening: Group Discussion
Assessment Available online in Assessments	Selection Test		
My Resources	A Unit 4 Answer Key is available online and in the Interactive Teacher's Edition.		

Media Complexity Rubric: The Theory of Multiple Intelligences Infographic

Quantitative Measures

Format and Length: Chart with graphics and text

Qualitative Measures

Knowledge Demands ① ② **③** ④ ⑤	In the text of the chart, terminology is used that may not be familiar (descriptions of types of intelligence), but they are partially defined within the chart.
Structure ① **②** ③ ④ ⑤	The chart is clear and easy to read, with each type of intelligence explained in text and associated with an icon that helps with the meaning.
Language Conventionality and Clarity ① ② **③** ④ ⑤	The text in the chart includes subject specific vocabulary (types of intelligence) and phrases to define it.
Levels of Meaning/Purpose ① **②** ③ ④ ⑤	Unfamiliar words are defined with familiar terms, making it easy to understand their meaning. They are also accompanied by icons that help to show the meaning.

FACILITATING

Jump Start

FIRST REVIEW Ask groups to consider and discuss the following prompts: *Why are some people naturally good at one thing while others are better at something else? Who do you know who is great with numbers? Who is athletically inclined? Who is always in tune with how others feel?*

The Theory of Multiple Intelligences Infographic

What are some of your favorite things to do? Which subject comes easiest for you in school? What hobbies or activities do you enjoy? What makes you good at these things? Modeling questions such as these will help students connect to "The Theory of Multiple Intelligences Infographic" and to the Performance Task assignment. Selection audio and print capability for the selection are available in the Interactive Teacher's Edition.

Media Vocabulary

Encourage groups to discuss the media vocabulary. *Have they seen the terms in texts before? Do they use any of them in their speech and writing?*

Encourage groups to discuss other words that are related to the media vocabulary and to add at least one additional occupation for each word in the chart.

● FIRST REVIEW

Have students perform the steps of the first review independently:

LOOK: Remind students to examine the labels in bold and the selected images for each type of intelligence.

NOTE: Encourage students to identify a key phrase or other element that helps them to better understand each type of intelligence.

CONNECT: Encourage students to make connections beyond the infographic. If they cannot make connections to their own lives, have them consider the different types of intelligences reflected in previous selections.

RESPOND: Students will answer questions to demonstrate understanding.

Point out to students that while they will always complete the Respond step at the end of the first read, the other steps will probably happen somewhat concurrently. You may wish to print copies of the **First-Review Guide: Media: Art and Photography** for students to use.

MAKING MEANING

About the Theorist

Howard Gardner (b. 1943) is an American psychologist and a professor at the Harvard Graduate School of Education. The child of Jewish parents who fled Germany before World War II, Gardner has been called "one of the 100 most influential public intellectuals in the world." Although he has published dozens of books and research articles, he remains best known for his theory of multiple intelligences, which he outlined in his book *Frames of Mind: The Theory of Multiple Intelligences*.

≡ STANDARDS

Reading Informational Text
By the end of the year, read and comprehend literary nonfiction at the high end of the grades 6–8 text complexity band independently and proficiently.

Language
Acquire and use accurately grade-appropriate general academic and domain-specific words and phrases; gather vocabulary knowledge when considering a word or phrase important to comprehension or expression.

The Theory of Multiple Intelligences Infographic

Media Vocabulary

The following words or concepts will be useful to you as you analyze, discuss, and write about infographics.

infographic: image used to present information, data, or knowledge quickly and clearly	• An infographic can help simplify a complicated subject and present it in an engaging way. • Infographics are structured to encourage readers to compare different ideas and information.
icons: symbols or graphic representations, often used in charts and on digital screens	• Icons are design to be simple, functional, and easily recognizable. • On digital screens, icons allow the user to easily identify and access files, programs, and applications.
labels and captions: short descriptive words or phrases that provide information	• Captions are used to briefly explain the content of an image. • Labels are often formatted to draw attention to specific content.

First Review MEDIA: INFOGRAPHIC

Apply these strategies as you conduct your first review. You will have an opportunity to complete a close review after your first review.

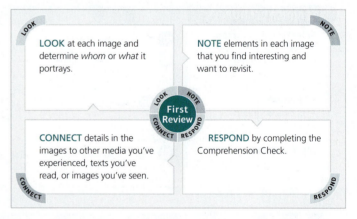

412 UNIT 4 • HUMAN INTELLIGENCE

👥 FACILITATING SMALL-GROUP CLOSE READING

CLOSE READ: Infographic As groups perform the close review, circulate and offer support as needed.

• Encourage groups to carefully read the text that accompanies the infographic. Have groups discuss the explicit and implicit information provided in the text and how it affects their understanding of the infographic.

• If a group is confused about why particular elements are important in the text or infographic, remind them to think about how the elements are related.

• Challenge groups to determine the main idea of the infographic and the specific details that refine the main idea.

DIGITAL PERSPECTIVES

MEDIA | INFOGRAPHIC

The Theory of Multiple Intelligences Infographic

Howard Gardner

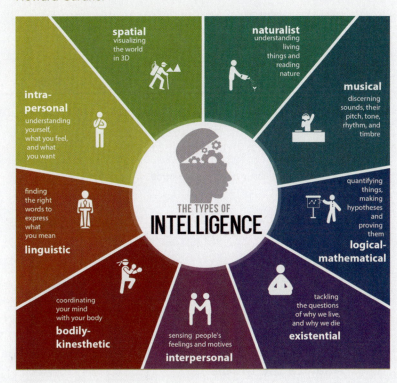

BACKGROUND

When Howard Gardner first developed his theory of multiple intelligences in 1983, he identified seven different ways that people can be intelligent. He added the naturalist and existential intelligences to his theory about a decade later. According to his theory, intelligence is not defined by a single ability, but by different types of related abilities. Gardner's theory claims that most people have a combination of these types of intelligences, but they will often display some types more strongly than others.

SCAN FOR MULTIMEDIA

NOTES

CLOSER REVIEW

Analyze Infographics

Circulate among groups as students conduct their first review. Suggest that groups review the infographic. Encourage them to talk about the notes they make. If needed, provide the following support.

NOTE: Have students note the details in the infographic that describe each type of intelligence, or work with small groups to have students participate while you note them together.

QUESTION: Guide students to consider what these details might tell them. Ask them to identify the graphic elements such as font, images, color choices, and spatial design.

Possible response: The designer uses all lowercase letters, the font and images are white, the lines are simple, and the background colors are dark.

CONCLUDE: Help students to formulate conclusions about the importance of these details in the infographic. Ask students why the designer might have included these details.

Possible response: The lowercase lettering and the white font and images are clean and simple against the darker-colored background. These choices make the infographic easy to read and understand.

Explain to students that **infographics** are used when a large amount of information must be displayed in a meaningful way. The design of an infographic can make it effective in showing the relationship between the ideas. It may demonstrate comparison-and-contrast, problem-and-solution, or cause-and-effect, or it may be used to show data or provide information.

PERSONALIZE FOR LEARNING

English Language Support

Domain-Specific Words: Science The domain-specific vocabulary that appears in "The Theory of Multiple Intelligences Infographic" may present challenges to English Learners. Support them in understanding the text:

- Encourage students to examine and discuss the action taking place in each of the images in the infographic.

- Ask students to compare and contrast the perceived actions with the definition or description of each type of intelligence.

- Have students select three domain-specific words that cause confusion, and create their own illustrated glossary of the words. **ALL LEVELS**

FACILITATING

Jump Start

CLOSE REVIEW Ask students to consider the following questions: *Do you have family members or friends who are particularly good at specific skills? What is it that they are great at doing? Which of the multiple intelligences do those people have that makes them so good those skills?*

Comprehension Check

Possible responses:

1. Linguistic intelligence is the ability to choose your words well to express your meaning.
2. The ability to understand yourself and your feelings is intrapersonal intelligence.
3. The ability to sense other people's feelings and emotions is associated with interpersonal intelligence.
4. Spatial intelligence is associated with the ability to picture the world in 3D.

Word Network
Possible Words: *musical, spatial, existential*

● CLOSE REVIEW

If needed, model close reviewing by using the Closer Review notes in the Interactive Teacher's Edition. Remind students to use Accountable Talk in their discussions and to support one another as they complete the close review.

Analyze the Media

1. **Possible response:** The captions and labels help to categorize and organize larger ideas in easier, more memorable ways. The captions provide examples that suit each intelligence.
2. Responses will vary by group but should clearly distinguish between advantages and disadvantages of the infographic as a medium.
3. Responses will vary by group.

FORMATIVE ASSESSMENT
Analyze the Media
If students struggle to close review the media, **then** provide the **The Theory of Multiple Intelligences Infographic: Media Questions** available online in the Interactive Teacher's Edition or Unit Resources. Answers and DOK levels are also available.

Media Vocabulary
If groups are struggling to use these words as they discuss and write about the infographic, **then** have students use each word in a sentence.

414 UNIT 4 • HUMAN INTELLIGENCE

MAKING MEANING

Comprehension Check
Complete the following items after you finish your first review. Review and clarify details with your group.

1. What ability is associated with linguistic intelligence?

2. Which type of intelligence is characterized by the ability to understand yourself and your feelings?

3. What ability is associated with interpersonal intelligence?

4. Which type of intelligence is shown by the ability to picture the world in 3D?

MEDIA VOCABULARY
Use these words as you discuss and write about the infographic.

infographic
icons
labels and captions

Close Review
With your group, review the infographic and your first-review notes. What **questions** do you have? What can you **conclude**?

WORD NETWORK
Add words related to human intelligence from the text to your Word Network.

Analyze the Media

CITE TEXTUAL EVIDENCE to support your answers.

Notebook Complete the activities.

1. **Analyze and Discuss** How do the captions and labels in the infographic enhance your understanding of the different ways in which people can be intelligent? Provide specific examples to support your response.

2. **Review and Synthesize** Review the infographic with your group. What are the advantages of presenting the information about multiple intelligences in an infographic? In what ways might presenting the information this way be disadvantageous?

3. **Essential Question:** *In what different ways can people be intelligent?* What has this infographic taught you about the different ways people can be intelligent? Discuss with your group.

STANDARDS
Reading Informational Text
Evaluate the advantages and disadvantages of using different mediums to present a particular topic or idea.

414 UNIT 4 • HUMAN INTELLIGENCE

EFFECTIVE EXPRESSION

Speaking and Listening

Assignment

Take part in a **group discussion** about the different types of intelligence shown on the infographic. Choose from the following topics:

☐ With your group, engage in a collaborative discussion in which you analyze the nine types of intelligence. Then, pick three or four types on which to focus. For each type of intelligence, identify a well-known person, from the past or present, who has demonstrated that type of intelligence in a particularly strong way. For example, Dr. Martin Luther King, Jr., is a good example of a person with substantial linguistic intelligence. Finally, write a sentence or two about each person you have identified, in which you explain how he or she has demonstrated that type of intelligence.

☐ With your group, engage in a collaborative discussion in which you analyze the nine types of intelligence. Then, pick three or four types on which to focus. For each type of intelligence, identify a fictional character from literature who demonstrates that type of intelligence in a particularly strong way. For example, Sherlock Holmes might be a good example of a character who demonstrates great logical-mathematical intelligence. Finally, write a sentence or two about each character, in which you explain how he or she demonstrates that type of intelligence.

THE THEORY OF MULTIPLE INTELLIGENCES INFOGRAPHIC

Notebook Record notes from your discussion in the chart.

PERSON/CHARACTER	TYPE OF INTELLIGENCE	WHY
(Person) Jackie Robinson	bodily-kinesthetic	His athletic ability helped him become a major league baseball player.
(Fictional Character) Sherlock Holmes	logical-mathematical	His logic helped him to solve many mysteries.

Holding the Discussion Be sure to come to the discussion prepared with ideas that are supported with evidence from the infographic. If you disagree with someone else's ideas or views, express your disagreement respectfully. Pose questions that connect the ideas of other speakers, and respond to questions from other group members with relevant observations supported by details from the text. When another group member provides information that is new to you, reflect on your own ideas, and decide whether the new information has changed your ideas about the subject matter.

EVIDENCE LOG

Before moving on to a new selection, go to your Evidence Log, and record what you learned from the infographic.

STANDARDS

Speaking and Listening
Engage effectively in a range of collaborative discussions with diverse partners on *grade 8 topics, texts, and issues*, building on others' ideas and expressing their own clearly.

a. Come to discussions prepared, having read or researched material under study; explicitly draw on that preparation by referring to evidence on the topic, text, or issue to probe and reflect on ideas under discussion.
b. Follow rules for collegial discussions and decision-making, track progress toward specific goals and deadlines, and define individual roles as needed.
c. Pose questions that connect the ideas of several speakers and respond to others' questions and comments with relevant evidence, observations, and ideas.
d. Acknowledge new information expressed by others, and, when warranted, qualify or justify their own views in light of the evidence presented.

The Theory of Multiple Intelligences Infographic 415

DIGITAL PERSPECTIVES

Speaking and Listening

Encourage groups to identify people or fictional characters who are likely to be familiar to their classmates. This will make the discussion regarding the types of intelligences much more meaningful for others. For more support, see **Speaking and Listening: Group Discussion.**

See possible responses in chart on student page.

Holding the Discussion Encourage students to make supportive comments about each speaker's words, ideas, and delivery.

Evidence Log Support students in completing their Evidence Log. This paced activity will help prepare them for the Performance-Based Assessment at the end of the unit.

FORMATIVE ASSESSMENT

Speaking and Listening

If groups struggle to identify a famous person or character that they are familiar with, **then** have them focus on a main character from a selection that everyone has read.

Selection Test

Administer the "The Theory of Multiple Intelligences Infographic" Selection Test, which is available in both print and digital formats online in Assessments.

PERSONALIZE FOR LEARNING

Strategic Support

Group Discussion Groups often struggle taking turns and ensuring that everyone has an opportunity to speak. To encourage everyone to participate in the group discussion and share ideas, encourage groups to track participation.

Have each group create a T-chart. Record the group members' names in the column on the left, and record the number of contributions to the conversation on the right. Encourage groups to track not only the contributions during their presentation but also the contributions during the other groups' discussions.

Ask students to review the data from the chart following the group discussion. You may wish to ask each student to write a personal reflection regarding what the data say about the discussion and what he or she may wish to do differently or the same in the next group discussion.

Small-Group Learning 415

PLANNING
SMALL-GROUP LEARNING • RETORT • *from* THE PEOPLE, YES

Retort • *from* The People, Yes

🔊 **AUDIO SUMMARIES**
Audio summaries of the poetry collection are available online in both English and Spanish in the Interactive Teacher's Edition or Unit Resources. Assigning these summaries prior to reading the selection may help students build additional background knowledge and set a context for their first read.

Summary
This selection consists of poems about intelligence.

"Retort" is a poem by Paul Laurence Dunbar. Written from the perspective of a man in love, it concerns the conflict between coldly rational thought and what we desire.

Carl Sandburg's *The People, Yes* is a book-length poem about knowledge. In this excerpt, a man claims he knows more than another, before being reminded that the amount that either of them knows is vast.

Insight
"Retort" argues that to ignore what you feel and refuse to be taken in by beauty is worse than foolish. To act as if emotional attachment is a trick to avoid is ridiculous.

The excerpt from *The People, Yes* shows that differences in people pale in comparison to what we all have yet to learn. Due to its simplicity, it may strike students as insensitive. The claim that the "white man" knows all things the "red man" does and more shouldn't go unchallenged.

ESSENTIAL QUESTION:
In what different ways can people be intelligent?

Connection to Essential Question
These poems relate to the essential question because they show different kinds of thinking: useful, desirable, or argumentative. They prompt readers to use introspection to better know themselves, how they think, and where blind spots are.

SMALL-GROUP LEARNING PERFORMANCE TASK
How does each selection highlight a different way to be intelligent?

Connection to Performance Tasks
Small-Group Learning Performance Task The poems in this collection focus on Gardner's "intrapersonal intelligence"—understanding what you feel and what you want.

UNIT PERFORMANCE-BASED ASSESSMENT
In what different ways can people be intelligent?

Unit Performance-Based Assessment The types of intelligence discussed here include the skill of reflection—thinking about what you think.

DIGITAL PERSPECTIVES | Audio | Video | Document | Annotation Highlights | EL Highlights | Online Assessment

LESSON RESOURCES

	Making Meaning	Language Development	Effective Expression
Lesson	First Read Close Read Analyze the Text Analyze Craft and Structure	Archaic Vocabulary Word Study Conventions	Speaking and Listening
Instructional Standards	**RL.10** By the end of the year, read and comprehend literature . . . **L.4** Determine or clarify the meaning of unknown and multiple-meaning words or phrases . . . **L.4.a** Use context as a clue . . . **RL.5** Compare and contrast the structure of two or more texts . . . **L.5** Demonstrate understanding of figurative language . . .	**RL.4** Determine the meaning of words and phrases . . . **L.4** Determine or clarify the meaning of unknown and multiple-meaning words and phrases . . . **L.4.c** Consult general and specialized reference materials . . . **L.5.b** Use the relationship between particular words . . . **L.1** Demonstrate command of the conventions . . . **L.1.a** Explain the function of verbals . . .	**SL.1** Engage effectively in a range of collaborative discussions . . . **SL.1.a** Come to discussions prepared. . . **SL.5** Integrate multimedia and visual displays . . .
STUDENT RESOURCES Available online in the Interactive Student Edition or Unit Resources	Selection Audio First-Read Guide: Poetry Close-Read Guide: Poetry	Word Network	Evidence Log
TEACHER RESOURCES **Selection Resources** Available online in the Interactive Teacher's Edition or Unit Resources	Audio Summaries Annotation Highlights EL Highlights English Language Support Lesson: Multiple-Meaning Words Poetry Collection: Text Questions Analyze Craft and Structure: Poetic Structures	Archaic Vocabulary and Word Study Conventions: Participial and Infinitive Phrases	Speaking and Listening: Multimedia Presentation
Reteach/Practice (RP) Available online in the Interactive Teacher's Edition or Unit Resources	Analyze Craft and Structure: Poetic Structures (RP)	Word Study: Multiple-Meaning Words (RP) Conventions: Participial and Infinitive Phrases (RP)	Speaking and Listening: Multimedia Presentation (RP)
Assessment Available online in Assessments	Selection Test		
My Resources	A Unit 4 Answer Key is available online and in the Interactive Teacher's Edition.		

PERSONALIZE FOR LEARNING

SMALL-GROUP LEARNING • RETORT • from THE PEOPLE, YES

Reading Support

Text Complexity Rubric: Retort • from The People, Yes

Quantitative Measures

Lexile: NP; NP   Text Length: 10 lines; 7 lines

Qualitative Measures

Knowledge Demands ①—②—**❸**—④—⑤	Some background context is needed to fully understand the poems, but sufficient information is given on the background page.
Structure ①—②—**❸**—④—⑤	"Retort" is a poem in two stanzas, with unusual but predictable rhyme scheme (AABAB); the excerpt from *The People, Yes* is a poem in the form of sentences.
Language Conventionality and Clarity ①—②—**❸**—④—⑤	Language in the poems is mostly easy to understand. "Retort" has some archaic expressions and syntax (*thou art*); *The People, Yes* has concrete, straightforward sentences.
Levels of Meaning/Purpose ①—②—**❸**—④—⑤	Both poems have multiple levels of meaning, using symbolic language and metaphors.

DECIDE AND PLAN

English Language Support

Provide English Learners with support for structure and language as they read the selection.

Structure For each poem, ask volunteers to read the poem aloud. Have the other students read along and note which words rhyme. Then pair students and have them practice reading the poems aloud, paying attention to the cadence of the phrases and the rhymes.

Language Have students identify the unfamiliar words in each of the poems. Remind students to look for explanations in the background information and footnotes. Discuss the meanings. Then have them reread the lines with those words in order to understand the meaning in context. Finally, have them reread the whole poems.

Strategic Support

Provide students with strategic support to ensure that they can successfully read the text.

Knowledge Demands For each poem, have students read the information on the background page about the author and the poem. Ask them to summarize in their own words what they learned. Then have a volunteer read the poem aloud. Ask questions to help students connect the poem and the background. For example, for "Retort," ask: *What did we learn about Phyllis?* (She could be a muse, someone who inspires him.)

Meaning Discuss the literal meanings of the lines of each poem. Then talk about the symbolism the lines could have.

Challenge

Provide students who need to be challenged with ideas for how they can go beyond a simple interpretation of the text.

Text Analysis Have each student choose one of the poems to memorize and recite for the group. Have them also prepare to talk about one or two lines from the poem that they find most interesting or want to discuss. After each reading, ask students to share their ideas about the lines they chose, their questions, interpretation, or why they chose them.

Written Response Have students look up and read other poems by either of the poets, or other excerpts from *The People, Yes*. Ask them to write background information about the poem they chose, what they liked about it, and their interpretation. Have students share their poems and writing.

TEACH

Read and Respond

Have groups read the selections and complete the Making Meaning and Language Development activities.

Standards Support Through Teaching and Learning Cycle

IDENTIFY NEEDS

Analyze results of the Beginning-of-Year Assessment, focusing on the items relating to Unit 4. Also take into consideration student performance to this point and your observations of where particular students struggle.

ANALYZE AND REVISE

- Analyze student work for evidence of student learning.
- Identify whether or not students have met the expectations in the standards.
- Identify implications for future instruction.

TEACH

Implement the planned lesson, and gather evidence of student learning.

DECIDE AND PLAN

- If students have performed poorly on items matching these standards, then provide selection scaffolds before assigning them the on-level lesson provided in the Student Edition.
- If students have done well on the Beginning-of-Year Assessment, then challenge them to keep progressing and learning by giving them opportunities to practice the skills in depth.
- Use the Selection Resources listed on the Planning pages for "Retort," and from The People, Yes to help students continually improve their ability to master the standards.

Instructional Standards: Retort • from The People, Yes

	Catching Up	This Year	Looking Forward
Reading	You may wish to administer the **Analyze Craft and Structure: Poetic Structures (RP)** worksheet to familiarize students with the different sound devices at use in the poems.	**RL.5** Compare and contrast the structure of two or more texts and analyze how the differing structure of each text contributes to its meaning and style. or allusions to other texts.	Work with students to identify any metaphors or similes they notice in the selections.
Speaking and Listening	You may wish to administer the **Speaking and Listening: Multimedia Presentation (RP)** worksheet to help students better prepare for their presentations.	**SL.5** Integrate multimedia and visual displays into presentations to clarify information, strengthen claims and evidence, and add interest.	Ask students to use multimedia in a way that enhances the topic rather than reiterates the ideas they are saying. (i.e., make it interactive.)
Language	Review the **Conventions: Participial and Infinitive Phrases (RP)** worksheet to help students understand the difference between participial and infinitive phrases. Review the **Word Study: Multiple-Meaning Words (RP)** worksheet to help students understand multiple-meaning words.	**L.1.a** Explain the function of verbals in general and their function in particular sentences. **L.4** Determine or clarify the meaning of unknown and multiple-meaning words or phrases based on *grade 8 reading and content*, choosing flexibly from a range of strategies.	Challenge students to locate any gerund phrases in the selections. Have students look up words they only know one meaning for, to determine whether they have multiple meanings.

FACILITATING

Jump Start

FIRST READ Ask students to consider the following questions: *What kind of intelligence do we value most? How can a poem help us question our ideas about intelligence?* Engage students in a discussion about how poetry can distill complicated ideas in condensed form with carefully chosen words.

Archaic Vocabulary

Encourage groups to discuss the three vocabulary words. Have they seen the words in texts before? Have they ever used any of the words in their speech or writing? Do they recognize any synonyms or antonyms for the words in the poems?

Point out to students that archaic words like these are used in works of literature that are hundreds of years old, like Shakespeare's plays. Explain that sometimes more modern poets use these archaic words to achieve a certain tone or effect. Support students as they search for synonyms and antonyms for the words, and discuss how these can help clarify meaning. Encourage students to think of another archaic word that they might encounter in a poem, and to name a synonym or antonym for it. (Possible response: *right* in line 9 of "Retort," synonym: *very*)

● FIRST READ

Students should perform the steps of the first read independently.

NOTICE: You may want to encourage students to notice the basic elements of the text to ensure they understand the message the author is trying to convey.

ANNOTATE: Remind students to mark passages that include sound devices such as rhyme, alliteration, or a strong rhythm.

CONNECT: Students should increase their understanding by connecting what they have read to other texts or personal experiences.

RESPOND: Students will answer questions to demonstrate understanding. Point out to students that while they will always complete the Respond step at the end of the first read, the other steps will probably happen somewhat concurrently. You may wish to print copies of the **First-Read Guide: Poetry** for students to use.

416 UNIT 4 • HUMAN INTELLIGENCE

MAKING MEANING

POETRY COLLECTION

Retort
from The People, Yes

Archaic Vocabulary

Just as the way we live changes over time, so, too, does the way we speak and use language. The vocabulary words are "archaic" words because, though once in common usage, they are no longer used regularly today, or the way in which they are used has changed. As you conduct your first read of these poems, you will encounter these words.

| art | tress | fair |

Context Clues To find the meaning of an unfamiliar word, look for clues in the context—words and phrases that appear in nearby text.

> **Example from "Life's Tragedy," by Paul Laurence Dunbar:**
> It may be misery never to be loved, / But deeper griefs than these **beset** the way.
>
> **Possible Meaning:** Because of the context clues "griefs" and "the way," I can infer that *beset* may mean "pose obstacles."

Apply your knowledge of context clues and other vocabulary strategies to determine the meanings of unfamiliar words you encounter during your first read.

First Read POETRY

Apply these strategies as you conduct your first read. You will have an opportunity to complete a close read after your first read.

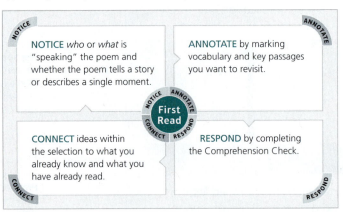

STANDARDS

Reading Literature
By the end of the year, read and comprehend literature, including stories, dramas, and poems, at the high end of grades 6–8 text complexity band independently and proficiently.

Language
Determine or clarify the meaning of unknown and multiple-meaning words or phrases based on *grade 8 reading and content*, choosing flexibly from a range of strategies.
  a. Use context as a clue to the meaning of a word or phrase.

416 UNIT 4 • HUMAN INTELLIGENCE

● FACILITATING SMALL-GROUP CLOSE READING

CLOSE READ: Poetry versus Prose As groups perform their close read, circulate and offer assistance as required.

Discuss with students the differences between poetry and prose. Help students note that the sounds made by the combination of words is much more important in poetry than in prose. In addition, poems tend to be shorter, and therefore must distill important ideas in carefully chosen words. Figurative language, including sound devices such as alliteration and rhyme, are much more common in poetry than in prose.

ESSENTIAL QUESTION: In what different ways can people be intelligent?

About the Poets

Paul Laurence Dunbar (1872–1906) was one of the first African American poets to achieve national prominence. The child of freed slaves from Kentucky, Dunbar often wrote stories and poems about plantation life, many of which were written in dialect. Despite being a fine student, Dunbar could not afford to pay for college, so he took a job as an elevator operator. In 1893, Dunbar self-published a collection of poems called *Oak and Ivy*. To help pay the publishing costs and gain an audience for his poetry, he sold the book for a dollar to people riding in his elevator.

Carl Sandburg (1878–1967) was a Pulitzer Prize–winning American poet, historian, and novelist. Born in Galesburg, Illinois, to Swedish immigrant parents, Sandburg decided at age six that he would be a writer. Although he had to quit school after eighth grade to go to work so he could help support his family, Sandburg continued to write. As he pursued writing, Sandburg worked in a variety of positions, from factory worker to newspaperman. He also became a well-known musician and political activist. The variety of Sandburg's experiences informed his writing, and Sandburg eventually gained recognition as an iconic American writer.

Backgrounds

Retort

In Greek mythology, the Muses were a group of goddesses who represented the arts and sciences. Currently, a muse can refer to any person who inspires an artist, writer, or musician and who may be a reoccurring focus of or subject in their work. Paul Laurence Dunbar addresses a woman named Phyllis, a possible muse, in this poem, as well as in several other poems, including "Phyllis" and "Response."

from The People, Yes

The excerpt in this section is part of a longer epic poem entitled *The People, Yes*. Carl Sandburg wrote this 300-page poem in the 1930s during the height of the Great Depression, a period when many people could not find work and lived in poverty. As a whole, the epic poem praises the perseverance and triumphs of the American people.

DIGITAL PERSPECTIVES

Retort • from The People, Yes

In "Retort," why is the head calling the heart a fool? Why does the heart reject the head's opinion? Modeling questions such as these will help students connect "Retort," and the excerpt from *The People, Yes* to the Small-Group Performance Task assignment. Selection audio and print capability for the selections are available in the Interactive Teacher's Edition.

FACILITATING

POETRY

Retort
Paul Laurence Dunbar

"Thou art a fool," said my head to my heart,
"Indeed, the greatest of fools thou art,
    To be led astray by the trick of a tress,
By a smiling face or a ribbon smart;"
5   And my heart was in sore distress.

Then Phyllis came by, and her face was fair,
The light gleamed soft on her raven hair;
    And her lips were blooming a rosy red.
Then my heart spoke out with a right bold air:
10   "Thou art worse than a fool, O head!"

NOTES

Mark context clues or indicate another strategy you used that helped you determine meaning.

art (ahrt) *v.*
MEANING:

tress (trehs) *n.*
MEANING:

fair (fair) *adj.*
MEANING:

Retort **419**

DIGITAL PERSPECTIVES

Archaic Vocabulary

ART If groups are struggling to define the word *art* in line 1, point out that identifying synonyms and antonyms can help them clarify the word's meaning. Students can use a thesaurus to find a synonym, and use a dictionary to check a word's meaning. Point out that using context clues ("Thou art a fool," line 1) will also help them identify the word's meaning.

Possible response: In this context, *art* means "are," which is a synonym for the word.

TRESS If groups are struggling to define the word *tress* in line 3, point out that identifying synonyms and antonyms can help them clarify the word's meaning. Students can use a thesaurus to find a synonym, and use a dictionary to check a word's meaning.

Possible response: *Tress* means "hair," which is a synonym for the word.

FAIR If groups are struggling to define the word *fair* in line 6, point out that identifying synonyms and antonyms can help them clarify the word's meaning. Students can use a thesaurus to find a synonym, and use a dictionary to check a word's meaning. Point out that using context clues (". . . and her face was fair," line 6) will also help them identify the word's meaning.

Possible response: In this context, *fair* means "pretty," which is a synonym for the word.

 Additional **English Language Support** is available in the Interactive Teacher's Edition.

VOCABULARY DEVELOPMENT

Multiple Meanings Tell students that the word *raven* (line 7) has multiple meanings. Discuss the following sentences with students.

1. The *raven* was black and flew nearby. (a large black bird)
2. Her *raven* eyes shone darkly. (the color black)
3. The dogs will *raven* the garbage. (eat eagerly)

Have students reread line 7: "The light gleamed soft on her raven hair." Guide them to identify which meaning is used in the sentence. Discuss how to use context clues to define a word with multiple meanings.

Small-Group Learning

FACILITATING

● **CLOSER LOOK**

Identify Sound Devices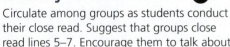

Circulate among groups as students conduct their close read. Suggest that groups close read lines 5–7. Encourage them to talk about the annotations they mark. If needed, provide the following support.

ANNOTATE: Have students mark details in lines 5–7 that show the author's use of sound devices such as alliteration, or work with small groups as you highlight them together.

QUESTION: Guide students to consider what these details might tell them. Ask what a reader can infer from the use of alliteration and accept student responses.

Possible response: The alliteration draws attention to certain actions and words, such as *stick* and *swept*.

CONCLUDE: Help students to formulate conclusions about the importance of these details in the text. Ask students why the author might have included these details.

Possible response: The author might have included these sound devices to create a musical effect, and to draw attention to certain words, especially the last two: *know nothing*.

Remind students that **sound devices** such as alliteration help establish a poem's mood and tone, and help convey the author's meaning. Other sound devices used in poetry are rhyme, repetition, and a strong rhythm or meter.

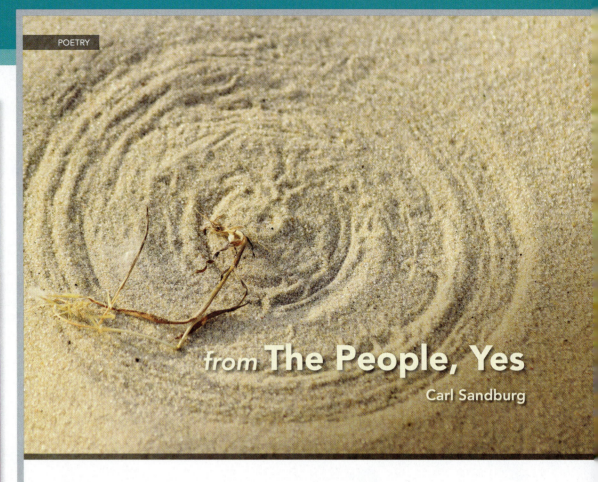

POETRY

from **The People, Yes**

Carl Sandburg

NOTES

The white man drew a small circle in the sand and told the red man, "This is what the Indian knows," and drawing a big circle around the small one, "This is what the white man knows."
5 The Indian took the stick and swept an immense ring around both circles: "This is where the white man and the red man know nothing."

WriteNow Express and Reflect

Parable Explain to students that in this excerpt from *The People, Yes*, the poet tells a parable, which is a short narrative that teaches a lesson. Have students discuss the lesson of the poem. Then ask them to write their own short parable that teaches a lesson.

Comprehension Check

Complete the following items after you finish your first read. Review and clarify details with your group.

RETORT

1. In the first stanza of the poem, how does the speaker's heart feel?

2. How does the speaker describe Phyllis's face?

3. What kind of "air" does the speaker's heart speak with?

from THE PEOPLE, YES

Draw the figure created by the circles described in the poem. Label each circle according to the details the speaker provides.

RESEARCH

Research to Clarify Choose at least one unfamiliar detail from one of the poems. Briefly research that detail. In what way does the information you learned shed light on an aspect of the poem?

DIGITAL PERSPECTIVES

Comprehension Check

Retort
Possible responses:
1. The speaker's heart feels distressed and ashamed.
2. The speaker states that "her face was fair."
3. The speaker's heart speaks with a "right bold" air.

from The People, Yes
Drawings will vary but should include a small circle labeled "What the Red Man Knows"; a bigger circle labeled "What the White Man Knows" that goes around the smaller circle; and a much larger circle labeled "Where the White Man and the Red Man Know Nothing," which goes around the two smaller circles.

Research

Research to Clarify If students struggle to come up with an unfamiliar detail, have them reread the poems and notice an idea or a concept that might be new to them, such as a *tress* or other archaic terms in "Retort."

PERSONALIZE FOR LEARNING

Challenge
Write a Poem Challenge students to write their own poems, based on either of the poems just read. Students can change the point of view; for instance, they might write as Phyllis in "Retort." Or they can take the situation in the excerpt from *The People, Yes*, and explain what the "white man" says or does next. Encourage students to use figurative language, including sound devices, as the poets do. As students share their poems, guide listeners to identify the themes and poetic techniques.

FACILITATING

Jump Start

CLOSE READ Invite students to consider the following questions: *How can poetry get inside a person's head? What is special about poetry's use of language to communicate ideas?* Engage students in a discussion about what makes poetry unique in addressing human intelligence. Are the ideas about intelligence in the poems different from those in other selections in the unit? If so, how?

Close Read the Text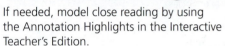

If needed, model close reading by using the Annotation Highlights in the Interactive Teacher's Edition.

Remind students to use Accountable Talk in their discussions and to support one another as they complete the close read.

Analyze the Text

1. **Possible response:** The two fools are the heart and the head. The heart, according to the head, is a fool to be distracted by a pretty young woman. The head, according to the heart, is a fool for not paying attention to the charming Phyllis.
2. **Passages will vary by group.** Remind students to explain their choices.
3. **Responses will vary by group.**

Archaic Vocabulary

Why These Words? Possible response: *Right* in the poem means "very." Today, it means "opposite of left" or "correct."

Practice

Possible responses: Thou *art* a scholar because you study so often. She kept a *tress* in her locket, and looked at the lock of hair when she was sad. Some called her *fair*, while others thought her plain.

Word Network

Possible words: *knows, thoughts, suspects*

Word Study

Possible responses: In the poem, *fair* means "beautiful." *Fair* can also mean (1) equitable, or following the rules; (2) light-skinned; (3) a carnival or event. For more support, see **Archaic Vocabulary and Word Study**.

POETRY COLLECTION

TIP

GROUP DISCUSSION
Make sure that everyone in the group has the opportunity to speak. Encourage quiet members to join the discussion.

WORD NETWORK
Add words related to human intelligence from the text to your Word Network.

STANDARDS

Reading Literature
• Determine the meaning of words and phrases as they are used in a text, including figurative and connotative meanings; analyze the impact of specific word choices on meaning and tone, including analogies or allusions to other texts.
• Compare and contrast the structure of two or more texts and analyze how the differing structure of each text contributes to its meaning and style.

Language
• Determine or clarify the meaning of unknown and multiple-meaning words or phrases based on *grade 8 reading and content*, choosing flexibly from a range of strategies.
 c. Consult general and specialized reference materials, both print and digital, to find the pronunciation of a word or determine or clarify its precise meaning or its part of speech.
• Demonstrate understanding of figurative language, word relationships, and nuances in word meanings.
 b. Use the relationship between particular words to better understand each of the words.

422 UNIT 4 • HUMAN INTELLIGENCE

MAKING MEANING

Close Read the Text

With your group, revisit sections of the text you marked during your first read. **Annotate** what you notice. What **questions** do you have? What can you **conclude**?

Analyze the Text

CITE TEXTUAL EVIDENCE to support your answers.

📓 **Notebook** Complete the activities.

1. **Review and Clarify** With your group, reread "Retort." Who are the two fools in the poem? Why are they both fools? How does Dunbar's poem connect to the idea of different types of intelligence?

2. **Present and Discuss** Now, work with your group to share lines from the poems that you found especially important. Take turns presenting your lines. Discuss what you noticed in the text, what questions you asked, and what conclusions you reached.

3. **Essential Question:** *In what different ways can people be intelligent?* What have these poems taught you about the different ways people can be intelligent? Discuss with your group.

LANGUAGE DEVELOPMENT

Archaic Vocabulary

| art | tress | fair |

Why These Words? The vocabulary words for these poems are all archaic words. Find at least one additional archaic word in the poems. Determine if the word you identified is no longer used in everyday English, or if it is used but its meaning has changed.

Practice

📓 **Notebook** Confirm your understanding of these words from the text by using each in a sentence. Provide context clues for each vocabulary word to demonstrate your understanding.

Word Study

📓 **Notebook Multiple-Meaning Words** In "Retort," the speaker describes Phyllis's face using the word *fair*—a word with multiple possible meanings. Write the meaning of the word as the speaker uses it. Then, write three other meanings of the word. If you have trouble thinking of three, use a dictionary to help you.

FORMATIVE ASSESSMENT

Analyze the Text
If students struggle to close read the text, **then** provide the **Poetry Collection: Text Questions** available online in the Interactive Teacher's Edition or Unit Resources. Answers and DOK levels are also available.

Archaic Vocabulary
If students struggle to identify archaic words, **then** have them reread "Retort," looking for words used in an unfamiliar way.

Word Study
If students struggle to find multiple-meaning words, **then** suggest that they reread the two poems to see if any of the words might be familiar in other contexts. For Reteach and Practice, see **Word Study: Multiple-Meaning Words (RP)**.

ESSENTIAL QUESTION: In what different ways can people be intelligent?

Analyze Craft and Structure

Author's Choices: Poetic Structures A **poetic form** is a set arrangement of poetic elements. A form may have a certain number of stanzas, lines, or both. It may require a pattern of rhyme, called a **rhyme scheme.** It may also use a certain meter, or pattern of stressed and unstressed syllables. Some forms of poetry have rules for all of these elements. This type of poetry is seen as having a formal structure. By contrast, **free verse** poetry does not follow any set pattern. A free verse poem may have rhyme or meter, but those elements will vary throughout the poem. Most poems—whether formal or free verse—include **sound devices.** These are combinations of words that emphasize the musical qualities of language. Common sound devices include the following types:

- **Alliteration:** repetition of consonant sounds at the beginnings of syllables, especially stressed syllables
  EXAMPLE: O wild West Wind

- **Consonance:** repetition of consonant sounds at the ends of syllables with different vowel sounds
  EXAMPLE: a quiet light, and then not even that

- **Assonance:** repetition of vowel sounds in stressed syllables that end with different consonant sounds
  EXAMPLE: pebbles resting in wet sand

Practice

CITE TEXTUAL EVIDENCE to support your answers.

Notebook Work with your group to analyze the poems in this collection. Use a chart like this one to record your ideas. Then, answer the questions that follow.

	RETORT	from THE PEOPLE, YES
Is the poem free verse or formal verse? How do you know?	formal verse fixed rhyme scheme and stanza structure	free verse no fixed patterns
What kind of sound devices are used? Identify the line(s) in which the sound devices appear.	alliteration line 1: head/heart line 3: trick/tress	assonance lines 1–2: man/sand/and/man line 7: know nothing

1. (a) A *retort* is a quick, sharp reply, especially one that turns the words of the previous speaker back upon that speaker. Reread "Retort," and identify the central idea of each stanza. (b) How does the structure of the poem reflect its title?

2. (a) In the excerpt from *The People, Yes*, what effect is created by the use of repetition? (b) How does use of sound devices enhance this poem's meaning?

Poetry Collection 423

DIGITAL PERSPECTIVES

Analyze Craft and Structure

Author's Choices: Poetic Structures Point out to students that rhyme scheme is the pattern of end rhyme in a poem. Each rhyme is assigned a different letter, as follows in the first four lines of "Invitation to Love" by Paul Laurence Dunbar:

Come when the nights are bright with stars	a
Or come when the moon is mellow;	b
Come when the sun his golden bars	a
Drops on the hay-field yellow.	b

These lines have the rhyme scheme ***abab.***

For more support, see **Analyze Craft and Structure: Poetic Structures.**

Practice

See possible responses in chart on student page.

1. (a) In the first stranza, the head tells the heart not to be interested in the woman. In the second stanza, the woman appears and the heart falls for her anyway. (b) The head calls the heart a fool for falling in love, and then the heart calls the head a fool for avoiding love.

2. (a) The repetition of the words *white man, red man,* and *circle* make the description of the event seem generic. (b) The alliteration of *stick, swept,* and *circle* make the people more musical. The assonance of the words *know* and *nothing* help to reinforce the ideas the words convey.

FORMATIVE ASSESSMENT

Analyze Craft and Structure

If students are unable to recognize sound devices, **then** review definitions of the devices and read the poems aloud so that students can listen for each device. For Reteach and Practice, see **Analyze Craft and Structure: Poetic Structures (RP).**

PERSONALIZE FOR LEARNING

English Language Support

Understanding Multiple-Meaning Words Provide students with a list of multiple-meaning words found in the selections. Tell students that they can use a dictionary to verify their meanings if they need help. Have students choose one of the multiple-meaning words and write its possible meanings. Then ask students to select which meaning fits the sentence. **EMERGING**

Have students choose one of the multiple-meaning words and write a sentence for each of its meanings. **EXPANDING**

Have students find a different multiple-meaning word in one of the selections or in another text. Then ask each student to write a sentence for each of the meanings of the word. **BRIDGING**

An expanded **English Language Support Lesson** on Multiple-Meaning Words is available in the Interactive Teacher's Edition.

Small-Group Learning 423

FACILITATING

Conventions

Participial and Infinitive Phrases As you discuss participial and infinitive phrases with students, provide the following examples:

- The man, **embarrassed by his feelings,** tried not to act on them.

In this sentence, "embarrassed by his feelings" is a participial phrase that modifies "the man."

- The man wanted **to draw a perfect circle.**

In this case, "to draw a perfect circle" is an infinitive phrase that acts as a noun. It answers the question *draw what?*

Encourage students to come up with their own examples of participial and infinitive phrases. For more support, see **Conventions: Participial and Infinitive Phrases.**

Read It

1. a. One *man*, having made his point, walked away happy. (modifies *man*)
   b. He saw the *woman* thinking very hard. (modifies *woman*)
2. a. To teach the man a lesson, he *drew* a larger circle. (functions as an adverb modifying *drew*)
   b. The professor agreed to reward his students. (functions as an adverb modifying *agreed*.)

Write It

Possible response: Coming into view of the speaker, Phyllis changes the speaker's mind about everything. To understand the poem, think about your own emotions.

FORMATIVE ASSESSMENT
Conventions

If students are unable to distinguish between participial and infinitive phrases, **then** review with them that infinitive phrases usually begin with the word *to,* and participial phrases usually begin with a verb ending in *-ing* or *-ed.* For Reteach and Practice, see **Conventions: Participial and Infinitive Phrases (RP).**

POETRY COLLECTION

LANGUAGE DEVELOPMENT

Conventions

Participial and Infinitive Phrases Participles and infinitives and the phrases they form can make writing more concise or add important information to sentences.

A **participle** is a verb form that acts as an adjective. A **participial phrase** is made up of a participle with its modifiers, such as adverbs, and complements, such as objects. These all act together as an adjective, modifying a noun or pronoun. Present participles end in *-ing,* and past participles of regular verbs end in *-ed*. Past participles of irregular verbs have a variety of endings, such as *-en* or *-t*.

An **infinitive** is a verb form that acts as a noun, an adjective, or an adverb. Infinitives usually begin with the word *to*. An **infinitive phrase** is made up of an infinitive with modifiers or complements, all acting together as a single part of speech.

The chart below shows examples of participial phrases and infinitive phrases. In the chart, participles and infinitives are underlined, and phrases are in boldface.

PARTICIPIAL PHRASES AND THE WORDS THEY MODIFY	INFINITIVE PHRASES AND THEIR FUNCTIONS
Moving quickly, he picked up a stick. (modifies the subject, *he*)	**To prove how much he knew** was the man's main goal. (functions as a noun)
The man, **bothered by his thoughts**, tried to clear his head. (modifies the subject, *man*)	He agreed with the request **to listen to his heart**. (functions as an adjective modifying *request*)
The poem is about people **fooling themselves**. (modifies the object of a preposition, *people*)	They practice **to improve their skills**. (functions as an adverb modifying *practice*)

Read It

1. Mark the participial phrase in each sentence, and identify the word it modifies.
   a. One man, having made his point, walked away happy.
   b. He saw the woman thinking very hard.
2. Mark the infinitive phrase in each sentence, and identify its function.
   a. To teach the man a lesson, he drew a larger circle.
   b. The professor agreed to reward his students.

Write It

Choose one of the poems, and write two sentences about it. Use a participial phrase in one and an infinitive phrase in the other.

STANDARDS
Language
Demonstrate command of the conventions of standard English grammar and usage when writing or speaking.
a. Explain the function of verbals in general and their function in particular sentences.

424 UNIT 4 • HUMAN INTELLIGENCE

PERSONALIZE FOR LEARNING

Challenge

Participial Phrases Point out to students that writers use participial phrases to vary sentence structure. Explain that in some cases, two sentences may be combined into one sentence by adding a participial phrase. Show students the following two sentences:

The poet used rhymes. She created a musical effect.

Point out that the two sentences could be combined using a participial phrase as follows:

Using rhymes, the poet created a musical effect.

Now challenge students to use a participial phrase to combine the following two sentences:

The speaker talked slowly. He held the audience's attention.

(Possible response: Talking slowly, the speaker held the audience's attention.)

EFFECTIVE EXPRESSION

Speaking and Listening

Assignment

With your group, develop a **multimedia presentation** of one of the poems from this collection. Make sure to come to your group's discussion prepared with ideas, and follow the rules for a friendly, productive discussion. Choose from the following options:

☐ With your group, identify a poem for a **dramatic reading**. Then, develop a plan for your presentation. Decide who will read each line, and determine how to read it. Which words should be emphasized? Should the line be read quickly or slowly? Softly or loudly? What type of emotions should the speaker show as he or she is reading the line? Remember to include multimedia elements, such as background music, props, and costumes.

☐ With your group, identify a poem for a **nonverbal multimedia presentation**. Then, discuss the poem, and develop a plan for your presentation in which you present the poem without words. Instead, convey the meaning of the poem by carefully arranging multimedia elements, such as music, video, dance, photos, original artwork, and mime.

Project Plan With your group, decide which members will carry out each task. Also, decide on the order of speakers or sequence of multimedia elements. You may wish to annotate a copy of the poem you chose in order to indicate what happens and when in the presentation it should occur. Use the chart to organize your presentation.

EVIDENCE LOG

Before moving on to a new selection, go to your Evidence Log, and record what you learned from "Retort" and the excerpt from *The People, Yes*.

STANDARDS

Speaking and Listening
Engage effectively in a range of collaborative discussions with diverse partners on *grade 8 topics, texts, and issues*, building on others' ideas and expressing their own clearly.
  a. Come to discussions prepared, having read or researched material under study; explicitly draw on that preparation by referring to evidence on the topic, text, or issue to probe and reflect on ideas under discussion.

• Integrate multimedia and visual displays into presentations to clarify information, strengthen claims and evidence, and add interest.

POEM LINE/STANZA	READER/ PERFORMER	MUSIC/SOUND	PROPS, COSTUMES, VISUALS	NOTES

DIGITAL PERSPECTIVES

Speaking and Listening

If students are having difficulty choosing which type of presentation to do, encourage them to consider which option plays to their strengths. For example, if students enjoy reading aloud, the dramatic reading might be the best option. Remind them that no matter which option they choose, all group members should participate in the project.

Project Plan Remind groups to consult the schedule for Small-Group activities as they create their Project Plan. Check to make sure each group has made assignments and that the work is divided evenly among group members. For more support, see **Speaking and Listening: Multimedia Presentation.**

Evidence Log Support students in completing their Evidence Log. This paced activity will help prepare them for the Performance-Based Assessment at the end of the unit.

FORMATIVE ASSESSMENT

Speaking and Listening

If groups struggle to create meaningful presentations, **then** review one stanza of each poem, asking students to think about the best option for sharing their insights with the class. For Reteach and Practice, see **Speaking and Listening: Multimedia Presentation (RP).**

Selection Test

Administer the "Poetry Collection" Selection Test, which is available in both print and digital formats online in Assessments.

PERSONALIZE FOR LEARNING

Strategic Support

Shifts in Tone or Meaning As students work in groups to prepare their presentations, encourage them to look at the poem line by line. Point out that students should look for places where there is a shift in tone or meaning. For example, in "Retort," the tone shifts in line 6, when Phyllis "came by," as the speaker's mood seems to improve, and it shifts again in lines 9 and 10, when the speaker's heart boldly calls the head a fool.

If students are working on a dramatic reading, make sure that each reader says their line with the proper tone. Media, such as music or images, should also shift to reflect the moods. If students are working on a nonverbal presentation, the shifts in tone should also be reflected in the music, video, dance, photos, artwork, or mime that is used.

FACILITATING

Deliver a Multimedia Presentation

Before groups begin work on their projects, have them clearly differentiate the role each group member will play. Remind groups to consult the schedule for Small-Group Learning to guide their work during the Performance Task.

Students should complete the assignment using presentation software to take advantage of text, graphics, and sound features.

Plan With Your Group

Analyze the Text Encourage students to try to note the topic of each selection. Then ask groups to reach a consensus on the main idea of each selection. Once they decide on the main idea, they can dig into the selection for evidence.

Gather Evidence and Media Examples Suggest that groups brainstorm about what to look for as they search for media to represent different types of intelligence found in the selections. For example, students might want to use video clips featuring Daniel Tammet discussing synesthesia or Howard Gardner discussing multiple intelligences. They might want to use photographs of the poets or recordings of people reading their poems as they discuss their points, or they could choose images that work well with the themes of the poems. Explain that while students may find many media examples, they should be strategic about what will work best in their presentations.

PERFORMANCE TASK: SPEAKING AND LISTENING FOCUS

SOURCES
- *from* BLUE NINES AND RED WORDS
- THE THEORY OF MULTIPLE INTELLIGENCES INFOGRAPHIC
- RETORT
- *from* THE PEOPLE, YES

Deliver a Multimedia Presentation

Assignment
In this section, you have analyzed various selections that explore the different ways people can be intelligent. Work with your group to develop a **multimedia presentation** that addresses this question:

> How does each selection highlight a different way to be intelligent?

Plan With Your Group

Analyze the Text With your group, discuss the ways in which the texts in this section explore different types of intelligence. Use the chart to list your ideas. For each selection, identify the type of intelligence featured. Note that in some selections more than one type of intelligence may be covered. Then, ask other group members questions you have about intelligence, and answer questions they may have. Work together to determine what each selection reveals about human intelligence.

SELECTION	TYPES OF INTELLIGENCE FEATURED
from Blue Nines and Red Words	
The Theory of Multiple Intelligences Infographic	
Retort	
from The People, Yes	

Gather Evidence and Media Examples Identify specific examples from the selections to support your group's ideas. Then, brainstorm about the types of multimedia you can use to clarify your ideas and emphasize key points. These may include charts, graphs, photos, video, or other visuals. Also, consider including audio elements, such as music. Allow each group member to make suggestions as to what multimedia content should be included, as well as how to sequence multimedia to engage your audience.

STANDARDS
Speaking and Listening
- Engage effectively in a range of collaborative discussions with diverse partners on *grade 8 topics, texts, and issues,* building on others' ideas and expressing their own clearly.
  a. Come to discussions prepared, having read or researched material under study; explicitly draw on that preparation by referring to evidence on the topic, text, or issue to probe and reflect on ideas under discussion.
  b. Follow rules for collegial discussions and decision-making, track progress toward specific goals and deadlines, and define individual roles as needed.
  c. Pose questions that connect the ideas of several speakers and respond to others' questions and comments with relevant evidence, observations, and ideas.
- Integrate multimedia and visual displays into presentations to clarify information, strengthen claims and evidence, and add interest.

426 UNIT 4 • HUMAN INTELLIGENCE

AUTHOR'S PERSPECTIVE Ernest Morrell, Ph.D.

Active Classroom Listening Teachers can help students participate in class more effectively by discussing how to ask critical questions in classroom conversations. Teachers can guide students to determine which questions are most important and will yield good answers by modeling questions that synthesize multiple viewpoints and tap critical thinking skills.

Here are some samples to use:
- What are the implications of . . . ?
- What is the difference between . . . and . . . ?
- What is the counterargument for . . . ?
- What are the strengths and weakness of . . . ?
- What is another way to look at . . . ?

Remind students to avoid yes/no questions because they cut off discussion. Teachers can also teach students to use *critical listening*—weighing what has been said to decide if they agree with it or not. Critical listening can help students identify the salient parts of each question and integrate these parts to formulate an idea or an opinion.

ESSENTIAL QUESTION: In what different ways can people be intelligent?

Organize Your Ideas As a group, decide who is responsible for each part of the presentation. Decide when each part of the presentation will begin, and record what the presenter will say. Use a chart like this one to organize your script.

MULTIMEDIA PRESENTATION SCRIPT	
Media Cues	Script
Presenter 1	
Presenter 2	
Presenter 3	

Rehearse With Your Group

Practice With Your Group As you work through the script for your presentation, use this checklist to evaluate the effectiveness of your group's first rehearsal. Then, use your evaluation and the instruction here to guide revisions to your presentation.

CONTENT	USE OF MEDIA	PRESENTATION TECHNIQUES
☐ The presentation clearly addresses the prompt.	☐ Media clarify and emphasize important points in the presentation.	☐ Speakers use adequate volume and maintain eye contact.
☐ Main ideas are supported with evidence from the texts.	☐ Media are sequenced to engage the audience and add interest to the presentation.	☐ Speakers use formal English and have an objective tone.

Fine-Tune the Content To make your presentation stronger, review your evidence to be sure you fully support your main points.

Improve Your Use of Media Review each piece of media to make sure it clarifies information effectively and adds interest to the presentation.

Brush Up on Your Presentation Techniques Make sure that your script includes only formal English, such as academic vocabulary and complete sentences. Avoid slang, idioms, contractions, run-on sentences, and sentence fragments. Practice delivering your presentation using a formal tone and proper English.

Present and Evaluate

Evaluate how well other presentations met the checklist criteria. Did other groups explore ideas you had not thought to include? After hearing the presentations of others, are there things you would do differently in your next presentation? In what ways? For what purpose?

STANDARDS
Speaking and Listening
- Engage effectively in a range of collaborative discussions with diverse partners on *grade 8 topics, texts, and issues*, building on others' ideas and expressing their own clearly.
  d. Acknowledge new information expressed by others, and, when warranted, qualify or justify their own views in light of the evidence presented.
- Present claims and findings, emphasizing salient points in a focused, coherent manner with relevant evidence, sound valid reasoning, and well-chosen details; use appropriate eye contact, adequate volume, and clear pronunciation.
- Integrate multimedia and visual displays into presentations to clarify information, strengthen claims and evidence, and add interest.
- Adapt speech to a variety of contexts and tasks, demonstrating command of formal English when indicated or appropriate.

Performance Task: Deliver a Multimedia Presentation **427**

PERSONALIZE FOR LEARNING

Strategic Support
Types of Intelligence Some groups may have difficulty identifying types of intelligence in the poems. Be prepared to assist these students with questions such as these:

- In "Retort," is the head or the heart smarter? What does each represent?

- In the excerpt from *The People, Yes,* what does the Indian recognize that the white man does not? How would you describe the Indian?
- In "Unsuspecting," how is the "kind of mind" described? Are such people intelligent, or do they just think that they are?

DIGITAL PERSPECTIVES

Organize Your Ideas Remind groups that all group members should have an opportunity to speak and that no one member should dominate the presentation.

Rehearse With Your Group

Practice With Your Group Remind students that each group member should come prepared, having practiced his or her part ahead of time. As members of the group listen to one another, they should provide constructive feedback. If there are problems with the timing of the presentation, have group members work together to solve the problems.

Fine-Tune the Content As students review content, encourage them to delete any text that is confusing and does not support their main points.

Improve Your Use of Media Encourage students to make sure that visuals are clearly visible to everyone in the classroom and that any audio is played at an appropriate sound level.

Brush Up on Your Presentation Techniques Remind students that they should be sure to speak with energy and conviction and that they should strive to make eye contact with the audience.

MAKE IT INTERACTIVE
Encourage groups to make video or audiotapes as they rehearse for their presentation. They can then view or listen to the tapes, and find where they need to improve the flow or content of their presentation.

Present and Evaluate

Before beginning the presentations, set expectations for the audience. You may wish to have students consider these questions as groups present.
- What claim about each selection did the group make?
- What were some of the supporting ideas?
- Which multimedia worked best to support the ideas?
- What presentation skills did this group excel at?

As students provide feedback to the presenting group, remind them that they should be polite and respectful when offering suggestions.

Small-Group Learning **427**

OVERVIEW

INDEPENDENT LEARNING

In what different ways can people be intelligent?

Encourage students to think carefully about what they have already learned and what more they want to know about the unit topic of human intelligence. This is a key first step to previewing and selecting the text they will read in Independent Learning.

Independent Learning Strategies

Review the Learning Strategies with students and explain that as they work through Independent Learning they will develop strategies to work on their own.

- Have students watch the video on Independent Learning Strategies.
- A video on this topic is available online in the Professional Development Center.

Students should include any favorite strategies that they might have devised on their own during Whole-Class and Small-Group Learning. For example, for the strategy "Create a schedule," students might include:

- Understand the goals and deadlines.
- Make a schedule for what to do each day.

Block Scheduling

Each day in this Pacing Plan represents a 40–50 minute class period. Teachers using block scheduling may combine days to reflect their class schedule. In addition, teachers may revise pacing to differentiate and support core instruction by integrating components and resources as students require.

Pacing Plan

OVERVIEW: INDEPENDENT LEARNING

ESSENTIAL QUESTION:

In what different ways can people be intelligent?

Human intelligence can be shown in small ways or in astonishing displays. In this section, you will complete your study of human intelligence by exploring an additional selection related to the topic. You'll then share what you learn with classmates. To choose a text, follow these steps.

Look Back Think about the selections you have already studied. What more do you want to know about human intelligence?

Look Ahead Preview the selections by reading the descriptions. Which one seems most interesting and appealing to you?

Look Inside Take a few minutes to scan through the text you chose. Choose a different one if this text doesn't meet your needs.

Independent Learning Strategies

Throughout your life, in school, in your community, and in your career, you will need to rely on yourself to learn and work on your own. Review these strategies and the actions you can take to practice them during Independent Learning. Add ideas of your own for each category.

STRATEGY	ACTION PLAN
Create a schedule	• Understand your goals and deadlines. • Make a plan for what to do each day. •
Practice what you have learned	• Use first-read and close-read strategies to deepen your understanding. • After you read, evaluate the usefulness of the evidence to help you understand the topic. • Consider the quality and reliability of the source. •
Take notes	• Record important ideas and information. • Review your notes before preparing to share with a group. •

428 UNIT 4 • HUMAN INTELLIGENCE

SCAN FOR MULTIMEDIA

DIGITAL PERSPECTIVES

CONTENTS

Choose one selection. Selections are available online only.

ARGUMENT
Is Personal Intelligence Important?
John D. Mayer

A psychologist argues that personal intelligence is important because it helps us solve our own problems and resolve conflicts that arise with others.

BLOG POST
Why Is Emotional Intelligence Important for Teens?
Divya Parekh

What is your EQ, or level of emotional intelligence?

EXPLANATORY ESSAY
The More You Know, the Smarter You Are?
Jim Vega

Everyone has different strengths, and this essay presents examples and explanations of the reasons for these variations, as well as ways in which to identify your own strengths.

EXPOSITORY NONFICTION
from The Future of the Mind
Michio Kaku

A physicist uses the example of Einstein's brain to discuss the question "Are geniuses made or born?"

PERFORMANCE-BASED ASSESSMENT PREP
Review Evidence for an Informative Essay
Complete your Evidence Log for the unit by evaluating what you have learned and synthesizing the information you have recorded.

SCAN FOR MULTIMEDIA

Overview: Independent Learning 429

Contents

Selections Encourage students to scan and preview the selections before choosing the one they would like to read or review. Suggest that they consider the genre and subject matter of each one before making their decision. You can use the information on the following Planning pages to advise students in making their choice.

> Remind students that the selections for Independent Learning are only available in the Interactive Student Edition. Allow students who do not have digital access at home to preview the selections using classroom or computer lab technology. Then either have students print the selection they choose or provide a printout for them.

Performance-Based Assessment Prep
Review Evidence for an Informative Essay Point out to students that collecting evidence during Independent Learning is the last step in completing their Evidence Log. After they finish their independent reading, they will synthesize all the evidence they have compiled in the unit.

The evidence students collect will serve as the primary source of information they will use to complete the writing and oral presentation for the Performance-Based Assessment at the end of the unit.

Independent Learning 429

PLANNING   INDEPENDENT LEARNING

SELECTION RESOURCES

- First-Read Guide: Nonfiction
- Close-Read Guide: Nonfiction
- Is Personal Intelligence Important?: Text Questions
- Audio Summaries
- Selection Audio
- Selection Test

Is Personal Intelligence Important?

Summary

In the argumentative essay "Is Personal Intelligence Important?" John D. Mayer argues that personal intelligence should be recognized and appreciated as one of several broad intelligence types. The author defines personal intelligence as the ability to reason about our own and other people's personalities. This includes thinking about the way that different people think and act based on their personality. Although all kinds of intelligences are important, they are not all the same. The author then examines how personal intelligence can help us, our loved ones, and society as a whole. Personal intelligence can help us to understand ourselves and evaluate honestly why we do things. Similarly, it can help us to understand why loved ones, friends, and co-workers do the things they do. Finally, it can help us to understand our own society in a way that promotes cooperation and assures that our society thrives.

Insight

Reading this selection will help students understand kinds of intelligences in general and personal intelligence specifically. Acknowledging and recognizing the value of personal intelligence will help students appreciate it in themselves and others. It will also help students to use it as an important criteria for choosing leaders, careers, and friends.

Connection to Essential Question

The Essential Question—In what different ways can people be intelligent?— is directly answered in this selection. The selection addresses the question by exploring the different kinds of intelligences and how each one adds value to the human experience. The writer discusses the value of personal intelligence.

Connection to Performance-Based Assessment

In the Performance-Based Assessment, students are asked to write an informative essay that addresses the following prompt: In what different ways can people be intelligent? This selection provides useful background information to help students understand the array of intelligences that research has identified.

Text Complexity Rubric: Is Personal Intelligence Important?	
Quantitative Measures	
Lexile: 1230 Text Length: 1,521 words	
Qualitative Measures	
Knowledge Demands ①—②—❸—④—⑤	Selection includes a number of subject-specific terms that may be unfamiliar. However, new concepts are well explained.
Structure ①—❷—③—④—⑤	Organization is very clear, explicit, and logical. Some subheadings are used to divide information. Bullet points are used in several sections to explain concepts in logical order.
Language Conventionality and Clarity ①—②—③—❹—⑤	Language is academic and complex; sentences are lengthy and include a lot of academic and subject-specific vocabulary.
Levels of Meaning/Purpose ①—②—❸—④—⑤	Purpose of article and main ideas are explicitly stated at beginning and end; supporting concepts and details are clearly explained throughout. Real-life examples are used to support the concepts.

UNIT 4 • HUMAN INTELLIGENCE

Why Is Emotional Intelligence Important for Teens?

Summary

"Why Is Emotional Intelligence Important for Teens?" is a blog/argument by Divya Parekh that defines emotional intelligence and explains why it is an important set of skills. Emotional intelligence, or EQ, is a person's ability to understand emotions and the way they impact how people behave. A person with strong emotional intelligence is self-aware, but also able to understand the actions and feelings of others. The writer argues that developing emotional intelligence is important for stress management. Lowering stress can reduce anxiety and depression and improve physical health. Teens who develop this skill can apply it to building stronger relationships, working in groups, conflict resolution, and working in teams.

Insight

Students may be familiar with IQ, which measures intelligence, but EQ is a newer type of measure score which considers interpersonal awareness. Students may find this information useful as they navigate the difficulties of adolescence and young adulthood.

SELECTION RESOURCES
- First-Read Guide: Nonfiction
- Close-Read Guide: Nonfiction
- Why Is Emotional Intelligence Important for Teens?: Text Questionst
- Audio Summaries
- Selection Audio
- Selection Test

Connection to Essential Question

The article directly addresses the Essential Question: In what different ways can people be intelligent? The blog writer's contention is that a powerful type of intelligence is within our control and is possibly even more important than all other types of intelligences.

Connection to Performance-Based Assessment

In the Performance-Based Assessment, students are asked to write an informative essay that addresses the following prompt: In what different ways can people be intelligent? The article provides background to help students see how emotional intelligence affects our lives and can benefit us personally, academically, and professionally.

Text Complexity Rubric: Why Is Emotional Intelligence Important for Teens?

Quantitative Measures

Lexile: 1120   Text Length: 522 words

Qualitative Measures

Knowledge Demands (2)	Beyond a general understanding of emotional awareness, the article requires no specialized knowledge.
Structure (1)	The structure is straightforward and easy to follow.
Language Conventionality and Clarity (3)	Language is straightforward, clear, and somewhat conversational. Some clinical terminology is used.
Levels of Meaning/Purpose (3)	Concepts are clearly explained and their importance is made relevant. The concept of emotional intelligence impacting future success is somewhat complex.

Independent Learning   430B

PLANNING INDEPENDENT LEARNING

The More You Know, the Smarter You Are?

SELECTION RESOURCES
- First-Read Guide: Nonfiction
- Close-Read Guide: Nonfiction
- The More You Know, the Smarter You Are?: Text Questions
- Audio Summaries
- Selection Audio
- Selection Test

Summary
Jim Vega's explanatory essay "The More You Know, the Smarter You Are?" questions the idea that collecting facts and information is an important aspect of being smart. He describes the work of Howard Gardner, a professor at Harvard University, as evidence. Gardner identified multiple kinds of human intelligence, including visual/spatial, musical, and interpersonal, among others. Gardner thought that too much emphasis had been placed on language and math abilities and that IQ was not the only way to measure intelligence. According to Gardner, we should start thinking of being "smart" in new ways. In addition to Gardner's ideas, the essay suggests that street smarts and wisdom are two additional types of intelligence. The author concludes that there are many ways to be smart. He urges readers to identify their intelligence strengths and to use their strengths to stretch their weaknesses.

Insight
Reading this essay will help students expand their ideas about intelligence. It will prod them to think about intelligence in people who perhaps do not have that much book knowledge. It will also lead them to assess their own intelligence in new ways.

Connection to Essential Question
The article directly addresses the Essential Question: In what different ways can people be intelligent? It does this by supplying evidence that there are many ways to be intelligent.

Connection to Performance-Based Assessment
In the Performance-Based Assessment, students are asked to write an informative essay that addresses the prompt: In what different ways can people be intelligent? The essay provides background to the question by suggesting that applying book and experiential knowledge to problems is essential to intelligence.

Text Complexity Rubric: The More You Know, the Smarter You Are?

Quantitative Measures

Lexile: 1190   Text Length: 733 words

Qualitative Measures

Knowledge Demands ①—②—**③**—④—⑤	Some familiarity with the idea of multiple intelligences is helpful for reading the text, though terms are explained.
Structure ①—**②**—③—④—⑤	Structure is easy to follow; after an introduction of the main ideas, Gardner's multiple intelligences are listed with examples. The rest of the article follows a clear organization with logical connections.
Language Conventionality and Clarity ①—②—**③**—④—⑤	Style of language is conversational, but there are many lengthy sentences with multiple ideas and clauses. Some vocabulary is academic and subject-specific.
Levels of Meaning/Purpose ①—②—**③**—④—⑤	Main purpose and concepts are explicitly stated, explained at the beginning, and summarized at end. Concepts cover a wide range of ideas, some of which are complex.

DIGITAL PERSPECTIVES

Audio · Video · Document · Annotation Highlights · EL Highlights · Online Assessment

from The Future of the Mind

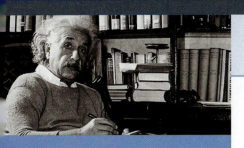

SELECTION RESOURCES

- First-Read Guide: Nonfiction
- Close-Read Guide: Nonfiction
- from The Future of the Mind: Text Questions
- Audio Summaries
- Selection Audio
- Selection Test

Summary

The expository essay by Michio Kaku, from *The Future of the Mind*, examines the desire to understand the origins of genius intelligence. In the case of Albert Einstein, Dr. Thomas Harvey of Princeton Hospital secretly preserved Einstein's brain so he could study it. Upon examination, what scientists discovered was interesting. There was one part of the brain that was larger than normal, but other than that, Einstein's brain was ordinary. Scientists did, however, draw some conclusions about roots of Einstein's genius. First, he spent most of his time engaging in thought experiments. Second, Einstein would spend up to ten years running a single thought experiment in his mind. Third, Einstein was prone to rebel against the theories of establishment physicists. And fourth, the time was right for the emergence of an Einstein. Einstein's personality, determination, and sheer focus helped him build his genius. The brain actually changes when people learn and practice.

Insight

Reading this essay will help students consider the many factors that may contribute to genius intelligence. Some students may have difficulty with the idea of autopsies and preserving human remains. Give them support as needed.

Connection to Essential Question

The article provides background for the Essential Question, "In what different ways can people be intelligent?" by exploring the unique genius of Albert Einstein, and proposing the multiple reasons for his success.

Connection to Performance-Based Assessment

In the Performance-Based Assessment, students are asked to write an informative essay on the prompt: In what different ways can people be intelligent? This selection may be helpful because the essay addresses factors other than brain structure that affect intelligence.

Text Complexity Rubric: from The Future of the Mind

Quantitative Measures

Lexile: 1190   Text Length: 1,986 words

Qualitative Measures

Knowledge Demands (1–2–3–**4**–5)	Readers need familiarity with Einstein and what he did. Selection contains multiple references to the topics of Einstein's work. However, these topics are not central to the content.
Structure (1–2–**3**–4–5)	Organization is clear and logical, but multiple ideas are included in dense text. Selection describes both events related to the study of Einstein's brain and exposition about what made Einstein unique.
Language Conventionality and Clarity (1–2–**3**–4–5)	Language has clear, straightforward style, but sentences are complex and often include multiple clauses. Vocabulary is academic and sometimes subject-specific.
Levels of Meaning/Purpose (1–2–3–**4**–5)	Purpose of article and meaning of concepts is clearly explained, but concepts are sophisticated, complex, and theoretical. Article pursues the nature vs. nurture debate.

Independent Learning   430D

DIGITAL PERSPECTIVES

 Audio Video Document Annotation Highlights EL Highlights ✓ Online Assessment

MY NOTES

ADVISING

You may wish to direct students to use the generic **First-Read** and **Close-Read Guides** in the Print Student Edition. Alternatively, you may wish to print copies of the genre-specific **First-Read** and **Close-Read Guides** for students. These are available online in the Interactive Student Edition or Unit Resources.

 **FIRST READ**

Students should perform the steps of the first read independently.

NOTICE: Students should focus on the basic elements of the text to ensure they understand what is happening.

ANNOTATE: Students should mark any passages they wish to revisit during their close read.

CONNECT: Students should increase their understanding by connecting what they've read to other texts or personal experiences.

RESPOND: Students will write a summary to demonstrate their understanding.

Point out to students that while they will always complete the Respond step at the end of the first read, the other steps will probably happen somewhat concurrently. Remind students that they will revisit their first-read annotations during the close read.

> After students have completed the First-Read Guide, you may wish to assign the Text Questions for the selection that are available in the Interactive Teacher's Edition.

Anchor Standards

In the first two sections of the unit, students worked with the whole class and in small groups to gain topical knowledge and greater understanding of the skills required by the anchor standards. In this section, they are asked to work independently, applying what they have learned and demonstrating increased readiness for college and career.

INDEPENDENT LEARNING

First-Read Guide

Use this page to record your first-read ideas.

Selection Title: _____

Tool Kit
First-Read Guide and Model Annotation

NOTICE new information or ideas you learn about the unit topic as you first read this text.

ANNOTATE by marking vocabulary and key passages you want to revisit.

CONNECT ideas within the selection to other knowledge and the selections you have read.

RESPOND by writing a brief summary of the selection.

STANDARD
Reading Read and comprehend complex literary and informational texts independently and proficiently.

430 UNIT 4 • HUMAN INTELLIGENCE

PERSONALIZE FOR LEARNING

Strategic Support
Writing a Summary Students may struggle with writing a summary for the Respond section of the First-Read Guide. Discuss the components of a successful summary, and have students create a checklist to help them review and revise their First-Read Guide entry.

- Explain that a summary should be short and should identify the title and author of a selection.
- The topic (for nonfiction selections) or genre (for literary selections) should be noted, followed by the main ideas in a nonfiction text or brief descriptions of the essential elements in literary selections (i.e., character, plot, setting, point of view, literary techniques).

Students should use their own words to describe, or restate, the ideas or elements of a selection. If they include exact words from the text, those words should be enclosed in quotation marks.

ESSENTIAL QUESTION: In what different ways can people be intelligent?

Close-Read Guide

Use this page to record your close-read ideas.

Tool Kit
Close-Read Guide and Model Annotation

Selection Title: _____

Close Read the Text

Revisit sections of the text you marked during your first read. Read these sections closely and **annotate** what you notice. Ask yourself **questions** about the text. What can you **conclude**? Write down your ideas.

Analyze the Text

Think about the author's choices of patterns, structure, techniques, and ideas included in the text. Select one, and record your thoughts about what this choice conveys.

QuickWrite

Pick a paragraph from the text that grabbed your interest. Explain the power of this passage.

STANDARD
Reading Read and comprehend complex literary and informational texts independently and proficiently.

Independent Learning **431**

DIGITAL PERSPECTIVES

CLOSE READ

Students should begin their close read by revisiting the annotations they made during their first read. Then students should analyze one of the author's choices regarding the following elements:

- **patterns,** such as repetition or parallelism
- **structure,** such as cause-and-effect or problem-solution
- **techniques,** such as description or dialogue
- **ideas,** such as the author's main idea or claim

MAKE IT INTERACTIVE
Group students according to the selection they have chosen. Then have students meet to discuss the selection in depth. Their discussions should be guided by their insights and questions.

PERSONALIZE FOR LEARNING

Strategic Support

QuickWrite To scaffold support for the QuickWrite, help students organize and develop their ideas about a specific paragraph in the text. Have them read aloud to a partner the paragraph they chose, summarize the main idea and supporting details, and point out specific examples in the writing that captured their interest. Students may point to specific vocabulary, direct quotations, dialogue, descriptions, imagery, or visuals and/or captions related to the paragraph they chose. Students should also talk with their partner about something more they'd like to know. For example, they might have questions about the main idea or details in the paragraph, or they might want to know more about how the writer decided to craft the paragraph.

Independent Learning 431

ADVISING

Share Your Independent Learning

Prepare to Share
Explain to students that sharing what they learned from their Independent Learning selection provides classmates who read a different selection with an opportunity to consider the text as a source of evidence during the Performance-Based Assessment. As students prepare to share, remind them to highlight how their selection contributed to their knowledge of the concept of human intelligence as well as how the selection connects to the question, *In what different ways can people be intelligent?*

Learn From Your Classmates
As students discuss the Independent Learning selections, direct them to take particular note of how their classmates' chosen selections align with their current position on the Performance-Based Assessment question.

Reflect
Students may want to add their reflection to their Evidence Log, particularly if their insight relates to a specific selection from the unit.

MAKE IT INTERACTIVE
Have students consider the Independent Learning selection they read and jot down whether or not they felt the text changed or challenged the way they define intelligence. In a class discussion, ask volunteers to share and explain their answers, and invite classmates to further the discussion by asking questions.

Evidence Log Support students in completing their Evidence Log. This paced activity will help prepare them for the Performance-Based Assessment at the end of the unit.

INDEPENDENT LEARNING

EVIDENCE LOG
Go to your Evidence Log, and record what you learned from the text you read.

Share Your Independent Learning

Prepare to Share
In what different ways can people be intelligent?

Even when you read something independently, you can continue to grow by sharing what you have learned with others. Reflect on the text you explored independently, and write notes about its connection to the unit. In your notes, consider why this text belongs in this unit.

Learn From Your Classmates
Discuss It Share your ideas about the text you explored on your own. As you talk with your classmates, jot down ideas that you learn from them.

Reflect
Review your notes, and mark the most important insight you gained from these writing and discussion activities. Explain how this idea adds to your understanding of the different ways in which people can be intelligent.

STANDARDS
Speaking and Listening
Engage effectively in a range of collaborative discussions with diverse partners on *grade 8 topics, texts, and issues*, building on others' ideas and expressing their own clearly.

AUTHOR'S PERSPECTIVE — Ernest Morrell, Ph.D.

Self-facing Notes Some students may not believe that they need to take notes because they'll remember what the teacher and their classmates said. However, taking notes can provide more than a memory jog. To reinforce the importance of taking good notes, teachers should remind students that they will need notes to learn effectively from their peers. In addition, self-facing notes may help students in discussion because these notes will help them prepare the key points they want to share. Point out that the Share Your Independent Learning activity will help students in these ways:

- **Provide Feedback:** Making self-facing notes will help students give classmates useful comments about their independent reading, which will result in deeper learning.

- **Share Key Ideas:** Model how to jot down information that is essential to understanding. Focus on identifying the main ideas and critical details. Students can use these notes to help them make valuable discussion contributions.

- **Expand on Others' Ideas:** Explain to students that effective notes help them cut to the heart of the matter and so provide a scaffolding for what others may have noticed in the reading.

PERFORMANCE-BASED ASSESSMENT PREP

Review Evidence for an Informative Essay

At the beginning of this unit, you responded to the following question:

> In what different ways can people be intelligent?

EVIDENCE LOG

Review your Evidence Log and your QuickWrite from the beginning of the unit. Have your ideas changed?

NOTES

Identify at least three pieces of evidence that interested you about the ways in which people demonstrate intelligence.

1.

2.

3.

Identify the way of demonstrating intelligence that made the strongest impression on you:

_____
_____

Develop your thoughts into a topic sentence for an informative essay. Complete this sentence starter:

One of the most unexpected ways in which people can show intelligence is _____
_____
_____

Evaluate Your Evidence Consider your ideas about intelligence prior to reading the texts in this unit. How did the texts you studied influence your ideas about intelligence? Note specific examples and key passages that piqued your curiosity.

STANDARDS

Writing
Write informative/explanatory texts, to examine a topic and convey ideas, concepts, and information through the selection, organization, and analysis of relevant content.

b. Develop the topic with relevant, well-chosen facts, definitions, concrete details, quotations, or other information and examples.

DIGITAL PERSPECTIVES

Review Evidence for an Informative Essay

Evidence Log Students should understand that their viewpoint can evolve as they learn more about the subject and are exposed to additional points of view. Point out that their original answer to the question *In what different ways can people be intelligent?* can change after careful consideration of their learning and evidence.

Evaluate Your Evidence Remind students that there are many different types of evidence they can use as support in their informative essays, such as the following:

- examples from texts
- facts
- quotations from authorities
- passages that challenged or changed their way of thinking
- passages or quotations that they think are memorable or inspiring

Students should select evidence from the text that directly supports their assertions. For example, they might include a quotation or passage from a text and explain how it changed their thinking, or they might note a fact or an anecdote that confirmed their thinking.

ASSESSING

Writing to Sources: Informative Essay

Students should complete the Performance-Based Assessment independently, with little to no input or feedback during the process. Students should use word processing software to take advantage of editing tools and features.

Prior to beginning the Assessment, ask students to think about how the different people or characters in the selections seem to acquire and/or improve their intelligence.

Review the Elements of Effective Informative Essay Students can review the work they did earlier in the unit as they complete the Performance-Based Assessment. They may also consult other resources, such as the following:

- the elements of an informative essay, including language, tone, and grammar, as well as how to organize an informative essay, available in Whole-Class Learning
- their Evidence Log
- their Word Network

Although students will use evidence from unit selections for their informative essays, they may need to collect additional evidence, including facts, statistics, anecdotes, quotations from authorities, or examples.

PERFORMANCE-BASED ASSESSMENT

SOURCES
- WHOLE CLASS SELECTIONS
- SMALL GROUP SELECTIONS
- INDEPENDENT-LEARNING SELECTION

WORD NETWORK
As you write and revise your informative essay, use your Word Network to help vary your word choices.

PART 1
Writing to Sources: Informative Essay

In this unit, you have read a variety of perspectives on human intelligence. Both fiction and nonfiction texts have offered new ideas and explanations about the ways we think about and define human intelligence.

> **Assignment**
> Write an **informative essay** in which you address the Essential Question:
>
> In what different ways can people be intelligent?
>
> Consider how each selection you read reveals a different perspective on what *intelligence* means. Make sure that you integrate relevant quotations, facts, and examples to support your ideas. Use a formal style and tone in your writing.

Reread the Assignment Review the assignment to be sure you fully understand it. The assignment may reference some of the academic words presented at the beginning of the unit. Be sure you understand each of the words given below in order to complete the assignment correctly. You may want to integrate some of the words into your essay.

Academic Vocabulary

| assimilate | tendency | integrate |
| observation | documentation | |

Review the Elements of an Effective Informative Essay Before you begin writing, read the Informative Essay Rubric. Once you have completed your first draft, check it against the rubric. If one or more of the elements is missing or not as strong as it could be, revise your essay to add or strengthen that component.

STANDARDS
Writing
- Write informative/explanatory texts to examine a topic and convey ideas, concepts, and information through the selection, organization, and analysis of relevant content.
- Draw evidence from literary or informational texts to support analysis, reflection, and research.
- Write routinely over extended time frames and shorter time frames for a range of discipline-specific tasks, purposes, and audiences.

ESSENTIAL QUESTION: In what different ways can people be intelligent?

DIGITAL PERSPECTIVES

Informative Essay Rubric

	Focus and Organization	Evidence and Elaboration	Conventions
4	The introduction engages the reader and states the topic in a compelling way. The essay is organized, and ideas progress logically. Transitions clearly show the relationships among ideas. The conclusion follows from the information in the essay and offers fresh insight into the topic.	The topic is developed with relevant facts, definitions, examples, and quotations. The style and tone of the essay are formal. The vocabulary is precise and suited to the topic, audience, and purpose.	The essay demonstrates mastery of standard English conventions of usage and mechanics.
3	The introduction is somewhat engaging and states the topic clearly. The essay is organized, and ideas progress somewhat logically. Some transitions are included to show the relationships among ideas. The conclusion follows from the information in the essay.	The topic is developed with facts, definitions, examples, and quotations. The style and tone of the essay are mostly formal. Vocabulary is generally suited to the topic, audience, and purpose.	The essay demonstrates accuracy in standard English conventions of usage and mechanics.
2	The introduction states the topic. The essay is somewhat organized, but not all ideas flow logically. A few transitions are included that show the relationship among ideas. The conclusion is somewhat related to the information in the essay.	The topic is developed with some facts, definitions, and quotations. The style and tone of the essay are occasionally formal. Vocabulary is somewhat suited to the topic, audience, and purpose.	The essay demonstrates some accuracy in standard English conventions of usage and mechanics.
1	The topic is not clearly stated. The essay is disorganized. Transitions are not included. The conclusion does not contain information that is related to the essay or is nonexistent.	Evidence is not used to develop the topic. The style and tone of the essay are informal. The vocabulary is not suited to the topic, audience, or purpose.	The essay contains mistakes in standard English conventions of usage and mechanics.

Informative Essay Rubric

As you review the Informative Essay Rubric with students, remind them that the rubric is a resource that can guide their revisions. Students should pay particular attention to the differences between a draft that contains all the elements of an informative essay (a score of 3) and one that is compelling and insightful (a score of 4).

PERSONALIZE FOR LEARNING

English Language Support
Define Key Terms Ask students to review key terms used in the lesson, for example, *informative*, *essay*, and *transitions*. Then have them find or review the definitions of the terms: *informative*—used to describe something that informs or explains; *essay*—a short nonfiction work on a particular subject; *transitions*—words and phrases that show the relationship between ideas. Discuss aspects of the words that will help students understand their meanings; for example, *informative* is related to *inform*. Have students use the words in sentences to demonstrate comprehension. **ALL LEVELS**

ASSESSING

Speaking and Listening: Speech

As student annotate their essays, encourage them to mark places where a pause will give the audience time to absorb a key point.

Remind students that the effectiveness of an oral informative essay relies on how the speaker establishes credibility with his or her audience. If a speaker comes across as confident and authoritative, it will be easier for the audience to give credence to the speaker's presentation.

Review the Rubric As you review the Oral Presentation Rubric with students, remind them that it is a valuable tool that can help them plan their presentation. They should strive to include all of the criteria required to achieve a score of 3. Draw their attention to some of the subtle differences between scores of 2 and 3.

PERFORMANCE-BASED ASSESSMENT

PART 2
Speaking and Listening: Speech

Assignment
After completing the final draft of your informative essay, use it as the foundation for a short **speech.**

Do not simply read your essay aloud. Instead, take the following steps to make your speech lively and engaging.

- Go back to your essay, and annotate its most important ideas and supporting details. Add details where needed to suit a listening audience.
- Refer to your annotated text to guide your presentation and keep it focused.
- Speak clearly and make eye contact with your audience.

Review the Rubric Before you deliver your presentation, check your plans against this rubric. If one or more of the elements is missing or not as strong as it could be, revise your presentation to improve it.

STANDARDS
Speaking and Listening
Present claims and findings, emphasizing salient points in a focused, coherent manner with relevant evidence, sound valid reasoning, and well-chosen details; use appropriate eye contact, adequate volume, and clear pronunciation.

	Content	Organization	Presentation Techniques
3	The introduction is engaging and establishes the topic in a compelling way. Ideas are clearly supported with relevant evidence. The conclusion offers fresh insight and follows from the rest of the presentation.	Ideas are organized and progress logically. Listeners can easily follow the presentation.	The speaker maintains effective eye contact. The speaker speaks clearly and with adequate volume.
2	The introduction establishes the topic. Ideas are usually supported with relevant evidence. The conclusion follows from the information in the presentation.	Ideas are organized. Listeners can mostly follow the presentation.	The speaker sometimes maintains eye contact. The speaker speaks somewhat clearly and usually with adequate volume.
1	The introduction does not clearly establish the topic. Ideas are not supported with relevant evidence. The information in the conclusion is not related to the presentation.	Ideas are disorganized. Listeners have difficulty following the presentation.	The speaker does not maintain eye contact. The speaker does not speak clearly or with adequate volume.

DIGITAL PERSPECTIVES

Preparing for the Assignment To help students understand what an effective oral presentation of an informative essay looks like, find examples on the Internet of teenagers or adults presenting information. Project the examples for the class, and have students note the techniques that make each speaker successful (that is, eye contact, pacing, tone, and so on). Suggest that students record themselves presenting their essays prior to presenting to the class so that they can practice incorporating some of the elements in the examples you showed them.

UNIT 4 REFLECTION

Reflect on the Unit
Now that you've completed the unit, take a few moments to reflect on your learning.

Reflect on the Unit Goals
Look back at the goals at the beginning of the unit. Use a different colored pen to rate yourself again. Then, think about readings and activities that contributed the most to the growth of your understanding. Record your thoughts.

Reflect on the Learning Strategies
Discuss It Write a reflection on whether you were able to improve your learning based on your Action Plans. Think about what worked, what didn't, and what you might do to keep working on these strategies. Record your ideas before joining a class discussion.

Reflect on the Text
Choose a selection that you found challenging, and explain what made it difficult.

Describe something that surprised you about a text in the unit.

Which activity taught you the most about human intelligence? What did you learn?

SCAN FOR MULTIMEDIA

Invention

UNIT 5

INTRODUCTION

Jump Start

Engage students in a discussion by asking them the following questions: *What if you were to invent something that changed how people live? What would the invention do, and what would people do differently by using your invention?*

Have students jot down answers to the questions. Ask for volunteers to share their answers to start a discussion about invention.

Invention

Ask students what the word *invention* suggests to them. Point out that as they work through this unit, they will read many examples about invention.

Video ▶

Project the introduction video in class, ask students to open the video in their interactive textbooks, or have students scan the Bounce Page icon with their phones to access the video.

Discuss It If you want to make this a digital activity, go online and navigate to the Discussion Board. Alternatively, students can share their responses in a class discussion.

Block Scheduling

Each day in this pacing calendar represents a 40–50 minute class period. Teachers using block scheduling may combine days to reflect their class schedule. In addition, teachers may revise pacing to differentiate and support core instruction by integrating components and resources as students require.

📅 **Pacing Plan**

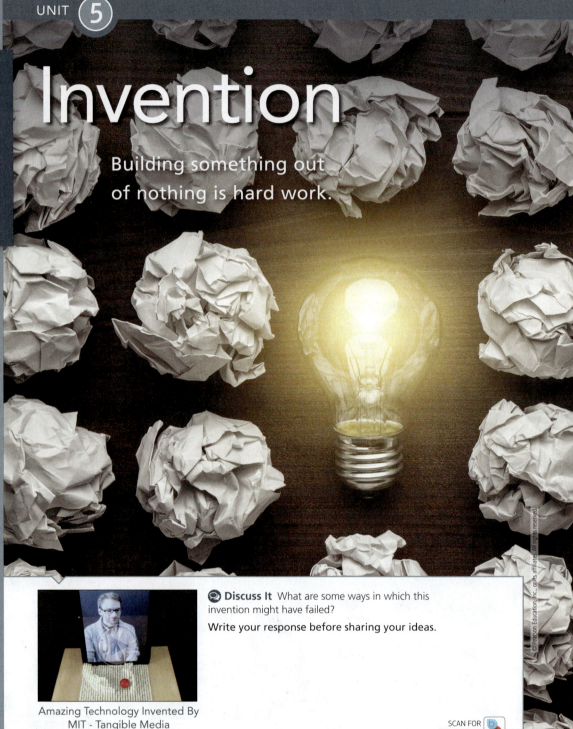

UNIT 5

Invention

Building something out of nothing is hard work.

Discuss It What are some ways in which this invention might have failed?

Write your response before sharing your ideas.

Amazing Technology Invented By MIT - Tangible Media

438

SCAN FOR MULTIMEDIA

Unit Introduction	Introduce Whole-Class Learning	Uncle Marcos	To Fly	Performance Task
1 2	3	4 5 6 7 8 9	10 11 12 13 14 15	16 17 18

438 UNIT 5 • INVENTION

DIGITAL PERSPECTIVES | Audio | Video | Document | Annotation Highlights | EL Highlights | Online Assessment

UNIT 5

UNIT INTRODUCTION

ESSENTIAL QUESTION: Are inventions realized through inspiration or perspiration?

LAUNCH TEXT ARGUMENT MODEL: Inspiration Is Overrated!

WHOLE-CLASS LEARNING

ANCHOR TEXT: NOVEL EXCERPT
Uncle Marcos
from The House of the Spirits
Isabel Allende, translated by Magda Bogin

ANCHOR TEXT: ESSAY
To Fly
from Space Chronicles
Neil deGrasse Tyson
▶ MEDIA CONNECTION: When I Look Up

SMALL-GROUP LEARNING

BIOGRAPHY
Nikola Tesla: The Greatest Inventor of All?
Vicky Baez

COMPARE

NOVEL EXCERPT
from The Invention of Everything Else
Samatha Hunt

SCIENCE ARTICLE
25 Years Later, Hubble Sees Beyond Troubled Start
Dennis Overbye

MEDIA: VIDEO
Sounds of a Glass Armonica

INDEPENDENT LEARNING

WEB ARTICLE
Ada Lovelace: A Science Legend
James Essinger

WEB ARTICLE
Fermented Cow Dung Air Freshener Wins Two Students Top Science Prize
Kimberley Mok

NEWS ARTICLE
Scientists Build Robot That Runs, Call It "Cheetah"
Rodrique Ngowi

NOVEL EXCERPT
from The Time Machine
H. G. Wells

MYTH
Icarus and Daedalus
retold by Josephine Preston Peabody

PERFORMANCE TASK
WRITING FOCUS:
Write an Argument

PERFORMANCE TASK
SPEAKING AND LISTENING FOCUS:
Conduct a Debate

PERFORMANCE-BASED ASSESSMENT PREP
Review Evidence for an Argument

PERFORMANCE-BASED ASSESSMENT

Argument: Essay and Speech
PROMPT:
Which invention described in this unit has had the biggest impact on humanity?

Are inventions realized through inspiration or perspiration?

Introduce the Essential Question and point out that students will respond to related prompts.

- **Whole-Class Learning** Which text—"Uncle Marcos" or "To Fly"—best describes the dream or fantasy of human flight?
- **Small-Group Learning** Are inventions realized through inspiration or perspiration?
- **Performance-Based Assessment** Which invention described in this unit has had the biggest impact on humanity?

Using Trade Books

Refer to the Teaching with Trade Books section in the Interactive Teacher's Edition for suggestions on how to incorporate the following thematically related titles into this unit:

- *The Time Machine* by H. G. Wells
- *20,000 Leagues Under the Sea* by Jules Verne
- *Boy: Tales of Childhood* by Roald Dahl

Current Perspectives

To increase student engagement, search online for stories about invention, and invite your students to recommend stories they find. Always preview content before sharing it with your class.

- **News Story: How Jeff Bezos and Other Billionaires Are Transforming Space Travel (Space.com)** An article by Mike Wall describes the enormous impact that billionaires have had on the space travel industry in recent years.
- **Video: Elon Musk: Greatest living inventor? (CNBC)** A video of James Fallows discusses the many hugely influential inventions by billionaire Elon Musk.

Introduce Small-Group Learning — Nikola Tesla: The Greatest Inventor of All? — from The Invention of Everything Else — 25 Years Later, Hubble Sees Beyond Troubled Start — Media: Sounds of a Glass Armonica — Performance Task — Introduce Independent Learning — Independent Learning — Performance-Based Assessment

| 19 | 20 | 21 | 22 | 23 | 24 | 25 | 26 | 27 | 28 | 29 | 30 | 31 | 32 | 33 | 34 | 35 | 36 |

Unit Introduction 439

INTRODUCTION

About the Unit Goals
These unit goals were backward designed from the Performance-Based Assessment at the end of the unit and the Whole-Class and Small-Group Performance Tasks. Students will practice and become proficient in many more standards over the course of this unit.

Unit Goals ▶
Review the goals with students and explain that as they read and discuss the selections in this unit, they will improve their skills in reading, writing, research, language, and speaking and listening.

- Have students watch the video on Goal Setting.
- A video on this topic is available online in the Professional Development Center.

Reading Goals Tell students they will read to learn about invention and inspiration. They will also read various genres to study the ways writers express ideas.

Writing and Research Goals Tell students that they will learn the elements of argumentative writing. They will write their own argument, and they will also write for a number of reasons, including to organize and share ideas, reflect on experiences, and gather evidence. They will conduct research to clarify and explore ideas.

Language Goal Tell students that they will study grammar and usage, including combining sentences using gerunds and participles.

Speaking and Listening Explain to students that they will work to develop consensus and communicate with one another.

HOME Connection ✉

A Home Connection letter to students' parents or guardians is available in the Interactive Teacher's Edition. The letter explains what students will be learning in this unit and how they will be assessed.

UNIT 5 INTRODUCTION

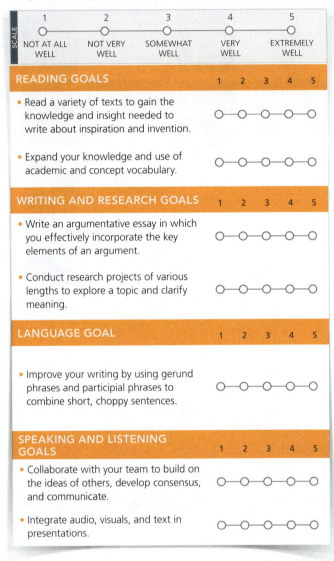

STANDARDS
Language
Acquire and use accurately grade-appropriate general academic and domain-specific words and phrases; gather vocabulary knowledge when considering a word or phrase important to comprehension or expression.

440 UNIT 5 • INVENTION

AUTHOR'S PERSPECTIVE Ernest Morrell, Ph.D.

How to Support Kids When They Have Trouble When setting goals with students, have them consider these questions:

1. What are the opportunities open to me if I achieve this goal?
2. What are the biggest challenges that I will face in attempting to achieve this goal?
3. What support will I need from others in order to achieve this goal and how will I ensure that I get that support?

The first question helps students see that setting goals helps them take control of their life and focus on the issues that matter to them. As a result, they are likely to make good decisions. The second question helps students understand that achieving goals take hard work, resilience, and determination. The third question reassures students that help is available and shows them the importance of seeking—and accepting—help when necessary.

ESSENTIAL QUESTION: Are inventions realized through inspiration or perspiration?

Academic Vocabulary: Argument

Understanding and using academic terms can help you read, write, and speak with precision and clarity. Here are five academic words that will be useful in this unit as you analyze and write arguments.

Complete the chart.

1. Review each word, its root, and the mentor sentences.
2. Use the information and your own knowledge to predict the meaning of each word.
3. For each word, list at least two related words.
4. Refer to the dictionary or other resources if needed.

TIP

FOLLOW THROUGH
Study the words in this chart, and mark them or their forms wherever they appear in the unit.

WORD	MENTOR SENTENCES	PREDICT MEANING	RELATED WORDS
opponent ROOT: *-pon-* "place"; "put"	1. He managed to win the game against a strong *opponent*. 2. I respect her even though she is my *opponent*.		postpone; component
position ROOT: *-pos-* "place"; "put"	1. His *position* that everyone receive a different amount angered the other children. 2. Our debate team took the *position* that cellphone use should be banned from classrooms.		
contradict ROOT: *-dic-* "speak"; "assert"	1. Even though Abby knew Kyle was wrong, she did not *contradict* him. 2. The results of this study *contradict* the findings from earlier studies.		
legitimate ROOT: *-leg-* "law"	1. It's a *legitimate* argument, but they pretended not to hear it. 2. The judge determined that the oldest son was the *legitimate* heir to the fortune.		
dissent ROOT: *-sent-* "feel"	1. The proposal caused *dissent* because the members were against it. 2. The whole family wanted to go to the beach, so there was no *dissent* this time.		

Unit Introduction 441

DIGITAL PERSPECTIVES

Academic Vocabulary: Argument

Introduce the blue words in the chart on the student page. Point out that the root of each word provides a clue to its meaning. Discuss the mentor sentences to ensure students understand each word's usage. Students should also use the mentor sentences as context to help them predict the meaning of each word. Check that students are able to fill the chart in correctly. Complete pronunciations, parts of speech, and definitions are provided for you. Students are only expected to provide the definition.

Possible responses:

opponent *n.* (uh POH nehnt)
Meaning: person on the other side in a game, debate, argument, etc.
Related words: oppose, opposing
Additional words related to root *-pon-*: proponent, respond

position *n., v.* (poh ZIH shuhn)
Meaning: *n.* location; *v.* to place
Related words: opposition, oppose
Additional words related to root *-pos-*: compose, deposit

contradict *v.* (kon truh DIHKT)
Meaning: to state the contrary or opposite; to deny
Related words: contradicted, contradictory
Additional words related to the root *-dic-*: dictate, verdict, diction

legitimate *adj.* (luh JIHT uh miht)
Meaning: allowed, legal, valid
Related words: legitimacy, legitimating
Additional words related to root *-leg-*: illegitimate, legislate

dissent: *n., v.* (dih SEHNT)
Meaning: *n.* disagreement; *v.* to disagree
Related words: dissenting, dissention
Additional words related to the root *-sent-*: consent, resent

---

PERSONALIZE FOR LEARNING

English Language Support
Cognates Many of the academic words have Spanish cognates. Use these cognates with students whose home language is Spanish.

opponent – oponente
proposition – proposición
contradict – contradecir
legitimate – legítimo
dissension – disensión

ALL LEVELS

INTRODUCTION

Purpose of the Launch Text
The Launch Text provides students with a common starting point to address the unit topic. After reading the Launch Text, all students will be able to participate in discussions about invention.

Lexile: 850 The easier reading level of this selection makes it perfect to assign for homework. Students will need little or no support to understand it.

Additionally, "Inspiration Is Overrated!" provides a writing model for the Performance-Based Assessment students complete at the end of the unit.

Launch Text: Argument Model
Have students pay attention to the structure of the text. They should note that in an argument, the author's position is usually stated in the first or second paragraph of the text, and that the paragraphs that follow provide details supporting that position. The concluding paragraph or paragraphs restate the author's position.

Encourage students to read this text on their own and annotate unfamiliar words and sections of text they think are particularly important.

🔊 AUDIO SUMMARIES
Audio summaries of "Inspiration Is Overrated!" are available in both English and Spanish in the Interactive Teacher's Edition or Unit Resources. Assigning these summaries before students read the Launch Text may help them build additional background knowledge and set a context for their reading.

UNIT 5 INTRODUCTION

LAUNCH TEXT | ARGUMENT MODEL

This text is an example of an **argument,** a type of writing in which an author states and defends a position on a topic. This is the type of writing you will develop in the Performance-Based Assessment at the end of the unit.

As you read, look at the way the writer builds a case. Mark the text to answer this question: What is the writer's position, and how is it supported?

Inspiration Is Overrated!

NOTES

1 Here's something that isn't on everyone's shopping list: a coffee mug that irons clothes. It's just one of a multitude of inventions that most of us have never heard of. Each of those forgotten contraptions was probably someone's bright idea—a flash of inspiration experienced while walking in the woods, an idea guaranteed to change the world. So what went wrong?

2 Some inventions are so much a part of everyday life we forget that they started off as someone's bright idea. Others are long forgotten or remembered only as being colossal duds.

3 For every invention that actually makes it to production, there are thousands that don't. The line between the bizarre and the ingenious is often very thin. History is filled with examples of new inventions that supporters thought would be transformational but turned out to be just minor fads.

4 Experts say that the odds are stacked astronomically against inventors, and that no amount of marketing can turn a situation around. The number of failed inventions reinforces how hard it is for inventors to make the leap from idea to marketable product.

5 Let's look at some figures. According to the U.S. Patent and Trademark Office, there are about 1.5 million products that have patents. Perhaps 3,000 of those make money. A noted business magazine states that only one in 5,000 inventions succeeds in the marketplace. This estimate is ten times lower than the one from the Trademark Office!

SCAN FOR MULTIMEDIA

442 UNIT 5 • INVENTION

PERSONALIZE FOR LEARNING

English Language Support

Descriptive Language Explain to students that when writers are trying to get their message across, word choice matters. Sometimes, writers use flowery language to make their argument more compelling or their story more interesting. In paragraphs 1 and 2, the writer describes types of ideas in a variety of ways, including "bright idea," "flash of Inspiration," and "colossal duds."

Ask students why the writer didn't just use the words *idea* or *failure*, eliciting that the article is more interesting because the writer used descriptive language. Discuss that the message is more likely to be remembered because exciting language is used. **ALL LEVELS**

ESSENTIAL QUESTION: Are inventions realized through inspiration or perspiration?

6   What explains the high rate of failure? Is there something the inventors failed to see? The answer is *yes*: They failed to see how much work is involved in getting a product off the ground. Someone once said that genius is one percent inspiration and ninety-nine percent perspiration. That is true for invention, too. Hard work is more important than a good idea.

7   Developing something new that actually works—and that people want—can take years. After an inventor has a brilliant idea, the hard part begins. A working model must be developed and tested. If the results are poor or inconsistent, the project may have to be rethought—or even scrapped. A good idea is necessary, but what comes after is more important.

8   When a working model is finally developed, the inventor must conduct what is called a "search for prior art." That means checking to make sure that there isn't a similar or even identical invention around. Sometimes it seems as if all the good ideas have been taken! That means more work.

9   When everything is ready to go, the inventor has to apply for a patent—a legal right to ownership of the invention. It's like a contract, and every single word has legal consequences. Many inventors hire patent lawyers to make sure their interests are protected. That means more work.

10 It's a common mistake to think that you can sell an idea. You can't. You can only sell an invention. Turning an idea into a viable invention takes work—time-consuming, tedious, and sometimes frustrating work!

11 If invention is one percent inspiration and ninety-nine percent perspiration, I'm putting my money on the ninety-nine percent.

NOTES

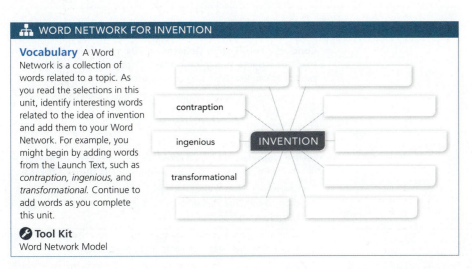

WORD NETWORK FOR INVENTION

Vocabulary A Word Network is a collection of words related to a topic. As you read the selections in this unit, identify interesting words related to the idea of invention and add them to your Word Network. For example, you might begin by adding words from the Launch Text, such as *contraption, ingenious,* and *transformational.* Continue to add words as you complete this unit.

Tool Kit
Word Network Model

Inspiration Is Overrated! **443**

INTRODUCTION

Summary

Have students read the introductory paragraph. Provide them with tips for writing a summary:
- Write in the present tense.
- Make sure to include the title of the work.
- Be concise: a summary should not be equal in length to the original text.
- If you need to quote the words of the author, use quotation marks.
- Don't put your own opinions, ideas, or interpretations into the summary. The purpose of writing a summary is to accurately represent what the author says, not to provide a critique.

If necessary, students can refer to the Tool Kit for help in understanding the elements of a good summary.

See possible summary on the student page.

Launch Activity

Explain to students that as they work on this unit, they will have many opportunities to discuss how they feel about the quotation "Inventing takes one percent inspiration and ninety-nine percent perspiration." Students may rely on their personal opinions as they choose their initial responses to the statement. Remind students that when they choose a side in an argument, they need to have facts to support their positions.

UNIT 5 INTRODUCTION

Summary

Write a summary of "Inspiration Is Overrated!" A **summary** is a concise, complete, and accurate overview of a text. It should not include a statement of your opinion or an analysis.

Possible response: In "Inspiration Is Overrated!" the author explains that for every invention we use in our lives, there are many more that people came up with that did not get produced. According to the author, the vast majority of patented projects don't make money, and thousands of other ideas for inventions never get patented at all. The author argues that coming up with a good idea is just the beginning. After that, the inventor must make a working model and make sure that the idea has not already been taken. According to the author, coming up with one good idea is not so hard. However, coming up with a unique idea and making it into something that people can use can take a lot of time and effort.

Launch Activity

Conduct a Four-Corner Debate Consider this statement: **Inventing takes one percent inspiration and ninety-nine percent perspiration.** Choose a position and explain why you feel this way.

☐ Strongly Agree ☐ Agree ☐ Disagree ☐ Strongly Disagree

- Join your classmates who chose the same response in one corner of the room. Together, formulate arguments for the class discussion.
- Share your group's ideas with your classmates. Then, ask questions or make comments. Remember to express your own point of view in a considerate, respectful way.
- After the debate, decide whether your opinion has changed. Go to the corner that best represents your new opinion.

ESSENTIAL QUESTION: Are inventions realized through inspiration or perspiration?

DIGITAL PERSPECTIVES

QuickWrite

Consider class discussions, the video, and the Launch Text as you think about the prompt. Record your first thoughts here.

PROMPT: Which invention has had the biggest impact on humanity?

Possible response: I think the biggest impact on humanity has come from the invention of the light bulb. It has allowed people to work longer hours and to gather with other people at times when they would have gone to sleep at night. This impact has been both positive and negative in its impact. It's positive because people can work longer hours and earn more money. However, it's negative because people are working too hard and not getting enough sleep or relaxation time.

EVIDENCE LOG FOR INVENTION

Review your QuickWrite. Summarize your point of view in one sentence to record in your Evidence Log. Then, record evidence from "Inspiration Is Overrated!" that supports your point of view.

Prepare for the Performance-Based Assessment at the end of the unit by completing the Evidence Log after each selection.

Title of Text: _____		Date: _____
CONNECTION TO PROMPT	TEXT EVIDENCE/DETAILS	ADDITIONAL NOTES/IDEAS

How does this text change or add to my thinking? Date: _____

Tool Kit
Evidence Log Model

SCAN FOR MULTIMEDIA

Unit Introduction 445

QuickWrite

In this QuickWrite, students should present their own response to the prompt based on the material they have read and viewed in the Unit Overview and Introduction or from their prior knowledge. This initial response will help inform their work when they complete the Performance-Based Assessment at the end of the unit. Students should make sure they present their position clearly and support it with well-reasoned evidence and accurate details.

See possible QuickWrite on the student page.

Evidence Log for Invention

Students should record their initial position in their Evidence Logs along with evidence from "Inspiration Is Overrated!" that support this position.

If you choose to print the Evidence Log, distribute it to students at this point so they can use it throughout the rest of the unit.

Performance-Based Assessment: Refining Your Thinking ▶

- Have students watch the video on Refining Your Thinking.
- A video on this topic is available online in the Professional Development Center.

PERSONALIZE FOR LEARNING

Strategic Support

Argument Students may struggle to decide which side of the argument to take. Create a class chart to help students organize their thoughts. Have students suggest thoughts and ideas for each side, and add them to the chart. Remind students that as they continue working on this idea, they will need evidence to support their arguments. Ask students to look at the suggestions added to the chart and decide which can be supported by evidence and which are emotion-based. Ask why it is important to be able to tell the difference.

"Inventions come from one percent inspiration and ninety-nine percent perspiration."

Agree	Disagree

Inspiration Is Overrated! 445

OVERVIEW

WHOLE-CLASS LEARNING

Are inventions realized through inspiration or perspiration?

Engage students in a conversation about some current inventions, such as smartphones, social media, and hybrid or electric cars. Ask students to think about how these inventions all started out as someone's inspired idea, and what kind of work must have gone into inventions that most of us take for granted.

Whole-Class Learning Strategies ▶

Review the Learning Strategies with students and explain that as they work through Whole-Class Learning they will develop strategies to work in large-group environments.

- Have students watch the video on Whole-Class Learning Strategies.
- A video on this topic is available online in the Professional Development Center.

You may wish to discuss some action items to add to the chart as a class before students complete it on their own. For example, for "Listen actively," you might solicit the following from students:

- Do not interrupt the speaker.
- Write down important points you can refer to later.

> **Block Scheduling**
>
> Each day in this Pacing Plan represents a 40–50 minute class period. Teachers using block scheduling may combine days to reflect their class schedule. In addition, teachers may revise pacing to differentiate and support core instruction by integrating components and resources as students require.

📅 **Pacing Plan**

OVERVIEW: WHOLE-CLASS LEARNING

ESSENTIAL QUESTION:

Are inventions realized through inspiration or perspiration?

How do people invent? Does an idea simply come in a flash, or is there a long struggle to find a solution to a particular problem? You will work with your whole class to explore the concept of invention. The selections you are going to read present insights into some aspects of the topic.

Whole-Class Learning Strategies

Throughout your life, in school, in your community, and in your career, you will continue to learn and work in large-group environments.

Review these strategies and the actions you can take to practice them as you work with your whole class. Add ideas of your own for each step. Get ready to use these strategies during Whole-Class Learning.

STRATEGY	ACTION PLAN
Listen actively	• Eliminate distractions. For example, put your cellphone away. • Keep your eyes on the speaker. •
Clarify by asking questions	• If you're confused, other people probably are, too. Ask a question to help your whole class. • If you see that you are guessing, ask a question instead. •
Monitor understanding	• Notice what information you already know and be ready to build on it. • Ask for help if you are struggling. •
Interact and share ideas	• Share your ideas and answer questions, even if you are unsure. • Build on the ideas of others by adding details or making a connection. •

SCAN FOR MULTIMEDIA

Unit Introduction | Introduce Whole-Class Learning | Uncle Marcos | To Fly | Performance Task

1 | 2 | 3 | 4 | 5 | 6 | 7 | 8 | 9 | 10 | 11 | 12 | 13 | 14 | 15 | 16 | 17 | 18

WHOLE-CLASS LEARNING

CONTENTS

ANCHOR TEXT: NOVEL EXCERPT

Uncle Marcos
from **The House of the Spirits**
Isabel Allende,
translated by Magda Bogin

Clara's favorite uncle is an unusual explorer and inventor.

ANCHOR TEXT: ESSAY

To Fly
from **Space Chronicles**
Neil deGrasse Tyson

A famous astrophysicist ponders the appeal and challenge of human flight.

▸ MEDIA CONNECTION: When I Look Up

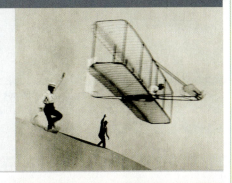

PERFORMANCE TASK
WRITING FOCUS

Write an Argument
The Whole-Class readings focus on human flight—as realized by both real and fictitious inventors. After reading, you will write an essay in which you express your position about which text best captures the power of human inventiveness.

Overview: Whole-Class Learning 447

DIGITAL PERSPECTIVES

Contents

Anchor Texts Preview the anchor texts and media with students to generate interest. Encourage students to discuss other texts they may have read or movies or television shows they may have seen that deal with the issues of invention.

You may wish to conduct a poll to determine which selection students think looks more interesting and discuss the reasons for their preference. Students can return to this poll after they have read the selections to see if their preference changed.

Performance Task

Write an Argument Explain to students that after they have finished reading the selections, they will write an essay that makes a claim as to which reading more effectively captures inventiveness. To help them prepare, encourage students to think about the topic as they progress through the selections and as they participate in the Whole-Class Learning experience.

PLANNING
WHOLE-CLASS LEARNING • UNCLE MARCOS

Uncle Marcos

🔊 **AUDIO SUMMARIES**
Audio summaries of "Uncle Marcos" are available online in both English and Spanish in the Interactive Teacher's Edition or Unit Resources. Assigning these summaries prior to reading the selection may help students build additional background knowledge and set a context for their first read.

Summary
"Uncle Marcos" is an excerpt from Isabel Allende's novel *The House of the Spirits*. During Clara's childhood, Uncle Marcos occasionally returns from journeys to faraway lands, bringing all manner of luggage, animals, and unusual items with him. During these visits to his sister's house, he might bring embarrassment to the family, as he does when he buys a barrel organ in order to publicly woo his cousin Antonieta. He also might bring excitement, as he does when he builds a flying machine that looks like a bird. Clara and Uncle Marcos share an interest in prophesying and develop a special bond.

Insight
Allende's *The House of the Spirits* is an example of magical realism, a genre of fiction that began with Latin American writers. Magical realism portrays fantastical events in an otherwise realistic tone. The flight Uncle Marcos takes in his airplane is an example of magical realism.

ESSENTIAL QUESTION:
Are inventions realized through inspiration or perspiration?

Connection to Essential Question
"Uncle Marcos" provides a unique connection to the Essential Question, *Are inventions realized through inspiration or perspiration?* Uncle Marcos is such a fantastical character that his inventions seem to be realized through inspiration. The reader does not become concerned with his effort to produce his creations. The focus is on his imagination and creativity.

WHOLE-CLASS LEARNING PERFORMANCE TASK
Which text—"Uncle Marcos" or "To Fly"— best describes the dream or fantasy of human flight?

UNIT PERFORMANCE-BASED ASSESSMENT
Which invention described in this unit has had the biggest impact on humanity?

Connection to Performance Tasks
Whole-Class Learning Performance Task To support students as they prepare for the Performance Task, ask them to note the way that this text describes the dream of human flight.

Unit Performance-Based Assessment Students will decide whether flight has had a greater or lesser impact on humanity than other inventions. While most selections in this unit focus on characters, both real and imagined, who toiled to overcome obstacles to achieve flight, the character of Uncle Marcos is encouraged by his imagination and sense of adventure. As this selection is a work of far-fetched fiction, it will serve students as a counterpoint in their arguments.

DIGITAL PERSPECTIVES

 Audio Video Document Annotation Highlights EL Highlights Online Assessment

LESSON RESOURCES

	Making Meaning	Language Development	Effective Expression
Lesson	First Read Close Read Analyze the Text Analyze Craft and Structure	Concept Vocabulary Word Study Conventions	Writing to Sources Speaking and Listening
Instructional Standards	**RL.10** By the end of the year, read and comprehend literature . . . **RL.1** Cite the textual evidence . . . **RL.3** Analyze how particular lines of dialogue . . .	**L.1** Demonstrate command of the conventions . . . **L.4** Determine or clarify the meaning of unknown and multiple-meaning words or phrases . . . **L.4.b** Use common, grade-appropriate Greek or Latin affixes and roots . . .	**W.1** Write arguments . . . **W.1.b** Support claim(s) . . . **W.1.c** Use words, phrases, and clauses . . . **RL.9** Analyze how a modern work of fiction draws on themes, patterns of events, or character types . . . **SL.1** Engage effectively in a range of collaborative discussions . . . **SL.1.a** Come to discussions prepared . . . **SL.1.c** Pose questions . . .
STUDENT RESOURCES Available online in the Interactive Student Edition or Unit Resources	Selection Audio First-Read Guide: Fiction Close-Read Guide: Fiction	Word Network	Evidence Log
TEACHER RESOURCES **Selection Resources** Available online in the Interactive Teacher's Edition or Unit Resources	Audio Summaries Annotation Highlights EL Highlights English Language Support Lesson: Plot Analyze Craft and Structure: Characters	Concept Vocabulary and Word Study Conventions: Subject Complements	Writing to Sources: Critical Review Speaking and Listening: Class Discussion
Reteach/Practice (RP) Available online in the Interactive Teacher's Edition or Unit Resources	Analyze Craft and Structure: Characters (RP)	Word Study: Latin Suffix –ity (RP) Conventions: Subject Complements (RP)	Writing to Sources: Critical Review (RP) Speaking and Listening: Class Discussion (RP)
Assessment Available online in Assessments	Selection Test		
My Resources	A Unit 5 Answer Key is available online and in the Interactive Teacher's Edition.		

Whole-Class Learning   448B

PERSONALIZE FOR LEARNING

WHOLE-CLASS LEARNING • UNCLE MARCOS

Reading Support

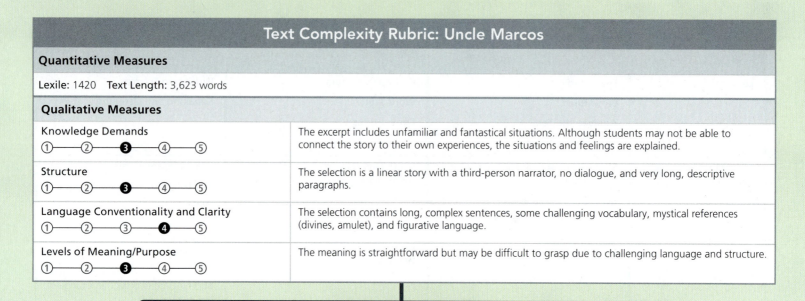

English Language Support

Provide English Learners with support for language and meaning as they read the selection.

Language Help students reword long and complex sentences. Using the language from the selection, suggest simpler sentences that convey the same meaning. Ask students to read the new sentences and discuss.

Meaning To help students sort out the events and ideas in the story, suggest that they keep a log of the main events, stating them in their own words.

Strategic Support

Provide students with strategic support to ensure that they can successfully read the text.

Knowledge Demands Using the background information, discuss the situation depicted in the story, asking what aspects of it are more likely for people to experience. Discuss which elements of the story are fantastical and which are realistic.

Language If students have difficulty with the long, complex sentences, work together to break down sentences into smaller chunks in order to understand their meaning. Ask students to highlight words or phrases that they don't understand. As a group, help define these unfamiliar words and phrases.

Challenge

Provide students who need to be challenged with ideas for how they can go beyond a simple interpretation of the text.

Text Analysis Have students discuss Clara's strong connection with Uncle Marcos. How is her relationship with Uncle Marcos different than others' relationship with him? Why does she feel such a close connection with him?

Written Response Challenge students to rewrite one of the paragraphs in the story from the perspective of Uncle Marcos. Ask students to imagine how Uncle Marcos's voice might sound. Have students share their paragraphs in small groups.

Read and Respond

Have students do their first read of the selection. Then have them complete their close read. Finally, work with them on the Making Meaning, Language Development, and Effective Expression activities.

Standards Support Through Teaching and Learning Cycle

IDENTIFY NEEDS

Analyze results of the Beginning-of-Year Assessment, focusing on the items relating to Unit 5. Also take into consideration student performance to this point and your observations of where particular students struggle.

DECIDE AND PLAN

- If students have performed poorly on items matching these standards, then provide selection scaffolds before assigning them the on-level lesson provided in the Student Edition.
- If students have done well on the Beginning-of-Year Assessment, then challenge them to keep progressing and learning by giving them opportunities to practice the skills in depth.
- Use the Selection Resources listed on the Planning pages for "Uncle Marcos" to help students continually improve their ability to master the standards.

Instructional Standards: Uncle Marcos

	Catching Up	This Year	Looking Forward
Reading	You may wish to administer the **Analyze Craft and Structure: Characters (RP)** worksheet to help students understand how authors construct characters who demonstrate variety in both personality and behavior.	**RL.3** Analyze how particular lines of dialogue or incidents in a story or drama propel the action, reveal aspects of a character, or provoke a decision.	Ask students to conduct analyses of the characters, defining their motivations and actions, and how these drive the plot.
Writing	You may wish to administer the **Writing to Sources: Critical Review (RP)** worksheet to help students prepare for their writing.	**W.1.b** Support claim(s) with logical reasoning and relevant evidence, using accurate, credible sources and demonstrating an understanding of the topic or text.	Have students consider possible counterclaims in their reviews.
Speaking and Listening	You may wish to administer the **Speaking and Listening: Class Discussion (RP)** worksheet to help students better prepare for their discussion.	**SL.1.a** Come to discussions prepared, having read or researched material under study; explicitly draw on that preparation by referring to evidence on the topic, text, or issue to probe and reflect on ideas under discussion.	Challenge students to conduct short, self-propelled, outside research while preparing to enhance the discussion.
Language	Review the **Word Study: Latin Suffix -ity (RP)** worksheet with students to ensure they understand the Latin suffix -ity means "state or quality of being." Review the **Conventions: Subject Complements (RP)** worksheet with students to better familiarize them with predicate nouns, predicate pronouns, and predicate adjectives.	**L.4.b** Use common, grade-appropriate Greek or Latin affixes and roots as clues to the meaning of a word. **L.1** Demonstrate command of the conventions of standard English grammar and usage when writing or speaking.	Work with students to identify other suffixes they recognize in the selection.

ANALYZE AND REVISE

- Analyze student work for evidence of student learning.
- Identify whether or not students have met the expectations in the standards.
- Identify implications for future instruction.

TEACH

Implement the planned lesson, and gather evidence of student learning.

TEACHING

Jump Start

FIRST READ Are you an explorer? Do you have an insatiable appetite for adventure? Where would you go? The world is a big place and there are so many adventures to be had.

Uncle Marcos

Who is Uncle Marcos? What is unique about him? Modeling the questions readers might ask as they read "Uncle Marcos" for the first time brings the text alive for students and connects it to the Whole-Class Performance Task assignment. Selection audio and print capability for the selection are available in the Interactive Teacher's Edition.

Concept Vocabulary

Support students as they rank their words. Ask if they've ever heard, read, or used them. Reassure them that the definitions for these words are listed in the selection.

FIRST READ

As they read, students should perform the steps of the first read:

NOTICE: You may want to encourage students to notice other characters' responses to Uncle Marcos.

ANNOTATE: Remind students to mark passages that contain particularly interesting images or details.

CONNECT: Encourage students to go beyond the text to make connections to their own lives or to larger-than-life characters they have encountered in stories or movies.

RESPOND: Students will answer questions and write a summary to demonstrate understanding.

Point out to students that while they will always complete the Respond step at the end of the first read, the other steps will probably happen somewhat concurrently. You may wish to print copies of the **First-Read Guide: Fiction** for students to use.

MAKING MEANING

About the Author

Isabel Allende (b. 1942) is a Chilean American novelist, essayist, and lecturer who has been called the world's most widely read Spanish-language author. Allende's novels combine elements of myth and realism ("magical realism") and are often based on her personal experiences. In 1992, after the tragic death of her daughter, she established a foundation dedicated to the protection and empowerment of women and children worldwide. Allende became a U.S. citizen in 1993 and, in 2014, was awarded the Presidential Medal of Freedom by President Barack Obama.

Tool Kit
First-Read Guide and Model Annotation

STANDARDS
Reading Literature
By the end of the year, read and comprehend literature, including stories, dramas, and poems, at the high end of grades 6–8 text complexity band independently and proficiently.

448 UNIT 5 • INVENTION

Uncle Marcos

Concept Vocabulary

As you conduct your first read of "Uncle Marcos," you will encounter these words. Before reading, note how familiar you are with each word. Then, rank the words in order from most familiar (1) to least familiar (6).

WORD	YOUR RANKING
decipher	
invincible	
contraption	
newfangled	
ingenuity	
improvisations	

After completing the first read, come back to the concept vocabulary and review your rankings. Mark changes to your original rankings as needed.

First Read FICTION

Apply these strategies as you conduct your first read. You will have an opportunity to complete the close-read notes after your first read.

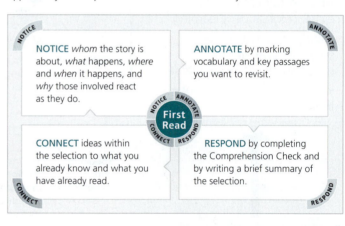

AUTHOR'S PERSPECTIVE Kelly Gallagher, M.Ed.

Reading Reasons Students often ask "Why should I read?" Increasingly, teachers see students who often give up easily when confronted with challenging reading material such as a biology textbook or a state-mandated exam. They are unable, or unwilling, to tackle difficult text. How do teachers turn around this apathy? How do teachers shelter fragile adolescent readers and help them grow into people for whom reading matters? Building reading motivation is complex, as there isn't a single correct motivational tool, but together, many of these techniques send the message that reading is rewarding.

- Give students access to high-interest reading material, which is provided in this program.
- Give students a time and place to read.

ANCHOR TEXT | NOVEL EXCERPT

Uncle Marcos
from The House of the Spirits

Isabel Allende

translated by
Magda Bogin

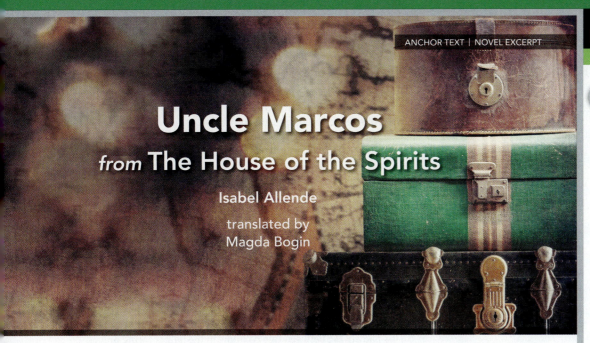

BACKGROUND
"Uncle Marcos" is from Isabel Allende's first novel, which began as a letter to her 100-year-old grandfather. This excerpt draws on the Greek myth of Icarus and Daedalus. In the myth, Daedalus invents a pair of wings and teaches his son how to use them, but warns him not to fly too close to the sun because the wax in the wings would melt. Icarus is too excited to listen, and he drowns in the ocean after his wings melt.

1   It had been two years since Clara had last seen her Uncle Marcos, but she remembered him very well. His was the only perfectly clear image she retained from her whole childhood, and in order to describe him she did not need to consult the daguerreotype[1] in the drawing room that showed him dressed as an explorer leaning on an old-fashioned double-barreled rifle with his right foot on the neck of a Malaysian tiger, the same triumphant position in which she had seen the Virgin standing between plaster clouds and pallid angels at the main altar, one foot on the vanquished devil. All Clara had to do to see her uncle was close her eyes and there he was, weather-beaten and thin, with a pirate's mustache through which his strange, sharklike smile peered out at her. It seemed impossible that he could be inside that long black box that was lying in the middle of the courtyard.

2   Each time Uncle Marcos had visited his sister Nívea's home, he had stayed for several months, to the immense joy of his nieces and nephews, particularly Clara, causing a storm in which the

---
1. **daguerreotype** (duh GEHR oh typ) *n.* early type of photograph.

NOTES

CLOSE READ
ANNOTATE: In paragraph 1, mark details that show how Clara pictures her uncle, particularly his mustache and smile.

QUESTION: Why does the author use these descriptive details?

CONCLUDE: What is the effect of these details?

Uncle Marcos 449

TEACHING

NOTES

sharp lines of domestic order blurred. The house became a clutter of trunks, of animals in jars of formaldehyde,[2] of Indian lances and sailor's bundles. In every part of the house people kept tripping over his equipment, and all sorts of unfamiliar animals appeared that had traveled from remote lands only to meet their death beneath Nana's irate broom in the farthest corners of the house. Uncle Marcos's manners were those of a cannibal, as Severo put it. He spent the whole night making incomprehensible movements in the drawing room; later they turned out to be exercises designed to perfect the mind's control over the body and to improve digestion. He performed alchemy[3] experiments in the kitchen, filling the house with fetid smoke and ruining pots and pans with solid substances that stuck to their bottoms and were impossible to remove. While the rest of the household tried to sleep, he dragged his suitcases up and down the halls, practiced making strange, high-pitched sounds on savage instruments, and taught Spanish to a parrot whose native language was an Amazonic dialect. During the day, he slept in a hammock that he had strung between two columns in the hall, wearing only a loincloth that put Severo in a terrible mood but that Nívea forgave because Marcos had convinced her that it was the same costume in which Jesus of Nazareth had preached. Clara remembered perfectly, even though she had been only a tiny child, the first time her Uncle Marcos came to the house after one of his voyages. He settled in as if he planned to stay forever. After a short time, bored with having to appear at ladies' gatherings where the mistress of the house played the piano, with playing cards, and with dodging all his relatives' pressures to pull himself together and take a job as a clerk in Severo del Valle's law practice, he bought a barrel organ and took to the streets with the hope of seducing his Cousin Antonieta and entertaining the public in the bargain. The machine was just a rusty box with wheels, but he painted it with seafaring designs and gave it a fake ship's smokestack. It ended up looking like a coal stove. The organ played either a military march or a waltz, and in between turns of the handle the parrot, who had managed to learn Spanish although he had not lost his foreign accent, would draw a crowd with his piercing shrieks. He also plucked slips of paper from a box with his beak, by way of selling fortunes to the curious. The little pink, green, and blue papers were so clever that they always divulged the exact secret wishes of the customers. Besides fortunes there were little balls of sawdust to amuse the children. The idea of the organ was a last desperate attempt to win the hand of Cousin Antonieta after more conventional means of courting her had failed. Marcos thought

2. **formaldehyde** (fawr MAL duh hyd) *n.* solution used as a preservative.
3. **alchemy** (AL kuh mee) *n.* early form of chemistry, with philosophical and magical associations.

450 UNIT 5 • INVENTION

PERSONALIZE FOR LEARNING

English Language Support

Sentence Structure The author uses long paragraphs and long sentences in her writing. This serves an important purpose in telling the story. These long sentences and paragraphs help create the chaotic mood of the home. Call students' attention to the sentence in paragraph 2 that begins, "After a short time, bored with having to appear . . ."

Read the sentence, using the commas as break points, and explain that several things happen in this sentence. Ask students to help make a list of each of the things that happen in the sentence, and have them consider why the writer included all this information in one sentence. **ALL LEVELS**

450 UNIT 5 • INVENTION

no woman in her right mind could remain impassive before a barrel-organ serenade. He stood beneath her window one evening and played his military march and his waltz just as she was taking tea with a group of female friends. Antonieta did not realize the music was meant for her until the parrot called her by her full name, at which point she appeared in the window. Her reaction was not what her suitor had hoped for. Her friends offered to spread the news to every salon[4] in the city, and the next day people thronged the downtown streets hoping to see Severo del Valle's brother-in-law playing the organ and selling little sawdust balls with a moth-eaten parrot, for the sheer pleasure of proving that even in the best of families there could be good reason for embarrassment. In the face of this stain to the family reputation, Marcos was forced to give up organ-grinding and resort to less conspicuous ways of winning over his Cousin Antonieta, but he did not renounce his goal. In any case, he did not succeed, because from one day to the next the young lady married a diplomat who was twenty years her senior; he took her to live in a tropical country whose name no one could recall, except that it suggested negritude,[5] bananas, and palm trees, where she managed to recover from the memory of that suitor who had ruined her seventeenth year with his military march and his waltz. Marcos sank into a deep depression that lasted two or three days, at the end of which he announced that he would never marry and that he was embarking on a trip around the world. He sold his organ to a blind man and left the parrot to Clara, but Nana secretly poisoned it with an overdose of cod-liver oil, because no one could stand its lusty glance, its fleas, and its harsh, tuneless hawking of paper fortunes and sawdust balls.

3   That was Marcos's longest trip. He returned with a shipment of enormous boxes that were piled in the far courtyard, between the chicken coop and the woodshed, until the winter was over. At the first signs of spring he had them transferred to the parade grounds, a huge park where people would gather to watch the soldiers file by on Independence Day, with the goosestep they had learned from the Prussians. When the crates were opened, they were found to contain loose bits of wood, metal, and painted cloth. Marcos spent two weeks assembling the contents according to an instruction manual written in English, which he was able to **decipher** thanks to his **invincible** imagination and a small dictionary. When the job was finished, it turned out to be a bird of prehistoric dimensions, with the face of a furious eagle, wings that moved, and a propeller on its back. It caused an uproar. The families of the oligarchy[6] forgot all about the barrel organ, and Marcos became the star attraction of the season.

---

4. **salon** (suh LON) *n.* regular gathering of distinguished guests that meets in a private home.
5. **negritude** (NEHG ruh tood) *n.* black people and their cultural heritage.
6. **oligarchy** (OL ih gahr kee) *n.* government ruled by only a few people.

NOTES

CLOSE READ
ANNOTATE: Mark the sentence in the latter part of paragraph 2 that suggests how Antonieta reacts to Marcos's barrel-organ music.

QUESTION: Why does the author provide so little description of her reaction?

CONCLUDE: What is the effect of this choice to suggest but not describe Antonieta's reaction?

decipher (dih SY fuhr) *v.* succeed in interpreting or understanding something

invincible (ihn VIHN suh buhl) *adj.* impossible to defeat

Uncle Marcos 451

Remind students to focus on syntax. You may wish to model the close read using the following think-aloud format. Possible responses to questions on the student page are included.

ANNOTATE: As I read paragraph 2, I mark the sentence that suggests Antonieta's reaction to Uncle Marcos's barrel-organ music.

QUESTION: The author's choice to provide so little description of Antonieta's reaction deliberately contrasts with both Uncle Marcos's and the reader's expectations. While the minimal description allows the reader to fill in the gaps, it also suggests Antonieta's indifference to Uncle Marcos and his efforts to woo her.

CONCLUDE: This choice creates humor by contrasting Uncle Marcos's elaborate overtures with Antonieta's indifference to them.

WriteNow Analyze and Interpret

Narrative Call attention to the sentence lengths in paragraph 2. The writer employs lengthy sentences as a tool to create an image of the frantic nature of life with Uncle Marcos. A single sentence can be four or five lines and contain several connected thoughts. These sentences, while long are grammatically correct, using wordy descriptions and dependent clauses to convey information. Have students write their own long sentence about a chaotic time during the school day. Then have volunteers share their writing. Discuss the effectiveness of the tool, as well as its drawbacks, in fiction writing.

Whole-Class Learning   451

TEACHING

CLOSER LOOK

Analyze Motivation

Students may have marked paragraph 3 during their first read. Encourage them to talk about the annotations that they marked. You may want to model a close read with the class based on the highlights shown in the text.

ANNOTATE: Have students mark details in paragraph 3 that hint at why Uncle Marcos decides to take this flight, or have students participate while you highlight them.

QUESTION: Guide students to consider what these details might tell them. Ask what a reader can infer about Uncle Marcos's reasons based on his actions and his reactions to others' interest.

Possible response: Uncle Marcus wants to cause a sensation by flying.

CONCLUDE: Help students to formulate conclusions about the importance of these details in the text. Ask students why the author might have included these details.

Possible response: The author wants the reader to know what motivates Uncle Marcos. Uncle Marcos is not just motivated by showmanship and a wish to be the center of attention. He is ambitious—he wants to restore his reputation with his family by achieving immortal fame with his flying machine.

Remind students that **motivation** is the reason or reasons for a character's actions. Motivation may arise from internal causes, such as love, loneliness, or jealousy, or from external causes, such as danger or poverty.

NOTES

contraption (kuhn TRAP shuhn) *n.* machine that seems strange or unnecessarily complicated

newfangled (NOO fang uhld) *adj.* invented only recently and, therefore, strange-seeming

People took Sunday outings to see the bird; souvenir vendors and strolling photographers made a fortune. Nonetheless, the public's interest quickly waned. But then Marcos announced that as soon as the weather cleared he planned to take off in his bird and cross the mountain range. The news spread, making this the most talked-about event of the year. The contraption lay with its stomach on terra firma,[7] heavy and sluggish and looking more like a wounded duck than like one of those newfangled airplanes they were starting to produce in the United States. There was nothing in its appearance to suggest that it could move, much less take flight across the snowy peaks. Journalists and the curious flocked to see it. Marcos smiled his immutable[8] smile before the avalanche of questions and posed for photographers without offering the least technical or scientific explanation of how he hoped to carry out his plan. People came from the provinces to see the sight. Forty years later his great-nephew Nicolás, whom Marcos did not live to see, unearthed the desire to fly that had always existed in the men of his lineage. Nicolás was interested in doing it for commercial reasons, in a gigantic hot-air sausage on which would be printed an advertisement for carbonated drinks. But when Marcos announced his plane trip, no one believed that his contraption could be put to any practical use. The appointed day dawned full of clouds, but so many people had turned out that Marcos did not want to disappoint them. He showed up punctually at the appointed spot and did not once look up at the sky, which was growing darker and darker with thick gray clouds. The astonished crowd filled all the nearby streets, perching on rooftops and the balconies of the nearest houses and squeezing into the park. No political gathering managed to attract so many people until half a century later, when the first Marxist candidate attempted, through strictly democratic channels, to become President. Clara would remember this holiday as long as she lived. People dressed in their spring best, thereby getting a step ahead of the official opening of the season, the men in white linen suits and the ladies in Italian straw hats that were all the rage that year. Groups of elementary-school children paraded with their teachers, clutching flowers for the hero. Marcos accepted their bouquets and joked that they might as well hold on to them and wait for him to crash, so they could take them directly to his funeral. The bishop himself, accompanied by two incense bearers, appeared to bless the bird without having been asked, and the police band played happy, unpretentious music that pleased everyone. The police, on horseback and carrying lances, had trouble keeping the crowds far enough away from the center of

---

7. **terra firma** (TEHR uh FUR muh) *n.* firm earth; solid ground (from Latin).
8. **immutable** (ih MYOOT uh buhl) *adj.* never changing.

the park, where Marcos waited dressed in mechanic's overalls, with huge racer's goggles and an explorer's helmet. He was also equipped with a compass, a telescope, and several strange maps that he had traced himself based on various theories of Leonardo da Vinci and on the polar knowledge of the Incas.[9] Against all logic, on the second try the bird lifted off without mishap and with a certain elegance, accompanied by the creaking of its skeleton and the roar of its motor. It rose flapping its wings and disappeared into the clouds, to a send-off of applause, whistlings, handkerchiefs, drumrolls, and the sprinkling of holy water. All that remained on earth were the comments of the amazed crowd below and a multitude of experts, who attempted to provide a reasonable explanation of the miracle. Clara continued to stare at the sky long after her uncle had become invisible. She thought she saw him ten minutes later, but it was only a migrating sparrow. After three days the initial euphoria that had accompanied the first airplane flight in the country died down and no one gave the episode another thought, except for Clara, who continued to peer at the horizon.

4   After a week with no word from the flying uncle, people began to speculate that he had gone so high that he had disappeared into outer space, and the ignorant suggested he would reach the moon. With a mixture of sadness and relief, Severo decided that his brother-in-law and his machine must have fallen into some hidden crevice of the *cordillera*,[10] where they would never be found. Nívea wept disconsolately and lit candles to San Antonio, patron of lost objects. Severo opposed the idea of having masses said, because he did not believe in them as a way of getting into heaven, much less of returning to earth, and he maintained that masses and religious vows, like the selling of indulgences, images, and scapulars,[11] were a dishonest business. Because of his attitude, Nívea and Nana had the children say the rosary[12] behind their father's back for nine days. Meanwhile, groups of volunteer explorers and mountain climbers tirelessly searched peaks and passes, combing every accessible stretch of land until they finally returned in triumph to hand the family the mortal remains of the deceased in a sealed black coffin. The intrepid traveler was laid to rest in a grandiose funeral. His death made him a hero and his name was on the front page of all the papers for several days. The same multitude that had gathered to see him off the day he flew away in his

---

NOTES

CLOSE READ
ANNOTATE: Toward the end of paragraph 3, mark details that describe how Marcos is dressed as he waits to begin his flight.

QUESTION: Why does the author mention these details?

CONCLUDE: What do these details show about Marcos's knowledge and experience?

---

9. **Leonardo da Vinci . . . Incas** Leonardo da Vinci (1452–1519) was an Italian painter, sculptor, architect, and scientist. The Incas were Native Americans who dominated ancient Peru until Spanish conquest.
10. **cordillera** (kawr dihl YAIR uh) *n.* system or chain of mountains.
11. **indulgences, images, and scapulars** Indulgences are pardons for sins. Images are pictures or sculptures of religious figures. Scapulars are garments worn by Roman Catholics as tokens of religious devotion.
12. **say the rosary** use a set of beads to say prayers.

TEACHING

● CLOSE READ ✎

Remind students to focus on Uncle Marcos's unusual behavior and beliefs. You may wish to model the close read using the following think-aloud format. Possible responses to questions on the student page are included.

ANNOTATE: As I read paragraph 5, I notice that the crystal ball seems magical because Uncle Marcos bought it at a Persian bazaar and it was from the East. It seems ordinary because it is actually a buoy from a fishing boat.

QUESTION: The author includes these contrasting elements to show that there are two ways to see a crystal ball—as a source of insight or as a tool of deception and fraud.

CONCLUDE: These details add humor to the description and help to further develop Uncle Marcos's character.

NOTES

bird paraded past his coffin. The entire family wept as befit the occasion, except for Clara, who continued to watch the sky with the patience of an astronomer. One week after he had been buried, Uncle Marcos, a bright smile playing behind his pirate's mustache, appeared in person in the doorway of Nívea and Severo del Valle's house. Thanks to the surreptitious[13] prayers of the women and children, as he himself admitted, he was alive and well and in full possession of his faculties, including his sense of humor. Despite the noble lineage of his aerial maps, the flight had been a failure. He had lost his airplane and had to return on foot, but he had not broken any bones and his adventurous spirit was intact. This confirmed the family's eternal devotion to San Antonio, but was not taken as a warning by future generations, who also tried to fly, although by different means. Legally, however, Marcos was a corpse. Severo del Valle was obliged to use all his legal **ingenuity** to bring his brother-in-law back to life and the full rights of citizenship. When the coffin was pried open in the presence of the appropriate authorities, it was found to contain a bag of sand. This discovery ruined the reputation, up till then untarnished, of the volunteer explorers and mountain climbers, who from that day on were considered little better than a pack of bandits.

5   Marcos's heroic resurrection made everyone forget about his barrel-organ phase. Once again he was a sought-after guest in all the city's salons and, at least for a while, his name was cleared. Marcos stayed in his sister's house for several months. One night he left without saying goodbye, leaving behind his trunks, his books, his weapons, his boots, and all his belongings. Severo, and even Nívea herself, breathed a sigh of relief. His visit had gone on too long. But Clara was so upset that she spent a week walking in her sleep and sucking her thumb. The little girl, who was only seven at the time, had learned to read from her uncle's storybooks and been closer to him than any other member of the family because of her prophesying powers. Marcos maintained that his niece's gift could be a source of income and a good opportunity for him to cultivate his own clairvoyance. He believed that all human beings possessed this ability, particularly his own family, and that if it did not function well it was simply due to a lack of training. He bought a crystal ball in the Persian bazaar, insisting that it had magic powers and was from the East (although it was later found to be part of a buoy from a fishing boat), set it down on a background of black velvet, and announced that he could tell people's fortunes, cure the evil eye, and improve the quality of dreams, all for the modest sum of five centavos. His first customers were the maids from around the neighborhood. One of them had been accused of stealing, because her employer had misplaced a valuable ring. The crystal ball revealed the

ingenuity (ihn juh NOO uh tee) *n.* quality of being original and clever

CLOSE READ
ANNOTATE: In paragraph 5, mark details that present the crystal ball as mysterious and magical. Mark other details that present it as ordinary.

QUESTION: Why does the author include these contrasting elements?

CONCLUDE: What is the effect of these details?

---

13. **surreptitious** (sur uhp TIHSH uhs) *adj.* secretive.

454 UNIT 5 • INVENTION

VOCABULARY DEVELOPMENT

Word Analysis Call students' attention to the concept vocabulary word *ingenuity* in paragraph 4. Point out that the Latin root of this word is *-gen-*, which indicates a connection to birth or heredity. Ask students to explain how this root is related to the meaning of *ingenuity* provided here. Then, ask students to create a list of other words that have the same root. Guide them to the words *genus* and *genius*. Have students look up the meanings of these words. Finally, discuss how they all relate to the Latin root.

exact location of the object in question: it had rolled beneath a wardrobe. The next day there was a line outside the front door of the house. There were coachmen, storekeepers, and milkmen; later a few municipal employees and distinguished ladies made a discreet appearance, slinking along the side walls of the house to keep from being recognized. The customers were received by Nana, who ushered them into the waiting room and collected their fees. This task kept her busy throughout the day and demanded so much of her time that the family began to complain that all there ever was for dinner was old string beans and jellied quince. Marcos decorated the carriage house with some frayed curtains that had once belonged in the drawing room but that neglect and age had turned to dusty rags. There he and Clara received the customers. The two divines wore tunics "the color of the men of light," as Marcos called the color yellow. Nana had dyed them with saffron powder, boiling them in pots usually reserved for rice and pasta. In addition to his tunic, Marcos wore a turban around his head and an Egyptian amulet around his neck. He had grown a beard and let his hair grow long and he was thinner than ever before. Marcos and Clara were utterly convincing, especially because the child had no need to look into the crystal ball to guess what her clients wanted to hear. She would whisper in her Uncle Marcos's ear, and he in turn would transmit the message to the client, along with any **improvisations** of his own that he thought pertinent. Thus their fame spread, because all those who arrived sad and bedraggled at the consulting room left filled with hope. Unrequited lovers were told how to win over indifferent hearts, and the poor left with foolproof tips on how to place their money at the dog track. Business grew so prosperous that the waiting room was always packed with people, and Nana began to suffer dizzy spells from being on her feet so many hours a day. This time Severo had no need to intervene to put a stop to his brother-in-law's venture, for both Marcos and Clara, realizing

improvisations (ihm pruh vy ZAY shuhnz) *n.* things that are created without any preparation

HOW LANGUAGE WORKS

Linking Verbs and Subject Complements
Use paragraph 5 to review this grammar concept with students. A linking verb is a verb that links the subject of a sentence to a noun or an adjective that identifies or describes the subject of the sentence. Linking verbs connect the subject with the subject complement, a noun, pronoun, or adjective that completes the thought. Read aloud the following sentence part from paragraph 5 of the text, noting that it can stand alone and function as a complete sentence: *Marcos and Clara were utterly convincing . . .*

Have students identify the linking verb (*were*) and the subject complement (*convincing*), and ask students to find other examples of linking verbs and subject complements in the text. Have several students share their example sentences. Then have other students identify the linking verbs and subject complements in the examples.

TEACHING

● CLOSE READ

Remind students to consider on Uncle Marcos's stories. You may wish to model the close read using the following think-aloud format. Possible responses to questions on the student page are included.

ANNOTATE: As I read paragraph 6, I notice and mark details that relate to the senses.

QUESTION: I think the author wanted to show the strong impression that Clara's uncle had made on her.

CONCLUDE: These details are used to build Marcos's larger-than-life character. They give readers a clearer look at Marcos's character.

NOTES

CLOSE READ
ANNOTATE: In the description of Marcos's stories in paragraph 6, mark details that relate to the senses of touch, sight, and hearing.

QUESTION: Why does the author include these sensory details?

CONCLUDE: What is the effect of these details?

that their unerring guesses could alter the fate of their clients, who always followed their advice to the letter, became frightened and decided that this was a job for swindlers. They abandoned their carriage-house oracle and split the profits, even though the only one who had cared about the material side of things had been Nana.

6 Of all the del Valle children, Clara was the one with the greatest interest in and stamina for her uncle's stories. She could repeat each and every one of them. She knew by heart words from several dialects of the Indians, was acquainted with their customs, and could describe the exact way in which they pierced their lips and earlobes with wooden shafts, their initiation rites, the names of the most poisonous snakes, and the appropriate antidotes for each. Her uncle was so eloquent that the child could feel in her own skin the burning sting of snakebites, see reptiles slide across the carpet between the legs of the jacaranda room divider, and hear the shrieks of macaws behind the drawing-room drapes. She did not hesitate as she recalled Lope de Aguirre's search for El Dorado[14], or the unpronounceable names of the flora and fauna her extraordinary uncle had seen; she knew about the lamas who take salt tea with yak lard and she could give detailed descriptions of the opulent women of Tahiti, the rice fields of China, or the white prairies of the North, where the eternal ice kills animals and men who lose their way, turning them to stone in seconds. Marcos had various travel journals in which he recorded his excursions and impressions, as well as a collection of maps and books of stories and fairy tales that he kept in the trunks he stored in the junk room at the far end of the third courtyard. From there they were hauled out to inhabit the dreams of his descendants, until they were mistakenly burned half a century later on an infamous pyre.

7 Now Marcos had returned from his last journey in a coffin. He had died of a mysterious African plague that had turned him as yellow and wrinkled as a piece of parchment. When he realized he was ill, he set out for home with the hope that his sister's ministrations and Dr. Cuevas's knowledge would restore his health and youth, but he was unable to withstand the sixty days on ship and died at the latitude of Guayaquil, ravaged by fever and hallucinating about musky women and hidden treasure. The captain of the ship, an Englishman by the name of Longfellow, was about to throw him overboard wrapped in a flag, but Marcos, despite his savage appearance and his delirium, had made so many friends on board and seduced so many women that the

---

14. **Lope de Aguirre's...El Dorado** Lope de Aguirre (LOH pay day ah GEER ray) was a Spanish adventurer (1510–1561) who journeyed through South America in search of the legendary city of El Dorado, which was supposedly rich in gold.

PERSONALIZE FOR LEARNING

Strategic Support

Choral Reading Call student attention to paragraph 7. Throughout this story, the author makes use of very long sentences to help create the mood of the story. She does this again in paragraph 7 by describing Uncle Marcos's final, real demise. Do a choral reading of the final paragraph. Have pairs of students read each sentence slowly and deliberately to create the mood the narrator is trying to evoke here. Ask students to discuss how the read-aloud differed from their original first read of the paragraph.

passengers prevented him from doing so, and Longfellow was obliged to store the body side by side with the vegetables of the Chinese cook, to preserve it from the heat and mosquitoes of the tropics until the ship's carpenter had time to improvise a coffin. At El Callao they obtained a more appropriate container, and several days later the captain, furious at all the troubles this passenger had caused the shipping company and himself personally, unloaded him without a backward glance, surprised that not a soul was there to receive the body or cover the expenses he had incurred. Later he learned that the post office in these latitudes was not as reliable as that of far-off England, and that all his telegrams had vaporized en route. Fortunately for Longfellow, a customs lawyer who was a friend of the del Valle family appeared and offered to take charge, placing Marcos and all his paraphernalia in a freight car, which he shipped to the capital to the only known address of the deceased: his sister's house....

NOTES

Comprehension Check
Complete the following items after you finish your first read.

1. How does Uncle Marcos try to win the hand of Cousin Antonieta?

2. What does Uncle Marcos make from the materials he brings back in "enormous boxes"?

3. What special power does Clara have that Marcos pretends to possess?

4. **Notebook** To confirm your understanding, write a summary of "Uncle Marcos."

RESEARCH

Research to Clarify Choose at least one unfamiliar detail from the text. Briefly research that detail. In what way does the information you learned shed light on an aspect of the story?

DIGITAL PERSPECTIVES

Comprehension Check

Possible responses:
1. He builds a barrel organ and serenades her.
2. He builds an airplane.
3. She has the power to predict the future.
4. Uncle Marcos is an adventurer who loves exploring the world. He also craves attention and does many things to gain it, including flying a primitive plane. He is a romantic, trying to win over Cousin Antonieta. He is a schemer, with his fortune-telling business.

Research

Research to Clarify If students struggle to decide on a detail to research, you may want to suggest that they focus on clairvoyance, alchemy, primitive flying machines, or Malaysian tigers.

PERSONALIZE FOR LEARNING

Challenge
Make Connections As suggested in paragraph 6, Uncle Marcos is a unique character. He is the relative that legends are made of, even if not everything about him was true or real. While it might be impossible to relate to an uncle like him, families are full of unique characters. Think about a unique character in your family or life. Write a short paragraph in the author's style to describe a moment in that person's life.

TEACHING

Jump Start

CLOSE READ Why are some adventure stories so exciting to read? Could it be because they satisfy some deep, unfulfilled desire for adventure in their readers? What adventure would be a dream come true for you?

Close Read the Text

Walk students through the Annotation Model on the student page. Encourage them to complete items 2 and 3 on their own. Review and discuss the sections students have marked. If needed, continue to model close reading by using the Annotation Highlights in the Interactive Teacher's Edition.

Analyze the Text

Possible responses:

1. Uncle Marcos stands out in Clara's memory because he was a remarkable figure. He traveled the world and brought back many stories. He also created adventures, such as building and flying in a winged machine. He also believed in her ability to prophesy, and they worked together to tell fortunes.

2. He took on the flying project after coming out of a depression, and it inspired him and kept him going. It reinforced the notion of him as a great adventurer for both him and his niece. **DOK 1**

3. In both cases Uncle Marcos wishes to be loved and admired—in the first by Cousin Antonieta and in the second by the people of the community. He is not successful at gaining love through the barrel organ incident, but he gets much attention and admiration through the mechanical bird incident.

4. Student responses will vary, but answers should include an explanation about what the story taught them about how and why inventions are created. Some students may see the importance of imagination to invention. **DOK 4**

FORMATIVE ASSESSMENT

Analyze the Text

- **If** students fail to cite evidence, **then** remind them to support their ideas with specific information.
- **If** students struggle to answer the questions, **then** revisit the sections of the text that will help them and discuss the unclear concepts.

458 UNIT 5 • INVENTION

MAKING MEANING

UNCLE MARCOS

Close Read the Text

1. This model, from paragraph 3 of the text, shows two sample annotations, along with questions and conclusions. Close read the passage, and find another detail to annotate. Then, write a question and your conclusion.

> **ANNOTATE:** These phrases have similar structures but present contrasting ideas.
> **QUESTION:** Why does the author use these similar phrases?
> **CONCLUDE:** The structure emphasizes the contrast and hints at the surprise of the successful lift-off.

Against all logic, on the second try the bird lifted off **without mishap** and **with a certain elegance,** accompanied by the creaking of its skeleton and the roar of its motor. It rose flapping its wings and disappeared into the clouds, to a send-off of **applause, whistlings, handkerchiefs, drumrolls, and the sprinkling of holy water.**

> **ANNOTATE:** This series of nouns indicates the reactions of the crowd.
> **QUESTION:** Why does the author present the crowd's reaction in this way?
> **CONCLUDE:** The series of nouns shows how different types of people respond. The nouns suggest their social roles.

Tool Kit
Close-Read Guide and Model Annotation

2. For more practice, go back into the text and complete the close-read notes.

3. Revisit a section of the text you found important during your first read. Read this section closely and **annotate** what you notice. Ask yourself **questions** such as "Why did the author make this choice?" What can you **conclude**?

Analyze the Text

CITE TEXTUAL EVIDENCE to support your answers.

📔 **Notebook** Respond to these questions.

1. **Analyze** Why might Uncle Marcos be "the only perfectly clear image" Clara remembers from her childhood? Explain.

2. **Interpret** What motivates Uncle Marcos to undertake the flying machine project? Explain your thinking.

3. **Compare and Contrast** In what ways is the barrel organ incident similar to and different from the incident with the mechanical bird?

4. **Essential Question:** *Are inventions realized through inspiration or perspiration?* What has this story taught you about the concept of invention?

STANDARDS
Reading Literature
- Cite the textual evidence that most strongly supports an analysis of what the text says explicitly as well as inferences drawn from the text.
- Analyze how particular lines of dialogue or incidents in a story or drama propel the action, reveal aspects of a character, or provoke a decision.

ESSENTIAL QUESTION: Are inventions realized through inspiration or perspiration?

DIGITAL PERSPECTIVES

Analyze Craft and Structure

Propelling the Action: Character A **character** is a personality that is part of a story. A character may be a person, an animal, or even an object. In all narratives, the **plot,** or sequence of related events, is moved by a conflict that characters face. The story involves the ways in which characters experience and solve the conflict.

- The **main character** is the most important character in the narrative, the one whose conflict drives the plot.
- **Character traits** are the qualities, attitudes, and values that a character has. For example, a character might be reliable, smart, selfish, or stubborn.
- A **round character** has many different traits, both good and bad. In contrast, a **flat character** is one-dimensional, displaying only a single trait.
- A **dynamic character** changes and learns. A **static character** does not change or learn.

Writers use a variety of techniques to portray characters. They describe what characters look like and how they behave. They reveal what characters want, feel, think, and say. **Dialogue,** or words characters say, is a tool most fiction writers use to help portray characters. Dialogue reflects the words as a character speaks them, and is set off with quotation marks. In this excerpt, Isabel Allende does not use dialogue in a traditional way. She refers to things characters say, but does not quote them directly.

Practice

CITE TEXTUAL EVIDENCE to support your answers.

Notebook Respond to these questions.

1. **(a)** What happens to Nívea's household when Uncle Marcos visits? Cite details that support your response. **(b)** What does his effect on the household tell you about Uncle Marcos's character?

2. **(a)** What does Clara do repeatedly after her uncle disappears on the flying machine? **(b)** How does her reaction differ from those of other family members? **(c)** What does Clara's reaction show about her character and relationship to Uncle Marcos? Explain.

3. Allende does not quote characters directly. However, she sometimes tells the reader what they say. Cite an example of a statement Uncle Marcos makes. Explain what this statement shows about his character.

4. Reread sections of the text that describe Clara and Uncle Marcos. **(a)** Determine whether each character is round or flat. **(b)** Determine whether each character is static or dynamic. For both (a) and (b), explain your responses and cite textual details that support them.

Analyze Craft and Structure

Propelling the Action: Character One way to think about characters is to think of how they drive the plot and reveal their personalities through emotions and behavior. For more support, see **Analyze Craft and Structure: Character.**

Practice

Possible responses:

1. (a) Uncle Marcos creates messes and chaos when he stays with his sister Nívea. For example, the grandmother has to stay on her feet all day to support the fortune-telling business. (b) They show that he acts in unconventional ways and does not care what others think.

2. (a) She continues to watch for his return. (b) Everyone else assumes he died. (c) Clara believes in her Uncle Marcos, unlike others.

3. Uncle Marcos refers to the fortune-telling tunics as "the color of the men of light," suggesting that yellow is a magical color. This example shows that he is persuasive and tricky.

4. (a) Both are round characters. (b) Clara is a dynamic character. Uncle Marcos is a static character. They are round characters because they have many traits. He is bold and exaggerates. She is loyal and has a sixth sense. Uncle Marcos is a static character because his personality remains unchanged throughout the selection. He continues his crazy antics and adventures even though they are usually unsuccessful. Clara is a dynamic character because she grows and learns from Uncle Marcos's stories and her experiences with her uncle.

FORMATIVE ASSESSMENT

Analyze Craft and Structure

If students struggle to identify the components of plot in "Uncle Marcos," **then** have them revisit the story together to find examples. For Reteach and Practice, see **Analyze Craft and Structure: Characters (RP).**

PERSONALIZE FOR LEARNING

English Language Support

Characters Ask students to choose a story that they have read recently that has clearly defined characters.

Have pairs of students discuss and collaborate on writing a few sentences that describe the difference between the characters. **EMERGING**

Have students retell the story by giving the characters additional traits. Then have them write a few sentences describing how the story and readers' reactions might change. **EXPANDING**

Ask students to rewrite the story with the addition of a few more characters. Then have them write a paragraph explaining why they added these characters and whether they are round/flat and dynamic/static. **BRIDGING**

An expanded **English Language Support Lesson** on Characters is available in the Interactive Teacher's Edition.

Whole-Class Learning

TEACHING

Concept Vocabulary

Why These Words?
Possible responses:
1. The vocabulary words help explain how Uncle Marcos makes and works on his devices.
2. *incomprehensible, alchemy, imagination, mechanic, clairvoyance, venture, excursions, impressions*

Practice
1. newfangled   4. ingenuity
2. decipher   5. contraption
3. improvisations   6. invincible

Word Network
Possible words: *equipment, unfamiliar, designed, improve, assembling*

Word Study
For more support, see **Concept Vocabulary and Word Study.**

Possible responses:
1. It tells you that the word refers to the state or quality of being able to do something.
2. The word *responsibility* refers to the quality of being responsible, or to something for which one is responsible. Taking care of a pet would be one example of a responsibility.

FORMATIVE ASSESSMENT

Concept Vocabulary
If students struggle to understand and apply the concept vocabulary, **then** review the words and meanings by finding them in the text.

Word Study
If students struggle to understand the suffix *-ity*, **then** help them to compose a short list of words that end in *-ity* and work together to determine what the words mean and how the suffix contributes to their meaning. For Reteach and Practice, see **Word Study: Latin Suffix -ity (RP).**

UNCLE MARCOS

LANGUAGE DEVELOPMENT

Concept Vocabulary

| decipher | contraption | ingenuity |
| invincible | newfangled | improvisations |

Why These Words? The concept vocabulary words are all related to cleverness and innovation. For example, Uncle Marcos manages to *decipher* an instruction manual written in English in order to build his flying machine. Severo must use his *ingenuity*, or original, clever thinking to restore Uncle Marcos's citizenship rights.

1. How does the concept vocabulary help the reader understand Uncle Marcos as an inventor?

2. What other words in the selection describe Uncle Marcos's inventions or inventiveness?

Practice

Notebook The concept vocabulary words appear in "Uncle Marcos." Complete each sentence with the correct word.

1. A person who prefers old-fashioned objects might not want something _____.
2. A spy might have to _____ a code to find the hidden message.
3. If things do not go according to plan, you might have to think quickly and make _____.
4. You might admire a creative person's _____ in solving problems.
5. People might call a strange or unusual machine a _____.
6. A superhero who is _____ has nothing to fear from a villain's attacks.

Word Study

Latin Suffix: -ity The Latin suffix *-ity* means "state or quality of being." The author of this story refers to Severo's legal *ingenuity*, or his quality of being *ingenious* (original, clever, and resourceful). Use what you know about the Latin suffix *-ity* to answer these questions.

1. How does the Latin suffix *-ity* help you understand the meaning of the word *ability* as it is used in paragraph 5?

2. Explain what the word *responsibility* means. Then, give an example of a situation in which a person demonstrates responsibility.

WORD NETWORK
Add words related to invention from the text to your Word Network.

STANDARDS
Language
- Demonstrate command of the conventions of standard English grammar and usage when writing or speaking.
- Determine or clarify the meaning of unknown and multiple-meaning words or phrases based on *grade 8 reading and content*, choosing flexibly from a range of strategies.
  b. Use common, grade-appropriate Greek or Latin affixes and roots as clues to the meaning of a word.

AUTHOR'S PERSPECTIVE — Elfrieda Hiebert, Ph.D.

Digital Tools As students develop and expand their Word Networks, remind them of the digital tools available and of their value. Explain what digital tools offer—pronunciation, audio, word families, definitions, links to synonyms and antonyms, interactive levels of complexity of synonyms and antonyms, and words in context sentences. Using digital tools to access word families is especially helpful in a cross-cultural context. A word family for science, for instance, might include the words *botanist, chemist, geneticist, neurologist, nutritionist, physicist,* and *zoologist,* as they all end with the suffix *-ist*. A word family for westward expansion might be organized around the common concept and so include the words *settler, heritage, mission,* and *manifest destiny*. To conclude, help students understand that digital tools also have drawbacks. For instance, the word family feature doesn't show how the words are related in meaning, only in sound.

ESSENTIAL QUESTION: Are inventions realized through inspiration or perspiration?

Conventions

Subject Complements One essential tool for Allende and other writers is the subject complement, which allows a writer to define or describe the subject of a sentence.

A **linking verb** connects its subject to a subject complement. A **subject complement** is a noun, a pronoun, or an adjective that follows a linking verb and tells something about the subject.

The most common linking verbs are forms of *be*, such as *am, is, are, was,* and *were*. Other verbs that function as linking verbs when they are followed by subject complements include *seem, look, feel, become, grow,* and *appear*. There are three types of subject complements:

- A **predicate noun** or **predicate pronoun** (also called **predicate nominatives**) follows a linking verb and identifies or renames the subject of a sentence.
- A **predicate adjective** follows a linking verb and describes the subject of a sentence.

PREDICATE NOUN	PREDICATE PRONOUN	PREDICATE ADJECTIVE
Ronnie *became* the <u>captain</u> of the team.	The winners *are* <u>they</u>.	The flight to Houston *seemed* <u>swift</u>.
The noun *captain* renames the subject, *Ronnie*.	*They* identifies the subject, *winners*.	*Swift* describes the subject, *flight*.

Read It

1. 📓 **Notebook** Identify the predicate noun, pronoun, or adjective in each sentence. Then, briefly describe its function in the sentence.
   a. The man who returned was really he, alive and well.
   b. Clara is a genuine fortune-teller.
   c. When Uncle Marcos leaves, Clara grows upset.
2. Reread paragraph 2 of "Uncle Marcos." Find and label at least one predicate noun and one predicate adjective.

Write It

1. Fill in each of the following sentences with a predicate noun or a phrase that includes a predicate noun.
   a. Uncle Marcos is a(n) _____.
   b. Clara is the _____.
2. Fill in each of the following sentences with a predicate adjective.
   a. When he works on his inventions, Uncle Marcos seems _____.
   b. The character of Clara appears _____.

Uncle Marcos 461

DIGITAL PERSPECTIVES

Conventions

Subject Complements Remind students that there are two main parts of a sentence: the subject and the predicate. The predicate modifies the subject. Subject complements are predicate nouns, predicate pronouns, and predicate adjectives. They all serve the purpose of giving the reader more information about the subject. For more support, see **Conventions: Subject Complements.**

Read It
Possible responses:
1. (a) The predicate pronoun *he* identifies the subject, *the man*. (b) The predicate noun *fortune-teller* renames the subject, *Clara*. (c) The predicate adjective *upset* tells something about the subject, *Clara*.
2. Predicate Noun: The machine was just a rusty <u>box</u> with wheels.
   Predicate Adjective: The little pink, green, and blue papers were so <u>clever</u>.

Write It
Possible responses:

a. inventor

b. person who cares most about Uncle Marcos

c. determined

d. mature for her age

FORMATIVE ASSESSMENT

Conventions

If students are unable to identify linking verbs and subject complements, **then** provide more examples for practice. For Reteach and Practice, see **Conventions: Subject Complements (RP).**

PERSONALIZE FOR LEARNING

English Language Support

Syntax Understanding sentence structure and sentence components will help students' comprehension and writing. To review subject complements, create the following chart. Review the completed example shown in item 1. Then, work with the class to complete items 2 and 3. **Answers:** (2) Subject: Sarah; Linking verb: was; Predicate noun, pronoun, or adjective: leader (predicate noun) (3) Subject: chef; Linking verb: is; Predicate noun, pronoun, or adjective: she (predicate pronoun) **ALL LEVELS**

Sentence	Subject	Linking verb	Predicate noun, pronoun, or adjective
1. The cheetah was fast.	cheetah	was	fast (predicate adjective)
2. Sarah was the leader of the band.			
3. The chef is she.			

Whole-Class Learning 461

TEACHING

Writing to Sources

A critical review is a writer's perspective on, and opinion about, another piece of writing. In order to be effective, the critical review makes a claim about the other piece of writing and must explain why the claim is valid. For more support, see **Writing to Sources: Critical Review.**

Reflect on Your Writing

1. **Responses will vary.** Students may note that both involve taking a position, offering support, and anticipating counterclaims.
2. **Responses will vary.** Students may have had difficulty making a claim, finding sufficient evidence to support their claim, and so on.
3. **Why These Words?** Responses will vary. Students should note specific word choices and the intended effect of those choices.

FORMATIVE ASSESSMENT
Writing to Sources

If students struggle to support their claims, **then** ask them to review the text and note direct quotations that reflect and support their ideas. For Reteach and Practice, see **Writing to Sources: Critical Review (RP).**

462 UNIT 5 • INVENTION

UNCLE MARCOS

EFFECTIVE EXPRESSION

Writing to Sources

A critical review is a type of argument in which a writer states and supports an interpretation or evaluation of a literary work.

> **Assignment**
> Write a **critical review** in which you state, explain, and support your understanding of the character of Uncle Marcos. In your view, is Uncle Marcos a dreamer, a crackpot, an innovator, a phony, just an unusual person, or something else? Your critical review should include the following elements:
> - a main claim in which you state your position about Uncle Marcos
> - an explanation of specific ways in which author Isabel Allende shows what Uncle Marcos is like
> - evidence, including quotations from the narrative, that supports your main claim
> - reasons that clarify your claim or show why it is valid

As you write your review, be clear about the ways in which your ideas fit together. Use words and phrases that show how one idea leads to the next, and how your evidence connects to the ideas. For example, words and phrases such as *because, as a result,* and *consequently* show cause-and-effect relationships. Words and phrases such as *like, similarly,* or *on the other hand* show comparison and contrast.

Vocabulary and Conventions Connection Consider including several of the concept vocabulary words. Also, remember to use subject complements correctly to strengthen your writing.

decipher	contraption	ingenuity
invincible	newfangled	improvisations

Reflect on Your Writing

After you have written your critical review, answer these questions.

1. How does stating a claim and finding support for it help you write a critical review?

2. What was the most difficult part of writing your critical review?

3. **Why These Words?** The words you choose make a difference in your writing. Which words did you specifically choose to clearly convey the connections between your ideas and evidence from the text?

STANDARDS
Writing
Write arguments to support claims with clear reasons and relevant evidence.
  b. Support claim(s) with logical reasoning and relevant evidence, using accurate, credible sources and demonstrating an understanding of the topic or text.
  c. Use words, phrases, and clauses to create cohesion and clarify the relationships between claim(s), counterclaims, reasons, and evidence.

462 UNIT 5 • INVENTION

WriteNow   Analyze and Interpret

Analyze an Argument Have students look at both sides of an argument related to "Uncle Marcos." Divide the class into two groups: One should argue that Uncle Marcos is an innovator, and the other should argue that he is an eccentric man with crazy ideas. Have students brainstorm evidence from the text to support each claim. Create a two-column chart with a claim at the top of each column. Have each group take turns providing evidence to support their claims. Add evidence to the chart in a point, counter-point fashion. Students can use the class chart to inform their writing for the assignment.

ESSENTIAL QUESTION: Are inventions realized through inspiration or perspiration?

Speaking and Listening

Assignment
Prepare for a **class discussion** about how the episode involving Uncle Marcos and his mechanical bird draws on themes from the Greek myth of Icarus.

1. **Prepare to Participate in Class Discussion** Find a version of the myth of Icarus online or in the Independent Learning section of this unit. Read the myth and jot down some notes about the key events. Then, skim paragraphs 3 and 4 of "Uncle Marcos" to review the episode involving the mechanical bird. Think about connections you see between the two stories.

2. **Cite Specific Text Evidence** As you begin the discussion, refer to your notes so that you can support your ideas with evidence from the texts. Make sure you can answer the following questions during the discussion.
   - How is Uncle Marcos similar to and different from Icarus?
   - What passages from "Uncle Marcos" support your ideas?
   - Why might the author have chosen to draw on the myth of Icarus in her portrayal of Uncle Marcos?

3. **Evaluate Discussion Participation** As you and your classmates contribute to the discussion, listen to one another attentively. Use an evaluation guide like the one shown to analyze the quality of the discussion.

DISCUSSION PARTICIPATION GUIDE

Rate each statement on a scale of 1 (not demonstrated) to 5 (demonstrated).

- ☐ The participants were prepared for the discussion.
- ☐ The participants cited specific passages and examples from the texts to support ideas.
- ☐ The participants built on one another's ideas and expressed their own clearly.
- ☐ The participants posed questions that connected ideas.
- ☐ The participants responded to questions and comments with relevant evidence, observations, and ideas.

EVIDENCE LOG
Before moving on to a new selection, go to your Evidence Log and record what you learned from "Uncle Marcos."

STANDARDS

Reading Literature
Analyze how a modern work of fiction draws on themes, patterns of events, or character types from myths, traditional stories, or religious works such as the Bible, including describing how the material is rendered new.

Speaking and Listening
Engage effectively in a range of collaborative discussions with diverse partners on *grade 8 topics, texts, and issues*, building on others' ideas and expressing their own clearly.
  a. Come to discussions prepared, having read or researched material under study; explicitly draw on that preparation by referring to evidence on the topic, text, or issue to probe and reflect on ideas under discussion.
  c. Pose questions that connect the ideas of several speakers and respond to others' questions and comments with relevant evidence, observations, and ideas.

PERSONALIZE FOR LEARNING

Strategic Support
Graphic Organizers Sometimes, organizing one's thoughts for a class discussion can be overwhelming. Graphic organizers are a useful tool to help students visualize what they want to say and how they want to say it. Have students create a chart to organize their points and their evidence to show how Clara and Uncle Marcos change and develop throughout the story.

They can make a two-column chart with each character at the top of a column, or they can set up a flowchart like this.

Clara

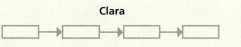

PLANNING
WHOLE-CLASS LEARNING • TO FLY

To Fly

Summary

In his essay "To Fly," Neil deGrasse Tyson addresses the long history of human interest in and fascination with flight. Though flying was long considered impossible, Tyson points out that flight today is limited only by the laws of physics and technological know-how.

The author traces the history of flight, including the Wright brothers in Kitty Hawk, North Carolina, in 1903. Attention to the possibilities of flight increased over time, and, by World War II, bomber airplanes were common, and the German V-2 missiles, which could be launched from hundreds of miles away from their targets, marked another turning point by bringing orbital technology within reach. By 1969, Apollo astronauts had landed on the moon. But what Tyson feels is the greatest achievement is that of Voyager 2, which is now in interstellar space.

Insight

Neil deGrasse Tyson's "To Fly" is an engaging part of a larger work, *Space Chronicles: Facing the Ultimate Frontier*. The essay and the book from which it comes are pleas for further exploration of space. The noted astrophysicist is an enthusiastic teacher, and the essay is just a small taste of a fascinating subject.

AUDIO SUMMARIES
Audio summaries of "To Fly" are available online in both English and Spanish in the Interactive Teacher's Edition or Unit Resources. Assigning these summaries prior to reading the selection may help students build additional background knowledge and set a context for their first read.

ESSENTIAL QUESTION:
Are inventions realized through inspiration or perspiration?

Connection to Essential Question

"To Fly" provides a clear-cut connection to the Essential Question, *Are inventions realized through inspiration or perspiration?* The accomplishments to achieve different forms of flight in the twentieth and twenty-first centuries have been largely due to extended and focused efforts to overcome historic obstacles and rigid thinking.

WHOLE-CLASS LEARNING PERFORMANCE TASK
Which text—"Uncle Marcos" or "To Fly"—best describes the dream or fantasy of human flight?

UNIT PERFORMANCE-BASED ASSESSMENT
Which invention described in this unit has had the biggest impact on humanity?

Connection to Performance Tasks

Whole-Class Learning Performance Task To support students as they prepare for the Performance Task, ask them to note the way that this text describes the dream of human flight.

Unit Performance-Based Assessment Tyson's chapter gives many examples of how human ingenuity has brought us varied forms of flight. However, most of the events and people involved are not examined in depth. What may interest students for their arguments might be the points Tyson makes about the world's taking so long to realize the importance of the Wright brothers' achievements in flight and the impact of flight on humanity.

DIGITAL PERSPECTIVES

 Audio   Video   Document   Annotation Highlights   EL Highlights ☑ Online Assessment

LESSON RESOURCES

	Making Meaning	Language Development	Effective Expression
Lesson	First Read Close Read Analyze the Text Analyze Craft and Structure	Concept Vocabulary Word Study Conventions	Writing to Sources Speaking and Listening
Instructional Standards	**RI.10** By the end of the year, read and comprehend literary nonfiction . . . **RI.3** Analyze how a text . . . **RI.4** Determine the meaning of words and phrases . . . **RI.5** Analyze in detail the structure . . . **L.5.a** Interpret figures of speech . . .	**L.2** Demonstrate command of the conventions. . . **L.2.c** Spell correctly . . . **L.4** Determine or clarify the meaning of unknown and multiple-meaning words or phrases . . . **L.4.b** Use common, grade-appropriate Greek or Latin affixes and roots . . .	**W.1** Write arguments . . . **W.1.b** Support claim(s) with logical reasoning . . . **W.1.e** Provide a concluding statement or section . . . **SL.4** Present claims and findings . . . **SL.5** Integrate multimedia and visual displays . . .
▶ STUDENT RESOURCES Available online in the Interactive Student Edition or Unit Resources	🔊 Selection Audio 📄 First-Read Guide: Nonfiction 📄 Close-Read Guide: Nonfiction	📄 Word Network	📄 Evidence Log
▶ TEACHER RESOURCES **Selection Resources** Available online in the Interactive Teacher's Edition or Unit Resources	🔊 Audio Summaries ✏️ Annotation Highlights 💬 EL Highlights 📄 English Language Support Lesson: Expository Writing 📄 Analyze Craft and Structure: Expository Writing	📄 Concept Vocabulary and Word Study 📄 Conventions: Capitalization	📄 Writing to Sources : Argumentative Essay 📄 Speaking and Listening: Informative Presentation
Reteach/Practice (RP) Available online in the Interactive Teacher's Edition or Unit Resources	📄 Analyze Craft and Structure: Expository Writing (RP)	📄 Word Study: Old English Prefix *fore-* (RP) 📄 Conventions: Capitalization (RP)	📄 Writing to Sources: Argumentative Essay (RP) 📄 Speaking and Listening: Informative Presentation (RP)
Assessment Available online in Assessments	📄 ☑ Selection Test		
My Resources	📄 A Unit 5 Answer Key is available online and in the Interactive Teacher's Edition.		

PERSONALIZE FOR LEARNING
WHOLE-CLASS LEARNING • TO FLY

Reading Support

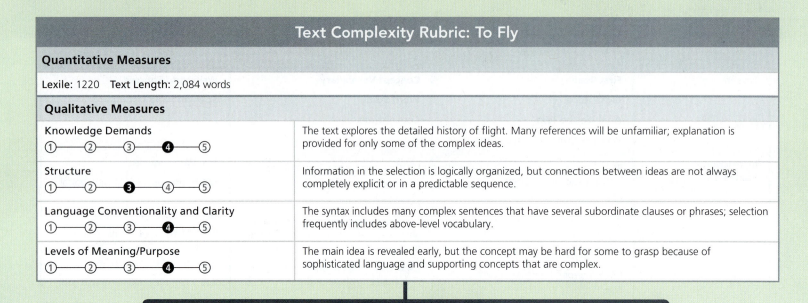

English Language Support
Provide English Learners with support for knowledge demands and language as they read the selection.

Knowledge Demands Before students read, make a list of some of the terms and phrases they will need to understand: *aerodynamics, sound barrier, propulsion, speed of light.* Discuss and define each term as needed.

Language If students have difficulty with some of the complex language, have them break down the sentences into smaller chunks. Then have them highlight any words that are confusing. Guide students to an understanding of the challenging concepts.

Strategic Support
Provide students with strategic support to ensure that they can successfully read the text.

Knowledge Demands Use the background information to discuss the history of human flight. Determine students' prior knowledge and experience with flying. Provide additional background if needed.

Language If students have difficulty with complex scientific concepts, work together to break down sentences into smaller chunks in order to understand their meaning. Ask students to highlight words or phrases that they don't understand. As a group, help to clarify some of the concepts they find difficult.

Challenge
Provide students who need to be challenged with ideas for how they can go beyond a simple interpretation of the text.

Text Analysis Discuss what it means to use language *figuratively* or *literally*. The selection does both. Ask students what they think these sentences mean in paragraph 17: *We Americans didn't build a space station; instead we went to the Moon. With this effort, our wing worship continued.* Ask them to explain what idea the author is trying to convey.

Written Response Challenge students to choose an historical aviator and write a research paper about him or her. Have students share their papers with the class.

TEACH

Read and Respond
Have students do their first read of the selection. Then have them complete their close read. Finally, work with them on the Making Meaning, Language Development, and Effective Expression activities.

Standards Support Through Teaching and Learning Cycle

IDENTIFY NEEDS

Analyze results of the Beginning-of-Year Assessment, focusing on the items relating to Unit 5. Also take into consideration student performance to this point and your observations of where particular students struggle.

DECIDE AND PLAN

- If students have performed poorly on items matching these standards, then provide selection scaffolds before assigning them the on-level lesson provided in the Student Edition.
- If students have done well on the Beginning-of-Year Assessment, then challenge them to keep progressing and learning by giving them opportunities to practice the skills in depth.
- Use the Selection Resources listed on the Planning pages for "To Fly" to help students continually improve their ability to master the standards.

Instructional Standards: To Fly

	Catching Up	This Year	Looking Forward
Reading	You may wish to administer the **Analyze Craft and Structure: Expository Writing (RP)** worksheet to help students understand the function of expository writing.	**RI.3** Analyze how a text makes connections among and distinctions between individuals, ideas, or events.	Ask students to consider the order in which Tyson gives the reader the information.
Writing	You may wish to administer the **Writing to Sources: Argumentative Essay (RP)** worksheet to help students prepare for their writing.	**W.1** Write arguments to support claims with clear reasons and relevant evidence.	Challenge students to consider possible counterclaims in their arguments.
Speaking and Listening	You may wish to administer the **Speaking and Listening: Informative Presentation (RP)** worksheet to help students prepare for their presentation.	**SL.4** Present claims and findings, emphasizing salient points in a focused, coherent manner with relevant evidence, sound valid reasoning, and well-chosen details; use appropriate eye contact, adequate volume, and clear pronunciation.	Challenge students to conduct short, self-propelled, outside research while preparing to enhance the presentation.
Language	Review the **Word Study: Old English Prefix fore- (RP)** worksheet with students to make sure they understand that the prefix fore- means "before," "toward," or "front." Review the **Conventions: Capitalization (RP)** worksheet with students to ensure they know when to capitalize.	**L.4** Determine or clarify the meaning of unknown and multiple–meaning words or phrases based on grade 8 reading and content, choosing flexibly from a range of strategies. **L.2** Demonstrate command of the conventions of standard English capitalization, punctuation, and spelling when writing.	Have students locate words in the text with other prefixes they recognize. Work with students to discuss whether is it necessary to capitalize in informal writing.

ANALYZE AND REVISE

- Analyze student work for evidence of student learning.
- Identify whether or not students have met the expectations in the standards.
- Identify implications for future instruction.

TEACH

Implement the planned lesson, and gather evidence of student learning.

TEACHING

Jump Start

FIRST READ Prior to students' first read, discuss what they already know about the history of aviation. Then, extend this discussion to include missions to explore space.

To Fly 🔊 📄

Why have people always been fascinated by the ability to fly? In the future, will we be able to accomplish flights that are thought to be impossible today? Modeling questions such as these will help students connect with "To Fly" and to the Performance Task assignment. Selection audio and print capability for the selection are available in the Interactive Teacher's Edition.

Concept Vocabulary

Support students as they rank the words. Ask if they've ever heard, read, or used them. Reassure them that the definitions for these words are listed in the selection.

⦿ FIRST READ

As they read, students should perform the steps of the first read:

NOTICE: You may want to encourage students to notice how Tyson links flying to other topics, such as mythology, history, popular culture, science, and fiction.

ANNOTATE: Remind students to mark text that expresses the main ideas of this selection.

CONNECT: Encourage students to make connections beyond the text. If they cannot make connections to their own lives or other texts, have them consider movies, TV shows, and news reports.

RESPOND: Students will answer questions and write a summary to demonstrate understanding.

Point out to students that while they will always complete the Respond step at the end of the first read, the other steps will probably happen somewhat concurrently. You may wish to print copies of the **First-Read Guide: Nonfiction** for students to use. 📄

Remind students that during their first read, they should not answer the close-read questions that appear in the selection.

464 UNIT 5 • INVENTION

MAKING MEANING

About the Author

Neil deGrasse Tyson (b. 1958) is an American astrophysicist, author, and science communicator, as well as the current director of the Hayden Planetarium's Rose Center for Earth and Space. From 2006 to 2011, he hosted the educational science show *NOVA ScienceNow* on PBS. Tyson grew up in the Bronx and attended the Bronx High School of Science from 1972 to 1976, where he was the editor-in-chief of "Physical Science," the school paper, and also the captain of the wrestling team.

🔧 **Tool Kit**
First-Read Guide and Model Annotation

📋 **STANDARDS**
Reading Informational Text
By the end of the year, read and comprehend literary nonfiction at the high end of the grades 6–8 text complexity band independently and proficiently.

464 UNIT 5 • INVENTION

To Fly
Concept Vocabulary

As you conduct your first read of "To Fly," you will encounter these words. Before reading, note how familiar you are with each word. Then, rank the words in order from most familiar (1) to least familiar (6).

WORD	YOUR RANKING
myopic	
foresight	
naiveté	
prescient	
enable	
seminal	

After completing the first read, come back to the concept vocabulary and review your rankings. Mark changes to your original rankings as needed.

First Read NONFICTION

Apply these strategies as you conduct your first read. You will have an opportunity to complete the close-read notes after your first read.

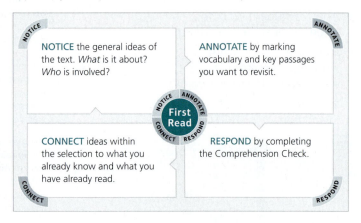

HOW LANGUAGE WORKS

Suffix -ic Call attention to the concept vocabulary word *myopic*. Help students understand the suffix *-ic*. Explain that words in which this suffix appears are usually adjectives, and adding this suffix to another word usually makes that word an adjective. This suffix can mean "having the character or form of" (*biographic*); "of or relating to" (*artistic*); "in the manner of" (*dramatic*); "associated, dealing with, or using" (*electronic*); "characterized by or affected" (*allergic*); or "caused by" (*volcanic*).

ANCHOR TEXT | ESSAY

To Fly
from Space Chronicles
Neil deGrasse Tyson

BACKGROUND
The history of human flight is closely tied to the history of speed—flying has meant setting speed records. Heavy flying vehicles, like airplanes, have to move very quickly in order to stay in the air, and space shuttles have to travel at a very high speed called "escape velocity" to get into space.

1   In ancient days two aviators procured to themselves wings. Daedalus flew safely through the middle air, and was duly honored in his landing. Icarus soared upwards to the sun till the wax melted which bound his wings, and his flight ended in a fiasco. In weighing their achievements perhaps there is something to be said for Icarus. The classic authorities tell us, of course, that he was only "doing a stunt"; but I prefer to think of him as the man who certainly brought to light a serious constructional defect in the flying-machines of his day [and] we may at least hope to learn from his journey some hints to build a better machine.
   —Sir Arthur Eddington, *Stars & Atoms* (1927)

TEACHING

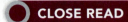

CLOSE READ

As students look for ways that the author compares and contrasts humans and birds, remind the class that comparing tells how things are alike and contrasting tells how they are different. You may wish to model the close read using the following think-aloud format. Possible responses to questions on the student page are included.

ANNOTATE: In paragraphs 2, 3, and 4, I notice that people may have been envious of birds' ability to fly, as shown by flying images on television and on money.

QUESTION: I think he wants to show that flying has always held a strong attraction for humans, because it's something we cannot do on our own. In paragraph 2, he says that we have "wing envy" or "wing worship."

CONCLUDE: I think these details emphasize that although humans think we are superior to birds, we are only able to fly with the help of technological innovation.

 Additional **English Language Support** is available in the Interactive Teacher's Edition.

NOTES

CLOSE READ
ANNOTATE: In paragraphs 2, 3, and 4, mark details that describe how people move about on Earth. Mark other details that describe how birds and other creatures fly.

QUESTION: Why does the author present such a strong contrast between walking and flying?

CONCLUDE: What point do these descriptive details emphasize?

myopic (my OP ihk) *adj.* nearsighted; unable to see clearly; showing a lack of understanding

foresight (FAWR syt) *n.* knowledge or insight gained by looking toward the future

2   For millennia, the idea of being able to fly occupied human dreams and fantasies. Waddling around on Earth's surface as majestic birds flew overhead, perhaps we developed a form of wing envy. One might even call it wing worship.

3   You needn't look far for evidence. For most of the history of broadcast television in America, when a station signed off for the night, it didn't show somebody walking erect and bidding farewell; instead it would play the "Star Spangled Banner" and show things that fly, such as birds soaring or Air Force jets whooshing by. The United States even adopted a flying predator as a symbol of its strength: the bald eagle, which appears on the back of the dollar bill, the quarter, the Kennedy half dollar, the Eisenhower dollar, and the Susan B. Anthony dollar. There's also one on the floor of the Oval Office in the White House. Our most famous superhero, Superman, can fly upon donning blue pantyhose and a red cape. When you die, if you qualify, you might just become an angel—and everybody knows that angels (at least the ones who have earned their wings) can fly. Then there's the winged horse Pegasus; the wing-footed Mercury; the aerodynamically unlikely Cupid; and Peter Pan and his fairy sidekick, Tinkerbell.

4   Our inability to fly often goes unmentioned in textbook comparisons of human features with those of other species in the animal kingdom. Yet we are quick to use the word "flightless" as a synonym for "hapless" when describing such birds as the dodo and the booby, which tend to find themselves on the wrong end of evolutionary jokes. We did, however, ultimately learn to fly because of the technological ingenuity afforded by our human brains. And of course, while birds can fly, they are nonetheless stuck with bird brains. But this self-aggrandizing line of reasoning is somewhat flawed, because it ignores all the millennia that we were technologically flightless.

5   I remember as a student in junior high school reading that the famed physicist Lord Kelvin, at the turn of the twentieth century, had argued the impossibility of self-propelled flight by any device that was heavier than air. Clearly this was a **myopic** prediction. But one needn't have waited for the invention of the first airplanes to refute the essay's premise. One merely needed to look at birds, which have no trouble flying and, last I checked, are all heavier than air.

6   If something is not forbidden by the laws of physics, then it is, in principle, possible, regardless of the limits of one's technological **foresight**. The speed of sound in air ranges from seven hundred to eight hundred miles per hour, depending

466 UNIT 5 • INVENTION

PERSONALIZE FOR LEARNING

English Language Support
Prefixes *in-*, *un-*, and *im-* Point out *inability* (paragraph 4), *unmentioned* (paragraph 4), and *impossibility* (paragraph 5). Help students better understand the prefixes *in-*, *un-*, and *im-*. Explain that as they're used in the text, these prefixes mean "not." Discuss the meaning of each word and how it is formed using a prefix. However, also explain that *in*, *un*, and *im* at the beginning of a word are not always prefixes. Point out the words *ingenuity* (paragraph 4), *invention* (paragraph 5), *unite*, and *importance* (paragraph 10). Explain that none of these words are made using these prefixes. **ALL LEVELS**

on the atmospheric temperature. No law of physics prevents objects from going faster than Mach 1,[1] the speed of sound. But before the sound "barrier" was broken in 1947 by Charles E. "Chuck" Yeager, piloting the Bell X-1 (a US Army rocket plane), much claptrap[2] was written about the impossibility of objects moving faster than the speed of sound. Meanwhile, bullets fired by high-powered rifles had been breaking the sound barrier for more than a century. And the crack of a whip or the sound of a wet towel snapping at somebody's buttocks in the locker room is a mini sonic boom, created by the end of the whip or the tip of the towel moving through the air faster than the speed of sound. Any limits to breaking the sound barrier were purely psychological and technological.

7   During its lifetime, the fastest winged aircraft by far was the space shuttle, which, with the aid of detachable rockets and fuel tanks, exceeded Mach 20[3] on its way to orbit. Propulsionless on return, it fell back out of orbit, gliding safely down to Earth. Although other craft routinely travel many times faster than the speed of sound, none can travel faster than the speed of light. I speak not from a **naiveté** about technology's future but from a platform built upon the laws of physics, which apply on Earth as they do in the heavens. Credit the Apollo astronauts who went to the Moon with attaining the highest speeds at which humans have ever flown: about seven miles per second at the end of the rocket burn that lifted their craft beyond low Earth orbit. This is a paltry 1/250 of one percent of the speed of light. Actually, the real problem is not the moat that separates these two speeds but the laws of physics that prevent any object from ever achieving the speed of light, no matter how inventive your technology. The sound barrier and the light barrier are not equivalent limits on invention.

8   The Wright brothers of Ohio are, of course, generally credited with being "first in flight" at Kitty Hawk, North Carolina, as that state's license-plate slogan reminds us. But this claim needs to be further delineated. Wilbur and Orville Wright were the first to fly a heavier-than-air, engine-powered vehicle that carried a human being—Orville, in this case—and that did not land at a lower elevation than its takeoff point. Previously, people had flown in balloon gondolas and in gliders and had executed controlled descents from the sides of cliffs, but none of those efforts would have made a bird jealous. Nor would Wilbur and Orville's first trip have turned any bird heads. The first of their four flights—at 10:35 A.M. eastern time on December 17, 1903—lasted twelve

NOTES

naiveté (nah eev TAY) *n.* quality of innocent simplicity

---

1. **Mach** (mok) **1** speed of sound in dry air; sound travels faster in denser substances.
2. **claptrap** *n.* nonsensical talk.
3. **Mach 20** twenty times the speed of sound.

DIGITAL PERSPECTIVES

Illuminating the Text To help students understand the early history of aviation and appreciate how far we've come, use the search term "Wright Brothers" to find photos of the Wright brothers' first flight or video of later flights. (Note: Be sure to preview any video before showing it to students.) Have students discuss what they see and how this helps them understand what Tyson is talking about in paragraph 8. Then, have students write a paragraph expressing their reaction to the images. What did they think as they were watching it? Did it change their ideas about this historic event? If it did, in what way? How does it feel to watch this as someone who lives in a time when flight is taken for granted? Ask volunteers to share their response with the class. **(Research to Clarify)**

TEACHING

🔴 **CLOSE READ** ✏️

You may wish to model the close read using the following think-aloud format. Possible responses to questions on the student page are included.

ANNOTATE: As I read paragraph 11, I mark the word "guy," which the author uses to refer to the writer of the passage quoted in paragraph 10.

QUESTION: I think the author uses this informal term to imply that even though the writer is clearly smart and observant, he is just like everyone else — and the impact of flying is felt by all of us.

CONCLUDE: I think the effect of this casual language is that it draws in the reader in a persuasive way. This is a very short sentence among much longer ones and it creates contrast.

NOTES

prescient (PREHSH uhnt) *adj.* having knowledge of things before they happen

enable (ehn AYB uhl) *v.* make possible

CLOSE READ
ANNOTATE: In paragraph 11, mark the word the author uses to refer to the writer of the passage quoted in paragraph 10.

QUESTION: Why does the author use this informal term?

CONCLUDE: What is the effect of this casual language?

---

seconds, at an average speed of 6.8 miles per hour against a 30-mile-per-hour wind. The Wright Flyer, as it was called, had traveled 120 feet, not even the length of one wing on a Boeing 747.

9   Even after the Wright brothers went public with their achievement, the media took only intermittent notice of it and other aviation firsts. As late as 1933—six years after Lindbergh's historic solo flight across the Atlantic—H. Gordon Garbedian ignored airplanes in the otherwise **prescient** introduction to his book *Major Mysteries of Science*:

> Present day life is dominated by science as never before. You pick up a telephone and within a few minutes you are talking with a friend in Paris. You can travel under sea in a submarine, or circumnavigate the globe by air in a Zeppelin. The radio carries your voice to all parts of the earth with the speed of light. Soon, television will **enable** you to see the world's greatest spectacles as you sit in the comfort of your living room.

10 But some journalists did pay attention to the way flight might change civilization. After the Frenchman Louis Blériot crossed the English Channel from Calais to Dover on July 25, 1909, an article on page three of the *New York Times* was headlined "Frenchman Proves Aeroplane No Toy." The article went on to delineate England's reaction to the event:

> Editorials in the London newspapers buzzed about the new world where Great Britain's insular[4] strength is no longer unchallenged; that the aeroplane is not a toy but a possible instrument of warfare, which must be taken into account by soldiers and statesmen, and that it was the one thing needed to wake up the English people to the importance of the science of aviation.

11 **The guy was right.** Thirty-five years later, not only had airplanes been used as fighters and bombers in warfare but the Germans had taken the concept a notch further and invented the V-2 to attack London. Their vehicle was significant in many ways. First, it was not an airplane; it was an unprecedentedly large missile. Second, because the V-2 could be launched several hundred miles from its target, it basically birthed the modern rocket. And third, for its entire airborne journey after launch, the V-2 moved under the influence of gravity alone; in other words, it was a suborbital ballistic missile, the fastest way to deliver a bomb from one location on Earth to another. Subsequently, Cold War "advances" in the design of missiles enabled military power to target cities on

---

4. **insular** (IHN suh luhr) *adj.* literally, related to being an island; figuratively, detached or isolated.

PERSONALIZE FOR LEARNING

English Language Support
Idioms Help students understand the idioms *buzzed* (paragraph 10) and [*take up*] *a notch* (paragraph 11). Explain that as it's used in the article, *buzzed* means "talked excitedly." (Reporters buzzed with anticipation when they heard the president was going to make an important speech.) As it's used in the article, *notch* means "degree, step." (Art took our idea of forming a team a notch further when he started making suggestions about who should be on the team.)
ALL LEVELS

opposite sides of the world. Maximum flight time? About forty-five minutes—not nearly enough time to evacuate a targeted city.

12   While we can say they're suborbital, do we have the right to declare missiles to be flying? Are falling objects in flight? Is Earth "flying" in orbit around the Sun? In keeping with the rules applied to the Wright brothers, a person must be onboard the craft and it must move under its own power. But there's no rule that says we cannot change the rules.

13   Knowing that the V-2 brought orbital technology within reach, some people got impatient. Among them were the editors of the popular, family-oriented magazine *Collier's*, which sent two journalists to join the engineers, scientists, and visionaries gathered at New York City's Hayden Planetarium on Columbus Day, 1951, for its seminal Space Travel Symposium. In the March 22, 1952, issue of *Collier's*, in a piece titled "What Are We Waiting For?" the magazine endorsed the need for and value of a space station that would serve as a watchful eye over a divided world:

> In the hands of the West a space station, permanently established beyond the atmosphere, would be the greatest hope for peace the world has ever known. No nation could undertake preparations for war without the certain knowledge that it was being observed by the ever-watching eyes aboard the "sentinel in space." It would be the end of the Iron Curtains[5] wherever they might be.

14   We Americans didn't build a space station; instead we went to the Moon. With this effort, our wing worship continued. Never mind that Apollo astronauts landed on the airless Moon, where wings are completely useless, in a lunar module named after a bird. A mere sixty-five years, seven months, three days, five hours, and forty-three minutes after Orville left the ground, Neil Armstrong gave his first statement from the Moon's surface: "Houston, Tranquility Base here. The Eagle has landed."

15   The human record for "altitude" does not go to anybody for having walked on the Moon. It goes to the astronauts of the ill-fated Apollo 13. Knowing they could not land on the Moon after the explosion in their oxygen tank, and knowing they did not have enough fuel to stop, slow down, and head back, they executed a single figure-eight ballistic trajectory around the Moon, swinging them back toward Earth. The Moon just happened to be near apogee, the farthest point from Earth in its elliptical orbit. No other Apollo mission (before or since) went to the Moon during apogee, which granted the Apollo 13 astronauts the human

---

NOTES

seminal (SEHM uh nuhl) *adj.* being the first of something that is later recognized as important

---

5. **Iron Curtains** figurative walls of secrecy and suspicion between the Soviet Union and non-communist countries during the Cold War.

CLOSER LOOK

Analyze Author's Style

Students may have marked text in paragraph 14 during their first read. Encourage them to talk about the annotations that they marked. You may want to model a close read with the class based on the highlights shown in the text.

ANNOTATE: Have students mark text in paragraph 14 that demonstrates Tyson's precision, or have students participate while you highlight them.

QUESTION: Guide students to consider what these details tell them. Ask why they think Tyson is so precise in this part of the text.

Possible response: Tyson is so precise in this part of the text to show how relatively quickly people reached the moon once the age of modern aviation began, and to draw attention to how important the moon landing was.

CONCLUDE: Help students to formulate conclusions about the importance of these details. Ask what bigger idea Tyson is communicating by being so precise in this part of the essay.

Possible response: The age of modern aviation began with the Wright brothers, whom Tyson mentions earlier in the essay. Landing on the moon is a major aviation milestone. By measuring the exact years, months, days, hours, and minutes from one event to the other, Tyson is emphasizing the relationship between these two accomplishments.

Point out that numbers and precision are part of **author's style**, which also includes an author's choice of words, sentence structure, and figurative language. Being so precise strengthens Tyson's credibility—he is writing about historical and scientific events, and as a good scientist and thorough researcher, he provides exact details to support his ideas.

VOCABULARY DEVELOPMENT

Domain-Specific Words Discuss the following space-related words in paragraph 15: *ballistic* ("related to the science of the motion of projectiles in flight"); *trajectory* ("the curve that a body [as a planet or comet in its orbit or a rocket] describes in space"); *apogee* ("the point farthest from a planet or a satellite [as the moon] reached by an object orbiting it"); *elliptical* ("of or relating to an oval-shaped path"). Encourage students to record and define other space- or aviation-related words in the selection.

TEACHING

CLOSE READ

You may wish to model the close read using the following think-aloud format. Possible responses to questions on the student page are included.

ANNOTATE: As I read paragraph 16, I mark the point at which the author stops using scientific words and phrases and begins to use poetic, emotional language: "earthly sounds of . . . the human heartbeat"; "So with our heart, if not our soul, we fly even farther."

QUESTION: I think the language changes dramatically at this point because Tyson is trying to persuade the reader that flight is not only about science—that it also has a strong impact on our emotions.

CONCLUDE: I think the effect of this change is to leave the reader with a feeling of hope and inspiration about the future possibilities of flight and its effect on us.

Media Connection

Project the media connection video in class, ask students to open the video in their interactive textbooks, or have students scan the Bounce Page icon with their phones to access the video.

Discuss It

Possible response: This video helped me understand the wonder of exploring the universe.

NOTES

altitude record. (After calculating that they must have reached about 245,000 miles "above" Earth's surface, including the orbital distance from the Moon's surface, I asked Apollo 13 commander Jim Lovell, "Who was on the far side of the command module as it rounded the Moon? That single person would hold the altitude record." He refused to tell.)

16 In my opinion, the greatest achievement of flight was not Wilbur and Orville's aeroplane, nor Chuck Yeager's breaking of the sound barrier, nor the Apollo 11 lunar landing. For me, it was the launch of Voyager 2, which ballistically[6] toured the solar system's outer planets. During the flybys, the spacecraft's slingshot trajectories stole a little of Jupiter's and Saturn's orbital energy to enable its rapid exit from the solar system. Upon passing Jupiter in 1979, Voyager's speed exceeded forty thousand miles an hour, sufficient to escape the gravitational attraction of even the Sun. Voyager passed the orbit of Pluto in 1993 and has now entered the realm of interstellar space. Nobody happens to be onboard the craft, but a gold phonograph record attached to its side is etched with the earthly sounds of, among many things, the human heartbeat. So with our heart, if not our soul, we fly ever farther.

CLOSE READ

ANNOTATE: In paragraph 16, mark the point at which the author stops using scientific words and phrases and begins to use poetic, emotional language.

QUESTION: Why does the language change so dramatically at this point?

CONCLUDE: What is the effect of this change, especially in a concluding paragraph?

---
6. **ballistically** (buh LIHS tihk lee) *adv.* like a thrown object.

MEDIA CONNECTION

When I Look Up

Discuss It How does viewing this video affect your thinking about space exploration?

Write your response before sharing your ideas.

SCAN FOR MULTIMEDIA

470 UNIT 5 • INVENTION

CROSS–CURRICULAR PERSPECTIVES

Science Challenge students to research the science of aviation and space travel. Have students answer questions such as the following, and ask volunteers to share their research with the class.

What is the "sound barrier"?

How are rockets different from airplanes?

What is involved in escaping Earth's gravity?

What challenges do astronauts face in zero gravity?

What are the effects of zero gravity on people?

What challenges are involved in extremely long space missions? **(Research to Explore)**

470 UNIT 5 • INVENTION

Comprehension Check

Complete the following items after you finish your first read.

1. According to Tyson, what idea occupied human fantasies for millennia?

2. According to Tyson, what two ideas did people once think were impossible, even though they do not defy any laws of physics?

3. In Tyson's opinion, what is the greatest achievement of human flight?

4. **Notebook** Create a rough timeline showing when the inventions discussed in the article were first created. Make sure the order is correct, even if you do not have an exact date for every invention.

RESEARCH

Research to Clarify Choose at least one unfamiliar detail from the text. Briefly research that detail. In what way does the information you learned shed light on an aspect of the essay?

Research to Explore Choose something that interested you from the text, and formulate a research question.

DIGITAL PERSPECTIVES

Comprehension Check

Possible responses:

1. The idea of flying
2. People once thought that it was impossible to have self-propelled flight by any device that was heavier than air and that objects could not move faster than the speed of sound.
3. In Tyson's opinion, the greatest achievement of human flight was Voyager 2, which explored the solar system's outer planets.
4. 1903: Wright Flyer; 1944: V-2 rocket; 1947: Bell X-1; ballistic missiles; lunar module

Research

Research to Clarify If students struggle to identify an unfamiliar detail, have them reread the text and notice scientific terms or nontechnical words that might be new to them.

Research to Explore Responses will vary. Students should identify something specific from the text and articulate a relevant research question.

PERSONALIZE FOR LEARNING

Challenge

Interpret Ask students to consider the last sentences of the article. "*Voyager* passed the orbit of Pluto in 1993 and has now entered the realm of interstellar space. Nobody happens to be onboard the craft, but a gold phonograph record attached to its side is etched with the earthly sounds of among many things, the human heartbeat. So with our heart, if not our soul, we fly ever farther." (You may have to explain what a phonograph record is.) Have students write a paragraph answering these questions: What does Tyson mean when he says "with our heart, if not our soul, we fly ever farther"? How does this idea connect to his statement at the beginning of the article: "For millennia, the idea of being able to fly occupied human dreams and fantasies"? Ask volunteers to share their response with the class.

TEACHING

Jump Start

CLOSE READ Have students consider the title of the selection, "To Fly." Why might Tyson have chosen such a short, simple title for an essay that is very complex and detailed? Ask students to consider what other titles they might suggest and then discuss whether they think Tyson's title works best.

Close Read the Text

Walk students through the Annotation Model on the student page. Encourage them to complete items 2 and 3 on their own. Review and discuss the sections students have marked. If needed, continue to model close reading by using the Annotation Highlights in the Interactive Teacher's Edition.

Analyze the Text

Possible responses:

1. Tyson's attitude is one of satisfaction. He notes: "A mere sixty-five years, seven months, three days, five hours, and forty-three minutes after Orville left the ground, Neil Armstrong gave his first statement from the Moon's surface" (paragraph 14); "the greatest achievement of flight...was the launch of *Voyager 2*" (paragraph 16); "with our heart...we fly ever farther" (paragraph 16) **DOK 3**

2. Responses will vary. Students should identify a specific achievement and support their response with relevant details from the text. **DOK 3**

3. Responses will vary. Students may conclude that people use past inventions to create new ones. **DOK 3**

FORMATIVE ASSESSMENT

Analyze the Text

- If students fail to cite evidence, **then** remind them to support their ideas with specific information from the text.
- If students fail to grasp key ideas in the text, **then** have them review relevant sections of the article.

472 UNIT 5 • INVENTION

MAKING MEANING

TO FLY

Close Read the Text

1. This model from the text shows two sample annotations, along with questions and conclusions. Close read the passage, and find another detail to annotate. Then, write a question and your conclusion.

ANNOTATE: These words and phrases have an informal, jokey quality.

QUESTION: Why does the author use an informal, lighthearted tone?

CONCLUDE: The author is presenting scientific information in a way that makes it entertaining for non-scientists.

> When you die, if you qualify, you might just become an angel—and everybody knows that angels (at least the ones who have earned their wings) can fly. Then there's the winged horse Pegasus; the wing-footed Mercury; the aerodynamically unlikely Cupid; and Peter Pan and his fairy sidekick, Tinkerbell.

ANNOTATE: This description applies a scientific term to a mythological figure.

QUESTION: Why does the author describe Cupid in this way?

CONCLUDE: The description is funny, and also reminds readers that scientific principles guide the technology of flight.

Tool Kit
Close-Read Guide and Model Annotation

2. For more practice, go back into the text, and complete the close-read notes.

3. Revisit a section of text you found important during your first read. **Annotate** what you notice. Ask **questions** such as "Why did the author make this choice?" What can you **conclude**?

Analyze the Text

CITE TEXTUAL EVIDENCE to support your answers.

Notebook Respond to these questions.

1. **Interpret** What is the author's attitude toward the achievements he describes? Explain your interpretation.

2. **Make a Judgment** Which of the achievements described in the article do you think is the most significant? Why? Cite details from the text to support your answer.

3. **Essential Question:** *Are inventions realized through inspiration or perspiration?* What have you learned about how inventions are created?

STANDARDS
Reading Informational Text
• Analyze how a text makes connections among and distinctions between individuals, ideas, or events.
• Determine the meaning of words and phrases as they are used in a text, including figurative, connotative, and technical meanings; analyze the impact of specific word choices on meaning and tone, including analogies or allusions to other texts.
• Analyze in detail the structure of a specific paragraph in a text, including the role of particular sentences in developing and refining a key concept.
Language
Interpret figures of speech in context.

472 UNIT 5 • INVENTION

PERSONALIZE FOR LEARNING

English Language Support

Multiple-Meaning Words Help students understand that the word *flight* (paragraph 1 and throughout the article) has several meanings. Explain that as it's used here, *flight* is a noun that means "an act or instance of passing through the air by the use of wings" or "a trip made by or in an airplane or spacecraft." *Flight* can also mean "a continuous series of stairs from one landing or floor to another" (We climbed a *flight* of stairs), "an act or instance of running away" (The captured bank robber was considered to be a *flight* risk), or "a brilliant, imaginative, or unrestrained exercise or display" (That's a nice idea, but it's really a *flight* of fancy.). **ALL LEVELS**

ESSENTIAL QUESTION: Are inventions realized through inspiration or perspiration?

DIGITAL PERSPECTIVES

Analyze Craft and Structure

Text Structure: Expository Writing The word *exposition* means "explanation." An **expository essay** is a brief work of nonfiction that explains a topic. That explanation may involve the presentation of information, discussion of ideas, or clarification of a process. In this essay, Neil deGrasse Tyson presents information and ideas related to human flight. He uses a variety of methods to make ideas and information clear to readers.

- **Allusions** are references in a text to well-known people, places, characters, myths, events, or works of literature or art. These references appear without explanation. They are designed to help readers make connections and expand their thinking about the writer's ideas.

- **Comparisons and contrasts** present similarities and differences among two or more items or ideas. By showing how one thing is like or unlike another, an expository writer clarifies the qualities of each item.

- **Description** uses words and phrases that appeal to the senses. In expository writing, description can help readers understand a topic by "showing" what something looks like, how it sounds or moves, and even what it smells or tastes like.

- **Cause-and-effect** relationships show how one situation can result from another and then lead to yet another. These connections help readers understand how or why a situation developed as it did.

Practice

CITE TEXTUAL EVIDENCE to support your answers.

📓 **Notebook** Answer these questions.

1. Reread paragraph 3. **(a)** What allusions does the author make? **(b)** What do these allusions have in common? **(c)** What idea do these allusions support? Explain.
2. Reread paragraph 4. **(a)** What two different things does the author compare and contrast? **(b)** What idea does this comparison-and-contrast help the author explain?
3. Reread paragraph 6. **(a)** What descriptive elements does this paragraph include? **(b)** What idea does the description help the author develop?
4. Reread paragraphs 11 to 13. **(a)** According to Tyson, under what circumstances was the German V-2 invented? **(b)** What was important about the V-2 at the time? **(c)** What changes in technology did the V-2 lead to or influence? Explain. **(d)** What idea does Tyson's example of the V-2 help develop or support?

To Fly 473

PERSONALIZE FOR LEARNING

English Language Support
Expository Writing To help students study one tool of expository writing, ask them to write a brief description of a person, place, or thing that includes an allusion.

Have pairs of students work together and remind them that allusions can be a literary, historical, or cultural reference. **EMERGING**

Have students also write a brief description of the person or event that they are alluding to. **EXPANDING**

Ask students to write two brief descriptions that include allusions—one historical allusion and one literary. **BRIDGING**

An expanded **English Language Support Lesson** on Expository Writing is available in the Interactive Teacher's Edition.

Analyze Craft and Structure

Text Structure: Expository Writing To help students study the methods of expository writing, use these discussion points:

- In paragraph 4, explain to students that Tyson alludes to the dodo and the booby to compare the brain power of birds and humans.
- Help students to locate the use of moat **imagery** in paragraph 7.
- Discuss an example of **comparison and contrast** in paragraph 6, where Tyson compares the official breaking of the "sound barrier" with the objects that had already been breaking the barrier—bullets and towel whips.
- Point out the **cause-and-effect** content in paragraph 1, which describes Icarus's fall.

For more support, see **Analyze Craft and Structure: Expository Writing.**

MAKE IT INTERACTIVE
Have students write a compare-and-contrast or a cause-and-effect paragraph in which they use description to build their explanation.

Practice
Possible responses:

1. (a) The author alludes to images of money, the flag, and Superman. (b) All of these allusions relate to popular images of flying. (c) The allusions support the idea that flying has been special to humans for a long time.
2. (a) The author compares birds and humans. (b) The comparison helps the author to explain that although birds can fly, their brains are small—and, interestingly, that the reason humans can fly is they can use their brains to develop technology.
3. (a) Paragraph 6 includes descriptive details about the speed of sound. (b) The author is developing an idea that suggests that humans were unaware of their ability to break the sound barrier.
4. (a) The Germans created the V-2 during World War II to enable them to attack London. (b) It could be launched from hundreds of miles away. (c) The V-2 allowed for the design of missiles that could be activated quickly and target cities that were far away. (d) It shows that once humans became interested in aviation, many things became.

FORMATIVE ASSESSMENT

Analyze Craft and Structure

- **If** students have difficulty identifying Tyson's use of comparison-and-contrast or cause-and-effect, **then** show them appropriate parts of the text and discuss these with elements.
- **If** students have difficulty with imagery or allusion, **then** review appropriate parts of the text and discuss the use of either device.

For Reteach and Practice, see **Analyze Craft and Structure: Expository Writing (RP).**

Whole-Class Learning 473

TEACHING

Concept Vocabulary
Why These Words?
Possible responses:
1. The concept vocabulary helps the reader better understand the inventions Tyson describes because these words describe what can result from both conventional thinking and innovative thinking. These words also help express the author's viewpoint that conventional thinking may be the enemy of innovation.
2. *classic* (paragraph 1), *ingenuity* (paragraph 4), *limits* (paragraph 6), *inventive* (paragraph 7), *unprecedentedly* (paragraph 13)

Practice
Possible responses:
1. Responses will vary.
2. innovative: *foresight, prescient, seminal, enable*
   conventional: *myopic, naivete*

The innovative words express looking forward and making advances; the conventional words express not making the same kind of progress.

Word Network
Possible words: *machine, advances, device, physics, faster, exceeded, achievement*

Word Study
For more support, see **Concept Vocabulary and Word Study.**

Possible responses:
1. in the front of the book
2. at the front of the animal

FORMATIVE ASSESSMENT
Concept Vocabulary
If students fail to see the connection among the words, **then** work as a class to use the words in sentences on a single topic and discuss why they are connected.

Word Study
If students have trouble answering the questions, **then** review the prefix *fore-* and discuss the words. Also discuss the words *foresee* and *forehead*. For Reteach and Practice, see **Word Study: Old English Prefix *fore-* (RP).**

LANGUAGE DEVELOPMENT

TO FLY

Concept Vocabulary

| enable | foresight | prescient |
| myopic | naivete | seminal |

Why These Words? These concept words help to show the contrast between innovative and conventional ways of thinking. For example, in paragraph 5, the author criticizes Lord Kelvin's limited vision of flight as *myopic*. This word vividly reveals the author's view of Kelvin's mistake.

1. How does the concept vocabulary help the reader better understand the author's attitude toward invention and the future?

2. What other words in the selection connect to innovative or conventional thinking?

Practice

Notebook The concept vocabulary words appear in "To Fly."

1. Write a paragraph in which you describe something that might *enable* someone to become a groundbreaking artist or musician. Use at least three of the concept vocabulary words in your paragraph.
2. Divide the concept vocabulary words into two categories: innovative thinking and conventional thinking. Explain why you placed each word in its category.

Word Study

Old English Prefix: *fore-* The prefix *fore-* means "before," "toward," or "front." In paragraph 6, the author notes that lack of *foresight*, or looking ahead, can be an obstacle to creating new inventions. Use what you know about the prefix *fore-* to answer these questions.

1. Where is a book's foreword located?

2. Where would you expect to find an animal's *foreleg*?

WORD NETWORK
Add words related to invention from the text to your Word Network.

STANDARDS
Language
- Demonstrate command of the conventions of standard English capitalization, punctuation, and spelling when writing.
  c. Spell correctly.
- Determine or clarify the meaning of unknown and multiple meaning words or phrases based on *grade 8 reading and content*, choosing flexibly from a range of strategies.
  b. Use common, grade-appropriate Greek or Latin affixes and roots as clues to the meaning of a word.

VOCABULARY DEVELOPMENT

Concept Vocabulary Reinforcement Students will benefit from additional examples and practice with the concept vocabulary. Reinforce their comprehension with "show-you-know" sentences. The first part of the sentence uses the vocabulary word in an appropriate context. The second part of the sentence—the show-you-know part—clarifies the first. Model the strategy with this example for *foresight*:

It was lucky that Joaquin had the *foresight* to bring his umbrella; when he walked outside, it started to pour.

Then, give students these sentence prompts, and coach them in creating the clarification part:
1. The *myopic* scientist's experiment kept failing; _____.

   Possible response: he couldn't see the solution even though it was right in front of him.

2. Myra's invention is *prescient*; _____.

   Possible response: it meets a need many people don't even know we have yet.

Conventions

Capitalization Capital letters signal the beginning of a sentence or quotation and identify proper nouns and proper adjectives. **Proper nouns** include the names of people, geographical locations, specific events and time periods, organizations, languages, documents, and religions. **Proper adjectives** are derived from proper nouns, as in *French* (from *France*) and *Canadian* (from *Canada*).

This chart shows examples of situations in which capitalization is required.

CAPITALIZE	EXAMPLES
the first letter of the first word in a sentence	**T**he blue jay is a very aggressive bird. **W**ait! **C**an you give me back my pen?
the beginning of the first word in a quotation that is a complete sentence; the beginning of the first word in a line of dialogue	Einstein said, "**A**nyone who has never made a mistake has never tried anything new."
the pronoun *I*	After swimming, **I** felt tired.
proper nouns, including people's names, people's titles when used as part of their names, place names, and names of organizations	**E**lsa went sailing down the **H**udson **R**iver with **M**s. **L**iu and her **G**irl **S**cout troop.
proper adjectives, or adjectives formed from proper nouns	Many people of **B**razilian background speak the **P**ortuguese language.

Read It

1. Identify the capital letters in each sentence, and explain why each one is capitalized.
   a. Superman, a famous American superhero, has the power to fly.
   b. Neil deGrasse Tyson studied physics at Harvard and Columbia.
   c. I believe that *Collier's* published editorials about building a space station.
2. **Notebook** In "To Fly," find examples of two types of capitalization, and explain why each word is capitalized.

Write It

Notebook Rewrite this paragraph, correcting errors in capitalization.

In this article, neil degrasse tyson starts by discussing birds and mythical flying figures, such as pegasus, mercury, and peter pan. he continues with the invention of the airplane by the wright brothers. Although tyson mainly focuses on american technology, he also discusses the german v-2 rocket. he writes, "their vehicle was significant in many ways."

To Fly **475**

PERSONALIZE FOR LEARNING

Strategic Support

Capitalization Review paragraph 15 with students. Have them identify the capital letters in the paragraph and tell you why each of these letters is capitalized. Explain that when *Moon* is capitalized, it refers specifically to Earth's moon; tell students that they will often see this word not capitalized, in which case it refers to any moon. Explain that *Earth* is capitalized when it refers to our planet, but there are times when it is not capitalized. (for example, when the word refers to soil: We shoveled a great deal of earth as we dug the enormous hole).

DIGITAL PERSPECTIVES

Conventions

Capitalization Review the rules of capitalization presented in the chart. Explain that capitalization is a convention that helps writers convey ideas clearly. For example, capital letters at the beginning of sentences help readers to understand the text; they signal the start of a new idea. Capitalization of proper nouns and adjectives helps to emphasize an important or specific thing. For more support, see **Conventions: Capitalization.**

MAKE IT INTERACTIVE
Have students write a single sentence that demonstrates correct capitalization for the first letter of the first word in a sentence, the beginning of the first word in a quotation that's a complete sentence, proper nouns, and proper adjectives, as in the following sentence: *When Janell asked me if I preferred speaking the English language or the French language, I said, "Both languages work equally well for me."*

Read It

1. (a) **S**uperman (proper noun and first word of sentence); **A**merican (proper adjective); (b) **N**eil de**G**rasse **T**yson (proper noun and first word of sentence); **H**arvard (proper noun); **C**olumbia (proper noun) (c) **C**ollier's (proper noun - title)

Possible responses:

2. **P**resent (first word of sentence); **Y**ou (first word of sentence); **P**aris (proper noun); **Y**ou (first word of sentence); **Z**eppelin (proper noun); **T**he (first word of sentence); **S**oon (first word of sentence)

Write It

In this article, Neil deGrasse Tyson starts by discussing birds and mythical flying figures, such as Pegasus, Mercury, and Peter Pan. He continues with the invention of the airplane by the Wright brothers. Although Tyson mainly focuses on American technology, he also discusses the German V-2 rocket. He writes, "Their vehicle was significant in many ways."

FORMATIVE ASSESSMENT

Conventions

If students have trouble understanding capitalization, **then** use another passage from a magazine or newspaper to review other examples of capitalization. For Reteach and Practice, see **Conventions: Capitalization (RP).**

Whole-Class Learning **475**

TEACHING

Writing to Sources

Discuss with students the importance of stating a clear position, supporting it with relevant, logical evidence, and including and addressing counterclaims. Encourage students to include details from the article in their essay. For more support, see **Writing to Sources: Argumentative Essay.**

Reflect on Your Writing

1. Responses will vary. Students should clearly answer the question, suggesting a revision for the claim they made.

2. Responses will vary. Students should suggest an effective revision for how they presented evidence in their essay.

3. **Why These Words?** Responses will vary. Have students list specific examples of words they chose that clearly convey their ideas.

FORMATIVE ASSESSMENT

Writing to Sources

If students have trouble articulating a position, **then** ask them to simply tell you, in one or two sentences, what their response to the questions is. Then, have them write their response. For Reteach and Practice, see **Writing to Sources: Argumentative Essay (RP).**

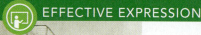

TO FLY

STANDARDS
Writing
Write arguments to support claims with clear reasons and relevant evidence.
  b. Support claim(s) with logical reasoning and relevant evidence, using accurate, credible sources and demonstrating an understanding of the topic or text.
  e. Provide a concluding statement or section that follows from and supports the argument presented.
Speaking and Listening
• Present claims and findings, emphasizing salient points in a focused, coherent manner with relevant evidence, sound valid reasoning, and well-chosen details; use appropriate eye contact, adequate volume, and clear pronunciation.
• Integrate multimedia and visual displays into presentations to clarify information, strengthen claims and evidence, and add interest.

476 UNIT 5 • INVENTION

EFFECTIVE EXPRESSION

Writing to Sources

In an argumentative essay, a writer states a position on a subject. He or she then defends or supports that position through the use of logical reasoning and relevant evidence.

Assignment
Tyson mentions the golden record that is attached to the side of the Voyager 2. That record includes music, voices, and other sounds that represent Earth and its occupants. Imagine that you are able to choose a sound to add to that record. What sound would it be? Write an **argumentative essay** in which you state and defend your choice. Follow these steps as you write:

• Clearly state your position, or claim, in an introductory paragraph. This should include both your choice of a sound and a broad reason for it.

• In the body of the essay, provide specific reasons for your choice, and support them with evidence from Tyson's essay, your own observations, or another source.

• Organize your reasons and evidence logically. Use transitional words and phrases, such as *because*, *instead*, and *after*, to clarify the relationships between your claims, your reasons, and the supporting evidence.

• Conclude with a strong closing statement that follows from and supports your argument.

Vocabulary and Conventions Connection Consider using several of the concept vocabulary words. Also, remember to use correct capitalization for proper nouns and proper adjectives.

| enable | foresight | prescient |
| myopic | naivete | seminal |

Reflect on Your Writing

After you have written your essay, answer the following questions.

1. How might you revise your claim to make it stronger?

2. How might you revise the way you present your evidence to help it more strongly support your claim?

3. **Why These Words?** The words you choose make a difference in your writing. Which words did you specifically choose to clearly convey your ideas?

PERSONALIZE FOR LEARNING

Challenge
Extend Review Tyson's use of allusion in paragraph 3. Have students write a paragraph about other examples of or allusions to birds, wings, or flying that are common in American culture. If students struggle to identify examples, have them conduct research online. Ask volunteers to share their responses with the class.

ESSENTIAL QUESTION: Are inventions realized through inspiration or perspiration?

Speaking and Listening

Assignment
Work with a partner to create and deliver an **informative presentation** on one of the historic flying feats or scientific principles that Neil deGrasse Tyson discusses in the text.

1. **Research Your Topic** Choose a science-related topic mentioned in the text. Divide up tasks between partners. Be sure that you know enough about the topic that you are able to explain it in easy-to-understand language.

2. **Plan Your Presentation** Once you have completed the research, decide how to best present the information. You may find and add images, or create your own graphics, such as a table or chart. As you create the presentation, keep the following in mind:
   - Clearly state your main idea and supporting ideas.
   - Identify interesting and relevant details to support your key points.
   - Select images that add useful information or illustrate your ideas.

3. **Prepare Your Delivery** Practice your presentation with your partner. Include the following performance techniques.
   - Vary your speaking volume to emphasize key points. Use eye contact appropriately to connect with your audience.
   - Present images at appropriate points.
   - Invite questions from listeners, and work to clarify any information they may not understand.

4. **Evaluate Presentations** As your classmates deliver their presentations, listen carefully. Use an evaluation guide like the one shown to analyze classmates' presentations.

PRESENTATION EVALUATION GUIDE

Rate each statement on a scale of 1 (not demonstrated) to 5 (demonstrated).

☐ The information was well organized and easy to understand.

☐ The presenters connected with their audience by maintaining eye contact and varying the volume of their voices.

☐ Relevant details provided support for the main ideas.

☐ Images fit well with the information and were presented in a way that made sense for the subject.

☐ Presenters allowed time for the audience to ask questions.

EVIDENCE LOG

Before moving on to a new selection, go to your Evidence Log and record what you learned from "To Fly."

To Fly **477**

DIGITAL PERSPECTIVES

Speaking and Listening

1. **Research Your Topic** Encourage students to take notes as they research, and to keep track of the sources that they use. Remind students that not all sources are trustworthy, and steer them to reliable sources.

2. **Plan Your Presentation** Encourage students to use the notes from their research to write their presentations. Remind them to think about the main point they are trying to make with each section of the presentation, and encourage them to think how each section fits in with the main idea of the whole presentation. Have students review each section to make sure that they have provided enough evidence to support the main point. Then support students as they take the time to find appropriate images, including photos, illustrations, tables, and charts, to make the presentation engaging and easier to understand.

3. **Prepare Your Delivery** Partners should practice their presentation in front of another pair of students before delivering the presentation before the whole class. This will allow students to give each other feedback before they do their final presentations.

4. **Evaluate Presentations** Encourage students to read through the Presentation Evaluation Guide before they begin listening to or giving presentations. Remind them that positive comments can be as valuable as critical comments.

For more support, see **Speaking and Listening: Informative Presentation.**

Evidence Log Support students in completing their Evidence Log. This paced activity will help prepare them for the Performance-Based Assessment at the end of the unit.

PERSONALIZE FOR LEARNING

Strategic Support

Extend In paragraph 16, Tyson says the gold phonograph record attached to *Voyager 2* has "earthly sounds of among many things, the human heartbeat." Have students write 1–2 paragraphs to consider these ideas:
- Why might scientists have included the human heartbeat on the record?
- What other sounds might be included on this record? Why?

Ask students to share their ideas with the class.

FORMATIVE ASSESSMENT

Speaking and Listening

- **If** students have trouble researching their topic, **then** have them try different key word searches that relate to their research project.
- **If** students are anxious about presenting in front of others, **then** have them spend more time practicing in front of a smaller group.

For Reteach and Practice, see **Speaking and Listening: Informative Presentation (RP).**

Selection Test

Administer the "To Fly" Selection Test, which is available in both print and digital formats online in Assessments.

Whole-Class Learning **477**

TEACHING

Jump Start

What makes an invention successful? Ask students to identify two things they have learned about the requirements needed for a successful invention after reading "Uncle Marcos" and "To Fly." Have students share their ideas and cite specific examples from the text to support their ideas.

Write an Argument

Remind students that they are going to formulate an opinion about which text best describes the dream or fantasy of human flight, based on the information they learned in this unit. Remind them to return to the text while gathering details.

Students should complete the assignment using word processing software to take advantage of editing tools and features.

Elements of an Argument

Students should begin their argumentative essays by making a claim and considering possible counterclaims. Point out that they need to support their claim with evidence from the text. Evidence and reasons to support the claim should be clear and relevant, and the argument should be organized in a logical manner. Also, students must have introductions and conclusions that make their argumentative essays cohesive and effective.

MAKE IT INTERACTIVE

Project "Inspiration Is Overrated!" and remind students of the writer's argument. Ask students to identify the elements that make up an effective argument. Ask volunteers to cite examples from the Launch Text, in preparation for writing their own arguments.

Academic Vocabulary

Ask students to use each of the academic vocabulary words in a sentence that could be either an introduction to an argument or a concluding sentence. For example: In order for legitimate flight to take place, the device must become airborne.

PERFORMANCE TASK: WRITE AN ARGUMENT

WRITING TO SOURCES
- UNCLE MARCOS
- TO FLY

ACADEMIC VOCABULARY

As you craft your argument, consider using some of the academic vocabulary you learned in the beginning of the unit.

opponent
position
contradict
legitimate
dissent

🔧 **Tool Kit**
Student Model of an Argument

STANDARDS
Writing
Write arguments to support claims with clear reasons and relevant evidence.

478 UNIT 5 • INVENTION

Write an Argument

You have just read two texts in which the authors explore the idea of human flight. In "Uncle Marcos," Uncle Marcos builds a flying machine and becomes a hero when he attempts to fly it over the mountains. In "To Fly," author Neil deGrasse Tyson discusses the development of human flight, from myths to airplanes and space travel. Now you will use your knowledge of these texts to explore your thoughts and write your own argument about human flight.

Assignment

Think about what flying means to people, both individually and collectively. Then, write an **argumentative essay** in which you make a claim that answers this question:

> Which text—"Uncle Marcos" or "To Fly"—best describes the dream or fantasy of human flight?

Be sure to clearly state your position and support it with logical reasoning and evidence from the texts.

Elements of an Argument

An **argument** is a logical way of presenting a viewpoint, belief, or stand on an issue. A well-written argument may convince the reader, change the reader's mind, or motivate the reader to take a certain action.

An effective argumentative essay about a literary work contains these elements:

- an analysis of the work, including its content and style
- a thesis statement or precise claim that expresses your interpretation of the work
- inclusion of a counterclaim, or alternate interpretation, and a discussion of why it is less convincing than yours
- textual evidence that supports your interpretation
- a logical organization, including a conclusion that follows from and supports your claim
- a formal style and objective tone appropriate for an academic purpose and audience
- error-free grammar, including correct use of gerunds and participles

Model Argument For a model of a well-crafted argument, see the Launch Text, "Inspiration Is Overrated!"

Challenge yourself to find all of the elements of an effective argument in the text. You will have an opportunity to review these elements as you prepare to write your own argument.

LAUNCH TEXT

AUTHOR'S PERSPECTIVE Kelly Gallagher, M.Ed.

Read, Analyze, Emulate Teachers can use scaffolding to help students grow as writers by studying good writing with them. When students recognize the qualities of good writing, they begin producing it.

Step 1: Read Provide students with excellent narratives from the text and direct them to "read like a writer" by paying attention to ideas, style, voice, and organization. Encourage students to look for the moves the writer made to elicit a response in readers.

Step 2: Analyze Focus on the ideas by asking students questions such as "What is the writer's theme? How did the writer develop it?" Then turn to style and voice, asking, "How did the writer develop the characters?" "What effect did the dialogue have?" "What sensory details did the writer use?" and "Where do you hear the author's distinctive voice?" Finally, ask questions about organization, such as "How did the writer pace events?" "What do you notice about the writer's paragraphing decisions?"

Step 3: Emulate Select one or two or the writer's moves to practice. Guide students to follow the models they studied as they write.

ESSENTIAL QUESTION: Are inventions realized through inspiration or perspiration?

Prewriting / Planning

Write a Working Claim You may already have a clear idea about which text you feel best portrays the dream of human flight. Start by writing a working claim. As you gather evidence that claim may shift or even change completely.

- Working Claim: _____

Identify Types of Details Your claim and supporting reasons determine the kinds of details you need to include. Consider these tips:

- **To analyze a text,** support your ideas with evidence from the selection.
- **To explain a personal response,** show how the work connects to your own experiences, observations, and ideas.
- **To refute an opposing point of view,** identify other interpretations of a text. Use the chart to gather textual details that support your position and could be used to refute, or argue against, a different opinion.

COUNTERCLAIM	RESPONSE WITH SUPPORTING EVIDENCE

Use Direct Quotations and Paraphrases When you write about literature, include textual details that show the accuracy of your interpretation. You may use direct quotations or paraphrases.

- A **direct quotation** is the inclusion of exact words from the text. Use a direct quotation when the words are especially powerful or unique.
- A **paraphrase** is a restatement of an author's ideas in your own words. You may choose to use a paraphrase because the exact words are not particularly interesting or you have so many direct quotations that your own words get lost. Make sure your paraphrase accurately reflects the meaning of the original.

Formatting Direct Quotations Shorter direct quotations appear within a sentence or paragraph. They are preceded by a comma or a colon. The page number on which the quotation appears is indicated in parentheses. Direct quotations that are four lines or longer are introduced with a colon, set apart, and indented ten spaces. The page number on which the quotation appears is always indicated in parentheses.

Direct Quotation in Running Text:
Rainsford is horrified when he realizes the truth of his situation: "The Cossack was the cat; he was the mouse" (232).

Direct Quotation Block Indented:
Rainsford breathes a sigh relief. Then, the horror hits him:

> Rainsford did not want to believe what his reason told him was true, but the truth was as evident as the sun that had by now pushed through the morning mists. The general was playing with him! (231)

EVIDENCE LOG
Review your Evidence Log and identify key details you may want to cite in your argument.

STANDARDS
Writing
Write arguments to support claims with clear reasons and relevant evidence.
a. Introduce claim(s), acknowledge and distinguish the claim(s) from alternate claims, and organize the reasons and evidence logically.
b. Support claim(s) with logical reasoning and relevant evidence, using accurate, credible sources and demonstrating an understanding of the topic or text.

DIGITAL PERSPECTIVES

Prewriting/Planning

Write a Working Claim Encourage students to take some notes about which text they feel best portrays the dream of human flight, so they can prepare a working claim.

Identify Types of Details Explain to students that their claims and supporting reasons will determine the details they need, such as evidence, connections to their experiences, or additional interpretations.

Use Direct Quotations and Paraphrases Remind students, as needed, that a direct quotation uses exact words to emphasize a point, and that a paraphrase restates the author's words.

Formatting Direct Quotations Assist students with formatting short or long direct quotations in a sentence or a paragraph.

PERSONALIZE FOR LEARNING

Strategic Support

Organization One of the most important parts of writing an effective argument is a logical organization of ideas. Suggest that students use index cards to organize their thoughts. Have them label one *Argument* for their main claim. Next, they should have *Claim and Evidence* cards, as well as *Counterclaim* cards. Finally, they should make a *Conclusion* card. Once they have completed all of their cards, students can easily organize and reorganize them to create the most impactful argument.

TEACHING

Drafting

Present Your Reasoning Explain to students that their argument should clearly state their position or claim. While completing the Argument Outline, students should think about the reasons for their claim and provide strong evidence for each reason. Restating the claim in the conclusion will further strengthen their argument.

Write a First Draft Students have been introduced to several organization tools for constructing an argument. Remind them to consider the tools they are using and draw on what they have learned about constructing a convincing argument. As students write their first draft, they should use their outline as a guide, making sure that their reasons and evidence are in a logical order and clearly support their claim.

 PERFORMANCE TASK: WRITE AN ARGUMENT

Drafting

Present Your Reasoning In a strong argument, reasons are supported by evidence and organized in an order that makes sense. Use an outline to help you plan your reasons and the evidence that supports them.

LAUNCH TEXT

Model: "Inspiration Is Overrated!"

CLAIM
Inspiration does not always produce successful inventions.

REASON
Many ideas for inventions never succeed.

EVIDENCE
One source says that only 3,000 products make money out of the 1.5 million products that have patents. Another says that only 1 in 5,000 products succeeds in the marketplace.

REASON
There is a reason many new inventions fail.

EVIDENCE
The author compares genius and invention by referring to the saying "genius is one percent inspiration and ninety-nine percent perspiration."

CONCLUSION
The conclusion restates and extends the claim: Successfully turning an idea into an invention requires a lot of hard work, not just inspiration.

Argument Outline

CLAIM

REASON

EVIDENCE

REASON

EVIDENCE

CONCLUSION

Write a First Draft As you write, use your outline as a guide.
- Start by writing an introduction that clearly introduces your claim about which text best captures the dream of human flight.
- Confirm that you have presented sufficient evidence from the texts, as well as personal experience or observations, to support your claim.
- Present your reasons and evidence in an order that makes sense.
- End with a concluding statement or section that briefly summarizes or extends your argument.

STANDARDS
Writing
Write arguments to support claims with clear reasons and relevant evidence.
  e. Provide a concluding statement or section that follows from and supports the argument presented.

AUTHOR'S PERSPECTIVE Jim Cummins, Ph.D.

Working in Pairs There is an important sense in which the development of academic expertise on the part of English Learners is a process of socialization rather than simply instruction. As a result, English writing development will be enhanced when students can work in pairs to create texts to share with others. That's because the process of collaboration and communication entails social interaction, which fosters language development.

- First, teachers can partner students to read, discuss, and react to a reading in the unit. Select a text, such as a nonfiction article, poem, or narrative.
- Have partners discuss the text, make notes about their ideas, and together write a response that highlights what they found important or responds to a prompt teachers provide. Encourage students to include specific details from the text in their drafts.

Then, teachers can invite partners to share their writing with the whole class. Guide students to explain how working together helped them express their ideas more effectively than working alone.

ESSENTIAL QUESTION: Are inventions realized through inspiration or perspiration?

DIGITAL PERSPECTIVES

LANGUAGE DEVELOPMENT: CONVENTIONS

Revising to Combine Sentences Using Gerunds and Participles

Gerunds and participles are **verbals**, or verb forms that are used as nouns or adjectives.

Identifying Gerunds A **gerund** is a verb form ending in *-ing* that acts as a noun. A **gerund phrase** is a gerund with modifiers or complements, all acting together as a noun. Like all nouns, gerunds and gerund phrases may be used in different parts of a sentence, as in these examples:

- **As a subject:** *Baking cookies* is Felice's hobby.
- **As a direct object:** Antoine enjoys *swimming*.
- **As a predicate noun:** David's greatest talent is *playing the piano*.
- **As the object of a preposition:** Greta never gets tired of *surfing*.

Identifying Participles A **participle** is a verb form that acts as an adjective. There are two kinds: present participles and past participles. A **participial phrase** is a participle with modifiers or complements, all acting together as an adjective.

- **Present participle:** The *chirping* canary sang sweetly.
- **Past participle in participial phrase:** The runner, *filled with hope*, raced toward the finish line.

Revising Sentences To combine sentences using gerunds and participles, first identify pairs of sentences that sound choppy and that relate to the same idea. Then, combine the sentences by using participles, gerunds, or participial or gerund phrases.

Read these choppy sentences: *The sisters like to draw and paint. They like to play together.* These sentences can be combined with two gerunds and a gerund phrase: *The sisters like drawing, painting, and playing together.*

Read It

These sentences from the Launch Text contain gerunds and participles. Describe the function of each verbal in the sentence shown.

- *Each of these* **forgotten** *contraptions was probably someone's bright idea, a flash of inspiration* **experienced while walking in the woods.** (past participle and past participial phrase)
- **Developing** *something new that actually works—and that people want—can take years.* (gerund)

Write It

As you draft your argument, find pairs of sentences that deal with the same subject. If they are too choppy or repetitive, combine them using gerund or participial phrases.

TIP

SPELLING
Make sure to spell verbs used as gerunds or participles correctly.

- Remember that when a verb ends in *e*, the *e* should almost always be dropped before adding *-ing*. For example, the verb *hike* becomes the gerund *hiking*.

- The past participles of regular verbs are the same as the past tense, which ends in *-ed*. For example, *remembered* is both the past tense and the past participle of *remember*.

- Irregular verbs form the past tense differently. Many of these verbs also have special forms for the past participle, such as *forgotten*. Make sure to use the correct form as your participle.

STANDARDS

Language
- Demonstrate command of the conventions of standard English grammar and usage when writing or speaking.
  a. Explain the function of verbals in general and their function in particular sentences.
- Demonstrate command of the conventions of standard English capitalization, punctuation, and spelling when writing.
  c. Spell correctly.

Revising to Combine Sentences Using Gerunds and Participles

Read It

Explain the function of gerunds and participles and how they are used to combine choppy sentences. Have students look at the examples of each type of gerund and participle provided before the *Read It* section on the student page. Ask them to provide alternative gerunds or participles for each sample sentence. The sentences must make sense.

MAKE IT INTERACTIVE

Point out the following sentence in paragraph 5 of the Launch Text:

A noted business magazine states that only one in 5,000 inventions succeeds in the marketplace.

Ask students to decide if there is a gerund or participle in this sentence and to identify it. Ask students to explain how they arrived at their conclusion. Have students find other examples in the Launch Text.

Write It

Provide students with additional sentences to combine for further practice.

At camp, Sam likes to swim and hike. Michael likes to paint and climb the rock wall.

In the evening, the chef cooks. He also prepares the food.

HOW LANGUAGE WORKS

Gerunds and Participial Phrases To reinforce student understanding of gerunds and participial phrases, copy the following chart on the board, and work with students to create example sentences for each category in the Verbal column.

Verbal	Sentence
Gerund as a subject	
Gerund as a direct object	
Gerund as a predicate noun	
Gerund as an object of a preposition	
Present participle	
Past participle	

TEACHING

Revising

Evaluating Your Draft
Before students begin revising their writing, they should first evaluate their draft to make sure that it contains all the required elements, is organized well, and adheres to the norms and conventions of written arguments.

Revising for Focus and Organization
Conclusion Remind students that while they may have provided a strong argument supported by reasons and evidence, the conclusion is the last thing that the reader reads and it is what is likely to stick with the reader most. Therefore, a well-planned conclusion can make the difference in constructing a convincing argument. Ask students to answer this question: What is the single most important idea I want my reader to take away from my argument?

Revising for Evidence and Elaboration
Use Language to Make Connections Provide students with opportunities to revise sentences using transitions effectively. Offer the following example. Ask students to use transitions to combine these three sentences into one:

The banana is the greatest piece of produce. It comes with its own wrapper. It provides you with potassium.

PERFORMANCE TASK: WRITE AN ARGUMENT

Revising

Evaluating Your Draft
Use the following checklist to evaluate the effectiveness of your first draft. Then, use your evaluation and the instruction on this page to guide your revision.

FOCUS AND ORGANIZATION	EVIDENCE AND ELABORATION	CONVENTIONS
☐ Presents a clearly stated claim that is distinguished from other possible claims.	☐ Uses relevant, logical evidence and reasons to support the main claim.	☐ Attends to the norms and conventions of the discipline, especially correct use of gerunds and participles.
☐ Organizes information in a logical way that makes connections between claims, counterclaims, reasons, and evidence.	☐ Considers and discusses possible counterclaims.	
☐ Presents ideas in a clear and formal style.	☐ Includes language that helps make connections among claims, counterclaims, and supporting details.	
☐ Includes a conclusion that logically supports or extends the argument.		

WORD NETWORK
Include interesting words from your Word Network in your argument.

Revising for Focus and Organization
Conclusion Make sure that your concluding statement or section logically supports or extends your argument. You may wish to restate your claim and summarize the strongest reasons and evidence that support it. You may also introduce a final quotation or example. If you wish to extend your argument, make sure the connection between what you have written and your new idea is clear and logical. Use transition words and other language to make connections and help readers understand your train of thought.

Revising for Evidence and Elaboration
Use Language to Make Connections Make sure you are using transitions effectively in your argument. Add new transition words and phrases if necessary to make connections and clarify the relationship between ideas. Use words such as *because* and *therefore* to make connections that establish clearly how one event or idea led to another. Use words and phrases such as *such as* and *for example* to introduce evidence and examples. Use words such as *before* and *later* to clarify when events occurred.

STANDARDS
Writing
Write arguments to support claims with clear reasons and relevant evidence.
  c. Use words, phrases, and clauses to create cohesion and clarify the relationships among claim(s), counterclaims, reasons, and evidence.
  e. Provide a concluding statement or section that follows from and supports the argument presented.

482 UNIT 5 • INVENTION

PERSONALIZE FOR LEARNING

English Language Support
Transitions Writing complex sentences that are not run-ons can be a challenge. Practice combining sentences will help students improve their writing. Provide students with a list of transition words. You can use the examples in this lesson or add others. Provide them with several short sentences on index cards or presented on a screen.
ALL LEVELS

482 UNIT 5 • INVENTION

ESSENTIAL QUESTION: Are inventions realized through inspiration or perspiration?

PEER REVIEW

Exchange essays with a classmate. Use the checklist to evaluate your classmate's essay and provide supportive feedback.

1. Is the claim clearly stated and distinguished from other possible claims and counterclaims?

   ☐ yes ☐ no   If no, suggest how the writer might improve it.

2. Are the reasons and evidence logical and relevant?

   ☐ yes ☐ no   If no, explain what the author might add or remove.

3. Does the organization make clear connections among claims, counterclaims, reasons, and evidence?

   ☐ yes ☐ no   If no, tell what you think might be missing.

4. What is the strongest part of your classmate's essay? Why?

Editing and Proofreading

Edit for Conventions Reread your draft for accuracy and consistency. Correct errors in grammar and word usage. Make sure you have correctly combined sentences using gerunds and participles.

Proofread for Accuracy Read your draft carefully, looking for errors in spelling and punctuation. As you proofread, make sure that you have used the correct spelling for gerunds and other verbs ending in –*ing*. Also check that you have used the correct form of any irregular past participles, such as *lit* and *broken*.

Publishing and Presenting

Post your final essay to a class or school website so classmates can read and comment on your ideas. Consider the ways in which other students' arguments are similar to and different from your own.

Reflecting

Reflect on what you learned as you wrote your argument. What did you learn about how ideas for inventions are realized? What was the most challenging aspect of composing your argument? Did you learn something from reviewing yours and others' work that might inform your writing process in the future?

STANDARDS

Writing
- Write arguments to support claims with clear reasons and relevant evidence.
- With some guidance and support from peers and adults, develop and strengthen writing as needed by planning, revising, editing, rewriting, or trying a new approach, focusing on how well purpose and audience have been addressed.

DIGITAL PERSPECTIVES

Peer Review

Remind students that the purpose of peer review is to provide useful feedback. Constructive feedback is written in a positive way but also provides useful information for improving an essay.

Editing and Proofreading

As students edit, remind them to identify sentences that could be combined using gerunds and participles. Students should look for grammar, spelling, and punctuation errors as they proofread their work.

Publishing and Presenting

Have students read several examples of other students' arguments. As a class, discuss the impact of reading the work of others. Did they find points they may have missed to support their own arguments? Did reading opposing viewpoints impact how they felt about their own points of view?

Reflecting

Explain that by reflecting on their arguments, students may gain a better sense of how to improve their writing and how to better present their ideas and evidence.

PERSONALIZE FOR LEARNING

Challenge

Write an Argument Ask students to suggest a current topic that has opposing viewpoints and have them write a brief argument related to the topic. Remind students to use what they have learned in this unit to construct an effective argument. Be sure they include claims, reasoning, and evidence, as well as a strong introduction and conclusion. Ask volunteers to share their arguments with the class.

OVERVIEW

SMALL-GROUP LEARNING

Are inventions realized through inspiration or perspiration?

Explain that most inventions are the result of someone's creative idea. Sometimes, inventions are "discovered" when the inventor is working on something else. During Small-Group Learning, students will read selections that explore innovative and groundbreaking inventors and their inventions that resulted from both inspired ideas and hard work.

Small-Group Learning Strategies ▶

Review the Learning Strategies with students and explain that as they work through Small-Group Learning they will develop strategies to work in small-group environments.

- Have students watch the video on Small-Group Learning Strategies.
- A video on this topic is available online in the Professional Development Center.

You may wish to discuss some action items to add to the chart as a class before students complete it on their own. For example, for "Support others," you might solicit the following from students:

- Encourage others in your group to elaborate on an idea.
- Invite others who have not yet spoken to join the discussion.

> ### Block Scheduling
> Each day in this Pacing Plan represents a 40–50 minute class period. Teachers using block scheduling may combine days to reflect their class schedule. In addition, teachers may revise pacing to differentiate and support core instruction by integrating components and resources as students require.

📅 **Pacing Plan**

OVERVIEW: SMALL-GROUP LEARNING

ESSENTIAL QUESTION:

Are inventions realized through inspiration or perspiration?

Can hard work alone—or a great idea alone—result in a successful invention? How much of an invention's success results from creativity as opposed to hard work? You will work in a group to continue your exploration of the process of invention.

Small-Group Learning Strategies

Throughout your life, you'll continue to develop strategies that make you a better learner. In school, in your community, and in your career, you will continue to learn and work in teams.

Review these strategies and the actions you can take to practice them as you work in teams. Add ideas of your own for each step. Use these strategies during Small-Group Learning.

STRATEGY	ACTION PLAN
Prepare	• Complete your assignments so that you are prepared for group work. • Organize your thinking so you can contribute to your group's discussions. •
Participate fully	• Make eye contact to signal that you are listening and taking in what is being said. • Use text evidence when making a point. •
Support others	• Build off ideas from others in your group. • Invite others who have not yet spoken to do so. •
Clarify	• Paraphrase the ideas of others to ensure that your understanding is correct. • Ask follow-up questions. •

484 UNIT 5 • INVENTION

SCAN FOR MULTIMEDIA

Unit Introduction | Introduce Whole-Class Learning | Uncle Marcos | To Fly | Performance Task

1 2 3 4 5 6 7 8 9 10 11 12 13 14 15 16 17 18

484 UNIT 5 • INVENTION

CONTENTS

COMPARE

BIOGRAPHY

Nikola Tesla: The Greatest Inventor of All?
Vicky Baez

How did history forget about one of its most visionary inventors?

NOVEL EXCERPT

from The Invention of Everything Else
Samantha Hunt

The combination of fact, fiction, biography, and history creates an engaging portrait of an under-appreciated inventor.

SCIENCE ARTICLE

25 Years Later, Hubble Sees Beyond Troubled Start
Dennis Overbye

In spite of its flaws, the Hubble Space Telescope remains a groundbreaking invention that has changed the way people see the universe.

MEDIA: VIDEO

Sounds of a Glass Armonica

Watch one of Benjamin Franklin's favorite inventions in action!

PERFORMANCE TASK

SPEAKING AND LISTENING FOCUS

Conduct a Debate

The Small-Group readings offer various ideas about the hard work and creative thinking that goes into inventions. After reading, your group will plan and conduct a debate on the Essential Question.

Overview: Small-Group Learning 485

DIGITAL PERSPECTIVES

Contents

Selections Circulate among groups as they preview the selections. You might encourage groups to discuss any knowledge they already have about any of the selections or the situations and settings shown in the photographs. Students may wish to take a poll within their group to determine which selections look the most interesting.

Remind students that communicating and collaborating in groups is an important skill that they will use throughout their lives—in school, in their careers, and in their community.

Performance Task

Conduct a Debate Give groups time to read about and briefly discuss the small-group debate they will create after reading. Encourage students to do some preliminary thinking about the types of media they may want to use. This may help focus their subsequent reading and group discussion.

Introduce Small-Group Learning

Nikola Tesla: The Greatest Inventor of All? — 19 20 21

from The Invention of Everything Else — 22 23 24 25

25 Years Later, Hubble Sees Beyond Troubled Start — 26 27 28

Media: Sounds of a Glass Armonica — 29 30

Performance Task — 31 32

Introduce Independent Learning

Independent Learning — 33 34

Performance-Based Assessment — 35 36

SMALL-GROUP LEARNING

OVERVIEW

SMALL-GROUP LEARNING

Working as a Team

1. **Take a Position** Remind groups to let all members share their responses. You may wish to set a time limit for this discussion.

2. **List Your Rules** You may want to have groups share their lists of rules and consolidate them into a master list to be displayed and followed by all groups.

3. **Apply the Rules** As you circulate among the groups, ensure that students are staying on task. Consider a short time limit for this step.

4. **Name Your Group** This task can be creative and fun. If students have trouble coming up with a name, suggest that they think of something related to the unit topic. Encourage groups to share their names with the class.

5. **Create a Communication Plan** Encourage groups to include in their plans agreed-upon times during the day to share ideas. They should also devise a method for recording and saving their communications.

Accountable Talk

You can post these Accountable Talk suggestions and encourage students to add their own. Students should:

Remember to . . . Ask clarifying questions.
Which sounds like . . .
Can you please repeat what you said?
Would you give me an example?
I think you said _____. Did I understand you correctly?

Remember to . . . Explain your thinking.
Which sounds like . . .
I believe _____ is true because _____.
I feel _____ because _____.

Remember to . . . Build on the ideas of others.
Which sounds like . . .
When _____ said _____, it made me think of _____.

OVERVIEW: SMALL-GROUP LEARNING

Working as a Team

1. **Take a Position** In your group, discuss the following question:

   Is an invention typically created by a single inventor, or is an invention usually the result of many minds working together?

   As you take turns sharing your thoughts, be sure to provide information and examples to support your ideas. After all group members have shared, discuss your responses. Did other group members' ideas change your own response? Why or why not?

2. **List Your Rules** As a group, decide on the rules that you will follow as you work together. Samples are provided; add two more of your own. You may add or revise rules based on your experience together.

   - Everyone should participate in group discussions.
   - People should not interrupt.
   - _____
   - _____

3. **Apply the Rules** Practice working as a group. Share what you have learned about invention. Make sure each person in the group contributes. Take notes and be prepared to share with the class one thing that you heard from another member of your group.

4. **Name Your Group** Choose a name that reflects the unit topic.

   Our group's name: _____

5. **Create a Communication Plan** Decide how you want to communicate with one another. For example, you might use online collaboration tools, email, or instant messaging.

   Our group's decision: _____

FACILITATING SMALL-GROUP LEARNING

Forming Groups You may wish to form groups for Small-Group Learning so that each consists of students with different learning abilities. Some students may be adept at organizing information whereas other may have strengths related to generating or synthesizing information. A good mix of abilities can make the experience of Small-Group Learning dynamic and productive.

ESSENTIAL QUESTION: Are inventions realized through inspiration or perspiration?

Making a Schedule

First, find out the due dates for the small-group activities. Then, preview the texts and activities with your group and make a schedule for completing the tasks.

SELECTION	ACTIVITIES	DUE DATE
Nikola Tesla: The Greatest Inventor of All?		
from The Invention of Everything Else		
25 Years Later, Hubble Sees Beyond Troubled Start		
Sounds of a Glass Armonica		

Working on Group Projects

As your group works together, you'll find it more effective if each person has a specific role. Different projects require different roles. Before beginning a project, discuss the necessary roles and choose one for each group member. Here are some possible roles; add your own ideas.

Project Manager: monitors the schedule and keeps everyone on task
Researcher: organizes research activities
Recorder: takes notes during group meetings

_____

_____

_____

_____

SCAN FOR MULTIMEDIA

DIGITAL PERSPECTIVES

Making a Schedule

Encourage groups to preview the reading selections and to consider how long it will take them to complete the activities accompanying each selection. Point out that they can adjust the due dates for particular selections as needed as they work on their small-group projects; however, they must complete all assigned tasks before the group Performance Task is due. Encourage groups to review their schedules upon completing the activities for each selection to make sure they are on track to meet the final due date.

Working on Group Projects

Point out to groups that the roles they assign can also be changed later. Students might have to make changes based on who is best at doing what. Try to make sure that there is no favoritism, cliquishness, or stereotyping by gender or other means in the assignment of roles.

Also, you should review the roles each group assigns to its members. Based on your understanding of students' individual strengths, you might find it necessary to suggest some changes.

AUTHOR'S PERSPECTIVE Kelly Gallagher, M.Ed.

Accountability in Group Work The teacher's role during group work is to serve as the facilitator rather than as the leader. This means that the teacher should support the thinking and discussion but not provide the answers or content direction. Problems can arise if a group is unfocused, if the task is not meaningful, or if there is no accountability. To help groups work together well, achieve their goals, and ensure accountability, teachers can follow these three steps:

1. First, define and clarify the task. Explain why it is valuable, and make sure students know what they are expected to do.
2. Let each group know that one student will be selected randomly to share the group's thinking. This randomness builds in accountability.
3. Pull the whole class back together to share information and to check learning.

If groups struggle, teachers can prod them with questions that support how they will get to the answer. For example, if they are unable to find the main point of the essay, ask them: "In this type of text, where might a reader look to find the main idea?"

PLANNING

SMALL-GROUP LEARNING • NIKOLA TESLA: THE GREATEST INVENTOR OF ALL?

Nikola Tesla: The Greatest Inventor of All?

🔊 AUDIO SUMMARIES
Audio summaries of "Nikola Tesla: The Greatest Inventor of All?" are available online in both English and Spanish in the Interactive Teacher's Edition or Unit Resources. Assigning these summaries prior to reading the selection may help students build additional background knowledge and set a context for their first read.

Summary
In "Nikola Tesla: The Greatest Inventor of All?" Vicky Baez tells the story of the genius behind much of modern electrical technology. Tesla came to America in 1884 to work with Thomas Edison. After he and Edison had a falling out, Tesla started his own company. There he developed the system of alternating current, which differed from Edison's direct current. (Both are used today.) Tesla invented many devices still in use. He also helped develop the electrical system used in modern cities. With George Westinghouse he created a power plant at Niagara Falls that provided power throughout New York State. Tesla died penniless and forgotten, but the electric vehicle he designed in 1882 is the forerunner of the Tesla, a modern electric car.

Insight
"Nikola Tesla: The Greatest Inventor of All?" provides students with a glimpse of the creative genius who invented many practical applications of electricity. The fact that Tesla was almost forgotten provides an interesting insight into the power of publicity and labeling. Modern electric companies bear Edison's name in spite of their use of alternating current and the technologies that Tesla invented.

ESSENTIAL QUESTION:
Are inventions realized through inspiration or perspiration?

Connection to Essential Question
For Nikola Tesla, the work behind an invention took place in his mind. He worked out the technology in his head before his invention took physical form. Unlike Edison, who made many models of an invention before he was satisfied—expending greater "perspiration"—Tesla was more dependent on inspiration for the realization of his invention.

SMALL-GROUP LEARNING PERFORMANCE TASK
Are inventions realized through inspiration or perspiration?

UNIT PERFORMANCE-BASED ASSESSMENT
Which invention described in this unit has had the biggest impact on humanity?

Connection to Performance Tasks

Small-Group Learning Performance Task "Nikola Tesla: The Greatest Inventor of All?" provides an interesting view of the creative process. The selection suggests that the realization of an invention is just as reliant on inspiration as it is on physical effort.

Unit Performance-Based Assessment The selection indicates that prolific creators are encouraged to invent by the connections their minds make between physical principles. Tesla was driven by his own creativity to demonstrate the practical application of the inventions he envisioned. In their essays, students will determine the impact of his work.

DIGITAL PERSPECTIVES

 Audio Video Document Annotation Highlights EL Highlights Online Assessment

LESSON RESOURCES

	Making Meaning	Language Development
Lesson	First Read Close Read Analyze the Text Analyze Craft and Structure	Concept Vocabulary Word Study Conventions
Instructional Standards	**RI.10** By the end of the year, read and comprehend literary nonfiction . . . **L.5** Demonstrate understanding of figurative language . . . **L.5.b** Use the relationship between particular words . . . **L.6** Acquire and use accurately grade-appropriate general academic and domain-specific words and phrases . . . **RI.3** Analyze how a text makes connections . . . **RI.5** Analyze in detail the structure of a specific paragraph . . .	**L.4** Determine or clarify the meaning of unknown and multiple-meaning words and phrases . . . **L.4.c** Consult general and specialized reference materials . . . **L.2** Demonstrate command of the conventions . . . **L.2.a** Use punctuation . . .

▷ STUDENT RESOURCES

Available online in the Interactive Student Edition or Unit Resources	🔊 Selection Audio 📄 First-Read Guide: Nonfiction 📄 Close-Read Guide: Nonfiction	📄 Word Network

▷ TEACHER RESOURCES

Selection Resources Available online in the Interactive Teacher's Edition or Unit Resources	🔊 Audio Summaries ✎ Annotation Highlights 💬 EL Highlights 📄 English Language Support Lesson: Cause and Effect 📄 Nikola Tesla: The Greatest Inventor of All?: Text Questions 📄 Analyze Craft and Structure: Biographical Writing	📄 Concept Vocabulary and Word Study 📄 Conventions: Commas and Semicolons
Reteach/Practice (RP) Available online in the Interactive Teacher's Edition or Unit Resources	📄 Analyze Craft and Structure: Biographical Writing (RP)	📄 Word Study: Multiple-Meaning Words (RP) 📄 Conventions: Commas and Semicolons (RP)
Assessment Available online in Assessments	📄✓ Selection Test	
My Resources	📄 A Unit 5 Answer Key is available online and in the Interactive Teacher's Edition.	

PERSONALIZE FOR LEARNING

SMALL-GROUP LEARNING • NIKOLA TESLA: THE GREATEST INVENTOR OF ALL?

Reading Support

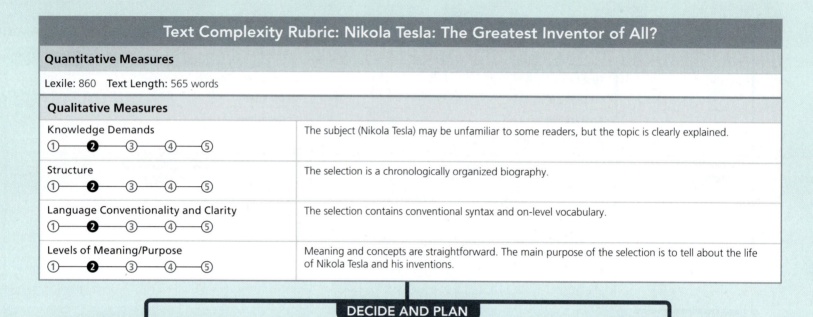

Text Complexity Rubric: Nikola Tesla: The Greatest Inventor of All?

Quantitative Measures

Lexile: 860   Text Length: 565 words

Qualitative Measures

Knowledge Demands ①—❷—③—④—⑤	The subject (Nikola Tesla) may be unfamiliar to some readers, but the topic is clearly explained.
Structure ①—❷—③—④—⑤	The selection is a chronologically organized biography.
Language Conventionality and Clarity ①—❷—③—④—⑤	The selection contains conventional syntax and on-level vocabulary.
Levels of Meaning/Purpose ①—❷—③—④—⑤	Meaning and concepts are straightforward. The main purpose of the selection is to tell about the life of Nikola Tesla and his inventions.

DECIDE AND PLAN

English Language Support
Provide English Learners with support for knowledge demands and structure as they read the selection.

Knowledge Demands Tell students that this selection is about the inventor Nikola Tesla. They should expect to see language that describes the inventions, electricity, and devices.

Structure If students have difficulty following the text, encourage them to keep a timeline of events as they read, noting the year of the event and the main thing that happened.

Strategic Support
Provide students with strategic support to ensure that they can successfully read the text.

Knowledge Demands Using the background information for the selection, discuss Nikola Tesla and Thomas Edison. Ask students to share their prior knowledge about these men and their inventions.

Meaning Pair students. Have them each take a paragraph and retell it to their partner, using their own descriptions without reading from the text. Encourage them to include details. They may refer to the text as needed to remember details, but they should use their own words.

Challenge
Provide students who need to be challenged with ideas for how they can go beyond a simple interpretation of the text.

Text Analysis Have students analyze how Edison is portrayed in the biography. What kind of person does he seem to be? What are his personality traits? Ask students to look for text evidence to support their ideas.

Written Response Ask students to research Tesla Motors. Have students write a short essay telling how the new company is honoring the legacy of Nikola Tesla.

TEACH

Read and Respond
Have the groups read the selection and complete the Making Meaning and Language Development activities.

Standards Support Through Teaching and Learning Cycle

IDENTIFY NEEDS

Analyze results of the Beginning-of-Year Assessment, focusing on the items relating to Unit 5. Also take into consideration student performance to this point and your observations of where particular students struggle.

DECIDE AND PLAN

- If students have performed poorly on items matching these standards, then provide selection scaffolds before assigning them the on-level lesson provided in the Student Edition.
- If students have done well on the Beginning-of-Year Assessment, then challenge them to keep progressing and learning by giving them opportunities to practice the skills in depth.
- Use the Selection Resources listed on the Planning pages for "Nikola Tesla: The Greatest Inventor of All?" to help students continually improve their ability to master the standards.

Instructional Standards: Nikola Tesla: The Greatest Inventor of All?

	Catching Up	This Year	Looking Forward
Reading	You may wish to administer the **Analyze Craft and Structure: Biographical Writing (RP)** worksheet to help students understand what tools and structures are available to biographical writers.	**RI.3** Analyze how a text makes connections among and distinctions between individuals, ideas, or events.	Ask students to analyze the order in which the information is given.
Language	Review the **Word Study: Multiple-Meaning Words (RP)** worksheet with students to help familiarize them with more multiple-meaning words. Review the **Conventions: Commas and Semicolons (RP)** worksheet with students to ensure they know the difference between these two punctuation marks.	**L.4** Determine or clarify the meaning of unknown and multiple-meaning words or phrases based on *grade 8 reading and content,* choosing flexibly from a range of strategies. **L.2** Demonstrate command of the conventions of standard English capitalization, punctuation, and spelling when writing.	Challenge students to look up words for which they know only one definition, to find out if they have multiple meanings. Work with students to discuss the differences between using semicolons, dashes, and ellipses.

ANALYZE AND REVISE

- Analyze student work for evidence of student learning.
- Identify whether or not students have met the expectations in the standards.
- Identify implications for future instruction.

TEACH

Implement the planned lesson, and gather evidence of student learning.

FACILITATING

Jump Start

FIRST READ Why do we sometimes fail to recognize a person's accomplishments? Who decides which names in history are remembered? Engage students in a conversation about recognizing achievement that sets the context for reading "Nikola Tesla: The Greatest Inventor of All?" As students share their thoughts, guide them to identify specific factors that affected their responses.

Nikola Tesla: The Greatest Inventor of All? 🔊 📄

Why do some inventions catch on while others fail? What makes one inventor more successful than another? Modeling questions such as these will help students connect to "Nikola Tesla: The Greatest Inventor of All?" and to the Small-Group Performance Task assignment. Selection audio and print capability for the selection are available in the Interactive Teacher's Edition.

Concept Vocabulary

Have students look closely at the example of a base word, or "inside word," and discuss how they can use base words to figure out the meanings of the concept vocabulary terms. Ask students to think of other examples of unfamiliar terms that have base words they know.

● FIRST READ

As they read, students should perform the steps of the first read:

NOTICE: You may want to encourage students to identify or infer key ideas in the text.

ANNOTATE: Remind students to mark passages that contrast Tesla's achievements with those of his peers.

CONNECT: Connect Tesla's achievements with those of other people you know or have heard of whose talent has been overlooked or underestimated.

RESPOND: Students will answer questions and write a summary to demonstrate understanding.

Point out to students that while they will always complete the Respond step at the end of the first read, the other steps will probably happen somewhat concurrently. You may wish to print copies of the **First-Read Guide: Nonfiction** for students to use. 📄

488 UNIT 5 • INVENTION

👥 MAKING MEANING

Comparing Texts

In this lesson, you will read and compare the biographical work "Nikola Tesla: The Greatest Inventor of All?" with an excerpt from *The Invention of Everything Else*, a fictional account of Tesla's life.

from THE INVENTION OF EVERYTHING ELSE

About the Author
Vicky Baez (b. 1971) was born in Albuquerque, New Mexico. In elementary school, one of Baez's teachers gave exciting science demonstrations that instilled in her a love of the subject, and she frequently writes about science and scientists. Her own science library currently exceeds 1,000 books.

Nikola Tesla: The Greatest Inventor of All?

Concept Vocabulary

As you perform your first read, you will encounter these words.

| engineer | generators | current |

Base Words If these words are unfamiliar, check to see if any of them contain a base word you know. Then, use context and your knowledge of the "inside" word to find the meanings of the concept words. Follow this strategy:

Unfamiliar Word: *equipment*

Familiar "Inside" Word: *equip*, which means "to supply with necessary items for a particular purpose"

Context: At each place where he worked, [Tesla] designed and made improvements to the **equipment**.

Conclusion: Tesla designed *equipment*, or items used for a purpose.

Apply your knowledge of base words and other vocabulary strategies to determine the meanings of words you encounter during your first read.

First Read NONFICTION

Apply these strategies as you conduct your first read. You will have an opportunity to complete a close read after your first read.

NOTICE the general ideas of the text. *What* is it about? *Who* is involved?

ANNOTATE by marking vocabulary and key passages you want to revisit.

CONNECT ideas within the selection to what you already know and what you have already read.

RESPOND by completing the Comprehension Check and by writing a brief summary of the selection.

▤ STANDARDS

Reading Informational Text
By the end of the year, read and comprehend literary nonfiction at the high end of the grades 6–8 text complexity band independently and proficiently.

Language
• Demonstrate understanding of figurative language, word relationships, and nuances in word meaning.
    b. Use the relationship between particular words to better understand each of the words.
• Acquire and use accurately grade-appropriate general academic and domain-specific words and phrases; gather vocabulary knowledge when considering a word or phrase important to comprehension or expression.

488 UNIT 5 • INVENTION

AUTHOR'S PERSPECTIVE   Jim Cummins, Ph.D.

Language Awareness Vocabulary knowledge is an extremely robust predictor of students' reading comprehension. The Frayer model is an effective tool for enabling students to extend their vocabulary knowledge in a systematic way. The tool aims to deepen students' knowledge of words and concepts by focusing their attention not only on simple definitions but also on characteristics of the concept and examples and non-examples of it.

Create an electronic template and have students work in groups of "language detectives" to enter new and interesting words onto the group's template. If time allows, encourage students to complete two to five words each day. Where multiple home languages are represented in a

Nikola Tesla: The Greatest Inventor of All?

Vicky Baez

BIOGRAPHY

BACKGROUND

At the end of the nineteenth century, electricity was a new technology. At this time, very few people had access to electric lighting, and most people used coal, gas, and steam power for energy. Today, electricity has become a common utility because of inventors like Nikola Tesla and Thomas Edison.

1 Nikola Tesla was born in 1856 to a Serbian family in the country that is now called Croatia. When Tesla was young, he was able to do such complex math problems in his head that his teachers thought he was cheating. He finished high school in 3 years instead of 4.

2 He started college, but didn't finish. However, he learned enough to go to work. He moved several times over the next few years, each time getting a job as an electrician. At each place where he worked, he designed and made improvements to the equipment.

3 In 1884, he moved to New York City. He came with a letter of recommendation to Thomas Edison from one of his bosses. The letter is claimed to have said, "I know two great men and you are one of them; the other is this young man." Edison hired Tesla, who began as an electrical **engineer**. He quickly became very important to the company, solving some of its most difficult problems. Tesla was able to use his mind to imagine how different methods worked. Edison always made a lot of models and tried them out, which took a lot longer.

4 In 1885, Tesla and Edison had a falling out. Tesla told Edison he could improve some of Edison's motors and **generators**. Edison told him he would pay him $50,000 if he did. This was quite a lot of money at that time. Tesla worked hard and spent months on the task. When he succeeded, he asked Edison for the reward, but Edison told him he had been joking. He said, "Tesla, you don't understand our American humor." He offered Tesla a $10 raise on his $18 weekly pay. Tesla quit the job.

5 Tesla started his own company in 1887, Tesla Electric Light and Manufacturing. There he worked on making a system called

NOTES

Mark base words or indicate another strategy that helped you determine meaning.

engineer (ehn jih NEER) *n.*
MEANING:

generators (JEHN uhr ray tuhrz) *n.*
MEANING:

FACILITATING

Concept Vocabulary

CURRENT If groups struggle to define the term *current* in paragraph 5, have them apply what they know about current related to electricity. Then have them discuss the difference between alternating and direct current.

Possible response: *Current* describes the flow of electricity. *Alternating current* means a "flow of electricity that switches sides or directions," while *direct current* is a "flow of electricity that moves in only one direction."

Comprehension Check

Possible responses:

1. Tesla could solve complex math problems in his head.
2. Edison did not pay him what he said he would.
3. Tesla Motors makes electric cars, and its first car used Tesla's design.
4. Summaries will vary but should include the following information: Tesla was born in what is now Croatia; though he was gifted in math, he didn't finish college but worked as an electrician, designing equipment; in 1884, he started to work for Edison in New York City; their working relationship ended when Edison refused to pay Tesla what he promised; Tesla started his own company and developed an "alternating current," while Edison used "direct current"; each claimed his system was better; Tesla died forgotten and penniless, but now he is celebrated as a great inventor.

Research

Research to Clarify If students have difficulty narrowing their research results on the unfamiliar details in the text, suggest they enter search terms as follows: *Tesla AND "X-rays," Tesla AND "fluorescent lights,"* and so on.

NOTES
Mark base words or indicate another strategy that helped you determine meaning.

current (KUR uhnt) *n.*
MEANING:

"alternating **current**" to produce electricity. Thomas Edison thought his system, called "direct current," was better and safer. The two became rivals. They each gave talks about why his particular method was better. They had public demonstrations to show people how they created electricity. This rivalry was referred to as the "War of the Currents."

6   Another rival of Edison's, George Westinghouse, had also been trying to create an electrical system. He bought some of Tesla's inventions and paid him $2,000 a month to consult with him. Tesla spent all his money on new inventions and ideas. He invented the Tesla coil, which carried electricity without wires. You can still see a Tesla coil at some museums today. Tesla invented or helped develop a long list of devices, including X-ray machines, radio, wireless remotes, fluorescent lights, and the system of electricity that is still used today in our cities. He helped create a power plant in Niagara Falls that provided power all the way to New York City. He was given many awards and honorary degrees from universities all over the world.

7   Sadly, Tesla died without a cent. People forgot about him, and remembered Edison, whose companies still exist and have his name, like Consolidated Edison, the electric company that powers New York City. In the 1990s, people started to write about Tesla, and now he is becoming better known again. The owner of a new car company named it Tesla Motors because they make electric cars. Their first car used Tesla's design from 1882 for an electric car.

Comprehension Check

Complete the following items after you finish your first read. Review and clarify details with your group.

1. Why did Tesla's teachers sometimes think he was cheating?
2. Why did Tesla leave Edison's company?
3. Why does Tesla Motors use Tesla's name?
4. 📓 **Notebook** Confirm your understanding of the biography by writing a short summary.

RESEARCH

Research to Clarify Choose at least one unfamiliar detail from the biography. Briefly research that detail. In what way does the information you learned shed light on an aspect of the biography?

490   UNIT 5 • INVENTION

PERSONALIZE FOR LEARNING

Challenge

Dramatize the "War of the Currents" Have students research the dispute between Tesla and Edison described in paragraph 5 and how it grew into the "War of the Currents." Students can work in groups to research the rivalry and write a play featuring Tesla, Edison, and possibly Westinghouse. Have students present their dramatizations, in which they should explain the technology that each inventor promoted. As a safety precaution, do not permit students to reproduce the two rivals' public demonstrations with real electricity.

ESSENTIAL QUESTION: Are inventions realized through inspiration or perspiration?

Close Read the Text

With your group, revisit sections of the text you marked during your first read. **Annotate** what you notice. What **questions** do you have? What can you **conclude**?

NIKOLA TESLA: THE GREATEST INVENTOR OF ALL?

Analyze the Text

CITE TEXTUAL EVIDENCE to support your answers.

📓 **Notebook** Complete the activities.

1. **Review and Clarify** With your group, reread paragraph 3. Discuss the differences between Edison's and Tesla's approaches to invention. Whose approach, Edison's or Tesla's, do you think is better? Why?

2. **Present and Discuss** Discuss what you noticed in the selection, what questions you asked, and what conclusions you reached.

3. **Essential Question:** *Are inventions realized through inspiration or perspiration?* What has this selection taught you about invention? Discuss with your group.

LANGUAGE DEVELOPMENT

Concept Vocabulary

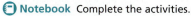

Why These Words? The three concept vocabulary words are related. With your group, discuss the words, and determine what they have in common. Write another word related to this concept.

Practice

📓 **Notebook** Confirm your understanding of these words by using them in sentences. Include context clues that hint at meaning.

Word Study

Multiple-Meaning Words Many English words have more than one meaning. In "Nikola Tesla: The Greatest Inventor of All?," the word *current* refers to an *electrical current,* which is the flow of electricity through a wire. In this context, *current* is a technical word with a definition specific to the fields of science, electricity, and physics. Use a dictionary to look up other definitions of the word *current,* and record the meaning and the part of speech for each.

© Pearson Education, Inc. or its affiliates. All rights reserved.

🗣 **GROUP DISCUSSION**

If you do not understand a group member's contribution, ask for clarification. Respond politely when others ask you for clarification, and try to state your point more simply and clearly.

🔗 **WORD NETWORK**

Identify words from the selection that relate to the concept of invention. Add these words to your Word Network.

📋 **STANDARDS**

Reading Informational Text
Analyze how a text makes connections among and distinctions between individuals, ideas, or events.

Language
• Determine or clarify the meaning of unknown and multiple-meaning words or phrases based on *grade 8 reading and content,* choosing flexibly from a range of strategies.

c. Consult general and specialized reference materials, both print and digital, to find the pronunciation of a word or determine or clarify its precise meaning or its part of speech.

Nikola Tesla: The Greatest Inventor of All? **491**

DIGITAL PERSPECTIVES

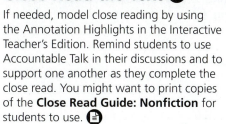

Jump Start

CLOSE READ Ask students to consider the following prompt: *Why do you think Edison is better remembered than Tesla?* As groups discuss, ask them to consider the relationship between genius and celebrity.

Close Read the Text

If needed, model close reading by using the Annotation Highlights in the Interactive Teacher's Edition. Remind students to use Accountable Talk in their discussions and to support one another as they complete the close read. You might want to print copies of the **Close Read Guide: Nonfiction** for students to use.

Analyze the Text

Possible responses:

1. Edison came up with ideas and created models until his idea worked. Tesla used his imagination to see how his ideas would work. Tesla's method seems more efficient but more difficult to share.

2. Remind students to explain the questions they asked and the conclusions they reached.

3. Students may note that Tesla seemed to be able to use his mind to come up with inventive solutions to practical problems.

Concept Vocabulary

Why These Words? Possible response: The words are all related to electrical engineering. Another word that fits this category is *electrician*.

Practice

Possible responses:
1. The *engineer* worked on restoring electricity after the storm.
2. Nikola Tesla worked on *generators* to convert energy into electricity.
3. The *current* running through the wires was very strong.

Word Network

Possible responses: *designed, methods, models*

Word Study

For more support, see **Concept Vocabulary and Word Study.**

Possible responses: *adjective:* "happening or existing in the present; popular"; *noun:* "the moving part of a fluid body of water"

FORMATIVE ASSESSMENT

Analyze the Text

If students struggle to close read the text, **then** provide the Nikola Tesla: The Greatest Inventor of All?: Text Questions available online in the Interactive Teacher's Edition or Unit Resources. Answers and DOK levels are also available.

Concept Vocabulary

If students struggle to understand the meanings of *alternating* and *direct current,* **then** suggest they search online for *alternating current vs. direct current.* Reading how the two currents are used differently may help students understand each more fully.

Word Study

If students have trouble with the multiple meanings of *current,* **then** have them use a dictionary to read the different definitions and write sample sentences that show they understand the various meanings. For Reteach and Practice, see **Word Study: Multiple-Meaning Words (RP).**

Small-Group Learning **491**

FACILITATING

Analyze Craft and Structure

Text Structure: Biographical Writing As students create their charts, remind them that information about the order of events—the chronology—should go under *Organization*. Insights about Tesla's early years and struggles should go under *Development of Ideas*. Also, students should think about different possible paragraph structures (chronological; comparison and contrast; cause and effect). For more support, see **Analyze Craft and Structure: Biographical Writing.**

Practice
Possible responses:
1. The author uses a cause-and-effect strategy to explain the "falling out" between Tesla and Edison. The strategy shows how the cause of the falling out—Tesla working hard to win a money reward that Edison refused to pay—led to the effect—Tesla quitting Edison's company.
2. In paragraphs 3 and 5, the author uses a comparison-and-contrast strategy to show key differences between Tesla and Edison—how they worked and, later, how their companies took different paths for the creation of electrical systems.

FORMATIVE ASSESSMENT

Analyze Craft and Structure

If students have trouble identifying the strategy used in a paragraph, **then** have them reread the paragraph and draw a diagram to show the key people and events. For Reteach and Practice, see **Analyze Craft and Structure: Biographical Writing (RP).**

MAKING MEANING

NIKOLA TESLA: THE GREATEST INVENTOR OF ALL?

Analyze Craft and Structure

Text Structure: Biographical Writing Biographical writing is a type of nonfiction in which the author tells about important events in the life of another person. Biographies provide factual information about the subject, and details and descriptions related to the person's life.

Most biographies are written in chronological order, describing key events in the subject's life. Individual paragraphs, however, may be organized differently, in order to provide information that supports a key idea. Here are some common paragraph structures:

- **chronological order:** the order in which events actually occur
- **comparison and contrast:** explanation and analysis of the similarities and differences between related subjects
- **cause and effect:** explanation of why something happens and how it affects other things

Practice
CITE TEXTUAL EVIDENCE to support your answers.

Notebook Use the chart to analyze the organization and development of ideas in the text. Model your analysis on the example. Then, answer the questions that follow.

PARAGRAPH	ORGANIZATION	DEVELOPMENT OF IDEAS
paragraph 1	chronological organization	• describes Tesla's early years • descriptive details provide information about early signs of Tesla's genius
paragraph 2	• chronological organization	• describes events leading Tesla to quit his job with Edison
paragraph 3	• cause and effect	
paragraph 4	• chronological	• comparing two scientists
paragraph 5	• compare and contrast	• comparing two approaches to developing electrical systems
paragraph 6		
paragraph 7		
paragraph 8		

1. What organizational strategy does the author use in paragraph 4? How does its organization link individuals, ideas, and events in the selection?

2. What organizational strategy does the author use in paragraphs 3 and 5? How does its organization help link ideas and events?

STANDARDS
Reading Informational Text
• Analyze how a text makes connections among and distinctions between individuals, ideas, or events.
• Analyze in detail the structure of a specific paragraph in a text, including the role of particular sentences in developing and refining a key concept.

492 UNIT 5 • INVENTION

PERSONALIZE FOR LEARNING

English Language Support

Biographical Writing To help students understand one organizational tool of biographical writing, have students think about the causes and effects that they learned about in the selection, "Nikola Tesla: The Greatest Inventor of All?"

Ask students to write down one cause and the effect of that cause from the selection. **EMERGING**

Ask students to write down two causes and the effects of those causes from the selection. **EXPANDING**

Have students write a brief argumentative essay in which they take a position on the information presented in the selection. Tell students to include causes and effects when making their argument. **BRIDGING**

An expanded **English Language Support Lesson** on Biographical Writing is available in the Interactive Teacher's Edition.

492 UNIT 5 • INVENTION

LANGUAGE DEVELOPMENT

Conventions

Commas and Semicolons Effective writers use commas and semicolons correctly. Here are some guidelines for using commas and semicolons.

- A **comma (,)** is a punctuation mark that signals a brief pause.
- A **semicolon (;)** may be used to join two independent clauses.

USE A COMMA	EXAMPLES
before a **coordinating conjunction** (*and, but, or, nor, for, so, yet*) that joins two independent clauses in a compound sentence	Tesla worked hard, **and** he invented many things.
between items in a series	He worked on **radio, fluorescent lights, and electric plants.**
between **coordinate adjectives,** adjectives of equal rank whose order may be switched	The **ingenious, inventive** products changed the world.
after introductory words, phrases, or clauses	**In his later years,** Tesla had little money.
to set off **nonrestrictive,** or nonessential, **phrases or clauses**	Edison's company, **which was in the United States,** hired Tesla.

USE A SEMICOLON	
to join independent clauses not connected by a coordinating conjunction	Edison did not pay Tesla $50,000**;** Tesla quit.
to separate independent clauses joined by adverbs such as *however* and *therefore*	Tesla had many great inventions**;** however, his fame faded over the years.

Read It

📓 **Notebook** Complete the following items by identifying a comma or semicolon in the selection paragraph and explaining the reason it is used in the sentence.

1. paragraph 1 (comma)
2. paragraph 3 (semicolon)
3. paragraph 5 (comma)
4. paragraph 7 (comma)

Write It

Correct each sentence by adding commas or semicolons as needed.

1. Tesla contributed many great electrical inventions to the world however he died a poor man.
2. Tesla invented or helped to develop X-ray machines wireless remotes fluorescent lights and the Tesla coil.
3. Edison preferred direct current he thought it was safer than alternating current.

> **EVIDENCE LOG**
> Before moving on to a new selection, go to your Evidence Log and record what you learned from "Nikola Tesla: The Greatest Inventor of All?"

> **TIP**
> **COLLABORATION TIP**
> To ensure that your group understands the correct use of commas and semicolons in different grammatical situations, challenge members to come up with examples of each type of sentence modeled in the charts.
>
> **STANDARDS**
> **Language**
> Demonstrate command of the conventions of standard English capitalization, punctuation, and spelling when writing.
> a. Use punctuation (comma, ellipsis, dash) to indicate a pause or break.

Nikola Tesla: The Greatest Inventor of All? **493**

DIGITAL PERSPECTIVES

Conventions

Commas and Semicolons As needed, add the following additional comma rules to those presented in the student chart:

- Do not place a comma before or after a list of items in a series
  INCORRECT: Before the test put, cell phones, calculators, and notebooks, in your backpack.
  CORRECT: Before the test, put cell phones, calculators, and notebooks in your backpack.
- Use a comma to introduce a quotation.
  Did Edison really say, "You don't understand American humor"?

For more support, see **Conventions: Commas and Semicolons.**

Read It
Possible responses:
1. Sentence 2: to set off an introductory clause
2. Sentence 3: to separate two independent clauses in a compound sentence
3. Sentence 1: to set off a nonrestrictive clause
4. Paragraph 7: sentence 1: to set off an introductory word

Write It
Correct answers:
1. Tesla contributed many great electrical inventions to the world; however, he died a poor man.
2. Tesla invented, or helped to develop, X-ray machines, wireless remote, fluorescent lights, and the Tesla coil.
3. Edison preferred the direct current; he thought it was safer than alternating current.

Evidence Log Support students in completing their Evidence Log. This paced activity will help prepare them for the Performance-Based Assessment at the end of the unit.

PERSONALIZE FOR LEARNING

Strategic Support
Analyzing Details Students may be confused about the seeming overlap between two items in the list of biographical elements: "factual information about the setting and context" and "details and description that help develop a subject's character."

Confirm that facts *do* include details—in the form of examples, names, dates, and statistics. The details associated with description, however, tend to be sensory details that paint an image in the reader's mind. Therefore, as students look for biographical elements, they should draw a distinction between details that explain (the "factual information" in the bulleted list) and details that describe ("details and description").

Ask groups to discuss whether the text uses descriptions or facts and examples to help explain the technical content.

FORMATIVE ASSESSMENT
Conventions

If students have trouble editing sentences 1 and 3, **then** suggest that they identify the types of sentences they are. Then ask them to find and study the rules for commas and semicolons that apply to independent clauses. For Reteach and Practice, see **Conventions: Commas and Semicolons (RP).**

Small-Group Learning **493**

PLANNING

SMALL-GROUP LEARNING • from THE INVENTION OF EVERYTHING ELSE

from The Invention of Everything Else

🔊 **AUDIO SUMMARIES**
Audio summaries of the excerpt from *The Invention of Everything Else* are available online in both English and Spanish in the Interactive Teacher's Edition or Unit Resources. Assigning these summaries prior to reading the selection may help students build additional background knowledge and set a context for their first read.

Summary
This excerpt from Samantha Hunt's novel *The Invention of Everything Else* is an interior monologue in which an aged Nikola Tesla reflects bitterly on his life as an inventor. At the age of 86, he lives in a hotel in New York City, lonely and impoverished, and interacts with the pigeons that congregate on his window ledge, feeding them and tending to their injuries. Tesla recalls one of his earliest inventions at age seven, a motor powered by May bugs, which was eaten by a local bully. He thinks angrily about Guglielmo Marconi, who he believes stole his patent for wireless transmission that became the radio. The reader is offered a glimpse into the mind of a brilliant inventor who has been largely forgotten by the world and has little to show for his life's work.

Insight
The excerpt from *The Invention of Everything Else* challenges the belief that Marconi invented the radio. Indeed, the Supreme Court in 1943 did invalidate some of Marconi's patents. Tesla had provided an idea for which Marconi found a practical application. Tesla was an extraordinary genius with such an active mind that he rarely bothered to take out patents on his work. Unlike other inventors, like Edison, Westinghouse, and Marconi, Tesla did not spend much time on public relations, so he was forgotten long before his death.

ESSENTIAL QUESTION:
Are inventions realized through inspiration or perspiration?

Connection to Essential Question
The modern controversy over the invention of the radio is directly related to the Essential Question regarding the realization of inventions. Although Tesla supplied some inspiration, Marconi expended the effort required to make radio a practical reality.

SMALL-GROUP LEARNING PERFORMANCE TASK
Are inventions realized through inspiration or perspiration?

Connection to Performance Tasks
Small-Group Learning Performance Task Students will find plenty of material in the excerpt from *The Invention of Everything Else* for a discussion of the realization of inventions. The learning task will require them to consider the relative importance of each aspect of invention.

UNIT PERFORMANCE-BASED ASSESSMENT
Which invention described in this unit has had the biggest impact on humanity?

Unit Performance-Based Assessment Some people might find inspiration a sufficient impetus to invent. Many scientists, including Tesla, provided information that led to the invention of the radio, but only Marconi put in the effort to make the device a reality. In their essays, students will evaluate the impact of the inventions they have read about.

DIGITAL PERSPECTIVES

 Audio   Video   Document   Annotation Highlights   EL Highlights   Online Assessment

LESSON RESOURCES

	Making Meaning	Language Development	Effective Expression
Lesson	First Read Close Read Analyze the Text Analyze Craft and Structure	Concept Vocabulary Word Study Conventions	Writing to Compare
Instructional Standards	**RL.10** By the end of the year, read and comprehend literature . . . **L.4** Determine or clarify the meaning of unknown and multiple-meaning words or phrases... **L.4.a** Use context as a clue... **L.5** Demonstrate understanding of figurative language . . . **RL.4** Determine the meaning of words and phrases . . . **L.5.a** Interpret figures of speech . . .	**L.4** Determine or clarify the meaning of unknown and multiple-meaning words or phrases . . . **L.5** Demonstrate understanding of figurative language . . . **L.5.c** Distinguish among the connotations . . . **L.1** Demonstrate command of the conventions . . .	**W.2** Write informative/explanatory texts . . . **W.9** Draw evidence from literary or informational texts . . .
▸ STUDENT RESOURCES			
Available online in the Interactive Student Edition or Unit Resources	🔊 Selection Audio 📄 First-Read Guide: Fiction 📄 Close-Read Guide: Fiction	📄 Word Network	📄 Evidence Log
▸ TEACHER RESOURCES			
Selection Resources Available online in the Interactive Teacher's Edition or Unit Resources	🔊 Audio Summaries ✏️ Annotation Highlights 👁 EL Highlights 📄 English Language Support Lesson: Compare-and-Contrast Essay 📄 from *The Invention of Everything Else:* Text Questions 📄 Analyze Craft and Structure: Figurative Language	📄 Concept Vocabulary and Word Study 📄 Conventions: Comparative and Superlative Forms of Adjectives and Adverbs	📄 Writing to Compare: Compare-and-Contrast Essay
Reteach/Practice (RP) Available online in the Interactive Teacher's Edition or Unit Resources	📄 Analyze Craft and Structure: Figurative Language (RP)	📄 Word Study: Denotation and Connotation (RP) 📄 Conventions: Comparative and Superlative Forms of Adjectives and Adverbs (RP)	
Assessment Available online in Assessments	📄 ✅ Selection Test		
My Resources	📄 A Unit 5 Answer Key is available online and in the Interactive Teacher's Edition.		

PERSONALIZE FOR LEARNING

SMALL-GROUP LEARNING • *from* THE INVENTION OF EVERYTHING ELSE

Reading Support

Text Complexity Rubric: *from* The Invention of Everything Else

Quantitative Measures

Lexile: 880 Text Length: 3,631 words

Qualitative Measures

Knowledge Demands ①—②—**❸**—④—⑤	The central situation may not be familiar to all students, but the situation and feelings are explained.
Structure ①—②—**❸**—④—⑤	Use of flashback to switch between present and past may cause some confusion.
Language Conventionality and Clarity ①—②—③—**❹**—⑤	Selection contains figurative language; complex descriptions.
Levels of Meaning/Purpose ①—②—③—**❹**—⑤	Multiple levels of meaning; description of events are interspersed with introspective comments by character and observations and generalizations about human nature; some sophisticated concepts.

DECIDE AND PLAN

English Language Support

Provide English Learners with support for language and structure as they read the selection.

Language Students may get confused reading passages with figurative language, for example, *All day thoughts of Marconi have been poking me in the ribs* (paragraph 8). Ask questions to guide students to understand that these are figurative rather than literal phrases.

Structure To help students sort out the events and ideas in the story, suggest that they keep a log of the main events, stating them in their own words.

Strategic Support

Provide students with strategic support to ensure that they can successfully read the text.

Knowledge Demands Using the background information, discuss the situation depicted in the story. Discuss that the selection has historical and fictional elements.

Structure Discuss what it means to use a flashback in a text. Explain that an author uses a flashback to relate events that occurred in the past. If students have difficulty with the time sequence, point out clues to transitions between past and present. When students reread, have them note each transition from past to present.

Challenge

Provide students who need to be challenged with ideas for how they can go beyond a simple interpretation of the text.

Text Analysis Ask students to describe the relationship Tesla has with the birds. How does the author use this relationship to reveal aspects of Tesla's personality and inner turmoil?

Written Response Ask students to speculate on what might have happened if Tesla had made different choices in his life. Have students reimagine his life if he had sent the wireless before Marconi.

TEACH

Read and Respond

Have groups read the selection and complete the Making Meaning, Language Development, and Effective Expression activities.

Standards Support Through Teaching and Learning Cycle

IDENTIFY NEEDS

Analyze results of the Beginning-of-Year Assessment, focusing on the items relating to Unit 5. Also take into consideration student performance to this point and your observations of where particular students struggle.

ANALYZE AND REVISE

- Analyze student work for evidence of student learning.
- Identify whether or not students have met the expectations in the standards.
- Identify implications for future instruction.

TEACH

Implement the planned lesson, and gather evidence of student learning.

DECIDE AND PLAN

- If students have performed poorly on items matching these standards, then provide selection scaffolds before assigning them the on-level lesson provided in the Student Edition.
- If students have done well on the Beginning-of-Year Assessment, then challenge them to keep progressing and learning by giving them opportunities to practice the skills in depth.
- Use the Selection Resources listed on the Planning pages for the excerpt from *The Invention of Everything Else* to help students continually improve their ability to master the standards.

Instructional Standards: *from* The Invention of Everything Else

	Catching Up	This Year	Looking Forward
Reading	You may wish to administer the **Analyze Craft and Structure: Figurative Language (RP)** worksheet to help students understand how personification, simile, and metaphor work.	**RL.4** Determine the meaning of words and phrases as they are used in a text, including figurative and connotative meanings; analyze the impact of specific word choices on meaning and tone, including analogies or allusions to other texts.	Work with students to analyze how the figurative language used in the texts affects the overall tone.
Language	Review the **Word Study: Denotation and Connotation (RP)** worksheet with students to help them understand the power of language beyond a word's literal meaning. Review the **Conventions: Comparative and Superlative Forms of Adjectives and Adverbs (RP)** worksheet with students to help them understand how to use positive, comparative, and superlative forms of adjectives and adverbs.	**L.5.c** Distinguish among the connotations of words with different denotations. **L.1** Demonstrate command of the conventions of standard English grammar and usage when writing or speaking.	Ask students to find a word with many synonyms and then discuss the connotation for each one. Challenge students to discuss the varying degrees of these adjectives/adverbs and when it is proper to use them.

FACILITATING

Jump Start

FIRST READ Engage students in a discussion about how a fictional account of a person might provide insight that a biography cannot. How might readers understand and relate to a fictional Tesla?

from The Invention of Everything Else

Why is Tesla living in a hotel? Why does he keep pigeons? Modeling the questions readers might ask as they read the excerpt from *The Invention of Everything Else* brings the text alive for students and connects it to the Small-Group Performance Task assignment. Selection audio and print capability for the selection are available in the Interactive Teacher's Edition.

Concept Vocabulary

Encourage groups to discuss the concept vocabulary. Have they seen the terms in texts before?

Ask groups to think about the word *context*. Explain that when something is said to be "in context," it is related to a larger concept. Suggest that during their first read, students think about context clues that can help them understand the meaning of unfamiliar words.

FIRST READ

As they read, students should perform the steps of the first read:

NOTICE: You may want to encourage students to notice the elderly Tesla and where he is living.

ANNOTATE: Remind students to mark passages that describe Tesla's reactions to events from the past.

CONNECT: Have students compare the thoughts and feelings of Tesla as he recalls what happened to what you read in the biography about Tesla's life.

RESPOND: Students will answer questions and write a summary to demonstrate understanding.

Point out to students that while they will always complete the Respond step at the end of the first read, the other steps will probably happen somewhat concurrently. You may wish to print copies of the **First-Read Guide: Fiction** for students to use.

MAKING MEANING

NIKOLA TESLA: THE GREATEST INVENTOR OF ALL?

Comparing Texts

You will now read an excerpt from the novel *The Invention of Everything Else*. First, complete the first-read and close-read activities for the excerpt. Then, you will analyze the differences in how a subject is portrayed in a work of nonfiction and in a work of fiction.

from THE INVENTION OF EVERYTHING ELSE

About the Author

Samantha Hunt (b. 1971) is an American novelist, essayist, and short story writer. Her award-winning stories and essays have appeared in many prestigious publications, including the *New Yorker*, the *New York Times Magazine*, and *Esquire*. In 2006, she won the National Book Foundation's *5 Under 35* award, which, each year, honors five young fiction writers for their excellence.

STANDARDS

Reading Literature
By the end of the year, read and comprehend literature, including stories, dramas, and poems, at the high end of grades 6–8 text complexity band independently and proficiently.

Language
Determine or clarify the meaning of unknown and multiple-meaning words or phrases based on grade 8 reading and content, choosing flexibly from a range of strategies.
 a. Use context as a clue to the meaning of a word or phrase.

from The Invention of Everything Else

Concept Vocabulary

As you perform your first read of the excerpt from *The Invention of Everything Else*, you will encounter these words.

| deficiencies | triumph | revolutionized |

Context Clues If these words are unfamiliar to you, try using context clues—words and phrases that surround an unfamiliar word in a text to determine their meanings. There are various types of context clues that you may encounter as you read.

> **Related Details:** I maintain a small **infirmary** for <u>injured and geriatric</u> pigeons.
>
> **Restatement:** So **plentiful** was the supply that the jar was <u>filled to the brim</u> in no time.

Apply your knowledge of context clues and other vocabulary strategies to determine the meanings of unfamiliar words you encounter during your first read.

First Read FICTION

Apply these strategies as you conduct your first read. You will have an opportunity to complete a close read after your first read.

NOTICE whom the story is about, *what* happens, *where* and *when* it happens, and *why* those involved react the way they do.

ANNOTATE by marking vocabulary and key passages you want to revisit.

CONNECT ideas within the selection to what you already know and what you have already read.

RESPOND by completing the Comprehension Check and by writing a brief summary of the selection.

VOCABULARY DEVELOPMENT

Concept Vocabulary Reinforcement To increase familiarity with the concept vocabulary, ask students to use each of the words in a sentence. Encourage students to include context clues in their own sentences to demonstrate knowledge of the word. If students are still struggling with the words, encourage them to identify the base word in each term, look up the base word in the dictionary, and then use the definition to come up with the meaning of the concept vocabulary word.

NOVEL EXCERPT

from The Invention of Everything Else

Samantha Hunt

BACKGROUND

In her novel, Samantha Hunt imagines the last days in the life of Nikola Tesla from the perspective of the famous inventor. This excerpt refers to Guglielmo Marconi, an inventor who sent the first wireless signal across an ocean and received a Nobel Prize for his work in 1911. However, he did so by using many key inventions that were initially developed by Nikola Tesla.

1   Lightning first, then the thunder. And in between the two I'm reminded of a secret. I was a boy and there was a storm. The storm said something muffled. Try and catch me, perhaps, and then it bent down close to my ear in the very same way my brother Dane used to do. Whispering. A hot, damp breath, a tunnel between his mouth and my ear. The storm began to speak. You want to know what the storm said? Listen.

FACILITATING

2   Things like that, talking storms, happen to me frequently. Take for example the dust here in my hotel room. Each particle says something as it drifts through the last rays of sunlight, pale blades that have cut their way past my closed curtains. Look at this dust. It is everywhere. Here is the tiniest bit of a woman from Bath Beach who had her hair styled two days ago, loosening a few small flakes of scalp in the process. Two days it took her to arrive, but here she is at last. She had to come because the hotel where I live is like the sticky tongue of a frog jutting out high above Manhattan, collecting the city particle by wandering particle. Here is some chimney ash. Here is some buckwheat flour blown in from a Portuguese bakery on Minetta Lane and a pellicle of curled felt belonging to the haberdashery[1] around the corner. Here is a speck of evidence from a shy graft inspector. Maybe he lived in the borough of Queens. Maybe a respiratory influenza killed him off in 1897. So many maybes, and yet he is still here. And, of course, so am I. Nikola Tesla, Serbian, world-famous inventor, once celebrated, once visited by kings, authors and artists, welterweight pugilists,[2] scientists of all stripes, journalists with their prestigious awards, ambassadors, mezzo-sopranos,[3] and ballerinas. And I would shout down to the dining hall captain for a feast to be assembled. "Quickly! Bring us the Stuffed Saddle of Spring Lamb. Bring us the Mousse of Lemon Sole and the Shad Roe Belle Meunière! Potatoes Raclette! String Bean Sauté! Macadamia nuts! A nice bourbon, some tonic, some pear nectar, coffees, teas, and please, please make it fast!"

3   That was some time ago. Now, more regularly, no one visits. I sip at my vegetable broth listening for a knock on the door or even footsteps approaching down the hallway. Most often it turns out to be a chambermaid on her rounds. I've been forgotten here. Left alone talking to lightning storms, studying the mysterious patterns the dust of dead people makes as it floats through the last light of day.

4   Now that I have lived in the Hotel New Yorker far longer than any of the tourists or businessmen in town for a meeting, the homogeneity[4] of my room, a quality most important to any hotel décor, has all but worn off. Ten years ago, when I first moved in, I constructed a wall of shelves. It still spans floor to ceiling. The wall consists of seventy-seven fifteen-inch-tall drawers as well as a number of smaller cubbyholes to fill up the odd spaces. The

---
1. **haberdashery** *n.* store that sells men's clothing, including hats made from felt.
2. **welterweight pugilists** (PYOO juh lihsts) *n.* professional boxers of intermediate weight, between lightweight and middleweight.
3. **mezzo-sopranos** (MEHT soh suh PRAN ohz) singers.
4. **homogeneity** (hoh muh juh NEE uh tee) *n.* similar and uniform quality.

PERSONALIZE FOR LEARNING

English Language Support

Syntax Call student attention to paragraph 2. Help students analyze the somewhat confusing sentence structure in the paragraph. Guide students' attention to the sentence beginning with "Nikola Tesla, Serbian, world-famous inventor, once celebrated, once visited by kings, authors and artists . . ." Point out that the sentence does not follow the usual subject/predicate/object structure. In fact, its verbs are used as adjectives. Explain that the entire sentence consists of a noun ("Nikola Tesla"), followed by words and phrases that describe him. Point out that the last of the identifying phrases ("authors and artists, welterweight pugilists . . . ") refer to the people who used to visit him. Explain that students can navigate the sentence by examining each word or phase that is separated by commas and determining how it relates to the rest of the sentence.
ALL LEVELS

top drawers are so high off the ground that even I, at over six feet tall, am forced to keep a wooden step stool behind the closet door to access them. Each drawer is stained a deep brown and is differentiated from the others by a small card of identification taped to the front. The labels have yellowed under the adhesive. COPPER WIRE. CORRESPONDENCE. MAGNETS. PERPETUAL MOTION. MISC.

5   Drawer #42. It sticks and creaks with the weather. This is the drawer where I once thought I'd keep all my best ideas. It contains only some cracked peanut shells. It is too dangerous to write my best ideas down. "Whoops. Wrong drawer. Whoops." I repeat the word. It's one of my favorites. If it were possible I'd store "Whoops" in the safe by my bed, along with "OK" and "Sure thing" and the documents that prove that I am officially an American citizen.

6   Drawer #53 is empty, though inside I detect the slightest odor of ozone. I sniff the drawer, inhaling deeply. Ozone is not what I am looking for. I close #53 and open #26. Inside there is a press clipping, something somebody once said about my work: "Humanity will be like an antheap stirred up with a stick. See the excitement coming!" The excitement, apparently, already came and went.

7   That is not what I'm looking for.

8   Somewhere in one of the seventy-seven drawers I have a clipping from an article published in the *New York Times*. The article includes a photo of the inventor Guglielmo Marconi riding on the shoulders of men, a loose white scarf held in his raised left hand, flagging the breeze. All day thoughts of Marconi have been poking me in the ribs. They often do whenever I feel particularly low or lonely or poorly financed. I'll shut my eyes and concentrate on sending Marconi a message. The message is, "Marconi, you are a thief." I focus with great concentration until I can mentally access the radio waves. As the invisible waves advance through my head I attach a few words to each—"donkey," and "worm," and "limacine," which is an adjective that I only recently acquired the meaning of, *like a slug*. When I'm certain that the words are fixed to the radio waves I'll send the words off toward Marconi, because he has stolen my patents.[5] He has stolen my invention of radio. He has stolen my notoriety. Not that either of us deserved it. Invention is nothing a man can own.

9   And so I am resigned.

---

5. **patents** *n.* documents that give an individual the right to make or sell new inventions or products; patents prevent others from making, using, or selling the inventions or products for a set period of time.

from The Invention of Everything Else

10   Out the window to the ledge, thirty-three stories above the street, I go legs first. This is no small feat. I am no small man. Imagine an oversized skeleton. I have to wonder what a skeleton that fell thirty-three stories, down to the street below, would look like. I take one tentative glance toward the ground. Years ago power lines would have stretched across the block in a mad cobweb, a net, because years ago, any company that wanted to provide New York with electricity simply strung its own decentralized power lines all about the city before promptly going out of business or getting forced out by J. P. Morgan.[6] But now there is no net. The power lines have been hidden underground.

11   That's not why I've come here. I have no interest in jumping. I'm not resigned to die. Most certainly not. No, I'm resigned only to leave humans to their humanness. Die? No. Indeed, I've always planned to see the far side of one hundred and twenty-five. I'm only eighty-six. I've got thirty-nine more years. At least.

12   "HooEEEhoo. HooEEEhoo." The birds answer the call. Gray flight surrounds me, and the reverse swing of so many pairs of wings, some iridescent, some a bit duller, makes me dizzy. The birds slow to a landing before me, beside me, one or two perching directly on top of my shoulders and head. Mesmerized by their feathers—such engineering!—I lose my balance. The ledge is

---

6. **J.P. Morgan** powerful businessman who merged several electrical companies to create one massive company in 1891.

DIGITAL PERSPECTIVES

Illuminating the Text Call student attention to the description of power lines in paragraph 10. Have students search online to locate and share images of New York City, circa late 1800s, that depict the power lines that were strung haphazardly across streets. This will help students understand both the author's metaphor of a "mad cobweb" and the enthusiasm with which people embraced electricity in the latter part of the century. After students have viewed the images, have them discuss how their ability to visualize the scene of a "mad cobweb" has changed. Ask them if the description was accurate and what other words or phrases they would use to describe the scene. Additionally, have them consider what the many power lines suggest about the way the public embraced electricity.

perhaps only forty-five centimeters wide. My shoulders lurch forward a bit, just enough to notice the terrific solidity of the sidewalks thirty-three stories down. Like a gasp for air, I pin my back into the cold stone of the window's casing. A few pigeons startle and fly away out over Eighth Avenue, across Manhattan. Catching my breath, I watch them go. I watch them disregard gravity, the ground, and the distance between us. And though an old feeling, one of wings, haunts my shoulder blades, I stay pinned to the window. I've learned that I cannot go with them.

13   Out on the ledge of my room, I maintain a small infirmary for injured and geriatric[7] pigeons. A few tattered boxes, some shredded newspaper. One new arrival hobbles on a foot that has been twisted into an angry knuckle, a pink stump. I see she wants nothing more to do with the hydrogen peroxide that bubbled fiercely in her wound last night. I let her be, squatting instead to finger the underside of another bird's wing. Beneath his sling the ball of his joint has finally stayed lodged in its orbit, and for this I am relieved. I turn my attention to mashing meal.

14   "Hello, dears." The air of New York this high up smells gray with just a hint of blue. I sniff the air. "It's getting chilly, hmm?" I ask the birds. "And what are your plans for the New Year tonight?" The hotel has been in a furor, preparing for the festivities all week. The birds say nothing. "No plans yet? No, me neither."

15   I stand, looking out into the darkening air. "HooEEEhoo?" It's a question. I stare up into the sky, wondering if she will show tonight. "HooEEEhoo?"

16   Having lived in America for fifty-nine years, I've nearly perfected my relationships with the pigeons, the sparrows, and the starlings of New York City. Particularly the pigeons. Humans remain a far greater challenge.

17   I sit on the ledge with the birds for a long while, waiting for her to appear. It is getting quite cold. As the last rays of sun disappear from the sky, the undersides of the clouds glow with a memory of the light. Then they don't anymore, and what was once clear becomes less so in the darkening sky. The bricks and stones of the surrounding buildings take on a deeper hue. A bird cuts across the periphery of my sight. I don't allow myself to believe it might be her. "HooEEEhoo?" Don't look, I caution my heart. It won't be her. I take a look just the same. A gorgeous checkered, his hackle purple and green. It's not her.

18   She is pale gray with white-tipped wings, and into her ear I have whispered all my doubts. Through the years I've told her of my childhood, the books I read, a history of Serbian battle songs, dreams of earthquakes, endless meals and islands, inventions,

---

7. **geriatric** (jehr ee AT rihk) *adj.* elderly.

from The Invention of Everything Else

FACILITATING

Concept Vocabulary

DEFICIENCIES If groups are struggling to define the word *deficiencies* in paragraph 20, point out that they can use context clues to infer the word's meaning. Draw their attention to the context clues "I don't have wings" and "I don't have magnetite in my head." Have students use these context clues to define the word. Encourage them to consider the word's connotation.

Possible response: In this context, *deficiencies* means "a lack of something."

NOTES

Mark context clues or indicate another strategy you used to help you determine connotations and denotations.

deficiencies (dih FIHSH uhn seez) *n.*
MEANING:

---

lost notions, love, architecture, poetry—a bit of everything. We've been together since I don't remember when. A long while. Though it makes no sense, I think of her as my wife, or at least something like a wife, inasmuch as any inventor could ever have a wife, inasmuch as a bird who can fly could ever love a man who can't.

19 Most regularly she allows me to smooth the top of her head and neck with my pointer finger. She even encourages it. I'll run my finger over her feathers and feel the small bones of her head, the delicate cage made of calcium built to protect the bit of magnetite[8] she keeps inside. This miraculous mineral powers my system of alternating-current electrical distribution. It also gives these birds direction, pulling north, creating a compass in their bodies, ensuring that they always know the way home.

20 I've not seen my own home in thirty-five years. There is no home anymore. Everyone is gone. My poor, torn town of Smiljan—in what was once Lika, then Croatia, now Yugoslavia. "I don't have wings," I tell the birds who are perched beside me on the ledge. "I don't have magnetite in my head." These **deficiencies** punish me daily, particularly as I get older and recall Smiljan with increasing frequency.

21 When I was a child I had a tiny laboratory that I'd constructed in an alcove of trees. I nailed tin candle sconces to the trunks so that I could work into the night while the candles' glow crept up the orange bark and filled my laboratory with odd shadows— the stretched fingers of pine needles as they shifted and grew in the wind.

22 There is one invention from that time, one of my very first, that serves as a measure for how the purity of thought can dwindle with age. Once I was clever. Once I was seven years old. The invention came to me like this: Smiljan is a very tiny town surrounded by mountains and rivers and trees. My house was part of a farm where we raised animals and grew vegetables. Beside our home was a church where my father was the minister. In this circumscribed[9] natural setting my ears were attuned to a different species of sounds: footsteps approaching on a dirt path, raindrops falling on the hot back of a horse, leaves browning. One night, from outside my bedroom window, I heard a terrific buzzing noise, the rumble of a thousand insect wings beating in concert. I recognized the noise immediately. It signaled the seasonal return of what people in Smiljan called May bugs, what people in America call June bugs. The insects' motions, their constant energy, kept me awake through the night, considering, plotting, and scheming. I roiled in my bed with the possibility these insects presented.

---

8. **magnetite** (MAG nuh tyt) *n.* type of iron that is strongly attracted by magnets.
9. **circumscribed** (suhr kuhm SKRYBD) *adj.* limited.

500 UNIT 5 • INVENTION

VOCABULARY DEVELOPMENT

Concept Vocabulary Reinforcement Students will benefit from additional examples and practice with the concept vocabulary. Reinforce their comprehension with "show-you-know" sentences. The first part of the sentence uses the vocabulary word in an appropriate context. The second part of the sentence—the show-you-know part—clarifies the first.

Model the strategy with this example for *deficiencies* from paragraph 20:

The thief's *deficiencies* were obvious: he had neither money nor honor.

Then, give students these sentence prompts and coach them in the clarification part:

1. At the end of the race, she raised her arms in *triumph*; _____.

Possible response: she had beaten her nearest rival by almost a meter.

2. Many people hope that in fifty years, electric cars will have *revolutionized* transportation; _____.

Possible response: they anticipate that one day, everyone will be driving electric cars.

23   Finally, just before the sun rose, I sneaked outside while my family slept. I carried a glass jar my mother usually used for storing stewed vegetables. The jar was nearly as large as my rib cage. I removed my shoes—the ground was still damp. I walked barefoot through the paths of town, stopping at every low tree and shrub, the leaves of which were alive with June bugs. Their brown bodies hummed and crawled in masses. They made my job of collection quite easy. I harvested the beetle crop, sometimes collecting as many as ten insects per leaf. The bugs' shells made a hard click when they struck against the glass or against another bug. So plentiful was the supply that the jar was filled to brimming in no time.

24   I returned to my pine-tree laboratory and set to work. First, by constructing a simple system of gear wheels, I made an engine in need of a power supply. I then studied the insects in the jar and selected those that demonstrated the most aggressive and muscular tendencies. With a dab of glue on their thorax undersides, I stuck my eight strongest beetles to the wheel and stepped back. The glue was good; they could not escape its harness. I waited a moment, and in that moment my thoughts grew dark. Perhaps, I thought, the insects were in shock. I pleaded with the bugs, "Fly away!" Nothing. I tickled them with a twig. Nothing. I stomped my small feet in frustration and stepped back prepared to leave the laboratory and hide away from the failed experiment in the fronds of breakfast, when, just then, the engine began to turn. Slowly at first, like a giant waking up, but once the insects understood that they were in this struggle together their speed increased. I gave a jump of **triumph** and was immediately struck by a vision of the future in which humans would exist in a kingdom of ease, the burden of all our chores and travails would be borne by the world of insects. I was certain that this draft of the future would come to pass. The engine spun with a whirling noise. It was brilliant, and for a few moments I burned with this brilliance.

25   In the time it took me to complete my invention the world around me had woken up. I could hear the farm animals. I could hear people speaking, beginning their daily work. I thought how glad my mother would be when I told her that she'd no longer have to milk the goats and cows, as I was developing a system where insects would take care of all that. This was the thought I was tumbling joyfully in when Vuk, a boy who was a few years older than me, entered into the laboratory. Vuk was the urchin son of an army officer. He was no friend of mine but rather one of the older children in town who, when bored, enjoyed needling

NOTES

Mark context clues or indicate another strategy you used to help you determine connotations and denotations.

triumph (TRY uhmf) *n.*
MEANING:

from *The Invention of Everything Else*

DIGITAL PERSPECTIVES

Concept Vocabulary

TRIUMPH If groups are struggling to define the word *triumph* in paragraph 24, point out that they can use context clues to infer the word's meaning. Draw their attention to the context clues "their speed increased," "a jump," and "was immediately struck by a vision of the future in which humans would exist in a kingdom of ease." Have students use these context clues to define the word. Encourage students to consider the word's connotation (positive) and list synonyms with neutral connotation (for example, *success*).

Possible response: In this context, *triumph* means "a great achievement."

HOW LANGUAGE WORKS

Comparative and Superlative Forms of Adjectives and Adverbs Explain to students that the comparative form of an adjective adds *–er* to the word or *more* before the word, while the comparative form of an adverb is preceded by *more*. Explain that the comparative form of an adjective is used when comparing two things, and that the superlative form is used when comparing three or more. For example, point to the superlative adjectives *most aggressive* and *strongest* in paragraph 24 and to the comparative adjective *older* in paragraph 25. Note that the second use of *older* (*older children*) is appropriate as the narrator is presumably comparing two groups of children—those who are older and those who are younger. Have students suggest sentences using the comparative form of *aggressive* and *strong* and the superlative form of *old*.

FACILITATING

Concept Vocabulary

REVOLUTIONIZED If groups are struggling to define the word *revolutionized* in paragraph 25, point out that they can use context clues to infer the word's meaning. Draw their attention to the context clue "how I had developed insect energy, the source that would soon be providing the world with cheap, replenishable power." Have students use this context clue to define the word. Encourage them to consider the word's connotation—is it positive, neutral, or negative?

Possible response: In this context, *revolutionized* means "changed dramatically." It has a positive connotation here.

> Additional **English Language Support** is available in the Interactive Teacher's Edition.

NOTES

Mark context clues or indicate another strategy you used to help you determine connotations and denotations.

revolutionized (rehv uh LOO shuh nyzd) *v.*
MEANING:

---

me, vandalizing the laboratory I had built in the trees. But that morning my delight was such that I was glad to see even Vuk. I was glad for a witness. Quickly I explained to him how I had just **revolutionized** the future, how I had developed insect energy, the source that would soon be providing the world with cheap, replenishable power. Vuk listened, glancing once or twice at the June bug engine, which, by that time, was spinning at a very impressive speed. His envy was thick; I could nearly touch it. He kept his eyes focused on the glass jar that was still quite full of my power source. Vuk twisted his face up to a cruel squint. He curled the corners of his fat lips. With my lecture finished, he nodded and approached the jar. Unscrewing the lid he eyed me, as though daring me to stop him. Vuk sank his hand, his filthy fingernails, down into the mass of our great future and withdrew a fistful of beetles. Before I could even understand the annihilation I was about to behold, Vuk raised his arm to his mouth, opened the horrid orifice, and began to chew. A crunching sound I will never forget ensued. Tiny exoskeletons mashed between molars, dark legs squirming for life against his chubby white chin. With my great scheme crashing to a barbarous end—I could never look at a June bug again—I ran behind the nearest pine tree and promptly vomited.

26   On the ledge the birds are making a noise that sounds like contentment, like the purr of the ocean from a distance. I forget Vuk. I forget all thoughts of humans. I even forget about what I was searching for in the wall of drawers until, staring out at the sky, I don't forget anymore.

27   On December 12, 1901, Marconi sent a message across the sea. The message was simple. The message was the letter *S*. The message traveled from Cornwall, England, to Newfoundland, Canada. This *S* traveled on air, without wires, passing directly through mountains and buildings and trees, so that the world thought wonders might never cease. And it was true. It was a magnificent moment. Imagine, a letter across the ocean without wires.

28   But a more important date is October 1893, eight years earlier. The young Marconi was seated in a crowded café huddled over, intently reading a widely published and translated article written by me, Nikola Tesla. In the article I revealed in exacting detail my system for both wireless transmission of messages and the wireless transmission of energy. Marconi scribbled furiously.

29   I pet one bird to keep the chill from my hands. The skin of my knee is visible through my old suit. I am broke. I have given AC electricity to the world. I have given radar, remote control, and

---

PERSONALIZE FOR LEARNING

Challenge

Personal Experience Review paragraph 25. Ask students to think about how young Tesla might have felt when Vuk ate his bugs and when Marconi stole his ideas. Then have students think of a time when something they were excited about didn't work out as they had planned. It could be an idea they'd had or a project that didn't turn out as they'd hoped. Students should write a paragraph describing their experience, how it made them feel, and what they learned from it.

radio to the world, and because I asked for nothing in return, nothing is exactly what I got. And yet Marconi took credit. Marconi surrounded himself with fame, strutting as if he owned the invisible waves circling the globe.

30   Quite honestly, radio is a nuisance. I know. I'm its father. I never listen to it. The radio is a distraction that keeps one from concentrating.

31   "HooEEEhoo?"

32   There is no answer.

33   I'll have to go find her. It is getting dark and Bryant Park is not as close as it once was, but I won't rest tonight if I don't see her. Legs first, I reenter the hotel, and armed with a small bag of peanuts, I set off for the park where my love often lives.

34   The walk is a slow one, as the streets are beginning to fill with New Year's Eve revelers. I try to hurry, but the sidewalks are busy with booby traps. One gentleman stops to blow his nose into a filthy handkerchief, and I dodge to the left, where a woman tilts her head back in a laugh. Her pearl earrings catch my eye. Just the sight of those monstrous jewels sets my teeth on edge, as if my jaws were being ground down to dull nubs. Through this obstacle course I try to outrun thoughts of Marconi. I try to outrun the question that repeats and repeats in my head, paced to strike with every new square of sidewalk I step on. The question is this: "If they are your patents, Niko, why did Marconi get word—well, not word but letter—why did he get a letter across the ocean before you?" I walk quickly. I nearly run. Germs be damned. I glance over my shoulder to see if the question is following. I hope I have outpaced it.

35   New York's streets wend their way between the arched skyscrapers. Most of the street-level businesses have closed their doors for the evening. Barbizon Hosiery. Conte's Salumeria, where a huge tomcat protects the drying sausages. Santangelo's Stationery and Tobacco. Wasserstein's Shoes. Jung's Nautical Maps and Prints. The Wadesmith Department Store. All of them closed for the holiday. My heels click on the sidewalks, picking up speed, picking up a panic. I do not want this question to catch me, and worse, I do not want the answer to this question to catch me. I glance behind myself one more time. I have to find her tonight.

> I do not want this question to catch me, and worse, I do not want the answer to this question to catch me.

FACILITATING

Comprehension Check

1. Tesla lives in the Hotel New Yorker in New York City. He originally lived in what became Yugoslavia.
2. Tesla uses the ledge outside his window as a place to treat old and injured pigeons.
3. Marconi stole his invention of the radio and has gained fame as a result.
4. The question is why Marconi progressed more quickly than Tesla in communicating across the ocean.
5. Students' summaries will vary but should include an indication of the conflict Tesla has with Marconi, his love of pigeons, and his current isolation in a hotel in New York City.

Research

Research to Clarify Students will likely be unfamiliar with many details in the story. If they have trouble figuring out what to focus on, you may want to suggest the following details: history of the Hotel New Yorker, how homing pigeons navigate, patents, June bugs.

NOTES

36   I turn one corner and the question is there, waiting, smoking, reading the newspaper. I pass a lunch counter and see the question sitting alone, slurping from a bowl of chicken soup. "If they are your patents, Niko, why did Marconi send a wireless letter across the ocean before you?"

37   The question makes me itch. I decide to focus my thoughts on a new project, one that will distract me. As I head north, I develop an appendix of words that begin with the letter *S*, words that Marconi's first wireless message stood for.

Comprehension Check

Complete the following items after you finish your first read. Review and clarify details with your group.

1. Where does Tesla live? In what country did he originally live?

2. What does Tesla use the ledge outside his window for?

3. For what reason is Tesla angry with Marconi?

4. What question does Tesla try to outrun?

Notebook Confirm your understanding of the text by writing a short summary.

RESEARCH

Research to Clarify Choose at least one unfamiliar detail from the excerpt. Briefly research that detail. In what way does the information you learned shed light on an aspect of the story?

504 UNIT 5 • INVENTION

PERSONALIZE FOR LEARNING

Challenge

Speculate The excerpt ends with Tesla asking himself why Marconi sent a wireless letter across the ocean before he, Tesla, did. Ask students to speculate on how Tesla's life might have been different if he had fought harder in the beginning for the credit he deserved for his inventions. Have students write a day in the life of Tesla at the age of 86—that is, a day that might have been if he had made different choices many years before.

ESSENTIAL QUESTION: Are inventions realized through inspiration or perspiration?

Close Read the Text

With your group, revisit sections of the text you marked during your first read. **Annotate** what you notice. What **questions** do you have? What can you **conclude**?

from THE INVENTION OF EVERYTHING ELSE

Analyze the Text

CITE TEXTUAL EVIDENCE to support your answers.

 Notebook Complete the activities.

1. **Review and Clarify** Reread paragraphs 21–25 of the excerpt. What is one of the first inventions Tesla made as a child? How does this **anecdote**, or short account, about his childhood experience with invention help to develop Tesla's character? What does it reveal about the nature of inventions? Discuss with your group.

2. **Present and Discuss** Discuss what you noticed in the selection, what questions you asked, and what conclusions you reached.

3. **Essential Question:** *Are inventions realized through inspiration or perspiration?* What have you learned about invention from reading this selection?

TIP

GROUP DISCUSSION
As you work with your group, make sure each member has an opportunity to contribute to the discussion. Be sensitive to the amount of time you spend speaking.

LANGUAGE DEVELOPMENT

Concept Vocabulary

| deficiencies | triumph | revolutionized |

Why These Words? The three concept vocabulary words are related. With your group, determine what the words have in common. Write your ideas, and add at least one other word that fits the category.

Practice

Notebook Confirm your understanding of these words from the text by using each word in a sentence. Share your sentences with your group.

Word Study

Denotation and Connotation A word's **denotation** is its dictionary meaning. Synonyms have nearly identical denotations. A word's **connotation** is the idea or emotion associated with the word. Often, words have positive or negative connotations that affect how people respond to them. Synonyms often have different connotations. For example, the concept vocabulary word *triumph* and the word *win* are synonyms, but *triumph* has a more positive, stronger connotation than *win*, which is more neutral. With your group, find a synonym for each of the other concept vocabulary words, and discuss the connotations of each pair.

WORD NETWORK

Identify words from the selection that relate to the concept of invention. Add these words to your Word Network.

STANDARDS

Language
• Determine or clarify the meaning of unknown and multiple-meaning words or phrases based on *grade 8 reading and content,* choosing flexibly from a range of strategies.
• Demonstrate understanding of figurative language, word relationships, and nuances in word meanings.
  c. Distinguish among the connotations of words with similar denotations.

from The Invention of Everything Else 505

FORMATIVE ASSESSMENT

Analyze the Text
If students struggle to close read the text, **then** provide the *from The Invention of Everything Else: Text Questions* available online in the Interactive Teacher's Edition or Unit Resources. Answers and DOK levels are also available.

Concept Vocabulary
If students fail to see a connection among the words, **then** ask them to use each in a sentence about invention.

Word Study
If students struggle to identify connotations, **then** have them use each synonym in a sentence and determine how those sentences differ from sentences that include the concept vocabulary words. For Reteach and Practice, see **Word Study: Denotation and Connotation (RP).**

DIGITAL PERSPECTIVES

Jump Start

CLOSE READ In what way can invention result in both great achievement and deep personal failure? As students discuss the prompt in their groups, have them consider what they learned about Tesla from both the biography and from the excerpt.

Close Read the Text

If needed, model close reading by using the Annotation Highlights in the Interactive Teacher's Edition.

Remind students to use Accountable Talk in their discussions and to support one another as they complete the close read. You may want to print copies of the **Close Read Guide: Fiction** for students to use.

Analyze the Text

1. **Possible response:** Tesla's first invention was an engine powered by bugs. The anecdote reveals that the invention is, in part, inspiration, as Tesla came up with the idea when he was kept awake by the noise of June bugs.

2. Responses will vary by group. Groups should support their choices.

3. Responses will vary by group.

Concept Vocabulary

Why These Words? Possible response: The concept vocabulary words relate to the reasons people invent and the results of their inventions. Two other words that fit the category are *scheming* and *frustration*.

Practice
Responses will vary.

Word Network
Possible words: *world-famous, patents, notoriety, brilliance*

Word Study

For more support, see **Concept Vocabulary and Word Study.**

Possible responses: *shortages* (deficiencies has a more negative connotation); *success* (triumph has a slightly more positive connotation); *changed* (revolutionized has a stronger, more positive connotation)

Small-Group Learning 505

FACILITATING

Analyze Craft and Structure

Word Choice: Figurative Language Discuss with students why authors use figurative language. Point out that by making comparisons to unlike things, the author can help readers visualize what they're reading. Explain that figurative language allows authors to use just a few words to create vivid pictures in the minds of readers. For more support, see **Analyze Craft and Structure: Figurative Language.**

MAKE IT INTERACTIVE
Choose an interesting image and project it for the class. Ask students to write down what the image looks like. For example, the tree looks like a man with outstretched hands. Then, ask students to discuss in their groups the different comparisons they made.

Practice See possible responses in the chart on the student page.

FORMATIVE ASSESSMENT

Analyze Craft and Structure

If students are unable to identify examples of similes, **then** remind them to look for the signal word *like* or *as*. For Reteach and Practice, see **Analyze Craft and Structure: Figurative Language. (RP)**

MAKING MEANING

from THE INVENTION OF EVERYTHING ELSE

Analyze Craft and Structure

Word Choice: Figurative Language In *The Invention of Everything Else*, the author uses **figurative language**—language not meant to be taken literally—to describe and compare things in imaginative ways. The chart defines several **figures of speech**, or types of figurative language, and provides an example for each type.

TYPE OF FIGURATIVE LANGUAGE	DEFINITION	EXAMPLE FROM THE TEXT
personification	comparison in which a nonhuman subject is given human characteristics	*The storm said something muffled. . . .* (paragraph 1)
simile	compares two unlike things using the words *like* or *as*	*She had to come because the hotel where I live is like the sticky tongue of a frog jutting out high above Manhattan, collecting the city particle by wandering particle. . . .* (paragraph 2)
metaphor	compares two unlike things by saying that one thing is the other	*Years ago power lines would have stretched across the block in a mad cobweb, a net, . . .* (paragraph 10)

Practice
CITE TEXTUAL EVIDENCE to support your answers.

Reread the excerpt and find other examples of figurative language. Gather your examples in the chart. With your group, analyze the ways in which the examples you noted deepen your understanding of the text and its subject, Nikola Tesla.

TYPE OF FIGURATIVE LANGUAGE	EXAMPLE FROM THE TEXT
personification	One new arrival **hobbles on a foot that has been twisted into an angry knuckle, a pink stump.** (paragraph 13)
simile	**Like a gasp for air,** I pin my back into the cold stone of the window's casing. (paragraph 12)
metaphor	. . . while the candles' glow crept up the orange bark . . . **the stretched fingers of pine needles as they shifted and grew in the wind.** (paragraph 21)

STANDARDS
Reading Literature
• Determine the meaning of words and phrases as they are used in a text, including figurative and connotative meanings; analyze the impact of specific word choices on meaning and tone, including analogies or allusions to other texts.

Language
Demonstrate understanding of figurative language, word relationships, and nuances in word meanings.
  a. Interpret figures of speech in context.

LANGUAGE DEVELOPMENT

Conventions

Comparative and Superlative Forms of Adjectives and Adverbs
Most adjectives and adverbs have three degrees of comparison, helping writers easily compare the qualities or conditions of their subjects.

- The **positive** degree is used when no comparison is made: Tesla was a *great* inventor.
- The **comparative** is used when two things are being compared: Some people believe that Tesla was a *greater* inventor than Edison.
- The **superlative** is used when three or more things are being compared: Perhaps, Tesla was the *greatest* inventor of all.

FORMING COMPARATIVE AND SUPERLATIVE ADJECTIVES AND ADVERBS	
Use *-er* or *more* to form the **comparative** degree.	*taller, sooner, more inventive, more quietly*
Use *-est* or *most* to form the **superlative** degree.	*sharpest, fastest, most colorful, most creatively*

Irregular adjectives and adverbs have special forms that must be memorized. This chart shows some commonly used irregular adjectives and adverbs.

POSITIVE	COMPARATIVE	SUPERLATIVE
bad, badly	worse	worst
good, well	better	best
many, much	more	most
little (small amount of)	less	least

Read It

1. Identify the adjective or adverb in each sentence. Then, identify the degree of comparison it indicates: *positive, comparative,* or *superlative*.
   a. Toward the end of his life, Tesla seemed happiest feeding pigeons.
   b. Tesla's supporters were convinced he was doing the most exciting work ever in the field of electrical engineering.
   c. Rather than admit he had dropped out of school, Tesla found it easier to pretend he had drowned.
2. Find three adjectives and adverbs in *The Invention of Everything Else* and indicate the degree of comparison each reflects.

Write It

Notebook Write a brief paragraph about Tesla's feelings toward Marconi. Your paragraph should have at least one adjective or adverb for each degree of comparison. Include at least one irregular adjective or adverb in your paragraph.

STANDARDS
Language
Demonstrate command of the conventions of standard English grammar and usage when writing or speaking.

from The Invention of Everything Else **507**

DIGITAL PERSPECTIVES

Conventions

Comparative and Superlative Forms of Adjectives and Adverbs Discuss with students how the positive form is simply the adjective or adverb. Then point out that the comparative, when it is used to compare two things that are stated in the sentence, usually includes the word *than* in the comparison. For example, *She arrived earlier **than** he did.* Explain, too, that when forming the superlative, always use *the*. For example, *He is **the** best dog ever.* For more support, see **Conventions: Comparative and Superlative Forms of Adjectives and Adverbs.**

Read It

MAKE IT INTERACTIVE
Have students write each sentence on a sentence strip using a different colored marker for the adjective or adverb, underlining comparative adjectives and adverbs, and circling superlative adjectives and adverbs.

Possible responses:
1. a. happiest, superlative
   b. most exciting, superlative
   c. easier, comparative
2. It is getting quite cold (positive); Here is the tiniest bit of a woman from Bath (superlative); Now, more regularly, no one visits (comparative).

Write It

Paragraphs will vary, but make sure that students use at least one adjective or adverb for each degree of comparison and that at least one of those is irregular.

FORMATIVE ASSESSMENT

Conventions

If students are unable to distinguish between comparative and superlative, **then** have them look for the endings *–er* or *–est* or for the words *more* or *most*. For Reteach and Practice, see **Conventions: Comparative and Superlative Forms of Adjectives and Adverbs (RP).**

PERSONALIZE FOR LEARNING

English Language Support

Commonly Confused Words Tell students that the word pairs *later* and *latest*, *latter* and *last* have different uses. Share the following definitions and examples with students:

Later: the comparative form of late; referring to time
He arrived later than she did.

Latest: the superlative form of late; referring to time
He was the latest arrival.

Latter: a comparative adjective that means occurring nearer to the end of something; refers to position
The latter half of the movie was boring.

Last: a superlative adjective that means occurring at the end of something; refers to position
The last scene in the movie was a surprise.

Invite students to work as a group to write a sentence for each word. **ALL LEVELS**

FACILITATING

Writing to Compare
As students prepare to compare the two selections on the life of Nikola Tesla, they will consider the legacy of his work.

Planning and Prewriting
Compare Text Details Encourage students to analyze the portrayal of Nikola Tesla in the selections and how they differ from one another.

EFFECTIVE EXPRESSION

NIKOLA TESLA: THE GREATEST INVENTOR OF ALL?

from THE INVENTION OF EVERYTHING ELSE

Writing to Compare
In this feature you read two selections about the inventor Nikola Tesla. In the biographical work "Nikola Tesla: The Greatest Inventor of All?," you learned factual information about Tesla and his life. In *The Invention of Everything Else*, you read a historical fiction account in which the author, Samantha Hunt, uses her imagination in combination with historical facts to develop the character of Nikola Tesla.

Assignment
Write a **compare-and-contrast essay** in which you analyze the ways in which each text reveals an aspect of Tesla's life and personality.

You will work with your group to analyze the texts and gather information to use in your essay. Then, you will write your essays individually.

Planning and Prewriting
Compare Text Details Work with your group to analyze the ways in which Nikola Tesla is portrayed in a nonfiction text and a work of fiction. Work as a group to fill in the chart with details from both texts.

DETAILS FROM THE TEXT	NIKOLA TESLA: THE GREATEST INVENTOR OF ALL?	from THE INVENTION OF EVERYTHING ELSE
Events from Tesla's life	a. Rivals with Edison; Discovered alternating current.	e. As an aging adult, lonely; Angry with Marconi for his success.
Tesla's character traits and personality	b. Brilliant; Died without success.	f. Brilliant; Strange.
Details about important places in Tesla's life	c. Worked on coils; Created a power plant; Tesla motors named for him.	g. Once famous; Invented a machine that used June bugs for energy.
Details about Tesla's accomplishments	d. This text provided more biographical detail.	h. This text provided emotional context that showed Tesla as a person.

 **Notebook** Respond to these questions.
- Which did you enjoy reading more? Which text more effectively portrayed Tesla? Which text provided more biographical detail?

PERSONALIZE FOR LEARNING

Challenge
Building Understanding Have groups discuss how the genres in the Small-Group Learning section affected students' understandings of the lessons presented throughout the unit. Encourage students to share which genre they found most understandable or thought-provoking. Remind students that there is no one genre that is better than another, and that a genre or format they find easier to understand may be challenging for another student.

ESSENTIAL QUESTION: Are inventions realized through inspiration or perspiration?

Drafting

Form a Thesis Focus your thoughts by creating a thesis statement that explains the point of your comparison. Here is a sentence starter to help you begin:

Thesis: When you compare and contrast these two treatments of Nikola Tesla's life, it becomes clear that

_____

_____

_____.

Organize Your Essay When you are satisfied with your thesis, determine how you should present the information. Develop an outline for your essay using the following strategies:

- Begin your essay by revealing your thesis and providing background for readers.
- Develop your comparison and contrast in one of two ways: Discuss one text and all its features in a series of paragraphs and then discuss the other text in the following paragraph. Alternatively, in each body paragraph, discuss one element as it is treated in both texts, and then discuss a second element, and so on.
- Create cohesion in your essay by using transitional words and phrases, such as *regardless*, *despite*, and *for this reason*, that connect your claims, reasons, and evidence.
- Conclude your essay with a paragraph in which you restate your thesis and summarize the main evidence that you presented in support of your thesis.

Review, Revise, and Edit

Add Details Review your draft and add supporting details where needed. Consider quoting materials from the texts as support. When you do so, be sure to use quotation marks and indicate the source of each quotation.

Use a Formal Style Once you are done drafting, review your essay to be sure you have maintained a formal style. Revise your writing to eliminate instances where you used informal language, such as contractions, slang, or clichés.

Proofread for Accuracy Carefully reread your essay. Fix spelling errors as well as any grammatical problems. Be sure to check all quoted material against the original source to be sure the quotes are accurate.

EVIDENCE LOG

Before moving on to a new selection, go to your Evidence Log and record what you have learned from reading "Nikola Tesla: The Greatest Inventor of All?" and *The Invention of Everything Else*.

STANDARDS

Writing
Write informative/explanatory texts to examine a topic and convey ideas, concepts, and information through the selection, organization, and analysis of relevant content.
- Draw evidence from literary or informational texts to support analysis, reflection, and research.

from The Invention of Everything Else **509**

DIGITAL PERSPECTIVES

Drafting
Organize Your Essay Remind students that an effective essay is well organized. Help them make an outline before they begin writing.

Review, Revise, and Edit
As students revise, encourage them to review their style. Ask them to review their word choice. Finally, remind students to check for grammar, usage, and mechanics.

For more support, see **Writing to Compare: Compare-and-Contrast Essay.**

Evidence Log Support students in completing their Evidence Log. This paced activity will help prepare them for the Performance-Based Assessment at the end of the unit.

FORMATIVE ASSESSMENT

Writing to Compare
If students struggle to provide specific examples and details, **then** ask them to skim the selections again with specific questions in mind.

Selection Test
Administer "The Invention of Everything Else" Selection Test, which is available in both print and digital formats online in Assessments.

PERSONALIZE FOR LEARNING

English Language Support
Compare-and-Contrast Essay Give students two short essays or articles that approach the same topic in different ways. Possibilities for topics are lengthened academic years, vehicle emission standards, or another topic of your choosing.

Ask pairs of students to take notes on how each essay approaches the topic and have partners discuss the differences. **EMERGING**

Ask pairs of students to take notes on how each essay approaches the topic and write a few sentences about which essay more effectively addresses the topic. Then have the students discuss their work. **EXPANDING**

Ask pairs of students to take notes on how each essay approaches the topic and write a few paragraphs about which essay more effectively addresses the topic. Have them prepare reasons as to why their position is correct. **BRIDGING**

An expanded **English Language Support Lesson** on Compare-and-Contrast Essay is available in the Interactive Teacher's Edition.

Small-Group Learning 509

PLANNING

SMALL-GROUP LEARNING • 25 YEARS LATER, HUBBLE SEES BEYOND TROUBLED START

25 Years Later, Hubble Sees Beyond Troubled Start

AUDIO SUMMARIES
Audio summaries of "25 Years Later, Hubble Sees Beyond Troubled Start" are available online in both English and Spanish in the Interactive Teacher's Edition or Unit Resources. Assigning these summaries prior to reading the selection may help students build additional background knowledge and set a context for their first read.

Summary

In "25 Years Later, Hubble Sees Beyond Troubled Start," Dennis Overbye recounts the initial difficulties and remarkable accomplishments of the Hubble Space Telescope. Launched into space in 1990, the telescope had initial technical problems that led to blurred images being sent back to Earth. Three years later, a NASA crew spent five days in space repairing the telescope. The Hubble began recording images of space that had never before been seen. Astronaut servicing crews kept the Hubble up to date, but in 2003, the *Columbia* space shuttle exploded. This led NASA to cancel a scheduled Hubble repair. The Hubble appeared to be doomed, but in 2009 a repair crew once again serviced it. Today the Hubble continues to record extraordinary images of our universe.

Insight

"25 Years Later, Hubble Sees Beyond Troubled Start" reveals that even the best scientific inspirations are often dependent on political realities. The article states that it took over three decades from the original proposal for the Hubble to come to fruition. The problems the scientists encountered and the delays in fixing them are the unfortunate realities of major scientific efforts.

ESSENTIAL QUESTION:
Are inventions realized through inspiration or perspiration?

Connection to Essential Question

Inventions like the Hubble Space Telescope are the work of many scientists, engineers, and astronauts. The newspaper article by Dennis Overbye suggests the amount of time and effort put into the creation of the telescope. Although the original idea was an inspiration, the "perspiration" was considerable.

SMALL-GROUP LEARNING PERFORMANCE TASK
Are inventions realized through inspiration or perspiration?

UNIT PERFORMANCE-BASED ASSESSMENT
Which invention described in this unit has had the biggest impact on humanity?

Connection to Performance Tasks

Small-Group Learning Performance Task "25 Years Later, Hubble Sees Beyond Troubled Start" is a demonstration of the amount of energy that must be devoted to making an inspiration a reality. For the Performance Task, students are asked to debate and take a position on the Essential Question.

Unit Performance-Based Assessment Science depends on new and improved ways to make discoveries about the universe. The article shows that the quest for more and different knowledge are reasons people invent. Students will evaluate these concepts as they determine which inventions had the greatest impact on humanity.

DIGITAL PERSPECTIVES Audio Video Document Annotation Highlights EL Highlights Online Assessment

LESSON RESOURCES

	Making Meaning	Language Development	Effective Expression
Lesson	First Read Close Read Analyze the Text Analyze Craft and Structure	Concept Vocabulary Word Study Conventions	Speaking and Listening
Instructional Standards	**RI.6** Determine an author's point of view or purpose in a text . . . . . . **RI.10** By the end of the year, read and comprehend literary nonfiction . . . **L.4** Determine or clarify the meaning of unknown and multiple-meaning words or phrases . . . **L.4.a** Use context as a clue . . .	**L.4** Determine or clarify the meaning of unknown and multiple-meaning words or phrases . . . **L.4.b** Use common, grade-appropriate Greek or Latin affixes and roots . . . **L.4.c** Consult general and specialized reference materials . . . **L.2** Demonstrate command of the conventions . . . **L.2.a** Use punctuation . . . **L.2.b** Use an ellipsis . . .	**SL.1** Engage effectively in a range of collaborative discussions . . . **SL.1.a** Come to discussions prepared . . . **SL.1.b** Follow rules for collegial discussions . . . **SL.1.c** Pose questions . . . **SL.1.d** Acknowledge new information . . . **SL.3** Delineate a speaker's argument . . .
STUDENT RESOURCES Available online in the Interactive Student Edition or Unit Resources	Selection Audio First-Read Guide: Nonfiction Close-Read Guide: Nonfiction	Word Network	Evidence Log
TEACHER RESOURCES **Selection Resources** Available online in the Interactive Teacher's Edition or Unit Resources	Audio Summaries Annotation Highlights EL Highlights English Language Support Lesson: Author's Purpose 25 Years Later, Hubble Sees Beyond: Text Questions Analyze Craft and Structure: Diction and Tone	Concept Vocabulary and Word Study Conventions: Dashes and Ellipses	Speaking and Listening: Debate
Reteach/Practice (RP) Available online in the Interactive Teacher's Edition or Unit Resources	Analyze Craft and Structure: Diction and Tone (RP)	Word Study: Latin Root *-vers-* (RP) Conventions: Dashes and Ellipses (RP)	Speaking and Listening: Debate (RP)
Assessment Available online in Assessments	Selection Test		
My Resources	A Unit 5 Answer Key is available online and in the Interactive Teacher's Edition.		

PERSONALIZE FOR LEARNING

SMALL-GROUP LEARNING • 25 YEARS LATER, HUBBLE SEES BEYOND TROUBLED START

Reading Support

Text Complexity Rubric: 25 Years Later, Hubble Sees Beyond Troubled Start

Quantitative Measures

Lexile: 1320   Text Length: 1,272 words

Qualitative Measures

Knowledge Demands (3 of 5)	Students may not be familiar with the Hubble Space Telescope. Most of the information in the selection is clearly explained.
Structure (3 of 5)	Organization is a straightforward sequence of events.
Language Conventionality and Clarity (4 of 5)	The syntax includes many complex sentences that have subordinate clauses or phrases. The selection has above-level vocabulary.
Levels of Meaning/Purpose (3 of 5)	The concept may be hard for some to grasp because of sophisticated language.

DECIDE AND PLAN

English Language Support

Provide English Learners with support for knowledge demands and language as they read the selection.

Knowledge Demands Before reading the text, have students summarize the background information. Making notes of what they know so far will help them as they read the text. Tell them they should expect to see language that describes space (cosmic, stellar, nebula…).

Language Students may have difficulty with the numerous complex sentences and above-level vocabulary. Instead of trying to understand every word, encourage students to scan for events in each paragraph that they understand. Ask them to write sentences restating the information they understood.

Strategic Support

Provide students with strategic support to ensure that they can successfully read the text.

Knowledge Demands After reading the background information, make sure students understand the subject that is the focus of the selection—the Hubble Space Telescope. Ask students to share prior knowledge they may have. Provide additional background information as needed.

Language/Clarity For students who may have difficulty with sophisticated concepts and complex sentences, encourage them to break each sentence down into smaller chunks or identify the meaning of unfamiliar words or phrases. Then have them reread the sentence.

Challenge

Provide students who need to be challenged with ideas for how they can go beyond a simple interpretation of the text.

Text Analysis Pair students. Have them each take a paragraph and retell it to their partner, using their own descriptions without reading from the text. Encourage them to include details and descriptive language. They may refer to the text as needed to remember details, but they should use their own words.

Written Response Ask students to research one of the "postcards" created by the Hubble Space Telescope. Have them prepare a visual presentation about the postcard and tell what the postcard shows.

TEACH

Read and Respond

Have groups read the selection and complete the Making Meaning, Language Development, and Effective Expression activities.

Standards Support Through Teaching and Learning Cycle

IDENTIFY NEEDS

Analyze results of the Beginning-of-Year Assessment, focusing on the items relating to Unit 5. Also take into consideration student performance to this point and your observations of where particular students struggle.

ANALYZE AND REVISE

- Analyze student work for evidence of student learning.
- Identify whether or not students have met the expectations in the standards.
- Identify implications for future instruction.

TEACH

Implement the planned lesson, and gather evidence of student learning.

DECIDE AND PLAN

- If students have performed poorly on items matching these standards, then provide selection scaffolds before assigning them the on-level lesson provided in the Student Edition.
- If students have done well on the Beginning-of-Year Assessment, then challenge them to keep progressing and learning by giving them opportunities to practice the skills in depth.
- Use the Selection Resources listed on the Planning pages for "25 Years Later, Hubble Sees Beyond Troubled Start" to help students continually improve their ability to master the standards.

Instructional Standards: 25 Years Later, Hubble Sees Beyond Troubled Start

	Catching Up	This Year	Looking Forward
Reading	You may wish to administer the **Analyze Craft and Structure: Diction and Tone (RP)** worksheet to help students understand how word choice affects tone.	**RI.10** By the end of the year, read and comprehend literary nonfiction at the high end of the grades 6–8 text complexity band independently and proficiently.	Challenge students to consider how the author may have used a different tone and how this would have affected the reading.
Speaking and Listening	You may wish to administer the **Speaking and Listening: Debate (RP)** worksheet to help students prepare for their debate.	**SL.1.c** Pose questions that connect the ideas of several speakers and respond to others' questions and comments with relevant evidence, observations, and ideas.	Have students ask questions that expand the debate to broader themes or ideas and actively incorporate others' statements into their own.
Language	Review the **Word Study: Latin Root -vers- (RP)** worksheet with students to make sure they understand the Latin root -vers- means "to turn." Review the **Conventions: Dashes and Ellipses (RP)** worksheet with students to ensure they know when to use these punctuation marks.	**L.4.b** Use common, grade-appropriate Greek or Latin affixes and roots as clues to the meaning of a word. **L.2.b** Use an ellipsis to indicate an omission.	Work with students to locate words in the text with other roots they recognize. Ask students to discuss when to use ellipses and dashes as opposed to commas, colons, semicolons, and parentheses.

Small-Group Learning   510D

FACILITATING

Jump Start

FIRST READ When you look up and see the stars, what do you notice? Mostly tiny, twinkling white dots. Between light pollution and great distance, there is a limit to what you can see with the naked eye. What do you think you could see if you had a telescope that was out in space?

25 Years Later, Hubble Sees Beyond Troubled Start 🔊 📄

What is the Hubble Space Telescope? Why was it such a big deal? What kind of images does it provide? Modeling the questions readers might ask as they read "25 Years Later, Hubble Sees Beyond Troubled Start" brings the text alive for students and connects it to the Small-Group Performance Task question. Selection audio and print capability for the selection are available in the Interactive Teacher's Edition.

Concept Vocabulary

Remind groups that when they come to an unfamiliar word as they read, one of the first things they should do is look for context clues. Have them find the word *deployed* in the text. Ask students to identify some clues within the text that hint at the word's meaning. Next, have them consider background knowledge. Have they heard of that word being used in a different way? Finally, have them consult a dictionary, if necessary.

▶ FIRST READ

As they read, students should perform the steps of the first read:

NOTICE: You may want to encourage students to notice the details provided about the history of the Hubble Space Telescope.

ANNOTATE: Remind students to mark passages that include details about the Hubble's rocky start and final outcome.

CONNECT: Encourage students to go beyond the text to make connections—What images of space have they seen in movies, books, magazines, or television?

RESPOND: Students will answer questions and write a summary to demonstrate understanding. Point out to students that while they will always complete the Respond step at the end of the first read, the other steps will probably happen somewhat concurrently. You may wish to print copies of the **First-Read Guide: Nonfiction** for students to use. 📄

510   UNIT 5 • INVENTION

👥 MAKING MEANING

About the Author

Dennis Overbye (b. 1944) is a science writer specializing in physics and cosmology, the science of the origin and development of the universe. In 1998, he joined the staff of the *New York Times* as deputy science editor, then switched to full-time writing. His articles have appeared in *Time, Science,* the *Los Angeles Times,* and the *New York Times,* among others. In 2014, he was a finalist for the Pulitzer Prize for Explanatory Reporting. Overbye lives in New York City with his wife, daughter, and two cats.

▤ STANDARDS

Reading Informational Text
By the end of the year, read and comprehend literary nonfiction at the high end of the grades 6–8 text complexity band independently and proficiently.

Language
Determine or clarify the meaning of unknown and multiple-meaning words or phrases based on *grade 8 reading and content,* choosing flexibly from a range of strategies.
  a. Use context as a clue to the meaning of a word or phrase.

510   UNIT 5 • INVENTION

25 Years Later, Hubble Sees Beyond Troubled Start

Concept Vocabulary

As you perform your first read of "25 Years Later, Hubble Sees Beyond Troubled Start," you will encounter these words.

| dismay | controversy | outcry |

Context Clues Sometimes you need to infer the meaning of an unfamiliar word by looking for context clues in the surrounding words.

Example from the selection:

> When the Hubble was finally deployed, NASA's **spinmasters** were instantly at the top of their game, <u>hailing it as the greatest advance in astronomy since Galileo.</u>

If you didn't know the meaning of the term *spinmasters,* you might infer from the underlined clues that *spinmasters* provide positive reviews to the public in order to boost the reputation of a business or organization.

First Read NONFICTION

Apply these strategies as you conduct your first read. You will have an opportunity to complete a close read after your first read.

- **NOTICE** the general ideas of the text. *What* is it about? *Who* is involved?
- **ANNOTATE** by marking vocabulary and key passages you want to revisit.
- **CONNECT** ideas within the selection to what you already know and what you have already read.
- **RESPOND** by completing the Comprehension Check and writing a brief summary of the selection.

First Read

PERSONALIZE FOR LEARNING

English Language Support

Make Predictions Have students read the title of the article. Ask a volunteer to predict what the article is going to be about. After they respond that it is about the Hubble, ask what else they can predict from the title. They should suggest that it started 25 years ago and there were some problems. Next, if they do not already know, tell them what the Hubble is. Ask them to again predict what they will learn as they read. **ALL LEVELS**

SCIENCE ARTICLE

25 Years Later, Hubble Sees Beyond Troubled Start

Dennis Overbye

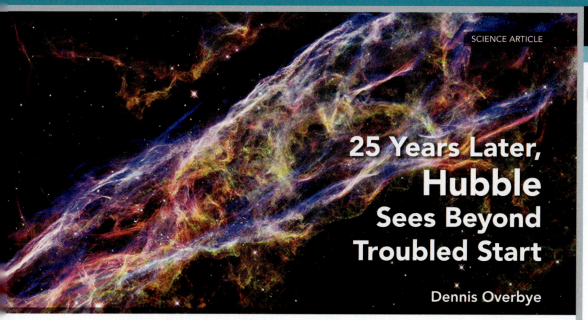

BACKGROUND

Lyman Spitzer Jr. (1914–1997), whose ideas inspired the creation of the Hubble Space Telescope, achieved great success as an astrophysicist. He studied space astronomy, star clusters, and the physics of stars. Not only did he propose the creation of a space telescope, he did so a decade before the first satellite had been launched.

1 Against all odds, it's 25 years in space and counting for the Hubble Space Telescope this month.[1]

2 Few icons of science have had such a perilous existence, surviving political storms, physical calamities, and the simple passage of time in the service of cosmic exploration.

3 In 1946, the astronomer Lyman Spitzer, Jr., had a dream. A telescope in space, above the unruly atmosphere, would be able to see stars unaffected by the turbulence that blurs them and makes them twinkle. It would be able to see ultraviolet and infrared emissions that are blocked by the atmosphere and thus invisible to astronomers on the ground.

4 It took more than three decades for the rest of the astronomical community, NASA, and Congress to buy into this dream, partly as a way to showcase the capabilities of the space shuttle, still in development then, and the ability of astronauts to work routinely in space. By the time the telescope was launched into space from the space shuttle *Discovery* on April 25, 1990, it had been almost canceled at least twice and then delayed following the explosion of the shuttle *Challenger* in 1986.

_____
1. **this month** This article was published in April 2015.

FACILITATING

Concept Vocabulary

DISMAY If groups are struggling to define the word *dismay* in paragraph 8, point out the context clues within the text that may help them define the word. Help students see that the paragraph describes a mistake with large consequences. The scientists were not happy to learn about this mistake.

Possible response: In this context, *dismay* means "alarm, concern, or distress."

NOTES

Mark context clues or indicate another strategy you used that helped you determine meaning.

dismay (diss MAY) *n.*
MEANING:

---

5 When the Hubble was finally deployed, NASA's spinmasters were instantly at the top of their game, hailing it as the greatest advance in astronomy since Galileo.[2]

6 And it might have been except for one problem: The telescope couldn't be focused. Instead, within days it became a laughingstock—a "technoturkey," in the words of some of its critics.

7 Designed using spy satellite technology, Hubble had an eight-foot mirror, just small enough to fit into the space shuttle cargo bay.

8 But because of a measuring error during a testing process that was hurried to save money, that big mirror wound up misshapen, polished four-millionths of an inch too flat, leaving the telescope with blurry vision. It was the kind of mistake, known as a spherical aberration, that an amateur astronomer might make, and it was a handful of astronomers who first recognized the flaw—to the disbelief and then the **dismay** of the engineers and contractors working for NASA.

9 For bright objects, astronomers could correct for the flaw with image processing software. But for the fainter parts of the universe, the Hubble needed glasses.

10 NASA scientists shrugged off their heartbreak and worked to figure out a way to provide corrective lenses.

11 Three years later, the space shuttle *Endeavour* and a repair crew led by Story Musgrave—astronaut, pilot, surgeon, spacewalker and Zen gardener—rode to the rescue.

12 In five tense days of spacewalks, they replaced the telescope's main camera and installed tiny mirrors designed to correct the Hubble's vision.

13 The rest of the universe snapped into crystalline focus. And NASA could stop holding its breath.

14 The Hubble was the first big-deal telescope of the Internet age, and its cosmic postcards captivated the world. Trained on a patch of sky known as the Hubble Ultra Deep Field in 2010, the telescope's keen eye discerned swarms of baby galaxies crawling out of the primordial[3] darkness as early as only 600 million years after the Big Bang.

15 And it took one of the first visible-light photos of a distant planet, Fomalhaut b, orbiting its star.

16 In perhaps its most iconic image, called "Pillars of Creation," the Hubble recorded baby stars burning their way out of biblical-looking mountains of gas and dust in a stellar nursery known as the Eagle nebula.

---

2. **Galileo** Galileo Galilei (1564–1642) was an Italian scientist and scholar who was the first person to use a telescope to observe space.
3. **primordial** *adj.* ancient; from the beginning of time.

HOW LANGUAGE WORKS

Dashes Direct students' attention to paragraph 6. Ask them to notice any unusual punctuation. Point out the punctuation after the word *laughingstock*. Ask if anyone can identify that mark. Explain that it is a dash. Ask students to suggest why the writer used it. Point out that a dash shows a strong, sudden break in thought or speech.

17 These postcards were not without **controversy**. The Hubble's camera records in black and white, through filters that isolate the characteristic light from different atoms, such as sulfur, hydrogen, and oxygen. Then the different layers are assigned whatever colors look good to the eye and best show off the underlying astrophysics rather than their natural colors.

18 "Pillars of Creation," for example, is presented in earth tones of green and brown and is oriented to look like a Turner landscape,[4] while the natural emissions from the nebula are shades of red.

19 Technological hiccups have also continued. In 1999, four of the six gyroscopes that keep the telescope pointed failed, and the Hubble went into "safe mode." A crew was hastily dispatched to replace the gyros. That was the first of what would be three trips to the telescope by John M. Grunsfeld, an astronaut, astronomer, and now NASA's associate administrator for science, who would win the sobriquet "Hubble Repairman" for his feats.

20 The telescope has been reborn again and again over the years, thanks to the efforts of astronaut servicing crews. Astronauts wearing the equivalent of boxing gloves have gradually learned how to do things the telescope's designers had never dared dream of, fiddling with its innards, replacing circuit boards and performing the equivalent of eye surgery and computer repairs in space.

21 The Hubble was hitting its stride, getting better and better, when the *Columbia* space shuttle disintegrated in 2003, killing all seven astronauts on board. That harkened the end of NASA's space shuttle dreams.

22 The agency's administrator, Sean O'Keefe, canceled what was to be the final Hubble servicing mission on the grounds that it was too risky. Without it, the telescope would be doomed to die in orbit within two or three years when its batteries and gyros failed again.

23 The decision was announced and defended by Dr. Grunsfeld, who was then NASA's chief scientist. "Being an astronaut, there are not a lot of things that have really shocked me in my life," Dr. Grunsfeld recalled later. "But I don't think anybody could ever prepare themselves for, you know, trying to bury something that they have said, 'Hey, this is worth risking my life for.'"

24 Mr. O'Keefe's decision ignited a national **outcry**. Schoolchildren offered to send their pennies to NASA to help pay for the telescope.

NOTES

Mark context clues or indicate another strategy you used that helped you determine meaning.

controversy (KON truh vuhr see) *n.*
MEANING:

Mark context clues or indicate another strategy you used that helped you determine meaning.

outcry ((OWT kry) *n.*
MEANING:

---

4. **Turner landscape.** J.M.W Turner was an artist famed for his use of color.

FACILITATING

CLOSER LOOK

Analyze Figurative Language

Circulate among groups as students conduct their close read. Suggest that groups read paragraph 27. Encourage them to talk about the annotations they mark. If needed, provide the following support.

ANNOTATE: Have students mark details in paragraph 27 that show the writer's use of personification, or work with small groups as you highlight them together.

QUESTION: Guide students to consider what these details might tell them. Ask what a reader can infer from the language used in this paragraph, and accept student responses.

Possible response: The writer gives the Hubble telescope human characteristics to help readers understand the connection Dr. Grunsfeld has to it and to show the importance of the information it has helped scientists discover.

CONCLUDE: Help students formulate conclusions about the importance of these details in the text. Ask students why the author might have included these details.

Possible response: The Hubble's images are not just pretty pictures. They help the world see how large the universe really is and how we are but a small part of it.

Reminds students that **personification** is a type of figurative language in which a nonhuman subject is given human characteristics. Remind students that personification is not meant to be interpreted literally but rather used to create vivid impressions by setting up comparisons between dissimilar things.

NOTES

25 Behind the scenes, however, Dr. Grunsfeld and other astronomers and NASA engineers were working on ways to save the Hubble, perhaps by sending robots to work on it.

26 The robotic approach was eventually rejected by a National Academy of Sciences panel, but it had served as a placeholder to keep the teams of engineers together. In the end, Mr. O'Keefe resigned, and his successor, Michael Griffin, reinstated a servicing mission.

27 In 2009, Dr. Grunsfeld led one last mission to the Hubble. He was the last human to touch the telescope, patting it as the shuttle *Atlantis* prepared to let it go again. But that does not mean the telescope has ceased to touch humanity. On the contrary, it continues to deliver news about this thing we are all part of—a universe—but barely understand.

28 Earlier this spring, astronomers announced that the Hubble had seen a sort of cosmic mirage known as an Einstein ring, in which they could view multiple reruns of a star that died in a stupendous supernova explosion more than nine billion years ago on the other side of the cosmos.

29 NASA is making a big deal of the Hubble anniversary, with a weeklong symposium[5] in Baltimore, where the Space Telescope Science Institute is based.

30 "This is a celebration partly about the telescope and partly about NASA," Dr. Grunsfeld said, "but much of it is a celebration of people doing science."

31 The Hubble today is more powerful than its designers ever dreamed, and it has a good chance of living long enough to share the universe with its designated successor, the James Webb Space Telescope, due to be launched in 2018. The Hubble's longevity is something few would have imagined 10 years ago, yet NASA is already planning a 30th-anniversary celebration in 2020, Dr. Grunsfeld said.

32 After a quarter-century, the telescope's future and promise are still as big as the sky and our ignorance of what lies behind it.

---

5. **symposium** *n.* conference where experts discuss a certain topic.

DIGITAL PERSPECTIVES

Illuminating the Text Have students go online to find images taken by the Hubble Space Telescope. Ask students to give their thoughts about the images. Ask them to compare what they see with what they might have seen in the sky on a clear night. Also, given what they read in paragraph 17, ask them what they notice and what they think about the colors in the images. **(Research to Clarify)**

Comprehension Check

Complete the following items after you finish your first read. Review and clarify details with your group.

1. When was the Hubble Space Telescope launched into space?

2. What advantage does a telescope in space have over one located on the ground?

3. A *laughingstock* is the subject of a joke or an object of ridicule. According to the article, what flaw made Hubble a "laughingstock"?

4. What is Hubble's most recent image?

5. **Notebook** Confirm your understanding of the article by writing a short summary.

RESEARCH

Research to Clarify Choose at least one unfamiliar detail from the text. Briefly research that detail. In what way does the information you learned shed light on an aspect of the article?

Research to Explore Conduct research on an aspect of the text you find interesting. For example, you may want to learn more about the Hubble's designated successor, the James Webb Space Telescope, due to be launched in 2018.

DIGITAL PERSPECTIVES

Comprehension Check

Possible responses:
1. The Hubble Space Telescope was launched into space on April 25, 1990.
2. A telescope in space would see more stars, unaffected by the atmosphere. It would also see the ultraviolet in infrared emissions blocked by the atmosphere.
3. The Hubble had a mistake, a spherical aberration, which caused it to have blurred images.
4. The Hubble saw a cosmic mirage known as an Einstein ring. With this, the Hubble saw multiple reruns of a star dying in a supernova explosion.
5. Summaries will vary but should include the following information: the Hubble launched in 1990; people were excited, but the Hubble's mirror had a flaw; a crew was sent in a space shuttle to fix the problem; the Hubble began sending back stunning images of planets and stars; NASA sent three more missions to repair the Hubble; the Hubble continues to send amazing images as NASA celebrates the telescope's 25 years in space.

Research

Research to Clarify If students struggle to decide on a detail to research, you may want to suggest that they focus on one of the following topics: Lyman Spitzer Jr, *Challenger, Discovery,* NASA, Galileo, *Endeavor,* "Pillars of Creation," John Grunsfeld, James Webb Space Telescope.

Research to Explore If students aren't sure how to go about formulating a research question, suggest that they use their findings from Research to Clarify as a starting point. For example, if students researched the James Webb Space Telescope, they might formulate a question such as, "What is unique about the James Webb Space Telescope?"

PERSONALIZE FOR LEARNING

Challenge

Timeline Have students use what they have learned in this article and do more research about the history of the Hubble Space Telescope. Have students create a timeline about the telescope, from its conception until today. Have students include images to enhance their timeline presentations. Then, display the timelines. Survey the timelines and find unique details included in some timelines. Ask those students to share the details with the class.

FACILITATING

Jump Start

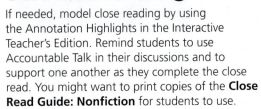

CLOSE READ Space exploration—books, television shows, and movies have all glorified this idea. In fact, it is a reality. People have been to space, landed on the moon, orbited Earth, lived on the International Space Station, and will someday go to Mars. Have students discuss why space exploration has such a hold on people's imagination.

Close Read the Text

If needed, model close reading by using the Annotation Highlights in the Interactive Teacher's Edition. Remind students to use Accountable Talk in their discussions and to support one another as they complete the close read. You might want to print copies of the **Close Read Guide: Nonfiction** for students to use.

Analyze the Text

Possible responses:
1. The error shows that even brilliant people working on a long-term project can make mistakes. Inventions are made by humans, who make mistakes.
2. Passages will vary by group. Remind students to explain why they chose the questions they asked and how they reached their conclusions.
3. Responses will vary by group.

Concept Vocabulary

Why These Words? Possible response: The concept words all have to do with the Hubble's flaws or shortcomings. Another word that has to do with this concept is *laughingstock*.

Practice

Possible responses: The scientist expressed dismay when the experiment failed. There is often a controversy over whether the country should spend a great deal of money on dangerous space missions. To prevent an outcry, be careful about the way you report your findings as not to alarm people.

Word Network

Possible words: *capabilities, corrective, discerned, engineers*

Word Study

For more support, see **Concept Vocabulary and Word Study.**

Possible responses: *Reverse:* opposite in direction or position; *subversive:* tending to undermine a position; *converse:* opposite in direction. The root *-vers-* means to turn, and all of these words have to do with making a change.

516 UNIT 5 • INVENTION

25 YEARS LATER, HUBBLE SEES BEYOND TROUBLED START

MAKING MEANING

Close Read the Text

With your group, revisit sections of the text you marked during your first read. **Annotate** what you notice. What **questions** do you have? What can you **conclude**?

Analyze the Text

CITE TEXTUAL EVIDENCE to support your answers.

Notebook Complete the activities.

1. **Review and Clarify** With your group, reread paragraphs 8–9 of the article. Discuss the specific problem that the Hubble had. What does this problem show about the nature of invention?
2. **Present and Discuss** Discuss what you noticed in the selection, what questions you asked, and what conclusions you reached.
3. **Essential Question:** *Are inventions realized through inspiration or perspiration?* What has this article taught you about invention? Discuss with your group.

TIP

GROUP DISCUSSION
Take time to review the meanings of unfamiliar words and technical terms before discussing the article with your group.

WORD NETWORK

Identify words from the article that relate to the concept of invention. Add these words to your Word Network.

STANDARDS

Language
Determine or clarify the meaning of unknown and multiple-meaning words or phrases based on *grade 8 reading and content*, choosing flexibly from a range of strategies.
b. Use common, grade-appropriate Greek or Latin affixes and roots as clues to the meaning of a word.
c. Consult general and specialized reference materials, both print and digital, to find the pronunciation of a word or determine or clarify its precise meaning or its part of speech.

516 UNIT 5 • INVENTION

LANGUAGE DEVELOPMENT

Concept Vocabulary

| dismay | controversy | outcry |

Why These Words? The concept vocabulary words from the text are related. With your group, determine what the words have in common. Write your ideas and add another word that fits the category.

Practice

Notebook Confirm your understanding of the concept vocabulary words by using each in a sentence. Provide context clues for the words.

Word Study

Latin Root: *-vers-* The word *controversy* contains the Latin root *-vers-* which means "to turn." It also includes a variation of the Latin prefix *contra-*, which means "against" or "in opposition." In the article, the author explains that the images from Hubble were the subject of a *controversy* because people had different opinions on their accuracy and usefulness. Based on the context and the Latin word parts, you can infer that a *controversy* is when people "turn against" each other. Use a dictionary to find the definitions of the following words that include the root *-vers-*: *reverse, subversive,* and *converse.* Briefly explain how the root *-vers-* contributes to the meaning of each word.

FORMATIVE ASSESSMENT

Analyze the Text

If students struggle to close read the text, **then** provide the **25 Years Later, Hubble Sees Beyond: Text Questions** available online in the Interactive Teacher's Edition or Unit Resources. Answers and DOK levels are also available.

Concept Vocabulary

If students struggle to understand the concept vocabulary, **then** review them in context again.

Word Study

If struggle to understand the Latin root *-vers-*, **then** review words that contain the root and how its meaning connects them. For Reteach and Practice, see **Word Study: Latin Root -vers- (RP).**

ESSENTIAL QUESTION: Are inventions realized through inspiration or perspiration?

DIGITAL PERSPECTIVES

Analyze Craft and Structure

Author's Purpose: Diction and Tone An author's purpose for writing is the reason he or she writes. For example, an author may write to inform, to persuade, or to entertain. In "25 Years Later, Hubble Sees Beyond Troubled Start," Dennis Overbye's purpose for writing can be inferred by studying his diction and tone.

Diction, or word choice, has a great impact on readers. Writers choose what information to convey and how to say it. Examining diction can help you identify an author's tone and purpose.

Tone is an author's attitude toward his or her subject and audience. Tone is created by an author's diction. Tone can usually be described using adjectives, such as *humorous, argumentative,* or *academic.* Identifying tone can also help you identify author's purpose.

Here is an example of how to analyze diction and tone:

PASSAGE	ANALYSIS OF DICTION	ANALYSIS OF TONE
The telescope has been reborn again and again over the years, thanks to the efforts of astronaut servicing crews.	"reborn," "thanks to the efforts" This passage conveys information but in an informal way.	grateful; positive

TIP

COLLABORATION
Some members of your group may have different ideas about the tone of the article. Reading a passage aloud may help you come to agreement.

STANDARDS
Reading Informational Text
• Determine an author's point of view or purpose in a text and analyze how the author acknowledges and responds to conflicting evidence or viewpoints.

Practice

CITE TEXTUAL EVIDENCE to support your answers.

Use this chart to analyze Dennis Overbye's diction and tone in "25 Years Later, Hubble Sees Beyond Troubled Start." Then, share your analysis with your group, and work together to determine Overbye's purpose for writing. The first row has been completed as an example.

PASSAGE	ANALYSIS OF DICTION	ANALYSIS OF TONE
Against all odds, it's 25 years in space and counting for the Hubble Space Telescope this month. Few icons of science have had such a perilous existence, surviving political storms, physical calamities, and the simple passage of time in the service of cosmic exploration.	"it's 25 years ... and counting" / "icons" / "service of" / "perilous" / "calamity" This passage uses contrasting language—informal words in Paragraph 1 and formal, difficult words in Paragraph 2.	dramatic; admiring
Paragraph 8	"Misshapen," and "amateur" imply the size of the problem.	The tone is critical.
Paragraphs 19 and 20	"Hiccups" and "repairman" imply that the Hubble had problems.	The tone is serious.
Paragraph 31	"Dreamed" and "longevity" suggest the success of the telescope.	The tone is optimistic.
Author's Purpose	The author shares information about the difficulties the Hubble has faced, and also celebrates its successes.	

Analyze Craft and Structure

Author's Purpose: Diction and Tone Tone is an important tool of a writer, even when the writer is sharing information rather than a piece of fiction. The tone of an article tells the reader how the writer feels. The writer's diction, or word choice, helps the writer create the tone. Often, the writer's opinion can be discerned from the writer's tone. For more support, see **Analyze Craft and Structure: Diction and Tone.**

Practice
See possible responses in the chart on the student page.

FORMATIVE ASSESSMENT
Analyze Craft and Structure
If students struggle to understand the author's use of tone and diction, **then** review examples from the article. For Reteach and Practice, see **Analyze Craft and Structure: Diction and Tone (RP).**

PERSONALIZE FOR LEARNING

English Language Support

Author's Purpose Remind students that an author may state his or her purpose directly, or simply indicate it through diction and tone. Ask students to choose a topic having to do with space travel about which they have a strong opinion. Also ask students to include adverbs and adjectives in their writing. Tell them that their writing should illustrate a specific tone based on their word choice.

Have students write one or two sentences about their chosen subject. Remind them that tone is the attitude of the author. It can be cheerful, sarcastic, serious, or cynical. **EMERGING** Ask students to write three or four sentences about their subject. Tell them to choose the tone that their writing will have before they begin to write so that they can choose their words carefully. **EXPANDING**

Have students write a brief explanatory essay on their subject, and then ask them to explain the tone that their writing has and the specific words that they chose to create that tone. **BRIDGING**

An expanded **English Language Support Lesson** on Author's Purpose is available in the Interactive Teacher's Edition.

FACILITATING

Conventions

Dashes and Ellipses Display the following sentences: "I saw what happened—a huge fight in the schoolyard. I wanted to tell the principal, but . . ." Ask students to explain why a dash and ellipsis might have been used here. Punctuation choice does have an impact on the meaning of writing. Understanding the purpose of different types of punctuation helps readers understand the text. For more support, see **Conventions: Dashes and Ellipses.**

Read It

Possible responses:
1. (a) "Few icons of science have had such a perilous existence, ..." (b) "The telescope has been reborn …, thanks to the efforts of astronaut servicing crews."
2. From paragraph 6: "Instead, within days it became a laughingstock—a 'technoturkey,' in the words of some of its critics." The author uses a dash in place of other words, such as *that is*. From paragraph 11, "Three years later, the space shuttle *Endeavor* and a repair crew led by Story Musgrave—astronaut, pilot, surgeon, spacewalker, and Zen gardener—rode to the rescue." The author uses a dash to set off a nonrestrictive element.

Write It

Students' paragraphs will vary but should use ellipses and dashes correctly.

FORMATIVE ASSESSMENT

Conventions

If students struggle to understand how dashes and ellipses are used, **then** review examples of sentences that use these conventions. For Reteach and Practice, see **Conventions: Dashes and Ellipses (RP).**

LANGUAGE DEVELOPMENT

25 YEARS LATER, HUBBLE SEES BEYOND TROUBLED START

Conventions

Dashes and Ellipses

- An **ellipsis** (. . .) shows something is missing from a quoted passage. It can also show a pause or an interruption in speech.
- A **dash** (—) shows a strong, sudden break in thought or speech.

This chart shows some common reasons why authors use an ellipsis or a dash.

USE AN ELLIPSIS	EXAMPLES
to show the reader that you have chosen to leave out a word or words from a quoted passage	As the inscription on the Statue of Liberty says, "Give me your tired, your poor. . . ."
to indicate a pause or an interruption in speech	The scientist said, "When I saw the telescope's pictures, I . . . I couldn't speak."

USE A DASH	EXAMPLES
to show the reader that there is a strong, sudden interruption in thought or speech	"I can't believe—hey, look at the meteor!—how gorgeous the night sky is."
in place of *in other words*, *namely*, or *that is* before an explanation	The astronaut wanted one thing—to explore space in his lifetime.
to set off nonrestrictive elements (modifiers or other elements that are not essential to the meaning of the sentence) when there is a sudden break in thought	Albert Einstein—the physicist who developed the theory of relativity—became an American citizen in 1940.

Read It

Work with your group to complete each of the following items.

1. The following quotations are passages from the news article. Use an ellipsis to omit a portion of each quotation without altering the meaning.
   a. "Few icons of science have had such a perilous existence, surviving political storms, physical calamities, and the simple passage of time in the service of cosmic exploration."
   b. "The telescope has been reborn again and again over the years, thanks to the efforts of astronaut servicing crews."
2. Review the selection, and find at least two sentences in which the author uses dashes. Record the sentence, and determine the reason the author used dashes based on the information in the chart.

Write It

Notebook Write a brief paragraph in which you explain what you learned from the news article about the Hubble Space Telescope. In your paragraph, use an ellipsis and a dash in at least three of the ways indicated in the chart.

STANDARDS
Language
Demonstrate command of the conventions of standard English capitalization, punctuation, and spelling when writing.
  a. Use punctuation to indicate a pause or break.
  b. Use an ellipsis to indicate an omission.

PERSONALIZE FOR LEARNING

Challenge

Time Travel Have students research articles written at the time the Hubble mistake was discovered. Have them report about how this problem was viewed by news outlets. Given what they know now, have students write a response letter to a news outlet from the future. Encourage them to use what they have learned about dashes and ellipses to enhance their writing.

EFFECTIVE EXPRESSION

Speaking and Listening

Assignment

With your group, conduct a **debate** in which you respond to one of the following propositions, or statements of opinion:

- [ ] **Proposition 1:** Learning about the universe with a space telescope, such as Hubble, is a worthwhile pursuit that should be endorsed and well funded.

- [ ] **Proposition 2:** The Hubble's flaws prevent it from providing humans with accurate and useful information about the universe.

Project Plan Decide which proposition your group will debate. With your group, determine which members will argue for the proposition and which members will argue against it. Choose a moderator to keep time and see that the debaters remain orderly and don't speak out of turn. Keep the following instructions in mind.

Preparing for the Debate

- Reread the article, and identify information from the selection that supports your proposition. Then, conduct research to find additional evidence to support your proposition, or argument.
- Analyze your evidence, and note specific details that support your proposition. Based on these notes, make logical connections between the evidence and your proposition. These connections are your reasons for arguing the position.
- Create a thesis, or statement of your position, from your notes. Present this thesis during your opening statement.
- Prior to the debate, prepare to address your opponents' arguments, or the **counterclaims** to your position, by thinking about the topic from the opposite perspective and considering the arguments that they might make.

Taking Part in the Debate

- During the debate, each participant should build on and respond to the arguments presented by the previous speaker.
- Use supporting evidence from the selection and from your research.
- Listen carefully to the opposing side during the debate so you can address their arguments and make counterclaims.
- Listen carefully and evaluate your opponents' arguments to see if they make sense. Identify when they do not present enough evidence to support their views or when the evidence they present is not well connected to their arguments.

EVIDENCE LOG

Before moving on to a new selection, go to your Evidence Log and record what you learned from "25 Years Later, Hubble Sees Beyond Troubled Start."

STANDARDS

Speaking and Listening

- Engage effectively in a range of collaborative discussions (one-on-one, in groups, and teacher-led) with diverse partners on *grade 8 topics, texts, and issues,* building on others' ideas and expressing their own clearly.
  a. Come to discussions prepared, having read or researched material under study; explicitly draw on that preparation by referring to evidence on the topic, text, or issue to probe and reflect on ideas under discussion.
  b. Follow rules for collegial discussions and decision-making, track progress toward specific goals and deadlines, and define individual roles as needed.
  c. Pose questions that connect the ideas of several speakers and respond to others' questions and comments with relevant evidence, observations, and ideas.
  d. Acknowledge new information expressed by others, and, when warranted, qualify or justify their own views in light of the evidence presented.

- Delineate a speaker's argument and specific claims, evaluating the soundness of the reasoning and relevance and sufficiency of the evidence and identifying when irrelevant evidence is introduced.

DIGITAL PERSPECTIVES

Speaking and Listening

Explain that a debate is an organized argument. Students should understand that they can choose a side that they disagree with and still successfully debate its merits. Remind them that there are many important parts of a successful debate. First, students need to have clear positions. They need to have evidence to back up their positions. Successful debaters also anticipate their opponents arguments and find counter-arguments.

Preparing for the Debate

Encourage groups to practice before the debate. Within each group, members can state their positions, make their arguments, and rebut counter-arguments. Other members can provide critiques focused on what was convincing and what wasn't.

Taking Part in the Debate

Remind students to be respectful of others' debate performances. For more support, see **Speaking and Listening: Debate.**

Evidence Log Support students in completing their Evidence Log. This paced activity will help prepare them for the Performance-Based Assessment at the end of the unit.

FORMATIVE ASSESSMENT

Speaking and Listening

If students struggle to identify the different parts of a successful debate, **then** review the components and some examples of each. For Reteach and Practice, see **Speaking and Listening: Debate (RP).**

Selection Test

Administer the "25 Years Later, Hubble Sees Beyond Troubled Start" Selection Test, which is available in both print and digital formats online in Assessments.

PERSONALIZE FOR LEARNING

Strategic Support

Graphic Organizer Have students prepare for their debates by creating a graphic organizer like this. This will help them develop a clear and organized presentation. It will force them to look at the other side of the argument as well.

Position:	
Point:	Counterpoint:
Point:	Counterpoint:
Point:	Counterpoint:
Conclusion:	

PLANNING

SMALL-GROUP LEARNING • SOUNDS OF A GLASS ARMONICA

Sounds of a Glass Armonica

AUDIO
Audio summaries of "Sounds of a Glass Armonica" are available online in both English and Spanish in the Interactive Teacher's Edition or Unit Resources. Assigning these summaries prior to watching the video may help students build additional background knowledge and set a context for their first review.

Summary
The media selection "Sounds of a Glass Armonica" presents composer and musician William Zeitler as he plays the glass armonica. Benjamin Franklin got the idea for his invention after seeing someone make music using wineglasses partially filled with water. The armonica shown in the video is made up of glass goblets attached horizontally to a slowly revolving rod that is propelled by a small motor. The player makes music by touching different goblets with his fingers, producing an ethereal melody.

Insight
"Sounds of a Glass Armonica" provides an insight into the wide range of creativity of one of America's earliest and most celebrated inventors. Not only was Franklin a creator of practical inventions, such as the Franklin stove and bifocals, but also he was a musician of some note. The glass armonica was very popular for musical occasions in which the room was small but there was no way to amplify the sound. Today, the armonica is increasing in popularity, aided by modern sound technology.

ESSENTIAL QUESTION:
Are inventions realized through inspiration or perspiration?

Connection to Essential Question
The glass armonica is an invention that was inspired by water filled wineglasses centuries ago. It began, no doubt, as an exploration of sound made by glasses containing different amounts of liquid. Once Benjamin Franklin observed the phenomenon, the invention of an actual instrument turned the experiment into a matter of applied physics. The inspiration was realized through perspiration.

SMALL-GROUP LEARNING PERFORMANCE TASK
Are inventions realized through inspiration or perspiration?

UNIT PERFORMANCE-BASED ASSESSMENT
Which invention described in this unit has had the biggest impact on humanity?

Connection to Performance Tasks
Small-Group Learning Performance Task Both inspiration and perspiration were involved in the invention of the armonica throughout its history. After viewing the video, students might appreciate the amount of perspiration involved in creating the instrument. For the Performance Task, students are asked to debate and take a position on the Essential Question.

Unit Performance-Based Assessment Many situations encourage people to invent. Franklin was probably encouraged to invent the glass armonica by his interest in music and by the intellectual challenge involved. In their essays, students will decide the impact of this invention as it relates to humanity.

DIGITAL PERSPECTIVES Audio Video Document Annotation Highlights EL Highlights Online Assessment

LESSON RESOURCES

	Making Meaning	Language Development	Effective Expression
Lesson	First Review Close Review Analyze the Media	Media Vocabulary	Research
Instructional Standards	**RI.10** By the end of the year, read and comprehend literary nonfiction . . . **L.6** Acquire and use accurately grade-appropriate general academic and domain-specific words and phrases . . . **SL.1** Engage effectively in a range of collaborative discussions . . .		**W.7** Conduct short research projects . . . **SL.1** Engage effectively in a range of collaborative discussions . . . **SL.1.a** Come to discussions prepared . . . **SL.1.b** Follow rules for collegial discussions . . . **SL.5** Integrate multimedia and visual displays . . .
▷ STUDENT RESOURCES			
Available online in the Interactive Student Edition or Unit Resources	Selection Audio First-Review Guide: Media Video Close-Review Guide: Media Video	Word Network	Evidence Log
▷ TEACHER RESOURCES			
Selection Resources Available online in the Interactive Teacher's Edition or Unit Resources	Audio Summaries Sounds of a Glass Armonica: Media Questions	Media Vocabulary	Research: Presentation
My Resources	A Unit 5 Answer Key is available online and in the Interactive Teacher's Edition.		

Media Complexity Rubric: Sounds of a Glass Armonica

Quantitative Measures

Format and Length: Approximately 2:17 minute video

Qualitative Measures

Knowledge Demands ①—②—**❸**—④—⑤	To fully understand the video, prior knowledge is needed about Benjamin Franklin. The video also contains reference to classical music (Mozart).
Structure ①—**❷**—③—④—⑤	The video is a demonstration of the instrument Franklin invented. Some verbal explanation is provided.
Language Conventionality and Clarity ①—②—**❸**—④—⑤	There is very little speaking in the video. There are some references to classical music that may need explanation.
Levels of Meaning/Purpose ①—**❷**—③—④—⑤	Meaning and concepts are straightforward and easy to grasp.

FACILITATING

Jump Start

FIRST REVIEW When the glass armonica was first played in the eighteenth century, the eerie sound it produced was said to drive some people mad. What kind of sound could do that? Why might it be easier for us, today, to hear such strange sounds and not go mad? Engage students in a discussion about how sound can affect our thoughts and emotions. As students discuss, urge them to also share the kinds of sounds that move them.

Sounds of a Glass Armonica

What would it be like to touch glass and create sound with your fingertip? What might you hear? Modeling questions such as these will help students connect to "Sounds of a Glass Armonica" and to the Small-Group Performance Task assignment. Audio for the selection is available in the Interactive Teacher's Edition.

Media Vocabulary

Encourage groups to discuss the media vocabulary. Have they seen or used these terms before? Do they use any of them in their speech or writing?

Ask groups to look closely at the three terms and ask how they relate to videos and films they see online every day. Have students discuss different ways that zoom and focus effects can be used.

FIRST REVIEW

As they review, students should perform the steps of the first review:

WATCH: Remind students to play close attention to what the narrator says—and how.

NOTE: Encourage students to make notes of any elements of the video they may want to revisit during their close review.

CONNECT: Encourage students to make connections beyond the video. If they cannot make connections to their own lives, have them consider music they have heard or strange instruments they've learned about.

RESPOND: Students will answer questions and write a summary to demonstrate understanding.

Point out to students that while they will always complete the Respond step at the end of the first review, the other steps will probably happen somewhat concurrently. You may wish to print copies of the **First-Review Guide: Media Video** for students to use.

520   UNIT 5 • INVENTION

MAKING MEANING

About the Musician
William Zeitler (b. 1954) earned his music degree from the California Institute of the Arts. He is a pianist, composer, and the author of a book on the history of the glass armonica. He is also one of the world's few professional armonica players and has released five albums of original armonica music.

STANDARDS

Reading Informational Text
By the end of the year, read and comprehend literary nonfiction at the high end of the grades 6–8 text complexity band independently and proficiently.

Language
Acquire and use accurately grade-appropriate general academic and domain-specific words and phrases; gather vocabulary knowledge when considering a word or phrase important to comprehension or expression.

520   UNIT 5 • INVENTION

Sounds of a Glass Armonica

Media Vocabulary

The following words will be useful to you as you analyze, discuss, and write about the video.

zoom: enlarge, magnify, or close in on an image	• Elements within the lens create the camera's zoom effect.
	• Zooming in on an image emphasizes its importance.
video clip: a short video, often part of a larger recording, that can be used on a website	• The term "video clip" is used to mean any video shorter than the length of a traditional program.
	• A video clip can contain video, audio, animation, graphics, or any other content.
focus: to aim the camera so that it creates a distinct image	• A shot that is out of focus can seem mysterious and eerie.
	• Some photographers prefer sharply focused images and bright colors.

First Review MEDIA: VIDEO

Review the video using these strategies. Take note of time codes as you watch the video so that you can revisit sections you find interesting or important.

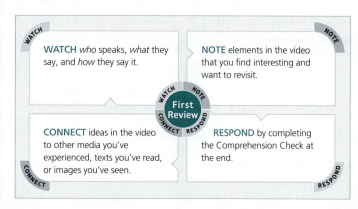

PERSONALIZE FOR LEARNING

English Language Support

Some students may have difficulty with the exact meaning of the word *zoom*, which describes something between a sound and a motion. Explain that the word *zoom* actually derived from the sound it describes. It was first used in the 1880s as a noun, but in World War I, aviators used it as a verb to describe the action of their planes. It wasn't until 1936 that the word was used to describe a camera lens—and the zooming action of moving in for a close up. Elicit that this means *zoom* is onomatopoeic, meaning the word sounds like what it is—like *splat* or *squish*.

MEDIA | VIDEO

Sounds of a Glass Armonica

BACKGROUND

Although Benjamin Franklin is well known for his role in the founding of the United States, he was also one of the era's foremost scientists. Among his numerous inventions were the "Franklin stove," the lightning rod, bifocals, the rocking chair, and a musical instrument called the armonica that premiered in 1762. At first Franklin named the instrument the "glassychord," but he soon changed it to *armonica*—based on the Italian word *armonia*, which means "harmony."

SCAN FOR MULTIMEDIA

NOTES

Sounds of a Glass Armonica **521**

DIGITAL PERSPECTIVES

CLOSER REVIEW

Analyze Zoom

Circulate among groups as students conduct their close review. Suggest that groups close review 0:52 to 1:05 in the video. Encourage them to talk about the notes they make. If needed, provide the following support.

NOTE: Have students note details about what happens in the video when the camera zooms, or work with small groups to have students participate while you note them together.

QUESTION: Guide students to consider what the details they noted might tell them. Ask what a viewer can infer from the zooming in, and accept possible responses.

Possible response: When the camera zooms in, the viewer can see exactly what the musician does with his hands.

CONCLUDE: Help students formulate conclusions about the importance of these details in the video. Ask students why the director might have included these details.

Possible response: The director probably wanted to remove some of the "mystery" of the glass armonica, which is very different from other instruments. By zooming in on the musician's hands and fingers, the director lets the viewer understand how the instrument is played.

Remind students that directors use camera techniques such as **zoom** to emphasize certain images and actions.

FACILITATING SMALL-GROUP CLOSE REVIEWING

CLOSE REVIEW: Video As groups perform the close review, circulate and offer support as needed.

- Remind groups that when they watch a video, they should pay close attention to anything being said—and the information those words may seek to convey.

- Encourage groups to work together to determine how camera angles help to share information with viewers.

- Ask students to think about the purpose of the video and to identify which details help them decide.

Small-Group Learning **521**

FACILITATING

Comprehension Check

1. Friction between the glass and a wet fingertip produces the sound.
2. It's there for the performer to wet his or her fingers.
3. Mozart

Close Review

If needed, model close reviewing by using the Closer Review note in the Interactive Teacher's Edition.

Remind students to use Accountable Talk in their discussions and to support one another as they complete the close review. You may want to print copies of the **Close Review Guide: Media-Video** for students to use.

Analyze the Media

Possible responses:

1. Responses will vary by group. Remind students to review their notes from the first review to get details that support their assertions before discussing with the group.
2. Responses will vary by group. Groups should support their assertions about how the glass armonica was invented and what went into the design process with specific reference to the video.
3. Responses will vary. Groups should conclude that some combination of perspiration and inspiration is required, though they may place emphasis on one or the other.

Media Vocabulary

Make sure that students use the words accurately. For more support, see **Media Vocabulary.**

Word Network

Students may suggest such words as *voila, custom-blown,* and *invention*.

FORMATIVE ASSESSMENT

Analyze the Media

If students struggle to close review the video, **then** provide the **Sounds of a Glass Armonica: Media Questions** available online in the Interactive Teacher's Edition or Unit Resources. Answers and DOK levels are also available.

Media Vocabulary

If students don't use the media vocabulary accurately, **then** have them reread the definitions and practice using the terms in sentences.

522 UNIT 5 • INVENTION

MAKING MEANING

Comprehension Check

Complete the following items after you finish your first review. Review and clarify details with your group.

1. What produces sound in the glass armonica?

2. What is the purpose of the bowl of water shown in the video?

3. What famous composer wrote for the glass armonica?

MEDIA VOCABULARY

Use these words as you discuss and write about the video.

zoom
video clip
focus

WORD NETWORK

Identify words from the video that relate to the concept of invention. Add these words to your Word Network.

STANDARDS
Speaking and Listening
Engage effectively in a range of collaborative discussions with diverse partners on *grade 8 topics, texts, and issues,* building on others' ideas and expressing their own clearly.

522 UNIT 5 • INVENTION

Close Review

Watch the video or parts of it again. Write any new observations that seem important. What **questions** do you have? What can you **conclude**?

Analyze the Media

CITE TEXTUAL EVIDENCE to support your answers.

Complete the activities.

1. **Present and Discuss** Choose the section of the video you found most interesting or powerful. Share your choice with the group, and explain what you noticed in the video, the questions it raised for you, and the conclusions you reached about it.

2. **Review and Synthesize** With your group, review the whole video. What did you learn about how the armonica was invented? What do you think went into the design process?

3. **Essential Question:** *Are inventions realized through inspiration or perspiration?* What has this video revealed about whether inventions are realized through inspiration or perspiration? Discuss with your group.

EFFECTIVE EXPRESSION

Research

Assignment
Create a **multimedia presentation** highlighting a homemade or unusual musical instrument. Choose from the following topics:

☐ Research and present information on another unusual musical instrument, such as the steel drum, the zither, or the theremin.

☐ Research and present information on a "homemade" instrument, such as the comb kazoo, the chopo choor, or the reed flute.

Set Project Goals Work with your group to form a plan for your presentation. Decide which instrument to focus on, what information and multimedia you will need, and the best way to present your information. Decide which group member will be responsible for each part of the presentation.

Conduct Research Begin the research process by finding details about the instrument your group chose—how it works, its origins, notable musicians who have played it, and memorable songs that feature it. Then, consider the types of multimedia that will best help your audience to visualize and understand how the instrument works and sounds. Since the presentation is about a musical instrument, you will need to include some audio components. For example, you might use audio or video recordings of the instrument being played, or you may choose to play the instrument yourself during the class presentation.

Organize Your Information It is important to sequence, or organize, your information effectively in a multimedia presentation. You must integrate text, visuals, and audio in a seamless, easy-to-follow manner. You will also have to consider the best time for information to be presented digitally, by a speaker, and through live performance. Once you have organized a sequence, rehearse your presentation with your group. Then, try rearranging the elements of your presentation, and practice presenting them in a different order. This will help you to determine whether you have selected the best organization for your presentation.

Use a chart like this to organize your ideas.

PRESENTER	SCRIPT	MEDIA

SOUNDS OF A GLASS ARMONICA

EVIDENCE LOG
Before moving on to a new selection, go to your Evidence Log and record what you learned from the video.

STANDARDS
Writing
Conduct short research projects to answer a question, drawing on several sources and generating additional related, focused questions that allow for multiple avenues of exploration.

Speaking and Listening
• Engage effectively in a range of collaborative discussions with diverse partners on grade 8 topics, texts, and issues, building on others' ideas and expressing their own clearly.
  a. Come to discussions prepared, having read or researched material under study; explicitly draw on that preparation by referring to evidence on the topic, text, or issue to probe and reflect on ideas under discussion.
  b. Follow rules for collegial discussions and decision-making, track progress toward specific goals and deadlines, and define individual roles as needed.
• Integrate multimedia and visual displays into presentations to clarify information, strengthen claims and evidence, and add interest.

DIGITAL PERSPECTIVES

Research

If groups have trouble deciding which task to take on, encourage them to try a democratic approach, discussing both topics first, then voting with a show of hands to find out which presentation is the most popular.

Set Project Goals Suggest to groups that doing some preliminary research to discover what the options are is a good way to proceed—whichever instrument the group finally decides upon. Once a group has found an array of possible instruments, the members can make a decision about which one they most want to investigate.

Conduct Research Encourage students to spend time researching how people play the instrument, and have them be sure that they can explain that in their presentation. If students are able to bring in an instrument, have them practice producing a few notes for the presentation.

Organize Your Information After students have done their initial organization, have them practice running through the segments of the presentation. Group members should give each other feedback and reorganize the order of the segments, and even who is presenting each segment, in order to strengthen the presentation. For more support, see **Research: Presentation.**

Evidence Log Support students in completing their Evidence Log. This paced activity will help prepare them for the Performance-Based Assessment at the end of the unit.

FORMATIVE ASSESSMENT
Research
If students are having difficulty choosing an instrument, **then** have them look up videos of people playing each instrument so that they can make a more informed decision.

PERSONALIZE FOR LEARNING

Strategic Support
Research Students may require support in finding out how to actually build a homemade instrument. Encourage them to check out educational sites on the Internet, or add the phrase "for kids" to a search to limit it to doable projects, as in "Make Your Own Zither for Kids." They can then sift through the results and possibly find sites with multiple, doable projects that can help them create their own instrument.

FACILITATING

Conduct a Debate

Before groups begin work on their projects, have them clearly differentiate the role each group member will play. Remind groups to consults the schedule for Small-Group Learning to guide their work during the Performance Task.

Students should complete the assignment using presentation software to take advantage of text, graphics, and sound features.

Plan With Your Group

Remind groups that although one selection may offer the most powerful evidence for their position, it is important that they consider evidence from all of the selections. Even if one selection does not seem to support the group's position at all, analyzing the selection will still be helpful for identifying potential counterclaims.

Gather Evidence and Media Examples Remind students that the position they are arguing for does not necessarily have to reflect their own personal viewpoint. Remind them to look for evidence that supports their group's chosen position, *not* their personal views. As students are looking for media to use, explain that some media may fit their presentation better than others.

PERFORMANCE TASK: SPEAKING AND LISTENING FOCUS

SOURCES

- NIKOLA TESLA: THE GREATEST INVENTOR OF ALL?
- from THE INVENTION OF EVERYTHING ELSE
- 25 YEARS LATER, HUBBLE SEES BEYOND TROUBLED START
- SOUNDS OF A GLASS ARMONICA

Tool Kit
Collaboration Checklist

STANDARDS
Speaking and Listening
- Engage effectively in a range of collaborative discussions with diverse partners on *grade 8 topics, texts, and issues*, building on others' ideas and expressing their own clearly.
  a. Come to discussions prepared, having read or researched material under study; explicitly draw on that preparation by referring to evidence on the topic, text, or issue to probe and reflect on ideas under discussion.
  b. Follow rules for collegial discussions and decision-making, track progress toward specific goals and deadlines, and define individual roles as needed.
- Delineate a speaker's argument and specific claims, evaluating the soundness of the reasoning and relevance and sufficiency of the evidence and identifying when irrelevant evidence is introduced.

Conduct a Debate

Assignment
The selections in this section have provided various perspectives on the subject of invention—the processes involved, the people behind them, and the inventions themselves. With your group, pair up with another group to conduct a **debate** in which each team takes a position on the Essential Question:

> Are inventions realized through inspiration or perspiration?

Plan With Your Group

Support your position with evidence and examples from reading, viewing, and analyzing the selections in this part of the unit. Use the chart to list your ideas. For each selection, identify evidence that relates to whether inventions are realized through inspiration or perspiration. Use the evidence to begin planning the argument you will make in the debate.

TITLE	SUPPORTING EVIDENCE
Nikola Tesla: The Greatest Inventor of All?	
from The Invention of Everything Else	
25 Years Later, Hubble Sees Beyond Troubled Start	
Sounds of a Glass Armonica	

Gather Evidence and Media Examples As a group, discuss your notes and ideas. Identify specific examples from the selections to support your group's position. As a group, assess whether you have sufficient evidence to support your position.

AUTHOR'S PERSPECTIVE Ernest Morrell, Ph.D.

Digital Speech Since "a picture is worth a thousand words," help students find and use effective images for oral presentations. Remind students to give full credit to visual sources, as they would for print ones. Teachers can guide students to create rhetorically powerful digital presentations such as slideshows, blogs, and online forums using these suggestions:

- *Keep it simple.* Choose one striking image rather than several smaller ones. Position the visual carefully, allowing "white space" to make the image stand out.
- *Go for quality.* Choose clear, high-quality images or take high-resolution photos.
- *Limit bullet points and text.* The most effective slideshows have limited text. Suggest that slides should have no more than six words across and six lines down of text.
- *Choose color and font carefully.* Cool colors (blues, greens) work best for backgrounds; warm colors (orange, red) work best for objects in the foreground. Use a simple, standard font such as Arial or Helvetica.

Last, teachers can help students create a rubric to assess presentations.

ESSENTIAL QUESTION: Are inventions realized through inspiration or perspiration?

Organize Your Ideas As a group, develop an outline for your argument. Clearly identify the claims you will make and the reasons and evidence that support them. Prepare for your opponents' arguments by considering their counterclaims to your position. Consider how you can respond, and have evidence ready to support your responses.

Set Debate Rules Assign one member of each group to moderate the debate and assign a designated time limit for each response. To show respect for your opponents, keep your responses within the designated time limit. Plan the discussion so you do not get cut off by the moderator when making a point.

Rehearse With Your Group

Practice With Your Group Within your group, practice delivering the points you will make in the debate. As each member practices his or her delivery, have other group members role-play as opponents. This will help you to identify places you need to strengthen your argument.

CONTENT	DEBATE TECHNIQUE	PRESENTATION TECHNIQUES
☐ Claims are presented clearly and supported by reasons and evidence.	☐ Each speaker keeps within the allotted time limit.	☐ Each speaker argues persuasively and confidently.
☐ Counterclaims are anticipated and addressed effectively.	☐ Points are clear and organized.	☐ Each speaker speaks clearly and makes eye contact with the person he or she is addressing.

Fine-Tune the Content Review your evidence to be sure it supports your claims. If your claim is not fully supported, work with your group members to find information that better supports your claim.

Improve Your Debate Technique As you review your outline, consider whether you have connected all of your ideas in the clearest way possible. If you are concerned you might be missing a connection, ask your teacher for guidance on how to better connect your ideas.

Present and Evaluate

As you listen to other groups' debates, evaluate how well they meet the checklist requirements. After the debate, discuss whether other groups' claims were well supported by reasons and evidence. Then, discuss and reflect on any new information you gained from the process and whether it changed your initial views on the subject.

STANDARDS
Speaking and Listening
- Engage effectively in a range of collaborative discussions with diverse partners on *grade 8 topics, texts, and issues,* building on others' ideas and expressing their own clearly.
  c. Pose questions that connect the ideas of several speakers and respond to others' questions and comments with relevant evidence, observations, and ideas.
  d. Acknowledge new information expressed by others, and, when warranted, qualify or justify their own views in light of the evidence presented.
- Present claims and findings, emphasizing salient points in a focused, coherent manner with relevant evidence, sound valid reasoning, and well-chosen details; use appropriate eye contact, adequate volume, and clear pronunciation.

DIGITAL PERSPECTIVES

Organize Your Ideas Remind groups that their thesis should be a concise sentence that clearly states their position. Encourage students to evaluate the strength and credibility of each piece of evidence they use. Explain to students that they should focus on a few main points. For every claim students make, they should carefully consider how they would address the counterarguments.

Rehearse With Your Group

Practice With Your Group Point out to students that their debate rehearsal allows their groups to practice presenting their claim and their main reasons and evidence. You may wish to pair groups so they can rehearse their debates with each other.

Improve Your Debate Technique Suggest that the moderator use a timer during the debate rehearsal to ensure that speakers stay within their allotted time limits. Moderators also might give speakers a cue when they have 30 seconds left.

Present and Evaluate

Before beginning the debates, set the expectations for the audience. You may wish to have students consider these questions as other groups debate:

- What is the group's thesis?
- What are the group's strongest supporting reasons and evidence?
- What debate techniques did this group excel at?

As students provide feedback to the presenting group, remind them that compliments are just as valuable as constructive criticism.

PERSONALIZE FOR LEARNING

Strategic Support

Counterclaims If some groups have trouble responding to potential counterclaims to their argument, suggest that they hold a "mini-debate" during the planning process. They should divide their group into two halves and have one half argue for the opposing side. As the first half presents their claims and evidence, the second half will attempt to rebut their arguments. This will help students anticipate the other group's arguments during the real debate. Explain that the act of arguing for the opposing side will help them expand their view of the topic.

OVERVIEW

INDEPENDENT LEARNING

Are inventions realized through inspiration or perspiration?

Encourage students to think carefully about what they have already learned and what more they want to know about the unit topic of invention. This is a key first step to previewing and selecting the text they will read in Independent Learning.

Independent Learning Strategies ▶

Review the Learning Strategies with students and explain that as they work through Independent Learning they will develop strategies to work on their own.

- Have students watch the video on Independent Learning Strategies.
- A video on this topic is available online in the Professional Development Center.

Students should include any favorite strategies that they might have devised on their own during Whole-Class and Small-Group Learning. For example, for the strategy "Create a schedule," students might include:

- Understand the goals and deadlines.
- Make a schedule for what to do each day.

Block Scheduling

Each day in this Pacing Plan represents a 40–50 minute class period. Teachers using block scheduling may combine days to reflect their class schedule. In addition, teachers may revise pacing to differentiate and support core instruction by integrating components and resources as students require.

📅 **Pacing Plan**

OVERVIEW: INDEPENDENT LEARNING

ESSENTIAL QUESTION:

Are inventions realized through inspiration or perspiration?

There is a story behind every invention, and the ideas, knowledge, and experiences that contributed to each one are different. In this section, you will complete your study of invention by exploring an additional selection related to the topic. Then, you will share what you have learned with your classmates. To choose a text, follow these steps.

Look Back Think about the selections you have already read. What more do you want to know about the topic of invention?

Look Ahead Preview the selections by reading the descriptions. Which one seems most interesting and appealing to you?

Look Inside Take a few minutes to scan through the text you chose. Make another selection if this text doesn't meet your needs.

Independent Learning Strategies

Throughout your life, in school, in your community, and in your career, you will need to rely on yourself to learn and work on your own. Review these strategies and the actions you can take to practice them during Independent Learning. Add ideas of your own for each category.

STRATEGY	ACTION PLAN
Create a schedule	• Understand your goals and deadlines. • Make a plan for what to do each day. •
Practice what you have learned	• Use first-read and close-read strategies to deepen your understanding. • After you read, evaluate the usefulness of the evidence to help you understand the topic. • Consider the quality and reliability of the source. •
Take notes	• Record important ideas and information. • Review your notes before preparing to share with a group. •

SCAN FOR MULTIMEDIA

Pacing Plan:
1 — Unit Introduction
2
3 — Introduce Whole-Class Learning
4–9 — Uncle Marcos
10–15 — To Fly
16–18 — Performance Task

UNIT 5 • INVENTION

CONTENTS

Choose one selection. Selections are available online only.

WEB ARTICLE

Ada Lovelace: A Science Legend
James Essinger

Why isn't the woman who wrote the first computer program—in the nineteenth century—famous?

WEB ARTICLE

Fermented Cow Dung Air Freshener Wins Two Students Top Science Prize
Kimberley Mok

Two Indonesian girls make something out of nothing by inventing a product using materials that nobody else wants.

NEWS ARTICLE

Scientists Build Robot That Runs, Call It "Cheetah"
Rodrique Ngowi

When scientists can't beat the inventions of Mother Nature, they often are inspired to imitate them.

NOVEL EXCERPT

from The Time Machine
H. G. Wells

The destination of this inventor's vehicle isn't *where*—it's *when*.

MYTH

Icarus and Daedalus
retold by Josephine Preston Peabody

Is an initial failure the basis for the future success of an invention?

PERFORMANCE-BASED ASSESSMENT PREP

Review Evidence for an Argument

Complete your Evidence Log for the unit by evaluating what you have learned and synthesizing the information you have recorded.

 SCAN FOR MULTIMEDIA

Overview: Independent Learning 527

DIGITAL PERSPECTIVES

Contents

Selections Encourage students to scan and preview the selections before choosing the one they would like to read. Suggest that they consider the genre and subject matter of each one before making their decision. You can use the information on the following Planning pages to advise students in making their choice.

> Remind students that the selections for Independent Learning are only available in the Interactive Student Edition. Allow students who do not have digital access at home to preview the selections or review the media selection(s) using classroom or computer lab technology. Then either have students print the selection they choose or provide a printout for them.

Performance-Based Assessment Prep

Review Evidence for an Argument Point out to students that collecting evidence during Independent Learning is the last step in completing their Evidence Log. After they finish their independent reading, they will synthesize all the evidence they have compiled in the unit.

The evidence students collect will serve as the primary source of information they will use to complete the writing and oral presentation for the Performance-Based Assessment at the end of the unit.

Independent Learning 527

PLANNING   INDEPENDENT LEARNING

SELECTION RESOURCES

- First-Read Guide: Nonfiction
- Close-Read Guide: Nonfiction
- Ada Lovelace: A Science Legend: Text Questions
- Audio Summaries
- Selection Audio
- Selection Test

Ada Lovelace: A Science Legend

Summary

This blog entry, "Ada Lovelace: A Science Legend," by James Essinger, provides a brief history of Ada Lovelace's life and genius. Lovelace, the only legitimate child of the poet Lord Byron, never knew her father. Guided by her mother into an education that emphasized mathematics, she had an active imagination. Her chance meeting with the inventor Charles Babbage introduced her to his "Analytical Engine," a nineteenth-century attempt to create a computer. Although Babbage rejected her help, Lovelace went on to write what is seen as the world's first computer program. Today Ada Lovelace is regarded as "one of the most insightful and visionary women in the history of science."

Insight

Reading about Ada Lovelace will show students that some inventors are handicapped by being born ahead of their time. Lovelace was a woman in an age that did not value women's intelligence or knowledge.

Connection to Essential Question

The Essential Question, *Are inventions realized through inspiration or perspiration?* may not apply in the case of Ada Lovelace. Lovelace's invention was not realized until more than a century after her death. However, students may decide that her intelligence was a combination of both inspiration and effort.

Connection to Performance-Based Assessment

The prompt asks, "Which invention described in this unit has had the biggest impact on humanity?" This selection suggests that many women were discouraged from inventing before the twentieth century. Society relegated women to less important activities and often did not take their ideas seriously. Students will note that Lovelace was interested in Babbage's ideas and wanted to work with him, documenting her own ideas as she translated his work. Students might discuss the impact of women's contributions to inventions.

Text Complexity Rubric: Ada Lovelace: A Science Legend

Quantitative Measures

Lexile: 1320   Text Length: 1,391 words

Qualitative Measures

Knowledge Demands ①—②—❸—④—⑤	Students may not know Ada Lovelace's background or the names of the others mentioned in this text, but the ideas are explained clearly. A general knowledge of the powers of computers and the timeline of their development is helpful.
Structure ①—❷—③—④—⑤	The selection is biographical and presented in chronological order.
Language Conventionality and Clarity ①—②—❸—④—⑤	Some sentences in the explanation are complex, with multiple clauses and difficult vocabulary. Simpler, more inviting conversational language is also used.
Levels of Meaning/Purpose ①—②—❸—④—⑤	Selection has only one level of meaning. The main concept and supporting ideas are clearly stated.

Fermented Cow Dung Air Freshener Wins Two Students Top Science Prize

Summary

Kimberley Mok's blog article "Fermented Cow Dung Air Freshener Wins Two Students Top Science Prize" reports on an organic air freshener made by treating cow dung. Most commercial air fresheners contain potentially harmful chemicals. Two Indonesian students decided to make a more organic product. The young women extracted the water from fermented manure and mixed it with coconut water. They then distilled the liquid to eliminate impurities. The result is an inexpensive natural air freshener with an herbal aroma. The cow dung air freshener won top prize for the two students in Indonesia's Science Project Olympiad.

Insight

The article will reinforce the idea that anyone with a creative idea can be an inventor. The students chose materials that are common and abundant in their environment and used them to make a product that is competitive with more expensive products with a similar purpose.

Connection to Essential Question

The Essential Question, *Are inventions realized through inspiration or perspiration?* is often answered with the word *both*. The students in the article went to some effort to create their product, but their inspiration was probably the result of study and research.

Connection to Performance-Based Assessment

Students may find the concept of this article helpful as they prepare to respond to the prompt, "Which invention described in this unit has had the biggest impact on humanity?" The invention of the cow dung air freshener may have been inspired by the urge to compete. Many inventions are the result of the desire to be first or best at producing something new, as well as the desire to have an impact.

SELECTION RESOURCES
- First-Read Guide: Nonfiction
- Close-Read Guide: Nonfiction
- Fermented Cow Dung Air Freshener Wins Two Students Top Science Prize: Text Questions
- Audio Summaries
- Selection Audio
- Selection Test

Text Complexity Rubric: Fermented Cow Dung Air Freshener Wins Two Students Top Science Prize

Quantitative Measures	
Lexile: 1460 Text Length: 292 words	
Qualitative Measures	
Knowledge Demands ①—②—❸—④—⑤	The topic will probably not be familiar to students, but the concept is explained clearly.
Structure ①—②—❸—④—⑤	The selection is logically organized and connections between ideas are clear.
Language Conventionality and Clarity ①—②—❸—④—⑤	Some sentences in the explanation are complex, with multiple clauses and difficult vocabulary. Text includes some figurative language.
Levels of Meaning/Purpose ①—②—❸—④—⑤	Selection has only one level of meaning. The main concept and supporting ideas are clearly stated.

PLANNING INDEPENDENT LEARNING

Scientists Build Robot That Runs, Call It "Cheetah"

Summary
Rodrique Ngowi's newspaper article "Scientists Build Robot That Runs, Call It 'Cheetah'" describes a robot that is controlled by video game technology and existing sensors from military equipment. However, key elements had to be invented during a five-year process. Scientists at the Massachusetts Institute of Technology created powerful lightweight motors. They devised complex algorithms to balance the robot and provide the appropriate amount of force to each leg. The final product weighs 70 pounds. Scientists hope to develop sensors that will make the robot be able to work independently. Funded by the U.S. Department of Defense, the final result of the research is intended both for military and civilian use.

SELECTION RESOURCES
- First-Read Guide: Nonfiction
- Close-Read Guide: Nonfiction
- Scientists Build Robot That Runs, Call it "Cheetah": Text Questions
- Audio Summaries
- Selection Audio
- Selection Test

Insight
This article about robot technology points out the variety of purposes that a robotic runner might serve. It also demonstrates that groups of scientists can use both established technology and creativity to produce a new generation of technology.

Connection to Essential Question
Reading "Scientists Build Robot That Runs, Call It 'Cheetah'" provides an answer to the Essential Question, *Are inventions realized through inspiration or perspiration?* Students will understand that the invention of a technology product can take years of hard work and many cases of trial and error.

Connection to Performance-Based Assessment
Students may answer the question "Which invention described in this unit has had the biggest impact on humanity?" by considering that the robot described in the article has a dual purpose—military and civilian. Ultimately, the scientists are encouraged to invent by the knowledge that the robot will someday save lives by traveling into places that humans might not be able to reach.

Text Complexity Rubric: Scientist Build Robot That Runs, Call It "Cheetah"

Quantitative Measures

Lexile: 1380   Text Length: 598 words

Qualitative Measures

Knowledge Demands ①—②—③—❹—⑤	Text explores complex topics associated with science and research that will be unfamiliar; explanation is provided for only some of the complex ideas.
Structure ①—②—❸—④—⑤	Information in the selection is logically organized, but connections between ideas are not always completely explicit or in a predictable sequence.
Language Conventionality and Clarity ①—②—③—❹—⑤	The syntax includes many complex sentences; selection has a lot of above-level and subject-specific vocabulary.
Levels of Meaning/Purpose ①—②—❸—④—⑤	The expository purpose of the article is clear and accessible.

| DIGITAL PERSPECTIVES | Audio | Video | Document | Annotation Highlights | EL Highlights | Online Assessment |

from The Time Machine

Summary
In this excerpt from H.G. Wells's novel *The Time Machine,* the Time Traveler explains his invention to a skeptical group of men with scientific backgrounds. The Time Traveler shows them a miniature version of his time machine. He invites the Psychologist to press the lever that sends the small machine through time. After all the men have expressed their amazement and disbelief, the Time Traveler shows them the full-size machine. They are still skeptical.

Insight
This excerpt from the famous novel by H.G. Wells illustrates the difficulty inventors sometimes face when making claims for their inventions. The novel is one of several works of the late nineteenth century that can be classified as science fiction. Many of the inventions in those early novels have since become a reality. Time travel is one of the few inventions that has yet to materialize.

SELECTION RESOURCES
- First-Read Guide: Fiction
- Close-Read Guide: Fiction
- *from* The Time Machine: Text Questions
- Audio Summaries
- Selection Audio
- Selection Test

Connection to Essential Question
Students will find that the excerpt from *The Time Machine* provides an enigmatic answer to the Essential Question, *Are inventions realized through inspiration or perspiration?* The reader does not know the extent of the effort expended by the Time Traveler, but one can imagine that it is considerable. As for inspiration, the invention was clearly a remarkable idea.

Connection to Performance-Based Assessment
The prompt question, "Which invention described in this unit has had the biggest impact on humanity?" has a clear answer when it comes to Wells's Time Traveler. He is curious and daring. He is encouraged to invent because he wants to test the limits of time. Students may wish to discuss the potential impacts of this invention.

Text Complexity Rubric: *from* The Time Machine

Quantitative Measures	
Lexile: 830 Text Length: 1,341 words	

Qualitative Measures	
Knowledge Demands ①—②—❸—④—⑤	Students may not be familiar with the concept of time travel, its constraints, or its consequences. Clear explanations are made of some of the elements in the selection.
Structure ①—②—❸—④—⑤	Organization of the first-person narrative is mostly sequential. Paragraphs contain a lot of information, but quotes break up the text somewhat.
Language Conventionality and Clarity ①—②—③—❹—⑤	Sentences are long with embedded clauses, above-level vocabulary, and challenging scientific concepts. Selection was written in the late 1800s, so some language styles and expressions may be unfamiliar.
Levels of Meaning/Purpose ①—②—❸—④—⑤	The main event of the narrative is not difficult, and the purpose of the text is clear.

Independent Learning   **528D**

PLANNING INDEPENDENT LEARNING

Icarus and Daedalus

Summary
"Icarus and Daedalus," from *Old Greek Folk-Stories Told Anew* by Josephine Preston Peabody, tells the story of Daedalus, a great inventor, and his son Icarus. They were prisoners in a maze, and Icarus begged to be free. Icarus convinced his father to build wings. Daedalus studied the wings of birds and then built his own, using feathers, string, and wax. He taught himself to fly, and then made wings for Icarus. Daedalus warned his son not to fly too high or too low because the wings would be destroyed. Both took flight and left Crete far behind them. But Icarus flew too close to the sun, and the wax in his wings melted. Icarus plunged to his death.

Insight
This is a classical story that warns about the danger of inventions. Although one might love to invent things, one must always consider the consequences. The fate of Icarus can be attributed to the anger of the gods at Daedalus's attempt to appear divine, or it might show that Daedalus did not take into account his son's impetuosity when he made the wings for him.

SELECTION RESOURCES
- First-Read Guide: Fiction
- Close-Read Guide: Fiction
- Icarus and Daedalus: Text Questions
- Audio Summaries
- Selection Audio
- Selection Test

Connection to Essential Question
The Essential Question is *Are inventions realized through inspiration or perspiration?* In the case of Daedalus, both idea and inspiration played a part. The inspiration was provided by intelligent observation. The realization of the invention depended on the practical application of Daedalus's genius.

Connection to Performance-Based Assessment
This myth provides an angle on the prompt, "Which invention described in this unit has had the biggest impact on humanity?" Daedalus invented to please his son who yearned to be free. The desire for freedom has inspired many inventors.

Text Complexity Rubric: Icarus and Daedalus	
Quantitative Measures	
Lexile: 1100 Text Length: 722 words	
Qualitative Measures	
Knowledge Demands ①—②—**❸**—④—⑤	The selection is a Greek myth that may be unfamiliar to students. Background information and context will be helpful, but the story is fairly straightforward.
Structure ①—②—**❸**—④—⑤	The text follows a linear plot line with some dialogue.
Language Conventionality and Clarity ①—②—**❸**—④—⑤	Selection has complex sentences with antiquated language, figurative language, and many descriptive passages.
Levels of Meaning/Purpose ①—②—**❸**—④—⑤	The myth can be read on a plot level or for its message and teachings.

MY NOTES

ADVISING

You may wish to direct students to use the generic **First-Read** and **Close-Read Guides** in the Print Student Edition. Alternatively, you may wish to print copies of the genre-specific **First-Read** and **Close-Read Guides** for students. These are available online in the Interactive Student Edition or Unit Resources.

FIRST READ

Students should perform the steps of the first read independently.

NOTICE: Students should focus on the basic elements of the text to ensure they understand what is happening.

ANNOTATE: Students should mark any passages they wish to revisit during their close read.

CONNECT: Students should increase their understanding by connecting what they've read to other texts or personal experiences.

RESPOND: Students will write a summary to demonstrate their understanding.

Point out to students that while they will always complete the Respond step at the end of the first read, the other steps will probably happen somewhat concurrently. Remind students that they will revisit their first-read annotations during the close read.

> After students have completed the First-Read Guide, you may wish to assign the Text Questions for the selection that are available in the Interactive Teacher's Edition.

Anchor Standards

In the first two sections of the unit, students worked with the whole class and in small groups to gain topical knowledge and greater understanding of the skills required by the anchor standards. In this section, they are asked to work independently, applying what they have learned and demonstrating increased readiness for college and career.

INDEPENDENT LEARNING

First-Read Guide

Use this page to record your first-read ideas.

Selection Title: _____

Tool Kit
First-Read Guide and Model Annotation

NOTICE new information or ideas you learn about the unit topic as you first read this text.

ANNOTATE by marking vocabulary and key passages you want to revisit.

CONNECT ideas within the selection to other knowledge and the selections you have read.

RESPOND by writing a brief summary of the selection.

STANDARD
Reading Read and comprehend complex literary and informational texts independently and proficiently.

528 UNIT 5 • INVENTION

PERSONALIZE FOR LEARNING

Challenge

Additional Questions To help students reflect on their first read and prepare for the close read, encourage them to think about what more they would like to know about a text. Ask students to write two to three questions they have about the text. Then, students can meet in small groups with others who have read the same selection. Each group can share First-Read Guides and their additional questions before proceeding to the Close Read.

ESSENTIAL QUESTION: Are inventions realized through inspiration or perspiration?

DIGITAL PERSPECTIVES

Close-Read Guide

Use this page to record your close-read ideas.

🔧 **Tool Kit**
Close-Read Guide and Model Annotation

Selection Title: _____

Close Read the Text

Revisit sections of the text you marked during your first read. Read these sections closely and **annotate** what you notice. Ask yourself **questions** about the text. What can you **conclude**? Write down your ideas.

Analyze the Text

Think about the author's choices of patterns, structure, techniques, and ideas included in the text. Select one, and record your thoughts about what this choice conveys.

QuickWrite

Pick a paragraph from the text that grabbed your interest. Explain the power of this passage.

▤ **STANDARD**
Reading Read and comprehend complex literary and informational texts independently and proficiently.

Independent Learning **529**

🔴 CLOSE READ

Students should begin their close read by revisiting the annotations they made during their first read. Then, students should analyze one of the author's choices regarding the following elements:

- **patterns,** such as repetition or parallelism
- **structure,** such as cause-and-effect or problem-solution
- **techniques,** such as description or dialogue
- **ideas,** such as the author's main idea or claim

MAKE IT INTERACTIVE
Group students according to the selection they have chosen. Then, have students meet to discuss the selection in depth. Their discussions should be guided by their insights and questions.

PERSONALIZE FOR LEARNING

Challenge

Group Review Have students who have read the same text collaborate to write a group review of the entire text. The review should include a summary and excerpts from each group member's Close-Read Guide. Group members should agree on contributions, the order in which the excerpts will appear, and how the excerpts will fit into paragraphs within the review. Together, group members should revise and edit the writing for coverage of the entire text and make sure ideas are logically organized and expressed clearly. They can use signal words and transitions to connect the ideas and writing of all the contributors. After editing and proofreading, the completed reviews may be posted in a blog or printed and distributed to the class.

Independent Learning **529**

ADVISING

Share Your Independent Learning

Prepare to Share
Explain to students that sharing what they learned from their Independent Learning selection provides classmates who read a different selection with an opportunity to consider the text as a source of evidence during the Performance-Based Assessment. As students prepare to share, remind them to highlight how their selection contributed to their knowledge of the concept of invention as well as how the selection connects to the Essential Question: *Are inventions realized through inspiration or perspiration?*

Learn From Your Classmates
As students discuss the Independent Learning selections, direct them to take particular note of how their classmates' chosen selections align with their current position on the Performance-Based Assessment question.

Reflect
Students may want to add their reflection to their Evidence Log, particularly if their insight relates to a specific selection from the unit.

MAKE IT INTERACTIVE
Have students research something they use on a daily basis to find out when the product was invented and who invented it. Then ask students to write down ideas for how they would improve the invention they chose. How would it change? What new features would it have, and what would it do? Have students volunteer their ideas and ask them what they think would need to happen to make the improvements they suggested.

Evidence Log Support students in completing their Evidence Log. This paced activity will help prepare them for the Performance-Based Assessment at the end of the unit.

INDEPENDENT LEARNING

📝 **EVIDENCE LOG**
Go to your Evidence Log and record what you learned from the text you read.

Share Your Independent Learning

Prepare to Share
Are inventions realized through inspiration or perspiration?

Even when you read something independently, your understanding continues to grow when you share what you have learned with others. Reflect on the text you explored independently and write notes about its connection to the unit. In your notes, consider why this text belongs in this unit.

Learn From Your Classmates
💬 **Discuss It** Share your ideas about the text you explored on your own. As you talk with your classmates, jot down ideas that you learn from them.

Reflect
Review your notes, and mark the most important insight you gained from these writing and discussion activities. Explain how this idea adds to your understanding of the topic of invention.

STANDARDS
Speaking and Listening
Engage effectively in a range of collaborative discussions with diverse partners on *grade 8 topics, texts, and issues,* building on others' ideas and expressing their own clearly.

AUTHOR'S PERSPECTIVE — Ernest Morrell, Ph.D.

Powerful Speaking in Small Groups Explain to students that learning how to speak with confidence, without over-compensating, will help them make and/or defend an argument and point of view in a small group. Point out that their goal is to be convincing, but not argumentative. To help build this skill, provide students with the following guidelines:

1. **Earn credibility.** Speakers who are prepared with evidence tailored to their audience's needs will sway their audience with the power of their proof. As a result, these speakers will have no need to try to harass or intimidate their listeners.

2. **Choose words carefully.** Effective speakers use the exact words they need, words that convey their precise meaning. Further, effective speakers avoid "loaded words" that attempt to sway an audience by appealing to stereotypes.

3. **Be audible, not loud.** Speakers who avoid shouting convey their point with greater confidence than those who do raise their voices.

PERFORMANCE-BASED ASSESSMENT PREP

Review Evidence for an Argument

At the beginning of this unit you took a position on the following question:

> Which invention described in this unit has had the biggest impact on humanity?

✎ EVIDENCE LOG

Review your Evidence Log and your QuickWrite from the beginning of the unit. Has your position changed?

☐ YES	☐ NO
Identify at least three pieces of evidence that convinced you to change your mind.	Identify at least three new pieces of evidence that reinforced your initial position.
1.	1.
2.	2.
3.	3.

State your position now: _____

Identify a possible counterclaim: _____

Evaluate the Strength of Your Evidence Consider your argument. Do you have enough evidence to support your claim? Do you have enough evidence to refute a counterargument? If not, make a plan.

- ☐ Do more research
- ☐ Reread a selection
- ☐ Talk with my classmates
- ☐ Ask an expert
- ☐ Other: _____

▤ STANDARDS
Writing
Write arguments to support claims with clear reasons and relevant evidence.
  a. Introduce claim(s), acknowledge and distinguish the claim(s) from alternate or opposing claims, and organize the reasons and evidence logically.
  b. Support claim(s) with logical reasoning and relevant evidence, using accurate, credible sources and demonstrating an understanding of the topic or text.

DIGITAL PERSPECTIVES

Review Evidence for an Argument

Evidence Log Students should understand that their position on an issue could evolve as they learn more about the subject and are exposed to additional points of view. Point out that just because they took an initial position on the question *Which invention described in this unit has had the biggest impact on humanity?* doesn't mean that their position can't change after careful consideration of their learning and evidence.

Evaluate the Strength of Your Evidence
Remind students that there are many different types of evidence they can use to support their argument, including:

- facts
- statistics
- anecdotes
- quotations from authorities
- examples

In addition to ensuring they have sufficient evidence to support their claim and address counterclaims, students should evaluate the reliability of their evidence. Discuss the characteristics that make evidence credible:

- reliable sources, including government, educational, and professional organizations
- degree to which experts have reviewed the evidence for accuracy
- credibility of references and confirmation provided by the source of the evidence

ASSESSING

Writing to Sources: Argument

Students should complete the Performance-Based Assessment independently, with little to no input or feedback during the process. Students should use word processing software to take advantage of editing tools and features.

Prior to beginning the Assessment, ask students to think about what motivates them to be creative. Suggest they consider different sources of inspiration, from being moved by the brilliant inventions of others to being confronted by problems that need solutions, or even just listening to music they like.

Review the Elements of Effective Argument Students can review the work they did earlier in the unit as they complete the Performance-Based Assessment. They may also consult other resources such as:
- the elements of an effective argument, including a clear claim, logical reasons, and relevant evidence, as well effective organization of an argument, available in Whole-Class Learning
- their Evidence Log
- their Word Network

Although students will use evidence from unit selections for their argument, they may need to collect additional evidence, including facts, statistics, anecdotes, quotations from authorities, or examples that support their position.

 PERFORMANCE-BASED ASSESSMENT

SOURCES
- WHOLE-CLASS SELECTIONS
- SMALL-GROUP SELECTIONS
- INDEPENDENT-LEARNING SELECTION

PART 1
Writing to Sources: Argument

In this unit, you read about various inventors and inventions, real and imaginary. In some cases, the inventors described seem like uniquely gifted individuals who also work hard. In other cases, inventors are presented as workers presented with a challenge who use what they know to solve practical problems.

Assignment
Write an **argument** in which you state and defend a claim about the following question:

> Which invention described in this unit has had the biggest impact on humanity?

Take a position on this question based on the knowledge you gained from reading and analyzing the selections in the unit. Use examples from the selections you read and viewed to support your claim, and organize your ideas so that they flow logically and are easy to follow. Address and refute counterclaims to limit dissent and ensure your argument is well received. Use an appropriately formal tone.

Reread the Assignment Review the assignment to be sure you fully understand it. The task may reference some of the academic words presented at the beginning of the unit. Be sure you understand each of the words given below to complete the assignment correctly.

Academic Vocabulary

| opponent | contradict | dissent |
| position | legitimate | |

Review the Elements of Effective Argument Before you begin writing, read the Argument Rubric. Once you have completed your first draft, check it against the rubric. If one or more of the elements is missing or not as strong as it could be, revise your essay to add or strengthen that element.

WORD NETWORK
As you write and revise your argument, use your Word Network to help vary your word choices.

STANDARDS
Writing
Write arguments to support claims with clear reasons and relevant evidence.
a. Introduce claim(s), acknowledge and distinguish the claim(s) from alternate or opposing claims, and organize the reasons and evidence logically.
b. Support claim(s) with logical reasoning and relevant evidence, using accurate, credible sources and demonstrating an understanding of the topic or text.
c. Use words, phrases, and clauses to create cohesion and clarify the relationships among claim(s), counterclaims, reasons, and evidence.
d. Establish and maintain a formal style.
e. Provide a concluding statement or section that follows from and supports the argument presented.

ESSENTIAL QUESTION: Are inventions realized through inspiration or perspiration?

Argument Rubric

	Focus and Organization	Evidence and Elaboration	Conventions
4	The introduction engages the reader and establishes a position in a compelling way. The position is supported by logical reasons and relevant evidence, and opposing claims are addressed. The reasons and evidence are organized logically so that the argument is easy to follow. Transitions clearly show the relationships among ideas. The conclusion follows from and supports the rest of the argument.	The sources of evidence are relevant and credible. The tone of the argument is formal and objective. Words are carefully chosen and suited to the audience and purpose.	The argument consistently uses standard English conventions of usage and mechanics.
3	The introduction is somewhat engaging and states the position clearly. The claim is supported by reasons and evidence, and opposing claims are acknowledged. Reasons and evidence are organized so that the argument is easy to follow. Transitions show the relationships among ideas. The conclusion restates the claim.	The sources are relevant. The tone of the argument is mostly formal and objective. Words are generally suited to the audience and purpose.	The argument demonstrates general accuracy in standard English conventions of usage and mechanics.
2	The introduction states a claim. The claim is supported by some reasons and evidence, and opposing claims may be briefly acknowledged. Reasons and evidence are organized somewhat logically. A few sentence transitions are used to orient readers. The conclusion relates to the claim.	Some sources are relevant. The tone of the argument is occasionally formal and objective. Words are somewhat suited to the audience and purpose.	The argument demonstrates some accuracy in standard English conventions of usage and mechanics.
1	The claim is not clearly stated. The claim is not supported by reasons and evidence, and opposing claims are not addressed. Reasons and evidence are disorganized and the argument is difficult to follow. No transitions are used. The conclusion does not restate the claim.	Reliable and relevant evidence is not included. The tone of the argument is informal. The vocabulary is ineffective.	The argument contains mistakes in standard English conventions of usage and mechanics.

DIGITAL PERSPECTIVES

Argument Rubric

As you review the Argument Rubric with students, remind them that the rubric is a resource that can guide their revisions. Students should pay particular attention to the differences between an argument that contains all of the required elements (a score of 3) and one that is comprehensive, engaging, and progresses in a logical and thoughtful manner (a score of 4).

ASSESSING

Speaking and Listening: Speech

Students should annotate their written argument in preparation for the oral presentation, marking the important elements (claim, reasons, evidence, and counterclaims) as well as critical anecdotes or facts.

Remind students that the effectiveness of an oral presentation relies on how the speaker establishes credibility with his or her audience. If a speaker comes across as confident and authoritative, it will be easier for the audience to give credence to the speaker's claim.

Review the Rubric As you review the Oral Presentation Rubric with students, remind them that it is a valuable tool that can help them plan their presentation. They should strive to include all of the criteria required to achieve a score of 3. Draw their attention to some of the subtle differences between scores of 2 and 3.

 PERFORMANCE-BASED ASSESSMENT

PART 2
Speaking and Listening: Speech

Assignment
After completing the final draft of your argument, use it as the foundation for a three- to five-minute **speech**.

Take the following steps to make your speech lively and engaging.

- Go back to your argument and annotate the most important claims and supporting details.
- Refer to your annotated text to guide your speech and keep it focused.
- Use appropriate eye contact, adequate volume, and clear pronunciation when speaking.
- Deliver your speech with conviction.

Review the Rubric Before you deliver your speech, check the rubric. If one or more of the elements is weak, revise your presentation.

📋 **STANDARDS**
Speaking and Listening
- Delineate a speaker's argument and specific claims, evaluating the soundness of the reasoning and relevance and sufficiency of the evidence and identifying when irrelevant evidence is introduced.
- Present claims and findings, emphasizing salient points in a focused, coherent manner with relevant evidence, sound valid reasoning, and well-chosen details; use appropriate eye contact, adequate volume, and clear pronunciation.

	Content	Organization	Presentation Techniques
3	The introduction engages the reader and establishes a claim in a compelling way. The presentation has strong, valid reasons and evidence to support the claim and answers counterclaims. The conclusion follows from and supports the rest of the argument.	Ideas progress logically, with clear transitions among ideas so that listeners can easily follow the argument.	The speaker maintains effective eye contact and speaks clearly and with adequate volume. The speaker presents with strong conviction and energy.
2	The introduction establishes a claim. The presentation includes some valid reasons and evidence to support the claim and acknowledges counterclaims. The conclusion offers some insight into the claim and restates important information.	Ideas progress logically with some transitions between ideas. Listeners can mostly follow the speaker's argument.	The speaker sometimes maintains effective eye contact and speaks somewhat clearly and with adequate volume. The speaker presents with some conviction and energy.
1	The introduction does not clearly state a claim. The presentation does not include reasons or evidence to support a claim or acknowledge counterclaims. The conclusion does not restate important information about a claim.	Ideas do not progress logically. Listeners have difficulty following the argument.	The speaker does not maintain effective eye contact or speak clearly with adequate volume. The speaker presents without conviction or energy.

DIGITAL PERSPECTIVES

Preparing for the Assignment To help students understand what an effective oral presentation of an essay looks and sounds like, have students find examples on the Internet of people presenting arguments. Project the examples for the class, and have students note the techniques that make each speaker successful (gesture, pacing, tone, and so on). Suggest that students record themselves presenting their explanatory essays so they can practice incorporating some of the elements from the examples you showed them.

UNIT 5 REFLECTION

Reflect on the Unit

Now that you've completed the unit, take a few moments to reflect on your learning. Use the questions below to think about where you succeeded, what skills and strategies helped you, and where you can continue to grow in the future.

Reflect on the Unit Goals

Look back at the goals at the beginning of the unit. Use a different colored pen to rate yourself again. Think about readings and activities that contributed the most to the growth of your understanding. Record your thoughts.

Reflect on the Learning Strategies

Discuss It Write a reflection on whether you were able to improve your learning based on your Action Plans. Think about what worked, what didn't, and what you might do to keep working on these strategies. Record your ideas before a class discussion.

Reflect on the Text

Choose a selection that you found challenging, and explain what made it difficult.

Describe something that surprised you about a text in the unit.

Which activity taught you the most about invention? What did you learn?

SCAN FOR MULTIMEDIA

DIGITAL PERSPECTIVES

Reflect on the Unit

- Have students watch the video on Reflecting on Your Learning.
- A video on this topic is available online in the Professional Development Center.

Reflect on the Unit Goals

Students should re-evaluate how well they met the unit goals now that they have completed the unit. You might ask them to provide a written commentary on the goal they made the most progress with as well as the goal they feel warrants continued focus.

Reflect on the Learning Strategies

Discuss It If you want to make this a digital activity, go online and navigate to the Discussion Board. Alternatively, students can share their learning strategies reflections in a class discussion.

Reflect on the Text

Consider having students share their text reflections with one another.

MAKE IT INTERACTIVE

Have students write one or two sentences that summarize their reflections on the unit. Then have students read their reflections to the class. Afterward, have students discuss the reflections. Were there any common themes?

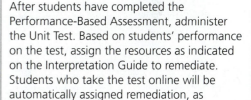

Unit Test and Remediation

After students have completed the Performance-Based Assessment, administer the Unit Test. Based on students' performance on the test, assign the resources as indicated on the Interpretation Guide to remediate. Students who take the test online will be automatically assigned remediation, as warranted by test results.

RESOURCES

CONTENTS

TOOL KIT

Close Reading R1
  Marking the Text
  First-Read Model and Guide
  Close-Read Model and Guide

Writing R6
  Argument Model
  Informative/Explanatory Model
  Narrative Model

Research R24
  Conducting Research
  Reviewing Research Findings
  Incorporating Research Into Writing
  MLA Style for Listing Sources

Program Resources R34
  Evidence Log Model
  Word Network Model

GLOSSARY

**Academic/
Concept Vocabulary** R36
  Vocabulario académico/
  Vocabulario de conceptos

Literary Terms Handbook R43
  Manual de términos literarios

Grammar Handbook R56

INDEXES

Index of Skills R66

**Index of Authors
and Titles** R72

ACKNOWLEDGMENTS

**Acknowledgments
and Credits** R75

CLOSE READING

Marking the Text: Strategies and Tips for Annotation

When you close read a text, you read for comprehension and then reread to unlock layers of meaning and to analyze a writer's style and techniques. Marking a text as you read it enables you to participate more fully in the close-reading process.

Following are some strategies for text mark-ups, along with samples of how the strategies can be applied. These mark-ups are suggestions; you and your teacher may want to use other mark-up strategies.

✱	Key Idea
!	I love it!
?	I have questions
◯	Unfamiliar or important word
----	Context Clues

Suggested Mark-Up Notations

WHAT I NOTICE	HOW TO MARK UP	QUESTIONS TO ASK
Key Ideas and Details	• Highlight key ideas or claims. • Underline supporting details or evidence.	• What does the text say? What does it leave unsaid? • What inferences do you need to make? • What details lead you to make your inferences?
Word Choice	• Circle unfamiliar words. • Put a dotted line under context clues, if any exist. • Put an exclamation point beside especially rich or poetic passages.	• What inferences about word meaning can you make? • What tone and mood are created by word choice? • What alternate word choices might the author have made?
Text Structure	• Highlight passages that show key details supporting the main idea. • Use arrows to indicate how sentences and paragraphs work together to build ideas. • Use a right-facing arrow to indicate foreshadowing. • Use a left-facing arrow to indicate flashback.	• Is the text logically structured? • What emotional impact do the structural choices create?
Author's Craft	• Circle or highlight instances of repetition, either of words, phrases, consonants, or vowel sounds. • Mark rhythmic beats in poetry using checkmarks and slashes. • Underline instances of symbolism or figurative language.	• Does the author's style enrich or detract from the reading experience? • What levels of meaning are created by the author's techniques?

CLOSE READING

First Read: NOTICE, ANNOTATE, CONNECT, RESPOND

* Key Idea
! I love it!
? I have questions
◯ Unfamiliar or important word
---- Context Clues

In a first read, work to get a sense of the main idea of a text. Look for key details and ideas that help you understand what the author conveys to you. Mark passages that prompt a strong response from you.

Here is how one reader marked up this text.

MODEL

INFORMATIONAL TEXT

from Classifying the Stars

Cecilia H. Payne

1 Sunlight and starlight are *composed of waves of various lengths,* which the eye, even aided by a telescope, is unable to separate. We must use more than a telescope. In order to sort out the *component colors,* the light must be dispersed by a prism, or split up by some other means. For instance, sunbeams passing through rain drops are transformed into the (myriad)-tinted rainbow. *The familiar rainbow spanning the sky is Nature's most glorious demonstration that light is composed of many colors.*

2 The *very beginning of our knowledge* of the nature of a star dates back to 1672, when *Isaac Newton* gave to the world the results of his experiments on passing sunlight through a prism. To describe the beautiful band of rainbow tints, produced when sunlight was dispersed by his three-cornered piece of glass, he took from the Latin the word *spectrum*, meaning an *appearance*. The rainbow is the (spectrum) of the Sun. . . .

3 *In 1814,* more than a century after Newton, the spectrum of the Sun was obtained in such purity that an *amazing detail* was seen and studied *by the German optician, Fraunhofer.* He saw that the multiple spectral tints, ranging from delicate violet to deep red, were crossed by hundreds of fine dark lines. In other words, there were narrow gaps in the spectrum where certain shades were wholly blotted out. We must remember that the word spectrum is applied not only to sunlight, but also to the light of any glowing substance when its rays are sorted out by a prism or a (grating).

MODEL

First-Read Guide

Use this page to record your first-read ideas.

Selection Title: _Classifying the Stars_

> You may want to use a guide like this to organize your thoughts after you read. Here is how a reader completed a First-Read Guide.

NOTICE
NOTICE new information or ideas you learned about the unit topic as you first read this text.

Light = different waves of colors. (Spectrum)

Newton - the first person to observe these waves using a prism.

Faunhofer saw gaps in the spectrum.

ANNOTATE
ANNOTATE by marking vocabulary and key passages you want to revisit.

Vocabulary
 myriad
 grating
 component colors

Different light types = different lengths

Isaac Newton also worked theories of gravity.

Multiple spectral tints? "colors of various appearance"

Key Passage:
Paragraph 3 shows that Fraunhofer discovered more about the nature of light spectrums: he saw the spaces in between the tints.

CONNECT
CONNECT ideas within the selection to other knowledge and the selections you have read.

I remember learning about prisms in science class.

Double rainbows! My favorite. How are they made?

RESPOND
RESPOND by writing a brief summary of the selection.

Science allows us to see things not visible to the naked eye. What we see as sunlight is really a spectrum of colors. By using tools, such as prisms, we can see the components of sunlight and other light. They appear as single colors or as multiple colors separated by gaps of no color. White light contains a rainbow of colors.

TOOL KIT: CLOSE READING

CLOSE READING

* Key Idea
! I love it!
? I have questions
◯ Unfamiliar or important word
---- Context Clues

In a close read, go back into the text to study it in greater detail. Take the time to analyze not only the author's ideas but the way that those ideas are conveyed. Consider the genre of the text, the author's word choice, the writer's unique style, and the message of the text.

Here is how one reader close read this text.

MODEL

INFORMATIONAL TEXT

from Classifying the Stars
Cecilia H. Payne

NOTES:
- explanation of sunlight and starlight
- What is light and where do the colors come from?
- This paragraph is about Newton and the prism.
- What discoveries helped us understand light?
- Fraunhofer and gaps in spectrum

1 Sunlight and starlight are **composed of waves of various lengths**, which the eye, even aided by a telescope, is unable to separate. We must use more than a telescope. In order to sort out the **component colors**, the light must be dispersed by a prism, or split up by some other means. For instance, sunbeams passing through rain drops are transformed into the (myriad)-tinted rainbow. **The familiar rainbow spanning the sky is Nature's most glorious demonstration that light is composed of many colors.**

2 The **very beginning of our knowledge** of the nature of a star dates back to 1672, when **Isaac Newton** gave to the world the results of his experiments on passing sunlight through a prism. To describe the beautiful band of rainbow tints, produced when sunlight was dispersed by his three-cornered piece of glass, he took from the Latin the word *spectrum*, meaning an **appearance**. The rainbow is the (spectrum) of the Sun. . . .

3 **In 1814**, more than a century after Newton, the spectrum of the Sun was obtained in such purity that an **amazing detail** was seen and studied **by the German optician, Fraunhofer**. He saw that the multiple spectral tints, ranging from delicate violet to deep red, **were crossed by hundreds of fine dark lines**. In other words, there were narrow gaps in the spectrum where certain shades were wholly blotted out. We must remember that the word spectrum is applied not only to sunlight, but also to the light of any glowing substance when its rays are sorted out by a prism or a (grating).

MODEL

Close-Read Guide

Use this page to record your close-read ideas.

Selection Title: _Classifying the Stars_

> You can use the Close-Read Guide to help you dig deeper into the text. Here is how a reader completed a Close-Read Guide.

Close Read the Text

Revisit sections of the text you marked during your first read. Read these sections closely and **annotate** what you notice. Ask yourself **questions** about the text. What can you **conclude?** Write down your ideas.

Paragraph 3: Light is composed of waves of various lengths. Prisms let us see different colors in light. This is called the spectrum. Fraunhofer proved that there are gaps in the spectrum, where certain shades are blotted out.

More than one researcher studied this and each built off the ideas that were already discovered.

Analyze the Text

Think about the author's choices of patterns, structure, techniques, and ideas included in the text. Select one, and record your thoughts about what this choice conveys.

The author showed the development of human knowledge of the spectrum chronologically. Helped me see how ideas were built upon earlier understandings. Used dates and "more than a century after Newton" to show time.

QuickWrite

Pick a paragraph from the text that grabbed your interest. Explain the power of this passage.

The first paragraph grabbed my attention, specifically the sentence "The familiar rainbow spanning the sky is Nature's most glorious demonstration that light is composed of many colors." The paragraph began as a straightforward scientific explanation. When I read the word "glorious," I had to stop and deeply consider what was being said. It is a word loaded with personal feelings. With that one word, the author let the reader know what was important to her.

WRITING

Argument

When you think of the word *argument,* you might think of a disagreement between two people, but the word has another meaning, too. An argument is a logical way of presenting a belief, conclusion, or stance. A good argument is supported with reasoning and evidence.

Argument writing can be used for many purposes, such as changing a reader's opinion or bringing about an action or a response from a reader.

Elements of an Argumentative Text

An **argument** sets forth a belief or stand on an issue. A well-written argument may convince the reader, change the reader's mind, or motivate the reader to take a certain action.

An effective argument contains these elements:

- a precise claim
- consideration of alternate claims, or opposing positions, and a discussion of their strengths and weaknesses
- logical organization that makes clear connections among claim, reasons, and evidence
- valid reasoning and evidence
- a concluding statement or section that follows from and supports the argument
- formal and objective language and tone
- error-free grammar, including accurate use of transitions

MODEL

ARGUMENT: SCORE 1

Celebrities Should Try to Be Better Role Models

A lot of Celebrities are singers or actors or actresses or athletes. Kids spend tons of time watching Celebrities on TV. They listen to their songs. They read about them. They watch them play and perform. No matter weather the Celebrities are good people or bad people. Kids still spend time watching them. The kids will try to imitate what they do. Some of them have parents or brothers and sisters who are famous also.

Celebrities don't seem to watch out what they do and how they live. Some say, *"Why do I care? It's none of you're business"*! Well, that's true. But it's bad on them if they do all kinds of stupid things. Because this is bad for the kids who look up to them.

Sometimes celebrity's say they wish they are not role models. *"I'm just an actor!" "I'm just a singer"!* they say. But the choice is not really up to them. If their on TV all the time, then kids' will look up to them, no matter what. It's stupid when Celebrities mess up and then nothing bad happens to them. That gives kids a bad lesson. Kids will think that you can do stupid things and be fine. That is not being a good role model.

Some Celebrities give money to charity. That's a good way to be a good role model. But sometimes it seems like Celebrities are just totally messed up. It's hard always being in the spotlight. That can drive Celebrities kind of crazy. Then they act out.

It is a good idea to support charities when you are rich and famous. You can do a lot of good. For a lot of people. Some Celebrities give out cars or houses or free scholarships. You can even give away your dresses and people can have an auction to see who will pay the most money for them. This can help for example the Humane Society. Or whatever charity or cause the celebrity wants to support.

Celebrities are fun to watch and follow, even when they mess up. I think they don't realize that when they do bad things, they give teens wrong ideas about how to live. They should try to keep that under control. So many teens look up to them and copy them, no matter what.

- The claim is not clearly stated in the introduction or elsewhere.
- Some of the ideas in the essay do not relate to the stated position or focus on the issue.
- The word choice in the essay is not effective and lends it an informal tone.
- The progression of ideas is not logical or well controlled.
- Errors in spelling, capitalization, punctuation, grammar, usage, and sentence boundaries are frequent. The fluency of the writing and effectiveness of the essay are affected by these errors.
- The conclusion does not clearly restate the claim.

WRITING

MODEL

ARGUMENT: SCORE 2

Celebrities Should Try to Be Better Role Models

Most kids spend tons of time watching celebrities on TV, listening to their songs, and reading about them. No matter how celebrities behave—whether they do good things or bad—they are role models for kids. They often do really dumb things, and that is not good considering they are role models.

Sometimes celebrity's say they wish they were not role models. *"I'm just an actor!"* or, *"I'm just a singer!"* they say. But the choice is not really up to them. If they are on TV all the time, then kids' will look up to them. No matter what. It's really bad when celebrities mess up and then nothing bad happens to them. That gives kids a false lesson because in reality there are bad things when you mess up. That's why celebrities should think more about what they are doing and what lessons they are giving to kids.

Some celebrities might say, *"Why do I care? Why should I be bothered?"* Well, they don't have to. But it's bad on them if they do all kinds of stupid things and don't think about how this affects the kids who look up to them. Plus, they get tons of money, much more even than inventors or scientists or other important people. Being a good role model should be part of what they have to do to get so much money.

When you are famous it is a good idea to support charities. Some celebrities give out cars, or houses, or free scholarships. They even sometimes give away their dresses and people have an auction to see who will pay the most money for them. This can help for example the Humane Society, or whatever charity or cause the celebrity wants to support.

Sometimes it seems like celebrities are more messed up than anyone else. That's in their personal lives. Imagine if people wanted to take pictures of you wherever you went, and you could never get away. That can drive celebrities kind of crazy, and then they act out.

Celebrities can do good things and they can do bad things. They don't realize that when they do bad things, they give teens wrong ideas about how to live. So many teens look up to them and copy them, no matter what. They should make an effort to be better role models.

- The introduction does not state the argument claim clearly enough.
- Errors in spelling, grammar, and sentence boundaries decrease the effectiveness of the essay.
- The word choice in the essay contributes to an informal tone.
- The writer does not make use of transitions and sentence connections.
- Some of the ideas in the essay do not relate to the stated position or focus on the issue.
- The essay has a clear conclusion.

MODEL

ARGUMENT: SCORE 3

Celebrities Should Try to Be Better Role Models

Kids look up to the celebrities they see on TV and want to be like them. Parents may not *want* celebrities to be role models for their children, but they are anyway. Therefore, celebrities should think about what they say and do and live lives that are worth copying. Celebrities should think about how they act because they are role models.

> The writer's word choice is good but could be better.

"I'm just an actor!" or, "I'm just a singer!" celebrities sometimes say. "Their parents and teachers are the ones who should be the role models!" But it would be foolish to misjudge the impact that celebrities have on youth. Kids spend hours every day digitally hanging with their favorite stars. Children learn by imitation, so, for better or worse, celebrities are role models. That's why celebrities should start modeling good decision-making and good citizenship.

> The introduction mostly states the claim.

> The ideas relate to the stated position and focus on the issue.

With all that they are given by society, celebrities owe a lot back to their communities and the world. Celebrities get a lot of attention, time, and money. Often they get all that for doing not very much: acting, singing, or playing a sport. It's true; some of them work very hard. But even if they work very hard, do they deserve to be in the news all the time and earn 100 or even 1000 times more than equally hard-working teachers, scientists, or nurses? I don't think so. After receiving all that, it seems only fair that celebrities take on the important job of being good role models for the young people who look up to them.

> The sentences are varied and well controlled and enhance the effectiveness of the essay.

Celebrities can serve as good role models is by giving back. Quite a few use their fame and fortune to do just that. They give scholarships, or even build and run schools; they help veterans; they visit hospitals; they support important causes such as conservation, and women's rights. They donate not just money but their time and talents too. This is a great way to be a role model.

> The progression of ideas is logical, but there could be better transitions and sentence connections to show how ideas are related.

Celebrities should recognize that as role models, they have a responsibility to try to make good decisions and be honest. Celebrities should step up so they can be a force for good in people's lives and in the world.

> The conclusion mostly follows from the claim.

Argument (Score 3) R9

WRITING

MODEL

ARGUMENT: SCORE 4

Celebrities Should Try to Be Better Role Models

Like it or not, kids look up to the celebrities they see on TV and want to be like them. Parents may not *want* celebrities to be role models for their children, but the fact is that they are. With such an oversized influence on young people, celebrities have a responsibility to think about what they say and do and to live lives that are worth emulating. In short, they should make an effort to be better role models.

Sometimes celebrities say they don't want to be role models. "I'm just an actor!" or "I'm just a singer!" they protest. "Their parents and teachers are the ones who should be guiding them and showing them the right way to live!" That is all very well, but it would be foolish to underestimate the impact that celebrities have on children. Kids spend hours every day digitally hanging out with their favorite stars. Children learn by imitation, so for better or worse, celebrities act as role models.

Celebrities are given a lot of attention, time, and money. They get all that for doing very little: acting, singing, or playing a sport very well. It's true some of them work very hard. But even if they work hard, do they deserve to be in the news all the time and earn 100 or even 1,000 times more than equally hardworking teachers, scientists, or nurses? I don't think so.

With all that they are given, celebrities owe a lot to their communities and the world. One way they can serve as good role models is by giving back, and quite a few celebrities use their fame and fortune to do just that. They give scholarships or even build and run schools; they help veterans; they entertain kids who are sick; they support important causes such as conservation and women's rights. They donate not just money but their time and talents too.

Celebrities don't have to be perfect. They are people too and make mistakes. But they should recognize that as role models for youth, they have a responsibility to try to make good decisions and be honest about their struggles. Celebrities should step up so they can be a force for good in people's lives.

- The writer has chosen words that contribute to the clarity of the essay.
- The writer clearly states the claim of the argument in the introduction.
- The essay is engaging and varied.
- There are no errors to distract the reader from the fluency of the writing and effectiveness of the essay.
- The writer uses transitions and sentence connections to show how ideas are related.
- The writer clearly restates the claim and the most powerful idea presented in the essay.

Argument Rubric

	Focus and Organization	Evidence and Elaboration	Conventions
4	The introduction is engaging and states the claim in a compelling way. The claim is supported by clear reasons and relevant evidence. Reasons and evidence are logically organized so that the argument is easy to follow. The conclusion clearly restates the claim and the most powerful idea.	Sources are effectively credible and accurate. The argument demonstrates an understanding of the thesis by providing strong examples. The tone of the argument is formal and objective.	The argument intentionally uses standard English conventions of usage and mechanics. The argument effectively uses words, phrases, and clauses to clarify the relationships among claim(s) and reasons.
3	The introduction is mostly engaging and states the claim. The claim is mostly supported by logical reasons and evidence. Reasons and evidence are organized so that the argument is mostly easy to follow. The conclusion mostly restates the claim.	Sources are mostly credible and accurate. The argument mostly demonstrates an understanding of the thesis by providing adequate examples. The tone of the argument is mostly formal and objective.	The argument mostly demonstrates accuracy in standard English conventions of usage and mechanics. The argument mostly uses words, phrases, and clauses to clarify the relationships among claim(s) and reasons.
2	The introduction somewhat states the claim. The claim is supported by some reasons and evidence. Reasons and evidence are organized somewhat logically with a few transitions to orient readers. The conclusion somewhat relates to the claim.	Some sources are relevant. The argument somewhat demonstrates an understanding of the thesis by providing some examples. The tone of the argument is occasionally formal and objective.	The argument demonstrates some accuracy in standard English conventions of usage and mechanics. The argument somewhat uses words, phrases, and clauses to clarify the relationships among claim(s) and reasons.
1	The claim is not clearly stated. The claim is not supported by reasons and evidence. Reasons and evidence are disorganized and the argument is difficult to follow. The conclusion does not include relevant information.	There is little or no reliable, relevant evidence The argument does not demonstrate an understanding of the thesis and does not provide examples. The tone of the argument is informal.	The argument contains mistakes in standard English conventions of usage and mechanics. The argument does not use words, phrases, and clauses to clarify the relationships among claim(s) and reasons.

WRITING

Informative/Explanatory Texts

Informative and explanatory writing should rely on facts to inform or explain. Informative writing can serve several purposes: to increase readers' knowledge of a subject, to help readers better understand a procedure or process, or to provide readers with an enhanced comprehension of a concept. It should also feature a clear introduction, body, and conclusion.

Informative/explanatory texts present facts, details, data, and other kinds of evidence to give information about a topic. Readers turn to informative and explanatory texts when they wish to learn about a specific idea, concept, or subject area, or when they want to learn how to do something.

An effective informative/explanatory text contains these elements:

- a topic sentence or thesis statement that introduces the concept or subject
- relevant facts, examples, and details that expand upon a topic
- definitions, quotations, and/or graphics that support the information given
- headings (if desired) to separate sections of the essay
- a structure that presents information in a direct, clear manner
- clear transitions that link sections of the essay
- precise words and technical vocabulary where appropriate
- formal and objective language and tone
- a conclusion that supports the information given and provides fresh insights

MODEL

INFORMATIVE: SCORE 1

Kids, School, and Exercise: Problems and Solutions

In the past, children ran around and even did hard physical labor. Today most kid's just sit most of the time. They don't know the old Outdoor Games. Like tether ball. and they don't have hard chores to do. Like milking the cows. But children should be Physically Active quite a bit every day. That doesn't happen very much any more. Not as much as it should anyway.

Even at home when kid's have a chance to run around, they choose to sit and play video games, for example. Some schools understand that it's a problem when students don't get enough exercise. Even though they have had to cut Physical Education classes. Some also had to make recess shorter.

But lots of schools are working hard to find ways to get kid's moving around again. Like they used to long ago.

Schools use volunteers to teach kid's old-fashioned games. Old-fashioned games are an awesome way to get kid's moving around like crazy people.

Some schools have before school activities. Such as games in the gym. Other schools have after school activities. Such as bike riding or outdoor games. They can't count on kid's to be active. Not even on their own or at home. So they do the activities all together. Kids enjoy doing stuff with their friends. So that works out really well.

If you don't exercise you get overweight. You can end up with high blood pressure and too much colesterol. Of course its also a problem if you eat too much junk food all the time. But not getting enough exercise is part of the problem too. That's why schools need to try to be part of the solution.

A break during class to move around helps. Good teachers know how to use exercise during classes. There are all kinds of ways to move in the classroom that don't mean you have to change your clothes. Classes don't have to be just about math and science.

Schools are doing what they can to get kids moving, doing exercise, being active. Getting enough exercise also helps kid's do better in school. Being active also helps kids get strong.

There are extensive errors in spelling, capitalization, punctuation, grammar, usage, and sentence boundaries.

Many of the ideas in the essay do not focus on the topic.

The word choice shows the writer's lack of awareness of the essay's purpose and tone.

The essay's sentences are not purposeful, varied, or well controlled. The writer's sentences decrease the effectiveness of the essay.

The essay is not well organized. Its structure does not support its purpose or respond well to the demands of the prompt.

The essay is not particularly thoughtful or engaging.

WRITING

MODEL

INFORMATIVE: SCORE 2

Kids, School, and Exercise: Problems and Solutions

In the past, children ran around a lot and did chores and other physical work. Today most kid's sit by a TV or computer screen or play with their phones. But children should be active for at least 60 minutes a day. Sadly, most don't get nearly that much exercise. And that's a big problem.

Some schools understand that it's a problem when students don't get enough exercise. Even though they have had to cut Physical Education classes due to budget cuts. Some also had to make recess shorter because there isn't enough time in the schedule. But they are working hard to find creative ways that don't cost too much or take up too much time to get kid's moving. Because there's only so much money in the budget, and only so much time in the day, and preparing to take tests takes lots of time.

Schools can use parent volunteers to teach kid's old-fashioned games such as kick-the-can, hopscotch, foursquare, tetherball, or jump rope. Kid's nowadays often don't know these games! Old-fashioned games are a great way to get kid's moving. Some schools have before school activities, such as games in the gym. Other schools have after school activities, such as bike riding or outdoor games. They can't count on kid's to be active on their own or at home.

A break during class can help students concentrate when they go back to work. There are all kinds of ways to move in the classroom. And you don't have to change your clothes or anything. Wiggling, stretching, and playing a short active game are all good ideas. Good teachers know how to squeeze in time during academic classes like math and language arts.

Not getting enough exercise is linked to many problems. For example, unhealthy wait, and high blood pressure and colesterol. When students don't' get enough exercise, they end up overweight.

Physical activity also helps kid's do better in school. Kids who exercise have better attendance rates. They have increased attention span. They act out less. They have less stress and learn more. Being active also helps muscles and bones. It increases strength and stamina.

Schools today are doing what they can to find a solution by being creative and making time for physical activity before, during, and after school. They understand that it is a problem when kid's don't get enough exercise.

Annotations:
- Not all the ideas in the essay focus on the topic.
- The writer uses some transitions and sentence connections.
- Some of the ideas in the essay are reasonably well developed. Some details and examples add substance to the essay.
- Some ideas are well developed. Some examples and details are well chosen and specific and add substance to the essay.
- Some details are specific and well chosen.
- There are errors in spelling, punctuation, grammar, usage, and sentence boundaries that decrease the effectiveness of the essay.
- The essay is not well organized. Its organizing structure does not support its purpose well or respond well to the demands of the prompt.

MODEL

INFORMATIVE: SCORE 3

Kids, School, and Exercise: Problems and Solutions

A 2008 report said school-age children should be physically active for at least 60 minutes a day. Sadly, most children don't get nearly that much exercise. Lots of schools have cut Physical Education classes because of money and time pressures. And there's less recess than there used to be. Even at home when kids have a chance to run around, many choose screen time instead. No wonder so many of us are turning into chubby couch potatoes!

Not getting exercise is linked to many problems, for example unhealthy weight, and high blood pressure and cholesterol. Studies show physical activity also helps students do better in school: it means better attendance rates, increased attention span, fewer behavioral problems, less stress, and more learning. Being active helps develop strong muscles and bones. It increases strength and stamina.

Many schools around the country get that there are problems when students are inactive. They are working hard to find creative solutions that don't cost too much or take up precious time in the school schedule.

Some schools are using parent volunteers to teach kids active games such as kick-the-can, hopscotch, foursquare, tetherball, or jump rope. These games are more likely to get kids moving than just sitting gossiping with your friends or staring at your phone. Some schools have before school activities such as run-around games in the gym. Other schools have after school activities such as bike riding or outdoor games. They can't count on kids to be active on their own.

There are all kinds of fun and healthy ways to move in the classroom, without changing clothes. An active break during class can help students concentrate when they go back to work. Creative teachers know how to squeeze in active time even during academic classes. Wiggling, stretching, and playing a short active game are all good ideas.

Schools today understand that it is a problem when kids don't get enough exercise. They are doing what they can to find a solution by being creative and making time for physical activity before, during, and after school.

Annotations:
- The essay is fairly thoughtful and engaging.
- Almost all the ideas focus on the topic.
- The ideas in the essay are well developed, with well-chosen and specific details and examples.
- The writer uses transitions and connections, such as "Not getting exercise is linked…" "Many schools …" "Some schools…" "Other schools…"
- Ideas in the essay are mostly well developed.
- Words are chosen carefully and contribute to the clarity of the essay.

WRITING

MODEL

INFORMATIVE: SCORE 4

Kids, School, and Exercise: Problems and Solutions

In 2008, the U.S. Department of Health and Human Services published a report stating that all school-age children need to be physically active for at least 60 minutes a day. Sadly, most children don't get nearly the recommended amount of exercise. Due to budget cuts and time pressure, many schools have cut Physical Education classes. Even recess is being squeezed to make room for more tests and test preparation.

The writer explains the problem and its causes.

Lack of exercise can lead to many problems, such as unhealthy weight, high blood pressure, and high cholesterol. Physical activity helps develop strong muscles and bones, and it increases strength and stamina. Studies show physical activity leads to better attendance rates, increased attention span, fewer behavioral problems, less stress, and more learning. When kids don't get enough physical activity, a lot is at stake!

The writer clearly lays out the effects of the problem.

Many schools around the country are stepping up to find innovative solutions—even when they don't have time or money to spare. Some have started before-school activities such as active games in the gym. Others have after-school activities such as bike riding or outdoor games. Just a few extra minutes a day can make a big difference!

The writer turns to the solution. The essay's organizing structure supports its purpose and responds to the demands of the prompt.

Some schools try to make the most of recess by using parent volunteers to teach kids active games such as kick-the-can, hopscotch, foursquare, tetherball, or jump rope. Volunteers can also organize races or tournaments—anything to get the kids going! At the end of recess, everyone should be a little bit out of breath.

The writer includes specific examples and well-chosen details.

Creative educators squeeze in active time even during academic classes. It could be a quick "brain break" to stretch in the middle of class, imaginary jump rope, or a game of rock-paper-scissors with legs instead of fingers. There are all kinds of imaginative ways to move in the classroom, without moving furniture or changing clothes. And research shows that an active break during class can help students focus when they go back to work.

The progression of ideas is logical and well controlled.

Details and examples add substance to the essay.

Schools today understand the problems that can arise when kids don't have enough physical activity in their lives. They are meeting the challenge by finding opportunities for exercise before, during, and after school. After all, if students do well on tests but end up unhealthy and unhappy, what is the point?

The essay is thoughtful and engaging.

R16 RESOURCES: TOOL KIT

Informative Rubric

	Focus and Organization	Evidence and Elaboration	Conventions
4	The introduction is engaging and sets forth the topic in a compelling way. The ideas progress logically. A variety of transitions are included to show the relationship among ideas. The conclusion follows from the rest of the essay.	The topic is developed with relevant facts, definitions, details, quotations, and examples. The tone of the essay is formal. The vocabulary is precise and relevant to the topic, audience, and purpose.	The essay uses standard English conventions of usage and mechanics.
3	The introduction is somewhat engaging and sets forth the topic in a way that grabs readers' attention. The ideas progress somewhat logically. Some transitions are included to show the relationship among ideas. The conclusion mostly follows from the rest of the essay.	The topic is developed with some relevant facts, definitions, details, quotations, and other examples. The tone of the essay is mostly formal. The vocabulary is generally appropriate for the topic, audience, and purpose.	The essay demonstrates general accuracy in standard English conventions of usage and mechanics.
2	The introduction sets forth the topic. More than one idea is presented. A few transitions are included that show the relationship among ideas. The conclusion does not completely follow from the rest of the essay.	The topic is developed with a few relevant facts, definitions, details, quotations, or other examples. The tone of the essay is occasionally formal. The vocabulary is somewhat appropriate for the topic, audience, and purpose.	The essay demonstrates some accuracy in standard English conventions of usage and mechanics.
1	The topic is not clearly stated. Ideas do not follow a logical progression. Transitions are not included. The conclusion does not follow from the rest of the essay.	The topic is not developed with reliable or relevant evidence. The tone is informal. The vocabulary is limited or ineffective.	The essay contains mistakes in standard English conventions of usage and mechanics.

Tool Kit

WRITING

Narrative

Narrative writing conveys an experience, either real or imaginary, and uses time order to provide structure. Usually its purpose is to entertain, but it can also instruct, persuade, or inform. Whenever writers tell a story, they are using narrative writing. Most types of narrative writing share certain elements, such as characters, setting, a sequence of events, and, often, a theme.

Elements of a Narrative Text

A **narrative** is any type of writing that tells a story, whether it is fiction, nonfiction, poetry, or drama.

An effective nonfiction narrative contains these elements:
- an engaging beginning in which characters and setting are established
- characters who participate in the story events
- a well-structured, logical sequence of events
- details that show time and place
- effective story elements such as dialogue, description, and reflection
- a narrator who relates the events from a particular point of view
- use of language that brings the characters and setting to life

An effective fictional narrative usually contains these elements:
- an engaging beginning in which characters, setting, or a main conflict is introduced
- a main character and supporting characters who participate in the story events
- a narrator who relates the events of the plot from a particular point of view
- details that show time and place
- narrative techniques such as dialogue, description, and suspense
- use of language that vividly brings to life characters and events

MODEL

NARRATIVE: SCORE 1

Mind Scissors

There's a bike race. Right away people start losing. But me and Thad were winning. Thad is the kid who always wins is who is also popular. I don't like Thad. I pumped pumping hard at my pedals, I knew the end was coming. I looked ahead and all I could see was Thad, and the woods.

I pedaled harder and then I was up to Thad. That was swinging at me, I swerved, I kept looking at him, I was worried!

That's stick had untied my shoelace and it was wrapped around my pedal! But I didn't know it yet.

We were out of the woods. I still wanted to win, I pedaled even faster. than my pedals stopped!

I saw with my mind the shoelace was caught in my pedal. No worries, I have the superpower of mind scissors. That's when my mind looked down and I used my mind scissors. I used the mind scissors to cut the shoelace my right foot was free.

That's how I became a superhero. I save people with my mind scissors now.

- The story's beginning is not clear or engaging.
- The narrative does not include sensory language and precise words to convey experiences and to develop characters.
- Events do not progress logically. The ideas seem disconnected, and the sentences do not include transitions.
- The narrative contains mistakes in standard English conventions of usage and mechanics.
- The conclusion does not connect to the narrative.

WRITING

MODEL

NARRATIVE: SCORE 2

Mind-Scissors

When I was a baby I wound up with a tiny pair of scissors in my head. What the doctors couldn't have predicted is the uncanny ability they would give me. This past summer that was when I discovered what I could do with my mind-scissors.

Every summer there's a bike race. The kid who always wins is Thad who is popular.

The race starts. Right away racers start losing. After a long time pumping hard at my pedals, I knew the end was coming. I looked ahead and all I could see was Thad, and the woods.

I pedaled harder than ever. I was up to Thad. I turned my head to look at him. He was swinging a stick at me, I swerved, I kept looking at him, boy was I worried.

We were now out of the woods. Still hopeful I could win, I pedaled even faster. Suddenly, my pedals stopped!

Oh no! Thad's stick had untied my shoelace and it was wrapped around my pedal!

I was going to crash my bike. That's when my mind looked down. That's when I knew I could use my mind-scissors. I used the mind scissors to cut the shoelace my right foot was free.

That's how I won the race.

The story's beginning introduces the main character.

Events in the narrative progress somewhat logically, and the writer use some transition words.

The writer uses some description in the narrative.

The narrative demonstrates some accuracy in standard English conventions of usage and mechanics.

The words vary between vague and precise. The writer uses some sensory language.

The conclusion is weak and adds very little to the narrative.

MODEL

NARRATIVE: SCORE 3

Mind-Scissors

When I was a baby I wound up with a tiny pair of scissors in my head. Lots of people live with pieces of metal in their heads. We just have to be careful. What the doctors couldn't have predicted is the uncanny ability they would give me.

> The story's beginning is engaging and clearly introduces the main character and situation.

Every summer there's a bike race that ends at the lake. The kid who always wins is Thad Thomas the Third, who is popular. This past summer that was about to change. It's also when I discovered what I could do with my mind-scissors.

The race starts. Right away racers start falling behind. After what seemed an eternity pumping hard at my pedals, I knew the end had to be in sight. I looked ahead and all I could see was Thad, and the opening to the woods—the last leg of the race.

> Events in the narrative progress logically, and the writer uses transition words frequently.

I felt like steam was coming off my legs. I could see Thad's helmet. I turned my head to flash him a look. Only, Thad was the one who was gloating! And then I saw it—he was holding a stick he had pulled off a low-hanging branch.

> The writer uses precise words and some sensory language to convey the experiences in the narrative and to describe the characters and scenes.

He jabbed it toward me. I swerved out of the way. I kept pedaling, shifting my eyes to the right, to see what he was going to do.

But I waited too long. Then Thad made a slashing motion. Then he tossed the stick aside, yelled, "Yes!" and zoomed forward.

> The writer uses some description and dialogue to add interest to the narrative and develop experiences and events.

What happened? I felt nothing. We were now out of the woods and into the clearing before the finish line. Still hopeful I could win, I pedaled even faster. Suddenly, there was a jerk. My pedals had stopped!

I looked down. Oh no! My shoelace was wrapped around my pedal! Thad's stick had untied it!

> The narrative demonstrates accuracy in standard English conventions of usage and mechanics.

I looked for a place to crash. That's when my head started tingling. I looked down at the shoelace. I concentrated really hard. I could see the scissors in my mind, floating just beside the pedal. Snip! The shoelace broke and my foot was free.

Thad was too busy listening to his fans cheer him on as I rode past him. Thanks to the mind-scissors, I won.

> The conclusion follows from the rest of the narrative.

WRITING

MODEL

NARRATIVE: SCORE 4

Mind-Scissors

As long as I wear my bike helmet, they say I'll be okay. Lots of people live with pieces of metal in their heads. We just have to be careful. When I was a baby I wound up with a tiny pair of scissors in mine. What the doctors couldn't have predicted is the uncanny ability they would give me.

Every summer there's a bike race that ends at the lake. The kid who always wins is Thad Thomas the Third, who is popular, but if you ask me, it's because he knows how to sweet-talk everyone. This past summer that was about to change. It's also when I discovered what I could do with my mind-scissors.

The race starts. Right away, racers start falling behind. After what seemed an eternity pumping hard at my pedals, I knew the end had to be in sight. I looked ahead and all I could see was Thad and the opening to the woods—the last leg of the race.

I put my stamina to the test—pedaling harder than ever, I felt like steam was coming off my legs. Thad's red helmet came into view. As I could sense I was going to overtake him any second, I turned my head to flash him a look. Only, to my befuddlement, Thad was the one who was gloating! And then I saw it—he was holding a stick he had pulled off a low-hanging branch.

He jabbed it toward me. I swerved out of the way. Was he trying to poke me with it? I kept pedaling, shifting my eyes to the right, to see what he was going to do.

But I waited too long. Thad made a slashing motion. Then he tossed the stick aside, yelled, "Yes!" and zoomed forward.

What happened? I felt nothing. We were now out of the woods and into the clearing before the finish line. Still hopeful I could win, I pedaled even faster. Suddenly, there was a jerk. My pedals had stopped!

I looked down. Oh no! My shoelace was wrapped around my pedal! Thad's stick had untied the shoelace!

I coasted as I looked for a place to crash. That's when my head started tingling. I got this funny notion to try something. I looked down. I had the tangled shoelace in my sights. I concentrated really hard. I could see the scissors in my mind, floating just beside the pedal. Snip! The shoelace broke and my right foot was free.

Thad was busy motioning his fans to cheer him on as I made my greatest effort to pedal back up to speed. Guess who made it to the finish line first?

- The story's beginning is engaging and introduces the main character and situation in a way that appeals to a reader.

- The writer uses techniques such as dialogue and description to add interest to the narrative and to develop the characters and events.

- Events in the narrative progress in logical order and are linked by clear transitions.

- Writer uses vivid description and sensory language to convey the experiences in the narrative and to help the reader imagine the characters and scenes.

- The writer uses standard English conventions of usage and mechanics.

- Writer's conclusion follows from the events in the narrative.

Narrative Rubric

	Focus and Organization	Development of Ideas/Elaboration	Conventions
4	The introduction is engaging and introduces the characters and situation in a way that appeals to readers. Events in the narrative progress in logical order and are linked by clear transitions. The conclusion effectively follows from and reflects on the narrated experiences or events.	The narrative effectively includes techniques such as dialogue and description to add interest and to develop the characters and events. The narrative effectively includes precise words and phrases, relevant descriptive details, and sensory language to convey experiences and events. The narrative effectively establishes voice through word choice, sentence structure, and tone.	The narrative intentionally uses standard English conventions of usage and mechanics. The narrative effectively varies sentence patterns for meaning, reader interest, and style.
3	The introduction is somewhat engaging and clearly introduces the characters and situation. Events in the narrative progress logically and are often linked by transition words. The conclusion mostly follows from and reflects on the narrated experiences or events.	The narrative mostly includes dialogue and description to add interest and develop experiences and events. The narrative mostly includes precise words and sensory language to convey experiences and events. The narrative mostly establishes voice through word choice, sentence structure, and tone.	The narrative mostly demonstrates accuracy in standard English conventions of usage and mechanics. The narrative mostly varies sentence patterns for meaning, reader interest, and style.
2	The introduction occasionally introduces characters. Events in the narrative progress somewhat logically and are sometimes linked by transition words. The conclusion adds very little to the narrated experiences or events.	The narrative includes some dialogue and descriptions. The words in the narrative vary between vague and precise, and some sensory language is included. The narrative occasionally establishes voice through word choice, sentence structure, and tone.	The narrative demonstrates some accuracy in standard English conventions of usage and mechanics. The narrative occasionally varies sentence patterns for meaning, reader interest, and style.
1	The introduction does not introduce characters and an experience or there is no clear introduction. The events in the narrative do not progress logically. The ideas seem disconnected and the sentences are not linked by transitions. The conclusion does not connect to the narrative or there is no conclusion.	Dialogue and descriptions are not included in the narrative. The narrative does not incorporate sensory language or precise words to convey experiences and to develop characters. The narrative does not establish voice through word choice, sentence structure, and tone.	The narrative contains mistakes in standard English conventions of usage and mechanics. The narrative does not vary sentence patterns for meaning, reader interest, and style.

RESEARCH

Conducting Research

You can conduct research to gain more knowledge about a topic. Sources such as articles, books, interviews, or the Internet have the facts and explanations that you need. Not all of the information that you find, however, will be useful—or reliable. Strong research skills will help you find accurate information about your topic.

Narrowing or Broadening a Topic

The first step in any research is finding your topic. Choose a topic that is narrow enough to cover completely. If you can name your topic in just one or two words, it is probably too broad. Topics such as mythology, hip hop music, or Italy are too broad to cover in a single report. Narrow a broad topic into smaller subcategories.

When you begin to research, pay attention to the amount of information available. If there is way too much information on your topic, you may need to narrow your topic further.

You might also need to broaden a topic if there is not enough information for your purpose. A topic is too narrow when it can be thoroughly presented in less space than the required size of your assignment. It might also be too narrow if you can find little or no information in library and media sources. Broaden your topic by including other related ideas.

Generating Research Questions

Use research questions to focus your research. Specific questions can help you avoid wasting time. For example, instead of simply hunting for information about Peter Pan, you might ask, "What inspired J. M. Barrie to write the story of Peter Pan?" or "How have different artists shown Peter Pan?"

A research question may also lead you to find your topic sentence. The question can also help you focus your research plan. Write your question down and keep it in mind while you hunt for facts. Your question can prevent you from gathering unnecessary details. As you learn more about your topic, you can always rewrite your original question.

Consulting Print and Digital Sources

An effective research project combines information from multiple sources. It is important not to rely too heavily on a single source. The creativity and originality of your research depends on how you combine ideas from many places. Plan to include a variety of these resources:

- **Primary and Secondary Sources:** Use both primary sources (firsthand or original accounts, such as interview transcripts and newspaper articles) and secondary sources (accounts that are not created at the time of an event, such as encyclopedia entries).
- **Print and Digital Resources:** The Internet allows fast access to data, but print resources are often edited more carefully. Plan to include both print and digital resources in order to guarantee that your work is accurate.
- **Media Resources:** You can find valuable information in media resources such as documentaries, television programs, podcasts, and museum exhibitions.
- **Original Research:** Depending on your topic, you may wish to conduct original research to include among your sources. For example, you might interview experts or eyewitnesses or conduct a survey of people in your community.

Evaluating Sources It is important to evaluate the credibility and accuracy of any information you find. Ask yourself questions such as these to evaluate other sources:

- **Authority:** Is the author well known? What are the author's credentials? Does the source include references to other reliable sources? Does the author's tone win your confidence? Why or why not?
- **Bias:** Does the author have any obvious biases? What is the author's purpose for writing? Who is the target audience?
- **Currency:** When was the work created? Has it been revised? Is there more current information available?

Using Online Encyclopedias

Online encyclopedias are often written by anonymous contributors who are not required to fact-check information. These sites can be very useful as a launching point for research, but should not be considered accurate. Look for footnotes, endnotes, or hyperlinks that support facts with reliable sources that have been carefully checked by editors.

Tool Kit **R25**

RESEARCH

Using Search Terms

Finding information on the Internet is easy, but it can be a challenge to find facts that are useful and trustworthy. If you type a word or phrase into a search engine, you will probably get hundreds—or thousands—of results. However, those results are not guaranteed to be relevant or accurate.

These strategies can help you find information from the Internet:

- Create a list of topic keywords before you begin using a search engine. Use a thesaurus to expand your list.
- Enter six to eight keywords.
- Choose unique nouns. Most search engines ignore articles and prepositions. Verbs may lead to sources that are not useful. Use modifiers, such as adjectives, when necessary to specify a category. For example, you might enter "ancient Rome" instead of "Rome."
- Use quotation marks to focus a search. Place a phrase in quotation marks to find pages that include exactly that phrase. Add several phrases in quotation marks to narrow your results.
- Spell carefully. Many search engines correct spelling automatically, but they cannot catch every spelling error.
- Scan search results before you click them. The first result isn't always the most useful. Read the text and notice the domain before make a choice.
- Consult more than one search engine.

Evaluating Internet Domains

Not everything you read on the Internet is true, so you have to evaluate sources carefully. The last three letters of an Internet URL identify the site's domain, which can help you evaluate the information of the site.

- **.gov**—Government sites are sponsored by a branch of the United States federal government and are considered reliable.
- **.edu**—Information from an educational research center or department is likely to be carefully checked, but may include student pages that are not edited or monitored.
- **.org**—Organizations are nonprofit groups and usually maintain a high level of credibility but may still reflect strong biases.
- **.com** and **.net**—Commercial sites exist to make a profit. Information might be biased to show a product or service in a good light.

R26 RESOURCES: Tool Kit

Taking Notes

Use different strategies to take notes:

- Use index cards to create notecards and source cards. On each source card, record information about each source you use—author, title, publisher, date of publication, and relevant page numbers. On each notecard, record information to use in your writing. Use quotation marks when you copy exact words, and indicate the page number(s) on which the information appears.
- Photocopy articles and copyright pages. Then, highlight relevant information. Remember to include the Web addresses of printouts from online sources.
- Print articles from the Internet or copy them directly into a "notes" folder.

You will use these notes to help you write original text.

Source Card

```
                                        [A]
Papp, Joseph,
and Elizabeth Kirkland

Shakespeare Alive!

Bantam Books, 1988
```

Notecard

```
Only the upper classes could read.

Most of the common people in
Shakespeare's time could not read.
Source Card: A, p. 5.
```

Quote Accurately Responsible research begins with the first note you take. Be sure to quote and paraphrase your sources accurately so you can identify these sources later. In your notes, circle all quotations and paraphrases to distinguish them from your own comments. When photocopying from a source, include the copyright information. Include the Web addresses of printouts from online sources.

RESEARCH

Reviewing Research Findings

You will need to review your findings to be sure that you have collected enough accurate and appropriate information.

Considering Audience and Purpose

Always keep your audience in mind as you gather information. Different audiences may have very different needs. For example, if you are writing a report for your class about a topic you have studied together, you will not need to provide background information in your writing. However, if you are writing about the topic for a national student magazine, you cannot assume that all of your readers have the same information. You will need to provide background facts from reliable sources to help inform those readers about your subject. When thinking about your research and your audience, ask yourself:

- Who are my readers? For whom am I writing?
- Have I collected enough information to explain my topic to this audience?
- Do I need to conduct more research to explain my topic clearly?
- Are there details in my research that I can leave out because they are already familiar to my audience?

Your purpose for writing will also affect your research review. If you are researching to satisfy your own curiosity, you can stop researching when you feel you understand the answer completely. If you are writing a research report that will be graded, you need to think about your assignment. When thinking about whether or not you have enough information, ask yourself:

- What is my purpose for writing?
- Will the information I have gathered be enough to achieve my purpose?
- If I need more information, where might I find it?

Synthesizing Sources

Effective research writing is more than just a list of facts and details. Good research synthesizes—gathers, orders, and interprets—those elements. These strategies will help you synthesize effectively:

- Review your notes. Look for connections and patterns among the details you have collected.
- Organize notes or notecards to help you plan how you will combine details.
- Pay close attention to details that emphasize the same main idea.
- Also look for details that challenge each other. For many topics, there is no single correct opinion. You might decide to conduct additional research to help you decide which side of the issue has more support.

Types of Evidence

When reviewing your research, also think about the kinds of evidence you have collected. The strongest writing combines a variety of evidence. This chart describes three of the most common types of evidence.

TYPE OF EVIDENCE	DESCRIPTION	EXAMPLE
Statistical evidence includes facts and other numerical data used to support a claim or explain a topic.	Statistical evidence are facts about a topic, such as historical dates, descriptions about size and number, and poll results.	Jane Goodall began to study chimpanzees when she was 26 years old.
Testimonial evidence includes any ideas or opinions presented by others. Testimonies might be from experts or people with special knowledge about a topic.	Firsthand testimonies present ideas from eyewitnesses to events or subjects being discussed.	Goodall's view of chimps has changed: "When I first started at Gombe, I thought the chimps were nicer than we are. But time has revealed that they are not. They can be just as awful."
	Secondary testimonies include commentaries on events by people who were not directly involved.	Science writer David Quammen points out that Goodall "set a new standard, a very high standard, for behavioral study of apes in the wild."
Anecdotal evidence presents one person's view of the world, often by describing specific events or incidents.	An anecdote is a story about something that happened. Personal stories can be part of effective research, but they should not be the only kind of evidence presented. Anecdotes are particularly useful for proving that broad generalizations are not accurate.	It is not fair to say that it is impossible for dogs to use tools. One researcher reports the story of a dog that learned to use a large bone as a back scratcher.

Tool Kit **R29**

RESEARCH

Incorporating Research Into Writing

Avoiding Plagiarism

Whether you are presenting a formal research paper or an opinion paper on a current event, you must be careful to give credit for any ideas or opinions that are not your own. Presenting someone else's ideas, research, or opinion as your own—even if you have phrased it in different words—is *plagiarism*, the equivalent of academic stealing, or fraud.

Do not use the ideas or research of others in place of your own. Read from several sources to draw your own conclusions and form your own opinions. Incorporate the ideas and research of others to support your points. Credit the source of the following types of support:

- Statistics
- Direct quotations
- Indirectly quoted statements of opinions
- Conclusions presented by an expert
- Facts available in only one or two sources

When you are drafting and revising, circle any words or ideas that are not your own. Follow the instructions on pages R32 and R33 to correctly cite those passages.

Reviewing for Plagiarism Take time to review your writing for accidental plagiarism. Read what you have written and take note of any ideas that do not have your personal writing voice. Compare those passages with your resource materials. You might have copied them without remembering the exact source. Add a correct citation to give credit to the original author. If you cannot find the questionable phrase in your notes, think about revising your word choices. You want to be sure that your final writing reflects your own thinking and not someone else's work.

Quoting and Paraphrasing

When including ideas from research into your writing, you will decide to quote directly or paraphrase.

Direct Quotation Use the author's exact words when they are interesting or persuasive. You might decide to include direct quotations in these situations:

- to share a strong statement
- to reference a historically significant passage
- to show that an expert agrees with your position
- to present an argument to which you will respond

Include complete quotations, without deleting or changing words. If you need to leave out words for space or clarity, use ellipsis points to show where you removed words. Enclose direct quotations in quotation marks.

Paraphrase A paraphrase restates an author's ideas in your own words. Be careful to paraphrase accurately. Beware of making sweeping generalizations in a paraphrase that were not made by the original author. You may use some words from the original source, but a good paraphrase does more than simply rearrange an author's phrases, or replace a few words with synonyms.

Original Text	"Some teens doing homework while listening to music and juggling tweets and texts may actually work better that way, according to an intriguing new study performed by two high-school seniors." Sumathi Reddy, "Teen Researchers Defend Media Multitasking"
Patchwork Plagiarism phrases from the original are rearranged, but they too closely follow the original text.	An intriguing new study conducted by two high-school seniors suggests that teens work better when they are listening to music and juggling texts and tweets.
Good Paraphrase	Two high-school students studied homework habits. They concluded that some people do better work while multitasking, such as studying and listening to music or checking text messages at the same time.

Maintaining the Flow of Ideas

Effective research writing is much more that just a list of facts. Maintain the flow of ideas by connecting research information to your own ideas. Instead of simply stating a piece of evidence, use transitions to connect information you found from outside resources and your own thinking. The transitions in the box on the page can be used to introduce, compare, contrast, and clarify.

Choosing an effective organizational strategy for your writing will help you create a logical flow of ideas. Once you have chosen a clear organization, add research in appropriate places to provide evidence and support.

Useful Transitions

When providing examples:

for example   for instance   to illustrate   in [name of resource], [author]

When comparing and contrasting ideas or information:

in the same way   similarly   however   on the other hand

When clarifying ideas or opinions:

in other words   that is   to explain   to put it another way

RESEARCH

ORGANIZATIONAL STRUCTURE	USES
Chronological order presents information in the sequence in which it happens.	historical topics; science experiments; analysis of narratives
Part-to-whole order examines how several categories affect a larger subject.	analysis of social issues; historical topics
Order of importance presents information in order of increasing or decreasing importance.	persuasive arguments; supporting a bold or challenging thesis
Comparison-and-contrast organization presents similarities and differences.	addressing two or more subjects

Formats for Citing Sources

When you cite a source, you acknowledge where you found your information and you give your readers the details necessary for locating the source themselves. Within the body of a paper, you provide a short citation, a footnote number linked to a footnote, or an endnote number linked to an endnote reference. These brief references show the page numbers on which you found the information. Prepare a reference list at the end of a research report to provide full bibliographic information on your sources. These are two common types of reference lists:

- A bibliography provides a listing of all the resources you consulted during your research.
- A works-cited list indicates the works your have referenced in your writing.

The chart on the next page shows the Modern Language Association format for crediting sources. This is the most common format for papers written in the content areas in middle school and high school. Unless instructed otherwise by your teacher, use this format for crediting sources.

Focus on Citations When you revise your writing, check that you cite the sources for quotations, factual information, and ideas that are not your own. Most word-processing programs have features that allow you to create footnotes and endnotes.

Identifying Missing Citations These strategies can help you find facts and details that should be cited in your writing:

- Look for facts that are not general knowledge. If a fact was unique to one source, it needs a citation.
- Read your report aloud. Listen for words and phrases that do not sound like your writing style. You might have picked them up from a source. If so, use you notes to find the source, place the words in quotation marks, and give credit.
- Review your notes. Look for ideas that you used in your writing but did not cite.

R32 RESOURCES: Tool Kit

MLA (8th Edition) Style for Listing Sources

Book with one author	Pyles, Thomas. *The Origins and Development of the English Language.* 2nd ed., Harcourt Brace Jovanovich, 1971. [Indicate the edition or version number when relevant.]
Book with two authors	Pyles, Thomas, and John Algeo. *The Origins and Development of the English Language.* 5th ed., Cengage Learning, 2004.
Book with three or more authors	Donald, Robert B., et al. *Writing Clear Essays.* Prentice Hall, 1983.
Book with an editor	Truth, Sojourner. *Narrative of Sojourner Truth.* Edited by Margaret Washington, Vintage Books, 1993.
Introduction to a work in a published edition	Washington, Margaret. Introduction. *Narrative of Sojourner Truth,* by Sojourner Truth, edited by Washington, Vintage Books, 1993, pp. v–xi.
Single work in an anthology	Hawthorne, Nathaniel. "Young Goodman Brown." *Literature: An Introduction to Reading and Writing,* edited by Edgar V. Roberts and Henry E. Jacobs, 5th ed., Prentice Hall, 1998, pp. 376–385. [Indicate pages for the entire selection.]
Signed article from an encyclopedia	Askeland, Donald R. "Welding." *World Book Encyclopedia,* vol. 21, World Book, 1991, p. 58.
Signed article in a weekly magazine	Wallace, Charles. "A Vodacious Deal." *Time,* 14 Feb. 2000, p. 63.
Signed article in a monthly magazine	Gustaitis, Joseph. "The Sticky History of Chewing Gum." *American History,* Oct. 1998, pp. 30–38.
Newspaper article	Thurow, Roger. "South Africans Who Fought for Sanctions Now Scrap for Investors." *Wall Street Journal,* 11 Feb. 2000, pp. A1+. [For a multipage article that does not appear on consecutive pages, write only the first page number on which it appears, followed by the plus sign.]
Unsigned editorial or story	"Selective Silence." Editorial. *Wall Street Journal,* 11 Feb. 2000, p. A14. [If the editorial or story is signed, begin with the author's name.]
Signed pamphlet or brochure	[Treat the pamphlet as though it were a book.]
Work from a library subscription service	Ertman, Earl L. "Nefertiti's Eyes." *Archaeology,* Mar.–Apr. 2008, pp. 28–32. *Kids Search,* EBSCO, New York Public Library. Accessed 7 Jan. 2017. [Indicating the date you accessed the information is optional but recommended.]
Filmstrips, slide programs, videocassettes, DVDs, and other audiovisual media	*The Diary of Anne Frank.* 1959. Directed by George Stevens, performances by Millie Perkins, Shelley Winters, Joseph Schildkraut, Lou Jacobi, and Richard Beymer, Twentieth Century Fox, 2004. [Indicating the original release date after the title is optional but recommended.]
CD-ROM (with multiple publishers)	Simms, James, editor. *Romeo and Juliet.* By William Shakespeare, Attica Cybernetics / BBC Education / Harper, 1995.
Radio or television program transcript	"Washington's Crossing of the Delaware." *Weekend Edition Sunday,* National Public Radio, 23 Dec. 2013. Transcript.
Web page	"Fun Facts About Gum." ICGA, 2005–2017, www.gumassociation.org/index.cfm/facts-figures/fun-facts-about-gum. Accessed 19 Feb. 2017. [Indicating the date you accessed the information is optional but recommended.]
Personal interview	Smith, Jane. Personal interview, 10 Feb. 2017.

All examples follow the style given in the MLA Handbook, 8th edition, published in 2016.

PROGRAM RESOURCES

MODEL

Evidence Log

Unit Title: _Discovery_

Perfomance-Based Assessment Prompt: _Do all discoveries benefit humanity?_

My initial thoughts: _Yes – all knowledge moves us forward._

> As you read multiple texts about a topic, your thinking may change. Use an Evidence Log like this one to record your thoughts, to track details you might use in later writing or discussion, and to make further connections.
>
> Here is a sample to show how one reader's ideas deepened as she read two texts.

Title of Text: _Classifying the Stars_ Date: _Sept. 17_

CONNECTION TO THE PROMPT	TEXT EVIDENCE/DETAILS	ADDITIONAL NOTES/IDEAS
Newton shared his discoveries and then other scientists built on his discoveries.	Paragraph 2: "Isaac Newton gave to the world the results of his experiments on passing sunlight through a prism." Paragraph 3: "In 1814 . . . the German optician, Fraunhofer . . . saw that the multiple spectral tints . . . were crossed by hundreds of fine dark lines."	It's not always clear how a discovery might benefit humanity in the future.

How does this text change or add to my thinking? _This confirms what I think._ Date: _Sept. 20_

Title of Text: _Cell Phone Mania_ Date: _Sept. 21_

CONNECTION TO THE PROMPT	TEXT EVIDENCE/DETAILS	ADDITIONAL NOTES/IDEAS
Cell phones have made some forms of communication easier, but people don't talk to each other as much as they did in the past.	Paragraph 7: "Over 80% of young adults state that texting is their primary method of communicating with friends. This contrasts with older adults who state that they prefer a phone call."	Is it good that we don't talk to each other as much? Look for article about social media to learn more about this question.

How does this text change or add to my thinking? _Maybe there are some downsides to discoveries. I still think that knowledge moves us forward, but sometimes there are negative effects._ Date: _Sept. 25_

TOOL KIT

MODEL

Word Network

A word network is a collection of words related to a topic. As you read the selections in a unit, identify interesting theme-related words and build your vocabulary by adding them to your Word Network.

Use your Word Network as a resource for your discussions and writings. Here is an example:

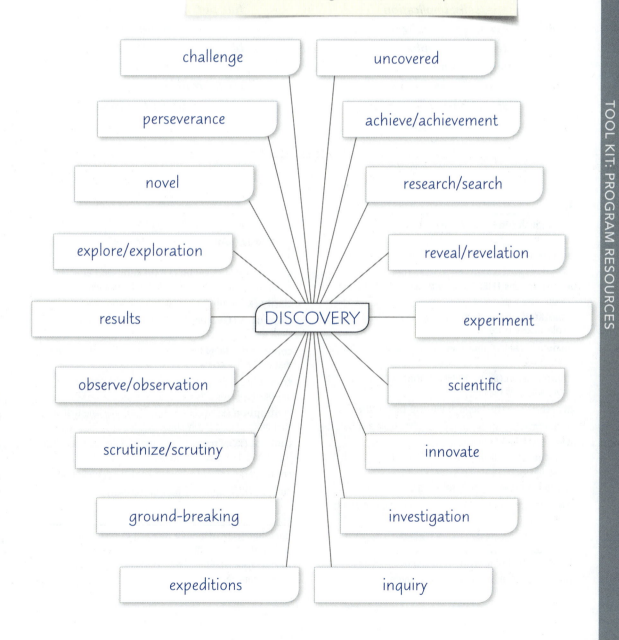

ACADEMIC / CONCEPT VOCABULARY

Academic vocabulary appears in **blue type**.

Pronunciation Key

Symbol	Sample Words	Symbol	Sample Words
a	at, catapult, Alabama	oo	boot, soup, crucial
ah	father, charms, argue	ow	now, stout, flounder
ai	care, various, hair	oy	boy, toil, oyster
aw	law, maraud, caution	s	say, nice, press
awr	pour, organism, forewarn	sh	she, abolition, motion
ay	ape, sails, implication	u	full, put, book
ee	even, teeth, really	uh	ago, focus, contemplation
eh	ten, repel, elephant	ur	bird, urgent, perforation
ehr	merry, verify, terribly	y	by, delight, identify
ih	it, pin, hymn	yoo	music, confuse, few
o	shot, hopscotch, condo	zh	pleasure, treasure, vision
oh	own, parole, rowboat		

A

accomplish (uh KOM plihsh) *v.* carry out; finish or complete

achieve (uh CHEEV) *v.* succeed in doing something you want to do

aesthetic (ehs THEHT ihk) *adj.* sensitive to art and beauty

annotated (AN uh tayt ihd) *adj.* containing explanatory notes

anxiously (ANGK shuhs lee) *adv.* in a nervous or worried way

apprehension (ap rih HEHN shuhn) *n.* fearful feeling about what will happen next

art (ahrt) *v.* archaic form of the verb *be*, used with *thou*

assimilate (uh SIHM uh layt) *v.* absorb, as a culture or ideas; make part of oneself

attribute (uh TRIHB yoot) *v.* indicate the cause of; give the origin of

audio (AW dee oh) *adj.* relating to the sound of a film

awakenings (uh WAY kuhn ihngz) *n.* acts of waking up from sleep

B

beaming (BEEM ihng) *v.* smiling broadly with happiness

bickering (BIHK uhr ihng) *n.* arguing over unimportant things

C

candid (KAN dihd) *adj.* very honest; informal; unposed

cautiously (KAW shuhs lee) *adv.* carefully, to avoid danger

chronological (kron uh LOJ uh kuhl) *adj.* arranged in a sequence that follows the time order of events

clarity (KLAR uh tee) *n.* state of thinking clearly

close-up (KLOHS uhp) *n.* camera shot taken from a short distance

confidently (KON fuh duhnt lee) *adv.* with the belief that one will succeed

contradict (kon truh DIHKT) *v.* say the opposite of what has been said; disagree

contraption (kuhn TRAP shuhn) *n.* machine that seems strange or unnecessarily complicated

contrast (KON trast) *n.* amount of difference between bright and dark elements in filming and viewing

controversy (KON truh vuhr see) *n.* quarrel or dispute

current (KUR uhnt) *n.* flow of electricity

D

decipher (dih SY fuhr) *v.* succeed in interpreting or understanding something

declaration (dehk luh RAY shuhn) *n.* announcement; formal statement

R36 GLOSSARY

deficiencies (dih FIHSH uhn seez) *n.* lackings; missing essentials

despised (dih SPYZD) *v.* hated; scorned

deterioration (dih tihr ee uh RAY shuhn) *n.* process of becoming worse

determination (dih tuhr muh NAY shuhn) *n.* quality of pursuing a goal even when it is difficult

dictate (DIHK tayt) *v.* give orders to control or influence something

dismay (dihs MAY) *n.* strong feeling of disappointment

dissent (dih SEHNT) *n.* difference in belief or opinion; disagreement

documentation (dok yuh muhn TAY shuhn) *n.* printed information; proof

E

enable (ehn AY buhl) *v.* make possible

encapsulation (ehn kap suh LAY shuhn) *n.* choice of which scenes to capture, or display, in panels

engineer (ehn jih NEER) *n.* person with scientific training who designs and builds machines, products, or systems

enumerate (ih NOO muh rayt) *v.* specify, as in a list; count

exemption (ehg ZEHMP shuhn) *n.* permission not to do or pay for something that others are required to do or pay

F

fair (fair) *adj.* beautiful; lovely

fatigue (fuh TEEG) *n.* physical or mental exhaustion

focus (FOH kuhs) *v.* aim the camera so that it creates a distinct image

forbidden (fuhr BIHD uhn) *v.* not permitted

foreboding (fawr BOH dihng) *n.* sudden feeling that something bad is going to happen

foresight (FAWR syt) *n.* knowledge or insight gained by looking toward the future

frail (frayl) *adj.* delicate; weak

G

generators (JEHN uh ray tuhrz) *n.* machines that produce electricity

gratifying (GRAT uh fy ihng) *adj.* satisfying; pleasing

H

horizon (huh RY zuhn) *n.* the distant line where the sky appears to meet the surface of the earth

humiliation (hyoo mihl ee AY shuhn) *n.* feeling of shame or embarassment

hysterically (hihs TEHR ihk lee) *adv.* in a way that shows uncontrolled emotion

I

icons (Y konz) *n.* symbols or graphic representations, often used in charts and on digital screens

immense (ih MEHNS) *adj.* very large; huge

implemented (IHM pluh mehnt ihd) *adj.* carried out; put into effect

impose ((ihm POHZ) *v.* force a law, idea, or belief on someone by using authority

improvisations (ihm pruh vy ZAY shuhnz) *n.* things that are created without any preparation

infographic (ihn foh GRAF ihk) *n.* image used to present information, data, or knowledge quickly and clearly

ingenuity (ihn juh NOO uh tee) *n.* quality of being original and clever

insistent (ihn SIHS tuhnt) *adj.* demanding that something should happen

inspire (ihn SPYR) *v.* stimulate to some creative or effective effort

integrate (IHN tuh grayt) *v.* bring together different parts

intentions (ihn TEHN shuhnz) *n.* purposes for or goals of one's actions

intervene (ihn tuhr VEEN) *v.* interfere with; take action to try to stop a dispute or conflict

introspective (ihn truh SPEHK tihv) *adj.* thoughtful; inward-looking

intuition (ihn too IHSH uhn) *n.* ability to see the truth of something immediately without reasoning

invincible (ihn VIHN suh buhl) *adj.* impossible to defeat

J

justifiable (juhs tuh FY uh buhl) *adj.* able to be defended as correct; reasonable and logical

L

labels and captions (LAY buhlz) (KAP shuhnz) *n.* short descriptive words or phrases that provide information

legitimate (luh JIHT uh miht) *adj.* allowed; legal; valid

M

majestic (muh JEHS tihk) *adj.* very grand; dignified; king-like

mandates (MAN dayts) *n.* orders or commands

misrepresentations (mihs rehp rih zehn TAY shuhnz) *n.* false statements

misunderstandings (mihs uhn duhr STAND ihngz) *n.* failures in coming to agreements; minor disputes

mounting (MOWN tihng) *adj.* increasing gradually; building up

myopic (my OP ihk) *adj.* nearsighted; unable to see clearly; showing a lack of understanding

N

naiveté (nah eev TAY) *n.* quality of innocent simplicity

narration (na RAY shuhn) *n.* commentary that accompanies a film

nervously (NUR vuhs lee) *adv.* in a manner that shows worry or fear

newfangled (NOO fang uhld) *adj.* invented only recently and, therefore, strange-seeming

notable (NOH tuh buhl) *adj.* worth noticing; important

numerous (NOO muhr uhs) *adj.* very many; existing in large numbers

O

obligations (ob lih GAY shuhnz) *n.* debts to someone due to past promises or favors

observation (ob suhr VAY shuhn) *n.* act of watching carefully to obtain information

opponent (uh POH nuhnt) *n.* person on the other side in a game, debate, argument, etc.

outcry (OWT kry) *n.* strong expression of anger in reaction to an event

P

pan (pan) *n.* vertical or horizontal camera motion used to follow a subject

panel (PAN uhl) *n.* individual frame of a graphic novel depicting a single moment

parallel (PAR uh lehl) *adj.* similar and happening at the same time

patronized (PAY truh nyzd) *v.* treated someone as inferior

peak (peek) *n.* highest level

performance (puhr FAWR muhns) *n.* entertainment presented before an audience, such as music or a drama

persecuted (PUR suh kyoo tihd) *v.* treated unfairly and cruelly

persistent (puhr SIHS tuhnt) *adj.* continuing; lasting, especially in the face of difficulty

personal account (PUR suh nuhl) (uh KOWNT) *n.* account of a personal experience, told from the first-person point of view

position (puh ZIH shuhn) *n.* point of view or stand taken on an issue

prescient (PREHSH uhnt) *adj.* having knowledge of things before they happen

principle (PRIHN suh puhl) *n.* moral rule or set of ideas about right or wrong that influences individuals to behave in a certain way

pronounce (pruh NOWNS) *v.* say a word in the correct way; officially announce

psychological (sy kuh LOJ ih kuhl) *adj.* of the mind; mental

purposeful (PUR puhs fuhl) *adj.* having a clear aim or goal

pursue (puhr SOO) *v.* continue doing an activity over a period of time

Q

quarrels (KWAWR uhlz) *n.* arguments; disagreements

R

rational (RASH uh nuhl) *adj.* able to make decisions based on reason rather than emotion; sensible

rectify (REHK tuh fy) *v.* correct; set right

regression (rih GREHSH uhn) *n.* return to a previous, less advanced state

restraining (rih STRAY nihng) *v.* holding back; controlling one's emotions

restrictions (rih STRIHK shuhnz) *n.* limitations; rules that limit activities

retort (rih TAWRT) *n.* witty, sharp reply

revolutionized (rehv uh LOO shuh nyzd) *v.* drastically changed; improved

rigid (RIHJ ihd) *adj.* stiff and unbending

S

sacrifices (SAK ruh fys ihz) *n.* acts of giving up needs or desires for a purpose

seminal (SEHM uh nuhl) *adj.* being the first of something that is later recognized as important

sheepishly (SHEEP ihsh lee) *adv.* in an embarrassed way

speculate (SPEHK yuh layt) *v.* make a guess about something unknown

speech balloon (speech) (buh LOON) *n.* display of what a character is speaking or thinking

spiral (SPY ruhl) *n.* winding circle around a central point

status quo (STAT uhs kwoh) *n.* existing state or condition at a particular time

straggled (STRAG uhld) *v.* hung in messy strands

subconscious (suhb KON shuhs) *n.* mental activity that occurs without someone's being aware of it

suspicion (suh SPIHSH uhn) *n.* feeling of doubt or mistrust

sustain (suh STAYN) *v.* maintain or keep up

sychronization, sync (sihng kruh nih ZAY shuhn) (sihngk) *n.* coordination of motion and sound

symmetrical (sih MEH trih kuhl) *adj.* having the same form on both sides of a dividing line

T

tackling (TAK lihng) *v.* dealing with or handling a problem or situation

tendency (TEHN duhn see) *n.* inclination; way of behaving that is likely or becoming common

tension (TEHN shuhn) *n.* nervous, worried, or excited condition that makes relaxation impossible

theorize (THEE uh ryz) *v.* form an explanation based on observation and reasoning; speculate

traumatized (TRAW muh tyzd) *adj.* severely hurt; suffering serious emotional injury

tress (trehs) *n.* a woman's or girl's hair

triumph (TRY uhmf) *n.* victory; success

U

unleashed (uhn LEESHT) *v.* released; set loose on the world

urgently (UR juhnt lee) *adv.* in a manner that requires immediate attention

V

verify (VEHR uh fy) *v.* prove to be true

video clip (VIHD ee oh) (klihp) *n.* short video, often part of a larger recording, that can be used on a website

volume and pacing (VOL yoom) (PAYS ihng) *n.* softness or loudness of one's voice and the rate at which one speaks

W

wearily (WEER uh lee) *adv.* in a tired way

Z

zoom (zoom) *v.* enlarge, magnify, or close in on an image

Academic / Concept Vocabulary

VOCABULARIO ACADÉMICO/ VOCABULARIO DE CONCEPTOS

El vocabulario académico está en **letra azul**.

A

accomplish / lograr *v.* alcanzar una meta; terminar

achieve / lograr *v.* tener éxito en algo que se quiere hacer

aesthetic / estético *adj.* sensible al arte y la belleza

annotated / comentado *adj.* marcado con notas explicativas

anxiously / ansiosamente *adv.* de manera nerviosa o con preocupación

apprehension / aprensión *s.* sentimiento de temor hacia lo que va a suceder

art / sois *v.* forma arcaica del verbo *ser*, usado con *vos*

assimilate / asimilar *v.* absorber una cultura o ideas

attribute / atribuir *v.* indicar la causa de; dar el origin de

audio / sonoro *adj.* relativo al sonido de una película

awakenings / despertares *s.* actos de despertarse

B

beaming / sonriente *adj.* que sonríe con alegría

bickering / reñir *v.* discutir por cosas sin importancia

C

candid / franco *adj.* muy honesto; informal, sin pretensiones

cautiously / cautelosamente *adv.* cuidadosamente, para evitar el peligro

chronological / cronológico *adj.* clasificado en una secuencia que sigue el orden en que ocurrieron eventos

clarity / claridad *s.* estado en el que se piensa claramente

close-up / primer plano *s.* toma de cámara a corta distancia

confidently / confiadamente *adv.* con la certeza de que se tendrá éxito

contradict / contradecir *v.* decir lo opuesto a lo que se ha dicho; discrepar

contraption / artilugio *s.* máquina que parece extraña o innecesariamente complicada

contrast / constraste *s.* cantidad de diferencia entre los elementos brillantes y oscuros de una película

controversy / controversia *s.* desacuerdo o disputa

current / corriente *s.* flujo de electricidad

D

decipher / descifrar *v.* interpretar o comprender algo desconocido

declaration / declaración *s.* anuncio; revelación formal

deficiencies / deficiencias *s.* insuficiencias; falta de lo esencial

despised / detestó *v.* odió; aborreció

deterioration / deterioro *s.* proceso de empeorar

determination / determinación *s.* cualidad de perseguir una meta aun cuando sea difícil

dictate / dictar *v.* dar órdenes para controlar o influir sobre algo

dismay / desaliento *s.* consternación o pena

documentation / documentación *s.* información impresa; prueba

E

enable / posibilitar *v.* permitir; hacer posible

encapsulation / encapsulación *s.* elección de escenas importantes para capturar, o mostrar, en paneles

engineer / ingeniero *s.* persona con entrenamiento científico que diseña y construye máquinas, productos o sistemas

enumerate / enumerar *v.* especificar en forma de lista; contar

exemption / exención *s.* permiso de no hacer o pagar por algo que los demás deben hacer o pagar

F

fair / hermoso *adj.* precioso; bonito

fatigue / fatiga *s.* agotamiento físico o mental

focus / enfocar *v.* apuntar la cámara para que forme una imagen nítida

forbidden / prohibido *v.* no permitido

foreboding / presagio *s.* ansiedad repentina de que va a suceder algo malo

foresight / previsión *s.* visión del futuro; consideración o provisión para el futuro

frail / frágil *adj.* delicado; débil

G

generators / generadores *s.* máquinas que producen electricidad

gratifying / gratificante *v.* que satisface o complace

H

horizon / horizonte *s.* la línea distante donde el cielo parece unirse a la superficie terrestre

humiliation / humillación *s.* sentimiento de vergüenza o turbación

hysterically / histéricamente *adv.* de forma que muestra emociones descontroladas

I

icons / íconos *s.* símbolos o representaciones gráficas que se usan con frecuencia en tablas y en pantallas digitales

immense / inmenso *adj.* muy grande; enorme

implemented / implementó *v.* llevó a cabo; realizó

impose / imponer *v.* obligar a otros a seguir una ley o idea por fuerza de autoridad

improvisations / improvisaciones *s.* cosas que se crean sin ninguna preparación

infographic / infografía *s.* imagen que se usa para presentar información y conocimientos de manera rápida y sencilla

ingenuity / ingenio *s.* calidad de ser original y listo

insistent / insistente *adj.* que exige que algo ocurra

inspire / inspirar *v.* estimular para lograr algún esfuerzo creativo o efectivo

integrate / integrar *v.* abolir la segregación; unir diferentes partes

intentions / intenciones *s.* propósitos o metas de las acciones de alguien

intervene / intervenir *v.* interferir con; tomar acción para tratar de detener una disputa o conflicto

introspective / introspectivo *adj.* reflexivo; introvertido

intuition / intuición *s.* capacidad de ver la verdad de algo inmediatamente, sin razonarlo

invincible / invencible *adj.* imposible de vencer

J

justifiable / justificable *adj.* capaz de ser defendido como correcto, razonable y lógico

L

labels and captions / rótulos y leyendas *s.* frases cortas y descriptivas que proveen información

legitimate / legítimo *adj.* permitido; legal; válido

M

majestic / majestuoso *adj.* muy grande; digno; de reyes

mandates / mandatos *s.* órdenes

misrepresentations / distorsiones *s.* declaraciones falsas

misunderstandings / malentendidos *s.* fracasos al intentar llegar a un acuerdo; disputas menores

mounting / creciente *adj.* que incrementa gradualmente; que se acumula

myopic / miope *adj.* que no puede ver bien de lejos; que ve sin claridad; falto de comprensión

N

naiveté / ingenuidad *s.* cualidad de la simplicidad inocente

narration / narración *s.* comentario que acompaña a una película

nervously / nerviosamente *adv.* mostrando preocupación o temor

newfangled / moderno *adj.* recién inventado y, a consecuencia, de aspecto extraño

notable / destacado *adj.* que merece atención; importante

numerous / numeroso *adj.* muchos; que existe en gran cantidad

O

obligations / obligaciones *s.* deudas que se le deben a alguien por promesas o favores pasados

observation / observación *s.* acto de mirar con atención para obtener información

opponent / oponente *s.* persona del otro lado del juego, debate, argumento, etc.

oughts / deberes *s.* obligaciones; compromisos

outcry / clamor *s.* expresión fuerte de protesta en contra de un evento

P

pan / paneo *s.* movimiento horizontal o vertical de la cámara

panel / viñeta *s.* cada uno de los recuadros de una novela gráfica en el que se representa una escena

parallel / paralelo *adj.* similar y que sucede al mismo tiempo

patronized / condescendió *v.* trató a alguien como inferior

peak / pico *s.* nivel más alto

penned / enjauló *v.* encerró a alguien como a un animal; encarceló

performance / representación *s.* entretenimiento musical, dramático o de otro tipo que se presenta ante un público

persecuted / acosó *v.* trató con injusticia y crueldad

persistent / persistente *adj.* duradero; que perdura, especialmente ante las dificultades

personal account / relato personal *s.* relato de una experiencia personal contado desde el punto de vista de primera persona

position / posición *s.* punto de vista tomado respecto de algo

prescient / profético *adj.* teniendo conocimiento de las cosas antes de que pasen

principle / principio *s.* regla moral o conjunto de ideas que influye sobre el comportamiento de individuos

pronounce / pronunciar *v.* decir una palabra de forma correcta; anunciar oficialmente

psychological / psicológico *adj.* de la mente; mental

purposeful / significante *adj.* que tiene una meta u objetivo claro

pursue / perseguir *v.* continuar una acción por un período de tiempo

Q

quarrels / peleas *s.* discusiones; desacuerdos

R

rational / racional *adj.* capaz de tomar decisiones basado en la razón; sensato

rectify / rectificar *v.* corregir; reparar

regression / regresión *s.* retroceso a un estado anterior menos avanzado

restraining / restringiendo *v.* reteniendo; controlando las emociones

restrictions / restricciones *s.* limitaciones; reglas que limitan las actividades

retort / réplica *s.* respuesta ingeniosa y brusca

revolutionized / revolucionó *v.* que cambió de forma drástica; mejoró

rigid / rígido *adj.* tieso e inflexible

S

sacrifices / sacrificios *s.* actos de abandonar las necesidades o deseos para lograr un propósito

seminal / trascendental *adj.* que es el primero o el más antiguo de algo

sheepishly / avergonzadamente *adv.* de manera vergonzosa

speculate / especular *v.* adivinar sobre lo desconocido

speech balloon / globo de diálogo *s.* espacio donde se contienen las palabras o pensamientos de un personaje

spiral / espiral *s.* círculos alrededor de un punto central

status quo / statu quo *s.* estado o condición de las cosas en un momento dado

straggled / desaliñó *v.* colocó de forma desaliñada o desordenada

subconscious / subconsciente *s.* actividad mental que ocurre sin que la persona la perciba

suspicion / sospecha *s.* sentimiento de duda; falta de confianza

sustain / sostener *v.* mantener o seguir el ritmo

sychronization, sync / sincronización *s.* coordinación de movimiento y sonido

symmetrical / simétrico *adj.* que tiene la misma forma a ambos lados de la recta que lo divide

T

tackling / afrontando *v.* lidiando con un problema o situación

tendency / tendencia *s.* inclinación; comportamiento probable o que se vuelve común

tensión / tensión *s.* estado de nerviosismo, preocupación o emoción que hace imposible la relajación

theorize / teorizar *v.* formar una explicación con base en la observación y razonamiento; especular

traumatized / traumatizado *adj.* herido o golpeado emocionalmente; gravemente afectado

tress / mechón *s.* cabello de una niña o mujer

triumph / triunfo *s.* victoria; éxito

U

unleashed / desató *v.* soltó; dio rienda suelta a

urgently / urgentemente *adv.* que requiere de atención inmediata

V

verify / verificar *v.* demostrar que es cierto

video clip / videoclip *s.* video corto, que suele ser parte de una grabación de mayor extensión, y que se puede usar en sitios web

volume and pacing / volumen y velocidad *s.* nivel de la voz y rapidez con que se habla

W

wearily / cansino *adv.* con aire cansado

Z

zoom / hacer zoom *v.* agrandar, magnificar o aumentar una imagen

LITERARY TERMS HANDBOOK

ALLITERATION *Alliteration* is the repetition of initial consonant sounds. Writers use alliteration to draw attention to certain words or ideas, to imitate sounds, and to create musical effects.

ALLUSION An *allusion* is a reference to a well-known person, event, place, literary work, or work of art. Allusions connect literary works to a larger cultural heritage. They allow the writer to express complex ideas without spelling them out. Understanding what a literary work is saying often depends on recognizing its allusions and the meanings they suggest.

ANALOGY An *analogy* makes a comparison between two or more things that are similar in some ways but otherwise unalike.

ANECDOTE An *anecdote* is a brief story about an interesting, amusing, or strange event. Writers tell anecdotes to entertain or to make a point.

ARGUMENT An *argument* is a logical way of presenting a belief, conclusion, or stance. A good argument must include at least one **claim** and be supported with reasoning and **evidence** that is **relevant**, or related, to the subject. If an author's beliefs and feelings are too prominent, the argument is less convincing and may seem **biased** or one-sided.

AUTHOR'S INFLUENCES An *author's influences* include his or her heritage, culture, and personal beliefs.

AUTHOR'S POINT OF VIEW The attitudes and approach that an author takes to a piece of informational writing shows the **author's point of view**, or the **author's perspective**.

AUTHOR'S PURPOSE An *author's purpose* is his or her main reason for writing. For example, an author may want to entertain, inform, or persuade the reader. Sometimes an author is trying to teach a moral lesson or reflect on an experience. An author may have more than one purpose for writing.

AUTHOR'S STYLE *Style* is an author's typical way of writing. Many factors determine a writer's style, including diction; tone; use of characteristic elements such as figurative language, dialect, rhyme, meter, or rhythmic devices; typical grammatical structures and patterns, typical sentence length, and typical methods of organization. Style comprises every feature of a writer's use of language.

AUTOBIOGRAPHY An *autobiography* is the story of the writer's own life, told by the writer. Autobiographical writing may tell about the person's whole life or only a part of it.

Because autobiographies are about real people and events, they are a form of nonfiction. Most autobiographies are written in the first person.

BIOGRAPHY A *biography* is a form of nonfiction in which a writer tells the life story of another person. Most biographies are written about famous or admirable people. Although biographies are nonfiction, the most effective ones share the qualities of good narrative writing.

BLURB A *blurb* is a short description of a piece of literature, often found on the back cover of a book.

CAUSE-AND-EFFECT ESSAY A *cause-and-effect essay* examines the relationship between events. Effective essays contain clearly stated thesis statements, with examples, evidence, and logic to support them.

CHARACTER A *character* is a person or an animal that takes part in the action of a literary work. The main, or **major**, character is the most important character in a story, poem, or play. A **minor** character is one who takes part in the action but is not the focus of attention.

Characters are sometimes classified as flat or round. A **flat character** is one-sided and often stereotypical. A **round character**, on the other hand, is fully developed and exhibits many traits—often both faults and virtues. Characters can also be classified as dynamic or static. A **dynamic character** is one who changes or grows during the course of the work. A **static character** is one who does not change.

CHARACTERIZATION *Characterization* is the act of creating and developing a character. Authors use two major methods of characterization—**direct** and **indirect**. When using **direct** characterization, a writer states the **character's traits**, or characteristics.

When describing a character **indirectly**, a writer depends on the reader to draw conclusions about the character's traits. Sometimes the writer tells what other participants in the story say and think about the character.

CHRONOLOGICAL ORDER Writers often sequence events in narratives using **chronological order**, so that one event proceeds to the next in the order in which they actually happened.

CHARACTER TRAITS *Character traits* are the qualities, attitudes, and values that a character has or displays—such as dependability, intelligence, selfishness, or stubbornness.

CLAIM A *claim* is a reasonable conclusion based on evidence. A **counterclaim** is an opposing position to a claim. Strong, specific, **narrow claims** are usually more effective than **broad claims** because they are easier to support with evidence.

CLIMAX The *climax,* also called the turning point, is the high point in the action of the plot. It is the moment of greatest tension, when the outcome of the plot hangs in the balance.

Literary Terms Handbook **R43**

COMPARE-AND-CONTRAST ESSAY An essay in which an author lays out the differences and similarities between two subjects is called a *compare-and-contrast essay*.

Compare-and-contrast essays can be organized using *point-by-point organization,* in which one aspect of both subjects is discussed, and then another aspect, and so on. *Block-method* organization presents all the details of one subject, and then all details about the next subject.

CONFLICT A *conflict* is a struggle between opposing forces. Conflict is one of the most important elements of stories, novels, and plays because it causes the action. There are two kinds of conflict: external and internal. An *external conflict* is one in which a character struggles against some outside force, such as another person. Another kind of external conflict may occur between a character and some force in nature.

An *internal conflict* takes place within the mind of a character. The character struggles to make a decision, take an action, or overcome a feeling.

CONNECTIONS Transition words show *clear connections* among claims, reasons, and evidence. *Unclear connections* can confuse and weaken arguments.

CONNOTATIONS The *connotation* of a word is the set of ideas associated with it in addition to its explicit meaning. The connotation of a word can be personal, based on individual experiences. More often, cultural connotations—those recognizable by most people in a group—determine a writer's word choices.

DENOTATION The *denotation* of a word is its *dictionary* meaning, independent of other associations that the word may have. The denotation of the word *lake*, for example, is "an inland body of water." "Vacation spot" and "place where the fishing is good" are connotations of the word *lake*.

DESCRIPTION A *description* is a portrait, in words, of a person, place, or object. Descriptive writing uses images that appeal to the five senses—sight, hearing, touch, taste, and smell.

DIALOGUE A *dialogue* is a conversation between characters. In poems, novels, and short stories, dialogue is usually set off by quotation marks to indicate a speaker's exact words.

In a play, dialogue follows the names of the characters, and no quotation marks are used.

DIARY A *diary* is a type of autobiographical writing. Entries to a diary or journal are made periodically over time.

DICTION *Diction* is a writer's or speaker's word choice. Diction is part of a writer's style and may be described as formal or informal, plain or fancy, ordinary or *technical*, sophisticated or down-to-earth, old-fashioned or modern.

DICTIONARY A *dictionary* is a reference resource that provides a word's meaning, its part of speech, pronunciation, and etymology.

DRAMA A *drama* is a story written to be performed by actors. Although a drama is meant to be performed, one can also read the script, or written version, and imagine the action. The *script* of a drama is made up of dialogue and stage directions. The *dialogue* is the words spoken by the actors. The *stage directions*, usually printed in italics, tell how the actors should look, move, and speak. They also describe the setting, sound effects, and lighting.

Dramas are often divided into parts called *acts.*

The acts are often divided into smaller parts called *scenes.*

DRAMA REVIEW A *drama review* is an evaluation of a dramatic performance. The writer's analysis and opinions are supported with examples.

ESSAY An *essay* is a short nonfiction work about a particular subject. Most essays have a single major focus and a clear introduction, body, and conclusion.

There are many types of essays. An *informal essay* uses casual, conversational language. A *historical essay* gives facts, explanations, and insights about historical events. An *expository essay* explains an idea by breaking it down. A *narrative essay* tells a story about a real-life experience. An *informational essay* explains a process. A *persuasive essay* offers an opinion and supports it. An *explanatory essay* is a short piece of nonfiction in which the author explains, defines, or interprets ideas, events, or processes. A *reflective essay* is a brief prose work in which an author presents his or her thoughts or feelings—or reflections—about an experience or an idea.

In an *argumentative essay* the writer states and supports a claim, based on factual evidence and logical reasoning. *Problem-and-solution essays* identify problems and make arguments, or claims about solutions.

EXAMPLE An *example* is a fact, idea, or event that supports an idea or insight.

EXPOSITION In the plot of a story or a drama, the *exposition,* or introduction, is the part of the work that introduces the characters, setting, and basic situation.

EXPLANATORY TEXT *Explanatory text* explains a process or provides directions.

EXPOSITORY WRITING *Expository writing* is a work that presents information, discusses ideas, or explains a process.

FACTS AND DETAILS *Facts and details* are forms of evidence a writer uses to support a thesis or opinion. Facts can be proven to be true.

FANTASY A *fantasy* is highly imaginative writing that contains elements not found in real life. Examples of

R44 GLOSSARY

fantasy include stories that involve supernatural elements, stories that resemble fairy tales, stories that deal with imaginary places and creatures, and science-fiction stories.

FICTION *Fiction* is prose writing that tells about imaginary characters and events. Short stories and novels are works of fiction. Some writers base their fiction on actual events and people, adding invented characters, dialogue, settings, and plots. Other writers rely on imagination alone.

FIGURATIVE LANGUAGE *Figurative language* is writing or speech that is not meant to be taken literally. The many types of figurative language are known as *figures of speech.* Common figures of speech include metaphor, personification, and simile. Writers use figurative language to state ideas in vivid and imaginative ways.

FORESHADOWING *Foreshadowing* is the author's use of clues to hint at what might happen later in the story. Writers use foreshadowing to build their readers' expectations and to create suspense.

FREE VERSE *Free verse* is poetry not written in a regular, rhythmical pattern, or meter. The poet is free to write lines of any length or with any number of stresses, or beats. Free verse is therefore less constraining than *metrical verse,* in which every line must have a certain length and a certain number of stresses.

GENRE A *genre* is a division or type of literature. Literature is commonly divided into three major genres: poetry, prose, and drama. Each major genre is, in turn, divided into lesser genres, as follows:

1. *Poetry:* lyric poetry, concrete poetry, dramatic poetry, narrative poetry, epic poetry
2. *Prose:* fiction (novels and short stories) and nonfiction (biography, autobiography, letters, essays, and reports)
3. *Drama:* serious drama and tragedy, comic drama, melodrama, and farce

HISTORICAL FICTION In *historical fiction,* real events, places, or people are incorporated into a fictional, or made-up, story.

HUMOR *Humor* is writing intended to evoke laughter or entertain. It can also be used to convey a serious theme.

IMAGERY *Imagery* is the use of vivid word pictures writers use to appeal to the five senses.

IMAGES *Images* are words or phrases that appeal to one or more of the five senses. Writers use images to describe how their subjects look, sound, feel, taste, and smell. Poets often paint images, or word pictures, that appeal to your senses. These pictures help you to experience the poem fully.

INFERENCE Making an educated guess about a character based on how he or she thinks, acts, or speaks is *making an inference*. Making an inference is sometimes referred to as *reading between the lines*.

INFORMATIVE TEXT *Informative text* provides information on a subject.

IRONY *Irony* is a contradiction between what happens and what is expected. There are three main types of irony. *Situational irony* occurs when something happens that directly contradicts the expectations of the characters or the audience. *Verbal irony* occurs when what is said is the exact opposite of what is meant. said. In *dramatic irony,* the audience is aware of something that the character or speaker is not.

JOURNAL A *journal* is a daily, or periodic, account of events and the writer's thoughts and feelings about those events. Personal journals are not normally written for publication, but sometimes they do get published later with permission from the author or the author's family.

LETTERS A *letter* is a written communication. In personal letters, the writer shares information and his or her thoughts and feelings with one other person or group. Although letters are not normally written for publication, they sometimes are published with the permission of the author or the author's family.

LOGICAL FALLACIES *Logical fallacies* are errors in reasoning that weaken an argument. Here are some examples: *Overgeneralization* is a false conclusion that ignores evidence to the contrary. A *slippery slope* assumes that B, C, and D, will happen because of A. *Ad populum* appeals to the audience's basic beliefs of right and wrong.

LYRIC POEM A *lyric poem* is a highly musical verse that expresses the observations and feelings of a single *speaker*. It creates a single, unified impression.

MAIN IDEA The *main idea* is the *central idea* or most important point in a text. To determine an *implied central* idea, make *inferences* based on what is known.

MEDIA Stories and information are shared using different forms of *media*. Books, magazines, film, television, and ebooks are all forms of media. A *multimedia presentation* contains a combination of words, images, sounds, and video.

MEDIA ACCOUNTS *Media accounts* are reports, explanations, opinions, or descriptions written for television, radio, newspapers, and magazines. While some media accounts report only facts, others include the writer's thoughts and reflections.

MEMOIR A *memoir* is a type of autobiography that focuses on a particularly meaningful period or series of events in the author's life. A memoir is typically written

Literary Terms Handbook **R45**

from the first-person point of view in which the author, or narrator, takes part in the story's events. The author will refer to himself or herself using the pronoun I.

METAPHOR A *metaphor* is a figure of speech in which something is described as though it were something else. A metaphor, like a simile, works by pointing out a similarity between two unlike things.

METER The *meter* of a poem is its rhythmical pattern. This pattern is determined by the number of *stresses*, or beats, in each line. To describe the meter of a poem, read it while emphasizing the beats in each line. Then, mark the stressed and unstressed syllables, as follows:

My fáth | ĕr wăs | thĕ first | tŏ hĕar |

As you can see, each strong stress is marked with a slanted line (´) and each unstressed syllable with a horseshoe symbol (˘). The weak and strong stresses are then divided by vertical lines (|) into groups called feet.

MONOLOGUE A *monologue* is a lengthy speech given by a character that expresses that character's point of view.

MOOD The *mood* is the feeling created in a reader by a piece of writing. Writers create mood by using imagery, word choice, and descriptive details.

MOTIVE A *motive* is a reason that explains or partially explains a character's thoughts, feelings, actions, or speech. Writers try to make their characters' motives, or *motivations*, as clear as possible. If the motives of a main character are not clear, then the character will not be well understood.

Characters are often driven by **external motivations** or needs, such as food and shelter. **Internal motivations** that drive characters are feelings, such as fear, love, and pride. Motives may be obvious or hidden.

MYTH A *myth* is a fictional tale that explains the actions of gods or heroes or the origins of elements of nature. Myths are part of the oral tradition. They are composed orally and then passed from generation to generation by word of mouth. Every ancient culture has its own mythology, or collection of myths. Greek and Roman myths are known collectively as **classical mythology.**

NARRATION *Narration* is writing that tells a story. The act of telling a story is also called narration. A story told in fiction, nonfiction, poetry, or even in drama is called a *narrative*.

NARRATIVE A *narrative* is a story. A narrative can be either fiction or nonfiction. Novels and short stories are types of fictional narratives. Biographies and autobiographies are nonfiction narratives. Poems that tell stories are also narratives. An author uses **narrative pacing** to regulate the speed and flow of information in a text.

NARRATIVE POEM A *narrative poem* is a story told in verse. Narrative poems often have all the elements of short stories, including characters, conflict, and plot.

NARRATOR A *narrator* is a speaker or a character who tells a story. The narrator's perspective is the way he or she sees things. A **third-person narrator** is one who stands outside the action and speaks about it. A **first-person narrator** is one who tells a story and participates in its action.

NONFICTION *Nonfiction* is prose writing that presents and explains ideas or that tells about real people, places, objects, or events. Autobiographies, biographies, essays, reports, letters, memos, and newspaper articles are all types of nonfiction.

NOVEL A *novel* is a long work of fiction. Novels contain such elements as characters, plot, conflict, and setting. The writer of novels, or novelist, develops these elements. In addition to its main plot, a novel may contain one or more subplots, or independent, related stories. A novel may also have several themes.

ONOMATOPOEIA *Onomatopoeia* is the use of words that imitate sounds. ***Crash, buzz, screech, hiss, neigh, jingle,*** and ***cluck*** are examples of onomatopoeia. ***Chickadee, towhee,*** and ***whippoorwill*** are onomatopoeic names of birds.

Onomatopoeia can help put the reader in the action of a poem.

OPINION An *opinion* is a person's judgment or belief. It may be supported by factual evidence, but it cannot be proved.

ORGANIZATION The *organization*, or structure of a text, depends on the topic and the author's purpose and reason for writing.

OXYMORON An *oxymoron* (pl. *oxymora*) is a figure of speech that links two opposite or contradictory words, to point out an idea or a situation that seems contradictory or inconsistent but on closer inspection turns out to be somehow true.

PARALLELISM *Parallelism* is the use of similar grammatical forms or patterns to express similar ideas. Parallelism adds rhythm and balance to writing and strengthens the connections among an author's ideas.

PARAPHRASE To *paraphrase* is to restate something you read or heard in your own words.

PERSONIFICATION *Personification* is a type of figurative language in which a nonhuman subject is given human characteristics.

PERSUASION *Persuasion* is used in writing or speech that attempts to convince the reader or listener to adopt a particular opinion or course of action. Newspaper editorials and letters to the editor use persuasion, as do advertisements and campaign speeches given by political candidates. Writers use a variety of persuasive techniques to argue their point of view. **Appeals to authority** use the statements of experts. **Appeals to emotion** use words that convey strong feelings. **Appeals to reason** use logical arguments supported by facts.

PLAYWRIGHT A *playwright* is a person who writes plays. William Shakespeare is regarded as the greatest playwright in English literature.

PLOT *Plot* is the sequence of events in a story. In most novels, dramas, short stories, and narrative poems, the plot involves both characters and a central conflict. The plot usually begins with an exposition that introduces the setting, the characters, and the basic situation. This is followed by the *inciting incident,* which introduces the central conflict. The conflict then increases during the *rising action,* until it reaches a high point of interest or suspense, the *climax.* The climax is followed by the *falling action,* or events that happen after the central conflict is resolved. The story's final outcome, in which remaining conflicts are resolved or left open, is the *resolution* or *denouement.*

Some plots do not have all of these parts. For example, some stories begin with the inciting incident and end with the resolution.

See **Conflict.**

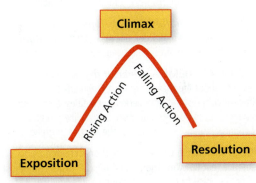

POETRY *Poetry* is one of the three major types of literature, the others being prose and drama. Most poems make use of highly concise, musical, and emotionally charged language. Many also make use of imagery, figurative language, and special devices of sound such as rhyme. Major types of poetry include *lyric poetry, narrative poetry,* and *concrete poetry.*

POINT OF VIEW *Point of view* is the perspective, or vantage point, from which a story is told. It is either a narrator outside the story or a character in the story. **First-person point of view** is told by a character who uses the first-person pronoun "I."

The two kinds of **third-person point of view,** limited and omniscient, are called "third person" because the narrator uses third-person pronouns such as "he" and "she" to refer to the characters. There is no "I" telling the story.

In stories told from the **omniscient third-person point of view,** the narrator knows and tells about what each character feels and thinks.

In stories told from the **limited third-person point of view,** the narrator relates the inner thoughts and feelings of only one character, and everything is viewed from this character's perspective.

PRESENTATION An *oral presentation* is a verbal form of presentation and can include other *visual presentation* forms such as charts, diagrams, illustrations, and photos. Video clips and slide-shows are included in *digital presentations,* which are created partly or entirely on a computer.

PROSE *Prose* is the ordinary form of written language. Most writing that is not poetry, drama, or song is considered prose. Prose is one of the major genres of literature and occurs in two forms—fiction and nonfiction.

QUOTATION *Quotations* are exact statements from personal interviews or conversations with the subjects of a narrative.

REPETITION *Repetition* is the use, more than once, of any element of language—a sound, word, phrase, clause, or sentence. Repetition is used in both prose and poetry.

RESOLUTION The *resolution* is the outcome of the conflict in a plot.

RESPONSES Any reaction to a set of events is called a *response*. *Internal responses* reveal a character's thoughts. *External responses* are actions.

RETELLING A *retelling* of a story can be either written or oral and should include a clear sequence of events and narrative techniques such as dialogue and descriptions.

RHYME *Rhyme* is the repetition of sounds at the ends of words. Poets use rhyme to lend a songlike quality to their verses and to emphasize certain words and ideas. Many traditional poems contain **end rhymes,** or rhyming words at the ends of lines.

Another common device is the use of **internal rhymes,** or rhyming words within lines. Internal rhyme also emphasizes the flowing nature of a poem.

RHYTHM *Rhythm* is the pattern of stressed and unstressed syllables in spoken or written language.

SCENE A *scene* is a section of uninterrupted action in the act of a drama.

Literary Terms Handbook **R47**

SCIENCE FICTION *Science fiction* combines elements of fiction and fantasy with scientific fact. Many science-fiction stories are set in the future.

SENSORY LANGUAGE *Sensory language* is writing or speech that appeals to one or more of the five senses.

SETTING The *setting* of a literary work is the time and place of the action. The setting includes all the details of a place and time—the year, the time of day, even the weather. The place may be a specific country, state, region, community, neighborhood, building, institution, or home. Details such as dialects, clothing, customs, and modes of transportation are often used to establish setting. In most stories, the setting serves as a backdrop—a context in which the characters interact. Setting can also help to create a feeling, or atmosphere.

SHORT STORY A *short story* is a brief work of fiction. Like a novel, a short story presents a sequence of events, or plot. The plot usually deals with a central conflict faced by a main character, or protagonist. The events in a short story usually communicate a message about life or human nature. This message, or central idea, is the story's theme.

SIMILE A *simile* is a figure of speech that uses *like* or *as* to make a direct comparison between two unlike ideas. Everyday speech often contains similes, such as "pale as a ghost," "good as gold," "spread like wildfire," and "clever as a fox."

STAGE DIRECTIONS *Stage directions* are notes included in a drama to describe how the work is to be performed or staged. Stage directions are usually printed in italics and enclosed within parentheses or brackets. Some stage directions describe the movements, costumes, emotional states, and ways of speaking of the characters.

STAGING *Staging* includes the setting, lighting, costumes, special effects, music, dance, and so on that go into putting on a stage performance of a drama.

SUMMARY A *summary* is a concise, complete, and accurate overview of a text.

SYMBOL A *symbol* is anything that stands for or represents something else. Symbols are common in everyday life. A dove with an olive branch in its beak is a symbol of peace. A blindfolded woman holding a balanced scale is a symbol of justice. A crown is a symbol of a king's or queen's status and authority.

SYMBOLISM *Symbolism* is the use of symbols. Symbolism plays an important role in many different types of literature. It can highlight certain elements the author wishes to emphasize and also add levels of meaning.

THEME The *theme* is a central message, concern, or purpose in a literary work. A *universal theme* can usually be expressed as a generalization, or a general statement, about human beings or about life. The theme of a work is not a summary of its plot. The theme is the writer's central idea. A *stated theme* is directly expressed. An *implied theme* is suggested by what happens to the characters.

Although a theme may be stated directly in the text, it is more often presented indirectly. When the theme is stated indirectly, or implied, the reader must figure out what the theme is by looking carefully at what the work reveals about people or about life.

THESAURUS A *thesaurus* is a reference resource that provides synonyms and antonyms of words.

TONE The *tone* of a literary work is the writer's attitude toward his or her audience and subject. The tone can often be described by a single adjective, such as *formal* or *informal, serious* or *playful, bitter,* or *ironic.* Factors that contribute to the tone are word choice, sentence structure, line length, rhyme, rhythm, and repetition.

TOPIC A text's *central idea* is its *topic*. The sentence that states the author's main idea about a topic is the *topic sentence* and is often the first sentence of the paragraph.

UNIVERSAL THEME A *universal theme* is a message about life that is expressed regularly in many different cultures and time periods. Folk tales, epics, and romances often address universal themes like the importance of courage, the power of love, or the danger of greed.

VOICE The unique *voice* of an author is created using sentence length, word choice, and tone. A writer can adjust his or her voice to the type of writing and audience.

WORD CHOICE An author's *word choice*—sometimes referred to as *diction*—is an important factor in creating the tone or mood of a literary work. Authors choose words based on the intended audience and the work's purpose.

MANUAL DE TÉRMINOS LITERARIOS

ALLITERATION / ALITERACIÓN La *aliteración* es la repetición de los sonidos consonantes iniciales. Los escritores usan la aliteración para llamar la atención sobre determinadas palabras o ideas, para imitar sonidos y para crear efectos de musicalidad.

ALLUSION / ALUSIÓN Una *alusión* es una referencia a una persona, lugar, hecho, obra literaria u obra de arte muy conocida. Las alusiones relacionan las obras literarias con una herencia cultural más extensa. Permiten al escritor expresar ideas complejas sin explicarlas con gran lujo de detalles. Comprender lo que dice una obra literaria a menudo depende de poder reconocer sus alusiones y los significados que sugieren.

ANALOGY / ANALOGÍA Una *analogía* establece una comparación entre dos o más cosas que son parecidas en algunos aspectos, pero se diferencian en otros.

ANECDOTE / ANÉCDOTA Una *anécdota* es un relato breve sobre un hecho interesante, divertido o extraño. Los escritores cuentan anécdotas con el fin de entretener o decir algo importante.

ARGUMENT ARGUMENTO Un *argumento* es una manera lógica de presentar una creencia, una conclusión o una postura. Un buen argumento debe incluir una *afirmación* y se respalda con razonamientos y *evidencias* que sean *relevantes*; es decir, que se relacionen con el tema. Si las creencias y el sentir del autor son obvios, el argumento es menos convincente y resulta *sesgado* o parcial.

AUTHOR'S INFLUENCES / INFLUENCIAS DEL AUTOR Las *influencias de un autor* son su herencia, su cultura y sus creencias personales.

AUTHOR'S POINT OF VIEW / PUNTO DE VISTA DEL AUTOR La actitud y postura que revela el autor de un texto informativo muestra el *punto de vista del autor*, o la *perspectiva del autor*.

AUTHOR'S PURPOSE / PROPÓSITO DEL AUTOR El *propósito del autor* es su razón principal para escribir. Por ejemplo, el autor puede tener como objetivo entretener, informar o persuadir al lector. En ocasiones el autor intenta dar una lección o hacer una reflexión sobre una experiencia. El autor puede tener más de un propósito para escribir.

AUTHOR'S STYLE / ESTILO DEL AUTOR El *estilo* de un autor es la manera típica en que escribe. Muchos factores determinan el estilo de un escritor, entre ellos la dicción, el tono, el uso que hace de elementos característicos como el lenguaje retórico, el dialecto, la rima, la métrica o los recursos rítmicos; las estructuras y patrones gramaticales típicos, la longitud de las oraciones y los métodos típicos de organización. El estilo comprende todas las características del uso del lenguaje de un escritor.

AUTOBIOGRAPHY / AUTOBIOGRAFÍA Una *autobiografía* es la historia de la vida del escritor contada por él mismo. Una autobiografía puede contar toda la vida de una persona o solo parte de ella.

Como las autobiografías tratan de personas y hechos reales, son una forma de no-ficción. La mayoría de las autobiografías están escritas en primera persona.

BIOGRAPHY / BIOGRAFÍA Una *biografía* es una forma de no-ficción en la que un escritor cuenta la vida de otra persona. La mayoría de las biografías tratan de personas famosas o admirables. Aunque las biografías son formas de no-ficción, las más efectivas comparten las cualidades de los buenos relatos.

CAUSE-AND-EFFECT ESSAY / ENSAYO DE CAUSA Y EFECTO Un *ensayo de causa y efecto* analiza la relación entre distintos sucesos. Los ensayos eficaces contienen una tesis clara, respaldada por ejemplos, evidencia y lógica.

CHARACTER / PERSONAJE Un *personaje* es una persona o animal que participa en la acción en una obra literaria. El personaje principal, o *protagonista*, es el personaje más importante del relato, poema u obra de teatro. Un personaje *secundario* es el que forma parte de la acción, pero no es el centro de la atención.

Los personajes se clasifican a veces como complejos o chatos. Un *personaje chato* muestra solo un rasgo y a menudo representa un estereotipo. Un *personaje complejo*, por el contrario, está totalmente desarrollado y muestra muchos rasgos diferentes, tanto faltas como virtudes.

Los personajes también se pueden clasificar como dinámicos o estáticos. Un *personaje dinámico* cambia o crece en el curso de la obra. Un *personaje estático* no cambia.

CHARACTERIZATION / CARACTERIZACIÓN La *caracterización* es el acto de crear y desarrollar un personaje. Los autores usan dos métodos principales de caracterización: *directa* e *indirecta*.

En una caracterización *directa*, el escritor expresa los *rasgos*, o características, *del personaje*.

Cuando describe a un personaje de manera *indirecta*, el escritor depende del lector para que saque conclusiones sobre los rasgos del personaje. Algunas veces, el autor cuenta lo que otros participantes del relato dicen y piensan del personaje.

CHARACTER TRAITS / RASGOS DEL PERSONAJE Los *rasgos de los personajes* son los atributos, actitudes y valores que un personaje tiene o exhibe, como la confiabilidad, la inteligencia, el egoísmo o la obstinación.

Manual de términos literarios **R49**

CHRONOLOGICAL ORDER / ORDEN CRONOLÓGICO Los escritores suelen ordenar los sucesos en las narraciones utilizando el *orden cronológico*, de manera que un suceso precede al siguiente en el orden en el que tuvieron lugar.

CLAIM / AFIRMACIÓN Una *afirmación* es una conclusión razonable que se basa en evidencia. Un *contraargumento* es una postura opuesta a la afirmación. Las *afirmaciones limitadas* son fuertes y específicas, por lo que suelen ser más eficaces que *las afirmaciones amplias* porque se pueden respaldar más fácilmente con evidencia.

CLIMAX / CLÍMAX El *clímax*, también llamado punto de inflexión, es el punto máximo en la acción de la trama. Es el momento de mayor tensión, cuando el resultado de la trama pende de un hilo.

COMPARE-AND-CONTRAST ESSAY / ENSAYO DE COMPARACIÓN Y CONTRASTE Se conoce como *ensayo de comparación y contraste* al ensayo en el que el autor expone las diferencias y similitudes entre dos asuntos.

Los ensayos de comparación y contraste pueden utilizar una *organización de punto por punto* en la que primero se trata un aspecto de los dos asuntos, después otro y así sucesivamente. También se puede emplear una *organización de método de bloques* en la que primero se presentan todos los detalles de uno de los asuntos, seguidos por los detalles del otro asunto.

CONFLICT / CONFLICTO Un *conflicto* es una lucha entre fuerzas opuestas. El conflicto es uno de los elementos más importantes de cuentos, novelas y obras de teatro porque causa la acción.

Hay dos tipos de conflicto: externos e internos. Un *conflicto externo* es aquel en el que un personaje lucha contra una fuerza externa, por ejemplo, otra persona. Otro tipo de conflicto externo puede ocurrir entre un personaje y alguna fuerza de la naturaleza.

Un *conflicto interno* tiene lugar dentro de la mente de un personaje, el cual lucha para tomar una decisión, realizar una acción o superar un sentimiento.

CONNECTORS / CONECTORES Los nexos o conectores son palabras que muestran *conexiones claras* entre las afirmaciones, las razones y las evidencias. Por el contrario, las *conexiones confusas* pueden complicar y debilitar los argumentos.

CONNOTATION / CONNOTACIÓN La *connotación* de una palabra es el conjunto de ideas que se asocian a ella, además de su significado explícito. La connotación de una palabra puede ser personal, esto es, basarse en experiencias personales. Más a menudo, las connotaciones culturales, es decir, las que la mayoría de un grupo reconoce, determinan la elección de palabras que hace el autor.

DENOTATION / DENOTACIÓN La *denotación* de una palabra es su significado en un *diccionario*, independientemente de otras asociaciones que la palabra suscita. Por ejemplo, la denotación de la palabra *lago* es "cuerpo de agua tierra adentro". "Lugar de vacaciones" y "lugar donde la pesca es buena" son connotaciones de la palabra *lago*.

DESCRIPTION / DESCRIPCIÓN Una *descripción* es un retrato en palabras de una persona, un lugar o un objeto. La escritura descriptiva utiliza imágenes que apelan a los cinco sentidos: la vista, el oído, el tacto, el gusto y el olfato.

DIALOGUE / DIÁLOGO Un *diálogo* es una conversación entre personajes. En poemas, novelas y cuentos, el diálogo en inglés usualmente se resalta con comillas para indicar las palabras exactas del hablante.

En una obra de teatro, el diálogo sigue a los nombres de los personajes y no se usan comillas.

DIARY / DIARIO Un *diario* es un tipo de texto autobiográfico. Las entradas de un diario se hacen de manera periódica a lo largo del tiempo.

DICTION / DICCIÓN La *dicción* comprende la elección de palabras que hace el autor o el hablante. La dicción es parte del estilo de un escritor y se puede describir como formal o informal, sencilla o elevada, coloquial o *técnica*, sofisticada o centrada, antigua o moderna.

DICTIONARY / DICCIONARIO Un *diccionario* es una obra de referencia que ofrece información sobre el significado de una palabra, su categoría gramatical y su etimología.

DRAMA / DRAMA Un *drama* es una historia escrita para ser representada por actores. Aunque la intención del drama es su representación, también se puede leer el guion, o versión escrita, e imaginar la acción. El *guion* de un drama está constituido por el diálogo y las acotaciones. El *diálogo* son las palabras que dicen los actores. Las *acotaciones*, por lo general impresas en cursivas, dicen cómo se ven, se mueven y hablan los actores. También describen la ambientación, los efectos sonoros y la iluminación.

Con frecuencia, los dramas se dividen en partes llamadas *actos*.

Los actos se dividen a menudo en partes más pequeñas llamadas *escenas*.

THEATRICAL CRITICISM / CRÍTICA TEATRAL La *crítica teatral* es una evaluación de una representación dramática. El análisis y las opiniones del escritor se respaldan con ejemplos.

ESSAY / ENSAYO Un *ensayo* es una obra breve de no-ficción sobre un tema en particular. La mayoría de los ensayos tienen un único punto central importante y una introducción, cuerpo y conclusión claras.

Hay muchos tipos de ensayos. Un *ensayo informal* usa lenguaje casual, coloquial. Un *ensayo histórico* brinda hechos, explicaciones y perspectivas de hechos históricos. Un *ensayo expositivo* explica una idea al descomponerla. Un *ensayo narrativo* cuenta una historia sobre una experiencia de la vida real. Un *ensayo informativo* explica un proceso. Un *ensayo persuasivo* ofrece una opinión y la apoya. Un *ensayo explicativo* es una pieza breve de no-ficción en la que el autor explica, define o interpreta ideas, eventos o procesos. Un *ensayo reflexivo* es una breve obra en prosa en la cual el autor presenta sus pensamientos o sentimientos (o reflexiones) sobre una experiencia o idea. En un *ensayo argumentativo* el escritor manifiesta y respalda una afirmación, basándose en evidencias y en razones lógicas. Los *ensayos de problema y solución* identifican un problema y presentan un argumento o afirmación sobre sus soluciones.

EXAMPLE / EJEMPLO Un *ejemplo* es un hecho, idea o suceso que respalda una opinión o percepción.

EXPOSITION / EXPOSICIÓN En la trama de un cuento o de un drama, la *exposición*, o introducción, es la parte de la obra donde se presenta a los personajes, la ambientación y la situación básica.

EXPLANATORY TEXT / TEXTO EXPLICATIVO Un *texto explicativo* explica un proceso o da instrucciones.

EXPOSITORY WRITING / ESCRITURA EXPOSITIVA La *escritura expositiva* es aquella que presenta información, discute ideas o explica un proceso.

FACTS AND DETAILS / HECHOS Y DETALLES Los *hechos y detalles* son un tipo de evidencia que el escritor usa para respaldar una tesis u opinión. Los hechos son datos cuya veracidad se puede demostrar.

FANTASY / LITERATURA FANTÁSTICA La *literatura fantástica* son escritos de gran imaginación que contienen elementos que no se encuentran en la vida real. Ejemplos de la literatura fantástica son los cuentos que incluyen elementos sobrenaturales, historias que recuerdan a los cuentos de hadas o las que tratan de lugares y criaturas imaginarias, y los relatos de ciencia ficción.

FICTION / FICCIÓN Una obra de *ficción* es un escrito en prosa que cuenta algo sobre personajes y hechos imaginarios. Los cuentos y las novelas son obras de ficción. Algunos escritores basan sus obras de ficción en hechos y personas reales, a los que agregan personajes, diálogos, ambientaciones y tramas de su propia invención. Otros autores dependen solo de su imaginación.

FIGURATIVE LANGUAGE / LENGUAJE FIGURADO El *lenguaje figurado* es un escrito o discurso que no se debe interpretar literalmente. Los muchos tipos de lenguaje figurado son conocidos como *figuras retóricas*. Las figuras retóricas comunes incluyen la metáfora, la personificación y los símiles. Los escritores usan el lenguaje figurado para expresar sus ideas de forma vívida y creativa.

FORESHADOWING / PREFIGURACIÓN La *prefiguración* es el uso que hace un autor de claves que sugieren hechos que van a suceder. Los escritores usan la prefiguración para desarrollar las expectativas de los lectores y crear suspenso.

FREE VERSE / VERSO LIBRE El *verso libre* es una forma poética en la que no se sigue un patrón, o métrica, regular ni rítmico. El poeta es libre de escribir los versos de cualquier longitud o con cualquier cantidad de énfasis o ritmos. Por consiguiente, el verso libre es menos restrictivo que el *verso métrico*, en el que cada verso debe tener una longitud determinada y un cierto número de acentos.

GENRE / GÉNERO Un *género* es una categoría o tipo de literatura. La literatura se divide por lo general en tres géneros principales: poesía, prosa y drama. Cada uno de estos géneros principales se divide a su vez en géneros más pequeños. Por ejemplo:

1. *Poesía*: poesía lírica, poesía concreta, poesía dramática, poesía narrativa y poesía épica
2. *Prosa*: ficción (novelas y cuentos) y no-ficción (biografía, autobiografía, cartas, ensayos, artículos)
3. *Drama*: drama serio y tragedia, comedia dramática, melodrama y farsa

HISTORICAL FICTION / FICCIÓN HISTÓRICA En la *ficción histórica* se incorporan hechos, lugares o personas reales a un relato ficticio o inventado.

HUMOR / HUMOR El *humor* es la escritura que tiene la intención de despertar la risa o entretener. También se puede usar para transmitir un tema serio.

IMAGERY / IMAGINERÍA La *imaginería* es el uso que hacen los escritores de imágenes vívidas creadas con palabras para apelar a los cinco sentidos.

IMAGES / IMÁGENES Las *imágenes* son las palabras vívidas que los autores usan para apelar a uno o más de los cinco sentidos. Los escritores usan imágenes para describir cómo se ven, suenan, sienten, gustan y huelen sus personajes. Los poetas a menudo pintan imágenes, o dibujos con palabras, que despiertan los sentidos. Estas imágenes ayudan a experimentar plenamente el poema.

INFERENCE / INFERENCIA Se conoce como *hacer una inferencia* al acto de hacer una conjetura o deducción sobre un personaje basándose en la manera en la que dicho personaje piensa, se comporta o habla. También se conoce como *leer entre líneas*.

INFORMATIVE TEXT / TEXTO INFORMATIVO Un *texto informativo* ofrece información sobre un tema.

Manual de términos literarios **R51**

IRONY / IRONÍA La *ironía* es una contradicción entre lo que se espera y lo que ocurre. Hay tres tipos principales de ironía. La *ironía situacional* se da cuando ocurre algo que contradice directamente las expectativas de los personajes o de la audiencia. La *ironía verbal* tiene lugar cuando lo que se dice es justo lo opuesto a lo que se quiere decir. En la *ironía dramática*, la audiencia sabe algo que el personaje o el que habla no sabe.

JOURNAL / DIARIO Un *diario* es un relato diario o periódico de sucesos y de los pensamientos y sentimientos que el escritor tiene sobre esos sucesos. Por lo general, los diarios personales no se escriben para publicarse, pero algunas veces se publican más tarde con la autorización del autor o de la familia del autor.

LETTERS / CARTAS Una *carta* es una comunicación escrita. En las cartas personales, el escritor comparte información y sus pensamientos y sentimientos con otra persona o grupo. Aunque las cartas por lo general no se escriben para su publicación, a veces se publican con la autorización del autor o de la familia del autor.

LOGICAL FALLACIES / FALACIAS LÓGICAS Las *falacias lógicas* son errores en el razonamiento que debilitan el argumento. Estos son algunos ejemplos: La *sobregeneralización* es una conclusión que no toma en cuenta una evidencia opuesta o contraria. En la *presuposición* se asume que B, C y D sucederán como consecuencia de A. Un *argumento ad populum* apela a las creencias fundamentales que tiene el público sobre lo que está bien y lo que está mal.

LYRIC POEM / POEMA LÍRICO Un *poema lírico* es una sucesión de versos de mucha musicalidad que expresan las observaciones y sentimientos de un único *hablante*. Crea una impresión única y unificada.

LOGICAL FALLACIES / FALACIAS LÓGICAS Las falacias lógicas son errores en el razonamiento que debilitan el argumento. Estos son algunos ejemplos: La *sobregeneralización* es una conclusión que no toma en cuenta una evidencia opuesta o contraria. En la *presuposición* se asume que B, C y D sucederán como consecuencia de A. Un *argumento ad populum* apela a las creencias fundamentales que tiene la audiencia sobre lo que están bien y lo que está mal.

MAIN IDEA / IDEA PRINCIPAL La *idea* principal es la *idea central*; es decir, el objetivo más importante de un texto. Se deben hacer *inferencias* basándose en lo que se sabe para poder determinar la *idea central implícita*.

MEDIA / MEDIOS DE COMUNICACIÓN Las historias y la información se divulgan a través de distintos *medios de comunicación*. Los libros, las revistas, las películas, la televisión y los libros electrónicos son medios de comunicación. Una *presentación multimedia* es el resultado de la combinación de palabras, imágenes, sonidos y video.

MEDIA ACCOUNTS / INFORMES DE MEDIOS DE COMUNICACIÓN Los *informes de los medios de comunicación* son reportes, explicaciones, opiniones o descripciones escritos para televisión, radio, periódicos y revistas. Aunque algunos informes de medios de comunicación se refieren solo a hechos, otros incluyen los pensamientos y reflexiones del escritor.

MEMOIR / MEMORIAS Un libro de *memorias* es un tipo de autobiografía que se centra en un período o serie de eventos particularmente significativos de la vida del autor. Por lo general, las memorias se escriben desde el punto de vista de la primera persona, en la que el autor, o narrador, forma parte de los eventos de la historia. El autor se refiere a sí mismo usando el pronombre *yo*.

METAPHOR / METÁFORA Una *metáfora* es una figura retórica en la que se describe algo como si fuera otra cosa. Una metáfora, al igual que el símil, destaca una similitud entre dos cosas disímiles.

METER / MÉTRICA La *métrica* de un poema es su patrón rítmico. Este patrón queda determinado por el número de *acentos*, o ritmos, en cada línea. Para describir la métrica de un poema en inglés, léelo enfatizando los acentos en cada línea. Luego, marca las sílabas acentuadas y las no acentuadas, como sigue:

My fáth | ĕr wás | thĕ fírst | tŏ héar |

Como puedes ver, en inglés cada acento fuerte se marca con una rayita inclinada, (´) y cada sílaba no acentuada con un símbolo de herradura (˘). Luego, los acentos débiles y fuertes se dividen con rayas verticales (|) en grupos llamados pies.

MONOLOGUE / MONÓLOGO Un *monólogo* es un parlamento extenso de uno de los personajes en el que dicho personaje expresa su punto de vista.

MOOD / ATMÓSFERA La *atmósfera* es la sensación que un texto produce en el lector. Los escritores crean la atmósfera mediante el uso de imaginería, su elección de palabras y los detalles descriptivos.

MOTIVE / MOTIVO Un *motivo* es una razón que explica del todo o parcialmente los pensamientos, sentimientos, acciones o discurso de un personaje. Los escritores tratan de hacer que los motivos, o *motivaciones*, de sus personajes sean lo más claros posible. Si los motivos de un personaje principal no están claros, entonces el personaje no será bien entendido.

A menudo, a los personajes los mueven *motivos externos*; es decir, necesidades como la alimentación y el cobijo. También los mueven *motivos internos*; es decir, sentimientos como el miedo, el amor y el orgullo. Los motivos pueden ser obvios o escondidos.

MYTH / MITO Un *mito* es un relato de ficción que explica las acciones de los dioses, los héroes o los orígenes de los elementos de la naturaleza. Los mitos forman parte de la tradición oral. Se componían oralmente y luego pasaban de boca en boca, de una generación a otra. Todas las culturas antiguas tienen su propia mitología, o recopilación de mitos. Los mitos griegos y romanos son conocidos en su conjunto como **mitología clásica**.

NARRATION / NARRACIÓN Una *narración* es un escrito que cuenta una historia. El acto de contar una historia de forma oral también se llama narración. Una historia contada en forma de ficción, no-ficción, poesía o incluso en forma de drama es un *relato*.

NARRATIVE / RELATO Se llama *relato* a la historia que se narra. Puede ser de ficción o de no-ficción. Las novelas y los cuentos son tipos de relatos de ficción. Las biografías y las autobiografías son relatos de no-ficción. Los poemas que cuentan historias también son relatos.

Los autores usan el *ritmo narrativo* para controlar la velocidad y el flujo de información de un texto.

NARRATIVE POEM / POEMA NARRATIVO Un *poema narrativo* es una historia contada en verso. Los poemas narrativos a menudo tienen todos los elementos de los cuentos, incluyendo los personajes, el conflicto y la trama.

NARRATOR / NARRADOR Un *narrador* es el hablante o el personaje que cuenta una historia. La perspectiva del narrador es la forma en que ve las cosas. Un *narrador en tercera persona* permanece fuera de la acción y habla de ella. Un *narrador en primera persona* es quien cuenta la historia y participa en su acción.

NONFICTION / NO-FICCIÓN La *no-ficción* es un escrito en prosa que presenta y explica ideas o cuenta algo acerca de personas, lugares, objetos o hechos reales. Las autobiografías, biografías, ensayos, informes, cartas, memorándums y artículos de periódico son tipos de no-ficción.

NOVEL / NOVELA Una *novela* es una obra extensa de ficción. Las novelas contienen elementos como personajes, trama, conflicto y ambientación. El escritor de novelas, o novelista, desarrolla estos elementos. Además de su trama principal, una novela puede contener una o más tramas secundarias, es decir, historias relacionadas independientes. Una novela también puede tener varios temas.

ONOMATOPOEIA / ONOMATOPEYA La *onomatopeya* es el uso de palabras que imitan sonidos. *Crash, pío-pío, tica-tac* y *psss* son ejemplos de onomatopeyas. *Cu-cú* es un nombre onomatopéyico de un pájaro.

La onomatopeya puede ayudar a meter al lector en la acción de un poema.

OPINION / OPINIÓN Una *opinión* es un juicio de valor o la creencia de una persona. Puede respaldarse con evidencias basadas en hechos, pero no se puede demostrar.

ORGANIZATION / ORGANIZACIÓN La *organización* o estructura de un texto depende del tema y del propósito o razón que tenga el escritor para escribir.

OXYMORON / OXÍMORON Un *oxímoron* (pl. *oxímora*) es una figura retórica que relaciona dos palabras opuestas o contradictorias para resaltar una idea o situación que parece contradictoria o incongruente, pero que, al analizar con más detalle, resulta tener algo de cierto.

PARALLELISM / PARALELISMO *Paralelismo* es el uso de formas o patrones gramaticales similares para expresar ideas parecidas. El paralelismo añade ritmo y equilibrio a la escritura y fortalece las relaciones entre las ideas del autor.

PARAPHRASE / PARÁFRASIS La *paráfrasis* es reescribir o volver a contar con nuestras propias palabras algo que hemos leído u oído.

PERSONIFICATION / PERSONIFICACIÓN La *personificación* es un tipo de figura retórica en la que se dota a una instancia no humana de características humanas.

PERSUASION / PERSUASIÓN La *persuasión* es un recurso escrito u oral por el que se intenta convencer al lector u oyente de que adopte una opinión en particular o actúe de determinada manera. Los editoriales de los periódicos y las cartas al editor utilizan la persuasión. También lo hacen los anuncios y los discursos de campaña que dan los candidatos políticos.

Los escritores emplean distintas técnicas persuasivas para defender sus opiniones. Las *apelaciones a la autoridad* usan lo que han dicho diversos expertos. Las *apelaciones a las emociones* usan palabras que transmiten sentimientos profundos. Las *apelaciones a la razón* utilizan argumentos lógicos fundamentados con datos.

PLAYWRIGHT / DRAMATURGO Un *dramaturgo* es una persona que escribe obras de teatro. William Shakespeare es reconocido como el mejor dramaturgo de la literatura inglesa.

PLOT / TRAMA o ARGUMENTO La *trama* o *argumento* es la secuencia de los sucesos de una historia. En la mayoría de las novelas, dramas, cuentos y poemas narrativos, la trama implica tanto a los personajes como al conflicto central. La trama por lo general empieza con una exposición que introduce la ambientación, los personajes y la situación básica. A ello le sigue el *suceso desencadenante*, que introduce el conflicto central. Este conflicto aumenta durante la *acción ascendente* hasta que alcanza el punto más alto de interés o suspenso, llamado *clímax*. Al clímax le sigue la *acción descendente*, o los sucesos que ocurren después de que se haya resuelto el conflicto central. El final de la historia, en el que se resuelven los conflictos que quedaban pendientes o se dejan abiertos, conforma el *desenlace,* o *resolución*.

Manual de términos literarios **R53**

Algunas tramas no tienen todas estas partes. Por ejemplo, algunas historias comienzan con el suceso desencadenante y terminan con el desenlace.

Ver **Conflicto**.

Presentación del conflicto

POETRY / POESÍA La *poesía* es uno de los tres géneros literarios más importantes. Los otros dos son la prosa y el drama. La mayoría de los poemas están escritos en un lenguaje altamente conciso, musical y emocionalmente rico. Muchos también hacen uso de imágenes, figuras retóricas y recursos especiales de sonido, como la rima. Los tipos principales de poesía incluyen la *poesía lírica*, la *poesía narrativa* y la *poesía concreta*.

POINT OF VIEW / PUNTO DE VISTA El *punto de vista* es la perspectiva, o enfoque, desde la cual se narran o describen los hechos. Es un narrador externo a la historia o un personaje del relato. El *punto de vista en primera persona* lo cuenta un personaje que usa el pronombre en primera persona "yo".

Los dos tipos de *punto de vista en tercera persona*, limitado y omnisciente, se llaman "tercera persona" porque el narrador usa pronombres de la tercera persona como "él" o "ella" para referirse a los personajes. No hay un "yo" que cuente la historia.

En los relatos contados desde el *punto de vista omnisciente en tercera persona*, el narrador sabe y cuenta lo que cada personaje siente y piensa.

En los relatos contados desde el *punto de vista limitado en tercera persona*, el narrador relata los pensamientos y sentimientos internos de solo un personaje, y todo se ve desde la perspectiva de este personaje.

PRESENTATION / PRESENTACIÓN Las *presentaciones orales* son un tipo de presentación verbal que puede incluir *presentaciones visuales* como tablas, diagramas, ilustraciones y fotos. Los videoclips y las presentaciones de diapositivas son parte de las llamadas *presentaciones digitales*, que se crean en parte o en su totalidad con computadora.

PROSE / PROSA La *prosa* es la forma común del lenguaje escrito. La mayoría de los escritos que no son poesía, drama, ni canciones, se consideran prosa. La prosa es uno de los géneros literarios más importantes y puede ser de dos formas: de ficción y de no-ficción.

QUOTE / CITA Las *citas* son enunciados exactos tomados de entrevistas y conversaciones personales con los individuos de una narración.

REPETITION / REPETICIÓN La *repetición* es el uso de cualquier elemento del lenguaje —un sonido, una palabra, una frase, una cláusula, o una oración— más de una vez. La repetición se usa tanto en prosa como en poesía.

RESPONSE / RESPUESTA Se conoce como *respuesta* a la reacción a un conjunto de sucesos. Las *respuestas internas* revelan los pensamientos del personaje. Las *respuestas externas* son acciones.

RESOLUTION / RESOLUCIÓN La *resolución* es el resultado del conflicto de una trama.

RETELL / VOLVER A CONTAR Las historias se pueden *volver a contar* de manera escrita u oral. Al volverse a contar una historia, se debe seguir una secuencia clara de los sucesos y utilizar técnicas narrativas como el diálogo y la descripción.

RHYME / RIMA La *rima* es la repetición de sonidos al final de las palabras. Los poetas usan la rima para prestar un atributo musical a sus versos y para enfatizar determinadas palabras e ideas. Muchos poemas tradicionales contienen *rimas finales*, o palabras que riman al final de los versos.

Otro recurso común es el uso de *rimas internas*, o palabras que riman dentro de los versos. La rima interna también enfatiza la naturaleza fluida de un poema.

RHYTHM / RITMO El *ritmo* es el patrón de sílabas acentuadas y no acentuadas en el lenguaje hablado o escrito.

SCENE / ESCENA Una *escena* es una sección de acciones ininterrumpidas en la representación de un drama.

SCIENCE FICTION / CIENCIA FICCIÓN La *ciencia ficción* combina elementos de ficción y fantasía con información científica. Muchos relatos de ciencia ficción están ambientados en el futuro.

SENSORY LANGUAGE / LENGUAJE SENSORIAL El *lenguaje sensorial* es un escrito o discurso que apela a uno o más de los cinco sentidos.

SETTING / AMBIENTACIÓN La *ambientación* de una obra literaria es la época y el lugar en el que se desarrolla la acción. Incluye todos los detalles del lugar y la época (el año, la hora del día, incluso el clima). El lugar puede ser un país, estado, región, comunidad, barrio, edificio, institución o casa específicos. Los detalles como dialectos, vestuario, costumbres y medios de transporte se usan a menudo para establecer la ambientación. En la mayoría de los relatos, la ambientación sirve como telón de fondo para la acción: un contexto en el que los personajes interactúan.

La ambientación también puede ayudar a crear un sentimiento o atmósfera.

SHORT STORY / CUENTO Un *cuento* es una obra breve de ficción. Como en la novela, un cuento presenta una secuencia de eventos, o trama. La trama por lo general trata de un conflicto central que enfrenta un personaje principal o protagonista. Los eventos de un cuento por lo general comunican un mensaje sobre la vida o la naturaleza humana. Este mensaje, o idea central, es el tema del cuento.

SIMILE / SÍMIL Un *símil* es una figura retórica en la que se usa la palabra *como* para establecer una comparación entre dos ideas disímiles. El habla cotidiana a menudo contiene símiles, como "pálido como un fantasma", "bueno como el oro", "se expandió como el fuego" y "astuto como un zorro".

STAGE DIRECTIONS / ACOTACIONES Las *acotaciones* son notas que se incluyen en una obra de teatro para describir cómo debe ser actuada o puesta en escena. Estas instrucciones suelen aparecer en cursivas y entre paréntesis o corchetes. Algunas acotaciones describen los movimientos, vestuario, estados emocionales y formas de hablar de los personajes.

STAGING / PUESTA EN ESCENA La *puesta en escena* incluye la ambientación, la iluminación, el vestuario, los efectos especiales, la música, el baile, etc. que forman parte de poner en un escenario la representación de un drama.

SUMMARY / RESUMEN Un *resumen* es una visión concisa, completa y precisa de un texto.

SYMBOL / SÍMBOLO Un *símbolo* es algo que representa otra cosa. Los símbolos son comunes en la vida diaria. Una paloma con una rama de olivo en el pico es un símbolo de paz. Una mujer con los ojos vendados que sostiene una balanza es un símbolo de la justicia. Una corona es un símbolo del estatus y la autoridad de un rey o una reina.

SYMBOLISM / SIMBOLISMO El *simbolismo* es el uso de los símbolos. El simbolismo desempeña un papel importante en muchos tipos diferentes de literatura. Puede destacar determinados elementos que el autor quiera enfatizar y también añadir niveles de significado.

THEME / TEMA El *tema* es el mensaje central, preocupación o propósito de una obra literaria. El *tema universal* puede expresarse como generalización, o enunciado general, sobre los seres humanos o sobre la vida. El tema de una obra no es un resumen de su trama. Es la idea central del autor. Un *tema explícito* es aquel que se expresa directamente. Un *tema implícito* se insinúa en lo que les sucede a los personajes.

Aunque el tema se puede expresar directamente en el texto, se presenta con más frecuencia de manera indirecta. Cuando se expresa indirectamente, o está implícito, el lector debe averiguar cuál es el tema analizando con cuidado lo que la obra revela sobre la gente o sobre la vida.

THESAURUS / TESAURO Un *tesauro* es una obra de referencia que incluye los sinónimos y los antónimos de las palabras.

TONE / TONO El *tono* de una obra literaria es la actitud del escritor hacia su tema y su audiencia. A menudo, el tono se puede describir con un solo adjetivo, como *formal* o *informal*, *serio* o *divertido*, *amargo* o *irónico*. Los factores que contribuyen al tono son la elección de las palabras, la estructura de las oraciones, la longitud de las líneas, la rima, el ritmo y la repetición.

TOPIC or ISSUE / TEMA o ASUNTO La *idea central* de un texto es su *tema o asunto*; es decir, nos indica de qué trata el texto. La oración que nos ofrece la idea principal del autor es la *oración temática* y suele ser la primera oración del párrafo.

UNIVERSAL THEME / TEMA UNIVERSAL Un *tema universal* es un mensaje sobre la vida que se expresa regularmente en muchas culturas y periodos diferentes. Las leyendas populares, la novela épica y los romances a menudo tratan temas universales como la importancia del valor, el poder del amor y el peligro de la avaricia.

VOICE / VOZ La *voz* distintiva de un autor se crea mediante la extensión de las oraciones, la elección de las palabras y el tono. El escritor puede modificar su voz según el tipo de texto y la audiencia.

WORD CHOICE / ELECCIÓN DE LAS PALABRAS La *elección de las palabras* que hace un autor (a veces conocida como *dicción*) es un factor importante en la creación del tono o atmósfera de la obra literaria. Los autores eligen las palabras con base en la audiencia a la que se dirigen y el propósito de la obra.

GRAMMAR HANDBOOK

PARTS OF SPEECH

Every English word, depending on its meaning and its use in a sentence, can be identified as one of the eight parts of speech. These are nouns, pronouns, verbs, adjectives, adverbs, prepositions, conjunctions, and interjections. Understanding the parts of speech will help you learn the rules of English grammar and usage.

Nouns A **noun** names a person, place, or thing. A **common noun** names any one of a class of persons, places, or things. A **proper noun** names a specific person, place, or thing.

Common Noun	Proper Noun
writer, country, novel	Charles Dickens, Great Britain, *Hard Times*

Pronouns A **pronoun** is a word that stands for one or more nouns. The word to which a pronoun refers (whose place it takes) is the **antecedent** of the pronoun.

A **personal pronoun** refers to the person speaking (first person); the person spoken to (second person); or the person, place, or thing spoken about (third person).

	Singular	Plural
First Person	I, me, my, mine	we, us, our, ours
Second Person	you, your, yours	you, your, yours
Third Person	he, him, his, she, her, hers, it, its	they, them, their, theirs

A **reflexive pronoun** reflects the action of a verb back on its subject. It indicates that the person or thing performing the action also is receiving the action.
> I keep *myself* fit by taking a walk every day.

An **intensive pronoun** adds emphasis to a noun or pronoun.
> It took the work of the president *himself* to pass the law.

A **demonstrative** pronoun points out a specific person(s), place(s), or thing(s).
> this, that, these, those

A **relative pronoun** begins a subordinate clause and connects it to another idea in the sentence.
> that, which, who, whom, whose

An **interrogative pronoun** begins a question.
> what, which, who, whom, whose

An **indefinite pronoun** refers to a person, place, or thing that may or may not be specifically named.
> all, another, any, both, each, everyone, few, most, none, no one, somebody

Verbs A **verb** expresses action or the existence of a state or condition.

An **action verb** tells what action someone or something is performing.
> gather, read, work, jump, imagine, analyze, conclude

A **linking verb** connects the subject with another word that identifies or describes the subject. The most common linking verb is *be*.
> appear, be, become, feel, look, remain, seem, smell, sound, stay, taste

A **helping verb**, or **auxiliary verb**, is added to a main verb to make a verb phrase.
> be, do, have, should, can, could, may, might, must, will, would

Adjectives An **adjective** modifies a noun or pronoun by describing it or giving it a more specific meaning. An adjective answers the questions:

What kind?	*purple* hat, *happy* face, *loud* sound
Which one?	*this* bowl
How many?	*three* cars
How much?	*enough* food

The articles *the*, *a*, and *an* are adjectives.

A **proper adjective** is an adjective derived from a proper noun.
> French, Shakespearean

Adverbs An **adverb** modifies a verb, an adjective, or another adverb by telling *where, when, how,* or *to what extent*.
> will answer *soon*, *extremely* sad, calls *more* often

Prepositions A **preposition** relates a noun or pronoun that appears with it to another word in the sentence.
> Dad made a meal *for* us. We talked *till* dusk. Bo missed school *because of* his illness.

Conjunctions A **conjunction** connects words or groups of words. A **coordinating conjunction** joins words or groups of words of equal rank.
> bread *and* cheese, brief *but* powerful

Correlative conjunctions are used in pairs to connect words or groups of words of equal importance.
> *both* Luis *and* Rosa, *neither* you *nor* I

R56 GLOSSARY

PARTS OF SPEECH continued

Subordinating conjunctions indicate the connection between two ideas by placing one below the other in rank or importance. A subordinating conjunction introduces a subordinate, or dependent, clause.

> We will miss her *if* she leaves. Hank shrieked *when* he slipped on the ice.

Interjections An **interjection** expresses feeling or emotion. It is not related to other words in the sentence.
> ah, hey, ouch, well, yippee

PHRASES AND CLAUSES

Phrases A **phrase** is a group of words that does not have both a subject and a verb and that functions as one part of speech. A phrase expresses an idea but cannot stand alone.

Prepositional Phrases A **prepositional phrase** is a group of words that begins with a preposition and ends with a noun or pronoun that is the **object of the preposition.**
> before dawn   as a result of the rain

An **adjective phrase** is a prepositional phrase that modifies a noun or pronoun.
> Eliza appreciates the beauty **of a well-crafted poem.**

An **adverb phrase** is a prepositional phrase that modifies a verb, an adjective, or an adverb.
> She reads Spenser's sonnets **with great pleasure.**

Appositive Phrases An **appositive** is a noun or pronoun placed next to another noun or pronoun to add information about it. An **appositive phrase** consists of an appositive and its modifiers.
> Mr. Roth, **my music teacher,** is sick.

Verbal Phrases A **verbal** is a verb form that functions as a different part of speech (not as a verb) in a sentence. **Participles, gerunds,** and **infinitives** are verbals.

A **verbal phrase** includes a verbal and any modifiers or complements it may have. Verbal phrases may function as nouns, as adjectives, or as adverbs.

A **participle** is a verb form that can act as an adjective. Present participles end in *-ing;* past participles of regular verbs end in *-ed*.

A **participial phrase** consists of a participle and its modifiers or complements. The entire phrase acts as an adjective.
> Jenna's backpack, **loaded with equipment,** was heavy.
> **Barking incessantly,** the dogs chased the squirrels out of sight.

A **gerund** is a verb form that ends in *-ing* and is used as a noun.

A **gerund phrase** consists of a gerund with any modifiers or complements, all acting together as a noun.
> **Taking photographs of wildlife** is her main hobby. [acts as subject]
> We always enjoy **listening to live music.** [acts as object]

An **infinitive** is a verb form, usually preceded by *to*, that can act as a noun, an adjective, or an adverb.

An **infinitive phrase** consists of an infinitive and its modifiers or complements, and sometimes its subject, all acting together as a single part of speech.
> She tries **to get out into the wilderness often.** [acts as a noun; direct object of *tries*]
> The Tigers are the team **to beat.** [acts as an adjective; describes *team*]
> I drove twenty miles **to witness the event.** [acts as an adverb; tells why I drove]

Clauses A **clause** is a group of words with its own subject and verb.

Independent Clauses An independent clause can stand by itself as a complete sentence.
> George Orwell wrote with extraordinary insight.

Subordinate Clauses A subordinate clause cannot stand by itself as a complete sentence. Subordinate clauses always appear connected in some way with one or more independent clauses.
> George Orwell, **who wrote with extraordinary insight,** produced many politically relevant works.

An **adjective clause** is a subordinate clause that acts as an adjective. It modifies a noun or a pronoun by telling *what kind* or *which one*. Also called relative clauses, adjective clauses usually begin with a **relative pronoun:** *who, which, that, whom,* or *whose*.
> "The Lamb" is the poem **that I memorized for class.**

An **adverb clause** is a subordinate clause that, like an adverb, modifies a verb, an adjective, or an adverb. An adverb clause tells *where, when, in what way, to what extent, under what condition,* or *why*.

Grammar Handbook **R57**

PHRASES AND CLAUSES continued

The students will read another poetry collection **if their schedule allows.**
When I recited the poem, Mr. Lopez was impressed.

A **noun clause** is a subordinate clause that acts as a noun.
William Blake survived on **whatever he made as an engraver.**

SENTENCE STRUCTURE

Subject and Predicate A **sentence** is a group of words that expresses a complete thought. A sentence has two main parts: a *subject* and a *predicate*.

A **fragment** is a group of words that does not express a complete thought. It lacks an independent clause.

The **subject** tells *whom* or *what* the sentence is about. The **predicate** tells what the subject of the sentence does or is.

A subject or a predicate can consist of a single word or of many words. All the words in the subject make up the **complete subject.** All the words in the predicate make up the **complete predicate.**

Complete Subject**Complete Predicate**
Both of those girls | have already read *Macbeth*.

The **simple subject** is the essential noun, pronoun, or group of words acting as a noun that cannot be left out of the complete subject. The **simple predicate** is the essential verb or verb phrase that cannot be left out of the complete predicate.
Both of those girls | **have** already **read** *Macbeth*.
[Simple subject: *Both;* simple predicate: *have read*]

A **compound subject** is two or more subjects that have the same verb and are joined by a conjunction.
Neither the horse nor the driver looked tired.

A **compound predicate** is two or more verbs that have the same subject and are joined by a conjunction.
She **sneezed and coughed** throughout the trip.

Complements A **complement** is a word or word group that completes the meaning of the subject or verb in a sentence. There are four kinds of complements: *direct objects, indirect objects, objective complements,* and *subject complements.*

A **direct object** is a noun, a pronoun, or a group of words acting as a noun that receives the action of a transitive verb.
We watched the **liftoff**.
She drove **Zach** to the launch site.

An **indirect object** is a noun or pronoun that appears with a direct object and names the person or thing to which or for which something is done.
He sold the **family** a mirror. [The direct object is *mirror.*]

An **objective complement** is an adjective or noun that appears with a direct object and describes or renames it.
The decision made her **unhappy**.
[The direct object is *her.*]
Many consider Shakespeare the greatest **playwright.** [The direct object is *Shakespeare.*]

A **subject complement** follows a linking verb and tells something about the subject. There are two kinds: *predicate nominatives* and *predicate adjectives.*

A **predicate nominative** is a noun or pronoun that follows a linking verb and identifies or renames the subject.
"A Modest Proposal" is a **pamphlet**.

A **predicate adjective** is an adjective that follows a linking verb and describes the subject of the sentence.
"A Modest Proposal" is **satirical**.

Classifying Sentences by Structure

Sentences can be classified according to the kind and number of clauses they contain. The four basic sentence structures are *simple, compound, complex,* and *compound-complex.*

A **simple sentence** consists of one independent clause.
Terrence enjoys modern British literature.

A **compound sentence** consists of two or more independent clauses. The clauses are joined by a conjunction or a semicolon.
Terrence enjoys modern British literature, but his brother prefers the classics.

A **complex sentence** consists of one independent clause and one or more subordinate clauses.
Terrence, who reads voraciously, enjoys modern British literature.

A **compound-complex sentence** consists of two or more independent clauses and one or more subordinate clauses.
Terrence, who reads voraciously, enjoys modern British literature, but his brother prefers the classics.

Classifying Sentences by Function

Sentences can be classified according to their function or purpose. The four types are *declarative, interrogative, imperative,* and *exclamatory.*

SENTENCE STRUCTURE continued

A **declarative sentence** states an idea and ends with a period.

An **interrogative sentence** asks a question and ends with a question mark.

An **imperative sentence** gives an order or a direction and ends with either a period or an exclamation mark.

An **exclamatory sentence** conveys a strong emotion and ends with an exclamation mark.

PARAGRAPH STRUCTURE

An effective paragraph is organized around one **main idea,** which is often stated in a **topic sentence.** The other sentences support the main idea. To give the paragraph **unity,** make sure the connection between each sentence and the main idea is clear.

Unnecessary Shift in Person

Do not change needlessly from one grammatical person to another. Keep the person consistent in your sentences.
   Max went to the bakery, but **you** can't buy mints there. [shift from third person to second person]
   Max went to the bakery, but **he** can't buy mints there. [consistent]

Unnecessary Shift in Voice

Do not change needlessly from active voice to passive voice in your use of verbs.
   Elena and I **searched** the trail for evidence, but no clues **were found.** [shift from active voice to passive voice]
   Elena and I **searched** the trail for evidence, but we **found** no clues. [consistent]

AGREEMENT

Subject and Verb Agreement

A singular subject must have a singular verb. A plural subject must have a plural verb.
   Dr. Boone uses a telescope to view the night sky.
   The **students use** a telescope to view the night sky.

A verb always agrees with its subject, not its object.
   Incorrect: The best part of the show were the jugglers.
   Correct: The best part of the show was the jugglers.

A phrase or clause that comes between a subject and verb does not affect subject-verb agreement.
   His **theory,** as well as his claims, **lacks** support.

Two subjects joined by *and* usually take a plural verb.
   The **dog** and the **cat are** healthy.

Two singular subjects joined by *or* or *nor* take a singular verb.
   The **dog** or the **cat is** hiding.

Two plural subjects joined by *or* or *nor* take a plural verb.
   The **dogs** or the **cats are** coming home with us.

When a singular and a plural subject are joined by *or* or *nor,* the verb agrees with the closer subject.
   Either the **dogs** or the **cat is** behind the door.
   Either the **cat** or the **dogs are** behind the door.

Pronoun and Antecedent Agreement

Pronouns must agree with their antecedents in number and gender. Use singular pronouns with singular antecedents and plural pronouns with plural antecedents.
   Doris Lessing uses **her** writing to challenge ideas about women's roles.
   Writers often use **their** skills to promote social change.

Use a singular pronoun when the antecedent is a singular indefinite pronoun such as *anybody, each, either, everybody, neither, no one, one,* or *someone.*
   Judge **each** of the articles on **its** merits.

Use a plural pronoun when the antecedent is a plural indefinite pronoun such as *both, few, many,* or *several.*
   Both of the articles have **their** flaws.

The indefinite pronouns *all, any, more, most, none,* and *some* can be singular or plural depending on the number of the word to which they refer.
   Most of the *books* are in **their** proper places.
   Most of the *book* has been torn from **its** binding.

Grammar Handbook **R59**

USING VERBS

Principal Parts of Regular and Irregular Verbs

A verb has four principal parts:

Present	Present Participle	Past	Past Participle
learn	learning	learned	learned
discuss	discussing	discussed	discussed
stand	standing	stood	stood
begin	beginning	began	begun

Regular verbs such as *learn* and *discuss* form the past and past participle by adding *-ed* to the present form. **Irregular verbs** such as *stand* and *begin* form the past and past participle in other ways. If you are in doubt about the principal parts of an irregular verb, check a dictionary.

The Tenses of Verbs

The different tenses of verbs indicate the time an action or condition occurs.

The **present tense** expresses an action that happens regularly or states a current condition or a general truth.
> Tourists **flock** to the site yearly.
> Daily exercise **is** good for your health.

The **past tense** expresses a completed action or a condition that is no longer true.
> The squirrel **dropped** the nut and **ran** up the tree.
> I **was** very tired last night by 9:00.

The **future tense** indicates an action that will happen in the future or a condition that will be true.
> The Glazers **will visit** us tomorrow.
> They **will be** glad to arrive from their long journey.

The **present perfect tense** expresses an action that happened at an indefinite time in the past or an action that began in the past and continues into the present.
> Someone **has cleaned** the trash from the park.
> The puppy **has been** under the bed all day.

The **past perfect tense** shows an action that was completed before another action in the past.
> Gerard **had revised** his essay before he turned it in.

The **future perfect tense** indicates an action that will have been completed before another action takes place.
> Mimi **will have painted** the kitchen by the time we finish the shutters.

USING MODIFIERS

Degrees of Comparison

Adjectives and adverbs take different forms to show the three degrees of comparison: the *positive*, the *comparative*, and the *superlative*.

Positive	Comparative	Superlative
fast	faster	fastest
crafty	craftier	craftiest
abruptly	more abruptly	most abruptly
badly	worse	worst

Using Comparative and Superlative Adjectives and Adverbs

Use comparative adjectives and adverbs to compare two things. Use superlative adjectives and adverbs to compare three or more things.
> This season's weather was **drier** than last year's.
> This season has been one of the **driest** on record.
> Jake practices **more often** than Jamal.
> Of everyone in the band, Jake practices **most often**.

USING PRONOUNS

Pronoun Case

The **case** of a pronoun is the form it takes to show its function in a sentence. There are three pronoun cases: *nominative, objective,* and *possessive*.

Nominative	Objective	Possessive
I, you, he, she, it, we, you, they	me, you, him, her, it, us, you, them	my, your, yours, his, her, hers, its, our, ours, their, theirs

Use the **nominative case** when a pronoun functions as a *subject* or as a *predicate nominative*.

> **They** are going to the movies. [subject]
> The biggest movie fan is **she**. [predicate nominative]

Use the **objective case** for a pronoun acting as a *direct object*, an *indirect object*, or the *object of a preposition*.
> The ending of the play surprised **me**. [direct object]
> Mary gave **us** two tickets to the play. [indirect object]
> The audience cheered for **him**. [object of preposition]

Use the **possessive case** to show ownership.
> The red suitcase is **hers**.

COMMONLY CONFUSED WORDS

Diction The words you choose contribute to the overall effectiveness of your writing. **Diction** refers to word choice and to the clearness and correctness of those words. You can improve one aspect of your diction by choosing carefully between commonly confused words, such as the pairs listed below.

accept, except

Accept is a verb that means "to receive" or "to agree to." *Except* is a preposition that means "other than" or "leaving out."

Please **accept** my offer to buy you lunch this weekend.

He is busy every day **except** the weekends.

affect, effect

Affect is normally a verb meaning "to influence" or "to bring about a change in." *Effect* is usually a noun meaning "result."

The distractions outside **affect** Steven's ability to concentrate.

The teacher's remedies had a positive **effect** on Steven's ability to concentrate.

among, between

Among is usually used with three or more items, and it emphasizes collective relationships or indicates distribution. *Between* is generally used with only two items, but it can be used with more than two if the emphasis is on individual (one-to-one) relationships within the group.

I had to choose a snack **among** the various vegetables.

He handed out the booklets **among** the conference participants.

Our school is **between** a park and an old barn.

The tournament included matches **between** France, Spain, Mexico, and the United States.

amount, number

Amount refers to overall quantity and is mainly used with mass nouns (those that can't be counted). *Number* refers to individual items that can be counted.

The **amount** of attention that great writers have paid to Shakespeare is remarkable.

A **number** of important English writers have been fascinated by the legend of King Arthur.

assure, ensure, insure

Assure means "to convince [someone of something]; to guarantee." *Ensure* means "to make certain [that something happens]." *Insure* means "to arrange for payment in case of loss."

The attorney **assured** us we'd win the case.

The rules **ensure** that no one gets treated unfairly.

Many professional musicians **insure** their valuable instruments.

bad, badly

Use the adjective *bad* before a noun or after linking verbs such as *feel, look,* and *seem*. Use *badly* whenever an adverb is required.

The situation may seem **bad**, but it will improve over time.

Though our team played **badly** today, we will focus on practicing for the next match.

beside, besides

Beside means "at the side of" or "close to." *Besides* means "in addition to."

The stapler sits **beside** the pencil sharpener in our classroom.

Besides being very clean, the classroom is also very organized.

can, may

The helping verb *can* generally refers to the ability to do something. The helping verb *may* generally refers to permission to do something.

I **can** run one mile in six minutes.

May we have a race during recess?

complement, compliment

The verb *complement* means "to enhance"; the verb *compliment* means "to praise."

Online exercises **complement** the textbook lessons.

Ms. Lewis **complimented** our team on our excellent debate.

compose, comprise

Compose means "to make up; constitute." *Comprise* means "to include or contain." Remember that the whole comprises its parts or is composed of its parts, and the parts compose the whole.

The assignment **comprises** three different tasks.

The assignment is **composed** of three different tasks.

Three different tasks **compose** the assignment.

different from, different than

Different from is generally preferred over *different than*, but *different than* can be used before a clause. Always use *different from* before a noun or pronoun.

Your point of view is so **different from** mine.

His idea was so **different from** [or **different than**] what we had expected.

farther, further

Use *farther* to refer to distance. Use *further* to mean "to a greater degree or extent" or "additional."

Chiang has traveled **farther** than anybody else in the class.

If I want **further** details about his travels, I can read his blog.

Grammar Handbook **R61**

COMMONLY CONFUSED WORDS continued

fewer, less

Use *fewer* for things that can be counted. Use *less* for amounts or quantities that cannot be counted. *Fewer* must be followed by a plural noun.

> **Fewer** students drive to school since the weather improved.
> There is **less** noise outside in the mornings.

good, well

Use the adjective *good* before a noun or after a linking verb. Use *well* whenever an adverb is required, such as when modifying a verb.

> I feel **good** after sleeping for eight hours.
> I did **well** on my test, and my soccer team played **well** in that afternoon's game. It was a **good** day!

its, it's

The word *its* with no apostrophe is a possessive pronoun. The word *it's* is a contraction of "it is."

> Angelica will try to fix the computer and **its** keyboard.
> **It's** a difficult job, but she can do it.

lay, lie

Lay is a transitive verb meaning "to set or put something down." Its principal parts are *lay, laying, laid, laid*. *Lie* is an intransitive verb meaning "to recline" or "to exist in a certain place." Its principal parts are *lie, lying, lay, lain*.

> Please **lay** that box down and help me with the sofa.
> When we are done moving, I am going to **lie** down.
> My hometown **lies** sixty miles north of here.

like, as

Like is a preposition that usually means "similar to" and precedes a noun or pronoun. The conjunction *as* means "in the way that" and usually precedes a clause.

> **Like** the other students, I was prepared for a quiz.
> **As** I said yesterday, we expect to finish before noon.

Use **such as**, not **like**, before a series of examples.

> Foods **such as** apples, nuts, and pretzels make good snacks.

of, have

Do not use *of* in place of *have* after auxiliary verbs such as *would, could, should, may, might,* or *must*. The contraction of *have* is formed by adding *-ve* after these verbs.

> I **would have** stayed after school today, but I had to help cook at home.
> Mom **must've** called while I was still in the gym.

principal, principle

Principal can be an adjective meaning "main; most important." It can also be a noun meaning "chief officer of a school." *Principle* is a noun meaning "moral rule" or "fundamental truth."

> His strange behavior was the **principal** reason for our concern.
> Democratic **principles** form the basis of our country's laws.

raise, rise

Raise is a transitive verb that usually takes a direct object. *Rise* is intransitive and never takes a direct object.

> Iliana and Josef **raise** the flag every morning.
> They **rise** from their seats and volunteer immediately whenever help is needed.

than, then

The conjunction *than* is used to connect the two parts of a comparison. The adverb *then* usually refers to time.

> My backpack is heavier **than** hers.
> I will finish my homework and **then** meet my friends at the park.

that, which, who

Use the relative pronoun *that* to refer to things or people. Use *which* only for things and *who* only for people.

That introduces a restrictive phrase or clause, that is, one that is essential to the meaning of the sentence. *Which* introduces a nonrestrictive phrase or clause—one that adds information but could be deleted from the sentence—and is preceded by a comma.

> Ben ran to the park **that** just reopened.
> The park, **which** just reopened, has many attractions.
> The man **who** built the park loves to see people smiling.

when, where, why

Do not use *when, where,* or *why* directly after a linking verb, such as *is*. Reword the sentence.

> *Incorrect:* The morning is when he left for the beach.
> *Correct:* He left for the beach in the morning.

who, whom

In formal writing, use *who* only as a subject in clauses and sentences. Use *whom* only as the object of a verb or of a preposition.

> **Who** paid for the tickets?
> **Whom** should I pay for the tickets?
> I can't recall to **whom** I gave the money for the tickets.

your, you're

Your is a possessive pronoun expressing ownership. *You're* is the contraction of "you are."

> Have you finished writing **your** informative essay?
> **You're** supposed to turn it in tomorrow. If **you're** late, **your** grade will be affected.

EDITING FOR ENGLISH LANGUAGE CONVENTIONS

Capitalization

First Words

Capitalize the first word of a sentence.
> Stories about knights and their deeds interest me.

Capitalize the first word of direct speech.
> Sharon asked, "Do you like stories about knights?"

Capitalize the first word of a quotation that is a complete sentence.
> Einstein said, "Anyone who has never made a mistake has never tried anything new."

Proper Nouns and Proper Adjectives

Capitalize all proper nouns, including geographical names, historical events and periods, and names of organizations.
> Thames River   John Keats   the Renaissance
> United Nations   World War II   Sierra Nevada

Capitalize all proper adjectives.
> Shakespearean play   British invasion
> American citizen   Latin American literature

Academic Course Names

Capitalize course names only if they are language courses, are followed by a number, or are preceded by a proper noun or adjective.
> Spanish   Honors Chemistry   History 101
> geology   algebra   social studies

Titles

Capitalize personal titles when followed by the person's name.
> Ms. Hughes   Dr. Perez   King George

Capitalize titles showing family relationships when they are followed by a specific person's name, unless they are preceded by a possessive noun or pronoun.
> Uncle Oscar   Mangan's sister   his aunt Tessa

Capitalize the first word and all other key words in the titles of books, stories, songs, and other works of art.
> Frankenstein   "Shooting an Elephant"

Punctuation

End Marks

Use a **period** to end a declarative sentence or an imperative sentence.
> We are studying the structure of sonnets.
> Read the biography of Mary Shelley.

Use periods with initials and abbreviations.
> D. H. Lawrence   Mrs. Browning
> Mt. Everest   Maple St.

Use a **question mark** to end an interrogative sentence.
> What is Macbeth's fatal flaw?

Use an **exclamation mark** after an exclamatory sentence or a forceful imperative sentence.
> That's a beautiful painting!   Let me go now!

Commas

Use a **comma** before a coordinating conjunction to separate two independent clauses in a compound sentence.
> The game was very close, but we were victorious.

Use commas to separate three or more words, phrases, or clauses in a series.
> William Blake was a writer, artist, and printer.

Use commas to separate coordinate adjectives.
> It was a witty, amusing novel.

Use a comma after an introductory word, phrase, or clause.
> When the novelist finished his book, he celebrated with his family.

Use commas to set off nonessential expressions.
> Old English, of course, requires translation.

Use commas with places and dates.
> Coventry, England   September 1, 1939

Semicolons

Use a **semicolon** to join closely related independent clauses that are not already joined by a conjunction.
> Tanya likes to write poetry; Heather prefers prose.

Use semicolons to avoid confusion when items in a series contain commas.
> They traveled to London, England; Madrid, Spain; and Rome, Italy.

Colons

Use a **colon** before a list of items following an independent clause.
> Notable Victorian poets include the following: Tennyson, Arnold, Housman, and Hopkins.

Use a colon to introduce information that summarizes or explains the independent clause before it.
> She just wanted to do one thing: rest.
> Malcolm loves volunteering: He reads to sick children every Saturday afternoon.

Quotation Marks

Use **quotation marks** to enclose a direct quotation.
> "Short stories," Ms. Hildebrand said, "should have rich, well-developed characters."

An **indirect quotation** does not require quotation marks.
> Ms. Hildebrand said that short stories should have well-developed characters.

Use quotation marks around the titles of short written works, episodes in a series, songs, and works mentioned as parts of collections.
> "The Lagoon"   "Boswell Meets Johnson"

Grammar Handbook **R63**

EDITING FOR ENGLISH LANGUAGE CONVENTIONS continued

Italics

Italicize the titles of long written works, movies, television and radio shows, lengthy works of music, paintings, and sculptures.

Howards End   *60 Minutes*   *Guernica*

For handwritten material, you can use underlining instead of italics.

The Princess Bride   Mona Lisa

Dashes

Use **dashes** to indicate an abrupt change of thought, a dramatic interrupting idea, or a summary statement.

I read the entire first act of *Macbeth*—you won't believe what happens next.

The director—what's her name again?—attended the movie premiere.

Hyphens

Use a **hyphen** with certain numbers, after certain prefixes, with two or more words used as one word, and with a compound modifier that comes before a noun.

seventy-two
self-esteem
president-elect
five-year contract

Parentheses

Use **parentheses** to set off asides and explanations when the material is not essential or when it consists of one or more sentences. When the sentence in parentheses interrupts the larger sentence, it does not have a capital letter or a period.

He listened intently (it was too dark to see who was speaking) to try to identify the voices.

When a sentence in parentheses falls between two other complete sentences, it should start with a capital letter and end with a period.

The quarterback threw three touchdown passes. (We knew he could do it.) Our team won the game by two points.

Apostrophes

Add an **apostrophe** and an *s* to show the possessive case of most singular nouns and of plural nouns that do not end in *-s* or *-es*.

Blake's poems   the mice's whiskers

Names ending in *s* form their possessives in the same way, except for classical and biblical names, which add only an apostrophe to form the possessive.

Dickens's   Hercules'

Add an apostrophe to show the possessive case of plural nouns ending in *-s* and *-es*.

the girls' songs   the Ortizes' car

Use an apostrophe in a contraction to indicate the position of the missing letter or letters.

She's never read a Coleridge poem she didn't like.

Brackets

Use **brackets** to enclose clarifying information inserted within a quotation.

Columbus's journal entry from October 21, 1492, begins as follows: "At 10 o'clock, we arrived at a cape of the island [San Salvador], and anchored, the other vessels in company."

Ellipses

Use three ellipsis points, also known as an **ellipsis,** to indicate where you have omitted words from quoted material.

Wollestonecraft wrote, "The education of women has of late been more attended to than formerly; yet they are still . . . ridiculed or pitied. . . ."

In the example above, the four dots at the end of the sentence are the three ellipsis points plus the period from the original sentence.

Use an ellipsis to indicate a pause or interruption in speech.

"When he told me the news," said the coach, "I was . . . I was shocked . . . completely shocked."

Spelling

Spelling Rules

Learning the rules of English spelling will help you make **generalizations** about how to spell words.

Word Parts

The three word parts that can combine to form a word are roots, prefixes, and suffixes. Many of these word parts come from the Greek, Latin, and Anglo-Saxon languages.

The **root word** carries a word's basic meaning.

Root and Origin	Meaning	Examples
-leg- (-log-) [Gr.]	to say, speak	*legal, logic*
-pon- (-pos-) [L.]	to put, place	*postpone, deposit*

A **prefix** is one or more syllables added to the beginning of a word that alter the meaning of the root.

Prefix and Origin	Meaning	Example
anti- [Gr.]	against	*antipathy*
inter- [L.]	between	*international*
mis- [A.S.]	wrong	*misplace*

EDITING FOR ENGLISH LANGUAGE CONVENTIONS continued

A **suffix** is a letter or group of letters added to the end of a root word that changes the word's meaning or part of speech.

Suffix and Origin	Meaning and Example	Part of Speech
-ful [A.S.]	full of: *scornful*	adjective
-ity [L.]	state of being: *adversity*	noun
-ize (-ise) [Gr.]	to make: *idolize*	verb
-ly [A.S.]	in a manner: *calmly*	adverb

Rules for Adding Suffixes to Root Words

When adding a suffix to a root word ending in *y* preceded by a consonant, change *y* to *i* unless the suffix begins with *i*.

 ply + -able = pliable   happy + -ness = happiness
 defy + -ing = defying   cry + -ing = crying

For a root word ending in *e*, drop the *e* when adding a suffix beginning with a vowel.

 drive + -ing = driving   move + -able = movable
 SOME EXCEPTIONS: traceable, seeing, dyeing

For root words ending with a consonant + vowel + consonant in a stressed syllable, double the final consonant when adding a suffix that begins with a vowel.

 mud + -y = muddy   submit + -ed = submitted
 SOME EXCEPTIONS: mixing, fixed

Rules for Adding Prefixes to Root Words

When a prefix is added to a root word, the spelling of the root remains the same.

 un- + certain = uncertain   mis- + spell = misspell

With some prefixes, the spelling of the prefix changes when joined to the root to make the pronunciation easier.

 in- + mortal = immortal   ad- + vert = avert

Orthographic Patterns

Certain letter combinations in English make certain sounds. For instance, *ph* sounds like *f*, *eigh* usually makes a long *a* sound, and the *k* before an *n* is often silent.

 pharmacy   n**eigh**bor   **k**nowledge

Understanding **orthographic patterns** such as these can help you improve your spelling.

Forming Plurals

The plural form of most nouns is formed by adding -*s* to the singular.

 computer**s**   gadget**s**   Washington**s**

For words ending in *s*, *ss*, *x*, *z*, *sh*, or *ch*, add -*es*.

 circus**es**   tax**es**   wish**es**   bench**es**

For words ending in *y* or *o* preceded by a vowel, add -*s*.

 key**s**   patio**s**

For words ending in *y* preceded by a consonant, change the *y* to an *i* and add -*es*.

 cit**ies**   enem**ies**   troph**ies**

For most words ending in *o* preceded by a consonant, add -*es*.

 echo**es**   tomato**es**

Some words form the plural in irregular ways.

 women   oxen   children   teeth   deer

Foreign Words Used in English

Some words used in English are actually foreign words that have been adopted. Learning to spell these words requires memorization. When in doubt, check a dictionary.

 sushi   enchilada   au pair   fiancé
 laissez faire   croissant

INDEX OF SKILLS

Analyzing Text
Analyze, 22, 152, 188, 270, 290, 381, 472, 473
   essential question, 50, 62, 72, 218, 226, 310, 408, 422, 491, 516
   media, 199
      analyze and discuss, 414
      essential question, 326, 414, 522
      present and discuss, 31, 240, 326, 522
      review and clarify, 240
      review and synthesize, 31, 326, 414, 522
   present and discuss, 50, 62, 72, 218, 226, 310, 320, 408, 422, 491, 505, 516
   review and clarify, 50, 62, 72, 218, 226, 310, 320, 408, 422, 491, 505, 516
Anecdotes, 505
Argument, 257, 258, 441, 442
Articles, 276
Author's argument, 283
   facts, 283
   opinions, 283
   relevant, 283
Author's perspective, 283
   bias, 283
Author's style, 220
   diary, 220
   parallelism, 312
   transitions, 37
   word choice, 220
Autobiography, 409
Cause and effect, 152
Cite textual evidence, 22, 23, 24, 50, 51, 62, 63, 72, 73, 152, 153, 188, 189, 199, 218, 219, 226, 227, 240, 270, 271, 282, 283, 290, 291, 310, 320, 321, 380, 381, 408, 409, 422, 423, 458, 459, 472, 473, 491, 492, 505, 506, 516, 517, 522
Close read, 14, 15, 16, 18, 19, 20, 102, 104, 105, 108, 111, 112, 114, 117, 121, 123, 127, 130, 134, 137, 141, 144, 148, 157, 160, 161, 164, 166, 171, 177, 179, 183, 186, 266, 267, 268, 277, 278, 279, 288, 289, 352, 355, 357, 359, 361, 363, 365, 368, 371, 373, 375, 377, 378, 449, 451, 453, 454, 456, 466, 468, 470
   annotate, 22, 152, 188, 270, 282, 290, 310, 320, 380, 458, 472
close-read guide, 81, 247, 333, 431, 529
conclude, 22, 50, 62, 72, 152, 188, 218, 226, 270, 282, 290, 310, 320, 380, 408, 422, 458, 472, 491, 505, 516
notice, 50, 62, 72, 218, 226, 408, 422, 491, 505, 516
questions, 22, 50, 62, 72, 152, 188, 218, 226, 270, 282, 290, 310, 320, 380, 408, 422, 458, 472, 491, 505, 516
Close review
   conclude, 31, 199, 240, 326, 387, 414
   notice, 240
   questions, 31, 199, 240, 326, 387, 414
   video, 522
Compare, 380, 458
Compare and contrast, 152, 199
Comparing texts
   articles, 276, 286
   nonfiction article and novel excerpts, 488
   novel excerpt and nonfiction, 494
   play and timeline, 100, 156
   short story and film, 350
   short story and video, 12
Comparing text to media
   play and timeline, 194
   video and short story, 28, 384
Conflict, 152
Connect, 290, 381
Craft and structure
   allusion, 381
   author's arguments, 283
      ad populum, 291
      conflicting, 291
      logical fallacies, 291
      overgeneralization, 291
      slippery slope, 291
   author's perspective, 283
   author's point of view, 227
      diction, 517
      tone, 517
   author's purpose, 227, 409, 492
   biographical writing
      direct quotations, 492
      pacing, 492
   central idea, 219
      implied, 219
      stated, 219
      topic sentence, 219
   characterization
      direct, 271
      indirect, 271
      in nonfiction, 271
   character's motivation, 189
      inference of, 189
      settings, 189
   descriptive writing
      author's purpose, 321
      mood, 321
      point of view, 321
      tone, 321
      voice, 321
      word choice, 321
   dialogue, 153, 459
      dramatic irony, 153
      mood, 153
   diction, 517
      connotations, 517
      technical language, 517
   dramatic irony, 153
   expository writing
      cause-and-effect, 473
      comparison-and-contrast, 473
      description, 473
   figurative language, 423, 506
      figures of speech, 506
      sound devices, 423
   figurative meaning, 23
   figures of speech, 506
      metaphor, 506
      personification, 506
      simile, 506
   forms of poetry, 63
   inference, 219
   informational texts
      memoir, 409
      reflective writing, 409
   make inferences, 271
   mood, 153
   persuasive techniques, 311
      appeals to authority, 311
      appeals to emotions, 311
      appeals to reason, 311
      repetition, 311
   plot, 459
      climax, 459
      conflict, 459

exposition, 459
falling action, 459
resolution, 459
rising action, 459
poetry
  forms of, 63
  lyric poem, 63
  narrative poem, 63
  speaker, 63
point of view, 73, 227
  first-person, 73
  limited, 73
  omniscient, 73
  third-person, 73
sound devices, 423
  alliteration, 423
  assonance, 423
  consonance, 423
structure
  biographical writing, 492
  cause and effect, 492
  chronological order, 492
  comparison and contrast, 492
  expository writing, 473
supporting details, 219
symbolism, 23
technical language, 517
theme, 381
  implied, 381
  stated, 381
  universal, 381
tone, 51, 63, 517
  connotation, 51
word choice
  connotations, 311
  denotations, 311
  figurative language, 506
  tone, 311
Deduce, 282
Diary, 213, 220
Diction, 220
Distinguish, 282
Drama, 100, 101, 156, 157, 194
Draw conclusions, 22, 152, 380
Essay
  explanatory, 91, 92
  expository, 473
Essential question, 10, 22, 40, 78, 96, 188, 199, 208, 244, 262, 270, 282, 290, 302, 330, 348, 396, 428, 446, 472, 484, 526
Evaluate, 22, 188, 381, 459
Explanatory essay, 91, 92
Expository essay, 473
Expository nonfiction, 465, 489

First read
  drama, 100, 156
  fiction, 12, 66, 350, 448, 494
  first-read guide, 80, 246, 332, 430, 528
  letter, 44
  nonfiction, 212, 222, 264, 276, 286, 306, 314, 400, 464, 488, 510
  poetry, 54, 416
First review media
  art and photography, 194, 230, 412
  video, 28, 324, 384, 520
Graphic novel, 231
Historical perspective, 98
Independent learning
  close-read guide, 81, 247, 333, 431, 529
  first-read guide, 80, 246, 332, 430, 528
  share learning, 82, 248, 334, 432, 530
  strategies
    apply strategies, 244
    create a schedule, 78, 330, 428, 526
    practice what you have learned, 78, 244, 330, 428, 526
    take notes, 78, 244, 330, 428, 526
Informational texts
  memoir, 409
  reflective writing, 409
Informative writing, 343, 344
Interpret, 22, 188, 199, 270, 282, 459
Letter, 44, 46
Make a judgment, 152, 188, 290, 380, 472
Make connections, 473
Make inferences, 290, 473
Media
  analyze, 199
    essential question, 326, 414, 522
    present and discuss, 31, 240, 326, 414, 522
    review and clarify, 240
    review and synthesize, 31, 326, 414, 522
  film, 350
  graphic novel, 231
  infographic, 413
  present and discuss, 387
  review and synthesize, 387
  timeline, 195
  video, 29, 324, 325, 384, 385, 520, 521
Memoir, 315, 401, 409
Mood, 104

Narrative nonfiction, 5
News article, 265, 511
Nonfiction, expository, 465, 489
Nonfiction narrative, 5, 6
Novel excerpt, 449, 495
Opinion piece, 277, 287
Paraphrase, 188, 270
Play, 100, 156
Poetry, 54, 56, 58, 416, 418, 419, 420
Point of view, 283
Reflective writing, 409
  central idea, 409
  conflicts, 409
Sentence structure, 220
Short story, 13, 67, 350, 351
Speech, 222, 223, 307
Summarize, 22, 472
Support, 282, 290, 381
Synthesize, 152
Timeline, 100, 156, 194, 195
Tone, 282
Video, 324, 325, 327
  direct quotations, 327
  external conflict, 327
  implies, 327
  internal conflict, 327

Assessment

Speaking and listening, oral presentation, 86, 252, 338, 436, 534
Writing to sources
  argument, 336, 532
  explanatory essay, 250
  informative essay, 434
  nonfiction narrative, 84

Language Conventions

Active voice, 393
Adjectives, 322
  capitalization of, 475
  comparative, 507
  irregular, 507
  predicate adjectives, 461
  proper, 475
  superlative, 507
Adverbs, 322
  comparative, 507
  irregular, 507
  superlative, 507
Capitalization, 475
  proper nouns and adjectives, 475
Clauses, 285
  adverb clauses, 285
  dependent (subordinate) clauses, 285,

Index of Skills R67

293
  independent clauses, 285, 293
  noun clauses, 285
  relative clauses, 285
Direct object, 383
  gerunds/gerund phrases as, 481
Gerund phrase, 481
Gerunds, 481
Indirect object, 383
Infinitive, 424
Infinitive phrase, 424
Linking verb, 461
Mood, 52, 64
  conditional, 64, 74
  imperative, 52, 64, 74
  indicative, 52, 64, 74
  interrogative, 52, 74
  subjunctive, 64, 74
Nouns, 273
  capitalization of, 475
  direct and indirect objects, 383
  possessive, 273
  predicate nouns, 461
  proper, 273, 475
Object of preposition, gerunds/gerund phrases as, 481
Participial phrase, 424, 481
Participle, 424, 481
  past, 481
  present, 481
Passive voice, 393
Phrases
  gerund, 481
  infinitive, 424
  participial, 424, 481
Plural words, 393
Predicate noun, gerunds/gerund phrases as, 481
Pronoun-antecedent agreement, 299
Pronoun case, 410
  nominative (subjective) case, 410
  objective case, 410
  possessive case, 410
Pronouns, 299
  antecedents, 299
  direct and indirect objects, 383
  indefinite pronouns, 299
  personal, 273
  possessive, 273
  predicate pronouns, 461
Punctuation
  commas, 493
  dashes, 518
  ellipses, 518
  semicolons, 493

Revising, pronoun-antecedent agreement, 299
Sentences
  combining, with gerunds and participles, 481
  mood, 52
    declarative sentences, 52
    imperative sentences, 52
    interrogative sentences, 52
Sentence structure, 293
  complex sentence, 293
  compound-complex sentence, 293
  compound sentence, 293
  simple sentence, 293
Singular words, 393
Subject, gerunds/gerund phrases as, 481
Subject complements, 461
  predicate adjectives, 461
  predicate nouns, 461
  predicate pronouns, 461
Subject-verb agreement, 393
Tenses
  future, 191
  future perfect, 228
  past, 191
  past perfect, 228
  perfect tenses, 228
  present, 191
  present perfect, 228
  simple, 191
Verbs
  active voice, 393
  irregular, 155
  linking, 461
  mood, 52, 64, 74
  passive voice, 393
  principal parts, 155
    past, 155
    past participle, 155
    present, 155
    present participle, 155
  regular, 155
  subject-verb agreement, 393
  tenses, 191, 228
  voice, 25
Voice
  active voice, 25, 393
  passive voice, 25, 393

Research

Direct quotations, 313
Informational report
  brief, 411
  traditional African healers, 75
  traditional family life in Zimbabwe, 75

Informative presentation, 241
Multimedia presentation, 523
Paraphrase, 313
Research plan, 346
Research report
  biographical report, 313
  historical report, 313
  informational report, 75
Research to clarify, 21, 49, 61, 71, 151, 187, 198, 217, 225, 239, 269, 281, 309, 319, 379, 407, 421, 457, 471, 490, 504, 515
Research to explore, 21, 151, 187, 198, 217, 239, 269, 281, 289, 379, 457, 471, 515

Speaking and Listening

Argument skit, 328
  plan, 328
  present and evaluate, 329
  rehearse, 329
Assessment, oral presentation, 86, 252, 338, 436, 534
Class discussion, 463
Debate
  four-corner, 444
  propositions, 519
  small-group, 524
    plan, 524
    present and evaluate, 525
    rehearse, 525
Discussion, 229
Dramatic reading, 193
Group discussion, 327, 415
  aspects of growing up, 65
  impact of author's tone, 65
Informative presentation, 477
Media connection, 71, 268, 470
Monologue, 27
Multimedia presentation, 425
  dramatic reading, 425
  nonverbal, 425
  plan, 426
  present and evaluate, 427
  rehearse, 427
Note taking, 28
Persuasive presentation, 275
Present an explanatory essay, 242
  plan, 242
  present and evaluate, 243
  rehearse, 243
Present a nonfiction narrative, 76
  plan, 76
  present and evaluate, 77
  rehearse, 77

Small-group learning
  making a schedule, 43, 211, 305, 399, 487
  strategies for
    clarify, 40, 208, 302, 396, 484
    participate fully, 40, 208, 302, 396, 484
    prepare, 40, 208, 302, 396, 484
    support others, 40, 208, 302, 396, 484
  working as a team
    apply the rules, 42, 210, 304, 486
    create a communication plan, 42, 210, 304, 398, 486
    list your rules, 42, 210, 304, 398, 486
    name your group, 42, 210, 304, 398, 486
    practice working as a group, 398
    roles for group projects, 43, 211, 305, 399, 487
    take a position, 42, 210, 304, 398, 486
Speeches, informative, 390
Visual presentation
  dance instructions, 53
  informational presentation, 53
  research presentation, 53
Whole-class learning strategies
  clarify by asking questions, 10, 96, 262, 348, 446
  interact and share ideas, 10, 96, 262, 348, 446
  listen actively, 10, 96, 262, 348, 446
  monitor understanding, 10, 96, 262, 348, 446

Vocabulary

Academic vocabulary
  assimilate, 343, 434
  attribute, 5, 34, 84
  candid, 257, 336
  contradict, 441, 478, 532
  declaration, 91, 202, 250
  documentation, 343, 434
  enumerate, 91, 202, 250
  gratifying, 5, 34, 84
  inspire, 5, 34, 84
  integrate, 343, 434
  legitimate, 441, 478, 532
  notable, 5, 34, 84
  observation, 343, 434
  opponent, 441, 478, 532
  persistent, 5, 34, 84
  position, 441, 478, 532
  pronounce, 91, 202, 250
  rectify, 257, 336
  retort, 257, 336
  speculate, 257, 336
  sustain, 91, 202, 250
  tendency, 343, 434
  theorize, 91, 202, 250
  verify, 257, 336
Archaic vocabulary
  art, 416, 418, 422
  fair, 416, 418, 422
  oughts, 416, 420, 422
  tress, 416, 418, 422
Concept vocabulary
  accomplish, 264, 267, 272
  achieve, 264, 266, 272
  aesthetic, 400, 404, 408
  anxiously, 100, 107, 154
  apprehension, 156, 162, 190
  awakenings, 54, 59, 62
  beaming, 54, 59, 62
  bickering, 100, 125, 154
  cautiously, 314, 319, 320
  clarity, 384, 385, 387
  confidently, 314, 316, 320
  contraption, 448, 452, 460, 462
  controversy, 510, 513, 516
  current, 488, 490, 491
  decipher, 448, 451, 460, 462
  deficiencies, 494, 500, 505
  despised, 350, 367, 382
  deterioration, 350, 372, 382
  determination, 264, 266, 272
  dictate, 286, 288, 292
  dismay, 510, 512, 516
  enable, 464, 474, 476
  engineer, 488, 489, 491
  exemption, 286, 288, 292
  fatigue, 12, 15, 24, 26
  forbidden, 212, 214, 218, 221
  foreboding, 156, 162, 190, 192
  foresight, 464, 466, 474, 476
  frail, 12, 15, 24, 26
  generators, 488, 489, 491
  horizon, 54, 59, 62
  humiliation, 222, 224, 226
  hysterically, 100, 149, 154
  immense, 44, 47, 50
  implemented, 286, 287, 292
  impose, 276, 277, 284
  improvisations, 448, 455, 460, 462
  ingenuity, 448, 454, 460, 462
  insistent, 156, 182, 190, 192
  intentions, 286, 288, 292
  intervene, 286, 287, 292
  introspective, 350, 374, 382
  intuition, 156, 169, 190, 192
  invincible, 448, 460, 462
  justifiable, 276, 278, 284
  majestic, 44, 47, 50
  mandates, 286, 287, 292
  misrepresentations, 306, 308, 310
  misunderstandings, 306, 308, 310
  mounting, 156, 175, 190, 192
  myopic, 464, 466, 474, 476
  naivete, 464, 467, 474, 476
  nervously, 314, 316, 320
  newfangled, 448, 452, 460, 462
  numerous, 44, 48, 50
  obligations, 66, 68, 72
  outcry, 510, 513, 516
  patronized, 66, 68, 72
  peak, 384, 385
  penned, 306, 308, 310
  persecuted, 222, 224, 226
  prescient, 464, 468, 474, 476
  principle, 276, 278, 284
  psychological, 66, 70, 72
  purposeful, 264, 267, 272
  pursue, 264, 266, 272
  quarrels, 100, 125, 154
  rational, 276, 278, 284
  regression, 350, 371, 382
  restraining, 100, 123, 154
  restrictions, 212, 214, 218, 221
  revolutionized, 494, 502, 505
  rigid, 156, 175, 190, 192
  sacrifices, 212, 215, 218, 221
  seminal, 464, 469, 474, 476
  sheepishly, 12, 16, 24, 26
  spiral, 400, 403, 408
  status quo, 276, 278, 284
  straggled, 12, 14, 24, 26
  subconscious, 350, 358, 382
  suspicion, 350, 363, 382
  symmetrical, 400, 403, 408
  tackling, 264, 267, 272
  tension, 100, 108, 154
  traumatized, 222, 224, 226
  triumph, 494, 501, 505
  unleashed, 384, 386, 387
  urgently, 314, 315, 320
  wearily, 12, 14, 24, 26
Media vocabulary
  adapted, 384, 387
  annotated, 194, 199
  audio, 28, 31
  chronological, 194, 199
  close-up, 28, 31

contrast, 28, 31
encapsulation, 230, 240
focus, 520, 522
icons, 412, 414
infographic, 412, 414
labels and captions, 412, 414
narration, 28, 31
pan, 28, 31
panel, 230, 240
parallel, 194, 199
performance, 324, 326
personal account, 324, 326
speech balloon, 230, 240
synchronization (sync), 28, 31
video clip, 520, 522
volume and pacing,
zoom, 520, 522
Word study skills
  antonyms, 24, 154, 284, 416
  base words, 400
  connotations, 494
  context clues, 44, 54, 66, 212, 306, 494, 510
  dictionary, 222, 314, 510
  etymology (word origin), 505
    horizon, 62
  Greek root
    -psych-, 72
    -trauma-, 226
  Latin prefix
    ex-, 292
    sub-, 382
  Latin root
    -just-, 284
    -strict-, 218
    -vers-, 516
  Latin suffix
    -ent, 190
    -ical, 408
    -ion, 154
    -ity, 460
    -ous, 50
  multiple-meaning words, 24, 422, 491
  Old English prefix
    fore-, 474
    mis-, 310
  Old English suffix
    -ful, 272
    -ly, 320
  synonym, 154, 284, 416
  thesaurus, 222, 314, 510
  word choice, 24, 26, 50, 62, 72, 154, 190, 192, 218, 226, 272, 274, 284,

292, 310, 320, 382, 408, 422, 460, 462, 474, 476, 491, 505, 516
Word Network, 7, 93, 259, 345, 443

Writing

Adjectives, 507
Adverbs, 507
Argumentative essay, 294, 508
Argument(s), 296, 478
  conflicting, 294
  counterclaims, 294, 478
  drafting, 298, 480
  editing and proofreading, 301, 483
  elements of, 296, 478
  model argument, 296, 478
  prewriting/planning, 297, 479
  problem-and-solution essay, 296
  publishing and presenting, 301, 483
  review evidence for, 335, 531
  revising, 300, 482
Blurb, 321
Body, 33
Claim, 274, 476
  broad, 295
  narrower, 295
Clauses, 293
Comparison-and-contrast essay, 32, 388
Conclusion, 38
Conjunctions, coordinating, 205
Description, 321
Dialogue, 39
Diary entry, 220
Diction, 220
Drafting, 33
  argumentative essay, 295, 509
  cause-and-effect essay, 201
  comparison-and-contrast essay, 389
  first draft, 36, 204, 298, 392, 480
  match organization to topic, 204
  organization, 392
    argument, 509
    cause-and-effect, 392
    compare-and-contrast, 392
    problem-and-solution, 392
  organize argument, 298
  present reasoning, 480
  prove connections, 204
    strong, 204
    weak, 204
  sequence of events, 36
    chronological order, 36
  thesis statements, 260
  transitions, 36

Drama review, 192
Editing for conventions, 39, 207, 301, 395, 483
Essay
  argumentative, 294, 476, 508
  cause-and-effect, 201
  comparison-and-contrast, 32, 388
  explanatory, 202, 249
  informative, 433
  problem-and-solution, 296
Evidence, 32, 274, 476
  anecdotes, 479
  for argument, 335
  draw conclusions about, 295
  examples, 203, 479
  facts and details, 203, 479
  quotations, 479
  statistics, 479
Evidence Log, 9, 33, 95, 261, 347, 445
Explanatory essay, 202
  drafting, 204
  editing and proofreading, 207
  elements of, 202
  model of, 202
  prewriting/planning, 203
  publishing and presenting, 207
  review evidence, 249
  revising, 206
Fictional retelling
  journal entry, 323
  letter, 323
Formal style, 509
Homophones, 301
Informative essay, 433
Informative speech, 390
  drafting, 392
  editing and proofreading, 395
  elements of, 390
  model for, 390
  prewriting/planning, 391
  publishing and presenting, 395
  revising, 394
Introduction, 33
Journal entry, 221, 323
Letter, 323
Mood
  imperative, 52, 74
  indicative, 52, 74
  subjunctive, 74
Nonfiction narrative, 34
  drafting, 36
  editing and proofreading, 39
  elements of, 34
  model for, 34

prewriting/planning, 35
publishing and presenting, 39
review evidence for, 83
revising, 38
transitions, 37
Paragraph, 507
   clauses
      dependent, 285
      independent, 285
   ellipses and dashes, 518
   parallel structure, 389
   present perfect tense, 228
   revising, 273
Parallelism, 312
Paraphrase, 203, 479
Peer review, 39, 207, 301, 395, 483
Precise language, 38
Prewriting/planning, 32
   cause-and-effect essay, 200
   characters, 35
   claim, 297, 479
   comparison-and-contrast essay, 388
   concluding statement, 391
   connect across texts, 35, 203, 297, 391, 479
   counterclaims, 297, 479
   focus on topic, 35
   gather evidence, 35, 203, 297, 391, 479
   paraphrase, 35
   working thesis, 203
Problem-and-solution essay, 296
Pronoun cases, 410
Proofreading for accuracy, 39, 207, 301, 395, 483
Publishing and collaborating, 509
Publishing and presenting, 207, 301, 395, 483
QuickWrite, 9, 81, 95, 247, 261, 333, 347, 431, 445, 529
Quotations, 479

exact, 203, 479
Reflect on writing, 26, 39, 192, 207, 221, 274, 301, 395, 462, 476, 483
Resolution, 38
Review and revise, 33
   argumentative essay, 295, 509
   cause-and-effect essay, 201
   comparison-and-contrast essay, 389
Revising
   capitalization, 475
   for clarity and cohesion, 295
   by combining with conjunctions, 205
   evaluating draft, 38, 206, 300, 394, 482
   for evidence and elaboration
      depth of support, 206
      fact and opinion, 206
      precise language, 38
      relevant, logical evidence, 300
      transitions, 394
      using language to make connections, 482
   nouns, 273
   pronouns, 273
   punctuation, 493
   for purpose and organization
      clear conclusion, 38
      conclusion, 482
      logical organization, 206
      maintain formal style, 300
      precise, formal word choice, 394
      strong introductory statement, 394
Rewrite
   mood, 74
   stage directions, 155, 191
   verb forms, 64
Sentences
   active voice, 25
   adjectives, 322
   adverbs, 322

combining, 481
direct and indirect objects, 383
participial and infinitive phrases, 424
predicate nouns, 461
Sentence structure
   clauses, 293
   diary entry, 220
Structure
   block method, 201
   point-by-point, 201
Subject-verb agreement, 393
Summary, 8, 94, 260, 346, 444
Thesis statement, 260
Transitions, 36, 389
Verbs, 64
Writing to compare
   argumentative essay, 294, 508
   cause-and-effect essay, 200
   comparison-and-contrast essay, 388
   video review and short story, 32
Writing to sources
   argument, 476
      claim, 476
      evidence, 476
      to support claim, 274
   assessment
      argument, 336, 532
      explanatory essay, 250
      informative essay, 434
      nonfiction narrative, 84
   critical review, 462
      claim, 462
   drama review, 192
   journal entry, 221
   point of view, 26

INDEX OF AUTHORS AND TITLES

The following authors and titles appear in the print and online versions of Pearson Literature.

A
Acceptance Speech for the Nobel Peace Prize, 223
Ada Lovelace: A Science Legend, 527
Allende, Isabel, 448, 449
Angelou, Maya, 79
Anne Frank: The Diary of a Young Girl, from, 213
Apache Girl's Rite of Passage, 29
Auden, W.H., 331

B
Baez, Vicky, 488, 489
Ban the Ban!, 287
Barrington Irving, Pilot and Educator, 265
Basu, Moni, 245
Bleckner, Jeff, 384, 385
Blue Nines and Red Words, from, 401
Bridges, Ruby, 331
Byers, Ann, 245

C
Childhood and Poetry, 79
Conly, Sarah, 276, 277
Cub Pilot on the Mississippi, 79

D
Diary of Anne Frank, The
   Act I, 101
   Act II, 157
Dirkx, Mary Helen, 245
Dunbar, Paul Laurence, 417, 418

E
Emden, Bloeme, 245
Essinger, James, 527

F
Fermented Cow Dung Air Freshener Wins Two Students Top Science Prize, 527
Flowers for Algernon, 351
Flowers for Algernon, from (TV movie), 385
Follow the Rabbit-Proof Fence, from, 315
Frank, Anne, 194, 212, 213
Future of the Mind, The, from, 429

G
Gardner, Howard, 412, 413
Goodrich, Frances, 100, 101, 156, 157
Great Adventure in the Shadow of War, A, 245

H
Hackett, Albert, 100, 101, 156, 157
Hanging Fire, 56
Harriet Tubman: Conductor on the Underground Railroad, 331
Herbach, Geoff, 45, 46
Ho, Minfong, 79
Hunt, Samantha, 494, 495

I
Icarus and Daedalus, 527
I Know Why the Caged Bird Sings, from, 79
I'll Go Fetch Her Tomorrow, from *Hidden Like Anne Frank,* 245
Invention of Everything Else, The, from, 495
Irena Sendler: Rescuer of the Children of Warsaw, 245
Is Personal Intelligence Important?, 429

J
Joseph, Chief, 306, 307
Just Be Yourself!, 48

K
Kaku, Michio, 429
Kazmi, Aleeza, 324, 325
Keyes, Daniel, 350, 351
Klein, Karin, 286, 287
Kroll, Chana, 245

L
Lorde, Audre, 55, 56

M
Maus, from, 231
Mayer, John D., 429
Medicine Bag, The, 13
Mok, Kimberly, 527
More You Know, the Smarter You Are, The?, 429
Moth Presents, The: Aleeza Kazmi, 325
Mungoshi, Charles, 66, 67

N
National Geographic, 28, 29, 264, 265
Neruda, Pablo, 79
Ngowi, Rodrique, 527
Nikola Tesla: The Greatest Inventor of All?, 489

O
Overbye, Dennis, 510, 511

P
Parekh, Divya, 429
Peabody, Josephine Preston, 527
Pellegrin, Stephanie, 45, 48
People, Yes, The, from, 419
Petry, Ann, 331
Pilkington, Doris, 314, 315

Q
Quiet Resistance, from *Courageous Teen Resisters,* 245
Quinceañera Birthday Bash Preserves Tradition, Marks Passage to Womanhood, 79

R
Remembering a Devoted Keeper of Anne Frank's Legacy, 245
Retort, 418
Rogers, David, 384, 385

S
St. John, Natalie, 79
Sandburg, Carl, 417, 420
Saving the Children, 245
Scientists Build Robot That Runs, Call It "Cheetah," 527
Setting Sun and the Rolling World, The, 67
Simon, Bob, 245
Sneve, Virginia Driving Hawk, 12, 13
Soda's a Problem but..., 287
Sounds of a Glass Armonica, 521
Spiegelman, Art, 230, 231
Stone, SidneyAnne, 286, 287

T
Tammet, Daniel, 400, 401
Theory of Multiple Intelligences Infographic, The, 413

Three Cheers for the Nanny State, 277
Through My Eyes, 331
Time Machine, The, from, 527
To Fly, from *Space Chronicles,* 465
Translating Grandfather's House, 58
Twain, Mark, 79
25 Years Later, Hubble Sees Beyond Troubled Start, 511
Tyson, Neil deGrasse, 464, 465

U
Uncle Marcos, from *The House of Spirits,* 449
Unknown Citizen, The, 331

V
Vega, E.J., 55, 58
Vega, Jim, 429

W
Wells, H.G., 527
Why Is Emotional Intelligence Important for Teens?, 429
Wiesel, Elie, 222, 223
Winter Hibiscus, The, 79
Words Do Not Pay, 307

Y
You Are the Electric Boogaloo, 46

ADDITIONAL SELECTIONS: AUTHOR AND TITLE INDEX

The following authors and titles appear in the Online Literature Library.

A
Ada Lovelace: A Science Legend
Angelou, Maya
Auden, W.H.

B
Basu, Moni
Bridges, Ruby
Byers, Ann

C
Childhood and Poetry
Cub Pilot on the Mississippi

D
Dirkx, Mary Helen

E
Emden, Bloeme
Essinger, James

F
Fermented Cow Dung Air Freshener Wins Two Students Top Science Prize
Future of the Mind, The, from

G
Great Adventure in the Shadow of War, A

H
Harriet Tubman: Conductor on the Underground Railroad
Hometown Product Marlen Esparza Given a Hero's Welcome
Ho Minfong

I
Icarus and Daedalus, from *Old Greek Folk-Stories Told Anew*
I Know Why the Caged Bird Sings, from
I'll Go Fetch Her Tomorrow, from *Hidden Like Anne Frank*
Irena Sendler: Rescuer of the Children of Warsaw
Is Personal Intelligence Important?

K
Kako, Michio
Kroll, Chana

M
Mayer, John D.
Mok, Kimberly
More You Know, the Smarter You Are, The?

N
Neruda, Pablo
Ngowi, Rodrique

O
Orozco, Y.C.

P
Parekh, Divya
Peabody, Josephine Preston
Petry, Ann

Q
Quiet Resistance, from *Courageous Teen Resisters*
Quinceañera Birthday Bash Preserves Tradition, Marks Passage to Womanhood

R
Remembering a Devoted Keeper of Anne Frank's Legacy

S
St. John, Natalie
Saving the Children
Scientists Build Robot That Runs, Call It "Cheetah"
Simon, Bob

T
Through My Eyes
Time Machine, The, from
Twain, Mark

U
Unknown Citizen, The

V
Vega, Jim

W
Wells, H.G.
Why Is Emotional Intelligence Important for Teens?
Winter Hibiscus, The

ACKNOWLEDGMENTS AND CREDITS

Acknowledgments

The following selections appear in Grade 8 of myPerspectives. Some selections appear online only.

Albion Press. "Words Do Not Pay," Excerpt from *In a Sacred Manner I Live: Native American Wisdom,* edited by Neil Philip. (The Albion Press Ltd., 1997).

Associated Press (Reprint Management Services). "Scientists Build Robot That Runs, Call It 'Cheetah'" used with permission of The Associated Press Copyright ©2015. All rights reserved.

BBC Worldwide Americas, Inc. *The Holocaust* ©BBC Worldwide Learning.

Carmen Balcells Agencia Literaria. "Uncle Marcos" from *The House of the Spirits* by Isabel Allende. Published by Jonathan Cape. Reprinted by permission of Carmen Balcells Agencia Literaria.

CBS News. "Saving the Children," ©CBS News.

Chabad Lubavitch Center. "Irena Sendler: Rescuer of the Children of Warsaw" by Chana Kroll; Used with permission.

Charlotte Sheedy Literary Agency, Inc. "Hanging Fire," Copyright ©1978, 1997 by Audre Lorde – from the collection BLACK UNICORN by Audre Lorde.

CNN. "Remembering a Devoted Keeper of Anne Frank's Legacy," From CNN.com, March 19, 2015 ©2015 Turner Broadcast Systems, Inc. All rights reserved. Used by permission and protected by the Copyright Laws of the United States. The printing, copying, redistribution, or retransmission of this Content without express written permission is prohibited.

Curtis Brown Ltd. "The Unknown Citizen." Copyright ©1940 by W. H. Auden, renewed. Reprinted by permission of Curtis Brown, Ltd.

ENSLOW PUBLISHING, LLC. "Quiet Resistance," *Courageous Teen Resisters* by Ann Byers, ©2010 by Enslow Publishers, Inc. and reprinted with permission.

Essinger, James. "Ada Lovelace: A Science Legend" by James Essinger, from *Huffington Post,* December 29, 2014. Used with permission of the author.

Flora Roberts, Inc. Entire Play from *Diary of Anne Frank* by Frances Goodrich and Albert Hackett, Copyright ©1956 by Albert Hackett, Frances Goodrich Hackett, and Otto Frank. Copyright renewed 1984 by Albert Hackett. Used by permission of Flora Roberts, Inc.

Funders and Founders. "The Types of Intelligences Infographic based on Howard Gardner's Theory of Multiple Intelligences"; http://fundersandfounders.com/9-types-of-intelligence/ by Mark Vital and Anna Vital. Used with permission of Funders and Founders.

Georges Borchardt Literary Agency. "Friends All of Us" from *Neruda and Vallego: Selected Poems* translated by Robert Bly. Translation Copyright ©1971, 1993 by Robert Bly. Reprinted by permission of Georges Borchardt, Inc., for Robert Bly.

Hannigan Salky Getzler Agency. "Harriet Tubman: Conductor of the Underground Railroad" reprinted by the permission of HSG Agency as agent for the author. Copyright ©1954, 1982, 2006 by Ann Petry.

Hear Africa Foundation. Hear Africa gives permission to Pearson Education for "Stories of Zimbabwean Women."

Houghton Mifflin Harcourt Publishing Co. Excerpt from *In a Sacred Manner I Live: Native American Wisdom,* edited by Neil Philip. Copyright ©1997 by The Albion Press Ltd. Reprinted by permission of Clarion Books, an imprint of Houghton Mifflin Harcourt Publishing Company. All rights reserved; Excerpted from *Flowers for Algernon* by Daniel Keyes. Copyright ©1966, 1959 and renewed 1994, 1987 by Daniel Keyes. Reprinted by permission of Houghton Mifflin Harcourt Publishing Company. All rights reserved; "Circles" from *The People, Yes* by Carl Sandburg. Copyright 1936 by Houghton Mifflin Harcourt Publishing Company. Copyright © renewed 1981 by Carl Sandburg. Reprinted by permission of Houghton Mifflin Harcourt Publishing Company. All rights reserved; Excerpt from *The Invention of Everything Else: A Novel* by Samantha Hunt. Copyright ©2008 by Samantha Hunt. Used by permission of Houghton Mifflin Harcourt Publishing Company. All rights reserved.

ITN Source. *Amazing Man Draws NYC from Memory* © ITN Source.

Jukin Media. *Dear Graduates—A Message From Kid President* Courtesy Jukin Media, Inc.

LA Times. "Soda's a Problem but Bloomberg Doesn't Have the Solution" by Karin Klein, from *LA Times,* March 15, 2013. Copyright ©2013 Los Angeles Times. Reprinted with Permission.

Little, Brown and Co. (UK). From *I Know Why the Caged Bird Sings* by Maya Angelou. Copyright ©1997. Used with permission of Little, Brown Book Group.

Mayer, John. "Is Personal Intelligence Important?" by John D. Mayer, *Psychology Today* blog, May 6, 2014; Used with permission of the author.

McIntosh & Otis. "Winter Hibiscus," Copyright ©1993 by Minfong Ho. Reprinted by permission of McIntosh & Otis, Inc.

Mok, Kimberly. "Fermented Cow Dung Air Freshener Wins Two Students Top Science Prize," ©Kimberly Mok.

Mungoshi, Jesesi. From *The Setting Sun and the Rolling World* by Charles Mungoshi, ©1989. Used with permission of Jesesi Mungoshi.

National Geographic Creative. *Girl's Rite of Passage* ©National Geographic Creative.

National Geographic Magazine. "Barrington Irving, Pilot and Educator" from National Geographic: Explorers, http://www.nationalgeographic.com/explorers/bios/barrington-irving/. NG Staff/National Geographic Creative.

Nobel Media AB. "Elie Wiesel Nobel Acceptance Speech," Copyright © The Nobel Foundation (1986). Source: Nobelprize.org.

Parekh, Divya. "Why Is Emotional Intelligence Important for Teens?" by Divya Parekh. Used with permission of the author.

PARS International Corporation. "A Great Adventure in the Shadow of War," From *Newsweek,* September 13, 2004 ©2004 IBT Media. All rights reserved. Used by permission and protected by the Copyright Laws of the United States. The printing, copying, redistribution, or retransmission of this Content without express written permission is prohibited; "Three Cheers for the Nanny State" from *The New York Times,* March 25, 2013 ©2013 The New York Times. All rights reserved. Used by permission and protected by the Copyright Laws of the United States. The printing, copying, redistribution, or retransmission of this Content without express written permission is prohibited; "25 Years Later, Hubble Sees Beyond Troubled Start" from *The New York Times,* April 24, 2015 ©2015 The New York Times. All rights reserved. Used by permission and protected by the Copyright

Acknowledgments and Credits **R75**

Laws of the United States. The printing, copying, redistribution, or retransmission of this Content without express written permission is prohibited.

Penguin Books, Ltd. (UK). From *The Diary of a Young Girl: The Definitive Edition* by Anne Frank, edited by Otto H. Frank and Mirjam Pressler, translated by Susan Massotty (Viking, 1997) copyright © The Anne Frank-Fonds, Basle, Switzerland, 1991. English translation copyright © Doubleday a division of Bantam Doubleday Dell Publishing Group Inc., 1995. Reproduced by permission of Penguin Books Ltd.; From THE COMPLETE MAUS by Art Spiegelman (Penguin Books, 2003). Copyright © Art Spiegelman, 1973, 1980, 1981, 1982, 1983, 1984, 1985, 1986, 1989, 1990, 1991. Reproduced by permission of Penguin Books Ltd.; "Einstein's Brain and Enhancing Our Intelligence" from *The Future of the Mind* by Michio Kaku (Penguin, 2015) Copyright © Michio Kaku, 2014. Reproduced by permission of Penguin Books Ltd.

Peppe, Holly. *Got 30 Dollars in my Pocket* Courtesy Barrington Irving.

Random House Group Ltd., Permissions Department. From *The Invention of Everything Else* by Samantha Hunt. Published by Harvill Secker. Reprinted by permission of The Random House Group Limited.

Random House UK Limited. "Uncle Marcos" from *The House of the Spirits* by Isabel Allende. Published by Jonathan Cape. Reprinted by permission of The Random House Group Limited.

Random House, Inc. Excerpt(s) from *I Know Why the Caged Bird Sings* by Maya Angelou, Copyright ©1969 and renewed 1997 by Maya Angelou. Used by permission of Random House, an imprint and division of Penguin Random House LLC. All rights reserved. Any third party use of this material, outside of this publication, is prohibited. Interested parties must apply directly to Penguin Random House LLC for permission; Entire Play from *Diary of Anne Frank* by Frances Goodrich and Albert Hackett, copyright ©1956 by Albert Hackett, Frances Goodrich Hackett, and Otto Frank. Copyright renewed 1984 by Albert Hackett. Used by permission of Random House, an imprint and division of Penguin Random House LLC. All rights reserved. Any third party use of this material, outside of this publication, is prohibited. Interested parties must apply directly to Penguin Random House LLC for permission; Excerpt(s) from *The Diary of a Young Girl: The Definitive Edition* by Anne Frank, edited by Otto H. Frank and Mirjam Pressler, translated by Susan Massotty, translation Copyright ©1995 by Doubleday, a division of Random House LLC. Used by permission of Doubleday, an imprint of the Knopf Doubleday Publishing Group, a division of Penguin Random House LLC. All rights reserved. Any third party use of this material, outside of this publication, is prohibited. Interested parties must apply directly to Penguin Random House LLC for permission; Graphic Novel excerpt from *The Complete Maus: A Survivor's Tale* by Art Spiegelman, Maus, Volume I copyright ©1973, 1980, 1981, 1982, 1983, 1984, 1985, 1986 by Art Spiegelman; Maus, Volume II copyright ©1986, 1989, 1990, 1991 by Art Spiegelman. Used by permission of Pantheon Books, an imprint of the Knopf Doubleday Publishing Group, a division of Penguin Random House LLC. All rights reserved. Any third party use of this material, outside of this publication, is prohibited. Interested parties must apply directly to Penguin Random House LLC for permission; "The Unknown Citizen," copyright ©1940 and renewed 1968 by W. H. Auden; from *W. H. Auden Collected Poems* by W. H. Auden. Used by permission of Random House, an imprint and division of Penguin Random House LLC. All rights reserved. Any third party use of this material, outside of this publication, is prohibited. Interested parties must apply directly to Penguin Random House LLC for permission; "What Happened During the Ice Storm" from *The One-Room Schoolhouse: Stories About the Boys* by Jim Heynen, copyright ©1993 by Jim Heynen. Used by permission of Alfred A. Knopf, an imprint of the Knopf Doubleday Publishing Group, a division of Penguin Random House LLC. All rights reserved; "Einstein's Brain and Enhancing Our Intelligence" excerpt(s) from *The Future of the Mind: The Scientific Quest to Understand, Enhance, and Empower the Mind* by Michio Kaku, copyright ©2013 by Michio Kaku. Used by permission of Doubleday, an imprint of the Knopf Doubleday Publishing Group, a division of Penguin Random House LLC. All rights reserved. Any third party use of this material, outside of this publication, is prohibited. Interested parties must apply directly to Penguin Random House LLC for permission.

Ricketson, James. *Phillipe Petit Tightrope Walk on The Sydney Harbour Bridge* 1973 - Part 2 © James Ricketson.

Scholastic, Inc. "I'll Go Fetch Her Tomorrow" from *Hidden Like Anne Frank* by Marcel Prins and Peter Kenk Steehuis, translated by Laura Watkinson. Copyright ©2001 by Marcel Prins and Peter Henk Steenhuis. Translation by Laura Watkinson copyright ©2014 by Scholastic, Inc. Reprinted by permission of Scholastic Inc.; From *Through My Eyes* by Ruby Bridges. Copyright ©1999 by Ruby Bridges. Reprinted by permission of Scholastic, Inc.

Simon & Schuster Inc. "Uncle Marcos" from *The House of the Spirits* by Isabel Allende. Copyright ©1982. Used with permission of Simon & Schuster, Inc.; "Blue Nines and Red Words" reprinted with the permission of Free Press, a Division of Simon & Schuster, Inc., from *Born on a Blue Day: Inside the Extraordinary Mind of an Autistic Savant* by Daniel Tammet. Copyright © 2006 by Daniel Tammet. Originally published in Great Britain in 2006 by Hodder & Stoughton. All rights reserved.

Sneve, Virginia. "The Medicine Bag" from *Grandpa Was a Cowboy & an Indian and Other Stories* by Virginia Driving Hawk Sneve. Used with permission.

Stone, SidneyAnne. "Ban the Ban!" from *Huffington Post,* May 12, 2013, by SidneyAnne Stone. Used with permission of the author.

The Andrew Lownie Literary Agency Ltd. "Blue Nines and Red Words" from *Born on a Blue Day* by Daniel Tammet. Copyright ©2009. Used with permission of Andrew Lownie Literary Agency.

The Daily News. "Quinceanera Birthday Bash Preserves Tradition, Marks Passage to Womanhood," Copyright ©July 28, 2012, Author: Natalie St. John, in *The Daily News.*

The Moth. The Moth Presents: Aleeza Kazmi © The Moth.

Toronto Star Newspapers Limited. Sounds of a Glass Armonica ©Mike Kelly/GetStock

University of Arizona Press. From *For a Girl Becoming* by Joy Harjo. ©2009 Joy Harjo and Mercedes McDonald. Reprinted by permission of the University of Arizona Press.

University of Queensland Press. From *Follow the Rabbit-Proof Fence* by Doris Pilkington. Copyright ©1996. Used with permission of University of Queensland Press.

Vega, Eddie. "Translating Grandfather's House" by Eddie Vega, from *Cool Salsa: Bilingual Poems on Growing Up Latino in the United States,* edited by Lori M. Carlson, Introduction by Oscar Hijuelos. Used with permission of Eddie Vega.

W. W. Norton & Co. "Hanging Fire." Copyright ©1978 by Audre

Lorde, from *The Collected Poems of Audre Lorde* by Audre Lorde. Used by permission of W.W. Norton & Company, Inc.; "To Fly" from *Space Chronicles: Facing the Ultimate Frontier* by Neil deGrasse Tyson, edited by Avis Lang. Copyright ©2012 by Neil deGrasse Tyson. Used by permission of W.W. Norton & Company.

WGBH Stock Sales. *Got 30 Dollars in my Pocket* Courtesy of the WGBH Media Library & Archives.

William Morris Endeavor Entertainment, LLC. Excerpted from *Flowers for Algernon* by Daniel Keyes. Copyright ©1966, 1959, and renewed 1994, 1987 by Daniel Keyes. Reprinted by permission of WME Entertainment, LLC.

Writers House. "Heartbeat" Copyright ©2005 David Yoo. Reprinted with permission of the author.

Wylie Agency. From *Maus* by Art Spiegelman. Copyright ©1973, 1980, 1981, 1982, 1983, 1984, 1985, 1986 by Art Spiegelman, used by permission of The Wylie Agency.

Zest Books. "Just Be Yourself!," reprinted from *Dear Teen Me: Authors Write Letters to Their Teen Selves* by E. Kristin Anderson and Miranda Kenneally, published by Zest Books © 2012; "You Are the Electric Boogaloo," reprinted from *Dear Teen Me: Authors Write Letters to Their Teen Selves* by E. Kristin Anderson and Miranda Kenneally, published by Zest Books, © 2012.

Credits

Photo locators denoted as follows Top (T), Center (C), Bottom (B), Left (L), Right (R), Background (Bkgd)

Cover: Lee Powers/Stone/Getty Images

vi Encyclopedia/Corbis; **viii** Josselin Dupont/Moment/Getty Images; **xii** David Malan/Photographer's Choice RF/Getty Images; **xiv** Ruslan Grumble/Shutterstock; **2** Encyclopedia/Corbis; **3** (BC) Paul Bruins Photography/Moment Open/Getty Images, (BCR) Christina Havis/EyeEm/Getty Images, (BR) Tetsuya Tanooka/a.collectionRF/Getty Images, (C) Amos Morgan/Photodisc/Getty Images, (CBR) Image Source/Photodisc/Getty Images, (CR) Library of Congress/Science Faction/Getty Images, (T) Michael Shay/Stockbyte/Getty Images, (TC) Kiselev Andrey Valerevich/Shutterstock, (TL) Claudia Kunin/The Image Bank/Getty Images, (TR) John Parrot/Stocktrek Images/Getty Images; **6** Michael Shay/Stockbyte/Getty Images; **11** (B) National Geographic Creative, (T) Claudia Kunin/The Image Bank/Getty Images; **12** (TL) Claudia Kunin/The Image Bank/Getty Images, (TR) National Geographic Creative; **13, 22, 24, 26, 28** (L), **32** (T) Claudia Kunin/The Image Bank/Getty Images; **17** Roberto A Sanchez/Getty Images; **28** (R), **29, 31, 32** (B) National Geographic Creative; **34** Michael Shay/Stockbyte/Getty Images; **41** (T), **44, 46** Kiselev Andrey Valerevich/Shutterstock, (B) Paul Bruins Photography/Moment Open/Getty Images, (C) Amos Morgan/Photodisc/Getty Images; **45** Photo by Katherine Warde; **48** Olaf Speier/Alamy; **54** Danita Delimont/Gallo Images/Getty Images; **55** (B) ©Eddie Vega, (T) Everett Collection Historical/Alamy; **56** Amos Morgan/Photodisc/Getty Images; **58** Danita Delimont/Gallo Images/Getty Images; **66** ©Jesesi Mungoshi; **67** Paul Bruins Photography/Moment Open/Getty Images; **72** Paul Bruins Photography/Moment Open/Getty Images; **74** Paul Bruins Photography/Moment Open/Getty Images; **79** (B) Tetsuya Tanooka/a.collectionRF/Getty Images, (BR) Christina Havis/EyeEm/Getty Images, (C) Image Source/Photodisc/Getty Images, (T) John Parrot/Stocktrek Images/Getty Images, (TR) Library of Congress; **88** Josselin Dupont/Moment/Getty Images; **89** (B) Dave Bartruff/Danita Delimont Photography/Newscom, (BC) Miquel Benitez/REX/Newscom, (BCL) Anne Frank Fonds Basel/Premium Archive/Getty Images, (BCR) DC Premiumstock/Alamy, (BL) Historical/Corbis, (C) Heritage Images/Glow Images, (CBR) Charlie Riedel/AP Images, (CL) Anne Frank Fonds Basel/Getty Images, (CR) Harvey Meston/Staff/Getty Images, (T) Age Fotostock/Alamy; (TC) Leo La Valle/epa/Corbis, (TL) John Cairns/Alamy, (TR) Pictorial Press Ltd/Alamy; **92** Age Fotostock/Alamy; **97** (B) Historical/Corbis, (BC) Anne Frank Fonds Basel/Premium Archive/Getty Images, (T) John Cairns/Alamy, (TC) Anne Frank Fonds Basel/Getty Images; **98** (B) Print Collector/Hulton Archive/Getty Images, (T) Hulton-Deutsch Collection/Corbis, (B) John Cairns/Alamy; **99** Galerie Bilderwelt/Hulton Archive/Getty Images; **100** (BL, CL) Nancy R. Schiff/Archive Photos/Getty Images, (TL) Anne Frank Fonds Basel/Getty Images, (TR) Historical/Corbis; **101, 105, 152, 154, 156** (TL),**157, 177, 188, 190, 192, 194** (L), **197** (TL), **200** (T), **212** Anne Frank Fonds Basel/Getty Images; **110** Bettmann/Corbis; **119** Desk/AFP/Getty Images; **127** Richard Sowersby/REX/Newscom; **134** UPPA/Photoshot/Newscom; **139** Ralph Crane/The Life Picture Collection/Getty Images; **145** CSP_RonaldWilfredJansen/AGE Fotostock; **150** Reuters Photographer/Reuters/Corbis; **156** (BL), (CL) Nancy R. Schiff/Archive Photos/Getty Images; **156** (TR), **194** (R), **196** (BL), **199, 200** (B) Historical/Corbis; Hulton Archive/Getty Images; **169** Leo La Valle/epa/Corbis; **196** (BC) Rieke Hammerich/Alamy, (BR) Hulton-Deutsch Collection/Corbis; **196** (T), **197** (BL) Bettmann/Corbis; **197** (BR) GPO/Hulton Archive/Getty Images, (TR) Richard Boot/Alamy; **202** Age Fotostock/Alamy; **209, 223, 226, 228** Heritage Images/Glow Images; **209, 213, 218, 220** Leo La Valle/epa/Corbis; **222** Ulf Andersen/Hulton Archive/Getty Images; **230** Aurora Photos/Alamy; **245** (B) Dave Bartruff/Danita Delimont Photography/Newscom, (BC) Miquel Benitez/REX/Newscom, (C) Charlie Riedel/AP Images, (CB) DC Premiumstock/Alamy, (T) Pictorial Press Ltd/Alamy, (TC) Harvey Meston/Staff/Getty Images; **254** Noah Seelam/Getty Images; **255** (B) Universal History Archive/Getty Images, (BR) Rawpixel/Shutterstock, (C) Paul Mayall/Paul Mayall imageBROKER/Newscom, (CL) Blend Images/Brand X Pictures/Getty Images, (CR) AP Images, (T) Jerry Horbert/Shutterstock,(TC) Washington State Historical Society/Art Resource, New York, (TL) MA1/MA1 Wenn Photos/Newscom, (TR) Jed Jacobsohn/Sports Illustrated/Getty Images; **258** Jerry Horbert/Shutterstock; **263** (C) Blend Images/Brand X Pictures/Getty Images, (T) MA1/MA1 Wenn Photos/Newscom; **265, 270, 272, 274** MA1/MA1 Wenn Photos/Newscom; **276** (B) Copyright Bowdoin College, (TL) Blend Images/Brand X Pictures/Getty Images; **277, 282, 284, 286, 294** Blend Images/Brand X Pictures/Getty Images; **296** Jerry Horbert/Shutterstock; **303** (B) ©The Moth, (C) Paul Mayall/Paul Mayall imageBROKER/Newscom, (T) Washington State Historical Society/Art Resource, New York; **306** Library of Congress, Prints & Photographs Division, LC-USZC4-5785; **307, 310, 312** Washington State Historical Society/Art Resource, New York; **314** Tom Kidd/Alamy; **315, 320, 322** Paul Mayall/Paul Mayall imageBROKER/Newscom; **324, 325, 327** ©The Moth; **331** (B) Universal History Archive/Getty Images, (BC) Rawpixel/Shutterstock, (T) Jed Jacobsohn/Sports Illustrated/Getty Images, (TC) AP Images; **340** David Malan/Photographer's Choice RF/Getty Images; **341** (B) Lucien Aigner/Corbis, (BC) Magann/YAY Media AS/Alamy, (BR) Vladyslav Starozhylov/Shutterstock, (T) DrAfter123/DigitalVision Vectors/Getty Images, (TC) Puckillustrations/Fotolia, (TL) Neil Lockhart/Shutterstock, (TR) Nopgraphic/Fotolia; **344, 390** DrAfter123/DigitalVision Vectors/Getty Images; **349, 350, 351, 380, 382, 388** Neil Lockhart/Shutterstock; **366** ABC Pictures/Photofest; **373** Everett Collection; **378** ClassicStock/Superstock; **384** (B) Ari Perilstein/Getty Images, (T) Neil Lockhart/Shutterstock; **397** (B) Magann/YAY Media AS/Alamy, (T) Puckillustrations/Fotolia; **400** Gerard Julien/AFP/Getty Images; **401, 408, 410** Puckillustrations/Fotolia; **404** Shutterstock; **412** J.L. Cereijido/epa/Corbis; **416, 418** Magann/YAY Media AS/Alamy; **417** (B) Library of Congress, Prints & Photographs Division, LC-USZ62-115064, (T) Anthony Barboza/Getty Images; **419** Olha Lavrenchuk/Shutterstock; **429** (B) Lucien Aigner/Corbis, (BC) Vladyslav Starozhylov/Shutterstock, (T) Nopgraphic/Fotolia; **438** Ruslan Grumble/Shutterstock; **439** (B) Pan Xunbin/Shutterstock, (BC) NASA/ESA/Hubble Heritage Team, (BCR) Fyle/Fotolia, (C) Imagophotodesign/Shutterstock, (CBR) Charles Krupa/AP Images, (CL) World History Archive/Alamy, (CR) AP Images, (T) Laborant/Shutterstock, (TC) Richard T. Nowitz/Corbis, (TL) MorganStudio/Shutterstock, (TR) Bill Pierce/The Life Images Collection/Getty Images; **442** Laborant/Shutterstock; **447** (B) World History Archive/Alamy, (T) MorganStudio/Shutterstock; **449** MorganStudio/Shutterstock; **455** Peter vd Rol/Shutterstock; **458, 460, 462** MorganStudio/Shutterstock; **464** Mike Coppola/Getty Images; **465, 472** World History Archive/Alamy; **474, 476** World History Archive/Alamy; **478** Laborant/Shutterstock; **485** (B) Mike Kelly/GetStock.com, (BC) NASA/ESA/Hubble Heritage Team, (TC) Imagophotodesign/Shutterstock, (T) Richard T. Nowitz/Corbis; Photo by Celine M Grouard; **488** (L) Richard T. Nowitz/Corbis; **488** (R) Imagophotodesign/Shutterstock; **489, 491, 492, 508** Richard T. Nowitz/Corbis; **494** (TL) Richard T. Nowitz/Corbis, (TR) Imagophotodesign/Shutterstock, (B) Marion Ettlinger/Corbis; **495, 505, 506** Imagophotodesign/Shutterstock; **498** Andrew Meyerson/Shutterstock; **510** Terry Ashe/The LIFE; Images Collection/Getty Images; **511, 516, 518** NASA/ESA/Hubble Heritage Team; **521, 523** Mike Kelly/GetStock.com; **527** (B) Pan Xunbin/Shutterstock, (BC) Fyle/Fotolia, (C) Charles Krupa/AP Images, (T) Bill Pierce/The Life Images Collection/Getty Images.

Credits for Images in Interactive Student Edition Only

Unit 1

Africa Studio/Shutterstock; AP Images; Christopher Dennis; Everett Historical/Shutterstock; Jedrzej Kaminski/EyeEm/Getty images; Ken Charnock/Getty Images; Natalie St. John copyright 2013; North Wind Picture Archives;

Unit 2

Courtesy CNN; Czarek Sokolowski/AP Images; Hulton-Deutsch Collection/Corbis; Jason Kempin/Getty Images; Piotr Latacha/Shutterstock; Wjarek/Shutterstock; ©Nancy Newberry; ©United States Holocaust Memorial Museum, Courtesy of Bloeme Evers-Emden. THE VIEWS OR OPINIONS EXPRESSED IN THIS (BOOK/ARTICLE/EXHIBIT/OTHER), AND THE CONTEXT IN WHICH THE IMAGES ARE USED, DO NOT NECESSARILY REFLECT THE VIEWS OR POLICY OF, NOR IMPLY APPROVAL OR ENDORSEMENT BY, THE UNITED STATES HOLOCAUST MEMORIAL MUSEUM;

Unit 3

The Underground Railroad, 1893 (oil on canvas), Webber, Charles T. (1825–1911)/Cincinnati Art Museum, Ohio, USA/Subscription Fund Purchase/Bridgeman Art Library; Walter Daran/The LIFE Images Collection/Getty Images; ZUMA Press,Inc./Alamy;

Unit 4

Anthony Barboza/Getty Images; Divya Parekh; Evan Agostini/AP Images; Kmiragaya/Fotolia; ©2013, The University of New Hampshire;

Unit 5

David Levenson/National Basketball Association/Getty Images; Kimberley Mok; Michael Nicholson/Corbis.